UNDERSTANDING
DRAMA

TWELVE PLAYS

By

CLEANTH BROOKS
Yale University

ROBERT B. HEILMAN
University of Washington

HOLT, RINEHART AND WINSTON
New York · Chicago · San Francisco · Toronto

2049500

CONTENTS

PART ONE
Problems of the Drama

PART TWO

Simpler Types

PART THREE

More Mature Types

PART FOUR

Special Studies in the Tragic Mode

LETTER TO TEACHER AND STUDENTS

This textbook represents an attempt to embody the following principles: (1) the primary task in teaching drama is to acquaint the student with the fundamental structure of drama—to teach the student to deal with drama not merely as literary history or the history of ideas or the expression of the author's personality, but as *drama*, a special form with methods and characteristics of its own; (2) such teaching can best be done by intensive analysis of specific examples; and (3) the examples may be studied most profitably when arranged in a scale of ascending difficulty. This book, therefore, is primarily a manual for reading drama, with the essentially modest aim that such a term connotes, though also with all the importance, the editors hasten to add, that the richest and fullest definition of *reading* must imply.

Whether or not the book succeeds in actually exemplifying the principles which have guided the editors, the teacher will have, of course, to determine for himself. But as to the validity of the principles themselves, the editors have absolute conviction. Indeed, in so far as they have failed to implement the principles, they rely upon the teacher to make good their failure, for they are under no illusion that a textbook can ever substitute for the teacher. The utmost that the editors of such a textbook as this may hope is to provide an effective instrument for the teacher, or at least one flexibly adapted to his use. It is in such a spirit that they make the following notes upon the plan of the book.

The book is divided into sections which carry the student from rather simple problems to increasingly complex ones. The plays are, therefore, arranged in a scheme of ascending difficulty, though in Part One there is a definite exception: *Lady Windermere's Fan* is obviously a more complex play than those which follow it in Part Two. Yet we feel that the exception can be justified—that the task of defining drama for the student (the special problem of Part One) can best be completed by placing before the student, as an initial example, a play which is rather fully developed and which is likely to be more interesting to him than a more primitive or "simple" example of the genre. Relatively simple plays, however, are met with in Part Two, and plays that involve more special or more difficult problems are relegated to Parts Three and Four.

In general, the order of the plays contained in Parts Three and Four continues the scale of increasing difficulty. But the editors are not disposed to set much store by the detail of their arrangement and would be willing to concede that some of the plays at the end of Part Three may possibly be more complex than some of those at the beginning of Part Four. The editors' general feeling in the matter is reflected in the titles which they have chosen for these last two sections, "More Mature Types" and "Special Studies in the Tragic Mode"—titles which suggest, rather than insist upon, a steadily increasing complexity.

Tragedy, it will be conceded, is more complex than comedy; and there is a good deal to be said for emphasizing tragedy in the final section of this manual. But here again the editors have preferred not to compartmentalize the two modes: Part Three is concerned principally, but not exclusively, with comedy; and Part Four itself admits a play which is not strictly a tragedy. The student's ability to distinguish comedy and tragedy is, of course, a matter of crucial importance. His ability to apply these terms with discrimination and at a high level might even constitute a significant test of his mastery of drama in general. But the editors would not have him use the terms mechanically, and they have preferred to avoid an arrangement of the plays which might appear to encourage such a mechanical use.

For most of the plays, comments and questions are inserted at the end of each act: this novel arrangement should provide a special stimulus to careful and intensive reading. But teachers who so prefer may easily have the play in question read first as a whole and may take up an act-by-act analysis only after the student has made a rapid over-all survey of the play. Each method has its own advantages.

As for the commentaries themselves, the editors naturally hope that most teachers will judge them to be basically sound; but the commentaries are certainly not meant to be prescriptive or to render the teacher's own comments superfluous. They offer *a* reading of the play, but this does not purport to be *the* reading. It is quite possible, indeed, that the commentaries may best serve a pedagogical purpose by furnishing the teacher with an account of the play which can be attacked or modified or discarded, or by stimulating the student to make his own interpretation. Yet the editors do have some confidence that the commentaries, even when taken at the lowest discount, do raise central questions which need to be raised with regard to drama in general and with regard to the plays here represented in particular.

For the use of classes whose teachers wish them to do more extensive reading (and who have time for such reading), questions and exercises on additional plays are provided in Appendix A. Most of these plays are readily accessible in various popular collections (notice of where they may be found is given in footnotes); suggestions for integrating them with the scheme of plays printed in the text are also given in Appendix A, though the teacher will naturally make his own disposition of the additional plays. The exercises provide in particular opportunities for special papers and reports which may demonstrate how well the student has absorbed the intensive reading methods proposed by the treatment of the plays printed in the body of the text.

In this connection, the editors wish to point out the possibility of using this text as an entry into Shakespeare, particularly into the Shakespearian tragedies. Notes and questions, in some cases rather elaborate, are provided for *Othello, Macbeth, Hamlet,* and *Antony and Cleopatra,* and there are numerous cross references to the other tragedies printed here—especially to *Dr. Faustus, Oedipus the King,* and *King Lear.* The relative ease in securing texts of Shakespeare's plays (including the twenty-five cent Pocket Books edition) makes this suggestion a thoroughly practical one.

An alphabetically arranged Glossary should make it easier for the student to master the basic critical terms which any discussion of the drama requires. As an additional feature the Glossary has been split into two parts: the second is the conventional lexicon, but the first, providing fuller discussion under a few major headings, gives a coherent summary account of the basic structural characteristics of drama. Though this volume does not purport to be a guide to play writing, it is possible that Part I of the Glossary, taken along with the analyses in the body of the book, may be useful to students interested in the writing of plays.

We have remarked that the first consideration of this manual has been the problem of reading drama with appreciation and understanding. But the editors do not intend to discount the claims of literary history. Much of the historical material, of course, will be provided by the teacher, and some teachers will wish to supplement this manual with readings in the history of the drama. Teachers who wish to stress the historical approach will find a succinct account of the history of the drama in Appendix B. Moreover, the plays printed and analyzed in this book, though chosen primarily to illustrate various dramatic modes and problems, do provide a rather full representation of the major developments in dramatic history.

Instructors and students should note the dual system of line-numbering. In plays which are in verse-form or largely in verse-form and in the prologues and epilogues written in verse, the lines are numbered consecutively; in prose plays, the line-numbering is by pages, and the numbers are in the middle space on the page. When the latter system of numbering is used, references to specific passages give first the page-number, then the column (*a* for left, *b* for right), then the line-number. Thus "p. 124a, 25-30" means "page 124, left-hand column, lines 25 to 30."

The index provides some guide not only to the subjects discussed recurrently throughout the book but also to plays, dramatists, and other literary works and figures mentioned briefly in the discussions.

New Haven, Conn.   C. B.
Seattle, Wash.   R. B. H.
February 1, 1948

PART ONE

PROBLEMS
of the
DRAMA

1. *Dialogue and Action*

ABOOK about the drama should perhaps begin with a definition of the drama. But in one sense the book could only end with such a definition: only by careful examination of various plays can we really understand the drama. Of course, there is another sense in which drama does not seem at all difficult to define, for some of its characteristics are easily recognized by everybody. On the obvious level its distinctions from prose, fictional or non-fictional, are as sharp as those of poetry. Everyone knows that in drama there is little or no place for "description" or for other comment made directly by the author; that the work consists almost entirely of words spoken directly by the characters, that is, of dialogue; that the work can be read or that it can be seen in the form of stage-presentation; that plays are often written in verse-form.

I. TYPES OF DIALOGUE

Of these generally familiar facts, the dialogue-form is to most people probably the distinguishing characteristic. At a superficial glance, it seems that a play consists, except for some stage directions, of conversation—people talking to each other directly—and that when this goes on long enough, we have a play. But have we? To answer that question, we need to do some looking into the nature of dialogue, and to try to see just what goes on there. Let us take first a sample of the interchange of question and answer which we find in a court-trial. We have all seen newspaper reproductions of such "dialogues"; in their printed form they do not look much different from the text of a play, for the trimmings that we find in fiction are all gone, and spoken words are the essence of the matter.

Courtroom Dialogue. In the trial in which the following actual dialogue took place, the physician (Dr. Armbruster) of a murdered man (Sir Henry Laurel) is being questioned by the Defense Attorney (Fermor Biggs):

"Was blood from the wounds on Laurel's head stopped or flowing when you examined the body?" Biggs asked.
"Stopped," the doctor replied.
"What was the condition of Sir Henry's face? Was it bloody?"
"There was a small clot of dry blood on the nostril and upper lip. There might have been a little oozing from a wound, but I am not sure."

3

Biggs handed Armbruster a photograph of the body showing a streak of blood across the face.

"The body must have been moved," the physician stated emphatically. "Blood will not flow uphill out of the ear and nostrils."

Jury Foreman Jacob Stone interrupted the questioning to ask the doctor if there was any indication of the body being lifted.

"I did not examine it sufficiently to answer that question," Armbruster replied

"Would you say that the burns you saw would have prevented Sir Henry from moving from the bed?" the juror continued.

"No, Sir Henry would have been capable of moving if the burns preceded the blows."

"Did he move after the blows?" Stone asked.

"In my opinion, Sir Henry did not move himself after the blows were struck," the doctor added.

Justice Sir Claude Weeks asked, "How long would it have taken a normal, healthy person to die then?"

"A normal, healthy person does not die," Armbruster responded candidly. The courtroom roared with laughter, including the white-wigged, red-robed Weeks.

As far as superficial matters are concerned, only a slight change or two would be necessary to arrange these lines as they would appear in a play. Instead of "Biggs asked" and "the doctor replied" we would find the names preceding the speeches. For the fifth paragraph, which describes the use of the photograph, there could be an extra line to this effect: "Take a look at this photograph of the body. You see that streak of blood across the face. What do you make of that?" Adverbs such as "emphatically" could be used as a part of stage directions, or alternatively, the emphasis could be indicated by changes in the present wording. Foreman Stone's interruption is obviously an interruption, and what he says could easily be a direct quotation. And so on.

Now from this it may appear that the composition of a play, or of dramatic dialogue, may be merely the product of a rearrangement of a series of speeches and actions into the form of direct discourse. But clearly this is not true. The excerpt from the report of the Laurel trial is obviously not drama at all. It may convey a certain excitement and even exhibit a mild tension—qualities which one expects of true drama, but still it is not drama. This fact, anyone can realize. But why is this true?

Is it not that the purpose of this passage is wholly different from any purpose which we could imagine drama to have? The purpose of the interchange is to *secure factual information*, whereas the securing or the giving of factual information is not the function of drama or any other literary form. This kind of exchange of lines could go on for three hundred pages, and we would still be essentially just where we had started. We would have a few more facts about a murder, but nothing more. Note that among the things not done by such a dialogue is the portrayal of *character*. Such questions and answers could go on indefinitely, and we would still know practically nothing about the attorney, the jurymen, the judge, or the witnesses. The bringing forth of great quantities of factual information would of course give us some ground for inferences, but we would not really see characters in action. The complex world of human motives and values would come into the picture only accidentally if it came in at all. Obviously, therefore, dialogue which is to do more than furnish a statistical record of conduct must be carefully managed; it cannot be arranged in a mere chronological order; and what goes into it must be determined by some more significant purpose than the discovery and clarification of a series of external facts. It must do more than fill the blanks in a questionnaire. Let us therefore look at another kind of dialogue, one in which, it is true, there are many questions and answers, but one in which we learn far more significant matters than in the account of the murder-trial.

The "Conversation." The following selection is from a type of work which the author himself, W. S. Landor, designated by the term *Conversation.* The date of this imaginary conversation is the seventeenth century; the participants are Bossuet, a famous bishop, and the Duchess de Fontanges, mistress of Louis XIV:

Bossuet: Mademoiselle, it is the King's desire that I compliment you on the elevation you have attained.

Fontanges: O monseigneur, I know very well what you mean. His Majesty is kind and polite to everybody. The last thing he said to me was, "Angélique! do not forget to compliment Monseigneur the Bishop on the dignity I have conferred upon him, of almoner to the Dauphiness. I desired the appointment for him only that he might be of rank sufficient to confess you, now you are Duchess. Let him be your confessor, my little girl. He has fine manners."

B.: I dare not presume to ask you, mademoiselle, what was your gracious reply to the condescension of our royal master.

F.: Oh! yes, you may! I told him I was almost sure I should be ashamed of confessing such naughty things to a person of high rank, who writes like an angel.

B.: The observation was inspired, mademoiselle, by your goodness and modesty.

F.: You are so agreeable a man, monseigneur, I will confess to you directly, if you like.

B.: Have you brought yourself to a proper frame of mind, young lady?

F.: What is that?

B.: Do you hate sin?

F.: Very much.

B.: Are you resolved to leave it off?

F.: I have left it off entirely since the King began to love me. I have never said a spiteful word of anybody since.

B.: In your opinion, mademoiselle, are there no other sins than malice?

F.: I never stole anything; I never committed adultery; I never coveted my neighbor's wife; I never killed any person, though several have told me they should die for me.

B.: Vain, idle talk! Did you listen to it?

F.: Indeed I did, with both ears; it seemed so funny.

B.: You have something to answer for, then.

F.: No, indeed, I have not, monseigneur. I have asked many times after them and found they were all alive; which mortified me.

B.: So, then! you would really have them die for you?

F.: Oh, no, no! but I wanted to see whether they were in earnest, or told me fibs; for, if they told me fibs I would never trust them again. I do not care about them; for the King told me I was only to mind *him*.

B.: Lowest and highest, we all owe to his Majesty our duty and submission.

F.: I am sure he has mine; so you need not blame me or question me on that. At first, indeed, when he entered the folding-doors, I was in such a flurry I could hear my heart beat across the chamber; by degrees I cared little about the matter; and at last, when I grew used to it, I liked it rather than not. Now, if this is not confession, what is?

B.: We must abstract the soul from every low mundane thought. Do you hate the world, mademoiselle?

F.: A good deal of it; all Picardy, for example, and all Sologne; nothing is uglier—and, oh, my life! What frightful men and women!

B.: I would say, in plain language, do you hate the flesh and the Devil?

F.: Who does not hate the Devil? If you will hold my hand the while, I will tell him so.—I hate you, beast! There now. As for flesh, I never could bear a fat man. Such people can neither dance nor hunt, nor do anything that I know of.

B.: Mademoiselle Marie-Angélique de Scoraille de Rousille, Duchess de Fontanges! do you hate titles and dignities and yourself?

F.: Myself! does anyone hate me? Why should I be the first? Hatred is the worst thing in the world: it makes one so very ugly.

B.: To love God, we must hate ourselves. We must detest our bodies, if we would save our souls.

F.: That is hard; how can I do it? I see nothing so detestable in mine! Do you? To love *is* easier . . .

F.: . . . And now let me tell you, my lord, you compose such pretty funeral sermons, I hope I shall have the pleasure of hearing you preach mine . . .

B.: To me the painful duty will, I trust, be spared: I am advanced in age; you are a child.

F.: Oh, no! I am seventeen.

B.: I should have supposed you younger by two years at least . . .

As in the previous quotations from the murder-trial record, a considerable part of this Conversation depends upon questions. But note the difference between the trial witness's answers and the Duchess's answers: every word the latter speaks gives some clue to her character, so that, by the end of even the short section here reprinted, we have a pretty clear notion of what sort of person she is. She is naive, with both the advantages and the disadvantages of naiveté: on the one hand, she is completely candid and without hypocrisy, and her pleasure in her own charms is a long way from adult vanity; on the other hand, her simplicity is such that she misses the real point of all the questions. She is well-meaning but tactless; she jumps to conclusions; she is completely literal-minded. She is unable to understand such simple and well-known figures of speech as "the world," "the flesh," and "the devil"; she has had, so to speak, no literary training or experience. Note, further, that as we read we also get some impression of the Bishop's character. In part he is the conventional clergyman; his pastoral inquiries and comments are mostly predetermined. But there is also some individualization: the almost exaggerated humility of the references to the king, the exasperation of tone in such phrases as "Vain, idle talk!" And above all he is a master of irony, as we see especially in his final remark about the Duchess's age.

So we see two characters developing before us, and since they are quite different, the contrast, we may say, is "dramatic"; that is, there is more "tension" than if the bishop were speaking to a conventional, devout adult. And now observe the way in which Landor complicates this contrast somewhat, that is, tries to keep it from being too simple and obvious, by having the Duchess tell about her "checking up" on the men who said that they would die for her. In her way, we see, she is *somewhat of a moralist* too; she is just a little more than the beautiful and stupid mistress of the king. This union of apparently contradictory qualities, this complexity, makes her a more complete and plausible character, not unlike one we might find in a good play or story.

Further, we may note that Landor is not quite content with mere conversation; at one place physical action is clearly implied. The Duchess will tell the devil she hates him if the Bishop will hold her hand. Then, "I hate you, beast! There now." This is just what is seen in plays: the meaning of the spoken lines is constantly supplemented by physical action.

Finally, we may note that, to use a phrase often found in literary study, the contrast of the two characters "says something." Behind the contrast of characters is a further contrast—we might even call it a philosophical one—between two ways of life: the contrast between devotion to a heavenly master and devotion to an earthly master. Yet even here we find a complication: the Duchess is completely devoted to the king, and yet sticks closely to the formulae of a religion with which her life is so inconsistent. The Bishop speaks as the servant of God, yet his devotion, we notice, is qualified by his devotion to an earthly master. So we get some sense of the conflicting claims to which man is subject and thus of the basic complexity of experience.

The Difference Between the "Conversation" and Drama. We have, then, the presentation of character, with some complexity in the characters; the dramatic contrast of characters; some implied physical action, such as we might see on the stage; and, behind it all, an implied commentary on the nature of human experience. In every one of these respects, Landor's Conversation is like drama. Yet it clearly is not drama; no one is likely to mistake it for a scene in a play. Why?

1. There is no "plot," no real action taking place. The scene displays the characters, but we do not see them in action. The relationship between the Bishop and the Duchess is only casual and formal; it is the product of a purely external matter, the king's wish. It is not organic; it is not the product of a situation in which both are involved. There is no development or change in character; no decisions are being made; no action will result from the interview. No situation is created which must develop to a logical conclusion. The future conduct and lives of the participants will be fundamentally unaffected by the interview, whereas in good drama each scene

has some definite influence or relation to what happens sul s..quently. Otherwise, a good dramatist would throw it out as "uneconomical." But this conversation exists for its own sake; it shows the characters for a minute, and that is all. Think how different the situation would be if the bishop were trying to persuade the duchess to leave the king or to use her influence to get the king to favor some duke or to deprive a count of an appointment. We would then look forward to the outcome of the situation; whereas here there is strictly speaking no "outcome" at all.

2. The Conversation does not have the directness and continuity which it would have as part of a play. It does have "form," of course; the formal series of questions partly determines its structure. But the structure is also influenced by the nature of conversation itself, by its tendency to go from subject to subject by association rather than by logic. For instance, the question, "Do you hate the world?" would logically follow close upon "Do you hate sin?" but the mention of sin leads the duchess off into the digression about her admirers. That is precisely what everyday conversations do. But this kind of "realistic" conversational fullness Landor could hardly use in a play, where he would have to stick—or give the appearance of ⌐ticking—very close to the business of advancing the action.

So, though we have many characteristics of the drama here, we do not have drama. We do not have central action which binds the parts together, unifies them, and gives them direction. What we need to do now, therefore, is to try to see what meaningful action is and how it works.

2. THE MEANING OF ACTION

By way of a preliminary glance at "action," we may try to see it in "pure" form, that is, isolated as much as possible from the other elements in drama. In fact, we can get at it in its elementary or physical form, though we must keep in mind that "action" includes a great deal more than physical movements. But an account of the physical actions of a group of characters will at least indicate some of the difference between a conversation and a drama. What follows is part of a movie script, and here, you will observe, we can see action reduced to the bare skeleton—indeed, to a sort of blueprint for action.

SHOOTING-SCRIPT FOR *THE GREAT McGINTY*[*]

The last title is imposed over a NIGHT SHOT of a drinking establishment. Now we HEAR some rumba music and we TRUCK FORWARD SLOWLY TOWARD THE CAFÉ . . . DISSOLVE TO:

A PRETTY RUMBA DANCER PERFORMING IN FRONT OF A BAND

We see a few customers IN THE FOREGROUND but they are not particularly interested. In other words, they ¿ive one look then turn away. Noticing the lack of interest she bends over and grabs her skirt.

[*] From Arthur Mizener's "Our Elizabethan Movies," *Kenyon Review*, 194? By permission of the author and publisher.

CUT TO:

THE RUMBA DANCER FROM WAIST DOWN

Slowly she starts to pull up her skirt. The CAMERA follows her

CUT TO:

LOW CAMERA SHOT UP AT THE TABLE OF MEN

They are not paying any attention. One of them is lighting a pipe. As he turns his head away to escape the cloud of smoke his eye catches the legs on the floor. There is a slight double-take, then he gives the legs his undivided attention. A second later the other men at the table follow his gaze. Now the whole table looks on stonily. In the BACKGROUND we see McGinty working at the bar but he is OUT OF FOCUS.

CUT TO:

THE GIRL'S LEGS AS SHE DANCES

CUT TO:

THE GIRL'S UPPER HALF

She looks around and is amused at the effect her legs are having.

This is pure action (or at least action about as pure as we shall ever get). It is not very dramatic. True, it would not be fair to say that it is meaningless, that it does not express something. It does: but as *action* it expresses very little; and even as acted out by a competent actress whose gesture and facial expression might conceivably add a good deal to the meaning of the scene, the "meaning" of the scene is blurred and vague. Obviously, this is a typical cheap café, on, so far as we can tell, a typical night. But we do not know enough about the characters—about the men at the table, or about the pretty rumba dancer—for the scene to have much more than the meaning which any "slice of life" would give us. Even a very competent actress, limited as here to mere gesture and facial expression, could not tell us much about what is going on in the pretty rumba dancer's mind. What the script thus far gives us is *pantomime*—a very old art and for certain types of material highly expressive, but an art which, deprived as it is of the use of words, can get at the inner life of its characters only very indirectly.

The Script and the Completed Movie. But, of course, as will have already occurred to the reader, it is hardly fair to take the shooting script of the movie in this kind of literal fashion. After all, the shooting script is only a set of directions and suggestions to be employed by the director as he makes the "movie" proper come to life on the film. This is all very true, though we ought to observe that *what the director will add here is a kind of commentary*, a kind of interpretation which, even though it does not make use of words, still is an interpretation over and above the "pure action" we have already considered.

Mr. Arthur Mizener has indicated some of the things which the movie camera will do to transform the recipe-for-action of the script into the meaningful completed picture. Let us reread the last lines of the section of shooting script quoted above, and then go on with his comments on what the camera is doing:

CUT TO:

THE GIRL'S UPPER HALF

She looks around and is amused at the effect her legs are having.

"Once more the camera," comments Mr. Mizener, "apparently about its simple narrative business, is unobtrusively stressing certain implications. It picks out and isolates the girl's legs, the only part of her that exists for the men at the table, and then cuts to the girl's face, as if to contrast the human intelligence, which does not exist for these men, with the legs which so emphatically do. The girl's amusement is a comment, not so much on the men's attitude, as on the ludicrousness of the whole situation."

In other words, the camera by arranging the "action" for us, by directing our attention, first to one detail, then to another, by suggesting contrasts, by repeating a detail for emphasis or by repeating it with a significant variation is actually suggesting to us how we are to "take the scene"— is suggesting to us what the scene "means." Words are not being used to do this, it is true, but it ought to be abundantly evident that we are not getting mere "action" either. The camera is sifting the material and arranging it for us in a meaningful pattern. It is making an interpretation of the scene.

Actually, the scene in question becomes, as the movie develops, even further removed from "raw" action. The McGinty who, as the script tells us, is to be shown working behind the bar, has gone up very far in the world. He has been gradually pushed up the political ladder by the Boss's machine, until he has been actually elected governor of the state. But there is a political fiasco. The Great McGinty, the Boss, the Politician, and the Boss's Bodyguard barely escape to a banana republic. Now the Great McGinty has a job, perhaps somewhat more appropriate to his talents, behind the bar in the "drinking establishment" where the scene we have already discussed opens.

The story of McGinty's rise and fall is told in flashback. The section of the shooting script which we have read introduces McGinty and the rumba dancer. The next shots pick up the other characters who will be important in the story.

TRUCKING SHOT—PAST THE TABLES AT RINGSIDE

The CAMERA represents the girl's eyes and sees what she sees as she dances by. In this way we pass the rest of the ringside tables, with all the occupants looking down under us. Be sure to have some bald heads here. The heads turn slowly as we pass. A waiter is circulating between the tables serving drinks but we do not see his face. [This waiter turns out to be The Politician.] The last table we see is back a little from the dance floor. Here seven men are playing poker. With their BACKS TO US and unrecognizable, are the Boss and Dr. Jarvis, the latter in a green eyeshade. Directly across the table in a strong light is a pale drunken young American, Thompson. [It is to Thompson and the rumba dancer that McGinty tells the main story.] Two American and two Spanish types complete the game. Behind Thompson stands Louie twiddling a toothpick. The top of the frame cuts him off at the necktie. (NOTE: this is the exact shot we use at the end of the picture except for Thompson who will have left the game.) A second after we come in on the SHOT Thompson throws down his cards disgustedly and gets to his feet unsteadily.

Mizener goes on to comment: "You see how economical and quietly purposeful this apparently casual opening is. Both the rumba dancer and Thompson . . . [to whom McGinty will tell the story of his rise and fall] have been placed for us, and distinct but not too easily recognizable images of all the leading figures of the main story have been fixed in our minds. These images will shadow the characters as we follow them through the main story, until the picture returns to this shot again at its close, and the two impressions of the characters merge. Furthermore, everything in this sequence is being used to set the tone, the slightly cynical, very amused attitude of the picture to its story. Our attitude toward the rumba dancer and her audience is our attitude toward the political world of the main story; we have seen The Boss, The Reformer, The Politician and The Bodyguard doing what they have always done, but now without hypocrisy, in a natural and fitting atmosphere. Best of all, perhaps, we have seen the shrewd, friendly, essentially simple McGinty at a job which is in itself almost a definition of his character."

The scene, then, properly understood, becomes, as the moving picture develops, a commentary on McGinty and the other characters. The cheap café is their natural haunt: McGinty is "naturally" a better bartender than he is a governor, and the political crash which has sent him behind the bar in this cheap cafe has put him where he will really be more comfortable—more thoroughly at home.

Action and Character. Action, then, apart from its reference to character is relatively meaningless. This wordless opening scene from the movie—even though it is wordless—does not violate the principle. Action, even violent and exciting action, unless it becomes the action of concrete characters, soon becomes tiresome. Not even the Western picture or the murder mystery is able to get by without a certain minimum of character. We are, as human beings, simply not able to get interested in the murder of one cipher by another. Nor are we interested in mere summaries of action. It is not enough to know that McGinty, for example, fell from the job of governor to that of bartender. If it were, the movie's first scene (which, we are told, is the same as the last) would be enough.

If it is true, then, that physical action can become dramatic only as it becomes meaningful, we shall have little difficulty in seeing why dialogue is of tremendous importance in drama. For language is perhaps our richest and most subtle means of significant expression. Gesture, though it goes hand and hand with dramatic dialogue—even the Landor Conversation demands gesture when the duchess takes the bishop's hand—gesture is highly limited. In the first place, the more subtle aspects of facial expression, for example, tend to be lost on most of the audience, who sit too far back from the stage to be able to see it clearly.

By means of the "close-up," it is true, movies may more or less overcome this particular handicap. And Mr. Mizener's comments on the script of

The Great McGinty have suggested some of the other special resources which the cinema has at its disposal. This is not the place to go into a thorough-going discussion of the differences between the cinema and the drama proper. It is possible that one should distinguish between the "cinematic" and the "dramatic" effect; it is also possible to argue that any art becomes most thoroughly an art when it is content to exploit its own special resources, and, therefore, argue further that the cinema is primarily a *visual* not an *auditory* art.

But regardless of whether the movies should make much or little use of dialogue, there can be no question that the legitimate drama is primarily an auditory art, and that the dialogue is its primary element. For drama, there-fore, costumes, setting, and even acting itself are, finally, secondary. It is the word which is primary here; and this fact may explain why a good play retains so much of its dramatic power even when merely read in the study or the classroom.

The Relation of Dialogue to Action. But though dialogue is primary in drama, the dialogue must, of course, be of a certain kind. In the courtroom dialogue which we first examined, we have dialogue which is definitely not dramatic, even though it concerns action, and violent action at that. The questions in that dialogue are concerned with eliciting information, with establishing what happened. *They have to do with the past;* they are deter-mined by the nature of past events. The only audience at which they are aimed is the jury.

In the Landor Conversation, the questions are not concerned with the past at all, for here there is no past. They are meant to lead the duchess to self-examination and thus to give the reader a sense of her character and of the differences between her character and the bishop's. Everything is *in the present.* In drama, on the other hand, the questions may elicit informa-tion about the past, and will certainly illustrate present character. But, primarily, they are concerned with the future; that is they are meant to be a *stimulus to further action.* In a play, every scene except the last is looking ahead: the play must be progressive.

The action develops and moves forward—however, it moves forward, not placidly, but with a sense of strain and conflict. There is struggle; forces come into collision; decisions are made. The action is not only meaningful action; it has the tensions of active conflict within it.

There is a sense, of course, in which all literature involves a certain amount of conflict. Yet, drama tends to accentuate conflict. And the fact that it does so often emphasize conflict is in accord with its special potenti-alities. As we shall see a little later, drama, compared with some of the other arts, is limited in its ability to change scene, in its ability to show the slow development of character, in its ability to show us a character from as many points of view as, say, a novel can. But it can deal powerfully with charac-ters in conflict: problems do come to a head at a particular time; conflicts occur in a particular place; and if the dramatist posts us there, he can dis-play to us with maximum immediacy and power the final struggle itself.

2. *Drama and Other Literary Forms*

I N DISCUSSING some of the characteristics of dramatic dialogue and action, we have said little that is true of the drama alone. The various points which we have made apply almost as well to all kinds of prose fiction. In fact, the term *dramatic*, which comes from the noun *drama*, can also be applied to poetry, not only to narrative poetry, such as that of Chaucer, which naturally has basic resemblances to drama and fiction, but also to lyric poetry, which is often thought of as being quite different from these forms. It may therefore be well to observe in a little more detail just what characteristics the drama shares with other literary forms. We will then be ready to see precisely wherein it differs from them and how it goes about meeting its own particular problems.

1. DRAMA AND FICTION

One way to do this is to examine a specific story and a specific poem and see how they resemble, and how they differ from, drama. Let us take the story first.

A SUM IN ADDITION*

William March

Collins said: "Sure there's a corkscrew in there. You'll find it chained to the wall. All hotels have 'em." And Menefee answered from the bathroom: "Well, there's not one in *here*. Look for yourselves if you boys don't believe me."

"That's a fine way to treat drummers," said Red Smith. "I'll write and complain to the management." He got up and stretched himself. "I'll look in the closet," he said. "Maybe I'll find something to open it with in there."

Menefee came back into the room and put the unopened bottle on the dresser, his head drawn backward and turned at an angle, his eyes squinting up. He ground out the cigarette that had been burning between his relaxed lips. "You boys keep your pants on," he said; "I'll go down and borrow a corkscrew off a bellhop." He put on his coat and went into the hall, closing the door behind him.

Collins sat back and rested his legs on the vacant chair, looking lazily over his shoulder at Red Smith. Red was pulling out drawers noisily, or standing tiptoe to peer at shelves just above his head. Then he stopped, picked up something and came into the room with it. It was a sheet of hotel stationery covered with writing and it had been crumpled into a ball and thrown into the closet.

Red opened the sheet and smoothed it flat, and when he had read it, he passed it to Collins, a peculiar look on his face. "Read this, Wade," he said.

---

* From *Some Like Them Short* by William March. Reprinted by permission of Little, Brown & Company.

Collins read slowly, the paper held close to his eyes. At the right of the sheet, and commencing it, was the following entry: "Cash on hand $17.45."
Then, to the left, were the following entries:

Expenses babyies funerel (about)	$148.00
Wifes hospital bill (about)	65.00
Owe to grocery store	28.17
Back Rent (2 mo.—make it 3)	127.25
Incidentals	25.00
	$394.42

A little farther down the paper were the following words: "Will borrow four hundred dollars from Mr. Sellwood." This sentence was repeated, like an exercise in penmanship, over and over, until the paper was filled with it. At first the words were written boldly, heavily, and there were places where the pen had broken through the paper behind the determination of the writer; but as the writing progressed, the man seemed less sure of himself, as if his courage and his certainty were fading away. The sentences were more perfect here, with an occasional mended letter; they were written more slowly, as if each letter were pondered. The last sentence was not finished at all. It dwindled thinly into wavering illegibility.

Collins had read the thing through and sat with it in his hands. He said sympathetically: "Tough! Tough!" then added: "He knew he couldn't work it out. He knew he was fooling himself; so he crumpled up the paper and threw it in the closet."

Red Smith sat down, resting his elbows on his knees, his bright, coppery hair shining in the light. Suddenly he had a picture of a shabby little man sitting in this same cheap hotel room, going over his problem, over and over, and finding no answer to it. Finally he said: "Don't you suppose Mr. Sellwood let him have the four hundred bucks after all? Why not?"

Collins sighed, the masonic emblem resting on his fat stomach, rising with his breath. He spoke mockingly: "Of course not, Little Sunshine. Of course not! Maybe our friend went to *see* Mr. Sellwood all right, but Mr. Sellwood said that times were hard right then and he had a lot of expenses of his own. I guess that's about the way it worked out."

Red lifted his alert face. "I think you're wrong, Wade, I think everything worked out all right."

But Collins shook his head. "Not a chance, young fellow!" he said. "Not a chance!"

Red replied: "Just the same, I think Mr. Sellwood let him have the four hundred bucks. He was an old friend of the family, you see. Then he got a good job for this fellow that paid more money, and this fellow came back home almost running. He came up the steps three at the time to tell his wife. Everything worked out fine for them after that."

"Maybe he met Santa Claus on the way home," said Wade heavily, "and old Santa slipped the money in his stocking." Then he said more seriously: "The fellow who wrote that is sitting in some other cheap hotel tonight still figuring, and still trying to find an answer, but he won't, because there isn't any answer for him to find."

The door opened then and Menefee stood before them, a corkscrew in his hand. "Everything's okay," he said. "Everything's all set."

"We'll leave it to Menefee," said Red Smith. "Give him the writing, Wade, and let's see what he thinks."

Collins passed over the paper and Menefee examined it carefully, as if he did not understand it, before he looked at the two men, puzzled a little.

"What's it all about? This don't make sense to me."

Collins shook his head. "Good old Menefee. Trust him."

Red laughed a little and said earnestly: "Don't you see the point, Menefee?"

Menefee read the thing through again, turned the paper over and examined the writing once more. "I'm damned if I do," he said helplessly. Then a moment later he added triumphantly: "Oh sure, sure, I see the point now! Sure I do: It's added up wrong."

Red Smith looked at Collins and they both laughed. "It *is* added up wrong!" said Menefee, indignant and a little hurt. "Eight and five are thirteen and eight are twenty-one . . . seven makes twenty-eight, and five thirty-three—not thirty-four, like it is here."

But Collins and Red Smith continued to laugh and to shake their heads.

"All right," said Menefee. "I'm dumb; I admit it." He pulled in his lips and spoke in a high, quavering voice: "Come on, boys: let your poor old grandmother in on the joke!" He picked up the bottle and poured three drinks into three tumblers, grumbling a little to himself. "I never saw such superior bastards in all my life as you two are," he said.

The Method of the Story. This story turns upon a rather simple contrast: into the humdrum evening of a group of salesmen in a cheap hotel tumbles a bit of pure pathos—the itemized list of expenses of some poor devil who had spent an evening in the same room trying to figure out a way of paying the bills incurred by his wife's illness and his baby's death. The story depends largely upon contrasts: the contrast between the misfortunes of the earlier occupant and the relative well-being of the salesmen, between the desperation of his evening and the casual gaiety of theirs, between the indifference which we may expect of them and the actual sympathy which they show, between the different responses to and understandings of the note.

The same hotel room is the scene of two totally different types of evening spent by people in wholly different circumstances. Yet the link between them is more than that of place: there is also a certain amount of sympathy. But the sympathy itself involves another contrast, for the salesmen are not particularly likely sources of sympathy. They have no personal regard for the former occupant; they do not even know him. And, hunting for a corkscrew in order to have drinks, they do not seem likely to be sensitive to the "still sad music of humanity."

By using contrast, the author gives the impression of being restrained and *objective*. He uses no device to help pump up sympathy. He lets the pathetic document speak for itself; he does not "play up" the pathos by choosing especially sensitive characters or a setting (a Christmas Eve scene, for instance) designed to catch the reader on his softer side. Hence the effect of the paper on the characters seems plausible, and we are induced to respond in like manner. In this connection, notice the author's use of Menefee, who is honestly puzzled by the note and can see nothing in it but a mistake in addition. The contrast between him and the other men is very important in creating the final effect of the story. For one thing, this contrast reinforces the objectivity of the story in that it serves further to avoid any impression that pathos is being artificially played up. That is, some people, like Menefee, simply don't have the understanding necessary for sympathy. Then his lack of understanding leads to the amusement of the others and to his irritation at their amusement: thus the author ends the story not on a note of sadness but on one of ironic amusement. He does not try to wring the last drop of pity from the situation; instead he returns the salesmen to the normal world of talk and banter. The sense of pity is gone. The characters are ordinary men, and they are not made to act in an extraordinary fashion.

Further, Menefee's lack of comprehension reinforces the ironic point of the story. Menefee does not think of himself as a callous man, nor do his friends regard him as callous. He would probably be affected by grief before his eyes, grief touching someone that he knew. But, like the Duchess de Fontanges in Landor's Conversation, he simple lacks the imagination necessary to grasp a case that is not close to home.

Through him, then, we get a glimpse of the world with which the writer of the note must struggle: not an essentially hard-hearted or cruel world, but a world too busy, too obsessed with its own concerns to be able to participate imaginatively in the plight of others. The author has already skillfully prepared us for this conclusion by presenting us with Collins's view of Mr. Sellwood as a possible helper of the note-writer. In both cases the stress is not on hardness and unfeelingness. Menefee can honestly see only the mistake in addition: ironically, he knows what it "adds up to" as far as the figures are concerned, but not in any more significant way. He habitually reads the world in terms of figures. But whatever the motive, the fact is that he—and the world—are still callous. We have a final sense of hopelessness because we realize that the callousness springs not from calculated cruelty but from the inability of human beings to break through their ordinary habits.

The Story as Drama. So much for the story itself. Now of what use is it in understanding drama? In many ways it is very much like drama: the method is *objective* (that is, the author refrains from comment on the situation), the effect depends upon *sharp contrasts*, there is very *little description*, and the situation is advanced almost entirely by *dialogue*. And, in addition to these matters which we have already seen, the story uses one important technical device in the same way that drama does. Menefee's failure to understand the paper, we have seen, really points the effect of the story. Now the story *"builds up to" this effect* just as a play might do it, for about a third of the story is spent on the other two men's talking about the paper before Menefee sees it. The author "holds" this part of the story because it establishes our attitude to the note and thus prepares for the shock caused by Menefee's incomprehension. This arrangement of materials is very important for the effect.

Now obviously the preparatory discussion of the note has to take place when Menefee is out of the room, and Menefee must be got out of the room—not in a forced or unnatural way but by a well "motivated" departure (later we shall discuss motivation at length). This is an ever-present problem in drama. Menefee goes for a corkscrew, and his departure seems perfectly plausible. But the plausibility is not an accident. March makes the departure seem logical by opening the story with a search for the corkscrew, and thus prevents the search from seeming an awkward afterthought, an expedient dragged in after the main business has been introduced. And the paper with the expenses, instead of being a starting point, also comes in very smoothly as a product of the hunt for the corkscrew. This very skillful management of materials shows exactly what the dramatist must do in articulating the parts of his play.

Hence this story might seem easily convertible into a play: we could have a single scene in a hotel room, and the three characters could speak most of the lines almost as they are given in the story, with Menefee going out and returning at the proper time. There would be no serious mechanical problems. But we would soon be aware that something was missing, that the dramatic version was a good deal less effective than the story version. Now, if we can see how a story so like drama still does not work very well as drama, we have taken the major step toward understanding the problems peculiar to drama.

The Difference Between Story and Play. In the first place, the story has very little "action"; what goes on consists almost entirely of the comments of the characters on a situation. Not much happens overtly. The characters talk about a situation instead of participating in it; they are not really influenced by it, and so what we have is a kind of photographic glimpse of static characters. The story is in this respect not unlike Landor's Conversation: characters are exhibited, and a general commentary on human experience is implied. But, in general, drama apparently works with greater success when characters act out a situation themselves instead of merely viewing it, even though they be very diverse and significant spectators.

Second, we should have to leave out one of the most important "characters" of all—the crumpled sheet of paper. Of course, the characters could tell us about it, but this second-hand presentation would deprive it of almost all vitality, besides being extremely awkward. The illiterate spelling tells us much about the man who wrote the note and has much to do with our ability to visualize him imaginatively. We should have to leave out the fact given to us so vividly, though unobtrusively, in the story, that the line "Will borrow four hundred dollars from Mr. Sellwood" is first written boldly and heavily, then less confidently, and finally in its last form was left unfinished. The sentence, "It dwindled thinly into wavering illegibility," a detail which suggests so eloquently the writer's final despair, we should have to forego entirely. One of the men could describe this, but we would then see it through him rather than directly. Further, it would have to be a cruder description, for the author's neatness and precision would be out of character in the men. Yet this one piece of economical literary expression is very useful in a story made up mostly of the colloquial dialogue of rather unpolished people.

Third, we should have to leave out—or else present very awkwardly in Red's words—the insight into Red's mind which the author uses: "Suddenly he had a picture of a shabby little man in this same cheap hotel, going over his problem, over and over, and finding no answer to it." The loss might not be fatal, but the omission of the passage, which establishes the concrete form of Red's imaginative sympathy with the man, might reduce the plausibleness of the sympathy. This passage shows what the omniscient author can do that a dramatist cannot do: give a direct, immediate account of mental operations.

In summary, we may observe that the second and third points are really amplifications of the first: because of what it cannot do, drama demands a more overt form of action. The ability of fiction to describe setting and properties of all kinds, to look both at the outer world of things and the inner world of the mind, to shift easily from present to past, means that it has a variety of resources with which to take an apparently slight or trivial situation and extend it, as it were, into a much fuller and richer meaning. It can take a difference of attitude which appears only at the level of casual conversation (*A Sum in Addition*) and give it dramatic substance. Lacking all these devices, drama must present the difference of attitude in an actual clash of character, where the words are not merely descriptive but are accompaniments of action or indications of action to come.

Another Story. Now take another kind of story, de Maupassant's *A Piece of String*, which can easily be made available for the student on the reserve shelf. It has more "action," but it presents still greater difficulties than *A Sum in Addition* to the dramatist. The action is in at least ten scenes, some of them "moving," and several requiring lengthy description. First we see people on "all the roads around Goderville" and then "in the public square of Goderville." Maître Hauchecorne finds the piece of string—a most important scene—as he is "directing his steps toward the public square." Then we have street scenes, an inn scene, and a scene at the Mayor's; and "moving scenes" as Hauchecorne moves about Goderville and Breaute talking to people. In fact, up until the deathbed scene, nearly all the action is of this kind. All this would provide insuperable difficulty to the dramatist. He could not deal with the large number of scenes without greatly expanding the materials; he could not do the crowd scenes which de Maupassant describes at length to establish the psychological and ethical atmosphere; he could not show Hauchecorne traveling around and buttonholing everybody to protest his innocence—a most important part of the story. Note also how many explanations there are about what goes on in Hauchecorne's mind—all very difficult to get into dialogue form.

Here, then, are further differences between story and drama. And we can easily imagine another type of story in which there is extended com ment by the author or a great deal of direct psychological analysis. Obviously drama would have to attack the subjects of such stories in a completely different way. Does this mean that drama is a cruder or less effective form than fiction? Not at all. It simply means that drama is a highly specialized form of literature which can do some things supremely well but which must handle matters in its own way. As we shall see, it has some positive advantages; but perhaps we can best learn about it at the start by looking further into what it cannot do.

2. DRAMA AND POETRY

To understand further the special ways in which the drama works, we may do well to compare it with another literary form, poetry. Here, the contrast is not quite on the same footing as that between fiction and drama. For, as we shall see later, drama and poetry can be combined. We may have, as in the plays of Shakespeare, great drama which is also great poetry. Yet the comparison between the treatment of a theme in drama and the treatment of it in a lyric poem may tell us much again about the nature of dramatic statement of theme.

TO A MOUSE

On Turning Her up in Her Nest with the Plough
November, 1785

Robert Burns

1

Wee, sleekit, cowrin, tim'rous beastie,
O, what a panic's in thy breastie!
Thou need na start awa sae hasty
    Wi' bickerin brattle!
I wad be laith to rin an' chase thee,   5
    Wi' murdering pattle!

2

I'm truly sorry man's dominion
Has broken Nature's social union,
An' justifies that ill opinion
    Which makes thee startle   10
At me, thy poor earth-born companion
    An' fellow mortal!

3

I doubt na, whyles, but thou may thieve;
What then? poor beastie, thou maun live!

1. *sleekit*, sleek. 4. *bickering brattle*, sudden scamper. 5. *laith to rin*, loath to run. 6. *pattle*, paddle. 13. *whyles*, sometimes. 14. *maun*, must.

A daimen icker in a thrave   15
    'S a sma' request;
I'll get a blessin wi' the lave,
    An' never miss 't!

                    4

Thy wee-bit housie, too, in ruin!
Its silly wa's the win's are strewin!   20
An' naething, now, to big a new ane,
    O' foggage green!
An' bleak December's win's ensuin
    Baith snell an' keen!

                    5

Thou saw the fields laid bare an' waste,   25
An' weary winter comin fast,
An' cozie here, beneath the blast,
    Thou thought to dwell,
Till crash! the cruel coulter past
    Out thro' thy cell.   30

                    6

That wee bit heap o' leaves an' stibble,
Has cost thee monie a weary nibble!
Now thou's turned out, for a' thy trouble,
    But house or hald,
To thole the winter's sleety dribble,   35
    An' cranreuch cauld!

                    7

But Mousie, thou are no thy lane,
In proving foresight may be vain:
The best-laid schemes o' mice an' men
    Gang aft a-gley,
An' lea'e us nought but grief an' pain,   40
    For promis'd joy!

                    8

Still thou art blest, compared wi' me!
The present only toucheth thee:
But och! I backward cast my e'e,   45
    On prospects drear!
An' forward, tho' I canna see,
    I guess an' fear!

The Method of the Poem. The theme of Burns's poem is closely related to that of March's story: the imaginative response to misfortune. But while in the story we have a dialogue about the misfortune, with different degrees

15. *daimen icker in a thrave,* occasional ear in a shock. 17. *lave,* rest. 21. *big a new ane,* build a new one. 22. *foggage,* grass. 24. *baith snell,* both sharp. 34. *But,* without. *hald,* dwelling. 35. *thole,* endure. 36. *cranreuch cauld,* hoar frost cold. 37. *no thy lane,* not alone. 40. *Gang aft a-gley,* go often awry.

of comprehension of it, Burns's poem takes the form of a meditation upon the misfortune. Both are dramatic: the story because of the concrete situation and the conflicts implied by and growing out of it; the poem because it also grows out of a special concrete occasion and because the meditation is addressed to the mouse. In fact, the meditation comes close to doing what Browning's dramatic monologues do, that is, introducing by implication the responses that the other character in the dialogue makes or might make. At least the plowman does imagine what goes on in the tiny creature's brain as it scampers away, and he goes on to make an apology as if the mouse actually were listening and could understand it. The apology is clearly on the whimsical side, but it is serious too, as we shall see. But first we should stress the whimsicalness or amusement of the speaker, the fact that, although he recognizes the pathos of the mouse's situation, he does not stress the pathos in a way that would produce a sentimental effect.

For one thing, the speaker's attitude is essentially intellectual: he is interested in the meaning of the situation rather than in the feeling it evokes. He does not express pity merely for the self-indulgent pleasure of feeling pity; the pity is, so to speak, merely introductory to the act of reflection. As early as stanza 2, Burns introduces a philosophical generalization which immediately lifts the poem out of the realm of mere "emoting." Then, too, if the speaker were a mere man of feeling, we might expect him to do something about remedying the mouse's situation so that he could enjoy the feeling of kindness; instead he accepts the situation as an accomplished fact, a subject for reflection. (Consider a similar device for the avoidance of sentimentality in *A Sum in Addition*.)

Second, the possible pathos is reduced by the humor of incongruity, which is very unobtrusively but clearly at work in the poem. The man addresses the tiny mouse—in part at least—as an equal. The man is represented as interfering in the life of the mouse, instead of vice versa, as is the usual view. The mouse has an "ill opinion" of the man instead of the reverse. The mouse is afraid when he need not be. This use of contradictions is a clear reversal of the sentimental, which depends upon familiar, expected responses. The author even carries his use of the incongruous into further details in the poem: the mouse has not only a house but also the human quality of "foresight." This is obviously in the mode of whimsy.

Finally we must note certain words which contribute to the effect: such words as *wee, beastie, housie, silly*. Three of these words are diminutives, a type of word often used with sentimental effect. But in view of the poet's objectivity—that is, his keeping his distance—and in view of his use of incongruity, these words actually contribute to the effect of humor. It is an affectionate humor, with a touch of condescension; but it is clearly not a way of stressing the "dearness" popular with sentimentalists.

If the poet were concerned only with feeling, there would not be much to do after the first stanza except repeat. But since, despite the whimsy, he has a serious comment to make, he can now go on with the development of his theme. His initial method is unusual, almost startling: he identifies himself with the mouse, despite the break between them. "Nature's social union" openly states the bond; the idea is reinforced at the end of stanza 2 with "me, thy poor, earth-born companion." Stanza 3 continues the theme by minimizing man's case against the mouse as a thief. Stanzas 4, 5, and 6 do two things: they present the fact that the mouse, like man, must have a house for protection against the weather; and the details make his plight concrete and real for us.

If this method seem far-fetched, it may be useful to recognize that Burns is only doing what Walt Disney has done on a much more elaborate scale with Mickey Mouse: Mickey is a mouse in form but otherwise is wholly endowed with human characteristics. He gives us a detached way of looking at ourselves, just as Burns's mouse provides the poet with a new way of looking at human experience.

The Climax. Now observe how the method is used at the climax of the poem: the final identification of man and mouse is in the possession of foresight and in the ironic experience of finding that the "best-laid schemes . . . Gang aft agley." (The imaginative success of the comparison is suggested by John Steinbeck's use of the phrase "of mice and men" as the title of a novel.) Both are victims. But, as we have seen, the endowment of the mouse with foresight is whimsical rather than a piece of serious psychology. For suddenly the whimsy is dropped; bare fact intervenes; the mouse, of course, does not have human foresight. "The present only touches thee." The mouse is the gainer; his absence of imagination is his comfort. Here Burns reverses his method: man and mouse change places. Earlier, man's experience was used to interpret the mouse's; now, the mouse illuminates man. The man who was formerly superior suddenly becomes worse off; he suffers, not in one, but in three dimensions—past, present, and future.

In summary, we may say that the last stanza very neatly does three things: 1. As we have seen, the note of whimsicality gives way to a deeper seriousness; 2. Attention is shifted from the mouse; to exploit the mouse further might seem forced, precious, disproportionate—and thus sentimental; 3. Attention is shifted to the man, who is the only really defined character and therefore the really important figure in the poem. The three functions work together: the seriousness of the man's situation gives point to the sympathy for the mouse and prevents the whimsy from seeming mere triviality; yet that the man's situation, the really important issue, can be presented with the partial amusement evoked by the mouse's misadventure, keeps the man's attitude to himself from seeming strained and sentimental.

The poem can be said to be *dramatic* in these ways: the emotion springs from some definite occasion; the play of thought and feeling is developed in terms of the occasion (rather than expressed in abstract terms); and the poet's attitude to the situation is carefully controlled, even involving dramatic shifts and sharp reversals (that is, it does not get out of hand, becoming sentimental, vague, or monotonous).

EXERCISE: Wordsworth's *Lines Written in Early Spring* is another poem written on the same theme. Is it closer to or farther from drama than *To a Mouse?*

The Poem Compared with Other Forms. Much good poetry is dramatic in the sense that Burns's is, and it is well to remember that these qualities which we call "dramatic" are important in all great literature. Yet, quite obviously, the poem differs sharply from both fiction and drama in the ways in which it get its effects. Burns's poem has even less of overt action than March's story, and less development of character in the usual sense of the word—a point sharply outlined for us by the similarity of the themes (in each case sympathy for another being is accidentally aroused. Because the creature in the poem is not human, the point is made more emphatically, but the poet's problem is more difficult: he must so develop the mouse's situation as to make it an adequate symbol of man's). The special quality of character on which both depend is the imaginative sympathy necessary to grasp the "meaning" of the misfortune which is encountered. The story shows this sympathy in two characters and its absence in a third, who are presented largely by dialogue and with little interior monologue and little direct handling of symbols. In the poem we have only the single character who speaks almost entirely to himself; the writer works rather through the situation of the mouse, which, by close control of imagery and rhythm (which we have not analyzed here), he develops into a rich and exact symbol of the position of man in the world.

It is obvious, then, that turning the poem into a play would present much greater difficulties than dramatizing the story. For, in the accepted sense of the word, nothing "happens." The action would be so slight as to seem meaningless; it would suggest a pretentious author. The meditation—which would be the "dialogue" of the drama—would seem of too trivial origin, and hence forced and sentimental. There is "drama" in the poem in the shifting of moods and the conflict between attitudes; but it is too *inward* to find adequate expression in the types of symbol which the drama uses. In the poem Burns gives this material a wide meaningfulness, whereas in the drama it could be saved from triviality—for it *could* be used—only by appearing as related to some more outward action. The man's meditation, for instance, might conceivably influence some decision which he was going to make. Drama and poetry are both concerned with presenting situations which will be meaningful. Poetry uses imagery, rhythm, symbols, statements, as the words of the author or of some character, spoken to himself or to someone else. Drama depends almost entirely on what people do and say to each other: meanings, thought, feelings must in the main be externalized in conduct (though the conduct need not be violent or sensational).

We have already remarked, however, that the differences between drama and poetry are in general not quite on the same level as those between drama and fiction, for actually great drama and great poetry can be united, as in the works of Shakespeare. Perhaps we can now begin to understand why this is so: in Shakespeare's great dramas the methods of poetry—a more intense treatment of imagery, rhythm, etc., than we ordinarily find in prose—everywhere work with and support (and are supported by) the means appropriate to drama: characters acting and speaking in situations which involve intense conflict.

3. THE ELEMENTS COMMON TO DRAMA AND OTHER FORMS

We can see, in conclusion, that drama, fiction, and poetry have certain common elements, characteristics which distinguish literature from such types of writing as history, biography, philosophy. All the forms of literature, we may say, "present a situation," which stimulates the reader's imagination and thus leads him to apprehend the meaning or meanings latent in it. The situation is specific; but the significance is more extensive: it is 'general." The situation is meant to elicit certain emotional responses, which the author is expected to control by means of his materials (for instance, the other men's laughing at Menefee, Burns's use of the mouse's "foresight"). The situation may be developed by contrast: we see it in Landor's Conversation, in the movie script, and in Burns's poem, and we shall shortly see it used very sharply in Oscar Wilde's *Lady Windermere's Fan* (in fact, as contrast is intensified, developed in emotional terms, and made overt, it becomes the conflict that we especially associate with drama). In drama and story, the situation involves characters talking and acting; poetry may, and often does, use the same materials. The action may be inner or outer, physical or psychological, or a combination of both, with different effects and to fit the medium. An ingredient in the situation is setting: Burns's poem is as closely identified with a rural scene as is March's story with a hotel room and as Wilde's play is with English upperclass homes. Finally, drama and poetry use the same devices of language (imagery, etc.), and drama and story share certain technical devices: focusing the reader's attention, preparing for subsequent effects, "motivating" the occurrences which develop the situation.

4. THE DIFFERENCES BETWEEN DRAMA AND OTHER FORMS

As we have seen, the dramatist cannot himself take a hand as can the novelist or poet. The latter two, of course, are governed by the effects they wish to produce; but the dramatist is restricted in a very special sense. For, whereas poetry *may* use characters speaking and fiction *does* use dialogue a good deal, drama can do nothing else. The author cannot intrude, unless a certain character acts as his mouthpiece; and this device is likely to be prohibitively awkward. Hence a vast amount of materials accessible to fiction and poetry are not accessible to drama.

1. There can be none of the *direct description*—of persons, places, sounds, sights, smells—upon which both fiction and poetry heavily depend; the characters' speeches can do little of this without becoming strained and implausible. As we have seen, drama has no way of letting us see directly the letter so important in March's story; this is true of many other such materials. In acted drama, of course, we have costumes, settings, and "properties"; but drama as literature has no such appurtenances. The absence of a technique of description will account partly for the fact that, in general, drama is much less free than fiction in making changes in place. As a problem either of practical stage-craft or of literary technique, the presenting of a number of places is of more trouble than value. It can hardly be done unobtrusively, and if not expert, it can interfere with the central dramatic effect by distracting attention from the human conflict.*

2. There can be no *direct comments* by the author, on the meaning of an action, a situation, an expression, a gesture, and so on. If made by a character, such comments are likely to be very awkward. It would, for instance, be most difficult to get into a dialogue de Maupassant's comment on Hauchecorne: ". . . with his Norman cunning, he was quite capable of doing the thing with which he was charged." Thus one whole method of giving clues, of suggesting deeper and richer meanings, is out.

3. There can be little direct use of action that is purely mental or psychological; some direct mental probing can be done, as in Shakespeare's soliloquies, but in general this will have to be occasional and subordinate. (Eugene O'Neill has tried to circumvent this difficulty by introducing a new convention: each character speaks not only the usual lines to other characters but also speaks his own thoughts aloud, it being understood that these lines are heard only by the audience.) The drama has no convenient way of letting us see Smith's mental picture of the man in debt, which March gives in a sentence; of letting us grasp the unuttered sensations and half-reflections of Hauchecorne in *A Piece of String;* of presenting the whole substance of Burns's poem; of using the "flashbacks" by which both fiction and the movies can skillfully present, simultaneously, both present and past time. All this does not mean that drama is not concerned with psychological action; far from it. But this action must come in the outer forms of dialogue and action, and what lies behind them must in general come only by implication. Poetry can deal directly with an *inward* situation; drama requires a more perceptible kind of movement.

This catalogue of limitations (fiction, we notice, comes closer to drama as it gives up its own special prerogatives) may make drama seem only a kind of literary shortcut, leading to blunt effects and incapable of much completeness or subtlety. But it is clear that poetry and fiction, for all their greater resources, may, and often do, produce crude and ineffective

* A marked exception is the practice of the Elizabethan drama, in which the use of a great variety of scenes was common. But in the Elizabethan theatre, scenery was at a minimum, and the change of place was effected largely by the imaginations of the audience. Here one can observe the principle of the "conventions of the theatre" in very extensive use. For a fuller discussion of *conventions,* see the Glossary.

work. It is less the wealth of materials than the skill of the user that is important. In proper hands, drama can make its own way very effectively. For instance, the very fact of its limitations (in extent, in ability to cover great reaches of time and space and to include large numbers of fully developed characters) gives it a special kind of concentration of effect. One's attention is focused on a relatively small area of human experience and held there firmly until it has been completely explored. We may extend matters far beyond that area by implications, but there is no room for direct elaboration of the larger world. We stay with our restricted action, and every stroke must count. If the characters may not speak as much as they do in a novel, they must in one sense speak with greater compression. Part of the effect of drama resides in the care with which the dramatist restricts the dialogue to the specific issue with which the play is concerned. Much is eliminated which in a novel would be a legitimate part of a fuller presentation of the characters' lives. Now this compression, this treatment of a bare conflict divested of all attendant circumstances, is itself a source of tension—that effect of "tightening up" which in a work denotes crucial events and in ourselves a heightened attention and concern. And this increase in tension means that the language naturally develops toward that of poetry—toward a more perceptible rhythm and the use of figures that is characteristic of heightened emotion. It has been argued that great drama must take poetic form.* Very frequently it does just that. And now the student will observe that our very discussion of the limitations of drama has gradually led us into another subject—the breaking of those limitations. That is, if drama seems on the one hand to give up so many means of expression that it must become blunt and fumbling, it at the same time makes compensating adjustments. For it gains the precision and exactness essential in literature, first, by the very act of eliminating everything but a bare central theme and, second, by dealing with that theme in the most expressive but at the same time the most controlled kind of language. So, ironically, in considering the special symbols of drama we have inevitably come around to an earlier point, its sharing of the symbols of poetry. One cannot strictly compartmentalize drama, for at its height it combines two modes of concentration.

---

* A character in T. S. Eliot's "A Dialogue on Dramatic Poetry" says, "The human soul, in intense emotion, strives to express itself in verse." Another character says, "All poetry tends toward drama, and all drama toward poetry."

3. *Special Problems of the Drama*

J UST as the drama has certain characteristics in common with other literary forms, so the dramatist has certain problems in common with other writers: he must find concrete ways of saying what he has to say; he must find specific situations through which he can control the responses of the reader; he must explore and develop these situations; he must find and develop characters who give a sense of reality. But because of the differences of drama from other forms, the dramatist must face certain problems. The problems arise out of the two main aspects of drama—the fact that it is limited in scope, and the fact that it works entirely through dialogue.

In theory, there is perhaps no reason why the drama should not be as long as a writer may choose to make it. In the twentieth century both Thomas Hardy and Eugene O'Neill have used the dramatic form in compositions which have far exceeded the traditional five, four, or three-act length. But the fact is that these are striking exceptions to a remarkably consistent practice. The length of drama has always been largely determined by the two or three hours conventionally allotted for public performance; and the influence of this form has been so strong that even writers of "closet" drama (plays not intended to be acted) have largely adhered to it. What we must now do is see what special characteristics the drama takes on because of this generally accepted limitation.*

I. PROBLEMS OF SCOPE

The Dramatic Situation. First of all, then, the dramatist must find a special kind of situation—one that is compact of its own nature or that can be made compact without vital loss. "Selection" is an important principle in the creative process of every artist, but the dramatist must utilize it most rigorously. He must get down to the bare center of a situation. *Hamlet* does not start with the original plot against Hamlet's father, nor *Lady Windermere's Fan* with the original difficulties of Lady Windermere's mother. In both works the experiences of the parents are quite important, and a novelist, for instance, might easily use them at length. But the plays must stick closely to the present and bring in the past only by suggestion.

---

* It is beyond the scope of this book to investigate whether the conventional length of drama has some justification more fundamental than theatrical practice. Such a conclusion is suggested by the general adherence of closet drama to this length. To have more than experimental existence, a longer drama would have to prove itself a better medium of expression than (1) the three-to-five act drama and (2) the average-length novel. This it has not yet done.

Drama works at the height of a situation; it must ignore earlier and later ramifications; if a situation does not have or cannot be made to have some high point, it is not a good one for drama. An obvious corollary is that the dramatist must work with relative rapidity; he must use fairly heavy emphasis in each step; he must cut out every possible suggestion of waste motion.

The student will recall, of course, that Shakespeare wrote a number of "chronicle plays" and that other dramatists have subsequently attempted to present rather complete dramatic records of men's lives. This kind of drama can, of course, be written. It is certain, however, that the problem is very difficult; that from such materials it is almost impossible to put together a "tight" and concentrated play; and that the few successes in the genre are triumphs of genius against all the probabilities. It would be impossible, for instance, to make a good dramatic version of Dickens's *Tale of Two Cities*. It is worth noting, in this connection, that Shakespeare's chronicle plays are less distinguished than his tragedies, which deal with material much more limited in time. In the latter he follows the general dramatic practice of restricting himself to the heart of a situation, the exploding point of a conflict.

Number of Characters. Similarly the dramatist is much more limited than the novelist in the number of characters he can use. In much fiction, of course, as in drama, the conflict tends to shape up between two, or among several, main characters. But while the novelist is under no obligation to accept such a form, the dramatist must center his main action in a character or two. For this reason it is most important that he select the right kind of "lead," that he recognize clearly just what the issue is and whose actions are really significant (later we shall see in Ibsen some tendency to lose sight of the main center of action and thus to get our attention focused on the wrong character). Perhaps we may express it thus: each character bears a greater symbolic weight than in fiction. For there is nothing (except sheer inability to utilize them advantageously) to hinder the novelist from developing as fully as he pleases as many characters as he pleases. In Dickens we often find numerous "main" characters, and in our day there has been developed the "multiplicity" novel involving the use of multiple points of view (e. g., Huxley's *Point Counter Point*). This the dramatist cannot do. If, like Wilde in *Lady Windermere's Fan*, he wishes to present a group of people (Society) whom he sees as not homogeneous but diverse, he will need a number of different characters to indicate the diversity, and his problem becomes this: if he uses as many characters as he wishes, they may be blurred because of inadequate treatment; if he uses a small enough number to permit some fullness of presentation, he may not create the variety he desires. You will shortly observe how Wilde copes with the problem. At any rate, the more numerous the characters, the more subordinate will most of them become; you will notice that the idea of minor or "supporting" characters is one which we associate principally with drama, not with fiction. Such characters exist purely in relationship to someone else's situation. In Dryden's *All for Love*, for example, the Roman general Ventidius has little to do besides try to get Antony away from Cleopatra. He has no independent existence, such as he might well have in a novel.

Place. The dramatist does not have the practically complete freedom in the use of place that the cinema and the novel do. While in theory* he is not restricted, in actual practice he finds it expedient to restrict himself. A tightly concentrated piece of action involving a limited number of characters is not normally spread over a dozen different places; i.e., the more protracted and inclusive in action, the more probable it is that it will have ramifications and echoes in different places; but the more it is cut down to climactic events, the more likely it is to be concentrated in a smaller number of places. The action may be appropriate to some general locale, which will be automatically determined for the dramatist (the action in *Macbeth* is obviously going to take place largely in Scottish castles). But then the dramatist must decide on which specific spots to use and must so work out the episodes that they will occur logically at these spots. As a part of his general problem of motivation, he must make the reader feel that the presence of characters at given spots, and their movement from one locality to another, is thoroughly logical. The more limited he is in space, the greater the demands of this kind that will be made upon him. The ironic fact for him is that if he does this well, we do not notice it; but if he does it badly, we feel that he is moving characters about arbitrarily and thus interfering with the effectiveness of his play.

2. PROBLEMS OF DIALOGUE

Further special problems arise from the fact that the dramatist must do everything in dialogue. As we have already seen, the dialogue must both characterize and lead on toward future action; it must be progressive. In addition to striving for this fundamental quality, the dramatist must face other problems of structure and method that arise from his dependence on dialogue.

Progression. Consider, for instance, the need of the dialogue to be progressive. In each scene the lines must not only be developing the situation with which that scene is concerned, but they must also be quietly directing us toward the future—quietly and yet rapidly, for we cannot have the leisureliness permitted by the amplitude of the novel. A scene that in a novel

* There once was an influential theory, known by the term "unity of place," which held that all the action of a drama had to occur in one place (variously interpreted as being one city, one building, or one room). One justification of the theory was that change of place would seem improbable to the audience. As Dr. Samuel Johnson pointed out, however, the human imagination is perfectly capable of making such transitions in place. But frequent change of place is likely to serve as a distraction, to make the action seem broken up into parts instead of unified, and thus to undermine concentration of effect. Shakespeare's extraordinary abilities enabled him to hold plays together despite unusual freedom in changing scenes. But two things are noteworthy: 1. The great tragedies are relatively compact in respect to place; 2. Even at his freest, Shakespeare is still more restricted in use of place than novelist or movie-writer would be.

might be an illuminating extension of the central action might in a play be only static. The dramatist is under pressure. But he cannot make his scene anticipatory in an artificial or strained way. In a melodrama we may accept a character's saying, "You will hear more of this later on," but in a play of serious intention that would be unbearably clumsy. Note how, in *Lady Windermere's Fan*, all of Act I points easily ahead toward Act II. For Act II presents a ball which various people are anticipating and to which they can therefore refer without giving the impression that the author is awkwardly pointing a finger ahead.

Exposition. The problem of dealing with the past, faced by all writers of narrative, becomes specialized when the sole medium is dialogue. This is the problem of "exposition," that is, of acquainting us with the background facts and the starting situation from which the main action moves forward. Fiction-writer and narrative-poet can begin with direct exposition or interpose it later, and fiction and cinema can both utilize different kinds of flashbacks. In drama the characters themselves must let us know what is what, and they must do it while they are talking about something else. They cannot inform us directly lest they speak for the author instead of themselves and thus get "out of character." What any person says must be consistent with his character generally, and with what he knows and what his auditor or auditors know. If characters are to be plausible, they cannot say things that to them would be stale or superfluous in order that the reader may secure certain information. The information must be implied in lines which are looking ahead rather than back; the dramatist must constantly keep two purposes in mind. He cannot make A. say to B.: "You remember, you came over to my house yesterday and gave me this subscription blank to sign and said that I should get it back to you by 2 o'clock this afternoon." This is easy exposition but entirely unnatural speech (unless we conceive of A. as making a statement of the facts for the sake of legal record). A. would probably say, "Well, here's your paper. I'm not giving you much, though." The reader must still find out the meaning of the paper, but the words "not giving you much" give him the clue from which he starts to make inferences.

The Use of Informative Devices. To a certain extent, presumably, the dramatist may attempt the use of devices which, as we have seen, work more easily in fiction—descriptions, comments, glances within, and other such clues. Older stage conventions (see the section on Conventions in the Glossary) gave him some help here; a good deal of "steering" could be done by the "aside" and by the solitary speaker's lines which were less a soliloquy than helpful hints to the audience. These are less reputable now. But even in their heyday they could not be used without limit; the dramatist had to depend on his standard dialogue to do double duty. As we have seen, description and comment are difficult, for, like everything else, they must not be obtrusive but must be consistent with character and situation. (Occasionally we find a character whose chief function is to interpret—like Enobarbus in Shakespeare's *Antony and Cleopatra*. But he is the exception rather than the rule.) The author's problem is to find circumstances under which explanatory lines—ones that are meant especially for the enlightenment of the reader—can come in without offending our sense of probability, or, still better, without our being aware of their presence. Ben Jonson manages this rather well in *Volpone*, in which Volpone, supposedly on his deathbed, is visited by a series of men who hope to be remembered in his will. Before these men come in, Volpone and his servant Mosca discuss them. This discussion is a zestful relishing of the deception to be practiced upon the visitors. It is perfectly plausible, but at the same time it serves most usefully to inform us about the intentions and characters of the visitors and to prepare us for the visits and make us the more sharply aware of the fluent hypocrisies which both sides speak. Or consider the soliloquy: plainly it cannot be introduced at any moment at which an inward glance may seem useful. Instead, the author must create a physical and psychological situation in which it is a logical mode of expression. Consider Faustus's soliloquy in the final scene of Marlowe's *Dr. Faustus*. Faustus has to face the devils alone, and his terror and despair naturally drive him into anguished expression. We need the aid of no convention to accept this probing of mind and feelings as plausible.

Plausibility. What lies behind this discussion is the necessity that the dialogue be plausible as dialogue, so that mechanical defects will not militate against its efficacy in presenting and developing the situation of the play. That is, dramatic dialogue is a specialized form of conversation and therefore to be effective has to have some of the generic qualities of conversation. Thus it will achieve "naturalness." Now this quality depends on two main things: (1) *what* is included in the conversation; (2) *how* it is said. (1) A "natural" aspect of spoken intercourse is its tendency to introduce irrelevancies, to wander, to be very inclusive. But drama, as we have seen, pares material down to the minimum, and its dialogue cannot wander (as Landor's *Conversation* can and to some extent does). Hence the dramatist really serves two masters. He must secure naturalness without admitting all the casualness and disorder of everyday speech, and yet concentrate on the subject without becoming strained and uneasy (a character must not sound like an orator reading from a prepared manuscript, which does stick to the subject at hand in a very formal way). You will observe, in fact, that most dramatists permit in the speeches of their characters a certain number of conversational tags, which by strict construction might be ruled out but which contribute some sense of ease (at least in the more "relaxed" scenes, before, and possibly after, those of climactic tension in which it is more natural to eliminate all excrescences). (2) In striving for plausible speech the dramatist finds his most useful ally in *how* people speak, and here he must depend on his own sense of language. He can make effective use of rhythm and of idiomatic vocabulary and constructions. In fact, to ignore such matters would produce a sense of serious constraint and unnaturalness. This is what we often find in melodrama, which is likely to depart sharply from normal idiom and rhythm.

Naturalness: Poetic Drama. We have so far spoken of *naturalness* as if it were a conventional, objective, easily identifiable quality of spoken English. Obviously it is not that, for what is natural at one time is not natural at another; what is natural for one person is not natural for another; and what is natural for one person on one occasion is not natural for him on another. There are different levels of speech and different kinds of rhythm, and of these the dramatist must be especially aware precisely because his medium is dialogue. Too much speed, too much slang, too much formality, too much ordinariness can ruin a scene, which depends always upon suitableness to the person, to the occasion, and to the effect to be secured. The dramatist must take into account all these claims, and his own tact rather than hard-and-fast rules must guide him. If his tact is insufficient, the dialogue will not work.

Consider, as a special case, the writing of drama in poetic form, which was the standard in ancient and modern times until the eighteenth century and of which there have been revivals in our own day. How does this cohere with our expectation that dialogue be "natural"? Someone may say, "People don't talk poetry," and it is true that in ordinary relationships they do not. But the fact is that in extraordinary circumstances they do tend toward poetic language. And here we get into another complication: in drama, people are not, strictly speaking, "natural." Drama is brief, compressed, concerned with crucial events; people are disturbed, unusually tense; there is a great increase in emotional pressure. John Dryden even defended the use of heroic couplets in tragedy on the ground that only they could represent the characteristic heightening of effect; therefore, said he, they are "natural." That is, people under pressure tend to speak in a more sharply accentuated rhythm and to use more figurative language ("It is a dream" or "You rat"—to use very commonplace examples—are metaphors which represent a heightened emotion in the speaker, who, whether he knows it or not, is speaking a simple form of poetry). So poetic language becomes natural in drama which achieves real intensity.

To put it in another way, we may say that poetic language is important among the symbols upon which drama relies. All discourse has to find effective symbols, and this symbol, since it springs from psychological necessity, is actually one of the least arbitrary. As a matter of fact, it should secure easier assent than some more familiar symbolic practices— such as saluting the flag. To say "People don't talk poetry" is like saying, "People don't venerate a piece of cloth that has a rather garish design in three colors."

It is clear that what has been said so far is particularly applicable to tragedy, where we especially find emotional pressure and intensity. In fact, it is even possible to argue that the shift from poetry to prose in the eighteenth century (Lillo's *London Merchant* unconsciously rebels against the change it inaugurates) marked the decline of the tragic sense. Shifting to another type, we find that comedy also has been written in verse. It is possible to secure in comedy a degree of tension comparable to that of tragedy, though with differences due to the different methods of the two forms (see the Glossary for Tragedy and Comedy). On the other hand, far more good comedy than tragedy has been written in prose, a fact which suggests that, whatever degree of intensity it may achieve, comedy is fundamentally closer to everyday affairs than is tragedy. On the evidence of language alone, in comedy man is taken at the relatively commonplace level of manners and customs. The tensions that arise perhaps find their best symbolic expression in witty repartee—the mode of Congreve, Sheridan, and Wilde. It is notable that when Wilde deserts epigram for more commonplace means of emotional expression, he tends to fall very flat. It is notable, too, that a verse comedy like Jonson's *Volpone* introduces such a profound sense of evil that the tensions created resemble those of tragedy.

However, whether the dramatist uses poetry as a symbolic language of tragedy or epigram as a symbolic language of comedy, he is still not exempted from the other demands of "naturalness." Heightened language still draws on the vocabulary, idioms, and constructions available to certain types of people at certain times. A dramatist of our day might very well endeavor to use Shakespeare's poetic method; but if he endeavored to use the language—the vocabulary and constructions—of Shakespeare he would produce something completely improbable. He cannot use *thee, fardels, meseems, hath, doth,* etc. Here the danger is that of being archaic and exotic. A comparable danger is that of commonplaceness, of depending on clichés. "O save me from the fate that's worse than death" is technically blank verse, but the words are stale and therefore ineffective. In either case we feel that the speech is rhetorical or declamatory, getting away from naturalness in the best sense of that word but failing to convey a heightened sense of reality (i.e., to achieve poetry). In comedy, too, it is possible to have a certain epigrammatic quality and yet to give to witty speech such a formal, stand-at-attention quality, and to embed it in passages characterized by such lack of ease and flexibility, that the whole effect is one of deadness and unreality.

A literary form which depends wholly upon dialogue obviously faces complex difficulties. Speeches must not only be plausible as speeches and convey the heightened tension of drama, and be always appropriate to time, place, and character; but they must also present character and situation, bring the past perceptibly into view, and progress toward the future.

Tempo. The quality by means of which the dialogue gives us the sense of moving forward we call its "movement" or "tempo." This movement may be barely perceptible, or it may be fairly rapid; it seems clear that, depending upon the author's intentions, the movement will be different in different plays or even in different parts of the same play (in general, for instance, it is likely to be rather slow in the early part of the play, where the author faces the large problems of exposition and of laying the groundwork for all the subsequent action. This is especially true in Congreve's *Way of the World*.). We all have some idea of what tempo is and hence of what it should be; we often complain, for instance, that a movie is "slow." By that we mean, really, that the producer has allotted too much time to events of secondary importance. Or in a play we may feel that the characters talk in such a way that the action is standing still or else moving forward very monotonously. So it is plain that a basic problem of the dramatist is giving to his dialogue that quality that will make it seem to move at a desirable speed and so allotting his limited space that we will not feel he has wasted any of it on less important materials.

For a fuller discussion of the ways in which the dramatist may accomplish these ends, the student may consult the Glossary.

4. *How the Problems Are Met*

DIFFERENT dramatists naturally find different answers to their common problems. We could not study all the answers even in an elaborate textbook, but we can understand certain representative ones. As a beginning, we shall make a rather careful study of a full-length comedy, Oscar Wilde's *Lady Windermere's Fan* (1892). Here we shall find various clues to the ways in which drama may work. These ways may not all be equally good ones, and our business will be to separate the more from the less successful devices.

If, as you read, you can succeed in finding for yourself answers to the question, "How would this be different if it were a short story or a novel?" you will be well on the way to grasping some fundamental truths about drama. Since certain aspects of dramatic structure appear in each act, each act will be followed by some preliminary discussion. The treatment of more extensive issues will be given at the end of the play.

I.

LADY WINDERMERE'S FAN

By OSCAR WILDE

DRAMATIS PERSONÆ

LORD WINDERMERE	LADY WINDERMERE
LORD DARLINGTON	THE DUCHESS OF BERWICK
LORD AUGUSTUS LORTON	LADY AGATHA CARLISLE
MR. DUMBY	LADY PLYMDALE
MR. CECIL GRAHAM	LADY STUTFIELD
MR. HOPPER	LADY JEDBURGH
PARKER, Butler	MRS. COWPER-COWPER
	MRS. ERLYNNE
	ROSALIE, Maid

THE SCENES OF THE PLAY

Act I.   Morning-room in Lord Windermere's House.
Act II. Drawing-room in Lord Windermere's House.
Act III. Lord Darlington's Rooms.
Act IV. Same as Act I.
Time: The Present.
Place: London.

[The action of the play takes place within twenty-four hours, beginning on a Tuesday afternoon at five o'clock, and ending the next day at 1:30 P.M.]

FIRST ACT

[SCENE. Morning-room of Lord Windermere's house in Carlton House Terrace. Doors C. and R. Bureau with books and papers R. Sofa with small tea-table L. Window opening on to terrace L. Table R.]

[Lady Windermere is at table R., arranging roses in a blue bowl.]

[Enter Parker.]

Parker: Is your ladyship at home this afternoon?

Lady Windermere: Yes—who has called?

Parker: Lord Darlington, my lady.

Lady Windermere: [Hesitates for a moment.] Show him up—and I'm at home to any one who calls.

P.: Yes, my lady. [Exit C.]

Lady W.: It's best for me to see him before to-night. I'm glad he's come.

[Enter Parker C.]

P.: Lord Darlington.

[Enter Lord Darlington C. Exit P.]

Lord Darlington: How do you do, Lady Windermere?

Lady W.: How do you do, Lord Darlington? No, I can't shake hands with you. My hands are all wet with these roses. Aren't they lovely? They came up from Selby this morning.

Lord D.: They are quite perfect. [Sees a fan lying on the table.] And what a wonderful fan! May I look at it?

Lady W.: Do. Pretty, isn't it! It's got my name on it, and everything. I have only just seen it myself. It's my hus-band's birthday present to me. You know to-day is my birthday?

Lord D.: No? Is it really?

Lady W.: Yes, I'm of age to-day. 5 Quite an important day in my life, isn't it? That is why I am giving this party to-night. Do sit down. [Still arranging flowers.]

Lord D.: [Sitting down.] I wish I had 10 known it was your birthday, Lady Windermere. I would have covered the whole street in front of your house with flowers for you to walk on. They are made for you. [A short pause.]

15 *Lady W.:* Lord Darlington, you annoyed me last night at the Foreign Office. I am afraid you are going to annoy me again.

Lord D.: I, Lady Windermere? [Enter 20 Parker and Footman C., with tray and tea things.]

Lady W.: Put it there, Parker. That will do. [Wipes her hands with her pocket-handkerchief, goes to tea-table L., and sits 25 down.] Won't you come over, Lord Darlington? [Exit Parker C.]

Lord D.: [Takes chair and goes across L.C.] I am quite miserable, Lady Windermere. You must tell me what I did. 30 [Sits down at table L.]

Lady W.: Well, you kept paying me elaborate compliments the whole evening.

Lord D.: [Smiling.] Ah, nowadays 35 we are all of us so hard up, that the only pleasant things to pay *are* compliments. They're the only things we *can* pay.

Lady W.: [*Shaking her head.*] No, I am talking very seriously. You mustn't laugh, I am quite serious. I don't like compliments, and I don't see why a man should think he is pleasing a woman enormously when he says to her a whole heap of things that he doesn't mean.

Lord D.: Ah, but I did mean them. [*Takes tea which she offers him.*]

Lady W.: [*Gravely.*] I hope not. I should be sorry to have to quarrel with you, Lord Darlington. I like you very much, you know that. But I shouldn't like you at all if I thought you were what most other men are. Believe me, you are better than most other men, and I sometimes think you pretend to be worse.

Lord D.: We all have our little vanities, Lady Windermere.

Lady W.: Why do you make that your special one? [*Still seated at table L.*]

Lord D.: [*Still seated L.C.*] Oh, nowadays so many conceited people go about Society pretending to be good, that I think it shows rather a sweet and modest disposition to pretend to be bad. Besides, there is this to be said. If you pretend to be good, the world takes you very seriously. If you pretend to be bad, it doesn't. Such is the astounding stupidity of optimism.

Lady W.: Don't you *want* the world to take you seriously, then, Lord Darlington?

Lord D.: No, not the world. Who are the people the world takes seriously? All the dull people one can think of, from the bishops down to the bores. I should like *you* to take me very seriously, Lady Windermere, *you* more than anyone else in life.

Lady W.: Why—why me?

Lord D.: [*After a slight hesitation.*] Because I think we might be great friends. Let us be great friends. You may want a friend some day.

Lady W.: Why do you say that?

Lord D.: Oh!—we all want friends at times.

Lady W.: I think we're very good friends already, Lord Darlington. We can always remain so as long as you don't—

Lord D.: Don't what?

Lady W.: Don't spoil it by saying extravagant, silly things to me. You think I am a Puritan, I suppose? Well, I have something of the Puritan in me. I was brought up like that. I am glad of it. My mother died when I was a mere child. I lived always with Lady Julia, my father's elder sister, you know. She was stern to me, but she taught me what the world is forgetting, the difference that there is between what is right and what is wrong. *She* allowed of no compromise. *I* allow of none.

Lord D.: My dear Lady Windermere!

Lady W.: [*Leaning back on the sofa.*] You look on me as being behind the age.—Well, I am! I should be sorry to be on the same level as an age like this.

Lord D.: You think the age very bad?

Lady W.: Yes. Nowadays people seem to look on life as a speculation. It is not a speculation. It is a sacrament. Its ideal is Love. Its purification is sacrifice.

Lord D.: [*Smiling.*] Oh, anything is better than being sacrificed!

Lady W.: [*Leaning forward.*] Don't say that.

Lord D.: I do say it. I feel it—I know it. [*Enter Parker C.*]

Parker: The men want to know if they are to put the carpets on the terrace for to-night, my lady?

Lady W.: You don't think it will rain. Lord Darlington, do you?

Lord D.: I won't hear of its raining on your birthday!

Lady W.: Tell them to do it at once, Parker. [*Exit Parker C.*]

Lord D.: [*Still seated.*] Do you think then—of course I am only putting an imaginary instance—do you think that in the case of a young married couple, say about two years married, if the husband suddenly becomes the intimate friend of a woman of—well, more than doubtful character—is always calling upon her, lunching with her, and probably paying her bills—do you think that the wife should not console herself?

Lady W.: [*Frowning.*] Console herself?

Lord D.: Yes, I think she should—I think she has the right.

Lady W.: Because the husband is vile —should the wife be vile also?

Lord D.: Vileness is a terrible word, Lady Windermere.

Lady W.: It is a terrible thing, Lord Darlington.

Lord D.: Do you know I am afraid that good people do a great deal of harm in this world. Certainly the greatest harm they do is that they make badness of such extraordinary importance. It is absurd to divide people into good and bad. People are either charming or tedious. I take the side of the charming, and you, Lady Windermere, can't help belonging to them.

Lady W.: Now, Lord Darlington. [*Rising and crossing R., front of him.*] Don't stir, I am merely going to finish my flowers. [*Goes to table R.C.*]

Lord D.: [*Rising and moving chair.*] And I must say I think you are very hard on modern life, Lady Windermere. Of course there is much against it, I admit. Most women, for instance, nowadays, are rather mercenary.

Lady W.: Don't talk about such people.

Lord D.: Well then, setting aside mercenary people, who, of course, are dreadful, do you think seriously that women who have committed what the world calls a fault should never be forgiven?

Lady W.: [*Standing at table.*] I think they should never be forgiven.

Lord D.: And men? Do you think that there should be the same laws for men as there are for women?

Lady W.: Certainly!

Lord D.: I think life too complex a thing to be settled by these hard-and-fast rules.

Lady W.: If we had "these hard-and-fast rules," we should find life much more simple.

Lord D.: You allow of no exceptions!

Lady W.: None!

Lord D.: Ah, what a fascinating Puritan you are, Lady Windermere!

Lady W.: The adjective was unnecessary, Lord Darlington.

Lord D.: I couldn't help it. I can resist everything except temptation.

Lady W.: You have the modern affectation of weakness.

Lord D.: [*Looking at her.*] It's only an affectation, Lady Windermere.

[*Enter Parker C.*]

Parker: The Duchess of Berwick and Lady Agatha Carlisle. [*Enter the Duchess of Berwick and Lady Agatha Carlisle C.*] [*Exit Parker C.*]

Duchess of Berwick: [*Coming down C., and shaking hands.*] Dear Margaret, I am so pleased to see you. You remember Agatha, don't you? [*Crossing L.C.*] How do you do, Lord Darlington? I won't let you know my daughter, you are far too wicked.

Lord D.: Don't say that, Duchess. As a wicked man I am a complete failure. Why, there are lots of people who say I have never really done anything wrong in the whole course of my life. Of course they only say it behind my back.

Duchess of B.: Isn't he dreadful? Agatha, this is Lord Darlington. Mind you don't believe a word he says. [*Lord Darlington crosses R.C.*] No, no tea, thank you, dear, [*Crosses and sits on sofa.*] We have just had tea at Lady Markby's. Such bad tea, too. It was quite undrinkable. I wasn't at all surprised. Her own son-in-law supplies it. Agatha is looking forward so much to your ball to-night, dear Margaret.

Lady W.: [*Seated L.C.*] Oh, you mustn't think it is going to be a ball, Duchess. It is only a dance in honour of my birthday. A small and early.

Lord D.: [*Standing L.C.*] Very small, very early, and very select, Duchess.

Duchess of B.: [*On sofa L.*] Of course it's going to be select. But we know *that*, dear Margaret, about *your* house. It is really one of the few houses in London where I can take Agatha, and where I feel perfectly secure about dear Berwick. I don't know what Society is coming to. The most dreadful people seem to go everywhere. They certainly come to my parties—the men get quite furious if one doesn't ask them. Really, some one should make a stand against it.

Lady W.: I will, Duchess. I will have no one in my house about whom there is any scandal.

Lord D.: [*R.C.*] Oh, don't say that, Lady Windermere. I should never be admitted! [*Sitting.*]

Duchess of B.: Oh, men don't matter. With women it is different. We're good. Some of us are, at least. But we are positively getting elbowed into the corner. Our husbands would really forget our existence if we didn't nag at them from time to time, just to remind them that we have a perfect legal right to do so.

Lord D.: It's a curious thing, Duchess, about the game of marriage—a game, by the way, that is going out of fashion—the wives hold all the honours, and invariably lose the odd trick.

Duchess of B.: The odd trick? Is that the husband, Lord Darlington?

Lord D.: It would be rather a good name for the modern husband.

Duchess of B.: Dear Lord Darlington, how thoroughly depraved you are!

Lady W.: Lord Darlington is trivial.

Lord D.: Ah, don't say that, Lady Windermere.

Lady W.: Why do you *talk* so trivially about life, then?

Lord D.: Because I think that life is far too important a thing ever to talk seriously about it. [*Moves up C.*]

Duchess of B.: What does he mean? Do, as a concession to my poor wits, Lord Darlington, just explain to me what you really mean.

Lord D.: [*Coming down back of table.*] I think I had better not, Duchess. Nowadays to be intelligible is to be found out. Good-bye! [*Shakes hands with Duchess.*] And now—[*goes up stage*],

Lady Windermere, good-bye. I may come to-night, mayn't I? Do let me come.

Lady W.: [*Standing up stage with Lord Darlington.*] Yes, certainly. But you are not to say foolish, insincere things to people.

Lord D.: [*Smiling.*] Ah! you are beginning to reform me. It is a dangerous thing to reform any one, Lady Windermere. [*Bows, and exit C.*]

Duchess of B.: [*Who has risen, goes C.*] What a charming, wicked creature! I like him so much. I'm quite delighted he's gone! How sweet you're looking! Where *do* you get your gowns? And now I must tell you how sorry I am for you, dear Margaret. [*Crosses to sofa and sits with Lady Windermere.*] Agatha, darling!

Lady Agatha: Yes, mamma. [*Rises.*]

Duchess of B.: Will you go and look over the photograph album that I see there?

Lady A.: Yes, mamma. [*Goes to table up L.*]

Duchess of B.: Dear girl! She is so fond of photographs of Switzerland. Such a pure taste, I think. But I really am so sorry for you, Margaret.

Lady W.: [*Smiling.*] Why, Duchess?

Duchess of B.: Oh, on account of that horrid woman. She dresses so well, too, which makes it much worse, sets such a dreadful example. Augustus—you know my disreputable brother—such a trial to us all—well, Augustus is completely infatuated about her. It is quite scandalous, for she is absolutely inadmissible into society. Many a woman has a past, but I am told that she has at least a dozen, and that they all fit.

Lady W.: Whom are you talking about, Duchess?

Duchess of B.: About Mrs. Erlynne.

Lady W.: Mrs. Erlynne? I never heard of her, Duchess. And what *has* she to do with me?

Duchess of B.: My poor child! Agatha, darling!

Lady A.: Yes, mamma.

Duchess of B.: Will you go out on the terrace and look at the sunset?

Lady A.: Yes, mamma. [*Exit through window L.*]

Duchess of B.: Sweet girl! So devoted to sunsets! Shows such refinement of feeling, does it not? After all, there is nothing like Nature, is there?

Lady W.: But what is it, Duchess? Why do you talk to me about this person?

Duchess of B.: Don't you really know? I assure you we're all so distressed about it. Only last night at dear Lady Fansen's every one was saying how extraordinary it was that, of all men in London, Windermere should behave in such a way.

Lady W.: My husband—what has *he* to do with any woman of that kind?

Duchess of B.: Ah, what indeed, dear? That is the point. He goes to see her continually, and stops for hours at a time, and while he is there she is not at home to any one. Not that many ladies call on her, dear, but she has a great many disreputable men friends—my own brother particularly, as I told you —and that is what makes it so dreadful about Windermere. We looked upon *him* as being such a model husband, but I am afraid there is no doubt about it. My dear nieces—you know the Saville girls, don't you?—such nice domestic creatures—plain, dreadfully plain, but so good—well, they're always at the window doing fancy work, and making ugly things for the poor, which I think so useful of them in these dreadful socialistic days, and this terrible woman has taken a house in Curzon Street, right opposite them—such a respectable street, too. I don't know what we're coming to! And they tell me that Windermere goes there four and five times a week—they *see* him. They can't help it—and although they never talk scandal, they—well, of course—they remark on it to every one. And the worst of it all is that I have been told that this woman has got a great deal of money

out of somebody, for it seems that she came to London six months ago without anything at all to speak of, and now she has this charming house in Mayfair, drives her ponies in the Park every afternoon and all well, all—since she has known poor dear Windermere.

Lady W.: Oh, I can't believe it!

Duchess of B.: But it's quite true, my dear. The whole of London knows it. That is why I felt it was better to come and talk to you, and advise you to take Windermere away at once to Homburg or to Aix, where he'll have something to amuse him, and where you can watch him all day long. I assure you, my dear, that on several occasions after I was first married, I had to pretend to be very ill, and was obliged to drink the most unpleasant mineral waters, merely to get Berwick out of town. He was so extremely susceptible. Though I am bound to say he never gave away any large sums of money to anybody. He is far too high-principled for that!

Lady W.: [*Interrupting.*] Duchess, Duchess, it's impossible! [*Rising and crossing stage to C.*] We are only married two years. Our child is but six months old. [*Sits in chair R. of L. table.*]

Duchess of B.: Ah, the dear pretty baby! How is the little darling? Is it a boy or a girl? I hope a girl—Ah, no I remember it's a boy! I'm so sorry. Boys are so wicked. My boy is excessively immoral. You wouldn't believe at what hours he comes home. And he's only left Oxford a few months—I really don't know what they teach them there.

Lady W.: Are *all* men bad?

Duchess of B.: Oh, all of them, my dear, all of them, without any exception. And they never grow any better. Men become old, but they never become good.

Lady W.: Windermere and I married for love.

Duchess of B.: Yes, we begin like that. It was only Berwick's brutal and incessant threats of suicide that made me accept him at all, and before the year was out, he was running after all kinds of petticoats, every colour, every shape, every material. In fact, before the honeymoon was over, I caught him winking at my maid, a most pretty, respectable girl. I dismissed her at once without a character.—No, I remember I passed her on to my sister; poor dear Sir George is so short-sighted, I thought it wouldn't matter. But it did, though—it was most unfortunate. [*Rises.*] And now, my dear child, I must go, as we are dining out. And mind you don't take this little aberration of Windermere's too much to heart. Just take him abroad and he'll come back to you all right.

Lady W.: Come back to me? [*C.*]

Duchess of B.: [*L.C.*] Yes, dear, these wicked women get our husbands away from us, but they always come back, slightly damaged, of course. And don't make scenes, men hate them!

Lady W.: It is very kind of you, Duchess, to come and tell me all this. But I can't believe that my husband is untrue to me.

Duchess of B.: Pretty child! I was like that once. Now I know that all men are monsters. [*Lady Windermere rings bell.*] The only thing to do is to feed the wretches well. A good cook does wonders, and that I know you have. My dear Margaret, you are not going to cry?

Lady W.: You needn't be afraid, Duchess, I never cry.

Duchess of B.: That's quite right, dear. Crying is the refuge of plain women but the ruin of pretty ones. Agatha, darling!

Lady A.: [*Entering L.*] Yes, mamma. [*Stands back of table L.C.*]

Duchess of B.: Come and bid good-bye to Lady Windermere, and thank her for your charming visit. [*Coming down again.*] And by the way, I must thank you for sending a card to Mr. Hopper—he's that rich young Australian people are taking such notice of just at present. His father made a great fortune by selling some kind of food in circular tins—most palatable, I believe —I fancy it is the thing the servants always refuse to eat. But the son is quite interesting. I think he's attracted by dear Agatha's clever talk. Of course, we should be very sorry to lose her, but I think that a mother who doesn't part with a daughter every season has no real affection. We're coming to-night, dear. [*Parker opens C. doors.*] And remember my advice, take the poor fellow out of town at once, it is the only thing to do. Good-bye, once more; come, Agatha. [*Exeunt Duchess and Lady Agatha C.*]

Lady W.: How horrible! I understand now what Lord Darlington meant by the imaginary instance of the couple not two years married. Oh! it can't be true—she spoke of enormous sums of money paid to this woman. I know where Arthur keeps his bank book—in one of the drawers of that desk. I might find out by that. I *will* find out. [*Opens drawer.*] No, it is some hideous mistake. [*Rises and goes C.*] Some silly scandal! He loves *me!* He loves *me!* But why should I not look? I am his wife, I have a right to look! [*Returns to bureau, takes out book and examines it page by page, smiles and gives a sigh of relief.*] I knew it! there is not a word of truth in this stupid story. [*Puts book back in drawer. As she does so, starts and takes out another book.*] A second book—private—locked! [*Tries to open it, but fails. Sees paper knife on bureau, and with it cuts cover from book. Begins to start at the first page.*] "Mrs. Erlynne—£600—Mrs. Erlynne —£700—Mrs. Erlynne—£400." Oh! it is true! it is true! How horrible! [*Throws book on floor.*] [*Enter Lord Windermere.*]

Lord W.: Well, dear, has the fan been sent home yet? [*Going R.C. Sees book.*] Margaret, you have cut open my bank book. You have no right to do such a thing!

Lady W.: You think it wrong that you are found out, don't you?

Lord W.: I think it wrong that a wife should spy on her husband.

Lady W.: I did not spy on you. I never knew of this woman's existence till half an hour ago. Some one who pitied me was kind enough to tell me what every one in London knows already—your daily visits to Curzon Street, your mad infatuation, the monstrous sums of money you squander on this infamous woman! [*Crossing L.*]

Lord W.: Margaret! don't talk like that of Mrs. Erlynne, you don't know how unjust it is!

Lady W.: [*Turning to him.*] You are very jealous of Mrs. Erlynne's honour. I wish you had been as jealous of mine.

Lord W.: Your honour is untouched, Margaret. You don't think for a moment that—[*Puts book back into desk.*]

Lady W.: I think that you spend your money strangely. That is all. Oh, don't imagine I mind about the money. As far as I am concerned, you may squander everything we have. But what I *do* mind is that you who have loved me, you who have taught me to love you, should pass from the love that is given to the love that is bought. Oh, it's horrible! [*Sits on sofa.*] And it is I who feel degraded! *you* don't feel anything. I feel stained, utterly stained. You can't realise how hideous the last six months seem to me now—every kiss you have given me is tainted in my memory.

Lord W.: [*Crossing to her.*] Don't say that, Margaret. I never loved any one in the whole world but you.

Lady W.: [*Rises.*] Who is this woman, then? Why do you take a house for her?

Lord W.: I did not take a house for her.

Lady W.: You gave her the money to do it, which is the same thing.

Lord W.: Margaret, as far as I have known Mrs. Erlynne—

Lady W.: Is there a Mr. Erlynne—or is he a myth?

Lord W.: Her husband died many years ago. She is alone in the world.

Lady W.: No relations? [*A pause.*]

Lord W.: None.

Lady W.: Rather curious, isn't it? [*L.*]

Lord W.: [*L.C.*] Margaret, I was saying to you—and I beg you to listen to me—that as far as I have known Mrs. Erlynne, she has conducted herself well. If years ago—

Lady W.: Oh! [*Crossing R.C.*] I don't want details about her life!

Lord W.: [*C.*] I am not going to give you any details about her life. I tell you simply this—Mrs. Erlynne was once honoured, loved, respected. She was well born, she had position—she lost everything—threw it away, if you like. That makes it all the more bitter. Misfortunes one can endure—they come from outside, they are accidents. But to suffer for one's own faults—ah!—there is the sting of life. It was twenty years ago, too. She was little more than a girl then. She had been a wife for even less time than you have.

Lady W.: I am not interested in her—and—you should not mention this woman and me in the same breath. It is an error of taste. [*Sitting R. at desk.*]

Lord W.: Margaret, you could save this woman. She wants to get back into society, and she wants you to help her. [*Crossing to her.*]

Lady W.: Me!

Lord W.: Yes, you.

Lady W.: How impertinent of her! [*A pause.*]

Lord W.: Margaret, I came to ask you a great favour, and I still ask it of you, though you have discovered what I had intended you should never have known, that I have given Mrs. Erlynne a large sum of money. I want you to send her an invitation for our party to-night. [*Standing L. of her.*]

Lady W.: You are mad! [*Rises.*]

Lord W.: I entreat you. People may chatter about her, do chatter about her, of course, but they don't know anything definite against her. She has been to several houses—not to houses where you would go, I admit, but still to houses where women who are in what is called Society nowadays do go. That does not content her. She wants you to receive her once.

Lady W.: As a triumph for her, I suppose?

Lord W.: No; but because she knows that you are a good woman—and that if she comes here once she will have a chance of a happier, a surer life than she has had. She will make no further effort to know you. Won't you help a woman who is trying to get back?

Lady W.: No! If a woman really repents, she never wishes to return to the society that has made or seen her ruin.

Lord W.: I beg of you.

Lady W.: [*Crossing to door R.*] I am going to dress for dinner, and don't mention the subject again this evening. Arthur [*going to him C.*], you fancy because I have no father or mother that I am alone in the world, and that you can treat me as you choose. You are wrong, I have friends, many friends.

Lord W.: [*L.C.*] Margaret, you are talking foolishly, recklessly. I won't argue with you, but I insist upon your asking Mrs. Erlynne to-night.

Lady W.: [*R.C.*] I shall do nothing of the kind. [*Crossing L.C.*]

Lord W.: You refuse? [*C.*]

Lady W.: Absolutely!

Lord W.: Ah, Margaret, do this for my sake; it is her last chance.

Lady W.: What has that to do with me?

Lord W.: How hard good women are!

Lady W.: How weak bad men are!

Lord W.: Margaret, none of us men may be good enough for the women we marry—that is quite true—but you don't imagine I would ever—oh, the suggestion is monstrous!

Lady W.: Why should *you* be different from other men? I am told that there is hardly a husband in London who does not waste his life over *some* shameful passion.

Lord W.: I am not one of them.

Lady W.: I am not sure of that!

Lord W.: You are sure in your heart.

But don't make chasm after chasm between us. God knows the last few minutes have thrust us wide enough apart. Sit down and write the card.

Lady W.: Nothing in the whole world would induce me.

Lord W.: [*Crossing to bureau.*] Then I will! [*Rings electric bell, sits and writes card.*]

Lady W.: You are going to invite this woman? [*Crossing to him.*]

Lord W.: Yes. [*Pause. Enter Parker.*] Parker!

Parker.: Yes, my lord. [*Comes down L.C.*]

Lord W.: Have this note sent to Mrs. Erlynne at No.. 84A Curzon Street. [*Crossing to L.C. and giving note to Parker.*] There is no answer! [*Exit Parker C.*]

Lady W.: Arthur, if that woman comes here, I shall insult her.

Lord W.: Margaret, don't say that.

Lady W.: I mean it.

Lord W.: Child, if you did such a thing, there's not a woman in London who wouldn't pity you.

Lady W.: There is not a *good* woman in London who would not applaud me. We have been too lax. We must make an example. I propose to begin to-night. [*Picking up fan.*] Yes, you gave me this fan to-day; it was your birthday present. If that woman crosses my threshold, I shall strike her across the face with it.

Lord W.: Margaret, you couldn't do such a thing.

Lady W.: You don't know me! [*Moves R.*] [*Enter Parker.*] Parker!

Parker: Yes, my lady.

Lady W.: I shall dine in my own room. I don't want dinner, in fact. See that everything is ready by half-past ten. And, Parker, be sure you pronounce the names of the guests very distinctly to-night. Sometimes you speak so fast that I miss them. I am particularly anxious to hear the names quite clearly, so as to make no mistake. You understand, Parker?

P.: Yes, my lady.

Lady W.: That will do! [Exit Parker C.] [Speaking to Lord Windermere.] Arthur, if that woman comes here—I warn you—

Lord W.: Margaret, you'll ruin us!

Lady W.: Us! From this moment my life is separate from yours. But if you wish to avoid a public scandal, write at once to this woman, and tell her that I forbid her to come here!

Lord W.: I will not—I cannot—she must come!

Lady W.: Then I shall do exactly as I have said. [Goes R.] You leave me no 5 choice. [Exit R.]

Lord W.: [Calling after her.] Margaret! Margaret! [A pause.] My God! What shall I do? I dare not tell her who this woman really is. The shame would 10 kill her. [Sinks down into a chair and buries his face in his hands.]

NOTES ON ACT I

Characterization. Act I introduces six characters. Since Wilde cannot describe them as he might in a novel or analyze their personalities for us, he depends upon arrangement to aid us in establishing their identity. By introducing them in terms of sharp contrast he distinguishes them superficially until we are better acquainted with them and can make more fundamental distinctions. For instance, we first meet a man and a woman, Lord Darlington and Lady Windermere, who have sharply divergent views of life. Using this one case as an example, the student should ask himself: What other use of sharp contrasts in Act I contributes to a quick preliminary identification of characters?

In place of the novelist's analysis, the dramatist can use self-analysis by a character; but then, of course, his problem is to justify the self-analysis. Note Lady W.'s speech beginning "Don't spoil it by saying, etc." (p. 36b, 5), a speech which is very useful in characterizing Lady W., but which does not seem forced. Why does it not seem forced and unnatural? Because it is a logical part of, and an explanation of, her protest to Lord D. Again, the Duchess of B. makes long speeches, in which, though she does not analyze herself, she gives herself away completely. With her, Wilde's problem is easier: a loquacious, insensitive person is very likely to speak freely about herself. Can you find other instances of characters' making revealing speeches about themselves without our feeling that the speeches are forced?

Exposition. Act I also carries a very heavy weight of exposition: we learn about the birthday, the fan, the coming party, Lord D.'s unsuccessful attentions to Lady W.; her position in society, the Duchess of B.'s ideas and her plans for her daughter, Lord W.'s mysterious interest in a mysterious Mrs. Erlynne whom Lady W. must entertain but whom she is not to identify. Wilde manages exposition so skillfully that we learn essential matters almost without knowing that we are learning them. For example, Lord D.'s comment on the fan is natural; hence we learn about the birthday; this fact, in turn, gives Lord D. an opening for making love—an excellent situation for characterizing the participants. Wilde has the Duchess of B. talk informatively, but he tries to keep her lines from seeming to the audience bald, intentional exposition. For one thing, the information about Lord W. is new to Lady W. as well as to us. Further, the Duchess's recital is so interlarded with gossip, autobiography, and consciously or unconsciously witty remarks, that it seems a natural speech, not a rough piece of exposition. Do you find other examples of well-managed exposition?

Motivation and Progression. Almost everything in the act points forward to something else in Act I or later in the play. Darlington's making love to Lady W. leads us to anticipate possible outcomes of this situation. Darlington's line, "You may want a friend some time," plus his evasion of her question, prepares for the Duchess's revelations. His question to Lady W. about forgiving women who have committed "a fault" and her firm assertion that "they should never be forgiven" look forward to the situation that comes up at the end of the act. The Duchess's revelations lead to Lady W.'s examining Lord W.'s bankbook; thus her attitude is established for the following scene with her husband.

The technique in terms of which parts of the action and conversation, however slight, anticipate subsequent actions, is called *motivation*. Good motivation shows that the author knows what he is going to do and can build up to his effects rather than introduce them crudely and unexpectedly. (See the Glossary for a further discussion.)

Besides skillfully preparing us for what is to follow, Wilde constantly compels us to look ahead. Take Lady W.'s coming party: see how many references to it you can find in the first two-thirds of Act I. Then, of course, there is the emphatic pointing to the party in the Windermeres' heated discussion of Mrs. Erlynne. Thus all our attention is focused on the coming events in Act II; all of Act I appears to progress toward it. Why is it, by the way, that it seems perfectly natural to us that Lady W. should threaten to use a fan (rather than some other object) to strike Mrs. Erlynne?

Note, finally, that we are made to look ahead even beyond Act II toward the solution of a basic situation on which we have certain hints. A number of small matters work together very unobtrusively: Lady W. is twenty-one years old; it was twenty years ago that Mrs. Erlynne committed her "fault"; Lord W. is hesitant in saying that Mrs. E. has no relations; Lady W. has "no father or mother"; and finally there is Lord W.'s speech that closes the act. Such lines, as they lead us on to make inferences about a situation, constitute *exposition*; as they suggest future developments, they help give us a sense of *progression*.

To give the reader certain hints about an unexplained situation is, you will observe, the method of the mystery story. When the unknown is a matter of *identity*, we have still more of the mystery manner. If an author depends too largely on such matters to gain his suspense, he writes *melodrama* (for further discussion, see the Glossary). Compare this kind of melodramatic suspense with the kind which Wilde has aroused with regard to the party to come in Act II: what Lady W. will do to Mrs. Erlynne is entirely a question of her *beliefs* and her *character*, not an external question of identity

Concentration. In Act I we already see the concentration characteristic of the drama; it seems clear, even at this stage, that a central event in the play is going to be the party in Act II. In fiction it is highly improbable that so much would hinge on a single occasion; or, if it did, the fiction-writer would permit himself a relatively elaborate build-up to the occasion. But Wilde's Act I exemplifies the tendency of drama to reduce the time represented—to deal only with the climax, when the situation is likely to be very tense. The events of Act I occur at 5 P.M. on the day of the party; Wilde could hardly start closer to his main event. In constricting his materials so sharply, he has to gamble somewhat on other matters. How can we accept as probable the two calls made so late on the day of the party? The Duchess's choice of such a time to make her revelations? The sureness and vigor and speed of Lady W.'s response? Lord W.'s waiting until so late to ask an invitation for Mrs. Erlynne? To an extent, of course, Wilde can rely upon our acceptance of dramatic *conventions* (for a fuller discussion, see the Glossary), that is, upon our agreeing to accept an acceleration of normal pace and to ignore certain actions which, from the point of view of "real life," may seem improbable. In dealing with all arts we must make some concessions—the "willing suspension of disbelief," as Coleridge called it. But no author can depend upon the conventions to gloss over *any* improbability; he must always be striving for the probable. So Wilde has the calls come at tea-time; the natural overlapping tends to obscure the fact that there are two calls; the callers are intimate acquaintances; Lord D.'s devotion would justify his presence. Thus, we are led on in such a way as to weaken our impulse to ask questions. The Duchess's tactless gossiping becomes plausible because of her unflagging, inclusive insensitiveness. Lady W.'s vigorous, energetic attempt to meet the situation is natural because we have already seen her as a person very sure of herself and her beliefs.

Another aspect of the concentration of the play is the apparently complex plot. We see three lines of action: the Darlington-Lady W. plot; the Erlynne-Windermeres plot; the Berwick-Agatha-Hopper sub-plot. Do they look like entirely separate plots? Or can you discern, even at this point, a thematic relationship among them, i.e., a relationship in terms of their meaning? Could all bear upon one central issue?

Note, finally, the climactic order in which Wilde has arranged the materials in Act I. What are the reasons why each part tends to produce higher tension than the one preceding?

SECOND ACT

[SCENE. Drawing-room in Lord Windermere's house. Door R.U. opening into ball-room, where band is playing. Door L. through which guests are entering. Door L.U. opens on to illuminated terrace. Palms, flowers, and brilliant lights. Room crowded with guests. Lady Windermere is receiving them.]

Duchess of B.: [*Up C.*] So strange Lord Windermere isn't here. Mr. Hopper is very late, too. You have kept those five dances for him, Agatha? [*Comes down.*]

Lady A.: Yes, mamma.

Duchess of B.: [*Sitting on sofa.*] Just let me see your card. I'm so glad Lady Windermere has revived cards.— They're a mother's only safeguard. You dear simple little thing! [*Scratches out two names.*] No nice girl should ever waltz with such particularly younger sons! It looks so fast! The last two dances you might pass on the terrace with Mr. Hopper. [*Enter Mr. Dumby and Lady Plymdale from the ball-room.*]

Lady A.: Yes, mamma.

Duchess of B.: [*Fanning herself.*] The air is so pleasant there.

Parker: Mrs. Cowper-Cowper. Lady Stutfield. Sir James Royston. Mr. Guy Berkeley. [*These people enter as announced.*]

Dumby: Good evening, Lady Stutfield. I suppose this will be the last ball of the season?

Lady Stutfield: I suppose so, Mr. Dumby. It's been a delightful season, hasn't it?

Dumby: Quite delightful! Good evening, Duchess. I suppose this will be the last ball of the season?

Duchess of B.: I suppose so, Mr. Dumby. It has been a very dull season, hasn't it?

D.: Dreadfully dull! Dreadfully dull!

Mrs. Cowper-Cowper: Good evening, Mr. Dumby. I suppose this will be the last ball of the season?

D.: Oh, I think not. There'll probably be two more. [*Wanders back to Lady Plymdale.*]

Parker: Mr. Rufford. Lady Jedburgh and Miss Graham. Mr. Hopper. [*These people enter as announced.*]

Hopper: How do you do, Lady Windermere? How do you do, Duchess? [*Bows to Lady Agatha.*]

Duchess of B.: Dear Mr. Hopper, how nice of you to come so early. We all know how you are run after in London.

Hopper: Capital place, London! They are not nearly so exclusive in London as they are in Sydney.

Duchess of B.: Ah! we know your value, Mr. Hopper. We wish there were more like you. It would make life so much easier. Do you know, Mr. Hopper, dear Agatha and I are so much interested in Australia. It must be so pretty with all the dear little kangaroos flying about. Agatha has found it on the map. What a curious shape it is! Just like a large packing case. However, it is a very young country, isn't it?

H.: Wasn't it made at the same time as the others, Duchess?

Duchess of B.: How clever you are, Mr. Hopper. You have a cleverness quite of your own. Now I mustn't keep you.

H.: But I should like to dance with Lady Agatha, Duchess.

Duchess of B.: Well, I *hope* she has a dance left. Have you a dance left, Agatha?

Lady A.: Yes, mamma.

Duchess of B.: The next one?

Lady A.: Yes, mamma.

H.: May I have the pleasure? [*Lady Agatha bows.*]

Duchess of B.: Mind you take great care of my little chatterbox, Mr. Hopper. [*Lady Agatha and Mr. Hopper pass into ball-room.*] [*Enter Lord Windermere L.*]

Lord W.: Margaret, I want to speak to you.

Lady W.: In a moment. [*The music stops.*]

P.: Lord Augustus Lorton. [*Enter Lord Augustus.*]

Lord Augustus: Good evening, Lady Windermere.

Duchess of B.: Sir James, will you take me into the ball-room? Augustus has been dining with us to-night. I really have had quite enough of dear Augustus for the moment. [*Sir James Royston gives the Duchess his arm and escorts her into the ball-room.*]

P.: Mr. and Mrs. Arthur Bowden. Lord and Lady Paisley. Lord Darlington. [*These people enter as announced.*]

Lord A.: [*Coming up to Lord Windermere.*] Want to speak to you particularly, dear boy. I'm worn to a shadow. Know I don't look it. None of us men do look what we really are. Demmed good thing, too. What I want to know is this. Who is she? Where does she come from? Why hasn't she got any demmed relations? Demmed nuisance, relations! But they make one so demmed respectable.

Lord W.: You are talking of Mrs. Erlynne, I suppose? I only met her six months ago. Till then, I never knew of her existence.

Lord A.: You have seen a good deal of her since then.

Lord W.: [*Coldly.*] Yes, I have seen a good deal of her since then. I have just seen her.

Lord A.: Egad! the women are very down on her. I have been dining with Arabella this evening! By Jove! you should have heard what she said about Mrs. Erlynne. She didn't leave a rag on her. . . . [*Aside.*] Berwick and I told her that didn't matter much as the lady in question must have an extremely fine figure. You should have seen Arabella's expression! . . . But, look here, dear boy. I don't know what to do about Mrs. Erlynne. Egad! I might be married to her: she treats me with such demmed indifference. She's deuced clever, too! She explains everything. Egad! she explains you. She has got any amount of explanations for you—and all of them different.

Lord W.: No explanations are neces-

sary about my friendship with Mrs. Erlynne.

Lord A.: Hem! Well, look here, dear old fellow. Do you think she will ever get into this demmed thing called Society? Would you introduce her to your wife? No use beating about the confounded bush. Would you do that?

Lord W.: Mrs. Erlynne is coming here to-night.

Lord A.: Your wife has sent her a card?

Lord W.: Mrs. Erlynne has received a card.

Lord A.: Then she's all right, dear boy. But why didn't you tell me that before? It would have saved me a heap of worry and demmed misunderstandings! [*Lady Agatha and Mr. Hopper cross and exeunt on terrace L.U.E.*]

P.: Mr. Cecil Graham! [*Enter Mr. Cecil Graham.*]

Cecil Graham: [*Bows to Lady Windermere, passes over and shakes hands with Lord Windermere.*] Good evening, Arthur. Why don't you ask me how I am? I like people to ask me how I am. It shows a widespread interest in my health. Now, to-night I am not at all well. Been dining with my people. Wonder why it is one's people are always so tedious? My father would talk morality after dinner. I told him he was old enough to know better. But my experience is that as soon as people are old enough to know better, they don't know anything at all. Hallo, Tuppy! Hear you're going to be married again; thought you were tired of that game.

Lord A.: You're excessively trivial, my dear boy, excessively trivial!

Cecil G.: By the way, Tuppy, which is it? Have you been twice married and once divorced, or twice divorced and once married? I say you've been twice divorced and once married. It seems so much more probable.

Lord A.: I have a very bad memory. I really don't remember which. [*Moves away R.*]

Lady Plymdale: Lord Windermere,

I've something most particular to ask you.

Lord W.: I am afraid—if you will excuse me—I must join my wife.

Lady P.: Oh, you mustn't dream of such a thing. It's most dangerous nowadays for a husband to pay any attention to his wife in public. It always makes people think that he beats her when they're alone. The world has grown so suspicious of anything that looks like a happy married life. But I'll tell you what it is at supper. [*Moves towards door of ball-room.*]

Lord W.: [*C.*] Margaret! I *must* speak to you.

Lady W.: Will you hold my fan for me, Lord Darlington? Thanks. [*Comes down to him.*]

Lord W.: [*Crossing to her.*] Margaret, what you said before dinner was, of course, impossible?

Lady W.: That woman is not coming here to-night!

Lord W.: [*R.C.*] Mrs. Erlynne is coming here, and if you in any way annoy or wound her, you will bring shame and sorrow on us both. Remember that! Ah, Margaret! only trust me! A wife should trust her husband!

Lady W.: [*C.*] London is full of women who trust their husbands. One can always recognise them. They look so thoroughly unhappy. I am not going to be one of them. [*Moves up.*] Lord Darlington, will you give me back my fan, please? Thanks. . . . A useful thing a fan, isn't it? . . . I want a friend to-night, Lord Darlington: I didn't know I would want one so soon.

Lord D.: Lady Windermere! I knew the time would come some day; but why to-night?

Lord W.: I *will* tell her. I must. It would be terrible if there were any scene. Margaret . . .

P.: Mrs. Erlynne! [*Lord Windermere starts. Mrs. Erlynne enters, very beautifully dressed and very dignified. Lady Windermere clutches at her fan, then lets it drop on the floor. She bows coldly to Mrs. Erlynne, who bows to her sweetly in turn, and sails into the room.*]

Lord D.: You have dropped your fan, Lady Windermere. [*Picks it up and hands it to her.*]

Mrs. Erlynne: [*C.*] How do you do, again, Lord Windermere? How charming your sweet wife looks! Quite a picture!

Lord W.: [*In a low voice.*] It was terribly rash of you to come!

Mrs. E.: [*Smiling.*] The wisest thing I ever did in my life. And, by the way, you must pay me a good deal of attention this evening. I am afraid of the women. You must introduce me to some of them. The men I can always manage. How do you do, Lord Augustus? You have quite neglected me lately. I have not seen you since yesterday. I am afraid you're faithless. Every one told me so.

Lord A.: [*R.*] Now really, Mrs. Erlynne, allow me to explain.

Mrs. E.: [*R.C.*] No, dear Lord Augustus, you can't explain anything. It is your chief charm.

Lord A.: Ah! if you find charms in me, Mrs. Erlynne—[*They converse together. Lord Windermere moves uneasily about the room watching Mrs. Erlynne.*]

Lord D.: [*To Lady Windermere.*] How pale you are!

Lady W.: Cowards are always pale!

Lord D.: You look faint. Come out on the terrace.

Lady W.: Yes. [*To Parker.*] Parker, send my cloak out.

Mrs. E.: [*Crossing to her.*] Lady Windermere, how beautifully your terrace is illuminated. Reminds me of Prince Doria's at Rome. [*Lady Windermere bows coldly, and goes off with Lord Darlington.*] Oh, how do you do, Mr. Graham? Isn't that your aunt, Lady Jedburgh? I should so much like to know her.

Cecil G.: [*After a moment's hesitation and embarrassment.*] Oh, certainly, if you wish it. Aunt Caroline, allow me to introduce Mrs. Erlynne.

Mrs. E.: So pleased to meet you, Lady Jedburgh. [*Sits beside her on the sofa.*] Your nephew and I are great friends. I am so much interested in his political career. I think he's sure to be a wonderful success. He thinks like a Tory, and talks like a Radical, and that's so important nowadays. He's such a brilliant talker, too. But we all know from whom he inherits that. Lord Allandale was saying to me only yesterday, in the Park, that Mr. Graham talks almost as well as his aunt.

Lady Jedburgh: [*R.*] Most kind of you to say these charming things to me! [*Mrs. Erlynne smiles, and continues conversation.*]

Dumby: [*To Cecil Graham.*] Did you introduce Mrs. Erlynne to Lady Jedburgh?

Cecil G.: Had to, my dear fellow. Couldn't help it! That woman can make one do anything she wants. How, I don't know.

D.: Hope to goodness she won't speak to me! [*Saunters towards Lady Plymdale.*]

Mrs. Erlynne: [*C. To Lady Jedburgh.*] On Thursday? With great pleasure. [*Rises, and speaks to Lord Windermere, laughing.*] What a bore it is to have to be civil to these old dowagers! But they always insist on it!

Lady P.: [*To Mr. Dumby.*] Who is that well-dressed woman talking to Windermere?

D.: Haven't got the slightest idea! Looks like an *édition de luxe* of a wicked French novel, meant specially for the English market.

Mrs. E.: So that is poor Dumby with Lady Plymdale? I hear she is frightfully jealous of him. He doesn't seem anxious to speak to me to-night. I suppose he is afraid of her. Those straw-coloured women have dreadful tempers. Do you know, I think I'll dance with you first, Windermere. [*Lord Windermere bites his lip and frowns.*] It will make Lord Augustus so jealous! Lord Augustus! [*Lord Augustus comes down.*]

Lord Windermere insists on my dancing with him first, and, as it's his own house, I can't well refuse. You know I would much sooner dance with you.

Lord A.: [*With a low bow.*] I wish I could think so, Mrs. Erlynne.

Mrs. E.: You know it far too well. I can fancy a person dancing through life with you and finding it charming.

Lord A.: [*Placing his hand on his white waistcoat.*] Oh, thank you, thank you. You are the most adorable of all ladies!

Mrs. Erlynne: What a nice speech! So simple and so sincere! Just the sort of speech I like. Well, you shall hold my bouquet. [*Goes towards ball-room on Lord Windermere's arm.*] Ah, Mr. Dumby, how are you? I am so sorry I have been out the last three times you have called. Come and lunch on Friday.

D.: [*With perfect nonchalance.*] Delighted! [*Lady Plymdale glares with indignation at Mr. Dumby. Lord Augustus follows Mrs. Erlynne and Lord Windermere into the ball-room holding bouquet.*]

Lady P.: [*To Mr. Dumby.*] What an absolute brute you are! I never can believe a word you say! Why did you tell me you didn't know her? What do you mean by calling on her three times running? You are not to go to lunch there; of course you understand that?

D.: My dear Laura, I wouldn't dream of going!

Lady P.: You haven't told me her name yet! Who is she?

D.: [*Coughs slightly and smooths his hair.*] She's a Mrs. Erlynne.

Lady P.: That woman!

D.: Yes; that is what every one calls her.

Lady P.: How very interesting! How intensely interesting! I really must have a good stare at her. [*Goes to door of ball-room and looks in.*] I have heard the most shocking things about her. They say she is ruining poor Windermere. And Lady Windermere, who goes in for being so proper, invites her! How extremely amusing! It takes a thoroughly good woman to do a thoroughly stupid thing. You are to lunch there on Friday!

D.: Why?

Lady P.: Because I want you to take my husband with you. He has been so attentive lately, that he has become a perfect nuisance. Now, this woman is just the thing for him. He'll dance attendance upon her as long as she lets him, and won't bother me. I assure you, women of that kind are most useful. They form the basis of other people's marriages.

D.: What a mystery you are!

Lady P.: [*Looking at him.*] I wish *you* were!

D.: I am—to myself. I am the only person in the world I should like to know thoroughly; but I don't see any chance of it just at present. [*They pass into the ball-room, and Lady Windermere and Lord Darlington enter from the terrace.*]

Lady W.: Yes. Her coming here is monstrous, unbearable. I know now what you meant to-day at tea time. Why didn't you tell me right out? You should have!

Lord D.: I couldn't! A man can't tell these things about another man! But if I had known he was going to make you ask her here to-night, I think I would have told you. That insult, at any rate, you would have been spared.

Lady W.: I did not ask her. He insisted on her coming—against my entreaties—against my commands. Oh! the house is tainted for me! I feel that every woman here sneers at me as she dances by with my husband. What have I done to deserve this? I gave him all my life. He took it—used it—spoiled it! I am degraded in my own eyes; and I lack courage—I am a coward! [*Sits down on sofa.*]

Lord D.: If I know you at all, I know that you can't live with a man who treats you like this! What sort of life would you have with him? You would feel that he was lying to you every moment of the day. You would feel that

the look in his eyes was false, his voice false, his touch false, his passion false. He would come to you when he was weary of others; you would have to comfort him. He would come to you when he was devoted to others; you would have to charm him. You would have to be to him the mask of his real life, the cloak to hide his secret.

Lady W.: You are right—you are terribly right. But where am I to turn? You said you would be my friend, Lord Darlington.—Tell me, what am I to do? Be my friend now.

Lord D.: Between men and women there is no friendship possible. There is passion, enmity, worship, love, but no friendship. I love you—

Lady W.: No, no! [*Rises.*]

Lord D.: Yes, I love you! You are more to me than anything in the whole world. What does your husband give you? Nothing. Whatever is in him he gives to this wretched woman, whom he has thrust into your society, into your home, to shame you before every one. I offer you my life—

Lady W.: Lord Darlington!

Lord D.: My life—my whole life. Take it, and do with it what you will.... I love you—love you as I have never loved any living thing. From the moment I met you I loved you, loved you blindly, adoringly, madly! You did not know it then—you know it now! Leave this house to-night. I won't tell you that the world matters nothing, or the world's voice, or the voice of society. They matter a great deal. They matter far too much. But there are moments when one has to choose between living one's own life, fully, entirely, completely—or dragging out some false, shallow, degrading existence that the world in its hypocrisy demands. You have that moment now. Choose! Oh, my love, choose!

Lady W.: [*Moving slowly away from him, and looking at him with startled eyes.*] I have not the courage.

Lord D.: [*Following her.*] Yes; you

have the courage. There may be six months of pain, of disgrace even, but when you no longer bear his name, when you bear mine, all will be well. Margaret, my love, my wife that shall be some day—yes, my wife! You know it! What are you now? This woman has the place that belongs by right to you. Oh! go—go out of this house, with head erect, with a smile upon your lips, with courage in your eyes. All London will know why you did it; and who will blame you? No one. If they do, what matter? Wrong? What is wrong? It's wrong for a man to abandon his wife for a shameless woman. It is wrong for a wife to remain with a man who so dishonours her. You said once you would make no compromise with things. Make none now. Be brave! Be yourself!

Lady W.: I am afraid of being myself. Let me think! Let me wait! My husband may return to me. [*Sits down on sofa.*]

Lord D.: And you would take him back! You are not what I thought you were. You are just the same as every other woman. You would stand anything rather than face the censure of a world whose praise you would despise. In a week you will be driving with this woman in the Park. She will be your constant guest—your dearest friend. You would endure anything rather than break with one blow this monstrous tie. You are right. You have no courage; none!

Lady W.: Ah, give me time to think. I cannot answer you now. [*Passes her hand nervously over her brow.*]

Lord D.: It must be now or not at all.

Lady W.: [*Rising from the sofa.*] Then, not at all! [*A pause.*]

Lord D.: You break my heart!

Lady W.: Mine is already broken. [*A pause.*]

Lord D.: To-morrow I leave England. This is the last time I shall ever look on you. You will never see me again. For one moment our lives met—our souls touched. They must never meet or touch again. Good-bye, Margaret. [*Exit.*]

Lady W.: How alone I am in life! How terribly alone! [*The music stops. Enter the Duchess of Berwick and Lord Paisley laughing and talking. Other guests come on from ball-room.*]

Duchess of B.: Dear Margaret, I've just been having such a delightful chat with Mrs. Erlynne. I am so sorry for what I said to you this afternoon about her. Of course, she must be all right if *you* invite her. A most attractive woman, and has such sensible views on life. Told me she entirely disapproved of people marrying more than once, so I feel quite safe about poor Augustus. Can't imagine why people speak against her. It's those horrid nieces of mine—the Saville girls—they're always talking scandal. Still, I should go to Homburg, dear, I really should. She is just a little too attractive. But where is Agatha? Oh, there she is! [*Lady Agatha and Mr. Hopper enter from terrace L.U.E.*] Mr. Hopper, I am very, very angry with you. You have taken Agatha out on the terrace, and she is so delicate.

Hopper: [*L.C.*] Awfully sorry, Duchess. We went out for a moment and then got chatting together.

Duchess of B.: [*C.*] Ah, about dear Australia, I suppose?

Hopper: Yes!

Duchess of B.: Agatha, darling! [*Beckons her over.*]

Lady A.: Yes, mamma!

Duchess of B.: [*Aside.*] Did Mr. Hopper definitely—

Lady A.: Yes, mamma.

Duchess of B.: And what answer did you give him, dear child?

Lady A.: Yes, mamma.

Duchess of B.: [*Affectionately.*] My dear one! You always say the right thing. Mr. Hopper! James! Agatha has told me everything. How cleverly you have both kept your secret.

Hopper: You don't mind my taking Agatha off to Australia, then, Duchess?

Duchess of B.: [*Indignantly.*] To Australia? Oh, don't mention that dreadful vulgar place.

H.: But she said she'd like to come with me.

Duchess of B.: [*Severely.*] Did you say that, Agatha?

Lady A.: Yes, mamma.

Duchess of B.: Agatha, you say the most silly things possible. I think on the whole that Grosvenor Square would be a more healthy place to reside in. There are lots of vulgar people live in Grosvenor Square, but at any rate there are no horrid kangaroos crawling about. But we'll talk about that to-morrow. James, you can take Agatha down. You'll come to lunch, of course, James. At half-past one, instead of two. The Duke will wish to say a few words to you, I am sure.

H.: I should like to have a chat with the Duke, Duchess. He has not said a single word to me yet.

Duchess of B.: I think you'll find he will have a great deal to say to you to-morrow. [*Exit Lady Agatha with Mr. Hopper.*] And now good-night, Margaret. I'm afraid it's the old, old story, dear. Love—well, not love at first sight, but love at the end of the season, which is so much more satisfactory.

Lady W.: Good-night, Duchess. [*Exit the Duchess of Berwick on Lord Paisley's arm.*]

Lady P.: My dear Margaret, what a handsome woman your husband has ben dancing with! I should be quite jealous if I were you! Is she a great friend of yours?

Lady W.: No!

Lady P.: Really? Good-night, dear. [*Looks at Mr. Dumby and exit.*]

D.: Awful manners young Hopper has!

Cecil G.: Ah! Hopper is one of Nature's gentlemen, the worst type of gentleman I know.

D.: Sensible woman, Lady Windermere. Lots of wives would have objected to Mrs. Erlynne coming. But Lady Windermere has that uncommon thing called common sense.

Cecil G.: And Windermere knows that nothing looks so like innocence as an indiscretion.

D.: Yes; dear Windermere is becoming almost modern. Never thought he would. [*Bows to Lady Windermere and exit.*]

Lady J.: Good-night, Lady Windermere. What a fascinating woman Mrs. Erlynne is! She is coming to lunch on Thursday, won't you come too? I expect the Bishop and dear Lady Merton.

Lady W.: I am afraid I am engaged, Lady Jedburgh.

Lady J.: So sorry. Come, dear. [*Exeunt Lady Jedburgh and Miss Graham.*] [*Enter Mrs. Erlynne and Lord Windermere.*]

Mrs. E.: Charming ball it has been! Quite reminds me of old days. [*Sits on sofa.*] And I see that there are just as many fools in society as there used to be. So pleased to find that nothing has altered! Except Margaret. She's grown quite pretty. The last time I saw her—twenty years ago, she was a fright in flannel. Positive fright, I assure you. The dear Duchess! and that sweet Lady Agatha! Just the type of girl I like! Well, really, Windermere, if I am to be the Duchess's sister-in-law—

Lord W.: [*Sitting L. of her.*] But are you—? [*Exit Mr. Cecil Graham with rest of guests Lady Windermere watches, with a look of scorn and pain, Mrs. Erlynne and her husband. They are unconscious of her presence.*]

Mrs. E.: Oh, yes! He's to call to-morrow at twelve o'clock! He wanted to propose to-night. In fact he did. He kept on proposing. Poor Augustus, you know how he repeats himself. Such a bad habit! But I told him I wouldn't give him an answer till to-morrow. Of course I am going to take him. And I dare say I'll make him an admirable wife, as wives go. And there is a great deal of good in Lord Augustus. Fortunately it is all on the surface. Just where good qualities should be. Of course you must help me in this matter.

Lord W.: I am not called on to encourage Lord Augustus, I suppose?

Mrs. E.: Oh, no! I do the encouraging. But you will make me a handsome settlement, Windermere, won't you?

Lord W.: [*Frowning.*] Is that what you want to talk to me about to-night?

Mrs. E.: Yes.

Lord W.: [*With a gesture of impatience.*] I will not talk of it here.

Mrs. E.: [*Laughing.*] Then we will talk of it on the terrace. Even business should have a picturesque background. Should it not, Windermere? With a proper background women can do anything.

Lord W.: Won't to-morrow do as well?

Mrs. E.: No, you see, to-morrow I am going to accept him. And I think it would be a good thing if I was able to tell him that I had—well, what shall I say?—£2000 a year left to me by a third cousin—or a second husband—or some distant relative of that kind. It would be an additional attraction, wouldn't it? You have a delightful opportunity now of paying me a compliment, Windermere. But you are not very clever at paying compliments. I am afraid Margaret doesn't encourage you in that excellent habit. It's a great mistake on her part. When men give up saying what is charming, they give up thinking what is charming. But seriously, what do you say to £2000? £2500, I think. In modern life margin is everything. Windermere, don't you think the world an intensely amusing place? I do! [*Exit on terrace with Lord Windermere. Music strikes up in ball-room.*]

Lady W.: To stay in this house any longer is impossible. To-night a man who loves me offered me his whole life. I refused it. It was foolish of me. I will offer him mine now. I will give him mine. I will go to him! [*Puts on cloak and goes to the door, then turns back. Sits down at table and writes a letter, puts it into an envelope, and leaves it on table.*] Arthur has never understood me. When he reads this, he will. He may do as he chooses now with his life. I have done

with mine as I think best, as I think right. It is he who has broken the bond of marriage—not I. I only break its bondage. [*Exit.*] [*Parker enters L. and crosses towards the ball-room R. Enter Mrs. Erlynne.*]

Mrs. E.: Is Lady Windermere in the ball-room?

P.: Her ladyship has just gone out.

Mrs. E.: Gone out? She's not on the terrace?

P.: No, madam. Her ladyship has just gone out of the house.

Mrs. E.: [*Starts, and looks at the servant with a puzzled expression in her face.*] Out of the house?

P.: Yes, madam—her ladyship told me she had left a letter for his lordship on the table.

Mrs. E.: A letter for Lord Windermere?

P.: Yes, madam.

Mrs. E.: Thank you. [*Exit Parker. The music in the ball-room stops.*] Gone out of her house! A letter addressed to her husband! [*Goes over to bureau and looks at letter. Takes it up and lays it down again with a shudder of fear.*] No, no! It would be impossible! Life doesn't repeat its tragedies like that! Oh, why does this horrible fancy come across me? Why do I remember now the one moment of my life I most wish to forget? Does life repeat its tragedies? [*Tears letter open and reads it, then sinks down into a chair with a gesture of anguish.*] Oh, how terrible! The same words that twenty years ago I wrote to her father! and how bitterly I have been punished for it! No; my punishment, my real punishment is to-night, is now! [*Still seated R.*] [*Enter Lord Windermere L.U.E.*]

Lord W.: Have you said good-night to my wife? [*Comes C.*]

Mrs. E.: [*Crushing letter in her hand.*] Yes.

Lord W.: Where is she?

Mrs. E.: She is very tired. She has gone to bed. She said she had a headache.

Lord W.: I must go to her. You'll excuse me?

Mrs. E.: [*Rising hurriedly.*] Oh, no! It's nothing serious. She's only very tired, that is all. Besides, there are people still in the supper-room. She wants you to make her apologies to them. She said she didn't wish to be disturbed. [*Drops letter.*] She asked me to tell you!

Lord W.: [*Picks up letter.*] You have dropped something.

Mrs. E.: Oh yes, thank you, that is mine. [*Puts out her hand to take it.*]

Lord W.: [*Still looking at letter.*] But it's my wife's handwriting, isn't it?

Mrs. E.: [*Takes the letter quickly.*] Yes, it's—an address. Will you ask them to call my carriage, please?

Lord W.: Certainly. [*Goes L. and Exit.*]

Mrs. E.: Thanks! What can I do? What can I do? I feel a passion awakening within me that I never felt before. What can it mean? The daughter must not be like the mother—that would be terrible. How can I save her? How can I save my child? A moment may ruin a life. Who knows that better than I? Windermere must be got out of the house; that is absolutely necessary. [*Goes L.*] But how shall I do it? It must be done somehow. Ah! [*Enter Lord Augustus R.U.E. carrying bouquet.*]

Lord. A.: Dear lady, I am in such suspense! May I not have an answer to my request?

Mrs. E.: Lord Augustus, listen to me. You are to take Lord Windermere down to your club at once, and keep him there as long as possible. You understand?

Lord A.: But you said you wished me to keep early hours!

Mrs. E.: [*Nervously.*] Do what I tell you. Do what I tell you.

Lord A.: And my reward?

Mrs. E.: Your reward? Your reward? Oh! ask me that to-morrow. But don't let Windermere out of your sight to-night. If you do I will never forgive you. I will never speak to you again. I'll have nothing to do with you. Remember you are to keep Windermere at your club, and don't let him come back to-night. [*Exit L.*]

Lord A.: Well, really, I might be her husband already. Positively I might. [*Follows her in a bewildered manner.*]

NOTES ON ACT II

Act II is the product of all the skillful preparations made in Act I. Note how all the lines of action established in Act I—those in which the Duchess, Lady W., and Mrs. Erlynne are the principals—have been followed up. Because of the carefulness and completeness of the prearrangements, everything appears to move ahead very smoothly.

But in writing Act II Wilde has more of a task than that of presenting the inevitable outcome of what was started in Act I. He has to arrange a complex set of materials in such a way that interest will be continuous, action progressive, and the effect climactic. Note his great initial advantage in having all the action take place at a ball: because of this fact the whole problem of exits and entrances becomes an easy one, and the author gains an unusual freedom in moving his characters about—in and out of the scene. He can devote all his energies to the effects he wishes to secure.

The Structure of Act II. The main structure of Act II is clear: Wilde arranges all the action around *three major points* of interest. So the whole Act moves in a recognizable *rhythm* of heightening and decreasing tension, reaching three climactic points, the third being the most sustained. This pattern is amplified further by Wilde's use of two moods, one quite serious, the other rather gay and witty. He alternates these not only for variety but also to support the basic pattern: the relaxation after a tense point usually takes the form of a lighter and gayer passage. The Act is written, as it were, in contrasting panels.

It is also written so as to present a logical progression from one high point to another: Lady W. has to be influenced by Mrs. Erlynne before she can listen to further proposals by Darlington, and she needs further persuasion by Darlington before she can decide to leave with him. Hence the Act seems tight and orderly in its construction.

The first high point is the arrival of Mrs. Erlynne, an incident toward which the latter part of Act I has been pointed. Notice how carefully Wilde sets the stage for Mrs. E.'s entry, toward which the first part of Act II moves in a crescendo. First, we have a general view of society. But in order to keep this from being detached and undramatic, Wilde uses, as a center for it, the already familiar Berwick-Agatha-Hopper action, which is developed a step further. Second, we have the dialogue between Lord Augustus and Lord Windermere, which not only focuses our attention on the coming arrival of Mrs. E., but also indicates Lord Augustus's interest in her and thus looks ahead toward other possibilities. Further, since Lord Augustus is the brother of the Duchess of Berwick, we find signs of a division in Society's attitude toward Mrs. Erlynne. Then, just before Mrs. E.'s arrival, Wilde skillfully focuses our attention by means of the fan. Why does he wish to make us very conscious of the fan? How does he set about doing it? What is the significance of Lady Windermere's dropping her fan at the climactic moment?

When Lady Windermere does not strike or assault Mrs. Erlynne, the issue is of course settled for the moment, tension relaxes, and Wilde introduces a panel of action in the lighter mood. But the contrast in tone does not obscure a real continuity: first Mrs. Erlynne faces her chief enemy, Lady Windermere, and then goes on to face the others. Matters become slightly more serious in the dialogue between Dumby and Lady Plymdale, which is brief but significant. What is Wilde getting at by indicating quite clearly the relationship between the two? The tone again becomes completely serious in the Darlington-Lady W. dialogue, which contains the second climactic moment of the Act—Lady W.'s refusal of Darlington.

Again we find a reduction of tension and a humorous panel—the completion of the Agatha-Hopper affair. Can you see by now how this secondary strand of action is woven into the theme? What, for instance, is the relation of this "love" affair to the love of Darlington for Lady W.? To Lady Berwick's suspicion of Mrs. Erlynne and of husbands in general? How does the Duchess contrast with Lady W.?

The third period of high tension is the most sustained, lasting from Lady W.'s decision to the end of the Act. Note how the three climaxes are related: since the second is more sustained than the first, and the third more than the second, we have an over-all rising movement; and further, at each climax, Lady W. is *making a decision*. In other words, the act is essentially hers, dramatizing her psychological development.

Evidences of Melodrama. After Lady W. leaves, however, and Mrs. Erlynne takes over the stage, we have a *shift in point of view*. That is, Wilde is not merely examining Lady W.'s internal conflict; rather he is interested in making a comparison. Hence we must learn about the comparable case. Since he wished to do it in this way, Wilde was doubtless willing to take the risk of the loss of continuity entailed in the shift of point of view.

Here is a good opportunity to note a difference between drama and other forms. Either a movie or a novel, for instance, could have kept both Lady W. and Mrs. Erlynne in view simultaneously and thus achieved some excellent effects. Drama cannot, so to speak, see things *simultaneously* but must present them *consecutively*. What it so loses is clear; but can you also see what it may gain? Further, how might the party of Act II have been handled differently by fiction or movie? What other events might have been presented directly? What might a movie have tended to overemphasize?

Note certain other problems at this point: (1) Lest Mrs. Erlynne's concern over Lady W. seem unmotivated, Wilde must make explanations. Why must Wilde use a soliloquy here? Now, we can accept the soliloquy as a *convention* (see Glossary), but beyond that we also can ask that it *work*. The question is not so much, Is it true to life?, as, Does it do what it is supposed to do? In this case, does Mrs. Erlynne's revelation seem easily and logically made, and does her emotion seem plausible? Or is it awkward and unconvincing, and even rather melodramatic? Does the management of this part of the act seem to indicate hasty or careless work on the part of Wilde? (2) Since Lord Augustus is Mrs. Erlynne's only available helper, it is he who must get Lord W. out of the house. But from what we have seen of Lord A. it is difficult to believe that he could get anybody to go anywhere (note, incidentally, that this little episode increases our knowledge of the relationship between Mrs. E. and Lord A.). (3) Mrs. Erlynne can discover and take part in what is going on only by finding and reading a letter addressed to someone else. Is not this the sort of device used in adventure and mystery stories, that is, in *melodrama*? (For a further discussion of this term, see the Glossary.)

In fact, do not all the difficulties here derive from the fact that Wilde is giving the play a melodramatic turn? He appears to lose interest in presenting the development of Lady W.'s character and to prefer, instead, to save her from the consequences of her mistake. That is, by turning from Lady W., he shows that he actually stops studying her beliefs and impulses; he turns from *analyzing* her to *rescuing* her. As Mrs. Erlynne takes charge of the situation, what we see coming up is precisely the last-minute rescue. Wilde gives up the problem of character and limits himself to purely external, mechanical matters. This is one of the ways of melodrama.

THIRD ACT

[SCENE. Lord Darlington's Rooms. A large sofa is in front of fireplace R. At the back of the stage a curtain is drawn across the window. Doors L. and R. Table R. with writing materials. Table C. with syphons, glasses, and Tantalus frame. Table L. with cigar and cigarette box. Lamps lit.]

Lady W.: [*Standing by the fireplace.*] Why doesn't he come? This waiting is horrible. He should be here. Why is he not here, to wake by passionate words some fire within me? I am cold—cold as a loveless thing. Arthur must have read my letter by this time. If he cared for me, he would have come after me, would have taken me back by force. But he doesn't care. He's entrammelled by this woman—fascinated by her—dominated by her. If a woman wants to hold a man, she has merely to appeal to what is worst in him. We make gods of men and they leave us. Others makes brutes of them and they fawn and are faithful. How hideous life is! . . . Oh! it was mad of me to come here, horribly mad. And yet, which is the worst, I wonder, to be at the mercy of a man who loves one, or the wife of a man who in one's own house dishonours one? What woman knows? What woman in the whole world? But will he love me always, this man to whom I am giving my life? What do I bring him? Lips that have lost the note of joy, eyes that are blinded by tears, chill hands and icy heart. I bring him nothing. I must go back—no; I can't go back, my letter has put me in their power—Arthur would not take me back! That fatal letter! No! Lord Darlington leaves England to-morrow. I will go with him—I have no choice. [*Sits down for a few moments. Then starts up and puts on her cloak.*] No, no! I will go back, let Arthur do with me what he pleases. I can't wait here. It has been madness my coming. I must go at once. As for Lord Darlington—Oh! here he is! What shall I do? What can I say to him? Will

he let me go away at all? I have heard that men are brutal, horrible . . . Oh! [*Hides her face in her hands.*] [*Enter Mrs. Erlynne L.*]

Mrs. E.: Lady Windermere! [*Lady Windermere starts and looks up. Then recoils in contempt.*] Thank Heaven I am in time. You must go back to your husband's house immediately.

Lady W.: Must?

Mrs. E.: [*Authoritatively.*] Yes, you must! There is not a second to be lost. Lord Darlington may return at any moment.

Lady W.: Don't come near me!

Mrs. E.: Oh! You are on the brink of ruin, you are on the brink of a hideous precipice. You must leave this place at once, my carriage is waiting at the corner of the street. You must come with me and drive straight home. [*Lady Windermere throws off her cloak and flings it on the sofa.*] What are you doing?

Lady W.: Mrs. Erlynne—if you had not come here, I would have gone back. But now that I see you, I feel that nothing in the whole world would induce me to live under the same roof as Lord Windermere. You fill me with horror. There is something about you that stirs the wildest—rage within me. And I know why you are here. My husband sent you to lure me back that I might serve as a blind to whatever relations exist between you and him.

Mrs. E.: Oh! You don't think that— you can't.

Lady W.: Go back to my husband, Mrs. Erlynne. He belongs to you and not to me. I suppose he is afraid of a scandal. Men are such cowards. They outrage every law of the world, and are afraid of the world's tongue. But he had better prepare himself. He shall have a scandal. He shall have the worst scandal there has been in London for years. He shall see his name in every vile paper, mine on every hideous placard.

Mrs. Erlynne: No—no—

Lady W.: Yes! he shall. Had he come

himself, I admit I would have gone back to the life of degradation you and he had prepared for me—I was going back—but to stay himself at home, and to send you as his messenger—oh! it was infamous—infamous.

Mrs. E.: [*C.*] Lady Windermere, you wrong me horribly—you wrong your husband horribly. He doesn't know you are here—he thinks you are safe in your own house. He thinks you are asleep in your own room. He never read the mad letter you wrote to him!

Lady W.: [*R.*] Never read it!

Mrs. E.: No—he knows nothing about it.

Lady W.: How simple you think me! [*Going to her.*] You are lying to me!

Mrs. E.: [*Restraining herself.*] I am not. I am telling you the truth.

Lady W.: If my husband didn't read my letter, how is it that you are here? Who told you I had left the house you were shameless enough to enter? Who told you where I had gone to? My husband told you, and sent you to decoy me back. [*Crosses L.*]

Mrs. E.: [*R.C.*] Your husband has never seen the letter. I—saw it, I opened it. I—read it.

Lady W.: [*Turning to her.*] You opened a letter of mine to my husband? You wouldn't dare!

Mrs. E.: Dare! Oh! to save you from the abyss into which you are falling, there is nothing in the world I would not dare, nothing in the whole world. Here is the letter. Your husband has never read it. He never shall read it. [*Going to fireplace.*] It should never have been written. [*Tears it and throws it into the fire.*]

Lady W.: [*With infinite contempt in her voice and look.*] How do I know that that was my letter after all? You seem to think the commonest device can take me in!

Mrs. E.: Oh! why do you disbelieve everything I tell you? What object do you think I have in coming here, except to save you from utter ruin, to save you

from the consequence of a hideous mistake? That letter that is burnt now *was* your letter. I swear it to you!

Lady W.: [*Slowly.*] You took good care to burn it before I had examined it. I cannot trust you. You, whose whole life is a lie, how could you speak the truth about anything? [*Sits down.*]

Mrs. E.: [*Hurriedly.*] Think as you like about me—say what you choose against me, but go back, go back to the husband you love.

Lady W.: [*Sullenly.*] I do *not* love him!

Mrs. E.: You do, and you know that he loves you.

Lady W.: He does not understand what love is. He understands it as little as you do—but I see what you want. It would be a great advantage for you to get me back. Dear Heaven! what a life I would have then! Living at the mercy of a woman who has neither mercy nor pity in her, a woman whom it is an infamy to meet, a degradation to know, a vile woman, a woman who comes between husband and wife!

Mrs. E.: [*With a gesture of despair.*] Lady Windermere, Lady Windermere, don't say such terrible things. You don't know how terrible they are, how terrible and how unjust. Listen, you must listen! Only go back to your husband, and I promise you never to communicate with him again on any pretext—never to see him—never to have anything to do with his life or yours. The money that he gave me, he gave me not through love, but through hatred, not in worship, but in contempt. The hold I have over him—

Lady W.: [*Rising.*] Ah! you admit you have a hold!

Mrs. E.: Yes, and I will tell you what it is. It is his love for you, Lady Windermere.

Lady W.: You expect me to believe that?

Mrs. E.: You must believe it! It is true. It is his love for you that has made him submit to—oh! call it what you like, tyranny, threats, anything **you** choose. But it is his love for you. His desire to spare you—shame, yes, shame and disgrace.

Lady W.: What do you mean? You are insolent! What have I to do with you?

Mrs. E.: [*Humbly.*] Nothing. I know it—but I tell you that your husband loves you—that you may never meet with such love again in your whole life —that such love you will never meet— and that if you throw it away, the day may come when you will starve for love and it will not be given to you, beg for love and it will be denied you—Oh! Arthur loves you!

Lady W.: Arthur? And you tell me there is nothing between you?

Mrs. E.: Lady Windermere, before Heaven your husband is guiltless of all offence towards you! And I—I tell you that had it ever occurred to me that such a monstrous suspicion would have entered your mind, I would have died rather than have crossed your life or his—oh! died, gladly died! [*Moves away to sofa R.*]

Lady W.: You talk as if you had a heart. Women like you have no hearts. Heart is not in you. You are bought and sold. [*Sits L.C.*]

Mrs. E.: [*Starts, with a gesture of pain. Then restrains herself, and comes over to where Lady Windermere is sitting. As she speaks, she stretches out her hands towards her, but does not dare to touch her.*] Believe what you choose about me. I am not worth a moment's sorrow. But don't spoil your beautiful young life on my account! You don't know what may be in store for you, unless you leave this house at once. You don't know what it is to fall into the pit, to be despised, mocked, abandoned, sneered at—to be an outcast! to find the door shut against one, to have to creep in by hideous byways, afraid every moment lest the mask should be stripped from one's face, and all the while to hear the laughter, the horrible laughter of the world, a thing more tragic than all the tears the world has ever shed. You don't know what it is. One pays for one's sin, and then one pays again, and all one's life one pays. You must never know that.— As for me, if suffering be an expiation, then at this moment I have expiated all my faults, whatever they have been; for to-night you have made a heart in one who had it not, made it and broken it. —But let that pass. I may have wrecked my own life, but I will not let you wreck yours. You—why, you are a mere girl, you would be lost. You haven't got the kind of brains that enables a woman to get back. You have neither the wit nor the courage. You couldn't stand dishonour! No! Go back, Lady Windermere, to the husband who loves you, whom you love. You have a child, Lady Windermere. Go back to that child who even now, in pain or in joy, may be calling to you. [*Lady Windermere rises.*] God gave you that child. He will require from you that you make his life fine, that you watch over him. What answer will you make to God if his life is ruined through you? Back to your house, Lady Windermere—your husband loves you! He has never swerved for a moment from the love he bears you. But even if he had a thousand loves, you must stay with your child. If he was harsh to you, you must stay with your child. If he ill-treated you, you must stay with your child. If he abandoned you, your place is with your child. [*Lady Windermere bursts into tears and buries her face in her hands.*] [*Rushing to her.*] Lady Windermere!

Lady W.: [*Holding out her hands to her, helplessly, as a child might do.*] Take me home. Take me home.

Mrs. E.: [*Is about to embrace her. Then restrains herself. There is a look of wonderful joy in her face.*] Come! Where is your cloak? [*Getting it from sofa.*] Here. Put it on. Come at once! [*They go to the door.*]

Lady W.: Stop! Don't you hear voices?

Mrs. E.: No, no! There is no one!

Lady W.: Yes, there is! Listen! Oh! that is my husband's voice! He is coming in! Save me! Oh, it's some plot! You have sent for him. [*Voices outside.*]

Mrs. E.: Silence! I'm here to save you, if I can. But I fear it is too late! There! [*Points to the curtain across the window.*] The first chance you have, slip out, if you ever get a chance!   10

Lady W.: But you?

Mrs. E.: Oh! never mind me. I'll face them. [*Lady Windermere hides herself behind the curtain.*]

Lord A.: [*Outside.*] Nonsense, dear 15 Windermere, you must not leave me!

Mrs. E.: Lord Augustus! Then it is I who am lost! [*Hesitates for a moment, then looks round and sees door R., and exit through it.*] [*Enter Lord Darlington,* 20 *Mr. Dumby, Lord Windermere, Lord Augustus Lorton, and Mr. Cecil Graham.*]

Dumby: What a nuisance their turning us out of the club at this hour! It's only two o'clock. [*Sinks into a chair.*] 25 The lively part of the evening is only just beginning. [*Yawns and closes his eyes.*]

Lord W.: It is very good of you, Lord Darlington, allowing Augustus to force 30 our company on you, but I'm afraid I can't stay long.

Lord D.: Really! I am so sorry! You'll take a cigar, won't you?

Lord W.: Thanks! [*Sits down.*]   35

Lord A.: [*To Lord Windermere.*] My dear boy, you must not dream of going. I have a great deal to talk to you about, of demmed importance, too. [*Sits down with him at L. table.*]   40

Cecil G.: Oh! We all know what that is! Tuppy can't talk about anything but Mrs. Erlynne!

Lord W.: Well, that is no business of yours, is it, Cecil?   45

Cecil G.: None! That is why it interests me. My own business always bores me to death. I prefer other people's.

Lord D.: Have something to drink, you fellows. Cecil, you'll have a whiskey 50 and soda?

Cecil G.: Thanks. [*Goes to table with Lord Darlington.*] Mrs. Erlynne looked very handsome to-night, didn't she?

Lord D.: I am not one of her ad- 5 mirers.

Cecil G.: I usen't to be, but I am now. Why! she actually made me introduce her to poor dear Aunt Caroline. I believe she is going to lunch there.

Lord D.: [*In surprise.*] No?

Cecil G.: She is, really.

Lord D.: Excuse me, you fellows. I'm going away to-morrow. And I have to write a few letters. [*Goes to writing table and sits down.*]

D.: Clever woman, Mrs. Erlynne.

Cecil G.: Hallo, Dumby! I thought you were asleep.

D.: I am, I usually am!

Lord A.: A very clever woman. Knows perfectly well what a demmed fool I am—knows it as well as I do myself. [*Cecil Graham comes towards him laughing.*] Ah, you may laugh, my boy, but it is a great thing to come across a woman who thoroughly understands one.

D.: It is an awfully dangerous thing They always end by marrying one.

Cecil G.: But I thought, Tuppy, you were never going to see her again! Yes! you told me so yesterday evening at the club. You said you'd heard—[*Whispering to him.*]

Lord A.: Oh, she's explained that.

Cecil G.: And the Wiesbaden affair?

Lord A.: She's explained that too.

Dumby: And her income, Tuppy? Has she explained that?

Lord A.: [*In a very serious voice.*] She's going to explain that to-morrow. [*Cecil Graham goes back to C. table.*]

D.: Awfully commercial, women nowadays. Our grandmothers threw their 45 caps over the mills, of course, but by Jove, their granddaughters only throw their caps over mills that can raise the wind for them.

Lord A.: You want to make her out a 50 wicked woman. She is not!

Cecil G.: Oh! Wicked women bother

one. Good women bore one. That is the only difference between them.

Lord A.: [*Puffing a cigar.*] Mrs. Erlynne has a future before her.

D.: Mrs. Erlynne has a past before her.

Lord A.: I prefer women with a past. They're always so demmed amusing to talk to.

Cecil G.: Well, you'll have lots of topics of conversation with *her*, Tuppy. [*Rising and going to him.*]

Lord A.: You're getting annoying, dear boy; you're getting demmed annoying.

Cecil G.: [*Puts his hands on his shoulders.*] Now, Tuppy, you've lost your figure and you've lost your character. Don't lose your temper; you have only got one.

Lord A.: My dear boy, if I wasn't the most good-natured man in London—

Cecil G.: We'd treat you with more respect, wouldn't we, Tuppy? [*Strolls away.*]

D.: The youth of the present day are quite monstrous. They have absolutely no respect for dyed hair. [*Lord Augustus looks round angrily.*]

Cecil G.: Mrs. Erlynne has a very great respect for dear Tuppy.

D.: Then Mrs. Erlynne sets an admirable example to the rest of her sex. It is perfectly brutal the way most women nowadays behave to men who are not their husbands.

Lord W.: Dumby, you are ridiculous, and Cecil, you let your tongue run away with you. You must leave Mrs. Erlynne alone. You don't really know anything about her, and you're always talking scandal against her.

Cecil G.: [*Coming towards him L.C.*] My dear Arthur, I never talk scandal. *I* only talk gossip.

Lord W.: What is the difference between scandal and gossip?

Cecil G.: Oh! gossip is charming! History is merely gossip. But scandal is gossip made tedious by morality. Now, I never moralise. A man who moralises is usually a hypocrite, and a woman who moralises is invariably plain. There is nothing in the whole world so unbecoming to a woman as a Nonconformist conscience. And most women know it, I'm glad to say.

Lord A.: Just my sentiments, dear boy, just my sentiments.

Cecil G.: Sorry to hear it, Tuppy; whenever people agree with me, I always feel I must be wrong.

Lord A.: My dear boy, when I was your age—

Cecil G.: But you never were, Tuppy, and you never will be. [*Goes up C.*] I say, Darlington, let us have some cards. You'll play. Arthur, won't you?

Lord W.: No, thanks, Cecil.

D.: [*With a sigh.*] Good heavens! how marriage ruins a man! It's as demoralising as cigarettes, and far more expensive.

Cecil G.: You'll play, of course, Tuppy?

Lord A.: [*Pouring himself out a brandy and soda at table.*] Can't, dear boy. Promised Mrs. Erlynne never to play or drink again.

Cecil G.: Now, my dear Tuppy, don't be led astray into the paths of virtue. Reformed, you would be perfectly tedious. That is the worst of women. They always want one to be good. And if we are good, when they meet us, they don't love us at all. They like to find us quite irretrievably bad, and to leave us quite unattractively good.

Lord D.: [*Rising from R. table, where he has been writing letters.*] They always do find us bad!

D.: I don't think we are bad. I think we are all good, except Tuppy.

Lord D.: No, we are all in the gutter, but some of us are looking at the stars. [*Sits down at C. table.*]

D.: We are all in the gutter, but some of us are looking at the stars? Upon my word, you are very romantic to-night, Darlington.

Cecil G.: Too romantic! You must be in love. Who is the girl?

Lord D.: The woman I love is not free, or thinks she isn't. [*Glances instinctively at Lord Windermere while he speaks.*]

Cecil G.: A married woman, then! Well, there's nothing in the world like the devotion of a married woman. It's a thing no married man knows anything about.

Lord D.: Oh! she doesn't love me. She is a good woman. She is the only good woman I have ever met in my life.

Cecil G.: The only good woman you have ever met in your life?

Lord D.: Yes!

Cecil G.: [*Lighting a cigarette.*] Well, you are a lucky fellow! Why, I have met hundreds of good women. I never seem to meet any but good women. The world is perfectly packed with good women. To know them is a middle-class education.

Lord D.: This woman has purity and innocence. She has everything we men have lost.

Cecil G.: My dear fellow, what on earth should we men do going about with purity and innocence? A carefully thought-out buttonhole is much more effective.

D.: She doesn't really love you then?

Lord D.: No, she does not!

D.: I congratulate you, my dear fellow. In this world there are only two tragedies. One is not getting what one wants, and the other is getting it. The last is much the worst, the last is a real tragedy! But I am interested to hear she does not love you. How long could you love a woman who didn't love you, Cecil?

Cecil G.: A woman who didn't love me? Oh, all my life!

D.: So could I. But it's so difficult to meet one.

Lord D.: How can you be so conceited, Dumby?

D.: I didn't say it as a matter of conceit. I said it as a matter of regret. I have been wildly, madly adored. I am sorry I have. It has been an immense nuisance. I should like to be allowed a little time to myself now and then.

Lord A.: [*Looking round.*] Time to educate yourself, I suppose.

D.: No, time to forget all I have learned. That is much more important, dear Tuppy. [*Lord Augustus moves uneasily in his chair.*]

Lord D.: What cynics you fellows are!

Cecil G.: What is a cynic? [*Sitting on the back of the sofa.*]

Lord D.: A man who knows the price of everything and the value of nothing.

Cecil G.: And a sentimentalist, my dear Darlington, is a man who sees an absurd value in everything, and doesn't know the market price of any single thing.

Lord D.: You always amuse me, Cecil. You talk as if you were a man of experience.

Cecil G.: I am. [*Moves up to front of fireplace.*]

Lord D.: You are far too young!

Cecil G.: That is a great error. Experience is a question of instinct about life. I have got it. Tuppy hasn't. Experience is the name Tuppy gives to his mistakes. That is all. [*Lord Augustus looks round indignantly.*]

D.: Experience is the name every one gives to their mistakes.

Cecil G.: [*Standing with his back to the fireplace.*] One shouldn't commit any. [*Sees Lady Windermere's fan on sofa.*]

D.: Life would be very dull without them.

Cecil G.: Of course you are quite faithful to this woman you are in love with, Darlington, to this good woman?

Lord D.: Cecil, if one really loves a woman, all other women in the world become absolutely meaningless to one. Love changes one—*I* am changed.

Cecil G.: Dear me! How very interesting! Tuppy, I want to talk to you. [*Lord Augustus takes no notice.*]

D.: It's no use talking to Tuppy. You might just as well talk to a brick wall.

Cecil G.: But I like talking to a brick

wall—it's the only thing in the world that never contradicts me! Tuppy!

Lord A.: Well, what is it? What is it? [*Rising and going over to Cecil Graham.*]

Cecil G.: Come over here. I want you particularly. [*Aside.*] Darlington has been moralising and talking about the purity of love, and that sort of thing, and he has got some woman in his rooms all the time.

Lord A.: No, really! really!

Cecil G.: [*In a low voice.*] Yes, here is her fan. [*Points to the fan.*]

Lord A.: [*Chuckling.*] By Jove! By Jove!

Lord W.: [*Up by door.*] I am really off now, Lord Darlington. I am sorry you are leaving England so soon. Pray call on us when you come back! My wife and I will be charmed to see you!

Lord D.: [*Up stage with Lord Windermere.*] I am afraid I shall be away for many years. Good-night!

Cecil G.: Arthur!

Lord W.: What?

Cecil G.: I want to speak to you for a moment. No, do come!

Lord W.: [*Putting on his coat.*] I can't —I'm off!

Cecil G.: It is something very particular. It will interest you enormously.

Lord W.: [*Smiling.*] It is some of your nonsense, Cecil.

Cecil G.: It isn't! It isn't really.

Lord A.: [*Going to him.*] My dear fellow, you mustn't go yet. I have a lot to talk to you about. And Cecil has something to show you.

Lord W.: [*Walking over.*] Well, what is it?

Cecil G.: Darlington has got a woman here in his rooms. Here is her fan. Amusing, isn't it? [*A pause.*]

Lord W.: Good God! [*Seizes the fan— Dumby rises.*]

Cecil G.: What is the matter?

Lord W.: Lord Darlington!

Lord D.: [*Turning round.*] Yes!

Lord W.: What is my wife's fan doing here in your rooms? Hands off, Cecil. Don't touch me.

Lord D.: Your wife's fan?

Lord W.: Yes, here it is!

Lord D.: [*Walking towards him.*] I don't know!

Lord W.: You must know. I demand an explanation. Don't hold me, you fool. [*To Cecil Graham.*]

Lord D.: [*Aside.*] She is here after all!

Lord W.: Speak, sir! Why is my wife's fan here? Answer me! By God! I'll search your rooms, and if my wife's here, I'll—[*Moves.*]

Lord D.: You shall not search my rooms. You have no right to do so. I forbid you!

Lord W.: You scoundrel! I'll not leave your room till I have searched every corner of it! What moves behind that curtain? [*Rushes towards the curtain C.*]

Mrs. E.: [*Enters behind R.*] Lord Windermere!

Lord W.: Mrs. Erlynne! [*Every one starts and turns round. Lady Windermere slips out from behind the curtain and glides from the room L.*]

Mrs. E.: I am afraid I took your wife's fan in mistake for my own, when I was leaving your house to-night. I am so sorry. [*Takes fan from him. Lord Windermere looks at her in contempt. Lord Darlington in mingled astonishment and anger. Lord Augustus turns away. The other men smile at each other.*]

NOTES ON ACT III

The Rhythm of Act III. Like Act II, Act III has several climactic points. What are they? How are they related to each other? How does Wilde work up to each one? Do we find any relaxation of tension after each climactic point, as in Act II? Is there any alternation of moods, as in Act II? Note the rather long witty passage between the arrival of the men and Cecil's discovery of the fan. Is this waste motion—simply so much repartee? Does the dialogue have any bearing on the theme? Is there, beneath the surface of the witty interchange, any contrast in mood? Is this part of the act "relaxed," or could it be argued that the wit itself maintains a kind of intellectual tension? Is this tension different from that of the first half of the Act?

The Melodramatic Tendency; Motivation. Here we see Wilde, though he does make some fight against it, continuing in his drift toward melodrama. For in general Act III goes on with a last-minute rescue, managed largely by forces *outside* the person being rescued; the force of which we see most is Mrs. E.'s resourcefulness. Lady W. does, of course, help to save herself. There is a real conflict between her and Mrs. E., she acquires new insight and undergoes a definite growth, and thus we have a genuine dramatic action. The ironic assurance with which Lady W. misjudges the intentions of Mrs. E. is an important part of the dramatic effect. There are, however, two ways in which the action might have produced a more profound sense of drama. If Lady W., with her ironic misunderstanding, had actually run away with Lord D., we would have had to come to grips with more fundamental complications. In that case, Lady W., the essentially good person with the *hamartia* or "tragic flaw" (terms frequently encountered in dramatic criticism), might have resembled closely the tragic "hero" defined by Aristotle (see Glossary). On the other hand, Act III might have been a very important step in a study of the growth of character of Mrs. Erlynne. But that purpose would have required a completely different orientation or "focus" (for a fuller discussion of this term, see the Glossary), with Mrs. E. in the central position and Lady W. "played down." The fact that our attention is now divided somewhat between the two indicates some lack of focus, some failure to get down to the basic problem of either of them.

Wilde, however, appears to prefer external complications. If he had wished to focus attention on Lady W.'s inner struggle, he might just as well—and perhaps better—have done it without all the to-do at Lord Darlington's, which shifts attention from the problem to the rescue. With his technical ingenuity, Wilde could certainly have managed to bring Lady W. and Mrs. E. together at Lady W.'s place. But he had evidently predetermined to have the excitement at Lord D's. Now notice all the difficulties he runs into in carrying out this plan.

First, he has no real reason for keeping Lord D. away from his apartment; indeed, we might expect him to be at home preparing to "leave England" next day. Second, Wilde has to rely on the accidental discovery of the letter to get Mrs. Erlynne to Lord D.'s apartment. Third, he has to rely on the accident of the men's arriving just at the climax of the scene between the women. Fourth, Wilde has no workable explanation of how the men happen to be there at all. Dumby says that they were put out of a club and that Lord Augustus "forced" them on Lord D., but *why* should it be Lord D. rather than someone else, and *how* could Lord Augustus, of all people, successfully do the forcing? Fifth, in order to have a double concealment, Wilde makes Mrs. Erlynne hide from Lord Augustus—although we have previously seen Mrs. Erlynne masterfully controlling Lord Augustus, and Lord Augustus overcome by Mrs. Erlynne's skill in explaining things.

Here we see a dramatist battling with certain problems of time and place, which we spoke about earlier in Part I (see p. 29). When he does not handle them very plausibly, we have a sense of poor *motivation*. Many readers will feel that here Wilde has arbitrarily decided on a certain type of scene and then has had to resort too much to trickery and unsubtle manipulation to bring it about.

A concealment scene may be used for legitimate and even brilliant dramatic effects, as we shall see when we come to read Sheridan's *School for Scandal*. Though we cannot now compare the two, we may suggest one or two contrasts. Note that, since none of Wilde's characters on the stage knows that anyone else is present, there can be none of the interaction which is a basic element in the corresponding Sheridan scene. Hence Wilde's scene is thinner, less dynamic; it is one-dimensional. Further, since the concealed women can actually *learn* nothing from what they overhear, the conversation on the stage can have no effect on them. Hence the scene depends for its effect entirely upon the possibility of discovery of the concealed persons. No real question of *character* is involved. The threat of discovery, the stress on the hairbreadth escape—this is the mood of melodrama, and to do him justice, Wilde makes the most of the possibility. Note how Wilde multiplies the threats in the last several pages of the scene. It is this rapid-fire series of thrills toward which he has directed the whole act. Does it not seem, in the long run, however, that to gain such an effect he has had to stay on a rather superficial level and proceed by too artificial means?

The Mother-Daughter Coincidence. The most striking coincidence is of course the resemblance between the experiences of mother and daughter, and the fact that the mother is present to aid her daughter at the critical moment. The danger here is that the author will seem to be more intent on a startling resemblance than on a study of character (for a comment on a somewhat similar handling of materials see the discussion of Somerset Maugham's *The Circle* in Appendix A). Wilde tries to reduce this danger in various ways: (1) By carefully preparing us for the fact that Mrs. Erlynne is Lady W.'s mother, he has endeavored to reduce the sense of surprise which would tend to reinforce our feeling that the situation is purely coincidental. (2) By introducing the irony of Lady W.'s unjustly suspecting Lord W. of having an affair with Mrs. Erlynne, he suggests that he is interested in more than a duplication for its own sake. (3) By making the experiences of mother and daughter come out very differently he reduces the appearance of having an improbable repetition. (4) By not making Mrs. Erlynne known to Lady W. he eliminates possible sentimental effects;

hence we are somewhat the more willing to acquit him of the charge of giving us a put-up job.

It is possible that Wilde, if questioned, would have justified his risk—of seeming to derive his major effects from an improbable coincidence—in this way. Lady W. is too inflexible and doctrinaire in her judgments. She can learn only from someone of wider experience. But it is precisely the person of worldly experience to whom she will not listen. Hence such a person must gain Lady W.'s trust by some striking act of devotion. This act of devotion, Wilde might argue, could be performed only by someone with maternal protectiveness and unselfishness. How plausible would you find this case?

FOURTH ACT

[SCENE. Same as in Act I.]

Lady W.: [*Lying on sofa.*] How can I tell him? I can't tell him. It would kill me. I wonder what happened after I escaped from that horrible room. Perhaps she told them the true reason of her being there, and the real meaning of that—fatal fan of mine. Oh, if he knows— how can I look him in the face again? He would never forgive me. [*Touches bell.*] How securely one thinks one lives —out of reach of temptation, sin, folly. And then suddenly—Oh! Life is terrible. It rules us, we do not rule it. [*Enter Rosalie R.*]

Rosalie: Did your ladyship ring for me?

Lady W.: Yes. Have you found out at what time Lord Windermere came in last night?

R.: His lordship did not come in till five o'clock.

Lady W.: Five o'clock? He knocked at my door this morning, didn't he?

R.: Yes, my lady—at half-past nine. I told him your ladyship was not awake yet.

Lady W.: Did he say anything?

R.: Something about your ladyship's fan. I didn't quite catch what his lordship said. Has the fan been lost, my lady? I can't find it, and Parker says it was not left in any of the rooms. He has looked in all of them and on the terrace as well.

Lady W.: It doesn't matter. Tell Parker not to trouble. That will do. [*Exit Rosalie.*]

Lady W.: [*Rising.*] She is sure to tell him. I can fancy a person doing a wonderful act of self-sacrifice, doing it spontaneously, recklessly, nobly—and afterwards finding out that it costs too much. Why should she hesitate between her ruin and mine? . . . How strange! I would have publicly disgraced her in my own house. She accepts public disgrace in the house of another to save me. . . . There is a bitter irony in things, a bitter irony in the way we talk of good and bad women. . . . Oh, what a lesson! and what a pity that in life we only get our lessons when they are of no use to us! For even if she doesn't tell, I must. Oh! the shame of it, the shame of it. To tell it is to live through it all again. Actions are the first tragedy in life, words are the second. Words are perhaps the worst. Words are merciless. . . . Oh! [*Starts as Lord Windermere enters.*]

Lord W.: [*Kisses her.*] Margaret— how pale you look!

Lady W.: I slept very badly.

Lord W.: [*Sitting on sofa with her.*] I am so sorry. I came in dreadfully late, and didn't like to wake you. You are crying, dear.

Lady W.: Yes, I am crying, for I have something to tell you, Arthur.

Lord W.: My dear child, you are not well. You've been doing too much. Let us go away to the country. You'll be all right at Selby. The season is almost over.

There is no use staying on. Poor darling! We'll go away to-day, if you like. [*Rises.*] We can easily catch the 3:40. I'll send a wire to Fannen. [*Crosses and sits down at table to write a telegram.*]

Lady W.: Yes; let us go away to-day. No; I can't go to-day, Arthur. There is some one I must see before I leave town—some one who has been kind to me.

Lord W.: [*Rising and leaning over sofa.*] Kind to you?

Lady W.: Far more than that. [*Rises and goes to him.*] I will tell you, Arthur, but only love me, love me as you used to love me.

Lord W.: Used to? You are not thinking of that wretched woman who came here last night? [*Coming round and sitting R. of her.*] You don't still imagine —no, you couldn't.

Lady W.: I don't. I know now I was wrong and foolish.

Lord W.: It was very good of you to receive her last night—but you are never to see her again.

Lady W.: Why do you say that? [*A pause.*]

Lord W.: [*Holding her hand.*] Margaret, I thought Mrs. Erlynne was a woman more sinned against than sinning, as the phrase goes. I thought she wanted to be good, to get back into a place that she had lost by a moment's folly, to lead again a decent life. I believed what she told me—I was mistaken in her. She is bad—as bad as a woman can be.

Lady W.: Arthur, Arthur, don't talk so bitterly about any woman. I don't think now that people can be divided into the good and the bad as though they were two separate races or creations. What are called good women may have terrible things in them, mad moods of recklessness, assertion, jealousy, sin. Bad women, as they are termed, may have in them sorrow, repentance, pity, sacrifice. And I don't think Mrs. Erlynne a bad woman—I know she's not.

Lord W.: My dear child, the woman's impossible. No matter what harm she tries to do us, you must never see her again. She is inadmissible anywhere.

Lady W.: But I want to see her. I want her to come here.

Lord W.: Never!

Lady W.: She came here once as *your* guest. She must come now as *mine*. That is but fair.

Lord W.: She should never have come here.

Lady W.: [*Rising.*] It is too late, Arthur, to say that now. [*Moves away.*]

Lord W.: [*Rising.*] Margaret, if you knew where Mrs. Erlynne went last night, after she left this house, you would not sit in the same room with her. It was absolutely shameless, the whole thing.

Lady W.: Arthur, I can't bear it any longer. I must tell you. Last night— [*Enter Parker with a tray on which lie Lady Windermere's fan and a card.*]

P.: Mrs. Erlynne has called to return your ladyship's fan which she took away by mistake last night. Mrs. Erlynne has written a message on the card.

Lady W.: Oh, ask Mrs. Erlynne to be kind enough to come up. [*Reads card.*] Say I shall be very glad to see her. [*Exit Parker.*] She wants to see me, Arthur.

Lord W.: [*Takes card and looks at it.*] Margaret, I *beg* you not to. Let me see her first, at any rate. She's a very dangerous woman. She is the most dangerous woman I know. You don't realise what you're doing.

Lady W.: It is right that I should see her.

Lord W.: My child, you may be on the brink of a great sorrow. Don't go to meet it. It is absolutely necessary that I should see her before you do.

Lady W.: Why should it be necessary? [*Enter Parker.*]

P.: Mrs. Erlynne. [*Enter Mrs. Erlynne.*] [*Exit Parker.*]

Mrs. E.: How do you do, Lady Windermere? [*To Lord Windermere.*] How do you do? Do you know, Lady Windermere, I am so sorry about your fan. I can't imagine how I made such a silly mistake. Most stupid of me. And as I was driving in your direction, I thought I would take the opportunity of returning your property in person with many apologies for my carelessness, and of bidding you good-bye.

Lady W.: Good-bye? [*Moves towards sofa with Mrs. Erlynne and sits down beside her.*] Are you going away, then, Mrs. Erlynne?

Mrs. E.: Yes; I am going to live abroad again. The English climate doesn't suit me. My—heart is affected here, and that I don't like. I prefer living in the south. London is too full of fogs and—and serious people, Lord Windermere. Whether the fogs produce the serious people or whether the serious people produce the fogs, I don't know, but the whole thing rather gets on my nerves, and so I'm leaving this afternoon by the Club Train.

Lady W.: This afternoon? But I wanted so much to come and see you.

Mrs. E.: How kind of you! But I am afraid I have to go.

Lady W.: Shall I never see you again, Mrs. Erlynne?

Mrs. E.: I am afraid not. Our lives lie too far apart. But there is a little thing I would like you to do for me. I want a photograph of you, Lady Windermere —would you give me one? You don't know how gratified I should be.

Lady W.: Oh, with pleasure. There is one on that table. I'll show it to you. [*Goes across to the table.*]

Lord W.: [*Coming up to Mrs. Erlynne and speaking in a low voice.*] It is monstrous your intruding yourself here after your conduct last night.

Mrs. E.: [*With an amused smile.*] My dear Windermere, manners before morals!

Lady W.: [*Returning.*] I'm afraid it is very flattering—I am not so pretty as that. [*Showing photograph.*]

Mrs. E.: You are much prettier. But haven't you got one of yourself with your little boy?

Lady W.: I *have.* Would you prefer one of those?

Mrs. E.: Yes.

Lady W.: I'll go and get it for you, if you'll excuse me for a moment. I have one upstairs.

Mrs. E.: So sorry, Lady Windermere, to give you so much trouble.

Lady W.: [*Moves to door R.*] No trouble at all, Mrs. Erlynne.

Mrs. E.: Thanks so much. [*Exit Lady Windermere R.*] You seem rather out of temper this morning, Windermere. Why should you be? Margaret and I get on charmingly together.

Lord W.: I can't bear to see you with her. Besides, you have not told me the truth, Mrs. Erlynne.

Mrs. E.: I have not told *her* the truth, you mean.

Lord W.: [*Standing C.*] I sometimes wish you had. I should have been spared then the misery, the anxiety, the annoyance of the last six months. But rather than my wife should know—that the mother whom she was taught to consider as dead, the mother whom she has mourned as dead, is living—a divorced woman, going about under an assumed name, a bad woman preying upon life, as I know you now to be—rather than that, I was ready to supply you with money to pay bill after bill, extravagance after extravagance, to risk what occurred yesterday, the first quarrel I have ever had with my wife. You don't understand what that means to me. How could you? But I tell you that the only bitter words that ever came from those sweet lips of hers were on your account, and I hate to see you next her. You sully the innocence that is in her. [*Moves L.C.*] And then I used to think that with all your faults you were frank and honest. You are not.

Mrs. E.: Why do you say that?

Lord W.: You made me get you an invitation to my wife's ball.

Mrs. E.: For my daughter's ball—yes.

Lord W.: You came, and within an hour of your leaving the house you are found in a man's rooms—you are disgraced before every one. [*Goes up stage C.*]

Mrs. E.: Yes.

Lord W.: [*Turning round on her.*] Therefore I have a right to look upon you as what you are—a worthless, vicious woman. I have the right to tell you never to enter this house, never to attempt to come near my wife—

Mrs. E.: [*Coldly.*] My daughter, you mean.

Lord W.: You have no right to claim her as your daughter. You left her, abandoned her when she was but a child in the cradle, abandoned her for your lover, who abandoned you in turn.

Mrs. E.: [*Rising.*] Do you count that to his credit, Lord Windermere—or to mine?

Lord W.: To his, now that I know you.

Mrs. E.: Take care—you had better be careful.

Lord W.: Oh, I am not going to mince words for you. I know you thoroughly.

Mrs. E.: [*Looking steadily at him.*] I question that.

Lord W.: I do know you. For twenty years of your life you lived without your child, without a thought of your child. One day you read in the papers that she had married a rich man. You saw your hideous chance. You knew that to spare her the ignominy of learning that a woman like you was her mother, I would endure anything. You began your blackmailing.

Mrs. E.: [*Shrugging her shoulders.*] Don't use ugly words, Windermere. They are vulgar. I saw my chance, it is true, and took it.

Lord W.: Yes, you took it—and spoiled it all last night by being found out.

Mrs. E.: [*With a strange smile.*] You are quite right, I spoiled it all last night.

Lord W.: And as for your blunder in taking my wife's fan from here and then leaving it about in Darlington's rooms, it is unpardonable. I can't bear the sight of it now. I shall never let my wife use it again. The thing is soiled for me. You should have kept it and not brought it back.

Mrs. E.: I think I *shall* keep it. [*Goes up.*] It's extremely pretty. [*Takes up fan.*] I shall ask Margaret to give it to me.

Lord W.: I hope my wife will give it you.

Mrs. E.: Oh, I'm sure she will have no objection.

Lord W.: I wish that at the same time she would give you a miniature she kisses every night before she prays—It's the miniature of a young innocent-looking girl with beautiful *dark* hair.

Mrs. E.: Ah, yes, I remember. How long ago that seems! [*Goes to sofa and sits down.*] It was done before I was married. Dark hair and an innocent expression were the fashion then, Windermere! [*A pause.*]

Lord W.: What do you mean by coming here this morning? What is your object? [*Crossing L.C. and sitting.*]

Mrs. E.: [*With a note of irony in her voice.*] To bid good-bye to my dear daughter, of course. [*Lord Windermere bites his under lip in anger. Mrs. Erlynne looks at him, and her voice and manner become serious. In her accents as she talks there is a note of deep tragedy. For a moment she reveals herself.*] Oh, don't imagine I am going to have a pathetic scene with her, weep on her neck and tell her who I am, and all that kind of thing. I have no ambition to play the part of a mother. Only once in my life have I known a mother's feelings. That was last night. They were terrible—they made me suffer—they made me suffer too much. For twenty years, as you say, I have lived childless,—I want to live childless still. [*Hiding her feelings with a trivial laugh.*] Besides, my dear Windermere, how on earth could I pose as a mother with a grown-up daughter?

Margaret is twenty-one, and I have never admitted that I am more than twenty-nine, or thirty at the most. Twenty-nine when there are pink shades, thirty when there are not. So you see what difficulties it would involve. No, as far as I am concerned, let your wife cherish the memory of this dead, stainless mother. Why should I interfere with her illusions? I find it hard enough to keep my own. I lost one illusion last night. I thought I had no heart. I find I have, and a heart doesn't suit me, Windermere. Somehow it doesn't go with modern dress. It makes one look old. [*Takes up hand-mirror from table and looks into it.*] And it spoils one's career at critical moments.

Lord W.: You fill me with horror— with absolute horror.

Mrs. E.: [*Rising.*] I suppose, Windermere, you would like me to retire into a convent, or become a hospital nurse, or something of that kind, as people do in silly modern novels. That is stupid of you, Arthur; in real life we don't do such things—not as long as we have any good looks left, at any rate. No—what consoles one nowadays is not repentance, but pleasure. Repentance is quite out of date. And besides, if a woman really repents, she has to go to a bad dressmaker, otherwise no one believes in her. And nothing in the world would induce me to do that. No; I am going to pass entirely out of your two lives. My coming into them has been a mistake—I discovered that last night.

Lord W.: A fatal mistake.

Mrs. E.: [*Smiling.*] Almost fatal.

Lord W.: I am sorry now I did not tell my wife the whole thing at once.

Mrs. E.: I regret my bad actions. You regret your good ones—that is the difference between us.

Lord W.: I don't trust you. I *will* tell my wife. It's better for her to know, and from me. It will cause her infinite pain —it will humiliate her terribly, but it's right that she should know.

Mrs. E.: You propose to tell her?

Lord W.: I am going to tell her.

Mrs. E.: [*Going up to him.*] If you do, I will make my name so infamous that it will mar every moment of her life. It will ruin her, and make her wretched. If you dare to tell her, there is no depth of degradation I will not sink to, no pit of shame I will not enter. You shall not tell her—I forbid you.

Lord W.: Why?

Mrs. E.: [*After a pause.*] If I said to you that I cared for her, perhaps loved her even—you would sneer at me, wouldn't you?

Lord W.: I should feel it was not true. A mother's love means devotion, unselfishness, sacrifice. What could you know of such things?

Mrs. E.: You are right. What could I know of such things? Don't let us talk any more about it—as for telling my daughter who I am, that I do not allow. It is my secret, it is not yours. If I make up my mind to tell her, and I think I will, I shall tell her before I leave the house—if not, I shall never tell her.

Lord W.: [*Angrily.*] Then let me beg of you to leave our house at once. I will make your excuses to Margaret. [*Enter Lady Windermere R. She goes over to Mrs. Erlynne with the photograph in her hand. Lord Windermere moves to back of sofa, and anxiously watches Mrs. Erlynne as the scene progresses.*]

Lady W.: I am so sorry, Mrs. Erlynne, to have kept you waiting. I couldn't find the photograph anywhere. At last I discovered it in my husband's dressing-room—he had stolen it.

Mrs. E.: [*Takes the photograph from her and looks at it.*] I am not surprised— it is charming. [*Goes over to sofa with Lady Windermere, and sits down beside her. Looks again at the photograph.*] And so that is your little boy! What is he called?

Lady W.: Gerard, after my dear father.

Mrs. E.: [*Laying the photograph down.*] Really?

Lady W.: Yes. If it had been a girl, I would have called it after my mother. My mother had the same name as myself, Margaret.

Mrs. E.: My name is Margaret too.

Lady W.: Indeed!

Mrs. E.: Yes. [*Pause.*] You are devoted to your mother's memory, Lady Windermere, your husband tells me.

Lady W.: We all have ideals in life. At least we all should have. Mine is my mother.

Mrs. E.: Ideals are dangerous things. Realities are better. They wound, but they're better.

Lady W.: [*Shaking her head.*] If I lost my ideals, I should lose everything.

Mrs. E.: Everything?

Lady W.: Yes. [*Pause.*]

Mrs. E.: Did your father often speak to you of your mother?

Lady W.: No, it gave him too much pain. He told me how my mother had died a few months after I was born. His eyes filled with tears as he spoke. Then he begged me never to mention her name to him again. It made him suffer even to hear it. My father—my father really died of a broken heart. His was the most ruined life I know.

Mrs. E.: [*Rising.*] I am afraid I must go now, Lady Windermere.

Lady W.: [*Rising.*] Oh no, don't.

Mrs. E.: I think I had better. My carriage must have come back by this time. I sent it to Lady Jedburgh's with a note.

Lady W.: Arthur, would you mind seeing if Mrs. Erlynne's carriage has come back?

Mrs. E.: Pray don't trouble, Lord Windermere.

Lady W.: Yes, Arthur, do go, please. [*Lord Windermere hesitates for a moment and looks at Mrs. Erlynne. She remains quite impassive. He leaves the room.*] [*To Mrs. Erlynne.*] Oh! What am I to say to you? You saved me last night? [*Goes towards her.*]

Mrs. E.: Hush—don't speak of it.

Lady W.: I must speak of it. I can't let you think that I am going to accept this sacrifice. I am not. It is too great. I am going to tell my husband everything. It is my duty.

Mrs. E.: It is not your duty—at least you have duties to others besides him. You say you owe me something?

Lady W.: I owe you everything.

Mrs. E.: Then pay your debt by silence. That is the only way in which it can be paid. Don't spoil the one good thing I have done in my life by telling it to any one. Promise me that what passed last night will remain a secret between us. You must not bring misery into your husband's life. Why spoil his love? You must not spoil it. Love is easily killed. Oh! how easily love is killed. Pledge me your word, Lady Windermere, that you will *never* tell him. I insist upon it.

Lady W.: [*With bowed head.*] It is your will, not mine.

Mrs. E.: Yes, it is my will. And never forget your child—I like to think of you as a mother. I like you to think of yourself as one.

Lady W.: [*Looking up.*] I always will now. Only once in my life I have forgotten my own mother—that was last night. Oh, if I had remembered her I should not have been so foolish, so wicked.

Mrs. E.: [*With a slight shudder.*] Hush, last night is quite over. [*Enter Lord Windermere.*]

Lord W.: Your carriage has not come back yet, Mrs. Erlynne.

Mrs. E.: It makes no matter. I'll take a hansom. There is nothing in the world so respectable as a good Shrewsbury and Talbot. And now, dear Lady Windermere, I am afraid it is really good-bye. [*Moves up C.*] Oh, I remember. You'll think me absurd, but do you know I've taken a great fancy to this fan that I was silly enough to run away with last night from your ball. Now, I wonder would you give it to me? Lord Windermere says you may. I know it is his present.

Lady W : Oh, certainly, if it will give you any pleasure. But it has my name on it. It has "Margaret" on it.

Mrs. E.: But we have the same Christian name.

Lady W.: Oh, I forgot. Of course, do have it. What a wonderful chance our names being the same!

Mrs. E.: Quite wonderful. Thanks—it will always remind me of you. [*Shakes hands with her.*] [*Enter Parker.*]

P.: Lord Augustus Lorton. Mrs. Erlynne's carriage has come. [*Enter Lord Augustus.*]

Lord A.: Good morning, dear boy. Good morning, Lady Windermere. [*Sees Mrs. Erlynne.*] Mrs. Erlynne!

Mrs. E. How do you do, Lord Augustus? Are you quite well this morning?

Lord A.: [*Coldly.*] Quite well, thank you, Mrs. Erlynne.

Mrs. E.: You don't look at all well, Lord Augustus. You stop up too late—it is so bad for you. You really should take more care of yourself. Good-bye, Lord Windermere. [*Goes towards door with a bow to Lord Augustus. Suddenly smiles and looks back at him.*] Lord Augustus! Won't you see me to my carriage? You might carry the fan.

Lord W.: Allow me!

Mrs. E.: No; I want Lord Augustus. I have a special message for the dear Duchess. Won't you carry the fan, Lord Augustus?

Lord A.: If you really desire it, Mrs. Erlynne.

Mrs. E.: [*Laughing.*] Of course I do. You'll carry it so gracefully. You would carry off anything gracefully, dear Lord Augustus. [*When she reaches the door she looks back for a moment at Lady Windermere. Their eyes meet. Then she turns, and exit C. followed by Lord Augustus.*]

Lady W.: You will never speak against Mrs. Erlynne again, Arthur, will you?

Lord W.: [*Gravely.*] She is better than one thought her.

Lady W.: She is better than I am.

Lord W.: [*Smiling as he strokes her hair.*] Child, you and she belong to different worlds. Into your world evil has never entered.

Lady W.: Don't say that, Arthur. There is the same world for all of us, and good and evil, sin and innocence, go through it hand in hand. To shut one's eyes to half of life that one may live securely is as though one blinded oneself that one might walk with more safety in a land of pit and precipice.

Lord W.: [*Moves down with her.*] Darling, why do you say that?

Lady W.: [*Sits on sofa.*] Because I, who had shut my eyes to life, came to the brink. And one who had separated us—

Lord W.: We were never separated.

Lady W.: We never must be again. O Arthur, don't love me less, and I will trust you more. I will trust you absolutely. Let us go to Selby. In the Rose Garden at Selby the roses are white and red. [*Enter Lord Augustus C.*]

Lord A.: Arthur, she has explained everything! [*Lady Windermere looks horribly frightened at this. Lord Windermere starts. Lord Augustus takes Windermere by the arm and brings him to front of stage. He talks rapidly and in a low voice. Lady Windermere stands watching them in terror.*] My dear fellow, she has explained every demmed thing. We all wronged her immensely. It was entirely for my sake she went to Darlington's rooms. Called first at the Club—fact is, wanted to put me out of suspense—and being told I had gone on—followed—naturally frightened when she heard a lot of us coming in—retired to another room—I assure you, most gratifying to me, the whole thing. We all behaved brutally to her. She is just the woman for me. Suits me down to the ground. All the conditions she makes are that we live entirely out of England. A very good thing too. Demmed clubs, demmed climate, demmed cooks, demmed everything. Sick of it all!

Lady W.: [*Frightened.*] Has Mrs. Erlynne—?

Lord A.: [*Advancing towards her with a low bow.*] Yes, Lady Windermere— Mrs. Erlynne has done me the honour of accepting my hand.

Lord W.: Well, you are certainly 5 marrying a very clever woman!

Lady W.: [*Taking her husband's hand.*] Ah, you're marrying a very good woman!

NOTES ON ACT IV

Wilde's Problems; Further Melodramatic Effects. Wilde's main problem in Act IV is that his play largely ended with Act III. What is left is largely a post-mortem, which has few dramatic possibilities. Hence Wilde must squeeze the materials dry to make the Act seem dramatic. Lady W.'s basic decision has been made, and the only problem left is that her husband may find out about her escapade. But this is only a matter of possible discomfort, not a real issue; it is irrelevant, and Wilde could not bring it in without getting off the subject. Hence his toying with the possibility of Lord W.'s finding out is really an introduction of false suspense. At the same time, however, Wilde ignores one subject that appears to call for treatment: why does Lord W. have no curiosity about his wife's change of attitude to Mrs. E.?

For suspense, too, Wilde introduces the possibility that Lady W. may find out who Mrs. E. is—another unreal threat. It is too late for the new theme that the identification would introduce. (Moreover, such a recognition scene is almost incurably melodramatic.) To secure a clash between Mrs. E. and Lord W. he makes Lord W. undergo an unmotivated change of mind about identifying Mrs. E. to Lady W.; a little later Wilde reverses Lord W.'s position and makes him angry at the possibility that Mrs. E. may identify herself. In fact, in an endeavor to keep up a sense of clash in Act IV, Wilde appears to move Lord W. around very arbitrarily. Consider, for example, his change of attitude to Mrs. Erlynne: we do not find adequate ground for his utter condemnation of her, a condemnation so much at variance with his earlier attacks on the hasty conclusions of others. So we constantly feel that he is angry without due cause. (One is almost tempted to suggest that Wilde has used him merely because he felt that an angry man would tone up the act.)

In reversing the feelings of both husband and wife to Mrs. Erlynne, Wilde is obviously striving for an ironic effect. But do we not feel that the irony is forced? That the reversal is too perfect? Are there any other instances of overplayed irony in the Act? Consider the speech in which Lord W. says to Mrs. E., "I should feel it was not true, etc." and that in which Lady W. says to Mrs. E., "Only once in my life have I forgotten my own mother—" (p. 70b, 16 ff.; p. 71b, 28 ff.).

Mrs. Erlynne's Part in Act IV. The only matter that is still dramatically incomplete is the fate of Mrs. Erlynne; perhaps Wilde could have secured his most solid dramatic effect by restricting Act IV to her and Lady W. At any rate, note certain aspects of Wilde's use of Mrs. Erlynne: (1) What change of tone occurs after she comes on the stage? Does her wit make for triviality after the heaviness of the Windermeres' dialogue? What is the effect of such a speech as this: "And, besides, if a woman really repents, she has to go to a bad dressmaker, otherwise no one believes in her"? (2) Wilde wishes Mrs. Erlynne to have separate interviews with both husband and wife. Do his devices for getting one or the other off the stage seem natural or labored? (3) Note several aspects of Lord Augustus's part in the Act. From one point of view, we have here another unmotivated entrance. On the other hand, the episode is very useful symbolically: it tells us again that Mrs. Erlynne can be convincing to part of society, enough so to achieve a comfortable *modus vivendi*. Lord Augustus is not an ideal catch, of course; if he were, we could have an inappropriate and unconvincing romantic ending. But to give Mrs. Erlynne a partially satisfactory existence is to avoid, on the other hand, a pathetic or sentimental ending that would be inconsistent with the comic tone which Wilde has adopted.

2. THE PLAY AS A WHOLE

Now that we can see the play as a whole, let us try to pick out some of the general problems faced by the writer of the play. The basic situation, we see, is the conflict between society and an individual who has flouted social conventions. What Wilde had to do first was to transform this vast, abstract subject into a compressed and concrete drama. That is, he had to pick a *specific* situation and impose on it various limitations that would bring it within the boundaries of the conventional play.

THE LIMITATIONS

The social outcast is represented by Mrs. Erlynne. Notice that Wilde has room only for the outcast who wants to get back into society and does something about it. There is no room for outcasts who are crushed or indifferent or resigned or inactive; nor do we see anything of Mrs. Erlynne's associates in exile. We see her only in her relation to society.

Further, we see that relationship exhibited in only one episode, and the episode centers in a single event, Lady Windermere's ball. Not only the action, but also the time and space are cut down: all the action takes place within twenty-four hours, and the events of three acts take place in one house. In order to see what a cut-down, specialized situation we have here, we have only to imagine how much time before and after the ball a movie or a novel would include (perhaps presenting directly Mrs. Erlynne's elopement of twenty years before), and how much movement in space they would show. This play illustrates, then, the general dramatic practice of cutting out everything but the climax of a situation.

The method offers special difficulties and special advantages. For one thing, the dramatist must make it plausible that so much crucial action should take place in so short a time. It is not easy to convince an audience that a prim Victorian lady will in a few hours' time decide to desert her husband. But under the high pressure which the drama maintains we do not seriously question the decision.

The nature of drama itself helps us out; for within its limits an unusually high tension can be maintained and an acceleration of the normal everyday tempo of life is not only natural but inevitable.

THE SYMBOLIC SITUATION

We are further helped in accepting this compressed action by the fact that we see it as *symbolic* action. Not that the play is primarily symbolic, but that the actions do become more than mere elements in a sequence. For instance, Lady W.'s ball symbolizes society in action; Mrs. E.'s experience there will symbolize her acceptance or rejection by society. Drama, because it can present only a very few of the complications which make up any human situation, must always rely on our grasping the symbolic import of what it does present. Conversely, the dramatist must find situations capable of taking on symbolic significance. If, for instance, Mrs. Erlynne simply called on Lady W. instead of coming to her party, it would be far more difficult to invest the episode with symbolic significance.

THE AUTHOR'S ATTITUDE

Thus far we have been considering the play almost entirely from the point of view of problems in *technique*, that is, relatively *mechanical* necessities and devices. And a very important problem still remains—a problem which is by no means separate from those already considered but which grows out of them. This is the problem of the meaning of the play. What is Wilde "saying"? How does he want us to feel about various characters? How can we discover his "attitude" toward them? To answer these questions we shall have to continue our consideration of how Wilde manages various mechanical aspects of the play. We are not so much changing our subject, perhaps, as shifting emphasis. In earlier sections we discussed technique from the point of view of theatrical limitations and effect, plausibility, and so on; now we turn to technique as an index of the author's attitude to his materials (see Glossary.)

Then another question comes up: shall we accept his attitude? It is clear that we need not agree with an author, but we certainly owe him a hearing; and though he may not bring us to accept his conclusion, he can do certain things to convince us that he is worth a hearing. He can show us that he has at least a *satisfactory grasp of experience;* that is, whatever his conclusions, he sees things with sufficient flexibility, comprehensiveness, and consistency. He can, for instance, guard against our accusing him of (1) oversimplifying the situation; (2) failing to grasp all the implications and ramifications; (3) arriving at too easy a solution; (4) being inaccurate through partisanship.

Now Wilde, in dealing with the conflict between Mrs. E. and society, might take one side and completely justify it. Conceivably he might thus write a successful play, but there would be strong likelihood of our seeing in it not so much a drama as a diatribe, an obvious piece of "poetic justice," or even what we now call propaganda, that is, over-simplification. Wilde clearly tries to avoid this as well as the other charges listed above. How does he go about it?

First of all, what is his view of society? It is very important that Wilde is unwilling to let the Windermeres alone stand for society. Despite the limitations of the dramatic form he provides a rather large number of characters to represent society. To secure this variety he is willing to face the great difficulty of trying to make these representatives of society recognizable as individuals, though none of them can have very large parts, and though he uses for all of them much the same epigrammatic style of speech. We have already seen (at the end of Act I) some of the devices which Wilde uses to distinguish the members of society. In general, how successful is he in meeting this problem?

The Treatment of Society. Wilde, then, prefers other risks to that of the oversimplification of presenting society as all of a piece. Rather, society is complex; it has many internal variations. Lady W. is "a good woman," but Wilde does not oversimplify her either. She is made too sure of herself and of her "hard-and-fast rules"; she is even priggish, as when she says to her husband, "—you should not mention this woman and me in the same breath. It is an error of taste." Thus Wilde informs us that he is not giving her unqualified approval; he is really saying that a strict "goodness" is not enough.

On the other hand we have the Duchess of Berwick, to whom the conventions are not so much the boundaries of right and wrong as they are a set of rules by which to play her own game of realistic power-politics. She delights in controlling her husband, daughter, and prospective son-in-law. With her lack of scruples, she might be a good object for outright satire; yet Wilde also qualifies his treatment of her. Her candor and wit and comic loquacity make her amusing rather than detestable.

Lady Plymdale has a small but very important part: she calls Mrs. Erlynne "*that* woman" but at the same time has contempt for Lady W., "who goes in for being so proper." And in her relations with Dumby it is clear that she is about as free with the moral rules as was Mrs. Erlynne. Then there is Lady Jedburgh, who shows society's susceptibility to flattery.

So society has both its admirable and unadmirable members: it is a complex mixture. In its way, it does the very things (or their equivalent) for which it condemns individuals. Wilde is not going to take the easy way out by either attacking it as a whole or defending it as a whole.

Treatment of Mrs. Erlynne. Nor is Wilde going to make Mrs. Erlynne either an unregenerate sinner or a romantic heroine who glorifies revolt. Wilde first gives us a bad report of her but then modifies it by the fact that Lord W. accepts her and that Lady W. is so unreasonably harsh in condemning her. Finally, she performs an act of generous devotion. But Wilde does not sentimentalize her: she has a strong sense of the value of money and a husband, and she can drive a hard bargain with Lord W. and manage Lord A. as suits her convenience. Nor does Wilde exculpate her: she neither denies that she erred nor blames society for ostracizing her. Wilde imposes on her the most severe penalty: her criticism of herself.

Mrs. Erlynne's attitude to society is important: if she were desperately anxious to re-enter a society which Wilde has presented as of somewhat uncertain merit, she would seem very superficial. Therefore, Wilde has her say in Act II (p. 52b, 19–20): "And I see there are just as many fools in society as there used to be." She is sensible and realistic: she sees society not as an end in itself, but, other things being equal, as a means to a more comfortable existence; and, still more important, she can discard this objective if an intrinsically better one makes a demand upon her.

Clearly, Wilde is avoiding a black-and-white world-view and striving for the qualifications needed at the adult level.

THE THEME

What, then, is the meaning of a conflict between two sides neither of which is ideal?

Consider the ending. Here Mrs. Erlynne is presented very sympathetically, and she has won a "victory" in that she has saved her daughter and secured a husband. But she cannot be acknowledged as a mother, and her relationships are so intricate that she has to give up her hope of living in English society. That is, Wilde presents dramatically the working-out of a complex life: neither the "good" nor the "bad" is wholly influential, but both affect the outcome. In a sense, the ending is a *compromise*.

Now notice how Lady W. is included in the compromise: in fact, it is she upon whom Wilde focuses our attention. *She has the last line in the play:* "Ah! you're marrying a very good woman." (note the echo (1) of the phrase first applied to Lady W. and (2) of Lord W.'s remark to Mrs. E. earlier in Act IV, "a worthless, vicious woman").

Her compromise is, finally, the chief event of the play. Mrs. Erlynne's primary function has been to provide an object lesson for Lady W.; the play is centered upon Lady W.'s learning process. And what has she learned? Not merely that Mrs. E. is a good woman. But the more general truth that good and evil are not easily determined by simple rules, that they do not often exist in pure form, so to speak; hence one must measure the evidence carefully and must avoid hasty conclusions.

As we look back, we find that Wilde has given us, in an unobtrusive part of the dialogue in Act I, an overt statement of the "moral." Lord D. says to Lady W., "I think life too complex a thing to be settled by these hard-and-fast rules" (p. 37a, 46–48). Then in Act IV Lady W. makes at least three direct applications of this principle. Mrs. Erlynne has shown her that life cannot be judged as simply as it had seemed.

Other Evidence. Other parts of the play help in the education of Lady W. She believes that a wife should not be "vile" because a husband is; yet when she discovers Lord W. in what she supposes is infidelity, she plans to elope with Lord Darlington. Further, when Lord D. proposes elopement, he does not speak in terms of a "hard-and-fast" romantic rule; instead he makes realistic qualifications. "I will not tell you that the world matters nothing," he says, "or the world's voice, or the voice of Society" (p. 50b, 36–38). There is no primrose path, no easy way out. So again the reader is reminded of the theme that all the complexities of a situation must be taken into account.

The Epigrammatic Style. Much of the repartee, of course, exists for its own sake or as a clue to the mind of the speaker, or as clue to the character of someone spoken about, e.g., "Many a woman has a past but I am told that she has at least a dozen, and that they all fit." But notice, on the other hand, that the wit makes a real contribution to the theme, particularly when it takes the form of *paradox*, that is, of turning upside down some conventional or accepted point of view or belief. The paradox implies a questioning, skeptical attitude; it means that the truth is more complex than it may appear at first glance. It helps create an atmosphere suitable to the over-turning of hard-and-fast rules. Consider some of the following epigrammatic lines:

"Oh, nowadays so many conceited people go about society pretending to be good, that I think it shows rather a sweet and modest disposition to pretend to be bad."
"Nowadays to be intelligible is to be found out."
'Life is far too important a thing ever to talk seriously about it."
"My father would talk morality after dinner. I told him he was old enough to know better."
"The youth of the present day are monstrous. They have absolutely no respect for dyed hair" (What is gained by substituting *dyed hair* for *grey hair* or *age?*)
"In this world there are only two tragedies. One is not getting what one wants, and the other is getting it."

What we get in such lines is not merely a breath-taking reversal of convention but actually a more complex insight into the truths which lie behind the conventions. It would be a very profitable exercise to make a study of all the wit in the play to see how much it does contribute to the meaning of the play, namely, that satisfactory judgments cannot be made in simple, cut-and-dried terms.

THE NATURE OF COMEDY

This is not the place to attempt a final definition of comedy, for which we need more evidence, but Wilde's play does point the way toward such a definition. Clearly it is not enough to say that this is comedy because it evokes laughter and has a happy ending, for, as Shakespeare shows, there can be laughter in a tragedy; and tragedy itself may on occasion have a happy ending. Besides, there are perfectly serious plays which are not tragedies. What, then, is the basic element in Wilde's play?

We have seen that Wilde hinges his action on the conventions, but he clearly does not equate the conventions with right—or, for that matter, with wrong. That is, he is not concerned with fundamental problems of good and evil; such matters as conscience and moral law are not primary in the play. He is concerned only with what society thinks at a given time, that is, with fashions in conduct. There are no profound issues to be decided, no vital choices to be made. Note that Lady W. does not have a *real choice* to make between Lord W. and Lord D. because what she desires is identical with what she feels is right: she starts to leave her husband for pique rather than principle, and she returns for practicality rather than principle. She has no decision to make; she is not a moral agent; and so serious issues are evaded.

What are the issues, then? Comfort, reputation, the conventions of society—matters which do not represent permanent values. This is the realm of sociology, of people's attitudes and opinions, which change from place to place and from time to time and hence need not be taken with ultimate seriousness. The problems are those of an external world, the world where matters can be managed and arranged, where compromises can be made, and agreeable solutions arrived at. In terms of this play, this is the world of comedy—a world of moral relativism. Here we do not have a world of moral absolutes, of fundamental principles of conduct, of an underlying moral structure that cannot be tampered with.

The Author's Choice. We should be clear that the author *chooses* to handle his materials in this way. Wilde *might* have presented Mrs. E.'s original desertion of her husband as of moral significance (the immediate starting-point in Aeschylus's tragic trilogy *Oresteia* is Clytemnestra's infidelity to Agamemnon), but instead he hurries over it as a mere mistake; her husband and lover are ignored; there have been no moral repercussions, no nemesis; Mrs. E. has merely undergone a certain amount of discomfort; and she has survived as a shrewd, resourceful, witty woman of the world. But she has not won the victory of real character—that is, of having got to the bottom of things. Wilde likewise makes Lady W.'s experience—relatively speaking, at least—only skin-deep, that is, comic. He might have had a real clash if there had been some vital, basic conflict between Lord and Lady W., or if Lady W. had actually loved Lord Darlington; in either case Lady W. would have run into the inescapable irreconcilability of two modes of life. She would have faced an actual crossroads. But there is no crossroads; Lady W. is merely in momentary danger of getting off on a sidetrack. It's all a mistake; not even a moral mistake, but a mere misunderstanding.

In tragedy, we may say, there is no easy way out, because the characters are coming to grips with what is permanently true. In tragedy, therefore, we expect to find symbols of permanent values. But Wilde is at pains to avoid such symbols. Society cannot embody the permanent, because Wilde by his ridicule deprives it of moral authority (even though he may tacitly admit that conventions are useful). Mrs. Erlynne's career might symbolize the good, perhaps—but she distinctly repudiates her own career. Lady W. starts by defending "hard-and-fast" rules, but it is the whole business of the play to wean her away from those rules. Does not the very matter of the play, then, preclude the possibility of tragedy? Wilde refuses to be concerned with the inevitable, with what must be; rather, he wishes to show the manysidedness of what is. (In one sense, he plays certain variations upon a theme. Note, for instance, the different varieties of relationship between the sexes which he presents in the course of the play.) The next play to which we come, *Everyman*, takes its stand firmly on the universal validity of certain truths. But Wilde, we see, tends to deny the existence of such a character as Everyman. Thus he makes tragedy impossible; and he gives us at least one pattern for comedy.

3. THE "WELL-MADE" PLAY

Wilde's play belongs, in some respects, to a type called the "well-made" play, a reaction against the romantic drama of the early nineteenth century. Writers of such plays wished to deal realistically with current society; they often dealt with "problems" like divorce; they wished to avoid accidents and surprises and to have instead a careful, plausible mechanical connection among the various parts; to achieve a skillful, logical motivation, preparation of effects, and bringing about of denouements.

In the earlier discussions we have seen how Wilde manages some technical problems very well, others less so. Here we may note one or two "well-made" devices of his, for instance, the careful use of various concrete articles or stage properties as means of (1) bringing about certain actions or (2) conveying certain meanings. There are the roses (Acts I and IV), the bankbook (I), the letter (II), the bouquet (II), the photographs (IV). Most striking, of course, is the fan, which Wilde considers important enough to use in the title. As it is put to different uses in one Act after another, it becomes a kind of connecting link; but, more than that, it has a series of symbolic meanings. Like other such properties when well used, a concrete symbol of this sort both seizes the attention and stimulates the imagination.

Such materials, of course, can be used too obviously: in Act I Lady W. "throws" down the bankbook just as her husband enters; in Act II Mrs. E. "drops letter"—a means of intensifying suspense; Lady W. not only takes the fan along on an elopement but is very careless about what she does with it. All this will seem to us somewhat less than "well-made." Since it once seemed "realistic," we can perhaps conclude that "realism" is relative and therefore not a very trustworthy guarantee of literary excellence. In fact, the manipulation of external matters is never of primary importance; some playwrights are very little concerned with this sort of thing. What is more important is sound sense of character and the values with which human beings must come to grips.

4. THE PROBLEM PLAY

This kind of play is also called the "problem play." In a sense, of course, almost any play involves a problem, but the term "problem play" is customarily used only with reference to plays treating a social problem class distinctions, conventions, women's rights, etc. (for a fuller discussion see the Glossary).

Wilde's play is unusual in that he deals with a social problem in the witty style generally associated with the comedy of manners (see Glossary) rather than in the solemn manner that one often finds in a problem play. Does the witty manner produce an effect of triviality? Consider Lord D.'s definition of a cynic in Act III. Does Wilde ever use wit inappropriately, or is it possible, on the other hand, that he gains by using the witty style? What is the influence of wit on potentially melodramatic scenes or on love-making scenes or on trite scenes? On the total effect of the screen scene in Act III? What tone might Mrs. E.'s lines in Act IV have had if they had been written "straight"?

A problem play is always under a handicap in that it usually derives from a specific transitory situation, and it is difficult for the play to survive the situation. It may of course, deal with a recurrent problem, or deal with a problem in terms of some universal human issue. Something of that sort is what we find in the next play to which we come, *Everyman*. It deals with a "problem," but in it we shall find none of the shifting social conventions out of which Wilde's play springs.

OTHER QUESTIONS

1. Why did Wilde have Mr. Erlynne desert Mrs. Erlynne? How would the play differ if they had got on and Mr. Erlynne were on the scene?

2. Aside from the change in his attitude toward her and the contrast between his and his wife's attitude toward her, what is ironic about Lord W.'s antagonistic attitude to Mrs. E. late in the play?

3. Does a witty passage create of its own nature a kind of tension? Compare this tension with that produced by an unsolved situation.

4. Can you discern any sort of "technique" or pattern in the witty passages? Do the best lines occur in a series or do you find them separated? How does Wilde focus attention on his best lines? Note the function of questions in a witty passage. Are these ever too obvious?

5. If Wilde were going to sustain society against Mrs. E., he would have to indicate that recognition of her would in some way be harmful to society. But instead he indicates that she cannot harm society. How? Assuming that the average reader will normally take the part of the group against the individual dubbed immoral, how does Wilde from the start prevent the reader's taking society's opinion of Mrs. E. very seriously?

6. Why is nothing seen of Lord D. after Act III?

7. What is the function of the Agatha-Hopper affair? Why are we shown so little of it directly?

8. What is shown by Lady B.'s change of attitude toward Australia?

9. How do you know at the start that Lady W. is wrong in her opinion of Lord W.'s relations with Mrs. E.?

10. Many of the speeches of Lord D., Cecil, and Dumby and the Duchess of Berwick are meant to evoke laughter from the reader. But is the laughter that the Duchess of B. gets the same as that evoked by the others? Analyze the difference.

11. Note the different attitudes of wives to husbands found throughout the play.

12. What is the relation of wit and emotion? Are they antithetical? What sort of effects would wit interfere with or prevent? Is the play a comedy because it contains wit?

13. What is the effect of Lady W.'s pun on *bond* and *bondage* in her last speech in Act II? Does it give an effect of frivolity?

PART TWO

SIMPLER TYPES

1. *Introduction*

IN PART I we have considered, in general, the problems which all dramatists face, and we have examined in detail one full-length modern play to see how one dramatist answers the various questions which confront him. We have endeavored also to see what the dramatist is "saying" and how this theme is related to the structure and form of the play. We should therefore have some idea of how drama in general works.

In Wilde's *Lady Windermere's Fan* we have seen a full-length play which combines, in a moderately complex way, elements of the comedy of wit, the problem play, and the "well-made" play. Our next step is to study three simpler dramatic forms in each of which a single element is dominant. In more advanced drama we are less likely to find plays in which the author has a single purpose so clearly evident as it is here and in which he goes so unmistakably to the point. So in Part II we ought to gain a fairly clearcut picture of certain types of dramatic procedure used when the author is intent upon one kind of stress rather than another. The objectives may be more or less commendable, and the procedures successful or unsuccessful; in either case we shall of course wish to know the reasons why.

In *Everyman* we find a play in which all the stress is upon the *idea* which the author wishes to develop. In that sense it may be called a problem play, and part of our business will be to see how it differs from *Lady Windermere's Fan*. Since some aspects of *Everyman* suggest the mode of tragedy, we shall also have a new kind of material to examine.

Plautus's *Menaechmi* is a comedy and therefore also subject to comparison with *Lady Windermere's Fan*. But it is a simpler kind of comedy, and Plautus is concerned with no problem. Hence the play will offer a quite different vantage point for the study of comedy.

Lillo's *George Barnwell* is a kind of tragedy which also contains some suggestions of the problem play; hence it may be useful to see how it differs from *Everyman*. Indeed, it is very interestingly different in materials and point of view; and in what it fails to do it should be very illuminating.

2. *Everyman*

*E*VERYMAN is of unknown authorship and of uncertain date: it is generally thought to belong to the late fifteenth century. It is the best-known example of the "morality play," a definite historical type which has as its primary purpose the teaching of a lesson. Though there were many variations of the form, the characteristic plot was based on a conflict of the Virtues and the Vices for the Soul of man.

EVERYMAN *

DRAMATIS PERSONÆ

Everyman	Kindred	Beauty
God: Adonai	Goods	Knowledge
Death	Good-Deeds	Confession
Messenger	Strength	Angel
Fellowship	Discretion	Doctor
Cousin	Five-Wits	

* Spelling is generally modernized.

Here beginneth a treatise how the high father of Heaven sendeth death to summon every creature to come and give account of their lives in this world and is in manner of a moral play. [*Enter a messenger who speaks the Prologue.*]

   Messenger: I pray you all give your
     audience,
And hear this matter with reverence,
By figure [1] a moral play:
The *Summoning of Everyman* called
   it is,
That of our lives and ending shows   5
How transitory we be all day.
This matter is wondrous precious,
But the intent of it is more gracious,
And sweet to bear away.
The story saith:—Man, in the begin-
     ning,   10
Look well, and take good heed to the
     ending,

Be you never so gay;
Ye think sin in the beginning full sweet,
Which in the end causeth the soul to
     weep,
When the body lieth in clay.   15
Here shall you see how Fellowship and
     Jollity,
Both Strength, Pleasure, and Beauty,
Will fade from thee as flower in May.
For we shall hear, how our heaven king
Calleth Everyman to a general reckon-
     ing: 20
Give audience, and hear what he doth
     say.   [*Exit.*]
   God speaketh [*from above*]: I per-
     ceive here in my majesty,
How that all creatures be to me unkind,
Living without dread in worldly pros-
     perity:
Of ghostly [2] sight the people be so blind,
Drowned in sin, they know me not for
     their God;   26

[1] In form.

[2] Spiritual.

In worldly riches is all their mind.
They fear not my rightwiseness, the sharp rod;
My law that I shewed, when I for them died,
They forget clean, and shedding of my blood red; 30
I hanged between two, it cannot be denied;
To get them life I suffered to be dead;
I healed their feet, with thorns hurt was my head;
I could do no more than I did truly,
And now I see the people do clean forsake me: 35
They use the seven deadly sins damnable,
As pride, covetise, wrath, and lechery,
Now in the world be made commendable,
And thus they leave of angels the heavenly company;
Every man liveth so after his own pleasure, 40
And yet of their life they be nothing sure:
I see the more that I them forbear
The worse they be from year to year;
All that liveth appaireth [3] fast;
Therefore I will in all the haste 45
Have a reckoning of every man's person.
For, and [4] I leave the people thus alone
In their life and wicked tempests,
Verily they will become much worse than beasts,
For now one would by envy another up eat; 50
Charity they all do clean forget.
I hoped well that every man
In my glory should make his mansion,
And thereto I had them all elect;
But now I see, like traitors deject, 55
They thank me not for the pleasure that I to them meant,
Nor yet for their being that I them have lent.
I proffered the people great multitude of mercy,
And few there be that asketh it heartily;

They be so cumbered with worldly riches, 60
That needs on them I must do justice,
On every man living without fear.
Where art thou, Death, thou mighty messenger?
[*Enter Death.*]
　　Death: Almighty God, I am here at your will,
Your commandment to fulfill. 65
　　God: Go thou to Everyman,
And show him in my name
A pilgrimage he must on him take,
Which he in no wise may escape;
And that he bring with him a sure reckoning. 70
Without delay or any tarrying.
　　　　　　　　[*God withdraws.*]
　　Death: Lord, I will in the world go run over all,
And cruelly outsearch both great and small;
Every man will I beset that liveth beastly
Out of God's laws, and dreadeth not folly. 75
He that loveth riches I will strike with my dart,
His sight to blind, and from heaven to depart,
Except that alms be his good friend,
In hell for to dwell, world without end.
Lo, yonder I see Everyman walking; 80
Full little he thinketh on my coming;
His mind is on fleshy lusts and his treasure,
And great pain it shall cause him to endure
Before the Lord, Heaven King.
Everyman, stand still; whither art thou going 85
Thus gayly? Hast thou thy Maker forgot? [*Death halts Everyman.*]
　　Everyman: Why askest thou?
Wouldst thou weet? [5]
　　Death: Yea, sir, I will show you;
In great haste I am sent to thee 90
From God, out of his majesty.
　　Everyman: What, sent to me?

---

[3] Decays.　　[4] If.　　　　　　　　[5] Know.

Death: Yea, certainly.
Though thou hast forgot him here,
He thinketh on thee in the heavenly
　　sphere,　　　　　　　　　　95
As, ere we depart, thou shalt know.
　　Everyman: What desireth God of me?
　　Death: That shall I show thee:
A reckoning he will needs have,
Without any longer respite.　　100
　　Everyman: To give a reckoning longer
　　　leisure I crave;
This blind matter troubleth my wit.
　　Death: On thee thou must take a long
　　journey:
Therefore thy book of count with thee
　　thou bring,
For turn again thou cannot by no way,
And look thou be sure of thy reckon-
　　ing,　　　　　　　　　　　106
For before God thou shalt answer, and
　　show
Thy many bad deeds and good but a
　　few,
How thou hast spent thy life, and in
　　what wise,
Before the chief lord of paradise.　110
Have ado we were in that way,[6]
For, weet thou well, thou shalt make
　　none attorney.
　　Everyman: Full unready I am such
　　　reckoning to give.
I know thee not; what messenger art
　　thou?
　　Death: I am Death, that no man
　　　dreadeth.　　　　　　　115
For every man I 'rest, and no man
　　spareth;
For it is God's commandment
That all to me should be obedient.
　　Everyman: O Death, thou comest
　　　when I had thee least in mind!
In thy power it lieth me to save;　120
Yet of my goods will I give thee, if thou
　　wilt be kind,
Yea, a thousand pound shalt thou have,
And defer this matter till another day.
　　Death: Everyman, it may not be by
　　　no way.
I set not by gold, silver, nor riches,　125

Nor by pope, emperor, king, duke, nor
　　princes.
For, and I would receive gifts great,
All the world I might get;
But my custom is clean contrary.
I give thee no respite; come hence, and
　　not tarry.　　　　　　　130
　　Everyman: Alas! shall I have no
　　　longer respite?
I may say, Death giveth no warning:
To think on thee, it maketh my heart
　　sick,
For all unready is my book of reckoning.
But twelve year and I might have abid-
　　ing,　　　　　　　　　　135
My counting book I would make so clear,
That my reckoning I should not need
　　to fear.
Wherefore, Death, I pray thee, for
　　God's mercy,
Spare me till I be provided of remedy.
　　Death: Thee availeth not to cry,
　　　weep, and pray:　　　　140
But haste thee lightly that thou wast
　　gone this journey,
And prove thy friends, if thou can.
For, weet thou well, the tide abideth no
　　man,
And in the world each living creature
For Adam's sin must die of nature.　145
　　Everyman: Death, if I should this
　　　pilgrimage take,
And my reckoning surely make,
Show me, for saint charity,
Should I not come again shortly?
　　Death: No, Everyman; and thou be
　　　once there,　　　　　　150
Thou mayst never more come here,
Trust me verily.
　　Everyman: O gracious God, in the high
　　　seat celestial,
Have mercy on me in this most need!
Shall I have no company from this vale
　　terrestrial　　　　　　　155
Of mine acquaintance that way me to
　　lead?
　　Death: Yea, if any be so hardy,
That would go with thee and bear thee
　　company.
Hie thee that thou were gone to God's
　　magnificence,

---

[6] Get ready that we may be on that road.

Thy reckoning to give before his presence. 160
What, weenest thou thy life is given thee,
And thy worldly goods also?
Everyman: I had wend [7] so, verily.
Death: Nay, nay; it was but lent thee;
For as soon as thou art gone, 165
Another awhile shall have it, and then go therefrom,
Even as thou hast done.
Everyman, thou art mad! Thou hast thy wits five,
And here on earth will not amend thy life!
For suddenly I do come. 170
Everyman: O wretched caitiff, whither shall I flee,
That I might scape this endless sorrow?
Now, gentle Death, spare me till to-morrow,
That I may amend me
With good advisement. 175
Death: Nay, thereto I will not consent,
Nor no man will I respite;
But to the heart suddenly I shall smite
Without any advisement.
And now out of thy sight I will me hie;
See thou make thee ready shortly, 181
For thou mayst say this is the day
That no man living may scape away.
[*Exit Death.*]
Everyman: Alas! I may well weep with sighs deep;
Now have I no manner of company
To help me in my journey, and me to keep; 186
And also my writing is full unready.
How shall I do now for to excuse me?
I would to God I had never be gete! [8]
To my soul a full great profit it had been; 190
For now I fear pains huge and great.
The time passeth; Lord, help, that all wrought!
For though I mourn, it availeth nought.
The day passeth, and is almost a-go;
I wot not well what for to do. 195

To whom were I best my complaint to make?
What and I to Fellowship thereof spake,
And showed him of this sudden chance?
For in him is all mine affiance [9];
We have in the world so many a day
Been good friends in sport and play.
I see him yonder, certainly; 202
I trust that he will bear me company;
Therefore to him will I speak to ease my sorrow. [*Enter Fellowship.*]
Well met, good Fellowship, and good morrow! 205
Fellowship: Everyman, good morrow! By this day,
Sir, why lookest thou so piteously?
If any thing be amiss, I pray thee me say,
That I may help to remedy.
Everyman: Yea, good Fellowship, yea,
I am in great jeopardy. 211
Fellowship: My true friend, show to me your mind;
I will not forsake thee, to my life's end,
In the way of good company.
Everyman: That was well spoken, and lovingly. 215
Fellowship: Sir, I must needs know your heaviness;
I have pity to see you in any distress.
If any have you wronged ye shall revenged be,
Though I on the ground be slain for thee,
Though that I know before that I should die. 220
Everyman: Verily, Fellowship, gramercy.
Fellowship: Tush! by thy thanks I set not a straw.
Show me your grief, and say no more.
Everyman: If I my heart should to you break,
And then you to turn your mind from me, 225
And would not me comfort, when ye hear me speak,
Then should I ten times sorrier be.
Fellowship: Sir, I say as I will do in deed.

---

[7] Thought. [8] Been born. [9] Trust.

Everyman: Then be you a good friend
  at need.
I have found you true here before. 230
  Fellowship: And so ye shall evermore;
For, in faith, and thou go to Hell,
I will not forsake thee by the way.
  Everyman: Ye speak like a good
  friend. I believe you well;
I shall deserve it, and I may.   235
  Fellowship: I speak of no deserving,
  by this day.
For he that will say and nothing do
Is not worthy with good company to go;
Therefore show me the grief of your
  mind,
As to your friend most loving and
  kind.   240
  Everyman: I shall show you how it is:
Commanded I am to go a journey,
A long way, hard and dangerous,
And give a straight count without delay
Before the high judge Adonai.   245
Wherefore I pray you, bear me company,
As ye have promised, in this journey.
  Fellowship: That is matter indeed!
  Promise is duty,
But, and I should take such a voyage
  on me,
I know it well, it should be to my pain;
Also it makes me afeard, certain. 251
But let us take counsel here as well as
  we can,
For your words would fear a strong
  man.
  Everyman: Why, ye said, if I had
  need,
Ye would me never forsake, quick nor
  dead,   255
Though it were to Hell, truly.
  Fellowship: So I said, certainly.
But such pleasures be set aside, the
  sooth to say:
And also, if we took such a journey,
When should we come again?   260
  Everyman: Nay, never again till the
  day of doom.
  Fellowship: In faith, then will not I
  come there!
Who hath you these tidings brought?
  Everyman: Indeed, Death was with
  me here.

  Fellowship: Now, by God that all
  hath bought,   265
If Death were the messenger,
For no man that is living today
I will not go that loath [10] journey—
Not for the father that begat me!
  Everyman: Ye promised otherwise,
  pardie.[11]   270
  Fellowship: I wot well I say so truly;
And yet if thou wilt eat, and drink, and
  make good cheer,
Or haunt to women the lusty company,
I would not forsake you, while the day
  is clear,
Trust me verily!   275
  Everyman: Yea, thereto ye would be
  ready;
To go to mirth, solace, and play,
Your mind will sooner apply,
Than to bear me company in my long
  journey.
  Fellowship: Now, in good faith, I will
  not that way.   280
But and thou will murder, or any man
  kill,
In that I will help thee with a good will!
  Everyman: O, that is a simple advice
  indeed!
Gentle fellow, help me in my necessity;
We have loved long, and now I need;
And now, gentle Fellowship, remem-
  ber me.   286
  Fellowship: Whether ye have loved
  me or no,
By Saint John, I will not with thee go.
  Everyman: Yet I pray thee, take the
  labor, and do so much for me
To bring me forward, for saint charity,
And comfort me till I come without
  the town.   291
  Fellowship: Nay, and thou would
  give me a new gown,
I will not a foot with thee go;
But and thou had tarried I would not
  have left thee so.
And as now, God speed thee in thy
  journey,   295
For from thee I will depart as fast as
  I may.

[10] Loathsome. [11] Certainly.

Everyman: Whither away, Fellow-
ship? will thou forsake me?
Fellowship: Yea, by my fay! to God I
betake [12] thee!
Everyman: Farewell, good Fellowship;
for this my heart is sore;
Adieu forever, I shall see thee no more.
Fellowship: In faith, Everyman, fare-
well now at the end; 301
For you I will remember that parting
is mourning. [*Exit Fellowship.*]
Everyman: Alack! shall we thus de-
part indeed?
Ah, Lady, help, without any more com-
fort,
Lo, Fellowship forsaketh me in my most
need. 305
For help in this world whither shall I
resort?
Fellowship herebefore with me would
merry make,
And now little sorrow for me doth he
take.
It is said, in prosperity men friends may
find,
Which in adversity be full unkind.
Now whither for succor shall I flee,
Sith [13] that Fellowship hath forsaken
me? 312
To my kinsmen I will truly,
Praying them to help me in my neces-
sity;
I believe that they will do so, 315
For kind [14] will creep where it may not
go.[15]
I will go say,[16] for yonder I see them go.
Where be ye now, my friends and kins-
men? [*Enter Kindred and Cousin.*]
Kindred: Here be we now at your
commandment.
Cousin, I pray you show us your in-
tent 320
In any wise, and not spare.
Cousin: Yea, Everyman, and to us
declare
If ye be disposed to go any whither,
For wit you well, we will live and die
together.

Kindred: In wealth and woe we will
with you hold, 325
For over his kin a man may be bold.
Everyman: Gramercy, my friends and
kinsmen kind;
Now shall I show you the grief of my
mind.
I was commanded by a messenger,
That is an high king's chief officer; 330
He bade me go a pilgrimage to my pain,
And I know well I shall never come
again;
Also I must give a reckoning straight,
For I have a great enemy, that hath me
in wait,[17]
Which intendeth me for to hinder. 335
Kindred: What account is that which
ye must render?
That would I know.
Everyman: Of all my works I must
show
How I have lived and my days spent;
Also of ill deeds, that I have used 340
In my time, sith life was me lent;
And of all virtues that I have refused.
Therefore I pray you go thither with me,
To help to make mine account, for saint
charity.
Cousin: What, to go thither? Is that
the matter? 345
Nay, Everyman, I had liefer fast bread
and water
All this five year and more.
Everyman: Alas, that ever I was born!
For now shall I never be merry
If that you forsake me. 350
Kindred: Ah, sir, what, ye be a merry
man!
Take good heart to you, and make no
moan.
But one thing I warn you, by Saint
Anne,
As for me, ye shall go alone.
Everyman: My Cousin, will you not
with me go? 355
Cousin: No, by our Lady! I have the
cramp in my toe.
Trust not to me, for, so God me speed,
I will deceive you in your most need.

---

[12] Commend. [13] Since. [14] Kinship.
[15] Walk. [16] Try

[17] Has me under observation.

Kindred: It availeth not us to tice.[18]
Ye shall have my maid with all my
heart;   360
She loveth to go to feasts, there to be
nice,[19]
And to dance, and abroad to start:
I will give her leave to help you in that
journey,
If that you and she may agree.
 Everyman: Now show me the very
effect of your mind,   365
Will you go with me, or abide be-
hind?
 Kindred: Abide behind? yea, that will
I and I may!
Therefore farewell till another day.
     [Exit Kindred.]
 Everyman: How should I be merry or
glad?
For fair promises men to me make, 370
But when I have most need, they me
forsake.
I am deceived; that maketh me sad.
 Cousin: Cousin Everyman, farewell
now,
For verily I will not go with you.
Also of mine own an unready reckoning
I have to account; therefore I make
tarrying.   376
Now, God keep thee, for now I go.
     [Exit Cousin.]
 Everyman: Ah, Jesus, is all come
hereto?
Lo, fair words maketh fools bain[20];
They promise and nothing will do cer-
tain.   380
My kinsmen promised me faithfully
For to abide with me steadfastly,
And now fast away do they flee:
Even so Fellowship promised me.
What friend were best me of to pro-
vide?   385
I lose my time here longer to abide.
Yet in my mind a thing there is;—
All my life I have loved riches;
If that my Goods now help me might,
He would make my heart full light. 390
I will speak to him in this distress.—
Where art thou, my Goods and Riches?

Goods: [*Within.*] Who calleth me?
Everyman? what hast thou haste?
I lie here in corners, trussed and piled so
high,
And in chests I am locked so fast, 395
Also sacked in bags, thou mayst see
with thine eye,
I cannot stir; in packs low I lie.
What would ye have, lightly me say.
 Everyman: Come hither, Goods, in all
the haste thou may,
For of counsel I must desire thee. 400
     [Enter Goods.]
 Goods: Sir, and ye in the world have
sorrow or adversity,
That can I help you to remedy shortly.
 Everyman: It is another disease that
grieveth me;
In this world it is not, I tell thee so.
I am sent for another way to go, 405
To give a straight account general
Before the highest Jupiter of all
And all my life I have had joy and
pleasure in thee,
Therefore I pray thee go with me;
For, peradventure, thou mayst before
God Almighty   410
My reckoning help to clean and purify;
For it is said ever among,
That money maketh all right that is
wrong.
 Goods: Nay, Everyman, I sing another
song,
I follow no man in such voyages; 415
For and I went with thee
Thou shouldst fare much the worse for
me.
For because on me thou didst set thy
mind,
Thy reckoning I have made blotted and
blind,
That thine account thou cannot make
truly;   420
And that hast thou for the love of me.
 Everyman: That would grieve me full
sore,
When I should come to that fearful
answer.
Up, let us go thither together.
 Goods: Nay, not so, I am too brittle,
I may not endure;   425

---

[18] To coax us. [19] Wanton. [20] Obedient.

I will follow no man one foot, be ye
   sure.
   Everyman: Alas, I have thee loved,
   and has great pleasure
All my life-days on good and treasure.
   Goods: That is to thy damnation
   without lesing,²¹
For my love is contrary to the love ever-
   lasting.   430
But if thou had me loved moderately
   during,²²
As to the poor give part of me,
Then shouldst thou not in this dolor be,
Nor in this great sorrow and care.
   Everyman: Lo, now was I deceived ere
   I was ware,   435
And all I may wyte²³ my spending of
   time.
   Goods: What, weenest thou I am thine?
   Everyman: I had wend so.
   Goods: Nay, Everyman, I say no;
As for a while I was lent thee,   440
A season thou hast had me in prosperity;
My condition is man's soul to kill;
If I save one, a thousand I do spill.²⁴
Weenest thou that I will follow thee?
Nay, from this world, not verily.   445
   Everyman: I had wend otherwise.
   Goods: Therefore to thy soul Goods is
   a thief;
For when thou art dead, this is my
   guise,²⁵
Another to deceive in the same wise
As I have done thee, and all to his soul's
   reprief.²⁶   450
   Everyman: O false Goods, cursed thou
   be!
Thou traitor to God, that hast de-
   ceived me,
And caught me in thy snare.
   Goods: Marry, thou brought thyself
   in care,
Whereof I am glad,   455
I must needs laugh, I cannot be sad.
   Everyman: Ah, Goods, thou hast had
   long my heartly love;
I gave thee that which should be the
   Lord's above.

But wilt thou not go with me indeed?
I pray thee truth to say.   460
   Goods: No, so God me speed,
Therefore farewell, and have good day.
                [Exit Goods.]
   Everyman: O, to whom shall I make
   my moan
For to go with me in that heavy jour-
   ney?
First Fellowship said he would with
   me go;   465
His words were very pleasant and gay,
But afterward he left me alone.
Then spake I to my kinsmen all in
   despair,
And also they gave me words fair,
They lacked no fair speaking,   470
But all forsake me in the ending.
Then went I to my Goods that I loved
   best,
In hope to have comfort, but there had
   I least;
For my Goods sharply did me tell
That he bringeth many into hell.   475
Then of myself I was ashamed,
And so I am worthy to be blamed;
Thus may I well myself hate.
Of whom shall I now counsel take?
I think that I shall never speed   480
Till that I go to my Good-Deeds;
But alas, she is so weak,
That she can neither go nor speak;
Yet will I venture on her now.—
My Good-Deeds, where be you?   485
   Good-Deeds: [*Speaking up from the
   ground.*] Here I lie, cold in the
   ground;
Thy sins hath me sore bound,
That I cannot stir.
   Everyman: O, Good-Deeds, I stand in
   fear;
I must you pray of counsel,   490
For help now should come right well.
   Good-Deeds: Everyman, I have un-
   derstanding
That ye be summoned account to make
Before Messias, of Jerusalem King;
And you do by me,²⁷ that journey with
   you will I take.   495

²¹ Lying.   ²² For the time being.   ²³ Lay
the blame upon.   ²⁴ Destroy.   ²⁵ Custom.
²⁶ Reproof.

²⁷ By my advice.

Everyman: Therefore I come to you,
  my moan to make;
I pray you that ye will go with me.
  Good-Deeds: I would full fain, but I
  cannot stand, verily.
  Everyman: Why, is there anything on
  you fall?
  Good-Deeds: Yea, sir, I may thank
  you of all,[28]   500
If ye had perfectly cheered me,
Your book of count full ready now had
  been.
Look, the books of your works and deeds
  eke;
Ah, see how they lie under the feet,
To your soul's heaviness.   505
  Everyman: Our Lord Jesus, help me!
For one letter here I cannot see.
  Good-Deeds: There is a blind reckon-
  ing in time of distress!
  Everyman: Good-Deeds, I pray you,
  help me in this need,
Or else I am forever damned indeed. 510
Therefore help me to make reckoning
Before the redeemer of all thing,
That king is, and was, and ever shall.
  Good-Deeds: Everyman, I am sorry of
  your fall,
And fain would I help you, and I were
  able.   515
  Everyman: Good-Deeds, your counsel
  I pray you give me.
  Good-Deeds: That shall I do verily;
Though that on my feet I may not go,
I have a sister, that shall with you also,
Called Knowledge, which shall with
  you abide,   520
To help you to make that dreadful reck-
  oning.   [*Enter Knowledge.*]
  Knowledge: Everyman, I will go with
  thee, and be thy guide,
In thy most need to go by thy side.
  Everyman: In good condition I am
  now in every thing,
And am wholly content with this good
  thing;   525
Thanked be God my Creator.
  Good-Deeds: And when she hath
  brought thee there,

Where thou shalt heal thee of thy smart,
Then go thou with thy reckoning and
  thy Good-Deeds together,
For to make thee joyful at heart   530
Before the blessed Trinity.
  Everyman: My Good-Deeds, gra-
  mercy;
I am well content, certainly,
With your words sweet.
  Knowledge: Now go we together lov-
  ingly,   535
To Confession, that cleansing river.
  Everyman: For joy I weep; I would
  we were there.
But, I pray you, give me cognition
Where dwelleth that holy man, Con-
  fession.
  Knowledge: In the house of salvation:
We shall find him in that place,   541
That shall us comfort by God's grace
                      [*Enter Confession.*]
Lo, this is Confession; kneel down and
  ask mercy,
For he is in good conceit with God Al-
  mighty.
  Everyman: [*kneeling.*] O glorious
  fountain that all uncleanness doth
  clarify,   545
Wash from me the spots of vice unclean,
That on me no sin may be seen.
I come with Knowledge for my re-
  demption,
Redempt with hearty and full contrition;
For I am commanded a pilgrimage to
  take,   550
And great accounts before God to make.
Now, I pray you, Shrift, mother of
  salvation,
Help my good deeds for my piteous ex-
  clamation.   [*He rises.*]
  Confession: I know your sorrow well,
  Everyman;
Because with Knowledge ye come to
  me,   555
I will you comfort as well as I can,
And a precious jewel I will give thee,
Called penance, voider of adversity;
Therewith shall your body chastised be,
With abstinence and perseverance in
  God's service: 560
            [*Gives Everyman a scourge.*]

----

[28] For everything.

Here shall you receive that scourge of me,
Which is penance strong, that ye must endure,
To remember thy Saviour was scourged for thee
With sharp scourges, and suffered it patiently;
So must thou, ere thou scape that painful pilgrimage;   565
Knowledge, keep him in this voyage,
And by that time Good-Deeds will be with thee.
But in any wise, be sure of mercy,
For your time draweth fast; and ye will saved be,
Ask God mercy, and He will grant truly.
When with the scourge of penance man doth him bind,   571
The oil of forgiveness then shall he find.
Everyman: Thanked be God for his gracious work,
For now I will my penance begin;
This hath rejoiced and lighted my heart,
Though the knots be painful and hard within.   576
Knowledge: Everyman, look your penance that ye fulfill,
What pain that ever it to you be,
And Knowledge shall give you counsel at will,
How your account ye shall make clearly.   580
[*Everyman kneels in prayer.*]
Everyman: O eternal God, O heavenly figure,
O way of rightwiseness, O goodly vision,
Which descended down in a virgin pure
Because he would Everyman redeem,
Which Adam forfeited by his disobedience,   585
O blessed Godhead, elect and high divine,
Forgive my grievous offence;
Here I cry thee mercy in this presence.
O ghostly treasure, O ransomer and redeemer,
Of all the world hope and conductor,
Mirror of joy, founder of mercy,   591
Which illumineth heaven and earth thereby,

Hear my clamorous complaint, though it late be!
Receive my prayers; unworthy in this heavy life
Though I be, a sinner most abominable,
Yet let my name be written in Moses' table.   596
O Mary, pray to the Maker of all thing,
Me for to help at my ending,
And save me from the power of my enemy,
For Death assaileth me strongly;   600
And, Lady, that I may by means of thy prayer
Of your Son's glory to be partner,
By the means of his passion I it crave,
I beseech you, help my soul to save!
[*He rises.*]
Knowledge, give me the scourge of penance,   605
My flesh therewith shall give acquaintance.
I will now begin, if God give me grace.
Knowledge: Everyman, God give you time and space:
Thus I bequeath you in the hands of our Saviour
Now may you make your reckoning sure.   610
Everyman: In the name of the Holy Trinity,
My body sore punished shall be:
[*He begins to scourge himself.*]
Take this, body, for the sin of the flesh;
Also thou delightest to go gay and fresh,
And in the way of damnation thou did me bring;   615
Therefore suffer now strokes of punishing.
Now of penance I will wade the water clear,
To save me from purgatory, that sharp fire.
[*Good-Deeds rises from the floor.*]
Good-Deeds: I thank God, now I can walk and go;
And am delivered of my sickness and woe.   620
Therefore with Everyman I will go, and not spare;

His good works I will help him to de-
clare.
Knowledge: Now, Everyman, be
merry and glad;
Your Good-Deeds cometh now, ye may
not be sad;
Now is your Good-Deeds whole and
sound,   625
Going upright upon the ground.
Everyman: My heart is light, and
shall be evermore;
Now will I smite faster than I did before.
Good-Deeds: Everyman, pilgrim, my
special friend,
Blessed be thou without end;   630
For thee is prepared the eternal glory.
Ye have me made whole and sound,
Therefore I will bide by thee in every
stound.[29]
Everyman: Welcome, my Good-
Deeds! Now I hear thy voice,
I weep for sweetness of love.   635
Knowledge: Be no more sad, but ever
rejoice;
God seeth thy living in his throne
above.
Put on this garment to thy behove,[30]
Which is wet with your tears,
Or else before God you may it miss,   640
When ye to your journey's end come
shall.
Everyman: Gentle Knowledge, what
do you it call?
Knowledge: It is a garment of sorrow,
From pain it will you borrow [31];
Contrition it is,   645
That getteth forgiveness;
It pleaseth God passing well.
Good-Deeds: Everyman, will you
wear it for your heal?
[*Everyman puts on the robe of contrition.*]
Everyman: Now blessed be Jesu,
Mary's Son,
For now have I on true contrition.   650
And let us go now without tarrying.
Good-Deeds, have we clear our reckon-
ing?
Good-Deeds: Yea, indeed I have them
here.

Everyman: Then I trust we need not
fear.
Now, friends, let us not part in twain.
Knowledge: Nay, Everyman, that will
we not, certain.   656
Good-Deeds: Yet must thou lead with
thee
Three persons of great might.
Everyman: Who should they be?
Good-Deeds: Discretion and Strength
they hight,[32]   660
And thy Beauty may not abide be-
hind.
Knowledge: Also ye must call to mind
Your Five-Wits as for your counsellors.
Good-Deeds: You must have them
ready at all hours.
Everyman: How shall I get them
hither?
Knowledge: You must call them all
together,   666
And they will hear you incontinent.
Everyman: My friends, come hither
and be present,
Discretion, Strength, my Five-Wits, and
Beauty.
[*Enter Discretion, Strength, Five-Wits,
and Beauty.*]
Beauty: Here at your will we be all
ready.   670
What will ye that we should do?
Good-Deeds: That ye would with
Everyman go,
And help him in his pilgrimage.
Advise you, will ye with him or not in
that voyage?
Strength: We will bring him all thither
To his help and comfort, ye may believe
me.   676
Discretion: So will we go with him all
together.
Everyman: Almighty God, loved
might thou be,
I give thee laud that I have hither
brought
Strength, Discretion, Beauty, and Five-
Wits; lack I nought;   680
And my Good-Deeds, with Knowledge
clear,

[29] Moment. [30] Benefit. [31] Ransom.   [32] Are called.

All be in my company at my will here;
I desire no more to my business.
   Strength: And I, Strength, will by
   you stand in distress,
Though thou would in battle fight on
   the ground. 685
   Five-Wits: And though it were
   through the world round,
We will not depart for sweet nor sour.
   Beauty: No more will I unto death's
   hour,
Whatsoever thereof befall.
   Discretion: Everyman, advise you first
   of all, 690
Go with a good advisement and delibera-
tion.
We all give you virtuous monition
That all shall be well.
   Everyman: My friends, hearken what
   I will tell:
I pray God reward you in his heavenly
   sphere. 695
Now hearken, all that be here,
For I will make my testament
Here before you all present.
In alms half my goods I will give with
   my hands twain
In the way of charity, with good intent,
And the other half still shall remain 701
In quethe [33] to be returned there it
   ought to be.
This I do in despite of the fiend of hell
To go quite out of his peril
Ever after and this day. 705
   Knowledge: Everyman, hearken what
   I say;
Go to priesthood, I you advise,
And receive of him in any wise
The holy sacrament and ointment to-
gether;
Then shortly see ye turn again hither;
We will all abide you here. 711
   Five-Wits: Yea, Everyman, hie you
   that ye ready were.
There is no emperor, king, duke, nor
   baron,
That of God hath commission,
As hath the least priest in the world
   being; 715

For of the blessed sacraments pure and
   benign
He beareth the keys, and thereof hath
   the cure
For man's redemption, it is ever sure,
Which God for our soul's medicine
Gave us out of his heart with great pain.
Here in this transitory life, for thee and
   me 721
The blessed sacraments seven there be:
Baptism, confirmation, with priesthood
   good,
And the sacrament of God's precious
   flesh and blood,
Marriage, the holy extreme unction,
   and penance; 725
These seven be good to have in re-
membrance,
Gracious sacraments of high divinity.
   Everyman: Fain would I receive that
   holy body,
And meekly to my ghostly [34] father I
   will go.   [*Exit Everyman.*]
   Five-Wits: Everyman, that is the best
   that ye can do. 730
God will you to salvation bring,
For priesthood exceedeth all other thing;
To us Holy Scripture they do teach,
And converteth man from sin, heaven
   to reach. 734
God hath to them more power given,
Than to any angel that is in heaven;
With five words he may consecrate
God's body in flesh and blood to make,
And handleth his maker between his
   hands.
The priest bindeth and unbindeth all
   bands, 740
Both in earth and in heaven.
Thou ministers all the sacraments seven.
Though we kiss thy feet thou were
   worthy;
Thou art surgeon that cureth sin deadly:
No remedy we find under God 745
But all only priesthood.
Everyman, God gave priests that dignity,
And setteth them in his stead among us
   to be;
Thus be they above angels in degree.

[33] Bequest.   [34] Spiritual.

Knowledge: If priests be good it is so
　　surely; 750
But when Jesus hanged on the cross
　　with great smart,
There he gave, out of his blessed heart,
The same sacrament in great torment;
He sold them not to us, that Lord Om-
　　nipotent.
Therefore Saint Peter the apostle doth
　　say 755
That Jesus' curse hath all they
Which God their Saviour do buy or sell,
Or they for any money do take or tell.[35]
Sinful priests giveth the sinners ex-
　　ample bad;
Their children sitteth by other men's
　　fires, I have heard, 760
And some haunteth women's company,
With unclean life, as lusts of lechery;
These be with sin made blind.
　　Five-Wits: I trust to God no such may
　　　　we find;
Therefore let us priesthood honor, 765
And follow their doctrine for our souls'
　　succor;
We be their sheep, and they shepherds be
By whom we all be kept in surety.
Peace, for yonder I see Everyman come,
Which hath made true satisfaction.
　　　　　　　[Re-enter Everyman.]
　　Good-Deeds: Methink it is he indeed.
　　Everyman: Now Jesu be our alder
　　　　speed.[36]
I have received the sacrament for my
　　redemption,
And then mine extreme unction:
Blessed be all they that counselled me to
　　take it! 775
And now, friends, let us go without
　　longer respite;
I thank God that ye have tarried so long.
Now set each of you on this rod [37] your
　　hand,
And shortly follow me:
I go before, there I would be; God be
　　our guide. 780
　　Strength: Everyman, we will not from
　　　　you go,
Till ye have gone this voyage long.

Discretion: I, Discretion, will bide by
　　you also.
Knowledge: And though this pilgrim-
　　age be never so strong,[38]
I will never part you from. 785
Everyman, I will be as sure by thee
As ever I did by Judas Maccabee.
　　　　[They walk together to the grave.]
　　Everyman: Alas, I am so faint I may
　　　　not stand,
My limbs under me do fold.
Friends, let us not turn again to this
　　land, 790
Not for all the world's gold,
For into this cave must I creep,
And turn to earth and there to sleep.
　　Beauty: What, into this grave? alas!
　　Everyman: Yea, there shall ye con-
　　　　sume more and less. 795
　　Beauty: And what, should I smother
　　　　here?
　　Everyman: Yea, by my faith, and
　　　　nevermore appear.
In this world live no more we shall,
But in heaven before the highest Lord
　　of all.
　　Beauty: I cross out all this! Adieu,
　　　　by Saint John! 800
I take my cap in my lap and am gone.
　　Everyman: What, Beauty, whither
　　　　will ye?
　　Beauty: Peace, I am deaf; I look not
　　　　behind me,
Not and thou wouldst give me all the
　　gold in thy chest. *[Exit Beauty.]*
　　Everyman: Alas, whereto may I trust?
Beauty goeth fast away from me, 806
She promised with me to live and die.
　　Strength: Everyman, I will thee also
　　　　forsake and deny;
Thy game liketh me not at all.
　　Everyman: Why, then ye will for-
　　　　sake me all! 810
Sweet Strength, tarry a little space.
　　Strength: Nay, sir, by the rood of
　　　　grace,
I will hie me from thee fast,
Though thou weep till thy heart do
　　brast.[39]

---

[35] Count. [36] The help of all of us. [37] Cross.

[38] Hard. [39] Burst.

Everyman: Ye would ever bide by me,
ye said. 815
Strength: Yea, I have you far enough
conveyed;
Ye be old enough, I understand,
Your pilgrimage to take on hand.
I repent me that I hither came.
Everyman: Strength, you do to dis-
please I am to blame; 820
Will you break promise that is debt?
Strength: In faith, as for that I care
not;
Thou art but a fool to complain,
You spend your speech and waste your
brain;
Go, thrust thee into the ground! 825
[*Exit Strength.*]
Everyman: I had wend surer I should
you have found.
But I see well, that trusteth in his
Strength,
She him deceiveth at the length.
Both Strength and Beauty forsaketh
me,
Yet they promised me fair and lov-
ingly.
Discretion: Everyman, I will after
Strength be gone, 831
As for me I will leave you alone.
Everyman: Why, Discretion, will ye
forsake me?
Discretion: Yea, in faith, I will go
from thee,
For when Strength goeth before 835
I follow after evermore.
Everyman: Yet, I pray thee, for love
of the Trinity,
Look in my grave once piteously.
Discretion: Nay, so nigh will I not
come.
Now farewell, fellows, every one! 840
[*Exit Discretion.*]
Everyman: O, all things faileth, save
God alone,
Beauty, Strength, and Discretion;
For when Death bloweth his blast,
They all run from me full fast.
Five-Wits: Everyman, my leave now
of thee I take; 845
I will follow the other, for here I thee
forsake.

Everyman: Alas! then may I wail and
weep,
For I took you for my best friend.
Five-Wits: I will no longer thee keep;
Now farewell, and here an end. 850
[*Exit Five-Wits.*]
Everyman: O Jesu, help! all hath for-
saken me!
Good-Deeds: Nay, Everyman, I will
bide with thee,
I will not forsake thee indeed;
Thou shalt find me a good friend at need.
Everyman: Gramercy, Good-Deeds,
now may I true friends see; 855
They have forsaken me every one;
I loved them better than my Good-
Deeds alone.
Knowledge, will ye forsake me also?
Knowledge: Yea, Everyman, when ye
to death shall go;
But not yet for no manner of danger.
Everyman: Gramercy, Knowledge,
with all my heart. 861
Knowledge: Nay, yet I will not from
hence depart,
Till I see where ye shall be come.
Everyman: Methink, alas, that I must
be gone,
To make my reckoning and my debts
pay, 865
For I see my time is nigh spent away.
Take example, all ye that this do hear
or see,
How they that I love best do forsake
me,
Except my Good-Deeds that bideth
truly.
Good-Deeds: All earthly things is but
vanity: 870
Beauty, Strength, and Discretion, do
man forsake,
Foolish friends and kinsmen that fair
spake,
All fleeth save Good-Deeds, and that
am I.
Everyman: Have mercy on me, God
most mighty,
And stand by me, thou Mother and
Maid, holy Mary. 875
Good-Deeds: Fear not, I will speak for
thee.

Everyman: Here I cry God mercy.
Good-Deeds: Short our end, and
  minish our pain;
Let us go and never come again.
  Everyman: Into thy hands, Lord, my
  soul I commend;   880
Receive it, Lord, that it be not lost!
As thou me boughtest, so me defend,
And save me from the fiend's boast,
That I may appear with that blessed
  host
That shall be saved at the day of doom.
In manus tuas [40]—of might's most   886
Forever—*commendo spiritum meum.*[41]
[*Everyman and Good-Deeds descend into
  the grave.*]
  Knowledge: Now hath he suffered that
  we all shall endure;
The Good-Deeds shall make all sure.
Now hath he made ending;   890
Methinketh that I hear angels sing
And make great joy and melody,
Where Everyman's soul received shall
  be.
  Angel: [*Within.*] Come, excellent
  elect spouse to Jesu;
Here above thou shalt go,   895
Because of thy singular virtue.
Now thy soul is taken thy body from,
Thy reckoning is crystal-clear.
Now shalt thou into the heavenly
  sphere,
Unto the which all ye shall come   900
That liveth well before the day of doom.
[*Exit Knowledge. Enter Doctor to speak
  the Epilogue.*]

[40] Into thy hands. [41] I commend my soul.

Doctor: This moral men may have in
  mind;
Ye hearers, take it of worth, old and
  young,
And forsake pride, for he deceiveth you
  in the end,
And remember Beauty, Five-Wits,
  Strength, and Discretion,   905
They all at the last do Everyman for-
  sake,
Save his Good-Deeds, there doth he
  take.
But beware, and they be small
Before God, he hath no help at all.
None excuse may be there for Every-
  man: 910
Alas, how shall he do then?
For after death amends may no man
  make,
For then mercy and pity do him for-
  sake.
If his reckoning be not clear when he
  doth come,
God will say—*ite maledicti in ignem ae-
  ternum.*[42]   915
And he that hath his account whole and
  sound,
High in heaven he shall be crowned;
Unto which place God bring us all
  thither,
That we may live body and soul to-
  gether.
Thereto help the Trinity!   920
Amen, say ye, for saint charity.
*Thus endeth this moral play of Every-
  man.*

[42] Go, ye accursed, into eternal fire.

NOTES ON *EVERYMAN*

I. THE NATURE OF PARABLE

Everyman may be regarded as a dramatized parable, and it therefore
introduces the problems inherent in the parable form. A parable may be
said to present some rather simple generalization by means of a concrete
example: it is a story which makes a point. It is primarily concerned with
theme or *idea*. For instance, if we turn to the New Testament, we find the
story of the foolish man who built his house on the sand and the wise man

who built his upon the rock. The storm comes, the foundations of the first house are swept away, and the whole fabric crumbles; but the house built upon the rock survives the storm.

Each feature of the story has a simple moral meaning. The house clearly is not a structure of wood or stone or brick, but a moral edifice. The physical storm symbolizes the doubts and difficulties of life. The sandy foundation represents frivolous or false beliefs, whereas the rock is eternal truth.

It would be possible, of course, to express the point of the parable still more simply by dropping the symbolism altogether and stating the implied generalization abstractly: that is, the man who lives in accordance with truth can endure the difficulties of life without suffering the collapse of the man who foolishly ignores the truth.

But the parable form of statement has distinct advantages: by making use of a concrete story it renders the point more vividly and emphatically. The reader's feelings and imagination are engaged as well as his mind— a matter that is important in two ways. For one thing, it may be useful in merely understanding the point; this is especially true of untrained or unsophisticated minds, which are naturally more accessible to emotional appeal than to abstract logical statements and therefore find the parable an easily grasped kind of expression. The statement, "John Doe's life was lived in accordance with false premises," may seem "dry" because, even though it seems to concern a specific case, it is abstract in form. But the concrete picture of the house built upon the sand is emotionally stirring and is immediate in its impact. We are prepared for an ironical mockery of such expensive folly, and we begin to feel some apprehension as we think of the weak foundation. But it should by now be clear that the parable is doing more than merely making a point understandable: in stimulating our emotions and imaginations, it is giving us a fuller and more complete experience than would the bare statement of fact. It is no longer a device of exposition for relatively untutored minds, but as it effectively engages our interest and our sympathies, it acts on the same level as works of literary art.

The Problem of the Parable Writer: the Relationship of Theme and Form. The parable writer, in other words, finds himself to some extent working in two fields at the same time. In one, he is writing a sermon, the aim of which is to convey a single, definite, clearcut idea; but as he goes on to give that idea the concrete narrative form which gains power from its appeal to our emotions, he introduces new elements which tend to widen and complicate the original forthright idea. Through our imaginations, which are necessarily brought into play by the story form, we naturally begin to see new meanings and implications. Thus, the theme of the sermon is expanded. For instance, the Biblical parable of the two houses might suggest to us such questions as the following: Was the man arrogantly foolish? Was he led into his folly by false appearance? Did he become criminally careless because he was preoccupied with other things? How will he feel when the house collapses—terrified, remorseful, or eager to blame someone else? And what of the innocent occupants of the house? What attitude are we to take toward them?

Now, as it happens, the author of this parable has taken steps to prevent such questions from becoming too prominent and thus interfering with the singleness of this theme. He simply says, "The man was foolish"; we are meant to accept this as adequate motivation of his action. Nor does the author say anything about the other occupants or give any real hints to stimulate our inquiring into the man's feelings after the fall of his house. In other words, the author has "protected" his thesis, so to speak; he has stuck quite close to the sermon form; he has not yielded very much to the demands of art, though he has used some of the devices of art.

When, however, the parable writer does use literary methods—action and character—to give his theme conviction and dramatic force, he does inevitably begin to surrender some of the simplicity of his theme. For the questions proposed by our imagination suggest *variations of the theme;* actually, we are tending to break down the abstract *generalization* into *concrete individual experiences.* The sermon gives us the generalization; the drama presents an experience. The particular circumstances of the experience begin to modify and qualify the simple, abstract statement. In conclusion, then, we come to this double principle, which is very important in dealing with the complex "parables" which drama involves: in proportion as we put an idea—any idea—as simply, generally, and abstractly as possible, we militate against dramatic effectiveness; and conversely, in proportion as we present a theme concretely and vividly, we tend, as a necessary consequence, to suggest a more complex interpretation of events than any simple, abstract statement will convey.

How We Become Aware of the "Meaning." Most important of all, we tend, in the concrete, dramatic presentation of the theme, to shift from the author's own unequivocal "meaning" as it may be stated by the author himself in his role as scientist, historian, or moralist to the total "meaning" of the events as presented to the audience or to the reader. To state the matter in slightly different terms: when we fictionalize or dramatize a generalization about life, the meaning tends to shift from the "say-so" of the author as an expert or authority to the meaning of the fictional or dramatic structure. The author speaks not directly but indirectly; he does not try to convince us by his logic or his authority, but offers us a group of events whose meaning we apprehend imaginatively.

Now the latter method does not mean that the author speaks any the less intelligibly; if he is a good artist, the novelist or dramatist or poet can successfully convey to us his interpretation. He may fail—just as the writer who speaks to us directly in his own person may fail by use of mistaken facts, bad logic, or muddled organization. But, with his more complex task, the artist has possibilities of full success. He selects and arranges the actions and the other dramatic materials in which we find a certain significance; when the arrangement and selection are done with sufficient skill and insight, what we see in them will presumably be very close to what he sees in them (we have already seen how the structure of *Lady Windermere's Fan* leads us definitely toward certain conclusions about Wilde's "meaning"). But at the same time that we are interpreting the structure of actions that constitute the play, we are also, as it were, participating in them and emotionally responding to them; the fact that we enter imaginatively into the story or play accounts for its superior immediacy and power.

2. THEME AND DRAMA IN *Everyman*

Although in the study of *Lady Windermere's Fan* we were finally able to come to some reasonably definite conclusions about "meaning," the theme was never in the foreground. What we were primarily conscious of was the conflict and interplay of a set of sharply characterized individuals. But in *Everyman* the situation is different: the theme is clearly before us from the start, and the characters and action are, in a sense, in a secondary position Hence our critical problem here is a different one.

We do not have to spend much time showing how the events of the play conform to the theme, for it is clear that the author has started out with the Christian account of life and adapted to it the particular set of circumstances that constitute the play. Rarely do we forget that he is expounding to us certain basic Christian values. The beginning and ending of the play and God's speech (ll. 22 ff.) present the theme almost to the exclusion of dramatic interest. The part of the play lying roughly between ll. 550 and 650 is largely a straightforward presentation, without conflict, of certain steps that the human being must go through on the way to salvation. Do you find other such relatively undramatic passages?

But the author has not chosen to write a sermon: he has written a dramatized parable. And the consequences of his use of the dramatic form are forcefully apparent. Here, then, is where our critical problem really lies: we want to see how much of an artist he was, that is, to what extent he made his drama a self-consistent presentation of a concrete experience and allowed his thesis to become subordinate to the more complex view of life entailed in the tracing of individual experiences.

Characterization. In a sense this play may be called an allegory; that is, each of the characters and events is definitely related to a system of abstract meanings. The names of the characters, of course, show their origin in abstractions—Knowledge, Discretion, Good Deeds, and so on. But they are not merely abstractions dressed up and walking around on the stage; some of them, at least, are three-dimensional beings that attain a degree of personality.

Death, for example, as far as the allegory is concerned, is merely what happens to all mortals, loss of life, which is the blotting out of the senses and the corruption of the body. Yet in the play, Death is presented as a person whose duty it is to summon Everyman before his Maker; but one notices that the author has done more than merely to dress Death up like a human being. The author has given him something of a personality as well. Death has the brisk, businesslike air of a deputy sheriff. He even appears to get a certain relish out of the stammering surprise which his descent provokes in his hitherto unsuspecting victim. Yet, on the other hand, his attitude is definitely not malicious. After all, he has no personal animus against his victim. To serve the summons on Everyman is simply his duty—part of the day's work.

If the student is inclined to feel that Death has been credited here with more personality than he actually achieves, it will surely be easy enough to show that some of the other characters do become personalities. Fellowship, the abstract quality, is represented by a typical goodfellow, who approaches his friend to cheer him up, who swears not to forsake him "to my life's end," but who adds cautiously "In the way of good company," and who finally leaves the friend in the lurch when he finds that really serious matters are afoot.

In the same way, Kindred—supported by Cousin—transcends the mere abstraction to become a typical kinsman, genuinely concerned about Everyman's melancholy, full of fatuous comment, willing to help him out—up to a point—but flatly refusing Everyman's great request.

The allegory is working itself out as the play develops: the play is saying that friends and even kinsmen cannot die for one. But the play makes its general point by attempting to give the illusion of life—the interplay of real people and concrete events.

Structure. Aside, then, from attempting to develop some of his characters as characters, the author goes a step further: he presents his actions in a more complex form than would be necessary if he were only making a point about Christian values. He has several climaxes, with resultant changes in tension and mood; he makes rather skillful use of irony; he uses different means of suspense. In other words, he is trying in every way he can to make us become emotionally concerned; he wants his story to be effective as a story—his plot to work as plot.

For the sake of the theme, all the author must do is show Everyman embracing Christian values and thus gaining everlasting life. But the author is not content with so simple a pattern: he wishes to present also Everyman's devotion to false values, and later his failure to distinguish, in the realm of sound values, between those which are only of earthly significance and those which relate directly to eternal salvation. Now these experiences have to come in a certain order, and as we observe what that order is, we really discover the structure of the play.

Although *Everyman* has no internal divisions such as acts or scenes, it is clearly divided into four parts which have a definite relationship to each other. In Part I we see Everyman in conflict with death, and losing the battle (to l. 183). In Part II Everyman unsuccessfully tries to find a companion for his journey (to l. 462). In Part III he is more successful in his search for companions, and the mood changes to one of joy and exaltation (to l. 770). In Part IV we have another turnabout: Everyman has a second major disappointment, and he finally meets death completely sobered and matured by his experiences. The author who conceived this fairly elaborate dramatic progression was doing much more than merely saying "Be good and you'll be happy."

Part I. Man's hearing that he must die would not on the face of it appear to have many dramatic possibilities. But the author does make it dramatic by showing Everyman trying to fight off Death as a concrete, personal enemy. Although the conclusion of the conflict is known in advance, the author maintains tension and interest with his vivid portrait of Everyman dashing quickly from one to another of the expedients by means of which human beings always greet or try to evade the unpleasant: incredulousness, the desire for delay, efforts to bribe, desire to do other things first, the naive hope that maybe it won't be so bad after all ("Should I not come again shortly?"), the hope for company, the final direct plea for grace. The author's acute psychological analysis of Everyman is much more than he needs to provide in order to develop his theme. But he wants to make his character alive.

Part II. In Part I we saw Everyman reduced from the brisk self-satisfaction of the undisturbed human being to the near-despair of one who must face death; now we see him experiencing several momentary recoveries of good spirits and then plunging into still deeper despair. In terms of action, Part II is connected with Part I by Everyman's acting on his expressed desire to find companionship. Now what the author might do is merely to run Everyman through a series of similar experiences, each of which has the same disappointing ending. But, actually, one should notice how much variety he has achieved in this scene, which might be repetitious and hence monotonous. First, he has Everyman take the most natural step for a human being—seek human companionship, that of friends and relatives. Then Everyman with his plea shifts to a wholly different kind of character, Goods. This gives us, on a superficial level, contrast, and, on a more profound level, a sense of deep irony: while Everyman thinks he is finding a more durable companion, we can see him making an even less discerning choice than before. As we examine in detail Everyman's dialogue with each of the characters whom he asks for help, we find that each little scene is handled in its own characteristic way. Note the difference in length: the first, that with Fellowship, is very fully developed; the second is only half so long; and that with Goods, where the theme receives a new twist, is longer again. The Fellowship scene is almost a playlet in itself, with the effect resting on irony: Everyman and Fellowship reach an enthusiastic height of good feeling based on the latter's helpfulness and the former's gratitude, and then comes the crash into reality. In the scene with Cousin and Kindred the author cannot use the same pattern of build-up and let-down; so here the refusal comes quite early (Everyman, partly disillusioned, is no longer so ambiguous about the journey he has to take). The author adds to the sense of freshness by the frivolity of Cousin's excuse, "I have the cramp in my toe"—a skillful picture of the ludicrously inadequate excuses which human beings give to justify their failures. Note also Kindred's line: "Ye shall have my maid . . ." Why is this dramatically effective? Compare, on the other hand, the excuse which Goods gives: does it merely repeat the scheme used in Cousin's excuse? Notice Goods's speech in ll. 401–402: what equivocation or "double talk" has the author woven into the words of the promise? Is this appropriate? What devices does the author use to make Goods a "realistic" character?

Once again, it is clear that the demands of the mere theme do not account for all the careful technical elaboration. With a good sense of drama, the author has gone on to present a full and vivid set of experiences. As a result, when we come to the end of Part II we do not feel that we are only being lectured, but we can genuinely grasp the depression of Everyman, who is a plausible human being.

Part III. Again the central element in Everyman's new experience is irony: by the author's use of irony we can see that he is avoiding the run-of-the-mill, routine, commonplace developments which the prominence of his theme might have led us to expect. Here, the irony lies in the fact that Everyman turns to his best help, not first, but only after he has been repulsed everywhere else. (Everyman's action here is typical of humanity's confusion about values.) Then, the easy and expected thing for the author to do would have been to have Good Deeds rescue Everyman from his plight immediately. But we have further irony: such on-the-spot assistance is impossible. And it may not be pushing the irony too far to point out that the reason in this case is the same reason given by Goods: Good Deeds is fettered—bound. Note that in each case the fetters are symbols, but symbols, of course, of different things: what are the symbolic meanings?

But Good Deeds, though, like Goods, she cannot go with Everyman, can send him to her sister Knowledge, who will tell him what to do; and the process of Everyman's salvation is thus begun. It is not necessary for us to follow in detail Everyman's changing situation. We should note, of course, that the subsequent episode with Confession and Penance has much less dramatic force than any scene which occurred thus far. Here the *sermon* takes precedence of the *drama:* the author is finishing one part of his theme and is looking forward to another part of it to be developed later.

But, on the whole, this part of the play still has considerable dramatic force, a dramatic force which grows out of the change of mood as Everyman feels overwhelming relief in his discovery at last, of trustworthy friends. In fact, here is a kind of summation and knitting together of the first three parts: the resolution of the original issue, which was Everyman's terror at being abandoned, at having to take a dreadful journey alone. He now feels comforted and strong. The author's bringing upon the stage a whole company of sympathetic counselors and friends builds up for the audience a sense of Everyman's increased security. They are the source of his changed feelings, and at the same time they become a kind of visible symbol of his new sense of security.

Note the effective touch of having Everyman assume the post of leader.

Everyman is no longer frightened and bewildered. Having received the sacrament, he is resolved and confident. "Follow me," he says; "I go before, there I would be."

It looks at this point as if everything is settled and the author is ready for a "happy ending."

Part IV: The Complication of Theme. But the author, as we have already suggested, has elected to introduce a further complication. The very company on whom Everyman has been instructed to rely on his journey to the grave begins to fall away as he approaches the grave. With regard to the theological meaning, this complication allows the author to make a further point about man's relation to death, namely, that at death man must give up not only physical but also certain more abstract endowments. But on the dramatic level, the complication is more important still: it permits the author to create another suspense which will take the place of the suspense which has been relaxed. In other words, the author has not wished to seem to take the fact of death too lightly: even in the contrite and repentant man, death begets a proper seriousness and a proper fear. The shrinking back of one pilgrim after another emphasizes this sense of fear and makes Everyman seem a *human* being with normal, human hopes and fears, and not a rather unreal—because incredibly complacent—convert.

The Growth of Everyman's Character. This process of humanizing Everyman is accompanied by a process of character development: Everyman, as he begins his journey to the grave, is no longer the rather callow and terrified person that he appeared to be at the beginning of the play. His eyes have now been opened; the ordinary illusions have fallen from him; he has knowledge of the slipperiness and falsity of the world; and, indeed, he has acquired a certain moral toughness.

This new quality comes out very plainly in the passage in which Beauty repudiates Everyman. Consider the whole passage (beginning with line 794). After the promises made to him by Strength, Discretion, and Knowledge, Everyman has been heartened for the journey and filled with joy by his sense of the loyalty manifested by his companions. But just at this high point of courage, when he addresses the company as friends and says to them "Let us not turn again to this land. . . . For into this cave must I creep"—just at this moment, Beauty starts back in fear with the exclamation: "What, into this grave?" Yet it is important to notice that it is Everyman who is now able to look the facts in the face and answer: "Yea, and there shall you consume more and less." The answer is a sorrowful one, but it is important to note that Everyman himself is here the instructor who can explain to Beauty the worst that can befall.

One may put the matter in somewhat different fashion by saying that in this part of the play the author is developing the process of disillusionment on a much higher level. For, now, at this point in the play, it is not the outside world which is deserting Everyman at the approach of death, but the very qualities and faculties of the man himself which are deserting him. The inner citadel, as it were, is going down under the attack.

Everyman's cry, "Now, Jesu help! all hath forsaken me!" comes therefore with special poignance. Everyman is, at this stage of the play, not the man easily disappointed; he has been chastened. For the same reason, Good Deeds's final promise to abide with him, too, comes with special force: it is a promise made in the face of full knowledge of the terror which has caused all the other supporters to flee.

What, then, of the refusal of Knowledge to accompany Everyman into the grave with Good Deeds? Truth to the allegory demands that the author have Knowledge refuse—a man cannot take his knowledge with him into the grave. Yet, dramatically considered, will not the refusal of Knowledge come as an anticlimax after the high point which we have reached with Good Deeds's promise not to forsake Everyman?

Significant Variation. Here, as we shall see, the author has given us a very fine example of *significant variation* (see Glossary). Throughout the play, we have witnessed Everyman's repeated plea for companionship, and have heard the request in all but one instance refused. When Everyman turns to Knowledge and asks whether Knowledge will forsake him, the reply, "Yea, Everyman, when ye to death shall go," on one level echoes the reply which we have heard so often throughout the play. But here it comes with very different effect. We may say that the refusal itself, here, turns into a sort of comforting assurance. Coming from Knowledge, who has been what might be called the presiding genius of the play, it cannot be equated with the cowardly and selfish refusals which superficially it resembles. Indeed, as Knowledge continues his speech, the refusal itself, as we have said, becomes a guarantee of continued watchfulness and supervision. Knowledge will not have to desert Everyman until the fact of death itself, and not before Knowledge has seen him safely through his ordeal. Man cannot take his knowledge with him into the grave, but by means of Knowledge, man can see what will happen to him beyond the grave.

Again, then, we see the allegory asserting itself, but, as before, being humanized and made dramatically meaningful. The author achieves a richer and more moving effect by having Knowledge unable to follow Everyman than he would have secured by having both Good Deeds and Knowledge descend with Everyman into the grave.

Summary. We began this analysis by saying that *Everyman* was a dramatized parable. We pointed out that the dramatization of a theme is more vivid and moving than is an abstract statement of the theme. We pointed out further that a theme is to some extent qualified and modified in the process of dramatization, and that the emotional power which the dramatization provides, itself springs from the fact that we are not *given* a statement but are forced to develop our own attitudes and to make our own interpretations.

How are these propositions illustrated by *Everyman?* Suppose that we consider the matter in this way. Had the author of *Everyman* conceived his play as propaganda for the Christian way of life even more narrowly than he has, he might have been tempted to leave out such bits of humor as

Cousin's reply to Everyman: "No, by our Lady; I have a cramp in my toe." Such humor, he might have felt, was unseemly in such a play, and might detract from the seriousness of the attitude he wishes to provoke in his audience. To pass on to a much more serious matter, he might have further decided that he ought not to play up the terror of death in Everyman *after* Everyman had repented and set his account in order.

It is perfectly true that, in the play as we have it, Everyman does go to his death with a deep and sincere confidence in the Christian hope of the resurrection. Yet a narrow propagandist might conceivably have felt that he ought not to seem to weaken Everyman's confidence at all. And certainly, in strict logic, Everyman ought to feel no qualms at all: yet in the play, having brought Everyman up to a height of confidence, the author has rather deliberately stripped the confidence from him. This is, of course, not to say, that there is any ambiguity as to the author's attitude toward Christianity. The play is a very fine and relatively uncomplicated treatment of the Christian theme. But it is important to observe that even so simple a treatment of the theme as one finds in this play is not so simple as a purely abstract account of it would be, and, concomitantly, that the play is as good a play as it is because the author was willing to write as a dramatist and not as a *mere propagandist*.

One may make the same general point in terms of the symbolism: the play is an allegory, which, though simple, is not purely mechanical. The author is willing and able to provide some hints of a richer and more fluid symbolism. The "meaning" is not exhausted by our referring each part of the play to its place in the allegorical scheme as we might with a key to the allegory. Allegory in the play there is, and the principal meaning of the play is allegorical, but we have the beginnings of that richer and more manysided symbolism which any good play involves, and which we find in its most magnificent form perhaps in some of the greater plays of Shakespeare.

To sum up: we may say that good drama is always meaningful, and probably is ultimately always moral; but the reader who is looking only for the "moral," or who indulges merely in "message-hunting," or, in general, is willing to see a play as merely the illustration of a special theme will be misreading the play.

Everyman AS TRAGEDY

We should, finally, give at least passing attention to those aspects of *Everyman* which may suggest that it should be called a "tragedy." The fact that the play deals with serious issues suggests a kinship with tragedy, and the fact that the protagonist dies will, for many people, clinch the assumption that it is a tragedy. It is probable, indeed, that many people feel that tragedy is synonymous with an unhappy ending; and the death of the protagonist, in terms of this same logic, is *per se* unhappy.

Yet *Everyman*, it ought to be pretty clearly evident, is not a tragedy, even though it does concern itself with serious issues. And it ought to be even more clearly evident that the conventional assumptions about tragedy which would make it a tragedy require drastic qualification. The death of Everyman, for instance—regardless of whether or not it is "tragic" —is certainly not "unhappy." There is a sense in which Everyman at his death is profoundly happy. We shall need much more precise definitions of tragedy than this if we are to come to any understanding of drama.

It is not wise at this point to attempt any elaborate discussion of the nature of tragedy. That can best be undertaken a little later in this manual and in connection with plays which raise the problem of tragedy in more explicit form. Yet even so, a few generalizations on the subject here may not be amiss.

In the first place the mere death of the protagonist has little to do with tragedy. For example, consider: the death of a good person who is the victim of malice; the death of a good person by a chance accident; the death of a gangster, either at the hand of the state or at the hands of another gangster; the death of a person who dies happily in a good cause. Could any of these taken as such be regarded as tragic? It ought to be clear that we cannot respond to all these deaths in the same way, but that they will affect us in a variety of ways. We may feel shocked; we may rejoice; we may remain indifferent; we may be moved to pity; our attitude may be not simple at all but may blend one feeling with another.

The fact of death, then, affects us in various ways and depends for its effect on the circumstances which attend it. Any definition of tragedy which depends, therefore, merely on the fact that the protagonist dies is hopelessly vague. The character of the protagonist and the nature of his struggle with circumstance or his fellows or with himself is much more to the point in developing a workable definition of tragedy.

A few generalizations, however, are so obvious that they can be made, here and now. First, the protagonist must struggle, for, if he is unable to struggle or is too passive to struggle, we can feel no more than pity for him. The death of a child, for example, may be pathetic, but it cannot be tragic. Second, we must feel some sympathy for the protagonist in his struggle: if his death merely gives us satisfaction or, worse still for the purposes of drama, leaves us indifferent, there can be no tragedy. Third, there must be in the protagonist some limitation or failure—else we shall probably feel no more than the pure pathos of his death, or that his death is unfair and and undeserved.

In the second play which follows, Lillo's *George Barnwell*, we shall have an opportunity to explore much more thoroughly what the character of the tragic protagonist must be and must not be. But even here we shall probably not find a complete answer to the nature of tragedy in the light of which we shall be able to see fully why *Everyman* is, though a serious play, not a tragedy. The full answer probably will have to wait upon our examination of other plays.

QUESTIONS

1. Beauty, in refusing to go with Everyman into the grave, uses the same oath ("By Saint John") that Fellowship has used earlier in the play in making the same refusal. What is gained by this parallelism? Does it help make the abstract character, Beauty, seem credibly human? Help enforce the essential loneliness of Everyman?

2. Review all the speeches of refusal to accompany Everyman. Note how many of the characters use homely turns of phrase ("I take my cap in my lap and am gone," "Thy game liketh me not at all") and understatement. What is gained by these devices?

3. As Everyman and Good Deeds prepare to descend into the grave, Good Deeds says, "Short our end, and minish our pain." Properly speaking Good Deeds does not suffer pain. Defend, on dramatic grounds, the author's use of *our* here.

4. We have pointed out that, although the play has no formal division into scenes, the play actually falls into four divisions. How has the author suggested these divisions by his arrangement of speeches or his management of the action?

5. Goods comes close to being the real villain of the piece. He mocks Everyman overtly in his last speech. Yet does not Goods really show a scrupulous neutrality? This may be very shrewd on the part of the author. He even makes Goods point out that he would have been transmuted into Everyman's true friend Good Deeds (with whom he is ironically linked by name) if only Everyman had "to the poor . . . give part of me." What is the effect of this paradox in emphasizing Everyman's own responsibility as a free agent? That is, does it lessen any impression we might have that Everyman is a victim of circumstances?

6. Primarily the author uses God, of course, to set up the moral issues of the play. Does the author attempt more than that in his initial presentation of God? Does he try to "characterize" Him at all? To make the first scene dramatic as well as homiletic?

7. Can you find any of the lines by which the author endeavors to suggest changes of place to the audience? How much care does he take in this matter?

8. What lines in the first scene point ahead to Everyman's interview with Goods?

9. Has the author succeeded at all in universalizing Fellowship? That is, in giving him qualities which we of a later generation find entirely recognizable? Are there any familiar idioms here (as well as elsewhere in the play)?

10. Is there anything ironic in the fact that Fellowship exclaims "in faith" in l. 232 and again "in good faith" in l. 280?

11. What do we learn about Fellowship from the fact that he says finally that he would not go with Everyman even if he were given a new gown (l. 292)?

3. Plautus, *The Twin Menaechmi*

W E TURN next to one of the best-known Roman comedies, Plautus's *Menaechmi*, the date of which is in
the neighborhood of 200 B.C. Here the student will
recognize the basic plot of Shakespeare's *Comedy of Errors*. In Plautus's
play we find in practically pure form the simple comic type known as farce.
As the student reads, he may find it useful to observe the ways in which its
effects differ from those of *Lady Windermere's Fan*.

THE TWIN MENAECHMI [1]

DRAMATIS PERSONÆ

BRUSH (PENICULUS), *a parasite*
MENAECHMUS I, *a young man of Epi-
damnus*
EROTIUM, *a courtesan*
CYLINDRUS, *cook of* EROTIUM
MENAECHMUS II (SOSICLES), *a young
man of Syracuse*
MESSENIO, *slave of* MENAECHMUS II
MAID *of* EROTIUM

WIFE *of* MENAECHMUS I
FATHER, *an old man, father-in-law of*
MENAECHMUS I
A DOCTOR
SLAVES
   [SCENE: A Street in Epidamnus in
front of the houses of Menaechmus I
and Erotium.]

PROLOGUE

Nor first and above all, spectators, I'm
   bringing a few
Of the best of good wishes to me—and
   then also to you;
I'm bringing you Plautus—by mouth,
   of course, not in person,
And therefore I pray you receive him
   with kindliest ears.
To the argument gird up your minds, as
   I babble my verse,   5
And I shall explain it—in briefest of
   terms, have no fears.
  And this is the thing that poets do in
   their plays:
The action has all taken place in Athens,
   they say,

That the setting will seem to be Greek
   to you all the more.
But from me you'll hear the truth—
   where it actually happened.   10
The plot of the play, to be sure, is Greek,
   but not
Of the Attic variety; Sicilian, rather.
I've given you now of the argument
   merely the preface;
And next the plot I'll generously pour out
Not merely by peck or bushel, but by
   the whole barn,   15
So kindly a nature I have for telling the
   plot.
  Now, an old merchant was living in
   Syracuse city,
And he by some chance had a couple of
   twin sons—yes, two of 'em—

---

[1] Reprinted by permission of Random House, Inc. The translation is by Edward C.
Weist and Richard W. Hyde: Acts II and V, by Weist; Acts I, III, and IV, by Hyde.

And they looked so alike that the nurse
couldn't tell (more's the pity)
Which one she gave suck to; no more
could their mother, for whom   20
The nurse was called in, no, not even
their mother who'd borne 'em.
Much later, the boys being now about
seven years old,
Their father filled up a big ship with a
lot of his goods
And, putting one twin in safekeeping
with them in the hold,
Betook himself off to Tarentum to
market, to turn 'em   25
To cash; and the other twin stayed at
home with his mother.
When they got there, Tarentum was
holding some games, as it hap-
pened,
And people were flocking to town, as
they do for the games.
The little boy strayed from his father
among all the crowds;
The lost was soon found by a rich Epi-
damnian merchant   30
Who seized him and took him off home.
But the father
Was sadly dejected at heart at the loss
of the boy,
And only a little while later he died of
despair.
Syracuse at last heard the bad news that
the father was dead
And that someone had stolen the twin
who had wandered away,   35
So the grandfather changed the remain-
ing twin's name then and there,
Since the other had been so beloved—
the one stolen away.
The other one's name he bestowed on
the twin safe at home,
And called him Menaechmus, the same
as the one I have said.
The grandfather's name was Menaechmus too, it so happened,   40
And with ease I remember the name, as
they called it aloud.
And lest you get muddled, both twins
now have the same name.
But now on the poet's rude feet I
must seek Epidamnus.

To speed on my tale. Should anyone
wish to have business
Transacted there, let him be bold and
speak forth and give me   45
The money with which I may carry out
all his commands.
But unless the money's forthcoming,
he's wasting his time,
And he's wasting his time even more,
should the money be given.
And while standing still I've returned to
my point of departure.
The old merchant I told you about,
who kidnapped the boy,   50
Had no children whatever, unless you
should count all his money.[2]
He adopted the stolen young twin as his
son, and to him
Gave a wife and a dowry, and made him
his heir when he died.
For, wandering into the country not far
from the town, the
Epidamnian stepped in a freshet, where
torrents of rain   55
Had been falling; the current caught
quickly the kidnapper's feet
And carried him off to the place where
he'll get his deserts.
So from him the young man inherits a
plentiful fortune,
And this is the house where the rich
kidnapped twin is now dwelling.
The other twin, living in Syracuse,
comes with his slave   60
To find his own twin brother here, for
whom he's been searching.
While the play's being acted, the town's
Epidamnus, you see;
When another play comes, 'twill turn
into some other town.
And then the families in the houses will
change;
The inhabitant is now a pander, and
now a youth,   65
Or a pauper, a beggar, a parasite, or a
prophet.

[2] There was apparently a jest here in the
Greek original (which lies behind Plautus'
Latin adaptation). The Greek word τόκος
means both "children" and "interest on
money."

ACT ONE. SCENE I

[*Enter Brush, who addresses audience.*]

Brush: My nickname's Brush, be- 5
cause when I eat I sweep the table clean.
People who keep prisoners in chains and
put shackles on runaway slaves do a
very foolish thing, if you ask me. You
see, if you add insult to injury, a poor 10
fellow will want all the more to escape
and go wrong. He'll get out of his chains
somehow, you can be sure—file away a
link, or knock out a nail with a stone.
That way's no good. If you really want 15
to keep somebody so he won't get away,
you'd better tie him with food and drink:
hitch his beak to a full dinnerpail. Give
him all he wants to eat and drink every
day, and he'll never try to run away, not 20
even if he's committed murder. The
bonds of food and drink are very elastic,
you know: the more you stretch them,
the tighter they hold you. [*Going towards the house of Menaechmus I.*] Now 25
take me—I'm on my way over to Menaechmus', where I've been doing a long
stretch; I'm giving myself up to let him
bind me. He doesn't only feed you, you
see: he builds you up and makes a new 30
man of you. There's no better doctor
alive. Just to show you what sort of
fellow he is—he has wonderful meals,
regular Thanksgiving dinners: he builds
up such skyscrapers of dishes you have 35
to stand on your couch if you want to
get anything off the top. But it's quite
a few days since I've been over there.
I've been kept at home with my dear
ones—I don't eat or buy anything but 40
what it's very dear. But now my army
of dear ones is deserting, and so I'm
going to see him. [*He approaches the
door.*] But the door's opening. There's
Menaechmus—he's coming out. [*With- 45
draws.*]

ACT ONE. SCENE II

[*Enter Menaechmus I from his house,
wearing a dress of his wife's under his own 50
cloak. He calls back to his wife inside.*]

Menaechmus I:
If you were not
Stubborn, bad,
Stupid, and a
Little mad,
What your husband hates, you'd see
And behave accordingly.
Act the way you have today
And back you go to dad to stay.
If I say I'm going out,
You're on hand to ask about
Where I'm going,
What to do,
What's my business,
What's for you.
I can't get out anywhere
But you want me to declare
All I've done and all I do.
Customs officer—that's you!
I've handled you with too much care;
Listen what I'm going to do:
Food I give you,
Maids, indeed,
Money, dresses—
All you need;
Now you'll keep your spying eyes
Off your husband, if you're wise.
And furthermore I'll see that you don't
have your watching for nothing: I'm
going to get even with you and take a
woman out to dinner somewhere.

Brush: [*Aside.*] The fellow pretends
he's cursing his wife, but he's really
cursing me. It's me he hurts if he eats
out, not his wife.

Menaechmus I: Gosh! At last I've
scolded my wife away from the door. [*To
the audience.*] Where are all you philan-
dering husbands? What are you waiting
for? Come on up and congratulate me
and reward me for the good fight I've
put up—I've just stolen this dress from
my wife in there and I'm taking it to
my mistress. This is a fine way to cheat
this clever guardian of mine. An excellent job, an honest job, an elegant job,
a workmanlike job! I risked my life and
robbed my wife, and the thing's going
to be a total loss. But I got the spoils
from the enemy and didn't lose a
man.

Brush: [*Accosting him.*] Hey, young fellow, is any of that stuff for me?

Menaechmus I: It's all over. I've fallen into a trap.

Brush: Oh no, sir, just into protective custody. Don't be alarmed.

Menaechmus I: Who are you?

Brush: Myself.

Menaechmus I: [*Turning.*] Why, you sight for sore eyes, you chance that comes once in a lifetime! Good morning.

Brush: Good morning.

Menaechmus I: What are you doing?

Brush: I'm shaking hands with my best friend.

Menaechmus I: You couldn't have come at a better time than this.

Brush: That's just like me: I'm quite an expert on opportune moments.

Menaechmus I: Want to see something gorgeous?

Brush: What cook cooked it? I'll know if he slipped up when I see what's left.

Menaechmus I: Say, did you ever see the painting on the temple wall where the eagle steals Ganymede, or where Venus gets away with Adonis?

Brush: Plenty of times. But what have those pictures got to do with me?

Menaechmus I: [*Revealing the dress.*] Take a look at me. Do I look like them at all?

Brush: What's that outfit you're wearing?

Menaechmus I: Say I'm a clever fellow.

Brush. When do we eat?

Menaechmus I. You just say what I tell you.

Brush. All right. "Clever Fellow."

Menaechmus I: Can't you add anything of your own?

Brush: Well—life of the party.

Menaechmus I: Go on, go on.

Brush: I certainly will not go on unless I know what I'm going to get out of it. You've had a quarrel with your wife and I'm staying on the safe side.

Menaechmus I: What do you say we find a place away from my wife where we can have a funeral—and then we burn up the day?

Brush: [*Enthusiastically.*] Wonderful! Let's get going. How soon do I light the pyre? The day's already dead up to the waist.

Menaechmus I: You'll wait if you interrupt me.

Brush: Knock my eye out, Menaechmus, if I say a word except when you tell me.

Menaechmus I: Come over here away from the door.

Brush: Sure.

Menaechmus I: Farther still.

Brush: All right.

Menaechmus I: Now come boldly away from the lion's den.

Brush: Say there, I've got an idea you'd make a good racing driver.

Menaechmus I: How come?

Brush: Well, you're always looking back to see that your wife isn't following you.

Menaechmus I: But what do you say—

Brush: What do I say? Why, anything you want, my friend.

Menaechmus I: I wonder if you could make a guess from the odor of a thing if you smelt it.

Brush: . . .[2] if you got the whole staff.

Menaechmus I: Well, take a sniff of this dress I've got. How does it smell? Don't hang back.

Brush: You ought to smell the top of a woman's dress; the smell down there is awful.

Menaechmus I: Then smell here, Brush. How dainty you are!

Brush: This is better.

Menaechmus I: How about it? What does it smell like? Tell me.

Brush: A moocher, a mistress, and a meal! . . .[1]

Menaechmus I: Now I'll take this to

[1] There is a short lacuna in the text here.

my lady Erotium here, and I'll order dinner for all three of us.

Brush: Swell!

Menaechmus I: After that we'll drink right through till daylight tomorrow.

Brush: Swell! You've said a mouthful. Do I knock now?

Menaechmus I: Go ahead. Or wait a minute.

Brush: Oh, you're holding up our drinking a mile.

Menaechmus I: Knock softly.

Brush: I suppose you're afraid the door is made of Samian ware.

Menaechmus I: Wait, for heaven's sake, wait! Look. She's coming out herself. Do you see how dim the sun is compared to the splendour of her beauty?

ACT ONE. SCENE III

[*Enter Erotium from her house.*]

Erotium: Good morning, Menaechmus, my sweet.

Brush: How about me?

Erotium: You don't count with me.

Brush: That's what usually happens to the reserves in an army.

Menaechmus I: I'd like you to do something for him and me over at your house—get ready a battle.

Erotium: It shall be done.

Menaechmus I: And we'll both drink in this battle, and which is the better battler will be found by the bottle. You're head of the army, and you'll decide which of us—you'll spend the night with. O my heart's delight, how I detest my wife when I set my eyes on you!

Erotium: [*Noticing the dress.*] Still, you can't keep from wearing her clothes. What's this?

Menaechmus I: Your dress and my wife's *un*dress, rosebud.

Erotium: You're an easy winner over all the others who possess me.

Brush: [*Aside.*] The woman flatters him as long as she sees what he's stolen. [*To Erotium.*] Now, if you really loved him, you'd have bitten his nose off with kisses.

Menaechmus I: Hold this, Brush. [*Handing him his cloak.*] I want to make the offering I have vowed.

Brush: Let's have it. But please, dance with that dress on like that.

Menaechmus I: Me dance? You're as crazy as they come.

Brush: Maybe you're the crazy one. But if you won't dance, take the thing off.

Menaechmus I: [*Removing dress.*] I took a big chance stealing this—bigger than Hercules did, I guess, when he stole Hippolyta's girdle. [*Handing the dress to Erotium.*] Here, my dear. You're the only one who really understands me.

Erotium: That's how true lovers should feel.

Brush: [*Aside.*] At least ones who are on their way to the poorhouse.

Menaechmus I: That cost me four minae last year when I bought it for my wife.

Brush: [*Aside.*] Four minae gone to the devil, when you add up your accounts.

Menaechmus I: Do you know what I want you to do?

Erotium: Tell me; I'll do anything you wish.

Menaechmus I: Then have a dinner for the three of us at your house. And get some fine food at the market—

The son of a glandule of pork,
The son of a fattened ham,
Or the jowl of a hog—
Some food of that sort
Which set on the table
Will tickle my palate
And give me the gorge of a kite.
And hurry up.

Erotium: Very well.

Menaechmus I: We'll go on downtown, but we'll be back soon. While the dinner's being cooked, we'll pass the time drinking.

Erotium: Come whenever you wish; everything will be ready.

Menaechmus I: Hurry now. [*To Brush.*] You follow me.

Brush: I'll watch you and follow you, all right. I wouldn't lose you for all the wealth of heaven. [*Menaechmus and Brush depart.*]

Erotium: [*To those inside.*] You in there, call out my cook Cylindrus at once.

ACT ONE. SCENE IV

[*Enter Cylindrus.*]

Erotium: Take a basket and some money. Here are three nummi.

Cylindrus: Yes, ma'am.

Erotium: Go and get some provisions. See that there's enough for three, not too little and not too much.

Cylindrus: What kind of people will they be?

Erotium: Menaechmus and his parasite and I.

Cylindrus: That makes ten, then, because a parasite does as well as eight ordinary men.

Erotium: I've told you the guests; take care of the rest.

Cylindrus: All right. Everything's done. Tell them dinner is served.

Erotium: Hurry back [*She goes into her house.*]

Cylindrus: I'm practically back now. [*Cylindrus departs.*]

ACT TWO. SCENE I

[*Enter Menaechmus II, and his slave Messenio carrying a bag, followed by sailors with luggage.*]

Menaechmus II: I think, Messenio, that there is no greater joy for sea travellers than sighting land.

Messenio: Yes, but it's still better if it's your own land. Why, I ask you, have we come here—why Epidamnus? We might as well be the ocean: we never miss a single island.

Menaechmus II: [*Sadly.*] We are searching for my twin brother.

Messenio: Is this search ever going to end? It's six years now that we've spent on it. We've seen 'em all—Istrians, Iberians, the people of Marseilles. Illyrians, the whole Adriatic, all of Magna Graecia, the whole Italian seacoast. If you'd been hunting for a needle you'd have found it long ago, if there had been one. We're looking for a dead man among the living; if he were alive you'd have found him long ago.

Menaechmus II: If I can find somebody who can prove that, who can say he knows for certain that my brother is dead, then I shall seek no further. But otherwise I shall go on as long as I live; I know how dear he is to my heart.

Messenio: You might as well try to find a knot in a bulrush. Let's clear out of here and go home. Or are we going to write a book—"Our Trip around the World"?

Menaechmus II: You do what you're told, take what's given you, and keep out of trouble. Don't annoy me. I'm running this, not you.

Messenio: [*Aside.*] Hm-m, that puts me in my place all right. Neat, complete; it can't be beat. But just the same, here I go again. [*Aloud.*] Look at our purse, Menaechmus; our money is feeling the heat: it's getting as thin as a summer shirt. If you don't go home, you'll be hunting for that blessed brother of yours without a cent to bless *yourself* with. That's what Epidamnus is like, full of rakes and tremendous drinkers; a lot of swindlers and spongers live here, and everybody knows their women are the most seductive in the whole world. That's why the place is called Epidamnus; scarcely anybody can come here without getting damned.

Menaechmus II: I'll take care of that: just hand the purse over to me.

Messenio: What for?

Menaechmus II: What you say makes me worried—about you.

Messenio: Makes you worried?

Menaechmus II: That you may get yourself damned in Epidamnus. You are very fond of the ladies, Messenio, and I have a bad temper and lose it very easily. So if I have the money, you get double protection: your foot doesn't slip, and my temper doesn't either.

Messenio: [Handing it over.] Take it, keep it; it's all right with me.

ACT TWO. SCENE II

[Enter Cylindrus the cook, with his market-basket.]

Cylindrus: [To himself.] I've done a good job of marketing—just what I like myself. I'll give the company a fine dinner.—Glory, there's Menaechmus! Now I'm in for it! Here are the guests at the door before I'm back from the market. I'll go up and speak to him. *[To Menaechmus II.]* Good day, Menaechmus.

Menaechmus II: Why, thank you. *[To Messenio.]* He seems to know my name. Who is he?

Messenio: I don't know.

Cylindrus: Where are the other guests?

Menaechmus II: What guests?

Cylindrus: [Grinning.] Your parasite.

Menaechmuse II: [To Messenio.] My parasite? The man's crazy.

Messenio: Didn't I tell you there were a lot of swindlers here?

Menaechmus II: [To Cylindrus.] What do you mean "my parasite," young man?

Cylindrus: Why, "Brush."

Messenio: [Peering into the bag.] Nonsense, I have your brush safe right here in the bag.

Cylindrus: You are a little early for dinner, Menaechmus; I'm just back from the market.

Menaechmus II: Tell me, young man: how much do pigs cost here? Grade A pigs, for sacrifice.

Cylindrus: A drachma.

Menaechmus II: Well, here's a drachma; go get yourself cured at my expense. Because you certainly must be crazy, what's-your-name, to be bothering a perfect stranger like me.

Cylindrus: "What's-your-name"! Don't you remember me? I'm Cylindrus.

Menaechmus II: The devil take you, whether your name is Cylinder or Colander. I don't know you, and I don't want to.

Cylindrus: [Persisting.] Your name is Menaechmus.

Menaechmus II: You're in your right mind when you call me by name, anyway. But where did you ever see me before?

Cylindrus: Where did I ever see you before—when my mistress, Erotium, is your mistress?

Menaechmus II: Confound it, she's not my mistress, and I don't know you, either.

Cylindrus: All the drinks I've poured for you in the house here, and you don't know me?

Messenio: I wish I had something to break his head with.

Menaechmus II: You pour my drinks for me, do you? When I've never set foot in Epidamnus before today and never even seen the place?

Cylindrus: You deny it?

Menaechmus II: Of course I deny it.

Cylindrus: Don't you live in that house over there?

Menaechmus II: The devil take the people that do!

Cylindrus: [Aside.] If he curses himself like this, *he's* crazy. *[Aloud.]* Menaechmus!

Menaechmus II: Well?

Cylindrus: If you ask me, you ought to take that drachma you—promised me a minute ago and order *yourself* a pig, because your head isn't on straight either, you know, if you curse your own self.

Menaechmus II: Confound your cheek, you chatterbox! *[Turns away.]*

Cylindrus: [Aside.] He likes to joke with me like this. Always full of laughs —when his wife's not there! *[To Menaechmus II.]* Well, sir—*[No response.]*

Well, sir—[*Menaechmus II turns.*] Is this enough for the three of you—you, the parasite, and the lady—or shall I get some more?

Menaechmus II: What "ladies"? What "parasites"?

Messenio: [*To Cylindrus.*] Here, what's the matter with you? Why are you pestering the gentleman?

Cylindrus: Who are you, and what's it to you? I'm talking to *him;* he's a friend of mine.

Messenio: You're cracked, that's certain.

Cylindrus: [*To Menaechmus II.*] I'll get these things into the pot right away, so don't wander off too far from the house. Anything else I can do for you?

Menaechmus II: Yes. Go to the devil.

Cylindrus: Oh, better that you should —go inside and make yourself comfortable on your couch, while Vulcan is getting violent with the food. I'll go in and tell Erotium that you're here. I know she'd rather take you in than make you wait outside. [*He goes into the house of Erotium.*]

Menaechmus II: Is he gone? Good, Whew! I see there was a lot in what you said.

Messenio: Yes, but look out. I think one of those fancy women lives here, just as that crackpot said.

Menaechmus II: All the same, I wonder how he knew my name.

Messenio: Nothing strange in that; it's just the way these women have. They send their maids and slave-boys to the harbour; and if a foreign ship comes in, they find out the name of the owner and where he's from, and then, bingo! they fasten onto him and stick to him like glue. If he falls for it, they send him home a ruined man. [*Pointing to house of Erotium.*] Now in that harbour rides a pirate craft, of which we must beware.

Menaechmus II: That's good advice.

Messenio: Yes, but it's no good unless you take it. [*The door starts to open.*]

Menaechmus II: Quiet a minute; I hear the door opening. Let's see who comes out.

Messenio: [*Putting down the bag.*] I'll set this down then. You sailors, keep an eye on the luggage.

ACT TWO. SCENE III

[*Enter Erotium from her house.*]

Erotium: [*To slaves within.*]
Go in, and do not close the door,
   I want it left just so.
See what there is to do inside
   And do it all—now go.
The couches must be spread, and perfumes burned:
Neatness entices lovers, I have learned.
Splendour to lovers' loss, to our gain is turned.   [*Coming forward.*]
But where is the man they said was before my door?
Ah, there he is; he's been of use before;
Yet is, as he deserves, my governor.
I'll go and speak to him myself.—My dear,
I am amazed to see you standing here;
My home is always yours when you appear.
Now all you ordered is prepared,
   The doors are opened wide,
Your dinner's cooked, and when you like
   Come take your place inside.

Menaechmus II: [*To Messenio.*] Who's this woman talking to?

Erotium: To you!

Menaechmus II: But why? We've never—

Erotium: Because it is the will of Venus that I exalt you above all others; and so I should, because you're the one who keeps me blooming with your loving favours.

Menaechmus II: [*To Messenio.*] This woman is either insane or drunk, Messenio. Such language, to a perfect stranger!

Messenio: [*To Menaechmus II.*] Didn't I tell you that was the way here? Why, these are just falling leaves; stay here a couple of days, and there'll be *trees* falling on you. These women look like pick-ups, but they're not; they're just stick-ups.—Let me talk to her. [*To Erotium.*] Listen, lady—

Erotium: What?

Messenio: Where did you get so familiar with the gentleman?

Erotium: In the same place where he got so familiar with me—here, in Epidamnus.

Messenio: In Epidamnus? He never set so much as his foot in the place until today.

Erotium: Oh, what a ravishing sense of humour! [*To Menaechmus II.*] Menaechmus dear, won't you come in? We can straighten this out so much better inside.

Menaechmus II: [*To Messenio.*] And now she calls me by name too. What's going on here?

Messenio: [*To Menaechmus II.*] She's got a whiff of that purse of yours.

Menaechmus II: [*To Messenio.*] You're probably right. Here, take it. [*Hands him the purse.*] Now I'll see which she loves, me or the money.

Erotium: Let's go in to dinner.

Menaechmus II: You are very kind, but [*backing away*] no, thank you.

Erotium: But you just told me to fix a dinner for you.

Menaechmus II: I told you to?

Erotium: Why, yes, for you and your parasite.

Menaechmus II: What parasite, confound it? [*To Messenio.*] She's crazy.

Erotium: Brush.

Menaechmus II: What is this brush you all keep talking about? You mean my shoe-brush?

Erotium: No, of course I mean the Brush who came with you when you brought me the dress you had stolen from your wife.

Menaechmus II: What? I gave you a dress that I had stolen from my wife? You're out of your mind! [*To Messenio.*] Why, this woman dreams standing up, like a horse.

Erotium: Why do you make fun of me, and deny what you did?

Menaechmus II: Well, what *did* I do?

Erotium: You gave me a dress of your wife's today.

Menaechmus II: I still deny it. I haven't got a wife and I never had one, and I never set foot in this house before. I had dinner on the boat, came ashore, walked by here, and ran into you.

Erotium: [*Frightened.*] Oh, my goodness, what boat?

Menaechmus II:

A wooden boat—oft sprung, oft plugged, oft struck with maul,

And peg lies close by peg, as in a furrier's frame.

Erotium: Oh, please stop joking and come in.

Menaechmus II: But madam, you are looking for somebody else, not me.

Erotium: Do you think I don't know Menaechmus, son of Moschus, born at Syracuse in Sicily where Agathocles was king, and then Phintia, and then Liparo, who left it to Hiero, who is king now?

Menaechmus II: That's all correct.

Messenio: [*To Menaechmus II.*] Good lord, the woman can't be from there herself, can she? She certainly has you down pat.

Menaechmus II: [*Weakening.*] You know, I don't see how I can refuse. [*He starts towards the door.*]

Messenio: Don't! If you go in there, you're done for!

Menaechmus II: Be quiet. Things are going nicely. Whatever she says, I'll agree to it, and see if I can pick up some entertainment! [*To Erotium.*] I've had a reason for contradicting you all this time: I was afraid this man would tell my wife about the dress and the dinner. But now let's go in, anytime you want.

Erotium: Are you going to wait for the parasite any longer?

Menaechmus II: No! I don't give a rap for him, and if he comes I don't want him let in.

Erotium: That's quite all right with

me. But there's something I wish you'd
do for me, will you?

Menaechmus II: Anything; command
me.

Erotium: That dress you just gave 5
me—take it to the place where they do
that lovely gold embroidery and get
them to fix it up and put on some new
trimming.

Menaechmus II: Splendid idea! And 10
that'll keep my wife from recognising it,
if she sees it on the street.

Erotium: You can take it with you
when you go.

Menaechmus II: I certainly will!

Erotium: Let's go in.

Menaechmus II: I'll be right with you.
I just want to speak to this man a minute. [*Erotium goes into her house.*] Hi
there, Messenio, come here. 20

Messenio: What's going on here?
Come to your senses!

Menaechmus II: What for!

Messenio: Because—

Menaechmus II: Oh, I know, don't 25
say it.

Messenio: So much the worse.

Menaechmus II: The booty is as good
as in my hands right now; the siege has
just begun! [*Pointing to the sailors.*] 30
Come on ,now, hustle these men off to
an inn somewhere, and then come back
for me here before sunset.

Messenio: Master, you don't know
what these women are! 35

Menaechmus II: None of that! If I do
anything foolish, it's my loss, not yours.
This woman is a silly fool. The way
things look so far, there's booty to be
had! [*He goes into the house of Ero-* 40
tium.]

Messenio: God help me! [*Calling after
Menaechmus II.*] Sir! [*To himself.*] God
help him, too! The pirate ship has got
the pinnace steered straight on the 45
rocks! But I'm a fool to expect to control my master. He bought me to obey
him, not to give him orders. [*To the
sailors.*] Come along you, so I can come
back and pick him up in time. Orders is 50
orders! [*They depart.*]

ACT THREE. SCENE I

[*Enter Brush from the forum.*]

Brush: [*To himself.*] Here I am over
thirty years old, but I never got into a
worse mess than I did today. I pushed
into the middle of the assembly, like a
darn fool, and while I was watching
things, Menaechmus sneaked away from
me. He probably went off to his mistress
and didn't want to take me.—Damn the
man who first got the idea of holding
assemblies and taking up the time of
busy men! Why couldn't they pick people who aren't tied up for this sort of
thing, and then if they didn't show up
when the roll was called, they could pay
a fine right off? There are plenty of
men who only eat once a day and never
get asked out to dinner or ask anyone
else in. They're the ones who ought to
have the job of sitting in assemblies and
law courts. If things were run that way,
I wouldn't have lost my dinner today.
As sure as I'm alive, he would have
given it to me.—I'll go on, anyway.
Maybe there'll be something left, and
just the idea makes my mouth water.
[*Enter Menaechmus II from Erotium's
house, carrying the dress, very drunk.*]
But what's this? There's Menaechmus
coming out with a wreath on. The dinner's over, and I've come just in time to
take him home. I'll see what he's up to,
and then go and speak to him. [*He withdraws.*]

ACT THREE. SCENE II

Menaechmus II. [*To Erotium within.*]
Oh, can't you keep quiet? I'll have it
nicely fixed for you, all right, and I'll
bring it back on time. I bet you won't
recognise it, it'll be so different.

Brush: [*Aside.*] He's taking the dress
to the embroiderer's. He's finished his
dinner, drunk his wine, and shut his
parasite outside. I'll get even for this
trick, all right, or my name's not Brush!
Just watch what's coming to him!

Menaechmus II: [*To himself.*] Gods above, did you ever give more luck in a single day to a man who didn't expect it? I wined and dined with the woman, and got away with this thing [*indicating the dress*], and she won't ever see it again.

Brush: I can't hear what he's saying from over here. Is he full of food and talking about me and my dinner?

Menaechmus II: She said I stole this from my wife and gave it to her. The moment I saw she was wrong, I began to agree with her, as if we'd had some sort of deal. Whatever the woman said, I said too. Why waste words? I never had a better time at less expense.

Brush: I'm going up to the fellow. I'm itching to smack him one.

Menaechmus II: Who's this coming towards me?

Brush: What are you talking about, you feather-weight, you scum, you crook, you disgrace to humanity, you sneak, you bum? What did I ever do to you that you should wipe me out? So you sneaked away from me downtown a while ago, did you? And you had the funeral of the dinner when I wasn't there? How did you have the nerve, when it was mine as much as it was yours?

Menaechmus II: See here, young fellow, what's the idea of going around and insulting a perfect stranger like me? Are you an idiot? Or do you want to get beaten up for your words?

Brush: Huh! After the beating you've already given me!

Menaechmus II: Tell me, young fellow, what's your name?

Brush: Are you making fun of me too, as if you didn't know my name?

Menaechmus II: Well, as far as I know, I never saw you or knew of you before today. But let me tell you, whoever you are, if you want to do the right thing, don't make a nuisance of yourself.

Brush: Menaechmus, wake up!

Menaechmus II: Damn it, I am awake as far as I know.

Brush: You don't know me?

Menaechmus II: I wouldn't deny it if I did.

Brush: You don't know your own parasite?

Menaechmus II: I think you're not all there, young fellow.

Brush: Answer me this: did you steal that dress from your wife today and give it to Erotium?

Menaechmus II: Damn it, I haven't got any wife, and I didn't give any dress to Erotium or steal one.

Brush: Are *you* all there? [*Aside.*] This thing's done for! [*To Menaechmus II.*] Didn't I see you come out of there with a dress on?

Menaechmus II: Go to the devil! Do you think everybody is a rotter just because you are? Do you mean to say that I had a dress on?

Brush: I do, all right.

Menaechmus II: Why don't you go where you belong, or else get yourself purified, you imbecile?

Brush: [*Furious.*] By God, no one will ever stop me from telling your wife the whole business, just the way it happened. All your insults will come back on you. I'll see to it that you don't get away with eating that dinner. [*He goes into house of Menaechmus I.*]

Menaechmus II: What's the matter? Why is it that everyone I meet makes fun of me? But I hear the door opening.

ACT THREE. SCENE III

[*Enter Maid from house of Erotium with a bracelet in her hand.*]

Maid: Menaechmus, Erotium says she would like to have you take this bracelet along to the jeweler's. She wants you to have an ounce of gold added to it and have it done over.

Menaechmus II: Tell her I'll tend to it and anything else she wants tended to, anything at all. [*He takes the bracelet.*]

Maid: Do you know what bracelet this is?

Menaechmus II: Only that it's a gold one.

Maid: It's the one you said once you stole from your wife's jewel-box.

Menaechmus II: I never did.

Maid: Come on, don't you remember? Give the bracelet back if you don't remember.

Menaechmus II: Wait a minute. Why, of course I remember. It must be the one I gave her. That's it. Where are the armlets I gave her with it?

Maid: You never gave her any.

Menaechmus II: Right you are; this was all I gave her.

Maid: I'll say you'll tend to it, then?

Menaechmus II: Yes, it'll be tended to. I'll see that the dress and the bracelet are brought back together.

Maid: [*Coaxingly.*] Please, Menaechmus dear, give me some earrings. Have them made to weigh two nummi. Then I'll be glad to see you when you come to see us.

Menaechmus II: Surely. Give me the gold and I'll pay for the work.

Maid: Oh, please, *you* give the gold, and I'll pay you back later.

Menaechmus II: No, you give it. Later I'll pay you back double.

Maid: I haven't got any.

Menaechmus II: Well, when you get some, give it to me then.

Maid: Anything else, sir?

Menaechmus II: Tell her I'll tend to the things, [*to himself, as the Maid goes inside*] and sell 'em for all they'll bring. Has she gone in? Yes; the door's shut. The gods are certainly supporting and supplying and sustaining me. But what am I waiting for when I've got a good chance to get away from this woman's place? Hurry up, Menaechmus. Forward, march! I'll take off this wreath and throw it away towards the left; then if they follow me, they'll think I've gone that way. I'll go and find my slave, if I can, and tell him myself about the luck the gods are giving me. [*He departs in the direction of the harbour.*]

ACT FOUR. SCENE I

[*Enter Wife and Brush from house of Menaechmus I.*]

Wife: How can I put up with married life any longer? My husband sneaks off with anything there is in the house and carries it off to his mistress.

Brush: Oh, keep quiet. I'll show you how to catch him with the goods. He had on a wreath, he was reeling drunk, and he was taking the dress he stole from you today to the embroiderer's. But look, there's the wreath. Now will you believe me? See, this is the way he went, if you want to track him down. [*Looking down the street.*] Well, for heaven's sake, there he is now, coming back. But he hasn't got the dress.

Wife: What'll I do to him now?

Brush: The same as usual—treat him rough. That's my advice. Let's get over here and hide from him. [*They step aside.*]

ACT FOUR. SCENE II

[*Enter Menaechmus I from the forum.*]

Menaechmus I: It's a very silly fashion and an awful nuisance, too,
That all of us obey, especially the well-to-do.
We want a lot of hangers-on, who may be good or bad:
Reputation doesn't matter when there's money to be had.
You may be poor and honest—as a fool you're sent away.
But if you're rich and wicked, you're a worthy protégé.
The lawless man, who when he's trusted with a thing will swear
He never saw it—that's the man for whom we patrons care:
The contentious man, the trickster, who by means of perjury
Or bribes supports a life of lawsuits, greed, and luxury.
But the patron has no holiday when law-days are decreed;

He must defend the guilty man and see
    that he is freed.
In just this way was I detained today by
    one poor sinner,
And now I've missed my mistress, to say 5
    nothing of my dinner.
I spoke before the aediles to allay their
    just suspicions,
And proposed a set of intricate and tor-
    tuous conditions   10
Which, if we could have proved 'em,
    would have surely won the case.
But then this brainless boob brought in
    a bondsman to the place!
I'm sure I never saw a man more clearly 15
    caught than he:
Three witnesses were there who swore
    to all his deviltry.
May heaven destroy the man who's
    made a ruin so complete   20
Of all my day—and me, who in the law-
    courts set my feet!
As soon as it was possible, I came di-
    rectly here.
I've ordered dinner, and she's waiting 25
    for me; yet I fear
She's mad at me now.
    But the dress ought to move her
That I stole from my wife
    And took to my lover.   30
Brush: [*Aside to Wife.*] What have
you got to say now?
Wife: I'm blessed with a bad mar-
riage and a bad husband.
Brush: Do you hear what he's saying 35
all right?
    Wife: I should say so.
Menaechmus I: Now the best thing
for me to do is to go in here where I can
have a good time. [*He starts towards* 40
Erotium's door, but Brush stops him.]
Brush: Just a minute. You'll have a
bad time first.
Wife: You'll pay interest on what you
stole, I promise you.   45
Brush: Now he's getting it.
Wife: So you thought you could get
away with all that crooked business, did
you?
Menaechmus I: What's the matter, 50
dear?

Wife: That's a fine thing to ask *me!*
Menaechmus I: Do you want me to
ask *him*, then? [*He attempts to fondle
Wife.*]
Wife: Cut out the pawing!
Brush: Keep after him, ma'am!
Menaechmus I: Why are you angry
at me?
Wife: You ought to know.
Brush: He does, the scum, but he's
making out he doesn't.
Menaechmus I: What's the matter?
Wife: A dress.
Menaechmus I: A dress?
Wife: A dress that someone—
Brush: What are you shaking about?
Menaechmus I: I'm not shaking about
anything.
Brush: Only this: the dress does im-
press!—You would sneak away from me
and eat dinner! [*To Wife.*] Keep after
the fellow!
Menaechmus I: Won't you shut up?
Brush: No, by George, I will not shut
up. [*To Wife.*] He's shaking his head at
me to shut up.
Menaechmus I: I am not, or winking
either.
Wife: Oh dear, I am an unhappy
woman!
Menaechmus I: Why unhappy? Tell
me about it.
Brush: What a nerve! Why, he won't
admit a thing is so when you can see
it is.
Menaechmus I: By Jupiter and all the
gods (Is that enough for you, dear?) I
swear I didn't shake my head at
him.
Brush: She'll believe you about that.
Now get back to business.
Menaechmus I: What business?
Brush: Oh, maybe the embroiderer's.
And give back the dress.
Menaechmus I: What dress are you
talking about?
Brush: Oh, I give up! He can't even
remember his own affairs.
Menaechmus I: [*To Wife.*] Has one
of the slaves been cutting up? Are the
maids or the menservants answering

back? Tell me. They won't get away with it.

Wife: Nonsense!

Menaechmus I: She's really mad. I don't like this much—

Wife: Nonsense!

Menaechmus I: You must be angry with one of the servants.

Wife: Nonsense!

Menaechmus I: Well, are you angry with me, then?

Wife: Now that's not nonsense.

Menaechmus I: What the devil! I haven't done anything.

Wife: More nonsense again!

Menaechmus I: Tell me, my dear, what's upsetting you?

Brush: Apple-sauce!

Menaechmus I: Can't you quit bothering me? Do you think I'm talking to you? [*He goes to Wife.*]

Wife: Take away your hand.

Brush: Now you're getting it. Go and eat dinner without me, will you? Then come out drunk, with a wreath on your head, and make fun of me in front of the house, will you?

Menaechmus I: What the devil! I haven't had dinner or set foot in that house today.

Brush: Do you mean to say that?

Menaechmus I: I certainly do.

Brush: This fellow's the worst yet. Didn't I just see you standing here in front of the house with a wreath on? You said I wasn't all there and you didn't know me and you were a foreigner.

Menaechmus I: See here, since I left you, I haven't been home until just now.

Brush: Oh, I know you. You didn't think I had any way of getting even with you. All right for you—I've told everything to your wife.

Menaechmus I: What did you tell her?

Brush: I don't know; ask her yourself.

Menaechmus I: [*To Wife.*] What's the matter, dear? What stories has he been telling you? What is it? Why don't you say something? Why don't you tell me what's the matter?

Wife: As if you didn't know! A dress has been stolen from me out of the house.

Menaechmus I: A dress has been stolen from you?

Wife: Are you asking me?

Menaechmus I: Well, I certainly wouldn't be asking you if I knew.

Brush: Look at the man! What a snake in the grass! You can't hide anything; she knows the whole story. I spilled everything, all right.

Menaechmus I: [*To Wife.*] What's the matter?

Wife: Well, since you're not ashamed and won't own up yourself, listen and learn. I'll explain what I'm angry about and what he told me. A dress has been stolen from me out of the house.

Menaechmus I: A dress has been stolen from me?

Brush: [*To Wife.*] See how the fellow's trying to catch you. [*To Menaechmus I.*] It was stolen from her, not from you. Now if it had really been stolen from you—it wouldn't be all right.

Menaechmus I: I'm not dealing with you. [*To Wife.*] What have you got to say, madam?

Wife: A dress, I tell you, is gone from the house.

Menaechmus I: Who stole it?

Wife: I expect the person who stole it knows that.

Menaechmus I: Who is this person?

Wife: Somebody named Menaechmus.

Menaechmus I: It's a dirty trick. But who is this Menaechmus?

Wife: You, I tell you.

Menaechmus I: Me?

Wife: Yes, you.

Menaechmus I: Who says so?

Wife: I do.

Brush: So do I. And you took the thing over to your friend Erotium.

Menaechmus I: What? I gave it to her?

Wife: Yes, you, you, I say.

Brush: Do you want us to get an owl to keep on saying, "You, you!" to you? We're getting tired, you see.

Menaechmus I: By Jupiter and all the

gods (Is that enough for you, my dear?)
I swear I didn't give—

Brush: All right, and we swear we're
not lying.

Menaechmus I: But I didn't give it to
her; I only lent it.

Wife: Maybe you did, but I certainly
never lend your dress suit or your overcoat to anybody. It's the wife's business
to lend her clothes, and the husband's
to lend his. Now go and bring that dress
back home.

Menaechmus I: I'll get it back.

Wife: Well, you'd better. You won't
get into this house again unless you
bring my dress with you. I'm going
home.

Brush: What do I get for going to so
much trouble for you?

Wife: You'll be repaid when something is stolen from your house. [*She
goes inside.*]

Brush: That'll never happen; I
haven't got anything at home to lose.
Damn the husband and the wife, too!
I'll go along downtown. I can see I'm
done with this family. [*He departs.*]

Menaechmus I: [*To himself.*] My wife
thinks she's punished me by shutting
me out—as if I didn't have a better
place to go where they'd let me in. If
you don't like me, that's your hard luck;
Erotium here likes me. She won't shut
me out from her; she'll shut me in *with*
her. Now I'll go and ask her to give back
that dress I gave her this morning. I'll
buy her a better one. [*Knocking at
Erotium's door.*] Hey, there, where's the
doorman? Open the door, somebody,
and call Erotium outside.

ACT FOUR. SCENE III

[*Enter Erotium from her house.*]

Erotium: Who is asking for me?

Menaechmus I: More of an enemy to
himself than to your tender years.

Erotium: Menaechmus, my love, why
are you standing out there? Come on in.

Menaechmus I: In just a minute. Do
you know what I've come to see you
for?

Erotium: Why, of course: to enjoy
yourself with me.

Menaechmus I: No; it's that dress I
gave you this morning. Be a good girl
and give it back to me. I'll buy you any
dress you want, twice as expensive.

Erotium: Why, I just gave it to you to
take to the embroiderer's. I gave you
the bracelet, you know, too, to take to
the jeweler's to be done over.

Menaechmus I: How could you have
given me the dress and the bracelet? I
gave you the dress just a little while ago
and went downtown, and this is the first
time I've come back and seen you since
then.

Erotium: Oh, I see your game. You're
trying to cheat me out of what I let you
take.

Menaechmus I: No, no, I'm not asking for the dress to cheat you. I tell you,
my wife's found out about it.

Erotium: [*Angrily.*] And I didn't ask
you to give it to me in the first place.
You brought it to me yourself, and you
gave it to me for a present. And now
you want it back. All right. Have the
old thing. Take it. Wear it yourself, or
let your wife wear it, or lock it up in a
trunk if you want to. After today you
won't set foot inside this house again—
don't fool yourself. You trifler with the
affections of an innocent woman! Unless
you bring me money, you haven't got a
chance to see me again. Now go and find
some other poor girl you can deceive.
[*She goes into her house.*]

Menaechmus I: Say, she's really mad
this time. [*Rushing to her door.*] Hey
there, wait a minute, I tell you. Come
back. Won't you stay? Won't you please
come back for my sake? [*To himself.*]
She's gone in and closed the door. Now
I am the most shut out of men! They
won't believe anything I say at home or
at my mistress's. I'll go and see what
my friends think I'd better do about
this. [*He departs in the direction of the
forum.*]

ACT FIVE. SCENE I

[*Enter Menaechmus II along the street; he still has the dress.*]

Menaechmus II: [*To himself.*] That was a fool thing I did a while ago, giving Messenio the purse with all my money in it. He's landed himself in a clip-joint somewhere, for sure. [*Enter Wife from her house.*]

Wife: [*To herself.*] I'll just have a look outside; that husband of mine should be back soon. Ah ha, there he is. And he's bringing back the dress. That's just fine.

Menaechmus II: [*To himself.*] I wonder where Messenio can be headed now.

Wife: [*To herself.*] I'll step up and give him the welcome he deserves. [*Aloud.*] You scoundrel, how dare you come into my sight with that dress?

Menaechmus II: Huh? What's the matter, lady, seen a ghost?

Wife: Impudence, how dare you utter one single syllable? How dare you speak to me?

Menaechmus II: Here, what have *I* done? Why shouldn't I?

Wife: You ask me! The cheek, the impudence of the man!

Menaechmus II: I suppose you know why the the Greeks used to call Hecuba the bitch?

Wife: No!

Menaechmus II: Because she acted just like you: she showered abuse on everybody in sight. That's how she got to be called the bitch—and she deserved it, too.

Wife: This is outrageous! I won't stand for it! No husband is worth it. It's outrageous!

Menaechmus II: What's it to me? You can't stand marriage, you're going to leave your husband—what is it, the custom of the country to babble this kind of nonsense to perfect strangers?

Wife: Babble? I won't stand for this a minute longer. I'll get a divorce.

Menaechmus II: Get a divorce. As far as I care, you can stay single till hell freezes over.

Wife: [*Pointing to the dress.*] And a minute ago you denied you stole this from me, and now you dangle it under my very nose. Haven't you any shame?

Menaechmus II: My God, woman, you certainly have an awful nerve. I didn't steal this dress from you. Another woman gave it to me; she wanted me to get it made over for her.

Wife: That settles it! I'm going to send for my father and tell him how outrageously you behave. [*Calls into the house to a slave.*] Decio! Go find my father and bring him here to me. Tell him it's important! [*To Menaechmus II.*] I'll tell him how outrageous you are.

Menaechmus II: Are you insane? What do you mean, outrageous?

Wife: You steal dresses and jewelry from your wife and take them to your mistress! And that's not babbling, either!

Menaechmus II: I wish you'd tell me some good medicine for me to take against that tongue of yours! I don't know who you think I am, but I don't know you from Hercules' wife's grandfather.

Wife: [*Pointing down the street.*] You may make fun of me, but not of him— my father! Here he comes. Look at him. Do you know *him*?

Menaechmus II: Oh yes, I remember meeting the two of you the same day I met Methuselah.

Wife: You deny you know me? And my father too?

Menaechmus II: And your grandfather too, if you want to drag him in.

Wife: You're impossible and always were.

ACT FIVE. SCENE II

[*Enter Father.*]

Father: As fast as my age will permit and this business requires, I'm getting along,

But if some of you think that it's easy
for me, very briefly I'll prove that
you're wrong.

My body's a burden, my nimbleness
gone, and of strength I've a notable 5
lack,

I'm quite overgrown with my years—oh,
confounded old age is a curse on the
back!

Why, if I were to tell all the terrible 10
evils that age, when it comes, brings
along,

I'm certain as certain can be that past
suitable limits I'd lengthen this
song. 15

However, my mind is a little disturbed
at this thing, for it seems a bit
queer

That my daughter should suddenly send
to my house with directions for me 20
to come here.

And how this affair is related to me, she
has not let me know up to now;

But I'm a good guesser, and I'm pretty
sure that her husband and she've 25
had a row.

That's what usually happens when men
are enslaved by their wives and
must come when they call;

And then it's the wives who are mostly 30
to blame, while the husbands aren't
guilty at all.

And yet there are bounds, which we all
must observe, to the things that a
wife can endure, 35

And a woman won't call in her father unless the offence of her husband is sure.

But I think very soon the suspense will
be over, and then I'll know what is
the matter— 40

But look, there's my daughter in front
of the door, and her husband; he's
not looking at her.

    It's just as I suspected. I'll start with 45
her.

    Wife: [*To herself.*] I'll go to meet
him. [*To father.*] How do you do, father.

    Father: How d'ye do, how d'ye do.
Now what's this how d'ye do? Why did 50
you send for me? What are you so sad

about? Why is he standing off from you
angry? The two of you have had a fight.
Tell me, which of you is in the wrong?
But be brief about it: no long speeches.

    Wife: I haven't done anything, not a
thing, believe me. But I can't live here,
I just can't stand it. Take me away!

    Father: Eh, what's this?

    Wife: He makes a laughingstock of me.

    Father: Who does?

    Wife: The man you entrusted me to—
my husband!

    Father: Tch, tch, tch! A squabble!
How many times have I told you not to
come to me with your complaints, either
of you?

    Wife: How can I help it, father?

    Father: You ask me that!

    Wife: [*Timidly.*] Yes.

    Father: I've told you often enough—
humour your husband; don't always
have your eye on what he's doing, where
he's going, what he's up to.

    Wife: But he has a mistress, right next
door!

    Father: Sensible man. And the more
you make of it, the more he'll love her.
No doubt of it.

    Wife: And he drinks there too.

    Father: Suppose it's there, suppose it's
somewhere else: can you stop him? Confound your impudence! Why not forbid
him to go out to dinner, or to have his
friends in for a meal? Do you want
husbands to be slaves? You might as
well give him piecework, and make him
sit with the maids and card wool.

    Wife: Father, I brought you here to
be *my* lawyer, not his; but now you're
arguing on his side instead of mine.

    Father: If he's been at fault in any
way, I'll be much harder on him that I
was on you. But he keeps you in clothes
and jewelry, and gives you proper food
and service, and so you oughtn't to be
so fussy about things, my girl.

    Wife: But he steals my jewelry and
dresses right out of the house! He takes
all my nice things and sneaks them off
to his mistress!

    Father: If he's up to that, he's up to

no good; if he's not up to that, *you're* up to no good; that would be slander.

Wife: But, father, he has the dress this very minute, and the bracelet he took her, too; he's bringing them back because I found out.

Father: I must have his account of it now. I'll speak to him. [*To Menaechmus II.*] Tell me, Menaechmus, what are you two quarreling for? What are you so sad about? Why is she standing off from you angry?

Menaechmus II: [*In legal style.*] Old man, whoever you may be, by highest Jupiter and the gods I swear—

Father: Well sworn. But what?

Menaechmus II: —firstly, that I have done no wrong to this your daughter who accuses me of stealing and purloining from her house this dress—

Wife: Perjury!

Menaechmus II: —and secondly, if I have ever set my foot within the house in which she lives, I pray that I may be the most miserable of miserable men.

Father: That's a fool's prayer, if you deny you ever set foot in the house you live in, you utter madman.

Menaechmus II: Old man, do you say I live in that house?

Father: Do you deny it?

Menaechmus II: I deny it and that's the truth.

Father: No, no, you deny it and it's *not* the truth. Unless, of course, you've moved since yesterday. [*To Wife.*] Come here, daughter. Tell me, you haven't moved, have you?

Wife: For goodness' sake, what for, and where to?

Father: I don't know.

Wife: He's playing games with you. Don't you see?

Father: Menaechmus, that's enough joking. Now get down to business.

Menaechmus II: [*Hotly.*] What business have we got to get down to? Who are you, anyway? You haven't got anything on me, and neither has that daughter of yours; and besides, she's a first-class pest.

Wife: [*Frightened, to Father.*] Look at the green in his eyes! He's getting green in the face! See how his eyes glitter!

Menaechmus II: [*Aside.*] Fine! They say I'm crazy: I'll pretend I *am*, and scare them away! [*He starts a mad-scene.*]

Wife: See how he stretches and gapes! What shall I do, father?

Father: Come over here, child; keep as far away from him as you can.

Menaechmus II: Hola, hola, Bromius! You call me to the forest, to the hunt? I hear; but I cannot leave this place: I am beset upon the left by this rabid bitch-woman, and behind her is that stinking goat who ruins innocent citizens with perjury.

Father: Woe to your head!

Menaechmus II: Lo! Apollo from his oracle bids me burn her eyes out with flaming torches!

Wife: Help, father! He's threatening to burn my eyes out!

Menaechmus II: [*Aside.*] Ha, they think I'm crazy, but they're the crazy ones.

Father: Psst! Daughter!

Wife: What?

Father: What shall we do? Suppose I get some slaves. Yes, they can grab him and chain him up in the house before he raises any more commotion.

Menaechmus II: [*Aside.*] Caught! If I don't work fast, they'll have me carried into the house with them. [*Aloud.*] Yes, Apollo? I must punch her face in with my fists unless she gets the hell out of my sight? I'll do your orders!

Father: Run home as fast as you can, or he'll smack you.

Wife: [*Retreating to her house.*] Please, father, watch him, don't let him get away! That I should live to hear such language! Poor me! [*She goes into her house.*]

Menaechmus II: [*Aside.*] I fixed her all right! Now for the other one. [*Aloud.*] Now this dirty wretch, this bearded tremulous Tithonus, this son of Cycnus; you want me to take that staff he has and beat him to pieces, joint from joint and bone from bone and limb from limb?

Father: [*Retreating.*] If you touch me or come a step closer, there'll be trouble.

Menaechmus II: I'll do your orders: I'll take a double axe and hack this old fellow's guts to mincemeat, down to the very bone.

Father: Then I must beware and take care of myself. The way he threatens me, I'm afraid he will do me harm.

Menaechmus II: New commands, Apollo! Now I am to yoke my wild ungovernable horses and mount my chariot, to trample down this stinking old toothless lion! Now I stand in the chariot; now I have the reins; now the goad is in my hand. Forward, my steeds! Ring out the clatter of your hoofs! Fleet feet, speed swift with tireless tumult!

Father: Threaten me with a chariot!

Menaechmus II: Another charge at him, Apollo, to the death? [*Pretending to have a change of fit.*] But who is this who drags me from the chariot by the hair? O edict of Apollo, thy command is maimed! [*He falls and is still.*]

Father: [*To himself.*] A violent and severe disease! . . .[1] The gods preserve us from the like. See now, how strong he was a moment since, and now is mad with sudden access of disease. I'll go and get a doctor, as fast as I can. [*He departs.*]

Menaechmus II: [*Rising.*] Are they out of sight, I wonder, these people that make me pretend I'm crazy? I'd better get back to the ship while the going is good. [*To the audience.*] Please, all of you, if the old man comes back, don't tell him which way I went. [*He departs. Considerable time is supposed to elapse before the next scene.*]

ACT FIVE. SCENE III

[*Enter Father.*]

Father: I've got pains in my back and pains in my eyes, waiting and watching

---

for the doctor to be free. He didn't want to leave his patients; I had a hard time persuading him to come. He says he set a broken leg for Aesculapius and a broken arm for Apollo.[1] Have I got a doctor, I wonder, or a joiner? Here he comes now. Get along, you ant!

ACT FIVE. SCENE IV

[*Enter the Doctor.*]

Doctor: Tell me, sir, what did you say was his disease? Has he hallucinations, or madness? Pray inform me. Has he the lethargy, or the subcutaneous humours?

Father: That's what I brought you here for: to tell me what's wrong with him, and cure him.

Doctor: Ah, that is quite simple. He shall be cured, I promise you.

Father: I want a careful treatment for him; spare no pains.

Doctor: No pains shall be spared; why, I will spend at least six hundred sighs a day on it.

Father: [*Seeing Menaechmus I approaching.*] Here he comes himself. Let's watch him.

ACT FIVE. SCENE V

[*Enter Menaechmus I, not seeing the others.*]

Menaechmus I: [*To himself.*] What a day! Everything going wrong, and getting me in wrong! I thought I was getting away with something; but that parasite of mine has let it all out and made a quaking criminal of me—the smart alec, biting the hand that feeds him. Sure as I live, it'll cost him his life. I'm a fool to call it *his* life though; it's mine: he lives on me and what I feed him. Well then, I'll cut his greedy throat. My mistress was just as bad; these girls are all alike. When I asked for

---

[1] There is a short lacuna in the text here.

[1] This is all the more amusing, since both Aesculapius and Apollo were gods of healing.

the dress so I could take it back to my wife, she pretended she'd given it to me already. Ugh! I certainly lead a miserable life!

Father: [*To Doctor.*] Can you hear what he's saying?

Doctor: He says he is miserable.

Father: Go on up to him.

Doctor: [*Complying.*] Good afternoon, Menaechmus. Tch, tch, why do you leave your arm uncovered like that? Don't you know how bad that is for a man in your condition?

Menaechmus I: Go hang yourself! [*The Doctor retreats.*]

Father: Notice anything?

Doctor: Notice anything! This case will take an *acre* of hellebore,[1] at least! [*Returning to Menaechmus I.*] Now, Menaechmus—

Menaechmus I: Well?

Doctor: Just a few questions, please. Do you drink red wine or white wine?

Menaechmus I: Why not ask about the bread I eat, if it's purple, pink, or scarlet? Or whether I eat scaly birds and feathered fish?

Father: My goodness, hear the way he raves! Hurry up and give him some medicine before he goes completely crazy.

Doctor: Just a minute; I want to finish my questions.

Father: You talk a man to death.

Doctor: [*To Menaechmus I.*] Tell me, are you ever troubled with a hardening of the eyes?

Menaechmus I: What, you idiot! Do you take me for a lobster?

Doctor: Tell me this: are you subject to rumbling of the bowels—as far as you know?

Menaechmus I: After a good meal, no; but if I'm hungry, then they do.

Doctor: [*Aside.*] Nothing crazy in that answer. [*To Menaechmus I.*] Do you sleep soundly all night? Do you fall asleep readily on retiring?

Menaechmus I: I sleep like a log—if

I've paid my bills! [*Losing his temper.*] Oh, the devil take you and all your questions!

Doctor: [*To Father.*] The madness is beginning. You hear the way he talks; be careful.

Father: Why he's talking like a perfect Nestor now, compared to the way he was a little while ago. Just a few minutes ago he called his wife a rabid bitch.

Menaechmus I: I said *what?*

Father: You were raving, I say.

Menaechmus I: *I* was raving?

Father: Yes, *you.* And you threatened to run over me with a chariot. I saw you; I accuse you.

Menaechmus I: [*Furious.*] And you stole a wreath out of the temple of Jupiter, I know, and you were thrown into jail for it, I know, and after you were let out of there you were strung up and whipped, I know, and you murdered your father and sold your mother into slavery, I know. Right back at you with your dirty insults! I'm sane enough for that, all right.

Father: For God's sake, doctor, hurry! Whatever you're going to do, do it. Don't you see the man is raving?

Doctor: The best thing for you to do is to have him taken to my house.

Father: You think so?

Doctor: Definitely. Then I'll have a free hand with his treatment.

Father: Just as you like.

Doctor: [*Gloatingly, to Menaechmus I.*] I'll have you drinking hellebore for something like three weeks!

Menaechmus I: [*Savagely.*] And I'll have you strung up and jabbed with ox-goads for a month!

Doctor: [*To Father.*] Get some men to bring him there.

Father: How many?

Doctor: Judging by the extent of his madness, four; no less.

Father: They'll be right here. [*Starts to go.*] Watch him, doctor.

Doctor: [*Hurriedly.*] No, no; I must go back and get things ready. Tell the slaves to bring him to me.

---

[1] Hellebore was used by the ancients as a remedy for insanity.

Father: I'll have him there right away.

Doctor: I'm on my way. [*The Doctor hurries down the street.*]

Father: Good-bye. [*The Father departs.*]

Menaechmus I: [*To himself.*] Father-in-law gone, doctor gone; now I'm alone. Good God, why do these people say I'm crazy? All my life I've never had a day's illness; I don't lose my head and pick fights, or law-suits either. I lead a normal life with normal people; I recognise my friends, and talk to them. Must be that *they're* crazy, the ones that say I am. What do I do now? I want to go home, but my wife won't have it. And I can't get in here. [*He points to the house of Erotium.*] A nice situation! I'll be stuck here forever! Well, maybe I'll get in at home by nightfall.

ACT FIVE. SCENE VI

[*Enter Messenio.*]

Messenio: [*To himself, not seeing Menaechmus I.*]
It's a proof of an excellent slave,
If, his master's belongings to save,
    He'll use as much care
    When his master's not there
As when master is watching the slave.

For his back and his shins he must fear,
The demands of his stomach not hear,
    And the punishment know
    Of the slothful and slow—
This servant whose conscience is clear.

There are beatings, and chains, and the mills,
Hunger, weariness, terrible chills—
    The reward of the lazy;
    But since I'm not crazy
I'm good, and avoid all these ills.

I can stand a tongue-lashing, but I don't like a whip-lashing; and I'd rather eat the meal than turn the mill. So I obey my master; it's worth my while. Others can take the easy way if they want to; I'll take the hard way. I'll keep out of trouble by worrying about being on the spot wherever my master needs me. Slaves who worry while they're *out* of trouble are the ones that serve their masters best: because the ones who don't worry then still have plenty to worry about when they're *in* trouble, but then the harm's done. But I don't have to worry much—my master will reward me before long. Beware of a beating, that's my motto. I've left the baggage and the slaves at an inn as he ordered, and now I'm back to meet him. I'll knock and let him know I'm here, in hopes I'm in time to get him safely out of this pirate lair. But I'm afraid the fight may be over already. [*He goes toward Erotium's door.*]

ACT FIVE. SCENE VII

[*Enter Father with Slaves. Messenio withdraws to one side.*]

Father: [*To slaves.*] Now by all that's holy, don't bungle your orders. I repeat: pick that man up and carry him to the doctor's, or your shanks and sides will smart for it. Pay no attention to his threats. Why do you stand there? What are you waiting for? You should have had him up and off already. I'm going to the doctor's; I'll be there when you come. [*He departs.*]

Menaechmus I: [*Finding himself surrounded.*] Good lord, what's going on here? Why are these men making for me? What do you want? What are you after? Why are you surrounding me? Why are you grabbing me? Where are you taking me? Murder! Help! Good folk of Epidamnus, help! Let me go!

Messenio: Great heaven, what is this I see? A gang of strangers carrying off my master! Shame!

Menaechmus I: Doesn't anybody dare help me?

Messenio: I do master, I dare most daringly! [*To the audience.*]

Oh! What an outrageous crime I see!
Epidamnians, this man was free,
My master, when he came today;
And now they're carrying him away,
While you're at peace, by light of day!
[*To the Slaves.*] Let go of him!

Menaechmus I: I implore you,
stranger, help me! Make them stop this
criminal outrage!

Messenio: You bet I will! I'll be your
helper, your defender, your ally! I won't
let them murder you; better me than
you. That one who has you by the
shoulder, gouge out his eye. I'll garden
up these fellows' faces and plant my
fists there. [*General scuffle.*] Try to kid-
nap him, would you? This is what you
get for it! Hands off him!

Menaechmus I: I've got him by the eye.

Messenio: Gouge it out! [*To Slaves.*]
Villains! Robbers! Bandits!

Slaves: Murder! Stop, for God's sake!

Messenio: Then let go of him! [*The
Slaves drop Menaechmus I.*]

Menaechmus I: Take your hands off
me! [*To Messenio.*] Keep on hoeing with
those fists.

Messenio: Go, beat it! Get the devil
out of here! Here's a prize for you, for
being the last to go! [*The Slaves run off.*]
I mapped out those faces pretty well, I
think! Well, master, I got here just in
time, didn't I?

Menaechmus I: May heaven reward
you, young man. If it hadn't been for
you, I'd never have lived to see the sun
go down today.

Messenio: Well then, if you did the
right thing, you'd set me free.

Menaechmus I: I'd set you free?

Messenio: Yes, master, because I
saved your life.

Menaechmus I: What is this? Young
man, you are mistaken.

Messenio: What do you mean?

Menaechmus I: By father Jupiter, I
swear I am not your master.

Messenio: You're joking!

Menaechmus I: No, I mean it. And no
slave of mine ever served me as well as
you have.

Messenio: Then if you say I don't belong to you, let me go free.

Menaechmus I: So far as I am concerned, I declare you free to go anywhere you want.

Messenio: My Patron! "Congratulations on your freedom, Messenio."
"Thank you." But please, Patron, I'm
still at your service just as much as
when I was your slave. I'll live with you
and go with you when you go back home.

Menaechmus I: [*To himself.*] I guess
not!

Messenio: I'll go to the inn now and
get your baggage and the money. The
purse and the passage-money are sealed
up safely in your bag. I'll have it all here
right away.

Menaechmus I: Do, by all means.

Messenio: I'll give it back to you all
safe, just as you gave it to me. Wait for
me here. [*He departs.*]

Menaechmus I: [*To himself.*] A lot of
strange things have certainly been happening to me today in strange ways.
People denying that I am I, and locking
me out of the house; and then this fellow
saying he was my slave, and I set him
free; and now he says he'll bring me a
bag of money. If he does, I'll tell him
he's free to go wherever he wants, so
that when he comes to his senses he
won't try to get the money back. And
my father-in-law and the doctor saying
I was insane! Heavens knows what it all
means; it all seems like a dream.—Well,
I'll try at Erotium's again. I suppose
she's still angry at me, but I've got to
try to get that dress and take it home.
[*He goes into the house of Erotium.*]

ACT FIVE. SCENE VIII

[*Enter Menaechmus II with Messenio.*]

Menaechmus II: You brazen rascal,
you dare tell me you've seen me anywhere today since I told you to come
here?

Messenio: Why, I rescued you just a

few minutes ago, when four men were carrying you off bodily, right in front of this very house. You were yelling for help to all heaven and earth, and I ran up and rescued you with my fists, in spite of them. And you set me free, because I saved your life. I said I'd get the money and the luggage, and then you doubled round the block so you could meet me and deny the whole thing!

Menaechmus II: I set you free?

Messenio: You did.

Menaechmus II: I'd turn slave myself sooner than free you. And that's that!

ACT FIVE. SCENE IX

[*Enter Menaechmus I from the house of Erotium.*]

Menaechmus I: [*To those within.*] Swear by your eyes if you want to, but you did *not* give me the dress or the bracelet either, you trollops!

Messenio: Immortal gods, what's this I see!

Menaechmus II: What do you see?

Messenio: Your mirror!

Menaechmus II: What's this?

Messenio: He's the very image of you, as like as can be.

Menaechmus II: Well! He's certainly not unlike me, now that I take stock of myself.

Menaechmus I: [*Catching sight of Messenio.*] Oh, the young man who saved my life. How are you?

Messenio: Please sir, if you don't mind, tell me what your name is, for goodness' sake!

Menaechmus I: Indeed I don't mind, after what you did for me. My name is Menaechmus.

Menaechmus II: No, that's *my* name.

Menaechmus I: I am a Sicilian, from Syracuse.

Menaechmus II: That's where *I* come from.

Menaechmus I: What's that?

Menaechmus II: That's the truth.

Messenio: [*Pointing to the wrong man,*] *Menaechmus I.*] This is the man I know, of course, this is my master. I'm his slave, but I thought I was that other man's. [*To Menaechmus I.*] I thought he was you, and bothered him. [*To Menaechmus II.*] Please excuse me if I said anything foolish without realising it.

Menaechmus II: You must be crazy. Don't you remember leaving the ship with me today?

Messenio: [*To Menaechmus II.*] You are right. *You* are my master. [*To Menaechmus I.*] *You* must look for another slave. [*To Menaechmus II.*] Greeting to you. [*To Menaechmus I.*] Goodbye to you. [*Pointing to Menaechmus II.*] I say *this* man is Menaechmus.

Menaechmus I: But I say *I* am.

Menaechmus II: What is this nonsense? *You* Menaechmus?

Menaechmus I: Yes; Menaechmus, son of Moschus.

Menaechmus II: The son of my father?

Menaechmus I: No, sir, mine, not yours. You may have your father; I don't want to deprive you of him.

Messenio: [*To himself.*] Immortal gods, fulfil this unhoped-for hope! Unless my mind has failed me, these are the two twin brothers! Both of them claim the same father and country. I'll tell my master about it first. [*Aloud.*] Menaechmus!

Menaechmus I and II: [*Together.*] What is it?

Messenio: I don't want both of you; just the one that came with me on the boat.

Menaechmus I: I didn't.

Menaechmus II: I did.

Messenio: Then it's you I want. [*Drawing him to one side.*] Come over here.

Menaechmus II: Well, what is it?

Messenio: That man is either a swindler or your twin brother! I never saw two men look so much alike. You're as hard to tell apart as two drops of water or two drops of milk. And besides, he claims the same father and the same country. We'd better ask him about this.

Menaechmus II: That's good advice, and thanks! Keep on helping, do! If you prove he is my brother, you shall be a free man.

Messenio: That's what I hope.

Menaechmus II: I hope so too.

Messenio: [*To Menaechmus I.*] You, sir: you said your name was Menaechmus, I believe.

Menaechmus I: Yes, it is.

Messenio: His name is Menaechmus too. You said you were born at Syracuse in Sicily; that's where he was born. Moschus was your father, you said; his too. Now both of you can help me, and help yourselves too.

Menaechmus I: I am in your debt; ask me whatever you want, and you shall have it. I'm at your service, just as if you had bought and paid for me.

Messenio: I hope to prove that you two are twin brothers, born on the same day to the same father and mother!

Menaechmus I: Amazing! I certainly wish you could prove that.

Messenio: I can. But come now, both of you, answer my questions.

Menaechmus I: Ask away, I'll answer; I won't conceal anything I know.

Messenio: [*Questioning each in turn.*] Your name is Menaechmus?

Menaechmus I: It is.

Messenio: And yours too?

Menaechmus II: Yes.

Messenio: You say you are the son of Moschus?

Menaechmus I: Quite so.

Menaechmus II: So am I.

Messenio: You are from Syracuse?

Menaechmus I: Yes.

Messenio: And you?

Menaechmus II: Of course.

Messenio: It checks very well so far. Now to proceed: what is the earliest thing you can remember of your life in Sicily?

Menaechmus I: Going with my father to the market in Tarentum; and then getting separated from him in the crowd, and being brought here.

Menaechmus II: God save us!

Messenio: [*To Menaechmus II.*] What are you shouting for? Be quiet. [*To Menaechmus I.*] How old were you when you went on this trip with your father?

Menaechmus I: Seven: I was just beginning to lose my teeth. I never saw my father again.

Messenio: Now then: how many sons did your father have at this time?

Menaechmus I: To the best of my recollection, two.

Messenio: Which was the older, you or the other one?

Menaechmus I: Both the same age.

Messenio: How is that possible?

Menaechmus I: We were twins.

Menaechmus II: Thank God!

Messenio: [*To Menaechmus II.*] If you interrupt, I'll stop.

Menaechmus II: No, no, I'll be quiet.

Messenio: [*To Menaechmus I.*] Tell me, did you both have the same name?

Menaechmus I: Oh, no. I was the one who was called Menaechmus then, as I still am. His name was Sosicles.

Menaechmus II: That's proof enough! No more delay! O my own twin brother, come to my arms! I am Sosicles!

Menaechmus I: [*Doubting.*] Then how does it come you're named Menaechmus?

Menaechmus II: After we got the news that you were lost . . . [1] and that our father was dead, our grandfather changed my name and gave me yours.

Menaechmus I: I believe you. But one more question.

Menaechmus II: Ask it.

Menaechmus I: What was the name of our mother?

Menaechmus II: Teuximarcha.

Menaechmus I: [*Convinced.*] Exactly so! Oh, welcome, beyond all hope, after all these years!

Menaechmus II: Welcome, dear brother! Sought with such misery and toil, and found with joy at last! [*They embrace.*]

---

[1] There is a lacuna of one verse here.

Messenio: [*To Menaechmus II.*] So that's why the woman here called you by name! She took you for him, and asked you to dinner.

Menaechmus I: Yes, I told her to have a dinner for me there today (putting one over on my wife), and I gave her a dress that I'd stolen from my wife too.

Menaechmus II: [*Producing the dress.*] Do you mean this dress?

Menaechmus I: That's the one! How did you get it?

Menaechmus II: The woman dragged me in to dinner and said the dress was mine, I'd given it to her. So after some excellent wine, women, and song, I took it away with me, and a gold bracelet too.

Menaechmus I: She thought she was getting *me* in, of course. But I'm certainly glad I got you fixed up so well.

Messenio: I suppose you're still willing to set me free as you promised?

Menaechmus I: A very good and fair request, brother; grant it for my sake.

Menaechmus II: [*Complying, with the correct legal formula.*] I declare you free.

Menaechmus I: Congratulations on your freedom, Messenio.

Messenio: I hope it lasts better this time.

Menaechmus II: Well, brother, now that everything has turned out the way we wanted, let's both go back to Syracuse.

Menaechmus I: Agreed! I'll have an auction and sell all my Epidamnus property. In the meantime, brother, won't you come in?

Menaechmus II: Good. [*They move towards the house of Menaechmus I.*]

Messenio: Do me a favour!

Menaechmus I: What is it?

Messenio: Give me the job of auctioneer.

Menaechmus I: You shall have it.

Messenio: You want the auction cried at once?

Menaechmus I: Yes, for a week from today. [*The brothers go into the house.*]

Messenio:

EXTRAORDINARY AUC—TION
WEEK FROM TODAY
MENAECHMUS SELLS HIS PROPERTY
CASH AND NO DELAY
ALL MUST GO—HOUSE AND LOT
SLAVES AND FURNITURE
WIFE GOES TOO IF ANY ONE
TAKES A FANCY TO HER

He'll be lucky if he gets a quarter of a million for the whole lot. [*To the audience.*] And now, spectators, fare ye well, and lustily applaud us all.

NOTES ON *THE TWIN MENAECHMI*

Since Plautus's play is, like Wilde's *Lady Windermere's Fan*, a "comedy," we naturally think first of all of the differences between the two. In both plays we have witty remarks, characters in difficult and embarrassing situations, domestic difficulties, and a "happy ending." But at the same time it is obvious that, despite his use of the comic mode, there is a wide difference between the two plays and that Wilde has vastly more serious intentions than Plautus. What we can observe at the outset, therefore, is that even some similarity in materials and method does not mean similarity of plays; we can learn the important fact that the author's attitude to his materials is what ultimately gives any play its distinctive character. What is the difference between Wilde's attitude and Plautus's will appear in the course of the discussion of *The Menaechmi*.

At the same time, it may be very helpful to make some comparison between *The Menaechmi* and *Everyman*, since both are relatively simple and even primitive plays. But the very dissimilarity between them should be enlightening.

Everyman is primarily concerned with an *idea* and subordinates plot and character to that: *The Twin Menaechmi* deals entirely in *amusing situations*, is little concerned with character, and not at all with ideas. Thus each play makes only a partial use of all the means available to drama. Ironically, however, *Everyman* looks very simple but turns out to have some complexity in its method, whereas Plautus's play, which looks very confused and complicated, is at bottom a quite simple thing.

I. THE NATURE OF FARCE

The Twin Menaechmi is as we have said an example of farce, a simple comic type always popular. When we say that it is concerned only with "amusing situations," what do we mean? Precisely what makes it farce?

1. The whole action springs from the mistaking of identical twins—clearly an "external" and a trivial situation. Since the plot demands that the twins be completely alike, not only in superficial appearance but also in character and personality, the whole problem of characterization is avoided. Plautus prefers the amusing confusions which he can get from the total identification of one twin with the other to the psychological problems which might be derived from other characters' perceiving the underlying differences between two people who happen to look alike. Thus, he does the simplest thing possible.

2. Note what Plautus does with the central dramatic problem of focusing, the problem of keeping some main theme, character, or characters in the foreground. We speak of a play's belonging to a character ("Hamlet's play," "Lady Windermere's play"), but *The Menaechmi* belongs to nobody. Our attention is focused mainly on the state of confusion into which all the characters fall. In other words, there is no main "conflict" but rather a series of minor differences. We see each person for only a short time, in flashes, not in a continuous action which, because it reveals the character and by revealing the character, becomes significant. The student will come to see, by the way, that one way to measure the relative maturity of various plays is to notice the degree to which the author of each play has succeeded in avoiding a scrambled and diffuse effect by a subordination of the characters which leaves the main action centered in one character alone. *The Menaechmi*, measured by this standard, lacks focus as compared with *Lady Windermere's Fan*, where, in spite of a larger number of characters, there is much better subordination to a central character. *Everyman*, whatever its deficiencies, also does excellently in relating everything to its central characters.

3. In *The Menaechmi*, the characters (since they are not very fully developed for us) cannot determine or influence the course of events: the action of the play progresses not because of what the characters *do*, but because of what *happens to* the characters. The characters themselves are

passive. To call attention to this fact is not, of course, to demand that every play must show man as the "master of his fate." Doubtless most of us, whether in drama or in life, are only to a degree masters of our fate. But in any significant drama, the characters must show some signs of struggle or else seem rather uninteresting. Even at the level of comedy, we expect men to use their wills, to attempt to use their intelligence, instead of merely getting knocked about by events toward which they can exhibit only a bewildered surprise. *Everyman*, as we have already observed, is a rather primitive play without very full character development. In it one might expect that the character Everyman, suddenly called by Death, would have to be regarded as the victim of an outer force. Yet even in this play, the drama hinges, not upon what fate does to Everyman, but on Everyman's efforts to cope with fate—to meet it satisfactorily. Everyman is not a merely passive character.

4. Thus, we may observe, the situations in farce do not *mean* anything: confusion and embarrassment are exhibited for their own sake. A character suffers embarrassment, not primarily because of what he is or does, but because his embarrassment is supposed to be amusing in itself. When Everyman, on the other hand, is upset by the summons of Death, his shocked surprise is not meant to be embarrassing in itself: it is dramatically effective because it represents the typical response of human beings to completely unforeseen predicaments. In *Lady Windermere's Fan* the conflict between Mrs. Erlynne and Lady Windermere is *symbolic* in the sense that it embodies a vast conflict between conventional society and an unconventional individual; it is meaningful because it involves much more than the single case. But a conflict between either Menaechmus and Erotium means merely that one Menaechmus has been mistaken for the other. That is all: there is no suggested or secondary value. The thing tends to be one-dimensional.

5. In fact, all farce is by its own nature one-dimensional. It exploits situations. Now when situations devoid of content demand our attention, how do they get it? By their variety, novelty, uniqueness—by being "different." Plautus's play depends on an extraordinary set of circumstances: identical twins who do not know each other are brought into proximity. We have to have the disappearance of a child, the hunt for him, the remarkable discovery of the needle in the haystack. The author trades in the rare, the unusual, the improbable.

He has to. If he started working in terms of character, he would be dealing in recognizable patterns of conduct, and the play would begin to veer from the unique to the universal. Aristotle insisted on the need of the "probable" in drama, that is, fidelity to human patterns as we understand them; the playwright, he said, should be concerned with what *may* happen. This is the universal. When an author decides to write farce and thus rules out the possibility of concentrating, by the treatment of character, wide ranges of human experience into the actions of an individual, he automatically commits himself to the novel, the untypical.

To return to comparison. *Everyman*, unlike *The Menaechmi*, deals with the universal—the human being's facing of death and consequent re-examination of his values. This does not inevitably make the play great, for *Everyman* has obvious faults—for instance, lack of sufficient indi-vidualization. Merely to introduce the universal is not enough; what is finally important is the author's method, the form which his conception takes. And here we come to a basic truth concerning all literary genres.

Any farce (and *The Menaechmi* is a good example) fails, by being funda-mentally off-center, to challenge greatness or even seriousness. Of course, the opposite method, dealing with the central, as in *Everyman*, is not of itself enough. The conclusion to be drawn from this comparison—and it may seem paradoxical at first glance—is this: a work of finest quality must be universal and individual at the same time. In a good author's work, says Samuel Johnson, "familiar things are made new," and events must be "surprising, and yet natural." The "surprising," however, is not the unex-pectedness of farce, for we do have expectation in good literary work (see *Motivation* in the Glossary); it is the "gripping" quality of a new but pro-found revelation. The theme of widest applicability and significance must be embodied in a unique form with sharply defined characters and situa-tion which entirely escape triteness; its quality is evinced in its coming across to us with a fine sense of freshness, even of uniqueness. There is a combination of novelty and expectation. An excellent theme, of course, may be treated so dully and stodgily as to be less successful than an un-pretentious but lively farce. Shakespeare's *Hamlet* embodies a great theme and succeeds in turning it into powerful drama. The situation in *Hamlet* is certainly as unusual as that of *The Menaechmi;* but on the other hand, whereas Menaechmus speaks only for himself, Hamlet is a sort of Every-man, painfully gaining insight into a complex world of good and evil.

The student, at this point, may be inclined to say: "Well, when Menaech-mus is mistreated or confused, he becomes angry; and surely that is uni-versal enough." To a degree, of course, this is true. For the figures of even the simplest farce must be, in some sense, universally human in their actions and responses. The characters could not be recognizably human unless they represented in some faint degree at least the basic patterns of human behavior. Literally, we overstate the case a little, perhaps, when we say that farce is absolutely one-dimensional. But the relative lack of another dimension in farce becomes clear enough when we realize that the actions of Menaechmus (either I or II—it does not matter) lack any but the thin-nest relevance to universal human nature. Menaechmus is not developing nor is he learning anything. He responds to a stimulus, only—one is tempted to say—automatically, like an eyelid that closes when something is waved in front of the eye. The response reveals nothing. Nothing is implied. There is no *symbolic situation*.

Thus, in spite of the fact that farce makes use of uncommon materials, farce is really *commonplace*. Serious drama is concerned with the common, but serious drama wins its title to seriousness, and when successful, to greatness, by avoiding, through its sharpness of insight and through its individuality of presentation, the commonplace.

6. The student should also note, as another aspect of the mechanical response which the characters of Plautus make to the situation, that they seem never to reason about what happens; they never use their heads. Like so many automatons, they register wonderment, anger, surprise, disgust, and so on, but they never make rational, adult inquiries. In Act III. ii, Menaechmus II accepts easily one incredible event after another; and the author does not even attempt to exploit, as a possible explanation of his credulity, the fact that he is too drunk to realize fully what is going on.

In general, the characters in farce tend to be abnormally insensitive to clues (cf. mystery melodramas, where one finds abnormal sensitiveness and abnormal insensitiveness side by side). This lack of normal inquisitiveness is an aspect of the rather sketchy characterization which the author has accorded them. If the characters in a typical farce did reason about events, the action of the farce would quickly come to an end. Thus, we may say that in farce the author must depend upon unalert, commonplace people in order to maintain his unusual situations.

2. THE QUALITY OF PLAUTUS'S FARCE

Yet, granted the limitations which inhere in the very nature of farce, how well has Plautus done within these limitations? How has he secured enough liveliness and tension—if he has in fact secured them—to keep his audience interested?

Since the very nature of farce precludes any significant study of character, that ordinarily rich source of interest is out of the question. As a substitute for it, and, indeed, in order to distract his audience from the lack of it, Plautus, in general, has attempted to play up the qualities of gusto, high animal spirits, and the sense of rapid movement. The incidents are exploited for their own sake with a boisterous and earthy humor, and we are hurried on to another surprising situation before the first situation has had time to pall on us or we have had time to raise embarrassing questions as to its general plausibility. One must remember too, that the liveliness and the successfulness of farce depend also on the ability of the comic actor to develop the humor fully with his facial expression, mimicry, and gesture. By such devices, as we know, an able comedian can frequently make very funny a part which in itself may seem rather wooden and flat. We may be sure that Plautus knew what he was doing, and that some of the rather obvious humor of the text was given point and meaning by the more able comic actors of the period, even as some such farce roles in the moving pictures are occasionally given point and meaning by the witty and talented comedian of today. But though the dramatist has a perfect right to depend upon the actor who has such devices at his command, it ought to be clear that his comedy, in so far as it does depend upon such devices, is moving away from drama proper and into the realm of pantomime, vaudeville, and musical comedy. It is with drama proper that this book is concerned. It is fair, therefore, to consider *The Menaechmi* with a full sense of its limitations as a drama, though this is not to forget that the other forms, such as pantomime, are worth having and may in their own right be thoroughly amusing.

Conventions. We have already remarked upon the need in this play to distract the audience from types of questions which ordinarily would arise with disastrous effect. But there are other problems—among them the problem of keeping a rather complicated plot moving smoothly without too much confusion in the minds of the audience. Here, by the way, Plautus' problem is greatly simplified by certain conventions of the Roman stage (see the section on *Conventions* in the Glossary). The stage regularly represented a street on which the houses of the principals could be represented as close together and where everyone could meet everyone else; thus, the whole logic of place was settled in advance, and the author had no problem such as those which arise for Wilde in Act III of *Lady Windermere's Fan.*

Exposition, too, was managed largely by conventional devices—the use of prologue; a character's introducing himself to the audience (I. i, I. ii, III. i, and IV. ii); asides (I. ii, I. iii ff.). Even when Plautus does use dialogue for exposition as in Act II. ii, he simply has the character give the desired information without bothering much about the dramatic logic involved. Since convention permitted characters not to see or hear other characters present on the stage, the usual problem of getting the stage free for necessary conversations is in this play perceptibly lessened; and since it was understood that one of the stage-exits led to the harbor, the other "downtown," the disposal of characters off-stage was pretty well predetermined.

In fairness to Plautus, the student should know and take into account the theatrical conventions which obtained in his day. Yet the student should also observe, in passing, that the greater the allowance which we have to make for theatrical conventions, the greater is our sense of the author's limitations. While some such allowances always have to be made, the fact is that one measure of artistic excellence is the ability of the artist to rise above the limitations of his own time and place, or else his ability to work through them to effects which transcend the mere fashions of his era. Plautus, in order to be acceptable to us, for example, demands a greater knowledge of his theater than do Sophocles and Shakespeare.

Yet, though his reliance on certain conventions is a measure of his relative weakness as a dramatist, the conventions, once apprehended, do give him a great freedom: he can devote nearly all his attention to securing the movement, liveliness, and variety that make for good farce, in which he is not unsuccessful. Note the following aspects of his method:

Variety. Plautus is careful to avoid monotony; he constantly shifts the characters on the stage, employing the introduction of the new character to give a new twist to the situation. If one runs through Acts I, II, and III, he will see how each new scene adds some novelty designed to maintain the curiosity of the audience. Note too that Plautus makes still greater use of variety later on—shifting from Menaechmus II to Menaechmus I, getting the latter into trouble with both his wife and Erotium, and then rapidly bringing in the father, the doctor, the insanity motif, the attempted arrest, the rescue by Messenio, and the issue of Messenio's emancipation. Plautus has no lack of inventiveness; but his method is to develop his situations, not by concentration, but by pursuing as many ramifications as possible. Note that in neither *Everyman* nor in *Lady Windermere's Fan* do we find mere variety for variety's sake; in *Everyman*, for example, the author uses variety as a means of making more effective what he has to say.

Climactic Arrangement. Plautus skillfully begins with a relatively mild confusion, that between Menaechmus II and Cylindrus in Act II, ii. In this case the mistake in identity is of very little consequence, and without too much strain it introduces the reader to the dominant theme of confusion. The next mistake in identity, however, that made by Erotium (II, iii), has more serious repercussions: and the confusion which involves Menaechmus II and Brush is more serious still; for, in his anger at what he regards as a slight, Brush brings in the wife of Menaechmus I. Indeed, relations become more and more confused until finally everybody is embroiled.

In connection with the crescendo of confusions, and as a factor which in itself contributes to the effect of crescendo, one should note that in Acts IV and V, the rapid shift of character and situation, plus the intensification of the feelings of the characters and their consequent tendency to express themselves more sharply and forcefully, gives an impression of much quicker movement than in the comparatively leisurely first part of the play. This change is called a change in "tempo" or an "increase in tempo," and it is obviously a factor which contributes to the total effect of the play. (See the section on *Tempo* in the Glossary.) Tempo can be heightened, too, by sudden decisions—impulsive leaps into action which can easily occur in a type of action which is not much concerned with motivation. As an example, notice the suddenness with which Menaechmus II (V, ii) decides to feign madness.

Language. As the excellent translation of this play makes clear, the characters of Plautus use a rapid-fire, colloquial, slangy speech suited to farce. Their speech is racy and even violent; farce depends, one remembers, on strong feelings, not thoughtfulness. Their wit takes the form of puns and word-play (*pick-ups* and *stick-ups*, Act II. iii; *Cylinder, Colander*, Act II. ii), which, because they depend on resemblances in sound rather than on double meaning, have the triviality appropriate to farce. Compare this wit with the kind found in the plays of Sheridan and Wilde.

Probability. Because of his plot Plautus has the difficult problem of keeping his audience from thinking, "I don't believe it." He is not dealing with character; hence he must achieve probability without using the best source of the probable.

First of all, he knows that the confusion of identity cannot last very long; so he represents it as lasting but a short time. In fact, the play comes very close to having the ideal "unity of time" which Renaissance critics called for—identity of the time of performance with the time of the actions represented.

Second, Plautus knows that he must make us accept the characters' initial failure to sense, or suspect, or do anything about the situation, and their subsequent acquiescence in incredible situation after incredible situation without any intelligent, mature effort to do something about it. If he can secure our assent at the start, his biggest battle is won; for, if we accept the situation as the author first presents it, we are, as it were, committed to it, and we tend to go along without undue questioning. So, as Plautus recognizes, II. ii and II. iii are crucial for the play, and the problem they present to the author is extremely difficult, for the author is faced with this dilemma: if Menaechmus really uses his head, there will be no plot: if he does not use his head at all, the situation will be wholly incredible.

Plautus gets out of the dilemma by having Menaechmus use his head, but use it *to make the wrong inference:* Menaechmus believes that he is the victim of a "racket." To strengthen this bid for our acceptance, Plautus spends most of Act II stressing the evil reputation of Epidamnus. The character of the city is skillfully built up *before* there has been any confusion, so that Messenio's speech. "Didn't I tell you there were a lot of swindlers here?" (II. ii) comes in logically, not as a clumsy after-thought. Besides, this comment is made very early in the scene so as to set Menaechmus's mind working immediately in the wrong direction.

(Has Plautus tried hard enough to convince us of Menaechmus's error? Should Messenio have a greater part in the scene? Why is Menaechmus surprised when Erotium addresses him in II. iii? Should he be presented as thinking that she is a part of the "racket"? Would this view justify his unquestioningly spending considerable time with her?)

Third, Plautus obviously must keep the brothers apart until the end of the play, and he must make us feel that their failure to run into each other is logical, is not merely the result of his own manipulation. Otherwise. we shall be the less willing to accept the play. Plautus has a good start here in that the speed and bustle and confusion of farce tend to distract our attention from weak connections and unsatisfactory causations. In a room full of noise and activity one is not likely to notice things that in calm and order would be easily apparent. Indeed, in farce (and melodrama) what we call motivation is generally subordinate to the quest for action, excitement, surprise, etc.

In stage terms, keeping the brothers apart is a matter of exits and entrances, and our problem, then, is to see how logical these are, how well motivated. The student might make a careful check of entrances and exits, to see whether on examination the brothers' movements are reasonably accounted for. Consider especially such a matter as Menaechmus I's not showing up for dinner on schedule. Before you begin, consult the section of the Glossary which discusses motivation. Remember that, since Plautus is not concerned with character, the problem of motivation is centered in his handling of technical matters of the sort we have discussed.

This should be very useful study: it should give the student some insight into a technical problem which every dramatist must face.

CONCLUSION

We have said that in various ways *The Menaechmi* is founded upon a basic improbability. One could go further and point out that the play is "unscientific": in view of the differing environments, the complete similarity of the twins is impossible. But this is not a relevant criticism of the play, for it is not the business of literature to be scientific. A work of literature makes its statements in its own way, which may or may not happen to be consistent with the scientific beliefs of the day (Milton, for instance, chose in *Paradise Lost* to run counter to astronomical knowledge). Aristotle said approximately this in his paradox-laden remark that in drama "the probable impossible" is preferable to the "possible improbable." A piece of literature may work quite successfully, for instance, in terms of fantasy, which has nothing at all to do with a scientific or a possible world, but which may achieve probability enough, as in *Gulliver's Travels*. The legitimate criticism of *The Menaechmi* is not that the twins are impossibly identical but that they do not behave like probable human beings.

The student may say, "Why should they be probable? Why should they be representative characters? Why should the play mean anything? Why should there be a 'symbolic situation'? It's fast and lively and amusing. Why not let it go at that? What if it is trivial, as you say?"

Well, all that is true enough, and we need not condemn Plautus for not being Congreve. But it is important to be able to distinguish Plautus from Congreve and Shakespeare, and it is with this general distinction that this analysis has been largely occupied. And doubtless there is a place for the enjoyment of Plautus and other writers of farce: the important thing is to know that it is *farce* and not to mistake it for high comedy. In seeing the movies one must especially be aware of this distinction.

But can one merely stop at a certain level and console himself with the thought that he can recognize the level for what it is? Can one be contented very long at the extremely unsophisticated level of farce? (It is worth noting, in fairness to Plautus, that his farces are less unsophisticated than a comparable group of Hollywood productions. There are, of course, the same simple characters, the same plot types, the same happy endings; but Plautus was far less restricted in the materials with which he could deal. He could cover a wider range of experience. Modern taboos have greatly increased the already considerable simplicity of farce.) To enjoy farce one has to make all sorts of allowances and concessions; one can rarely expect characters to be intelligent, discriminating, sensitive or representative—one can look for no meaning or significance. That is, one has to eliminate a great deal of one's power of perception; only a few of one's faculties are functioning. So one really gives up adult status. And whereas it may be delightful and healthfully refreshing to go slumming occasionally or to take a critical holiday, to habituate oneself to the naïve is to become naïve oneself.

QUESTIONS

1. What problems of exposition does the author eliminate by his use of the prologue?

2. Can you find any justification for Plautus's giving the last scene to Messenio? What effect is he striving for when he has Messenio speak commandingly to the brothers?

3. What similarities do you find between this play and modern theatrical performances? Musical plays?

4. How much use does Plautus make of coincidence? Is this consistent with the tone and manner of farce?

5. How early in the play is the tone of levity established?

6. Does Plautus give us any clues which would lead us to expect Brush's betrayal of his patron?

7. Can you find any evidence of dialogue which seems to be presented for immediate amusement rather than for advancing the action of the play?

8. Note the continuing use of military metaphor in Act I. What is accomplished by this?

9. In Act II. iii what is gained by the careful handing back and forth of the purse?

10. What contribution is made to the plot by Menaechmus II's deciding, at the end of Act II, to see what "booty" he can get in Epidamnus?

11. Does Menaechmus's drunkenness help characterize him at all? Or is it just introduced for whatever comic effect it may have?

12. Is the plot helped by the maid's coaxing Menaechmus II for a gift in Act III. iii?

13. Is there any evidence that the wife's quarrel with her husband is the result of real moral conviction on her part? Or is it just tossed in as a conventional comic device? How can you tell? Consider, in this connection, Menaechmus I's evasion of her in Act IV. ii.

14. Note the various quick turns at the climax of Act IV. ii. Are these characteristic of farce?

15. Is the double lockout of Menaechmus I in Act IV. iii effective? Why?

16. Why, in more serious plays, do we rarely find a main character introduced as late as Menaechmus I's father-in-law is introduced (IV. ii)?

17. How does Plautus keep the father-in-law from being a too obvious character?

18. In Act V. v does Plautus show any psychological insight which suggests a comic level better than that of farce?

19. We have seen (under *Probability*) how Plautus carefully prepares for

Menaechmus II's mistaken inference about his experiences. In *Lady Windermere's Fan* Lady W.'s mistaken inference about her husband's conduct was also important. Compare the efforts of the two dramatists to motivate these mistakes.

20. Does Plautus's play seem to be more or less "well-made" than Wilde's?

FOR FURTHER STUDY

See the analysis of and the questions on Shakespeare's *Comedy of Erro:* in Appendix A.

4. George Lillo. *The London Merchant; or the History of George Barnwell*

WHEN we turn from *The Menaechmi* to *The London Merchant*, we find a very sharp difference in mood; whereas Plautus wanted only to provide a gay entertainment, it is clear from the first scene that Lillo has very serious intentions. Indeed, he is aiming at tragedy, and in terms of the theater he was once very successful. After its first presentation in 1731 the play remained popular for a century; it even had some influence on French and German drama. In reading the play, the student will find it useful to try to discover the reason why the play is no longer the popular theater piece it once was.

THE LONDON MERCHANT;

OR,

THE HISTORY OF GEORGE BARNWELL

DRAMATIS PERSONÆ

THOROWGOOD	BLUNT
BARNWELL, *Uncle to George*	MARIA
GEORGE BARNWELL	MILLWOOD
TRUEMAN	LUCY

Officers with their Attendants, Keeper, and Footmen

[SCENE: London, and an adjacent Village.]

PROLOGUE

The tragic muse, sublime, delights to show
Princes distressed, and scenes of royal woe;
In awful pomp, majestic, to relate
The fall of nations or some hero's fate,
That sceptered chiefs may by example know 5
The strange vicissitude of things below;
What danger on security attend;
How pride and cruelty in ruin end;
Hence Providence supreme to know; and own
Humanity adds glory to a throne. 10
    In ev'ry former age, and foreign tongue,
With native grandeur thus the goddess sung.
Upon our stage indeed with wished success
You've sometimes seen her in a humbler dress,
Great only in distress. When she complains 15
In Southerne's, Rowe's, or Otway's moving strains
The brilliant drops that fall from each bright eye,
The absent pomp with brighter gems supply. 18
Forgive us then, if we attempt to show
In artless strains a tale of private woe.
A London prentice ruined is our theme,
Drawn from the famed old song that bears his name.
We hope your taste is not so high to scorn
A moral tale esteemed e'er you were born,
Which for a century of rolling years 25
Has filled a thousand-thousand eyes with tears.
If thoughtless youth to warn and shame the age
From vice destructive well becomes the stage,
If this example innocence secure, 29
Prevents our guilt, or by reflection cure,
If Millwood's dreadful guilt, and sad despair,
Commend the virtue of the good and fair,
Though art be wanting, and our numbers fail,
Indulge th' attempt in justice to the tale.

ACT I

[SCENE I.   A room in Thorowgood's house.]

[*Enter Thorowgood and Trueman.*]

Trueman: Sir, the packet from Genoa is arrived. [*Gives letters.*]

Thorowgood: Heaven be praised, the storm that threatened our royal mistress, 10 pure religion, liberty, and laws is for a time diverted; the haughty and revengeful Spaniard, disappointed of the loan on which he depended from Genoa, must now attend the slow return of wealth 15 from his new world to supply his empty coffers, e'er he can execute his purposed invasion of our happy island; by which means time is gained to make such preparations on our part as may, heaven concurring, prevent his malice or turn the meditated mischief on himself.

5 *Trueman:* He must be insensible indeed who is not affected when the safety of his country is concerned.—Sir, may I know by what means,—if I am too bold—

Thorowgood: Your curiosity is laudable; and I gratify it with the greater pleasure because from thence you may learn how honest merchants, as such, may sometimes contribute to the safety 15 of their country as they do at all times to its happiness; that if hereafter you should be tempted to any action that has the appearance of vice or meanness in it, upon reflecting on the dignity of our profession, you may with honest scorn reject whatever is unworthy of it.

Trueman: Should Barnwell or I, who have the benefit of your example, by our ill conduct bring any imputation on that honorable name, we must be left without excuse.

Thorowgood: You compliment, young man—[*Trueman bows respectfully.*] Nay, I'm not offended. As the name of merchant never degrades the gentleman, so by no means does it exclude him; only take heed not to purchase the character of complaisant at the expense of your sincerity.—But to answer your question,—the bank of Genoa had agreed, at excessive interest and on good security, to advance the King of Spain a sum of money sufficient to equip his vast armada, of which our peerless Elizabeth (more than in name the mother of her people), being well informed, sent Walsingham,[1] her wise and faithful secretary, to consult the merchants of this loyal city, who all agreed to direct their several agents to influence, if possible, the Genoese to break their contract with the Spanish court. 'Tis done, the state and bank of Genoa, having maturely weighed and rightly judged of their true interest, prefer the friendship of the merchants of London to that of a monarch who proudly styles himself King of both Indies.

Trueman: Happy success of prudent councils. What an expense of blood and treasure is here saved!—Excellent queen! O how unlike to former princes, who made the danger of foreign enemies a pretense to oppress their subjects, by taxes great and grievous to be borne.

Thorowgood: Not so our gracious queen, whose richest exchequer is her people's love as their happiness her greatest glory.

Trueman: On these terms to defend us, is to make our protection a benefit

worthy her who confers it, and well worth our acceptance. Sir, have you any commands for me at this time?

Thorowgood: Only to look carefully over the files to see whether there are any tradesmen's bills unpaid; and if there are, to send and discharge 'em. We must not let artificers lose their time, so useful to the public and their families, in unnecessary attendance. [*Exit Trueman.*]

Scene II

[*Thorowgood and Maria, who enters.*]

Thorowgood: Well, Maria, have you given orders for the entertainment? I would have it in some measure worthy the guests. Let there be plenty, and of the best, that the courtiers, though they should deny us citizens politeness, may at least commend our hospitality.

Maria: Sir, I have endeavored not to wrong your well-known generosity by an ill-timed parsimony.

Thorowgood: Nay, 'twas a needless caution; I have no cause to doubt your prudence.

Maria: Sir! I find myself unfit for conversation at present. I should but increase the number of the company, without adding to their satisfaction.

Thorowgood: Nay, my child, this melancholy must not be indulged.

Maria: Company will but increase it. I wish you would dispense with my absence; solitude best suits my present temper.

Thorowgood: You are not insensible that it is chiefly on your account these noble lords do me the honor so frequently to grace my board; should you be absent, the disappointment may make them repent their condescension and think their labor lost.

Maria: He that shall think his time or honor lost in visiting you, can set no real value on your daughter's company, whose only merit is that she is yours. The man of quality, who chooses to con-

[1] Sir Francis Walsingham (*c.* 1530–1590), Elizabeth's secretary of state.

verse with a gentleman and merchant of your worth and character, may confer honor by so doing, but he loses none.

Thorowgood: Come, come, Maria, I need not tell you that a young gentleman may prefer your conversation to mine, yet intend me no disrespect at all; for though he may lose no honor in my company, 'tis very natural for him to expect more pleasure in yours. I re-10 member the time when the company of the greatest and wisest man in the kingdom would have been insipid and tiresome to me, if it had deprived me of an opportunity of enjoying your mother's. 15

Maria: Yours no doubt was as agreeable to her; for generous minds know no pleasure in society but where 'tis mutual.

Thorowgood: Thou know'st I have no 20 heir, no child, but thee; the fruits of many years' successful industry must all be thine. Now it would give me pleasure great as my love, to see on whom you would bestow it. I am daily solicited by 25 men of the greatest rank and merit for leave to address you, but I have hitherto declined it, in hopes that by observation I should learn which way your inclination tends; for as I know love to be 30 essential to happiness in the marriage state, I had rather my approbation should confirm your choice than direct it.

Maria: What can I say? How shall I 35 answer as I ought this tenderness, so uncommon even in the best of parents; but you are without example; yet had you been less indulgent, I had been most wretched. That I look on the crowd of 40 courtiers that visit here with equal esteem but equal indifference you have observed, and I must needs confess; yet had you asserted your authority, and insisted on a parent's right to be obeyed, 45 I had submitted, and to my duty sacrificed my peace.

Thorowgood: From your perfect obedience in every other instance, I feared as much; and therefore would leave you 50 without a bias in an affair wherein your happiness is so immediately concerned.

Maria: Whether from a want of that just ambition that would become your 5 daughter or from some other cause I know not; but I find high birth and titles don't recommend the man who owns them, to my affections.

Thorowgood: I would not that they 10 should, unless his merit recommends him more. A noble birth and fortune, though they make not a bad man good, yet they are a real advantage to a worthy one, and place his virtues in the fairest 15 light.

Maria: I cannot answer for my inclinations, but they shall ever be submitted to your wisdom and authority; and as you will not compel me to marry where I cannot love, so love shall never make me act contrary to my duty. Sir, have I your permission to retire?

Thorowgood: I'll see you to your chamber. [*Exeunt.*]

[SCENE III. A room in Millwood's house.]

[*Discovered Millwood. Lucy waiting.*]

Millwood: How do I look today, Lucy?

Lucy: O, killingly, madam!—A little more red, and you'll be irresistible!— But why this more than ordinary care of your dress and complexion? What new conquest are you aiming at?

Millwood: A conquest would be new indeed!

Lucy: Not to you, who make 'em every day,—but to me.—Well! 'tis what I'm never to expect,—unfortunate as I am:—But your wit and beauty—

Millwood: First made me a wretch, 45 and still continue me so.—Men, however generous or sincere to one another, are all selfish hypocrites in their affairs with us. We are no otherwise esteemed or regarded by them, but as we contribute 50 to their satisfaction.

Lucy: You are certainly, madam, on

the wrong side in this argument. Is not the expense all theirs? And I am sure it is our own fault if we haven't our share of the pleasure.

Millwood: We are but slaves to men.

Lucy: Nay, 'tis they that are slaves most certainly; for we lay them under contribution.

Millwood: Slaves have no property; no, not even in themselves.—All is the victor's.

Lucy: You are strangely arbitrary in your principles, madam.

Millwood: I would have my conquests complete, like those of the Spaniards in the New World, who first plundered the natives of all the wealth they had, and then condemned the wretches to the mines for life to work for more.

Lucy: Well, I shall never approve of your scheme of government. I should think it much more politic, as well as just, to find my subjects an easier employment.

Millwood: It's a general maxim among the knowing part of mankind that a woman without virtue, like a man without honor or honesty, is capable of any action, though never so vile; and yet what pains will they not take, what arts not use, to seduce us from our innocence and make us contemptible and wicked even in their own opinions? Then is it not just, the villains, to their cost, should find us so?—But guilt makes them suspicious, and keeps them on their guard; therefore we can take advantage only of the young and innocent part of the sex, who, having never injured women, apprehend no injury from them.

Lucy: Ay, they must be young indeed.

Millwood: Such a one, I think, I have found.—As I've passed through the City, I have often observed him receiving and paying considerable sums of money; from thence I conclude he is employed in affairs of consequence.

Lucy: Is he handsome?

Millwood: Ay, ay, the stripling is well made.

Lucy: About—

Millwood: Eighteen—

Lucy: Innocent, handsome, and about eighteen.—You'll be vastly happy.— Why, if you manage well, you may keep him to yourself these two or three years.

Millwood: If I manage well, I shall have done with him much sooner; having long had a design on him, and meeting him yesterday, I made a full stop and, gazing wishfully on his face, asked him his name. He blushed, and bowing very low, answered, George Barnwell. I begged his pardon for the freedom I had taken, and told him that he was the person I had long wished to see, and to whom I had an affair of importance to communicate at a proper time and place. He named a tavern; I talked of honor and reputation, and invited him to my house. He swallowed the bait, promised to come, and this is the time I expect him. [*Knocking at the door.*] Somebody knocks,—d'ye hear? I am at home to nobody today, but him.—[*Exit Lucy.*]

Scene IV

Millwood

Millwood: Less affairs must give way to those of more consequence; and I am strangely mistaken if this does not prove of great importance to me and him, too, before I have done with him.—Now, after what manner shall I receive him? Let me consider—What manner of person am I to receive?—He is young, innocent, and bashful; therefore I must take care not to shock him at first.— But then, if I have any skill in physiognomy, he is amorous, and, with a little assistance, will soon get the better of his modesty.—I'll trust to nature, who does wonders in these matters.—If to seem what one is not, in order to be the better liked for what one really is; if to speak one thing, and mean the direct contrary, be art in a woman, I know nothing of nature.

Scene V

[*Enter to her, Barnwell bowing very low, and Lucy at a distance.*]

Millwood: Sir, the surprise and joy!—
Barnwell: Madam.—
Millwood: This is such a favor,—[*Advancing.*]
Barnwell: Pardon me, madam,—
Millwood: So unhoped for,—[*Still advances. Barnwell salutes her, and retires in confusion.*]
Millwood: To see you here—Excuse the confusion— 15
Barnwell: I fear I am too bold.—
Millwood: Alas, sir! All my apprehensions proceed from my fears of your thinking me so. Please, sir, to sit.—I am as much at a loss how to receive this 20 honor as I ought, as I am surprised at your goodness in conferring it.
Barnwell: I thought you had expected me. I promised to come.
Millwood: That is the more surprising; 25 few men are such religious observers of their word.
Barnwell: All who are honest are.
Millwood: To one another: But we silly women are seldom thought of con- 30 sequence enough to gain a place in your remembrance. [*Laying her hand on his, as by accident.*]
Barnwell: [*Aside.*] Her disorder is so great, she don't perceive she has laid her 35 hand on mine.—Heaven! how she trembles!—What can this mean!
Millwood: The interest I have in all that relates to you (the reason of which you shall know hereafter) excites my 40 curiosity; and, were I sure you would pardon my presumption, I should desire to know your real sentiments on a very particular affair.
Barnwell: Madam, you may com- 45 mand my poor thoughts on any subject; —I have none that I would conceal.
Millwood: You'll think me bold.
Barnwell: No, indeed.
Millwood: What then are your 50 thoughts of love?

Barnwell: If you mean the love of women, I have not thought of it [at] all. —My youth and circumstances make such thoughts improper in me yet. But 5 if you mean the general love we owe to mankind, I think no one has more of it in his temper than myself.—I don't know that person in the world whose happiness I don't wish, and wouldn't 10 promote, were it in my power.—In an especial manner I love my uncle, and my master, but above all my friend.
Millwood: You have a friend then whom you love?
Barnwell: As he does me, sincerely. 15
Millwood: He is, no doubt, often blessed with your company and conversation.—
Barnwell: We live in one house to- 20 gether, and both serve the same worthy merchant.
Millwood: Happy, happy youth!— Who e'er thou art, I envy thee, and so must all who see and know this youth. 25 What I have lost, by being formed a woman!—I hate my sex, myself.—Had I been a man, I might, perhaps, have been as happy in your friendship as he who now enjoys it: But as it is, 30 Oh!—
Barnwell: [*Aside.*] I never observed women before, or this is sure the most beautiful of her sex.—You seem disordered, madam! May I know the 35 cause?
Millwood: Do not ask me.—I can never speak it, whatever is the cause;— I wish for things impossible;—I would be a servant, bound to the same master 40 as you are, to live in one house with you.
Barnwell: [*Aside.*] How strange, and yet how kind, her words and actions are! —And the effect they have on me is as 45 strange.—I feel desires I never knew before;—I must be gone, while I have power to go. [*To Millwood.*]—Madam, I humbly take my leave.—
Millwood: You will not sure leave me 50 so soon!
Barnwell: Indeed I must.

Millwood: You cannot be so cruel!—I have prepared a poor supper, at which I promised myself your company.

Barnwell: I am sorry I must refuse the honor that you designed me;—but my duty to my master calls me hence.—I never yet neglected his service. He is so gentle and so good a master that should I wrong him, though he might forgive me, I never should forgive myself.

Millwood: Am I refused, by the first man, the second favor I ever stooped to ask?—Go then, thou proud, hard-hearted youth.—But know, you are the only man that could be found, who would let me sue twice for greater favors.

Barnwell: [*Aside.*] What shall I do!—How shall I go or stay!

Millwood: Yet do not, do not, leave me. I wish my sex's pride would meet your scorn; but when I look upon you, when I behold those eyes,—oh! spare my tongue, and let my blushes speak. This flood of tears to that will force their way, and declare—what woman's modesty should hide.

Barnwell: Oh, heavens! she loves me, worthless as I am; her looks, her words, her flowing tears confess it. And can I leave her then? Oh, never, never! Madam, dry up those tears. You shall command me always; I will stay here for ever, if you'd have me.

Lucy: [*Aside.*] So! she has wheedled him out of his virtue of obedience already and will strip him of all the rest one after another till she has left him as few as her ladyship or myself.

Millwood: Now you are kind, indeed; but I mean not to detain you always: I would have you shake off all slavish obedience to your master;—but you may serve him still.

Lucy: Serve him still!—Aye, or he'll have no opportunity of fingering his cash, and then he'll not serve your end, I'll be sworn.

Scene VI

[*Enter to them Blunt.*]

Blunt: Madam, supper's on the table.

Millwood: Come, sir, you'll excuse all defects. My thoughts were too much employed on my guest to observe the entertainment. [*Exeunt Millwood and Barnwell.*]

Scene VII

[*Manent Lucy and Blunt.*]

Blunt: What! is all this preparation, this elegant supper, variety of wines and music, for the entertainment of that young fellow!

Lucy: So it seems.

Blunt: What, is our mistress turned fool at last! She's in love with him, I suppose.

Lucy: I suppose not, but she designs to make him in love with her if she can.

Blunt: What will she get by that? He seems under age, and can't be supposed to have much money.

Lucy: But his master has; and that's the same thing, as she'll manage it.

Blunt: I don't like this fooling with a handsome young fellow; while she's endeavoring to ensnare him, she may be caught herself.

Lucy: Nay, were she like me, that would certainly be the consequence;—for, I confess, there is something in youth and innocence that moves me mightily.

Blunt: Yes, so does the smoothness and plumpness of a partridge move a mighty desire in the hawk to be the destruction of it.

Lucy: Why, birds are their prey, as men are ours; though, as you observed, we are sometimes caught ourselves. But that, I dare say, will never be the case with our mistress.

Blunt: I wish it may prove so; for you know we all depend upon her.

Should she trifle away her time with a young fellow that there's nothing to be got by, we must all starve.

Lucy: There's no danger of that, for I am sure she has no view in this affair but interest.

Blunt: Well, and what hopes are there of success in that?

Lucy: The most promising that can be.—'Tis true, the youth has his scruples; but she'll soon teach him to answer them, by stifling his conscience.—O, the lad is in a hopeful way, depend upon't. [*Exeunt.*]

[Scene VIII. Another room in Millwood's house.]

[*Discovered Barnwell and Millwood at an entertainment.*]

Barnwell: What can I answer! All that I know is, that you are fair and I am miserable.

Millwood: We are both so, and yet the fault is in ourselves.

Barnwell: To ease our present anguish, by plunging into guilt, is to buy a moment's pleasure with an age of pain.

Millwood: I should have thought the joys of love as lasting as they are great. If ours prove otherwise, 'tis your inconstancy must make them so.

Barnwell: The law of heaven will not be reversed; and that requires us to govern our passions.

Millwood: To give us sense of beauty 5 and desires, and yet forbid us to taste and be happy, is cruelty to nature. Have we passions only to torment us!

Barnwell: To hear you talk, tho' in the cause of vice, to gaze upon your 10 beauty, press your hand, and see your snow-white bosom heave and fall, enflames my wishes; my pulse beats high, my senses all are in a hurry, and I am on the rack of wild desire; yet for a 15 moment's guilty pleasure, shall I lose my innocence, my peace of mind, and hopes of solid happiness?

Millwood: Chimeras all,—
Come on with me and prove,
20 No joy's like woman, kind, nor heaven
like love.

Barnwell: I would not, yet I must on.
Reluctant thus, the merchant quits his
ease
25 And trusts to rocks and sands and
stormy seas;
In hopes some unknown golden coast to
find,
Commits himself, tho' doubtful, to the 30
wind,
Longs much for joys to come, yet mourns
those left behind. [*Exeunt.*]

QUESTIONS ON ACT I

1. What does Lillo appear to be doing in Scene I? Could the scene be omitted without loss?

2. Where does the exposition first get under way? Is it gracefully done?

3. Does Lillo inadvertently convict Thorowgood of snobbery?

4. In Scene ii, why does Lillo have Thorowgood say, "Thou know'st I have no heir, no child but thee, etc."? Is the speech convincing?

5. Note the abstract, generalized words and forms of expression used by Maria in her last two speeches in Scene ii. How do such words influence the effectiveness of what she says?

6. In Scene iii, would Lillo gain anything by having Barnwell mentioned earlier in the scene?

7. Is there any awkwardness in the way in which Lillo carries out his intentions in Scene iii?

8. Could you make a case for having the first part of the play deal with a

Barnwell who has already seen Millwood and is struggling with temptation? How might this reduce some of the difficulties faced in Scene v?

ACT II

[SCENE I. A room in Thorowgood's
house.]

[*Enter Barnwell.*]

Barnwell: How strange are all things
round me! Like some thief, who treads
forbidden ground, fearful I enter each
apartment of this well-known house. To
guilty love, as if that was too little, already have I added breach of trust. A
thief! Can I know myself that wretched
thing, and look my honest friend and injured master in the face? Though hypocrisy may a while conceal my guilt, at
length it will be known, and public
shame and ruin must ensue. In the
meantime, what must be my life? Ever
to speak a language foreign to my heart;
hourly to add to the number of my
crimes in order to conceal 'em. Sure,
such was the condition of the grand
apostate, when first he lost his purity;
like me disconsolate he wandered, and
while yet in Heaven, bore all his future
hell about him. [*Enter Trueman.*]

SCENE II

[*Barnwell and Trueman.*]

Trueman: Barnwell! O how I rejoice
to see you safe! So will our master and
his gentle daughter, who during your
absence often inquired after you.

Barnwell: [*Aside.*] Would he were
gone, his officious love will pry into the
secrets of my soul.

Trueman: Unless you knew the pain
the whole family has felt on your account, you can't conceive how much
you are beloved. But why thus cold and
silent? When my heart is full of joy for
your return, why do you turn away?
Why thus avoid me? What have I done?
How am I altered since you saw me

last? Or rather what have you done, and
why are you thus changed, for I am still
the same?

Barnwell: [*Aside.*] What have I done
indeed?

Trueman: Not speak nor look upon
me.

Barnwell: [*Aside.*] By my face he will
discover all I would conceal; methinks
already I begin to hate him.

Trueman: I cannot bear this usage
from a friend, one whom till now I ever
found so loving, whom yet I love,
though this unkindness strikes at the
root of friendship, and might destroy it
in any breast but mine.

Barnwell: I am not well. [*Turning to
him.*] Sleep has been a stranger to these
eyes since you beheld them last.

Trueman: Heavy they look indeed,
and swollen with tears; now they o'er-
flow; rightly did my sympathizing heart
forebode last night when thou wast absent something fatal to our peace.

Barnwell: Your friendship engages
you too far. My troubles, whate'er they
are, are mine alone; you have no interest
in them, nor ought your concern for me
give you a moment's pain.

Trueman: You speak as if you knew
of friendship nothing but the name. Before I saw your grief I felt it. Since we
parted last I have slept no more than
you, but, pensive in my chamber, sat
alone and spent the tedious night in
wishes for your safety and return; e'en
now, though ignorant of the cause, your
sorrow wounds me to the heart.

Barnwell: 'Twill not be always thus.
Friendship and all engagements cease, as
circumstances and occasions vary; and
since you once may hate me, perhaps it
might be better for us both that now
you loved me less.

Trueman: Sure I but dream! Without
a cause would Barnwell use me thus?
Ungenerous and ungrateful youth, fare-

well.—I shall endeavor to follow your advice,—[*Going.*] Yet stay, perhaps I am too rash, and angry when the cause demands compassion. Some unforeseen calamity may have befallen him, too great to bear.

Barnwell: [*Aside.*] What part am I reduced to act; 'tis vile and base to move his temper thus, the best of friends and men.

Trueman: I am to blame, prithee forgive me, Barnwell. Try to compose your ruffled mind, and let me know the cause that thus transports you from yourself, my friendly counsel may restore your peace.

Barnwell: All that is possible for man to do for man, your generous friendship may effect; but here even that's in vain.

Trueman: Something dreadful is laboring in your breast. O give it vent and let me share your grief! 'Twill ease your pain should it admit no cure and make it lighter by the part I bear.

Barnwell: Vain supposition! My woes increase by being observed; should the cause be known they would exceed all bounds.

Trueman: So well I know thy honest heart, guilt cannot harbor there.

Barnwell: [*Aside.*] O torture insupportable!

Trueman: Then why am I excluded? Have I a thought I would conceal from you?

Barnwell: If still you urge me on this hated subject, I'll never enter more beneath this roof, nor see your face again.

Trueman: 'Tis strange. But I have done; say but you hate me not.

Barnwell: Hate you!—I am not that monster yet.

Trueman: Shall our friendship still continue?

Barnwell: It's a blessing I never was worthy of, yet now must stand on terms; and upon conditions can confirm it.

Trueman: What are they?

Barnwell: Never hereafter, though you should wonder at my conduct, desire to know more than I am willing to reveal.

Trueman: 'Tis hard, but upon any conditions I must be your friend.

Barnwell: Then, as much as one lost to himself can be another's, I am yours. [*Embracing.*]

Trueman: Be ever so, and may Heaven restore your peace.

Barnwell: Will yesterday return? We have heard the glorious sun, that till then incessant rolled, once stopped his rapid course and once went back. The dead have risen; and parched rocks poured forth a liquid stream to quench a people's thirst. The sea divided and formed walls of water while a whole nation passed in safety through its sandy bosom. Hungry lions have refused their prey; and men unhurt have walked amidst consuming flames; but never yet did time once past, return.

Trueman: Though the continued chain of time has never once been broke, nor ever will, but uninterrupted must keep on its course till lost in eternity it ends there where it first begun; yet as Heaven can repair whatever evils time can bring upon us, he who trusts heaven ought never to despair. But business requires our attendance, business the youth's best preservative from ill, as idleness [is] his worst of snares. Will you go with me?

Barnwell: I'll take a little time to reflect on what has past, and follow you. [*Exit Trueman.*]

Scene III

Barnwell

Barnwell: I might have trusted Trueman to have applied to my uncle to have repaired the wrong I have done my master; but what of Millwood? Must I expose her too? Ungenerous and base! Then heaven requires it not. But heaven requires that I forsake her. What! Never see her more! Does heaven require that! I hope I may see her, and heaven not be offended. Presumptuous hope!

Dearly already have I proved my frailty; should I once more tempt heaven, I may be left to fall never to rise again. Yet shall I leave her, forever leave her, and not let her know the cause? She who loves me with such a boundless passion? Can cruelty be duty? I judge of what she then must feel, by what I now endure. The love of life and fear of shame, opposed by inclination strong as death or shame, like wind and tide in raging conflict met, when neither can prevail, keep me in doubt. How then can I determine? [*Enter Thorowgood.*]

Scene IV

[Thorowgood and Barnwell.]

Thorowgood: Without a cause assigned, or notice given, to absent yourself last night was a fault, young man, and I came to chide you for it, but hope I am prevented. That modest blush, the confusion so visible in your face, speak grief and shame. When we have offended heaven, it requires no more; and shall man, who needs himself to be forgiven, be harder to appease? If my pardon or love be of moment to your peace, look up, secure of both.

Barnwell: [*Aside.*] This goodness has o'ercome me.—O sir! You know not the nature and extent of my offence; and I should abuse your mistaken bounty to receive 'em. Though I had rather die than speak my shame; though racks could not have forced the guilty secret from my breast, your kindness has.

Thorowgood: Enough, enough! What-e'er it be, this concern shows you're convinced, and I am satisfied. How painful is the sense of guilt to an ingenuous mind!—some youthful folly, which it were prudent not to enquire into. When we consider the frail condition of humanity, it may raise our pity, not our wonder, that youth should go astray; when reason, weak at the best when opposed to inclination, scarce formed, and wholly unassisted by experience, faintly contends, or willingly becomes the slave of sense. The state of youth is much to be deplored, and the more so because they see it not; they being then to danger most exposed, when they are least prepared for their defence.

Barnwell: It will be known, and you recall your pardon and abhor me.

Thorowgood: I never will; so heaven confirm to me the pardon of my offences. Yet be upon your guard in this gay, thoughtless season of your life; now, when the sense of pleasure's quick, and passion high, the voluptuous appetites, raging and fierce, demand the strongest curb; take heed of a relapse. When vice becomes habitual, the very power of leaving it is lost.

Barnwell: Hear me, then, on my knees confess.

Thorowgood: I will not hear a syllable more upon this subject; it were not mercy, but cruelty, to hear what must give you such torment to reveal.

Barnwell: This generosity amazes and distracts me.

Thorowgood: This remorse makes thee dearer to me than if thou hadst never offended; whatever is your fault, of this I'm certain, 'twas harder for you to offend than me to pardon. [*Exit Thorowgood.*]

Scene V

[Barnwell.]

Barnwell: Villain, villain, villain! basely to wrong so excellent a man. Should I again return to folly?—detested thought!—But what of Millwood then? Why, I renounce her; I give her up; the struggle's over, and virtue has prevailed. Reason may convince, but gratitude compels. This unlooked for generosity has saved me from destruction. [*Going.*]

Scene VI

[To him a Footman.]

Footman: Sir, two ladies, from your uncle in the country, desire to see you.

Barnwell: [*Aside.*] Who should they be? Tell them I'll wait upon 'em.

Scene VII

[*Barnwell.*]

Barnwell: Methinks I dread to see 'em. Guilt, what a coward hast thou made me? Now everything alarms me. [*Exit.*]

Scene VIII

[Another room in Thorowgood's house.]

[*Discovered Millwood and Lucy, and to them enters a Footman.*]

Footman: Ladies, he'll wait upon you immediately.

Millwood: 'Tis very well. I thank you. [*Enter Barnwell.*]

Scene IX

[*Barnwell, Millwood, and Lucy.*]

Barnwell: Confusion! Millwood!

Millwood: That angry look tells me that here I'm an unwelcome guest; I feared as much,—the unhappy are so everywhere.

Barnwell: Will nothing but my utter ruin content you?

Millwood: Unkind and cruel! lost myself, your happiness is now my only care.

Barnwell: How did you gain admission?

Millwood: Saying we were desired by your uncle to visit and deliver a message to you, we were received by the family without suspicion, and with much respect directed here.

Barnwell: Why did you come at all?

Millwood: I never shall trouble you more; I'm come to take my leave forever. Such is the malice of my fate, I go hopeless, despairing ever to return. This hour is all I have left me. One short hour is all I have to bestow on love and you, for whom I thought the longest life too short.

Barnwell: Then we are met to part forever?

Millwood: It must be so; yet think not that time or absence ever shall put a period to my grief or make me love you less; though I must leave you, yet condemn me not.

Barnwell: Condemn you? No, I approve your resolution, and rejoice to hear it; 'tis just, 'tis necessary. I have well weighed, and found it so.

Lucy: [*Aside.*] I'm afraid the young man has more sense than she thought he had.

Barnwell: Before you came I had determined never to see you more.

Millwood: [*Aside.*] Confusion!

Lucy: [*Aside.*] Ay! we are all out; this is a turn so unexpected, that I shall make nothing of my part; they must e'en play the scene betwixt themselves.

Millwood: 'Twas some relief to think, though absent, you would love me still; but to find, though fortune had been kind, that you, more cruel and inconstant, had resolved to cast me off. This, as I never could expect, I have not learnt to bear.

Barnwell: I am sorry to hear you blame in me a resolution that so well becomes us both.

Millwood: I have reason for what I do, but you have none.

Barnwell: Can we want a reason for parting, who have so many to wish we never had met?

Millwood: Look on me, Barnwell; am I deformed or old, that satiety so soon succeeds enjoyment? Nay, look again; am I not she whom yesterday you thought the fairest and the kindest of her sex, whose hand, trembling with ecstasy, you pressed and molded thus, while on my eyes you gazed with such delight, as if desire increased by being fed?

Barnwell: No more! Let me repent my former follies, if possible, without remembering what they were.

Millwood: Why?

Barnwell: Such is my frailty that 'tis dangerous.

Millwood: Where is the danger, since we are to part?

Barnwell: The thought of that already is too painful.

Millwood: If it be painful to part, then I may hope at least you do not hate me?

Barnwell: No,—no,—I never said I did!—O my heart!

Millwood: Perhaps you pity me?

Barnwell: I do, I do, indeed, I do.

Millwood: You'll think upon me?

Barnwell: Doubt it not while I can think at all.

Millwood: You may judge an embrace at parting too great a favor, though it would be the last? [*He draws back.*] A look shall then suffice,—farewell forever. [*Exeunt Millwood and Lucy.*]

Scene X

[*Barnwell.*]

Barnwell: If to resolve to suffer be to conquer, I have conquered. Painful victory!

Scene XI

[*Barnwell; Millwood and Lucy who return.*]

Millwood: One thing I had forgot. I never must return to my own house again. This I thought proper to let you know, lest your mind should change, and you should seek in vain to find me there. Forgive me this second intrusion; I only came to give you this caution, and that, perhaps, was needless.

Barnwell: I hope it was, yet it is kind, and I must thank you for it.

Millwood: My friend, your arm. [*To Lucy.*] Now I am gone forever. [*Going.*]

Barnwell: One thing more;—sure, there's no danger in my knowing where you go? If you think otherwise—

Millwood: Alas! [*Weeping.*]

Lucy: [*Aside.*] We are right I find, that's my cue.—Ah; dear sir, she's going she knows not whither; but go she must.

Barnwell: Humanity obliges me to wish you well; why will you thus expose yourself to needless troubles?

Lucy: Nay, there's no help for it. She must quit the town immediately, and the kingdom as soon as possible; it was no small matter, you may be sure, that could make her resolve to leave you.

Millwood: No more, my friend; since he for whose dear sake alone I suffer, and am content to suffer, is kind and pities me. Where'er I wander through wilds and deserts, benighted and forlorn, that thought shall give me comfort.

Barnwell: For my sake! O tell me how; which way am I so cursed as to bring such ruin on thee?

Millwood: No matter, I am contented with my lot.

Barnwell: Leave me not in this incertainty.

Millwood: I have said too much.

Barnwell: How, how am I the cause of your undoing?

Millwood: 'Twill but increase your troubles.

Barnwell: My troubles can't be greater than they are.

Lucy: Well, well, sir, if she won't satisfy you, I will.

Barnwell: I am bound to you beyond expression.

Millwood: Remember, sir, that I desired you not to hear it.

Barnwell: Begin, and ease my racking expectation.

Lucy: Why you must know, my lady here was an only child; but her parents dying while she was young, left her and her fortune, (no inconsiderable one, I assure you) to the care of a gentleman who has a good estate of his own.

Millwood: Ay, ay, the barbarous man is rich enough;—but what are riches when compared to love?

Lucy: For a while he performed the office of a faithful guardian, settled her in a house, hired her servants;—but you have seen in what manner she lived, so I need say no more of that.

Millwood: How I shall live hereafter, heaven knows.

Lucy: All things went on as one could wish, till, some time ago, his wife dying, he fell violently in love with his charge, and would fain have married her. Now the man is neither old nor ugly, but a good, personable sort of a man, but I don't know how it was, she could never endure him, that he brought in an account of his executorship, wherein he makes her debtor to him.—

Millwood: A trifle in itself, but more than enough to ruin me, whom, by this unjust account, he had stripped of all before.

Lucy: Now she having neither money nor friend, except me, who am as unfortunate as herself, he compelled her to pass his account, and give bond for the sum he demanded; but still provided handsomely for her and continued his courtship, till, being informed by his spies (truly I suspect some in her own family) that you were entertained at her house, and stayed with her all night, he came this morning raving, and storming like a madman, talks no more of marriage (so there's no hopes of making up matters that way) but vows her ruin, unless she'll allow him the same favor that he supposes she granted you.

Barnwell: Must she be ruined, or find her refuge in another's arms?

Millwood: He gave me but an hour to resolve in, that's happily spent with you;—and now I go.—

Barnwell: To be exposed to all the rigors of the various seasons; the summer's parching heat, and winter's cold; unhoused to wander friendless through the unhospitable world, in misery and want; attended with fear and danger, and pursued by malice and revenge, wouldst thou endure all this for me, and can I do nothing, nothing to prevent it?

Lucy: 'Tis really a pity, there can be no way found out.

Barnwell: O where are all my resolutions now? Like early vapors, or the morning dew, chased by the sun's warm beams they're vanished and lost, as though they had never been.

Lucy: Now I advised her, sir, to comply with the gentleman, that would not only put an end to her troubles, but make her fortune at once.

Barnwell: Tormenting fiend, away!— I had rather perish, nay, see her perish, than have her saved by him; I will myself prevent her ruin, though with my own. A moment's patience, I'll return immediately.—[*Exit.*]

SCENE XII

[*Millwood and Lucy.*]

Lucy: 'Twas well you came, or, by what I can perceive, you had lost him.

Millwood: That, I must confess, was a danger I did not foresee; I was only afraid he should have come without money. You know a house of entertainment like mine, is not kept with nothing.

Lucy: That's very true; but then you should be reasonable in your demands; 'tis pity to discourage a young man. [*Enter Barnwell.*]

SCENE XIII

[*Barnwell, Millwood, and Lucy.*]

Barnwell: [*Aside.*] What am I about to do! Now you, who boast your reason all sufficient, suppose yourselves in my condition, and determine for me, whether it's right to let her suffer for my faults, or, by this small addition to my guilt, prevent the ill effects of what is past.

Lucy: [*Aside.*] These young sinners think everything in the ways of wickedness so strange,—but I could tell him that this is nothing but what's very common; for one vice as naturally begets another, as a father a son. But he'll find out that himself, if he lives long enough.

Barnwell: Here take this, and with it purchase your deliverance; return to your house, and live in peace and safety.

Millwood: So I may hope to see you there again.

Barnwell: Answer me not,—but fly,—

lest, in the agonies of my remorse, I take again what is not mine to give, and abandon thee to want and misery.

Millwood: Say but you'll come.—

Barnwell: You are my fate, my heaven, or my hell. Only leave me now, dispose of me hereafter as you please. [*Exeunt Millwood and Lucy.*]

Scene XIV

[*Barnwell.*]

What have I done? Were my resolutions founded on reason, and sincerely made? why then has heaven suffered me 15 to fall? I sought not the occasion; and, if my heart deceives me not, compassion and generosity were my motives. Is virtue inconsistent with itself, or are vice and virtue only empty names? Or do they depend on accidents beyond our 5 power to produce, or to prevent, wherein we have no part, and yet must be determined by the event?—But why should I attempt to reason? All is confusion, horror, and remorse;—I find I 10 am lost, cast down from all my late erected hopes and plunged again in guilt, yet scarce know how or why—

Such undistinguished horrors make my brain,
Like hell, the seat of darkness, and of pain. [*Exit.*]

QUESTIONS ON ACT II

1. Note Thorowgood's last speech in Scene iv. Why does it make for a sentimental effect?

2. What effect is produced by the method which Lucy and Millwood use in Scene xi to win back Barnwell?

3. Study Barnwell's next-to-last speech in Scene ii. How successful is Lillo in conveying Barnwell's feelings? Is the method right?

4. In Thorowgood's first speech in Scene iv, what is the matter with his use of the phrase, "When we have offended Heaven"? With his heavy use, in later speeches, of such abstract nouns as *folly, reason, pleasure*, etc.?

5. Do Barnwell's soliloquies in Scenes i, iii, and xiv accomplish what the author intends? Why?

6. What does Lillo intend to indicate by the near-quarrel in Scene ii? Is the embrace the proper outcome for this scene? How can we account for the author's using such an ending?

7. In this act we see the extremes to which an old style of breaking up the act was carried: with each change of persons on the stage, a new scene is indicated. What is the objection to this method of division?

ACT III

Scene I

[*Enter Thorowgood and Trueman.*]

Thorowgood: Methinks I would not have you only learn the method of merchandize and practise it hereafter merely as a means of getting wealth. 'Twill be well worth your pains to study it as a science. See how it is founded in reason and the nature of things. How it has promoted humanity, as it has opened and yet keeps up an intercourse between nations far remote from one another in 5 situation, customs, and religion; promoting arts, industry, peace and plenty by mutual benefits diffusing mutual love from pole to pole.

Trueman: Something of this I have 10 considered, and hope, by your assistance, to extend my thoughts much farther. I have observed those countries where trade is promoted and encouraged do not make discoveries to destroy, but to improve mankind by love and friendship, to tame the fierce, and polish the most savage, to teach them the advantages of honest traffic by taking from them with their own consent their useless superfluities, and giving them in return what, from their ignorance in manual arts, their situation, or some other accident they stand in need of.

Thorowgood: 'Tis justly observed. The populous east, luxuriant, abounds with glittering gems, bright pearls, aromatic spices, and health-restoring drugs. The late found western world glows with unnumbered veins of gold and silver ore. On every climate, and on every country, heaven has bestowed some good peculiar to itself. It is the industrious merchant's business to collect the various blessings of each soil and climate, and, with the product of the whole, to enrich his native country.

Well! I have examined your accounts. They are not only just, as I have always found them, but regularly kept, and fairly entered. I commend your diligence. Method in business is the surest guide. He who neglects it frequently stumbles, and always wanders perplexed, uncertain, and in danger. Are Barnwell's accounts ready for my inspection? He does not use to be the last on these occasions.

Trueman: Upon receiving your orders he retired, I thought in some confusion. If you please, I'll go and hasten him. I hope he hasn't been guilty of any neglect.

Thorowgood: I'm now going to the Exchange; let him know, at my return, I expect to find him ready. [*Exeunt.*]

Scene II

[*Enter Maria with a book; she sits and reads.*]

Maria: How forcible is truth! The weakest mind, inspired with love of that, fixed and collected in itself, with indifference beholds the united force of earth and hell opposing. Such souls are raised above the sense of pain, or so supported that they regard it not. The martyr cheaply purchases his heaven. Small are his sufferings, great is his reward; not so the wretch who combats love with duty, when the mind, weakened and dissolved by the soft passion, feeble and hopeless opposes its own desire. What is an hour, a day, a year of pain, to a whole life of tortures, such as these? [*Enter Trueman.*]

Scene III

[*Trueman and Maria.*]

Trueman: O, Barnwell! O, my friend, how art thou fallen!

Maria: Ha! Barnwell! What of him? Speak, say what of Barnwell?

Trueman: 'Tis not to be concealed. I've news to tell of him that will afflict your generous father, yourself, and all who knew him.

Maria: Defend us, Heaven!

Trueman: I cannot speak it.—See there [*Gives a letter, Maria reads.*]

Maria:

Trueman,

I know my absence will surprise my honored master, and yourself; and the more, when you shall understand that the reason of my withdrawing, is my having embezzled part of the cash with which I was entrusted. After this, 'tis needless to inform you that I intend never to return again. Though this might have been known by examining my accounts; yet, to prevent that unnecessary trouble, and to cut all fruitless expectations of my return, I have left this from the lost

George Barnwell.

Trueman: Lost indeed! Yet how he should be guilty of what he there charges himself withal, raises my wonder equal to my grief. Never had youth a higher sense of virtue. Justly he thought, and as he thought he practised; never was

life more regular than his; an understanding uncommon at his years; an
open, generous, manliness of temper; his
manners easy, unaffected and engaging.

Maria: This and much more you
might have said with truth.—He was
the delight of every eye, and joy of
every heart that knew him.

Trueman: Since such he was, and was
my friend, can I support his loss? See,
the fairest and happiest maid this
wealthy city boasts, kindly condescends
to weep for thy unhappy fate, poor,
ruined Barnwell!

Maria: Trueman, do you think a soul
so delicate as his, so sensible of shame,
can e'er submit to live a slave to vice?

Trueman: Never, never! So well I
know him, I'm sure this act of his, so
contrary to his nature, must have been
caused by some unavoidable necessity.

Maria: Is there no means yet to preserve him?

Trueman: O! that there were!—But
few men recover reputation lost, a merchant never. Nor would he, I fear,
though I should find him, ever be
brought to look his injured master in
the face.

Maria: I fear as much,—and therefore would never have my father know it.

Trueman: That's impossible.

Maria: What's the sum?

Trueman: 'Tis considerable.—I've
marked it here, to show it, with the
letter, to your father, at his return.

Maria: If I should supply the money,
could you so dispose of that, and the
account, as to conceal this unhappy
mismanagement from my father?

Trueman: Nothing more easy.—But
can you intend it? Will you save a helpless wretch from ruin? Oh! 'twere an act
worthy such exalted virtue as Maria's.
—Sure, heaven in mercy to my friend
inspired the generous thought!

Maria: Doubt not but I would purchase so great a happiness at a much
dearer price.—But how shall he be
found?

Trueman: Trust to my diligence for

that.—In the meantime, I'll conceal his
absence from your father, or find such
excuses for it, that the real cause shall
never be suspected.

Maria: In attempting to save from
shame, one whom we hope may yet return to virtue, to heaven and you, the
judges of this action, I appeal, whether
I have done anything misbecoming my
sex and character.

Trueman: Earth must approve the
deed, and heaven, I doubt not, will reward it.

Maria: If heaven succeed it, I am
well rewarded. A virgin's fame is sullied
by suspicion's slightest breath; and
therefore as this must be a secret from
my father and the world for Barnwell's
sake; for mine, let it be so to him.

Scene IV

[Millwood's house.]

[*Discovered Lucy and Blunt.*]

Lucy: Well! what do you think of
Millwood's conduct now?

Blunt: I own it is surprising. I don't
know which to admire most, her feigned,
or his real passion, though I have sometimes been afraid that her avarice would
discover her:—But his youth and want
of experience make it the easier to impose on him.

Lucy: No, it is his love. To do him
justice, notwithstanding his youth, he
don't want understanding; but you men
are much easier imposed on in these
affairs than your vanity will allow you
to believe. Let me see the wisest of you
all as much in love with me as Barnwell
is with Millwood, and I'll engage to
make as great a fool of him.

Blunt: And all circumstances considered, to make as much money of
him, too.

Lucy: I can't answer for that. Her
artifice in making him rob his master at
first, and the various stratagems, by
which she has obliged him to continue in
that course, astonish even me, who
know her so well.

Blunt: But then you are to consider that the money was his master's.

Lucy: There was the difficulty of it. Had it been his own, it had been nothing. Were the world his, she might have it for a smile. But these golden days are done; he's ruined, and Millwood's hopes of farther profits there are at an end.

Blunt: That's no more than we all expected.

Lucy: Being called by his master to make up his accounts, he was forced to quit his house and service, and wisely flies to Millwood for relief and entertainment.

Blunt: I have not heard of this before! How did she receive him?

Lucy: As you would expect. She wondered what he meant, was astonished at his impudence, and, with an air of modesty peculiar to herself swore so heartily that she never saw him before that she put me out of countenance.

Blunt: That's much indeed! But how did Barnwell behave?

Lucy: He grieved, and at length, enraged at this barbarous treatment, was preparing to be gone; and, making toward the door, showed a bag of money, which he had stolen from his master,— the last he's ever like to have from thence.

Blunt: But then Millwood?

Lucy: Aye, she, with her usual address, returned to her old arts of lying, swearing, and dissembling. Hung on his neck, and wept, and swore 'twas meant in jest, till the easy fool, melted into tears, threw the money into her lap, and swore he had rather die than think her false.

Blunt: Strange infatuation!

Lucy: But what followed was stranger still. As doubts and fears followed by reconcilement ever increase love where the passion is sincere, so in him it caused so wild a transport of excessive fondness, such joy, such grief, such pleasure, and such anguish, that nature in him seemed sinking with the weight, and the charmed soul disposed to quit his breast for hers.—Just then, when every passion with lawless anarchy prevailed, and reason was in the raging tempest lost, the cruel, artful Millwood prevailed upon the wretched youth to promise what I tremble but to think on.

Blunt: I am amazed! What can it be?

Lucy: You will be more so to hear it is to attempt the life of his nearest relation, and best benefactor.

Blunt: His uncle, whom we have often heard him speak of as a gentleman of a large estate and fair character in the country where he lives?

Lucy: The same. She was no sooner possessed of the last dear purchase of his ruin, but her avarice, insatiate as the grave, demands this horrid sacrifice, Barnwell's near relation; and unsuspected virtue must give too easy means to seize the good man's treasure, whose blood must seal the dreadful secret, and prevent the terrors of her guilty fears.

Blunt: Is it possible she could persuade him to do an act like that! He is, by nature, honest, grateful, compassionate, and generous. And though his love and her artful persuasions have wrought him to practise what he most abhors; yet we all can witness for him with what reluctance he has still complied! So many tears he shed o'er each offence, as might, if possible, sanctify theft, and make a merit of a crime.

Lucy: 'Tis true, at the naming the murder of his uncle, he started into rage; and, breaking from her arms, where she till then had held him with well dissembled love and false endearments, called her cruel monster, devil; and told her she was born for his destruction. She thought it not for her purpose to meet his rage with rage, but affected a most passionate fit of grief, railed at her fate, and cursed her wayward stars, that still her wants should force her to press him to act such deeds as she must needs abhor as well as he; but told him necessity had no law and love no bounds; that therefore he never truly loved, but meant in her necessity to forsake her. Then kneeled and swore, that since by his refusal he had given her cause to doubt his love, she never would see him more, unless, to prove it true, he robbed his uncle to supply her wants and murdered him to keep it from discovery.

Blunt: I am astonished! What said he?

Lucy: Speechless he stood; but in his face you might have read that various passions tore his very soul. Oft he in anguish threw his eyes towards heaven, and then as often bent their beams on her; then wept and groaned and beat his breast; at length, with horror not to be expressed, he cried, "Thou cursed fair! have I not given dreadful proofs of love? What drew me from my youthful innocence to stain my then unspotted soul but love? What caused me to rob my gentle master but cursed love? What makes me now a fugitive from his service, loathed by myself, and scorned by all the world, but love? What fills my eyes with tears, my soul with torture, never felt on this side death before? Why love, love, love! And why, above all, do I resolve (for, tearing his hair, he cried, I do resolve!) to kill my uncle?"

Blunt: Was she not moved? It makes me weep to hear the sad relation.

Lucy: Yes, with joy that she had gained her point. She gave him no time to cool, but urged him to attempt it instantly. He's now gone; if he performs it and escapes, there's more money for her; if not, he'll ne'er return, and then she's fairly rid of him.

Blunt: 'Tis time the world was rid of such a monster.—

Lucy: If we don't do our endeavors to prevent this murder, we are as bad as she.

Blunt: I'm afraid it is too late.

Lucy: Perhaps not. Her barbarity to Barnwell makes me hate her. We've run too great a length with her already. I did not think her or myself so wicked, as I find upon reflection we are.

Blunt: 'Tis true, we have all been too much so. But there is something so horrid in murder that all other crimes seem nothing when compared to that. I

would not be involved in the guilt of that for all the world.

Lucy: Nor I, heaven knows; therefore let us clear ourselves by doing all that is in our power to prevent it. I have just thought of a way that, to me, seems probable. Will you join with me to detect this cursed design?

Blunt: With all my heart. How else shall I clear myself? He who knows of a murder intended to be committed and does not discover it in the eye of the law and reason is a murderer.

Lucy: Let us lose no time; I'll acquaint you with the particulars as we go.

Scene V

[A walk at some distance from a county seat.]

[Enter Barnwell.]

Barnwell: A dismal gloom obscures the face of day; either the sun has slipped behind a cloud, or journeys down the west of heaven with more than common speed to avoid the sight of what I'm doomed to act. Since I set forth on this accursed design, where'er I tread, methinks, the solid earth trembles beneath my feet. Yonder limpid stream, whose hoary fall has made a natural cascade, as I passed by, in doleful accents seemed to murmur, "Murder." The earth, the air, the water, seem concerned; but that's not strange, the world is punished, and nature feels the shock when Providence permits a good man's fall! Just heaven! Then what should I be! for him that was my father's only brother, and since his death has been to me a father, who took me up an infant, and an orphan, reared me with tenderest care, and still indulged me with most paternal fondness; yet here I stand avowed his destined murderer!—I stiffen with horror at my own impiety; 'tis yet unperformed. What if I quit my bloody purpose and fly the place! [*Going, then stops.*]—But whither, O whither, shall I fly! My master's once friendly doors are ever shut against me; and without money Millwood will never see me more, and life is not to be endured without her! She's got such firm possession of my heart, and governs there with such despotic sway! Aye, there's the cause of all my sin and sorrow. 'Tis more than love; 'tis the fever of the soul and madness of desire. In vain does nature, reason, conscience, all oppose it; the impetuous passion bears down all before it, and drives me on to lust, to theft, and murder.—Oh conscience! feeble guide to virtue, who only shows us when we go astray, but wants the power to stop us in our course.—Ha! in yonder shady walk I see my uncle. He's alone. Now for my disguise. [*Plucks out a visor.*] This is his hour of private meditation. Thus daily he prepares his soul for heaven, whilst I— but what have I to do with heaven!—Ha! No struggles, Conscience.—

Hence! Hence remorse, and ev'ry
    thought that's good;
The storm that lust began must end in
    blood.
    [*Puts on the visor, and draws a pistol.*]

SCENE VI

[*A close walk in a wood.*]

[*Enter Uncle.*]

Uncle: If I was superstitious, I should fear some danger lurked unseen, or death were nigh. A heavy melancholy clouds my spirits; my imagination is filled with gashly [1] forms of dreary graves, and bodies changed by death, when the pale lengthened visage attracts each weeping eye, and fills the musing soul at once with grief and horror, pity and aversion. I will indulge the thought. The wise man prepares himself for death by making it familiar to his mind. When strong reflections hold the mirror near, and the living in the dead behold their future selves, how does each inordinate

[1] Ghastly.

passion and desire cease or sicken at the view! The mind scarce moves; the blood, curdling and chilled, creeps slowly through the veins, fixed, still, and motionless, like the solemn object of our thoughts. We are almost at present what we must be hereafter, till curiosity awakes the soul, and sets it on inquiry.—

SCENE VII

[*Uncle; enter George Barnwell at a distance.*]

Uncle: O death, thou strange mysterious power, seen every day, yet never understood but by the incommunicative dead, what art thou? The extensive mind of man, that with a thought circles the earth's vast globe, sinks to the center, or ascends above the stars; that worlds exotic finds, or thinks it finds, thy thick clouds attempts to pass in vain; lost and bewildered in the horrid gloom, defeated she returns more doubtful than before; of nothing certain, but of labor lost. [*During this speech, Barnwell sometimes presents the pistol, and draws it back again; at last he drops it,— at which his uncle starts, and draws his sword.*]

Barnwell. Oh, 'tis impossible!

Uncle: A man so near me, armed and masked!

Barnwell: Nay, then there's no retreat. [*Plucks a poinard from his bosom, and stabs him.*]

Uncle: Oh! I am slain! All gracious heaven, regard the prayer of thy dying servant! Bless with thy choicest blessings my dearest nephew, forgive my murderer, and take my fleeting soul to endless mercy. [*Barnwell throws off his mask, runs to him, and, kneeling by him, raises and chafes him.*]

Barnwell: Expiring saint! Oh, murdered, martyred uncle! Lift up your dying eyes, and view your nephew in your murderer. O do not look so tenderly upon me! Let indignation lighten from your eyes, and blast me ere you die. By heaven, he weeps in pity of my

woes. Tears, tears, for blood! The murdered, in the agonies of death, weeps for
his murderer! O, speak your pious purpose, pronounce my pardon then, and
take me with you!—He would, but
cannot. O why, with such fond affection
do you press my murdering hand!—
What! will you kiss me! [*Kisses him.*—
Uncle groans and dies.] He's gone forever, and oh! I follow.—[*Swoons away
upon his uncle's dead body.*] Do I still
live to press the suffering bosom of the
earth? Do I still breathe, and taint with
my infectious breath the wholesome air?
Let heaven, from its high throne, in
justice or in mercy, now look down on
that dear murdered saint, and me the
murderer. And, if his vengeance spares,
let pity strike and end my wretched
being.—Murder the worst of crimes,
and parricide the worst of murders, and
this the worst of parricides! Cain, who

stands on record from the birth of time,
and must to its last final period, as accursed, slew a brother favored above
him. Detested Nero, by another's hand,
dispatched a mother, that he feared and
hated. But I, with my own hand, have
murdered a brother, mother, father, and
a friend; most loving and beloved. This
execrable act of mine's without a parallel.—O may it ever stand alone!—the
last of murders, as it is the worst.—

The rich man thus, in torment and de-
   spair,
Preferred his vain, but charitable prayer.
The fool, his own soul lost, would fain
   be wise
For others' good; but heaven his suit
   denies.
By laws and means well known we stand
   or fall,
And one eternal rule remains for all.

QUESTIONS ON ACT III

1. Would there be any advantage, from the point of view of play construction, of having Barnwell murder Thorowgood, whom the reader
knows, instead of an unknown uncle? Would this justify giving the victim
the amount of space the uncle has in Scenes vi and vii?

2. Is the Lucy-Blunt dialogue in Scene iv a piece of subtle and well-
managed exposition?

3. What is the effect of Blunt's last speech in Scene iv? Does such a plan
of action make for tragic or melodramatic effects?

4. In Scene v, what is the effect of Barnwell's speaking of himself in
such terms as "doomed" to commit murder? Of his deciding to go on with
the murder because he has nowhere to go?

5. Compare Barnwell's dropping the gun in Scene vii with Lady Windermere's dropping the fan in Act II of Wilde's play. Which is more dramatically effective? Why?

6. How relevant is Scene i?

7. Does Scene iv suggest to you any dramatic possibilities that Lillo
missed?

8. Is there any motivation for Millwood's demanding the "horrid
sacrifice" that we learn about in Scene iv?

ACT IV

Scene I

[Thorowgood's house.]

[*Enter Maria.*]

Maria: How falsely do they judge who censure or applaud, as we're afflicted or rewarded here! I know I am unhappy, yet cannot charge myself with any crime more than the common frailties of our kind that should provoke just heaven to mark me out for sufferings so uncommon and severe. Falsely to accuse ourselves, heaven must abhor; then it is just and right that innocence should suffer, for heaven must be just in all its ways. Perhaps by that they are kept from moral evils, much worse than penal, or more improved in virtue; or may not the lesser ills that they sustain, be the means of greater good to others? Might all the joyless days and sleepless nights that I have passed, but purchase peace for thee—
Thou dear, dear cause of all my grief and pain,
Small were the loss, and infinite the gain:
Tho' to the grave in secret love I pine,
So life, and fame, and happiness were
      thine.   [*Enter Trueman.*]

Scene II

[*Trueman and Maria.*]

Maria: What news of Barnwell?

Trueman: None.—I have sought him with the greatest diligence, but all in vain.

Maria: Doth my father yet suspect the cause of his absenting himself?

Trueman: All appeared so just and fair to him, it is not possible he ever should; but his absence will no longer be concealed. Your father's wise; and though he seems to hearken to the friendly excuses, I would make for Barnwell, yet, I am afraid, he regards 'em only as such, without suffering them to influence his judgment.

Maria: How does the unhappy youth defeat all our designs to serve him! Yet I can never repent what we have done. Should he return, 'twill make his reconciliation with my father easier, and preserve him from future reproach from a malicious, unforgiving world.

Scene III

[*Enter to them Thorowgood and Lucy.*]

Thorowgood: This woman here has given me a sad, (and bating some circumstances) too probable account of Barnwell's defection.

Lucy: I am sorry, sir, that my frank confession of my former unhappy course of life should cause you to suspect my truth on this occasion.

Thorowgood: It is not that; your confession has in it all the appearance of truth. [*To them.*] Among many other particulars, she informs me that Barnwell had been influenced to break his trust, and wrong me, at several times, of considerable sums of money; now, as I know this to be false, I would fain doubt the whole of her relation, too dreadful to be willingly believed.

Maria: Sir, your pardon; I find myself on a sudden so indisposed, that I must retire.—[*Aside.*] Providence opposes all attempts to save him.—Poor ruined Barnwell!—Wretched lost Maria!— [*Exit Maria.*]

Scene IV

[*Thorowgood, Trueman and Lucy.*]

Thorowgood: How am I distressed on every side! Pity for that unhappy youth, fear for the life of a much valued friend —and then my child—the only joy and hope of my declining life. Her melancholy increases hourly and gives me painful apprehensions of her loss.—O Trueman! this person informs me, that your friend, at the instigation of an impious woman, is gone to rob and murder his venerable uncle.

Trueman: O execrable deed! I am blasted with the horror of the thought.

Lucy: This delay may ruin all.

Thorowgood: What to do or think I know not; that he ever wronged me, I 5 know is false; the rest may be so too, there's all my hope.

Trueman: Trust not to that, rather suppose all true than lose a moment's time; even now the horrid deed may be 10 a-doing—dreadful imagination! or it may be done, and we are vainly debating on the means to prevent what is already past.

Thorowgood: [*Aside.*] This earnest- 15 ness convinces me that he knows more than he has yet discovered. What ho! Without there! who waits?

Scene V   20

[*Enter to them a Servant.*]

Thorowgood: Order the groom to saddle the swiftest horse, and prepare himself to set out with speed. An affair of 25 life and death demands his diligence. [*Exit Servant.*]

Scene VI

[*Thorowgood, Trueman and Lucy.*]

Thorowgood: For you, whose behavior on this occasion I have no time to commend as it deserves, I must engage your farther assistance.—Return and observe 35 this Millwood till I come. I have your directions, and will follow you as soon as possible. [*Exit Lucy.*]

Scene VII

[*Thorowgood and Trueman.*]

Thorowgood: Trueman, you, I am sure, would not be idle on this occasion. [*Exit Thorowgood.*]

Scene VIII

[*Trueman.*]

Trueman: He only who is a friend can 50 judge of my distress. [*Exit.*]

Scene IX

[Millwood's house.]

[*Enter Millwood.*]

Millwood: I wish I knew the event of his design; the attempt without success would ruin him. Well! what have I to apprehend from that? I fear too much. The mischief being only intended, his friends, in pity of his youth, turn all their rage on me. I should have thought of that before. Suppose the deed done; then, and then only, I shall be secure; or what if he returns without attempting it at all?

Scene X

[*Millwood, and Barnwell bloody.*]

Millwood: But he is here, and I have done him wrong; his bloody hands show he has done the deed, but show he wants the prudence to conceal it.

Barnwell: Where shall I hide me? Whither shall I fly to avoid the swift unerring hand of justice?

Millwood: Dismiss those fears; though thousands had pursued you to the door, yet being entered here, you are safe as innocence; I have such a cavern, by art so cunningly contrived, that the piercing eyes of jealousy and revenge may search in vain, nor find the entrance to the safe retreat. There will I hide you if any danger's near.

Barnwell: O hide me from myself if it be possible, for while I bear my conscience in my bosom, tho' I were hid where man's eye never saw, nor light e'er dawned, 'twere all in vain. For that inmate, that impartial judge, will try, convict, and sentence me for murder; and execute me with never-ending torments. Behold these hands all crimsoned o'er with my dear uncle's blood! Here's a sight to make a statue start with horror or turn a living man into a statue.

Millwood: Ridiculous! Then it seems you are afraid of your own shadow; or what's less than a shadow, your conscience.

Barnwell: Though to man unknown I did the accursed act, what can we hide from heaven's omniscient eye?

Millwood: No more of this stuff; what advantage have you made of his death, or what advantage may yet be made of it? Did you secure the keys of his treasure? Those no doubt were about him? What gold, what jewels, or what else of value have you brought me?

Barnwell: Think you I added sacrilege to murder? Oh! had you seen him as his life flowed from him in a crimson flood, and heard him praying for me by the double name of nephew and of murderer; alas, alas! he knew not then that his nephew was his murderer; how would you have wished as I did, tho' you had a thousand years of life to come, to have given them all to have lengthened his one hour. But being dead, I fled the sight of what my hands had done, nor could I, to have gained the empire of the world, have violated by theft his sacred corpse.

Millwood: Whining preposterous canting villain! to murder your uncle, rob him of life, nature's first, last, dear prerogative, after which there's no injury—then fear to take what he no longer wanted! and bring to me your penury and guilt. Do you think I'll hazard my reputation, nay my life, to entertain you?

Barnwell: Oh!—Millwood!—This from thee?—But I have done, if you hate me, if you wish me dead; then are you happy,—for oh! 'tis sure my grief will quickly end me.

Millwood: [*Aside.*] In his madness he will discover all, and involve me in his ruin; we are on a precipice from whence there's no retreat for both.—Then to preserve myself—[*Pauses.*] There is no other way;—'tis dreadful, but reflection comes too late when danger's pressing, and there's no room for choice. It must be done. [*Stamps.*]

SCENE XI

[*Enter to them a Servant.*]

Millwood: Fetch me an officer and seize this villain; he has confessed himself a murderer. Should I let him escape, I justly might be thought as bad as he. [*Exit Servant.*]

SCENE XII

[*Millwood and Barnwell.*]

Barnwell: O Millwood! sure thou dost not, cannot mean it. Stop the messenger, upon my knees I beg you, call him back. 'Tis fit I die indeed, but not by you. I will this instant deliver myself into the hands of justice; indeed I will, for death is all I wish. But thy ingratitude so tears my wounded soul, 'tis worse ten thousand times than death with torture!

Millwood: Call it what you will, I am willing to live; and live secure; which nothing but your death can warrant.

Barnwell: If there be a pitch of wickedness that seats the author beyond the reach of vengeance, you must be secure. But what remains for me but a dismal dungeon, hard-galling fetters, an awful trial, and ignominious death, justly to fall unpitied and abhorred?—After death to be suspended between heaven and earth, a dreadful spectacle, the warning and horror of a gaping crowd. This I could bear, nay wish not to avoid, had it but come from any hand but thine.—[*Enter Blunt, Officer and Attendants.*]

SCENE XIII

[*Millwood, Barnwell, Blunt, Officer and Attendants.*]

Millwood: Heaven defend me! Conceal a murderer! Here, sir, take this youth into your custody; I accuse him of murder and will appear to make good my charge. [*They seize him.*]

Barnwell: To whom, of what, or how shall I complain? I'll not accuse her; the

hand of heaven is in it, and this, the
punishment of lust and parricide! Yet
heaven, that justly cuts me off, still
suffers her to live, perhaps to punish
others. Tremendous mercy! So friends 5
are cursed with immortality to be the
executioners of heaven—
Be warned, ye youths, who see my sad
    despair,
Avoid lewd women, false as they are fair; 10
By reason guided, honest joys pursue;
The fair, to honor, and to virtue true,
Just to herself, will ne'er be false to
    you.
By my example learn to shun my fate, 15
(How wretched is the man who's wise
    too late!)
Ere innocence, and fame, and life be lost,
Here purchase wisdom cheaply, at my
    cost.   [*Exeunt.*] 20

Scene XIV

[*Manent Millwood and Blunt.*]

Millwood: Where's Lucy? Why is she 25
absent at such a time?
Blunt: Would I had been so too, thou
devil!
Millwood: Insolent! This to me?
Blunt: The worst that we know of the 30
devil is, that he first seduces to sin, and
then betrays to punishment. [*Exit
Blunt.*]

Scene XV

[*Millwood.*]

Millwood: They disapprove of my
conduct, and mean to take this opportunity to set up for themselves. My ruin
is resolved; I see my danger, but scorn 40
both it and them. I was not born to fall
by such weak instruments. [*Enter Thorowgood.*]

Scene XVI

[*Thorowgood and Millwood.*]

Thorowgood: Where is the scandal of 45
her own sex, and curse of ours?
Millwood: What means this insolence?
Who do you seek?
Thorowgood: Millwood.

Millwood: Well, you have found her
then. I am Millwood.
Thorowgood: Then you are the most
impious wretch that e'er the sun beheld.
Millwood: From your appearance I
should have expected wisdom and moderation, but your manners belie your
aspect. What is your business here? I
know you not.
Thorowgood: Hereafter you may know
me better; I am Barnwell's master.
Millwood: Then you are master to a
villain, which, I think, is not much to
your credit.
Thorowgood: Had he been as much
above thy arts as my credit is superior
to thy malice, I need not blush to own
him.
Millwood: My arts? I don't understand you, sir! If he has done amiss, 20
what's that to me? Was he my servant,
or yours? You should have taught him
better.
Thorowgood: Why should I wonder to
find such uncommon impudence in one 25
arrived to such a height of wickedness!
When innocence is banished, modesty
soon follows. Know, sorceress, I'm not
ignorant of any of your arts by which
you first deceived the unwary youth. I 30
know how, step by step, you've led him
on, reluctant and unwilling, from crime
to crime to this last horrid act which you
contrived and by your cursed wiles even
forced him to commit, and then be- 35
trayed him.
Millwood: [*Aside.*] Ha! Lucy has got
the advantage of me, and accused me
first; unless I can turn the accusation,
and fix it upon her and Blunt, I am lost. 40
Thorowgood: Had I known your cruel
design sooner, it had been prevented. To
see you punished as the law directs, is all
that now remains. Poor satisfaction, for
he, innocent as he is compared to you, 45
must suffer too. But heaven, who knows
our frame, and graciously distinguishes
between frailty and presumption, will
make a difference, though man cannot,
who sees not the heart, but only judges 50
by the outward action.

Millwood: I find, sir, we are both unhappy in our servants. I was surprised at such ill treatment, from a gentleman of your appearance without cause, and therefore too hastily returned it, for which I ask your pardon. I now perceive you have been so far imposed on, as to think me engaged in a former correspondence with your servant, and, some way or other, accessory to his undoing.

Thorowgood: I charge you as the cause, the sole cause of all his guilt, and all his suffering, of all he now endures, and must endure, till a violent and shameful death shall put a dreadful period to his life and miseries together.

Millwood: 'Tis very strange; but who's secure from scandal and detraction? So far from contributing to his ruin, I never spoke to him till since that fatal accident, which I lament as much as you. 'Tis true, I have a servant, on whose account he has of late frequented my house; if she has abused my good opinion of her, am I to blame? Hasn't Barnwell done the same by you?

Thorowgood: I hear you; pray go on.

Millwood: I have been informed he had a violent passion for her, and she for him; but I always thought it innocent; I know her poor and given to expensive pleasures. Now who can tell but she may have influenced the amorous youth to commit this murder, to supply her extravagancies? It must be so. I now recollect a thousand circumstances that confirm it. I'll have her and a man servant that I suspect as an accomplice, secured immediately. I hope, sir, you will lay aside your ill-grounded suspicions of me, and join to punish the real contrivers of this bloody deed. [*Offers to go.*]

Thorowgood: Madam, you pass not this way. I see your design, but shall protect them from your malice.

Millwood: I hope you will not use your influence and the credit of your name to screen such guilty wretches. Consider, sir, the wickedness of persuading a thoughtless youth to such a crime.

Thorowgood: I do, and of betraying him when it was done.

Millwood: That which you call betraying him, may convince you of my innocence. She who loves him, though she contrived the murder, would never have delivered him into the hands of justice, as I, struck with the horror of his crimes, have done.

Thorowgood: [*Aside.*] How should an unexperienced youth escape her snares? The powerful magic of her wit and form might betray the wisest to simple dotage and fire the blood that age had froze long since. Even I, that with just prejudice came prepared, had, by her artful story, been deceived, but that my strong conviction of her guilt makes even a doubt impossible.—Those whom subtly you would accuse, you know are your accusers; and what proves unanswerably, their innocence, and your guilt—they accused you before the deed was done, and did all that was in their power to have prevented it.

Millwood: Sir, you are very hard to be convinced; but I have such a proof, which, when produced, will silence all objections. [*Exit.*]

Scene XVII

[*Thorowgood, and enter Lucy, Trueman, Blunt, Officers, &c.*]

Lucy: Gentlemen, pray place yourselves, some on one side of that door, and some on the other; watch her entrance, and act as your prudence shall direct you.—This way—[*to Thorowgood*] and note her behavior; I have observed her, she's driven to the last extremity, and is forming some desperate resolution.—I guess at her design.—

Scene XVIII

[*Enter to them, Millwood with a pistol, —Trueman secures her.*]

Trueman: Here thy power of doing mischief ends, deceitful, cruel, bloody woman!

Millwood: Fool, hypocrite, villain!—Man! thou can'st not call me that.

Trueman: To call thee woman were to wrong the sex, thou devil!

Millwood: That imaginary being is an emblem of thy cursed sex collected. A mirror, wherein each particular man may see his own likeness and that of all mankind!

Trueman: Think not, by aggravating the fault of others, to extenuate thy own, of which the abuse of such uncommon perfections of mind and body is not the least.

Millwood: If such I had, well may I curse your barbarous sex, who robbed me of 'em, ere I knew their worth, then left me, too late, to count their value by their loss! Another and another spoiler came, and all my gain was poverty and reproach. My soul disdained, and yet disdains, dependence and contempt. Riches, no matter by what means obtained, I saw, secured the worst of men from both; I found it therefore necessary to be rich; and, to that end, I summoned all my arts. You call 'em wicked; be it so, they were such as my conversation with your sex had furnished me withal.

Thorowgood: Sure none but the worst of men conversed with thee.

Millwood: Men of all degrees and all professions I have known, yet found no difference, but in their several capacities; all were alike wicked to the utmost of their power. In pride, contention, avarice, cruelty, and revenge, the reverend priesthood were my unerring guides. From suburb-magistrates, who live by ruined reputations, as the unhospitable natives of Cornwall do by shipwrecks, I learned that to charge my innocent neighbors with my crimes was to merit their protection; for to screen the guilty, is the less scandalous, when many are suspected, and detraction, like darkness and death, blackens all objects and levels all distinction. Such are your venal magistrates, who favor none but such as, by their office, they are sworn to punish.

With them, not to be guilty is the worst of crimes; and large fees privately paid is every needful virtue.

Thorowgood: Your practice has sufficiently discovered your contempt of laws, both human and divine; no wonder then that you should hate the officers of both.

Millwood: I hate you all, I know you, and expect no mercy; nay, I ask for none; I have done nothing that I am sorry for; I followed my inclinations and that the best of you does every day. All actions are alike natural and indifferent to man and beast, who devour, or are devoured, as they meet with others weaker or stronger than themselves.

Thorowgood: What pity it is, a mind so comprehensive, daring and inquisitive, should be a stranger to religion's sweet, but powerful charms.

Millwood: I am not fool enough to be an atheist, though I have known enough of men's hypocrisy to make a thousand simple women so. Whatever religion is in itself, as practised by mankind, it has caused the evils you say it was designed to cure. War, plague, and famine have not destroyed so many of the human race, as this pretended piety has done, and with such barbarous cruelty, as if the only way to honor heaven were to turn the present world into hell.

Thorowgood: Truth is truth, though from an enemy and spoke in malice. You bloody, blind, and superstitious bigots, how will you answer this?

Millwood: What are your laws, of which you make your boast, but the fool's wisdom and the coward's valor; the instrument and screen of all your villainies, by which you punish in others what you act yourselves, or would have acted, had you been in their circumstances? The judge who condemns the poor man for being a thief had been a thief himself had he been poor. Thus you go on deceiving and being deceived, harassing, plaguing, and destroying one another; but women are your universal prey.

Women, by whom you are, the source
of joy,
With cruel arts you labor to destroy.
A thousand ways our ruin you pursue,
Yet blame in us those arts, first taught
by you.
O may, from hence, each violated maid,
By flattering, faithless, barb'rous man
betrayed; 6

When robbed of innocence and virgin
fame
From your destruction raise a nobler
name;
To right their sex's wrongs devote their
mind,
And future Millwoods prove to plague
mankind. 10

QUESTIONS ON ACT IV

1. The striking thing about Scene x is the irony; there is a relatively small amount of direct homily. Does Lillo serve his purpose, which is to teach a lesson, more or less effectively in this scene?

2. Comment on Thorowgood's first speech in Scene xvi.

3. How dramatic is the soliloquy in Scene i?

4. Point out the irony in Scene ii. Is it effective?

5. Does Scene iv accomplish anything?

6. Is there anything in Scene x which might lead you to think that Lillo may have been modeling Millwood on Lady Macbeth? If that was his purpose, how well does he succeed?

7. Is Lillo on the right track in Barnwell's speech in Scene xiii?

8. In Scene xviii Lillo is about as far as possible from tragic effect. Study the scene with care. What is wrong with the various speeches of Thorowgood, especially the last?

ACT V

SCENE I

[A room in a prison.]

[*Enter Thorowgood, Blunt and Lucy.*]

Thorowgood: I have recommended to Barnwell a reverend divine whose judgment and integrity I am well acquainted with; nor has Millwood been neglected, but she, unhappy woman, still obstinate, refuses her assistance.

Lucy: This pious charity to the afflicted well becomes your character; yet pardon me, sir, if I wonder you were not at their trial.

Thorowgood: I knew it was impossible to save him, and I and my family bear so great a part in his distress, that to have been present would have aggravated our sorrows without relieving his.

Blunt: It was mournful, indeed.

Barnwell's youth and modest deportment as he passed drew tears from every eye. When placed at the bar and arraigned before the reverend judges, with many tears and interrupting sobs he confessed and aggravated his offences, without accusing, or once reflecting on, Millwood, the shameless author of his ruin, who, dauntless and unconcerned, stood by his side, viewing with visible pride and contempt the vast assembly, who all with sympathizing sorrow wept for the wretched youth. Millwood, when called upon to answer, loudly insisted upon her innocence, and made an artful and a bold defence; but finding all in vain, the impartial jury and the learned bench concurring to find her guilty, how did she curse herself, poor Barnwell, us, her judges, all mankind; but what could that avail? She was condemned, and is this day to suffer with him.

Thorowgood: The time draws on; I am

going to visit Barnwell, as you are Mill-wood.

Lucy: We have not wronged her, yet I dread this interview. She's proud, impatient, wrathful, and unforgiving. To be the branded instruments of vengeance, to suffer in her shame, and sympathize with her in all she suffers, is the tribute we must pay for our former ill-spent lives, and long confederacy with her in wickedness.

Thorowgood: Happy for you it ended when it did. What you have done against Millwood, I know, proceeded from a just abhorrence of her crimes, free from interest, malice, or revenge. Proselytes to virtue should be encouraged. Pursue your proposed reformation, and know me hereafter for your friend.

Lucy: This is a blessing as unhoped for as unmerited, but heaven, that snatched us from impending ruin, sure intends you as its instrument to secure us from apostasy.

Thorowgood: With gratitude to impute your deliverance to heaven is just. Many, less virtuously disposed than Barnwell was, have never fallen in the manner he has done,—may not such owe their safety rather to Providence than to themselves? With pity and compassion let us judge him. Great were his faults, but strong was the temptation. Let his ruin learn us diffidence, humanity and circumspection; for we, who wonder at his fate, perhaps had we like him, been tried,—like him, we had fallen, too.

Scene II

[A dungeon, a table and lamp.]

[*Enter Thorowgood, to Barnwell reading.*]

Thorowgood: See there the bitter fruits of passion's detested reign and sensual appetite indulged. Severe reflections, penitence, and tears!

Barnwell: [*Rising.*] My honored, injured master, whose goodness has covered me a thousand times with shame, forgive this last unwilling disrespect,— indeed I saw you not.

Thorowgood: 'Tis well. I hope you were better employed in viewing of yourself; your journey's long, your time for preparation almost spent. I sent a reverend divine to teach you to improve it and should be glad to hear of his success.

Barnwell: The word of truth, which he recommended for my constant companion in this my sad retirement, has at length removed the doubts I labored under. From thence I've learned the infinite extent of heavenly mercy; that my offences, though great, are not unpardonable; and that 'tis not my interest only, but my duty, to believe and to rejoice in that hope. So shall heaven receive the glory, and future penitents the profit of my example.

Thorowgood: Go on. How happy am I who live to see this!

Barnwell: 'Tis wonderful that words should charm despair, speak peace and pardon to a murderer's conscience; but truth and mercy flow in every sentence, attended with force and energy divine. How shall I describe my present state of mind? I hope in doubt, and trembling I rejoice. I feel my grief increase, even as my fears give way. Joy and gratitude now supply more tears than the horror and anguish of despair before.

Thorowgood: These are the genuine signs of true repentance, the only preparatory, certain way to everlasting peace. O the joy it gives to see a soul formed and prepared for heaven! For this the faithful minister devotes himself to meditation, abstinence, and prayer, shunning the vain delights of sensual joys, and daily dies that others may live forever. For this he turns the sacred volumes o'er, and spends his life in painful search of truth. The love of riches and the lust of power, he looks on with just contempt and detestation; who only counts for wealth the souls he wins, and whose highest ambition is to serve mankind. If the reward of all his pains be to preserve one soul from wandering or turn one from the error of his ways, how does he then rejoice and own his little labors over-paid!

Barnwell: What do I owe for all your generous kindness! But though I cannot, [5] heaven can, and will, reward you.

Thorowgood: To see thee thus is joy too great for words. Farewell! Heaven strengthen thee! Farewell!

Barnwell: Oh, sir, there's something I [10] could say, if my sad swelling heart would give me leave.

Thorowgood: Give it vent a while and try.

Barnwell: I had a friend ('tis true I [15] am unworthy) yet methinks your generous example might persuade—could I not see him once before I go from whence there's no return?

Thorowgood: He's coming, and as [20] much thy friend as ever; but I'll not anticipate his sorrow. [*Aside.*] Too soon he'll see the sad effect of his contagious ruin. This torrent of domestic misery bears too hard upon me; I must [25] retire to indulge a weakness I find impossible to overcome.—Much loved—and much lamented youth,—farewell!! Heaven strengthen thee! Eternally farewell!

Barnwell: The best of masters and of [30] men, farewell!—While I live, let me not want your prayers!

Thorowgood: Thou shalt not;—thy peace being made with Heaven, death's already vanquished; bear a little longer [35] the pains that attend this transitory life, and cease from pain forever. [*Exit.*]

SCENE III

[*Barnwell.*]

Barnwell: I find a power within that bears my soul above the fears of death, and, spite of conscious shame and guilt, gives me a taste of pleasure more than [45] mortal.

SCENE IV

[*Enter to him Trueman and Keeper.*]

Keeper: Sir, there's the prisoner. [50] [*Exit.*]

SCENE V

[*Barnwell and Trueman.*]

Barnwell: Trueman,—my friend, whom I so wished to see, yet now he's here I dare not look upon him. [*Weeps.*]

Trueman: O Barnwell! Barnwell!

Barnwell: Mercy! Mercy! gracious heaven! for death, but not for this, was I prepared!

Trueman: What have I suffered since I saw you last!—What pain has absence given me! But oh! to see thee thus!

Barnwell: I know it is dreadful! I feel the anguish of thy generous soul,—but I was born to murder all who love me. [*Both weep.*]

Trueman: I came not to reproach you; —I thought to bring you comfort,—but I'm deceived, for I have none to give;— I came to share thy sorrow, but cannot bear my own.

Barnwell: My sense of guilt, indeed, you cannot know; 'tis what the good and innocent like you can ne'er conceive; but other griefs at present I have none but what I feel for you. In your sorrow I read you love me still, but yet methinks 'tis strange, when I consider what I am.

Trueman: No more of that. I can remember nothing but thy virtue, thy honest, tender friendship, our former happy state and present misery. O had you trusted me when first the fair seducer tempted you, all might have been prevented!

Barnwell: Alas, thou know'st not what a wretch I've been! Breach of friendship was my first and least offence. So far was I lost to goodness,—so devoted to the author of my ruin,—that had she insisted on my murdering thee,—I think, —I should have done it.

Trueman: Prithee, aggravate thy faults no more.

Barnwell: I think I should! Thus good and generous as you are, I should [50] have murdered you!

Trueman: We have not yet embraced,

and may be interrupted. Come to my arms.

Barnwell: Never, never will I taste such joys on earth; never will I so soothe my just remorse. Are those honest arms and faithful bosom fit to embrace and to support a murderer? These iron fetters only shall clasp and flinty pavement bear me. [*Throwing himself on the ground.*] Even these too good for such a bloody monster!

Trueman: Shall fortune sever those whom friendship joined! Thy miseries cannot lay thee so low, but love will find thee. [*Lies down by him.*] Upon this rugged couch then let us lie, for well it suits our most deplorable condition. Here will we offer to stern calamity, this earth the altar, and ourselves the sacrifice. Our mutual groans shall echo to each other through the dreary vault. Our sighs shall number the moments as they pass,—and mingling tears communicate such anguish as words were never made to express.

Barnwell: Then be it so. Since you propose an intercourse of woe, pour all your griefs into my breast,—and in exchange take mine. [*Embracing.*] Where's now the anguish that you promised? You've taken mine, and make me no return.—Sure peace and comfort dwell within these arms, and sorrow can't approach me while I'm here! This, too, is the work of Heaven, who, having before spoke peace and pardon to me, now sends thee to confirm it. O take, take some of the joy that overflows my breast!

Trueman: I do, I do. Almighty Power, how have you made us capable to bear, at once, the extremes of pleasure and pain?

Scene VI

[*Enter to them, Keeper.*]

Keeper: Sir.
Trueman: I come. [*Exit Keeper.*]

Scene VII

[*Barnwell and Trueman.*]

Barnwell: Must you leave me? Death would soon have parted us forever.

Trueman: O, my Barnwell, there's yet another task behind:—Again your heart must bleed for others' woes.

Barnwell: To meet and part with you, I thought was all I had to do on earth! What is there more for me to do or suffer?

Trueman: I dread to tell thee, yet it must be known.—Maria—

Barnwell: Our master's fair and virtuous daughter!

Trueman: The same.

Barnwell: No misfortune, I hope, has reached that lovely maid! Preserve her, Heaven, from every ill, to show mankind that goodness is your care.

Trueman: Thy, thy misfortunes, my unhappy friend, have reached her. Whatever you and I have felt, and more, if more be possible, she feels for you.

Barnwell: [*Aside.*] I know he doth abhor a lie, and would not trifle with his dying friend.—This is, indeed, the bitterness of death!

Trueman: You must remember, for we all observed it, for some time past, a heavy melancholy weighed her down. Disconsolate she seemed, and pined and languished from a cause unknown; till hearing of your dreadful fate, the long stifled flame blazed out. She wept, she wrung her hands, and tore her hair, and in the transport of her grief discovered her own lost state, whilst she lamented yours.

Barnwell: Will all the pain I feel restore thy ease, lovely unhappy maid? [*Weeping.*] Why didn't you let me die and never know it?

Trueman: It was impossible; she makes no secret of her passion for you, and is determined to see you ere you die. She waits for me to introduce her. [*Exit.*]

Scene VIII

[*Barnwell.*]

Barnwell: Vain busy thoughts be still! What avails it to think on what I might have been. I now am what I've made myself.

Scene IX

[*Enter to him, Trueman and Maria.*]

Trueman: Madam, reluctant I lead you to this dismal scene. This is the seat of misery and guilt. Here awful justice reserves her public victims. This is the entrance to shameful death.

Maria: To this sad place, then, no improper guest, the abandoned, lost Maria brings despair; and see! the subject and the cause of all this world of woe! Silent and motionless he stands, as if his soul had quitted her abode, and the lifeless form alone was left behind; yet that so perfect, that beauty and death, ever at enmity, now seem united there.

Barnwell: I groan, but murmur not. Just Heaven, I am your own; do with me what you please.

Maria: Why are your streaming eyes still fixed below as though thou'dst give the greedy earth thy sorrows, and rob me of my due? Were happiness within your power, you should bestow it where you please; but in your misery I must and will partake.

Barnwell: Oh! say not so, but fly, abhor, and leave me to my fate. Consider what you are! How vast your fortune, and how bright your fame! Have pity on your youth, your beauty, and unequalled virtue, for which so many noble peers have sighed in vain. Bless with your charms some honorable lord. Adorn with your beauty; and, by your example, improve the English court, that justly claims such merits; so shall I quickly be to you as though I had never been.

Maria: When I forget you, I must be so, indeed. Reason, choice, virtue, all forbid it. Let women like Millwood if there be more such women smile in prosperity and in adversity forsake. Be it the pride of virtue to repair or to partake the ruin such have made.

Trueman: Lovely, ill-fated maid! Was there ever such generous distress before? How must this pierce his grateful heart and aggravate his woes!

Barnwell: Ere I knew guilt or shame, when fortune smiled, and when my youthful hopes were at the highest; if then to have raised my thoughts to you, had been presumption in me, never to have been pardoned, think how much beneath yourself you condescend to regard me now.

Maria: Let her blush, who, professing love, invades the freedom of your sex's choice and meanly sues in hopes of a return. Your inevitable fate hath rendered hope impossible as vain. Then why should I fear to avow a passion so just and so disinterested?

Trueman: If any should take occasion from Millwood's crimes to libel the best and fairest part of the creation, here let them see their error. The most distant hopes of such a tender passion from so bright a maid might add to the happiness of the most happy and make the greatest proud. Yet here 'tis lavished in vain. Though by the rich present the generous donor is undone, he on whom it is bestowed receives no benefit.

Barnwell: So the aromatic spices of the East, which all the living covet and esteem, are with unavailing kindness wasted on the dead.

Maria: Yes, fruitless is my love, and unavailing all my sighs and tears. Can they save thee from approaching death, from such a death? O terrible idea! What is her misery and distress, who sees the first last object of her love, for whom alone she'd live, for whom she'd die a thousand, thousand deaths if it were possible, expiring in her arms? Yet she is happy, when compared to me. Were millions of worlds mine, I'd gladly give them in exchange for her condition. The most consummate woe is light to mine. The last of curses to other miserable maids, is all I ask; and that's denied me.

Trueman: Time and reflection cure all ills.

Maria: All but this; his dreadful catastrophe virtue herself abhors. To give a holiday to suburb slaves; and, passing, entertain the savage herd who, elbowing each other for a sight, pursue and press upon him like his fate. A mind with piety and resolution armed may smile on death. But public ignominy! everlasting shame! shame the death of souls! to die a thousand times and yet survive even death itself, in never-dying infamy, is this to be endured? Can I, who live in him, and must each hour of my devoted life feel all these woes renewed, can I endure this!—

Trueman: Grief has impaired her spirits; she pants, as in the agonies of death.

Barnwell: Preserve her, Heaven, and restore her peace,—nor let her death be added to my crime,—[*Bell tolls.*] I am summoned to my fate.

Scene X

[*Enter to them, Keeper.*]

Keeper: The officers attend you, sir. Mrs. Millwood is already summoned.

Barnwell: Tell 'em I'm ready. And now, my friend, farewell. [*Embracing.*] Support and comfort the best you can this mourning fair. No more. Forget not to pray for me. [*Turning to Maria.*] Would you, bright excellence, permit me the honor of a chaste embrace, the last happiness this world could give were mine. [*She inclines towards him; they embrace.*] Exalted goodness! O turn your eyes from earth and me to heaven, where virtue like yours is ever heard. Pray for the peace of my departing soul. —Early my race of wickedness began, and soon has reached the summit, ere nature has finished her work, and stamped me man. Just at the time that others begin to stray, my course is fin-

ished! Though short my span of life, and few my days, yet count my crimes for years, and I have lived whole ages. Justice and mercy are in heaven the same. Its utmost severity is mercy to the whole, thereby to cure man's folly and presumption, which else would render even infinite mercy vain and ineffectual. Thus justice in compassion to mankind cuts off a wretch like me,—by one such example to secure thousands from future ruin.

If any youth, like you, in future times,
Shall mourn my fate, though he abhor my crimes;
Or tender maid, like you, my tale shall hear,
And to my sorrow gives a pitying tear:
To each such melting eye, and throbbing heart,
Would gracious heaven this benefit impart,
Never to know my guilt, nor feel my pain;
Then must you own, you ought not to complain;
Since you nor weep, nor shall I die, in vain.

[*Exeunt Keeper and Barnwell.*]

Scene XI

[*Trueman, Blunt and Lucy.*]

Lucy: Heart-breaking sight! O wretched, wretched Millwood!

Trueman: You came from her then— how is she disposed to meet her Fate?

Blunt: Who can describe unalterable woe?

Lucy: She goes to death encompassed with horror, loathing life, and yet afraid to die; no tongue can tell her anguish and despair.

Trueman: Heaven be better to her than her fears; may she prove a warning to others, a monument of mercy in herself.

Lucy: O sorrow insupportable! Break, break, my heart!

Trueman: In vain
With bleeding hearts and weeping eyes we show
A human gen'rous sense of others' woe;
Unless we mark what drew their ruin on,
And by avoiding that, prevent our own.

EPILOGUE

Written by *Colley Cibber, Esq.;* and Spoken by *Maria*

Since Fate has robbed me of the hopeless youth,
For whom my heart had hoarded up its truth;
By all the laws of love and honor, now,
I'm free again to choose,—and one of you.

But soft! With caution first I'll round me peep; 5
Maids, in my case, should look before they leap:
Here's choice enough, of various sorts, and hue,
The cit, the wit, the rake cocked up in cue,
The fair spruce mercer, and the tawny Jew.

Suppose I search the sober gallery. No, 10
There's none but prentices,—and cuckolds all a row;
And these, I doubt, are those that make 'em so.
[*Points to the boxes.*]

'Tis very well, enjoy the jest. But you,
Fine powdered sparks, nay, I'm told 'tis true,
Your happy spouses—can make cuckolds too. 15

'Twixt you and them, the diff'rence this perhaps,
The cit's ashamed whene'er his duck he traps;
But you, when madam's tripping, let her fall,
Cock up your hats, and take no shame at all.

What if some savored poet I could meet? 20
Whose love would lay his laurels at my feet?
No,—painted passion real love abhors,—
His flame would prove the suit of creditors.

Not to detain you then with longer pause,
In short; my heart to this conclusion draws, 25
I yield it to the hand, that's loudest in applause.

QUESTIONS ON ACT V

1. Note the large number of satisfying emotional exercises Barnwell is able to engage in in Act V. How does this fact influence the tragic tone?

2. It has been said that Act V really rewards the criminal, that it is likely to stimulate people to desire to spend their last days in jail. At what aspects of the Act is such a criticism aimed?

3. In Scene ix, what is wrong with Maria's saying, "Let women like Millwood . . . smile in prosperity, etc."?

4. In Scene ii Barnwell reappears for the first time since Act IV. xiii. Is his reappearance dramatic?

5. Analyze the source of the sentimentality of Barnwell's last speech in Scene v.

NOTES ON *THE LONDON MERCHANT*

Before we have finished reading the play we become aware of two things: that Lillo is trying to write a tragedy, and that it is not successful. We realize, of course, that he does improve on the murder-mystery melodrama (in Appendix A, Exercises on Additional Plays, the student will find an analysis of a play of this type, Morton's *Speed the Plough*); for Lillo's play does attempt to deal with character. On the other hand, it definitely falls short of such well-known English tragedies as Marlowe's *Dr. Faustus* and Shakespeare's *Macbeth*, which appeared more than a century earlier, but with which it may be compared in that the leading characters in all of these plays go down in pursuit of something that they cannot morally attain. But, whereas Marlowe and Shakespeare move us strongly, Lillo leaves us indifferent and, at times, even amused or annoyed. Our business is to find out why.

I. LACK OF FOCUS

At the outset we can see that Lillo has difficulties in keeping our attention directed toward Barnwell. His problem is one of focus, which we have already considered elsewhere. In *Lady Windermere's Fan* we could see that Wilde tended, in Acts II and III, to lose sight of both his central theme and his central character, though we argued that he did eventually succeed in pulling the play back into focus; in Plautus's *Menaechmi* we saw the attention split up between two main characters and not even held upon them with consistency. With regard to his difficulty in keeping Barnwell in the spotlight, Lillo probably falls somewhere between Wilde and Plautus. Barnwell speaks, as a matter of fact, about 26% of the lines of the play. Here some comparisons will be useful: Macbeth has about 31% of the lines of Shakespeare's play; Everyman, 41% of the lines in *Everyman;* and Faustus, 42% of the lines in Marlowe's play. Though the difference between the percentage of lines spoken by Barnwell and Macbeth is not large, and though each appears in about half of the scenes of his play, Macbeth is still the center of his play in a way that Barnwell is not the center of his. Macbeth's life sets the tone for and determines, so to speak, the life of the other characters; they are so bound up with his fate that their scenes are really a dramatic amplification of his career. But Barnwell exercises no real influence on the lives of his associates; he and they, unlike Macbeth and the Scottish lords, do not share a common political and moral existence; his friends are merely *observers*. Therefore, when they have the stage, we do not feel that we are seeing Barnwell's influence on a world of which he is the center, but rather that we are watching somebody—and a not too interesting somebody—watch the main action. Note how Act III. iii and iv give the stage over to secondary characters at a crucial time in the main character's career. Can you find other scenes of the sort?

In *Everyman* and *Dr. Faustus*, on the other hand, the hero is very much in the spotlight. In each play he has over 40% of the lines; except for two short passages, Everyman is present throughout the play; Dr. Faustus appears in ten of the fourteen scenes into which the play is often divided. Here, clearly, we find situations not unlike that in *The London Merchant:* the fate of the hero is less closely interwoven with that of the other characters than in *Macbeth.* Hence we find a number of characters—such as Friendship and Kindred in *Everyman*, and the other Scholars in *Dr. Faustus* —who are observers or outsiders, essentially uninfluenced by the hero's career. We feel, therefore, that Lillo should have organized his play like *Everyman* or *Dr. Faustus*, for Barnwell's own struggle is the central issue, and therefore his role should have received the emphasis which would be conferred by fuller development. Instead, Lillo makes Barnwell share our attention with too many other people, none of them essential to our understanding of Barnwell. That is, he uses a form more suitable to depicting the *state of a society* than the *struggles of an individual.* Why does he fall into this error? The following paragraphs will suggest some answers to this question.

2. MULTIPLICITY OF OBJECTIVES

When we examine the author's attitude to his material, which is always a matter of central importance, we find that Lillo was evidently not clear about what he was doing. In fact, it is obvious that he was *trying to do several things at once* and that the different objectives do not fit well together. The very fact that the different objectives can be identified and described separately is fairly convincing evidence that the play is not integrated. Let us notice what these objectives are.

1. There is of course the main problem of the development of Barnwell, which we shall discuss in detail later. For the time being, we may note that Lillo makes his greatest effort to center attention on Barnwell in the soliloquies, which are meant to be Shakespearian, in Act III. v and vii.

2. But Lillo is unable to let Barnwell's experience speak for itself or to see that the dramatist's job properly ends with his showing how Barnwell's moral decision has worked out. Instead, he adds, with a nagging pertinacity, direct, pointed, and wholly unnecessary moral lessons.

a. Most obvious are the moralizing couplets at the end of various scenes. Lillo actually points up his annoying shift to the undramatic by changing from prose to meter and rhyme.

b. In Act III. iv Lucy and Blunt are made, practically without motivation, to turn against Millwood. Lillo wishes, in this way, to stress her viciousness, a trait which of course might well have been left to speak for itself. He does try to account for the shift by letting Lucy describe (III. iv) a Barnwell scene which should be presented directly. Thus he scrimps on Barnwell's role and gives the other roles undue prominence; besides, too much of the speeches of the other characters is devoted to tedious moralizing. Act V. i and xi show his wandering off the track. What by the way is wrong with Lucy's last line: "Oh, sorrow insupportable! Break, break, my heart!"?

c. To stress the moral, Thorowgood, Trueman, and Maria are used to demonstrate the threefold loss suffered by Barnwell in the realms of business, friendship, and love, respectively. Thus their whole function is didactic ("Crime doesn't pay") and external. Second, Thorowgood is the good employer, and Trueman the good apprentice, both in contrast with Barnwell, but Lillo overplays the contrast and makes them too good; Trueman, especially, becomes an annoying prig instead of an effective foil. This is what comes of making a point explicitly instead of implicitly through an exploration of character; the meaning of Barnwell's acts is pointed enough, without trite exclamations from Thorowgood and Trueman. Hence their parts are overstuffed (see Acts II. iv, IV. xvi, and most of Act V). Note, finally, that Trueman often speaks (for instance, in Act III. iii) in the style of the "sentiment" (see the analysis of *The School for Scandal*), the kind of generalized remark which suggests that the speaker has few real feelings but wants to say something "appropriate."

d. Lillo uses even Millwood to moralize: in Act IV. xviii she defends religion while attacking bad church practices and social conditions! Notice how this takes the play away from tragedy, which is concerned with the individual's relation to problems of good and evil (see *Tragedy* in the Glossary), and into the realm of the problem play, which is concerned with the issues faced by a given society at a given time. Aside from having her make such undramatic speeches, Lillo uses Millwood in a very obvious way to illustrate the influence of evil in human life. Note two technical mistakes of Lillo here: (1) In his eagerness to have a complete record of moral decline from good life to ignominious death, Lillo includes too much of the relationship between Millwood and Barnwell. He starts too early and thus does not have time enough to trace plausibly gradual development in Barnwell (I. v; I. viii; II. i). (2) To show how "one vice . . . begets another," as Lucy says, Lillo has Millwood deliberately lead Barnwell on to murder, though this involves a moral and psychological leap which is simply not motivated. Perhaps his hesitance to present this step directly (it is given by report) shows Lillo's awareness of the difficulty that he runs into here. But Lillo does know that Millwood must be presented as a human being, not as a mere personification of evil. Note what qualities he gives her to this end; note especially how her wit and cleverness suggest a hard reality that makes her in some ways a more plausible character than Trueman.

3. Besides moralizing, Lillo wants to justify his innovation of basing a tragedy on middle-class characters instead of on royalty or nobility; one of the first crusaders for this type of tragedy, he lets his arguments flow over from preface and prologue, where they may legitimately appear, into the play itself, where they do not belong. Since, for his middle-class characters, he picks a merchant and his associates, he lets himself bog down in an

irrelevant defense of merchandizing. Act I. i is an unconnected discourse which sounds like a Chamber of Commerce pamphlet; Acts I. ii and III. i dilute their propaganda with only slight suggestions of dramatic situation. A subtler damage occurs in that all the talk about commerce somehow manages to suggest that Barnwell's deeds are an offense, not so much against morality, as against good business. One of the dismally anticlimactic spots in the play is Trueman's line in Act III. iii, "But few men recover reputations lost—a merchant never." The profit motive and tragedy are irreconcilable.

4. Though he doesn't recognize it, Lillo allows himself to be further distracted from tragedy by a kind of scientific or sociological interest. He likes to work out social processes and social causes in too much detail, as in tracing the relationship of Millwood and Barnwell. Act I. iii, for instance, gives too much attention to Millwood—the *means* by which the tragic hero is to be influenced. Act IV. xvi harps on Millwood as strategist, a subject which needs no further demonstration at this late point. Worse than that, Lillo waters down his tragedy when he has Thorowgood accuse Millwood of being "sole cause" of Barnwell's trouble. To evade responsibility and look for a scapegoat constitutes a muddleheaded flight from the moral responsibility with which tragedy is concerned. Macbeth, for example, does not blame Lady Macbeth, nor Faustus, Mephistopheles; Shakespeare and Marlowe know that the problem is ultimately an inner one. Lillo, however, carries matters even a step further in Act IV. xviii when he starts absolving the "sole cause" by blaming society for Millwood's state. When he gets to the origins of prostitution, he is writing sociology, or, in literary terms, the problem play (note, in this connection, certain resemblances between Millwood and Mrs. Erlynne in *Lady Windermere's Fan.*) He is scientist rather than artist when he describes the impact of society on Millwood instead of exploring the qualitative differences which make her and other women behave differently in response to the same impact. Thus, he eliminates the element of choice which we shall see is so essential in *Faustus* and *Macbeth*. The study of Millwood as a social product and a social influence gets away from the subject and attitude proper to tragedy.

5. Lillo knows, however, that above all his play must work in emotional terms. The emotional effect should, and in some parts does, come naturally from the development of Barnwell, but Lillo consciously plays for our emotions in other ways also. His use of Trueman and Maria constantly betrays him.

Consider Maria, whom we are supposed to pity and admire. One notices that, actually, she is extraneous; her situation *does nothing* in the play. Compare Shakespeare's use of Ophelia in *Hamlet:* through Hamlet's attitude to her, we learn a great deal about Hamlet. But before Act V Barnwell shows not the slightest consciousness of Maria's existence, so that she becomes merely a little added emotional flavoring. Again, compare her with Octavia in Shakespeare's *Antony and Cleopatra* and in Dryden's *All for Love.* In the former, Octavia has a small part, but it is effective: she is shown in direct relationship with her husband and is thus an organic part of the play. In Dryden's play, Octavia becomes a principal force, appearing in direct conflict with Cleopatra. But Maria is not a major character nor is she even a minor character that is integrated with the rest of the play. Take Act V. ix. Since her emotions are not reciprocated, they and her appearance in jail both lack dignity; all she can do is talk about her feelings, an act which combines bad taste with irrelevance. As Barnwell is only a static listener, the play is out of focus again.

With Trueman, who, in general, is too much the mere observer and commentator (I. i; III. i), Lillo does a better job, at least in Act II. ii; there is direct interplay between him and Barnwell, and through him Barnwell's state of mind is exhibited. But note the excessive stress on their friendship, which is meant to be very touching, but which is still a side issue. The climactic embrace of Barnwell and Trueman produces a wrong effect by focusing attention on what, considering the seriousness of Barnwell's problem, is a triviality. Yet it is supposed to be very heart-warming. For reasons of this sort the play is often called a "sentimental tragedy."

Consider Act III. iii. Here the action does advance, but Lillo avoids presenting the advance directly. Instead of sharing in the emotions of Barnwell as he absconds, we are asked to be moved by the exclamations of Trueman and Maria. The effect is one of sentimentality (see Glossary) because we are removed from the source of the emotion. Their praise of Barnwell ("a soul so delicate") is too easy; we see no basis for their enthusiasm. Maria's concealment of the theft is totally unrelated to Barnwell's central problem but is presented merely in order to emphasize her benevolence—a method which is always likely to produce a sentimental effect.

3. THE TREATMENT OF BARNWELL

Lillo's main business, of course, is with Barnwell, to whom he should have given more space. Not until Act II does Lillo begin to take enough care in presenting Barnwell's inner disturbance, and he effectively restrains his tendency to sentimentalism when he introduces several good ironic scenes: Act II. iv, where, from intended kindness, Thorowgood refuses to hear a confession that might save Barnwell; and Act II. ix–xiv, where Barnwell returns to Millwood after thinking he has conquered his passion for her (II. v). Here, too, Lillo is able to keep his play on the psychological rather than the didactic level, as Barnwell's saying he has won a "painful victory" indicates.

Lillo makes his strongest effort to get inside Barnwell's mind at the time of the murder, Act III. v ff. Yet notice, first of all, the mistakes Lillo makes here. He gives too much emphasis to the uncle, whom we do not know, and whose premonitions, apostrophe to death, and prayer are simply artificial, "theatrical" means for working up an effect. Here we see the unsteadiness of focus revealing itself again. Lillo becomes preoccupied with the stock devices of melodrama, such as the disguise, pistol, poniard, and sword, and thus allows his dramatic effect to degenerate into triviality. He falls back into sentimentality by stressing the uncle's benevolence, which is too simple to be plausible; we need to know that the author does not consider a kindly kiss the only possible or likely response to a death-blow, or we again accuse him of arrant tear-jerking. He becomes maudlin by having Barnwell swoon, pointlessly, on his uncle's body. Compare, for instance, Juliet's falling on Romeo's body as she dies—an act both symbolic and ironic.

Barnwell's Language. But aside from this bogging down in the *circumstances* surrounding the tragic action, Lillo makes a decided effort to deal with Barnwell directly, and here we must consider the kind of language Barnwell speaks. Lillo tries hard to suggest a real struggle: Barnwell's speeches are developed with some fullness.

They use specific images (darkness of day, the sound of the stream) and comparisons (Nero, Cain), though Lillo does not make much effort to unite these images in a coherent pattern of meaning. But if we go on to compare Barnwell's soliloquies with those of Macbeth (I. vii and II. i), who is also being impelled to crime by ambition, we find differences. In Shakespeare, the situation speaks for itself; in Lillo, we have the usual moralizing lines. Shakespeare uses blank verse, which he controls as a part of the total means of giving expression to the situation; Lillo appears to be using prose, but (as in many parts of the play) the actual rhythm is not that of prose but of blank verse—a fact readily revealed by printing part of the speech as verse:

> A dismal gloom obscures the face of day;
> either the sun has slipped behind a cloud,
> or journeys down the west of heaven with more
> than common speed to avoid the sight of what
> I'm doomed to act. Since I set forth on this
> accursed design, where'er I tread, methinks,
> the solid earth trembles beneath my feet.

The unacknowledged meter serves as an artificial heightening device, a little like the tears to which Lillo is much addicted.

Moreover, though he makes some effort at concreteness, Lillo gives Barnwell lines full of abstract and conventional expressions which suggest a sermon about someone else rather than a setting forth of his own emotions. He speaks of Virtue, Conscience, nature, and reason; of "madness of desire" and "impetuous passion." Compare Shakespeare's single, original image for Macbeth's motive:

> I have no spur
> To prick the sides of my intent, but only
> Vaulting ambition, which o'erleaps itself
> And falls on the other—

Or take *murder*. Barnwell hears a stream "murmur 'Murder'"; in Act III. vii he talks about "murdering hand," "murdered saint," "murder the worst of crimes," as if Lillo thought that repetition of the word *murder* were enough. Compare *Macbeth* (II. i):

> . . . wither'd Murder,
> Alarum'd by his sentinel, the wolf,
> Whose howl's his watch, thus with his stealthy pace,
> With Tarquin's ravishing strides, towards his design
> Moves like a ghost.

And in Act II. ii:

> "Macbeth does murder sleep," the innocent sleep,
> Sleep that knits up the ravell'd sleave of care, . . .
>
> "Glamis hath murder'd sleep, and therefore Cawdor
> Shall sleep no more; Macbeth shall sleep no more."

Again, Barnwell and Macbeth state certain arguments against the projected murder—their relationship to, and the character of, the victim. Then Barnwell says, "I stiffen with horror at my own impiety"—a conventional and generalized phrase which suggests only that he is trying to feel horrified. Compare Macbeth on Duncan:

> . . . his virtues
> Will plead like angels, trumpet-tongu'd, against
> The deep damnation of his taking-off;
> And pity, like a naked new-born babe,
> Striding the blast, or heaven's cherubin, hors'd
> Upon the sightless couriers of the air,
> Shall blow the horrid deed in every eye,
> That tears shall drown the wind. . . .

By seeing the situation concretely in terms of the inevitable aftermath, Macbeth shows real, not merely verbal, horror. Shakespeare develops one figure into a full, direct, dramatic expression of his idea; Lillo describes it, talks about it, repeats it, and insists on it—and still stays unconvincingly outside it. In Act IV. x Millwood really seems more right than Lillo intends when she calls Barnwell a "whining . . . canting villain," for *whining* describes the effect produced by Lillo's vast but inept efforts to whip up horror. When Barnwell says, "Think you I added sacrilege to murder?" he actually dilutes the sense of evil by the implied praise of his own forbearance; we feel that he should have gone on and stolen the money with a kind of sardonic satisfaction in the increase of his moral debt. Or note the subtle self-exoneration in "Behold these hands all crimsoned o'er with my dear uncle's blood! Here's a sight to make a statue start with horror, or to turn a living man into a statue." The *dear* stresses his own affectionate nature, though he should hardly have the presumption to mention it here; the balanced structure of the second sentence makes it sound like a mere exercise in public speaking, especially when we realize that Barnwell has not turned into a statue. Compare Macbeth (II. iii):

What hands are here? Ha! they pluck out mine eyes.
Will all great Neptune's ocean wash this blood
Clean from my hand? No, this my hand will rather
The multitudinous seas incarnadine,
Making the green one red.

Here is no talk about "dear Duncan" or about what a terrible sight this is. Instead the blood comes to symbolize a crime too monstrous to be expunged.

The Problem of Acts IV and V. But these Barnwell-Millwood scenes (IV. x–xiv) are good at least to the extent that the outcome of them is ironic for Barnwell. And his disillusionment, added to his sense of iniquity, really ends the play. But Lillo's muddled sense of tragedy, which leads him to dispose of Millwood at a disproportionate length which gets the play out of focus again, also leads him into a needless Act V which is full of the didactic and the sentimental. Scenes i and xi are purely didactic, and Scene ii is largely for edification; Scene ix is devoted to the supposed pathos of Maria—all sheer loss. Two other scenes demand attention.

Scenes v–vii show how gushing emotions, which are not the right ones and which come too easily, produce a terribly maudlin effect. Barnwell's moral anguish is barely suggested; instead we have large doses of forgiveness and lovingkindness and such an ecstatic relish of friendly love that this seems to be an end in itself. The embracing on the ground is bathos: its lack of dignity and restraint is wholly incompatible with tragic effect. All the tears are too easy; we feel that the characters are actually relishing their emotions rather than that the emotions spring naturally from the situation. For a really guilty man, Barnwell is too happy in friendship. By insisting that he would have murdered Trueman, Barnwell takes easy credit for a sense of guilt; but he shows no authenticating repulsion. Trueman's insistence on an embrace shows Lillo's misguided determination to present an emotional act that is unnecessary and overdone. Barnwell's rolling on the ground is an easy, showy way of suggesting abasement; a more real and hard way would have been to refuse to see Trueman or to accept his affection. So what we have is an emotional orgy: a frantic "revival" scene, so to speak, but no real conversion.

In Scene x, Barnwell's speech has the set quality of a commencement address; he loses dramatic reality both by showing no real feelings and by joining the audience in pointing at himself (for a real sense of what goes on in the mind of a condemned man we must go to the end of *Faustus* or the banquet scene in *Macbeth*). The embraces are again irrelevant emotional acts, especially his embracing Maria; to introduce the symbol of an emotional state when the state does not exist is sentimental. Maria, of course, is in love, but under the circumstances she seems to lack both dignity and good taste.

CONCLUSION

Lillo's constant tendency to wander into the extraneous is illustrated, finally, by the way in which Barnwell's fate comes to be identified with trial and hanging: note the contents of Acts IV. xii, V. i, and V. ix, and the staging of a needless Act V in a dungeon. Greek and Shakespearian tragedy, by contrast, are not concerned with police courts and jails, which belong to problem plays or to comedy; and on the rare occasions when we do find such scenes in successful tragedy, external matters are carefully subordinated to meaning. But Lillo has *confused the legal and the moral*. He bases Act V on the following assumption: since Barnwell is legally caught up with and lessons are publicly drawn, evil is properly punished, and we are free to stress Barnwell's excellence. It may be said for Lillo that he knows that the tragic character must be complex, not a mere villain. His difficulty is that he cannot dramatize the complexity as a whole, in all its difficulty, as he must do. He breaks it down: he shows the evil and punishes it, and then goes on to admire the good. This he does by having Barnwell's acquaintances come to jail to show great friendliness and grief. The result is thoroughly sentimental:

1. To stress one side of the hero upsets the psychological effect of tragedy. If, as Aristotle says, the tragic incidents evoke pity and terror, the trouble here is that all the stress falls on pity: we do not have the balance or fusion of the two (just as we do not have the fusion of the different sides of Barnwell) that is essential (compare sentimental comedy, where the stress is rather on virtuous conduct than on the folly which is to be satirized.)

2. The hero's merits can be stressed here only by having other people insist on them. In fact, throughout the play that is the method: we never see Barnwell convincingly act the "good" man. Lillo tries to *talk* an effect rather than *dramatize* it—the essence of sentimentality. To praise Barnwell, Trueman and Maria have to ignore his most significant piece of conduct, so that, rather than serving as trustworthy witnesses, they seem bent on an emotional orgy.

3. Finally, it is difficult at best to secure a valid emotional effect in Act V because no decisive action is taking or can take place. Everything is settled, and all we have is a loquacious post-mortem. When Lillo, in the course of that post-mortem, starts using "strong" emotional words, we remain indifferent.

In sum, Lillo is unable to deal adequately with his central problem. Here, as throughout the play, he shows only a partial conception of what tragedy is. In trying to do many things he has fallen down. Lamb doubtless felt something of the sort when he called the play a "nauseous sermon" that still made "uncle-murder too trivial."

QUESTIONS

1. Some years after its original appearance *The London Merchant* was presented with an additional scene which portrayed the place of execution. A crowd is present and the gallows is visible. Lucy and Blunt talk about the terrors of death. Most of the lines are spoken by Barnwell, urging Millwood to repent, and by Millwood refusing to do so. Does it appear to you that such a scene would be a valuable dramatic addition?

2. Note that in Act V there are constant references to "Millwood's crime," as if she had especial responsibility. What is the effect of such references?

3. Would Lillo's efforts to universalize the middle class have greater likelihood of success if he did not let his play get involved in "propaganda" for the commercial classes?

4. In point of quantity, at least, Macbeth's crimes are "worse" than Barnwell's; yet there is no moralizing in *Macbeth*. Would this fact appear to make Shakespeare a less morally sensitive playwright than Lillo? Could you defend the position that Macbeth is actually made a more attractive, a more humanly understandable character than Barnwell?

5. Without pushing the matter too far, we can see that Millwood and Cleopatra (in Shakespeare's *Antony and Cleopatra*) have similarities. Notice, however, that Millwood moralizes and Cleopatra does not. How does this fact influence the characterization of each?

6. Note what slight change in stress would be necessary to change the Maria-Barnwell story into the Maria-Charles story of *The School for Scandal*. Are the tendencies toward sentimentality similar?

7. In what passages other than those discussed do you find Lillo writing blank verse or something much like it? Does this tendency appear more strongly in any particular kind of passage?

8. Make a detailed list of the speeches in the play which appear to be written primarily to glorify the business man. Include not only those which directly reflect Lillo's interest in trade but also those in which there are indirect indications of that interest.

FOR FURTHER STUDY

Look up Morton's *Speed the Plough* under Exercises on Additional Plays. *Speed the Plough*, like *The London Merchant*, tries to achieve tragedy but actually is melodrama. At the same time, it has farcical effects like those of Plautus's *Menaechmi*. As a hodge-podge of various dramatic motifs, it provides interesting material for study.

PART THREE

MORE MATURE TYPES

1. *Introduction*

PART three presents more mature types of the drama than those which we have studied in Part Two. Here we find, in general, that the dramatists have chosen subjects and methods more likely to lead to successful results at a mature level. This is not to say that the dramatists to be considered have been uniformly successful; the reader will doubtless discover various shortcomings in the plays to be read. But he will certainly be aware that the dramatists have had, in general, profounder and more complex objectives than those which we studied in Part Two. In the latter group of plays we found fairly simple patterns: the morality play with a relatively uninvolved theme; the farce with its transparent scheme of making the most of mistakes of identity, the would-be tragedy in which the author's own confusion about what he was doing could hardly obscure from the reader his fundamentally oversimple conception of the nature of tragedy. In Part Three, however, the patterns are far less simple.

Sheridan's *School for Scandal* is obviously a much more complex comedy than the *Menaechmi;* with it, we return to wit and satire of the sort found in Wilde's *Lady Windermere's Fan.* We shall find that it resembles that play further in that it seeks, beneath the surface of amusement, to make certain serious suggestions about human experience. But Sheridan's mode of treatment of these matters involves several special complications and will force us to glance, at least briefly, at that spurious type of comedy which dominated the period in which Sheridan wrote—"sentimental comedy."

Ibsen's *Rosmersholm*, on the contrary, is an entirely serious play. In one respect it resembles the "problem play" aspect of *Lady Windermere's Fan;* in another aspect, it will compel us to examine again the nature of tragedy and to develop some of the considerations of this topic already raised by the study of *Everyman* and *The London Merchant;* still another aspect of the play involves dramatic techniques as such and will afford an opportunity to consider on an even higher level of refinement some of the skills we have noted already in Wilde.

Shakespeare's *Henry IV, Part I*, combines comedy with what will be for us the new material of historic drama; hence the play brings up an entirely new kind of problem. Indeed, the comedy element here will itself offer us new material, for, in contrast with the satirical intentions of Wilde and Sheridan, Shakespeare is primarily concerned with the comedy inherent in character.

Congreve's *Way of the World* provides a climax to our study of comedy since it offers the most polished example we have of the comedy of manners. Yet *The Way of the World* is much more than merely a brilliant example of a special mode. We shall find it to be one of the most complex plays which we are studying, and, as such, a "serious" play as well as an entertaining comedy.

2. Sheridan, *The School for Scandal*

*T*HE SCHOOL FOR SCANDAL, 1777, ante-dates *Lady Windermere's Fan* by 115 years. Yet the plays are in some respects markedly similar—in their satire of society, their use of witty dialogue, their employment of large numbers of characters. Even here, however, the reader will discern some difference—the difference of effect that results, for instance, from the contrast between Wilde's attitudes to the two chief antagonists in his play, Lady Windermere and Mrs. Erlynne, and Sheridan's attitude toward the Surface brothers, the corresponding pair in his play. If the student will give attention to this contrast as he reads, he will find some of the main clues to what Sheridan is doing.

In pursuing the contrast between the two, the student will also come upon one of the matters which do reflect a significant difference growing out of the difference in time between the two plays. For in the latter eighteenth century, when Sheridan wrote, dramatists were less concerned with satire than with what is called "sentimental comedy," the method of which, in general, was to *praise good* rather than *ridicule folly*. So the tendency was to stress the characters that were amiable and admirable rather than those who were laughable, the plays ended frequently in scenes of reform and reward, and the tone was more likely to be edifying than amusing.

This revulsion against the traditional function of comedy did not occur unchallenged. Yet the spirit of the times was on the side of the sentimental comedy. The rise of the middle classes, the reaction against the brilliant comedy of the Restoration, the attempt to refine manners and improve morals—all tended to favor the praise of virtue and the cultivation of sentiment.

In the latter part of the eighteenth century, Goldsmith and Sheridan carried out a conscious attack on the sentimental comedy, though not with unqualified success. With regard to *The School for Scandal*, therefore, this question arises: has Sheridan succeeded in completely freeing himself from the limitations of sentimental comedy? More specifically, has Sheridan tended to focus our attention on the ought-to-be, on rewards, on edification rather than on the ridicule of folly?

THE SCHOOL FOR SCANDAL

DRAMATIS PERSONÆ

Sir Peter Teazle
Sir Oliver Surface
Joseph Surface
Charles Surface
Crabtree
Sir Benjamin Backbite
Rowley
Moses
Trip

Snake
Careless
Sir Toby Bumper

Lady Teazle
Maria
Lady Sneerwell
Mrs. Candour

PROLOGUE

Written by Mr. Garrick

A school for scandal! tell me, I beseech
    you,
Needs there a school this modish art to
    teach you?
No need of lessons now, the knowing
    think;
We might as well be taught to eat and
    drink.
Caused by a dearth of scandal, should
    the vapors   5
Distress our fair ones, let them read the
    papers;
Their powerful mixtures such disorders
    hit,
Crave what you will,—there's *quantum
    sufficit.*
"Lord!" cries my Lady Wormwood,
    who loves tattle
And puts much salt and pepper in her
    prattle,   10
Just risen at noon, all night at cards
    when threshing
Strong tea and scandal,—"Bless me,
    how refreshing!
Give me the papers, Lisp,—how bold
    and free!   [*Sips.*]
Last night Lord L. [*sips*] *was caught
    with Lady D.*
For aching head what charming sal
    volatile!   [*Sips.*]
If Mrs. B. will still continue flirting,   16
We hope she'll draw, *or we'll* undraw *the
    curtain.*

Fine satire, poz![1] In public all abuse it,
But by ourselves [*sips*] our praise we
    can't refuse it.
Now, Lisp, read you,—there at that
    dash and star."   20
"Yes, ma'am. *A certain lord has best be-
    ware,*
*Who lives not twenty miles from Grosvenor
    Square,*
For, should he Lady W. find willing,
Wormwood is bitter " "Oh! that's me!
    the villain!
Throw it behind the fire and never more
Let that vile paper come within my
    door."   26
Thus at our friends we laugh, who feel
    the dart;
To reach our feelings, we ourselves must
    smart.
Is our young bard so young to think
    that he
Can stop the full spring-tide of calumny?
Knows he the world so little, and its
    trade?   31
Alas! the devil's sooner raised than laid.
So strong, so swift, the monster there's
    no gagging;
Cut Scandal's head off, still the tongue
    is wagging.
Proud of your smiles once lavishly be-
    stowed,   35

[1] Positively.

Again our young Don Quixote takes the
road;
To show his gratitude he draws his pen
And seeks this hydra, Scandal, in his
den.
For your applause all perils he would
through,—
He'll fight (that's write) a cavalliero
true,
Till every drop of blood (that's ink) is
spilt for you.

ACT I

[SCENE I. Lady Sneerwell's house.]

[*Discovered, Lady Sneerwell at the
dressing table; Snake drinking chocolate.*]

Lady Sneerwell: The paragraphs, you
say, Mr. Snake, were all inserted?

Snake: They were, madam; and as I
copied them myself in a feigned hand,
there can be no suspicion whence they
came.

Lady Sneerwell: Did you circulate the
report of Lady Brittle's intrigue with
Captain Boastall?

Snake: That's in as fine a train as your
ladyship could wish. In the common
course of things, I think it must reach
Mrs. Clackitt's ears within four-and-
twenty hours; and then, you know, the
business is as good as done.

Lady Sneerwell: Why, truly, Mrs.
Clackitt has a very pretty talent and a
great deal of industry.

Snake: True, madam, and has been
tolerably successful in her day. To my
knowledge, she has been the cause of six
matches being broken off and three sons
being disinherited; of four forced elope-
ments and as many close confinements;
nine separate maintenances and two di-
vorces. Nay, I have more than once
traced her causing a *tête-à-tête* in the
Town and Country Magazine [1] when the
parties, perhaps, had never seen each
other's face before in the course of their
lives.

---

[1] This magazine ran "imaginary" character sketches, often scandalous in tone.

Lady Sneerwell: She certainly has talents, but her manner is gross.

Snake: 'Tis very true. She generally
designs well, has a free tongue and a
bold invention; but her coloring is too
dark and her outlines often extravagant.
She wants that delicacy of tint and mellowness of sneer which distinguish your
ladyship's scandal.

Lady Sneerwell: You are partial,
Snake.

Snake: Not in the least; everybody allows that Lady Sneerwell can do more
with a word or look than many can with
the most labored detail, even when they
happen to have a little truth on their
side to support it.

Lady Sneerwell: Yes, my dear Snake;
and I am no hypocrite to deny the satisfaction I reap from the success of my
efforts. Wounded myself in the early
part of my life by the envenomed tongue
of slander, I confess I have since known
no pleasure equal to the reducing others
to the level of my own reputation.

Snake: Nothing can be more natural.
But, Lady Sneerwell, there is one affair
in which you have lately employed me,
wherein, I confess, I am at a loss to guess
your motives.

Lady Sneerwell: I conceive you mean
with respect to my neighbor, Sir Peter
Teazle, and his family?

Snake: I do. Here are two young men
to whom Sir Peter has acted as a kind of
guardian since their father's death, the
eldest possessing the most amiable character and universally well spoken of,
the youngest, the most dissipated and
extravagant young fellow in the kingdom, without friends or character; the
former an avowed admirer of your ladyship and apparently your favorite; the
latter attached to Maria, Sir Peter's
ward, and confessedly beloved by her.
Now, on the face of these circumstances,
it is utterly unaccountable to me why
you, the widow of a city knight,[2] with a
good jointure, should not close with the

---

[2] A merchant, knighted because of an
office which he held.

passion of a man of such character and expectations as Mr. Surface; and more so, why you should be so uncommonly earnest to destroy the mutual attachment subsisting between his brother Charles and Maria.

Lady Sneerwell: Then at once to unravel this mystery, I must inform you that love has no share whatever in the intercourse between Mr. Surface and me.

Snake: No!

Lady Sneerwell: His real attachment is to Maria, or to her fortune; but finding in his brother a favored rival, he has been obliged to mask his pretensions and profit by my assistance.

Snake: Yet still I am more puzzled why you should interest yourself in his success.

Lady Sneerwell: Heavens! how dull you are! Cannot you surmise the weakness which I hitherto, through shame, have concealed even from you? Must I confess that Charles, that libertine, that extravagant, that bankrupt in fortune and reputation,—that he it is for whom I am thus anxious and malicious, and to gain whom I would sacrifice everything?

Snake: Now, indeed, your conduct appears consistent; but how came you and Mr. Surface so confidential?

Lady Sneerwell: For our mutual interest. I have found him out a long time since. I know him to be artful, selfish, and malicious,—in short, a sentimental knave, while with Sir Peter, and indeed with all his acquaintance, he passes for a youthful miracle of prudence, good sense, and benevolence.

Snake: Yes! Yet Sir Peter vows he has not his equal in England; and, above all, he praises him as a man of sentiment.

Lady Sneerwell: True; and with the assistance of his sentiment and hypocrisy he has brought Sir Peter entirely into his interest with regard to Maria, while poor Charles has no friend in the house, though I fear he has a powerful one in Maria's heart, against whom we must direct our schemes. [*Enter Servant.*]

Servant: Mr. Surface.

Lady Sneerwell: Show him up. [*Exit Servant. Enter Joseph Surface.*]

Joseph Surface: My dear Lady Sneerwell, how do you do today? Mr. Snake, your most obedient.

Lady Sneerwell: Snake has just been rallying me on our mutual attachment; but I have informed him of our real views. You know how useful he has been to us, and, believe me, the confidence is not ill placed.

Joseph Surface: Madam, it is impossible for me to suspect a man of Mr. Snake's sensibility and discernment.

Lady Sneerwell: Well, well, no compliments now; but tell me when you saw your mistress, Maria,—or what is more material to me, your brother.

Joseph Surface: I have not seen either since I left you; but I can inform you that they never meet. Some of your stories have taken a good effect on Maria.

Lady Sneerwell: Ah, my dear Snake, the merit of this belongs to you. But do your brother's distresses increase?

Joseph Surface: Every hour. I am told he has had another execution in the house yesterday. In short, his dissipation and extravagance exceed anything I have ever heard of.

Lady Sneerwell: Poor Charles!

Joseph Surface: True, madam, notwithstanding his vices, one can't help feeling for him. Poor Charles! I'm sure I wish it were in my power to be of any essential service to him, for the man who does not share in the distresses of a brother, even though merited by his own misconduct, deserves—

Lady Sneerwell: O lud! you are going to be moral and forget that you are among friends.

Joseph Surface: Egad, that's true! I'll keep that sentiment till I see Sir Peter. However, it is certainly a charity to rescue Maria from such a libertine, who, if he is to be reclaimed, can be so only by a person of your ladyship's superior accomplishments and understanding.

Snake: I believe, Lady Sneerwell, here's company coming. I'll go and copy the letter I mentioned to you. Mr. Surface, your most obedient.

Joseph Surface: Sir, your very devoted.—[*Exit Snake.*] Lady Sneerwell, I am very sorry you have put any farther confidence in that fellow.

Lady Sneerwell: Why so?

Joseph Surface: I have lately detected him in frequent conference with old Rowley, who was formerly my father's steward and has never, you know, been a friend of mine.

Lady Sneerwell: And do you think he would betray us?

Joseph Surface: Nothing more likely. Take my word for 't, Lady Sneerwell, that fellow hasn't virtue enough to be faithful even to his own villainy. Ah, Maria! [*Enter Maria.*]

Lady Sneerwell: Maria, my dear, how do you do? What's the matter?

Maria: Oh! there's that disagreeable lover of mine, Sir Benjamin Backbite, has just called at my guardian's with his odious uncle, Crabtree; so I slipped out and ran hither to avoid them.

Lady Sneerwell: Is that all?

Joseph Surface: If my brother Charles had been of the party, madam, perhaps you would not have been so much alarmed.

Lady Sneerwell: Nay, now you are too severe, for I dare swear the truth of the matter is, Maria heard you were here. But, my dear, what has Sir Benjamin done that you should avoid him so?

Maria: Oh, he has done nothing; but 'tis for what he has said. His conversation is a perpetual libel on all his acquaintance.

Joseph Surface: Ay, and the worst of it is, there is no advantage in not knowing him, for he'll abuse a stranger just as soon as his best friend; and his uncle's as bad.

Lady Sneerwell: Nay, but we should make allowance; Sir Benjamin is a wit and a poet.

Maria: For my part, I own, madam, wit loses its respect with me when I see it in company with malice. What do you think, Mr. Surface?

Joseph Surface: Certainly, madam. To smile at the jest which plants a thorn in another's breast is to become a principal in the mischief.

Lady Sneerwell: Psha, there's no possibility of being witty without a little ill nature. The malice of a good thing is the barb that makes it stick. What's your opinion, Mr. Surface?

Joseph Surface: To be sure, madam, that conversation where the spirit of raillery is suppressed will ever appear tedious and insipid.

Maria: Well, I'll not debate how far scandal may be allowable; but in a man, I am sure, it is always contemptible. We have pride, envy, rivalship, and a thousand motives to depreciate each other; but the male slanderer must have the cowardice of a woman before he can traduce one. [*Enter Servant.*]

Servant: Madam, Mrs. Candour is below and, if your ladyship's at leisure, will leave her carriage.

Lady Sneerwell: Beg her to walk in. [*Exit Servant.*] Now, Maria, here is a character to your taste, for though Mrs. Candour is a little talkative, everybody allows her to be the best natured and best sort of woman.

Maria: Yes, with a very gross affectation of good nature and benevolence, she does more mischief than the direct malice of old Crabtree.

Joseph Surface: I' faith that's true, Lady Sneerwell. Whenever I hear the current running against the characters of my friends, I never think them in such danger as when Candour undertakes their defence.

Lady Sneerwell: Hush!—Here she is. [*Enter Mrs. Candour.*]

Mrs. Candour: My dear Lady Sneerwell, how have you been this century? Mr. Surface, what news do you hear,— though indeed it is no matter, for I think one hears nothing else but scandal.

Joseph Surface: Just so, indeed ma'am.

Mrs. Candour: Oh, Maria, child! What, is the whole affair off between you and Charles? His extravagance, I presume—the town talks of nothing else.

Maria: I am very sorry, ma'am, the town is not better employed.

Mrs. Candour: True, true, child; but there's no stopping people's tongues. I own I was hurt to hear it, as I indeed was to learn from the same quarter that your guardian, Sir Peter, and Lady Teazle have not agreed lately as well as could be wished.

Maria: 'Tis strangely impertinent for people to busy themselves so.

Mrs. Candour: Very true, child, but what's to be done? People will talk; there's no preventing it. Why, it was but yesterday I was told that Miss Gadabout had eloped with Sir Filigree Flirt. But, Lord, there's no minding what one hears, though, to be sure, I had this from very good authority.

Maria: Such reports are highly scandalous.

Mrs. Candour: So they are, child,— shameful, shameful! But the world is so censorious, no character escapes. Lord, now who would have suspected your friend, Miss Prim, of an indiscretion? Yet such is the ill nature of people that they say her uncle stopped her last week just as she was stepping into the York diligence with her dancing master.

Maria: I'll answer for 't there are no grounds for that report.

Mrs. Candour: Ah, no foundation in the world, I dare swear; no more probably than for the story circulated last month of Mrs. Festino's affair with Colonel Cassino,—though, to be sure, that matter was never rightly cleared up.

Joseph Surface: The license of invention some people take is monstrous indeed.

Maria: 'Tis so; but in my opinion those who report such things are equally culpable.

Mrs. Candour: To be sure they are; tale bearers are as bad as the tale makers. 'Tis an old observation and a very true one; but what's to be done, as I said before? How will you prevent people from talking? Today, Mrs. Clackitt assured me Mr. and Mrs. Honeymoon were at last become mere man and wife like the rest of their acquaintance. She likewise hinted that a certain widow in the next street had got rid of her dropsy and recovered her shape in a most surprising manner. And at the same time Miss Tattle, who was by, affirmed that Lord Buffalo had discovered his lady at a house of no extraordinary fame; and that Sir H[arry] Boquet and Tom Saunter were to measure swords on a similar provocation. But, Lord, do you think I would report these things! No, no! Tale bearers as I said before, are just as bad as the tale makers.

Joseph Surface: Ah! Mrs. Candour, if everybody had your forbearance and good nature!

Mrs. Candour: I confess, Mr. Surface, I cannot bear to hear people attacked behind their backs; and when ugly circumstances come out against our acquaintance, I own I always love to think the best. By the by, I hope 'tis not true that your brother is absolutely ruined.

Joseph Surface: I am afraid his circumstances are very bad indeed, ma'am.

Mrs. Candour: Ah, I heard so; but you must tell him to keep up his spirits. Everybody almost is in the same way. Lord Spindle, Sir Thomas Splint, Captain Quinze, and Mr. Nickit,—all up,[3] I hear, within this week; so, if Charles is undone, he'll find half his acquaintance ruined too; and that, you know, is a consolation.

Joseph Surface: Doubtless, ma'am, a very great one. [*Enter Servant.*]

Servant: Mr. Crabtree and Sir Benjamin Backbite. [*Exit.*]

Lady Sneerwell: So, Maria, you see

[3] Arrested for debt.

your lover pursues you. Positively you shan't escape. [*Enter Crabtree and Sir Benjamin Backbite.*]

Crabtree: Lady Sneerwell, I kiss your hand. Mrs. Candour, I don't believe you 5 are acquainted with my nephew, Sir Benjamin Backbite? Egad, ma'am, he has a pretty wit and is a pretty poet too, isn't he, Lady Sneerwell?

Sir Benjamin: Oh, fie, uncle! 10

Crabtree: Nay, egad, it's true; I back him at a rebus or a charade against the best rhymer in the kingdom. Has your ladyship heard the epigram he wrote last week on Lady Frizzle's feather catching 15 fire?—Do, Benjamin, repeat it, or the charade you made last night extempore at Mrs. Drowzie's *conversazione.* Come, now, your first is the name of a fish, your second a great naval commander, and— 20

Sir Benjamin: Uncle, now, prithee—

Crabtree: I' faith, ma'am, 'twould surprise you to hear how ready he is at all these sort of things.

Lady Sneerwell: I wonder, Sir Benja- 25 min, you never publish anything.

Sir Benjamin: To say truth, ma'am, 'tis very vulgar to print; and, as my little productions are mostly satires and lampoons on particular people, I find they 30 circulate more by giving copies in confidence to the friends of the parties. However, I have some love elegies, which, when favored with this lady's smiles, I mean to give the public. [*Bow-* 35 *ing to Maria.*]

Crabtree: 'Fore heaven, ma'am, they'll immortalize you!—You will be handed down to posterity like Petrarch's Laura or Waller's Sacharissa. 40

Sir Benjamin: Yes, madam, I think you will like them when you shall see them on a beautiful quarto page, where a neat rivulet of text shall meander through a meadow of margin. 'Fore gad 45 they will be the most elegant things of their kind!

Crabtree: But, ladies, that's true— Have you heard the news?

Mrs. Candour: What, sir, do you 50 mean the report of—

Crabtree: No, ma'am, that's not it, Miss Nicely is going to be married to her own footman.

Mrs. Candour: Impossible!

Crabtree: Ask Sir Benjamin.

Sir Benjamin: 'Tis very true, ma'am. Everything is fixed and the wedding liveries bespoke.

Crabtree: Yes; and they do say there were pressing reasons for it.

Lady Sneerwell: Why, I have heard something of this before.

Mrs. Candour: It can't be—And I wonder anyone should believe such a story of so prudent a lady as Miss Nicely.

Sir Benjamin: O lud! ma'am, that's the very reason 'twas believed at once. She has always been so cautious and so reserved that everybody was sure there was some reason for it at bottom.

Mrs. Candour: Why, to be sure, a tale of scandal is as fatal to the credit of a prudent lady of her stamp as a fever is generally to those of the strongest constitutions. But there is a sort of puny, sickly reputation that is always ailing, yet will outlive the robuster characters of a hundred prudes.

Sir Benjamin: True, madam, there are valetudinarians in reputation as well as in constitution, who, being conscious of their weak part, avoid the least breath of air and supply their want of stamina by care and circumspection.

Mrs. Candour: Well, but this may be all a mistake. You know, Sir Benjamin, very trifling circumstances often give rise to the most injurious tales.

Crabtree: That they do, I'll be sworn, ma'am. Did you ever hear how Miss Piper came to lose her lover and her character last summer at Tunbridge? Sir Benjamin, you remember it?

Sir Benjamin: Oh, to be sure,—the most whimsical circumstance.

Lady Sneerwell: How was it, pray?

Crabtree: Why, one evening at Mrs. Ponto's assembly the conversation happened to turn on the breeding of Nova Scotia sheep in this country. Says a young lady in company, "I have known instances of it, for Miss Letitia Piper, a first cousin of mine, had a Nova Scotia sheep that produced her twins." "What," cries the Lady Dowager Dundizzy, who, you know, is as deaf as a post, "has Miss Piper had twins?" This mistake, as you may imagine, threw the whole company into a fit of laughter. However, 'twas next morning everywhere reported, and in a few days believed by the whole town, that Miss Letitia Piper had actually been brought to bed of a fine boy and a girl; and in less than a week there were some people who could name the father and the farmhouse where the babies were put to nurse.

Lady Sneerwell: Strange, indeed!

Crabtree: Matter of fact, I assure you. —O lud, Mr. Surface, pray is it true that your uncle, Sir Oliver, is coming home?

Joseph Surface: Not that I know of, indeed, sir.

Crabtree: He has been in the East Indies a long time. You can scarcely remember him, I believe? Sad comfort, whenever he returns, to hear how your brother has gone on.

Joseph Surface: Charles has been imprudent, sir, to be sure; but I hope no busy people have already prejudiced Sir Oliver against him. He may reform.

Sir Benjamin: To be sure, he may. For my part, I never believed him to be so utterly void of principle as people say; and, though he has lost all his friends, I am told nobody is better spoken of by the Jews.

Crabtree: That's true, egad, nephew. If the Old Jewry was a ward, I believe Charles would be an alderman. No man is more popular there, 'fore gad! I hear he pays as many annuities as the Irish tontine [4]; and that whenever he is sick, they have prayers for the recovery of his health in all the synagogues.

Sir Benjamin: Yet no man lives in greater splendor. They tell me that when

he entertains his friends he will sit down to dinner with a dozen of his own securities, have a score of tradesmen waiting in the antechamber, and an officer behind every guest's chair.

Joseph Surface: This may be entertaining to you, gentlemen, but you pay very little regard to the feelings of a brother.

Maria: [*Aside.*] Their malice is intolerable!—Lady Sneerwell, I must wish you a good morning; I'm not very well. [*Exit.*]

Mrs. Candour: O dear, she changes color very much!

Lady Sneerwell: Do, Mrs. Candour, follow her. She may want assistance.

Mrs. Candour: That I will, with all my soul, ma'am. Poor dear girl, who knows what her situation may be! [*Exit.*]

Lady Sneerwell: 'Twas nothing but that she could not bear to hear Charles reflected on, notwithstanding their difference.

Sir Benjamin: The young lady's *penchant* is obvious.

Crabtree: But, Benjamin, you must not give up the pursuit for that. Follow her and put her into good humor. Repeat her some of your own verses. Come, I'll assist you

Sir Benjamin: Mr. Surface, I did not mean to hurt you; but depend on 't your brother is utterly undone.

Crabtree: O lud, ay! Undone as ever man was! Can't raise a guinea!

Sir Benjamin: And everything sold, I'm told, that was moveable.

Crabtree: I have seen one that was at his house. Not a thing left but some empty bottles that were overlooked and the family pictures, which I believe are framed in the wainscots.

Sir Benjamin: And I'm very sorry also to hear some bad stories against him. [*Going.*]

Crabtree: Oh, he has done many mean things, that's certain.

Sir Benjamin: But, however, as he's your brother— [*Going.*]

---

[4] Government loans based upon the sale of annuities, so named because invented by the Italian banker, Tonti.

Crabtree: We'll tell you all another opportunity. [*Exeunt Crabtree and Sir Benjamin.*]

Lady Sneerwell: Ha! ha! 'tis very hard for them to leave a subject they have not quite run down.

Joseph Surface: And I believe the abuse was no more acceptable to your ladyship than Maria.

Lady Sneerwell: I doubt her affections 10 are farther engaged than we imagine. But the family are to be here this evening; so you may as well dine where you are and we shall have an opportunity of observing farther. In the meantime, I'll 15 go and plot mischief and you shall study sentiment. [*Exeunt.*]

[Scene II. Sir Peter's house.]

[*Enter Sir Peter.*]

Sir Peter: When an old bachelor marries a young wife, what is he to expect? 'Tis now six months since Lady Teazle 25 made me the happiest of men,—and I have been the most miserable dog ever since! We tiffed a little going to church and fairly quarreled before the bells had done ringing. I was more than once 30 nearly choked with gall during the honeymoon and had lost all comfort in life before my friends had done wishing me joy. Yet I chose with caution,—a girl bred wholly in the country, who never 35 knew luxury beyond one silk gown nor dissipation above the annual gala of a race ball. Yet she now plays her part in the extravagant fopperies of the fashion and the town with as ready a grace as if 40 she never had seen a bush or a grass-plot out of Grosvenor Square. I am sneered at by all my acquaintance and paragraphed in the newspapers. She dissipates my fortune and contradicts all my 45 humors; yet the worst of it is, I doubt [1] I love her, or I should never bear all this. However, I'll never be weak enough to own it. [*Enter Rowley.*]

[1] Fear.

Rowley: Oh, Sir Peter, your servant! How is it with you, sir?

Sir Peter: Very bad, Master Rowley, very bad. I meet with nothing but 5 crosses and vexations.

Rowley: What can have happened to trouble you since yesterday?

Sir Peter: A good question to a married man!

Rowley: Nay, I'm sure your lady, Sir Peter, can't be the cause of your uneasiness.

Sir Peter: Why, has anybody told you she was dead?

Rowley: Come, come, Sir Peter, you love her, notwithstanding your tempers don't exactly agree.

Sir Peter: But the fault is entirely hers, Master Rowley. I am myself the 20 sweetest tempered man alive and hate a teasing temper; and so I tell her a hundred times a day.

Rowley: Indeed!

Sir Peter: Ay; and what is very extraordinary in all our disputes she is always in the wrong. But Lady Sneerwell and the set she meets at her house encourage the perverseness of her disposition. Then, to complete my vexation, 30 Maria, my ward, whom I ought to have the power over, is determined to turn rebel too and absolutely refuses the man whom I have long resolved on for her husband, meaning, I suppose, to bestow 35 herself on his profligate brother.

Rowley: You know, Sir Peter, I have always taken the liberty to differ with you on the subject of these two young gentlemen. I only wish you may not be 40 deceived in your opinion of the elder. For Charles, my life on 't, he will retrieve his errors yet. Their worthy father, once my honored master, was at his years nearly as wild a spark; 45 yet when he died, he did not leave a more benevolent heart to lament his loss.

Sir Peter: You are wrong, Master Rowley. On their father's death, you 50 know, I acted as a kind of guardian to them both till their uncle Sir Oliver's liberality gave them an early independence. Of course, no person could have more opportunities of judging of their hearts, and I was never mistaken in my life. Joseph is indeed a model for the young men of the age. He is a man of sentiment and acts up to the sentiments he professes; but for the other, take my word for 't, if he had any grain of virtue by descent, he has dissipated it with the rest of his inheritance. Ah! my old friend Sir Oliver will be deeply mortified when he finds how part of his bounty has been misapplied.

Rowley: I am sorry to find you so violent against the young man, because this may be the most critical period of his fortune. I came hither with news that will surprise you.

Sir Peter: What? Let me hear!

Rowley: Sir Oliver is arrived and at this moment in town.

Sir Peter: How! You astonish me! I thought you did not expect him this month.

Rowley: I did not; but his passage has been remarkably quick.

Sir Peter: Egad, I shall rejoice to see my old friend. 'Tis fifteen years since we met. We have had many a day together. But does he still enjoin us not to inform his nephews of his arrival?

Rowley: Most strictly. He means, before it is known, to make some trial of their dispositions.

Sir Peter: Ah! There needs no art to discover their merits. He shall have his way; but, pray, does he know I am married?

Rowley: Yes, and will soon wish you joy.

Sir Peter: What, as we drink health to a friend in a consumption? Ah! Oliver will laugh at me. We used to rail at matrimony together, and he has been steady to his text. Well, he must be soon at my house, though—I'll instantly give orders for his reception. But, Master Rowley, don't drop a word that Lady Teazle and I ever disagree.

Rowley: By no means.

Sir Peter: For I should never be able to stand Noll's jokes; so I'll have him think, Lord forgive me! that we are a very happy couple.

Rowley: I understand you; but then you must be very careful not to differ while he is in the house with you.

Sir Peter: Egad, and so we must,—and that's impossible. Ah! Master Rowley, when an old bachelor marries a young wife, he deserves—No, the crime carries its punishment along with it. [*Exeunt.*]

QUESTIONS ON ACT I

1. Reread the section entitled "Exposition" in the discussion which follows Act I of *Lady Windermere's Fan*. Does Sheridan manage his exposition as successfully as Wilde? Consider especially the early part of Scene i.

2. How rapidly does characterization proceed in Scene i?

3. What is the advantage of using certain terms from art to discuss gossip in Scene i, p. 196 b, 3 ff.? Analyze the phrase "mellowness of sneer," as well as Lady Sneerwell's remark to Joseph (p. 197 b, 43) "O lud! you are going to be moral, and forget that you are among friends."

4. What is the dramatic function of Joseph's remark to Lady Sneerwell about Charles and old Rowley (p. 198 a, 7 ff.)? Of the reference to Sir Oliver's return in Scene ii (p. 203 a, 21–22)?

5. What is the source of the wit in Joseph's remark that Sir Benjamin will "abuse a stranger just as soon as his best friend" (p. 198 a, 45)?

6. Who is the winner in the little interchange between Lady Sneerwell and Sir Benjamin which begins "I wonder, Sir Benjamin. . . ." (p. 200 a, 27 ff.)?

7. Do you find any puns in Scene i?

8. By what means is Charles characterized in Scene i?

9. Keeping in mind the skillful way in which Wilde makes all of his first act lead up to and focus our attention on the contents of Act II, determine whether Sheridan is equally successful in initiating action and in pointing ahead.

ACT II

[SCENE I. Sir Peter's house.]

[Enter Sir Peter and Lady Teazle.]

Sir Peter: Lady Teazle, Lady Teazle, I'll not bear it!

Lady Teazle: Sir Peter, Sir Peter, you may bear it or not as you please; but I ought to have my own way in everything, and, what's more, I will, too. What though I was educated in the country, I know very well that women of fashion in London are accountable to nobody after they are married.

Sir Peter: Very well, ma'am, very well; so a husband is to have no influence, no authority?

Lady Teazle: Authority! No, to be sure! If you wanted authority over me, you should have adopted me and not married me. I am sure you were old enough.

Sir Peter: Old enough! Ay, there it is. Well, well, Lady Teazle, though my life may be made unhappy by your temper, I'll not be ruined by your extravagance.

Lady Teazle: My extravagance! I'm sure I'm not more extravagant than a woman of fashion ought to be.

Sir Peter: No, no, madam, you shall throw away no more sums on such unmeaning luxury. 'Slife! to spend as much to furnish your dressing-room with flowers in winter as would suffice to turn the Pantheon[1] into a greenhouse and give a *fête champêtre* at Christmas.

Lady Teazle: And am I now to blame, Sir Peter, because flowers are dear in cold weather? You should find fault with the climate, and not with me. For my part, I'm sure I wish it was spring all the year round and that roses grew under our feet!

Sir Peter: Oons, madam! If you had been born to this, I shouldn't wonder at your talking thus; but you forget what your situation was when I married you.

Lady Teazle: No, no, I don't. 'Twas a very disagreeable one, or I should never have married you.

Sir Peter: Yes, yes, madam, you were then in somewhat a humbler style,— the daughter of a plain country squire. Recollect, Lady Teazle, when I saw you first, sitting at your tambour[2] in a pretty figured linen gown with a bunch of keys at your side, your hair combed smooth over a roll and your apartment hung round with fruits in worsted of your own working.

Lady Teazle: Oh, yes! I remember it very well, and a curious life I led. My daily occupation to inspect the dairy, superintend the poultry, make extracts from the family receipt-book, and comb my Aunt Deborah's lap-dog.

Sir Peter: Yes, yes, ma'am, 'twas so indeed.

Lady Teazle: And then you know, my evening amusements! To draw patterns for ruffles, which I had not materials to make up; to play Pope Joan[3] with the curate; to read a sermon to my aunt; or to be stuck down to an old spinet to

---

[1] A concert hall, a favorite resort of the fashionable world at this time.

[2] Embroidery frame. [3] An old game of cards.

strum my father to sleep after a fox-chase.

Sir Peter: I am glad you have so good a memory. Yes, madam, these were the recreations I took you from; but now you must have your coach,—*vis-à-vis*,[4]—and three powdered footmen before your chair, and in the summer a pair of white cats[5] to draw you to Kensington Gardens. No recollection, I suppose, when you were content to ride double behind the butler on a docked coach-horse.

Lady Teazle: No—I swear I never did that. I deny the butler and the coach-horse.

Sir Peter: This, madam, was your situation; and what have I done for you? I have made you a woman of fashion, of fortune, of rank,—in short, I have made you my wife.

Lady Teazle: Well, then, and there is but one thing more you can make me to add to the obligation, that is—

Sir Peter: My widow, I suppose?

Lady Teazle: Hem! hem!

Sir Peter: I thank you, madam; but don't flatter yourself; for, though your ill conduct may disturb my peace, it shall never break my heart, I promise you. However, I am equally obliged to you for the hint.

Lady Teazle: Then why will you endeavor to make yourself so disagreeable to me and thwart me in every little elegant expense?

Sir Peter: 'Slife, madam, I say; had you any of these little elegant expenses when you married me?

Lady Teazle: Lud, Sir Peter, would you have me be out of the fashion?

Sir Peter: The fashion, indeed! What had you to do with the fashion before you married me?

Lady Teazle: For my part, I should think you would like to have your wife thought a woman of taste.

Sir Peter: Ay! There again! Taste! Zounds, madam, you had no taste when you married me!

Lady Teazle: That's very true, indeed, Sir Peter; and, having married you, I should never pretend to taste again, I allow. But now, Sir Peter, since we have finished our daily jangle, I presume I may go to my engagement at Lady Sneerwell's.

Sir Peter: Ay, there's another precious circumstance! A charming set of acquaintance you have made there!

Lady Teazle: Nay, Sir Peter, they are all people of rank and fortune and remarkably tenacious of reputation.

Sir Peter: Yes, egad, they are tenacious of reputation with a vengeance, for they don't choose anybody should have a character but themselves! Such a crew! Ah, many a wretch has rid on a hurdle[6] who has done less mischief than these utterers of forged tales, coiners of scandal, and clippers of reputation.

Lady Teazle: What, would you restrain the freedom of speech!

Sir Peter: Ah! they have made you just as bad as any one of the society.

Lady Teazle: Why, I believe I do bear a part with a tolerable grace. But I vow I bear no malice against the people I abuse. When I say an ill-natured thing, 'tis out of pure good humor; and I take it for granted they deal exactly in the same manner with me. But, Sir Peter, you know you promised to come to Lady Sneerwell's, too.

Sir Peter: Well, well, I'll call in just to look after my own character.

Lady Teazle: Then, indeed, you must make haste after me, or you'll be too late. So good by to ye! [*Exit.*]

Sir Peter: So I have gained much by my intended expostulation! Yet with what a charming air she contradicts everything I say, and how pleasantly she shows her contempt for my authority! Well, though I can't make her love me, there is great satisfaction in quarreling with her; and I think she never appears to such advantage as when she is doing everything in her power to plague me. [*Exit.*]

[4] A coach in which the occupants sat so as to face one another. [5] Ponies.

[6] Rail.

[SCENE II. At Lady Sneerwell's.]

[*Enter Lady Sneerwell, Mrs. Candour, Crabtree, Sir Benjamin Backbite, and Joseph Surface.*]

Lady Sneerwell: Nay, positively, we will hear it.

Joseph Surface: Yes, yes, the epigram, by all means.

Sir Benjamin: O plague on it, uncle! 'Tis mere nonsense.

Crabtree: No, no! 'Fore gad, very clever for an extempore!

Sir Benjamin: But, ladies, you should be acquainted with the circumstance. You must know that one day last week as Lady Betty Curricle was taking the dust in Hyde Park in a sort of duodecimo phaëton, she desired me to write some verses on her ponies, upon which I took out my pocketbook and in one moment produced the following:—

Sure never were seen two such beautiful ponies;
Other horses are clowns, but these macaronies.
To give them this title I'm sure can't be wrong,
Their legs are so slim and their tails are so long.

Crabtree: There, ladies, done in the smack of a whip and on horseback too!

Joseph Surface: A very Phœbus mounted! Indeed, Sir Benjamin!

Sir Benjamin: Oh, dear sir! Trifles, trifles. [*Enter Lady Teazle and Maria.*]

Mrs. Candour: I must have a copy.

Lady Sneerwell: Lady Teazle, I hope we shall see Sir Peter?

Lady Teazle: I believe he'll wait on your ladyship presently.

Lady Sneerwell: Maria, my love, you look grave. Come, you shall sit down to piquet with Mr. Surface.

Maria: I take very little pleasure in cards; however I'll do as you please.

Lady Teazle: [*Aside.*] I am surprised Mr. Surface should sit down with her; I thought he would have embraced this opportunity of speaking to me before Sir Peter came.

Mrs. Candour: Now, I'll die; but you are so scandalous I'll forswear your society.

Lady Teazle: What's the matter, Mrs. Candour?

Mrs. Candour: They'll not allow our friend Miss Vermilion to be handsome.

Lady Sneerwell: Oh, surely she is a pretty woman.

Crabtree: I am very glad you think so, ma'am.

Mrs. Candour: She has a charming, fresh color.

Lady Teazle: Yes, when it is fresh put on.

Mrs. Candour: Oh, fie! I'll swear her color is natural. I have seen it come and go.

Lady Teazle: I dare swear you have, ma'am; it goes off at night and comes again in the morning.

Sir Benjamin: True, ma'am, it not only comes and goes; but what's more, egad, her maid can fetch and carry it!

Mrs. Candour: Ha, ha, ha! How I hate to hear you talk so! But surely, now, her sister is, or was, very handsome.

Crabtree: Who? Mrs. Evergreen? O Lord! She's six-and-fifty if she's an hour!

Mrs. Candour: Now positively you wrong her; fifty-two or fifty-three in the utmost,—and I don't think she looks more.

Sir Benjamin: Ah! There's no judging by her looks unless one could see her face.

Lady Sneerwell: Well, well, if Mrs. Evergreen does take some pains to repair the ravages of time, you must allow she effects it with great ingenuity; and surely that's better than the careless manner in which the widow Ochre chalks her wrinkles.

Sir Benjamin: Nay, now, Lady Sneerwell, you are severe upon the widow. Come, come, 'tis not that she paints so ill; but, when she has finished her face, she joins it so badly to her neck that she looks like a mended statue in which the connoisseur may see at once that the head's modern though the trunk's antique.

Crabtree: Ha! ha! ha! Well said, nephew!

Mrs. Candour: Ha! ha! ha! Well, you make me laugh; but I vow I hate you for it. What do you think of Miss Simper?

Sir Benjamin: Why, she has very pretty teeth.

Lady Teazle: Yes; and on that account, when she is neither speaking nor laughing, which very seldom happens, she never absolutely shuts her mouth, but leaves it always on a-jar, as it were; thus—[*Shows her teeth.*]

Mrs. Candour: How can you be so ill natured?

Lady Teazle: Nay, I allow even that's better than the pains Mrs. Prim takes to conceal her losses in front. She draws her mouth till it positively resembles the aperture of a poor's-box,[1] and all her words appear to slide out edgewise, as it were; thus: *How do you do, madam? Yes, madam.*

Lady Sneerwell: Very well, Lady Teazle. I see you can be a little severe.

Lady Teazle: In defence of a friend it is but justice. But here comes Sir Peter to spoil our pleasantry. [*Enter Sir Peter.*]

Sir Peter: Ladies, your most obedient. —[*Aside.*] Mercy on me, here is the whole set! A character dead at every word, I suppose.

Mrs. Candour: I am rejoiced you are come, Sir Peter. They have been so censorious, and Lady Teazle as bad as any one.

Sir Peter: That must be very distressing to you, Mrs. Candour, I dare swear.

Mrs. Candour: Oh, they will allow good qualities to nobody, not even good nature to our friend Mrs. Pursy.

Lady Teazle: What, the fat dowager who was at Mrs. Quadrille's last night?

Mrs. Candour: Nay, her bulk is her misfortune; and, when she takes so much pains to get rid of it, you ought not to reflect on her.

Lady Sneerwell: That's very true, indeed.

Lady Teazle: Yes, I know she almost lives on acids and small whey; laces herself by pulleys; and often in the hottest noon in summer you may see her on a little squat pony, with her hair plaited up behind like a drummer's and puffing round the Ring[2] on a full trot.

Mrs. Candour: I thank you, Lady Teazle, for defending her.

Sir Peter: Yes, a good defence, truly.

Mrs. Candour: Truly, Lady Teazle is as censorious as Miss Sallow.

Crabtree: Yes, and she is a curious being to pretend to be censorious, an awkward gawky without any one good point under heaven.

Mrs. Candour: Positively you shall not be so very severe. Miss Sallow is a near relation of mine by marriage, and, as for her person, great allowance is to be made; for, let me tell you, a woman labors under many disadvantages who tries to pass for a girl of six-and-thirty.

Lady Sneerwell: Though, surely, she is handsome still; and for the weakness in her eyes, considering how much she reads by candlelight, it is not to be wondered at.

Mrs. Candour: True, and then as to her manner; upon my word, I think it is particularly graceful, considering she never had the least education; for you know her mother was a Welsh milliner and her father a sugar-baker at Bristol.

Sir Benjamin: Ah! you are both of you too good natured!

Sir Peter: [*Aside.*] Yes, damned good natured! This their own relation! Mercy on me!

Mrs. Candour: For my part, I own I cannot bear to hear a friend ill spoken of.

Sir Peter: No, to be sure!

Sir Benjamin: Oh, you are of a moral turn. Mrs. Candour and I can sit for an

---

[1] A collection box with a slit in the top.

[2] In Hyde Park.

hour and hear Lady Stucco talk sentiment.

Lady Teazle: Nay, I vow Lady Stucco is very well with the dessert after dinner, for she's just like the French fruit one cracks for mottoes, made up of paint and proverb.

Mrs. Candour: Well, I never will join in ridiculing a friend; and so I constantly tell my cousin Ogle, and you all know what pretensions she has to be critical on beauty.

Crabtree: Oh, to be sure, she has herself the oddest countenance that ever was seen; 'tis a collection of features from all the different countries of the globe.

Sir Benjamin: So she has, indeed! An Irish front—

Crabtree: Caledonian locks—

Sir Benjamin: Dutch nose—

Crabtree: Austrian lips—

Sir Benjamin: Complexion of a Spaniard—

Crabtree: And teeth *à la Chinoise*—

Sir Benjamin: In short, her face resembles a *table d'hôte* at Spa,—where no two guests are of a nation—

Crabtree: Or a congress at the close of a general war,—wherein all the members, even to her eyes, appear to have a different interest, and her nose and chin are the only parties likely to join issue.

Mrs. Candour: Ha! ha! ha!

Sir Peter: [*Aside.*] Mercy on my life! A person they dine with twice a week!

Lady Sneerwell: Go, go! You are a couple of provoking toads.

Mrs. Candour: Nay, but I vow you shall not carry the laugh off so, for give me leave to say that Mrs. Ogle—

Sir Peter: Madam, madam, I beg your pardon. There's no stopping these good gentlemen's tongues. But when I tell you, Mrs. Candour, that the lady they are abusing is a particular friend of mine, I hope you'll not take her part.

Lady Sneerwell: Ha! ha! ha! Well said, Sir Peter! But you are a cruel creature, —too phlegmatic yourself for a jest, and too peevish to allow wit in others.

Sir Peter: Ah, madam, true wit is more nearly allied to good nature than your ladyship is aware of.

Lady Teazle: True, Sir Peter. I believe they are so near akin that they can never be united.

Sir Benjamin: Or rather, madam, suppose them to be man and wife because one seldom sees them together.

Lady Teazle: But Sir Peter is such an enemy to scandal I believe he would have it put down by parliament.

Sir Peter: 'For heaven, madam, if they were to consider the sporting with reputation of as much importance as poaching on manors and pass an act for the preservation of fame, I believe I would thank them for the bill.

Lady Sneerwell: O lud, Sir Peter, would you deprive us of our privileges?

Sir Peter: Ay, madam; and then no person should be permitted to kill characters and run down reputations but qualified old maids and disappointed widows.

Lady Sneerwell: Go, you monster!

Mrs. Candour: But, surely, you would not be quite so severe on those who only report what they hear!

Sir Peter: Yes, madam, I would have law merchant [3] for them, too; and in all cases of slander currency, whenever the drawer of the lie was not to be found, the injured parties should have a right to come on any of the indorsers.

Crabtree: Well, for my part, I believe there never was a scandalous tale without some foundation.

Sir Peter: O, nine out of ten of the malicious inventions are founded on some ridiculous misrepresentation.

Lady Sneerwell: Come, ladies, shall we sit down to cards in the next room? [*Enter Servant, who whispers Sir Peter.*]

Sir Peter: [*To Servant.*] I'll be with them directly. [*Exit Servant. Aside.*] I'll get away unperceived.

Lady Sneerwell: Sir Peter, you are not going to leave us?

---

[3] Commercial law.

Sir Peter: Your ladyship must excuse me; I'm called away by particular business. But I leave my character behind me. [*Exit.*]

Sir Benjamin: Well—certainly, Lady Teazle, that lord of yours is a strange being. I could tell you some stories of him would make you laugh heartily if he were not your husband.

Lady Teazle: Oh, pray don't mind that; come, do let's hear them. [*Joins the rest of the company going into the next room, who exeunt, except Joseph Surface and Maria.*]

Joseph Surface: Maria, I see you have no satisfaction in this society.

Maria: How is it possible I should? If to raise malicious smiles at the infirmities or misfortunes of those who have never injured us be the province of wit or humor, Heaven grant me a double portion of dulness!

Joseph Surface: Yet they appear more ill-natured than they are; they have no malice at heart.

Maria: Then is their conduct still more contemptible; for, in my opinion, nothing could excuse the intemperance of their tongues but a natural and uncontrollable bitterness of mind.

Joseph Surface: Undoubtedly, madam; and it has always been a sentiment of mine that to propagate a malicious truth wantonly is more despicable than to falsify from revenge. But can you, Maria, feel thus for others and be unkind to me alone? Is hope to be denied the tenderest passion?

Maria: Why will you distress me by renewing this subject?

Joseph Surface: Ah, Maria, you would not treat me thus and oppose your guardian, Sir Peter's will, but that I see that profligate Charles is still a favored rival.

Maria: Ungenerously urged! But whatever my sentiments are for that unfortunate young man, be assured I shall not feel more bound to give him up because his distresses have lost him the regard even of a brother.

Joseph Surface: Nay, but, Maria, do not leave me with a frown. By all that's honest I swear—[*Kneels. Enter Lady Teazle. Aside.*] Gad's life, here's Lady Teazle.—You must not—no, you shall not—for though I have the greatest regard for Lady Teazle—

Maria: Lady Teazle!

Joseph Surface: Yet were Sir Peter to suspect—[*Lady Teazle comes forward.*]

Lady Teazle: [*Aside.*] What is this, pray? Does he take her for me?—Child, you are wanted in the next room. [*Exit Maria.*] What is all this, pray?

Joseph Surface: Oh, the most unlucky circumstance in nature! Maria has somehow suspected the tender concern I have for your happiness and threatened to acquaint Sir Peter with her suspicions, and I was just endeavoring to reason with her when you came in.

Lady Teazle: Indeed! but you seemed to adopt a very tender mode of reasoning. Do you usually argue on your knees?

Joseph Surface: Oh, she's a child and I thought a little bombast—But, Lady Teazle, when are you to give me your judgment on my library, as you promised?

Lady Teazle: No, no; I begin to think it would be imprudent, and you know I admit you as a lover no farther than fashion sanctions.

Joseph Surface: True—a mere Platonic *cicisbeo*,[4]—what every wife is entitled to.

Lady Teazle: Certainly, one must not be out of the fashion. However, I have so many of my country prejudices left that, though Sir Peter's ill humor may vex me ever so, it shall never provoke me to—

Joseph Surface: The only revenge in your power. Well, I applaud your moderation.

Lady Teazle: Go! You are an insinuating wretch! But we shall be missed. Let us join the company.

[4] Gallant.

Joseph Surface: But we had best not return together.

Lady Teazle: Well, don't stay, for Maria shan't come to hear any more of your reasoning, I promise you. [*Exit.*]

Joseph Surface: A curious dilemma my politics have run me into! I wanted at first only to ingratiate myself with Lady Teazle that she might not be my enemy with Maria; and I have, I don't know how, become her serious lover. Sincerely I begin to wish I had never made such a point of gaining so very good a character, for it has led me into so many cursed rogueries that I doubt I shall be exposed at last. [*Exit.*]

[SCENE III. Sir Peter Teazle's house.]

[*Enter Rowley and Sir Oliver Surface.*]

Sir Oliver: Ha! ha! ha! so my old friend is married, hey? A young wife from the country! Ha! ha! ha! that he should have stood bluff [1] to old bachelor so long and sink into a husband at last!

Rowley: But you must not rally him on the subject, Sir Oliver; 'tis a tender point, I assure you, though he has been married only seven months.

Sir Oliver: Then he has been just half a year on the stool of repentance! Poor Peter! But you say he has entirely given up Charles—never sees him, hey?

Rowley: His prejudice against him is astonishing, and I am sure greatly increased by a jealousy of him with Lady Teazle, which he has industriously been led into by a scandalous society in the neighborhood who have contributed not a little to Charles's ill name. Whereas the truth is, I believe, if the lady is partial to either of them, his brother is the favorite.

Sir Oliver: Ay, I know there are a set of malicious, prating, prudent gossips, both male and female, who murder characters to kill time and will rob a young fellow of his good name before he has years to know the value of it. But I am not to be prejudiced against my nephew by such, I promise you. No, no; if Charles has done nothing false or mean, I shall compound for his extravagance.

Rowley: Then, my life on 't, you will reclaim him. Ah, sir, it gives me new life to find that your heart is not turned against him and that the son of my good old master has one friend, however, left.

Sir Oliver: What! Shall I forget, Master Rowley, when I was at his years myself? Egad, my brother and I were neither of us very prudent youths; and yet I believe you have not seen many better men than your old master was?

Rowley: Sir, 'tis this reflection gives me assurance that Charles may yet be a credit to his family. But here comes Sir Peter.

Sir Oliver: Egad, so he does. Mercy on me, he's greatly altered and seems to have a settled, married look! One may read *husband* in his face at this distance. [*Enter Sir Peter.*]

Sir Peter: Ha! Sir Oliver, my old friend! Welcome to England a thousand times!

Sir Oliver: Thank you, thank you, Sir Peter! And i' faith I am glad to find you well, believe me!

Sir Peter: Oh, 'tis a long time since we met,—fifteen years, I doubt, Sir Oliver, and many a cross accident in the time.

Sir Oliver: Ay, I have had my share. But, what! I find you are married, hey? Well, well, it can't be helped; and so—I wish you joy with all my heart!

Sir Peter: Thank you, thank you, Sir Oliver. Yes, I have entered into—the happy state; but we'll not talk of that now.

Sir Oliver: True, true, Sir Peter. Old friends should not begin on grievances at first meeting. No, no, no.

Rowley: [*Aside to Sir Oliver.*] Take care, pray, sir.

Sir Oliver: Well, so one of my nephews is a wild fellow, hey?

Sir Peter: Wild! Ah, my old friend, I

---

[1] Firm.

grieve for your disappointment there. He's a lost young man, indeed. However, his brother will make you amends; Joseph is, indeed, what a youth should be,—everybody in the world speaks well of him.

Sir Oliver: I am sorry to hear it; he has too good a character to be an honest fellow. "Everybody speaks well of him!" Psha! then he has bowed as low to knaves and fools as to the honest dignity of genius and virtue.

Sir Peter: What, Sir Oliver! Do you blame him for not making enemies?

Sir Oliver: Yes, if he has merit enough to deserve them.

Sir Peter: Well, well,—you'll be convinced when you know him. 'Tis edification to hear him converse; he professes the noblest sentiments.

Sir Oliver: Oh, plague of his sentiments! If he salutes me with a scrap of morality in his mouth, I shall be sick directly. But, however, don't mistake me, Sir Peter; I don't mean to defend Charles's errors; but before I form my judgment of either of them, I intend to make a trial of their hearts; and my old friend Rowley and I have planned something for the purpose.

Rowley: And Sir Peter shall own for once he has been mistaken.

Sir Peter: Oh, my life on Joseph's honor!

Sir Oliver: Well, come, give us a bottle of good wine, and we'll drink the lads' health and tell you our scheme.

Sir Peter: Allons, then!

Sir Oliver: And don't, Sir Peter, be so severe against your old friend's son. Odds, my life! I am not sorry that he has run out of the course a little. For my part, I hate to see prudence clinging to the green suckers of youth; 'tis like ivy round a sapling and spoils the growth of the tree. [*Exeunt.*]

QUESTIONS ON ACT II

1. Is the disagreement between the Teazles in Scene i supposed to be comic simply because a husband and wife disagree? Or does the reader see more in it than the mere quarrel? Does it contain any irony? Any satire?

2. Analyze the influence of the wit upon the total impression which we have of the gossips. If we consider them the "villains" of the piece, does their wit tend to make them more simple or more complex characters?

3. Do the exit and re-entry of Lady Teazle, near the end of Scene ii, seem adequately motivated? Why does Sheridan want Lady T. back on the stage at this particular point?

4. How much sense of progression does Act II give you? Note how Scene iii points ahead to a future action. Does this have the same effectiveness as the way in which Wilde's Act I leads up to his Act II?

5. See the analysis of Act II of Wilde's play and then decide whether Sheridan's Act II has a comparable rhythm and tightness of structure.

ACT III

[SCENE I. Sir Peter Teazle's house.]

[*Enter Sir Peter Teazle, Sir Oliver Surface, and Rowley.*]

Sir Peter: Well, then, we will see this fellow first and have our wine afterwards. But how is this, Master Rowley? I don't see the jet [1] of your scheme.

Rowley: Why, sir, this Mr. Stanley, whom I was speaking of, is nearly related to them by their mother. He was once a merchant in Dublin but has been ruined by a series of undeserved misfortunes. He has applied by letter to both Mr. Surface and Charles. From the former he has received nothing but evasive promises of future service, while Charles has done all that his extravagance has left him power to do; and he is at this time endeavoring to raise a sum of money, part of which, in the midst of his own distresses, I know he intends for the service of poor Stanley.

Sir Oliver: Ah! he is my brother's son.

Sir Peter: Well, but how is Sir Oliver personally to—

Rowley: Why, sir, I will inform Charles and his brother that Stanley has obtained permission to apply personally to his friends; and, as they have neither of them ever seen him, let Sir Oliver assume his character and he will have a fair opportunity of judging at least of the benevolence of their dispositions. And, believe me, sir, you will find in the youngest brother one who, in the midst of folly and dissipation, has still, as our immortal bard expresses it,—

a heart to pity and a hand,
Open as day for melting charity.[2]

Sir Peter: Psha! What signifies his having an open hand or purse either when he has nothing left to give? Well, well, make the trial, if you please. But where is the fellow whom you brought for Sir Oliver to examine relative to Charles's affairs?

Rowley: Below, waiting his commands, and no one can give him better intelligence. This, Sir Oliver, is a friendly Jew, who, to do him justice, has done everything in his power to bring your nephew to a proper sense of his extravagance.

Sir Peter: Pray, let us have him in.

Rowley: [*Apart to Servant.*] Desire Mr. Moses to walk upstairs.

Sir Peter: But, pray, why should you suppose he will speak the truth?

Rowley: Oh, I have convinced him that he has no chance of recovering certain sums advanced to Charles but through the bounty of Sir Oliver, who, he knows, has arrived, so that you may depend on his fidelity to his own interests. I have also another evidence in my power, one Snake, whom I have detected in a matter little short of forgery and shall speedily produce him to remove some of your prejudices.

Sir Peter: I have heard too much on that subject.

Rowley: Here comes the honest Israelite. [*Enter Moses.*] This is Sir Oliver.

Sir Oliver: Sir, I understand you have lately had great dealings with my nephew Charles.

Moses: Yes, Sir Oliver, I have done all I could for him; but he was ruined before he came to me for assistance.

Sir Oliver: That was unlucky, truly, for you have had no opportunity of showing your talents.

Moses: None at all. I hadn't the pleasure of knowing his distresses till he was some thousands worse than nothing.

Sir Oliver: Unfortunate, indeed! But I suppose you have done all in your power for him, honest Moses?

Moses: Yes, he knows that. This very evening I was to have brought him a gentleman from the city who does not know him and will, I believe, advance him some money.

---

[1] Point. [2] Slightly misquoted from *Henry IV, Part 2*, IV, iv, 31–32.

Sir Peter: What, one Charles has ever had money from before!

Moses: Yes. Mr. Premium, of Crutched Friars, formerly a broker.

Sir Peter: Egad, Sir Oliver, a thought strikes me! Charles, you say, does not know Mr. Premium?

Moses: Not at all.

Sir Peter: Now then, Sir Oliver, you may have a better opportunity of satisfying yourself than by an old, romancing tale of a poor relation. Go with my friend Moses and represent Premium, and then, I'll answer for it, you'll see your nephew in all his glory.

Sir Oliver: Egad, I like this idea better than the other, and I may visit Joseph afterwards as old Stanley.

Sir Peter: True,—so you may.

Rowley: Well, this is taking Charles rather at a disadvantage, to be sure. However, Moses, you understand Sir Peter and will be faithful?

Moses: You may depend upon me. This is near the time I was to have gone.

Sir Oliver: I'll accompany you as soon as you please, Moses. But hold! I have forgot one thing,—how the plague shall I be able to pass for a Jew?

Moses: There's no need. The principal is Christian.

Sir Oliver: Is he? I'm very sorry to hear it; but then, again, an't I rather too smartly dressed to look like a moneylender?

Sir Peter: Not at all; 'twould not be out of character, if you went in your own carriage, would it, Moses?

Moses: Not in the least.

Sir Oliver: Well, but how must I talk? There's certainly some cant of usury and mode of treating that I ought to know.

Sir Peter: Oh, there's not much to learn. The great point, as I take it, is to be exorbitant enough in your demands. Hey, Moses?

Moses: Yes, that's a very great point.

Sir Oliver: I'll answer for 't I'll not be wanting in that. I'll ask him eight or ten per cent. on the loan at least.

Moses: If you ask him no more than that, you'll be discovered immediately.

Sir Oliver: Hey! what, the plague! how much then?

Moses: That depends upon the circumstances. If he appears not very anxious for the supply, you should require only forty or fifty per cent.; but if you find him in great distress and want the moneys very bad, you may ask double.

Sir Peter: A good honest trade you're learning, Sir Oliver!

Sir Oliver: Truly, I think so,—and not unprofitable.

Moses: Then you know, you haven't the moneys yourself but are forced to borrow them of an old friend.

Sir Oliver: Oh! I borrow it of a friend, do I?

Moses: And your friend is an unconscionable dog; but you can't help that.

Sir Oliver: My friend an unconscionable dog, is he?

Moses: Yes, and he himself has not the moneys by him but is forced to sell stock at a great loss.

Sir Oliver: He is forced to sell stock at a great loss, is he? Well, that's very kind of him.

Sir Peter: I' faith, Sir Oliver—Mr. Premium, I mean—you'll soon be master of the trade. But, Moses, would not you have him run out a little against the annuity bill? [3] That would be in character, I should think.

Moses: Very much.

Rowley: And lament that a young man now must be at years of discretion before he is suffered to ruin himself?

Moses: Ay, great pity!

Sir Peter: And abuse the public for allowing merit to an act whose only object is to snatch misfortune and imprudence from the rapacious gripe of usury and give the minor a chance of inheriting his estate without being undone by coming into possession.

[3] Designed to protect minors against the sellers of annuities. It was passed in 1777.

Sir Oliver: So, so—Moses shall give me farther particulars as we go together.

Sir Peter: You will not have much time, for your nephew lives hard by.

Sir Oliver: Oh, never fear! My tutor appears so able that though Charles lived in the next street, it must be my own fault if I am not a complete rogue before I turn the corner. [*Exit with Moses.*]

Sir Peter: So, now, I think Sir Oliver will be convinced. You are partial, Rowley, and would have prepared Charles for the other plot.

Rowley: No, upon my word, Sir Peter.

Sir Peter: Well, go bring me this Snake, and I'll hear what he has to say presently. I see Maria and want to speak with her. [*Exit Rowley.*] I should be glad to be convinced my suspicions of Lady Teazle and Charles were unjust. I have never yet opened my mind on this subject to my friend Joseph. I am determined I will do it; he will give me his opinion sincerely. [*Enter Maria.*] So, child, has Mr. Surface returned with you?

Maria: No, sir. He was engaged.

Sir Peter: Well, Maria, do you not reflect the more you converse with that amiable young man what return his partiality for you deserves?

Maria: Indeed, Sir Peter, your frequent importunity on this subject distresses me extremely. You compel me to declare that I know no man who has ever paid me a particular attention whom I would not prefer to Mr. Surface.

Sir Peter: So—here's perverseness! No, no, Maria, 'tis Charles only whom you would prefer. 'Tis evident his vices and follies have won your heart.

Maria: This is unkind, sir. You know I have obeyed you in neither seeing or corresponding with him. I have heard enough to convince me that he is unworthy my regard. Yet I cannot think it culpable, if, while my understanding severely condemns his vices, my heart suggests some pity for his distresses.

Sir Peter: Well, well, pity him as much as you please, but give your heart and hand to a worthier object.

Maria: Never to his brother.

Sir Peter: Go, perverse and obstinate! But take care, madam; you have never yet known what the authority of a guardian is. Don't compel me to inform you of it.

Maria: I can only say, you shall not have just reason. 'Tis true, by my father's will I am for a short period bound to regard you as his substitute, but must cease to think you so when you would compel me to be miserable. [*Exit.*]

Sir Peter: Was ever man so crossed as I am, everything conspiring to fret me! I had not been involved in matrimony a fortnight before her father, a hale and hearty man, died, on purpose, I believe, for the pleasure of plaguing me with the care of his daughter.—But here comes my helpmate! She appears in great good humor. How happy I should be if I could tease her into loving me, though but a little! [*Enter Lady Teazle.*]

Lady Teazle: Lud, Sir Peter, I hope you haven't been quarreling with Maria? It is not using me well to be ill-humored when I am not by.

Sir Peter: Ah, Lady Teazle, you might have the power to make me good numored at all times.

Lady Teazle: I am sure I wish I had, for I want you to be in a charming, sweet temper at this moment. Do be good humored now and let me have two hundred pounds, will you?

Sir Peter: Two hundred pounds! What, ain't I to be in a good humor without paying for it? But speak to me thus and, i' faith, there's nothing I could refuse you. You shall have it, but seal me a bond for the repayment.

Lady Teazle: Oh, no! There,—my note of hand will do as well. [*Offering her hand.*]

Sir Peter: And you shall no longer reproach me with not giving you an independent settlement. I mean shortly rc surprise you. But shall we always live thus, hey?

Lady Teazle: If you please. I'm sure I don't care how soon we leave off quarreling provided you'll own you were tired first.

Sir Peter: Well, then let our future contest be who shall be most obliging.

Lady Teazle: I assure you, Sir Peter, good nature becomes you. You look now as you did before we were married, when you used to walk with me under the elms and tell me stories of what a gallant you were in your youth and chuck me under the chin and ask me if I thought I could love an old fellow who would deny me nothing—didn't you?

Sir Peter: Yes, yes, and you were as kind and attentive—

Lady Teazle: Ay, so I was, and would always take your part when my acquaintance used to abuse you and turn you into ridicule.

Sir Peter: Indeed!

Lady Teazle: Ay, and when my cousin Sophy has called you a stiff, peevish old bachelor and laughed at me for thinking of marrying one who might be my father, I have always defended you and said I didn't think you so ugly by any means; and I dared say you'd make a very good sort of husband.

Sir Peter: And you prophesied right; and we shall now be the happiest couple—

Lady Teazle: And never differ again?

Sir Peter: No, never. Though at the same time, indeed, my dear Lady Teazle, you must watch your temper very seriously, for in all our quarrels, my dear, if you recollect, my love, you always began first.

Lady Teazle: I beg your pardon, my dear Sir Peter. Indeed you always gave the provocation.

Sir Peter: Now see, my angel! Take care! Contradicting isn't the way to keep friends.

Lady Teazle: Then don't you begin it, my love.

Sir Peter: There, now, you—you—

are going on. You don't perceive, my life, that you are just doing the very thing which you know always makes me angry.

Lady Teazle: Nay, you know if you will be angry without any reason, my dear—

Sir Peter: There, now you want to quarrel again.

Lady Teazle: No, I'm sure I don't; but if you will be so peevish—

Sir Peter: There now! Who begins first?

Lady Teazle: Why, you to be sure. I said nothing; but there's no bearing your temper.

Sir Peter: No, no, madam! The fault's in your own temper.

Lady Teazle: Ay, you are just what my cousin Sophy said you would be.

Sir Peter: Your cousin Sophy is a forward, impertinent gipsy.

Lady Teazle: You are a great bear, I'm sure, to abuse my relations.

Sir Peter: Now may all the plagues of marriage be doubled on me if ever I try to be friends with you any more!

Lady Teazle: So much the better.

Sir Peter: No, no, madam. 'Tis evident you never cared a pin for me and I was a madman to marry you,—a pert, rural coquette that had refused half the honest squires in the neighborhood.

Lady Teazle: And I am sure I was a fool to marry you,—an old dangling bachelor, who was single at fifty only because he never could meet with anyone who would have him.

Sir Peter: Ay, ay, madam; but you were pleased enough to listen to me. You never had such an offer before.

Lady Teazle: No? Didn't I refuse Sir Tivy Terrier, who everybody said would have been a better match, for his estate is just as good as yours and he has broke his neck since we have been married?

Sir Peter: I have done with you, madam! You are an unfeeling, ungrateful—But there's an end of everything. I believe you capable of everything that is bad. Yes, madam, I now believe the reports relative to you and Charles, madam. Yes, madam, you and Charles are, not without grounds—

Lady Teazle: Take care, Sir Peter! You had better not insinuate any such thing! I'll not be suspected without cause, I promise you.

Sir Peter: Very well, madam, very well! A separate maintenance as soon as you please. Yes, madam, or a divorce! I'll make an example of myself for the benefit of all old bachelors. Let us separate, madam.

Lady Teazle: Agreed, agreed! And now, my dear Sir Peter, we are of a mind once more, we may be the happiest couple and never differ again, you know. Ha, ha, ha! Well, you are going to be in a passion, I see, and I shall only interrupt you; so bye, bye! [*Exit.*]

Sir Peter: Plagues and tortures! Can't I make her angry either? Oh, I am the most miserable fellow! But I'll not bear her presuming to keep her temper. No! She may break my heart, but she shan't keep her temper. [*Exit.*]

[SCENE II. Charles Surface's house.]

[*Enter Trip, Moses, and Sir Oliver Surface.*]

Trip: Here, Master Moses! If you'll stay a moment, I'll try whether— What's the gentleman's name?

Sir Oliver: [*Aside to Moses.*] Mr. Moses, what is my name?

Moses: Mr. Premium.

Trip: Premium. Very well. [*Exit, taking snuff.*]

Sir Oliver: To judge by the servants, one wouldn't believe the master was ruined. But what! Sure, this was my brother's house?

Moses: Yes, sir; Mr. Charles bought it of Mr. Joseph, with the furniture, pictures, &c., just as the old gentleman left it. Sir Peter thought it a piece of extravagance in him.

Sir Oliver: In my mind, the other's economy in selling it to him was more reprehensible by half. [*Enter Trip.*]

Trip: My master says you must wait, gentlemen. He has company and can't speak with you yet.

Sir Oliver: If he knew who it was wanted to see him, perhaps he would not send such a message?

Trip: Yes, yes, sir; he knows you are here. I did not forget little Premium. No, no, no.

Sir Oliver: Very well; and I pray, sir, what may be your name?

Trip: Trip, sir; my name is Trip, at your service.

Sir Oliver: Well, then, Mr. Trip, you have a pleasant sort of place here, I guess.

Trip: Why, yes. Here are three or four of us pass our time agreeably enough; but then our wages are sometimes a little in arrear, and not very great either, but fifty pounds a year and find our own bags and bouquets.[1]

Sir Oliver: [*Aside.*] Bags and bouquets! Halters and bastinadoes!

Trip: And *à propos*, Moses, have you been able to get me that little bill discounted?

Sir Oliver: [*Aside.*] Wants to raise money too! Mercy on me! has his distresses too, I warrant, like a lord and affects creditors and duns.

Moses: 'Twas not to be done, indeed, Mr. Trip.

Trip: Good lack, you surprise me! My friend Brush has indorsed it, and I thought when he put his name at the back of a bill 'twas the same as cash.

Moses: No, 'twouldn't do.

Trip: A small sum,—but twenty pounds. Harkee, Moses, do you think you couldn't get it me by way of annuity?

Sir Oliver: [*Aside.*] An annuity! Ha, ha! A footman raise money by way of annuity! Well done, luxury, egad!

Moses: Well, but you must insure your place.

Trip: Oh, with all my heart! I'll insure my place and my life too, if you please.

---

[1] Provide their own bag wigs and shoulder bouquets, worn by footmen.

Sir Oliver: [*Aside.*] It's more than I would your neck.

Moses: But is there nothing you could deposit?

Trip: Why, nothing capital of my master's wardrobe has dropped lately; but I could give you a mortgage on some of his winter clothes with equity of redemption before November; or you shall have the reversion of the French velvet or a post-obit on the blue and silver. These I should think, Moses, with a few pairs of point ruffles as collateral security—Hey, my little fellow?

Moses: Well, well. [*Bell rings.*]

Trip: Egad, I heard the bell! I believe, gentlemen, I can now introduce you. Don't forget the annuity, little Moses. This way, gentlemen; I'll insure my place, you know.

Sir Oliver: [*Aside.*] If the man be a shadow of the master, this is a temple of dissipation indeed. [*Exeunt.*]

[SCENE III. Another room.]

[*Charles Surface, Careless, &c., &c., at a table with wine, &c.*]

Charles: 'Fore heaven, 'tis true! There's the great degeneracy of the age. Many of our acquaintance have taste, spirit, and politeness; but, plague on't, they won't drink.

Careless: It is so, indeed, Charles. They go into all the substantial luxuries of the table and abstain from nothing but wine and wit. Oh, certainly society suffers by it intolerably, for now instead of the social spirit of raillery that used to mantle over a glass of bright Burgundy, their conversation is become just like the Spa-water they drink, which has all the pertness and flatulency of champagne without the spirit or flavor.

1st Gentleman: But what are they to do who love play better than wine?

Careless: True! There's Sir Harry diets himself for gaming and is now under a hazard regimen.

Charles. Then he'll have the worst of it. What! you wouldn't train a horse for the course by keeping him from corn? For my part, egad, I am never so successful as when I am a little merry. Let me throw on a bottle of champagne and I never lose.

Careless: At least I never feel my losses, which is exactly the same thing.

2d Gentleman: Ay, that I believe.

Charles: And then, what man can pretend to be a believer in love who is an abjurer of wine? 'Tis the test by which the lover knows his own heart. Fill a dozen bumpers to a dozen beauties and she that floats atop is the maid that has bewitched you.

Careless: Now then, Charles, be honest and give us your real favorite.

Charles: Why, I have withheld her only in compassion to you. If I toast her, you must give a round of her peers, which is impossible—on earth.

Careless: Oh, then, we'll find some canonized vestals or heathen goddesses that will do, I warrant!

Charles: Here, then, bumpers, you rogues! Bumpers! Maria! Maria!

Sir [*Toby*] *Bumper:* Maria who?

Charles: Oh, damn the surname! 'Tis too formal to be registered in love's calendar. But now, Sir [Toby], beware! We must have beauty superlative.

Careless: Nay, never study, Sir [Toby]. We'll stand to the toast though your mistress should want an eye and you know you have a song will excuse you.

Sir [*Toby*]: Egad, so I have, and I'll give him the song instead of the lady. [*Sings.*]

Here's to the maiden of bashful fifteen;
  Here's to the widow of fifty;
Here's to the flaunting, extravagant quean,
  And here's to the housewife that's thrifty.
CHORUS.   Let the toast pass,
        Drink to the lass,—
I'll warrant she'll prove an excuse for the glass!

Here's to the charmer whose dimples we prize;
  Now to the maid who has none, sir!

Here's to the girl with a pair of blue eyes,
  And here's to the nymph with but one, sir!
CHORUS.   Let the toast pass, &c.

Here's to the maid with a bosom of snow!
  Now to her that's as brown as a berry!
Here's to the wife with a face full of woe,
  And now to the girl that is merry!
CHORUS.   Let the toast pass, &c.

For let 'em be clumsy, or let 'em be slim,
  Young or ancient, I care not a feather;
So fill a pint bumper quite up to the brim,
  And let us e'en toast them together!
CHORUS.   Let the toast pass, &c.

All: Bravo! Bravo! [*Enter Trip and whispers Charles Surface.*]

Charles: Gentlemen, you must excuse me a little. Careless, take the chair, will you?

Careless: Nay, pr'ythee, Charles, what now? This is one of your peerless beauties, I suppose, has dropped in by chance?

Charles: No, faith! To tell you the truth, 'tis a Jew and a broker, who are come by appointment.

Careless: Oh, damn it, let's have the Jew in.

1st Gentleman: Ay, and the broker too, by all means.

2d Gentleman: Yes, yes, the Jew and the broker!

Charles: Egad, with all my heart! Trip, bid the gentlemen walk in. [*Exit Trip.*] Though there's one of them a stranger, I can tell you.

Careless: Charles, let us give them some generous Burgundy and perhaps they'll grow conscientious.

Charles: Oh, hang 'em, no! Wine does but draw forth a man's natural qualities; and to make them drink would only be to whet their knavery. [*Enter Trip, Sir Oliver, and Moses.*]

Charles: So, honest Moses! Walk in, pray, Mr. Premium. That's the gentleman's name, isn't it, Moses?

Moses: Yes, sir.

Charles: Set chairs, Trip.—Sit down, Mr. Premium.—Glasses, Trip.—Sit down, Moses.—Come, Mr. Premium,

I'll give you a sentiment: here's *Success to usury!* Moses, fill the gentleman a bumper.

Moses: Success to usury! [*Drinks.*]

Careless: Right, Moses! Usury is prudence and industry, and deserves to succeed.

Sir Oliver: Then—here's—all the success it deserves! [*Drinks.*]

Careless: No, no, that won't do! Mr. Premium, you have demurred at the toast and must drink it in a pint bumper.

1st Gentleman: A pint bumper at least!

Moses: Oh, pray, sir, consider! Mr. Premium's a gentleman.

Careless: And therefore loves good wine.

2d Gentleman: Give Moses a quart glass. This is mutiny and a high contempt for the chair.

Careless: Here, now for 't! I'll see justice done, to the last drop of my bottle.

Sir Oliver: Nay, pray, gentlemen! I did not expect this usage.

Charles: No, hang it, you shan't. Mr. Premium's a stranger.

Sir Oliver: [*Aside.*] Odd! I wish I was well out of their company.

Careless: Plague on 'em then! If they won't drink, we'll not sit down with them. Come, Toby, the dice are in the next room. Charles, you'll join us when you have finished your business with the gentlemen?

Charles: I will! I will! [*Exeunt Gentlemen.*] Careless!

Careless: [*Returning.*] Well?

Charles: Perhaps I may want you.

Careless: Oh, you know I am always ready. Word, note, or bond, 'tis all the same to me! [*Exit.*]

Moses: Sir, this is Mr. Premium, a gentleman of the strictest honor and secrecy, and always performs what he undertakes. Mr. Premium, this is—

Charles: Psha! Have done! Sir, my friend Moses is a very honest fellow but a little slow at expression. He'll be an hour giving us our titles. Mr. Premium, the plain state of the matter is this: I am an extravagant young fellow who wants to borrow money; you I take to be a prudent old fellow who have got money to lend. I am blockhead enough to give fifty per cent. sooner than not have it; and you, I presume, are rogue enough to take a hundred if you can get it. Now, sir, you see we are acquainted at once and may proceed to business without farther ceremony.

Sir Oliver: Exceeding frank, upon my word. I see, sir, you are not a man of many compliments.

Charles: Oh, no, sir! Plain dealing in business I always think best.

Sir Oliver: Sir, I like you the better for it. However, you are mistaken in one thing. I have no money to lend, but I believe I could procure some of a friend; but then he's an unconscionable dog, isn't he, Moses?

Moses: But you can't help that.

Sir Oliver: And must sell stock to accommodate you, mustn't he, Moses?

Moses: Yes, indeed! You know I always speak the truth and scorn to tell a lie.

Charles: Right! People that speak truth generally do. But these are trifles, Mr. Premium. What, I know money isn't to be bought without paying for 't!

Sir Oliver: Well, but what security could you give? You have no land, I suppose?

Charles: Not a mole-hill, nor a twig, but what's in the bough-pots [1] out of the window!

Sir Oliver: Nor any stock, I presume?

Charles: Nothing but live stock,—and that's only a few pointers and ponies. But, pray, Mr. Premium, are you acquainted at all with any of my connections?

Sir Oliver: Why, to say truth, I am.

Charles: Then you must know that I have a devilish rich uncle in the East Indies, Sir Oliver Surface, from whom I have the greatest expectations.

Sir Oliver: That you have a wealthy uncle, I have heard; but how your expectations will turn out is more, I believe, than you can tell.

Charles: Oh, no! There can be no doubt! They tell me I'm a prodigious favorite and that he talks of leaving me everything.

Sir Oliver: Indeed! This is the first I've heard of it.

Charles: Yes, yes, 'tis just so. Moses knows 'tis true, don't you, Moses?

Moses: Oh, yes! I'll swear to't.

Sir Oliver: [*Aside.*] Egad, they'll persuade me presently I'm at Bengal.

Charles: Now I propose, Mr. Premium, if it's agreeable to you, a post-obit on Sir Oliver's life, though at the same time the old fellow has been so liberal to me that I give you my word I should be very sorry to hear that anything had happened to him.

Sir Oliver: Not more than I should, I assure you. But the bond you mention happens to be just the worst security you could offer me,—for I might live to a hundred and never see the principal.

Charles: Oh, yes, you would! The moment Sir Oliver dies, you know, you would come on me for the money.

Sir Oliver: Then I believe I should be the most unwelcome dun you ever had in your life.

Charles: What! I suppose you're afraid that Sir Oliver is too good a life?

Sir Oliver: No, indeed I am not, though I have heard he is as hale and healthy as any man of his years in Christendom.

Charles: There, again, now you are misinformed. No, no, the climate has hurt him considerably, poor uncle Oliver. Yes, yes, he breaks apace, I'm told, and is so much altered lately that his nearest relations don't know him.

Sir Oliver: No! Ha, ha, ha! So much altered lately that his nearest relations don't know him! Ha, ha, ha! Egad! Ha, ha, ha!

Charles: Ha, ha! You're glad to hear that, little Premium?

Sir Oliver: No, no, I'm not.

---

[1] Window-boxes.

Charles: Yes, yes, you are! Ha, ha, ha! You know that mends your chance.

Sir Oliver: But I'm told Sir Oliver is coming over. Nay, some say he is actually arrived.

Charles: Psha! sure I must know better than you whether he's come or not. No, no, rely on't, he's at this moment at Calcutta, isn't he, Moses?

Moses: Oh, yes, certainly.

Sir Oliver: Very true, as you say, you must know better than I, though I have it from pretty good authority, haven't I, Moses?

Moses: Yes, most undoubted!

Sir Oliver: But, sir, as I understand you want a few hundreds immediately, is there nothing you could dispose of?

Charles: How do you mean?

Sir Oliver: For instance, now, I have heard that your father left behind him a great quantity of massy old plate.

Charles: O lud! that's gone long ago. Moses can tell you how better than I can.

Sir Oliver: [*Aside.*] Good lack, all the family race-cups and corporation bowls![2] —Then it was also supposed that his library was one of the most valuable and compact.

Charles: Yes, yes, so it was,—vastly too much so for a private gentleman. For my part, I was always of a communicative disposition; so I thought it a shame to keep so much knowledge to myself.

Sir Oliver: [*Aside.*] Mercy upon me! Learning that had run in the family like an heirloom!—Pray what are become of the books?

Charles: You must inquire of the auctioneer, Master Premium, for I don't believe even Moses can direct you.

Moses: I know nothing of books.

Sir Oliver: So, so, nothing of the family property left, I suppose?

Charles: Not much, indeed, unless you have a mind to the family pictures. I have got a room full of ancestors above; and if you have a taste for paintings, egad, you shall have 'em a bargain.

Sir Oliver: Hey! What the devil? Sure, you wouldn't sell your forefathers, would you?

Charles: Every man of them to the best bidder.

Sir Oliver: What! Your great-uncles and aunts?

Charles: Ay, and my great-grandfathers and grandmothers too.

Sir Oliver: [*Aside.*] Now I give him up!—What the plague, have you no bowels for your own kindred? Odd's life, do you take me for Shylock in the play that you would raise money of me on your own flesh and blood?

Charles: Nay, my little broker, don't be angry. What need you care if you have your money's worth?

Sir Oliver: Well, I'll be the purchaser. I think I can dispose of the family canvas. [*Aside.*] Oh, I'll never forgive him for this, never! [*Enter Careless.*]

Careless: Come, Charles; what keeps you?

Charles: I can't come yet. I' faith, we are going to have a sale above stairs. Here's little Premium will buy all my ancestors.

Careless: Oh, burn your ancestors!

Charles: No, he may do that afterwards if he pleases. Stay, Careless, we want you. Egad, you shall be auctioneer; so come along with us.

Careless: Oh, have with you, if that's the case. Handle a hammer as well as a dice-box!

Sir Oliver: [*Aside.*] Oh, the profligates!

Charles: Come, Moses, you shall be appraiser if we want one. Gad's life, little Premium, you don't seem to like the business.

Sir Oliver: Oh, yes, I do, vastly! Ha, ha, ha! Yes, yes, I think it a rare joke to sell one's family by auction. Ha, ha! [*Aside.*] Oh, the prodigal!

Charles: To be sure! When a man wants money, where the plague should he get assistance if he can't make free with his own relations? [*Exeunt.*]

[2] Testimonial bowls presented by the city for distinguished services.

QUESTIONS ON ACT III

1. In what way does the use of a character like Rowley, in Scene i, considerably ease the problems of the author of the play? Does the use of Rowley provide too easy solutions?

2. What is the technique by which Sheridan manages to introduce some satire of money-lending in Scene i without our feeling that it is irrelevant?

3. How does the wit of Moses influence the impression which he makes upon us? How does it influence the tone of the actual money-lending scene?

4. Does the Teazle argument advance the action in any way? Analyze the effectiveness of Sir Peter's final remark in Scene i, "I'll not bear her presuming to keep her temper."

5. In the narrow technical sense the scene of Trip's borrowing money (Scene ii) is irrelevant. Is there another sense, however, in which the scene might be justified? What do we learn through it?

6. Why do Charles's friends in Scene iii insist on having the money-lenders in? Note the use of irony in the rest of this scene.

7. How does Sheridan endeavor to create a sense of movement forward at the end of Act III?

ACT IV

[SCENE I. Picture room at Charles's.]

[*Enter Charles Surface, Sir Oliver Surface, Moses, and Careless.*]

Charles: Walk in, gentlemen, pray walk in. Here they are, the family of the Surfaces up to the Conquest.

Sir Oliver: And, in my opinion, a goodly collection.

Charles: Ay, ay, these are done in the true spirit of portrait-painting; no *volontière grâce* or expression. Not like the works of your modern Raphaels, who give you the strongest resemblance, yet contrive to make your portrait independent of you, so that you may sink the original and not hurt the picture. No, no; the merit of these is the inveterate likeness,—all stiff and awkward as the originals and like nothing in human nature besides.

Sir Oliver: Ah! We shall never see such figures of men again.

Charles: I hope not! Well, you see, Master Premium, what a domestic character I am; here I sit of an evening surrounded by my family. But come, get into your pulpit, Mr. Auctioneer; here's an old, gouty chair of my grandfather's will answer the purpose.

5 *Careless:* Ay, ay, this will do. But, Charles, I haven't a hammer; and what's an auctioneer without his hammer!

Charles: Egad, that's true! What parchment have we here? Oh, our gene-10 alogy in full. Here, Careless, you shall have no common bit of mahogany; here's the family tree for you, you rogue! This shall be your hammer, and now you may knock down my ancestors with 15 their own pedigree.

Sir Oliver: [*Aside.*] What an unnatural rogue! An *ex post facto* parricide!

Careless: Yes, yes, here's a list of your generation, indeed. Faith, Charles, 20 this is the most convenient thing you could have found for the business, for 'twill serve not only as a hammer but a catalogue into the bargain. Come, begin! A-going, a-going, a-going!

25 *Charles:* Bravo, Careless! Well, here's my great-uncle, Sir Richard Raveline, a marvellous good general in his day, I assure you. He served in all the Duke of Marlborough's wars and got that cut

over his eye at the battle of Malplaquet.[1] What say you, Mr. Premium? Look at him. There's a hero! Not cut out of his feathers as your modern clipped captains are, but enveloped in wig and regimentals as a general should be. What do you bid?

Moses: Mr. Premium would have you speak.

Charles: Why, then, he shall have him for ten pounds, and I'm sure that's not dear for a staff officer.

Sir Oliver: [*Aside.*] Heaven deliver me! His famous uncle Richard for ten pounds!—Very well, sir, I take him at that.

Charles: Careless, knock down my uncle Richard.—Here, now, is a maiden sister of his, my great-aunt Deborah, done by Kneller,[2] thought to be in his best manner, and a very formidable likeness. There she is, you see, a shepherdess feeding her flock. You shall have her for five pounds ten,—the sheep are worth the money.

Sir Oliver: [*Aside.*] Ah, poor Deborah, a woman who set such a value on herself!—Five pounds ten—She's mine.

Charles: Knock down my aunt Deborah! Here, now, are two that were a sort of cousins of theirs. You see, Moses, these pictures were done some time ago when beaux wore wigs and the ladies their own hair.

Sir Oliver: Yes, truly, head-dresses appear to have been a little lower in those days.

Charles: Well, take that couple for the same.

Moses: 'Tis a good bargain.

Charles: Careless!—This now, is a grandfather of my mother's, a learned judge, well known on the western circuit. What do you rate him at, Moses?

Moses: Four guineas.

Charles: Four guineas! Gad's life, you don't bid me the price of his wig. Mr. Premium, you have more respect for the

woolsack.[3] Do let us knock his lordship down at fifteen.

Sir Oliver: By all means.

Careless: Gone!

Charles: And these are two brothers of his, William and Walter Blunt, Esquires, both members of parliament and noted speakers; and what's very extraordinary, I believe this is the first time they were ever bought or sold.

Sir Oliver: That is very extraordinary, indeed! I'll take them at your own price for the honor of parliament.

Careless: Well said, little Premium! I'll knock them down at forty.

Charles: Here's a jolly fellow! I don't know what relation, but he was mayor of Manchester; take him at eight pounds.

Sir Oliver: No, no; six will do for the mayor.

Charles: Come, make it guineas,[4] and I'll throw you the two aldermen there into the bargain.

Sir Oliver: They're mine.

Charles: Careless, knock down the mayor and aldermen. But, plague on 't, we shall be all day retailing in this manner. Do let us deal wholesale, what say you, little Premium? Give me three hundred pounds for the rest of the family in the 'ump.

Careless: Ay, ay, that will be the best way.

Sir Oliver: Well, well, anything to accommodate you. They are mine. But there is one portrait which you have always passed over.

Careless: What, that ill-looking little fellow over the settee?

Sir Oliver: Yes, sir, I mean that, though I don't think him so ill-looking a little fellow by any means.

Charles: What, that? Oh, that's my uncle Oliver. 'Twas done before he went to India.

Careless: Your uncle Oliver! Gad,

---

[1] Victory won over the French in 1709.
[2] Sir Godfrey Kneller (1648–1723).

[3] On which the Lord Chancellor sits in the House of Lords; hence a symbol here of the legal profession. [4] The pound is twenty shillings; the guinea, twenty-one.

then you'll never be friends, Charles. That, now, is as stern a looking rogue as ever I saw, an unforgiving eye and a damned disinheriting countenance! An inveterate knave, depend on't, don't you think so, little Premium?

Sir Oliver: Upon my soul, sir, I do not. I think it is as honest a looking face as any in the room, dead or alive. But I suppose uncle Oliver goes with the rest of the lumber?

Charles: No, hang it! I'll not part with poor Noll. The old fellow has been very good to me, and, egad, I'll keep his picture while I've a room to put it in.

Sir Oliver: [*Aside.*] The rogue's my nephew after all!—But, sir, I have somehow taken a fancy to that picture.

Charles: I'm sorry for't, for you certainly will not have it. Oons, haven't you got enough of them?

Sir Oliver: [*Aside.*] I forgive him for everything!—But, sir, when I take a whim in my head, I don't value money. I'll give you as much for that as for all the rest.

Charles: Don't tease me, master broker. I tell you I'll not part with it, and there's an end of it.

Sir Oliver: [*Aside.*] How like his father the dog is!—Well, well, I have done. [*Aside.*] I did not perceive it before, but I think I never saw such a striking resemblance.—Here's a draft for your sum.

Charles: Why, 'tis for eight hundred pounds!

Sir Oliver: You will not let Sir Oliver go?

Charles: Zounds, no! I tell you once more.

Sir Oliver: Then never mind the difference, we'll balance that another time. But give me your hand on the bargain. You are an honest fellow, Charles—I beg pardon, sir, for being so free.— Come, Moses.

Charles: Egad, this is a whimsical old fellow!—But hark'ee, Premium, you'll prepare lodgings for these gentlemen.

Sir Oliver: Yes, yes, I'll send for them in a day or two.

Charles: But hold! Do, now, send a genteel conveyance for them, for, I assure you, they were most of them used to ride in their own carriages.

Sir Oliver: I will, I will,—for all but little Oliver.

Charles: Ay, all but the little nabob.

Sir Oliver: You're fixed on that?

Charles: Peremptorily.

Sir Oliver: [*Aside.*] A dear extravagant rogue!—Good day! Come, Moses. [*Aside.*] Let me hear now who dares call him profligate! [*Exeunt Sir Oliver and Moses.*]

Careless: Why, this is the oddest genius of the sort I ever met with.

Charles: Egad, he's the prince of brokers, I think. I wonder how Moses got acquainted with so honest a fellow. Ha! here's Rowley.—Do, Careless, say I'll join the company in a few moments.

Careless: I will, but don't let that old blockhead persuade you to squander any of that money on old, musty debts or any such nonsense, for tradesmen, Charles, are the most exorbitant fellows.

Charles: Very true, and paying them is only encouraging them.

Careless: Nothing else.

Charles: Ay, ay, never fear. [*Exit Careless.*] So, this was an odd old fellow, indeed. Let me see, two-thirds of this is mine by right, five hundred and thirty odd pounds. 'Fore heaven, I find one's ancestors are more valuable relations than I took them for! [*Bowing to the pictures.*] Ladies and gentlemen, your most obedient and very grateful servant. [*Enter Rowley.*] Ha, old Rowley! Egad, you are just come in time to take leave of your old acquaintance.

Rowley: Yes, I heard they were a-going. But I wonder you can have such spirits under so many distresses.

Charles: Why, there's the point, my distresses are so many that I can't afford to part with my spirits; but I shall be rich and splenetic, all in good time. However, I suppose you are surprised that I am not more sorrowful at parting with so many near relations. To be sure, 'tis very affecting; but you see they never move a muscle; so why should I?

Rowley: There's no making you serious a moment.

Charles: Yes, faith, I am so now. Here, my honest Rowley, here get me this changed directly and take a hundred pounds of it immediately to old Stanley.

Rowley: A hundred pounds! Consider only—

Charles: Gad's life, don't talk about it! Poor Stanley's wants are pressing and, if you don't make haste, we shall have someone call that has a better right to the money.

Rowley: Ah, there's the point! I never will cease dunning you with the old proverb—

Charles: "Be just before you're generous."—Why, so I would if I could; but Justice is an old, lame, hobbling beldame, and I can't get her to keep pace with Generosity for the soul of me.

Rowley: Yet, Charles, believe me, one hour's reflection—

Charles: Ay, ay, that's very true; but hark'ee, Rowley, while I have, by heaven I'll give; so damn your economy. And now for hazard! [*Exeunt.*]

[SCENE II. The parlor.]

[*Enter Sir Oliver Surface and Moses.*]

Moses: Well, sir, I think, as Sir Peter said, you have seen Mr. Charles in high glory; 'tis great pity he's so extravagant.

Sir Oliver: True, but he would not sell my picture.

Moses: And loves wine and women so much.

Sir Oliver: But he would not sell my picture.

Moses: And games so deep.

Sir Oliver: But he would not sell my picture. Oh, here's Rowley! [*Enter Rowley.*]

Rowley: So, Sir Oliver, I find you have made a purchase—

Sir Oliver: Yes, yes, our young rake has parted with his ancestors like old tapestry.

Rowley: And here he has commissioned me to re-deliver you part of the purchase money. I mean, though, in your necessitous character of old Stanley.

Moses: Ah, there's the pity of all; he is so damned charitable.

Rowley: And left a hosier and two tailors in the hall, who, I'm sure, won't be paid; and this hundred would satisfy them.

Sir Oliver: Well, well, I'll pay his debts and his benevolence, too. But now I am no more a broker, and you shall introduce me to the elder brother as old Stanley.

Rowley: Not yet awhile. Sir Peter, I know, means to call there about this time. [*Enter Trip.*]

Trip: Oh, gentlemen, I beg pardon for not showing you out. This way.— Moses, a word. [*Exit with Moses.*]

Sir Oliver: There's a fellow for you! Would you believe it, that puppy intercepted the Jew on our coming and wanted to raise money before he got to his master!

Rowley: Indeed!

Sir Oliver: Yes, they are now planning an annuity business. Ah, Master Rowley, in my days servants were content with the follies of their masters when they were worn a little threadbare, but now they have their vices like their birthday clothes,[1] with the gloss on. [*Exeunt.*]

[SCENE III. A library in Joseph Surface's house.]

[*Enter Joseph Surface and Servant.*]

Joseph Surface: No letter from Lady Teazle?

Servant: No, sir.

Joseph Surface: I am surprised she has not sent if she is prevented from coming. Sir Peter certainly does not

[1] Costumes worn for the celebration of the birthday.

suspect me. Yet I wish I may not lose the heiress through the scrape I have drawn myself into with the wife. However, Charles's imprudence and bad character are great points in my favor. 5

[*Knocking heard without.*]

Servant: Sir, I believe that must be Lady Teazle.

Joseph Surface: Hold! See whether it is or not before you go to the door. I 10 have a particular message for you if it should be my brother.

Servant: 'Tis her ladyship, sir. She always leaves her chair at a milliner's in the next street. 15

Joseph Surface: Stay, stay! Draw that screen before the window. That will do. My opposite neighbor is a maiden lady of so curious a temper. [*Servant draws the screen and exit.*] I have a difficult 20 hand to play in this affair. Lady Teazle has lately suspected my views on Maria, but she must by no means be let into that secret,—at least, till I have her more in my power. [*Enter Lady Teazle.*] 25

Lady Teazle: What, sentiment in soliloquy now? Have you been very impatient? O lud! don't pretend to look grave. I vow I couldn't come before.

Joseph Surface: O madam, punctual- 30 ity is a species of constancy very unfashionable in a lady of quality.

Lady Teazle: Upon my word, you ought to pity me. Do you know Sir Peter is grown so ill-natured to me of late, and 35 so jealous of Charles too! That's the best of the story, isn't it?

Joseph Surface: [*Aside.*] I am glad my scandalous friends keep that up.

Lady Teazle: I am sure I wish he 40 would let Maria marry him and then, perhaps, he would be convinced; don't you, Mr. Surface?

Joseph Surface: [*Aside.*] Indeed I do not.—Oh, certainly I do! for then my 45 dear Lady Teazle would also be convinced how wrong her suspicions were of my having any design on the silly girl.

Lady Teazle: Well, well, I'm inclined to believe you. But isn't it provoking to 50 have the most ill-natured things said of

one? And there's my friend Lady Sneerwell has circulated I don't know how many scandalous tales of me, and all without any foundation too. That's what vexes me. 5

Joseph Surface: Ay, madam, to be sure, that's the provoking circumstance, —without foundation. Yes, yes, there's the mortification, indeed; for, when a scandalous story is believed against one, 10 there certainly is no comfort like the consciousness of having deserved it.

Lady Teazle: No, to be sure, then I'd forgive their malice. But to attack me, who am really so innocent and who 15 never say an ill-natured thing of anybody,—that is, of any friend; and then Sir Peter, too, to have him so peevish and so suspicious, when I know the integrity of my own heart,—indeed, 'tis 20 monstrous!

Joseph Surface: But, my dear Lady Teazle, 'tis your own fault if you suffer it. When a husband entertains a groundless suspicion of his wife and withdraws 25 his confidence from her, the original compact is broken; and she owes it to the honor of her sex to endeavor to outwit him.

Lady Teazle: Indeed! So that, if he 30 suspects me without cause, it follows that the best way of curing his jealousy is to give him reason for it?

Joseph Surface: Undoubtedly,—for your husband should never be deceived 35 in you; and in that case it becomes you to be frail in compliment to his discernment.

Lady Teazle: To be sure, what you say is very reasonable, and when the con- 40 sciousness of my innocence—

Joseph Surface: Ah, my dear madam, there is the great mistake! 'Tis this very conscious innocence that is of the greatest prejudice to you. What is it makes 45 you negligent of forms and careless of the world's opinion? Why, the consciousness of your own innocence. What makes you thoughtless in your conduct and apt to run into a thousand little impru- 50 dences? Why, the consciousness of your own innocence. What makes you impatient of Sir Peter's temper and outrageous at his suspicions? Why, the consciousness of your own innocence.

Lady Teazle: 'Tis very true.

Joseph Surface: Now, my dear Lady Teazle, if you would but make a trifling *faux pas*, you can't conceive how cautious you would grow and how ready to humor and agree with your husband.

Lady Teazle: Do you think so?

Joseph Surface: Oh, I am sure on't! And then you would find all scandal cease at once, for, in short, your character at present is like a person in a plethora, absolutely dying from too much health.

Lady Teazle: So, so; then I perceive your prescription is that I must sin in my own defense and part with my virtue to preserve my reputation?

Joseph Surface: Exactly so, upon my credit, ma'am.

Lady Teazle: Well, certainly this is the oddest doctrine and the newest receipt for avoiding calumny!

Joseph Surface: An infallible one, believe me. Prudence, like experience, must be paid for.

Lady Teazle: Why, if my understanding were once convinced—

Joseph Surface: Oh, certainly, madam, your understanding should be convinced. Yes, yes,—heaven forbid I should persuade you to do anything you thought wrong. No, no, I have too much honor to desire it.

Lady Teazle: Don't you think we may as well leave honor out of the question?

Joseph Surface: Ah, the ill effects of your country education, I see, still remain with you.

Lady Teazle: I doubt they do, indeed; and I will fairly own to you that if I could be persuaded to do wrong, it would be by Sir Peter's ill usage sooner than your honorable logic after all.

Joseph Surface: Then, by this hand, which he is unworthy of—[*Taking her hand. Enter Servant.*] 'Sdeath, you blockhead, what do you want?

Servant: I beg your pardon, sir, but I thought you would not choose Sir Peter to come up without announcing him.

Joseph Surface: Sir Peter! Oons,—the devil!

Lady Teazle: Sir Peter! O lud! I'm ruined! I'm ruined!

Servant: Sir, 'twasn't I let him in.

Lady Teazle: Oh, I'm quite undone! What will become of me now, Mr. Logic? Oh, he's on the stairs—I'll get behind here, and if ever I'm so imprudent again—[*Goes behind the screen.*]

Joseph Surface: Give me that book. [*Sits down. Servant pretends to adjust his chair.*] [*Enter Sir Peter Teazle.*]

Sir Peter: Ay, ever improving himself! Mr. Surface, Mr. Surface—

Joseph Surface: Oh, my dear Sir Peter, I beg your pardon. [*Gaping, throws away the book.*] I have been dozing over a stupid book. Well, I am much obliged to you for this call. You haven't been here, I believe, since I fitted up this room. Books, you know, are the only things I am a coxcomb in.

Sir Peter: 'Tis very neat indeed. Well, well, that's proper; and you can make even your screen a source of knowledge,—hung, I perceive, with maps.

Joseph Surface: Oh, yes, I find great use in that screen.

Sir Peter: I dare say you must, certainly, when you want to find anything in a hurry.

Joseph Surface: [*Aside.*] Ay, or to hide anything in a hurry either.

Sir Peter: Well, I have a little private business—

Joseph: [*To Servant.*] You need not stay.

Servant: No, sir. [*Exit.*]

Joseph Surface: Here's a chair, Sir Peter. I beg—

Sir Peter: Well, now we are alone, there's a subject, my dear friend, on which I wish to unburden my mind to you, a point of the greatest moment to my peace; in short, my good friend, Lady Teazle's conduct of late has made me very unhappy.

Joseph Surface: Indeed! I am very sorry to hear it.

Sir Peter: Ay, 'tis but too plain she has not the least regard for me; but, what's worse, I have pretty good authority to suppose she has formed an attachment to another.

Joseph Surface: Indeed! You astonish me!

Sir Peter: Yes, and, between ourselves, I think I've discovered the person.

Joseph Surface: How! You alarm me exceedingly.

Sir Peter: Ay, my dear friend, I knew you would sympathize with me!

Joseph Surface: Yes, believe me, Sir Peter, such a discovery would hurt me just as much as it would you.

Sir Peter: I am convinced of it Ah, it is a happiness to have a friend whom we can trust even with one's family secrets. But have you no guess who I mean?

Joseph Surface: I haven't the most distant idea. It can't be Sir Benjamin Backbite!

Sir Peter: Oh, no! What say you to Charles?

Joseph Surface: My brother? Impossible!

Sir Peter: Oh, my dear friend, the goodness of your own heart misleads you. You judge of others by yourself.

Joseph Surface: Certainly, Sir Peter, the heart that is conscious of its own integrity is ever slow to credit another's treachery.

Sir Peter: True, but your brother has no sentiment. You never hear him talk so.

Joseph Surface: Yet I can't but think Lady Teazle herself has too much principle.

Sir Peter: Ay, but what is principle against the flattery of a handsome, lively young fellow?

Joseph Surface: That's very true.

Sir Peter: And then, you know, the difference of our ages makes it very improbable that she should have any great affection for me; and, if she were to be frail, and I were to make it public, why, the town would only laugh at me, the foolish old bachelor who had married a girl.

Joseph Surface: That's true, to be sure. They would laugh.

Sir Peter: Laugh, ay! And make ballads and paragraphs and the devil knows what of me.

Joseph Surface: No, you must never make it public.

Sir Peter: But then, again, that the nephew of my old friend, Sir Oliver, should be the person to attempt such a wrong, hurts me more nearly.

Joseph Surface: Ay, there's the point. When ingratitude barbs the dart of injury, the wound has double danger in it.

Sir Peter: Ay! I that was, in a manner, left his guardian, in whose house he had been so often entertained, who never in my life denied him—my advice!

Joseph Surface: Oh, 'tis not to be credited! There may be a man capable of such baseness, to be sure; but, for my part, till you can give me positive proofs, I cannot but doubt it. However, if it should be proved on him, he is no longer a brother of mine, I disclaim kindred with him; for the man who can break the laws of hospitality and tempt the wife of his friend, deserves to be branded as the pest of society.

Sir Peter: What a difference there is between you! What noble sentiments!

Joseph Surface: Yet I cannot suspect Lady Teazle's honor.

Sir Peter: I am sure I wish to think well of her and to remove all ground of quarrel between us. She has lately reproached me more than once with having made no settlement on her, and, in our last quarrel, she almost hinted that she should not break her heart if I was dead. Now, as we seem to differ in our ideas of expense, I have resolved she shall have her own way and be her own mistress in that respect for the future; and, if I were to die, she will find I have not been inattentive to her interest while living. Here, my friend, are the drafts of two deeds, which I wish to have your opinion on. By one, she will enjoy eight hundred a year independent while I live; and, by the other, the bulk of my fortune at my death.

Joseph Surface: This conduct, Sir Peter, is indeed truly generous. [*Aside.*] I wish it may not corrupt my pupil.

Sir Peter: Yes, I am determined she shall have no cause to complain, though I would not have her acquainted with the latter instance of my affection yet awhile.

Joseph Surface: [*Aside.*] Nor I, if I could help it.

Sir Peter: And now, my dear friend, if you please, we will talk over the situation of your hopes with Maria.

Joseph Surface: [*Softly.*] Oh, no, Sir Peter! Another time, if you please.

Sir Peter: I am sensibly chagrined at the little progress you seem to make in her affections.

Joseph Surface: [*Softly.*] I beg you will not mention it. What are my disappointments when your happiness is in debate! [*Aside.*] 'Sdeath, I shall be ruined every way!

Sir Peter: And though you are averse to my acquainting Lady Teazle with your passion for Maria, I'm sure she's not your enemy in the affair.

Joseph Surface: Pray, Sir Peter, now oblige me. I am really too much affected by the subject we have been speaking of to bestow a thought on my own concerns. The man who is entrusted with his friend's distresses can never—[*Enter Servant.*] Well, sir?

Servant: Your brother, sir, is speaking to a gentleman in the street and says he knows you are within.

Joseph Surface: 'Sdeath, you blockhead! I'm not within. I'm out for the day.

Sir Peter: Stay—Hold! A thought has struck me. You shall be at home.

Joseph Surface: Well, well, let him up. [*Exit Servant. Aside.*] He'll interrupt Sir Peter, however.

Sir Peter: Now, my good friend, oblige me, I entreat you. Before Charles comes, let me conceal myself somewhere; then do you tax him on the point we have been talking, and his answer may satisfy me at once.

Joseph Surface: Oh, fie, Sir Peter! Would you have me join in so mean a trick? To trepan my brother too!

Sir Peter: Nay, you tell me you are sure he is innocent. If so, you do him the greatest service by giving him an opportunity to clear himself, and you will set my heart at rest. Come, you shall not refuse me. Here, behind the screen will be —Hey! What the devil! There seems to be one listener here already! I'll swear I saw a petticoat!

Joseph Surface: Ha! ha! ha! Well, this is ridiculous enough. I'll tell you, Sir Peter, though I hold a man of intrigue to be a most despicable character, yet, you know, it does not follow that one is to be an absolute Joseph either.[2] Hark'ee, 'tis a little French milliner, a silly rogue that plagues me; and having some character to lose, on your coming, sir, she ran behind the screen.

Sir Peter: Ah, you rogue,—But, egad, she has overheard all I have been saying of my wife.

Joseph Surface: Oh, 'twill never go any farther, you may depend upon it!

Sir Peter: No? Then, faith, let her hear it out.—Here's a closet will do as well.

Joseph Surface: Well, go in there.

Sir Peter: Sly rogue! Sly rogue! [*Going into the closet.*]

Joseph Surface: A narrow escape, indeed! And a curious situation I'm in, to part man and wife in this manner.

Lady Teazle: [*Peeping.*] Couldn't I steal off?

Joseph Surface: Keep close, my angel!

Sir Peter: [*Peeping.*] Joseph, tax him home!

Joseph Surface: Back, my dear friend!

Lady Teazle: [*Peeping.*] Couldn't you lock Sir Peter in?

[2] See the story of Joseph and Potiphar's wife in *Genesis,* 39.

Joseph Surface: Be still, my life!

Sir Peter: [*Peeping.*] You're sure the little milliner won't blab?

Joseph Surface: In, in, my good Sir Peter!—'Fore gad, I wish I had a key to the door! [*Enter Charles Surface.*]

Charles: Holla, brother, what has been the matter? Your fellow would not let me up at first. What, have you had a Jew or a wench with you?

Joseph Surface: Neither, brother, I assure you.

Charles: But what has made Sir Peter steal off? I thought he had been with you.

Joseph Surface: He was, brother; but, hearing you were coming, he did not choose to stay.

Charles: What, was the old gentleman afraid I wanted to borrow money of him?

Joseph Surface: No, sir; but I am sorry to find, Charles, you have lately given that worthy man grounds for great uneasiness.

Charles: Yes, they tell me I do that to a great many worthy men. But how so, pray?

Joseph Surface: To be plain with you, brother, he thinks you are endeavoring to gain Lady Teazle's affections from him.

Charles: Who, I? O lud, not I, upon my word. Ha! ha! ha! ha! so the old fellow has found out that he has got a young wife, has he? Or, what's worse, Lady Teazle has found out she has an old husband?

Joseph Surface: This is no subject to jest on, brother. He who can laugh—

Charles: True, true, as you were going to say—Then, seriously, I never had the least idea of what you charge me with, upon my honor.

Joseph Surface: [*Aloud.*] Well, it will give Sir Peter great satisfaction to hear this.

Charles: To be sure, I once thought the lady se   ' to have taken a fancy to me;   '   my soul, I never gave !   ncouragement Be-

sides, you know my attachment to Maria.

Joseph Surface: But, sure, brother, even if Lady Teazle had betrayed the fondest partiality for you—

Charles: Why, look'ee, Joseph, I hope I shall never deliberately do a dishonorable action; but if a pretty woman was purposely to throw herself in my way, and that pretty woman married to a man old enough to be her father—

Joseph Surface: Well?

Charles: Why, I believe I should be obliged to borrow a little of your morality, that's all. But, brother, do you know now that you surprise me exceedingly by naming me with Lady Teazle; for, i' faith, I always understood you were her favorite.

Joseph Surface: Oh, for shame, Charles! This retort is foolish.

Charles: Nay, I swear I have seen you exchange such significant glances—

Joseph Surface: Nay, nay, sir, this is no jest.

Charles: Egad, I'm serious! Don't you remember one day when I called here—

Joseph Surface: Nay, pr'ythee, Charles—

Charles: And found you together—

Joseph Surface: Zounds, sir, I insist—

Charles: And another time when your servant—

Joseph Surface: Brother, brother, a word with you! [*Aside.*] Gad, I must stop him.

Charles: Informed, I say, that—

Joseph Surface: Hush! I beg your pardon, but Sir Peter has overheard all we have been saying. I knew you would clear yourself, or I should not have consented.

Charles: How, Sir Peter! Where is he?

Joseph Surface: Softly! There! [*Points to the closet.*]

Charles: Oh, 'fore heaven, I'll have him out. Sir Peter, come forth!

Joseph Surface: No, no—

Charles: I say, Sir Peter, come into court! [*Pulls in Sir Peter.*] What! My old guardian! What, turn inquisitor and take evidence *incog.?*

Sir Peter: Give me your hand, Charles. I believe I have suspected you wrongfully; but you mustn't be angry with Joseph. 'Twas my plan.

Charles: Indeed!

Sir Peter: But I acquit you. I promise you I don't think near so ill of you as I did. What I have heard has given me great satisfaction.

Charles: Egad, then, 'twas lucky you didn't hear any more. [*Apart to Joseph.*] Wasn't it, Joseph?

Sir Peter: Ah, you would have retorted on him.

Charles: Ah, ay, that was a joke.

Sir Peter: Yes, yes, I know his honor too well.

Charles: But you might as well have suspected him as me in this matter, for all that. [*Apart to Joseph.*] Mightn't he, Joseph?

Sir Peter: Well, well, I believe you.

Joseph Surface: [*Aside.*] Would they were both out of the room! [*Enter Servant and whispers Joseph.*]

Sir Peter: And in future, perhaps, we may not be such strangers. [*Exit Servant.*]

Joseph Surface: Gentlemen, I beg pardon. I must wait on you down stairs. Here is a person come on particular business.

Charles: Well, you can see him in another room. Sir Peter and I have not met a long time, and I have something to say to him.

Joseph Surface: [*Aside.*] They must not be left together.—I'll send this man away and return directly. [*Apart to Sir Peter and goes out.*] Sir Peter, not a word of the French milliner.

Sir Peter: [*Apart to Joseph.*] I! Not for the world.—Ah, Charles, if you associated more with your brother, one might indeed hope for your reformation. He is a man of sentiment. Well, there is nothing in the world so noble as a man of sentiment.

Charles: Psha, he is too moral by half;

and so apprehensive of his good name, as he calls it, that I suppose he would as soon let a priest into his house as a wench.

Sir Peter: No, no! Come, come! You wrong him. No, no, Joseph is no rake, but he is no such saint either, in that respect. [*Aside.*] I have a great mind to tell him. We should have such a laugh at Joseph.

Charles: Oh, hang him, he's a very anchorite, a young hermit.

Sir Peter: Hark'ee, you must not abuse him. He may chance to hear of it again, I promise you.

Charles: Why, you won't tell him?

Sir Peter: No, but—This way. [*Aside.*] Egad, I'll tell him.—Hark'ee, have you a mind to have a good laugh at Joseph?

Charles: I should like it, of all things.

Sir Peter: Then, i' faith, we will! I'll be quit with him for discovering me. He had a girl with him when I called.

Charles: What! Joseph? You jest.

Sir Peter: Hush! A little French milliner, and the best of the jest is she's in the room now.

Charles: The devil she is!

Sir Peter: Hush, I tell you! [*Points.*]

Charles: Behind the screen? 'Slife let's unveil her!

Sir Peter: No, no, he's coming. You shan't, indeed!

Charles: Oh, egad, we'll have a peep at the little milliner!

Sir Peter: Not for the world! Joseph will never forgive me.

Charles: I'll stand by you—

Sir Peter: Odds, here he is! [*Joseph Surface enters just as Charles Surface throws down the screen.*]

Charles: Lady Teazle, by all that's wonderful!

Sir Peter: Lady Teazle, by all that's damnable!

Charles: Sir Peter, this is one of the smartest French milliners I ever saw. Egad, you seem all to have been diverting yourselves here at hide and seek, and I don't see who is out of the secret.

Shall I beg your ladyship to inform me? Not a word! Brother, will you be pleased to explain this matter? What! Is morality dumb too? Sir Peter, though I found you in the dark, perhaps you are not so now! All mute!—Well, though I can make nothing of the affair, I suppose you perfectly understand one another; so I'll leave you to yourselves. [*Going.*] Brother, I'm sorry to find you have given that worthy man grounds for so much uneasiness. Sir Peter, there's nothing in the world so noble as a man of sentiment! [*Exit Charles. They stand for some time looking at each other.*]

Joseph Surface: Sir Peter, notwithstanding—I confess, that appearances are against me,—if you will afford me your patience, I make no doubt—but I shall explain everything to your satisfaction.

Sir Peter: If you please, sir.

Joseph Surface: The fact is, sir, that Lady Teazle, knowing my pretensions to your ward Maria,—I say, sir, Lady Teazle, being apprehensive of the jealousy of your temper,—and knowing my friendship to the family,—she, sir, I say —called here,—in order that—I might explain these pretensions; but on your coming,—being apprehensive,—as I said,—of your jealousy, she withdrew; and this, you may depend on it, is the whole truth of the matter.

Sir Peter: A very clear account, upon my word, and I dare swear the lady will vouch for every particle of it.

Lady Teazle: For not one word of it, Sir Peter.

Sir Peter: How! Don't you think it worth while to agree in the lie?

Lady Teazle: There is not one syllable of truth in what that gentleman has told you.

Sir Peter: I believe you, upon my soul, ma'am.

Joseph Surface: [*Aside.*] 'Sdeath, madam, will you betray me?

Lady Teazle: Good Mr. Hypocrite, by your leave, I'll speak for myself.

Sir Peter: Ay, let her alone, sir; you'll find she'll make out a better story than you, without prompting.

Lady Teazle: Hear me, Sir Peter! I came here on no matter relating to your ward and even ignorant of this gentleman's pretensions to her. But I came, seduced by his insidious arguments, at least to listen to his pretended passion, if not to sacrifice your honor to his baseness.

Sir Peter: Now, I believe the truth is coming, indeed.

Joseph Surface: The woman's mad!

Lady Teazle: No, sir; she has recovered her senses and your own arts have furnished her with the means. Sir Peter, I do not expect you to credit me, but the tenderness you expressed for me when I am sure you could not think I was a witness to it has so penetrated to my heart that had I left this place without the same of this discovery my future life should have spoken the sincerity of my gratitude. As for that smooth-tongued hypocrite, who would have seduced the wife of his too credulous friend while he affected honorable addresses to his ward, I behold him now in a light so truly despicable that I shall never again respect myself for having listened to him. [*Exit.*]

Joseph Surface: Notwithstanding all this, Sir Peter, heaven knows—

Sir Peter: That you are a villain, and so I leave you to your conscience. [*Exit.*]

Joseph Surface: [*Following Sir Peter.*] You are too rash, Sir Peter. You shall hear me. The man who shuts out conviction by refusing to—[*Exit.*]

QUESTIONS ON ACT IV

1. How does Sheridan avoid oversimplifying the money-lending scenes in Acts III and IV? Or, to put the question in another way, how is the tension secured?

2. What is the complexity of meaning implied by the lines spoken by Sir Oliver just before his exit (p. 224 b, 32 ff.)?

3. What is accomplished by Scene ii?

4. In Scene iii what is the technical significance of Joseph's referring to a possible call from his brother (p. 225 a, 11–12)?

5. Note the reference to the screen early in the scene. Is the handling of this in any way comparable to Wilde's management of the fan?

6. Do you find *double entendre* in any of Joseph's remarks during the screen scene?

7. Is the means by which Joseph is got out of the room wholly satisfactory? Why does Sheridan want Joseph out of the room?

8. In movement, concentration, and climactic development, how does this act compare with the preceding ones?

ACT V

[Scene I. The library.]

[*Enter Joseph Surface and Servant.*]

Joseph Surface: Mr. Stanley! And why should you think I would see him? You must know he comes to ask something.

Servant: Sir, I should not have let him in, but that Mr. Rowley came to the door with him.

Joseph Surface: Psha, blockhead! To suppose that I should now be in a temper to receive visits from poor relations! Well, why don't you show the fellow up?

Servant: I will, sir. Why, sir, it was not my fault that Sir Peter discovered my lady—

Joseph Surface: Go, fool! [*Exit Servant.*] Sure, Fortune never played a man of my policy such a trick before. My character with Sir Peter, my hopes with Maria, destroyed in a moment! I'm in a rare humor to listen to other people's distresses. I shan't be able to bestow even a benevolent sentiment on Stanley. —So here he comes and Rowley with him. I must try to recover myself and put a little charity into my face, how

ever. [*Exit.*] [*Enter Sir Oliver Surface and Rowley.*]

Sir Oliver: What, does he avoid us? That was he, was it not?

Rowley: It was, sir. But I doubt you are come a little too abruptly. His nerves are so weak that the sight of a poor relation may be too much for him. I should have gone first to break it to him.

Sir Oliver: Oh, plague of his nerves! Yet this is he whom Sir Peter extols as a man of the most benevolent way of thinking.

Rowley: As to his way of thinking, I cannot pretend to decide; for, to do him justice, he appears to have as much speculative benevolence as any private gentleman in the kingdom, though he is seldom so sensual as to indulge himself in the exercise of it.

Sir Oliver: Yet he has a string of charitable sentiments at his fingers' ends.

Rowley: Or, rather, at his tongue's end, Sir Oliver, for I believe there is no sentiment he has such faith in as that "Charity begins at home."

Sir Oliver: And his, I presume, is of that domestic sort which never stirs abroad at all.

Rowley: I doubt you'll find it so. But he's coming. I mustn't seem to interrupt you; and you know immediately as you leave him, I come in to announce your arrival in your real character.

Sir Oliver: True, and afterwards you'll meet me at Sir Peter's.

Rowley: Without losing a moment. [*Exit.*]

Sir Oliver: I don't like the complaisance of his features. [*Enter Joseph Surface.*]

Joseph Surface: Sir, I beg you ten thousands pardons for keeping you a moment waiting. Mr. Stanley, I presume.

Sir Oliver: At your service.

Joseph Surface: Sir, I beg you will do me the honor to sit down. I entreat you, sir.

Sir Oliver: Dear sir,—there's no occasion. [*Aside.*] Too civil by half.

Joseph Surface: I have not the pleasure of knowing you, Mr. Stanley, but I am extremely happy to see you look so well. You were nearly related to my mother, I think, Mr. Stanley?

Sir Oliver: I was, sir; so nearly that my present poverty, I fear, may do discredit to her wealthy children, else I should not have presumed to trouble you.

Joseph Surface: Dear sir, there needs no apology! He that is in distress, though a stranger, has a right to claim kindred with the wealthy. I am sure I wish I was of that class and had it in my power to offer you even a small relief.

Sir Oliver: If your uncle, Sir Oliver, were here, I should have a friend.

Joseph Surface: I wish he was, sir, with all my heart. You should not want an advocate with him, believe me, sir.

Sir Oliver: I should not need one; my distresses would recommend me. But I imagined his bounty would enable you to become the agent of his charity.

Joseph Surface: My dear sir, you were strangely misinformed. Sir Oliver is a worthy man, a very worthy man; but

avarice, Mr. Stanley, is the vice of age. I will tell you, my good sir, in confidence what he has done for me has been a mere nothing, though people I know have thought otherwise; and, for my part, I never chose to contradict the report.

Sir Oliver: What! Has he never transmitted you bullion, rupees, pagodas? [1]

Joseph Surface: Oh, dear sir, nothing of the kind! No, no, a few presents now and then,—china, shawls, congou tea, [2] avadavats, [3] and Indian crackers, [4]—little more, believe me.

Sir Oliver: [*Aside.*] Here's gratitude for twelve thousand pounds! Avadavats and Indian crackers!

Joseph Surface: Then, my dear sir, you have heard, I doubt not, of the extravagance of my brother. There are very few who would credit what I have done for that unfortunate young man.

Sir Oliver: [*Aside.*] Not I, for one!

Joseph Surface: The sums I have lent him! Indeed I have been exceedingly to blame; it was an amiable weakness; however, I don't pretend to defend it; and now I feel it doubly culpable since it has deprived me of the pleasure of serving you, Mr. Stanley, as my heart dictates.

Sir Oliver: [*Aside.*] Dissembler!— Then, sir, you can't assist me?

Joseph Surface: At present it grieves me to say I cannot; but whenever I have the ability, you may depend upon hearing from me.

Sir Oliver: I am extremely sorry—

Joseph Surface: Not more than I, believe me. To pity without the power to relieve is still more painful than to ask and be denied.

Sir Oliver: Kind sir, your most obedient, humble servant!

Joseph Surface: You leave me deeply affected, Mr. Stanley.—William, be ready to open the door.

Sir Oliver: Oh, dear sir, no ceremony.

[1] The pagoda, like the rupee, is an Indian coin. [2] A black, Chinese tea. [3] A kind of Indian song-bird. [4] Small firecrackers.

Joseph Surface: Your very obedient!

Sir Oliver: Sir, your most obsequious.

Joseph Surface: You may depend upon hearing from me whenever I can be of service.

Sir Oliver: Sweet sir, you are too good!

Joseph Surface: In the meantime I wish you health and spirits.

Sir Oliver: Your ever grateful and 10 perpetual humble servant!

Joseph Surface: Sir, yours as sincerely!

Sir Oliver: [*Aside.*] Charles, you are my heir! [*Exit.*]

Joseph Surface: This is one bad effect of a good character; it invites application from the unfortunate, and there needs no small degree of address to gain the reputation of benevolence without 20 incurring the expense. The silver ore of pure charity is an expensive article in the catalogue of a man's good qualities, whereas the sentimental French plate I use instead of it, makes just as good a 25 show and pays no tax. [*Enter Rowley.*]

Rowley: Mr. Surface, your servant! I was apprehensive of interrupting you, though my business demands immediate attention, as this note will inform you. 30

Joseph Surface: Always happy to see Mr. Rowley. [*Reads the letter.*] Sir Oliver Surface! My uncle arrived!

Rowley: He is, indeed; we have just parted. Quite well after a speedy voyage 35 and impatient to embrace his worthy nephew.

Joseph Surface: I am astonished!— William, stop Mr. Stanley, if he's not gone! 40

Rowley: Oh, he's out of reach, I believe.

Joseph Surface: Why did you not let me know this when you came in together?

Rowley: I thought you had particular business. But I must be gone to inform your brother and appoint him here to meet your uncle. He will be with you in a quarter of an hour. 50

Joseph Surface: So he says. Well, I am strangely overjoyed at his coming. [*Aside.*] Never, to be sure, was anything so damned unlucky!

Rowley: You will be delighted to see 5 how well he looks.

Joseph Surface: Ah, I'm overjoyed to hear it.—[*Aside.*] Just at this time!

Rowley: I'll tell him how impatiently you expect him.

Joseph Surface: Do, do! Pray give him my best duty and affection. Indeed, I cannot express the sensations I feel at the thought of seeing him. [*Exit Rowley.*] Certainly his coming just at this time 15 is the cruellest piece of ill fortune. [*Exit.*]

[SCENE II. Sir Peter Teazle's.]

[*Enter Mrs. Candour and Maid.*]

Maid: Indeed, ma'am, my lady will see nobody at present.

Mrs. Candour: Did you tell her it was her friend Mrs. Candour?

Maid: Yes, ma'am; but she begs you 25 will excuse her.

Mrs. Candour: Do go again. I shall be glad to see her if it be only for a moment, for I am sure she must be in great distress. [*Exit Maid.*] Dear heart, how 30 provoking! I'm not mistress of half the circumstances! We shall have the whole affair in the newspapers with the names of the parties at length before I have dropped the story at a dozen houses. 35 [*Enter Sir Benjamin Backbite.*] Oh, Sir Benjamin, you have heard, I suppose—

Sir Benjamin: Of Lady Teazle and Mr. Surface—

Mrs. Candour: And Sir Peter's dis- 40 covery—

Sir Benjamin: Oh, the strangest piece of business, to be sure!

Mrs. Candour: Well, I never was so surprised in my life. I am so sorry for all 45 parties, indeed.

Sir Benjamin: Now, I don't pity Sir Peter at all; he was so extravagantly partial to Mr. Surface.

Mrs. Candour: Mr. Surface! Why, 50 'twas with Charles Lady Teazle was detected:

Sir Benjamin: No, no, I tell you; Mr. Surface is the gallant.

Mrs. Candour: No such thing! Charles is the man. 'Twas Mr. Surface brought Sir Peter on purpose to discover them.

Sir Benjamin: I tell you I had it from one—

Mrs. Candour: And I have it from one—

Sir Benjamin: Who had it from one, who had it—

Mrs. Candour: From one immediately. But here comes Lady Sneerwell; perhaps she knows the whole affair. [*Enter Lady Sneerwell.*]

Lady Sneerwell: So, my dear Mrs. Candour, here's a sad affair of our friend Lady Teazle.

Mrs. Candour: Ay, my dear friend, who would have thought—

Lady Sneerwell: Well, there is no trusting appearances, though, indeed, she was always too lively for me.

Mrs. Candour: To be sure, her manners were a little too free; but then she was so young!

Lady Sneerwell: And had, indeed, some good qualities.

Mrs. Candour: So she had, indeed. But have you heard the particulars?

Lady Sneerwell: No; but everybody says that Mr. Surface—

Sir Benjamin: Ay, there, I told you Mr. Surface was the man.

Mrs. Candour: No, no; indeed, the assignation was with Charles.

Lady Sneerwell: With Charles? You alarm me, Mrs. Candour!

Mrs. Candour: Yes, yes; he was the lover. Mr. Surface, to do him justice, was only the informer.

Sir Benjamin: Well, I'll not dispute with you, Mrs. Candour; but, be it which it may, I hope that Sir Peter's wound will not—

Mrs. Candour: Sir Peter's wound! Oh, mercy! I didn't hear a word of their fighting.

Lady Sneerwell: Nor I, not a syllable.

Sir Benjamin: No? What, no mention of the duel?

Mrs. Candour: Not a word.

Sir Benjamin: Oh, yes. They fought before they left the room.

Lady Sneerwell: Pray let us hear.

Mrs. Candour: Ay, do oblige us with the duel.

Sir Benjamin: "Sir," says Sir Peter, immediately after the discovery, "you are a most ungrateful fellow."

Mrs. Candour: Ay, to Charles—

Sir Benjamin: No, no, to Mr. Surface. "A most ungrateful fellow; and old as I am, sir," says he, "I insist on immediate satisfaction."

Mrs. Candour: Ay, that must have been to Charles, for 'tis very unlikely Mr. Surface should fight in his own house.

Sir Benjamin: Gad's life, ma'am, not at all,—"giving me immediate satisfaction!" On this, ma'am, Lady Teazle, seeing Sir Peter in such danger, ran out of the room in strong hysterics and Charles after her calling out for hartshorn and water; then, madam, they began to fight with swords— [*Enter Crabtree.*]

Crabtree: With pistols, nephew, pistols! I have it from undoubted authority.

Mrs. Candour: Oh, Mr. Crabtree, then it is all true?

Crabtree: Too true, indeed, madam, and Sir Peter is dangerously wounded—

Sir Benjamin: By a thrust in second [1] quite through his left side—

Crabtree: By a bullet lodged in the thorax.

Mrs. Candour: Mercy on me! Poor Sir Peter!

Crabtree: Yes, madam, though Charles would have avoided the matter if he could.

Mrs. Candour: I knew Charles was the person.

Sir Benjamin: My uncle, I see, knows nothing of the matter.

---

[1] A term denoting a position in fencing.

Crabtree: But Sir Peter taxed him with the basest ingratitude—

Sir Benjamin: That I told you, you know—

Crabtree: Do, nephew, let me speak! And insisted on immediate—

Sir Benjamin: Just as I said—

Crabtree: Odd's life, nephew, allow others to know something too! A pair of pistols lay on the bureau (for Mr. Sur-face, it seems, had come home the night before late from Salthill,[2] where he had been to see the Montem with a friend who has a son at Eton) so, unluckily, the pistols were left charged.

Sir Benjamin: I heard nothing of this.

Crabtree: Sir Peter forced Charles to take one, and they fired, it seems, pretty nearly together. Charles's shot took effect, as I tell you, and Sir Peter's missed; but what is very extraordinary, the ball struck a little bronze Shake-speare that stood over the fireplace, grazed out of the window at a right angle and wounded the postman, who was just coming to the door with a double letter[3] from Northamptonshire.

Sir Benjamin: My uncle's account is more circumstantial, I confess; but I believe mine is the true one, for all that.

Lady Sneerwell: [*Aside.*] I am more interested in this affair than they im-agine and must have better information. [*Exit.*]

Sir Benjamin: Ah, Lady Sneerwell's alarm is very easily accounted for.

Crabtree: Yes, yes, they certainly do say—- But that's neither here nor there.

Mrs. Candour: But, pray, where is Sir Peter at present?

Crabtree: Oh, they brought him home, and he is now in the house, though the servants are ordered to deny him.

Mrs. Candour: I believe so, and Lady Teazle, I suppose, attending him.

Crabtree: Yes, yes; and I saw one of the faculty[4] enter just before me.

Sir Benjamin: Hey! Who comes here?

[2] A hill near Eton. [3] A letter heavy enough to require double postage fees. [4] Medical pro-fession.

Crabtree: Oh, this is he, the physician, depend on't.

Mrs. Candour: Oh, certainly, it must be the physician; and now we shall know. [*Enter Sir Oliver Surface.*]

Crabtree: Well, doctor, what hopes?

Mrs. Candour: Ay, doctor, how's your patient?

Sir Benjamin: Now, doctor, isn't it a wound with a smallsword?

Crabtree: A bullet lodged in the thorax, for a hundred!

Sir Oliver: Doctor? A wound with a smallsword? And a bullet in the thorax?—Oons, are you mad, good people?

Sir Benjamin: Perhaps, sir, you are not a doctor?

Sir Oliver: Truly, I am to thank you for my degree, if I am.

Crabtree: Only a friend of Sir Peter's, then, I presume. But, sir, you must have heard of his accident.

Sir Oliver: Not a word.

Crabtree: Not of his being dangerously wounded?

Sir Oliver: The devil he is!

Sir Benjamin: Run through the body—

Crabtree: Shot in the breast—

Sir Benjamin: By one Mr. Surface—

Crabtree: Ay, the younger—

Sir Oliver: Hey, what the plague! You seem to differ strangely in your accounts; however you agree that Sir Peter is dangerously wounded.

Sir Benjamin: Oh, yes, we agree there.

Crabtree: Yes, yes, I believe there can be no doubt of that.

Sir Oliver: Then, upon my word, for a person in that situation he is the most imprudent man alive, for here he comes, walking as if nothing at all was the matter. [*Enter Sir Peter Teazle.*] Odd's heart, Sir Peter, you are come in good time, I promise you, for we had just given you over.

Sir Benjamin: [*Aside to Crabtree.*] Egad, uncle, this is the most sudden recovery!

Sir Oliver: Why, man, what do you

out of bed with a smallsword through your body and a bullet lodged in your thorax?

Sir Peter: A smallsword and a bullet!

Sir Oliver: Ay! These gentlemen would have killed you without law or physic, and wanted to dub me a doctor to make me an accomplice.

Sir Peter: Why, what is all this?

Sir Benjamin: We rejoice, Sir Peter, that the story of the duel is not true and are sincerely sorry for your other misfortune.

Sir Peter: [*Aside.*] So, so! All over the town already.

Crabtree: Though, Sir Peter, you were certainly vastly to blame to marry at your years?

Sir Peter: Sir, what business is that of yours?

Mrs. Candour: Though, indeed, as Sir Peter made so good a husband, he's very much to be pitied.

Sir Peter: Plague on your pity, ma'am! I desire none of it.

Sir Benjamin: However, Sir Peter, you must not mind the laughing and jests you will meet with on the occasion.

Sir Peter: Sir, sir, I desire to be master in my own house.

Crabtree: 'Tis no uncommon case, that's one comfort.

Sir Peter: I insist on being left to myself. Without ceremony, I insist on your leaving my house directly.

Mrs. Candour: Well, well, we are going; and depend on't, we'll make the best report of it we can. [*Exit.*]

Sir Peter: Leave my house!

Crabtree: And tell how hardly you've been treated. [*Exit.*]

Sir Peter: Leave my house!

Sir Benjamin: And how patiently you bear it. [*Exit.*]

Sir Peter: Fiends! Vipers! Furies! Oh, that their own venom would choke them!

Sir Oliver: They are very provoking indeed, Sir Peter. [*Enter Rowley.*]

Rowley: I heard high words. What has ruffled you, sir?

Sir Peter: Psha, what signifies asking? Do I ever pass a day without my vexations?

Rowley: Well, I'm not inquisitive.

Sir Oliver: Well, Sir Peter, I have seen both my nephews in the manner we proposed.

Sir Peter: A precious couple they are!

Rowley: Yes, and Sir Oliver is convinced that your judgment was right, Sir Peter.

Sir Oliver: Yes, I find Joseph is indeed the man, after all.

Rowley: Ay, as Sir Peter says, he is a man of sentiment.

Sir Oliver: And acts up to the sentiments he professes.

Rowley: It certainly is edification to hear him talk.

Sir Oliver: Oh, he's a model for the young men of the age! But how's this, Sir Peter, you don't join us in your friend Joseph's praise as I expected?

Sir Peter: Sir Oliver, we live in a damned wicked world, and the fewer we praise the better.

Rowley: What, do you say so, Sir Peter, who were never mistaken in your life?

Sir Peter: Psha! Plague on you both! I see by your sneering you have heard the whole affair. I shall go mad among you!

Rowley: Then, to fret you no longer, Sir Peter, we are indeed acquainted with it all. I met Lady Teazle coming from Mr. Surface's so humbled that she deigned to request me to be her advocate with you.

Sir Peter: And does Sir Oliver know all this?

Sir Oliver: Every circumstance.

Sir Peter: What? Of the closet and the screen, hey?

Sir Oliver: Yes, yes, and the little French milliner. Oh, I have been vastly diverted with the story! Ha! ha! ha!

Sir Peter: 'Twas very pleasant.

Sir Oliver: I never laughed more in my life, I assure you. Ah! ah! ah!

Sir Peter: Oh, vastly diverting! Ha! ha! ha!

Rowley: To be sure, Joseph with his sentiments! Ha! ha! ha!

Sir Peter: Yes, yes, his sentiments! Ha! ha! ha! Hypocritical villain!

Sir Oliver: Ay, and that rogue Charles to pull Sir Peter out of the closet! Ha! ha! ha!

Sir Peter: Ha! ha! 'Twas devilish entertaining, to be sure!

Sir Oliver: Ha! ha! ha! Egad, Sir Peter, I should like to have seen your face when the screen was thrown down! Ha! ha!

Sir Peter: Yes, yes, my face when the screen was thrown down! Ha! ha! ha! Oh, I must never show my head again!

Sir Oliver: But come, come, it isn't fair to laugh at you neither, my old friend, though, upon my soul, I can't help it.

Sir Peter: Oh, pray don't restrain your mirth on my account. It does not hurt me at all. I laugh at the whole affair myself. Yes, yes, I think being a standing jest for all one's acquaintance a very happy situation. Oh, yes, and then of a morning to read the paragraphs about Mr. S—, Lady T—, and Sir P— will be so entertaining.

Rowley: Without affectation, Sir Peter, you may despise the ridicule of fools. But I see Lady Teazle going towards the next room. I am sure you must desire a reconciliation as earnestly as she does.

Sir Oliver: Perhaps my being here prevents her coming to you. Well, I'll leave honest Rowley to mediate between you; but he must bring you all presently to Mr. Surface's, where I am now returning, if not to reclaim a libertine, at least to expose hypocrisy.

Sir Peter: Ah, I'll be present at your discovering yourself there with all my heart, though 'tis a vile unlucky place for discoveries.

Rowley: We'll follow. [*Exit Sir Oliver.*]

Sir Peter: She is not coming here, you see, Rowley.

Rowley: No, but she has left the door of that room open, you perceive. See, she is in tears.

Sir Peter: Certainly a little mortification appears very becoming in a wife. Don't you think it will do her good to let her pine a little?

Rowley: Oh, this is ungenerous in you!

Sir Peter: Well, I know not what to think. You remember the letter I found of hers evidently intended for Charles?

Rowley: A mere forgery, Sir Peter, laid in your way on purpose. This is one of the points which I intend Snake shall give you conviction of.

Sir Peter: I wish I were once satisfied of that. She looks this way. What a remarkably elegant turn of the head she has! Rowley, I'll go to her.

Rowley: Certainly.

Sir Peter: Though, when it is known that we are reconciled, people will laugh at me ten times more.

Rowley: Let them laugh and retort their malice only by showing them you are happy in spite of it.

Sir Peter: I' faith, so I will! And, if I'm not mistaken, we may yet be the happiest couple in the country.

Rowley: Nay, Sir Peter, he who once lays aside suspicion—

Sir Peter: Hold, Master Rowley! If you have any regard for me, never let me hear you utter anything like a sentiment. I have had enough of them to serve me the rest of my life. [*Exeunt.*]

[SCENE III. The library.]

[*Enter Joseph Surface and Lady Sneerwell.*]

Lady Sneerwell: Impossible! Will not Sir Peter immediately be reconciled to Charles and, of course, no longer oppose his union with Maria? The thought is distraction to me!

Joseph Surface: Can passion furnish a remedy?

Lady Sneerwell: No, nor cunning neither. Oh, I was a fool, an idiot, to league with such a blunderer!

Joseph Surface: Sure, Lady Sneerwell, I am the greatest sufferer; yet you see I bear the accident with calmness.

Lady Sneerwell: Because the disappointment doesn't reach your heart; your interest only attached you to Maria. Had you felt for her what I have for that ungrateful libertine, neither your temper nor hypocrisy could prevent your showing the sharpness of your vexation.

Joseph Surface: But why should your reproaches fall on me for this disappointment?

Lady Sneerwell: Are you not the cause of it? Had you not a sufficient field for your roguery in imposing upon Sir Peter and supplanting his brother but you must endeavor to seduce his wife? I hate such an avarice of crimes. 'Tis an unfair monopoly and never prospers.

Joseph Surface: Well, I admit I have been to blame. I confess I deviated from the direct road of wrong, but I don't think we're so totally defeated neither.

Lady Sneerwell: No?

Joseph Surface: You tell me you have made a trial of Snake since we met and that you still believe him faithful to us?

Lady Sneerwell: I do believe so.

Joseph Surface: And that he has undertaken, should it be necessary, to swear and prove that Charles is at this time contracted by vows and honor to your ladyship, which some of his former letters to you will serve to support?

Lady Sneerwell: This, indeed, might have assisted.

Joseph Surface: Come, come; it is not too late yet. [*Knocking at the door.*] But hark! This is probably my uncle, Sir Oliver. Retire to that room; we'll consult farther when he is gone.

Lady Sneerwell: Well, but if he should find you out, too?

Joseph Surface: Oh, I have no fear of that. Sir Peter will hold his tongue for his own credit's sake. And you may depend on it I shall soon discover Sir Oliver's weak side.

Lady Sneerwell: I have no diffidence [1]

of your abilities; only be constant to one roguery at a time. [*Exit.*]

Joseph Surface: I will, I will! So! 'Tis confounded hard, after such bad fortune, to be baited by one's confederate in evil. Well, at all events, my character is so much better than Charles's that I certainly—Hey! What! This is not Sir Oliver but old Stanley again. Plague on't that he should return to tease me just now! I shall have Sir Oliver come and find him here, and—[*Enter Sir Oliver Surface.*] Gad's life, Mr. Stanley, why have you come back to plague me at this time? You must not stay now, upon my word.

Sir Oliver: Sir, I hear your uncle Oliver is expected here and, though he has been so penurious to you, I'll try what he'll do for me.

Joseph Surface: Sir, 'tis impossible for you to stay now; so I must beg—Come any other time and I promise you, you shall be assisted.

Sir Oliver: No. Sir Oliver and I must be acquainted.

Joseph Surface: Zounds, sir! Then I must insist on your quitting the room directly.

Sir Oliver: Nay, sir—

Joseph Surface: Sir, I insist on 't!—Here William, show this gentleman out. Since you compel me, sir, not one moment—This is such insolence! [*Going to push him out.*] [*Enter Charles Surface.*]

Charles: Heyday! What's the matter now? What the devil? Have you got hold of my little broker here! Zounds, brother, don't hurt little Premium. What's the matter, my little fellow?

Joseph Surface: So, he has been with you too, has he?

Charles: To be sure, he has. Why, he's as honest a little—But sure, Joseph, you have not been borrowing money too, have you?

Joseph Surface: Borrowing? No! But, brother, you know we expect Sir Oliver here every—

Charles: O Gad, that's true! Noll

---

[1] Doubt.

mustn't find the little broker here, to be sure!

Joseph Surface: Yet Mr. Stanley insists—

Charles: Stanley! Why his name's Premium.

Joseph Surface: No, sir, Stanley.

Charles: No, no, Premium!

Joseph Surface: Well, no matter which, but—

Charles: Ay, ay, Stanley or Premium, 'tis the same thing, as you say; for I suppose he goes by half a hundred names besides A. B. at the coffee-house. [*Knocking.*]

Joseph Surface: 'Sdeath, here's Sir Oliver at the door! Now, I beg, Mr. Stanley—

Charles: Ay, ay, and I beg, Mr. Premium—

Sir Oliver: Gentlemen—

Joseph Surface: Sir, by heaven, you shall go!

Charles: Ay, out with him, certainly!

Sir Oliver: This violence—

Joseph Surface: Sir, 'tis your own fault.

Charles: Out with him, to be sure! [*Both forcing Sir Oliver out.*] [*Enter Sir Peter and Lady Teazle, Maria, and Rowley.*]

Sir Peter: My old friend, Sir Oliver— Hey! What in the name of wonder? Here are two dutiful nephews! Assault their uncle at a first visit!

Lady Teazle: Indeed, Sir Oliver, 'twas well we came in to rescue you.

Rowley: Truly it was, for I perceive, Sir Oliver, the character of old Stanley was no protection to you.

Sir Oliver: Nor of Premium either. The necessities of the former could not extort a shilling from that benevolent gentleman; and, now, egad, I stood a chance of faring worse than my ancestors and being knocked down without being bid for.

Joseph Surface: Charles!

Charles: Joseph!

Joseph Surface: 'Tis now complete!

Charles: Very!

Sir Oliver: Sir Peter, my friend, and Rowley, too, look on that elder nephew of mine. You know what he has already received from my bounty; and you know how gladly I would have regarded half my fortune as held in trust for him. Judge then my disappointment in discovering him to be destitute of faith, charity, and gratitude!

Sir Peter: Sir Oliver, I should be more surprised at this declaration if I had not myself found him to be mean, treacherous, and hypocritical.

Lady Teazle: And if the gentleman pleads not guilty to these, pray let him call me to his character.

Sir Peter: Then, I believe, we need add no more. If he knows himself, he will consider it as the most perfect punishment that he is known to the world.

Charles: [*Aside.*] If they talk this way to honesty, what will they say to me, by and by?

Sir Oliver: As for that prodigal, his brother there—

Charles: [*Aside.*] Ay, now comes my turn. The damned family pictures will ruin me!

Joseph Surface: Sir Oliver—uncle, will you honor me with a hearing?

Charles: [*Aside.*] Now, if Joseph would make one of his long speeches, I might recollect myself a little.

Sir Oliver: [*To Joseph.*] I suppose you would undertake to justify yourself entirely?

Joseph Surface: I trust I could.

Sir Oliver: [*To Charles.*] Well, sir, and you could justify yourself, too, I suppose?

Charles: Not that I know of, Sir Oliver.

Sir Oliver: What? Little Premium has been let too much into the secret, I suppose?

Charles: True, sir; but they were family secrets and should not be mentioned again, you know.

Rowley: Come, Sir Oliver, I know you cannot speak of Charles's follies with anger.

Sir Oliver: Odd's heart, no more I can, nor with gravity either. Sir Peter, do you know the rogue bargained with me for all his ancestors, sold me judges and generals by the foot and maiden aunts as cheap as broken china?

Charles: To be sure, Sir Oliver, I did make a little free with the family canvas, that's the truth on 't. My ancestors may rise in judgment against me, there's no denying it; but believe me sincere when I tell you, and upon my soul I would not say so if I was not, that if I do not appear mortified at the exposure of my follies, it is because I feel at this moment the warmest satisfaction in seeing you, my liberal benefactor.

Sir Oliver: Charles, I believe you. Give me your hand again. The ill-looking little fellow over the settee has made your peace.

Charles: Then, sir, my gratitude to the original is still increased.

Lady Teazle: Yet I believe, Sir Oliver, here is one whom Charles is still more anxious to be reconciled to.

Sir Oliver: Oh, I have heard of his attachment there; and, with the young lady's pardon, if I construe right, that blush—

Sir Peter: Well, child, speak your sentiments!

Maria: Sir, I have little to say, but that I shall rejoice to hear that he is happy. For me, whatever claim I had to his attention, I willingly resign to one who has a better title.

Charles: How, Maria!

Sir Peter: Heyday! What's the mystery now? While he appeared an incorrigible rake, you would give your hand to no one else; and now that he is likely to reform I'll warrant you won't have him!

Maria: His own heart and Lady Sneerwell know the cause.

Charles: Lady Sneerwell!

Joseph Surface: Brother, it is with great concern I am obliged to speak on this point, but my regard for justice compels me, and Lady Sneerwell's injuries can no longer be concealed. [*Opens the door. Enter Lady Sneerwell.*]

Sir Peter: So! Another French milliner! Egad, he has one in every room in the house, I suppose!

Lady Sneerwell: Ungrateful Charles! Well may you be surprised and feel for the indelicate situation your perfidy has forced me into.

Charles: Pray, uncle, is this another plot of yours? For, as I have life, I don't understand it.

Joseph Surface: I believe, sir, there is but the evidence of one person more necessary to make it extremely clear.

Sir Peter: And that person, I imagine, is Mr. Snake. Rowley, you were perfectly right to bring him with us, and pray let him appear.

Rowley: Walk in, Mr. Snake. [*Enter Snake.*] I thought his testimony might be wanted; however, it happens unluckily that he comes to confront Lady Sneerwell, not to support her.

Lady Sneerwell: A villain! Treacherous to me at last! Speak, fellow, have you, too, conspired against me?

Snake: I beg your ladyship ten thousand pardons. You paid me extremely liberally for the lie in question, but I unfortunately have been offered double to speak the truth.

Sir Peter: Plot and counter-plot, egad!

Lady Sneerwell: The torments of shame and disappointment on you all!

Lady Teazle: Hold, Lady Sneerwell! Before you go, let me thank you for the trouble you and that gentleman have taken in writing letters from me to Charles and answering them yourself; and let me also request you to make my respects to the scandalous college, of which you are president, and inform them that Lady Teazle, licentiate, begs leave to return the diploma they granted her, as she leaves off practice and kills characters no longer.

Lady Sneerwell: You too, madam! Provoking! Insolent! May your husband live these fifty years! [*Exit.*]

Sir Peter: Oons, what a fury!

Lady Teazle: A malicious creature, indeed!

Sir Peter: Hey! Not for her last wish?

Lady Teazle: Oh, no!

Sir Oliver: Well, sir, and what have you to say now?

Joseph Surface: Sir, I am so confounded to find that Lady Sneerwell could be guilty of suborning Mr. Snake in this manner to impose on us all that I know not what to say. However, lest her revengeful spirit should prompt her to injure my brother, I had certainly better follow her directly. [*Exit.*]

Sir Peter: Moral to the last drop!

Sir Oliver: Ay, and marry her, Joseph, if you can. Oil and vinegar! Egad you'll do very well together.

Rowley: I believe we have no more occasion for Mr. Snake at present?

Snake: Before I go, I beg pardon once for all, for whatever uneasiness I have been the humble instrument of causing to the parties present.

Sir Peter: Well, well, you have made atonement by a good deed at last.

Snake: But I must request of the company that it shall never be known.

Sir Peter: Hey! What the plague! Are you ashamed of having done a right thing once in your life?

Snake: Ah, sir, consider. I live by the badness of my character. I have nothing but my infamy to depend on; and, if it were once known that I had been betrayed into an honest action, I should lose every friend I have in the world.

Sir Oliver: Well, well, we'll not traduce you by saying anything in your praise, never fear. [*Exit Snake.*]

Sir Peter: There's a precious rogue!

Lady Teazle: See, Sir Oliver, there needs no persuasion now to reconcile your nephew and Maria.

Sir Oliver: Ay, ay, that's as it should be; and, egad, we'll have the wedding tomorrow morning.

Charles: Thank you, dear uncle.

Sir Peter: What, you rogue! Don't you ask the girl's consent first?

Charles: Oh, I have done that a long time—a minute ago, and she has looked yes.

Maria: For shame, Charles! I protest Sir Peter, there has not been a word—

Sir Oliver: Well then, the fewer the better. May your love for each other never know abatement!

Sir Peter: And may you live as happily together as Lady Teazle and I intend to do!

Charles: Rowley, my old friend, I am sure you congratulate me; and I suspect that I owe you much.

Sir Oliver: You do, indeed, Charles.

Rowley: If my efforts to serve you had not succeeded, you would have been in my debt for the attempt; but deserve to be happy and you overpay me!

Sir Peter: Ay, honest Rowley always said you would reform.

Charles: Why, as to reforming, Sir Peter, I'll make no promises, and that I take to be a proof that I intend to set about it. But here shall be my monitor, my gentle guide. Ah, can I leave the virtuous path those eyes illumine?

Though thou, dear maid, shouldst waive
    thy beauty's sway,
Thou still must rule, because I will obey.
An humble fugitive from Folly view,
No sanctuary near but love and you.
                [*To the audience.*]
You can, indeed, each anxious fear remove,
For even Scandal dies, if you approve!

EPILOGUE

By Mr. Colman

Spoken by Lady Teazle

I, who was late so volatile and gay,
Like a trade-wind must now blow all
    one way,
Bend all my cares, my studies, and my
    vows,
To one dull, rusty weathercock,—my
    spouse!
So wills our virtuous bard,—the motley
    Bayes   5
Of crying epilogues and laughing plays!
Old bachelors who marry smart young
    wives

Learn from our play to regulate your lives;
Each bring his dear to town, all faults upon her,—
London will prove the very source of honor. 10
Plunged fairly in, like a cold bath it serves,
When principles relax, to brace the nerves.
Such is my case; and yet I must deplore
That the gay dream of dissipation's o'er.
And say, ye fair, was ever lively wife,
Born with a genius for the highest life,
Like me untimely blasted in her bloom,
Like me condemned to such a dismal doom? 18
Save money, when I just knew how to waste it!
Leave London, just as I began to taste it!
Must I then watch the early-crowing cock,
The melancholy ticking of a clock;
In a lone rustic hall forever pounded,[1]
With dogs, cats, rats, and squalling brats surrounded? 24
With humble curate can I now retire,
(While good Sir Peter boozes with the squire)
And at backgammon mortify my soul,
That pants for loo or flutters at a vole?[2]
Seven's near the main![3] Dear sound that must expire,
Lost at hot cockles[4] round a Christmas fire. 30

[1] Confined in a pound. [2] Loo, a game of cards, in which a vole was the taking of all the tricks. [3] The "point" to be thrown in a game of dice; to throw seven was, of course, to lose. [4] An old game.

The transient hour of fashion too soon spent,
Farewell the tranquil mind, farewell content![5]
Farewell the plumèd head, the cushioned *tête*,
That takes the cushion from its proper seat!
That spirit-stirring drum! Card drums, I mean, 35
Spadille, odd trick, pam, basto, king and queen!
And you, ye knockers that with brazen throat
The welcome visitors' approach denote,
Farewell all quality of high renown,
Pride, pomp, and circumstance of glorious town! 40
Farewell! Your revels I partake no more,
And Lady Teazle's occupation's o'er!
All this I told our bard; he smiled and said 'twas clear,
I ought to play deep tragedy next year.
Meanwhile he drew wise morals from his play, 45
And in these solemn periods stalked away:—
"Blessed were the fair like you, her faults who stopped,
And closed her follies when the curtain dropped!
No more in vice or error to engage
Or play the fool at large on life's great stage." 50

[5] Compare the passage which begins here with *Othello*, III, iii, 347–357.

NOTES ON *THE SCHOOL FOR SCANDAL*

At the beginning of the play we suggested two methods of approach to the problem offered by Sheridan: first, a comparison of him with Wilde; second, an examination of *The School for Scandal* with especial reference to the sentimental style of comedy which was very influential at the time. Though the two methods constantly overlap, we may for the sake of convenience attempt a partial separation of the two. In making comparisons, also, we may profitably include Plautus and other dramatists within the field of comparison. This two-way comparison should be enlightening.

1. SHERIDAN AND OTHER DRAMATISTS:
STRUCTURE AND MECHANICS

Though we have spoken of both the Wilde and the Sheridan plays as satirical comedies, a little examination will reveal considerable difference between them. Wilde, as we saw, is primarily concerned with the conflict between society and a woman who has violated society's rules; in commenting on that conflict, he found that it suited his purpose to view society with a satirical eye. His satire, then, occupies a secondary position, although it appears throughout a large part of the play. Sheridan, on the other hand, clearly begins his play, and develops the greater part of it, with a satirical intention: most of the first two acts are concerned with the society whose vices he primarily intends to ridicule. His satire—at least initially—is in the foreground.

Theme and Form. As a result, Sheridan makes a different selection and arrangement of his basic materials from that which Wilde adopts: as a writer whose primary intention is satirical, he sets up a much sharper contrast among characters than does Wilde. Wilde's initial contrast of the social "ins" and the social "outs" becomes rapidly dissolved into a picture of humanity in which the distribution of moral and intellectual qualities takes no account of who is in and who is out. But Sheridan's primary arrangement of his characters into the "good" and the "bad" holds throughout the play, as it must do in an atmosphere in which satire is dominant. On the one hand we have the "villains"—the various gossips with their special abilities, and Joseph Surface, the hypocrite. (We can easily see to what extent Sheridan has used exaggeration, which is a regular part of the technique of satire, in his presentation of these people.) On the other hand we have Maria, the honest, decent person who sees through the gossips; Lady Teazle, who, at first deceived by the gossips, later is enlightened and helps satirize them; Sir Peter, whose role is approximately that of innocent bystander; and Charles, who is directly contrasted with Joseph. The other characters are essentially outside the main conflict, which they serve to comment upon or to judge. The management of the "good" people and the commentators sheds further light upon the technique of satire. One notices that all the "good" characters are in one way or other, at one time or another, victims of the "bad" characters; this is a standard satirical device, since our sympathy with the victims always strengthens our detestation of the victimizers. As for the observers or commentators, they also serve to heighten the point the author is making. (Wilde, by the way, makes use of no such characters. Sheridan perhaps felt that his point needed the additional strengthening which such a device would give.)

Characterization. What we have said so far suggests that Sheridan has depended somewhat upon the hard-and-fast segregation of characters into good and bad which we associate with melodrama. There are indeed such resemblances to melodrama. Sheridan, of course, obviously tries to secure a redeeming complication of character; in a sense he starts out by saying that his characters "are not what they seem." Joseph seems a thoughtful, generous, honest man; he is actually the opposite. Charles seems an irresponsible and loose-lived playboy; but he turns out to possess a redeeming generosity and candor. Thus in one sense both men are complex. Yet as we go further we realize that this complexity of character is somewhat synthetic: Joseph's "good" side is entirely imaginary, and Charles's "bad" side is insignificant. One is plain bad, the other good. Actually, therefore, it appears that Sheridan's characters are conceived at a less mature level than Wilde's. In Wilde's play, for example, neither Lady W. nor Mrs. Erlynne is wholly justified. In a crude paraphrase of the play such as we have made here, of course, Sheridan is likely to sound worse than he is; in the full play, the naïveté implied by this blueprint is to a considerable extent overcome by Sheridan's wit and suavity. But our oversimplified blueprint is justified if it allows us to see how he achieves his effects—and in spite of what handicaps.

Focus. Notice how Sheridan, with almost twice as many characters as Lillo used in *Barnwell*, keeps them much better in hand than Lillo. Most of what happens is centered in the actions of Joseph and Charles, from whom our attention is not led astray at inopportune moments. The two brothers even provide most of the materials for the gossips, who are related to the intention of the play in a far more integral manner than are Barnwell's friends in the Lillo play. On the other hand, we notice that Sheridan is not quite so successful as Wilde in subordinating everything to the principal characters. He is very fond of complications that have a way of getting out of hand and befogging the central issues. Joseph is engaged in a variety of pursuits which constantly need clarifying (see for instance, his speech which closes Act II. ii); Lady Sneerwell's implausible passion for Charles is an avoidable excrescence; the Teazles tend to get too much into the limelight; Sir Oliver, Stanley, Moses, and Trim extend our interest in still other directions. Yet this tendency, it must be remarked, is less of an esthetic handicap than it would be in tragedy, which by its nature requires unremitting attention to the mind and soul of the protagonist. Comedy, as we have seen in our analysis of Wilde's play, is concerned primarily with the operations of society; therefore, having less need of intensity and depth, it can risk a greater spread of interest than can tragedy.

Sheridan and Farce. When we compare Sheridan's play with that of Plautus, certain obvious differences emerge: Plautus, as we have seen, keeps our attention focused on the confusion and hurly-burly, whereas Sheridan focuses our attention on character. As we move from plays in which farce-elements predominate to those which more truly deserve the name of *comedy*, we ascend into the realm of meaningfulness. For example, compare the marital troubles of Menaechmus with those of the Teazles. The former result from a mistake and mean nothing; the latter provides an index to the social life which Sheridan is satirizing. Sheridan does not ask us to feel amused simply because a husband and wife quarrel with each other; the quarrel is amusing, to be sure, but it is amusing, finally, because it reflects the characters of the two people and the nature of the society which influences them.

To illustrate with another comparison, consider the "screen scene" (IV. iii), which on the face of it certainly depends a good deal on physical or external situation, that is, upon Plautus's own favorite device. Sheridan, it is true, has made some effort to prepare for the various calls upon Joseph (can you find the evidence?). Yet the fact remains that he has to depend heavily upon coincidence (1) to get Lady Teazle, Sir Peter, and Charles all present in the right order; (2) to get Joseph out; (3) to bring Joseph in again at the climactic moment. Yet the scene as a whole is highly success-ful—and on the level of comedy rather than that of farce. It will be in-teresting to try to see why. The wit of the Joseph-Lady Teazle scene, for one thing, serves to keep us conscious of characters and ideas rather than of physical movements and, so to speak, of scene-shifting; that is, there is a minimum of emphasis on the mechanics involved in contriving the scene, and our attention is rapidly focused on the scene itself. But what serves more importantly to "save" the scene is its symbolic value: the scene becomes a *perfect embodiment of Joseph's basic duplicity, of his being all things to all men*. That is, it is meaningful; it is more than an artificial device meant to bring about the sort of farcical surprises and confusion upon which Plautus depends. Furthermore, development within the scene, the movement forward, are the result of the direct interaction of the charac-ters, not, as in some other parts of the play, of a third person's plotting. Charles's accusations of Joseph follow quite naturally upon Joseph's remarks to him about Lady Teazle; these accusations compel Joseph to confess that Sir Peter is in hiding; Charles's high spirits and sense of humor account plausibly for the disclosure of Sir Peter. Thus, Sheridan has logically and plausibly brought about the situation necessary for the climax of the scene. And that climax comes through the character of Sir Peter rather than through some mechanical device. Finally, any feeling we might have that all this is contrived is pretty well submerged in our awareness of the admirable succession of ironies; Sir Peter's inconsistently being willing to forgive an irregularity and then discovering something he can't forgive; his wanting to play a trick on Joseph but actually bringing pain to himself; Joseph's being found guilty of what Charles was suspected of. Plautus's farce—and indeed farce in general—fails to make use of such dramatic irony.

In fact, by virtue of its symbolic significance, Sheridan's scene is probably more effective than the corresponding scene in Act III of *Lady Winder-mere's Fan*. For Wilde's scene, as we have said (see p. 64), stresses rather the *threat of discovery* than *presentation of character*.

Melodramatic Tendencies. We have seen, however, that Sheridan does exhibit some tendency to use the devices of melodrama. In one respect, for instance, he works like Plautus: he depends rather heavily upon the discovery of certain *matters of fact*. In the screen scene itself there is a rather mechanical disclosure of information—for instance, that about Sir Peter's deed to his wife. Farce and melodrama are always fond of such "discoveries." The tendency to rely upon discoveries, the manipulation of wills and deeds, and the like, naturally leads away from character and away, indeed, from the direct interaction or conflict of character. Even in *The School for Scandal*, for all of its admirable quality, this distraction occurs. The issue between Charles and Joseph is not really settled by a series of clashes between them comparable to the series of meetings between Mrs. Erlynne and Lady Windermere, especially to that in Lord D.'s rooms; though they do meet, of course, the conflict is settled largely by the simple decision of the uncle, an outsider. He makes certain discoveries of fact—examines the boys' report cards, as it were—and decides who gets the money. Now, though Sheridan is able to mitigate the crudeness of procedure stressed by this paraphrase, to mitigate it by the wit and satirical impact of the last act (just as he succeeds in mitigating the dependence on sheer coincidence in the screen scene), we should not lose sight of what he is doing. For is not Sheridan, after all, resorting to the aid of the old *deus ex machina* (see Glossary) of melodrama? We should note, too, that this convenient savior first comes in disguise—a standard expedient of melodrama.*

To say that there are melodramatic elements in *The School for Scandal* is not, of course, finally to condemn the play. But it should indicate that the author tends to do things superficially rather than profoundly. For it is very easy indeed to have a character like Sir Oliver who not only gets everything straight but also has the power to set everything straight. It is certainly easier for the dramatist to do this than to let the characters, as it were, fight it out among themselves, and to have the outcome determined entirely by the clash of their minds and personalities. It would be finer drama still to indicate the inner development of the characters as a result of the impact of circumstances and conflict upon them. When we consider these possibilities, we can see that Sheridan's way of settling matters by an easy, external device such as the winning of a legacy does not really settle them at all but rather tends to evade the real issue.

In Wilde's play, on the other hand, we have seen that matters of fact (for instance, Mrs. Erlynne's identity) are subordinated to matters of understanding (the matter of Mrs. Erlynne's character and personality). Wilde offers us direct clashes: between Mrs. Erlynne and the Windermeres. There is no know-it-all and fix-it-all; there is no easy way out, no master solution. There is greater complexity, better dramatic logic. This is not to say, of course, that Wilde always sticks to the strait and narrow path of character-delineation. As we have seen, he definitely tends, in his third Act, to deviate from his study of Lady Windermere to a "rescue" of Lady Windermere, so that the effects are precisely those of melodrama (the

---

* The student should consult, in Appendix A, the analysis of Morton's *Speed the Plough*, a play which exemplifies the use of typical devices of melodrama.

situation is not unlike Sir Oliver's rescue of Charles). But Wilde does finally pull the play back into line, and the final note is upon Lady Windermere's growth in wisdom. Mrs. Erlynne comes out comfortably enough: at least she is not punished. But Sheridan tends to justify one side completely (except for a casual renunciation of his former conduct by Charles) and to reject the other completely.

Despite, however, some reliance on melodramatic method, Sheridan is much less crude than he might be; if Sir Oliver is the *deus ex machina*, he is at least not used to mystify and surprise us. His arrival is prepared for in I. i; and, as a matter of fact, the announcement functions ironically in that Joseph refuses to believe a report which might have helped him a good deal. Here Sheridan certainly relinquishes a standard privilege of melodrama. He actually takes us backstage with Sir Oliver and lets us relish the ironic situations into which Sir Oliver puts other people. An author content with mere melodrama would keep us in the dark; Sheridan strives for illuminating ironies. The former is content to shock; the latter wants to enlighten. Here the constant wit is his ally; it suggests mental alertness in the characters rather than the mere susceptibility to sensational effect characteristic of melodrama.

Another similarity to melodrama, yet with a difference, is Sheridan's Rowley—a too-easy stage standby, the old-faithful servitor, who sees all, hears all, knows all, and arranges all; he comes from what is called "intrigue comedy"—a kind of comedy of situation. When Rowley enlightens Oliver on the Surface situation (II. iii) or Sir Peter on his wife's change of heart (V. ii), Sheridan is really avoiding the problem—and the more probable situation—of having characters acquire essential knowledge the hard way, by themselves (note the means by which Lady Windermere comes to understand Mrs. Erlynne: there is no intermediary). That would take more effort and skill, and the tone would be less trivial. But though Sheridan takes the easy way, he is still unwilling to depend wholly on the easy, but essentially undramatic, way: Sir Oliver does go on to make his own tests, however thorough or valid these tests may or may not be.

2. SHERIDAN'S ATTITUDE: THEME: THE SENTIMENTAL TENDENCY

The latter half of the play is concerned with the means by which Sir Oliver tests and judges his nephews, that is, with his conception of good and bad conduct. Hence we must consider what the action implies about the author's point of view. This subject will bring us, also, to a consideration of the second general point which we mentioned at the beginning of this discussion, namely, Sheridan's relationship to the sentimental drama which was very popular in his day.

So far we have been considering Sheridan's dramatic methods. What has been already implied in most of this discussion is the fact that he is writing social satire. When we say this, we automatically say something about his point of view: Sheridan is discerning enough to detect, beneath the accepted normal conduct of society, a pettiness, vindictiveness, and hypocrisy which he finds deserving of satire. In his satire of Joseph we must note the especial use he makes of Joseph's "sentiments"—the point at which he first runs counter to what may be called the "sentimental tradition." These sentiments are generalized statements implying a strong sense of duty or propriety in the speaker; in the drama of the period which stressed edification, this kind of speech was frequently uttered by the characters meant to be admired. (We have already noticed the tendency in *The London Merchant.*) In giving such speeches to a hypocrite, therefore, Sheridan is obviously having a little fun with the sentimental tradition (Lady Sneerwell calls Joseph a "sentimental knave"). We can go on to look for other influences of that tradition.

Let us see what Sheridan has to say when he is speaking positively rather than negatively. A convenient introduction to the subject lies in the way Sir Oliver expresses his approval or disapproval.

Sir Oliver's Reward. Sir Oliver says, first of all, that if Charles pleases him, he will "compound for his extravagance" (II. iii). Charles has been counting on Sir Oliver's money (III. i, III. iii). Act III is almost entirely concerned with pecuniary matters. Twice again Sir Oliver speaks of paying Charles's debts (IV. ii, V. i), and he implies that Joseph is going to be cut off without a shilling (V. iii). So, although the final note is one of happy love, the major issue—hypocrisy—is dealt with largely in terms of monetary loss and gain. Now the effect of this is to give a tone of triviality which all the wit and satirical insight cannot quite obscure. If, as we are bound to feel, the author can think only in terms of a money reward, can we take his judgment of human values very seriously? Is he at the level of comedy of character or of farce (like the *Menaechmi*), where everything depends on *changes in external situation?* Again, what conception of human excellence is it that can be adequately expressed in terms of a pounds-and-shillings pay-off? It might be argued that we are taking the matter of inheritance too literally and that this inheritance should be regarded only as symbol. But we should have to reply that it is the wrong kind of symbol; it can denote only a trivial, commercial view of life. Further, it is doubtful whether the acquisition or loss of money, unless it represents an act of will, can symbolize an inner condition at all. As used in this play, the money simply shows the attitude of another person (Sir Oliver), who may or may not be right.

The Treatment of Charles. That brings us to the distinction between the brothers. In Joseph, Sheridan presents his belief that the proprieties and conventions may conceal very bad behavior; in Charles, that the absence of the conventional virtues may not mean the absence of such real virtues as candor, honesty, "goodness of heart."

In his presentation of Charles, Sheridan shows his method of dealing with a problem that confronts every satirist: the need of presenting, directly or by suggestion, his conception of the positive good from which the satire works (consider, for instance, the passages in which the authors of two famous satires, Swift's *A Modest Proposal* and Pope's *The Rape of the Lock*, indicate what they think are sound values for the societies which they ridicule). Unless he makes some such indication, the author may seem to present a despairing or cynical view of a wholly vicious world. He needs a foil of some kind; it is the main source of his dramatic tension. In dealing with the gossips Sheridan finds his foil in Maria, who is truthful and sensible; and Sir Peter makes a significant speech insisting on the relationship between wit and good nature (II. ii). But in dealing with Joseph, Sheridan not only finds a foil in Charles's honesty and unpretentiousness, which would do all that is needed; but he also goes on to give Charles a "good heart," which shows itself in fine feelings and generous actions. This appears especially in his generosity to "Stanley." Is this convincing? Or does it seem that the author is manipulating matters to create a sharp, high-lighted contrast with Joseph? Does not this bring us to the verge of comedy of situation? Further, does not this bring us very close to sentimental comedy? Consider the following matters:

1. In showing Charles's generosity and his final "reform," the author is directly displaying what is admirable, what is "virtuous," rather than keeping our attention upon what is ridiculous. Joseph becomes secondary to Charles, instead of *Charles's being secondary to Joseph, as satire demands*. Now this is precisely the pattern of sentimental comedy. Or, to put it in another way, we might say that this is a case of comedy's getting out of its relativistic world and endeavoring to make ethical pronouncements of a sort that are esthetically satisfactory only in the wholly different atmosphere of tragedy (see the section entitled "The Nature of Comedy" in the analysis of Wilde's play). Though this whole point may be very concisely stated, it should not be underemphasized, for it goes to the heart of the sentimental comedy that has flourished from Richard Steele in the eighteenth century to Saroyan in the twentieth: we are asked to admire the good rather than laugh at the bad. In its worst forms this method leads us into a very simple view of life: "Just see how good the world is after all." When we speak of a thing as "sentimental" we always mean, among other things, that it treats matters in entirely too simple a way.

2. In using this pattern, Sheridan is appealing less to the audience's sense of the laughable, less to their good sense, we might say, or, as the eighteenth century would have said, to their "judgment," than to their feelings, to an unconsidered emotional *relish* of kindness and good-heartedness. This is the psychological pattern that sentimental comedy follows. In its least restrained form this method results in simply pointing out delightful examples of kindness and goodheartedness and in rejecting any complexities that might interfere with the zestful inhaling of the fragrance of the examples. It is possible, indeed, that most sentimentality functions in this way. Notice that, like farce, it demands that the reader respond to situations in a very naïve way.

3. Finally, notice that Sheridan makes Charles's good actions come not from his reason and will, or from any training or discipline of which we are aware, but simply from his feelings, which, we must assume, are a sort of natural gift that functions autonomously. For, though this may seem rather surprising to the reader, the evidence suggests that Sheridan actually distrusts reason and finds the "good heart" a safer guide to action. Notice that it is Joseph who possesses powers of reason, not Charles; and that Sheridan makes Joseph use his reason entirely as an aid to selfish and acquisitive designs. Thus Sheridan says, dramatically, that reason is untrustworthy; conversely, by endowing Charles with feelings that on the whole lead him to pleasing and generous conduct, he demonstrates his conviction that feelings may be relied on in the conduct of life. This is what is often called sentimental ethics—which, as we have already seen, tends to interfere with proper comic effects (this aspect of the play should be compared with Congreve's *Way of the World*, which does not make a point of admiring, and finding goodness in, unreasonableness). Now when an author implicitly sets forth a code of conduct, he naturally invites us to consider the quality of his thought, its thoroughness. We need not attempt, of course, to give a final answer to the question: Are the feelings a trustworthy guide to conduct? The problem is one of vast philosophical extent. But we may ask how the quality of the thought affects the play, and whether Sheridan's theme is convincing in terms of the play. Consider Charles's gift to Stanley; suppose, for the sake of argument, that it is plausible. Still, is it enough to indicate that Charles is fundamentally a well-conducted person? Is an act of charity a guarantee of general decency? Does it compensate adequately for other failures in conduct? Or is it a pleasant gesture misleading us to draw a general conclusion which the evidence will not support? Is it not possible even to argue that Charles's gesture is a piece of self-deception, and that what appears as generosity may actually be prompted by a relish of sensation which might just as well lead him into conduct less admirable from a conventional point of view? What about the feelings which led Charles to spend all his time in drinking and gambling and getting into debt? Is it not highly likely, also, that these feelings would prompt the addition of women to a party which, as the play is written, is so conspicuously restricted to the enjoyment of only wine and song? By omitting this subject—and consequently all the complications to which it might lead—Sheridan, we may feel, is taking an overly simple view of his subject. As for the drinking and gambling, we should of course not be unduly solemn about them and treat them as though they were irrevocably vicious. That is not the point. The point is that Charles relies on his feelings, which for a long time have kept him immersed in youthful follies: will they be easily changed or eradicated? Will no restraint, no element besides pleasant feelings, be necessary? Might we not expect to find the habit of youthful follies very strongly upon him? And the happy outcome of his escapades leading him to feel that he should go right on with youthful follies? Is Sheridan, then, unconsciously whitewashing Charles?

Aside from his generosity to Stanley, Charles proves his quality only by refusing to sell Sir Oliver's picture. But is not Sir Oliver rather hasty in reaching conclusions? Is not this actually a case of a "sentiment" as evidence of general probity? Might not Sir Oliver just as reasonably disinherit Charles because Charles rudely pushes him out in Act V. iii? In fact, it appears that Sheridan actually set up, but failed to use, a good opportunity to satirize Sir Oliver also.

One of Charles's key speeches is the next-to-last in Act IV. i, where he praises Generosity and disparages Justice. Charles's rather flattering picture of himself, plus his eagerness "for hazard," may leave us in some doubt about his deserving great plaudits. And will his thinking bear examination? It happens that just about a decade before the play, Goldsmith had written *The Good-Natured Man*, a play which provides some very shrewd commentary on just this theme of Generosity vs. Justice. Goldsmith's hero is also in trouble—but *because* of his good heart (and lack of sense) and *not in spite of it;* and he is also rescued, not because of his good heart, but in spite of it, and upon his recognition that good sense is an important ingredient in adult behavior.

So even in his satire of sentimentalism Sheridan is not wholly able to escape its effects. It influences him just enough to prevent his treating the subject with completeness and maturity. On the other hand, he is by no means victimized by sentimentalism; even in the Charles-Joseph action there is so much wit that some of the less successful parts are concealed. The appeal of Charles's witty gaiety is strong, and Joseph's wit prevents his being the tritely sinister melodrama-villain. Notice his attempted seduction of Lady Teazle (IV. iii), where the stress is not on sex nor on her danger (as it would be in melodrama) but on the extraordinary logic of Joseph, and where the effect depends upon the brilliantly paradoxical use of reason in behalf of conduct which reason might be expected to oppose. Joseph's cleverness, you will note, draws attention from his intentions to the working of his mind; his speech on "conscious innocence" is itself rather satirical of a kind of sentimental literature; add his suavity, and you find Joseph here a character of considerable picaresque appeal, and certainly one of greater complexity than a "straight" villain.

3. OTHER INFLUENCES ON THE TONE

If the play consisted entirely of the Joseph-Charles action, its reputation as comedy would certainly be less than it is. But much of the effect depends upon the treatment of the gossips. True, their connection with the Surface-plot is not very convincing; the professed passions of Backbite and Lady Sneerwell are hardly real. But the very unreality of any emotions save love of gossip is a means of excluding any suggestion of the sentimental and of keeping a tone of brilliant satire. The gossips determine the tone of all Act I until, at the end, Rowley's part suggests the sentimental; but his part is overshadowed by Sir Peter's domestic trouble and his ironic cocksureness about the Surfaces. Note how irony always acts as an antidote for sentimentality. Again, Act II is composed almost entirely of satirical materials, except for some lines praising Charles. Note how much less effective these lines are than the anti-Joseph speeches.

Try to decide which parts of the rest of the play tend toward, or work against, a sentimental effect; note especially the big satirical scenes—of Joseph's hypocrisy (IV. iii) and of the gossips' lying (V. ii). Note how Sheridan gets speed and drive in the latter scene; how skillfully interruptions are used to suggest the irresistible pressure of rival minds pushing into an orgy of gossip. Consider the paradoxical fact that the gossips' almost disinterested, artistic devotion to making a good story gives them a kind of admirableness, just as, throughout the play, their wit makes them something more than the simple, hateful villains of melodrama. Thus Sheridan achieves a kind of balance.

Note the means primarily used to secure the satirical effect of the final gossip scene (V. ii): (1) It depends upon the reader's *knowledge of the facts* about which the gossips are telling immense lies. We can contrast this with the method of farce and especially melodrama, which depends largely upon the reader's *ignorance of the facts*. In the present play the reader relishes the irony of the continuous unfolding of the gossips' mendacity; without this knowledge he could experience merely a short-lived, and much less meaningful, shock or surprise, which is characteristic of melodrama and exists largely for its own sake. We can almost make it a law that for mature literary effects the author finds a better ally in the reader's knowledge than in his ignorance. Coleridge, for example, praises Shakespeare for using "expectation" rather than "surprise." (2) When Sneerwell says that she "must have better information," she climaxes the satire: the gossips have been repudiated by one of themselves.

Now, when we put together the fact that we have seen a skillful exposition of unscrupulous scandalmongering and the contrasting fact that the scandalmongers have done their job with a captivating zeal and imaginativeness, we see, not an easy black-and-white presentation, but a picture of such complexity as to explain in considerable part the durability of the play: or, in other words, the work of an author who combines artistic detachment and moral perception and so avoids the opposite extremes of moralizing on the one hand and indifference on the other.

Note that, except for several aspects of the treatment of Charles (e.g., his "reform"), Sheridan keeps Act V. iii on a very firm comic level. Indeed, Charles appears at his most consistent when he helps Joseph throw out Sir Oliver instead of "goodheartedly" protecting "little Premium." Sneerwell and Joseph are kept consistent; the former is given a brilliant final exit, as is Snake, with his paradoxical insistence that his good deed be kept secret. If Charles "reforms," at least the others do not.

SUMMARY

Sheridan, as we have seen, does not satirize gossip and hypocrisy with equal success. In dealing with gossip he is content with the standard comic method of presenting the vice and implying the opposite virtue. But in dealing with hypocrisy he tries to present a complete alternative way of life, that is, to make Charles a "hero" instead of letting him stay at the level of suggestion at which we see Maria. Thus he interferes with his tone: we are asked to admire rather than laugh—the mode of sentimental comedy. Further, since he is true enough to the nature of comedy to do Joseph at full-length, Sheridan lacks space in which to present Charles's virtue convincingly. Again, the desire to contrast the brothers sharply has led him to impute to Charles habits which we are not sure, as a matter of consistency of character, can be so easily dismissed. These matters, plus the fact that the judgment between Joseph and Charles is made largely in monetary terms, push Sheridan closer to comedy of situation than to comedy of character. Unsatisfactory, too, is the fact that the deciding judgment of Charles is not objective and disinterested; essentially, Sir Oliver is flattered into deciding that Charles is a fine fellow. Finally, we note that in so far as there is any mental activity in the play, it is Joseph's; Charles functions entirely in terms of feeling. Sheridan comes very close to stating outright that he does not believe in intelligence.

QUESTIONS

1. Sir Peter is presented as a comparatively innocent victim of the gossip circle. But at the same time he is shown as an irascible, dogmatic husband. Is anything gained by this? What would be the effect if he were presented as a thoroughly admirable husband?

2. What is the purpose of having Sir Peter mistaken in his judgment of Joseph and Charles? Is there any relationship between Sir Peter's function in this part of the plot and his function in the plot concerned primarily with the gossips? What is the justification for giving Sir Peter a relatively large part in the play? Is it too large?

3. Joseph Wood Krutch, the well-known modern critic, has referred to Sheridan's treatment of Lady Teazle as a "notorious whitewashing." Do you agree with this judgment? Consider her final speech in Act IV as well as the situation in the latter part of Act V. ii.

4. We have spoken of Sheridan's satire as having two objectives—gossip and hypocrisy. There are, of course, various mechanical connections between the gossips and the hypocritical Joseph (a study of all these mechanical connections will illustrate the complexity of the plot). What more fundamental relationship is there between them? At the same time, what different views of life are implied by the conduct of each?

5. Has Sheridan characterized the different gossips sufficiently to permit

us to make clear distinctions among them? What distinguishing marks can you find?

6. Throughout Acts I and II there is a sequence of remarks about ill-nature and good-nature. The regular recurrence of these terms suggests that they are there for a purpose. How do they contribute to the development of the theme?

7. Study Sheridan's use of soliloquies throughout the play. Do any of them seem justifiable dramatic devices? Do any of them seem hastily seized upon as the easiest means of exposition?

8. Does the contrast between Charles and Joseph seem too simple and symmetrical? Do they represent a logical scheme rather than sufficiently complex human beings?

9. We have said that Sheridan creates almost no direct clash between Charles and Joseph. He might have developed such a clash out of a rivalry for Maria. Why might he have avoided this method?

10. At different times both Sir Peter and Rowley give Sir Oliver characterizations of his nephews. Aside from the mere fact that they have different opinions, how does one such scene of assurance differ from another in tone?

11. What is the relationship between the literary satire (in Acts I. i, II. ii, and other scenes where Backbite is present) and the other satirical parts of the play? Or is the literary satire irrelevant?

12. Note how very late in the play Charles makes his entrance. Major characters in a play often do not come in at the start. Can you find any justification for this?

13. The satire of usury in Act III seems rather far removed from the main issue of the play. Could you, however, make a case for it as related to the satire of the gossips or of Joseph? Consider the points made by Moses in Act III. i.

14. Analyze the wit of Sneerwell's command to Joseph in Act V. iii: "only be constant to one roguery at a time."

15. In Act V. ii note the very minute details with which the gossips embellish their imaginary tales. Why are these details effective? Analyze especially Crabtree's final speech before Lady Sneerwell's exit. What is Sheridan's reason for making Candour say what she does just before Backbite's entry near the beginning of the scene? (p. 234 b, 31 ff.)

16. What is the dramatic function of Joseph's extreme politeness in Act V. i? Consider how much the effectiveness of this scene depends upon facts which the reader knows but which Joseph does not know.

17. In the early part of Act V. iii how does Sheridan avoid sentimentality in the relations between Charles and Stanley (Sir Oliver)? After the exposure, when Charles protests how glad he is to see Sir Oliver and Sir Oliver believes him, is the reader convinced that Sheridan has actually presented a cause capable of producing the given effect?

18. Analyze the effectiveness of Snake's lines at the end.

3. Ibsen, *Rosmersholm*

ROSMERSHOLM (1886) is an almost immediate contemporary of *Lady Windermere's Fan*, and the student may therefore find it useful to make some rough comparisons as he reads. We find each play, for instance, depending at least in part on a clash between an individual and a social group; but—with a diversity of method that should be interesting to observe—one is comedy, the other moves toward tragedy. There are, besides, two other respects in which the plays are eligible for comparison.

Ibsen is often said to have ended the reign of the "well-made" play, by which, as we saw, Wilde was influenced. That is, he got rid of many artificial technical devices for advancing action and producing effects, devices which often seem to us not "well-made" at all. He aspired instead to a more simple, natural, lifelike presentation of his themes (for instance, he worked very hard to manage all his exposition without the asides and soliloquies that we see in both Wilde and Sheridan), and in that respect he was vastly influential on a great deal of the drama of the subsequent half-century. As he reads, the student should try to estimate whether Ibsen does seem to have his play moving ahead in an easier and more plausible way than Wilde.

Again, both plays are often thought of as "problem plays"—that is, plays that focus attention on some particular problem which especially concerned the society of the time. There is a sense, of course, in which every play deals with a problem, and every play must reflect in some degree the thinking of its time. But the term "problem play" is used in a more special sense to denote a topical interest, with the further implication that the dramatist is using his play as a social and political instrument to direct the attention of society to its problems and to stir it to adopt a solution. It is certainly true that under Ibsen's influence succeeding dramatists have tended to give the problem play this narrower meaning.

But we shall do well to consider whether any really profoundly conceived play exhausts its meaning when it is taken as a mere tract, and whether any really great play does not have to transcend the framework of ideas of its own time. Moreover, Ibsen himself disclaimed more than once any intention of dealing merely or even primarily with "problems." Rather, he said, it is the dramatist's business to ask questions instead of answering them. He wrote specifically of his *Hedda Gabler:* "It was not my desire to deal in this play with so-called problems. What I wanted to do was to depict human beings, human emotions, and human destinies, upon a groundwork of certain of the social conditions and principles of the present day." The student will find it of interest to see whether this remark seems also to cover Ibsen's purpose in *Rosmersholm.*

ROSMERSHOLM

DRAMATIS PERSONÆ

JOHANNES ROSMER of Rosmersholm, formerly clergyman of the parish.

REBECCA WEST, in charge of Rosmer's household.

RECTOR [1] KROLL, Rosmer's brother-in-law.

ULRIC BRENDEL.

PETER MORTENSGÅRD.[2]

MADAM HELSETH, housekeeper at Rosmersholm.

The action takes place at Rosmersholm, an old family seat near a small coast town in the west of Norway.

[1] "Rector" in the Scotch and Continental sense of headmaster of a school, not in the English sense of a beneficed clergyman. [2] Pronounce *Mortensgore.*

ACT FIRST

[Sitting-room at Rosmersholm; spacious, old-fashioned, and comfortable. In front, on the right, a stove decked with fresh birch-branches and wild flowers. Farther back, on the same side, a door. In the back wall, folding-doors opening into the hall. To the left, a window, and before it a stand with flowers and plants. Beside the stove a table with a sofa and easy chairs. On the walls, old and more recent portraits of clergymen, officers, and government officials in uniform. The window is open; so are the door into the hall and the house door beyond. Outside can be seen an avenue of fir e old trees, leading up to the house. It is a summer evening, after sunset.]

[*Rebecca West is sitting in an easy-chair by the window, and crocheting a large white woollen shawl, which is nearly finished. She now and then looks out expectantly through the leaves of the plants. Madam Helseth presently enters from the right.*]

Madam Helseth: I suppose I had better begin to lay the table, Miss?

Rebecca West: Yes, please do. The Pastor must soon be in now.

Madam Helseth: Don't you feel the draught, Miss, where you're sitting?

Rebecca: Yes, there is a little draught. Perhaps you had better shut the window. [*Madam Helseth shuts the door into the hall, and then comes to the window.*]

Madam Helseth: [*About to shut the window, looks out.*] Why, isn't that the Pastor over there?

Rebecca: [*Hastily.*] Where? [*Rises.*] Yes, it is he. [*Behind the curtain.*] Stand aside—don't let him see us.

Madam Helseth: [*Keeping back from the window.*] Only think, Miss—he's beginning to take the path by the mill again.

Rebecca: He went that way the day before yesterday too. [*Peeps out between the curtains and the window-frame.*] But let us see whether—

Madam Helseth: Will he venture across the foot-bridge?

Rebecca: That is what I want to see. [*After a pause.*] No, he is turning. He is going by the upper road again. [*Leaves the window.*] A long way round.

Madam Helseth: Dear Lord, yes. No wonder the Pastor thinks twice about setting foot on that bridge. A place where a thing like that has happened—

Rebecca: [*Folding up her work.*] They cling to their dead here at Rosmersholm.

Madam Helseth: Now *I* would say, Miss, that it's the dead that clings to Rosmersholm.

Rebecca: [*Looks at her.*] The dead?

Madam Helseth: Yes, it's almost as if they couldn't tear themselves away from the folk that are left.

Rebecca: What makes you fancy that?

Madam Helseth: Well, if it wasn't for that, there would be no White Horse, I suppose.

Rebecca: Now what is all this about the White Horse, Madam Helseth?

Madam Helseth: Oh, I don't like to talk about it. And, besides, you don't believe in such things.

Rebeccca: Do you believe in it, then?

Madam Helseth: [*Goes and shuts the window.*] Oh, you'd only be for laughing at me, Miss. [*Looks out.*] Why, isn't that Mr. Rosmer on the mill-path again—?

Rebecca: [*Looks out.*] That man there? [*Goes to the window.*] No, that's the Rector!

Madam Helseth: Yes, so it is.

Rebecca: This is delightful. You may be sure he's coming here.

Madam Helseth: He goes straight over the foot-bridge, he does. And yet she was his sister, his own flesh and blood. Well, I'll go and lay the table then, Miss West. [*She goes out to the right. Rebecca stands at the window for a short time; then smiles and nods to some one outside. It begins to grow dark.*]

Rebecca: [*Goes to the door on the right.*] Oh, Madam Helseth, you might let us have some little extra dish for supper. You know what the Rector likes best.

Madam Helseth: [*Outside.*] Oh yes, Miss, I'll see to it.

Rebecca: [*Opens the door to the hall.*] At last—! How glad I am to see you, my dear Rector.

Rector Kroll: [*In the hall, laying down his stick.*] Thanks. Then I am not disturbing you?

Rebecca: You? How can you ask?

Kroll: [*Comes in.*] Amiable as ever. [*Looks around.*] Is Rosmer upstairs in his room?

Rebecca: No, he is out walking. He has stayed out rather longer than usual; but he is sure to be in directly. [*Motioning him to sit on the sofa.*] Won't you sit down till he comes?

Kroll: [*Laying down his hat.*] Many thanks. [*Sits down and looks about him.*]

Why, how you have brightened up the old room! Flowers everywhere!

Rebecca: Mr. Rosmer is so fond of having fresh, growing flowers about him.

Kroll: And you are too, are you not?

Rebecca: Yes; they have a delightfully soothing effect on me. We had to do without them, though, till lately.

Kroll: [*Nods sadly.*] Yes, their scent was too much for poor Beata.

Rebecca: Their colours, too. They quite bewildered her—

Kroll: I remember, I remember. [*In a lighter tone.*] Well, how are things going out here?

Rebecca: Oh, everything is going its quiet, jog-trot way. One day is just like another.—And with you? Your wife—?

Kroll: Ah, my dear Miss West, don't let us talk about my affairs. There is always something or other amiss in a family; especially in times like these.

Rebecca: [*After a pause, sitting down in an easy-chair beside the sofa.*] How is it you haven't once been near us during the whole of the holidays?

Kroll: Oh, it doesn't do to make oneself a nuisance—

Rebecca: If you knew how we have missed you—

Kroll: And then I have been away—

Rebecca: Yes, for the last week or two. We have heard of you at political meetings.

Kroll: [*Nods.*] Yes, what do you say to that? Did you think I would turn political agitator in my old age, eh?

Rebecca: [*Smiling.*] Well, you have always been a bit of an agitator, Rector Kroll.

Kroll: Why, yes, just for my private amusement. But henceforth it is to be no laughing matter, I can tell you.—Do you ever see those radical newspapers?

Rebecca: Well yes, my dear Rector, I can't deny that—

Kroll: My dear Miss West, I have nothing to say against it—nothing in your case.

Rebecca: No, surely not. One likes to

know what's going on—to keep up with the time—

Kroll: And of course I should not think of expecting you, as a woman, to side actively with either party in the civil contest—I might almost say the civil war—that is raging among us.— But you have seen then, I suppose, how these gentlemen of "the people" have been pleased to treat me? What infamous abuse they have had the audacity to heap on me?

Rebecca: Yes; but it seems to me you gave as good as you got.

Kroll: So I did, though I say it that I shouldn't. For now I have tasted blood; and they shall soon find to their cost that I am not the man to turn the other cheek—[*Breaks off.*] But come, come —don't let us get upon that subject this evening—it's too painful and irritating.

Rebecca: Oh no, don't let us talk of it.

Kroll: Tell me now—how do you get on at Rosmersholm, now that you are alone? Since our poor Beata—

Rebecca: Thank you, I get on very well. Of course one feels a great blank in many ways—a great sorrow and longing. But otherwise—

Kroll: And do you think of remaining here?—permanently, I mean.

Rebecca: My dear Rector, I really haven't thought about it, one way or the other. I have got so used to the place now, that I feel almost as if I belonged to it.

Kroll: Why, of course you belong to it.

Rebecca: And so long as Mr. Rosmer finds that I am of any use or comfort to him—why, so long, I suppose, I shall stay here.

Kroll: [*Looks at her with emotion.*] Do you know,—it is really fine for a woman to sacrifice her whole youth to others as you have done.

Rebecca: Oh, what else should I have had to live for?

Kroll: First, there was your untiring devotion to your paralytic and exacting foster-father—

Rebecca: You mustn't suppose that

Dr. West was such a charge when we were up in Finmark. It was those terrible boat-voyages up there that broke him down. But after we came here—well yes, the two years before he found rest were certainly hard enough.

Kroll: And the years that followed— were they not even harder for you?

Rebecca: Oh how can you say such a thing? When I was so fond of Beata— and when she, poor dear, stood so sadly in need of care and forbearance.

Kroll: How good it is of you to think of her with so much kindness!

Rebecca: [*Moves a little nearer.*] My dear Rector, you say that with such a ring of sincerity that I cannot think there is any ill-feeling lurking in the background.

Kroll: Ill-feeling? Why, what do you mean?

Rebecca: Well, it would be only natural if you felt it painful to see a stranger managing the household here at Rosmersholm.

Kroll: Why, how on earth—!

Rebecca: But you have no such feeling? [*Takes his hand.*] Thanks, my dear Rector, thank you again and again.

Kroll: How on earth did you get such an idea into your head?

Rebecca: I began to be a little afraid when your visits became so rare.

Kroll: Then you have been on a totally wrong scent, Miss West. Besides —after all, there has been no essential change. Even while poor Beata was alive —in her last unhappy days—it was you, and you alone, that managed everything.

Rebecca: That was only a sort of regency in Beata's name.

Kroll: Be that as it may—. Do you know, Miss West—for my part, I should have no objection whatever if you—. But I suppose I mustn't say such a thing.

Rebecca: What must you not say?

Kroll: If matters were to shape so that you took the empty place—

Rebecca: I have the only place I want, Rector.

Kroll: In fact, yes; but not in—

Rebecca: [*Interrupting gravely.*] For shame, Rector Kroll. How can you joke about such things?

Kroll: Oh well, our good Johannes Rosmer very likely thinks he has had more than enough of married life already. But nevertheless—

Rebecca: You are really too absurd, Rector.

Kroll: Nevertheless—. Tell me, Miss West—if you will forgive the question— what is your age?

Rebecca: I'm sorry to say I am over nine-and-twenty, Rector; I am in my thirtieth year.

Kroll: Indeed. And Rosmer—how old is he? Let me see: he is five years younger than I am, so that makes him well over forty-three. I think it would be most suitable.

Rebecca: [*Rises.*] Of course, of course; most suitable.—Will you stay to supper this evening?

Kroll: Yes, many thanks; I thought of staying. There is a matter I want to discuss with our good friend.—And I suppose, Miss West, in case you should take fancies into your head again, I had better come out pretty often for the future—as I used to in the old days.

Rebecca: Oh yes, do—do. [*Shakes both his hands.*] Many thanks—how kind and good you are!

Kroll: [*Gruffly.*] Am I? Well, that's not what they tell me at home. [*Johannes Rosmer enters by the door on the right.*]

Rebecca: Mr. Rosmer, do you see who is here?

Johannes Rosmer: Madam Helseth told me. [*Rector Kroll has risen.*]

Rosmer: [*Gently and softly, pressing his hands.*] Welcome back to this house, my dear Kroll. [*Lays his hands on Kroll's shoulders and looks into his eyes.*] My dear old friend! I knew that sooner or later things would come all right between us.

Kroll: Why, my dear fellow—do you mean to say you too have been so foolish as to fancy there was anything wrong?

Rebecca: [*To Rosmer.*] Yes, only think,—it was nothing but fancy after all!

Rosmer: Is that really the case, Kroll? Then why did you desert us so entirely?

Kroll: [*Gravely, in a low voice.*] Because my presence would always have been reminding you of the years of your happiness, and of—the life that ended in the mill-race.

Rosmer: Well, it was a kind thought— you were always considerate. But it was quite unnecessary to remain away on that account.—Come, sit here on the sofa. [*They sit down.*] No, I assure you, the thought of Beata has no pain for me. We speak of her every day. We feel almost as if she were still one of the household.

Kroll: Do you really?

Rebecca: [*Lighting the lamp.*] Yes, indeed we do.

Rosmer: It is quite natural. We were both so deeply attached to her. And both Rebec—both Miss West and I know that we did all that was possible for her in her affliction. We have nothing to reproach ourselves with.—So I feel nothing but a tranquil tenderness now at the thought of Beata.

Kroll: You dear, good people! Henceforward, I declare I shall come out and see you every day.

Rebecca: [*Seats herself in an arm chair.*] Mind, we shall expect you to keep your word.

Rosmer: [*With some hesitation.*] My dear Kroll—I wish very much that our intercourse had never been interrupted. Ever since we have known each other, you have seemed predestined to be my adviser—ever since I went to the University.

Kroll: Yes, and I have always been proud of the office. But is there anything particular just now—?

Rosmer: There are many things that I would give a great deal to talk over with you, quite frankly—straight from the heart.

Rebecca: Ah yes, Mr. Rosmer—that

must be such a comfort—between old friends—

Kroll: Oh I can tell you I have still more to talk to you about. I suppose you know I have turned a militant politician?

Rosmer: Yes, so you have. How did that come about?

Kroll: I was forced into it in spite of myself. It is impossible to stand idly looking on any longer. Now that the Radicals have unhappily come into power, it is high time something should be done,—so I have got our little group of friends in the town to close up their ranks. I tell you it is high time!

Rebecca: [*With a faint smile.*] Don't you think it may even be a little late?

Kroll: Unquestionably it would have been better if we had checked the stream at an earlier point in its course. But who could foresee what was going to happen? Certainly not I. [*Rises and walks up and down.*] But now I have had my eyes opened once for all; for now the spirit of revolt has crept into the school itself.

Rosmer: Into the school? Surely not into your school!

Kroll: I tell you it has into my own school. What do you think? It has come to my knowledge that the sixth-form boys—a number of them at any rate—have been keeping up a secret society for over six months; and they take in Mortensgård's paper!

Rebecca: The "Beacon"?

Kroll: Yes; nice mental sustenance for future government officials, is it not? But the worst of it is that it's all the cleverest boys in the form that have banded together in this conspiracy against me. Only the dunces at the bottom of the class have kept out of it.

Rebecca: Do you take this so very much to heart, Rector?

Kroll: Do I take it to heart! To be so thwarted and opposed in the work of my whole life! [*Lower.*] But I could almost say I don't care about the school—for there is worse behind. [*Looks round.*] I suppose no one can hear us?

Rebecca: Oh no, of course not.

Kroll: Well, then, I must tell you that dissension and revolt have crept into my own house—into my own quiet home. They have destroyed the peace of my family life.

Rosmer: [*Rises.*] What! Into your own house—?

Rebecca: [*Goes over to the Rector.*] My dear Rector, what has happened?

Kroll: Would you believe that my own children— In short, it is Laurits that is the ringleader of the school conspiracy; and Hilda has embroidered a red portfolio to keep the "Beacon" in.

Rosmer: I should certainly never have dreamt that, in your own house—

Kroll: No, who would have dreamt of such a thing? In my house, the very home of obedience and order—where one will, and one only, has always prevailed—

Rebecca: How does your wife take all this?

Kroll: Why, that is the most incredible part of it. My wife, who all her life long has shared my opinions and concurred in my views, both in great things and small she is actually inclined to side with the children on many points. And she blames me for what has happened. She says I tyrannise over the children. As if it weren't necessary to —. Well, you see how my house is divided against itself. But of course I say as little about it as possible. Such things are best kept quiet. [*Wanders up the room.*] Ah, well, well, well. [*Stands at the window with his hands behind his back, and looks out.*]

Rebecca: [*Comes up close to Rosmer, and says rapidly and in a low voice, so that the Rector does not hear her.*] Do it now!

Rosmer: [*Also in a low voice.*] Not this evening.

Rebecca: [*As before.*] Yes, just this evening. [*Goes to the table and busies herself with the lamp.*]

Kroll: [*Comes forward.*] Well, my dear Rosmer, now you know how the spirit of the age has overshadowed both my domestic and my official life. And am I to refrain from combating this pernicious, subversive, anarchic spirit, with any weapons I can lay my hands on? Fight it I will, trust me for that; both with tongue and pen.

Rosmer: Have you any hope of stemming the tide in that way?

Kroll: At any rate I shall have done my duty as a citizen in defence of the State. And I hold it the duty of every right-minded man with an atom of patriotism to do likewise. In fact—that was my principal reason for coming out here this evening.

Rosmer: Why, my dear Kroll, what do you mean—? What can I—?

Kroll: You can stand by your old friends. Do as we do. Lend a hand, with all your might.

Rebecca: But, Rector Kroll, you know Mr. Rosmer's distaste for public life.

Kroll: He must get over his distaste. You don't keep abreast of things, Rosmer. You bury yourself alive here, with your historical collections. Far be it from me to speak disrespectfully of family trees and so forth; but, unfortunately, this is no time for hobbies of that sort. You cannot imagine the state things are in, all over the country. There is hardly a single accepted idea that hasn't been turned topsy-turvy. It will be a gigantic task to get all the errors rooted out again.

Rosmer: I have no doubt of it. But I am the last man to undertake such a task.

Rebecca: And besides, I think Mr. Rosmer has come to take a wider view of life than he used to.

Kroll: [*With surprise.*] Wider?

Rebecca: Yes; or freer, if you like—less one-sided.

Kroll: What is the meaning of this? Rosmer—surely you are not so weak as to be influenced by the accident that the leaders of the mob have won a temporary advantage?

Rosmer: My dear Kroll, you know

how little I understand of politics. But I confess it seems to me that within the last few years people are beginning to show greater independence of thought.

Kroll: Indeed! And you take it for granted that that must be an improvement! But in any case you are quite mistaken, my friend. Just inquire a little into the opinions that are current among the Radicals, both out here and in the town. They are neither more nor less than the wisdom that's retailed in the "Beacon."

Rebecca: Yes; Mortensgård has great influence over many people hereabouts.

Kroll: Yes, just think of it! A man of his foul antecedents—a creature that was turned out of his place as a schoolmaster on account of his immoral life! A fellow like that sets himself up as a leader of the people! And succeeds too! Actually succeeds! I hear he is going to enlarge his paper. I know on good authority that he is on the lookout for a capable assistant.

Rebecca: I wonder that you and your friends don't set up an opposition to him.

Kroll: That is the very thing we are going to do. We have to-day bought the "County News"; there was no difficulty about the money question. But — [*Turns to Rosmer.*] Now I come to my real errand. The difficulty lies in the conduct of the paper—the editing— Tell me, Rosmer,—don't you feel it your duty to undertake it, for the sake of the good cause?

Rosmer: [*Almost in consternation.*] I?

Rebecca: Oh, how can you think of such a thing?

Kroll: I can quite understand your horror of public meetings, and your reluctance to expose yourself to their tender mercies. But an editor's work is less conspicuous, or rather—

Rosmer: No, no, my dear friend, you must not ask me to do this.

Kroll: I should be quite willing to try my own hand at that style of work too; but I couldn't possibly manage it. I have such a multitude of irons in the fire already. But for you, with no profession to tie you down— Of course the rest of us would give you as much help as we could.

Rosmer: I cannot, Kroll. I am not fitted for it.

Kroll: Not fitted? You said the same thing when your father preferred you to the living here—

Rosmer: And I was right. That was why I resigned it.

Kroll: Oh, if only you are as good an editor as you were a clergyman, we shall not complain.

Rosmer: My dear Kroll—I tell you once for all—I cannot do it.

Kroll: Well, at any rate, you will lend us your name.

Rosmer: My name?

Kroll: Yes, the mere name, Johannes Rosmer, will be a great thing for the paper. We others are looked upon as confirmed partisans—indeed I hear I am denounced as a desperate fanatic—so that if we work the paper in our own names, we can't reckon upon its making much way among the misguided masses. You, on the contrary, have always kept out of the fight. Everybody knows and values your humanity and uprightness —your delicacy of mind—your unimpeachable honour. And then the prestige of your former position as a clergyman still clings to you; and, to crown all, you have your grand old family name!

Rosmer: Oh, my name—

Kroll: [*Points to the portraits.*] Rosmers of Rosmersholm—clergymen and soldiers; government officials of high place and trust; gentlemen to the finger-tips, every man of them—a family that for nearly two centuries has held its place as the first in the district. [*Lays his hand on Rosmer's shoulder.*] Rosmer —you owe it to yourself and to the traditions of your race to take your share in guarding all that has hitherto been held sacred in our society. [*Turns round.*] What do you say, Miss West?

Rebecca: [*Laughing softly, as if to her-*

self.] My dear Rector—I can't tell you how ludicrous all this seems to me.

Kroll: What do you say? Ludicrous?

Rebecca: Yes, ludicrous. For you must let me tell you frankly—

Rosmer: [*Quickly.*] No, no—be quiet! Not just now!

Kroll: [*Looks from one to the other.*] My dear friends, what on earth—? [*Interrupting himself.*] H'm. [*Madam Helseth appears in the doorway on the right.*]

Madam Helseth: There's a man out in the kitchen passage that says he wants to see the Pastor.

Rosmer: [*Relieved.*] Ah, very well. Ask him to come in.

Madam Helseth: Into the sitting-room?

Rosmer: Yes, of course.

Madam Helseth: But he looks scarcely the sort of man to bring into the sitting-room.

Rebecca: Why, what does he look like, Madam Helseth?

Madam Helseth: Well, he's not much to look at, Miss, and that's a fact.

Rosmer: Did he not give his name?

Madam Helseth: Yes—I think he said his name was Hekman or something of the sort.

Rosmer: I know nobody of that name.

Madam Helseth: And then he said he was called Uldric, too.

Rosmer: [*In surprise.*] Ulric Hetman! Was that it?

Madam Helseth: Yes, so it was— Hetman.

Kroll: I've surely heard that name before—

Rebecca: Wasn't that the name he used to write under—that strange being —

Rosmer: [*To Kroll.*] It is Ulric Brendel's pseudonym.

Kroll: That black sheep Ulric Brendel's—of course it is.

Rebecca: Then he is still alive.

Rosmer: I heard he had joined a company of strolling players.

Kroll: When last I heard of him, he was in the House of Correction.

Rosmer: Ask him to come in, Madam Helseth.

Madam Helseth: Oh, very well. [*She goes out.*]

Kroll: Are you really going to let a man like that into your house?

Rosmer: You know he was once my tutor.

Kroll: Yes, I know he went and crammed your head full of revolutionary ideas, until your father showed him the door—with his horsewhip.

Rosmer: [*With a touch of bitterness.*] Father was a martinet at home as well as in his regiment.

Kroll: Thank him in his grave for that, my dear Rosmer.—Well! [*Madam Helseth opens the door on the right for Ulric Brendel, and then withdraws, shutting the door behind him. He is a handsome man, with grey hair and beard; somewhat gaunt, but active and well set up. He is dressed like a common tramp; threadbare frock-coat; worn-out shoes; no shirt visible. He wears an old pair of black gloves, and carries a soft, greasy felt hat under his arm, and a walking-stick in his hand.*]

Ulric Brendel: [*Hesitates at first, then goes quickly up to the Rector, and holds out his hand.*] Good evening, Johannes!

Kroll: Excuse me—

Brendel: Did you expect to see me again? And within these hated walls, too?

Kroll: Excuse me— [*Pointing.*] There——

Brendel: [*Turns.*] Right. There he is. Johannes—my boy—my best-beloved —!

Rosmer: [*Takes his hand.*] My old teacher.

Brendel: Notwithstanding certain painful memories, I could not pass by Rosmersholm without paying you a flying visit.

Rosmer: You are heartily welcome here now. Be sure of that.

Brendel: Ah, this charming lady—? [*Bows.*] Mrs. Rosmer, of course.

Rosmer: Miss West.

Brendel: A near relation, no doubt. And yonder unknown—? A brother of the cloth, I see.

Rosmer: Rector Kroll.

Brendel: Kroll? Kroll? Wait a bit?— Weren't you a student of philology in your young days?

Kroll: Of course I was.

Brendel: Why *Donnerwetter*, then I knew you!

Kroll: Pardon me—

Brendel: Weren't you—

Kroll: Pardon me—

Brendel: —one of those myrmidons of morality that got me turned out of the Debating Club?

Kroll: Very likely. But I disclaim any closer acquaintanceship.

Brendel: Well, well! *Nach Belieben*, Herr Doctor. It's all one to me. Ulric Brendel remains the man he is for all that.

Rebecca: You are on your way into town, Mr. Brendel?

Brendel: You have hit it, gracious lady. At certain intervals, I am constrained to strike a blow for existence. It goes against the grain; but—*enfin*— imperious necessity—

Rosmer: Oh, but, my dear Mr. Brendel, you must allow me to help you. In one way or another, I am sure—

Brendel: Ha, such a proposal to me! Would you desecrate the bond that unites us? Never, Johannes, never!

Rosmer: But what do you think of doing in town? Believe me, you won't find it easy to—

Brendel: Leave that to me, my boy. The die is cast. Simple as I stand here before you, I am engaged in a comprehensive campaign—more comprehensive than all my previous excursions put together. [*To Rector Kroll.*] Dare I ask the Herr Professor—*unter uns*—have you a tolerably decent, reputable, and commodious Public Hall in your estimable city?

Kroll: The hall of the Workmen's Society is the largest.

Brendel: And has the Herr Professor

any official influence in this doubtless most beneficent Society?

Kroll: I have nothing to do with it.

Rebecca: [*To Brendel.*] You should apply to Peter Mortensgård.

Brendel: Pardon, madame—what sort of an idiot is he?

Rosmer: What makes you take him for an idiot?

Brendel: Can't I tell at once by the name that it belongs to a plebeian?

Kroll: I did not expect that answer.

Brendel: But I will conquer my reluctance. There is no alternative. When a man stands—as I do—at a turning-point in his career—. It is settled. I will approach this individual—will open personal negotiations—

Rosmer: Are you really and seriously standing at a turning-point?

Brendel: Surely my own boy knows that, stand he where he may, Ulric Brendel always stands really and seriously. Yes, Johannes, I am going to put on a new man—to throw off the modest reserve I have hitherto maintained——

Rosmer: How—?

Brendel: I am about to take hold of life with a strong hand; to step forth; to assert myself. We live in a tempestuous, an equinoctial age.—I am about to lay my mite on the altar of Emancipation.

Kroll: You, too?

Brendel: [*To them all.*] Is the local public at all familiar with my occasional writings?

Kroll: No, I must candidly confess that—

Rebecca: I have read several of them. My adopted father had them in his library.

Brendel: Fair lady, then you have wasted your time. For, let me tell you, they are so much rubbish.

Rebecca: Indeed!

Brendel: What you have read, yes. My really important works no man or woman knows. No one—except myself.

Rebecca: How does that happen?

Brendel: Because they are not written.

Rosmer: But, my dear Mr. Brendel——

Brendel: You know, my Johannes, that I am a bit of a Sybarite—a *Feinschmecker.* I have been so all my days. I like to take my pleasures in solitude; for then I enjoy them doubly—tenfold. So, you see, when golden dreams descended and enwrapped me—when new, dizzy, far-reaching thoughts were born in me, and wafted me aloft on their sustaining pinions—I bodied them forth in poems, visions, pictures—in the rough, as it were, you understand.

Rosmer: Yes, yes.

Brendel: Oh, what pleasures, what intoxications I have enjoyed in my time! The mysterious bliss of creation—in the rough, as I said—applause, gratitude, renown, the wreath of bays—all these I have garnered with full hands quivering with joy. I have sated myself, in my secret thoughts, with a rapture—oh! so intense, so inebriating—!

Kroll: H'm.

Rosmer: But you have written nothing down?

Brendel: Not a word. The soulless toil of the scrivener has always aroused a sickening aversion in me. And besides, why should I profane my own ideals, when I could enjoy them in their purity by myself? But now they shall be offered up. I assure you I feel like a mother who delivers her tender daughters into their bridegrooms' arms. But I will offer them up, none the less. I will sacrifice them on the altar of Emancipation. A series of carefully elaborated lectures—over the whole country—!

Rebecca: [*With animation.*] This is noble of you, Mr. Brendel! You are yielding up the dearest thing you possess.

Rosmer: The only thing.

Rebecca: [*Looking significantly at Rosmer.*] How many are there who do as much—who dare do as much?

Rosmer: [*Returning the look.*] Who knows?

Brendel: My audience is touched. That does my heart good—and steels my will. So now I will proceed to action. Stay—one thing more. [*To the Rector.*] Can you tell me, Herr Preceptor,—is there such a thing as a Temperance Society in the town? A Total Abstinence Society? I need scarcely ask,

Kroll: Yes, there is. I am the president, at your service.

Brendel: I saw it in your face! Well, it is by no means impossible that I may come to you and enroll myself as a member for a week.

Kroll: Excuse me—we don't receive members by the week.

Brendel: A la bonne heure, Herr Pedagogue. Ulric Brendel has never forced himself into that sort of Society. [*Turns.*] But I must not prolong my stay in this house, so rich in memories. I must get on to the town and select a suitable lodging. I presume there is a decent hotel in the place.

Rebecca: Mayn't I offer you anything before you go?

Brendel: Of what sort, gracious lady?

Rebecca: A cup of tea, or—

Brendel: I thank my bountiful hostess —but I am always loath to trespass on private hospitality. [*Waves his hand.*] Farewell, gentlefolks all! [*Goes towards the door, but turns again.*] Oh, by the way—Johannes—Pastor Rosmer—for the sake of our ancient friendship, will you do your former teacher a service?

Rosmer: Yes, with all my heart.

Brendel: Good. Then lend me—for a day or two—a starched shirt—with cuffs.

Rosmer: Nothing else?

Brendel: For you see I am travelling on foot—at present. My trunk is being sent after me.

Rosmer: Quite so. But is there nothing else?

Brendel: Well, do you know—perhaps you could spare me an oldish, well-worn summer overcoat.

Rosmer: Yes, yes; certainly I can.

Brendel: And if a respectable pair of boots happened to go along with the coat—

Rosmer: That we can manage, too. As soon as you let us know your address, we will send the things in.

Brendel: Not on any account. Pray do not let me give you any trouble! I will take the bagatelles with me.

Rosmer: As you please. Come upstairs with me then.

Rebecca: Let me go. Madam Helseth and I will see to it.

Brendel: I cannot think of suffering this distinguished lady to—

Rebecca: Oh, nonsense! Come along, Mr. Brendel. [*She goes out to the right.*]

Rosmer: [*Detaining him.*] Tell me—is there nothing else I can do for you?

Brendel: Upon my word, I know of nothing more. Well, yes, damn it all— now that I think of it—! Johannes, do you happen to have eight crowns in your pocket?

Rosmer: Let me see. [*Opens his purse.*] Here are two ten-crown notes.

Brendel: Well, well, never mind! I can take them. I can always get them changed in the town. Thanks in the meantime. Remember it was two tenners you lent me. Good-night my own dear boy. Good-night, respected Sir. [*Goes out to the right. Rosmer takes leave of him, and shuts the door behind him.*]

Kroll: Merciful Heaven—so that is the Ulric Brendel people once expected such great things of.

Rosmer: [*Quietly.*] At least he has had the courage to live his life his own way. I don't think that is such a small matter either.

Kroll: What? A life like his! I almost believe he has it in him to turn your head afresh.

Rosmer: Oh, no. My mind is quite clear now, upon all points.

Kroll: I wish I could believe it, my dear Rosmer. You are so terribly impressionable.

Rosmer: Let us sit down. I want to talk to you.

Kroll: Yes, let us. [*They seat themselves on the sofa.*]

Rosmer: [*After a slight pause.*] Don't

you think we lead a pleasant and comfortable life here?

Kroll: Yes, your life is pleasant and comfortable now—and peaceful. You have found yourself a home, Rosmer. And I have lost mine.

Rosmer: My dear friend, don't say that. The wound will heal again in time.

Kroll: Never; never. The barb will always rankle. Things can never be as they were.

Rosmer: Listen to me, Kroll. We have been fast friends for many and many a year. Does it seem to you conceivable that our friendship should ever go to wreck?

Kroll: I know of nothing in the world that could estrange us. What puts that into your head?

Rosmer: You attach such paramount importance to uniformity of opinions and views.

Kroll: No doubt; but we two are in practical agreement—at any rate on the great essential questions.

Rosmer: [*In a low voice.*] No; not now.

Kroll: [*Tries to spring up.*] What is this?

Rosmer: [*Holding him.*] No, you must sit still—I entreat you, Kroll.

Kroll: What can this mean? I don't understand you. Speak plainly.

Rosmer: A new summer has blossomed in my soul. I see with eyes grown young again. And so now I stand—

Kroll: Where—where, Rosmer?

Rosmer: Where your children stand.

Kroll: You? You! Impossible! Where do you say you stand?

Rosmer: On the same side as Laurits and Hilda.

Kroll: [*Bows his head.*] An apostate! Johannes Rosmer an apostate!

Rosmer: I should have felt so happy—so intensely happy, in what you call my apostasy. But, nevertheless, I suffered deeply; for I knew it would be a bitter sorrow to you.

Kroll: Rosmer—Rosmer! I shall never get over this! [*Looks gloomily at him.*] To think that you, too, can find it in your heart to help on the work of corruption and ruin in this unhappy land.

Rosmer: It is the work of emancipation I wish to help on.

Kroll: Oh, yes, I know. That is what both the tempters and their victims call it. But do you think there is any emancipation to be expected from the spirit that is now poisoning our social life?

Rosmer: I am not in love with the spirit that is in the ascendant, nor with either of the contending parties. I will try to bring together men from both sides—as many as I can—and to unite them as closely as possible. I will devote my life and all my energies to this one thing—the creation of a true democracy in this country.

Kroll: So you don't think we have democracy enough already! For my part it seems to me we are all in a fair way to be dragged down into the mire, where hitherto only the mob have been able to thrive.

Rosmer: That is just why I want to awaken the democracy to its true task.

Kroll: What task?

Rosmer: That of making all the people of this country noble.

Kroll: All the people—? ·

Rosmer: As many as possible, at any rate.

Kroll: By what means?

Rosmer: By freeing their minds and purifying their wills.

Kroll: You are a dreamer, Rosmer. Will you free them? Will you purify them?

Rosmer: No, my dear friend—I will only try to arouse them to their task. They themselves must accomplish it.

Kroll: And you think they can?

Rosmer: Yes.

Kroll: By their own strength?

Rosmer: Yes, precisely by their own strength. There is no other.

Kroll: [*Rises.*] Is this becoming language for a priest?

Rosmer: I am no longer a priest.

Kroll: Well but—the faith of your fathers—?

Rosmer: It is mine no more.

Kroll: No more—!

Rosmer: [*Rises.*] I have given it up. I had to give it up, Kroll.

Kroll: [*Controlling his agitation.*] Oh, indeed— Yes, yes, yes. I suppose one thing goes with another. Was this, then, your reason for leaving the Church?

Rosmer: Yes. As soon as my mind was clear—as soon as I was quite certain that this was no passing attack of scepticism, but a conviction I neither could nor would shake off—then I at once left the Church.

Kroll: So this has been your state of mind all this time! And we—your friends—have heard nothing of it. Rosmer—Rosmer—how could you hide the miserable truth from us!

Rosmer: Because it seemed to me a matter that concerned myself alone. And besides, I did not wish to give you and my other friends any needless pain. I thought I might live on here, as before, quietly, serenely, happily. I wanted to read, to bury myself in all the studies that until then had been sealed books to me. I wanted to make myself thoroughly at home in the great world of truth and freedom that has been revealed to me.

Kroll: Apostate! Every word proves it. But why, then, do you confess your secret apostasy after all? And why just at this time?

Rosmer: You yourself have driven me to it, Kroll.

Kroll: I? Have I driven you—?

Rosmer: When I heard of your violence on the platform—when I read all the rancorous speeches you made—your bitter onslaughts on your opponents— the contemptuous invectives you heaped on them—oh, Kroll, to think that you— you—could come to this!—then my duty stood imperatively before me. Men are growing evil in this struggle. Peace and joy and mutual forbearance must once more enter into our souls. That is why I now intend to step forward and openly avow myself for what I am. I,

too, will try my strength. Could not you—from your side—help me in this, Kroll?

Kroll: Never so long as I live will I make peace with the subversive forces in society.

Rosmer: Then at least let us fight with honourable weapons—since fight we must.

Kroll: Whoever is not with me in the essential things of life, him I no longer know. I owe him no consideration.

Rosmer: Does that apply to me, too?

Kroll: It is you that have broken with me, Rosmer.

Rosmer: Is this a breach then?

Kroll: This! It is a breach with all who have hitherto been your friends. You must take the consequences. [*Rebecca West enters from the right, and opens the door wide.*]

Rebecca: There now; he is on his way to his great sacrifice. And now we can go to supper. Will you come in, Rector?

Kroll: [*Takes up his hat.*] Good-night, Miss West. I have nothing more to do here.

Rebecca: [*Eagerly.*] What is this? [*Shuts the door and comes forward.*] Have you spoken?

Rosmer: He knows everything.

Kroll: We will not let you go, Rosmer. We will force you to come back to us.

Rosmer: I can never stand where I did.

Kroll: We shall see. You are not the man to endure standing alone.

Rosmer: I shall not be so completely alone after all.—There are two of us to bear the loneliness together.

Kroll: Ah—. [*A suspicion appears in his face.*] That too! Beata's words —!

Rosmer: Beata's—?

Kroll: [*Shaking off the thought.*] No, no—that was vile. Forgive me.

Rosmer: What? What do you mean?

Kroll: Don't ask. Bah! Forgive me! Good-bye! [*Goes towards the entrance door.*]

Rosmer: [*Follows him.*] Kroll! Our

friendship must not end like this. I will come and see you to-morrow.

Kroll: [*In the hall, turns.*] You shall never cross my threshold again. [*He takes up his stick and goes out.*] [*Rosmer stands for a moment in the doorway; then shuts the door and walks up to the table.*]

Rosmer: It does not matter, Rebecca. We will see it out, we two faithful friends—you [1] and I.

Rebecca: What do you think he meant when he said "That was vile"?

Rosmer: Don't trouble about that, dear. He himself didn't believe what was in his mind. To-morrow I will go and see him. Good-night!

Rebecca: Are you going upstairs so early to-night? After this?

Rosmer: To-night as usual. I feel so relieved, now it is over. You see—I am quite calm, Rebecca. Do you, too, take it calmly. Good-night!

Rebecca: Good-night, dear friend! Sleep well! [*Rosmer goes out by the hall door; his steps are heard ascending the staircase.*] [*Rebecca goes and pulls a bell-rope near the stove. Shortly after, Madam Helseth enters from the right.*]

Rebecca: You can take away the supper things, Madam Helseth. Mr. Rosmer doesn't want anything, and the Rector has gone home.

Madam Helseth: Has the Rector gone? What was the matter with him?

Rebecca: [*Takes up her crochet work.*] He said he thought there was a heavy storm brewing——

Madam Helseth: What a strange notion! There's not a cloud in the sky this evening.

Rebecca: Let us hope he mayn't meet the White Horse! I'm afraid we shall soon be hearing something from the bogies now.

Madam Helseth: Lord forgive you, Miss! Don't say such awful things.

Rebecca: Well, well, well—

Madam Helseth: [*Softly.*] Do you really think some one is to go soon, Miss?

Rebecca: No; why should I think so? But there are so many sorts of white horses in this world, Madam Helseth.— Well, good-night. I shall go to my room now.

Madam Helseth: Good-night, Miss. [*Rebecca goes out to the right, with her crochet work.*]

Madam Helseth: [*Turns the lamp down, shaking her head and muttering to herself.*] Lord—Lord! That Miss West! The things she does say!

---

[1] From this point, and throughout when alone, Rosmer and Rebecca use the *du* of intimate friendship in speaking to each other.

THE MECHANICS OF ACT I

Act I manages the introduction of the characters, the general exposition, and the statement of the problem very skillfully—more skillfully, indeed, than any of the plays we have read except *Lady Windermere's Fan*. This skill is characteristic of Ibsen, who was intensely concerned with technical problems, and Act I well illustrates his methods. By now the student should be able to recognize most of the methods used, and this discussion, therefore, consists largely of questions and suggestions.

1. Minor characters, especially servants, are frequently used for exposition. Here Madam Helseth is so used at the beginning. Is her conversation with Rebecca forced or natural? Trace the steps by which Ibsen works ahead from a minor action to an important subject of conversation.

2. What parts of this dialogue begin the characterization of Rebecca?

3. Notice how Ibsen introduces very concrete images—the footbridge and the white horse. How does this technique start us moving forward,

introduce "suspense"? How does Ibsen especially focus our attention on the footbridge?

4. Why does Ibsen so arrange matters that Kroll talks alone with Rebecca before Rosmersholm arrives? Does this facilitate the exposition? Note with what naturalness the subject of Beata is first introduced. What is the purpose of having Kroll twice make references to his domestic situation before he really discusses it? Why does Kroll's discussion of the political situation seem perfectly suitable? What is the justification for cutting short this discussion and then reintroducing it later in the Act? Why is Ibsen so careful to establish ages?

5. What does the Kroll-Rebecca dialogue do by way of characterization? Why is Ibsen at pains to indicate that Kroll is perfectly willing to accept Rebecca as Rosmer's wife, and that he has no bitterness because of Beata? How does Ibsen especially stress this fact so that we will remember it later? Note how this matter provides a connecting link with the new dialogue that begins after Rosmer's entry.

6. Why is it necessary at this point to have Rosmer and Rebecca speak openly and easily of Beata? What would be the effect if they appeared to avoid the subject?

7. Note the irony (in view of later developments) of Kroll's saying that he must come out to see these "dear, good" people every day. Is there any other irony in Act I? What is the point of having Kroll tell Rebecca that of course she, as a woman, will be taking no part in civil troubles?

8. How does Ibsen attempt to make Rebecca's "aside" to Rosmer, "Do it now," look natural and not forced? What do we begin to learn about the character of Rebecca and about the relationship between her and Rosmer?

9. Does Ibsen suggest that in Kroll there are other elements besides his devotion to an ideal? Consider what he says about his "will" at home. What is suggested by his sense of the "prestige-value" of Rosmer to his political group?

10. Ibsen indicates that Rosmer is "relieved" when Madam Helseth announces a visitor. Why? Why does Ibsen introduce some talk about Brendel before he appears on the stage? Does this appear to help develop a theme already introduced? Is it possible that Ibsen, who usually makes careful advance preparations for what is to happen, is relying too much on coincidence in the matter of Brendel's arrival? Do any lines spoken by Brendel help to explain his presence at this moment in the town?

There is still another possibility to consider, namely, that the *meaning* of Brendel's visit tends to cover up the fact that it is somewhat unprepared for. We might reason that Brendel *represents an influence* which is bound to be present in some form, and that the details of making the influence felt are less important than the influence itself.

Ibsen gives almost a quarter of the act to Brendel—a large amount of space for a secondary character—and thus shows what importance he attaches to Brendel. What is that importance? His very poverty shows that he has made no compromise with conventional life. Rosmer, we have seen, is diffident, hesitant to commit himself, but Brendel's spirit drives him to act. He too has acquired the spirit of no-compromise; perhaps Brendel's presence is to symbolize what happens, and must happen, to Rosmer. That, at any rate, is one possible approach to the problem.

But Brendel is used in several other ways: (1) He shows further the influence of past on present. (2) He helps characterize Kroll, and his effect on Rebecca sheds further light on her. (3) We learn more about Rosmer through the reference to his home life in the past. (4) Brendel's initial mistaking of Kroll for Rosmer has a strong suggestive value. (5) Brendel's reference to the charm and beauty of Rebecca prepare for what he is to say about her later. (6) His sardonic tone and the severity of his humor provide an excellent contrast to the relative straightforwardness of Kroll and Rosmer. (7) Brendel's rapidity in going to the heart of things, which is appropriate to his character, provides a good example of the foreshortening characteristic of drama.

11. Note the structure of the act: each scene helps lead up to the climactic dialogue between Kroll and Rosmer. There is, however, another complication in the structure of the act. Kroll's final lines, "You shall never cross my threshold again," would, by most stage conventions, close the act admirably. But Ibsen adds two short scenes, milder in tone. What is accomplished in the brief scene between Rosmer and Rebecca? By that between Rebecca and Madam Helseth? Does it foreshadow future events? Is the symbolic meaning of the white horse becoming clear? Is there any dramatic usefulness in the contrast between Rebecca and Madam Helseth?

Could it be argued that the final scenes show that Ibsen wishes not only to focus our attention on the main clash but to go right ahead to consider the meaning and probable consequences of the clash?

12. That meaning, we can see taking shape in the nature of the basic conflict. This conflict, it is already suggested, is one between tradition and "emancipation," orthodoxy and rationalism, "blood" and intellect. What other conflicting elements do you find suggested? What are the passages which especially call attention to the conflict? Very early in the play Rebecca and Madam Helseth talk about the relationship between the living and the dead at Rosmersholm. Does this interchange give us an early clue to the conflict? What is the significance, with regard to the whole complex of meanings involved in the conflict, of: (1) Kroll's ironic change of mind about seeing Rosmer and Rebecca again? (2) Kroll's ironic change of mind about the relationship between Rosmer, Rebecca, and Beata? (3) Kroll's telling Rosmer that he is "impressionable" and that the conservatives will win him back? Consider what light is shed on the matter by Rebecca's manner with Rosmer.

ACT SECOND

[JOHANNES ROSMER'S study. Entrance door on the left. At the back, a doorway with a curtain drawn aside, leading into Rosmer's bedroom. On the right a window, and in front of it a writing-table covered with books and papers. Book-shelves and cases round the room. The furniture is simple. On the left, an old-fashioned sofa, with a table in front of it.]

[*Johannes Rosmer, in an indoor jacket, is sitting in a high-backed chair at the writing-table. He is cutting and turning over the leaves of a pamphlet, and reading a little here and there. There is a knock at the door on the left*].

Rosmer: [*Without moving.*] Come in.

Rebecca West: [*Enters, dressed in a morning gown.*] Good morning.

Rosmer: [*Turning the leaves of the pamphlet.*] Good morning, dear. Do you want anything?

Rebecca: I only wanted to hear if you had slept well.

Rosmer: Oh, I have had a beautiful, peaceful night. [*Turns.*] And you?

Rebecca: Oh, yes, thanks—towards morning—

Rosmer: I don't know when I have felt so light-hearted as I do now. I am so glad I managed to speak out at last.

Rebecca: Yes, it is a pity you remained silent so long, Rosmer.

Rosmer: I don't understand myself how I could be such a coward.

Rebecca: It wasn't precisely cowardice—

Rosmer: Oh, yes, dear—when I think the thing out, I can see there was a touch of cowardice at the bottom of it.

Rebecca: All the braver, then, to make the plunge at last. [*Sits on a chair at the writing-table, close to him.*] But now I want to tell you of something I have done—and you mustn't be vexed with me about it.

Rosmer: Vexed? How can you think —?

Rebecca: Well, it was perhaps rather indiscreet of me but—

Rosmer: Let me hear what it was.

Rebecca: Yesterday evening, when Ulric Brendel was leaving—I gave him a note to Peter Mortensgård.

Rosmer: [*A little doubtful.*] Why, my dear Rebecca— Well, what did you say?

Rebecca: I said that he would be doing you a service if he would look after that unfortunate creature a little, and help him in any way he could.

Rosmer: Dear, you shouldn't have done that. You have only done Brendel harm. And Mortensgård is not a man I care to have anything to do with. You know of that old episode between us.

Rebecca: But don't you think it would be as well to make it up with him again?

Rosmer: I? With Mortensgård? In what way do you mean?

Rebecca: Well, you know you can't feel absolutely secure now—after this breach with your old friends.

Rosmer: [*Looks at her and shakes his head.*] Can you really believe that Kroll or any of the others would try to take revenge on me? That they would be capable of—?

Rebecca: In the first heat of anger, dear—. No one can be sure. I think— after the way the Rector took it—

Rosmer: Oh, you ought surely to know him better than that. Kroll is a gentleman, to the backbone. I am going into town this afternoon to talk to him. I will talk to them all. Oh, you shall see how easily it will all go—[*Madam Helseth appears at the door on the left.*]

Rebecca: [*Rises.*] What is it, Madam Helseth?

Madam Helseth: Rector Kroll is downstairs in the hall.

Rosmer: [*Rises hastily.*] Kroll!

Rebecca: The Rector! Is it possible—

Madam Helseth: He wants to know if he may come upstairs, Mr. Rosmer.

Rosmer: [*To Rebecca.*] What did I tell

you?—Of course he may. [*Goes to the door and calls down the stairs.*] Come up, dear friend! I am delighted to see you. [*Rosmer stands holding the door open. Madam Helseth goes out. Rebecca draws the curtain before the doorway at the back, and then begins arranging things in the room.*] [*Rector Kroll enters, with his hat in his hand.*]

Rosmer: [*With quiet emotion.*] I knew it couldn't be the last time—

Kroll: I see things to-day in quite a different light from yesterday.

Rosmer: Ah yes, Kroll; I was sure you would, now that you have had time to reflect.

Kroll: You misunderstand me completely. [*Lays his hat on the table beside the sofa.*] It is of the utmost importance that I should speak to you, alone.

Rosmer: Why may not Miss West —?

Rebecca: No no, Mr. Rosmer. I will go.

Kroll: [*Looks at her from head to foot.*] And I must ask Miss West to excuse my coming at such an untimely hour— taking her unawares before she has had had time to—

Rebecca: [*Surprised.*] What do you mean? Do you see any harm in my wearing a morning gown about the house?

Kroll: Heaven forbid! I know nothing of what may now be customary at Rosmersholm.

Rosmer: Why, Kroll—you are not yourself to-day!

Rebecca: Allow me to wish you good morning, Rector Kroll. [*She goes out to the left.*]

Kroll: By your leave—[*Sits on sofa.*]

Rosmer: Yes, Kroll, sit down, and let us talk things out amicably. [*He seats himself in a chair directly opposite to the Rector.*]

Kroll: I haven't closed an eye since yesterday. I have been lying thinking and thinking all night.

Rosmer: And what do you say to things to-day?

Kroll: It will be a long story, Rosmer. Let me begin with a sort of introduction. I can give you news of Ulric Brendel.

Rosmer: Has he called on you?

Kroll: No. He took up his quarters in a low public-house—in the lowest company of course—and drank and stood treat as long as he had any money. Then he began abusing the whole company as a set of disreputable blackguards—and so far he was quite right—whereupon they thrashed him and pitched him out into the gutter.

Rosmer: So he is incorrigible after all.

Kroll: He had pawned the coat, too; but I am told that has been redeemed for him. Can you guess by whom?

Rosmer: Perhaps by you?

Kroll: No; by the distinguished Mr. Mortensgård.

Rosmer: Ah, indeed.

Kroll: I understand that Mr. Brendel's first visit was to the "idiot" and "plebeian."

Rosmer: Well, it was lucky for him—

Kroll: To be sure it was. [*Leans over the table towards Rosmer.*] And that brings me to a matter it is my duty to warn you about, for our old—for our former friendship's sake.

Rosmer: My dear Kroll, what can that be?

Kroll: It is this: there are things going on behind your back in this house.

Rosmer: How can you think so? Is it Reb—is it Miss West you are aiming at?

Kroll: Precisely. I can quite understand it on her part. She has so long been accustomed to have everything her own way here. But nevertheless—

Rosmer: My dear Kroll, you are utterly mistaken. She and I—we have no concealments from each other on any subject whatever.

Kroll: Has she told you, then, that she has entered into correspondence with the editor of the "Beacon"?

Rosmer: Oh, you are thinking of the few lines she sent by Ulric Brendel?

Kroll: Then you have found it out. And do you approve of her entering into relations with a scurrilous scribbler, who never lets a week pass without holding me up to ridicule, both as a schoolmaster and as a public man?

Rosmer: My dear Kroll, I don't 5 suppose that side of the matter ever entered her head. And besides, of course she has full liberty of action, just as I have.

Kroll: Indeed? Ah, no doubt that follows from your new line of thought. 10 For Miss West presumably shares your present standpoint?

Rosmer: Yes, she does. We two have worked our way forward in faithful comradeship.   15

Kroll: [*Looks at him and slowly shakes his head.*] Oh, you blind, deluded being!

Rosmer: I? Why do you say that?

Kroll: Because I dare not—I will not think the worst. No no, let me say my 20 say out.—You really do value my friendship, Rosmer? And my respect too? Do you not?

Rosmer: I surely need not answer that question.   25

Kroll: Well, but there are other questions that do require an answer—a full explanation on your part.—Will you submit to a sort of investigation—?

Rosmer: Investigation?   30

Kroll: Yes; will you let me question you about certain things it may pain you to be reminded of? You see—this apostasy of yours—well, this emancipation, as you call it—is bound up with 35 many other things that for your own sake you must explain to me.

Rosmer: My dear Kroll, ask what questions you please. I have nothing to conceal.   40

Kroll: Then tell me—what do you think was the real, the ultimate reason why Beata put an end to her life?

Rosmer: Can you have any doubt on the subject? Or, rather, can you ask for 45 reasons for what an unhappy, irresponsible invalid may do?

Kroll: Are you certain that Beata was completely irresponsible for her actions? The doctors, at any rate, were by no 50 means convinced of it.

Rosmer: If the doctors had ever seen her as I have so often seen her, for days and nights together, they would have had no doubts.

Kroll: I had no doubts either—then.

Rosmer: Oh, no, unhappily, there wasn't the smallest room for doubt. I have told you of her wild frenzies of passion—which she expected me to return. Oh, how they appalled me! And then her causeless, consuming self-reproaches during the last few years.

Kroll: Yes, when she had learnt that she must remain childless all her life.

Rosmer: Yes, just think of that! Such terrible, haunting agony of mind about a thing utterly beyond her control—! How could you call her responsible for her actions?

Kroll: H'm—. Can you remember whether you had any books in the house at that time treating of the rationale of marriage—according to the "advanced" ideas of the day?

Rosmer: I remember Miss West lending me a work of the kind. The Doctor left her his library, you know. But, my dear Kroll, you surely cannot suppose we were so reckless as to let my poor 30 sick wife get hold of any such ideas? I can solemnly assure you that the fault was not ours. It was her own distempered brain that drove her into these wild aberrations.

Kroll: One thing at any rate I can tell you; and that is, that poor, overstrung, tortured Beata put an end to her life in order that you might live happily—live freely, and—after your own heart.

Rosmer: [*Starts half up from his chair.*] What do you mean by that?

Kroll: Listen to me quietly, Rosmer; for now I can speak of it. In the last year of her life she came to me twice to pour 45 forth all her anguish and despair.

Rosmer: On this same subject?

Kroll: No. The first time she came, it was to declare that you were on the road to perversion—that you were going 50 to break with the faith of your fathers.

Rosmer: [*Eagerly.*] What you say is

impossible, Kroll. Absolutely impossible! You must be mistaken.

Kroll: And why?

Rosmer: Because while Beata was alive I was still wrestling with myself in doubt. And that fight I fought out alone and in utter silence. I don't think even Rebecca—

Kroll: Rebecca?

Rosmer: Oh, well—Miss West. I call her Rebecca for convenience' sake.

Kroll: So I have remarked.

Rosmer: So it is inconceivable to me how Beata could have got hold of the idea. And why did she not speak to me about it? She never did—she never said a single word.

Kroll: Poor creature—she begged and implored me to talk to you.

Rosmer: And why did you not?

Kroll: At that time I never for a moment doubted that she was out of her mind. Such an accusation against a man like you!—And then she came again—about a month later. This time she seemed outwardly calmer; but as she was going she said: "They may soon expect the White Horse at Rosmersholm now."

Rosmer: Yes, yes. The White Horse— she often spoke of it.

Kroll: And when I tried to divert her mind from such melancholy fancies, she only answered: "I have not long to live; for Johannes must marry Rebecca at once."

Rosmer: [*Almost speechless.*] What do you say? I marry—?

Kroll: That was on a Thursday afternoon—. On the Saturday evening she threw herself from the bridge into the mill-race.

Rosmer: And you never warned us—!

Kroll: You know very well how often she used to say that she felt her end was near.

Rosmer: Yes, I know. But nevertheless—you should have warned us!

Kroll: I did think of it; but not till too late.

Rosmer: But afterwards, why did you not—? Why have you said nothing about all this?

Kroll: What good would it have done for me to come torturing and harassing you still further? I took all she said for mere wild, empty ravings—until yesterday evening.

Rosmer: Then you have now changed your opinion?

Kroll: Did not Beata see quite clearly when she declared you were about to desert the faith of your fathers?

Rosmer: [*Looks fixedly, straight before him.*] I cannot understand it. It is the most incomprehensible thing in the world.

Kroll: Incomprehensible or not— there it is. And now I ask you, Rosmer, —how much truth is there in her other accusation? The last one, I mean.

Rosmer: Accusation? Was that an accusation?

Kroll: Perhaps you did not notice the way she worded it. She had to go, she said—why?

Rosmer: In order that I might marry Rebecca—

Kroll: These were not precisely her words. Beata used a different expression. She said: "I have not long to live; for Johannes must marry Rebecca at once."

Rosmer: [*Looks at him for a moment; then rises.*] Now I understand you, Kroll.

Kroll: And what then? What is your answer?

Rosmer: [*Still quiet and self-restrained.*] To such an unheard-of—? The only fitting answer would be to point to the door.

Kroll: [*Rises.*] Well and good.

Rosmer: [*Stands in front of him.*] Listen to me. For more than a year— ever since Beata left us—Rebecca West and I have lived alone here at Rosmersholm. During all that time you have known of Beata's accusation against us. But I have never for a moment noticed that you disapproved of Rebecca's living in my house.

Kroll: I did not know till yesterday

evening that it was an unbelieving man who was living with an—emancipated woman.

Rosmer: Ah—! Then you do not believe that purity of mind is to be found among the unbelieving and the emancipated? You do not believe that morality may be an instinctive law of their nature!

Kroll: I have no great faith in the morality that is not founded on the teachings of the Church.

Rosmer: And you mean this to apply to Rebecca and me? To the relation between us two—?

Kroll: Not even out of consideration for you two can I depart from my opinion that there is no unfathomable gulf between free thought and—h'm—

Rosmer: And what?

Kroll: —and free love,—since you will have it.

Rosmer: [*In a low voice.*] And you are not ashamed to say this to me! You, who have known me from my earliest youth!

Kroll: For that very reason. I know how easily you are influenced by the people you associate with. And this Rebecca of yours—well, Miss West then—we really know little or nothing about her. In short, Rosmer—I will not give you up. And you—you must try to save yourself in time.

Rosmer: Save myself? How—? [*Madam Helseth peeps in at the door on the left.*]

Rosmer: What do you want?

Madam Helseth: I wanted to ask Miss West to step downstairs.

Rosmer: Miss West is not up here.

Madam Helseth: Isn't she? [*Looks round the room.*] Well, that's strange. [*She goes.*]

Rosmer: You were saying—?

Kroll: Listen to me. I am not going to inquire too closely into the secret history of what went on here in Beata's lifetime—and may still be going on. I know that your marriage was a most unhappy one; and I suppose that must be taken as some sort of excuse—

Rosmer: Oh, how little you really know me—!

Kroll: Don't interrupt me. What I mean is this: if your present mode of life with Miss West is to continue, it is absolutely necessary that the change of views—the unhappy backsliding— brought about by her evil influence, should be hushed up. Let me speak! Let me speak! I say, if the worst comes to the worst, in Heaven's name think and believe whatever you like about everything under the sun. But you must keep your views to yourself. These things are purely personal matters, after all. There is no need to proclaim them from the housetops.

Rosmer: I feel it an absolute necessity to get out of a false and equivocal position.

Kroll: But you have a duty towards the traditions of your race, Rosmer! Remember that! Rosmersholm has, so to speak, radiated morality and order from time immemorial—yes, and respectful conformity to all that is accepted and sanctioned by the best people. The whole district has taken its stamp from Rosmersholm. It would lead to deplorable, irremediable confusion if it were known that you had broken with what I may call the hereditary idea of the house of Rosmer.

Rosmer: My dear Kroll, I cannot see the matter in that light. I look upon it as my imperative duty to spread a little light and gladness here, where the Rosmer family has from generation to generation been a centre of darkness and oppression.

Kroll: [*Looks at him severely.*] Yes, that would be a worthy life-work for the last of your race! No, Rosmer; let such things alone; you are the last man for such a task. You were born to be a quiet student.

Rosmer: Perhaps so. But for once in a way I mean to bear my part in the battle of life.

Kroll: And do you know what that battle of life will mean for you? It will mean a life-and-death struggle with all your friends.

Rosmer: [*Quietly.*] They cannot all be such fanatics as you.

Kroll: You are a credulous creature, Rosmer. An inexperienced creature, too. You have no conception of the overwhelming storm that will burst upon you. [*Madam Helseth looks in at the door on the left.*]

Madam Helseth: Miss West wants to know—

Rosmer: What is it?

Madam Helseth: There's a man downstairs wanting to have a word with the Pastor.

Rosmer: Is it the man who was here yesterday evening?

Madam Helseth: No, it's that Mortensgård.

Rosmer: Mortensgård?

Kroll: Aha! So it has come to this, has it?—Already!

Rosmer: What does he want with me? Why didn't you send him away?

Madam Helseth: Miss West said I was to ask if he might come upstairs.

Rosmer: Tell him I'm engaged—

Kroll: [*To Madam Helseth.*] Let him come up, Madam Helseth. [*Madam Helseth goes.*]

Kroll: [*Takes up his hat.*] I retire from the field—for the moment But the main battle has yet to be fought.

Rosmer: On my honour, Kroll—I have nothing whatever to do with Mortensgård.

Kroll: I do not believe you. On no subject and in no relation whatever will I henceforth believe you. It is war to the knife now. We will try whether we cannot disarm you.

Rosmer: Oh, Kroll—how low—how very low you have sunk!

Kroll: I? And you think you have the right to say that to me! Remember Beata!

Rosmer: Still harping upon that?

Kroll: No. You must solve the enigma of the mill-race according to your own conscience—if you have any-

thing of the sort left. [*Peter Mortensgård enters softly and quietly from the left. He is a small, wiry man with thin reddish hair and beard.*]

Kroll: [*With a look of hatred.*] Ah, here we have the "Beacon"—burning at Rosmersholm! [*Buttons his coat.*] Well, now I can no longer hesitate what course to steer.

Mortensgård: [*Deferentially.*] The "Beacon" may always be relied upon to light the Rector home.

Kroll: Yes; you have long shown your goodwill. To be sure there's a commandment about bearing false witness against your neighbour—

Mortensgård: Rector Kroll need not instruct me in the commandments.

Kroll: Not even in the seventh?

Rosmer: —Kroll—!

Mortensgård: If I needed instruction, it would rather be the Pastor's business.

Kroll: [*With covert sarcasm.*] The Pastor's? Oh, yes, unquestionably Pastor Rosmer is the man for that.—Good luck to your conference, gentlemen! [*Goes out and slams the door behind him.*]

Rosmer: [*Keeps his eyes fixed on the closed door and says to himself.*] Well, well—so be it then. [*Turns.*] Will you be good enough to tell me, Mr. Mortensgård, what brings you out here to me?

Mortensgård: It was really Miss West I came to see. I wanted to thank her for the friendly note I received from her yesterday.

Rosmer: I know she wrote to you. Have you seen her then?

Mortensgård: Yes, for a short time. [*Smiles slightly.*] I hear there has been a certain change of views out here at Rosmersholm.

Rosmer: My views are altered in many respects. I might almost say in all.

Mortensgård: So Miss West told me; and that's why she thought I had better come up and talk things over with the Pastor.

Rosmer: What things, Mr. Mortensgård?

Mortensgård: May I announce in the

"Beacon" that there has been a change in your views—that you have joined the party of freedom and progress?

Rosmer: Certainly you may. In fact, I beg you to make the announcement.

Mortensgård: Then it shall appear in to-morrow's paper. It will cause a great sensation when it's known that Pastor Rosmer of Rosmersholm is prepared to take up arms for the cause of light, in that sense, too.

Rosmer: I don't quite understand you.

Mortensgård: I mean that the moral position of our party is greatly strengthened whenever we gain an adherent of serious, Christian principles.

Rosmer: [*With some surprise.*] Then you do not know—? Did not Miss West tell you that, too?

Mortensgård: What, Pastor Rosmer? Miss West was in a great hurry. She said I was to go upstairs and hear the rest from yourself.

Rosmer: Well, in that case I may tell you that I have emancipated myself entirely, and on every side. I have broken with all the dogmas of the Church. Henceforth they are nothing to me.

Mortensgård: [*Looks at him in amazement.*] Well—if the skies were to fall I couldn't be more—! Pastor Rosmer himself announces—.

Rosmer: Yes, I now stand where you have stood for many years. That, too, you may announce in the "Beacon" to-morrow.

Mortensgård: That too? No, my dear Pastor—excuse me— I don't think it would be wise to touch on that side of the matter.

Rosmer: Not touch on it?

Mortensgård: Not at present, I mean.

Rosmer: I don't understand—

Mortensgård: Well, you see, Pastor Rosmer—you probably don't know the ins and outs of things so well as I do. But, since you have come over to the party of freedom—and, as I hear from Miss West, you intend to take an active share in the movement—I presume you would like to be of as much service as possible, both to the cause in general and to this particular agitation.

Rosmer: Yes, that is my earnest wish.

Mortensgård: Good. But now I must tell you, Pastor Rosmer, that if you openly declare your defection from the Church, you tie your own hands at the very outset.

Rosmer: Do you think so?

Mortensgård: Yes; believe me, you won't be able to do much for the cause, in this part of the country at any rate. And besides—we have plenty of freethinkers already, Pastor Rosmer—I might almost say too many. What the party requires, is a Christian element—something that every one must respect. That is what we are sadly in need of. And, therefore, I advise you to keep your own counsel about what doesn't concern the public. That's my view of the matter, at least.

Rosmer: I understand. Then if I openly confess my apostasy, you dare not have anything to do with me?

Mortensgård: [*Shaking his head.*] I scarcely like to risk it, Pastor Rosmer. I have made it a rule for some time past not to support any one or anything that is actively opposed to the Church.

Rosmer: Then you have yourself returned to the Church?

Mortensgård: That concerns no one but myself.

Rosmer: Ah, so that is it. Now I understand you.

Mortensgård: Pastor Rosmer—you ought to remember that I—I in particular—have not full liberty of action.

Rosmer: What hampers you?

Mortensgård: The fact that I am a marked man.

Rosmer: Ah—indeed.

Mortensgård: A marked man, Pastor Rosmer. You, above all men, should remember that; for I have chiefly you to thank for the scandal that branded me.

Rosmer: If I had then stood where I stand now, I should have dealt more gently with your offence.

Mortensgård: That I don't doubt. But

it is too late now. You have branded me once for all—branded me for life. I suppose you can scarcely understand what that means. But now you may perhaps come to feel the smart of it yourself, Pastor Rosmer.

Rosmer: I?

Mortensgård: Yes. You surely don't suppose that Rector Kroll and his set will ever forgive a desertion like yours? I hear the "County News" is going to be very savage in future. You, too, may find yourself a marked man before long.

Rosmer: In personal matters, Mr. Mortensgård, I feel myself secure from attack. My life is beyond reproach.

Mortensgård: [*With a sly smile.*] That's a large word, Mr. Rosmer.

Rosmer: Perhaps; but I have a right to use it.

Mortensgård: Even if you were to scrutinise your conduct as closely as you once scrutinised mine?

Rosmer: Your tone is very curious. What are you hinting at? Anything definite?

Mortensgård: Yes, something definite. Only one thing. But that might be bad enough, if malicious opponents got wind of it.

Rosmer: Will you have the kindness to let me hear what it is?

Mortensgård: Cannot you guess for yourself, Pastor?

Rosmer: No, certainly not. I have not the slightest idea.

Mortensgård: Well, well, I suppose I must come out with it then.—I have in my possession a strange letter, dated from Rosmersholm.

Rosmer: Miss West's letter, do you mean? Is it so strange?

Mortensgård: No, there's nothing strange about that. But I once received another letter from this house.

Rosmer: Also from Miss West?

Mortensgård: No, Mr. Rosmer.

Rosmer: Well then, from whom? From whom?

Mortensgård: From the late Mrs. Rosmer.

Rosmer: From my wife! You received a letter from my wife!

Mortensgård: I did.

Rosmer: When?

Mortensgård: Towards the close of Mrs. Rosmer's life. Perhaps about a year and a half ago. That is the letter I call strange.

Rosmer: I suppose you know that my wife's mind was affected at that time.

Mortensgård: Yes; I know many people thought so. But I don't think there was anything in the letter to show it. When I call it strange, I mean in another sense.

Rosmer: And what in the world did my poor wife take it into her head to write to you about?

Mortensgård: I have the letter at home. She begins to the effect that she is living in great anxiety and fear; there are so many malicious people about here, she says; and they think of nothing but causing you trouble and injury.

Rosmer: Me?

Mortensgård: Yes, so she says. And then comes the strangest part of all. Shall I go on, Pastor Rosmer?

Rosmer: Assuredly! Tell me everything, without reserve.

Mortensgård: The deceased lady begs and implores me to be magnanimous. She knows, she says, that it was her husband that had me dismissed from my post as teacher; and she conjured me by all that's sacred not to avenge myself.

Rosmer: How did she suppose you could avenge yourself?

Mortensgård: The letter says that if I should hear rumours of sinful doings at Rosmersholm, I am not to believe them; they are only spread abroad by wicked people who wish to make you unhappy.

Rosmer: Is all that in the letter?

Mortensgård: You may read it for yourself, sir, when you please.

Rosmer: But I don't understand—! What did she imagine the rumours to be about?

Mortensgård: Firstly, that the Pastor had deserted the faith of his fathers.

Your wife denied that absolutely—
then. And next—h'm—

Rosmer: Next?

Mortensgård: Well, next she writes—
rather confusedly—that she knows
nothing of any sinful intrigue at Rosmersholm; that she has never been
wronged in any way. And if any such
rumours should get about, she implores
me to say nothing of the matter in the
"Beacon."

Rosmer: Is no name mentioned?

Mortensgård: None.

Rosmer: Who brought you the letter?

Mortensgård: I have promised not to
say. It was handed to me one evening,
at dusk.

Rosmer: If you had made inquiries at
the time, you would have learnt that my
poor, unhappy wife was not fully accountable for her actions.

Mortensgård: I did make inquiries,
Pastor Rosmer. But I must say that was
not the impression I received.

Rosmer: Was it not?—But what is
your precise reason for telling me now
about this incomprehensible old letter?

Mortensgård: To impress on you the
necessity for extreme prudence, Pastor
Rosmer.

Rosmer: In my life, do you mean?

Mortensgård: Yes. You must remember that from to-day you have ceased to
be a neutral.

Rosmer: Then you have quite made
up your mind that I must have something to conceal?

Mortensgård: I don't know why an
emancipated man should refrain from
living his life out as fully as possible.
But, as I said before, be exceedingly
cautious in future. If anything should
get abroad that conflicts with current
prejudices, you may be sure the whole
liberal movement will have to suffer for
it.—Good-bye, Pastor Rosmer.

Rosmer: Good-bye.

Mortensgård: I shall go straight to the
office and have the great news put into
the "Beacon."

Rosmer: Yes; omit nothing.

Mortensgård: I shall omit nothing
that the public need know. [*He bows and
goes out. Rosmer remains standing in the
doorway while he goes down the stairs.
The outer door is heard to close.*]

Rosmer: [*In the doorway, calls softly.*]
Rebecca! Re— H'm. [*Aloud.*] Madam
Helseth,—is Miss West not there?

Madam Helseth: [*From the hall.*] No,
Pastor Rosmer, she's not here. [*The
curtain at the back is drawn aside. Rebecca appears in the doorway.*]

Rebecca: Rosmer!

Rosmer: [*Turns.*] What! Were you in
my room? My dear, what were you
doing there?

Rebecca: [*Goes up to him.*] I was listening.

Rosmer: Oh, Rebecca, how could you?

Rebecca: I could not help it. He said
it so hatefully—that about my morning
gown—

Rosmer: Then you were there when
Kroll—?

Rebecca: Yes. I wanted to know what
was lurking in his mind.

Rosmer: I would have told you.

Rebecca: You would scarcely have
told me all. And certainly not in his own
words.

Rosmer: Did you hear everything,
then?

Rebecca: Nearly everything, I think.
I had to go downstairs for a moment
when Mortensgård came.

Rosmer: And then you came back
again—?

Rebecca: Don't be vexed with me,
dear friend!

Rosmer: Do whatever you think right.
You are mistress of your own actions.—
But what do you say to all this, Rebecca
—? Oh, I seem never to have needed
you so much before!

Rebecca: Both you and I have been
prepared for what must happen some
time.

Rosmer: No, no—not for this.

Rebecca: Not for this?

Rosmer: I knew well enough that
sooner or later our beautiful, pure

friendship might be misinterpreted and soiled. Not by Kroll—I could never have believed such a thing of him—but by all those other people with the coarse souls and the ignoble eyes. Oh yes—I had reason enough for keeping our alliance so jealously concealed. It was a dangerous secret.

Rebecca: Oh, why should we care what all those people think! We know in our own hearts that we are blameless.

Rosmer: Blameless? I? Yes, I thought so—till to-day. But now—now, Rebecca—?

Rebecca: Well, what now?

Rosmer: How am I to explain Beata's terrible accusation?

Rebecca: [*Vehemently.*] Oh, don't speak of Beata! Don't think of Beata any more! You were just beginning to shake off the hold she has upon you, even in the grave.

Rosmer: Since I have heard all this, she seems, in a ghastly sort of way, to be alive again.

Rebecca: Oh no—not that, Rosmer! Not that!

Rosmer: Yes, I tell you. We must try to get to the bottom of this. What can possibly have led her to misinterpret things so fatally?

Rebecca: You are surely not beginning to doubt that she was on the very verge of insanity?

Rosmer: Oh yes—that is just what I can't feel quite certain of any longer. And besides—even if she was—

Rebecca: If she was? Well, what then?

Rosmer: I mean—where are we to look for the determining cause that drove her morbid spirit over the borderline of madness?

Rebecca: Oh, why brood over problems no one can solve?

Rosmer: I cannot help it, Rebecca. I cannot shake off these gnawing doubts, however much I may wish to.

Rebecca: But it may become dangerous—this eternal dwelling upon one miserable subject.

Rosmer: [*Walks about restlessly, in thought.*] I must have betrayed myself in one way or another. She must have noticed how happy I began to feel from the time you came to us.

Rebecca: Yes but, dear, even if she did—?

Rosmer: Be sure it didn't escape her that we read the same books—that the interest of discussing all the new ideas drew us together. Yet I cannot understand it! I was so careful to spare her. As I look back, it seems to me I made it the business of my life to keep her in ignorance of all our interests. Did I not, Rebecca?

Rebecca: Yes, yes; certainly you did.

Rosmer: And you too. And yet—! Oh, it's terrible to think of! She must have gone about here—full of her morbid passion—saying never a word—watching us—noting everything—and misinterpreting everything.

Rebecca: [*Pressing her hands together.*] Oh, I should never have come to Rosmersholm!

Rosmer: To think of all she must have suffered in silence! All the foulness her sick brain must have conjured up around us! Did she never say anything to you to put you at all on the alert?

Rebecca: [*As if startled.*] To me! Do you think I should have stayed a day longer if she had?

Rosmer: No, no, of course not.—Oh, what a battle she must have fought! And alone too, Rebecca; desperate and quite alone!—and then, at last, that heart-breaking, accusing victory—in the mill-race. [*Throws himself into the chair by the writing-table, with his elbows on the table and his face in his hands.*]

Rebecca: [*Approaches him cautiously from behind.*] Listen, Rosmer. If it were in your power to call Beata back—to you—to Rosmersholm—would you do it?

Rosmer: Oh, how do I know what I would or would not do? I can think of nothing but this one thing—that cannot be recalled.

Rebecca: You were just beginning to

live, Rosmer. You had begun. You had freed yourself—on every side. You felt so buoyant and happy—

Rosmer: Oh yes—I did indeed.—And now this crushing blow falls on me.

Rebecca: [Behind him, rests her arms on the chair-back.] How beautiful it was when we sat in the twilight, in the room downstairs, helping each other to lay out our new life-plans! You were to set resolutely to work in the world—the living world of to-day, as you said. You were to go as a messenger of emancipation from home to home; to win over minds and wills; to create noble-men around you in wider and wider circles. Noble-men.

Rosmer: Happy noble-men.

Rebecca: Yes—happy.

Rosmer: For it is happiness that ennobles, Rebecca.

Rebecca: Should you not say—sorrow as well? A great sorrow?

Rosmer: Yes—if one can get through it—over it—away from it.

Rebecca: That is what you must do.

Rosmer: [Shakes his head gloomily.] I shall never get over this—wholly. There will always be a doubt—a question left. I can never again know that luxury of the soul which makes life so marvellously sweet to live!

Rebecca: [Bends over his chair-back, and says more softly.] What is it you mean, Rosmer?

Rosmer: [Looking up at her.] Peaceful, happy innocence.

Rebecca: [Recoils a step.] Yes. Innocence. [A short pause.]

Rosmer: [With his elbow on the table, leaning his head on his hand, and looking straight before him.] And what extraordinary penetration she showed! How systematically she put all this together! First she begins to doubt my orthodoxy —— How could that occur to her? But it did occur to her; and then it grew to be a certainty. And then—yes, then of course it was easy for her to think all the rest possible. [Sits up in his chair and runs his hands through his hair.] Oh, all these horrible imaginings! I shall never get rid of them. I feel it. I know it. At any moment they will come rushing in upon me, and bring back the thought of the dead!

Rebecca: Like the White Horse of Rosmersholm.

Rosmer: Yes, like that. Rushing forth in the darkness—in the silence.

Rebecca: And because of this miserable figment of the brain, you will let slip the hold you were beginning to take upon the living world?

Rosmer: You may well think it hard. Yes, hard, Rebecca. But I have no choice. How could I ever leave this behind me?

Rebecca: [Behind his chair.] By entering into new relations.

Rosmer: [Surprised, looks up.] New relations?

Rebecca: Yes, new relations to the outside world. Live, work, act. Don't sit here brooding and groping among insoluble enigmas.

Rosmer: [Rises.] New relations? [Walks across the floor, stops at the door and then comes back.] One question occurs to me. Has it not occurred to you too, Rebecca?

Rebecca: [Drawing breath with difficulty.] Let me—hear—what it is.

Rosmer: What form do you think our relations will take after to-day?

Rebecca: I believe our friendship will endure—come what may.

Rosmer: That is not exactly what I meant. The thing that first brought us together, and that unites us so closely— our common faith in a pure comradeship between man and woman——

Rebecca: Yes, yes—what of that?

Rosmer: I mean, that such a relation —as this of ours—does it not presuppose a quiet, happy, peaceful life—?

Rebecca: What then?

Rosmer: But the life I must now look forward to is one of struggle and unrest and strong agitations. For I will live my life, Rebecca! I will not be crushed to earth by horrible possibilities. I will not have my course of life forced upon me, either by the living or by—any one else.

Rebecca: No, no—do not! Be an absolutely free man, Rosmer!

Rosmer: But can you not guess what is in my mind? Do you not know? Don't you see how I can best shake off all gnawing memories—all the unhappy past?

Rebecca: How?

Rosmer: By opposing to it a new, a living reality.

Rebecca: [*Feeling for the chair-back.*] A living— What do you mean?

Rosmer: [*Comes nearer.*] Rebecca—if I were to ask you—will you be my second wife?

Rebecca: [*For a moment speechless, then cries out with joy.*] Your wife! Your—! I!

Rosmer: Come; let us try it. We two will be one. The place of the dead must stand empty no longer.

Rebecca: I—in Beata's place—!

Rosmer: Then she will be out of the saga—completely—for ever and ever.

Rebecca: [*Softly, trembling.*] Do you believe that, Rosmer?

Rosmer: It must be so! It must! I cannot—I will not go through life with a dead body on my back. Help me to cast it off, Rebecca. And let us stifle all memories in freedom, in joy, in passion. You shall be to me the only wife I have ever had.

Rebecca: [*With self-command.*] Never speak of this again. I will never be your wife.

Rosmer: What! Never! Do you not think you could come to love me? Is there not already a strain of love in our friendship?

Rebecca: [*Puts her hands over her ears*

as if in terror.] Don't speak so, Rosmer! Don't say such things!

Rosmer: [*Seizes her arm.*] Yes, yes— there is a growing promise in our relation. Oh, I can see that you feel it too. Do you not, Rebecca?

Rebecca: [*Once more firm and calm.*] Listen to me. I tell you—if you persist in this, I will go away from Rosmersholm.

Rosmer: Go away! You! You cannot. It is impossible.

Rebecca: It is still more impossible that I should be your wife. Never in this world can I marry you.

Rosmer. [*Looks at her in surprise.*] You say "can"; and you say it so strangely. Why can you not?

Rebecca. [*Seizes both his hands.*] Dear friend—both for your own sake and for mine—do not ask why. [*Lets go his hands.*] Do not, Rosmer. [*Goes towards the door on the left.*]

Rosmer: Henceforth I can think of nothing but that one question—why?

Rebecca: [*Turns and looks at him.*] Then it is all over.

Rosmer: Between you and me?

Rebecca: Yes.

Rosmer: It will never be all over between us two. You will never leave Rosmersholm.

Rebecca: [*With her hand on the door-handle.*] No, perhaps I shall not. But if you ask me again—it is all over.

Rosmer: All over? How—?

Rebecca: For then I will go the way that Beata went. Now you know it, Rosmer.

Rosmer: Rebecca—?

Rebecca: [*In the doorway, nods slowly.*] Now you know it. [*She goes out.*]

Rosmer: [*Stares, thunderstruck, at the door, and says to himself.*] What—is— this?

WHAT THE STRUCTURE OF ACT II INDICATES

Although Act II, on first reading, may seem complex or even confused, it has a definite structure, and the meaning is clarified by the structure. After the brief "prologue" between Rebecca and Rosmer, Ibsen divides the rest of the act into three scenes—Rosmer and Kroll, Rosmer and Mortensgård, and Rosmer and Rebecca. Thus we can see pretty clearly what Ibsen is doing: he is showing Rosmer, the "liberal" idealist, under the impact of three different influences—that of the belligerent conservative, that of the crusading liberal journalist, and that of an intimate friend, also a liberal. Whereas in Act I it looked as if the play might hinge on a *direct conflict between conservative and liberal*, we now see, by the form of Act II, that Ibsen is venturing into a far more complicated situation and showing the idealist faced with a whole series of conflicts, of different kinds. Secondly, the fact that all these interviews take place at Rosmersholm and that Rosmer is the center of attention throughout show that Ibsen is concerned not with the town conflict but with what happens to the mind and spirit of Rosmer under various stresses. Further, the climactic scene of the act is that between Rebecca and Rosmer: what occurs between them is, of all the actions in the play, the most remote from the political battle in the town.

How does Ibsen intend us to view the characters in this manysided situation? Take, first of all, Rosmer. In Act I we saw him as decent, well-intentioned, kindly, truthful, idealistic. He is trusting: he has no idea that anyone will misconstrue his relationship with Rebecca. In Act II we see that he believes in the gentlemanliness of the combatants; he is willing to be examined by Kroll and to tell the whole truth; he is shocked by the suggestion of "free love"; he is willing to publish every detail of his change of principle; he had planned to create "happy noble-men." But above all, as a liberal he believes in complete freedom of action; he says to Rebecca, "Do whatever you think is right. You are the mistress of your own actions." Ibsen then throws this liberal idealist into an actual world of combat and invites us to observe how he fares in such a world.

Irony in Act II. The whole act is suffused with the irony of Rosmer's miscalculations of the way of the world. (Later on, in another play, we shall see Congreve handling the matter differently—endeavoring to show a type of idealism maintaining itself in an actual world. But there the mode is comic.) First, he finds that his old friend Kroll is willing to put the worst possible interpretation upon his conduct; what is still more ironic, Kroll will even *accept* the worst, if Rosmer will only keep quiet about it. Kroll shifts from principle to expediency, and he is ready for "war to the knife."

Notice how neatly Ibsen relates this interview to the next. Rosmer expects better things of the liberal Mortensgård. But it is ironical that Mortensgård too is for expediency, wants to hush things up, and isn't concerned about Rosmer's private life. In what other details does Mortensgård resemble Kroll?

Thus, Ibsen suggests a still more basic irony: that Kroll and Mortensgard actually have more in common than Rosmer has with either of them. Rosmer's devotion to quiet reasonableness is made to appear naïve in a world of merciless competing factions that are willing to use any weapons, reasonable or not, that they can get their hands on. Rosmer takes an overly simple view of life, and he receives an education in the complexities of an actual world.

The Past. Ibsen goes on to find a still heavier complication for Rosmer: Rosmer has to contend not only with the present but also with the past. Here, too, Ibsen uses irony in developing the situation, for Rosmer had thought he was escaping from the past. We recall Madam Helseth's remarking early in Act I that the dead cling to Rosmersholm; in this act Rebecca complains that Beata has not lost her hold upon Rosmer. Both turn out to be right—and in an unforeseen sense.

Several technical questions arise here. Does Ibsen seem to stack the cards against Rosmer? Is it necessary to give him a "past"? Or may we say rather that Rosmer does not really have a "past" more than any other man—that the past with which he is saddled is, in a sense, the creation of men seeking the most dangerous weapons and unscrupulous in their search? In that sense, any man has a "past"; the whole record of his life may in some way be used against him. Rosmer, we might argue, then, is not a special but a universal figure.

Second, Ibsen has carefully motivated this use of Rosmer's past. He informed us of it at the start, and very early in the play Rosmer and Rebecca showed relief that Kroll was not antagonistic to them. The revelation concerning Beata is not used for melodramatic surprise.

Third, Beata has important symbolic value. "The Past" (rather than "a past") is part of every man, so to speak; it cannot be escaped and it must be faced. More specifically, of course, Beata represents the more orthodox phase of Rosmer's life, just as Rebecca represents the new, liberal phase; Rebecca's antagonism to Beata (aside from its psychological meaning) suggests the philosophical split in Rosmer himself. Rational liberalism, Ibsen implies, can never be wholly separate from the old orthodoxy, or at least from its influence. This is the most pervasive irony of the play.

Finally, how does Ibsen introduce the dead Beata into the current situation? Here, the student can largely evaluate the techniques himself. Why is it natural for Kroll to start talking about Beata in Act II, to question Rosmer about her, and to pass on new information to him? In the Mortensgård scene, Ibsen has a slightly harder problem. In the first place, Ibsen has to bring the conversation around naturally to the subject of Rosmer's private life, not a wholly natural or easy one for Mortensgård. Notice the steps by which he does this. Second, we have to accept the fact that Beata actually wrote a letter to Mortensgård. What facts tend to make this plausible? What is ironic about the fact that she did write to him?

To show further the effect of the past, Ibsen introduces Rosmer's past censure of Mortensgård. Why does this not seem unmotivated when Mortensgård speaks of it? Notice precisely how it complicates Rosmer's career as a liberal: Rosmer cannot come completely into the open *because* Mortensgård cannot tell the whole truth *because* he is a marked man *because* of the criticism which Rosmer, in his conservative days, had brought down upon him. How does the influence of the Mortensgård heritage parallel the influence of the Beata heritage? Note how both combine to re-emphasize Rosmer's oversimplified view of life; as a man of reason he has separated things into reasonable little compartments—private life, public life. But in practice, facts will not behave according to such logical distinctions.

The Scene with Rebecca. To make clear what Ibsen is doing, we have, for the purpose of this discussion, broken down the act into strands of action which, in the play itself, actually do not appear separately but are closely interwoven. After two-thirds of Act II we see Rosmer facing, and almost crushed by, a world of unforeseen complexity. Ibsen now uses the last part of Act II to show Rosmer trying to accommodate himself to this world—a personal, private experience in which only Rebecca participates. But Ibsen conceives of the scene dramatically: it consists not only of Rosmer's talking matters over with Rebecca and himself, but rather of a readjustment of his relations with Rebecca. Note the ironic contrast between this dialogue and his final dialogue with Rebecca in Act I.

Even in presenting this effort at clarification and adjustment, Ibsen maintains the ironic tone: the complications keep piling up—both in Rebecca and in himself. Rebecca, for instance, has been eavesdropping, a fact which, though he appears willing to accept it, obviously disappoints him. She is irritable on the subject of Beata. But most of all, she responds in a peculiar way to his proposal of marriage; the act ends with Rosmer's expression of shocked incomprehension of a new element in Rebecca. Ibsen's climactic irony is the new complication within Rosmer himself: all the other events in the act have come to make him doubt his own innocence. He is less able than ever to face the outer world because he cannot now face himself. In his uncertainty, he takes another step, which in the light of preceding events shows itself to involve reversal: he asks Rebecca to marry him. Thus the man whose relationship with a woman has been pure, who has not even been conscious of being in love with her, who is proudly aware of the wrong done him by the suspicions of Kroll and Mortensgård, now does the one thing which will be calculated to confirm those suspicions.

Forward Movement. Aside from keeping Act II moving forward by creating new situations that will have to be dealt with, Ibsen also introduces a kind of undercurrent of anticipation of which we should be aware. First of all, there is Rosmer's shock at Beata's having apparently known of his growing religious skepticism, a fact of which no explanation is made to us here. Second, there is Beata's understanding of the relationship between Rebecca and Rosmer; Beata seems to have gone far beyond the apparently available evidence. Then there is Rebecca's irritation when Rosmer talks of Beata, a matter which Ibsen certainly wishes us to notice. When Rosmer asks Rebecca whether Beata ever said anything which would put her on the alert, Ibsen gives, with Rebecca's reply, a stage direction which is very important—"As if startled." (Here we see an unusual responsibility placed upon the actress; her interpretation of the line would be very important

in stimulating the imagination. The words alone do not convey much.)
Finally, there is Rebecca's mysterious refusal of Rosmer's offer of marriage,
not to mention her threat to go "the way that Beata went." By all of these
unexplained matters Ibsen is arousing our expectations of things to come.

QUESTIONS

1. Is it plausible to have Rosmer propose to Rebecca just after hearing
Kroll's and Mortensgård's aspersions upon his relationship with her and
after feeling shocked remorse at thinking about what Beata must have
suffered in believing he was in love with Rebecca? Rosmer defends himself
against the charge that he is in love with Rebecca; then he declares his
love to her. Does this reversal violate probability for the sake of a striking
effect? In attempting to frame an answer, the student might consider the
following matters: (1) Rosmer is the sort of man who accepts relationships
unconsciously without defining them overtly to himself. (2) In a sense
Kroll and Mortensgård actually give Rosmer the idea of marriage; their
accusations, even though Rosmer is to deny them sincerely, do make him
conscious of marriage as a possibility. (3) But this suggestion of marriage,
once made, is accidentally carried on by Rebecca herself when she answers
Rosmer's despairing, "How could I ever leave this behind me?" by saying
"By entering into new relations." (4) Rosmer needs to lean on someone;
his recent shocks increase the need, and perhaps cause the need to assert
itself overtly here. The student must decide whether, in the light of such
considerations, Ibsen has motivated the step adequately, whether he has
shrewdly penetrated the psychology of the "noble" but essentially weak
man.

2. Notice the various lines—especially those by Kroll—which are intended to indicate that Rosmer is weak. Does Ibsen intend to imply that
all pure, theoretical liberalism is weak? Does Rosmer seem typical, or a
special case? Are we supposed to despise him? Or are there reasons for our
admiring him at the same time that we may regret his weakness?

Note, in this connection, the treatment of Brendel, who at some points
is not unlike Rosmer. In Act II we learn that he has failed (how, by the
way, is his drunkenness prepared for in Act I?). Could this news be intended to foreshadow any future events?

3. We have thus far stressed consistently the interrelationship of past
and present in which Rosmer is involved. A similar interrelationship is
that of private and public life. Where does Rosmer fail to foresee and understand this relationship?

4. Perhaps all the ironies of the play might be summarized under one
head. Rosmer is a "liberal" who wants to "free" men's minds. That is, he
has used his reason to shake off old beliefs, and he wants other men likewise
to use their reason. But the world of actual conflict is not one of cold
reason: for irrationality flourishes here just as in the old orthodoxy. Note
how this comes out especially in the Mortensgård dialogue.

5. After studying Act II we may find several things in Act I more meaningful. Once Rosmer says to Kroll (p. 267b, 10 ff.), "I am not in love with the spirit that is in the ascendant, nor with either of the contending parties. I will try to bring together men from both sides—" Again, "Men are growing evil in this struggle. Peace and joy and mutual forbearance must once more enter into our souls" (p. 268a, 46 ff.). What connections can you find between such lines and later events?

6. In the brief opening scene between Rosmer and Rebecca, what is done that is necessary to make the rest of the act work out as it does? Do we learn anything more about the character of Rebecca? Does it fit in with what we saw of her in Act I?

7. Is the symbolism of the white horse made any clearer in this act? Does the use of the symbol seem to point toward future events?

8. What is the significance of Mortensgård's not committing himself about his membership in the church? With what does this contrast?

9. We have spoken of Beata as symbolizing the orthodox phase of Rosmer's career. Can you find any evidence for or against this interpretation? Might Rosmer's childlessness be intended to be symbolic? In Act I Kroll remarked that Rebecca had filled the house with flowers, whereas Beata could not stand flowers. Again, Rosmer says to Kroll (Act I, p. 267a, 33–35), "A new summer has blossomed in my soul. I see with my eyes grown young again." What do such lines suggest? Can you find others with similar suggestiveness?

10. We have spoken of Rosmer's ironic inability to understand how other people will react to a situation. Note how this is suggested even by his earlier conduct—in the relations among Beata, Rebecca, and himself. What is ironic about his belief in the purity of his own motives?

11. What aspects of liberalism appear to be represented by Brendel, Rosmer, Rebecca, Mortensgård?

ACT THIRD

[The sitting-room at Rosmersholm. The window and the entrance door are open. The sun is shining outside. Forenoon.]

[*Rebecca West, dressed as in the first Act, stands at the window, watering and arranging the flowers. Her crochet-work lies in the arm-chair. Madam Helseth is moving about, dusting the furniture with a feather-brush.*]

Rebecca: [*After a short silence.*] I can't understand the Pastor remaining so long upstairs to-day.

Madam Helseth: Oh, he often does that. But he'll soon be down now, I should think.

Rebecca: Have you seen anything of him?

Madam Helseth: I caught a glimpse of him when I went upstairs with his coffee. He was in his bedroom, dressing.

Rebecca: I asked because he was a little out of sorts yesterday.

Madam Helseth. He didn't look well. I wonder if there isn't something amiss between him and his brother-in-law.

Rebecca: What do you think it can be?

Madam Helseth: I couldn't say. Perhaps it's that Mortensgård that has been setting them against each other.

Rebecca: Likely enough.—Do you know anything of this Peter Mortensgård?

Madam Helseth: No indeed. How could you think so, Miss? A fellow like him?

Rebecca: Do you mean because he edits such a low paper?

Madam Helseth: Oh, it's not only that.—You must have heard, Miss, that he had a child by a married woman that had been deserted by her husband?

Rebecca: Yes, I have heard of it. But it must have been long before I came here.

Madam Helseth: It's true he was very young at the time; and she should have known better. He wanted to marry her too; but of course he couldn't do that. And I don't say he hasn't paid dear for it.—But, good Lord, Mortensgård has got on in the world since those days. There's a many people run after him now.

Rebecca: Yes, most of the poor people bring their affairs to him when they're in any trouble.

Madam Helseth: Ah, and others too, perhaps, besides the poor folk—

Rebecca: [*Looks at her furtively.*] Indeed.

Madam Helseth: [*By the sofa, dusting away vigorously.*] Perhaps the last people you would think likely to, Miss.

Rebecca: [*Busy with the flowers.*] Come, now, that's only an idea of yours, Madam Helseth. You can't be sure of what you're saying.

Madam Helseth: You think I can't, Miss? But I can tell you I am. Why—if you must know it—I once took a letter in to Mortensgård myself.

Rebecca: [*Turning.*] No—did you?

Madam Helseth: Yes, indeed I did. And a letter that was written here at Rosmersholm too.

Rebecca: Really, Madam Helseth?

Madam Helseth: Yes, that it was. And it was on fine paper, and there was a fine red seal on it too.

Rebecca: And it was given to you to deliver? Then, my dear Madam Helseth, it's not difficult to guess who wrote it.

Madam Helseth: Well?

Rebecca: It must have been something that poor Mrs. Rosmer, in her morbid state—

Madam Helseth: It's you that say that, Miss, not me.

Rebecca: But what was in the letter? Oh, I forgot—you can't know that.

Madam Helseth: H'm; what if I did know it, all the same?

Rebecca: Did she tell you what she was writing about?

Madam Helseth: No, she didn't exactly do that. But Mortensgård, when he'd read it, he began questioning me backwards and forwards and up and down, so that I soon guessed what was in it.

Rebecca: Then what do you think it was? Oh my dear good Madam Helseth, do tell me.

Madam Helseth: Oh no, Miss. Not for the whole world.

Rebecca: Oh you can surely tell me. We two are such good friends.

Madam Helseth: Lord preserve me from telling you anything about that, Miss. I can only tell you that it was something horrible that they'd got the poor sick lady to believe.

Rebecca: Who had got her to believe it?

Madam Helseth: Wicked people, Miss West. Wicked people.

Rebecca: Wicked— ?

Madam Helseth: Yes, I say it again. They must have been real wicked people.

Rebecca: And who do you think it could have been?

Madam Helseth: Oh, I know well enough what to think. But Lord forbid I should say anything. To be sure there's a certain lady in the town—h'm!

Rebecca: I can see that you mean Mrs. Kroll.

Madam Helseth: Ah, she's a fine one, she is. She has always been the great lady with me. And she's never had any too much love for you neither.

Rebecca: Do you think Mrs. Rosmer was in her right mind when she wrote that letter to Mortensgård?

Madam Helseth: It's a queer thing a person's mind, Miss. Clean out of her mind I don't think she was.

Rebecca: But she seemed to go distracted when she learned that she must always be childless. It was that that unsettled her reason.

Madam Helseth: Yes, poor lady, that was a dreadful blow to her.

Rebecca: [*Takes up her crochet and sits in a chair by the window.*] But after all—don't you think it was a good thing for the Pastor, Madam Helseth?

Madam Helseth: What, Miss?

Rebecca: That there were no children. Don't you think so?

Madam Helseth: H'm, I'm sure I don't know what to say about that.

Rebecca: Oh yes, believe me, it was fortunate for him. Pastor Rosmer is not the man to have crying children about his house.

Madam Helseth: Ah, Miss, little children don't cry at Rosmersholm.

Rebecca: [*Looks at her.*] Don't cry?

Madam Helseth: No. As long as people can remember, children have never been known to cry in this house.

Rebecca: That's very strange.

Madam Helseth: Yes; isn't it? But it runs in the family. And then there's another strange thing. When they grow up, they never laugh. Never, as long as they live.

Rebecca: Why, how extraordinary—

Madam Helseth: Have you ever once heard or seen the Pastor laugh, Miss?

Rebecca: No—now that I think of it, I almost believe you are right. But I don't think any one laughs much in this part of the country.

Madam Helseth: No, they don't. They say it began at Rosmersholm. And then I suppose it spread round about, as if it was catching-like.

Rebecca: You are a very wise woman, Madam Helseth.

Madam Helseth: Oh, Miss, you mustn't sit there and make fun of me. [*Listens.*] Hush, hush—here's the Pastor coming down. He doesn't like to see dusting going on. [*She goes out to the right.*] [*Johannes Rosmer, with his hat and stick in his hand, enters from the hall.*]

Rosmer: Good morning, Rebecca.

Rebecca: Good morning, dear. [*A moment after—crocheting.*] Are you going out?

Rosmer: Yes.

Rebecca: It's a beautiful day.

Rosmer: You didn't look in on me this morning.

Rebecca: No, I didn't. Not to-day.

Rosmer: Do you not intend to in future?

Rebecca: Oh, I don't know yet, dear.

Rosmer: Has anything come for me?

Rebecca: The "County News" has come.

Rosmer: The "County News"?

Rebecca: There it is on the table.

Rosmer: [*Puts down his hat and stick.*] Is there anything—?

Rebecca: Yes.

Rosmer: And you didn't send it up?

Rebecca: You will read it soon enough.

Rosmer: Oh, indeed? [*Takes the paper and reads, standing by the table.*]—What! —"We cannot warn our readers too earnestly against unprincipled renegades."[*Looks at her.*] They call me a renegade, Rebecca.

Rebecca: They mention no names.

Rosmer: That makes no difference. [*Reads on.*] "Secret traitors to the good cause."—"Judas-natures, who make brazen confession of their apostasy as soon as they think the most convenient and—profitable moment has arrived." "Ruthless befouling of a name honoured through generations"—"in the confident hope of a suitable reward from the party in momentary power." [*Lays down the paper on the table.*] And they can say such things of me!—Men who have known me so long and so well! Things they themselves don't believe.

Things they know there is not a word of truth in—they print them all the same.

Rebecca: That is not all.

Rosmer: [*Takes up the paper again.*] "Inexperience and lack of judgment the only excuse"—"pernicious influence—possibly extending to matters which, for the present, we do not wish to make subjects of public discussion or accusation." [*Looks at her.*] What is this?

Rebecca: It is aimed at me, plainly enough.

Rosmer: [*Lays down the paper.*] Rebecca,—this is the conduct of dishonourable men.

Rebecca: Yes, they need scarcely be so contemptuous of Mortensgård.

Rosmer: [*Walks about the room.*] Something must be done. All that is good in human nature will go to ruin, if this is allowed to go on. But it shall not go on! Oh, what a joy—what a joy it would be to me to let a little light into all this gloom and ugliness!

Rebecca: [*Rises.*] Ah yes, Rosmer. In that you have a great and glorious object to live for.

Rosmer: Only think, if I could rouse them to see themselves as they are; teach them to repent and blush before their better natures; bring them together in mutual forbearance—in love, Rebecca!

Rebecca: Yes, put your whole strength into that, and you must succeed.

Rosmer: I think success must be possible. Oh, what a delight it would be then to live one's life! No more malignant wrangling; only emulation. All eyes fixed on the same goal. Every mind, every will pressing forward—upward—each by the path its nature prescribes for it. Happiness for all—through all. [*Happens to look out of the window, starts, and says sadly.*] Ah! Not through me.

Rebecca: Not——? Not through you?

Rosmer: Nor for me.

Rebecca: Oh Rosmer, do not let such doubts take hold of you.

Rosmer: Happiness—dear Rebecca—

happiness is above all things the calm, glad certainty of innocence.

Rebecca: [*Looks straight before her.*] Yes, innocence—

Rosmer: Oh, you cannot know what guilt means. But I—

Rebecca: You least of all!

Rosmer: [*Points out of the window.*] The mill-race.

Rebecca: Oh Rosmer—! [*Madam Helseth looks in at the door.*]

Madam Helseth: Miss West!

Rebecca: Presently, presently. Not now.

Madam Helseth: Only a word, Miss. [*Rebecca goes to the door. Madam Helseth tells her something. They whisper together for a few moments. Madam Helseth nods and goes out.*]

Rosmer: [*Uneasily.*] Was it anything for me?

Rebecca: No, only something about the house-work.—You ought to go out into the fresh air, dear Rosmer. You should take a good long walk.

Rosmer: [*Takes up his hat.*] Yes, come. Let us go together.

Rebecca: No, dear, I can't just now. You must go alone. But shake off all these gloomy thoughts. Promise me.

Rosmer: I am afraid I shall never shake them off.

Rebecca: Oh, that such baseless fancies should take so strong a hold of you—!

Rosmer: Not so baseless I am afraid, Rebecca. I lay awake all night thinking it over and over. Perhaps Beata saw clearly after all.

Rebecca: In what?

Rosmer: In her belief that I loved you, Rebecca.

Rebecca: Right in that!

Rosmer: [*Lays his hat down on the table.*] The question that haunts me is this: were we two not deceiving ourselves all the time—when we called our relation friendship?

Rebecca: You mean that it might as well have been called—?

Rosmer: —love. Yes, Rebecca, that

is what I mean. Even while Beata was alive, all my thoughts were for you. It was you alone I longed for. It was when you were by my side that I felt the calm gladness of utter content. If you think it over, Rebecca—did we not feel for each other from the first a sort of sweet, secret child-love—desireless, dreamless? Was it not so with you? Tell me.

Rebecca: [*Struggling with herself.*] Oh —I don't know what to answer

Rosmer: And it was this close-linked life in and for each other that we took for friendship. No, Rebecca—our bond has been a spiritual marriage—perhaps from the very first. That is why there is guilt on my soul. I had no right to such happiness—it was a sin against Beata.

Rebecca: No right to live happily? Do you believe that, Rosmer?

Rosmer: She looked at our relation with the eyes of her love—judged it after the fashion of her love. Inevitably. Beata could not have judged otherwise than she did.

Rebecca: But how can you accuse yourself because of Beata's delusion?

Rosmer: It was love for me—her kind of love—that drove her into the mill-race. That is an immovable fact, Rebecca. And that is what I can never get over.

Rebecca: Oh, think of nothing but the great, beautiful task you have devoted your life to.

Rosmer: [*Shakes his head.*] It can never be accomplished, dear. Not by me. Not after what I have come to know.

Rebecca: Why not by you?

Rosmer: Because no cause ever triumphs that has its origin in sin.

Rebecca: [*Vehemently.*] Oh, these are only ancestral doubts—ancestral fears—ancestral scruples. They say the dead come back to Rosmersholm in the shape of rushing white horses. I think this shows that it is true.

Rosmer: Be that as it may; what does it matter, so long as I cannot rid myself of the feeling? And believe me, Rebecca, it is as I tell you. The cause that is to win a lasting victory must have for its champion a happy, an innocent man.

Rebecca: Is happiness so indispensable to you, Rosmer?

Rosmer: Happiness? Yes, dear,—it is.

Rebecca: To you, who can never laugh?

Rosmer: Yes, in spite of that. Believe me, I have a great capacity for happiness.

Rebecca: Now go for your walk, dear. A good long walk. Do you hear?—See, here is your hat. And your stick too.

Rosmer: [*Takes both.*] Thanks. And you won't come with me?

Rebecca: No, no; I can't just now.

Rosmer: Very well, then. You are with me none the less. [*He goes out by the entrance door. Rebecca waits a moment, cautiously watching his departure from behind the open door; then she goes to the door on the right.*]

Rebecca: [*Opens the door, and says in a low tone.*] Now, Madam Helseth. You can show him in now. [*Goes towards the window.*] [*A moment after, Rector Kroll enters from the right. He bows silently and formally, and keeps his hat in his hand.*]

Kroll: He has gone out?

Rebecca: Yes.

Kroll: Does he usually stay out long?

Rebecca: Yes, he does. But one cannot count on him to-day. So if you don't care to meet him—

Kroll: No, no. It is you I want to speak to,—quite alone.

Rebecca: Then we had better not lose time. Sit down, Rector. [*She sits in the easy-chair by the window. Rector Kroll sits on a chair beside her.*]

Kroll: Miss West—you can scarcely imagine how deeply and painfully I have taken this to heart—this change in Johannes Rosmer.

Rebecca: We expected it would be so—at first.

Kroll: Only at first?

Rebecca: Rosmer was confident that sooner or later you would join him.

Kroll: I?

Rebecca: You and all his other friends.

Kroll: Ah, there you see! That shows the infirmity of his judgment in all that concerns men and practical life.

Rebecca: But after all—since he feels it a necessity to emancipate himself on all sides—

Kroll: Yes, but wait—that is just what I do not believe.

Rebecca: What do you believe then?

Kroll: I believe that you are at the bottom of it all.

Rebecca: It is your wife who has put that in your head, Rector Kroll.

Kroll: No matter who has put it in my head. What is certain is that I feel a strong suspicion—an exceedingly strong suspicion—when I think things over, and piece together all I know of your behaviour ever since you came here.

Rebecca: [*Looks at him.*] I seem to recollect a time when you felt an exceedingly strong faith in me, dear Rector. I might almost call it a warm faith.

Kroll: [*In a subdued voice.*] Whom could you not bewitch—if you tried?

Rebecca: Did I try—?

Kroll: Yes, you did. I am no longer such a fool as to believe that there was any feeling in the matter. You simply wanted to get a footing at Rosmersholm —to strike root here—and in that I was to serve you. Now I see it.

Rebecca: You seem utterly to have forgotten that it was Beata who begged and implored me to come out here?

Kroll: Yes, when you had bewitched her too. Can the feeling she came to entertain for you be called friendship? It was adoration—almost idolatry. It developed into—what shall I call it?— a sort of desperate passion.—Yes, that is the right word for it.

Rebecca: Be so good as to recollect the state your sister was in. So far as I am concerned, I don't think any one can accuse me of being hysterical.

Kroll: No; that you certainly are not. But that makes you all the more danger-ous to the people you want to get into

your power. It is easy for you to weigh your acts and calculate consequences— just because your heart is cold.

Rebecca: Cold? Are you so sure of that?

Kroll: I am quite certain of it now. Otherwise you could never have lived here year after year without faltering in the pursuit of your object. Well, well— you have gained your end. You have got him and everything into your power. But in order to do so, you have not scrupled to make him unhappy.

Rebecca: That is not true. It is not I— it is you yourself that have made him unhappy.

Kroll: I?

Rebecca: Yes, when you led him to imagine that he was responsible for Beata's terrible end.

Kroll: Does he feel that so deeply, then?

Rebecca: How can you doubt it? A mind so sensitive as his—

Kroll: I thought that an emancipated man, so-called, was above all such scruples.—But there we have it! Oh yes —I admit I knew how it would be. The descendant of the men that look down on us from these walls—how could he hope to cut himself adrift from all that has been handed down without a break from generation to generation?

Rebecca: [*Looks down thoughtfully.*] Johannes Rosmer's spirit is deeply rooted in his ancestry. That is very certain.

Kroll: Yes, and you should have taken that fact into consideration, if you had felt any affection for him. But that sort of consideration was no doubt beyond you. There is such an immeasurable difference between your antecedents and his.

Rebecca: What antecedents do you mean?

Kroll: I am speaking of your origin— your family antecedents, Miss West.

Rebecca: Oh, indeed! Yes, it is quite true that I come of very humble folk. Nevertheless—

Kroll: I am not thinking of rank and position. I allude to your moral antecedents.

Rebecca: Moral—? In what sense?

Kroll: The circumstances of your birth.

Rebecca: What do you mean?

Kroll: I only mention the matter because it accounts for your whole conduct.

Rebecca: I do not understand this. You must explain.

Kroll: I really did not suppose you could require an explanation. Otherwise it would have been very odd that you should have let Dr. West adopt you—

Rebecca: [*Rises.*] Ah! Now I understand.

Kroll: —and that you should have taken his name. Your mother's name was Gamvik.

Rebecca: [*Walks across the room.*] My father's name was Gamvik, Rector Kroll.

Kroll: Your mother's business must have brought her very frequently into contact with the parish doctor.

Rebecca: Yes, it did.

Kroll: And then he takes you into his house—as soon as your mother dies. He treats you harshly; and yet you stay with him. You know that he won't leave you a halfpenny—as a matter of fact, you only got a case full of books—and yet you stay on; you bear with him; you nurse him to the last.

Rebecca: [*Stands by the table, looking scornfully at him.*] And you account for all this by assuming that there was something immoral—something criminal about my birth?

Kroll: I attribute your care for him to involuntary filial instinct. Indeed I believe your whole conduct is determined by your origin.

Rebecca: [*Vehemently.*] But there is not a single word of truth in what you say! And I can prove it! Dr. West did not come to Finmark till after I was born.

Kroll: Excuse me, Miss West. He

settled there the year before. I have assured myself of that.

Rebecca: You are mistaken, I say! You are utterly mistaken.

Kroll: You told me the day before yesterday that you were nine-and-twenty—in your thirtieth year.

Rebecca: Indeed! Did I say so?

Kroll: Yes, you did. And I can calculate from that—

Rebecca: Stop! You needn't calculate. I may as well tell you at once: I am a year older than I give myself out to be.

Kroll: [*Smiles incredulously.*] Really! I am surprised! What can be the reason of that?

Rebecca: When I had passed twenty-five, it seemed to me I was getting altogether too old for an unmarried woman. And so I began to lie about my age.

Kroll: You? An emancipated woman! Have you prejudices about the age for marriage?

Rebecca: Yes, it was idiotic of me—idiotic and absurd. But some folly or other will always cling to us, not to be shaken off. We are made so.

Kroll: Well, so be it; but my calculation may be right, none the less. For Dr. West was up there on a short visit the year before he got the appointment.

Rebecca: [*With a vehement outburst.*] It is not true!

Kroll: Is it not true?

Rebecca: No. My mother never spoke of any such visit.

Kroll: Did she not?

Rebecca: No, never. Nor Dr. West either; not a word about it.

Kroll: Might not that be because they both had reasons for suppressing a year? Just as you have done, Miss West. Perhaps it is a family foible.

Rebecca: [*Walks about clenching and wringing her hands.*] It is impossible. You want to cheat me into believing it. This can never, never be true. It cannot! Never in this world—

Kroll: [*Rises.*] My dear Miss West— why in heaven's name are you so terribly excited? You quite frighten me! What am I to think—to believe—?

Rebecca: Nothing! You are to think and believe nothing.

Kroll: Then you must really tell me how you can take this affair—this possibility—so terribly to heart.

Rebecca: [*Controlling herself.*] It is perfectly simple, Rector Kroll. I have no wish to be taken for an illegitimate child.

Kroll: Indeed! Well well, let us be satisfied with that explanation—in the meantime. But in that case you must still have a certain—prejudice on that point too?

Rebecca: Yes, I suppose I have.

Kroll: Ah, I fancy it is much the same with most of what you call your "emancipation." You have read yourself into a number of new ideas and opinions. You have got a sort of smattering of recent discoveries in various fields—discoveries that seem to overthrow certain principles which have hitherto been held impregnable and unassailable. But all this has only been a matter of the intellect, Miss West—a superficial acquisition. It has not passed into your blood.

Rebecca: [*Thoughtfully.*] Perhaps you are right.

Kroll: Yes, look into your own mind, and you will see! And if this is the case with you, one may easily guess how it must be with Johannes Rosmer. It is sheer, unmitigated madness—it is running blindfold to destruction—for him to think of coming openly forward and confessing himself an apostate! Only think—a man of his sensitive nature! Imagine him disowned and persecuted by the circle of which he has always formed a part—exposed to ruthless attacks from all the best people in the community! He is not—he never can be the man to endure all that.

Rebecca: He must endure it! It is too late now for him to retreat.

Kroll: Not at all too late. By no means. What has happened can be hushed up—or at least explained away

as a mere temporary aberration, however deplorable. But—one measure is certainly indispensable.

Rebecca: And what is that?

Kroll: You must get him to legalise the position, Miss West.

Rebecca: His position towards me?

Kroll: Yes. You must make him do that.

Rebecca: Then you absolutely cannot clear your mind of the idea that our position requires to be—legalised, as you call it?

Kroll: I would rather not go into the matter too closely. But I believe I have noticed that it is nowhere easier to break through all so-called prejudices than in —h'm—

Rebecca: In the relation between man and woman, you mean?

Kroll: Yes,—to speak plainly—I think so.

Rebecca: [*Wanders across the room and looks out at the window.*] I could almost say—I wish you were right, Rector Kroll.

Kroll: What do you mean by that? You say it so strangely.

Rebecca: Oh well—please let us drop the subject. Ah,—there he comes.

Kroll: Already! Then I will go.

Rebecca: [*Goes towards him.*] No— please stay. There is something I want you to hear.

Kroll: Not now. I don't feel as if I could bear to see him.

Rebecca: I beg you to say. Do! If not, you will regret it by-and-by. It is the last time I shall ask you for anything.

Kroll: [*Looks at her in surprise and puts down his hat.*] Very well, Miss West —so be it, then. [*A short silence. Then Johannes Rosmer enters from the hall.*]

Rosmer: [*Sees the Rector, and stops in the doorway.*] What!—Are you here?

Rebecca: He did not wish to meet you, dear.[1]

Kroll: [*Involuntarily.*] "Dear!"

[1] In the original, Rebecca here addresses Rosmer as "*du*" for the first time in Kroll's presence.

Rebecca: Yes, Rector Kroll, Rosmer and I say "dear" to each other. That is one result of our "position."

Kroll: Was that what you wanted me to hear?

Rebecca: That—and a little more.

Rosmer: [*Comes forward.*] What is the object of this visit?

Kroll: I wanted to try once more to stop you and win you back to us.

Rosmer: [*Points to the newspaper.*] After what appears in that paper?

Kroll: I did not write it.

Rosmer: Did you make the slightest effort to prevent its appearance?

Kroll: That would have been to betray the cause I serve. And, besides, it was not in my power.

Rebecca: [*Tears the paper into shreds, crushes up the pieces and throws them behind the stove.*] There! Now it is out of sight. And let it be out of mind too. For there will be nothing more of that sort, Rosmer.

Kroll: Ah, if you could only make sure of that!

Rebecca: Come, let us sit down, dear. All three of us. And then I will tell you everything.

Rosmer: [*Seats himself mechanically.*] What has come over you, Rebecca? This unnatural calmness—what is it?

Rebecca: The calmness of resolution. [*Seats herself.*] Pray sit down too, Rector. [*Rector Kroll seats himself on the sofa.*]

Rosmer: Resolution, you say? What resolution?

Rebecca: I am going to give you back what you require in order to live your life. Dear friend, you shall have your happy innocence back again!

Rosmer: What can you mean?

Rebecca: I have only to tell you something. That will be enough.

Rosmer: Well!

Rebecca: When I came down here from Finmark—along with Dr. West—it seemed to me that a great, wide new world was opening up before me. The Doctor had taught me all sorts of things

—all the fragmentary knowledge of life that I possessed in those days. [*With a struggle and in a scarcely audible voice.*] And then—

Kroll: And then?

Rosmer: But Rebecca—I know all this.

Rebecca: [*Mastering herself.*] Yes, yes—you are right. You know enough about this.

Kroll: [*Looks hard at her.*] Perhaps I had better go.

Rebecca: No, please stay where you are, my dear Rector. [*To Rosmer.*] Well, you see, this was how it was—I wanted to take my share in the life of the new era that was dawning, with all its new ideas.—Rector Kroll told me one day that Ulric Brendel had had great influence over you while you were still a boy. I thought it must surely be possible for me to carry on his work.

Rosmer: You came here with a secret design—?

Rebecca: We two, I thought, should march onward in freedom, side by side. Ever onward. Ever farther and farther to the front. But between you and perfect emancipation there rose that dismal, insurmountable barrier.

Rosmer: What barrier do you mean?

Rebecca: I mean this, Rosmer. You could grow into freedom only in the clear, fresh sunshine—and here you were pining, sickening in the gloom of such a marriage.

Rosmer: You have never before spoken to me of my marriage in that tone.

Rebecca: No, I did not dare to, for I should have frightened you.

Kroll: [*Nods to Rosmer.*] Do you hear that?

Rebecca: [*Goes on.*] But I saw quite well where your deliverance lay—your only deliverance. And then I went to work.

Rosmer: Went to work? In what way?

Kroll: Do you mean that—?

Rebecca: Yes, Rosmer— [*Rises.*] Sit still. You too, Rector Kroll. But now it must ou . It was not you, Rosmer. You are innocent. It was I that lured— that ended in luring Beata out into the paths of delusion—

Rosmer: [*Springs up.*] Rebecca!

Kroll: [*Rises from the sofa.*] The paths of delusion!

Rebecca: The paths—that led to the mill-race. Now you know it both of you.

Rosmer: [*As if stunned.*] But I don't understand— What is it she is saying? I don't understand a word—!

Kroll: Oh yes, Rosmer, I am beginning to understand.

Rosmer: But what did you do? What can you possibly have told her? There was nothing—absolutely nothing to tell!

Rebecca: She came to know that you were working yourself free from all the old prejudices.

Rosmer: Yes, but that was not the case at that time.

Rebecca: I knew that it soon would be.

Kroll: [*Nods to Rosmer.*] Aha!

Rosmer: And then? What more? I must know all now.

Rebecca: Some time after—I begged and implored her to let me go away from Rosmersholm.

Rosmer: Why did you want to go— then?

Rebecca: I did not want to go; I wanted to stay here, where I was. But I told her that it would be best for us all— that I should go away in time. I gave her to understand that if I stayed here any longer, I could not—I could not tell—what might happen.

Rosmer: Then this is what you said and did!

Rebecca: Yes, Rosmer.

Rosmer: This is what you call "going to work."

Rebecca: [*In a broken voice.*] I called it so, yes.

Rosmer: [*After a pause.*] Have you confessed all now, Rebecca?

Rebecca: Yes.

Kroll: Not all.

Rebecca: [*Looks at him in fear.*] What more should there be?

Kroll: Did you not at last give Beata to understand that it was necessary— not only that it would be wisest, but that it was necessary—both for your own sake and Rosmer's, that you should go away somewhere—as soon as possible? Well?

Rebecca: [*Low and indistinctly.*] Perhaps I did say something of the sort.

Rosmer: [*Sinks into the arm-chair by the window.*] And this tissue of lies and deceit she—my unhappy, sick wife believed in! Believed in it so firmly! So immovably! [*Looks up at Rebecca.*] And she never turned to me. Never said one word to me! Oh, Rebecca,—I can see it in your face—you dissuaded her from it!

Rebecca: She had conceived a fixed idea that she, as a childless wife, had no right to be here. And then she imagined that it was her duty to you to efface herself.

Rosmer: And you—you did nothing to disabuse her of the idea?

Rebecca: No.

Kroll: Perhaps you confirmed her in it? Answer me! Did you not?

Rebecca: I believe she may have understood me so.

Rosmer: Yes, yes—and in everything she bowed before your will. And she did efface herself! [*Springs up.*] How could you—how could you play this ghastly game!

Rebecca: It seemed to me I had to choose between your life and hers, Rosmer.

Kroll: [*Severely and impressively.*] That choice was not for you to make.

Rebecca: [*Vehemently.*] You think then that I was cool and calculating and self-possessed all the time! I was not the same woman then that I am now, as I stand here telling it all. Besides, there are two sorts of will in us I believe! I wanted Beata away, by one means or another; but I never really believed that it would come to pass. As I felt my way forward, at each step I ventured, I seemed to hear something within me cry out: No farther! Not a step farther! And yet I could not stop. I had to venture the least little bit farther. Only one hair's-breadth more. And then one more—and always one more.—And then it happened.—That is the way such things come about. [*A short silence.*]

Rosmer: [*To Rebecca.*] What do you think lies before you now? After this?

Rebecca: Things must go with me as they will. It doesn't greatly matter.

Kroll: Not a word of remorse! Is it possible you feel none?

Rebecca: [*Coldly putting aside his question.*] Excuse me, Rector Kroll—that is a matter which concerns no one but me. I must settle it with myself.

Kroll: [*To Rosmer.*] And this is the woman you are living under the same roof with—in the closest intimacy! [*Looks round at the pictures.*] Oh if those that are gone could see us now!

Rosmer: Are you going back to town?

Kroll: [*Takes up his hat.*] Yes. The sooner the better.

Rosmer: [*Does the same.*] Then I will go with you.

Kroll: Will you? Ah yes, I was sure we had not lost you for good.

Rosmer: Come then, Kroll! Come! [*Both go out through the hall without looking at Rebecca.*] [*After a moment, Rebecca goes cautiously to the window and looks out through the flowers.*]

Rebecca: [*Speaks to herself under her breath.*] Not over the foot-bridge to-day either. He goes round. Never across the mill-race. Never. [*Leaves window.*] Well, well, well! [*Goes and pulls the bell-rope; a moment after, Madam Helseth enters from the right.*]

Madam Helseth: What is it, Miss?

Rebecca: Madam Helseth, would you be so good as to have my trunk brought down from the garret?

Madam Helseth: Your trunk?

Rebecca: Yes—the brown sealskin trunk, you know.

Madam Helseth: Yes, yes. But, Lord preserve us—are you going on a journey, Miss?

Rebecca: Yes—now I am going on a journey, Madam Helseth.

Madam Helseth: And immediately!

Rebecca: As soon as I have packed up.

Madam Helseth: Well, I've never heard the like of that! But you'll come back again soon, Miss, of course?

Rebecca: I shall never come back again.

Madam Helseth: Never! Dear Lord, what will things be like at Rosmersholm when you're gone, Miss? And the poor Pastor was just beginning to be so happy and comfortable.

Rebecca: Yes, but I have taken fright to-day, Madam Helseth.

Madam Helseth: Taken fright! Dear, dear! how was that?

Rebecca: I thought I saw something like a glimpse of white horses.

Madam Helseth: White horses! In broad daylight!

Rebecca: Oh, they are abroad early and late—the white horses of Rosmersholm. [*With a change of tone.*] Well,—about the trunk, Madam Helseth.

Madam Helseth: Yes, yes. The trunk. [*Both go out to the right.*]

QUESTIONS ON ACT III

1. This act may be conveniently divided into five scenes. Find the dividing lines and try to determine the general contribution of each scene to the forward movement. Are all the exits and entrances adequately motivated? How does Ibsen try to make plausible the necessary departure of Rosmer?

2. Who is the most important character in the act? To whom does the act "belong"? Does Ibsen seem to be changing "focus," to be getting off on a side issue? Or can you justify his way of handling things here?

3. When Ibsen has Madam Helseth talk further about Beata's letter to Mortensgård, it is clear that he wished again to direct our attention to the fact. Why? Is the matter brought up naturally? Do we learn anything more about the character of Mortensgård? Are the references to Mrs. Kroll used later?

4. In talking with Madam Helseth, Rebecca is made to insist on two things: (1) the unsound mind of Beata; (2) the general rightness, for Rosmer, of the way things have gone. What does Ibsen intend to suggest here? Does what she says continue any of the suggestions made in Act II or anticipate later developments in Act II?

5. Madam Helseth's story that children never cry and adults never laugh at Rosmersholm may be taken at one level, of course, as folklore. May we assume that Ibsen also intends us to see a symbolic meaning? Is it a means of attacking the traditional life at Rosmersholm? Or, simply a way of suggesting that a man is bound by his tradition, whether or not one can think of "rational" ways of improving it (for instance, by introducing more laughter)?

6. How does Rosmer's dialogue with Rebecca develop logically from the substance of Act II? What new stage of development does Rosmer reach here? Is the development "in character"? Is it consistent of Rebecca to wish to charge Rosmer's doubts up to "ancestral doubts—ancestral fears—ancestral scruples"? How does this argument re-emphasize the basic conflict of the play?

7. Trace the steps by which the conversation between Kroll and Rebecca comes plausibly around to the subject of Rebecca's background and past. In what way do the events here develop an ironic parallel with events in Act II?

8. Is Rebecca's confession a melodramatic surprise, or is there evidence that Ibsen has been trying to make us foresee it?

9. How is this scene rendered more meaningful by the fact that we have already been given a very clear picture of Ulric Brendel?

10. Note the various references to white horses in this act. What does Ibsen intend to do by means of these references?

11. The reference to the foot-bridge picks up a matter first mentioned in the first scene in Act I. Study the two passages and see what meaning you find in them at this point.

ACT FOURTH

[The sitting-room at Rosmersholm. Late evening. A lighted lamp, with a shade over it, on the table.]

[*Rebecca West stands by the table, pack-* 5 *ing some small articles in a hand-bag. Her cloak, hat, and the white crocheted* shawl *are hanging over the back of the sofa. Madam Helseth enters from the right.*]

Madam Helseth: [*Speaks in a low voice and appears ill at ease.*] All your things have been taken down, Miss. They are in the kitchen passage.

Rebecca: Very well. You have ordered the carriage?

Madam Helseth: Yes. The coachman

wants to know what time he ought to be here.

Rebecca: About eleven o'clock, I think. The steamer starts at midnight.

Madam Helseth: [*Hesitates a little.*] But the Pastor? If he shouldn't be home by that time?

Rebecca: I shall go all the same. If I don't see him, you can tell him that I will write to him—a long letter. Tell him that.

Madam Helseth: Yes, writing—that may be all very well. But, poor Miss West—I do think you should try to speak to him once more.

Rebecca: Perhaps so. And yet—perhaps not.

Madam Helseth: Well—that I should live to see this! I never thought of such a thing.

Rebecca: What did you think then, Madam Helseth?

Madam Helseth: Well, I certainly thought Pastor Rosmer was a more dependable man than this.

Rebecca: Dependable?

Madam Helseth: Yes, that's what *I* say.

Rebecca: Why, my dear Madam Helseth, what do you mean?

Madam Helseth: I mean what's right and true, Miss. He shouldn't get out of it in this way, that he shouldn't.

Rebecca: [*Looks at her.*] Come now, Madam Helseth, tell me plainly: what do you think is the reason I am going away?

Madam Helseth: Well, Heaven forgive us, I suppose it can't be helped, Miss. Ah, well, well, well! But I certainly don't think the Pastor's behaving handsome-like. Mortensgård had some excuse; for her husband was alive, so that they two couldn't marry, however much they wanted to. But as for the Pastor—h'm!

Rebecca: [*With a faint smile.*] Could you have believed such a thing of Pastor Rosmer and me?

Madam Helseth: No, never in this world. At least, I mean—not until to-day.

Rebecca: But to-day, then—?

Madam Helseth: Well,—after all the horrible things that they tell me the papers are saying about the Pastor—

Rebecca: Aha!

Madam Helseth: For the man that can go over to Mortensgård's religion—good Lord, I can believe anything of him.

Rebecca: Oh yes, I suppose so. But what about me? What have you to say about me?

Madam Helseth: Lord preserve us, Miss—I don't see that there's much to be said against you. It's not so easy for a lone woman to be always on her guard, that's certain.—We're all of us human, Miss West.

Rebecca: That's very true, Madam Helseth. We are all of us human.—What are you listening to?

Madam Helseth: [*In a low voice.*] Oh Lord,—if I don't believe that's him coming.

Rebecca: [*Starts.*] After all then—? [*Resolutely.*] Well well; so be it. [*Johannes Rosmer enters from the hall.*]

Rosmer: [*Sees the hand-bag, etc., turns to Rebecca, and asks:*] What does this mean?

Rebecca: I am going.

Rosmer: At once?

Rebecca: Yes. [*To Madam Helseth.*] Eleven o'clock then.

Madam Helseth: Very well, Miss. [*Goes out to the right.*]

Rosmer: [*After a short pause.*] Where are you going to, Rebecca?

Rebecca: North, by the steamer.

Rosmer: North? What takes you to the North?

Rebecca: It was there I came from.

Rosmer: But you have no ties there now.

Rebecca: I have none here either.

Rosmer: What do you think of doing?

Rebecca: I don't know. I only want to have done with it all.

Rosmer: To have done with it?

Rebecca: Rosmersholm has broken me.

Rosmer: [*His attention aroused.*] Do you say that?

Rebecca: Broken me utterly and hopelessly.—I had a free and fearless will when I came here. Now I have bent my neck under a strange law.—From this day forth, I feel as if I had no courage for anything in the world.

Rosmer: Why not? What is the law that you say you have—?

Rebecca: Dear, don't let us talk of that just now.—What happened between you and the Rector?

Rosmer: We have made peace.

Rebecca: Ah yes; so that was the end.

Rosmer: He gathered all our old friends together at his house. They have made it clear to me that the work of ennobling the minds of men—is not for me.—And besides, it is hopeless in itself, Rebecca.—I shall let it alone.

Rebecca: Yes, yes—perhaps it is best so.

Rosmer: Is that what you say now? Do you think so now?

Rebecca: I have come to think so—in the last few days.

Rosmer: You are lying, Rebecca.

Rebecca: Lying—!

Rosmer: Yes, you are lying. You have never believed in me. You have never believed that I was man enough to carry the cause through to victory.

Rebecca: I believed that we two together could do it.

Rosmer: That is not true. You thought that you yourself could do something great in life; and that you could use me to further your ends. I was to be a serviceable instrument to you— that is what you thought.

Rebecca: Listen to me, Rosmer—

Rosmer: [*Seats himself listlessly on the sofa.*] Oh, what is the use? I see through it all now—I have been like a glove in your hands.

Rebecca: Listen, Rosmer. Hear what I have to say. It will be for the last time. [*Sits in a chair close to the sofa.*] I intended to write you all about it—when I was back in the North. But I daresay it is best that you should hear it at once.

Rosmer: Have you more confessions to make?

Rebecca: The greatest of all is to come.

Rosmer: The greatest?

Rebecca: What you have never suspected. What gives light and shade to all the rest.

Rosmer: [*Shakes his head.*] I don't understand you at all.

Rebecca: It is perfectly true that I once schemed to gain a footing at Rosmersholm. I thought I could not fail to turn things to good account here. In one way or the other you understand.

Rosmer: Well, you accomplished your ends.

Rebecca: I believe I could have accomplished anything, anything in the world—at that time. For I had still my fearless, free-born will. I knew no scruples—I stood in awe of no human tie.— But then began what has broken my will —and cowed me so pitiably for all my days.

Rosmer: What began? Do not speak in riddles.

Rebecca: It came over me,—this wild, uncontrollable passion—. Oh, Rosmer—!

Rosmer: Passion? You—! For what?

Rebecca: For you.

Rosmer: [*Tries to spring up.*] What is this?

Rebecca: [*Stops him.*] Sit still, dear; there is more to tell.

Rosmer: And you mean to say—that you have loved me—in that way!

Rebecca: I thought that it should be called love—then. Yes, I thought it was love. But it was not. It was what I said. It was a wild, uncontrollable passion.

Rosmer: [*With difficulty.*] Rebecca, is it really you—you yourself—that you are speaking of?

Rebecca: Yes, would you believe it, Rosmer?

Rosmer: Then it was because of this— under the influence of this—that you— that you "went to work," as you call it?

Rebecca: It came upon me like a storm on the sea. It was like one of the storms we sometimes have in the North in the winter time. It seizes you—and whirls you along with it—wherever it will. There is no resisting it.

Rosmer: And so it swept the unhappy Beata into the mill-race.

Rebecca: Yes; for it was a life-and-death struggle between Beata and me at that time.

Rosmer: Assuredly you were the strongest at Rosmersholm. Stronger than Beata and I together.

Rebecca: I judged you rightly in so far that I was sure I could never reach you until you were a free man, both in circumstances—and in spirit.

Rosmer: But I don't understand you, Rebecca. You—yourself—your whole conduct is an insoluble riddle to me. I am free now—both in spirit and in circumstances. You have reached the very goal you aimed at from the first. And yet—

Rebecca: I have never stood farther from my goal than now.

Rosmer: And yet I say—when I asked you yesterday—begged you to be my wife—you cried out, as if in fear, that it could never be.

Rebecca: I cried out in despair, Rosmer.

Rosmer: Why?

Rebecca: Because Rosmersholm has sapped my strength. My old fearless will has had its wings clipped here. It is crippled! The time is past when I had courage for anything in the world. I have lost the power of action, Rosmer.

Rosmer: Tell me how this has come about.

Rebecca: It has come about through my life with you.

Rosmer: But how? How?

Rebecca: When I was left alone with you here,—and when you had become yourself again—

Rosmer: Yes, yes?

Rebecca: —for you were never quite yourself so long as Beata lived—

Rosmer: I am afraid you are right there.

Rebecca: But when I found myself sharing your life here,—in quiet—in solitude,—when you showed me all your thoughts without reserve—every tender and delicate feeling, just as it came to you—then the great change came over me. Little by little, you understand. Almost imperceptibly—but at last with such overwhelming force that it reached to the depths of my soul.

Rosmer: Oh, is this true, Rebecca?

Rebecca: All the rest—the horrible sense-intoxicated desire—passed far, far away from me. All the whirling passions settled down into quiet and silence. Rest descended on my soul—a stillness as on one of our northern bird-cliffs under the midnight sun.

Rosmer: Tell me more of this. Tell me all you can.

Rebecca: There is not much more, dear. Only this—it was love that was born in me. The great self-denying love, that is content with life, as we two have lived it together.

Rosmer: Oh, if I had only had the faintest suspicion of all this!

Rebecca: It is best as it is. Yesterday —when you asked me if I would be your wife—I cried out with joy—

Rosmer: Yes, did you not, Rebecca! I thought that was the meaning of your cry.

Rebecca: For a moment, yes. I had forgotten myself. It was my old buoyant will that was struggling to be free. But it has no energy left now—no power of endurance.

Rosmer: How do you account for what has happened to you?

Rebecca: It is the Rosmer view of life —or your view of life, at any rate—that has infected my will.

Rosmer: Infected?

Rebecca: And made it sick. Enslaved it to laws that had no power over me before. You—life with you—has ennobled my mind—

Rosmer: Oh that I could believe it!

Rebecca: You may safely believe it! The Rosmer view of life ennobles. But — [*Shaking her head.*] But—but—
Rosmer: But—? Well?
Rebecca: —but it kills happiness.
Rosmer: Do you think so, Rebecca?
Rebecca: My happiness, at any rate.
Rosmer: Yes, but are you so certain of that? If I were to ask you again now—? If I were to beg and entreat you—?
Rebecca: Dear,—never speak of this again! It is impossible—! For you must know, Rosmer, I have a—a past behind me.
Rosmer: More than what you have told me?
Rebecca: Yes. Something different and something more.
Rosmer: [*With a faint smile.*] Is it not strange, Rebecca? Some such idea has crossed my mind now and then.
Rebecca: It has? And yet—? Even so—?
Rosmer: I never believed it. I only played with it—in my thoughts, you understand.
Rebecca: If you wish it, I will tell you all, at once.
Rosmer: [*Turning it off.*] No, no! I will not hear a word. Whatever it may be—I can forget it.
Rebecca: But I cannot.
Rosmer: Oh Rebecca—!
Rebecca: Yes, Rosmer—this is the terrible part of it: that now, when all life's happiness is within my grasp—my heart is changed, and my own past cuts me off from it.
Rosmer: Your past is dead, Rebecca. It has no hold on you any more—it is no part of you—as you are now.
Rebecca: Oh, you know that these are only phrases, dear. And innocence? Where am I to get that from?
Rosmer: [*Sadly.*] Ah,—innocence.
Rebecca: Yes, innocence. That is the source of peace and happiness. That was the vital truth you were to implant in the coming generation of happy noble-men—

Rosmer: Oh, don't remind me of that. It was only an abortive dream, Rebecca —an immature idea, that I myself no longer believe in.—Ah no, we cannot be ennobled from without, Rebecca.
Rebecca: [*Softly.*] Not even by tranquil love, Rosmer?
Rosmer: [*Thoughtfully.*] Yes—that would be the great thing—the most glorious in life, almost—if it were so. [*Moves uneasily.*] But how can I be certain of that? How convince myself?
Rebecca: Do you not believe me, Rosmer?
Rosmer: Oh Rebecca—how can I believe in you, fully? You who have all this while been cloaking, concealing such a multitude of things!—Now you come forward with something new. If you have a secret purpose in all this, tell me plainly what it is. Is there anything you want to gain by it? You know that I will gladly do everything I can for you.
Rebecca: [*Wringing her hands.*] Oh this killing doubt—! Rosmer—Rosmer—!
Rosmer: Yes, is it not terrible, Rebecca? But I cannot help it. I shall never be able to shake off the doubt. I can never be absolutely sure that you are mine in pure and perfect love.
Rebecca: Is there nothing in the depths of your own heart that bears witness to the transformation in me? And tells you that it is due to you—and you alone?
Rosmer: Oh Rebecca—I no longer believe in my power of transforming any one. My faith in myself is utterly dead. I believe neither in myself nor in you.
Rebecca: [*Looks darkly at him.*] Then how will you be able to live your life?
Rosmer: That I don't know. I cannot imagine how. I don't think I can live it. —And I know of nothing in the world that is worth living for.
Rebecca: Oh, life—life will renew itself. Let us hold fast to it, Rosmer.— We shall leave it soon enough.
Rosmer: [*Springs up restlessly.*] Then give me my faith again! My faith in you,

Rebecca! My faith in your love! Proof! I must have proof!

Rebecca: Proof? How can I give you proof—?

Rosmer: You must! [*Walks across the room.*] I cannot bear this desolation—this horrible emptiness—this—this— [*A loud knock at the hall door.*]

Rebecca: [*Starts up from her chair.*] Ah—did you hear that? [*The door opens. Ulric Brendel enters. He has a white shirt on, a black coat and a good pair of boots, with his trousers tucked into them. Otherwise he is dressed as in the first act. He looks excited.*]

Rosmer: Ah, is it you, Mr. Brendel?

Brendel: Johannes, my boy—hail—and farewell!

Rosmer: Where are you going so late?

Brendel: Downhill.

Rosmer: How—?

Brendel: I am going homewards, my beloved pupil. I am home-sick for the mighty Nothingness.

Rosmer: Something has happened to you, Mr. Brendel! What is it?

Brendel: So you observe the transformation? Yes—well you may. When I last set foot in these halls—I stood before you as a man of substance, and slapped my breast-pocket.

Rosmer: Indeed! I don't quite understand—

Brendel: But as you see me this night, I am a deposed monarch on the ash-heap that was my palace.

Rosmer: If there is anything *I* can do for you—

Brendel: You have preserved your child-like heart, Johannes. Can you grant me a loan?

Rosmer: Yes, yes, most willingly!

Brendel: Can you spare me an ideal or two?

Rosmer: What do you say?

Brendel: One or two cast-off ideals. It would be an act of charity. For I'm cleaned out, my boy. Ruined, beggared.

Rebecca: Have you not delivered your lecture?

Brendel: No, seductive lady. What do you think? Just as I am standing ready to pour forth the horn of plenty, I make the painful discovery that I am bankrupt.

Rebecca: But all your unwritten works—?

Brendel: For five-and-twenty years I have sat like a miser on his double-locked treasure-chest. And then yesterday—when I open it and want to display the treasure—there's none there! The teeth of time had ground it into dust. There was nix and nothing in the whole concern.

Rosmer: But are you so sure of that?

Brendel: There's no room for doubt, my dear fellow. The President has convinced me of it.

Rosmer: The President?

Brendel: Well well—His Excellency then. *Ganz nach Belieben.*

Rosmer: What do you mean?

Brendel: Peter Mortensgård, of course.

Rosmer: What?

Brendel: [*Mysteriously.*] Hush, hush, hush! Peter Mortensgård is the lord and leader of the future. Never have I stood in a more august presence. Peter Mortensgård has the secret of omnipotence. He can do whatever he will.

Rosmer: Oh, don't believe that.

Brendel: Yes, my boy! For Peter Mortensgård never wills more than he can do. Peter Mortensgård is capable of living his life without ideals. And that, do you see—that is just the mighty secret of action and of victory. It is the sum of the whole world's wisdom. *Basta!*

Rosmer: [*In a low voice.*] Now I understand—why you leave here poorer than you came.

Brendel: *Bien!* Then take a *Beispiel* by your ancient teacher. Rub out all that he once imprinted on your mind. Build not thy house on shifting sand. And look ahead—and feel your way—before you build on this exquisite creature, who here lends sweetness to your life.

Rebecca: Is it me you mean?

Brendel: Yes, my fascinating mermaid.

Rebecca: Why am I not to be built on?

Brendel: [*Comes a step nearer.*] I gather that my former pupil has a great cause to carry forward to victory.

Rebecca: What then—?

Brendel: Victory is assured. But—mark me well—on one indispensable condition.

Rebecca: Which is—?

Brendel: [*Taking her gently by the* 10 *wrist.*] That the woman who loves him shall gladly go out into the kitchen and hack off her tender, rosy-white little finger—here—just here at the middle joint. Item, that the aforesaid loving 15 woman—again gladly—shall slice off her incomparably-moulded left ear. [*Lets her go, and turns to Rosmer.*] Farewell, my conquering Johannes.

Rosmer: Are you going now? In the 20 dark night?

Brendel: The dark night is best. Peace be with you. [*He goes. There is a short silence in the room.*]

Rebecca: [*Breathes heavily.*] Oh, how 25 close and sultry it is here! [*Goes to the window, opens it, and remains standing by it.*]

Rosmer. [*Sits down in the arm-chair by the stove.*] There is nothing else for it 30 after all, Rebecca. I see it. You must go away.

Rebecca: Yes, I see no choice.

Rosmer: Let us make the most of our last hour. Come here and sit by me. 35

Rebecca: [*Goes and sits on the sofa.*] What do you want to say to me, Rosmer?

Rosmer: First, I want to tell you that you need not feel any anxiety about 40 your future.

Rebecca: [*Smiles.*] H'm, my future.

Rosmer: I have long ago arranged for everything. Whatever may happen, you are provided for. 45

Rebecca: That too, my dear one?

Rosmer: You might surely have known that.

Rebecca: It is many a long day since I have given a thought to such things. 50

Rosmer: Yes, yes—you thought things would always remain as they were between us.

Rebecca: Yes, I thought so.

Rosmer: So did I. But if I were to go—

Rebecca: Oh, Rosmer—you will live longer than I.

Rosmer: Surely my worthless life lies in my own hands.

Rebecca: What is this? You are never thinking of—!

Rosmer: Do you think it would be so strange? After this pitiful, lamentable defeat! I, who was to have borne a great cause on to victory—have I not fled from the battle before it was well begun?

Rebecca: Take up the fight again, Rosmer! Only try—and you shall see, you will conquer. You will ennoble hundreds—thousands of minds. Only try!

Rosmer: Oh Rebecca—I, who no longer believe in my own mission!

Rebecca: But your mission has stood the test already. You have ennobled one human being at least—me you have ennobled for the rest of my days.

Rosmer: Oh—if I dared believe you.

Rebecca: [*Pressing her hands together.*] Oh Rosmer,—do you know of nothing—nothing that could make you believe it?

Rosmer: [*Starts as if in fear.*] Don't speak of that! Keep away from that, Rebecca! Not a word more.

Rebecca: Yes, this is precisely what we must speak about. Do you know of anything that would kill the doubt? For *I* know of nothing in the world.

Rosmer: It is well for you that you do not know.—It is well for both of us.

Rebecca: No, no.—I will not be put off in this way! If you know of anything that would absolve me in your eyes, I claim as my right to be told of it.

Rosmer: [*As if impelled against his will to speak.*] Then let us see. You say that a great love is in you; that through me your mind has been ennobled. Is it so? Is your reckoning just, Rebecca? Shall we try to prove the sum? Say?

Rebecca: I am ready.

Rosmer: At any time?

Rebecca: Whenever you please. The sooner the better.

Rosmer: Then let me see, Rebecca,—if you for my sake—this very evening—[*Breaks off.*] Oh, no, no, no!

Rebecca: Yes, Rosmer! Yes! Tell me, and you shall see.

Rosmer: Have you the courage—have you the will—gladly, as Ulric Brendel said—for my sake, to-night—gladly—to go the same way that Beata went?

Rebecca: [*Rises slowly from the sofa; almost voiceless.*] Rosmer—!

Rosmer: Yes, Rebecca—that is the question that will for ever haunt me—when you are gone. Every hour in the day it will return upon me. Oh, I seem to see you before my very eyes. You are standing out on the foot-bridge—right in the middle. Now you are bending forward over the railing—drawn dizzily downwards, downwards towards the rushing water! No—you recoil. You have not the heart to do what she dared.

Rebecca: But if I had the heart to do it? And the will to do it gladly? What then?

Rosmer: I should have to believe you then. I should recover my faith in my mission. Faith in my power to ennoble human souls. Faith in the human soul's power to attain nobility.

Rebecca: [*Takes up her shawl slowly, and puts it over her head; says with composure.*] You shall have your faith again.

Rosmer: Have you the will and the courage—for this, Rebecca?

Rebecca: That you shall see to-morrow—or afterwards—when they find my body.

Rosmer: [*Puts his hand to his forehead.*] There is a horrible fascination in this—!

Rebecca: For I don't want to remain down there. Not longer than necessary. You must see that they find me.

Rosmer: [*Springs up.*] But all this—is nothing but madness. Go—or stay! I will take your bare word this time too.

Rebecca: Phrases, Rosmer! Let us have no more cowardly subterfuges, dear! How can you believe me on my bare word after this day?

Rosmer: I shrink from seeing your defeat, Rebecca!

Rebecca: It will be no defeat.

Rosmer: Yes, it will. You will never bring yourself to go Beata's way.

Rebecca: Do you think not?

Rosmer: Never. You are not like Beata. You are not under the dominion of a distorted view of life.

Rebecca: But I am under the dominion of the Rosmersholm view of life—now. What I have sinned—it is fit that I should expiate.

Rosmer: [*Looks at her fixedly.*] Is that your point of view?

Rebecca: Yes.

Rosmer: [*With resolution.*] Well then, I stand firm in our emancipated view of life, Rebecca. There is no judge over us; and therefore we must do justice upon ourselves.

Rebecca: [*Misunderstanding him.*] Yes, that is true—that too. My going away will save what is best in you.

Rosmer: Oh, there is nothing left to save in me.

Rebecca: Yes, there is. But I—after to-day, I should only be a sea-troll dragging down the ship that is to carry you forward. I must go overboard. Why should I remain here in the world, trailing after me my own crippled life? Why brood and brood over the happiness that my past has forfeited for ever? I must give up the game, Rosmer.

Rosmer: If you go—I go with you.

Rebecca: [*Smiles almost imperceptibly, looks at him, and says more softly.*] Yes, come with me—and see—.

Rosmer: I go with you, I say.

Rebecca: To the foot-bridge, yes. You know you never dare go out upon it.

Rosmer: Have you noticed that?

Rebecca: [*Sadly and brokenly.*] Yes.— It was that that made my love hopeless.

Rosmer: Rebecca,—now I lay my hand on your head— [*does so*]—and I wed you as my true wife.

Rebecca: [*Takes both his hands, and bows her head towards his breast.*] Thanks, Rosmer. [*Lets him go.*] And now I will go—gladly.

Rosmer: Man and wife should go together.

Rebecca: Only to the bridge, Rosmer.

Rosmer: Out on to it, too. As far as you go—so far shall I go with you. For now I dare.

Rebecca: Are you absolutely certain—that this way is the best for you?

Rosmer: I am certain that it is the only way.

Rebecca: If you were deceiving yourself? If it were only a delusion? One of those white horses of Rosmersholm?

Rosmer: It may be so. For we can never escape from them—we of this house.

Rebecca: Then stay, Rosmer!

Rosmer: The husband shall go with his wife, as the wife with her husband.

Rebecca: Yes, but first tell me this: Is it you who follow me? Or is it I who follow you?

Rosmer: We shall never think that question out.

Rebecca: But I should like to know.

Rosmer: We go with each other, Rebecca—I with you, and you with me.

Rebecca: I almost think that is the truth.

Rosmer: For now we two are one.

Rebecca: Yes. We are one. Come! We go gladly. [*They go out hand in hand through the hall, and are seen to turn to the left. The door remains open. The room stands empty for a little while. Then the door to the right is opened by Madam Helseth.*]

Madam Helseth: Miss West—the carriage is— [*Looks round.*] Not here? Out together at this time of night? Well—I must say—! H'm! [*Goes out into the hall, looks round, and comes in again.*] Not on the garden seat. Ah, well well. [*Goes to the window and looks out.*] Oh, good God! that white thing there—! My soul! They're both of them out on the bridge! God forgive the sinful creatures—if they're not in each other's arms! [*Shrieks aloud.*] Oh—down—both of them! Out into the millrace! Help! Help! [*Her knees tremble; she holds on to the chair-back, shaking all over; she can scarcely get the words out.*] No. No help here.—The dead wife has taken them.

NOTES ON *ROSMERSHOLM*

I. STRUCTURE AND THEME IN ACT III

As we have seen, in Acts I and II Ibsen is primarily concerned with Rosmer's inner conflict. The first part of Act III stresses further the ironic outcome of the conflict: Rosmer is more sure than ever that he has lost his innocence and therefore cannot go on as emancipator. In other words, Rosmer has not really broken with his traditions—they include a sense of guilt—and the grip of the irrational is still strong upon him.

At this point Ibsen suddenly shifts his attention to Rebecca and makes her the central figure—a complex figure who demands in her own right all of our attention. As we learn how completely she has managed things, we feel almost as if Rosmer were being shunted into a secondary role. Ibsen runs a great risk here: in Act III he actually seems to be starting off another play. It is doubtful, indeed, whether he does successfully handle this problem of structure—a matter which we shall discuss further in Section 6, on Tragedy.

In the meantime, however, we see that the Kroll-Rebecca dialogue does have a certain structural role: it is *parallel with* Act II. There, Rosmer learned about his past; here, Rebecca is reminded of hers. He could not escape his past; nor can the woman who encouraged him to try to do so escape hers. He is bound by the irrational, and so is she: she is worried about her age ("We are made so"), and she retains enough conventional scruples not to wish to be known as an illegitimate child. Thus the symmetry of the two acts is a means of stressing a theme. Ibsen pushes this symmetry still further when he has Kroll make the same shift from principles to expediency that Kroll has revealed in advising Rosmer: the relationship of Rosmer and Rebecca, he says, should be "legalised." Then there is the final impressive parallel: Rosmer renounces his career as emancipator, Rebecca renounces her hold on Rosmer. But whereas Rosmer retreats, Rebecca moves forward: her act, since she wishes to save Rosmer for liberalism, requires high courage and devotion.

2. IRONY IN ACT III

Irony again dominates—irony employed not to produce a mere sense of shock, but as a means of exhibiting the latent realities of a situation which is more complex than it appears on the surface:

1. Rebecca admits to Kroll the hold of the past upon Rosmer (the student should find the lines)—and thus, really, the failure of her whole mission.

2. Since Rebecca is stronger than Rosmer, the recoil of her past upon her is even more bitterly ironic than the corresponding experience of Rosmer's.

3. Kroll's insistence that Rosmer and Rebecca marry again sets up a richly ironic situation: Kroll wants the marriage for the sake of expediency; Rosmer wants it as an answer to his own need; and Rebecca wants the marriage because of her love for Rosmer, but she cannot go on with it because of her own conviction that she loved Rosmer with a guilty love in the past. Her own past thus comes to bear upon her in another way.

4. Seeing failure in every direction, she makes a final heroic gesture· she tries to give back to Rosmer a saving sense of innocence by admitting her own responsibility for Beata's death. But instead of freeing Rosmer she only throws him back into Kroll's arms. By this time we can see an ironic similarity between her renunciation and that made by Beata, which also failed to accomplish its purpose.

Through irony, then, we become aware that the characters have been acting upon false—or at least inadequate—premises. One line of Rebecca's points to the human truth that underlies the failures of Rosmer and Rebecca: "Besides, there are two sorts of will in us I believe" (p. 297b, 44–45).

3. THE STRUCTURE AND IRONY OF ACT IV

The function of Act IV is to push on to a logical and final settlement the complex relationship between Rosmer and Rebecca. Here Ibsen runs the risk of presenting us with merely an undramatic post-mortem (a risk which Wilde does not wholly escape in his Act IV). But notice how Ibsen (1) makes the act an integral part of the play and (2) gives the act a definite forward movement.

1. Rebecca's confession is really necessary to clarify a matter still obscure—her motives. We have seen her both as an idealist associate of Rosmer and as a not overly scrupulous wielder of power. The conflict between these aspects of her character is resolved by her passion for Rosmer, a passion which helps explain both the selfish and unselfish sides of her. Do we feel at this point that Ibsen has, like a mystery-writer, been unnecessarily withholding a piece of vital information? Probably not: Rebecca would not confess the truth while things seemed to be going well. Her confession is a sign of failure—but at the same time an evidence of the change of character she has undergone.

Again the effect is ironical. Rebecca has not conquered, but is conquered by, the "Rosmer view of life"; Rosmer, if he has influenced no one else, has ennobled her, brought her to *tranquil love;* so there grows upon her the very sense of guilt that had plagued him. Finally, Rosmer assumes her old role, assures her that her "past is dead."

2. But Ibsen still has to deal with Rosmer's conflict. Even while assuring Rebecca that her past is dead, Rosmer shifts back to his problem: how can he regain his sense of innocence, what evidence is there of disinterestedness in Rebecca's love? (The student will find it useful to trace the steps by which this transition to Rosmer's problem is made naturally.) Note how strongly Ibsen conveys to us Rosmer's distrust of Rebecca: we have seen her character unfold just as Rosmer has, exposing one unexpected layer after another. We share his uncertainty of her. In the resolution of that uncertainty lies the forward movement of the play.

The Significance of Brendel. Just as before, Brendel is used to point the way or to suggest a line of action. After seeing him in Act I, Rosmer went on uncompromisingly to make his break with Kroll. In Act IV, Brendel even speaks symbolically (Rebecca must cut off her finger and ear): he points to the need of complete, uncompromising renunciation. The only proof of love is ultimate selflessness.

After an interval of relatively flat conversation, which Ibsen perhaps intended to seem flat in order to suggest temporary inability or unwillingness to act upon Brendel's cue, Rosmer finally suggests that Rebecca's dying, as Beata had died, would finally give substance to her love for him. This is a very daring piece of craftsmanship by Ibsen, for it asks us to accept something which runs counter to all our usual ways of looking at things. We are not used to such absolute action; we do not easily think of the voluntary yielding of life except in great and heroic causes. Two matters are noteworthy, however. Ibsen has in a way prepared us for this by the fact that the whole play is concerned with the devoting of a life to a cause—Rosmer's to emancipation, Rebecca's to Rosmer. Second, we are so aware of Rebecca's interference in Rosmer's life that we feel she owes him heavy reparation. Further, Ibsen aids our acceptance of the situation by presenting Rebecca as accepting it: this is her formal act of purification, her search for salvation.

Rosmer's Proposal of the Sacrifice. Perhaps the greatest difficulty in the way of the reader's acceptance lies in the fact that Rosmer, the potential beneficiary, makes the request. If Rebecca made the suggestion first, or if a third person made it, or if Rosmer were a heroic or Christ-like figure who demanded a sacrifice to something greater than himself, there would be little difficulty. But as it is, the reader may feel that Rosmer seems intolerably self-centered.

Ibsen has, however, obviously attempted to manage the scene so as not to make Rosmer seem incredibly selfish. In the first place, Rosmer has certainly not planned to make any such proposal to Rebecca. Earlier in the scene he says that he has provided for her future; evidently he expects her to survive him. Second, even before making his proposal he is thinking of his own death, as his phrase "whatever may happen" and his statement, "My worthless life lies in my own hands," indicate plainly. Rebecca's exclamation, "What is this? You are never thinking—" shows that she thinks he is hinting at suicide.

Third, the proposal as Rosmer first makes it is *purely hypothetical*. He has learned such a distrust of himself and of her that only the most desperate action can bring him around. Moreover, and this is highly important, Rosmer is really convinced that Rebecca could not *logically* do such a thing; it is the one thing that the "emancipated," perfectly rational view of life would rule out. As he states the case to her, then, he is not so much making a serious suggestion as thinking aloud, commenting on his own desperation: it is impossible for me to regain confidence; I am at an impasse; your view of life makes impossible the one thing—an act like Beata's—that could restore my confidence in you.

He is hesitant even to say so much. His words, "There is a horrible fascination in this—" indicate his recognition that the whole proposal is fantastic and unthinkable. When he says, "Never. You are not Beata. You are not under the dominion of a distorted view of life," he is not taunting her with lack of character; he simply sees her as *belonging to a different school of thought from Beata.*

The student will judge for himself whether this interpretation is sound, or he may decide that it is perhaps what Ibsen ought to have done but did not really succeed in conveying to the reader. But another difficulty comes to the fore in what follows the last speech quoted. Even assuming that the interpretation suggested above is correct, the reader may feel that Rosmer's transition from fanciful hypothesis to serious proposal and acceptance of the sacrifice is entirely too easy.

How has Ibsen meant to present that transition? Rosmer says—Ibsen adds the stage direction "*(With resolution.)*"—"Well, then, I stand firm in our emancipated view of life, Rebecca. There is no judge over us; and therefore we must do justice on ourselves." Ibsen prefaces Rebecca's answer with the significant stage direction— "(*Misunderstanding him*)." How does she misunderstand him? By taking him to mean that he is going to persist in his emancipation after all, for she goes on to say, "My going away will save what is best in you." But Rosmer, as the rest of the scene reveals, means something quite different. He evidently means: even judged by the new morality of emancipation we—that is, the individual—must do what Beata did. What I am proposing is not a reversion to my old orthodoxy. I stand firm in the emancipated view—and it is from this viewpoint that I am executing judgment on myself.

But, again, this view of the action may claim too much for what is in the text. Ibsen certainly, most readers will agree, has put a heavy burden of interpretation upon the actor and actress who are to play this scene.

One thing is clear, however: when Rosmer does execute judgment on himself, and Rebecca is no longer a solitary victim, some of the early difficulties of the scene disappear. This self-judgment is part of a powerfully ironic conclusion. Rebecca dies by the Rosmersholm tradition— expiation of sin; Rosmer by the "emancipated view." This, ironically, is the *only real application of his modernity*. Then, there is the symbolic marriage just before death: indeed, death is ironically their marriage.

4. THE RELATION OF CHARACTERIZATION TO MEANING

Of the two preceding plays that resembled or aspired to be tragedy, one, *Everyman*, may be said to have a hero, and the other, *The London Merchant*, a "villain" (*The School for Scandal*, a comedy, also has a villain). *Rosmersholm* has neither; in all his major characters Ibsen consistently presents a complex mixture of "good" and "bad." His unwillingness to mould this mixture toward any conventional expectations gives the play maturity, and likewise some difficulty. The complexity of character makes greater demands of us than the relatively simple inner contradictions in Everyman, Barnwell, and Charles Surface. Rebecca's union of noble ends and doubtful means we have already discussed. In Rosmer we see fine idealism mixed with weakness and naïveté. Brendel is an uncompromising liberal of fine insight, whose drunkenness is the equivalent of Rosmer's weakness. Mortensgård stands for a noble cause, perhaps, but his means are less noble than expedient. Kroll, who combines great strength with remarkable understanding of character, tends to be hard, overbearing, and not overscrupulous in his methods of combat.

The inner complexity of the characters points toward complexity of meaning: Ibsen is not taking sides but is endeavoring to present in a lifelike way the multiplicity of forces and demands to which all individuals are subject. Rosmer and Rebecca view life a little too simply in wanting to be "free," to be reasonable, to ennoble men. Absolute freedom is not possible, nor absolute reason; and there are other roads to nobility besides emancipation. It is not that freedom is bad, but that Rosmer and Rebecca misinterpret freedom; their real problem is not to escape from the past but to use the past constructively in the present. They try to do too much, and so they fail. On the other hand Ibsen does not suggest that reliance on the past—that is, the traditional way of life, as symbolized by Rosmersholm—will of itself lead to perfection and happiness; we hear much of the gloom and oppression at Rosmersholm, and Kroll, though he gains strength and certainty from following a marked-out path, scarcely exhibits an invitingly serene wisdom. But there are no easy choices; the human being always runs into conflicting demands. Here it is well to recall Ibsen's insistence that his business was asking questions, not answering them.

5. LANGUAGE

This complexity of character and meaning is not easily grasped; it may be said, perhaps, that when it is all finished, we still feel a certain unsatisfactoriness about Ibsen's performance. One of the reasons for this is discussed in the following section on Tragedy. But at this point we may suggest that what Ibsen has to say would probably have come across more successfully in poetic form. Poetic language, with its suggestiveness and allusiveness, its taking full advantage of the richness of meanings, is almost essential to the expression of so complex a conception as that of *Rosmersholm*. Here we have several levels of activity in several characters—that which appears on the surface and those which, for whatever reason, are concealed. Poetic language could represent all the levels simultaneously; prose, which is relatively flat and one-dimensional, has to do them one at a time—as in the case of Rebecca, in whom we sense ambiguities almost to the end. We are left to effect our own synthesis, which can never be as satisfactory as the author's own. Ibsen, indeed, is working toward the method of poetry when he uses such a symbol as the foot-bridge and when he has Brendel say, "slice off her incomparably moulded left ear"; he might well have gone further. When we come to the plays of Marlowe and Shakespeare, for instance, we can see how fully the poetic language supports and intensifies the dramatic meaning.

6. *ROSMERSHOLM* AS TRAGEDY

Is the play a tragedy? Before we try to answer this question, it may be well to make sure that we agree *whose* play it is. Whose story is it? One is inclined to say that it is Rosmer's. In him the forces of orthodoxy and radicalism, rationality and irrationality, are headed up. It is over him that the others contend. Yet if it is his story, one must conclude that the play is hardly a tragedy. Rosmer is too weak to be a tragic hero. The difficulty is not that he lacks violence or has little picturesqueness. These qualities are not necessary in a tragic hero. The tragic protagonist can be a quiet man; in appearance, even an unprepossessing man. But strength *is* necessary. The tragic protagonist must put up a struggle, but Rosmer struggles only feebly. He is foredoomed to give in; the collapse of his program, fore-shadowed early in the play, is complete by the end of Act III. The decisive actions are taken without his knowledge, and as soon as he hears what they are, he gives up. As he says to Rebecca in Act IV, "Assuredly you were the strongest at Rosmersholm. Stronger than Beata and I together." Rosmer is right. It is Rebecca who decided to free Rosmer, who pushed Beata to suicide, who encouraged Rosmer to declare his emancipation. One can make a case for the play's being her tragedy. Rosmer's case is pathetic rather than tragic: he is the man whose fate is determined by forces of which his will is not one. He tends to be—in Aristotle's terms—the good man who suffers and who cannot therefore be the tragic protagonist. Rebecca, on the other hand, is not extraordinarily good or bad. She represents a mixture, and she has humanity, pluck, and daring. Yet there are difficulties in the way of considering her the tragic protagonist.

First, the author has hardly focused the play on her. In Acts I and II she plays a decidedly secondary role; she dominates most of Act III but only part of IV. That the play might be hers comes to the reader almost as an afterthought. The author has not had us live with her through the process of thought and emotion by which she reaches the decision to inter-fere with the lives of the Rosmers, or to visualize dramatically the effect upon her when she realizes that, because Beata has drowned herself, she has been successful. Her confession scene is dramatic enough, but then we see the earlier act as a *fait accompli*. She is now a different woman.

Second, if we argue that the great dramatic decision of the play is not Rebecca's decision to destroy Beata but rather Rebecca's deciding to free Rosmer finally from Beata by showing him that she can die for his good as well as Beata, and if we argue that we do participate imaginatively in the decisive act, which is indeed enacted before our eyes, it would have to be answered that, although the act is dramatic, Rebecca has now become Aristotle's "good man." Her act is entirely sacrificial; the struggle is over.

This is not to say that the end is ineffective or devoid of tragic elements. The fact that the struggle is internal, and that the conflict is between basic elements in human experience, certainly brings the play close to tragedy. It is obviously much better than *Barnwell;* yet if we compare it with *Lear* or *Oedipus* we shall have to say that it falls short of the tragic quality of these plays. Treated from the beginning as Rebecca's tragedy, it might have reached a high level. Certainly, it has the essential ingredients: Rebecca has a mixture of motives (though none of them is crass), she embarks on a great project, she fails, and she is ironically pulled down by the very forces from which she would save Rosmer. She can transcend them and win him from them only by complying with them and suffering from the same death into which she had forced Beata.

Why has Ibsen not worked it out in this way? In other words, why has he spent so much time on Rosmer? At this we can only conjecture. But it is worth noting that Rosmer is more closely related to the village situation than Rebecca, and the village situation suggests the "problem play" which, though he protest against it, Ibsen tends to write. Perhaps it is not too fantastic to suggest that he began the play at the problem level where he would be likely to deal with purely transitory problems—and then gradually, but a little bit too late, found himself shifting over to the tragic implication of his materials.

7. *ROSMERSHOLM* AS PROBLEM PLAY

The situation which we have suggested in the preceding paragraph is one which we do often find in modern drama: th preoccupation of the dramatist with a problem—such as prohibition, or race relations, or politics—often ties him to a temporary situation, the passing of which exhausts the meaning of the play.

All tragedy involves problems, of course. But the playwright who is primarily concerned with the solution of the problem, or who may even hope to assist in a certain kind of solution, is likely to miss the universal issues involved in the problem—the issues which he must find if the play is to be of perennial value. The danger is particularly great if, in his desire to move the public to *do something* about a problem (lynching, political corruption, cruelty of employers), the playwright presents his protagonist as a victim of circumstances beyond his control. This is to strike at the roots of tragedy by cutting the protagonist off from any meaningful struggle. He is not responsible for his downfall; he is not involved in guilt, as the tragic protagonist to a degree always is. Our emotions are rather simple: righteous anger against the circumstances, the environment, the state of affairs, whatever is responsible for the protagonist's sufferings. Such a concentration of emotions is logical if all the author wants to do is arouse resentment at certain conditions. But this method leads away from tragedy.

Since "problem plays" and tragedies are both concerned with problems, the crucial issue is what the author does with the character in treating the problem. If he regards the problem as providing merely a setting for the investigation of the complexities of character—and even the most topical issue can be so treated—he is on the road to tragedy. If he takes the goodness and badness of his characters for granted, he is going to secure much less profound effects. The choice is up to the author: What treatment will choose to make? Shakespeare, for instance might easily have made *Hamlet* into a rather trashy problem play if he had been dealing merely with the problem of preventing the usurpation of thrones.

Rosmersholm, we have suggested, falls short of tragedy. But we owe it to Ibsen to make clear that he has gone a long way beyond the mere problem—whether the conservatives or liberals shall determine the life of the community—and, by his concern with problems of character, has approached tragedy. He is concerned with moral rather than social problems: Rebecca, at least, has a certain freedom of will; both leading characters are responsible. Ibsen's plays do not always work out in this way. Shaw's, likewise, tend to become mere problem plays. And many modern plays, including

O'Neill's serious plays, are too much like mere clinical studies in environment or psychology.

We have no right, of course, to demand that every play be a tragedy—either in intention or in fact. We have to be grateful for the sensitive and intelligent play wherever we are so fortunate as to find it. We should be the poorer for the loss of such plays. We need not cease to enjoy them, though we acquire a finer discrimination of the nature of tragedy. Yet the fact that our age rarely produces tragedy, in spite of its evident dramatic talent, may tell us something about the nature of our age and of ourselves.

8. THE UNITIES

The action of the play all occurs on the last three days of the lives of Rosmer and Rebecca; all of it occurs at Rosmersholm—three acts in one room. That this is not an artificial limitation of time and place simply for the sake of adhering to the "unities" is apparent from our not feeling that the action is managed in a forced or awkward way. Ibsen has no difficulty in getting his characters where he wants them at a given time, or in making them seem to develop naturally within the time used.

The compactness of his play, then, is clearly the result, not of an artificial and inflexible theory of time and place, but of the way in which Ibsen conceives of his problem. This play—as well as others by Ibsen—suggests that he conceives of drama as essentially concerned only with the critical high point of an action, even though it may have roots and ramifications which may go far back in time. These earlier developments, of course, may have to be recalled in some detail and by one device or another introduced into the play (note with what skill past events are introduced in *Rosmersholm;* the play is never held up to permit exposition), but the direct presentation of them is outside the scope of the play. The play itself deals only with the climactic moment; hence the "unity of time" and the "unity of place," instead of having some intrinsic value, actually derive from the unity of the action—that is from its brevity, compactness, singleness. Indeed, Ibsen's management of these problems represents a very interesting application of the principles set forth in Part One, under "Problems of Scope," which it may be useful to review briefly (pp. 27–29).

QUESTIONS ON *ROSMERSHOLM*

1. What ironic effect does Ibsen secure in the short scene between Madam Helseth and Rebecca at the beginning of Act IV? Does Madam Helseth's thinking in any way resemble Kroll's? Does Madam Helseth's attitude to Rebecca in any way influence our own? Consider the final scene in Act III.

2. Brendel's speeches are often characterized by sardonic wit. Does this style seem appropriate to his character?

3. Does the Brendel scene accomplish anything else besides indicating a line of action for Rebecca and Rosmer? What do we learn from Brendel's references to Mortensgård?

4. Does Rosmer's statement to Rebecca, "Ah no, we cannot be ennobled from without" amplify the meaning of the play in any way?

5. What is the dramatic value of Rebecca's lines, "Then how will you be able to live your life?" and "Let us hold fast to it, Rosmer.—We shall leave it soon enough"?

6. What is ironic about Rosmer's telling Rebecca he has arranged for her "future"? Does this remark in any way suggest Madam Helseth?

7. Work out fully the meaning of the foot-bridge as it appears in the dialogue near the end of Act IV (p. 306a, 20 ff.). What was it that made Rebecca's love "hopeless"? Why does Rosmer feel that he can wed Rebecca at this point? Consider also the use made of the foot-bridge later.

8. What is the final use made of the white horses?

9. For a good deal of the play Rebecca regards Rosmer's sense of sin as an evil effect of tradition. Does Ibsen appear to intend this as an attack on traditionalism?

10. What additional meaning is suggested by the fact that Rebecca once "bewitched" Kroll?

11. We have discussed the complexity of the characters rather fully. In the light of all we have seen of Kroll, what should be made of the references, in Act I (p. 264b, 14–16 and p. 266a, 7–8), to his having been a very "moral" head of a college debating society and his being, now, president of the Temperance Society?

12. How are we to interpret Rebecca's remark, ". . . Rosmersholm has sapped my strength"? Can we recognize a universal human experience here? If so, what?

13. We have suggested that by poetic language Ibsen could gain a more full and precise statement of the complexities which he discerns. Note, for instance, the series of statements in which Rebecca tells Rosmer that Rosmersholm has "enslaved" her, has "ennobled" her mind, but killed her "happiness." Now here is a series of bold statements which appear flatly contradictory. Take just the latter two; to be ennobled cannot in any real sense lead to unhappiness. Does Ibsen mean that she is so evil a character that nobility actually makes her unhappy? Hardly that. What does he mean then? That she is experiencing several feelings at once— perhaps a more tranquil, more refined sense of the good life, plus a real sense of loss at the disappearance of an earlier zestful combativeness? But at best this is an awkward synthesis: metaphor could so fuse these meanings that we could have awareness of conflict without sense of contradiction. What is the problem raised by the use of the word *enslaved* in the next context?

14. The play depends to some extent, as we have seen, upon the clash between Rosmer's ideals and "the way of the world"—a theme also used by Congreve in *The Way of the World*. Notice that the same theme appears in *Lady Windermere's Fan*: there Mrs. Erlynne runs counter to the "way." In a sense, too, we may say that the "way of the world" has a certain influence in *Everyman*. Can you by examining the plays determine the

various roles played by the "way of the world"? Whether one kind of treatment or another leads to comedy or tragedy?

15. In Act II Rebecca eavesdrops upon the Rosmer-Kroll conversation. Thus we have another "screen scene." How does it compare with those in the plays by Wilde and Sheridan? Does it have as important an influence upon the action?

16. Compare Rebecca's "farewell" scene early in Act IV with Mill-wood's "farewell" scene in Act II. xi of *The London Merchant*. What similarities are there? What essential differences?

17. We have stressed the ironies in the last lines and actions of Rosmer and ˌRebecca. Could you argue that at the end Rosmer again, ironically, becomes a pastor? What act of his sugggests this interpretation?

SUGGESTED READING

Euripides' *Alcestis* is another play which has, as a central part of the action, the voluntary death of a woman to save a man. In the Greek play, a queen dies in place of her husband, who had been called upon to die. Euripides, however, treats the material rather differently from Ibsen. Study his play and account for the difference in effect. And, while studying *Alcestis*, you may wish to compare the attitude to the summons of death in that play with the attitude shown in *Everyman*.

4. Shakespeare, *Henry IV, Part One*

*H*ENRY IV, PART ONE (1596–97), has long been admired because of the presence in it of the character of Falstaff, who was a great favorite in Elizabethan times and who has since then come to be regarded as one of the great comic characters of all time. He has been compared with Don Quixote, and, on the level of imaginative insight, even with a great tragic character—Hamlet. He is certainly one of the greatest creations of Shakespeare's imagination. *Henry IV, Part One* is, of the several plays in which Falstaff appears, that one in which Falstaff is at his best, and, in the opinion of many readers, in which he is most truly and characteristically himself.

One view of the play, indeed, is that it is rather stodgy history redeemed only by Falstaff and the tavern scenes. Another view would argue for the brilliance of the central portraits of Prince Hal and of Hotspur and would tend to see the presence of Falstaff as destroying the unity of the play. The material of the play, it is true, is exceedingly diverse, and it is possible, of course, that the student may conclude after even a careful reading that the play lacks any real unity.

Still, it will not do for us to begin by assuming that this is so. There is abundant evidence that Shakespeare strove here as elsewhere for a total unity. The play will be more interesting—and, as a matter of fact, the character of Falstaff himself will seem the more brilliant—if we are able to see how he fits into the play as a whole than if we take him merely as a brilliant excrescence on the play, to be enjoyed for his own sake.

In this connection, the student should be aware of the detail of the poetry and particularly of Falstaff's witty "prose poetry." The latter is rewarding even if detached from the context. But, on careful examination, it may come to suggest deeper implications: it may suggest a kind of commentary on the world of the play, and thus indicate the positive function which the character of Falstaff has in the play; it may help us see more clearly what is the attitude of Shakespeare toward the characters and events of the play and the attitude toward them which he expects us as readers to adopt. Least of all with Shakespeare are we justified in thinking of the poetry as a kind of external decoration, applied to the surface of the play. The poetry is an integral part of the play itself; and this generalization applies in full measure to Falstaff's witty sallies and asides.

THE FIRST PART OF KING HENRY THE FOURTH

DRAMATIS PERSONÆ

KING HENRY THE FOURTH
HENRY, Prince of Wales ⎫ sons to the
JOHN OF LANCASTER ⎭ King
EARL OF WESTMORELAND
SIR WALTER BLUNT
THOMAS PERCY, Earl of Worcester
HENRY PERCY, Earl of Northumberland
HENRY PERCY, surnamed HOTSPUR, his son
EDMUND MORTIMER, Earl of March
RICHARD SCROOP, Archbishop of York
ARCHIBALD, Earl of Douglas
OWEN GLENDOWER
SIR RICHARD VERNON

SIR JOHN FALSTAFF
SIR MICHAEL, a friend to the Archbishop of York
POINS
GADSHILL
PETO
BARDOLPH
LADY PERCY, wife to Hotspur, and sister to Mortimer
LADY MORTIMER, daughter to Glendower, and wife to Mortimer
MISTRESS QUICKLY, hostess of a tavern in Eastcheap

Lords, Officers, Sheriff, Vintner, Chamberlain, Drawers, two Carriers, Travellers, and Attendants

SCENE—ENGLAND

[*Time of action*—Thirteen months—from the defeat of Mortimer by Glendower June 22, 1402, to the battle of Shrewsbury, July 21, 1403.]

ACT I

[SCENE I—London. The palace.]

[*Enter King Henry, Lord John of Lancaster, the Earl of Westmoreland, Sir Walter Blunt, and others.*]

King: So shaken as we are, so wan with care,
Find we a time for frighted peace to pant,
And breathe short-winded accents of new broils
To be commenced in stronds afar remote.
No more the thirsty entrance of this soil
Shall daub her lips with her own children's blood;   6
No more shall trenching war channel her fields,
Nor bruise her flowerets with the armed hoofs
Of hostile paces: those opposed eyes,[1]
Which, like the meteors of a troubled heaven,   10
All of one nature, of one substance bred,
Did lately meet in the intestine shock
And furious close of civil butchery
Shall now, in mutual well-beseeming ranks,
March all one way and be no more opposed   15
Against acquaintance, kindred and allies [2]:
The edge of war, like an ill-sheathed knife,
No more shall cut his master. Therefore, friends,
As far as to the sepulchre of Christ,
Whose soldier now, under whose blessed cross   20
We are impressed and engaged to fight,
Forthwith a power of English shall we levy;
Whose arms were moulded in their mother's womb

---

[1] The eyes of the opposing forces. [2] A reference to the civil wars which resulted in the deposing of Richard II and the crowning of Henry IV in his place.

To chase these pagans in those holy fields
Over whose acres walk'd those blessed feet   25
Which fourteen hundred years ago were nail'd
For our advantage on the bitter cross.
But this our purpose now is twelve month old,
And bootless 'tis to tell you we will go:
Therefore we meet not now. Then let me hear   30
Of you, my gentle cousin Westmoreland,
What yesternight our council did decree
In forwarding this dear expedience.[3]
  West.: My liege, this haste was hot in question,
And many limits of the charge set down
But yesternight: when all athwart there came   36
A post from Wales loaden with heavy news;
Whose worst was, that the noble Mortimer,
Leading the men of Herefordshire to fight
Against the irregular and wild Glen dower,   40
Was by the rude hands of that Welshman taken,
A thousand of his people butchered;
Upon whose dead corpse there was such misuse,
Such beastly shameless transformation,
By whose Welshwomen done as may not be   45
Without much shame retold or spoken of.
  King: It seems then that the tidings of this broil
Brake off our business for the Holy Land.
  West.: This match'd with other did, my gracious lord;
For more uneven and unwelcome news
Came from the north and thus it did import: 51
On Holy-rood day, the gallant Hotspur there,

---

[3] Enterprise, especially an enterprise which requires haste.

Young Harry Percy and brave Archi-
bald,
That ever-valiant and approved Scot,
At Holmedon met,
Where they did spend a sad and bloody
hour;   55
As by discharge of their artillery,
And shape of likelihood, the news was
told;
For he that brought them, in the very
heat
And pride of their contention did take
horse,
Uncertain of the issue any way.   60
    King: Here is a dear, a true industri-
ous friend,
Sir Walter Blunt, new lighted from his
horse,
Stain'd with the variation of each soil
Betwixt that Holmedon and this seat of
ours;
And he hath brought us smooth and wel-
come news.   65
The Earl of Douglas is discomfited:
Ten thousand bold Scots, two and
twenty knights,
Balk'd [4] in their own blood did Sir
Walter see
On Holmedon's plains. Of prisoners,
Hotspur took
Mordake the Earl of Fife, and eldest son
To beaten Douglas; and the Earl of
Athol,   71
Of Murray, Angus, and Menteith:
And is not this an honourable spoil?
A gallant prize? ha, cousin, is it not?
    West.: In faith,   75
It is a conquest for a prince to boast of.
    King: Yea, there [5] thou makest me
sad and makest me sin
In envy that my Lord Northumberland
Should be the father to so blest a son,
A son who is the theme of honour's
tongue;   80
Amongst a grove, the very straightest
plant;
Who is sweet Fortune's minion [6] and her
pride:

Whilst I, by looking on the praise of
him,
See riot and dishonour stain the brow
Of my young Harry. O that it could be
proved   85
That some night-tripping fairy had ex-
changed
In cradle-clothes our children where
they lay,
And call'd mine Percy, his Plantagenet!
Then would I have his Harry, and he
mine.
But let him from my thoughts. What
think you, coz,   90
Of this young Percy's pride? the pris-
oners,
Which he in this adventure hath sur-
prised,
To his own use he keeps; and sends me
word,
I shall have none but Mordake Earl of
Fife.
    West.: This is his uncle's teaching:
this is Worcester,   95
Malevolent to you in all aspects;
Which makes him prune himself, and
bristle up
The crest of youth against your dignity.
    King: But I have sent for him to
answer this;
And for this cause awhile we must
neglect   100
Our holy purpose to Jerusalem.
Cousin, on Wednesday next our council
we
Will hold at Windsor; so inform the
lords;
But come yourself with speed to us
again;
For more is to be said and to be done
Than out of anger can be uttered. 106
    West.: I will, my liege.   [*Exeunt.*]

[SCENE II—London. An apartment
of the Prince's.]

[*Enter the Prince of Wales and Falstaff.*]

    Fal.: Now, Hal, what time of day is
it, lad?
    Prince: Thou art so fat-witted, with

---

[4] Heaped up in balks or ridges. [5] At the
mention of *prince.* [6] Favorite, darling.

drinking of old sack and unbuttoning thee after supper and sleeping upon benches after noon, that thou hast forgotten to demand that truly which thou wouldst truly know. What a devil hast thou to do with the time of the day? Unless hours were cups of sack and minutes capons and clocks the tongues of bawds and dials the signs of leaping-houses and the blessed sun himself a fair hot wench in flame-coloured taffeta, I see no reason why thou shouldst be so superfluous to demand the time of the day.   17

Fal.: Indeed, you come near me now, Hal; for we that take purses go by the moon and the seven stars, and not by Phœbus, he, "that wandering knight so fair." And, I prithee, sweet wag, when thou art king, as, God save thy grace,— majesty I should say, for grace thou wilt have none,—   25

Prince: What, none?

Fal.: No, by my troth, not so much as will serve to be prologue to an egg and butter.[1]

Prince: Well, how then? come, roundly, roundly.   31

Fal.: Marry, then, sweet wag, when thou art king, let not us that are squires of the night's body be called thieves of the day's beauty[2]: let us be Diana's foresters, gentlemen of the shade, minions of the moon; and let men say we be men of good government, being governed, as the sea is, by our noble and chaste mistress the moon, under whose countenance we steal.   41

Prince: Thou sayest well, and it holds well too; for the fortune of us that are the moon's men doth ebb and flow like the sea, being governed, as the sea is, by the moon. As, for proof, now: a purse of gold most resolutely snatched on Monday night and most dissolutely spent on Tuesday morning; got with swearing "Lay by" and spent with cry-

ing "Bring in"; now in a slow an ebb as the foot of the ladder [3] and by and by in as high a flow as the ridge of the gallows.   54

Fal.: By the Lord, thou sayest true, lad. And is not my hostess of the tavern a most sweet wench?

Prince: As the honey of Hybla, my old lad of the castle. And is not a buff jerkin [4] a most sweet robe of durance [4]?

Fal.: How now, how now, mad wag! what, in thy quips and thy quiddities? what a plague have I to do with a buff jerkin?   64

Prince: Why, what a pox have I to do with my hostess of the tavern?

Fal.: Well, thou hast called her to a reckoning many a time and oft.

Prince: Did I ever call for thee to pay thy part?   70

Fal.: No; I'll give thee thy due, thou hast paid all there.

Prince: Yea, and elsewhere, so far as my coin would stretch; and where it would not, I have used my credit.

Fal.: Yea, and so used it that, were it not here apparent that thou art heir apparent [5]—But, I prithee, sweet wag, shall there be gallows standing in England when thou art king? and resolution thus fobbed as it is with the rusty curb of old father antic [6] the law? Do not thou, when thou art king, hang a thief.

Prince: No; thou shalt.   84

Fal.: Shall I? O rare! By the Lord, I'll be a brave judge.

Prince: Thou judgest false already: I mean, thou shalt have the hanging of the thieves and so become a rare hangman.

Fal.: Well, Hal, well; and in some sort it jumps with my humour as well as waiting in the court, I can tell you. 92

Prince: For obtaining of suits?

Fal.: Yea, for obtaining of suits,[7]

[3] By which the criminal ascended the gallows. [4] A leather jacket which would "endure" well but was also worn by prisoners in "duress vile." [5] Probably so pronounced as to yield a play on "here apparent." [6] Mountebank, buffoon. [7] Suits as favors granted to a courtier and as suits of clothes.

[1] Grace said before a meager, Lenten breakfast. [2] "Squires of the night's body" may be a euphemism for highwaymen; "thieves of the day's beauty," for loafers.

whereof the hangman hath no lean wardrobe. 'Sblood, I am as melancholy as a gib cat or a lugged bear.[8]

Prince: Or an old lion, or a lover's lute.

Fal.: Yea, or the drone of a Lincolnshire bagpipe. 101

Prince: What sayest thou to a hare, or the melancholy of Moor-ditch?

Fal.: Thou hast the most unsavoury similes and art indeed the most comparative, rascalliest, sweet young prince. But, Hal, I prithee, trouble me no more with vanity. I would to God thou and I knew where a commodity of good names were to be bought. An old lord of the council rated me the other day in the street about you, sir, but I marked him not; and yet he talked very wisely, but I regarded him not; and yet he walked wisely, and in the street too.

Prince: Thou didst well; for wisdom cries out in the streets, and no man regards it. 118

Fal.: O, thou hast damnable iteration and art indeed able to corrupt a saint. Thou hast done much harm upon me, Hal; God forgive thee for it! Before I knew thee, Hal, I knew nothing; and now am I, if a man should speak truly, little better than one of the wicked. I must give over this life, and I will give it over: by the Lord, an I do not, I am a villain; I'll be damned for never a king's son in Christendom.

Prince: Where shall we take a purse to-morrow, Jack? 131

Fal.: 'Zounds, where thou wilt, lad; I'll make one; an I do not, call me villain and baffle me.

Prince: I see a good amendment of life in thee; from praying to purse-taking. 137

Fal.: Why, Hal, 'tis my vocation, Hal; 'tis no sin for a man to labour in his vocation. [*Enter Poins.*] Poins! Now shall we know if Gadshill have set a match. O, if men were to be saved by merit, what hole in hell were hot enough

for him? This is the most omnipotent villain that ever cried "Stand" to a true man.[9] 146

Prince: Good morrow, Ned.

Poins: Good morrow, sweet Hal. What says Monsieur Remorse? what says Sir John Sack and Sugar? Jack! how agrees the devil and thee about thy soul, that thou soldest him on Good-Friday last for a cup of Madeira and a cold capon's leg? 154

Prince: Sir John stands to his word, the devil shall have his bargain; for he was never yet a breaker of proverbs: he will give the devil his due.

Poins: Then art thou damned for keeping thy word with the devil. 160

Prince: Else he had been damned for cozening[10] the devil.

Poins: But, my lads, my lads, to-morrow morning, by four o'clock, early at Gadshill! there are pilgrims going to Canterbury with rich offerings, and traders riding to London with fat purses: I have vizards[11] for you all; you have horses for yourselves: Gadshill lies to-night in Rochester: I have bespoke supper to-morrow night in Eastcheap: we may do it as secure as sleep. If you will go, I will stuff your purses full of crowns; if you will not, tarry at home and be hanged. 175

Fal.: Hear ye, Yedward; if I tarry at home and go not, I'll hang you for going.

Poins: You will, chops?[12]

Fal.: Hal, wilt thou make one? 180

Prince: Who, I rob? I a thief? not I, by my faith.

Fal.: There's neither honesty, manhood, nor good fellowship in thee, nor thou camest not of the blood royal,[13] if thou darest not stand for ten shillings.

Prince: Well then, once in my days I'll be a madcap.

Fal.: Why, that's well said.

Prince: Well, come what will, I'll tarry at home. 191

[8] A baited bear.

[9] "Halt" to an honest man. [10] Cheating. [11] Masks. [12] Chubby cheeks. [13] A royal was also a coin worth ten shillings.

Fal.: By the Lord, I'll be a traitor then, when thou art king.

Prince: I care not.

Poins: Sir John, I prithee, leave the prince and me alone: I will lay him down such reasons for this adventure that he shall go.   198

Fal.: Well, God give thee the spirit of persuasion and him the ears of profiting, that what thou speakest may move and what he hears may be believed, that the true prince may, for recreation sake, prove a false thief; for the poor abuses of the time want countenance. Farewell: you shall find me in Eastcheap.

Prince: Farewell, the latter spring! farewell, All-hallown summer! [*Exit Falstaff.*]   209

Poins: Now, my good sweet honey lord, ride with us to-morrow: I have a jest to execute that I cannot manage alone. Falstaff, Bardolph, Peto, and Gadshill shall rob those men that we have already waylaid; yourself and I will not be there; and when they have the booty, if you and I do not rob them, cut this head off from my shoulders.   218

Prince: How shall we part with them in setting forth?

Poins: Why, we will set forth before or after them, and appoint them a place of meeting, wherein it is at our pleasure to fail, and then will they adventure upon the exploit themselves; which they shall have no sooner achieved, but we'll set upon them.   227

Prince: Yea, but 'tis like that they will know us by our horses, by our habits, and by every other appointment, to be ourselves.   231

Poins: Tut! our horses they shall not see; I'll tie them in the wood; our vizards we will change after we leave them: and, sirrah, I have cases of buckram for the nonce, to immask our noted outward garments.   237

Prince: Yea, but I doubt they will be too hard for us.   239

Poins: Well, for two of them, I know them to be as true-bred cowards as ever

turned back; and for the third, if he fight longer than he sees reason, I'll forswear arms. The virtue of this jest will be, the incomprehensible lies that this same fat rogue will tell us when we meet at supper: how thirty, at least, he fought with; what wards, what blows, what extremities he endured; and in the reproof of this lies the jest.   250

Prince: Well, I'll go with thee: provide us all things necessary and meet me to-morrow night in Eastcheap; there I'll sup. Farewell.

Poins: Farewell, my lord. [*Exit.*]

Prince: I know you all, and will
    awhile uphold
The unyoked humour of your idleness:
Yet herein will I imitate the sun,
Who doth permit the base contagious
    clouds
To smother up his beauty from the
    world,   260
That, when he please again to be him-
    self,
Being wanted, he may be more won-
    der'd at,
By breaking through the foul and ugly
    mists
Of vapours that did seem to strangle
    him.
If all the year were playing holidays,
To sport would be as tedious as to work;
But when they seldom come, they wish'd
    for come,   267
And nothing pleaseth but rare accidents.
So, when this loose behaviour I throw off
And pay the debt I never promised,
By how much better than my word I am,
By so much shall I falsify men's hopes [14];
And like bright metal on a sullen ground,
My reformation, glittering o'er my fault,
Shall show more goodly and attract
    more eyes   275
Than that which hath no foil to set it off.
I'll so offend, to make offence a skill;
Redeeming time when men think least
    I will.   [*Exit.*]

---

[14] Deceive men's expectations

[SCENE III—London. The palace.]

[*Enter the King, Northumberland, Worcester, Hotspur, Sir Walter Blunt, with others.*]

King: My blood hath been too cold and temperate,
Unapt to stir at these indignities,
And you have found me [1]; for accordingly
You tread upon my patience: but be sure
I will from henceforth rather be myself,
Mighty and to be fear'd, than my condition [2]; 6
Which hath been smooth as oil, soft as young down,
And therefore lost that title of respect
Which the proud soul ne'er pays but to the proud.
Wor.: Our house, my sovereign liege, little deserves 10
The scourge of greatness to be used on it;
And that same greatness too which our own hands
Have holp to make so portly.[3]
North.: My lord,—
King: Worcester, get thee gone; for I do see 15
Danger and disobedience in thine eye:
O, sir, your presence is too bold and peremptory,
And majesty might never yet endure
The moody frontier of a servant brow.
You have good leave to leave us: when we need 20
Your use and counsel, we shall send for you. [*Exit Wor.*]
You were about to speak. [*To North.*]
North.: Yea, my good lord.
Those prisoners in your highness' name demanded,
Which Harry Percy here at Holmedon took,
Were, as he says, not with such strength denied 25

As is deliver'd to your majesty:
Either envy, therefore, or misprision
Is guilty of this fault and not my son.
Hot.: My liege, I did deny no prisoners.
But I remember, when the fight was done, 30
When I was dry with rage and extreme toil,
Breathless and faint, leaning upon my sword,
Came there a certain lord, neat, and trimly dress'd,
Fresh as a bridegroom; and his chin new reap'd
Show'd like a stubble-land at harvesthome; 35
He was perfumed like a milliner;
And 'twixt his finger and his thumb he held
A pouncet-box,[4] which ever and anon
He gave his nose and took 't away again;
Who therewith angry, when it next came there, 40
Took it in snuff [5]; and still he smiled and talk'd,
And as the soldiers bore dead bodies by,
He call'd them untaught knaves, unmannerly,
To bring a slovenly unhandsome corse
Betwixt the wind and his nobility. 45
With many holiday and lady terms
He question'd me; amongst the rest, demanded
My prisoners in your majesty's behalf.
I then, all smarting with my wounds being cold,
To be so pester'd with a popinjay, 50
Out of my grief and my impatience,
Answer'd neglectingly I know not what,
He should, or he should not; for he made me mad
To see him shine so brisk and smell so sweet
And talk so like a waiting-gentlewoman
Of guns and drums and wounds,—God save the mark!— 56
And telling me the sovereign'st thing on earth

---

[1] Found me out. [2] Follow my natural temper. [3] Majestic.

[4] Perfume box. [5] A play upon "snuffed it up" and "became angry."

Was parmaceti for an inward bruise;
And that it was great pity, so it was,
This villainous salt-petre should be
digg'd
Out of the bowels of the harmless earth,
Which many a good tall fellow had
destroy'd   62
So cowardly; and but for these vile guns,
He would himself have been a soldier.
This bald unjointed chat of his, my lord,
I answer'd indirectly, as I said;   66
And I beseech you, let not his report
Come current for an accusation
Betwixt my love and your high maj-
esty.
   Blunt: The circumstance consider'd,
good my lord,   70
Whate'er Lord Harry Percy then had
said
To such a person and in such a place,
At such a time, with all the rest retold,
May reasonably die and never rise
To do him wrong or any way impeach
What then he said, so he unsay it now.
   King: Why, yet he doth deny his
prisoners,   77
But with proviso and exception,[6]
That we at our own charge shall ransom
straight
His brother-in-law, the foolish Morti-
mer;   80
Who, on my soul, hath wilfully betray'd
The lives of those that he did lead to
fight
Against that great magician, damn'd
Glendower,
Whose daughter, as we hear, the Earl of
March
Hath lately married. Shall our coffers,
then,   85
Be emptied to redeem a traitor home?
Shall we buy treason? and indent with
fears,
When they have lost and forfeited
themselves?
No, on the barren mountains let him
starve;
For I shall never hold that man my
friend   90

Whose tongue shall ask me for one penny
cost
To ransom home revolted Mortimer.
   Hot.: Revolted Mortimer!
He never did fall off, my sovereign liege,
But by the chance of war: to prove that
true   95
Needs no more but one tongue for all
those wounds,
Those mouthed wounds, which valiantly
he took,
When on the gentle Severn's sedgy
bank,
In single opposition, hand to hand,
He did confound [7] the best part of an
hour   100
In changing hardiment with great Glen-
dower:
Three times they breathed and three
times did they drink,
Upon agreement, of swift Severn's flood;
Who then, affrighted with their bloody
looks,
Ran fearfully among the trembling
reeds,   105
And hid his crisp head in the hollow
bank
Bloodstained with these valiant com-
batants.
Never did base and rotten policy
Colour her working with such deadly
wounds;   109
Nor never could the noble Mortimer
Receive so many, and all willingly:
Then let not him be slander'd with re-
volt.
   King: Thou dost belie him, Percy,
thou dost belie him;
He never did encounter with Glendower:
I tell thee,   115
He durst as well have met the devil
alone
As Owen Glendower for an enemy.
Art thou not ashamed? But, sirrah,
henceforth
Let me not hear you speak of Mortimer:
Send me your prisoners with the speedi-
est means,   120
Or you shall hear in such a kind from me

[6] Except with reservations.   [7] Spend.

As will displease you. My Lord Northumberland,
We license your departure with your son.
Send us your prisoners, or you will hear of it.
[*Exeunt King Henry, Blunt, and train.*]
   Hot.: An if the devil come and roar for them,   125
I will not send them: I will after straight
And tell him so; for I will ease my heart,
Albeit I make a hazard of my head.
   North.: What, drunk with choler?
stay and pause awhile:
Here comes your uncle.
               [*Re-enter Worcester.*]
   Hot.:   Speak of Mortimer!   130
'Zounds, I will speak of him; and let my soul
Want mercy, if I do not join with him:
Yea, on his part I'll empty all these veins,
And shed my dear blood drop by drop in the dust,
But I will lift the down-trod Mortimer
As high in the air as this unthankful king,   136
As this ingrate and canker'd Bolingbroke.
   North.: Brother, the king hath made your nephew mad.
   Wor.: Who struck this heat up after I was gone?
   Hot.: He will, forsooth, have all my prisoners;   140
And when I urged the ransom once again
Of my wife's brother, then his cheek look'd pale,
And on my face he turn'd an eye of death,[8]
Trembling even at the name of Mortimer.
   Wor.: I cannot blame him: was not he proclaim'd   145
By Richard that dead is the next of blood?
   North.: He was; I heard the proclamation:

And then it was when the unhappy king,—
Whose wrongs in us God pardon!—did set forth
Upon his Irish expedition;   150
From whence he intercepted did return
To be deposed and shortly murdered.
   Wor.: And for whose death we in the world's wide mouth
Live scandalized and foully spoken of.
   Hot.: But, soft, I pray you; did King Richard then   155
Proclaim my brother Edmund Mortimer
Heir to the crown?
   North.:   He did; myself did hear it.
   Hot.: Nay, then I cannot blame his cousin king
That wish'd him on the barren mountains starve.
But shall it be, that you, that set the crown   160
Upon the head of this forgetful man
And for his sake wear the detested blot
Of murderous subornation, shall it be,
That you a world of curses undergo,
Being the agents, or base second means,
The cords, the ladder, or the hangman rather?   166
O, pardon me that I descend so low,
To show the line and the predicament [9]
Wherein you range under this subtle king;
Shall it for shame be spoken in these days,   170
Or fill up chronicles in time to come,
That men of your nobility and power
Did gage [10] them both in an unjust behalf,
As both of you—God pardon it!—have done,
To put down Richard, that sweet lovely rose,   175
And plant this thorn, this canker,[11] Bolingbroke?
And shall it in more shame be further spoken,
That you are fool'd discarded and shook off

---

[8] Eye threatening death.

[9] Category. [10] Pledge. [11] Wild rose.

By him for whom these shames ye un-
derwent?
No; yet time serves wherein ye may re-
deem   180
Your banish'd honours and restore your-
selves
Into the good thoughts of the world again,
Revenge the jeering and disdain'd con-
tempt
Of this proud king, who studies day and
night
To answer [12] all the debt he owes to you
Even with the bloody payment of your
deaths: 186
Therefore, I say,—
   Wor.:   Peace, cousin, say
no more:
And now I will unclasp a secret book,
And to your quick-conceiving discon-
tents
I'll read you matter deep and danger-
ous,   190
As full of peril and adventurous spirit
As to o'er-walk a current roaring loud
On the unsteadfast footing of a spear.
   Hot.: If he fall in, good-night! or sink
or swim:
Send danger from the east unto the
west,   195
So honour cross it from the north to
south,
And let them grapple: O, the blood more
stirs
To rouse a lion than to start a hare!
   North.: Imagination of some great ex-
ploit
Drives him beyond the bounds of pa-
tience.   200
   Hot.: By heaven, methinks it were an
easy leap,
To pluck bright honour from the pale-
faced moon,
Or dive into the bottom of the deep,
Where fathom-line could never touch
the ground,
And pluck up drowned honour by the
locks;   205
So he that doth redeem her thence
might wear

Without corrival all her dignities:
But out upon this half-faced fellowship!
   Wor.: He apprehends a world of
figures [13] here,
But not the form of what he should
attend.   210
Good cousin, give me audience for a
while.
   Hot.: I cry you mercy.
   Wor.   Those same noble Scots
That I have prisoners, —
   Hot.:   I'll keep them
all;
By God, he shall not have a Scot of
them;
No, if a Scot would save his soul, he
shall not: 215
I'll keep them, by this hand.
   Wor.:   You start
away
And lend no ear unto my purposes.
Those prisoners you shall keep.
   Hot.:   Nay, I
will; that's flat.
He said he would not ransom Mortimer;
Forbad my tongue to speak of Morti-
mer;   220
But I will find him when he lies asleep,
And in his ear I'll holla "Mortimer!"
Nay,
I'll have a starling shall be taught to
speak
Nothing but "Mortimer," and give it
him,   225
To keep his anger still in motion.
   Wor.: Hear you, cousin; a word.
   Hot.: All studies here I solemnly defy,
Save how to gall and pinch this Boling-
broke:
And that same sword-and-buckler Prince
of Wales,   230
But that I think his father loves him not
And would be glad he met with some
mischance,
I would have him poison'd with a pot of
ale.
   Wor.: Farewell, kinsman: I'll talk to
you
When you are better temper'd to attend.

---

[12] Pay.   [13] Fancies.

North.: Why, what a wasp-stung and
impatient fool   236
Art thou to break into this woman's
mood,
Tying thine ear to no tongue but thine
own!
Hot.: Why, look you, I am whipp'd
and scourged with rods,
Nettled and stung with pismires, when I
hear   240
Of this vile politician, Bolingbroke.
In Richard's time,—what do you call
the place?—
A plague upon it, it is in Gloucester-
shire;
'Twas where the madcap duke his uncle
kept,
His uncle York; where I first bow'd my
knee   245
Unto this king of smiles, this Boling-
broke,—
'Sblood!—
When you and he came back from
Ravenspurgh.
North.: At Berkley castle.
Hot.: You say true: 250
Why, what a candy deal of courtesy
This fawning greyhound then did proffer
me!
Look, "when his infant fortune came to
age,"
And "gentle Harry Percy," and "kind
cousin";
O, the devil take such cozeners! God
forgive me!   255
Good uncle, tell your tale; I have done.
Wor.: Nay, if you have not, to it
again;
We will stay your leisure.
Hot.:   I have done,
i' faith.
Wor.: Then once more to your Scot-
tish prisoners.
Deliver them up without their ransom
straight,   260
And make the Douglas' son your only
mean
For powers in Scotland; which, for
divers reasons
Which I shall send you written, be as-
sured,

Will easily be granted. You, my lord,
                [*To Northumberland.*]
Your son in Scotland being thus em-
ploy'd,   265
Shall secretly into the bosom creep
Of that same noble prelate, well be-
loved,
The archbishop,
Hot.: Of York, is it not?
Wor.: True; who bears hard   270
His brother's death at Bristol, the Lord
Scroop.
I speak not this in estimation,[14]
As what I think might be, but what I
know
Is ruminated, plotted and set down,
And only stays but to behold the face
Of that occasion that shall bring it on.
Hot.: I smell it: upon my life, it will
do well.   277
North.: Before the game is afoot, thou
still let'st slip.
Hot.: Why, it cannot choose but be a
noble plot:
And then the power of Scotland and of
York,   280
To join with Mortimer, ha?
Wor.:   And so they
shall.
Hot.: In faith, it is exceedingly well
aim'd.
Wor.: And 'tis no little reason bids us
speed,
To save our heads by raising of a head;
For, bear ourselves as even as we can,
The king will always think him in our
debt,   286
And think we think ourselves unsatis-
fied,
Till he hath found a time to pay us
home:
And see already how he doth begin
To make us strangers to his looks of
love.   290
Hot.: He does, he does: we'll be re-
venged on him.
Wor.: Cousin, farewell: no further go
in this
Than I by letters shall direct your course.

[14] Conjecturally.

When time is ripe, which will be suddenly,
I'll steal to Glendower and Lord Mortimer; 295
Where you and Douglas and our powers
at once,
As I will fashion it, shall happily meet,
To bear our fortunes in our own strong
arms,

Which now we hold at much uncertainty.
North.: Farewell, good brother: we
shall thrive, I trust. 300
Hot.: Uncle, adieu: O, let the hours
be short
Till fields and blows and groans applaud
our sport. [*Exeunt.*]

NOTES AND QUESTIONS ON ACT I

The first act of this play, like the first act of most other plays, must be
devoted to exposition and the introduction of characters. The historical
material with which Shakespeare works in this play (and in other "history"
plays) is usually regarded as relatively intractable material—difficult for
the dramatist to reduce to dramatic form and unity. This fact, plus the
fact that the play treats a relatively large body of characters, may seem
to render Shakespeare's problem almost insoluble. And indeed, at a first
glance the play does seem lacking in fundamental unity, and the first act,
in particular, confused and confusing. We meet many people—and very
diverse people at that; and their concerns do not appear to have any
fundamental relation to each other.

Yet a closer observation will indicate that the act is a sort of minor
triumph of exposition. We do meet many people, but the scenes which
introduce them reveal them in characteristic activity. There is the king,
burdened with affairs of state, wearing his crown with something of an
uneasy conscience, hoping to redeem the way in which he gained his power
by going on a crusade, yet prevented now once more by rebellions and
rumors of rebellion. There is Prince Hal, roistering with his tavern companions, indulging, indeed, in the very activities which cause sorrow to
the king and which seem a judgment on his own life: that is, the king is
ironically rebuked by Providence, for the crown, which he has gained with
difficulty and by violent means, is to be passed on to a son who is not in the
least kingly. In the last place, there is Percy ("Hotspur," as he is called),
whose indignation at his rebuff by the king throws him into the mood of
outraged pride out of which the new rebellion against the king will grow.
He exhibits at once the chivalrous fire which produces envy in the king that
his own son is not more like him, but which, on another level, and because
he is *not* the king's son, will cause the king future anxieties.

The three basic groupings of characters, then, the court group, the
tavern group, and the group of rebels, dominate Scenes i, ii, and iii, respectively. (The three groups, though they have interconnections, of
course, will not be brought fully together until they meet at the Battle of
Shrewsbury at the end of the play.)

But Shakespeare has gone further still in emphasizing the parallels and
contrasts between the various characters—parallels and contrasts which
exhibit them in meaningful relation to each other in terms of the purposes

of the play. In Scene i, the king reveals that he has a private problem and a public problem—as a man, and as a ruler. Scene ii goes on to exhibit the first; Scene iii, the second. But if Scenes ii and iii seem to contrast (from the standpoint of the king, ironically) the frivolousness of Hal and the warlike spirit of Hotspur, the two scenes are linked together—and linked with Scene i itself—by an ironic parallelism: all three scenes include councils: Scene i, the formal council of the king; Scene iii, Percy Hotspur's informal council with the other disaffected lords; and Scene ii, the "council" at the Boar's-Head Tavern which formulates plans for the Gadshill robbery. Finally, two of the councils hatch plots—though of different kinds—against the law and order for which the king stands. Thus, if we do have, in Act I, three different groups of characters that seem either unrelated or loosely related, the fact is that already there are patterns of relationship which we may expect to become more clearly defined later.

1. Why is it ironic that this act should open with the king's statement of satisfaction that England will be no longer convulsed with civil war?

2. Does the king, in Scenes i and ii, do anything to justify Hotspur's characterization of him as "this vile politician, Bolingbroke"?

3. The speech of Percy (Sc. iii, 29 ff.) about the "popinjay" lord is a speech which ordinarily might be expected to procure him the king's pardon—it impresses Blunt favorably. It does not, however, produce this effect. Could we attribute its failure to the fact that it may have seemed to the king to be a sneer at the Prince of Wales, about whose unwarlike conduct the king has already shown himself so sensitive?

4. Enumerate the puns in Falstaff's speeches in Scene ii (ll. 32–41 and 76–83). Note that in the first of these speeches there is a play on "night" and perhaps on "beauty" and "booty"; in the second, on "here apparent" and "heir apparent." Is it possible to say that there is a kind of poetry in Falstaff's speech as well as bantering good humor? That is, is there a secondary level of meaning for which we must look and which is more than mere fun?

5. In what ways does Falstaff show that he is thoroughly aware of the charge that he is corrupting the prince? What is the effect upon us of this disclosure of his awareness?

6. In what ways has Shakespeare played down the seriousness of the Gadshill robbery as a crime: in the case of the prince? In the case of Falstaff?

7. Consider carefully Falstaff's speech in Scene ii (ll.199–206). Falstaff imitates the phraseology of the Puritans as he expresses the pious hope that the prince will be moved by Poins's good counsel to take part in the robbery. He wishes that "the true prince may, for recreation sake, prove a false thief." Does the antithesis between *true* and *false* insist: (1) upon the irony of the prince's becoming a false thief ("false" in the sense that all thieves are false; the word is used in this sense several times elsewhere in this play); or (2) upon the fact that the true prince, stealing "for recreation sake" will not be a genuine thief but a false one—a spurious thief, a

"play" thief; or (3) upon the fact that since he is the true prince—he will eventually be king, and the king can do no wrong—he can only pretend to be a thief, that is, can be only a "false" thief; or (4) upon the suggestion that Hal is so truly the prince that he will betray the other thieves, as, indeed, a little later in the play he does? Is it possible that all four meanings are hinted at? Note that the meanings which this passage suggests may be prepared for, and hinted at, by other lines in Act I. ii. Hal tells Falstaff (l. 87), "Thou judgest *false* already . . ."; Falstaff says of Poins (ll. 144–45) "This is the most omnipotent villain that ever cried 'Stand' to a *true* man." Later, Poins describes Falstaff and the others (l. 241) as "*true*-bred cowards," and, in his final speech in Scene ii, Hal, promising to turn out a better man than he appears now, says, "By so much shall I *falsify* men's hopes" (l. 272). You will observe that in the latter two passages there is the paradoxical tone that distinguishes the true-prince-false-thief passage.

8. The king is bitterly disapproving of Hal's conduct. Yet, considering the first part of Scene iii, might not the king profit by some use of his son's talents for easy camaraderie and geniality? Notice that Sir Walter Blunt, whose loyalty to the king is unquestioned, deprecates the charges made against Percy and attempts to excuse him before the king.

9. The speech which ends Scene ii is held by some critics to show that the prince is rather coldly calculating as he deliberately plans to use his reputation for idleness to his advantage later. The speech, on the other hand, has been defended as a necessary piece of exposition: that is, the Prince's sudden reformation at the end of the play must not seem unmotivated. The audience must have some hint that the prince, all the time, had a better nature and intended to realize that nature when the time of trial came. It has been further argued that for an Elizabethan audience in particular it was necessary to save the prince's consistency of character— a consistency which would have been violated for them if the prince had undergone any real "change" in the course of the play.

Yet cannot one think of a further defense still, and one which does not depend so heavily on the conventions of Elizabethan thought? Does the speech not represent a young man whose conscience hurts him even in the midst of his trifling, and who is attempting to justify his conduct to himself? In other words, may the speech not be taken dramatically, not so much as an address to the audience (which might have better been spoken by another character or an agency such as the Greek chorus. See the Glossary) but rather as an argument addressed to himself as he attempts to justify to himself the latest—and most dangerous—madcap escapade, into which he has just consented to go?

ACT II

[SCENE I—Rochester. An inn yard.]

[*Enter a Carrier with a lantern in his hand.*]

First Car.: Heigh-ho! an it be not four by the day, I'll be hanged: Charles' wain [1] is over the new chimney, and yet our horse not packed. What, ostler!
Ost.: [*Within.*] Anon, anon.   5
First Car.: I prithee, Tom, beat Cut's saddle, put a few flocks in the point [2]; poor jade, is wrung in the withers out of all cess.[3] [*Enter another Carrier.*]   9
Sec. Car.: Peas and beans are as dank here as a dog, and that is the next way to give poor jades the bots: this house is turned upside down since Robin Ostler died.   14
First Car.: Poor fellow, never joyed since the price of oats rose; it was the death of him.
Sec. Car.: I think this be the most villainous house in all London road for fleas: I am stung like a tench.   20
First Car.: Like a tench! by the mass, there is ne'er a king christen could be better bit than I have been since the first cock. What, ostler! come away and be hanged! come away.   25
Sec. Car.: I have a gammon of bacon and two razes [4] of ginger, to be delivered as far as Charing-cross.
First Car.: God's body! the turkeys in my pannier are quite starved. What, ostler! A plague on thee! hast thou never an eye in thy head? canst not hear? An 't were not as good deed as drink, to break the pate on thee, I am a very villain. Come, and be hanged! hast no faith in thee? [*Enter Gadshill.*]   36
Gads.: Good morrow, carriers. What's o'clock?
First Car.: I think it be two o'clock.
Gads.: I prithee, lend me thy lantern, to see my gelding in the stable.   41
First Car.: Nay, by God, soft; I know a trick worth two of that, i' faith.

[1] The Great Bear. [2] Pommel of the saddle.
[3] Beyond all measure. [4] Roots.

Gads.: I pray thee, lend me thine.
Sec. Car.: Ay, when? canst tell? Lend me thy lantern, quoth he? marry, I'll see thee hanged first.
Gads.: Sirrah carrier, what time do you mean to come to London?   49
Sec. Car.: Time enough to go to bed with a candle, I warrant thee. Come, neighbour Mugs, we'll call up the gentlemen: they will along with company, for they have great charge. [*Exeunt Carriers.*]   55
Gads.: What, ho! chamberlain!
Cham.: [*Within.*] At hand, quoth pick-purse.
Gads.: That's even as fair as—at hand, quoth the chamberlain; for thou variest no more from picking of purses than giving direction doth from labouring; thou layest the plot how. [*Enter Chamberlain.*]   64
Cham.: Good morrow, Master Gadshill. It holds current that I told you yesternight: there's a franklin in the wild of Kent hath brought three hundred marks with him in gold: I heard him tell it to one of his company last night at supper; a kind of auditor; one that hath abundance of charge too, God knows what. They are up already, and call for eggs and butter: they will away presently.   75
Gads.: Sirrah, if they meet not with Saint Nicholas' clerks,[5] I'll give thee this neck.
Cham.: No, I'll none of it: I pray thee, keep that for the hangman; for I know thou worshippest Saint Nicholas as truly as a man of falsehood may.   82
Gads.: What talkest thou to me of the hangman? if I hang, I'll make a fat pair of gallows; for if I hang, old Sir John hangs with me, and thou knowest he is no starveling. Tut! there are other Trojans that thou dreamest not of, the which for sport sake are content to do the profession some grace; that would, if matters should be looked into, for their own credit sake, make all whole. I am

[5] Highwaymen.

joined with no foot land-rakers,[6] no long-staff sixpenny strikers,[7] none of these mad mustachio purple-hued malt-worms [8]; but with nobility and tranquillity, burgomasters and great oneyers,[9] such as can hold in, such as will strike sooner than speak, and speak sooner than drink, and drink sooner than pray: and yet, 'zounds, I lie; for they pray continually to their saint, the commonwealth; or rather, not pray to her, but prey on her, for they ride up and down on her and make her their boots.   106

Cham.: What, the commonwealth their boots? will she hold out water in foul way?   109

Gads.: She will, she will; justice hath liquored her. We steal as in a castle, cock-sure; we have the receipt of fern-seed,[10] we walk invisible.

Cham.: Nay, by my faith, I think you are more beholding to the night than to fern-seed for your walking invisible. 116

Gads.: Give me thy hand: thou shalt have a share in our purchase, as I am a true man.

Cham.: Nay, rather let me have it, as you are a false thief.   121

Gads.: Go to; "homo" is a common name to all men. Bid the ostler bring my gelding out of the stable. Farewell, you muddy knave. [*Exeunt.*]   125

[6] Roving vagabonds. [7] Men armed with staves, robbing for paltry sums. [8] Drunkards.
[9] Perhaps a burlesque formation meaning "great ones" on the analogy of law*yers*.
[10] Fern-seed, in the popular superstition, would make one invisible.

[SCENE II—The highway, near Gads-hill.]

[*Enter Prince Henry and Poins.*]

Poins: Come, shelter, shelter: I have removed Falstaff's horse, and he frets like a gummed velvet.[1]

Prince: Stand close. [*Enter Falstaff.*]

[1] Gum was sometimes used to give a gloss to velvet, though it made the cloth "fret" or wear out easily.

Fal.: Poins! Poins, and be hanged! Poins!   6

Prince: Peace, ye fat-kidneyed rascal! what a brawling dost thou keep!

Fal.: Where's Poins, Hal?

Prince: He is walked up to the top of the hill: I'll go seek him.   11

Fal.: I am accursed to rob in that thief's company: the rascal hath removed my horse, and tied him I know not where. If I travel but four foot by the squier [2] further afoot, I shall break my wind. Well, I doubt not but to die a fair death for all this, if I 'scape hanging for killing that rogue. I have forsworn his company hourly any time this two and twenty years, and yet I am bewitched with the rogue's company. If the rascal have not given me medicines to make me love him, I'll be hanged; it could not be else; I have drunk medicines. Poins! Hal! a plague upon you both! Bardolph! Peto! I'll starve ere I'll rob a foot further. An 't were not as good a deed as drink, to turn true man and to leave these rogues, I am the veriest varlet that ever chewed with a tooth. Eight yards of uneven ground is threescore and ten miles afoot with me; and the stony-hearted villains know it well enough: a plague upon it when thieves cannot be true one to another! [*They whistle.*] Whew! A plague upon you all! Give me my horse, you rogues; give me my horse, and be hanged!   39

Prince: Peace, ye fat-guts! lie down; lay thine ear close to the ground and list if thou canst hear the tread of travellers.

Fal.: Have you any levers to lift me up again, being down? 'Sblood, I'll not bear mine own flesh so far afoot again for all the coin in thy father's exchequer. What a plague mean ye to colt [3] me thus?   48

Prince: Thou liest; thou art not colted, thou art uncolted.

Fal.: I prithee, good Prince Hal, help me to my horse, good king's son.

Prince: Out, ye rogue! shall I be your ostler?   54

[2] Foot-rule. [3] Cheat.

Fal.: Go, hang thyself in thine own heir-apparent garters! If I be ta'en, I'll peach for this. An I have not ballads made on you all and sung to filthy tunes, let a cup of sack be my poison: when a jest is so forward, and afoot too! I hate it. [*Enter Gadshill, Bardolph and Peto with him.*]   62

Gads.: Stand.

Fal.: So I do, against my will.

Poins: O, 'tis our setter [4]: I know his voice. Bardolph, what news?   66

Bard.: Case ye, case ye; on with your vizards: there's money of the king's coming down the hill; 'tis going to the king's exchequer.   70

Fal.: You lie, you rogue; 'tis going to the king's tavern.

Gads.: There's enough to make us all.

Fal.: To be hanged.   74

Prince: Sirs, you four shall front them in the narrow lane; Ned Poins and I will walk lower: if they 'scape from your encounter, then they light on us.

Peto: How many be there of them?

Gads.: Some eight or ten.   80

Fal.: 'Zounds, will they not rob us?

Prince: What, a coward, Sir John Paunch?

Fal.: Indeed, I am not John of Gaunt, your grandfather; but yet no coward, Hal.   86

Prince: Well, we leave that to the proof.

Poins: Sirrah Jack, thy horse stands behind the hedge: when thou needest him, there thou shalt find him. Farewell, and stand fast.   92

Fal.: Now cannot I strike him, if I should be hanged.

Prince: Ned, where are our disguises?

Poins: Here, hard by: stand close. [*Exeunt Prince and Poins.*]   97

Fal.: Now, my masters, happy man be his dole, say I: every man to his business. [*Enter the Travellers.*]   100

First Trav.: Come, neighbour: the boy shall lead our horses down the hill; we'll walk afoot awhile, and ease our legs.

Thieves: Stand!   104

Travellers: Jesus bless us!

Fal.: Strike; down with them; cut the villains' throats: ah! whoreson caterpillars! bacon-fed knaves! they hate us youth: down with them: fleece them.

Travellers: O, we are undone, both we and ours for ever!   111

Fal.: Hang ye, gorbellied knaves, are ye undone? No, ye fat chuffs [5]; I would your store were here! On, bacons, on! What, ye knaves! young men must live. You are grandjurors, are ye? we'll jure ye, faith. [*Here they rob them and bind them. Exeunt.*] [*Re-enter Prince Henry and Poins.*]   119

Prince: The thieves have bound the true men. Now could thou and I rob the thieves and go merrily to London, it would be argument for a week, laughter for a month and a good jest for ever.

Poins: Stand close; I hear them coming. [*Enter the Thieves again.*]   126

Fal.: Come, my masters, let us share, and then to horse before day. An the Prince and Poins be not two arrant cowards, there's no equity stirring: there's no more valour in that Poins than in a wild-duck.   132

Prince: Your money!

Poins: Villains! [*As they are sharing, the Prince and Poins set upon them; they all run away; and Falstaff, after a blow or two, runs away too, leaving the booty behind them.*]

Prince: Got with much ease. Now
   merrily to horse: 139
The thieves are all scatter'd and possess'd with fear
So strongly that they dare not meet each other;
Each takes his fellow for an officer.
Away, good Ned. Falstaff sweats to death,
And lards the lean earth as he walks along: 144
Were't not for laughing, I should pity him.

Poins: How the rogue roar'd!
[*Exeunt.*]

---

[4] The thieves' decoy—here, Gadshill.   [5] Churls.

[SCENE III—Warkworth castle.]

[*Enter Hotspur, solus, reading a letter.*]

Hot.: "But, for mine own part, my lord, I could be well contented to be there, in respect of the love I bear your house." He could be contented: why is he not, then? In respect of the love he bears our house: he shows in this, he loves his own barn better than he loves our house. Let me see some more. "The purpose you undertake is dangerous"; —why, that's certain: 'tis dangerous to take a cold, to sleep, to drink; but I tell you, my lord fool, out of this nettle, danger, we pluck this flower, safety. "The purpose you undertake is dangerous; the friends you have named uncertain; the time itself unsorted; and your whole plot too light for the counterpoise of so great an opposition." Say you so, say you so? I say unto you again, you are a shallow cowardly hind, and you lie. What a lack-brain is this! By the Lord, our plot is a good plot as ever was laid; our friends true and constant; a good plot, good friends, and full of expectation; an excellent plot, very good friends. What a frosty-spirited rogue is this! Why, my lord of York commends the plot and the general course of the action. 'Zounds, an I were now by this rascal, I could brain him with his lady's fan. Is there not my father, my uncle and myself? lord Edmund Mortimer, my lord of York and Owen Glendower? is there not besides the Douglas? have I not all their letters to meet me in arms by the ninth of the next month? and are they not some of them set forward already? What a pagan rascal is this! an infidel! Ha! you shall see now in very sincerity of fear and cold heart, will he to the king and lay open all our proceedings. O, I could divide myself and go to buffets, for moving such a dish of skim milk with so honourable an action! Hang him! let him tell the king: we are prepared. I will set forward tonight. [*Enter Lady Percy.*] How now,

Kate! I must leave you within these two hours.   49

Lady: O, my good lord, why are you thus alone?
For what offence have I this fortnight been
A banish'd woman from my Harry's bed?
Tell me, sweet lord, what is 't that takes from thee
Thy stomach, pleasure and thy golden sleep?
Why dost thou bend thine eyes upon the earth,   55
And start so often when thou sit'st alone?
Why hast thou lost the fresh blood in thy cheeks;
And given my treasures and my rights of thee
To thick-eyed musing and cursed melancholy?
In thy faint slumbers I by thee have watch'd,   60
And heard thee murmur tales of iron wars;
Speak terms of manage to thy bounding steed;
Cry "Courage! to the field!" And thou hast talk'd
Of sallies and retires, of trenches, tents,
Of pasiladoes, frontiers, parapets,   65
Of basilisks, of cannon, culverin,
Of prisoners' ransom and of soldiers slain,
And all the currents of a heady fight.
Thy spirit within thee hath been so at war
And thus hath so bestirr'd thee in thy sleep,   70
That beads of sweat have stood upon thy brow,
Like bubbles in a late-disturbed stream;
And in thy face strange motions have appear'd,
Such as we see when men restrain their breath
On some great sudden hest.[1] O, what portents are these?   75

---

[1] Command.

Some heavy business hath my lord in
hand,
And I must know it, else he loves me not.
Hot.: What, ho!
    [*Enter Servant.*]
            Is Gilliams with the
packet gone?
Serv.: He is, my lord, an hour ago.
Hot.: Hath Butler brought those
horses from the sheriff?   80
Serv.: One horse, my lord, he brought
even now.
Hot.: What horse? a roan, a crop-ear,
is it not?
Serv.: It is, my lord.
Hot.:   That roan shall
be my throne.
Well, I will back him straight: O esper-
ance! [2]
Bid Butler lead him forth into the park.
            [*Exit Servant.*]
Lady: But hear you, my lord.   86
Hot.: What say'st thou, my lady?
Lady: What is it carries you away?
Hot.: Why, my horse, my love, my
horse.
Lady: Out, you mad-headed ape! 90
A weasel hath not such a deal of spleen
As you are toss'd with. In faith,
I'll know your business, Harry, that I
will.
I fear my brother Mortimer doth stir
About his title, and hath sent for you
To line [3] his enterprize: but if you go,—
Hot.: So far afoot, I shall be weary,
love.   97
Lady: Come, come, you paraquito,
answer me
Directly unto this question that I ask:
In faith, I'll break thy little finger,
Harry,   100
An if thou wilt not tell me all things true.
Hot.: Away,
Away, you trifler! Love! I love thee not,
I care not for thee, Kate: this is no
world
To play with mammets [4] and to tilt with
lips: 105

[2] The motto of the Percy family. [3] Support. [4] Dolls.

We must have bloody noses and crack'd
crowns,[5]
And pass them current too. God's me,[6]
my horse!
What say'st thou, Kate? what would'st
thou have with me?
Lady: Do you not love me? do you
not, indeed?
Well, do not then; for since you love me
not,   110
I will not love myself. Do you not love
me?
Nay, tell me if you speak in jest or no.
Hot.: Come, wilt thou see me ride?
And when I am o' horseback, I will swear
I love thee infinitely. But hark you, Kate;
I must not have you henceforth ques-
tion me   116
Whither I go, nor reason whereabout:
Whither I must, I must; and, to conclude,
This evening must I leave you, gentle
Kate.
I know you wise, but yet no farther wise
Than Harry Percy's wife: constant you
are,   121
But yet a woman: and for secrecy,
No lady closer; for I well believe
Thou wilt not utter what thou dost not
know;
And so far will I trust thee, gentle Kate.
Lady: How! so far?   126
Hot.: Not an inch further. But hark
you, Kate:
Whither I go, thither shall you go too;
To-day will I set forth, to-morrow you.
Will this content you, Kate?
Lady: It must of
force.   [*Exeunt.*] 130

[5] The crown of the head, but also the
coin as "And pass them current too" suggests. [6] God is for me.

[SCENE IV—The Boar's-Head Tavern, Eastcheap.]

    [*Enter the Prince and Poins.*],

Prince: Ned, prithee, come out of
that fat [1] room, and lend me thy hand
to laugh a little.
Poins: Where hast been, Hal?
[1] Stuffy.

Prince: With three or four loggerheads amongst three or four score hogsheads. I have sounded the very base-string of humility. Sirrah, I am sworn brother to a leash of drawers; and can call them all by their christen names, as Tom, Dick, and Francis. They take it already upon their salvation, that though I be but Prince of Wales, yet I am the king of courtesy; and tell me flatly I am no proud Jack, like Falstaff, but a Corinthian,[2] a lad of mettle, a good boy, by the Lord, so they call me, and when I am king of England, I shall command all the good lads in Eastcheap. They call drinking deep, dyeing scarlet; and when you breathe in your watering, they cry "hem!" and bid you play it off. To conclude, I am so good a proficient in one quarter of an hour, that I can drink with any tinker in his own language during my life. I tell thee, Ned, thou hast lost much honour, that thou wert not with me in this action. But, sweet Ned,—to sweeten which name of Ned, I give thee this pennyworth of sugar, clapped even now into my hand by an under-skinker,[3] one that never spoke other English in his life than "Eight shillings and sixpence," and "You are welcome," with this shrill addition, "Anon, anon, sir! Score a pint of bastard[4] in the Halfmoon," or so. But, Ned, to drive away the time till Falstaff come, I prithee, do thou stand in some by-room, while I question my puny drawer to what end he gave me the sugar; and do thou never leave calling "Francis," that his tale to me may be nothing but "Anon." Step aside, and I'll show thee a precedent.

Poins: Francis!   45
Prince: Thou art perfect.
Poins: Francis! [*Exit Poins.*] [*Enter Francis.*]
Fran.: Anon, anon, sir. Look down into the Pomgarnet,[5] Ralph.   50
Prince: Come hither, Francis.
Fran.: My lord?

[2] A good fellow, a hearty drinker. [3] Tapster's boy. [4] A sweet wine of Spain. [5] Pomegranate.

Prince: How long hast thou to serve, Francis?
Fran.: Forsooth, five years, and as much as to—   56
Poins: [*Within.*] Francis!
Fran.: Anon, anon, sir.
Prince: Five year! by 'r lady, a long lease for the clinking of pewter. But, Francis, darest thou be so valiant as to play the coward with thy indenture and show it a fair pair of heels and run from it?   64
Fran.: O Lord, sir, I'll be sworn upon all the books in England, I could find in my heart.
Poins: [*Within.*] Francis!
Fran.: Anon, sir.
Prince: How old art thou, Francis?
Fran.: Let me see—about Michaelmas next I shall be—   72
Poins: [*Within.*] Francis!
Fran.: Anon, sir. Pray stay a little, my lord.   75
Prince: Nay, but hark you, Francis: for the sugar thou gavest me, 'twas a pennyworth, was't not?
Fran.: O Lord, I would it had been two!   80
Prince: I will give thee for it a thousand pound: ask me when thou wilt, and thou shalt have it.
Poins: [*Within.*] Francis!
Fran.: Anon, anon.   85
Prince: Anon, Francis? No, Francis; but to-morrow, Francis; or Francis, o' Thursday; or indeed, Francis, when thou wilt. But, Francis!
Fran.: My lord?   90
Prince: Wilt thou rob this leathern jerkin, crystal-button, not-pated,[6] agate-ring, puke-stocking,[7] caddis-garter,[8] smooth-tongue, Spanish-pouch,[9]—   94
Fran.: O Lord, sir, who do you mean?
Prince: Why, then, your brown bastard is your only drink; for look you, Francis, your white canvas doublet will sully: in Barbary, sir, it cannot come to so much.   100

[6] Crop-headed. [7] Stockings of a dull gray color. [8] A garter of worsted. [9] Of Spanish leather.

Fran.: What, sir?

Poins: [*Within.*] Francis!

Prince: Away, you rogue! dost thou not hear them call? [*Here they both call him; the drawer stands amazed, not knowing which way to go.*] [*Enter Vintner.*]   107

Vint.: What, standest thou still, and hearest such a calling? Look to the guests within. [*Exit Francis.*] My lord, old Sir John, with half-a-dozen more, are at the door: shall I let them in?   113

Prince: Let them alone awhile, and then open the door. [*Exit Vintner.*] Poins! [*Re-enter Poins.*]   116

Poins: Anon, anon, sir.

Prince: Sirrah, Falstaff and the rest of the thieves are at the door: shall we be merry?   120

Poins: As merry as crickets, my lad. But hark ye; what cunning match have you made with this jest of the drawer? come, what's the issue?   124

Prince: I am now of all humours that have showed themselves humours since the old days of goodman Adam to the pupil age of this present twelve o'clock at midnight. [*Re-enter Francis.*] What's o'clock, Francis?

Fran.: Anon, anon, sir. [*Exit.*]   131

Prince: That ever this fellow should have fewer words than a parrot, and yet the son of a woman! His industry is up-stairs and down-stairs; his eloquence the parcel of a reckoning. I am not yet of Percy's mind, the Hotspur of the north; he that kills me some six or seven dozen of Scots at a breakfast, washes his hands, and says to his wife "Fie upon this quiet life! I want work." "O my sweet Harry," says she, "how many hast thou killed to-day?" "Give my roan horse a drench," says he; and answers "Some fourteen," an hour after; "a trifle, a trifle." I prithee, call in Falstaff: I'll play Percy, and that damned brawn shall play Dame Mortimer his wife. "Rivo!" [10] says the drunkard. Call in ribs, call in tallow. [*Enter Falstaff, Gads-*

[10] An exclamation used at drinking-bouts.

hill, Bardolph, and Peto; Francis follow-ing with wine.]   152

Poins: Welcome, Jack: where hast thou been?

Fal.: A plague of all cowards, I say, and a vengeance too! marry, and amen! Give me a cup of sack, boy. Ere I lead this life long, I'll sew nether stocks [11] and mend them and foot them too. A plague of all cowards! Give me a cup of sack, rogue. Is there no virtue extant? [*He drinks.*]   162

Prince: Didst thou ever see Titan [12] kiss a dish of butter? pitiful-hearted [creature], that melted at the sweet tale of the sun's! if thou didst, then behold that compound.   167

Fal.: You rogue, here's lime in this sack too: there is nothing but roguery to be found in villainous man: yet a coward is worse than a cup of sack with lime in it. A villainous coward! Go thy ways, old Jack; die when thou wilt, if man-hood, good manhood, be not forgot upon the face of the earth, then am I a shotten herring. [13] There live not three good men unhanged in England; and one of them is fat and grows old: God help the while! a bad world, I say. I would I were a weaver; I could sing psalms or any thing. A plague of all cowards, I say still.   182

Prince: How now, wool-sack! what mutter you?

Fal.: A king's son! If I do not beat thee out of thy kingdom with a dagger of lath, and drive all thy subjects afore thee like a flock of wild-geese, I'll never wear hair on my face more. You Prince of Wales!

Prince: Why, you whoreson round man, what's the matter?   192

Fal.: Are not you a coward? answer me to that: and Poins there?

Poins: 'Zounds, ye fat paunch, an ye call me coward, by the Lord, I'll stab thee.

Fal.: I call thee coward! I'll see thee damned ere I call thee coward: but I would give a thousand pound I could

[11] Stockings. [12] The sun. [13] A herring that has spawned.

run as fast as thou canst. You are straight enough in the shoulders, you care not who sees your back: call you that backing of your friends? A plague upon such backing! give me them that will face me. Give me a cup of sack: I am a rogue, if I drunk to-day.   206
Prince: O villain! thy lips are scarce wiped since thou drunkest last.
Fal.: All's one for that. [*He drinks.*] A plague of all cowards, still say I.   210
Prince: What's the matter?
Fal.: What's the matter! there be four of us here have ta'en a thousand pound this day morning.   214
Prince: Where is it, Jack? where is it?
Fal.: Where is it! taken from us it is: a hundred upon poor four of us.
Prince: What, a hundred, man?
Fal.: I am a rogue, if I were not at half-sword with a dozen of them two hours together. I have 'scaped by miracle. I am eight times thrust through the doublet, four through the hose; my buckler cut through and through; my sword hacked like a hand-saw—ecce signum! I never dealt better since I was a man: all would not do. A plague of all cowards! Let them speak: if they speak more or less than truth, they are villains and the sons of darkness.   230
Prince: Speak, sirs; how was it?
Gads.: We four set upon some dozen—
Fal.: Sixteen, at least, my lord.
Gads.: And bound them.   234
Peto: No, no, they were not bound.
Fal.: You rogue, they were bound, every man of them; or I am a Jew else, an Ebrew Jew.
Gads.: As we were sharing, some six or seven fresh men set upon us—   240
Fal.: And unbound the rest, and then come in the other.
Prince: What, fought you with them all?
Fal.: All! I know not what you call all; but if I fought not with fifty of them, I am a bunch of radish: if there were not two or three and fifty upon poor old Jack, then am I no two-legged creature.   250

Prince: Pray God you have not murdered some of them.
Fal.: Nay, that's past praying for: I have peppered two of them; two I am sure I have paid, two rogues in buckram suits. I tell thee what, Hal, if I tell thee a lie, spit in my face, call me horse. Thou knowest my old ward [14]; here I lay, and thus I bore my point. Four rogues in buckram let drive at me—   260
Prince: What, four? thou saidst but two even now.
Fal.: Four, Hal; I told thee four.
Poins: Ay, ay, he said four.   264
Fal.: These four came all a-front, and mainly thrust at me. I made me no more ado but took all their seven points in my target, thus.
Prince: Seven? why, there were but four even now.   270
Fal.: In buckram.
Poins: Ay, four, in buckram suits.
Fal.: Seven, by these hilts, or I am a villain else.
Prince: Prithee, let him alone; we shall have more anon.   276
Fal.: Dost thou hear me, Hal?
Prince: Ay, and mark thee too, Jack.
Fal.: Do so, for it is worth listening to. These nine in buckram that I told thee of—   281
Prince: So, two more already.
Fal.: Their points being broken,—
Poins: Down fell their hose.[15]
Fal.: Began to give me ground: but I followed me close, came in foot and hand; and with a thought seven of the eleven I paid.
Prince: O monstrous! eleven buckram men grown out of two!   290
Fal.: But, as the devil would have it, three misbegotten knaves in Kendal green came at my back and let drive at me; for it was so dark, Hal, that thou couldst not see thy hand.   295
Prince: These lies are like their father that begets them; gross as a mountain, open, palpable. Why, thou clay-brained

[14] Guard, in fencing. [15] There is a play here on points (of the swords) and "points," laces used for holding up the hose.

guts, thou knotty-pated fool, thou whoreson, obscene, greasy tallow-ketch,[16]—
    Fal.: What, art thou mad? art thou
mad? is not the truth the truth?   302
    Prince: Why, how couldst thou know
these men in Kendal green, when it was
so dark thou couldst not see thy hand?
come, tell us your reason: what sayest
thou to this?   307
    Poins: Come, your reason, Jack, your
reason.
    Fal.: What, upon compulsion?
'Zounds, an I were at the strappado,[17]
or all the racks in the world, I would not
tell you on compulsion. Give you a
reason on compulsion! if reasons were as
plentiful as blackberries, I would give
no man a reason upon compulsion, I.
    Prince: I'll be no longer guilty of this
sin; this sanguine coward, this bed-
presser, this horse-back-breaker, this
huge hill of flesh,—   320
    Fal.: 'Sblood, you starveling, you elf-
skin, you dried neat's[18] tongue, you
bull's pizzle, you stock-fish![19] O for
breath to utter what is like thee! you
tailor's-yard, you sheath, you bow-case,
you vile standing-tuck,[20]—   326
    Prince: Well, breathe awhile, and
then to it again: and when thou hast
tired thyself in base comparisons, hear
me speak but this.   330
    Poins: Mark, Jack.
    Prince: We two saw you four set on
four and bound them, and were masters
of their wealth. Mark now, how a plain
tale shall put you down. Then did we
two set on you four; and, with a word,
out-faced you from your prize, and have
it; yea, and can show it you here in the
house: and, Falstaff, you carried your
guts away as nimbly, with as quick
dexterity, and roared for mercy and still
run and roared, as ever I heard bull-calf.
What a slave art thou, to hack thy
sword as thou hast done, and then say
it was in fight! What trick, what device,
what starting-hole, canst thou now find

    [16] Tub of tallow. [17] A Spanish torture.
[18] Ox-tongue. [19] A dried fish. [20] Sword set upright.

out to hide thee from this open and
apparent shame?   348
    Poins: Come, let's hear, Jack; what
trick hast thou now?   350
    Fal.: By the Lord, I knew ye as well
as he that made ye. Why, hear you, my
masters: was it for me to kill the heir-
apparent? should I turn upon the true
prince? why, thou knowest I am as
valiant as Hercules: but beware instinct; the lion will not touch the true
prince. Instinct is a great matter; I was
now a coward on instinct. I shall think
the better of myself and thee during my
life; I for a valiant lion, and thou for a
true prince. But, by the Lord, lads, I am
glad you have the money. Hostess, clap
to the doors: watch to-night, pray to-
morrow. Gallants, lads, boys, hearts of
gold, all the titles of good fellowship
come to you! What, shall we be merry?
shall we have a play extempore?   368
    Prince: Content; and the argument
shall be thy running away.
    Fal.: Ah, no more of that, Hal, an
thou lovest me! [*Enter Hostess.*]
    Host.: O Jesu, my lord the prince!
    Prince: How now, my lady the
hostess! what sayest thou to me?   375
    Host.: Marry, my lord, there is a
nobleman of the court at door would
speak with you: he says he comes from
your father.   379
    Prince: Give him as much as will
make him a royal man, and send him
back again to my mother.
    Fal.: What manner of man is he?
    Host.: An old man.   384
    Fal.: What doth gravity out of his
bed at midnight? Shall I give him his
answer?
    Prince: Prithee, do, Jack.
    Fal.: 'Faith, and I'll send him pack-
ing. [*Exit.*]   390
    Prince: Now, sirs: by'r lady, you
fought fair; so did you, Peto; so did you,
Bardolph: you are lions too, you ran
away upon instinct, you will not touch
the true prince; no, fie!   395
    Bard.: 'Faith, I ran when I saw others
run.

Prince: 'Faith, tell me now in earnest, how came Falstaff's sword so hacked?

Peto: Why, he hacked it with his dagger, and said he would swear truth out of England but he would make you believe it was done in fight, and persuaded us to do the like. 404

Bard.: Yea, and to tickle our noses with spear-grass to make them bleed, and then to beslubber our garments with it and swear it was the blood of true men. I did that I did not this seven year before, I blushed to hear his monstrous devices. 411

Prince: O villain, thou stolest a cup of sack eighteen years ago, and wert taken with the manner, and ever since thou hast blushed extempore. Thou hadst fire and sword on thy side, and yet thou rannest away: what instinct hadst thou for it? 418

Bard.: My lord, do you see these meteors? do you behold these exhalations?

Prince: I do. 422

Bard.: What think you they portend?

Prince: Hot livers and cold purses.

Bard.: Choler,[21] my lord, if rightly taken. 426

Prince: No, if rightly taken, halter. [*Re-enter Falstaff.*] Here comes lean Jack, here comes bare-bone. How now, my sweet creature of bombast! How long is't ago, Jack, since thou sawest thine own knee? 432

Fal.: My own knee! when I was about thy years, Hal, I was not an eagle's talon in the waist; I could have crept into any alderman's thumb-ring: a plague of sighing and grief! it blows a man up like a bladder. There's villainous news abroad: here was Sir John Bracy from your father; you must to the court in the morning. That same mad fellow of the north, Percy, and he of Wales, that gave Amamon[22] the bastinado and made Lucifer cuckold and swore the devil his true liegeman upon

the cross of a Welsh hook—what a plague call you him? 447

Poins: O, Glendower.

Fal.: Owen, Owen, the same; and his son-in-law Mortimer, and old Northumberland, and that sprightly Scot of Scots, Douglas, that runs o'horseback up a hill perpendicular,— 453

Prince: He that rides at high speed and with his pistol kills a sparrow flying.

Fal.: You have hit it.

Prince: So did he never the sparrow.

Fal.: Well, that rascal hath good mettle in him; he will not run. 459

Prince: Why, what a rascal art thou then, to praise him so for running!

Fal.: O'horseback, ye cuckoo; but afoot he will not budge a foot.

Prince: Yes, Jack, upon instinct. 464

Fal.: I grant ye, upon instinct. Well, he is there too, and one Mordake, and a thousand blue-caps more: Worcester is stolen away to-night; thy father's beard is turned white with the news: you may buy land now as cheap as stinking mackerel. 471

Prince: Why, then, it is like, if there come a hot June, and this civil buffeting hold, we shall buy maidenheads as they buy hob-nails, by the hundreds. 475

Fal.: By the mass, lad, thou sayest true; it is like we shall have good trading that way. But tell me, Hal, art not thou horrible afeard? thou being heir-apparent, could the world pick thee out three such enemies again as that fiend Douglas, that spirit Percy, and that devil Glendower? Art thou not horribly afraid? doth not thy blood thrill at it?

Prince: Not a whit, i' faith; I lack some of thy instinct. 486

Fal.: Well, thou wilt be horribly chid to-morrow when thou comest to thy father: if thou love me, practise an answer. 490

Prince: Do thou stand for my father, and examine me upon the particulars of my life.

Fal.: Shall I? content: this chair shall be my state, this dagger my sceptre, and this cushion my crown. 496

---

[21] There is a pun on *choler*, anger, and *collar*. [22] The name of a fiend.

Prince: Thy state is taken for a joined-stool, thy golden sceptre for a leaden dagger, and thy precious rich crown for a pitiful bald crown!   500

Fal.: Well, an the fire of grace be not quite out of thee, now shalt thou be moved. Give me a cup of sack to make my eyes look red, that it may be thought I have wept; for I must speak in passion, and I will do it in King Cambyses' vein.[23]   507

Prince: Well, here is my leg.[24]

Fal.: And here is my speech. Stand aside, nobility.   510

Host.: O Jesu, this is excellent sport, i' faith!

Fal.: Weep not, sweet queen; for trickling tears are vain.

Host.: O, the father, how he holds his countenance!   515

Fal.: For God's sake, lords, convey my tristful queen;

For tears do stop the flood-gates of her eyes.

Host.: O Iesu, he doth it as like one of these harlotry [25] players as ever I see!

Fal.: Peace, good pint-pot; peace, good tickle-brain. Harry, I do not only marvel where thou spendest thy time, but also how thou art accompanied: for though the camomile, the more it is trodden on the faster it grows, yet youth, the more it is wasted the sooner it wears. That thou art my son, I have partly thy mother's word, partly my own opinion, but chiefly a villainous trick of thine eye and a foolish hanging of thy nether lip, that doth warrant me. If then thou be son to me, here lies the point; why, being son to me, art thou so pointed at? Shall the blessed sun of heaven prove a micher[26] and eat blackberries? a question not to be asked. Shall the son of England prove a thief and take purses? a question to be asked. There is a thing, Harry, which thou hast often heard of and it is known to many in our land by

the name of pitch: this pitch, as ancient writers do report, doth defile; so doth the company thou keepest: for, Harry, now I do not speak to thee in drink but in tears, not in pleasure but in passion, not in words only, but in woes also: and yet there is a virtuous man whom I have often noted in thy company, but I know not his name.   549

Prince: What manner of man, an it like your majesty?

Fal.: A goodly portly man, i' faith, and a corpulent; of a cheerful look, a pleasing eye and a most noble carriage; and, as I think, his age some fifty, or, by'r lady, inclining to three score; and now I remember me, his name is Falstaff: if that man should be lewdly given, he deceiveth me; for, Harry, I see virtue in his looks. If then the tree may be known by the fruit, as the fruit by the tree, then, peremptorily I speak it, there is virtue in that Falstaff: him keep with, the rest banish. And tell me now, thou naughty varlet, tell me, where hast thou been this month?   566

Prince: Dost thou speak like a king? Do thou stand for me, and I'll play my father.

Fal.: Depose me? if thou dost it half so gravely, so majestically, both in word and matter, hang me up by the heels for a rabbit-sucker [27] or a poulter's hare.   574

Prince: Well, here I am set.

Fal.: And here I stand: judge, my masters.

Prince: Now, Harry, whence come you?   579

Fal.: My noble lord, from Eastcheap.

Prince: The complaints I hear of thee are grievous.

Fal.: 'Sblood, my lord, they are false: nay, I'll tickle ye for a young prince, i' faith.   585

Prince: Swearest thou, ungracious boy? henceforth ne'er look on me. Thou art violently carried away from grace: there is a devil haunts thee in the likeness of an old fat man; a tun of man is

---

[23] A reference to the bombastic style of an early Elizabethan tragedy, the *Lamentable Tragedy of . . . Cambises.* [24] An elaborate bow. [25] Scurvy, good-for-nothing. [26] Truant.

[27] Suckling rabbit.

thy companion. Why dost thou converse with that trunk of humours, that bolting-hutch [28] of beastliness, that swollen parcel of dropsies, that huge bombard [29] of sack, that stuffed cloak-bag of guts, that roasted Manningtree ox with the pudding in his belly, that reverend vice, that grey iniquity, that father ruffian, that vanity in years? Wherein is he good, but to taste sack and drink it? wherein neat and cleanly, but to carve a capon and eat it? wherein cunning, but in craft? wherein crafty, but in villainy? wherein villainous, but in all things? wherein worthy, but in nothing?   605

Fal.: I would your grace would take me with you [30]: whom means your grace?

Prince: That villainous abominable misleader of youth, Falstaff, that old white-bearded Satan.   610

Fal.: My lord, the man I know.

Prince: I know thou dost.

Fal.: But to say I know more harm in him than in myself, were to say more than I know. That he is old, the more the pity, his white hairs do witness it; but that he is, saving your reverence, a whoremaster, that I utterly deny. If sack and sugar be a fault, God help the wicked! if to be old and merry be a sin, then many an old host that I know is damned: if to be fat be to be hated, then Pharaoh's lean kine are to be loved. No, my good lord; banish Peto, banish Bardolph, banish Poins: but for sweet Jack Falstaff, kind Jack Falstaff, true Jack Falstaff, valiant Jack Falstaff, and therefore more valiant, being, as he is, old Jack Falstaff, banish not him thy Harry's company, banish not him thy Harry's company: banish plump Jack, and banish all the world.   632

Prince: I do, I will. [*A knocking heard. Exeunt Hostess, Francis, and Bardolph. Re-enter Bardolph, running.*]

Bard.: O, my lord, my lord! the sheriff with a most monstrous watch is at the door.   638

Fal.: Out, ye rogue! Play out the play: I have much to say in the behalf of that Falstaff. [*Re-enter the Hostess.*]

Host.: O Jesu, my lord, my lord!   642

Fal.: Heigh, heigh! the devil rides upon a fiddlestick: what's the matter?

Host.: The sheriff and all the watch are at the door: they are come to search the house. Shall I let them in?

Fal.: Dost thou hear, Hal? never call a true piece of gold a counterfeit: thou art essentially mad, without seeming so.

Prince: And thou a natural coward, without instinct.   652

Fal.: I deny your major [31]: if you will deny the sheriff, so; if not, let him enter: if I become not a cart as well as another man, a plague on my bringing up! I hope I shall as soon be strangled with a halter as another.   658

Prince: Go, hide thee behind the arras: the rest walk up above. Now, my masters, for a true face and good conscience.

Fal.: Both which I have had: but their date is out, and therefore I'll hide me.   665

Prince: Call in the sheriff. [*Exeunt all except the Prince and Peto.*] [*Enter Sheriff and the Carrier.*]

Now, master sheriff, what is your will with me?

Sher.: First, pardon me, my lord. A hue and cry   670
Hath follow'd certain men unto this house.

Prince: What men?

Sher.· One of them is well known, my gracious lord,
A gross fat man.

Car.:   As fat as butter.

Prince: The man, I do assure you, is not here;   675
For I myself at this time have employ'd him.
And, sheriff, I will engage my word to thee
That I will, by to-morrow dinner-time,
Send him to answer thee, or any man,

---

[28] Sifting-bin. [29] A large drinking-vessel made of leather. [30] I . . . would explain what you mean.

[31] Major premise, with perhaps a pun on *mayor*.

For any thing he shall be charged withal: And so let me entreat you leave the house.   681
Sher.: I will, my lord. There are two gentlemen
Have in this robbery lost three hundred marks.
Prince: It may be so: if he have robb'd these men,
He shall be answerable; and so farewell.
Sher.: Good night, my noble lord.
Prince: I think it is good morrow, is it not?   688
Sher.: Indeed, my lord, I think it be two o'clock. [*Exeunt Sheriff and Carrier.*]   691
Prince: This oily rascal is known as well as Paul's.[32] Go, call him forth.
Peto: Falstaff!—Fast asleep behind the arras, and snorting like a horse. 695
Prince: Hark, how hard he fetches breath. Search his pockets. [*He searcheth his pockets, and findeth certain papers.*] What hast thou found?
Peto: Nothing but papers, my lord.

[32] St. Paul's Cathedral.

Prince: Let's see what they be: read them.   702
Peto: [*Reads.*]
Item, A capon, . . . 2*s.* 2*d.*
Item, Sauce,. 4*d.* 705
Item, Sack, two gallons 5*s.* 8*d.*
Item, Anchovies and sack after supper, . 2*s.* 6*d.*
Item Bread, ... *ob.* 709
Prince: O monstrous! but one half-pennyworth of bread to this intolerable deal of sack! What there is else, keep close; we'll read it at more advantage: there let him sleep till day. I'll to the court in the morning. We must all to the wars, and thy place shall be honourable. I'll procure this fat rogue a charge of foot; and I know his death will be a march of twelve-score.[33] The money shall be paid back again with advantage. Be with me betimes in the morning; and so, good morrow, Peto.
Peto: Good morrow, good my lord. [*Exeunt.*]

[33] Twelve-score paces.

NOTES AND QUESTIONS ON ACT II

1. With regard to Scene iii, may it be said that Percy is careless and impetuous with regard to momentous events, preparing for them far less carefully than the prince and his friends prepare for the really well-planned Gadshill robbery? If so, how does this anticipate later events?

2. Is Scene i justified? If so, in what terms: as necessary exposition? To provide suspense? Could it be omitted without loss? If so, why might we suppose Shakespeare to have included it?

3. Analyze Falstaff's speeches in Scene ii and notice the amount of ironic reversal that is involved: e.g., "I'll starve ere I'll rob a foot further"— as if Falstaff were slaving away at an honest occupation; "Hang ye, gor-bellied knaves, are ye undone? No, ye fat chuffs"—as if Falstaff himself were lean as a rail, etc., etc. Shakespeare, of course, has Falstaff reverse his real role for humorous effect. But what does this constant reversal tell us about the nature of Falstaff's humor? Does it reflect a knowing or a naïve attitude toward the world? Toward himself? Compare the constant re-versals which are the basis of a good deal of the wit in *Lady Windermere's Fan*, and the use to which Wilde puts them.

4. In Falstaff's speech in Scene iv (ll. 176–77) what is the implication of the statement that "there live not three good men unhanged in Eng-

land"? What is the force of the expression "good men" here? What sort of "good men" are hanged? Is this another one of the many hints that Falstaff is constantly suggesting a "transvaluation of values"?

5. Consider Falstaff's speech in Scene iv (ll. 197–206). Notice the number of ways in which each sentence may be read: e.g., he tells Poins, "but I would give a thousand pound I could run as fast as thou canst. You are straight enough in the shoulders, you care not who sees your back: call you that backing of your friends?" Primarily, of course, Falstaff is retorting to the charge that he ran away, by means of the child's repartee of "You did it too." He does not bother to deny that he ran away; he only wishes that he could run as fast as Poins can. Poins has a good enough back: he wouldn't care whether anyone saw *him* run away. Poins cares only for the figure he cuts and for his own skin—such matters as loyalty to friends are beyond him. Perhaps his style of backing up his friends is to show them his back. But in expressing the wish that he could run away as fast as Poins, Falstaff by implication admits the charge that he has run away.

In the same way, his statement, "I am a rogue, if I drunk today," is primarily an emphatic way of asserting his thirst. But taken literally, it is a gross and obvious falsehood. Falstaff hardly intends to be taken literally, and when he is taken literally, he does not attempt to argue the point: "All's one for that," he says. But the literal meaning is perfectly true: Falstaff is a rogue—though a very pleasant rogue.

It is with precisely this same expression that Falstaff begins the account of his adventures at Gadshill: "I am a rogue, if I were not at half-sword with a dozen of them two hours together." And the expression is used to introduce what, it must be obvious to any of his hearers, is another barefaced lie. Falstaff would hardly attempt seriously to convince Hal that he and his three companions had actually fought with a "hundred." Does not the subsequent piling up of the exaggeration surely point up the fact that Falstaff is making no real attempt to convince his hearers?

What, then, does Falstaff intend? To exaggerate in order to make a good story? To prove that he is really unruffled by events by showing that he is able to drink and lie as powerfully as ever? To tell a story that will be certain to draw contradictions from the prince and thus make the prince reveal what really happened to him and Poins? To brazen out his humiliation by turning the joke on himself—that is, by pretending to make a hero of himself, and yet, by so obviously exaggerating the heroism to absurdity that he shows he is perfectly aware of the total situation, and indeed remains the master of the situation? Or is Falstaff's motive a combination of a number of these possibilities? Suppose Falstaff's brazening out of the situations were done without his wit: how would the tone of Scene iv be changed?

Falstaff has been charged with being a coward and has been vehemently defended against the charge, first by Maurice Morgann in the later eighteenth century, and since that time by numerous critics on down to the present day. Actually the charge and the defense tend to miss the whole point.

If it is a little absurd to attempt to prove in the face of the Gadshill scene that Falstaff is a valiant man, it is only a little less absurd to use the scene to prove Falstaff's cowardice. Even a thief possessed of a good measure of personal valor will make good his escape if there is a good chance that standing his ground will increase the risk of his identification or capture. Even a rather brave thief, in Falstaff's position, might have run, for to be attacked themselves was the last thing that the successful thieves counted on.

Falstaff is no braver than he should be, doubtless, but he is certainly not a fool. He knows that a bag of gold filched without too much risk is one thing, but that the same bag, if it involves the risk of hanging, is quite another. He knows. on the other hand, as he recovers his breath after making good his escape, that it is a likely tale to turn up with—this story that he had made good the robbery and then by strange coincidence was at once robbed himself. He hacks his sword and tickles his nose with spear grass to prepare supporting evidence for a story that—whatever its merits—will have a better chance than the other. But Falstaff knows how much that story will bear—he sizes up the situation quickly and expertly—and he is able to shift his ground rapidly enough to remain in command of the situation at the end. For, when the prince in triumph asks, "What trick, what device, what starting-hole, canst thou now find out to hide thee from this open and apparent shame?" Falstaff is not even for a moment at a loss. His story about being brave by instinct is absurd, of course (he uses *instinct* as if it were a technical term, without moral significance, the use of which could remove his act from the realm of moral significance); but the "instinct" that prompts the story is not absurd at all. Falstaff is completely at home now. He never lacks a device. The gold is safe, after all, he now knows. First things first. The lads have the money; the joke has been a good joke; and Falstaff has capped the joke for them. "What, shall we be merry! shall we have a play extempore?"

6. How does the byplay between Percy and his wife (Scene iii) balance the merriment of the tavern scenes? What does it tell the reader about the real attitude of these two people to each other? Does Percy love his wife?

7. Prince Hal has been accused of snobbish cruelty in his treatment of Francis, the serving boy. Discuss the merits of this charge. Does the Francis scene have any real function in the play? Does the humor remind you in any way of that found in Plautus's *The Twin Menaechmi?* Does the prince's speech suggest modern "double-talk" comedy?

8. The speech which Falstaff as "king" makes to his errant son would be doubly amusing to an Elizabethan audience because it involves a clever parody of the style of John Lyly's short fiction *Euphues,* the highly artificial and elaborate style of which had recently been the rage in England. For an audience unfamiliar with *Euphues,* the element of parody, of course, is lost; but how are the elaborate formality, the carefully contrived antitheses, the references to "unnatural natural history," and the sententious treatment of the obvious, appropriate to a take-off on the formality of the

court? Is the speech typical of Falstaff's humor in that it scores points against the pretensions and hypocrisies always associated with a world which takes itself with too much seriousness? What would be shown, then, by the fact that Hal, when he is acting the part of the king, concludes his speech in the same Euphuistic style?

9. Notice, too, that the theme of the prince's keeping bad company appears as the theme of the "play extempore," and that Falstaff, when he plays the role of Hal, is still occupied with a defense of himself. The defense is made in jest; it is made for the occasion. To what extent, however, may it be taken as a serious defense?

10. What does Shakespeare gain, if anything, by having, at the height of the merriment, a messenger from the court bring the prince news that the rebellion has broken out? What do we learn about Falstaff from his reaction to the news? What about Prince Hal, from his reaction? Is Falstaff serious when he asks Hal ". . . art thou not horribly afraid"?

11. When the sheriff calls at the tavern seeking Falstaff, Falstaff's fate rests in the prince's hands. Mr. Dover Wilson, in a recent book, argues that Falstaff's speech (ll. 653–58) is "a magnificent display of stoutness of heart, which looks Death straight in the eyes without blinking or turning aside." But does Falstaff really have any doubt as to what the prince will do?

12. Falstaff and his companions, as we have seen, have most of the act. The relatively short Scene iii seems intended, on the surface, to do little more than remind us of the political activities which are shortly to become more important in the play. We see a further contrast between Hal and Hotspur, and we see a further step taken in one "plot" while the other "plot" is almost completed.

Perhaps, however, Shakespeare is doing a little more than merely, as it were, reserving a future place for Hotspur. As Hotspur reads the letter, for instance, we see, in the relationship among the conspirators, certain parallels to the relationship among the hold-up men. The letter-writer says, for instance, that Hotspur's plot is "too light" to meet "so great an opposition"; when Peto had asked, "How many be there of them?" and Gadshill had answered "Some eight or ten," Falstaff had replied, "'Zounds, will they not rob us?" (Sc. ii, 81). That is, both great and small plots tend, ironically, to evoke the same thoughts and attitudes.

The comparison goes a step further: just after the passage quoted above, Hotspur calls the writer "cowardly hind" and "frosty-spirited rogue"; and just after Falstaff expresses his fear, Hal taunts him with being a coward. Then, with some shift of characters, the parallel becomes more complex. When he first enters after the robbery, Falstaff introduces a new refrain, "A plague on all cowards!" (he says it four times), addressing his words to the men he thought had *not* participated in the hold-up—Hal and Poins (here *they* are comparable to the writer of the letter to Hotspur). And a great deal more is said about cowardice. Does Shakespeare not appear, then, to be carrying on the theme of cowardice which runs through all the rest of the act and which, as we have seen (see question 5 above), is a very complex one? Not only is cowardice not easy to define, but, ironically, the same charges are called forth by both comic and serious plots.

Hotspur's next sentence appears to provide a still more marked continuation of a theme that runs through the first two acts: his friends, he says, are "*true* and constant . . . good friends . . . very good friends,"and the writer of the letter is "an *infidel*." It is difficult not to believe that Shakespeare is here picking up a concept which was first introduced in Act I, as we saw, when Falstaff said that the "*true* prince" might become a "*false* thief" (see Act I, question 7). If these words were used only in these two places, we would have to be most hesitant about trying to find a connection between them, but the fact is that there is a sort of *true-false* chorus running all through Act II. In Scene i the Chamberlain says to Gadshill, "I know thou worshippest Saint Nicholas as *truly* as a man of *falsehood* may" (ll. 79–82); Gadshill says, ". . . I am a *true* man," and the Chamberlain replies, ". . . rather . . . you are a *false* thief" (ll. 119–21). In Scene ii Falstaff says it might be a good thing to become a "*true* man," especially when "thieves cannot be *true* to one another!" (ll. 29, 36). After the first robbery, Hal comments to Poins that the "thieves have bound the *true* men" (Sc. ii, 120). Then comes the Hotspur scene which we have already quoted. Next we see Hal informing Falstaff what had actually happened at the robbery—and what phrase does Falstaff keep repeating in his following speech? "The *true* prince"—three times, an epithet true in one sense and, in another, ironic. Hal playfully echoes the phrase a little later (Sc. iv, 395), and then Bardolph, referring to the blood that came from their "tickled" noses, says Falstaff would have them "swear it was the blood of *true* men" (l. 408). In the mock-trial scene Falstaff avers that the complaints against him are *false* and refers to himself as "*true* Jack Falstaff" (ll. 583 and 626). Finally, when, a moment later, the sheriff arrives, Falstaff exhorts Hal, ". . . never call a *true* piece of gold a *counterfeit*" (ll. 648–49); but he laughs at himself when Hal, about to admit the sheriff and his men, says, "Now . . . for a *true* face . . ." (l. 661).

In some of these passages the words *true* and *false* are clearly meant in a literal sense; elsewhere they are ironic. But whatever the tone, the very frequency of use—which the actors probably called attention to by their reading of the lines—suggests that the words occur by design rather than by accident. What might be the design?

May it not be a reminder, perhaps, of the complexities one runs into when one sets out to define *true* and *false* (like the difficulties presented by the word *coward*)? What *is* truth? If Falstaff's fellow-hold-up men do not observe their commitments to him, they are in one sense not *true;* if Hotspur's party do not stick to him, they are not *true.* But if the associates are not *true* to Falstaff and Hotspur respectively, are they not, in another sense, the more *true* to the king? It may be just to suggest that here we have a *relativistic* view of what is true and false; if that is so, it immediately leads us to ask the question, "Is Shakespeare, in presenting the complexities of truth, going to be content to say that it is relative, or, in the political world about which he writes here, will he present, finally, an *absolute truth?*" The answer, of course, we must find in the rest of the play, and, it is clear, we must find it in the conduct of Hal. In what way will he be *true?* Or will he be *true* in several ways at once?

13. Notice the speech in Scene iv in which Hal makes fun of Hotspur (ll. 136–46). In one sense the ridicule might be interpreted as what we now call a "defense mechanism." Is there, on the other hand, anything valid in the ridicule? Does Hal hit off any Hotspur foibles with skill? Note the relationship of this speech to the contents of Scene iii. May Hal's speech, "Give my roan horse a drench" be taken as an echo of Hotspur's "That roan shall be my throne"? (ll. 143–44 and iii, 83).

14. We have already seen Falstaff making a pun on *heir apparent* (see Act I, question 4). Note that Falstaff keeps using this phrase throughout Act II. Find the passages in question. Note that, although at all these places the words might be used literally, they could also be read in an ironic sense. A skilled actor could give them very effective emphasis. What would be suggested by such emphasis?

ACT III

[SCENE I—Bangor. The Archdeacon's house.]

[*Enter Hotspur, Worcester, Mortimer, and Glendower.*]
Mort.: These promises are fair, the parties sure,
And our induction full of prosperous hope.
Hot.: Lord Mortimer, and cousin Glendower,
Will you sit down? 4
And uncle Worcester: a plague upon it!
I have forgot the map.
Glend.: No, here it is.
Sit, cousin Percy; sit, good cousin Hotspur,
For by that name as oft as Lancaster
Doth speak of you, his cheek looks pale and with
A rising sigh he wisheth you in heaven.
Hot.: And you in hell as often as he hears 11
Owen Glendower spoke of.
Glend.: I cannot blame him: at my nativity
The front of heaven was full of fiery shapes,

Of burning cressets [1]; and at my birth
The frame and huge foundation of the earth 16
Shaked like a coward.
Hot.: Why, so it would have done at the same season, if your mother's cat had but kittened, though yourself had never been born.
Glend.: I say the earth did shake when I was born. 22
Hot.: And I say the earth was not of my mind,
If you suppose as fearing you it shook.
Glend.: The heavens were all on fire, the earth did tremble. 25
Hot.: O, then the earth shook to see the heavens on fire,
And not in fear of your nativity.
Diseased nature oftentimes breaks forth
In strange eruptions; oft the teeming earth
Is with a kind of colic pinch'd and vex'd 31
By the imprisoning of unruly wind
Within her womb; which, for enlargement striving,
Shakes the old beldam [2] earth and topples down
Steeples and moss-grown towers. At your birth

[1] Lamps on poles. [2] Grandmother.

Our grandam earth, having this distem-
perature,   35
In passion shook.
Glend.:   Cousin, of many men
I do not bear these crossings. Give me
leave
To tell you once again that at my birth
The front of heaven was full of fiery
shapes,
The goats ran from the mountains, and
the herds   40
Were strangely clamorous to the frighted
fields.
These signs have mark'd me extraordi-
nary;
And all the courses of my life do show
I am not in the roll of common men.
Where is he living, clipp'd in with the
sea   45
That chides the banks of England, Scot-
land, Wales,
Which calls me pupil, or hath read to
me?
And bring him out that is but woman's
son
Can trace me in the tedious ways of art
And hold me pace in deep experiments.
Hot.: I think there's no man speaks
better Welsh.   51
I'll to dinner.
Mort.: Peace, cousin Percy; you will
make him mad.
Glend.: I can call spirits from the
vasty deep.
Hot.: Why, so can I, or so can any
man;   55
But will they come when you do call for
them?
Glend.: Why, I can teach you, cousin,
to command
The devil.
Hot.: And I can teach thee, coz, to
shame the devil
By telling truth: tell truth and shame
the devil.   60
If thou have power to raise him, bring
him hither,
And I'll be sworn I have power to shame
him hence.
O, while you live, tell truth and shame
the devil!

Mort.: Come, come, no more of this
unprofitable chat.
Glend.: Three times hath Henry Bol-
ingbroke made head   65
Against my power; thrice from the banks
of Wye
And sandy-bottom'd Severn have I sent
him
Bootless [3] home and weather-beaten
back.
Hot.: Home without boots, and in
foul weather too!
How 'scapes he agues, in the devil's
name?   70
Glend.: Come, here's the map: shall
we divide our right
According to our threefold order ta'en?
Mort.: The archdeacon hath divided it
Into three limits very equally:
England, from Trent and Severn
hitherto,   75
By south and east is to my part as-
sign'd:
All westward, Wales beyond the Severn
shore,
And all the fertile land within that
bound,
To Owen Glendower: and, dear coz, to
you
The remnant northward, lying off from
Trent.   80
And our indentures tripartite are drawn;
Which being sealed interchangeably,
A business that this night may execute,
To-morrow, cousin Percy, you and I
And my good Lord of Worcester will set
forth   85
To meet your father and the Scottish
power,
As is appointed us, at Shrewsbury.
My father Glendower is not ready yet,
Nor shall we need his help these fourteen
days.
Within that space you may have drawn
together   90
Your tenants, friends and neighbouring
gentlemen.
Glend.: A shorter time shall send me
to you, lords:

[3] Without profit.

And in my conduct shall your ladies come;
From whom you now must steal and take no leave,
For there will be a world of water shed
Upon the parting of your wives and you.   96
Hot.: Methinks my moiety, north from Burton here,
In quantity equals not one of yours:
See how this river comes me cranking [4] in,
And cuts me from the best of all my land
A huge half-moon, a monstrous cantle [5] out.   101
I'll have the current in this place damm'd up;
And here the smug and silver Trent shall run
In a new channel, fair and evenly;
It shall not wind with such a deep indent,   105
To rob me of so rich a bottom here.
Glend.: Not wind? it shall, it must; you see it doth.
Mort.: Yea, but
Mark how he bears his course, and runs me up
With like advantage on the other side;
Gelding the opposed continent as much
As on the other side it takes from you.
Wor.: Yea, but a little charge will trench him here   113
And on this north side win this cape of land;
And then he runs straight and even.
Hot.: I'll have it so: a little charge will do it.   116
Glend.: I'll not have it alter'd.
Hot.:   Will not you?
Glend.: No, nor you shall not.
Hot.:   Who shall say me nay?
Glend.: Why, that will I.
Hot.: Let me not understand you, then; speak it in Welsh.   120
Glend.: I can speak English, lord, as well as you;

For I was train'd up in the English court;
Where, being but young, I framed to the harp
Many as English ditty lovely well
And gave the tongue a helpful ornament,
A virtue that was never seen in you. 126
Hot.: Marry,
And I am glad of it with all my heart:
I had rather be a kitten and cry mew
Than one of these same metre ballad-mongers;   130
I had rather hear a brazen canstick [6] turn'd,
Or a dry wheel grate on the axle-tree;
And that would set my teeth nothing on edge,
Nothing so much as mincing poetry:
'Tis like the forced gait of a shuffling nag.   135
Glend.: Come, you shall have Trent turn'd.
Hot.: I do not care: I'll give thrice so much land
To any well-deserving friend;
But in the way of bargain, mark ye me,
I'll cavil on the ninth part of a hair. 140
Are the indentures drawn? shall we be gone?
Glend.: The moon shines fair; you may away by night:
I'll haste the writer and withal
Break with your wives of your departure hence: 144
I am afraid my daughter will run mad,
So much she doteth on her Mortimer.
                [*Exit.*]
Mort.: Fie, cousin Percy! how you cross my father!
Hot.: I cannot choose: sometime he angers me
With telling me of the moldwarp [7] and the ant,
Of the dreamer Merlin and his prophecies,   150
And of a dragon and a finless fish,
A clip-wing'd griffin and a moulten raven,

---

[4] Winding. [5] Corner-piece.

[6] A brazen candlestick turned on the lathe.
[7] Mole.

A couching lion and a ramping cat,
And such a deal of skimble-skamble [8]
 stuff
As puts me from my faith. I tell you
 what: 155
He held me last night at least nine hours
In reckoning up the several devils'
 names
That were his lackeys: I cried "hum,"
 and "well, go to,"
But mark'd him not a word. O, he is as
 tedious
As a tired horse, a railing wife;   160
Worse than a smoky house: I had
 rather live
With cheese and garlic in a windmill,
 far,
Than feed on cates and have him talk
 to me
In any summer-house in Christendom.
 Mort.: In faith, he is a worthy gentle-
 man,   -   165
Exceedingly well read, and profited
In strange concealments, valiant as a
 lion
And wondrous affable and as bountiful
As mines of India. Shall I tell you,
 cousin?
He holds your temper in a high respect
And curbs himself even of his natural
 scope   171
When you come 'cross his humour; faith,
 he does:
I warrant you, that man is not alive
Might so have tempted him as you have
 done,   174
Without the taste of danger and reproof:
But do not use it oft, let me entreat you.
 Wor.: In faith, my lord, you are too
 wilful-blame [9];
And since your coming hither have done
 enough
To put him quite beside his patience.
You must needs learn, lord, to amend
 this fault: 180
Though sometimes it show greatness,
 courage, blood,—
And that's the dearest grace it renders
 you, —

Yet oftentimes it doth present harsh
 rage,
Defect of manners, want of government,
Pride, haughtiness, opinion and disdain:
The least of which haunting a nobleman
Loseth men's hearts and leaves behind a
 stain   187
Upon the beauty of all parts besides,
Beguiling them of commendation.[10]
 Hot.: Well, I am school'd: good man-
 ners be your speed!   190
Here come our wives, and let us take
 our leave.
 [*Re-enter Glendower with the ladies.*]
 Mort.: This is the deadly spite that
 angers me;
My wife can speak no English, I no
 Welsh.
 Glend.: My daughter weeps: she will
 not part with you;
She'll be a soldier too, she'll to the wars.
 Mort.: Good father, tell her that she
 and my aunt Percy   196
Shall follow in your conduct speedily.
 [*Glendower speaks to her in Welsh, and she
 answers him in the same.*]
 Glend.: She is desperate here; a peev-
 ish self-will'd harlotry,[11] one that no
 persuasion can do good upon. [*The lady
 speaks in Welsh.*]   201
 Mort.: I understand thy looks: that
 pretty Welsh
Which thou pour'st down from these
 swelling heavens
I am too perfect in; and, but for shame,
In such a parley should I answer thee.
 [*The lady speaks again in Welsh.*]
I understand thy kisses and thou mine,
And that's a feeling disputation: 207
But I will never be a truant, love,
Till I have learn'd thy language; for thy
 tongue
Makes Welsh as sweet as ditties highly
 penn'd,   210
Sung by a fair queen in a summer's
 bower,
With ravishing division, to her lute.
 Glend.: Nay, if you melt, then will

she run mad. [*The lady speaks again in Welsh.*]

Mort.: O, I am ignorance itself in this!

Glend.: She bids you on the wanton [12] rushes lay you down   215
And rest your gentle head upon her lap,
And she will sing the song that pleaseth you
And on your eyelids crown the god of sleep,
Charming your blood with pleasing heaviness,
Making such difference 'twixt wake and sleep   220
As is the difference betwixt day and night
The hour before the heavenly-harness'd team
Begins his golden progress in the east.

Mort.: With all my heart I'll sit and hear her sing:
By that time will our book, I think, be drawn.   225

Glend.: Do so;
And those musicians that shall play to you
Hang in the air a thousand leagues from hence,
And straight they shall be here: sit, and attend.

Hot.: Come, Kate, thou art perfect in lying down: come, quick, quick, that I may lay my head in thy lap.   232

Lady P.: Go, ye giddy goose. [*The music plays.*]

Hot.: Now I perceive the devil understands Welsh;
And 'tis no marvel he is so humorous.[13]
By'r lady, he is a good musician.   237

Lady P.: Then should you be nothing but musical, for you are altogether governed by humours. Lie still, ye thief, and hear the lady sing in Welsh.   241

Hot.: I had rather hear Lady, my brach,[14] howl in Irish.

Lady P.: Wouldst thou have thy head broken?   245

Hot.: No.

Lady P.: Then be still.

Hot.: Neither; 'tis a woman's fault.

Lady P.: Now God help thee! What's that?

Hot.: Peace! she sings. [*Here the lady sings a Welsh song.*]   252

Hot.: Come, Kate, I'll have your song too.

Lady P.: Not mine, in good sooth.

Hot.: Not yours, in good sooth! Heart! you swear like a comfit-maker's [15] wife. "Not you, in good sooth," and "as true as I live," and "as God shall mend me," and "as sure as day."   260
And givest such sarcenet surety [16] for thy oaths,
As if thou never walk'st further than Finsbury.
Swear me, Kate, like a lady as thou art,
A good mouth-filling oath, and leave "in sooth,"
And such protest of pepper-gingerbread,
To velvet-guards and Sunday-citizens.
Come, sing.   267

Lady P.: I will not sing.

Hot.: 'Tis the next way to turn tailor, or be red-breast teacher.[17] An the indentures be drawn, I'll away within these two hours; and so, come in when ye will. [*Exit.*]   273

Glend.: Come, come, Lord Mortimer; you are as slow
As hot Lord Percy is on fire to go.
By this our book is drawn; we'll but seal, and then to horse immediately.   277

Mort. With all my heart. [*Exeunt.*]

[SCENE II—London. The palace.]

[*Enter the King, Prince of Wales, and others.*]

King: Lords, give us leave; the Prince of Wales and I
Must have some private conference: but be near at hand,
For we shall presently have need of you.
          [*Exeunt Lords.*]
I know not whether God will have it so,

---

[12] Luxurious.   [13] Whimsical, capricious.
[14] Bitch, named Lady.

[15] Confectioner's.   [16] Feeble surety—sarcenet was a light silk cloth.   [17] Tailors were noted for singing at their work.

For some displeasing service I have
done, 5
That, in his secret doom, out of my
blood
He'll breed revengement and a scourge
for me;
But thou dost in thy passages of life
Make me believe that thou art only
mark'd
For the hot vengeance and the rod of
heaven 10
To punish my mistreadings. Tell me else,
Could such inordinate and low desires,
Such poor, such bare, such lewd, such
mean attempts,
Such barren pleasures, rude society,
As thou art match'd withal and grafted
to, 15
Accompany the greatness of thy blood
And hold their level with thy princely
heart?
 Prince: So please your majesty, I
would I could
Quit all offences with as clear excuse
As well as I am doubtless I can purge
Myself of many I am charged withal:
Yet such extenuation let me beg, 22
As, in reproof of many tales devised,
Which oft the ear of greatness needs
must hear,
By smiling pick-thanks [1] and base news-
mongers, 25
I may, for some things true, wherein my
youth
Hath faulty wander'd and irregular,
Find pardon on my true submission.
 King: God pardon thee! yet let me
wonder, Harry,
At thy affections, which do hold a wing
Quite from the flight of all thy ancestors.
Thy place in council thou hast rudely
lost, 32
Which by thy younger brother is sup-
plied,
And art almost an alien to the hearts
Of all the court and princes of my blood:
The hope and expectation of thy time
Is ruin'd, and the soul of every man
Prophetically doth forethink thy fall.

[1] Tattling sycophants.

Had I so lavish of my presence been,
So common-hackney'd in the eyes of
men, 40
So stale and cheap to vulgar company,
Opinion, that did help me to the crown,
Had still kept loyal to possession
And left me in reputeless banishment,
A fellow of no mark nor likelihood. 45
By being seldom seen, I could not stir
But like a comet I was wonder'd at;
That men would tell their children "This
is he";
Others would say "Where, which is
Bolingbroke?"
And then I stole all courtesy from
heaven, 50
And dress'd myself in such humility
That I did pluck allegiance from men's
hearts,
Loud shouts and salutations from their
mouths,
Even in the presence of the crowned
king.
Thus did I keep my person fresh and
new; 55
My presence, like a robe pontifical,
Ne'er seen but wonder'd at: and so my
state,
Seldom but sumptuous, showed like a
feast
And wan [2] by rareness such solemnity.
The skipping king, he ambled up and
down 60
With shallow jesters and rash bavin [3]
wits,
Soon kindled and soon burnt; carded [4]
his state,
Mingled his royalty with capering fools,
Had his great name profaned with their
scorns
And gave his countenance, against his
name, 65
To laugh at gibing boys and stand the
push
Of every beardless vain comparative,
Grew a companion to the common
streets,

[2] Won. [3] Brush-wood faggots—wits as
easily lighted and as soon burnt out as kin-
dling wood. [4] Debased—to "card" was to
adulterate by mixing.

Enfeoff'd himself to popularity;
That, being daily swallow'd by men's
eyes,   70
They surfeited with honey and began
To loathe the taste of sweetness, whereof
a little
More than a little is by much too much.
So when he had occasion to be seen,
He was but as the cuckoo is in June,
Heard, not regarded; seen, but with such
eyes   76
As, sick and blunted with community,[5]
Afford no extraordinary gaze,
Such as is bent on sun-like majesty
When it shines seldom in admiring eyes;
But rather drowsed and hung their eye-
lids down,   81
Slept in his face and render'd such aspect
As cloudy [6] men use to their adversaries,
Being with his presence glutted, gorged
and full.
And in that very line, Harry, standest
thou;   85
For thou hast lost thy princely privilege
With vile participation: not an eye
But is a-weary of thy common sight,
Save mine, which hath desired to see
thee more;
Which now doth that I would not have
it do,   90
Make blind itself with foolish tender-
ness.
Prince: I shall hereafter, my thrice
gracious lord,
Be more myself.
King: For all the world
As thou art to this hour was Richard
then
When I from France set foot at Ravens-
purgh,   95
And even as I was then is Percy now.
Now, by my sceptre and my soul to boot,
He hath more worthy interest to the
state
Than thou the shadow of succession;
For of no right,[7] nor colour like to right,
He doth fill fields with harness in the
realm,   101

Turns head against the lion's armed
jaws,
And, being no more in debt to years
than thou,
Leads ancient lords and reverend bish-
ops on
To bloody battles and to bruising arms.
What never-dying honour hath he got
Against renowned Douglas! whose high
deeds,   107
Whose hot incursions and great name in
arms
Holds from all soldiers chief majority [8]
And military title capital   110
Through all the kingdoms that acknowl-
edge Christ:
Thrice hath this Hotspur, Mars in
swathling clothes,
This infant warrior, in his enterprizes
Discomfited great Douglas, ta'en him
once,
Enlarged him and made a friend of him,
To fill the mouth of deep defiance up
And shake the peace and safety of our
throne.   117
And what say you to this? Percy, North-
umberland,
The Archbishop's grace of York, Doug-
las, Mortimer,
Capitulate against us [9] and are up.   120
But wherefore do I tell these news to
thee?
Why, Harry, do I tell thee of my foes,
Which art my near'st and dearest
enemy?
Thou that art like enough, through
vassal fear,   124
Base inclination and the start of spleen,
To fight against me under Percy's pay,
To dog his heels and curtsy at his frowns,
To show how much thou art degenerate.
Prince: Do not think so; you shall not
find it so:
And God forgive them that so much
have sway'd   130
Your majesty's good thoughts away
from me!
I will redeem all this on Percy's head

[5] Familiarity. [6] Sullen. [7] For though without any legal right.

[8] Preëminence. [9] Draw up their grievances
against us.

And in the closing of some glorious day
Be bold to tell you that I am your son;
When I will wear a garment all of blood
And stain my favours [10] in a bloody
mask,   136
Which, wash'd away, shall scour my
shame with it;
And that shall be the day, whene'er it
lights,
That this same child of honour and re-
nown,
This gallant Hotspur, this all-praised
knight,   140
And your unthought-of Harry chance to
meet.
For every honour sitting on his helm,
Would they were multitudes, and on my
head
My shames redoubled! for the time will
come
That I shall make this northern youth
exchange   145
His glorious deeds for my indignities.
Percy is but my factor,[11] good my lord,
To engross up glorious deeds on my be-
half;
And I will call him to so strict account,
That he shall render every glory up,
Yea, even the slightest worship of his
time,   151
Or I will tear the reckoning from his heart.
This, in the name of God, I promise here:
The which if He be pleased I shall per-
form,
I do beseech your majesty may salve
The long-grown wounds of my intem-
perance: 156
If not, the end of life cancels all bands;
And I will die a hundred thousand
deaths
Ere break the smallest parcel of this vow.
    King: A hundred thousand rebels die
    in this: 160
Thou shalt have charge and sovereign
trust herein. [*Enter Blunt.*]
How now, good Blunt? thy looks are full
of speed.
    Blunt: So hath the business that I
come to speak of.

Lord Mortimer of Scotland hath sent
word
That Douglas and the English rebels met
The eleventh of this month at Shrews-
bury: 166
A mighty and a fearful head they are,
If promises be kept on every hand,
As ever offer'd foul play in a state.
    King: The Earl of Westmoreland set
    forth to-day;   170
With him my son, Lord John of Lan-
caster;
For this advertisement is five days old:
On Wednesday next, Harry, you shall
set forward;
On Thursday we ourselves will march:
our meeting
Is Bridgenorth: and, Harry, you shall
march   175
Through Gloucestershire; by which ac-
count,
Our business valued, some twelve days
hence
Our general forces at Bridgenorth shall
meet.
Our hands are full of business: let's
away;   179
Advantage feeds him fat, while men delay.   [*Exeunt.*]

[SCENE III—Eastcheap. The Boar's-
Head Tavern.]

[*Enter Falstaff and Bardolph.*]

Fal.: Bardolph, am I not fallen away
vilely since this last action? do I not
bate? do I not dwindle? Why, my skin
hangs about me like an old lady's loose
gown; I am withered like an old apple-
john.[1] Well, I'll repent, and that suddenly, while I am in some liking; I shall
be out of heart shortly, and then I shall
have no strength to repent. An I have
not forgotten what the inside of a church
is made of, I am a peppercorn, a brew-
er's horse: the inside of a church! Company, villainous company, hath been the
spoil of me.   14

[10] Features. [11] Agent.

[1] A kind of apple, the skin of which
shrivels in keeping.

Ban'.: Sir Jonn, you are so fretful, you cannot live long.

Fal.: Why, there is it: come sing me a song; make me merry. I was as virtuously given as a gentleman need to be; virtuous enough; swore little; diced not above seven times a week; paid money that I borrowed, three or four times; lived well and in good compass: and now I live out of all order, out of all compass.   25

Bard.: Why, you are so fat, Sir John, that you must needs be out of all compass, out of all reasonable compass, Sir John.   29

Fal.: Do thou amend thy face, and I'll amend my life: thou art our admiral,[2] thou bearest the lantern in the poop, but 'tis in the nose of thee; thou art the Knight of the Burning Lamp.   34

Bard.: Why, Sir John, my face does you no harm.

Fal.: No, I'll be sworn; I make as good use of it as many a man doth of a Death's-head or a memento mori: I never see thy face but I think upon hellfire and Dives that lived in purple; for there he is in his robes, burning, burning. If thou wert any way given to virtue, I would swear by thy face; my oath should be " By this fire, that's God's angel"; but thou art altogether given over; and wert indeed, but for the light in thy face, the son of utter darkness. When thou rannest up Gadshill in the night to catch my horse, if I did not think thou hadst been an ignis fatuus or a ball of wildfire, there's no purchase in money. O, thou art a perpetual triumph, an everlasting bonfire-light! Thou hast saved me a thousand marks in links and torches, walking with thee in the night betwixt tavern and tavern: but the sack that thou hast drunk me would have bought me lights as good cheap at the dearest chandler's in Europe. I have maintained that salamander of yours with fire any time this two and thirty years; God reward me for it.   63

Bard.: 'Sblood, I would my face were in your belly!

Fal.: God-a-mercy! so should I be sure to be heart-burned. [*Enter Hostess.*] How now, Dame Partlet the hen! have you inquired yet who picked my pocket?

Host.: Why, Sir John, what do you think, Sir John? do you think I keep thieves in my house? I have searched, I have inquired, so has my husband, man by man, boy by boy, servant by servant: the tithe of a hair was never lost in my house before.   76

Fal.: Ye lie, hostess: Bardolph was shaved and lost many a hair; and I'll be sworn my pocket was picked. Go to, you are a woman, go.   80

Host.: Who, I? no; I defy thee: God's light, I was never called so in mine own house before.

Fal.: Go to, I know you well enough.

Host.: No, Sir John; you do not know me, Sir John. I know you, Sir John: you owe me money, Sir John; and now you pick a quarrel to beguile me of it: I bought you a dozen of shirts to your back.   90

Fal.: Dowlas,[3] filthy dowlas: I have given them away to bakers' wives, and they have made bolters of them.

Host.: Now, as I am a true woman, holland[4] of eight shillings an ell. You owe money here besides, Sir John, for your diet and by-drinkings, and money lent you, four and twenty pound.   98

Fal.: He had his part of it; let him pay.

Host.: He? alas, he is poor; he hath nothing.

Fal.: How! poor? look upon his face; what call you rich? let them coin his nose, let them coin his cheeks: I'll not pay a denier. What, will you make a younker[5] of me? shall I not take mine ease in mine inn but I shall have my pocket picked? I have lost a seal-ring of my grandfather's worth forty mark. 110

Host.: O Jesu, I have heard the prince

---

[2] Admiral's ship, flagship.

[3] A kind of coarse linen. [4] Finely woven lawn. [5] A greenhorn, a "sucker."

tell him, I know not how oft, that that ring was copper!

Fal.: How! the prince is a Jack, a sneak-cup: 'sblood, an he were here, I would cudgel him like a dog, if he would say so. [*Enter the Prince and Peto, marching, and Falstaff meets them playing on his truncheon like a fife.*] How now, lad! is the wind in that door, i' faith? must we all march?   121

Bard.: Yea, two and two, Newgate fashion.[6]

Host.: My lord, I pray you, hear me.

Prince: What sayest thou, Mistress Quickly? How doth thy husband? I love him well; he is an honest man.   127

Host.: Good my lord, hear me.

Fal.: Prithee, let her alone, and list to me.   130

Prince: What sayest thou, Jack?

Fal.: The other night I fell asleep here behind the arras and had my pocket picked: this house is turned bawdy-house; they pick pockets.   135

Prince: What didst thou lose, Jack?

Fal.: Wilt thou believe me, Hal? three or four bonds of forty pound a-piece, and a seal-ring of my grand-father's.   140

Prince: A trifle, some eight-penny matter.

Host.: So I told him, my lord; and I said I heard your grace say so: and, my lord, he speaks most vilely of you, like a foul-mouthed man as he is; and said he would cudgel you.   147

Prince: What! he did not?

Host.: There's neither faith, truth, nor womanhood in me else.   150

Fal.: There's no more faith in thee than in a stewed prune; nor no more truth in thee than in a drawn fox [7]; and for womanhood, Maid Marian may be the deputy's wife of the ward to thee. Go, you thing, go.   156

Host.: Say, what thing? what thing?

Fal.: What thing! why, a thing to thank God on.   159

[6] Like criminals conveyed to Newgate prison. [7] A fox drawn from his hole, trying to throw the dogs off his trail.

Host.: I am no thing to thank God on, I would thou shouldst know it; I am an honest man's wife: and, setting thy knighthood aside, thou art a knave to call me so.   164

Fal.: Setting thy womanhood aside, thou art a beast to say otherwise.

Host.: Say, what beast, thou knave, thou?

Fal.: What beast! why, an otter.

Prince: An otter, Sir John! why an otter?   171

Fal.: Why, she's neither fish nor flesh; a man knows not where to have her.

Host.: Thou art an unjust man in saying so: thou or any man knows where to have me, thou knave, thou!   176

Prince: Thou sayest true, hostess; and he slanders thee most grossly.

Host.: So he doth you, my lord; and said this other day you ought [8] him a thousand pound.   181

Prince: Sirrah, do I owe you a thousand pound?

Fal.: A thousand pound, Hal! a million: thy love is worth a million: thou owest me thy love.   186

Host.: Nay, my lord, he called you Jack, and said he would cudgel you.

Fal.: Did I, Bardolph?

Bard.: Indeed, Sir John, you said so.

Fal.: Yea, if he said my ring was copper.   192

Prince: I say 'tis copper: darest thou be as good as thy word now?

Fal.: Why, Hal, thou knowest, as thou art but man, I dare: but as thou art prince, I fear thee as I fear the roaring of the lion's whelp.   198

Prince: And why not as the lion?

Fal.: The king himself is to be feared as the lion: dost thou think I'll fear thee as I fear thy father? nay, an I do, I pray God my girdle break.   203

Prince: O, if it should, how would thy guts fall about thy knees! But, sirrah, there's no room for faith, truth, nor honesty in this bosom of thine; it is filled up with guts and midriff. Charge an

[8] Owed.

honest woman with picking thy pocket! why, thou impudent, embossed [9] rascal, if there were anything in thy pocket but tavern-reckonings, and one poor penny-worth of sugar-candy to make thee long-winded, if thy pocket were en-riched with any other injuries but these, I am a villain: and yet you will stand to it; you will not pocket up wrong: art thou not ashamed? 218
Fal.: Dost thou hear, Hal? thou knowest in the state of innocency Adam fell; and what should poor Jack Falstaff do in the days of villainy? Thou seest I have more flesh than another man, and therefore more frailty. You confess then, you picked my pocket? 225
Prince: It appears so by the story.
Fal.: Hostess, I forgive thee: go, make ready breakfast; love thy husband, look to thy servants, cherish thy guests: thou shalt find me tractable to any honest reason: thou seest I am pacified still. Nay, prithee, begone. [*Exit Hostess.*] Now, Hal, to the news at court: for the robbery, lad, how is that answered? 235
Prince: O, my sweet beef, I must still be good angel to thee: the money is paid back again.
Fal.: O, I do not like that paying back; 'tis a double labour. 240
Prince: I am good friends with my father and may do any thing.
Fal.: Rob me the exchequer the first
[9] Swollen

thing thou doest, and do it with un-washed hands too. 245
Bard.: Do, my lord.
Prince: I have procured thee, Jack, a charge of foot.
Fal.: I would it had been of horse. Where shall I find one that can steal well? O for a fine thief, of the age of two and twenty or thereabouts! I am heinously unprovided. Well, God be thanked for these rebels, they offend none but the virtuous: I laud them, I praise them. 256
Prince: Bardolph!
Bard.: My lord?
Prince: Go bear this letter to Lord John of Lancaster, to my brother John; this to my Lord of Westmoreland. [*Exit Bardolph.*] Go, Peto, to horse, to horse; for thou and I have thirty miles to ride yet ere dinner time. [*Exit Peto.*] Jack, meet me to-morrow in the Temple hall at two o'clock in the after-noon. 267
There shalt thou know thy charge; and there receive
Money and order for their furniture.
The land is burning; Percy stands on high;
And either we or they must lower lie. [*Exit.*]
Fal.: Rare words! brave world! Hos-tess, my breakfast, come! 271
O, I could wish this tavern were my drum! [*Exit.*]

QUESTIONS ON ACT III

1. Scene i shows the rebels in apparent amity, settling the division of the kingdom among them. In what ways, however, has Shakespeare managed to indicate the essential lack of unity among the rebels?

2. Hotspur's teasing of Glendower parallels Falstaff's "ragging" of the oversolemn and dignified people of the court. How does it differ from Falstaff's?

3. Hotspur in this scene delights in deflating Glendower's superstitious-ness and delights, too, in playing a realistic counterpoint to the romantic exchanges between Mortimer and his wife. Yet may it be said that, in his way, Hotspur is less realistic in his attitude toward the world than either of them?

4. Worcester's lecture to Hotspur (Sc. i, 177 ff.) furnishes a parallel to the lecture which the king reads to Hal in Scene ii. What effect is gained by the parallelism?

5. Scene ii is largely occupied with the king's sermon to Hal. Notice that the king shows some evidence of bad conscience at the way in which he won the crown (not by lineal descent but by deposing Richard II. See Shakespeare's play, *Richard II*). Notice that he reproves Hal for repeating the mistakes of Richard, who

> carded his state,
> Mingled his royalty with capering fools,
> Had his great name profaned with their scorns, . . .

It is perhaps natural that the king, obsessed by the memory of the king whom he deposed, should see Hal's conduct as inviting the same kind of disaster. Yet is the king's speech really relevant? One hardly needs to know much about the character of Richard II to see that Prince Hal resembles him little, if at all. For example, is the impression which we get of Hal from the play that of a man who has lost his "princely privilege/With vile participation," a man who has made the populace weary of seeing him, as the king suggests? Or is he not rather a man who has given himself, in the opinion of the world, too exclusively to a clique of low associates?

6. Do not the king's speeches indicate that he is a man too much obsessed with what he takes to be his own narrow formula of success—namely, that he won out over Richard because he made himself strange and unfamiliar? Are not the king's own present difficulties the result, in part, of making himself too haughty and of standing too proudly on his own dignity? Hal does not make this criticism, to be sure. He has hardly earned the right to make any criticism of his father. But the fact that Shakespeare does not have him make it need not mean that Shakespeare does not intend us, as audience, to be cognizant of it.

7. It is ironic, however, that Prince Hal has already resolved on a course which involves an improvement on his father's advice. In Scene ii, 29–91, the latter tells his son not to be *like* Richard, who was

> seen, but with such eyes
> As, sick and blunted with community,
> Afford no extraordinary gaze,
> Such as is bent on sun-like majesty
> When it shines seldom in admiring eyes. . . .

But, earlier (in I. ii, ll. 256 ff.) Hal had promised himself that he would "imitate the sun," which permits itself to be hidden by clouds only to burst forth in unexpected brilliance. He will, in short, not use a Richard for a foil but will employ as a foil his own former self. To sum up, is not Hal a better politician than his father, though his genuine delight in Falstaff may redeem him, for many readers, from the charge that he is what Percy calls his father, "a vile politician"?

8. Falstaff's exclamation, when told that the prince has procured him a

charge of foot, is: "Well, God be thanked for these rebels, they offend none but the virtuous: I laud them, I praise them." The comment, of course, primarily expresses his high spirits: that is, Falstaff is saying that it's an ill wind that blows nobody good; the rebels have at least been a cause of profit to him. Does not the statement, however, convey a hint of Falstaff's real attitude toward the state and toward matters of responsibility in general?

9. Here again, as in Act I, we see three different panels of action. Do we feel by now that these panels are closely enough related to give us a sense of essential unity in Act III? How does Act III advance the different phases of the action; that is, how does it fit into the structure of the play?

10. Does the fact that Hal settles up the robbery plot by having the stolen money repaid suggest to us anything about Hal's probable conduct with regard to the Percy plot?

ACT IV

[SCENE I—The rebel camp near Shrewsbury.]

[*Enter Hotspur, Worcester, and Douglas.*]

Hot.: Well said, my noble Scot: if speaking truth
In this fine age were not thought flattery,
Such attribution [1] should the Douglas have,
As not a soldier of this season's stamp
Should go so general current through the world. 5
By God, I cannot flatter; I do defy
The tongues of soothers; but a braver place
In my heart's love hath no man than yourself:
Nay, task me to my word; approve me, lord.
Doug.: Thou art the king of honour:
No man so potent breathes upon the ground 11
But I will beard him.
Hot.:   Do so, and 'tis well. [*Enter a Messenger with letters.*]
What letters hast thou there?—I can but thank you.

Mess.: These letters come from your father.
Hot.: Letters from him! why comes he not himself? 15
Mess.: He cannot come, my lord; he is grievous sick.
Hot.: 'Zounds! how has he the leisure to be sick
In such a justling [2] time? Who leads his power?
Under whose government come they along?
Mess.: His letters bear his mind, not I, my lord. 20
Wor.: I prithee, tell me, doth he keep his bed?
Mess.: He did, my lord, four days ere I set forth;
And at the time of my departure thence
He was much fear'd by his physicians.
Wor.: I would the state of time had first been whole 25
Ere he by sickness had been visited:
His health was never better worth than now.
Hot.: Sick now! droop now! this sickness doth infect
The very life-blood of our enterprise;
'Tis catching hither, even to our camp.
He writes me here, that inward sickness— 31

---

[1] Tribute, praise.

[2] Jostling.

And that his friends by deputation could
    not
So soon be drawn, nor did he think it
    meet
To lay so dangerous and dear a trust
On any soul removed but on his own.
Yet doth he give us bold advertisement,
That with our small conjunction we
    should on,   37
To see how fortune is disposed to us;
For, as he writes, there is no quailing
    now,
Because the king is certainly possess'd
Of all our purposes. What say you to it?
    Wor.: Your father's sickness is a maim
    to us.   42
    Hot.: A perilous gash, a very limb
lopp'd off:
And yet, in faith, it is not; his present
    want
Seems more than we shall find it: were
    it good
To set the exact wealth of all our states
All at one cast? to set so rich a main [3]
On the nice hazard of one doubtful hour?
It were not good; for therein should we
    read   49
The very bottom and the soul of hope,
The very list, the very utmost bound
Of all our fortunes.
    Doug.:   'Faith, and so we
    should;
Where now remains a sweet reversion [4]:
We may boldly spend upon the hope of
    what
Is to come in: 55
A comfort of retirement lives in this.
    Hot.: A rendezvous, a home to fly
    unto,
If that the devil and mischance look big
Upon the maidenhead of our affairs.
    Wor.: But yet I would your father
had been here.   60
The quality and hair [5] of our attempt
Brooks no division: it will be thought
By some, that know not why he is away,
That wisdom, loyalty and mere dislike
Of our proceedings kept the earl from
    hence: 65

[3] Stake, wager. [4] Inheritance still to be
realized. [5] Nature, character.

And think how such an apprehension
May turn the tide of fearful faction
And breed a kind of question in our
    cause;
For well you know we of the offering side
Must keep aloof from strict arbitrement,
And stop all sight-holes, every loop [6]
    from whence   71
The eye of reason may pry in upon us:
This absence of your father's draws a
    curtain,
That shows the ignorant a kind of fear
Before not dreamt of.
    Hot.:   You strain too
    far.   75
I rather of his absence make this use:
It lends a lustre and more great opinion,
A larger dare to our great enterprise,
Than if the earl were here; for men must
    think,
If we without his help can make a head
To push against a kingdom, with his
    help   81
We shall o'erturn it topsy-turvy down.
Yet all goes well, yet all our joints are
    whole.
    Doug.: As heart can think: there is
    not such a word
Spoke of in Scotland as this term of fear.
    [*Enter Sir Richard Vernon.*]
    Hot.: My cousin Vernon! welcome,
    by my soul.   86
    Ver.: Pray God my news be worth a
    welcome, lord.
The Earl of Westmoreland, seven thou-
    sand strong,
Is marching hitherwards; with him
    Prince John.
    Hot.: No harm: what more?
    Ver.:   And further, I have learn'd,
The king himself in person is set forth,
Or hitherwards intended speedily,   92
With strong and mighty preparation.
    Hot.: He shall be welcome too. Where
    is his son,
The nimble-footed madcap Prince of
    Wales,   95
And his comrades, that daff'd the world
    aside,
And bid it pass?
    [6] Loophole.

Ver.: All furnish'd, all in arms;
All plumed like estridges [7] that with the wind
Bated,[8] like eagles having lately bathed;
Glittering in golden coats, like images;
As full of spirit as the month of May,
And gorgeous as the sun at midsummer;
Wanton as youthful goats, wild as young bulls. 103
I saw young Harry, with his beaver on,
His cuisses on his thighs, gallantly arm'd,
Rise from the ground like feather'd Mercury,
And vaulted with such ease into his seat,
As if an angel dropp'd down from the clouds, 108
To turn and wind a fiery Pegasus
And witch [9] the world with noble horsemanship. 110
Hot.: No more, no more: worse than the sun in March,
This praise doth nourish agues. Let them come;
They come like sacrifices in their trim,
And to the fire-eyed maid of smoky war
All hot and bleeding will we offer them:
The mailed Mars shall on his altar sit
Up to the ears in blood. I am on fire
To hear this rich reprisal is so nigh 118
And yet not ours. Come, let me taste my horse,
Who is to bear me like a thunderbolt
Against the bosom of the Prince of Wales; 121
Harry to Harry shall, hot horse to horse,
Meet and ne'er part till one drop down a corse.
O that Glendower were come!
Ver.: There is more news:
I learn'd in Worcester, as I rode along,
He cannot draw his power this fourteen days. 126
Doug.: That's the worst tidings that I hear of yet.
Wor.: Ay, by my faith, that bears a frosty sound.
Hot.: What may the king's whole battle reach unto?

Ver.: To thirty thousand.
Hot.: Forty let it be:
My father and Glendower being both away, 131
The powers of us may serve so great a day.
Come, let us take a muster speedily:
Doomsday is near; die all, die merrily.
Doug.: Talk not of dying: I am out of fear 135
Of death or death's hand for this one-half year. [*Exeunt.*]

[SCENE II—A public road near Coventry.]

[*Enter Falstaff and Bardolph.*]

Fal: Bardolph, get thee before to Coventry; fill me a bottle of sack: our soldiers shall march through; we'll to Sutton Co'fil' to-night.
Bard.: Will you give me money, captain? 6
Fal.: Lay out, lay out.
Bard.: This bottle makes an angel.
Fal.: An if it do, take it for thy labour; and if it make twenty, take them all; I'll answer the coinage. Bid my lieutenant Peto meet me at town's end. 12
Bard.: I will, captain: farewell. [*Exit.*]
Fal.: If I be not ashamed of my soldiers, I am a soused gurnet.[1] I have misused the king's press [2] damnably. I have got, in exchange of a hundred and fifty soldiers, three hundred and odd pounds. I press me none but good householders, yeomen's sons; inquire me out contracted bachelors, such as had been asked twice on the banns; such a commodity of warm slaves, as had as lieve hear the devil as a drum; such as fear the report of a caliver [3] worse than a struck fowl or a hurt wild-duck. I pressed me none but such toasts-and-butter,[4] with hearts in their bellies no bigger than pins' heads, and they have bought out their services; and now my whole charge consists of ancients,[5] corporals,

[7] Goshawks. [8] Beat or fluttered their wings.
[9] Charm, enchant.

[1] Pickled fish. [2] Commission to impress ("draft") soldiers. [3] Musket. [4] Cf. Caspar Milquetoast. [5] Ensigns.

lieutenants, gentlemen of companies, slaves as ragged as Lazarus in the painted cloth, where the glutton's dogs licked his sores; and such as indeed were never soldiers, but discarded unjust serving-men, younger sons to younger brothers, revolted tapsters and ostlers trade-fallen, the cankers of a calm world and a long peace, ten times more dishonourabie ragged than an old faced ancient: and such have I, to fill up the rooms of them that have bought out their services, that you would think that I had a hundred and fifty tattered prodigals lately come from swine-keeping, from eating draff and husks. A mad fellow met me on the way and told me I had unloaded all the gibbets and pressed the dead bodies. No eye hath seen such scarecrows. I'll not march through Coventry with them, that's flat: nay, and the villains march wide betwixt the legs, as if they had gyves [6] on; for indeed I had the most of them out of prison. There's but a shirt and a half in all my company; and the half shirt is two napkins tacked together and thrown over the shoulders like an herald's coat without sleeves; and the shirt, to say the truth, stolen from my host at Saint Alban's, or the red-nose innkeeper of Daventry. But that's all one; they'll find linen enough on every hedge. [*Enter the Prince and Westmoreland.*]　　65

Prince: How now, blown Jack! how now, quilt!

Fal.: What, Hal! how now, mad wag! what a devil dost thou in Warwickshire? My good Lord of Westmoreland, I cry you mercy: I thought your honour had already been at Shrewsbury.　　72

West.: Faith, Sir John, 'tis more than time that I were there, and you too; but my powers are there already. The king, I can tell you, looks for us all: we must away all night.　　77

Fal.: Tut, never fear me: I am as vigilant as a cat to steal cream.

Prince: I think, to steal cream in-

deed, for thy theft hath already made thee butter. But tell me, Jack, whose fellows are these that come after?　　83

Fal.: Mine, Hal, mine.

Prince: I did never see such pitiful rascals.

Fal.: Tut, tut; good enough to toss; food for powder, food for powder; they'll fill a pit as well as better: tush, man, mortal men, mortal men.　　90

West.: Ay, but, Sir John, methinks they are exceeding poor and bare, too beggarly.

Fal.: 'Faith, for their poverty, I know not where they had that; and for their bareness, I am sure they never learned that of me.　　97

Prince: No, I'll be sworn; unless you call three fingers on the ribs bare.[7] But, sirrah, make haste: Percy is already in the field.　　101

Fal.: What, is the king encamped?

West.: He is, Sir John: I fear we shall stay too long.

Fal.: Well,
To the latter end of a fray and the beginning of a feast　　105
Fits a dull fighter and a keen guest.
　　　　　　　　　　　　　　[*Exeunt.*]

[SCENE III—The rebel camp near Shrewsbury.]

[*Enter Hotspur, Worcester, Douglas, and Vernon.*]

Hot.: We'll fight with him to-night.

Wor.:　　　　　　　　　It may not be.

Doug.: You give him then advantage.

Ver.:　　　　　　　　　Not a whit.

Hot.: Why say you so? looks he not for supply?

Ver.: So do we.

Hot.: His is certain, ours is doubtful.

Wor.: Good cousin, be advised; stir not to-night.　　6

Ver.: Do not, my lord.

Doug.:　　　　　　　　　You do not counsel well:
You speak it out of fear and cold heart.

---

[6] Fetters.

[7] Fat three finger-widths thick.

Ver.: Do me no slander, Douglas: by my life,
And I dare well maintain it with my life,
If well-respected honour bid me on,   11
I hold as little counsel with weak fear
As you, my lord, or any Scot that this day lives:
Let it be seen to-morrow in the battle
Which of us fears.
    Doug.:   Yea, or to-night.
    Ver.:   Content.
    Hot.: To-night, say I.   16
    Ver.: Come, come, it may not be. I wonder much,
Being men of such great leading as you are,
That you foresee not what impediments
Drag back our expedition: certain horse
Of my cousin Vernon's are not yet come up: 21
Your uncle Worcester's horse came but to-day;
And now their pride and mettle is asleep,
Their courage with hard labour tame and dull,
That not a horse is half the half of himself.   25
    Hot.: So are the horses of the enemy
In general, journey-bated and brought low:
The better part of ours are full of rest.
    Wor.: The number of the king exceedeth ours:
For God's sake, cousin, stay till all come in. [*The trumpet sounds a parley.*]
                [*Enter Sir Walter Blunt.*]
    Blunt: I come with gracious offers from the king,   31
If you vouchsafe me hearing and respect.
    Hot.: Welcome, Sir Walter Blunt; and would to God
You were of our determination!
Some of us love you well; and even those some   35
Envy your great deservings and good name,
Because you are not of our quality,
But stand against us like an enemy.
    Blunt: And God defend but still I should stand so,

So long as out of limit and true rule   40
You stand against anointed majesty.
But to my charge. The king hath sent to know
The nature of your griefs, and whereupon
You conjure from the breast of civil peace
Such bold hostility, teaching his duteous land   45
Audacious cruelty. If that the king
Have any way your good deserts forgot,
Which he confesseth to be manifold,
He bids you name your griefs; and with all speed
You shall have your desires with interest
And pardon absolute for yourself and these   51
Herein misled by your suggestion.
    Hot.: The king is kind; and well we know the king
Knows at what time to promise, when to pay.
My father and my uncle and myself
Did give him that same royalty he wears;   56
And when he was not six and twenty strong,
Sick in the world's regard, wretched and low,
A poor unminded outlaw sneaking home,
My father gave him welcome to the shore;   60
And when he heard him swear and vow to God
He came but to be Duke of Lancaster,
To sue his livery [1] and beg his peace,
With tears of innocency and terms of zeal,
My father, in kind heart and pity moved,   65
Swore him assistance and perform'd it too.
Now when the lords and barons of the realm
Perceived Northumberland did lean to him,

_____
[1] Sue for the delivery of his inheritance.

The more and less came in with cap and
knee [2]   69
Met him in boroughs, cities, villages,
Attended him on bridges, stood in lanes,
Laid gifts before him, proffer'd him
their oaths,
Gave him their heirs as pages; follow'd
him
Even at the heels in golden multitudes.
He presently, as greatness knows itself,
Steps me a little higher than his vow
Made to my father, while his blood was
poor,   77
Upon the naked shore at Ravenspurgh;
And now, forsooth, takes on him to re-
form
Some certain edicts and some strait de-
crees   80
That lie too heavy on the common-
wealth,
Cries out upon abuses, seems to weep
Over his country's wrongs; and by this
face,
This seeming brow of justice, did he win
The hearts of all that he did angle for;
Proceeded further; cut me off the heads
Of all the favourites that the absent
king   87
In deputation left behind him here,
When he was personal [3] in the Irish war.
Blunt: Tut, I came not to hear this.
Hot.:   Then to the point.
In short time after, he deposed the king;
Soon after that, deprived him of his life;
And in the neck of that,[4] task'd [5] the
whole state;   93
To make that worse, suffer'd his kins-
man March,
Who is, if every owner were well placed,
Indeed his king, to be engaged in Wales,
There without ransom to lie forfeited;
Disgraced me in my happy victories,
Sought to entrap me by intelligence;
Rated mine uncle from the council-
board;   100
In rage dismiss'd my father from the
court;
Broke oath on oath, committed wrong
on wrong,

[2] Cap in hand, kneeling. [3] Present in person. [4] Immediately after that. [5] Taxed.

And in conclusion drove us to seek out
This head of safety; and withal to pry
Into his title, the which we find   105
Too indirect for long continuance.
Blunt: Shall I return this answer to
the king?
Hot.: Not so, Sir Walter: we'll with-
draw awhile.
Go to the king; and let there be im-
pawn'd   109
Some surety for a safe return again,
And in the morning early shall my uncle
Bring him our purposes; and so farewell.
Blunt: I would you would accept of
grace and love.
Hot.: And may be so we shall.
Blunt: Pray God you do.
                              [*Exeunt.*]

[Scene IV—York. The Archbishop's
palace.]

[*Enter the Archbishop of York and
Sir Michael.*]

Arch.: Hie, good Sir Michael; bear
this sealed brief
With winged haste to the lord marshal;
This to my cousin Scroop, and all the
rest
To whom they are directed. If you knew
How much they do import, you would
make haste.   5
Sir M.: My good lord,
I guess their tenour.
Arch.:   Like enough you do.
To-morrow, good Sir Michael, is a day
Wherein the fortune of ten thousand
men
Must bide the touch [1]; for, sir, at
Shrewsbury,   10
As I am truly given to understand,
The king with mighty and quick-raised
power
Meets with Lord Harry: and, I fear, Sir
Michael,
What with the sickness of Northumber-
land,
Whose power was in the first proportion,
And what with Owen Glendower's ab-
sence thence,   16

[1] Must be put to the test.

Who with them was a rated sinew too
And comes not in, o'er-ruled by prophe-
cies,
I fear the power of Percy is too weak
To wage an instant trial with the king.
Sir M.: Why, my good lord, you need
not fear;   21
There is Douglas and Lord Mortimer.
Arch.: No, Mortimer is not there.
Sir M.: But there is Mordake, Ver-
non, Lord Harry Percy,
And there is my Lord of Worcester and
a head   25
Of gallant warriors, noble gentlemen.
Arch.: And so there is: but yet the
king hath drawn
The special head of all the land together:
The Prince of Wales, Lord John of Lan-
caster,
The noble Westmoreland and warlike
Blunt;   30

And many moe [2] corrivals and dear men
Of estimation and command in arms.
Sir M.: Doubt not, my lord, they
shall be well opposed.
Arch.: I hope no less, yet needful 'tis
to fear;
And, to prevent the worst, Sir Michael,
speed: 35
For if Lord Percy thrive not, ere the
king
Dismiss his power, he means to visit
us,
For he hath heard of our confederacy,
And 'tis but wisdom to make strong
against him:
Therefore make haste. I must go write
again   40
To other friends; and so farewell, Sir
Michael.   [*Exeunt.*]

[2] More.

QUESTIONS ON ACT IV

1. Is it in character for Percy Hotspur to suggest that perhaps the rebels will accept the king's terms? One remembers that throughout this act each piece of bad news which the rebels receive only spurs on his reso- lution to stand and fight the king. He argues that there will be the more glory if they can defeat the king without the aid of Northumberland and of Glendower. Why does Shakespeare have him reply to Blunt's

I would you would accept of grace and love

with "And may be so we shall"? Shakespeare goes further than this: in the next act he has Worcester refuse to tell Hotspur of the king's later offer of pardon for fear that he will accept it. Is the point this: that Percy, if he must fight, will welcome a turning of the odds against him as making his conduct more glorious; but that, on the other hand, he will be easily touched by any show of chivalry on the part of the king, his "liberal and kind offer" as Worcester terms it? In other words, is the mainspring of Hotspur's character a desire for "honor" or a desire for power? Does Hot- spur want an apology from the king which will satisfy his honor, or does he want the political power which overthrowing the king will give him?

2. Is the defection of Northumberland and Glendower adequately motivated?

3. What is the structural function of Act IV?

ACT V

[SCENE I—The King's camp near Shrewsbury.]

[*Enter the King, Prince of Wales, Lord John of Lancaster, Sir Walter Blunt, and Falstaff.*]

King: How bloodily the sun begins to peer
Above yon busky [1] hill! the day looks pale
At his distemperature.
Prince: The southern wind
Doth play the trumpet to his purposes,
And by his hollow whistling in the leaves
Foretells a tempest and a blustering day.
King: Then with the losers let it sympathise,   7
For nothing can seem foul to those that win   [*The trumpet sounds.*]
[*Enter Worcester and Vernon.*]
How now, my lord of Worcester! 'tis not well
That you and I should meet upon such terms   10
As now we meet. You have deceived our trust
And made us doff our easy robes of peace,
To crush our old limbs in ungentle steel:
This is not well, my lord, this is not well.
What say you to it? will you again unknit   15
This churlish knot of all-abhorred war?
And move in that obedient orb again
Where you did give a fair and natural light,
And be no more an exhaled meteor,
A prodigy of fear and a portent   20
Of broached mischief to the unborn times?
Wor.: Hear me, my liege:
For mine own part, I could be well content
To entertain the lag-end of my life
With quiet hours; for I do protest,   25
I have not sought the day of this dislike.
King: You have not sought it! how comes it, then?

Fal.: Rebellion lay in his way, and he found it.
Prince: Peace, chewet,[2] peace!
Wor.: It pleased your majesty to turn your looks   30
Of favour from myself and all our house;
And yet I must remember you, my lord,
We were the first and dearest of your friends.
For you my staff of office did I break
In Richard's time; and posted day and night   35
To meet you on the way, and kiss your hand,
When yet you were in place and in account
Nothing so strong and fortunate as I.
It was myself, my brother and his son,
That brought you home and boldly did outdare   40
The dangers of the time. You swore to us,
And you did swear that oath at Doncaster,
That you did nothing purpose 'gainst the state;
Nor claim no further than your new-fall'n right,[3]
The seat of Gaunt, dukedom of Lancaster: 45
To this we swore our aid. But in short space
It rain'd down fortune showering on your head;
And such a flood of greatness fell on you,
What with our help, what with the absent king,
What with the injuries of a wanton time,   50
The seeming sufferances that you had borne,
And the contrarious winds that held the king
So long in his unlucky Irish wars
That all in England did repute him dead: 54
And from this swarm of fair advantages
You took occasion to be quickly woo'd

---

[1] Bushy.

[2] Chough, a chattering bird.   [3] A right newly fallen due.

To gripe the general sway into your hand;
Forgot your oath to us at Doncaster;
And being fed by us you used us so 59
As that ungentle gull,[4] the cuckoo's bird,
Useth the sparrow; did oppress our nest;
Grew by our feeding to so great a bulk
That even our love durst not come near your sight
For fear of swallowing; but with nimble wing
We were enforced, for safety sake, to fly
Out of your sight and raise this present head; 66
Whereby we stand opposed by such means
As you yourself have forged against yourself
By unkind usage, dangerous countenance,
And violation of all faith and troth 70
Sworn to us in your younger enterprise.
  King: These things indeed you have articulate,
Proclaim'd at market-crosses, read in churches,
To face [5] the garment of rebellion
With some fine colour that may please the eye 75
Of fickle changelings and poor discontents,
Which gape and rub the elbow at the news
Of hurlyburly innovation:
And never yet did insurrection want
Such water-colours to impaint his cause;
Nor moody beggars, starving for a time
Of pellmell havoc and confusion. 82
  Prince: In both your armies there is many a soul
Shall pay full dearly for this encounter,
If once they join in trial. Tell your nephew, 85
The Prince of Wales doth join with all the world
In praise of Henry Percy: by my hopes,
This present enterprise set off his head,
I do not think a braver gentleman,

More active-valiant or more valiant-young, 90
More daring or more bold, is now alive
To grace this latter age with noble deeds.
For my part, I may speak it to my shame
I have a truant been to chivalry; 94
And so I hear he doth account me too;
Yet this before my father's majesty—
I am content that he shall take the odds
Of his great name and estimation,
And will, to save the blood on either side,
Try fortune with him in a single fight.
  King: And, Prince of Wales, so dare we venture thee, 101
Albeit considerations infinite
Do make against it. No, good Worcester, no,
We love our people well; even those we love
That are misled upon your cousin's part;
And, will they take the offer of our grace,
Both he and they and you, yea, every man 107
Shall be my friend again and I'll be his:
So tell your cousin, and bring me word
What he will do: but if he will not yield,
Rebuke and dread correction wait on us
And they shall do their office. So, be gone; 112
We will not now be troubled with reply:
We offer fair; take it advisedly.
  [*Exeunt Worcester and Vernon.*]
  Prince: It will not be accepted, on my life: 115
The Douglas and the Hotspur both together
Are confident against the world in arms.
  King: Hence, therefore, every leader to his charge;
For, on their answer, will we set on them:
And God befriend us, as our cause is just! 120
  [*Exeunt all but the Prince of Wales and Falstaff.*]
  Fal.: Hal, if thou see me down in the battle and bestride me,[6] so; 'tis a point of friendship.
  Prince: Nothing but a colossus can do thee that friendship. Say thy prayers, and farewell. 126

---

[4] Nestling. [5] Trim.

[6] Stand over and defend me.

Fal.: I would 'twere bed-time, Hal, and all well.

Prince: Why, thou owest God a death. [*Exit.*]   130

Fal.: 'Tis not due yet; I would be loath to pay him before his day. What need I be so forward with him that calls not on me? Well, 'tis no matter; honour pricks me on. Yea, but how if honour prick me off when I come on? how then? Can honour set to a leg? no: or an arm? no: or take away the grief of a wound? no. Honour hath no skill in surgery, then? no. What is honour? a word. What is in that word honour? what is that honour? air. A trim reckoning! Who hath it? he that died o' Wednesday. Doth he feel it? no. Doth he hear it? no. 'Tis insensible, then? Yea, to the dead. But will it not live with the living? no. Why? detraction will not suffer it. Therefore I'll none of it. Honour is a mere scutcheon: and so ends my catechism. [*Exit.*]

[SCENE II—The rebel camp.]

[*Enter Worcester and Vernon.*]

Wor.: O, no, my nephew must not know, Sir Richard,
The liberal and kind offer of the king.

Ver.: 'Twere best he did.

Wor.:   Then are we all undone.
It is not possible, it cannot be,
The king should keep his word in loving us;   5
He will suspect us still and find a time
To punish this offence in other faults:
Suspicion all our lives shall be stuck full of eyes;
For treason is but trusted like the fox,
Who, ne'er so tame, so cherish'd and lock'd up,   10
Will have a wild trick of his ancestors,
Look how we can, or sad or merrily,
Interpretation will misquote our looks,
And we shall feed like oxen at a stall,
The better cherish'd, still the nearer death.   15
My nephew's trespass may be well forgot;

It hath the excuse of youth and heat of blood,
And an adopted name of privilege,
A hare-brain'd Hotspur, govern'd by a spleen:
All his offences live upon my head   20
And on his father's; we did train him on,
And, his corruption being ta'en from us,
We, as the spring of all, shall pay for all.
Therefore, good cousin, let not Harry know,
In any case, the offer of the king.   25

Ver.: Deliver what you will; I'll say 'tis so.
Here comes your cousin.

[*Enter Hotspur and Douglas.*]

Hot.: My uncle is return'd:
Deliver up my Lord of Westmoreland.
Uncle, what news?   30

Wor.: The king will bid you battle presently.

Doug.: Defy him by the Lord of Westmoreland.

Hot.: Lord Douglas, go you and tell him so.

Doug.: Marry, and shall, and very willingly. [*Exit.*]

Wor.: There is no seeming mercy in the king.   35

Hot.: Did you beg any? God forbid!

Wor.: I told him gently of our grievances,
Of his oath-breaking; which he mended thus,
By now forswearing that he is forsworn:
He calls us rebels, traitors; and will scourge   40
With haughty arms this hateful name in us.

[*Re-enter Douglas.*]

Doug.: Arm, gentlemen; to arms! for I have thrown
A brave defiance in King Henry's teeth,
And Westmoreland, that was engaged, did bear it;
Which cannot choose but bring him quickly on.   45

Wor.: The Prince of Wales stepp'd forth before the king,
And, nephew, challenged you to single fight.

Hot.: O, would the quarrel lay upon our heads,
And that no man might draw short breath to-day
But I and Harry Monmouth! Tell me, tell me, 50
How show'd his tasking? seem'd it in contempt?
Ver.: No, by my soul; I never in my life
Did hear a challenge urged more modestly,
Unless a brother should a brother dare
To gentle exercise and proof of arms.
He gave you all the duties of a man:
Trimm'd up your praises with a princely tongue, 57
Spoke your deservings like a chronicle,
Making you ever better than his praise
By still dispraising praise valued with you; 60
And, which became him like a prince indeed,
He made a blushing cital [1] of himself;
And chid his truant youth with such a grace
As if he master'd there a double spirit
Of teaching and of learning instantly.
There did he pause: but let me tell the world, 66
If he outlive the envy of this day,
England did never owe so sweet a hope,
So much misconstrued in his wantonness.
Hot.: Cousin, I think thou art enamoured 70
On his follies: never did I hear
Of any prince so wild a libertine.
But be he as he will, yet once ere night
I will embrace him with a soldier's arm,
That he shall shrink under my courtesy.
Arm, arm with speed: and, fellows, soldiers, friends, 76
Better consider what you have to do
Than I, that have not well the gift of tongue,
Can lift your blood up with persuasion.
        [*Enter a Messenger.*]
Mess.: My lord, here are letters for you. 80

Hot.: I cannot read them now.
O gentlemen, the time of life is short!
To spend that shortness basely were too long,
If life did ride upon a dial's point,
Still ending at the arrival of an hour.
An if we live, we live to tread on kings;
If die, brave death, when princes die with us! 87
Now, for our consciences, the arms are fair,
When the intent of bearing them is just.
        [*Enter another Messenger.*]
Mess.: My lord, prepare; the king comes on apace. 90
Hot.: I thank him, that he cuts me from my tale,
For I profess not talking; only this—
Let each man do his best: and here draw I
A sword, whose temper I intend to stain
With the best blood that I can meet withal 95
In the adventure of this perilous day.
Now, Esperance! Percy! and set on.
Sound all the lofty instruments of war,
And by that music let us all embrace;
For, heaven to earth, some of us never shall 100
A second time do such a courtesy.
        [*The trumpets sound. They embrace and exeunt.*]

[SCENE III—Plain between the camps.]

[*The King enters with his power. Alarum to the battle. Then enter Douglas and Sir Walter Blunt.*]

Blunt: What is thy name, that in the battle thus
Thou crossest me? what honour dost thou seek
Upon my head?
Doug.:   Know then, my name is Douglas;
And I do haunt thee in the battle thus
Because some tell me that thou art a king.
Blunt: They tell thee true. 6
Doug.: The Lord of Stafford dear to-day hath bought

---

[1] Recital, statement.

Thy likeness, for instead of thee, King
    Harry,
This sword hath ended him: so shall it
    thee,
Unless thou yield thee as my prisoner.
  Blunt: I was not born a yielder, thou
    proud Scot;   11
And thou shalt find a king that will re-
    venge
Lord Stafford's death.
      [They fight. Douglas kills Blunt.]
             [Enter Hotspur.]
  Hot.: O Douglas, hadst thou fought at
    Holmedon thus,
I never had triumph'd upon a Scot. 15
  Doug.: All's done, all's won; here
    breathless lies the king.
  Hot.: Where?
  Doug.: Here.
  Hot.: This, Douglas? no: I know this
    face full well:
A gallant knight he was, his name was
    Blunt;   20
Semblably furnish'd [1] like the king him-
    self.
  Doug.: A fool go with thy soul,
    whither it goes!
A borrow'd title hast thou bought too
    dear:
Why didst thou tell me that thou wert a
    king?
  Hot.: The king hath many marching
    in his coats.   25
  Doug.: Now, by my sword, I will kill
    all his coats;
I'll murder all his wardrobe, piece by
    piece,
Until I meet the king.
  Hot.:   Up, and away!
Our soldiers stand full fairly for the day.
                    [Exeunt.]
  [Alarum. Enter Falstaff, solus.]
  Fal.: Though I could 'scape shot-
free [2] at London, I fear the shot here;
here's no scoring but upon the pate.
Soft! who are you? Sir Walter Blunt:
there's honour for you! here's no vanity!
I am as hot as molten lead, and as heavy

---

[1] Resembling in arms and equipment. [2] A
pun on *shot* in the sense of "bullet" and
of "tavern-reckoning" or score.

too: God keep lead out of me! I need no
more weight than mine own bowels. I
have led my ragamuffins where they are
peppered: there's not three of my hundred and fifty left alive; and they are
for the town's end, to beg during life.
But who comes here? *[Enter the Prince.]*
  Prince: What, stand'st thou idle here?
    lend me thy sword: 43
Many a nobleman lies stark and stiff
Under the hoofs of vaunting enemies,
Whose deaths are yet unrevenged: I
    prithee, lend me thy sword.   46
  Fal.: O Hal, I prithee, give me leave
to breathe awhile. Turk Gregory never
did such deeds in arms as I have done
this day. I have paid Percy, I have
made him sure.   51
  Prince: He is, indeed; and living to
kill thee. I prithee, lend me thy sword.
  Fal.: Nay, before God, Hal, if Percy
be alive, thou get'st not my sword; but
take my pistol, if thou wilt.   56
  Prince: Give it me: what, is it in the
case?
  Fal.: Ay, Hal; 'tis hot, 'tis hot; there's
that will sack a city. *[The Prince draws
it out, and finds it to be a bottle of sack.]*
  Prince: What, is it a time to jest and
dally now? *[He throws the bottle at him.
Exit.]*   64
  Fal.: Well, if Percy be alive, I'll pierce
him. If he do come in my way, so: if he
do not, if I come in his willingly, let him
make a carbonado [3] of me. I like not
such grinning honour as Sir Walter hath:
give me life: which if I can save, so; if
not, honour comes unlooked for, and
there's an end. *[Exit.]*   72

  *[Scene IV—Another part of the
field.]*

  *[Alarum. Excursions. Enter the King,
the Prince, Lord John of Lancaster, and
Earl of Westmoreland.]*

  King: I prithee,
Harry, withdraw thyself; thou bleed'st
    too much.

---

[3] Meat scored across and broiled.

Lord John of Lancaster, go you with him.

Lan.: Not I, my lord, unless I did bleed too.

Prince: I beseech your majesty, make up, 5
Lest your retirement do amaze your friends.

King: I will do so.
My Lord of Westmoreland, lead him to his tent.

West.: Come, my lord, I'll lead you to your tent.

Prince: Lead me, my lord? I do not need your help: 10
And God forbid a shallow scratch should drive
The Prince of Wales from such a field as this,
Where stain'd nobility lies trodden on,
And rebels' arms triumph in massacres!

Lan.: We breathe too long: come, cousin Westmoreland, 15
Our duty this way lies; for God's sake, come.

[*Exeunt Prince John and Westmoreland.*]

Prince: By God, thou has deceived me, Lancaster;
I did not think thee lord of such a spirit:
Before, I loved thee as a brother, John;
But now, I do respect thee as my soul.

King: I saw him hold Lord Percy at the point 21
With lustier maintenance[1] than I did look for
Of such an ungrown warrior.

Prince: O, this boy
Lends mettle to us all!   [*Exit.*]

[*Enter Douglas.*]

Doug.: Another king! they grow like Hydra's heads: 25
I am the Douglas, fatal to all those
That wear those colours on them: what art thou,
That counterfeit'st the person of a king?

King: The king himself; who, Douglas, grieves at heart 29
So many of his shadows thou hast met

And not the very king. I have two boys
Seek Percy and thyself about the field.
But, seeing thou fall'st on me so luckily,
I will assay thee: so, defend thyself.

Doug.: I fear thou art another counterfeit; 35
And yet, in faith, thou bear'st thee like a king:
But mine I am sure thou art, whoe'er thou be,
And thus I win thee.

[*They fight; the King being in danger,
re-enter Prince of Wales.*]

Prince: Hold up thy head, vile Scot, or thou art like
Never to hold it up again! the spirits 40
Of valiant Shirley, Stafford, Blunt, are in my arms:
It is the Prince of Wales that threatens thee;
Who never promiseth but he means to pay.   [*They fight: Douglas flies.*]
Cheerly, my lord: how fares your grace?
Sir Nicholas Gawsey hath for succour sent, 45
And so hath Clifton: I'll to Clifton straight.

King: Stay, and breathe awhile:
Thou has redeem'd thy lost opinion,
And show'd thou makest some tender of[2] my life,
In this fair rescue thou hast brought to me. 50

Prince: O God! they did me too much injury
That ever said I hearken'd for your death.
If it were so, I might have let alone
The insulting hand of Douglas over you,
Which would have been as speedy in your end 55
As all the poisonous potions in the world
And saved the treacherous labour of your son.

King: Make up to Clifton: I'll to Sir Nicholas Gawsey.   [*Exit.*]

[*Enter Hotspur.*]

Hot.: If I mistake not, thou art Harry Monmouth.

---

[1] Endurance.

[2] Thou hast some regard for.

Prince: Thou speak'st as if I would deny my name.   60
Hot.: My name is Harry Percy.
Prince: Why, then I see
A very valiant rebel of the name.
I am the Prince of Wales; and think not, Percy,
To share with me in glory any more:
Two stars keep not their motion in one sphere;   65
Nor can one England brook a double reign,
Of Harry Percy and the Prince of Wales.
Hot.: Nor shall it, Harry; for the hour is come
To end the one of us; and would to God
Thy name in arms were now as great as mine!   70
Prince: I'll make it greater ere I part from thee;
And all the budding honours on thy crest
I'll crop, to make a garland for my head.
Hot.: I can no longer brook thy vanities.   [*They fight.*]
      [*Enter Falstaff.*]
Fal.: Well said, Hal! to it, Hal! Nay, you shall find no boy's play here, I can tell you. [*Re-enter Douglas; he fights with Falstaff, who falls down as if he were dead, and exit Douglas. Hotspur is wounded, and falls.*]   80
Hot.: O, Harry, thou hast robb'd me of my youth!
I better brook the loss of brittle life
Than those proud titles thou hast won of me;
They wound my thoughts worse than thy sword my flesh:
But thought's the slave of life, and life time's fool;   85
And time, that takes survey of all the world,
Must have a stop. O, I could prophesy,
But that the earthy and cold hand of death
Lies on my tongue: no, Percy, thou art dust,
And food for— [*Dies.*]   90
Prince: For worms, brave Percy: fare thee well, great heart!

Ill-weaved ambition, how much art thou shrunk!
When that this body did contain a spirit,
A kingdom for it was too small a bound;
But now two paces of the vilest earth
Is room enough: this earth that bears thee dead   96
Bears not alive so stout a gentleman.
If thou wert sensible of courtesy,
I should not make so dear a show of zeal:
But let my favours hide thy mangled face;   100
And, even in thy behalf, I'll thank myself
For doing these fair rites of tenderness.
Adieu, and take thy praise with thee to heaven!
Thy ignominy sleep with thee in the grave,
But not remember'd in thy epitaph!
    [*He spieth Falstaff on the ground.*]
What, old acquaintance! could not all this flesh   106
Keep in a little life? Poor Jack, farewell!
I could have better spared a better man:
O, I should have a heavy miss of thee,
If I were much in love with vanity!   110
Death hath not struck so fat a deer to-day,
Though many dearer, in this bloody fray.
Embowell'd [3] will I see thee by and by:
Till then in blood by noble Percy lie.
           [*Exit.*]
Fal.: [*Rising up.*] Embowelled! if thou embowel me to-day, I'll give you leave to powder me and eat me to-morrow. 'Sblood, 'twas time to counterfeit, or that hot termagant [4] Scot had paid me scot and lot too. Counterfeit? I lie, I am no counterfeit: to die, is to be a counterfeit; for he is but the counterfeit of a man who hath not the life of a man: but to counterfeit dying, when a man thereby liveth, is to be no counterfeit, but the true and perfect image of life indeed. The better part of valour

[3] As a preparation for embalming.   [4] Furious, like the supposed deity of the Saracens, Termagant.

is discretion; in the which better part
I have saved my life. 'Zounds, I am
afraid of this gunpowder Percy, though
he be dead: how, if he should counterfeit
too and rise? by my faith, I am afraid
he would prove the better counterfeit.
Therefore I'll make him sure; yea, and
I'll swear I killed him. Why may not he
rise as well as I? Nothing confutes me
but eyes, and nobody sees me. Therefore, sirrah [*stabbing him*], with a
new wound in your thigh, come you
along with me. [*Takes up Hotspur on his
back.*] [*Re-enter the Prince of Wales and
Lord John of Lancaster.*]   142
    Prince: Come, brother John; full
bravely hast thou flesh'd
Thy maiden sword.
    Lan.:   But, soft! whom
have we here?
Did you not tell me this fat man was
dead?   145
    Prince: I did; I saw him dead,
Breathless and bleeding on the ground.
    Art thou alive?
Or is it fantasy that plays upon our
    eyesight?
I prithee, speak; we will not trust our
    eyes
Without our ears: thou art not what
    thou seem'st.   150
    Fal.: No, that's certain; I am not a
double man: but if I be not Jack Falstaff, then am I a Jack. There is Percy
[*throwing the body down*]: if your father
will do me any honour, so; if not, let
him kill the next Percy himself. I look
to be either earl or duke, I can assure
you.   158
    Prince: Why, Percy I killed myself
and saw thee dead.
    Fal.: Didst thou? Lord, Lord, how
this world is given to lying! I grant you
I was down and out of breath; and so
was he: but we rose both at an instant
and fought a long hour by Shrewsbury
clock. If I may be believed, so; if not,
let them that should reward valour bear
the sin upon their own heads. I'll take it
upon my death, I gave him this wound
in the thigh: if the man were alive and

would deny it, 'zounds, I would make
him eat a piece of my sword.   171
    Lan.: This is the strangest tale that
ever I heard.
    Prince: This is the strangest fellow,
brother John.
Come, bring your luggage nobly on your
    back: 174
For my part, if a lie may do thee grace,
I'll gild it with the happiest terms I
    have.   [*A retreat is sounded.*]
The trumpet sounds retreat; the day is
    ours.
Come, brother, let us to the highest of
    the field,
To see what friends are living, who are
    dead.   179
[*Exeunt Prince of Wales and Lancaster.*]
    Fal.: I'll follow, as they say, for re-
ward. He that rewards me, God reward
him! If I do grow great, I'll grow less;
for I'll purge, and leave sack, and live
cleanly as a nobleman should do. [*Exit.*]

[SCENE V—Another part of the field.]

    [*The trumpets sound. Enter the King,
Prince of Wales, Lord John of Lancaster,
Earl of Westmoreland, with Worcester and
Vernon prisoners.*]

    King: Thus ever did rebellion find re-
buke.
Ill-spirited Worcester! did not we send
    grace,
Pardon and terms of love to all of you?
And wouldst thou turn our offers con-
    trary?
Misuse the tenour of thy kinsman's
    trust?   5
Three knights upon our party slain to-
    day,
A noble earl and many a creature else
Had been alive this hour,
If like a Christian thou hadst truly
    borne
Betwixt our armies true intelligence.
    Wor.: What I have done my safety
urged me to;   11
And I embrace this fortune patiently,
Since not to be avoided it falls on me.

King: Bear Worcester to the death
and Vernon too:
Other offenders we will pause upon. 15
[*Exeunt Worcester and Vernon guarded.*]
How goes the field?
Prince: The noble Scot, Lord Doug-
las, when he saw
The fortune of the day quite turn'd from
him,
The noble Percy slain, and all his men
Upon the foot of fear, fled with the
rest; 20
And falling from a hill, he was so bruised
That the pursuers took him. At my tent
The Douglas is; and I beseech your grace
I may dispose of him.
King: With all my heart.
Prince: Then, brother John of Lan-
caster, to you 25
This honourable bounty shall belong:
Go to the Douglas, and deliver him
Up to his pleasure, ransomless and free:
His valour shown upon our crests to-
day

Hath taught us how to cherish such high
deeds 30
Even in the bosom of our adversaries.
Lan.: I thank your grace for this high
courtesy,
Which I shall give away immediately.
King: Then this remains, that we di-
vide our power.
You, son John, and my cousin West-
moreland 35
Towards York shall bend you with your
dearest speed,
To meet Northumberland and the pre-
late Scroop,
Who, as we hear, are busily in arms:
Myself and you, son Harry, will towards
Wales,
To fight with Glendower and the Earl of
March. 40
Rebellion in this land shall lose his sway,
Meeting the check of such another day:
And since this business so fair is done,
Let us not leave till all our own be won.
[*Exeunt.*]

NOTES ON *HENRY IV*, *PART I*

I. THE PROBLEM OF UNITY

As was pointed out earlier, the salient problem in this play must be the problem of unity. To most readers at least, the most important general question which presents itself is this: does the play achieve a real dramatic unity, or is it, after all, merely a not-too-interesting "history" play to which Shakespeare has added, in the interest of amusement, the Falstaff tavern scenes? To state the problem with special reference to Act V, does this last act really succeed in uniting the various threads of interest that run through the play?

The "history" plot is, of course, brought to a conclusion in this act with the decision gained in the Battle of Shrewsbury.* But what of the comic underplot? Does it come here into any organic relation with the other elements of the play, or does it remain isolated? What happens to Hotspur

* To a temporary conclusion at least, for Shakespeare continued the story in *Henry IV*, *Part 2*, which the student should read. The two-part arrangement in itself raises the problem of unity in a special form. Suffice it to say here that, whatever the total unity which the two parts taken together may have, this first part has its own special unity which it is our immediate problem here to attempt to define.

Falstaff's death is mentioned in *Henry V*, and he is the central figure in *The Merry Wives of Windsor;* but in this latter play, most critics and scholars agree that he comes closer to the mere buffoon—that he lacks the special quality of character shown in the *Henry* plays.

when he comes within the orbit of Falstaff? Or what, for that matter, happens to Falstaff when he comes between the "fell incensed points/ Of mighty opposites"? If he affords no more than comic relief, then we are perhaps justified in holding that as a character he is a lucky accident, a character who was, in Shakespeare's original plans, to have figured as a sort of jester, but who became something richer and more imaginative than intended. As a matter of fact, one might, pushing this line of argument a step further, contend that Falstaff has actually so far outgrown the needs of the play, strictly considered, that he comes close to destroying it.

It is possible, however, to see Falstaff's role as a more positive one than that of merely diverting us *from* the more serious concerns of the play. It is possible that his function is to define—as well as enrich—the theme of the play. But to explore this possibility will involve a rather careful consideration of his relation to the other characters in the play and a further inquiry into the theme—the total "meaning" of the play.

2. THE SYSTEM OF CONTRASTS IN THE PLAY

If *Henry IV, Part I* does have a principle of unity, it is obviously one which allows for, and makes positive use of, an amazing amount of contrast. Many of these contrasts have already been noted in the questions which come at the end of each act. There is the contrast between the king's hopes for his son and the life which Prince Hal has actually been leading; the contrast between the pomp and state of the councils at court which are called to debate the state of the realm and those other councils at the Boar's Head which take measures for the better lifting of travelers' purses. Moreover, as we have remarked earlier, Prince Hal and Percy Hotspur are obvious foils for each other, they are specifically contrasted again and again throughout the play. But one of the most important contrasts developed in the play is that between Falstaff and Percy Hotspur.

On one level, it ought to be pretty obvious, the play involves a study in the nature of kingship—not an unduly solemn study, to be sure—but a study, nevertheless, of what makes a good king. In this study, of course, Prince Hal is the central figure, and the play becomes, then, the study of his development.

On this level of consideration, Percy Hotspur not only is Hal's rival but also furnishes an ideal of conduct toward which Hal might aspire (and toward which his father, the king, actually wishes him to aspire). Falstaff represents another ideal of conduct—and here, consequently, finds his foil in Hotspur. (If the pairing of Falstaff and Hotspur seems, at first glance, forced, nevertheless we shall presently see that there is abundant evidence that Shakespeare thought the contrast important and relevant to his purpose.)

Indeed, as Mr. R. P. Warren has pointed out, it is almost as if Shakespeare were following, consciously or unconsciously, the theme of Aristotle's Nichomachaean ethics: virtue as the mean between two extremes of conduct. This suggestion can be used to throw a good deal of light on the relationship of the characters of Falstaff, Prince Hal, and Hotspur to each other.

Consider the matter of honor. Hotspur represents one extreme, Falstaff, the other. Hotspur declares characteristically

> By heaven, methinks it were an easy leap,
> To pluck bright honour from the pale-faced moon, . . .
>   (I. iii, 201–02)

Falstaff speaks just as characteristically when he argues in his famous speech on honor: "Well, 'tis no matter; honour pricks me on. Yea, but how if honour prick me off when I come on? how then? Can honour set to a leg? no: or an arm? no: or take away the grief of a wound? no . . . (V. i)

Falstaff's common sense is devastating; but it is also crippling—or would be to a prince or ruler. If it does not cripple Falstaff, it is because Falstaff frankly refuses to accept the responsibilities of leadership. Perhaps he chooses wisely in so refusing. By refusing he achieves a vantage point from which he can perceive the folly and pretentiousness which, to a degree, always tend to associate themselves with authority of any kind.

But Hotspur's chivalry is crippling too. He wants to fight for honor's sake: he will not wait for reinforcements because it will beget more honor to fight without waiting for them; but, on the other hand, he will not fight at all (Worcester fears) if he hears of the king's mollifying offer, for then his pride will be saved, his honor preserved, and the political aspects of the rebellion can go hang; for Hotspur has little or no interest in them. Indeed, Hotspur can rely on the obvious fact that he is fighting merely for honor to gain the forgiveness of the king, though Worcester fears that the forgiveness extended to himself will be only a nominal forgiveness and that the king will be on the lookout for later excuses to injure him.

If one assumes the necessity for leadership (and there is little doubt that the Elizabethan audience and Shakespeare did), then Hotspur points to an extreme which the truly courageous leader must avoid quite as clearly as he must avoid the other extreme represented by Falstaff. True courage, we may say, has as one frontier an unthinking impetuousness like that of Hotspur: it has as its other frontier a kind of calculation, which, if not cowardice, at least results in actions which look very much like cowardice. Falstaff is too "practical"; Hotspur, not "practical" enough.

3. THE "IMMATURITY" OF FALSTAFF AND HOTSPUR

Yet Shakespeare does not give us an oversimplified picture of either extreme. Falstaff redeems himself for most of us by his humor, by his good nature, by his love of life, and perhaps, most of all, by a thoroughgoing intellectual honesty. Hotspur also has his attractive side. There is a kind of abandon, a kind of light-hearted gaiety—in his whole-souled commitment to the pursuit of honor, in his teasing of his wife, and in his laughing at the pompous mystery-mongering of Glendower—which puts him, like Falstaff, *above* the plots and counter-plots that fill up the play.

Yet—if we assume the necessity for leadership and authority—both Falstaff and Hotspur are *below* the serious concerns that fill the play. About both of them there is a childlike quality which relieves them of the responsibility of mature life, a frankness which is the opposite of the pretense and hypocrisy so apparent in the adult world.*

This suggestion that there is something childlike and immature about Falstaff and Hotspur must, of course, be heavily qualified. There is a sense in which Hotspur is the epitome of manliness and aggressive masculinity, and certainly he thinks of himself as anything but childish. Moreover, Falstaff, in spite of the war cry with which he sets upon the travelers, "They hate us youth: down with them; fleece them," is old in the ways of vice, and indeed possesses a kind of wisdom which makes the solemn concerns of Henry IV's court appear callow and naïve beside it.

And yet, even so, the pair do not stand quite on the level of the adult world where there are jobs to be done and duties to be performed. They are either below it or else they transcend it; and Shakespeare is wise enough to let them—particularly Falstaff—do both. That is, they appear sometimes *childish* in their attitudes and sometimes *childlike*, for Shakespeare exploits both aspects of their characters in the play.

The childlike qualities, of course, are found predominantly in Falstaff—in his vitality and in his preservation of a kind of innocence. But Hotspur, too, has a kind of innocence which sets him apart from the more calculating of his fellow-conspirators. He is impulsive where they are Machiavellian; boyish, in his love of adventure, where they are playing coldly for high stakes. But the childlike innocence (or, if one prefers, the boyish impulsiveness) merges into childish foolhardiness when he insists on fighting the king at Shrewsbury before reinforcements can be brought up.

4. FALSTAFF AT THE BATTLE OF SHREWSBURY

Falstaff is, of course, a far more complex character than Hotspur, or, for that matter, than any other character in the play. But an examination of the childish-childlike aspects of his nature may, even if it will not wholly account for the richness of his personality, lead the student into a further knowledge of that richness. Certainly, it may give us one of the most important clues as to how his character is related to the central problems of the play.

Falstaff as Philosopher. Falstaff, we may say, is like the child in the story who alone was able to detect the fact that the emperor's new clothes were entirely imaginary. With a clarity of vision that is unclouded by reverence towards authority of any kind, the child sees that the emperor is

---

* If the student, remembering, for example, how "damnably" Falstaff has "misused the king's press," feels disposed to challenge this observation, he should be reminded that the matter in question is not Falstaff's goodness but his frankness and irresponsibility. He has the child's honest selfishness and the child's lack of conscience as he frankly goes after his own ends.

naked, and says so. (Falstaff strips Henry IV quite naked in his famous parody of the king's speech in Act II. iv. King Henry's concern for his son's wicked ways, as we see in Act III, is more than half an extension of his own self-conceit. His son's reputation disturbs him because he regards it as a reflection upon himself.)

Falstaff's clarity of vision, however, is not an effect of cynicism. The spectacle of the world in its nakedness, stripped of its pretensions, does not move Falstaff to bitterness. He can laugh in thorough good humor. And Falstaff does laugh continually through the play as he sees through what is glibly called "honor," through self-righteousness, through the pretensions of royalty. In this sense, like the child, he is fundamentally a moral anarchist. But Falstaff is—again like the child—not a missionary anarchist. He does not for a moment intend to convert others to his views; he is not the moralist, certainly, nor the inverted moralist, the cynic.

In short, in spite of the fact that he speaks merely to amuse himself and others, Falstaff supplies a brilliant and what is—up to a point—a perfectly true commentary upon the world about him. Falstaff is doubtless the last man in the world to set up for a philosopher; yet his humor, because it does have point and does make a rich commentary upon the world about him, does have a philosophical quality.

Falstaff as Man of Action. But in Act V we see Falstaff as man of action, and this action tests him even as the world of action is tested by Falstaff's commentary. On a battlefield the committed man of action must be prepared to die, but Falstaff does not feel the need to die for any man. He frankly sees no point in dying by Douglas's sword for King Henry. King Henry himself, as Falstaff well knows, is scarcely likely to appreciate such a devotion on Falstaff's part. Hal himself will not lose or retain his chances for the crown by Falstaff's death alone; and the issue, when Douglas challenges him, is certainly death; for Falstaff, in spite of his playful boasting, has absolutely no illusions about his own prowess as a warrior.

Falstaff loses no time in resolving his problem: he contents himself with playing 'possum. From one point of view, this is simply cowardice; from another, Falstaff is being perfectly consistent, and, to be so, risking the imputation of cowardice. In the same situation Blunt declares heroically, "I was not born a yielder, thou proud Scot"; he believes in honor, and so he has his reward, even in death. Falstaff is equally consistent because he does not believe in honor; for him, heroics would be a pretense—phony honor.

The Parallelism of Falstaff and Hotspur. If the student has had any difficulty in seeing and accepting the parallelism between Falstaff and Hotspur, he might reflect that in this last act of the play the author himself has taken some pains to point it up, and may be said to have allowed at least Prince Hal, among the characters, to see it. In this connection Hal's speech over the dead body of Hotspur and his remarks over Falstaff's "dead" body, which he discovers a moment later, are worth careful consideration.

William Empson has pointed out (in his *English Pastoral Poetry*) that Hal's remarks here involve a series of puns applying both to largeness of body and to greatness of spirit. Of Hotspur the prince says:

> When that this body did contain a spirit,
> A kingdom for it was too small a bound. . . .
> . . . . this earth that bears the dead
> Bears not alive so stout a gentleman.

A few lines later, he is saying of Falstaff:

> What, old acquaintance! could not all this flesh
> Keep in a little life? Poor Jack, farewell!
> I could have better spared a better man:
> O, I should have a heavy miss of thee,
> If I were much in love with vanity!
> Death hath not struck so fat a deer to-day, . . .

Hotspur has had too much spirit for the flesh; Falstaff has had so much flesh that it is ironical that the spirit has escaped at all. (The irony is increased, of course, by our knowing that Prince Hal little realizes how truly he speaks: the flesh that Falstaff so comfortably hugs about himself has *not*, as a matter of fact, allowed the spirit to escape.)

Moreover, it is significant that the prince, although he thinks that Falstaff has died in battle, refers to him as a "deer," a hunted animal, who would not fight back but would try to escape from the pursuit of death. From the standpoint of the huntsman (death) he is a fine animal ("so fat a deer"), and to the prince a "heavy loss" (another pun) though "better men" have died for his cause that day.

Is the prince mocking and cold-hearted? Hardly; the jesting farewell is the sort which accords with the jesting and affectionate companionship of the two in the past. It conveys a depth of feeling that perhaps would not be conveyed by a more solemn tribute.

At least Falstaff, who of course hears the prince's tribute, suffers no hurt feelings from the nature of the tribute. He has no shame and no qualms. In fact, only the word "Embowelled" runs the shivers up and down his back. The idea of being embalmed and given a fine burial by the prince stirs no regrets in him that he did not stand his ground and die honorably. Falstaff values his bowels. He is far from done with his gorbelly. Hotspur may have the prince's compliment and the noble burial which, doubtless, the prince intends for him. Falstaff is perfectly satisfied to abide by the choice which he has made.

Falstaff's Failure. Still, from the point of view of the need for responsibility and authority, Falstaff's conduct is childishly frivolous, if not much worse—as is his conduct throughout the battle. On one level, it is very funny when Prince Hal reaches into Falstaff's holster and pulls out a bottle of sack; and the prince himself doubtless smiles as he delivers his reprimand. But the reprimand is deserved: Falstaff won't realize that the battlefield is no place for joking. Indeed, though Shakespeare allows Falstaff his due even here, he has made the case against Falstaff very plain. Consider the incident in Act V. iv. An Elizabethan audience would not have missed the point when, just after Falstaff has stabbed the dead Hotspur, Prince Hal came on the scene with his younger brother, Prince John, and says to him

> Come, brother John; full bravely hast thou flesh'd
> Thy maiden sword.

The commendation of Prince John applies ironically to "Brother" John Falstaff—here in full view of the audience—whose sword is a "maiden" sword too, which he has just "flesh'd" safely in the dead Percy. The boy prince John has shown himself a man: Sir John Falstaff has shown himself a child.

5. FALSTAFF AND THE WORLD OF HISTORY

The student may possibly object to so heavy an emphasis upon the battlefield scenes: yet our search for the unity of the play demands that we consider carefully this one group of scenes in which all the characters come together. Besides bringing all the characters together, too, the battle scenes subordinate Falstaff, for all his delightfulness, to something larger (somewhat to the resentment of readers to whom Falstaff is a kind of demigod); and this subordination itself is a unifying process.

But the battle scenes do not cancel out the more widely discussed tavern scenes; they qualify the tavern scenes. We may now return to reconsider the tavern scenes in the light of these qualifications.

It is perhaps significant that Falstaff is introduced to us with the line: "Now, Hal, what time of day is it, lad?"—a question which the prince answers with a jest: ". . . What a devil hast thou to do with the time of the day? Unless hours were cups of sack and minutes capons and clocks the tongues of bawds and dials the signs of leaping-houses and the blessed sun himself a fair hot wench in flame-coloured taffeta, I see no reason why thou shouldst be so superfluous to demand the time of the day." The jesting in the prince's speech may not come quite up to the better efforts of Falstaff himself; but the speech, quite apart from the jesting, is perfectly true. It is true in a deeper sense than even the prince realizes.

It is indeed an absurdity for Falstaff to ask the time of day, for Falstaff has properly nothing to do with the world of time. He transcends the time-ridden world of important affairs—the world of appointments to be kept, of tasks to be performed, of responsibilities to be undertaken. Time does not exist in his world. This is not to say, of course, that Falstaff's world is one in which nothing ever happens. For Falstaff, that world is interesting and even exciting. But in it, one is not dogged by time just as the child is not dogged by time in his world.

Falstaff and the King. For Falstaff, each day is a new day, lived for itself. The future does not cast a cloud over the present. This characteristic Shakespeare has emphasized by pointing up a sharp contrast between

Falstaff and the king. The king is bedeviled with insomnia; Falstaff is not. Even with the bailiff at the door looking for a "gross fat man" suspected of robbery, Falstaff behind the arras drops off to sleep as naturally as would an exhausted child. Falstaff has nothing to do with time; but Henry, the king, is obsessed with time. The king not only makes history—his life *is* history. In the great tavern scene (II. iv) in which Falstaff plays the part of the king, Falstaff, as we have earlier observed (see Question 8 on Act II), parodies the sententious Euphuistic style which was popular in the period. But the parody involves more than a mere topical allusion: Falstaff is using the parody of style as an instrument for a deeper parody. He is mocking at the kind of seriousness with which authority has to express— and *take*—itself: the carefully balanced antitheses, the allusions to natural history, the appeal to learned authorities, the labored truisms—e.g., "There is a thing, Harry, which thou hast often heard of, and it is known to many in our land by the name of pitch: this pitch, as ancient writers do report, doth defile; . . ." The fun is good-humored; but the criticism which it turns upon the institutions of authority is penetrating, and, as far as it goes, perfectly fair. Falstaff as "king" in the tavern is a delightful comedian *because* he is a recognizable monarch; that is, he does not use the pose of royalty merely for slap-stick effects.

But Shakespeare, whom we see constantly balancing scene against scene, has the king "counterfeited" once more in the play on the battlefield, where knights and nobles wear the king's armor. Sir Walter Blunt, so dressed, is accosted by Douglas with "some tell me that thou art a king," and replies with the noble lie, "They tell thee true." He fights with Douglas and dies for the king—doubly. Falstaff appears on the scene immediately and, noticing Blunt's dead body, remarks "there's honour for you!" No aping of the king for him! The king's robes in the tavern play are one thing; the king's coat of arms on the battlefield, quite another.[*]

6. SHAKESPEARE'S ATTITUDE TOWARD FALSTAFF AND THE PRINCE

Here we come to the crucial problem of unity: what attitude, finally, are we to adopt toward Falstaff and the prince? Which is right? With which

[*] There has been of late a tendency to defend Falstaff even here: to say that Falstaff in his debunking of honor is right after all; that Falstaff sees truly through the empty conventions of "honor"; that he refuses to be taken in by the vainglorious pretensions of the usurper, Henry Bolingbroke, to "honor" and to a legitimacy which he does not deserve. Such critics go on to point out that the device of clothing a number of knights so as to counterfeit the king makes rather hollow all the talk about chivalry and honor that goes on with regard to the battle.

But to take this position is to read into the play far more than the play warrants. If the dynastic pretensions of various people in fifteenth-century England seem trivial enough to us, they did not seem so to Shakespeare's audience or to Shakespeare himself. There is nothing in the play to warrant the belief that Shakespeare is bitterly denying the reality of honor and chivalry. Falstaff never rises to a philosophic indictment which will issue in his calling down a "plague on both your houses."

of the two are our sympathies finally to rest? Those readers who have felt the charm of Falstaff and who have sensed the fact that Shakespeare is not disposed to defend the duplicities of the king are surely right in refusing to dismiss Falstaff as a coward or buffoon. Furthermore, they may be right in feeling that Shakespeare has even revealed in Prince Hal himself a certain cold-blooded calculation.

The probability is that we shall miss the play if we assume that Shakespeare is forcing upon us a choice of the *either-or* variety. Is it not possible that Shakespeare is not asking us to choose at all, but rather to contemplate, with understanding and some irony, a world very much like the world that we know, a world in which compromises have to be made, a world in which the virtues of Falstaff become, under changed conditions, vices, and the vices of the Prince Hal become, under certain conditions, necessary, and thus, in a sense, accommodated to virtue? (One might well reverse the form of this statement. From the point of view of an Elizabethan audience, one would almost certainly have to reverse it thus: Falstaff's vices partake of virtue and the virtues of the prince—an easy camaraderie, a genial understanding, an unwillingness to stand on a haughty dignity—are revealed to him ultimately as vices which must be put away.)

The Two Worlds of the Play. Human beings live in a world of time, and a world in which—except at rare heroic moments—compromises have to be made. Falstaff lives, as we have already suggested, in a world of the eternal present, a timeless world which stands apart from the time-harried world of adult concerns. Yet Shakespeare keeps the balance with complete fairness. Each world has its claims. For the prince to be able to retire for awhile into Falstaff's world is worth something to him. It testifies to his humanity, since Falstaff's world is a part of the human world. It probably makes him a better king than he would be if he followed his more calculating and limited father's wishes. Bathed in the light of Falstaff's world, the coldness, the pomposity, the pretentiousness of the world of high concerns is properly exposed. Yet, after all, men must act; responsibilities must be assumed. To remain in Falstaff's world is to deny the reality of the whole world of adult concerns.

It is ironic, of course, that the human being is thus divided between the claims of two aspects of life. It is ironic, from one point of view, that men must grow up at all—must grow away from the innocence of the timeless and amoral world of childhood into the adult world, where except when crises evoke extraordinary devotion and resolution, compromises and scheming are a regular, and perhaps inevitable, part of human experience. Prince Hal, for example, in entering into the world of affairs, loses something as well as gains something—a matter which the play (particularly in its second part) rather clearly indicates. Falstaff may belong to a world unshadowed by time, but it is not for nothing that Prince Hal appears in a "history" play. He belongs to history—to the world of time—and in the Battle of Shrewsbury he enters into history.

7. HENRY IV AS MATURE COMEDY

The problem of Shakespeare's attitude toward Hal and Falstaff has been argued for a long time, and doubtless will continue to be argued. At the end of *Henry IV, Part Two* the prince, on being crowned, publicly rejects Falstaff, and thus makes formal and explicit what is hinted at at the end of *Part One*. Having arrived at kingship with its serious duties, he can have no more time for such play as the Boar's-Head Tavern afforded. Delightful as Falstaff is, he must now be put by.

The Two Interpretations of Shakespeare's Attitude. With regard to Shakespeare's attitude toward this relationship there have been, in general, two courses taken. The first considers the two plays as constituting a study in the discipline of a young king, a king who was to be celebrated as the ideal king in Shakespeare's *Henry V*. According to this interpretation, the two plays present Falstaff as undergoing a gradual degeneration of character. Thus, it is argued, we lose some of our sympathy for him and are reconciled to the young king's rejection of him.

The second interpretation reverses the first. Here it is argued that Falstaff retains our sympathies to the end. Hal's conduct, on the other hand, is regarded as having, from the beginning, something of Machiavellian policy in it. Hal delights in Falstaff's company during his carefree youth but dashes the old man's hopes rather brutally at the end by publicly disowning him and reading him a rather smug sermon on the subject of good conduct.

Few critics have, of course, accepted either view without some reservations and qualifications, but it may make the issues clearer to state the views in extreme form as is here done. That the matter of our attitude toward the Falstaff-Hal relationship is important comes out clearly if we consult the most recent book on the subject, Dover Wilson's *Falstaff*. Wilson sees the plays as involving basically a study in kingship. Falstaff has to be rejected. Though, for Wilson, he remains brilliantly witty, even through the whole of *Henry IV, Part Two*, he becomes more boastful, with a correspondent weakening of our sympathy for him. And Wilson defends the terms of the rejection: Hal is not a "cad or a prig." Falstaff, after all, is not visited with a heavy punishment. The king sees to it that he, along with his other "wonted followers," is "very well provided for."

Shakespeare's Balance. To repeat, the present analysis agrees on the need of having the matter both ways. Surely, Wilson is at his soundest when he argues that Shakespeare keeps the balance most impartially between Hal and Falstaff; but perhaps he might, on the whole, have made out a more convincing case had he pressed this argument further still instead of trying to mitigate the terms of Falstaff's rejection or to argue that the later Falstaff becomes less attractive than the earlier Falstaff. Is not the real point this: that in Hal's rejection of Falstaff something is lost as well as gained—that a good king, one grants, must reject Falstaff, but that in the process by which a man becomes a good king, something else—

something spontaneous, something in itself good and attractive—must be sacrificed; that growing up is something which man must do and yet that even in growing up he loses, necessarily, something that is valuable?

Shakespeare does not sentimentalize the situation. The rejection is necessary if Hal is to become the king that he ought to be and that England doubtless needs; and yet Falstaff's dashed hopes are presented with due pathos. The sentimentalist will doubtless need to blacken Falstaff's character a little—suppress his sympathy for him—in order to be able to accept his being turned off; or, if he is unable to do this, he will, in order to justify Falstaff's rejection, doubtless have to blacken the prince's character, reading into it more of the "vile politician Bolingbroke" than Shakespeare ever intended. The stern moralist (and he is nearer allied to the sentimentalist than is usually suspected) will do much the same: he will probably applaud the rejection of Falstaff whole-heartedly, or, just possibly and perversely, he will condemn the prince for his acceptance of pomp and power and for his cold heart.

Neither the sentimentalist nor the moralist, then, will be able to accept the play in its fullness. It is possible, of course, that even for the mature reader, the play finally lacks unity—that the balancing of attitudes which has been argued for in this analysis is something which perhaps Shakespeare should have attempted to accomplish but did not, for one reason or another, actually succeed in accomplishing. This, of course, each reader must decide for himself. For the reader who remains unconvinced of any totality of effect, the play will probably remain a collection of brilliant but ill-assorted fragments—the wonderful tavern scenes juxtaposed oddly with passages of dull and pawky history.

For the reader, however, for whom the play does achieve a significant unity it may well seem that here Shakespeare has given us one of the wisest and fullest commentaries on human action possible to the comic mode—a view which scants nothing, which covers up nothing, and which takes into account in making its affirmations the most searching criticism of that which is affirmed. For such a reader, Shakespeare has no easy moral to draw, no simple generalization to make.

Shakespeare's Irony. Moreover, it will be evident that Shakespeare's final attitude toward his characters (and toward the human predicament, generally) is one of a very complex irony, though it is an irony which will be either missed altogether, or easily misinterpreted as an indifferent relativism—that is, a mere balancing of two realms of conduct and a refusal to make any judgment between them. The world which Shakespeare portrays here is a world of contradictions and of mixtures of good and evil. His vision of that world is ultimately a comic vision—if not gaily comic, and surely not bitterly comic, yet informed with the insights of mature comedy, nonetheless. For the comic writer does not attempt to transcend the world of compromises, even though the more thoughtful writer of comedy, as here, may be fully aware of the seriousness of the issues Comedy, after all, does not treat the lives of saints or heroes: it does not attempt to portray the absolute commitment to ultimate issues—the total commitment which transcends, tragically and heroically, the everyday world that we know. Shakespeare does not present Prince Hal (as he might conceivably do in a tragic treatment) as a callous man, the scion of the "vile politician Bolingbroke." Hal will make a good ruler, and Falstaff would undoubtedly make a very bad ruler. Nor, on the other hand, is Falstaff portrayed as a villain: Falstaff, too, has his case. Falstaff's wit—most of it at least—is not merely amusing, trifling. It constitutes a criticism of the world of serious affairs, a criticism which, on certain levels, is thoroughly valid. The rulers of the world had better not leave it totally out of account.

If the prince must choose between two courses of action—and, of course, he must choose—we as readers are not forced to choose: indeed, perhaps the core of Shakespeare's ironic insight comes to this: that man must choose and yet that the choice can never be a wholly satisfactory one. If the play is a comedy in this sense, then the "comic" scenes of the play turn out to be only an aspect of, though an important aspect of, the larger comedy. To repeat, the reader must decide for himself whether he can accept the play as a fully unified organism. But the reader who can so accept it may well feel that it represents Shakespeare's most sophisticated level of comedy, a comedy, indeed, more fine-grained and "serious" than the romantic comedies such as *As You Like It* and written with a surer touch than the "bitter" comedies such as *All's Well That Ends Well*.

QUESTIONS

1. By way of summary, notice how many characters Falstaff is, at one time or another, contrasted with or balanced against. Does this structure tend to create or prevent an artificial symmetry? Does it suggest that the meaning of Falstaff is narrow and easily definable, or rich and elusive?

2. Is Falstaff's account of his battle with Hotspur (V. iv) anticipated by his account of the hold-up in II. iv? How, in each case, does he remain "master of the situation"?

3. Note how the word *counterfeit* keeps echoing through V. iv. You will find it, on one occasion, balanced against the word *true*, and you will also find other terms suggesting the same antithesis. Do such passages suggest to you a continued treatment of the problem suggested by the *true-false* chorus in Acts I and II? Consult Act II, Question 12.

4. We have said that Shakespeare's treatment of his theme is essentially comic—rather than sentimental or moralistic. In fact, the entire discussion of what the play "says" implies that the play is comedy and implies, at the same time, a definition of comedy. By way of taking a further step toward a definition of comedy, the student should re-read, in this connection, the section "The Nature of Comedy" in the analysis of *Lady Winder-mere's Fan*. In each play he will find a tendency to contemplate, in a balanced, objective manner, the merits of certain contrasting claims to

which human beings are subject. Elsewhere we have suggested, further, that "the way of the world" is a key phrase to the nature of comedy. Does *Henry IV* tend to strengthen or diminish the merits of that suggestion?

5. It may have occurred to the student that a discussion of *Henry IV, Part One* as a kind of comedy is really irrelevant since the play is technically not a comedy or tragedy but a "history." (The first folio of Shakespeare's plays divides the plays into these three categories and places the Henry IV plays among the "histories.") Yet even if we assume that there is a distinct *genre* called history, still, is not the matter of the author's attitude toward his characters and their doings relevant and important? Is it not obviously of great importance in this play? And do not comedy and tragedy involve most importantly the matter of attitude—the degree of seriousness, the degree of sympathy, the degree of ironical qualificacion with which the author would have his audience take the materials in question?

6. The student should read *Henry IV, Part Two* and then attempt to answer the following questions: Is there further development in the character of Prince Hal? Does the character of Falstaff suffer any degeneration? Are the comic scenes in this part as funny as those in *Part One*? Do the history elements and the comedy elements in this play form a unity? If so, in what terms? What is the special role of Prince John in this play? Consider, in answering this question, the fact that Prince John ensnares the rebels by a piece of sharp dealing. Does this have any effect on our attitude toward the "honor" and chivalry of those who support the crown? Does the absence of any figure like Hotspur on the rebel side affect our attitude toward the rebels? What attitude are we to take toward the rejection of Falstaff at the end of the play? In general, test your theories about Falstaff and Hal and about the general theme of *Part One* against the substance of *Part Two*. (In this connection read the first scenes of *Henry V* recounting the death of Falstaff. How does this last comment by Shakespeare on Falstaff affect, if at all, the total picture of Falstaff?)

7. The student should read *The Merry Wives of Windsor*. Why have most scholars and critics agreed that the Falstaff here depicted differs from the Falstaff of the Henry plays? In what respects is he different? For what is his humor used in this play? Would it be fair to say that the comedy of this play approaches farce? Is it possible that *The Merry Wives* constitutes evidence that, since Falstaff is a more brilliant comic character in the "history" plays, the serious material, though superficially incongruous, is necessary after all? In other words, does not *The Merry Wives* suggest that the apparently incongruous mixture of history and comedy is justified since Falstaff, against a purely comic background, is really not so comic as Falstaff against the background of serious concerns?

5. Congreve, *The Way of the World*

WILLIAM CONGREVE'S *The Way of the World* (1700) is usually thought of, despite its late date, as belonging to "Restoration Comedy"—the witty, satirical comedy characteristic of the period after the restoration of the Stuart line to the British throne in 1660. Indeed, Congreve's play is often described as the last and best production of that period of English comedy.

Although posterity has consistently made some such evaluation of the play, *The Way of the World* was not successful when it was first presented. As he reads, the student should try to discover the reasons why the play did fail, and at the same time why it has since been much admired. Two aspects of the play which the student will very soon notice are the complexity of the plot and the brilliance of the wit, and in these perhaps, all the answers may be found.

It has been somewhat of a fashion to say that the plot can be ignored, more or less, and the witty passages simply read for their own sake; and it may be of service to the student to keep this dictum in mind as he reads. If he decides that the plot is indeed only a frothy addition to the conversation, he will of course have to conclude that the play falls short of dramatic perfection. But if he finds that he can make a case for the plot, he will obviously feel that Congreve has produced not only a witty, but also an integrated, work.

At any rate, the student should not neglect the plot from the outset. To judge the play, he must see clearly what is going on, and he may do very well to give the play, before he attempts further study, the two careful readings which are needed if the plot is to be got straight. Nor will repetition detract from appreciation of the repartee.

It may well be that the student, as he begins to read this play, will find himself reminded of Sheridan's *The School for Scandal*. The fact that he has read Sheridan's play may, indeed, make the reading of Congreve's comedy somewhat easier, for some of the resemblances between the plays are very real, and some are significant on a deeper level. But though the world of 1700, like that of 1777, was a world of coffee-houses, periwigs, and brilliant fashion, the England of 1700 differs in some very important regards from the England of 1777. What is even more to the purpose, however, is that the plays differ even more—in mood, in atmosphere, in tone, in quality of intention. The student should obviously use his acquaintance with Sheridan's play to illuminate Congreve's: he should not, however, allow it to blind him to highly important differences which exist between them.

THE WAY OF THE WORLD

DRAMATIS PERSONÆ

FAINALL, *in love with Mrs. Marwood*
MIRABELL, *in love with Mrs. Millamant*
WITWOUD \
PETULANT / *followers of Mrs. Millamant*
SIR WILFULL WITWOUD, *half-brother to Witwoud, and nephew to Lady Wishfort*
WAITWELL, *servant to Mirabell*
Dancers, Footmen, and Attendants
LADY WISHFORT, *enemy to Mirabell, for having falsely pretended love to her*
MRS. MILLAMANT, *a fine lady, niece to Lady Wishfort, and loves Mirabell*

MRS. MARWOOD, *friend to Mr. Fainall, and likes Mirabell*
MRS. FAINALL, *daughter to Lady Wishfort, and wife to Fainall, formerly friend to Mirabell*
FOIBLE, *woman to Lady Wishfort*
MINCING, *woman to Mrs. Millamant*
[BETTY, *waiting-maid at a chocolate-house*]
[PEG, *maid to Lady Wishfort*]
[Singer]

SCENE: *London*

PROLOGUE

Of those few fools who with ill stars are
    cursed,
Sure scribbling fools called poets, fare
    the worst:
For they're a sort of fools which Fortune
    makes,
And after she has made 'em fools, for-
    sakes.
With Nature's oafs 'tis quite a different
    case,   5
For Fortune favors all her idiot-race.
In her own nest the cuckoo-eggs we find,
O'er which she broods to hatch the
    changeling-kind.
No portion for her own she has to spare,
So much she dotes on her adopted care.
    Poets are bubbles, by the town drawn
    in,   11
Suffered at first some trifling stakes to
    win;
But what unequal hazards do they ⎫
    run!   ⎪
Each time they write they venture all ⎪
    they've won: ⎬
The squire that's buttered [1] still, is ⎪
    sure to be undone.   15 ⎭
This author heretofore has found your
    favor;
But pleads no merit from his past behav-
    ior.

To build on that might prove a vain pre-
    sumption,
Should grants, to poets made, admit re-
    sumption: 19
And in Parnassus he must lose his seat,
If that be found a forfeited estate.

    He owns with toil he wrought the fol-
    lowing scenes;
But, if they're naught, ne'er spare him
    for his pains:
Damn him the more; have no com-
    miseration
For dullness on mature deliberation.   25
He swears he'll not resent one hissed- ⎫
    off scene,   ⎪
Nor, like those peevish wits, his play ⎬
    maintain,   ⎪
Who, to assert their sense, your taste ⎪
    arraign. ⎭
Some plot we think he has, and some
    new thought;
Some humor too, no farce—but that's a
    fault.   30
Satire, he thinks, you ought not to ex-
    pect;
For so reformed a town who dares cor-
    rect?
To please, this time, has been his sole
    pretence,
He'll not instruct, lest it should give of-
    fence.

---

[1] Compare the modern slang term.

Should he by chance a knave or fool expose,   35
That hurts none here; sure, here are none
  of those.
In short, our play shall (with your leave   5
  to show it)
Give you one instance of a passive poet,
Who to your judgments yields all resignation;
So save or damn, after your own discre-   10
  tion.   40

ACT I

[SCENE: A chocolate-house.]

[*Mirabell and Fainall rising from cards,
Betty waiting.*]

Mirabell: You are a fortunate man,
Mr. Fainall!

Fainall: Have we done?

Mirabell: What you please. I'll play
on to entertain you.

Fainall: No, I'll give you your revenge
another time, when you are not so indifferent; you are thinking of something   25
else now, and play too negligently. The
coldness of a losing gamester lessens the
pleasure of the winner. I'd no more play
with a man that slighted his ill fortune
than I'd make love to a woman who   30
undervalued the loss of her reputation.

Mirabell: You have a taste extremely
delicate, and are for refining on your
pleasures.

Fainall: Prithee, why so reserved?   35
Something has put you out of humor.

Mirabell: Not at all. I happen to be
grave to-day, and you are gay; that's all.

Fainall: Confess, Millamant and you
quarrelled last night after I left you; my   40
fair cousin has some humors that would
tempt the patience of a stoic. What,
some coxcomb came in, and was well
received by her, while you were by?

Mirabell: Witwoud and Petulant; and   45
what was worse, her aunt, your wife's
mother, my evil genius; or to sum up all
in her own name, my old Lady Wishfort
came in.

Fainall: Oh, there it is then! She has   50
a lasting passion for you, and with

reason.—What, then my wife was
there?

Mirabell: Yes, and Mrs. Marwood,
and three or four more, whom I never
saw before. Seeing me, they all put on
their grave faces, whispered one another; then complained aloud of the
vapors [2] and after fell into a profound
silence.

Fainall: They had a mind to be rid of   10
you.

Mirabell: For which reason I resolved
not to stir. At last the good old lady broke
through her painful taciturnity with an
invective against long visits. I would   15
not have understood her, but Millamant
joining in the argument, I rose, and with
a constrained smile, told her I thought
nothing was so easy as to know when a
visit began to be troublesome. She   20
reddened, and I withdrew without expecting her reply.

Fainall: You were to blame to resent
what she spoke only in compliance with
her aunt.   25

Mirabell: She is more mistress of herself than to be under the necessity of
such a resignation.

Fainall: What! though half her fortune depends upon her marrying with   30
my lady's approbation?

Mirabell: I was then in such a humor,
that I should have been better pleased if
she had been less discreet.

Fainall: Now I remember, I wonder   35
not they were weary of you; last night
was one of their cabal nights. They
have 'em three times a week, and meet
by turns at one another's apartments,
where they come together like the coro-   40
ner's inquest, to sit upon the murdered
reputations of the week. You and I are
excluded, and it was once proposed that
all the male sex should be excepted; but
somebody moved that, to avoid scandal, 45
there might be one man of the community, upon which motion Witwoud
and Petulant were enrolled members.

Mirabell: And who may have been the
foundress of this sect? My Lady Wisha-   50
  [2] The blues.

fort, I warrant, who publishes her detestation of mankind, and, full of the vigor of fifty-five, declares for a friend and ratafia [3]; and let posterity shift for itself, she'll breed no more.

Fainall: The discovery of your sham addresses to her, to conceal your love to her niece, has provoked this separation; had you dissembled better, things might have continued in the state of nature.

Mirabell: I did as much as man could, with any reasonable conscience; I proceeded to the very last act of flattery with her, and was guilty of a song in her commendation. Nay, I got a friend to put her into a lampoon and compliment her with the imputation of an affair with a young fellow, which I carried so far that I told her the malicious town took notice that she was grown fat of a sudden; and when she lay in of a dropsy, persuaded her she was reported to be in labor. The devil's in't, if an old woman is to be flattered further, unless a man should endeavor downright personally to debauch her; and that my virtue forbade me. But for the discovery of this amour I am indebted to your friend, or your wife's friend, Mrs. Marwood.

Fainall: What should provoke her to be your enemy unless she has made you advances which you have slighted? Women do not easily forgive omissions of that nature.

Mirabell: She was always civil to me till of late. I confess I am not one of those coxcombs who are apt to interpret a woman's good manners to her prejudice, and think that she who does not refuse 'em everything, can refuse 'em nothing.

Fainall: You are a gallant man, Mirabell; and though you may have cruelty enough not to satisfy a lady's longing, you have too much generosity not to be tender of her honor. Yet you speak with an indifference which seems to be affected and confesses you are conscious of a negligence.

[3] A liqueur flavored with fruit or fruit kernels.

Mirabell: You pursue the argument with a distrust that seems to be unaffected and confesses you are conscious of a concern for which the lady is more indebted to you than is your wife.

Fainall: Fie, fie, friend! If you grow censorious I must leave you.—I'll look upon the gamesters in the next room.

Mirabell: Who are they?

Fainall: Petulant and Witwoud.—[*To Betty.*] Bring me some chocolate. [*Exit Fainall.*]

Mirabell: Betty, what says your clock?

Betty: Turned of the last canonical hour,[4] sir. [*Exit Betty.*]

Mirabell: How pertinently the jade answers me!—[*Looking on his watch.*]—Ha? almost one o'clock!—Oh, y'are come! [*Enter a Servant.*] Well, is the grand affair over? You have been something tedious.

Servant: Sir, there's such coupling at Pancras [5] that they stand behind one another, as 'twere in a country dance. Ours was the last couple to lead up, and no hopes appearing of dispatch—besides, the parson growing hoarse, we were afraid his lungs would have failed before it came to our turn; so we drove round to Duke's-place [6] and there they were riveted in a trice.

Mirabell: So, so! You are sure they are married?

Servant: Married and bedded, sir; I am witness.

Mirabell: Have you the certificate?

Servant: Here it is, sir.

Mirabell: Has the tailor brought Waitwell's clothes home, and the new liveries?

Servant: Yes, sir.

Mirabell: That's well. Do you go home again, d'ye hear, and adjourn the consummation till further orders. Bid Waitwell shake his ears, and Dame Partlet rustle up her feathers and meet me at

[4] Hour of legal marriage in a parish church.
[5] St. Pancras Church, where marriages were performed without a license at any time.
[6] Site of St. James's church, where many irregular marriages took place.

one o'clock by Rosamond's Pond,[7] that I may see her before she returns to her lady; and as you tender your ears be secret. [*Exit Servant.*] [*Enter Fainall and Betty.*]

Fainall: Joy of your success, Mirabell; you look pleased.

Mirabell: Aye; I have been engaged in a matter of some sort of mirth, which is not yet ripe for discovery. I am glad this is not a cabal night. I wonder, Fainall, that you, who are married and of consequence should be discreet, will suffer your wife to be of such a party.

Fainall: Faith, I am not jealous. Besides, most who are engaged are women and relations; and for the men, they are of a kind too contemptible to give scandal.

Mirabell: I am of another opinion. The greater the coxcomb, always the more the scandal; for a woman who is not a fool, can have but one reason for associating with a man who is one.

Fainall: Are you jealous as often as you see Witwoud entertained by Millamant?

Mirabell: Of her understanding I am, if not of her person.

Fainall: You do her wrong; for, to give her her due, she has wit.

Mirabell: She has beauty enough to make any man think so; and complaisance enough not to contradict him who shall tell her so.

Fainall: For a passionate lover, methinks you are a man somewhat too discerning in the failings of your mistress.

Mirabell: And for a discerning man, somewhat too passionate a lover; for I like her with all her faults—nay, like her for her faults. Her follies are so natural, or so artful, that they become her; and those affectations which in another woman would be odious, serve but to make her more agreeable. I'll tell thee, Fainall, she once used me with that insolence, that in revenge I took her to pieces, sifted her, and separated her

[7] In St. James's Park, scene of Act II.

failings; I studied 'em, and got em by rote. The catalogue was so large that I was not without hopes one day or other to hate her heartily: to which end I so used myself to think of 'em, that at length, contrary to my design and expectation, they gave me every hour less and less disturbance, till in a few days it became habitual to me to remember 'em without being displeased. They are now grown as familiar to me as my own frailties, and, in all probability, in a little time longer I shall like 'em as well.

Fainall: Marry her, marry her! Be half as well acquainted with her charms as you are with her defects, and my life on't, you are your own man again.

Mirabell: Say you so?

Fainall: Aye, aye, I have experience: I have a wife, and so forth. [*Enter Messenger.*]

Messenger: Is one Squire Witwoud here?

Betty: Yes, what's your business?

Messenger: I have a letter for him from his brother Sir Wilfull, which I am charged to deliver into his own hands.

Betty: He's in the next room, friend—that way. [*Exit Messenger.*]

Mirabell: What, is the chief of that noble family in town—Sir Wilfull Witwoud?

Fainall: He is expected to-day. Do you know him?

Mirabell: I have seen him; he promises to be an extraordinary person. I think you have the honor to be related to him.

Fainall: Yes; he is half-brother to this Witwoud by a former wife, who was sister to my Lady Wishfort, my wife's mother. If you marry Millamant, you must call cousins too.

Mirabell: I had rather be his relation than his acquaintance.

Fainall: He comes to town in order to equip himself for travel.

Mirabell: For travel! Why, the man that I mean is above forty.

Fainall: No matter for that; 'tis for

the honor of England, that all Europe should know we have blockheads of all ages.

Mirabell: I wonder there is not an act of parliament to save the credit of the 5 nation, and prohibit the exportation of fools.

Fainall: By no means; 'tis better as 'tis. 'Tis better to trade with a little loss, than be quite eaten up with being 10 overstocked.

Mirabell: Pray, are the follies of this knight-errant and those of the squire his brother anything related?

Fainall: Not at all; Witwoud grows 15 by the knight, like a medlar [8] grafted on a crab. One will melt in your mouth, and t'other set your teeth on edge; one is all pulp, and the other all core.

Mirabell: So one will be rotten before 20 he be ripe, and the other will be rotten without ever being ripe at all.

Fainall: Sir Wilfull is an odd mixture of bashfulness and obstinacy.—But when he's drunk, he's as loving as the 25 monster in *The Tempest*,[9] and much after the same manner. To give t'other his due, he has something of good nature, and does not always want wit.

Mirabell: Not always; but as often as 30 his memory fails him, and his commonplace of comparisons. He is a fool with a good memory and some few scraps of other folks' wit. He is one whose conversation can never be approved; yet 35 it is now and then to be endured. He has indeed one good quality—he is not exceptious; for he so passionately affects the reputation of understanding raillery, that he will construe an affront into a 40 jest, and call downright rudeness and ill language, satire and fire.

Fainall: If you have a mind to finish his picture, you have an opportunity to do it at full length.—Behold the 45 original! [*Enter Witwoud.*]

Witwoud: Afford me your compas-

[8] Fruit resembling the crab-apple; edible only when it begins to decay. [9] Caliban; cf. the Dryden-Davenant version of the play, 50 Act III.

sion, my dears! Pity me, Fainall! Mirabell, pity me!

Mirabell: I do, from my soul.

Fainall: Why, what's the matter?

Witwoud: No letters for me, Betty?

Betty: Did not a messenger bring you one but now, sir?

Witwoud. Aye, but no other?

Betty: No, sir.

Witwoud: That's hard, that's very hard.—A messenger, a mule, a beast of burden! He has brought me a letter from the fool my brother, as heavy as a panegyric in a funeral sermon, or a copy of commendatory verses from one poet to another. And what's worse, 'tis as sure a forerunner of the author as an epistle dedicatory.

Mirabell: A fool,—and your brother, Witwoud!

Witwoud: Aye, aye, my half-brother. My half-brother he is, no nearer, upon honor.

Mirabell: Then 'tis possible he may be but half a fool.

Witwoud: Good, good, Mirabell, *le drôle!* Good, good; hang him, don't let's talk of him.—Fainall, how does your lady? Gad, I say anything in the world to get this fellow out of my head. I beg pardon that I should ask a man of pleasure and the town, a question at once so foreign and domestic. But I talk like an old maid at a marriage; I don't know what I say. But she's the best woman in the world.

Fainall: 'Tis well you don't know what you say, or else your commendation would go near to make me either vain or jealous.

Witwoud: No man in town lives well with a wife but Fainall.—Your judgment, Mirabell?

Mirabell: You had better step and ask his wife if you would be credibly informed.

Witwoud: Mirabell?

Mirabell: Aye.

Witwoud: My dear, I ask ten thousand pardons—gad, I have forgot what I was going to say to you!

Mirabell: I thank you heartily, heartily.

Witwoud: No, but prithee, excuse me—my memory is such a memory.

Mirabell: Have a care of such apologies, Witwoud; for I never knew a fool but he affected to complain either of the spleen [10] or his memory.

Fainall: What have you done with Petulant?

Witwoud: He's reckoning his money —my money it was. I have no luck today.

Fainall: You may allow him to win of you at play, for you are sure to be too hard for him at repartee. Since you monopolize the wit that is between you, the fortune must be his, of course.

Mirabell: I don't find that Petulant confesses the superiority of wit to be your talent, Witwoud.

Witwoud: Come, come, you are malicious now, and would breed debates.—Petulant's my friend, and a very honest fellow, and a very pretty fellow, and has a smattering—faith and troth, a pretty deal of an odd sort of a small wit. Nay, I'll do him justice. I'm his friend, I won't wrong him. And if he had any judgment in the world, he would not be altogether contemptible. Come, come, don't detract from the merits of my friend.

Fainall: You don't take your friend to be over-nicely bred?

Witwoud: No, no, hang him, the rogue has no manners at all, that I must own —no more breeding than a bumbaily, that I grant you—'tis pity, faith; the fellow has fire and life.

Mirabell: What, courage?

Witwoud: Hum, faith I don't know as to that; I can't say as to that. Yes, faith, in a controversy, he'll contradict anybody.

Mirabell: Though 'twere a man whom he feared, or a woman whom he loved?

Witwoud: Well, well, he does not always think before he speaks—we have all our failings. You're too hard upon him—you are, faith. Let me excuse him. I can defend most of his faults, except one or two. One he has, that's the truth on't; if he were my brother, I could not acquit him—that, indeed, I could wish were otherwise.

Mirabell: Aye, marry, what's that, Witwoud?

Witwoud: O pardon me!—Expose the infirmities of my friend?—No, my dear, excuse me there.

Fainall: What! I warrant he's unsincere, or 'tis some such trifle.

Witwoud: No, no, what if he be? 'Tis no matter for that; his wit will excuse that. A wit should no more be sincere than a woman constant; one argues a decay of parts, as t'other of beauty.

Mirabell: Maybe you think him too positive?

Witwoud: No, no, his being positive is an incentive to argument, and keeps up conversation.

Fainall: Too illiterate?

Witwoud: That? That's his happiness: his want of learning gives him the more opportunities to show his natural parts.

Mirabell: He wants words?

Witwoud: Aye, but I like him for that, now; for his want of words gives me the pleasure very often to explain his meaning.

Fainall: He's impudent?

Witwoud: No, that's not it.

Mirabell: Vain?

Witwoud. No.

Mirabell: What! He speaks unseasonable truths sometimes, because he has not wit enough to invent an evasion?

Witwoud: Truths! ha! ha! ha! No, no; since you will have it—I mean, he never speaks truth at all—that's all. He will lie like a chambermaid, or a woman of quality's porter. Now, that is a fault. [*Enter Coachman.*]

Coachman: Is Master Petulant here, mistress?

Betty: Yes.

Coachman: Three gentlewomen in a coach would speak with him.

[10] Melancholy; bad humor.

Fainall: O brave Petulant!—three!

Betty: I'll tell him.

Coachman: You must bring two dishes of chocolate and a glass of cinnamon-water. [*Exit Coachman.*]

Witwoud: That should be for two fasting strumpets, and a bawd troubled with wind. Now you may know what the three are.

Mirabell: You are very free with your friend's acquaintance.

Witwoud: Aye, aye, friendship without freedom is as dull as love without enjoyment, or wine without toasting. But to tell you a secret, these are trulls whom he allows coachhire, and something more, by the week, to call on him once a day at public places.

Mirabell: How!

Witwoud: You shall see he won't go to 'em, because there's no more company here to take notice of him.—Why, this is nothing to what he used to do; before he found out this way, I have known him call for himself.

Fainall: Call for himself! What dost thou mean?

Witwoud: Mean! Why, he would slip you out of this chocolate-house just when you had been talking to him; as soon as your back was turned—whip, he was gone!—then trip to his lodging, clap on a hood and scarf and a mask, slap into a hackney-coach, and drive hither to the door again in a trice, where he would send in for himself, that is, I mean—call for himself, wait for himself; nay, and what's more, not finding himself, sometimes leave a letter for himself.

Mirabell: I confess this is something extraordinary —I believe he waits for himself now, he is so long a-coming.—Oh! I ask his pardon. [*Enter Petulant.*]

Betty: Sir, the coach stays.

Petulant: Well, well; I come.—'Sbud, a man had as good be a professed midwife as a professed whoremaster, at this rate! To be knocked up and raised at all hours, and in all places! Pox on 'em, I won't come!—D'ye hear, tell 'em I won't come—let 'em snivel and cry their hearts out.

Fainall: You are very cruel, Petulant.

Petulant: All's one, let it pass. I have a humor to be cruel.

Mirabell: I hope they are not persons of condition that you use at this rate.

Petulant: Condition! condition's a dried fig if I am not in humor!—By this hand, if they were your—a—a—your what-d'ye-call-'ems themselves, they must wait or rub off, if I want appetite.

Mirabell: What-d'ye-call-'ems! What are they, Witwoud?

Witwoud: Empresses, my dear: by your what-d'ye-call-'ems he means sultana queens.

Petulant: Aye, Roxolanas.[11]

Mirabell: Cry you mercy.

Fainall: Witwoud says they are—

Petulant: What does he say th' are?

Witwoud: I? Fine ladies, I say.

Petulant: Pass on, Witwoud.— Hark'ee, by this light, his relations—two co-heiresses, his cousins, and an old aunt who loves caterwauling better than a conventicle.[12]

Witwoud: Ha, ha, ha! I had a mind to see how the rogue would come off.—Ha, ha, ha! Gad, I can't be angry with him if he had said they were my mother and my sisters.

Mirabell: No?

Witwoud: No; the rogue's wit and readiness of invention charm me. Dear Petulant!

Betty: They are gone, sir, in great anger.

Petulant: Enough; let 'em trundle. Anger helps complexion—saves paint.

Fainall: This continence is all dissembled; this is in order to have something to brag of the next time he makes court to Millamant and swear he has abandoned the whole sex for her sake.

Mirabell: Have you not left off your

[11] Sultana in Davenant's *The Siege of Rhodes.* [12] A non-conformist religious gathering, reputedly fond of loud worship.

impudent pretensions there yet? I shall cut your throat some time or other, Petulant, about that business.

Petulant: Aye, aye, let that pass—there are other throats to be cut.

Mirabell: Meaning mine, sir?

Petulant: Not I—I mean nobody—I know nothing. But there are uncles and nephews in the world—and they may be rivals—what then? All's one for that.

Mirabell: How! Hark'ee, Petulant, come hither—explain, or I shall call your interpreter.

Petulant: Explain? I know nothing. Why, you have an uncle, have you not, lately come to town, and lodges by my Lady Wishfort's?

Mirabell: True.

Petulant: Why, that's enough—you and he are not friends; and if he should marry and have a child you may be disinherited, ha?

Mirabell: Where hast thou stumbled upon all this truth?

Petulant: All's one for that; why, then, say I know something.

Mirabell: Come, thou art an honest fellow, Petulant, and shalt make love to my mistress; thou sha't, faith. What ha.t thou heard of my uncle?

Petulant: I? Nothing, I. If throats are to be cut, let swords clash! snug's the word; I shrug and am silent.

Mirabell: Oh, raillery, raillery! Come, I know thou art in the women's secrets.—What, you're a cabalist; I know you stayed at Millamant's last night after I went. Was there any mention made of my uncle or me? Tell me. If thou hadst but good nature equal to thy wit, Petulant, Tony Witwoud, who is now thy competitor in fame, would show as dim by thee as a dead whiting's eye by a pearl of orient; he would no more be seen by thee than Mercury is by the sun. Come, I'm sure thou wo't tell me.

Petulant: If I do, will you grant me common sense then, for the future?

Mirabell: Faith, I'll do what I can for thee, and I'll pray that Heaven may grant it thee in the meantime.

Petulant: Well, hark'ee. [*Mirabell and Petulant talk apart.*]

Fainall: [*To Witwoud.*] Petulant and you both will find Mirabell as warm a rival as a lover.

Witwoud: Pshaw! pshaw! that she laughs at Petulant is plain. And for my part, but that it is almost a fashion to admire her, I should—hark'ee—to tell you a secret, but let it go no further—between friends, I shall never break my heart for her.

Fainall: How!

Witwoud: She's handsome; but she's a sort of an uncertain woman.

Fainall: I thought you had died for her.

Witwoud: Umh—no—

Fainall: She has wit.

Witwoud: 'Tis what she will hardly allow anybody else. Now, demme! I should hate that, if she were as handsome as Cleopatra. Mirabell is not so sure of her as he thinks for.

Fainall: Why do you think so?

Witwoud: We stayed pretty late there last night, and heard something of an uncle to Mirabell, who is lately come to town—and is between him and the best part of his estate. Mirabell and he are at some distance, as my Lady Wishfort has been told; and you know she hates Mirabell worse than a Quaker hates a parrot, or than a fishmonger hates a hard frost. Whether this uncle has seen Mrs. Millamant or not, I cannot say, but there were items of such a treaty being in embryo; and if it should come to life, poor Mirabell would be in some sort unfortunately fobbed,[13] i'faith.

Fainall: 'Tis impossible Millamant should hearken to it.

Witwoud: Faith, my dear, I can't tell; she's a woman, and a kind of humorist.[14]

Mirabell: [*To Petulant.*] And this is the sum of what you could collect last night?

Petulant: The quintessence. Maybe Witwoud knows more, he stayed longer.

---

[13] Cheated. [14] Odd or unpredictable person.

Besides, they never mind him; they say anything before him.

Mirabell: I thought you had been the greatest favorite.

Petulant: Aye, *tête-à-tête*, but not in public, because I make remarks. 5

Mirabell: Do you?

Petulant: Aye, aye; pox, I'm malicious, man! Now, he's soft, you know; they are not in awe of him—the fellow's well-bred; he's what you call a—what-d'ye-call-'em, a fine gentleman.—But he's silly withal.

Mirabell: I thank you. I know as much as my curiosity requires.—Fainall, are you for the Mall? [15]

Fainall: Aye, I'll take a turn before dinner.

Witwoud: Aye, we'll all walk in the Park; the ladies talked of being there.

Mirabell: I thought you were obliged to watch for your brother Sir Wilfull's arrival.

Witwoud: No, no; he comes to his aunt's, my Lady Wishfort. Pox on him! I shall be troubled with him, too; what shall I do with the fool?

Petulant: Beg him for his estate, that I may beg you afterwards, and so have but one trouble with you both. 30

Witwoud: Oh, rare Petulant! Thou art as quick as fire in a frosty morning.

[15] Along St. James's Park.

Thou shalt to the Mall with us, and we'll be very severe.

Petulant: Enough! I'm in a humor to be severe.

Mirabell: Are you? Pray then, walk by yourselves: let not us be accessory to your putting the ladies out of countenance with your senseless ribaldry, which you roar out aloud as often as they pass by you; and when you have made a handsome woman blush, then you think you have been severe.

Petulant: What, what? Then let 'em either show their innocence by not understanding what they hear, or else show their discretion by not hearing what they would not be thought to understand.

Mirabell: But has not thou then sense enough to know that thou oughtest to be most ashamed thyself when thou hast put another out of countenance?

Petulant: Not I, by this hand!—I always take blushing either for a sign of guilt or ill breeding.

Mirabell: I confess you ought to think so. You are in the right, that you may plead the error of your judgment in defence of your practice.

Where modesty's ill manners, 'tis but fit

That impudence and malice pass for wit. [*Exeunt.*]

NOTES AND QUESTIONS ON ACT I

This first act serves to give us some glimpse into the world in which the action of the play takes place. It is the London of the late seventeenth century: it is a world of coffee-houses and periwigs and elaborately formal dress. But the world of the play is particularized further still: it is an upper-class world, a world of fine ladies and attractive, idle gallants. The world of farms and shops lies all about it but does not enter into it. True, there are servants who bob in and out of it, and later there will appear a rough and hearty squire from the country. But the world is essentially one of fashionable people, gaming, gossiping, pursuing their amours.

The scene revealed in the first act specializes this world one degree further still: certain aspects of the world of society are heightened and emphasized. It is a world which not only sets a great deal of store by brilliance, but also succeeds, to a great degree, in being brilliant. The conversation is filled with epigrams and neat retorts. Moreover, it is a knowing and sophisticated conversation, full of shrewd and frequently cynical observations on the way in which human beings behave. The characters plume themselves on knowing the "way of the world."

1. In the period in which the action of the play takes place, the coffeehouses and chocolate-houses were very important centers of male society. How does placing the opening scene in a chocolate-house help to indicate the nature of the world of the play?

2. Act I is devoted largely to exposition: of Mirabell's courtship of Millamant; the anger of Lady Wishfort, Millamant's aunt, at Mirabell because of his pretended love for her; the fact that Millamant will lose half her fortune if she marries without her aunt's consent; Marwood's antagonism to Mirabell; there is also a slight hint of a Marwood-Fainall liaison, and even of Fainall's hoping to get Millamant's money. Find the passages in which we are informed about these matters and decide whether the information is conveyed easily and "naturally." Note which matters Congreve tries to clarify by mentioning them more than once.

Note that the information extends, beyond the mere facts, to the tone of the society and therefore of the play which deals with that society. It is a society of complex relationships and schemings; at this point we may well wonder whether such a world—and the play—is capable of greater depths than those of intrigue. What can Congreve do with it? Mirabell wants to marry Millamant; presumably he wishes to keep her fortune; he must come to terms with a scheming world, a brilliant world that is hard on fools; he seems a critical observer rather than an ardent lover, and Millamant sounds rather fashionable than romantic. In what terms can a love-story flourish in this milieu? Merely as another trick in a tricky plot? Or in a really convincing, significant way?

3. Why does not the author confine the act to the conversation of two persons, Mirabell and Fainall? Why does he bring in Petulant and Witwoud, who seem to have no major part in the action? What do they add, if anything?

4. Is the wittiness of the conversation meant, in part at least, to keep the retailing of the necessary exposition from becoming dull? Is it successful in this regard? What else does the incessant play of wit do?

5. Are the appearance of the footman and his conversation about his marriage at Pancras merely a bit of mystery-mongering? Mirabell's eagerness to make sure that the marriage has taken place and his evident satisfaction on confirming the news, a satisfaction which Fainall notices, would indicate that Mirabell is planning some sort of scheme. Does this liven up the mere retailing of the exposition in this opening act? Does it add forward movement?

6. What is gained, if anything, by having Mirabell appear as the rather studiedly critical lover (p. 393a, 32 ff.)? What is Mirabell's real attitude toward Millamant? Does his attitude heighten or diminish the possibility of the love-plot's producing a sentimental effect?

7. What is gained by Congreve's postponing our introduction to the heroine, Millamant? Of our introduction to her aunt, Lady Wishfort?

8. Analyze the wit in Mirabell's account of his making love to Lady Wishfort and in the passage characterizing Sir Wilfull. Is it in any way reminiscent of the wit in *Lady Windermere's Fan?*

ACT II

[SCENE: St. James's Park.]

[*Enter Mrs. Fainall and Mrs. Marwood.*]

Mrs. Fainall: Aye, aye, dear Marwood, if we will be happy, we must find the means in ourselves and among ourselves. Men are ever in extremes—either 10 doting or averse. While they are lovers, if they have fire and sense, their jealousies are insupportable; and when they cease to love—(we ought to think at least) they loathe; they look upon us 15 with horror and distaste; they meet us like the ghosts of what we were, and as from such, fly from us.

Mrs. Marwood: True, 'tis an unhappy circumstance of life, that love should 20 ever die before us and that the man so often should outlive the lover. But say what you will, 'tis better to be left than never to have been loved. To pass our youth in dull indifference, to refuse 25 the sweets of life because they once must leave us, is as preposterous as to wish to have been born old because we one day must be old. For my part, my youth may wear and waste, but it shall 30 never rust in my possession.

Mrs. Fainall: Then it seems you dissemble an aversion to mankind only in compliance to my mother's humor?

Mrs. Marwood: Certainly. To be free; 35 I have no taste of those insipid dry discourses with which our sex of force must entertain themselves apart from men. We may affect endearments to each other, profess eternal friendships, and 40 seem to dote like lovers; but 'tis not in our natures long to persevere. Love will resume his empire in our breasts and every heart, or soon or late, receive and readmit him as its lawful tyrant. 45

Mrs. Fainall: Bless me, how have I been deceived! Why, you profess a libertine.

Mrs. Marwood: You see my friendship 5 by my freedom. Come, be as sincere; acknowledge that your sentiments agree with mine.

Mrs. Fainall: Never!

Mrs. Marwood: You hate mankind?

Mrs. Fainall: Heartily, inveterately.

Mrs. Marwood: Your husband?

Mrs. Fainall: Most transcendently; aye, though I say it, meritoriously.

Mrs. Marwood: Give me your hand upon it. 15

Mrs. Fainall: There.

Mrs. Marwood: I join with you; what I have said has been to try you.

Mrs. Fainall: Is it possible? Dost thou 20 hate those vipers, men?

Mrs. Marwood: I have done hating 'em, and am now come to despise 'em; the next thing I have to do, is eternally to forget 'em.

Mrs. Fainall: There spoke the spirit 25 of an Amazon, a Penthesilea!

Mrs. Marwood: And yet I am thinking sometimes to carry my aversion further.

Mrs. Fainall: How? 30

Mrs. Marwood: Faith, by marrying; if I could but find one that loved me very well and would be thoroughly sensible of ill usage, I think I should do 35 myself the violence of undergoing the ceremony.

Mrs. Fainall: You would not make him a cuckold?

Mrs. Marwood: No; but I'd make him 40 believe I did, and that's as bad.

Mrs. Fainall: Why had not you as good do it?

Mrs. Marwood: Oh, if he should ever discover it, he would ther know the 45 worst and be out of his pain; but I would have him ever to continue upon the rack of fear and jealousy.

Mrs. Fainall: Ingenious mischief! would thou wert married to Mirabell.

Mrs. Marwood: Would I were!

Mrs. Fainall: You change color.

Mrs. Marwood: Because I hate him.

Mrs. Fainall: So do I, but I can hear him named. But what reason have you to hate him in particular?

Mrs. Marwood: I never loved him; he is, and always was, insufferably proud.

Mrs. Fainall: By the reason you give for your aversion, one would think it dissembled; for you have laid a fault to his charge, of which his enemies must acquit him.

Mrs. Marwood: Oh, then it seems you are one of his favorable enemies! Methinks you look a little pale—and now you flush again.

Mrs. Fainall: Do I? I think I am a little sick o' the sudden.

Mrs. Marwood: What ails you?

Mrs. Fainall: My husband. Don't you see him? He turned short upon me unawares, and has almost overcome me.

[*Enter Fainall and Mirabell.*]

Mrs. Marwood: Ha, ha, ha! He comes opportunely for you.

Mrs. Fainall: For you, for he has brought Mirabell with him.

Fainall: [*To Mrs. Fainall.*] My dear!

Mrs. Fainall: My soul!

Fainall: You don't look well to-day, child.

Mrs. Fainall: D'ye think so?

Mirabell: He is the only man that does, madam.

Mrs. Fainall: The only man that would tell me so, at least, and the only man from whom I could hear it without mortification.

Fainall: Oh, my dear, I am satisfied of your tenderness; I know you cannot resent anything from me, especially what is an effect of my concern.

Mrs. Fainall: Mr. Mirabell, my mother interrupted you in a pleasant relation last night; I would fain hear it out.

Mirabell: The persons concerned in that affair have yet a tolerable reputation. I am afraid Mr. Fainall will be censorious.

Mrs. Fainall: He has a humor more prevailing than his curiosity, and will willingly dispense with the hearing of one scandalous story, to avoid giving an occasion to make another by being seen to walk with his wife. This way, Mr. Mirabell, and I dare promise you will oblige us both. [*Exeunt Mrs. Fainall and Mirabell.*]

Fainall: Excellent creature! Well, sure if I should live to be rid of my wife, I should be a miserable man.

Mrs. Marwood: Aye?

Fainall: For having only that one hope, the accomplishment of it, of consequence, must put an end to all my hopes; and what a wretch is he who must survive his hopes! Nothing remains when that day comes but to sit down and weep like Alexander when he wanted other worlds to conquer.

Mrs. Marwood: Will you not follow 'em?

Fainall: Faith, I think not.

Mrs. Marwood: Pray, let us; I have a reason.

Fainall: You are not jealous?

Mrs. Marwood: Of whom?

Fainall: Of Mirabell.

Mrs. Marwood: If I am, is it inconsistent with my love to you that I am tender of your honor?

Fainall: You would intimate, then, as if[there] were a fellow-feeling between my wife and him.

Mrs. Marwood: I think she does not hate him to that degree she would be thought.

Fainall: But he, I fear, is too insensible.

Mrs. Marwood: It may be you are deceived.

Fainall: It may be so. I do not now begin to apprehend it.

Mrs. Marwood: What?

Fainall: That I have been deceived, madam, and you are false

Mrs. Marwood: That I am false! What mean you?

Fainall: To let you know I see through all your little arts.—Come, you both love him, and both have equally dissembled your aversion. Your mutual jealousies of one another have made you clash till you have both struck fire. I have seen the warm confession reddening on your cheeks and sparkling from your eyes.

Mrs. Marwood: You do me wrong.

Fainall: I do not. 'Twas for my ease to oversee and wilfully neglect the gross advances made him by my wife, that by permitting her to be engaged, I might continue unsuspected in my pleasures and take you oftener to my arms in full security. But could you think, because the nodding husband would not wake, that e'er the watchful over slept?

Mrs. Marwood: And wherewithal can you reproach me?

Fainall: With infidelity, with loving another—with love of Mirabell.

Mrs. Marwood: 'Tis false! I challenge you to show an instance that can confirm your groundless accusation. I hate him!

Fainall: And wherefore do you hate him? He is insensible, and your resentment follows his neglect. An instance!— the injuries you have done him are a proof—your interposing in his love. What cause had you to make discoveries of his pretended passion?—to undeceive the credulous aunt, and be the officious obstacle of his match with Millamant?

Mrs. Marwood: My obligations to my lady urged me. I had professed a friendship to her, and could not see her easy nature so abused by that dissembler.

Fainall: What, was it conscience, then? Professed a friendship! Oh, the pious friendships of the female sex!

Mrs. Marwood: More tender, more sincere, and more enduring than all the vain and empty vows of men, whether professing love to us or mutual faith to one another.

Fainall: Ha, ha, ha! You are my wife's friend, too.

Mrs. Marwood: Shame and ingratitude! Do you reproach me? You, you upbraid me? Have I been false to her, through strict fidelity to you, and sacrificed my friendship to keep my love inviolate? And have you the baseness to charge me with the guilt, unmindful of the merit? To you it should be meritorious that I have been vicious: and do you reflect that guilt upon me which should lie buried in your bosom?

Fainall: You misinterpret my reproof. I meant but to remind you of the slight account you once could make of strictest ties when set in competition with your love to me.

Mrs. Marwood: 'Tis false; you urged it with deliberate malice! 'Twas spoken in scorn, and I never will forgive it.

Fainall: Your guilt, not your resentment, begets your rage. If yet you loved, you could forgive a jealousy; but you are stung to find you are discovered.

Mrs. Marwood: It shall be all discovered.—You too shall be discovered; be sure you shall. I can but be exposed. —If I do it myself I shall prevent your baseness.

Fainall: Why, what will you do?

Mrs. Marwood: Disclose it to your wife; own what has passed between us.

Fainall: Frenzy!

Mrs. Marwood: By all my wrongs I'll do't!—I'll publish to the world the injuries you have done me, both in my fame and fortune! With both I trusted you,—you, bankrupt in honor, as indigent of wealth.

Fainall: Your fame I have preserved. Your fortune has been bestowed as the prodigality of your love would have it, in pleasures which we both have shared. Yet, had not you been false, I had ere this repaid it—'tis true. Had you permitted Mirabell with Millamant to have stolen their marriage, my lady had been incensed beyond all means of reconcilement; Millamant had forfeited the moiety of her fortune, which then would have descended to my wife—and wherefore did I marry but to make lawful prize of a rich widow's wealth, and squander it on love and you?

Mrs. Marwood: Deceit and frivolous pretence!

Fainall: Death, am I not married? What's pretence? Am I not imprisoned, fettered? Have I not a wife?—nay, a wife that was a widow, a young widow, a handsome widow; and would be again a widow, but that I have a heart of proof, and something of a constitution to bustle through the ways of wedlock and this world! Will you yet be reconciled to truth and me?

Mrs. Marwood: Impossible. Truth and you are inconsistent—I hate you, and shall forever.

Fainall: For loving you?

Mrs. Marwood: I loathe the name of love after such usage; and next to the guilt with which you would asperse me, I scorn you most. Farewell!

Fainall: Nay, we must not part thus.

Mrs. Marwood: Let me go.

Fainall: Come, I'm sorry.

Mrs. Marwood: I care not—let me go —break my hands, do! I'd leave 'em to get loose.

Fainall: I would not hurt you for the world. Have I no other hold to keep you here?

Mrs. Marwood: Well, I have deserved it all.

Fainall: You know I love you.

Mrs. Marwood: Poor dissembling!— Oh, that—well, it is not yet—

Fainall: What? What is it not? What is it not yet? It is not yet too late—

Mrs. Marwood: No, it is not yet too late—I have that comfort.

Fainall: It is, to love another.

Mrs. Marwood: But not to loathe, detest, abhor mankind, myself, and the whole treacherous world.

Fainall: Nay, this is extravagance!— Come, I ask your pardon—no tears—I was to blame, I could not love you and be easy in my doubts. Pray, forbear—I believe you; I'm convinced I've done

you wrong, and any way, every way will make amends. I'll hate my wife yet more, damn her! I'll part with her, rob her of all she's worth, and we'll retire somewhere—anywhere—to another world. I'll marry thee—be pacified.— 'Sdeath, they come! Hide your face, your tears.—You have a mask; wear it a moment. This way, this way—be persuaded. [*Exeunt.*] [*Enter Mirabell and Mrs. Fainall.*]

Mrs. Fainall: They are here yet.

Mirabell: They are turning into the other walk.

Mrs. Fainall: While I only hated my husband, I could bear to see him; but since I have despised him, he's too offensive.

Mirabell: Oh, you should hate with prudence.

Mrs. Fainall: Yes, for I have loved with indiscretion.

Mirabell: You should have just so much disgust for your husband as may be sufficient to make you relish your lover.

Mrs. Fainall: You have been the cause that I have loved without bounds, and would you set limits to that aversion of which you have been the occasion? Why did you make me marry this man?

Mirabell: Why do we daily commit disagreeable and dangerous actions? To save that idol, reputation. If the familiarities of our loves had produced that consequence of which you were apprehensive, where could you have fixed a father's name with credit but on a husband? I knew Fainall to be a man lavish of his morals, an interested and professing friend, a false and a designing lover, yet one whose wit and outward fair behavior have gained a reputation with the town enough to make that woman stand excused who has suffered herself to be won by his addresses. A better man ought not to have been sacrificed to the occasion, a worse had not answered to the purpose. When you are weary of him, you know your remedy.

Mrs. Fainall: I ought to stand in some degree of credit with you, Mirabell.

Mirabell: In justice to you, I have made you privy to my whole design, and put it in your power to ruin or advance my fortune.

Mrs. Fainall: Whom have you instructed to represent your pretended uncle?

Mirabell: Waitwell, my servant.

Mrs. Fainall: He is an humble servant[1] to Foible, my mother's woman, and may win her to your interest.

Mirabell: Care is taken for that—she is won and worn by this time. They were married this morning.

Mrs. Fainall: Who?

Mirabell: Waitwell and Foible. I would not tempt any servant to betray me by trusting him too far. If your mother, in hopes to ruin me, should consent to marry my pretended uncle, he might, like Mosca in *The Fox*,[2] stand upon terms; so I made him sure beforehand.

Mrs. Fainall: So if my poor mother is caught in a contract, you will discover the imposture betimes, and release her by producing a certificate of her gallant's former marriage.

Mirabell: Yes, upon condition that she consent to my marriage with her niece, and surrender the moiety of her fortune in her possession.

Mrs. Fainall: She talked last night of endeavoring at a match between Millamant and your uncle.

Mirabell: That was by Foible's direction and my instruction, that she might seem to carry it more privately.

Mrs. Fainall: Well, I have an opinion of your success; for I believe my lady will do anything to get a husband; and when she has this which you have provided for her, I suppose she will submit to anything to get rid of him.

Mirabell: Yes, I think the good lady would marry anything that resembled a man, though 'twere no more than what a butler could pinch out of a napkin.

Mrs. Fainall: Female frailty! We must all come to it if we live to be old and feel the craving of a false appetite when the true is decayed.

Mirabell: An old woman's appetite is depraved like that of a girl—'tis the green sickness of a second childhood, and, like the faint offer of a latter spring, serves but to usher in the fall and withers in an affected bloom.

Mrs. Fainall: Here's your mistress.

[*Enter Mrs. Millamant, Witwoud, and Mincing.*]

Mirabell: Here she comes, i'faith, full sail, with her fan spread and her streamers out, and a shoal of fools for tenders. Ha, no, I cry her mercy!

Mrs. Fainall: I see but one poor empty sculler, and he tows her woman after him.

Mirabell: [*To Mrs. Millamant.*] You seem to be unattended, madam. You used to have the *beau monde* throng after you, and a flock of gay fine perukes hovering round you.

Witwoud: Like moths about a candle. —I had like to have lost my comparison for want of breath.

Mrs. Millamant: Oh, I have denied myself airs to-day. I have walked as fast through the crowd—

Witwoud: As a favorite just disgraced, and with as few followers.

Mrs. Millamant: Dear Mr. Witwoud, truce with your similitudes; for I'm as sick of 'em—

Witwoud: As a physician of a good air. —I cannot help it, madam, though 'tis against myself.

Mrs. Millamant: Yet again! Mincing, stand between me and his wit.

Witwoud: Do, Mrs. Mincing, like a screen before a grate fire.—I confess I do blaze to-day; I am too bright.

Mrs. Fainall: But, dear Millamant, why were you so long?

Mrs. Millamant: Long! Lord, have I not made violent haste? I have asked every living thing I met for you; I have inquired after you as after a new fashion.

[1] Devoted to. [2] See Ben Jonson's *Volpone*, V. v.

Witwoud: Madam, truce with your similitudes.—No, you met her husband, and did not ask him for her.

Mrs. Millamant: By your leave, Witwoud, that were like inquiring after an old fashion, to ask a husband for his wife.

Witwoud: Hum, a hit! a hit! a palpable hit! I confess it.

Mrs. Fainall: You were dressed before I came abroad.

Mrs. Millamant: Aye, that's true.— Oh, but then I had Mincing, what had I? Why was I so long?

Mincing: O mem, your la'ship stayed to peruse a pecket of letters.

Mrs. Millamant: Oh, aye, letters—I had letters—I am persecuted with letters—I hate letters.—Nobody knows how to write letters—and yet one has 'em, one does not know why. They serve one to pin up one's hair.

Witwoud: Is that the way? Pray, madam, do you pin up your hair with all your letters? I find I must keep copies.

Mrs. Millamant: Only with those in verse, Mr. Witwoud; I never pin up my hair with prose. I think I tried once, Mincing.

Mincing: O mem, I shall never forget it.

Mrs. Millamant: Aye, poor Mincing tift and tift [3] all the morning.

Mincing: Till I had the cremp in my fingers, I'll vow, mem; and all to no purpose. But when your la'ship pins it up with poetry, it sits so pleasant the next day as anything, and is so pure and so crips.

Witwoud: Indeed, so "crips"?

Mincing: You're such a critic, Mr. Witwoud.

Mrs. Millamant: Mirabell, did you take exceptions last night? Oh, aye, and went away—now I think on't I'm angry—No, now I think on't I'm pleased—for I believe I gave you some pain.

² Arranged.

Mirabell: Does that please you?

Mrs. Millamant: Infinitely; I love to give pain.

Mirabell: You would affect a cruelty which is not in your nature; your true vanity is in the power of pleasing.

Mrs. Millamant: Oh, I ask your pardon for that—one's cruelty is one's power; and when one parts with one's cruelty, one parts with one's power; and when one has parted with that, I fancy one's old and ugly.

Mirabell: Aye, aye, suffer your cruelty to ruin the object of your power, to destroy your lover—and then how vain, how lost a thing you'll be! Nay, 'tis true: you are no longer handsome when you've lost your lover; your beauty dies upon the instant, for beauty is the lover's gift. 'Tis he bestows your charms— your glass is all a cheat. The ugly and the old, whom the looking-glass mortifies, yet after commendation can be flattered by it and discover beauties in it; for that reflects our praises, rather than your face.

Mrs. Millamant: Oh, the vanity of these men! Fainall, d'ye hear him? If they did not commend us, we were not handsome! Now you must know they could not commend one, if one was not handsome. Beauty the lover's gift!— Lord, what is a lover, that it can give? Why, one makes lovers as fast as one pleases, and they live as long as one pleases, and they die as soon as one pleases: and then, if one pleases, one makes more.

Witwoud: Very pretty. Why, you make no more of making of lovers, madam, than of making so many cardmatches.

Mrs. Millamant: One no more owes one's beauty to a lover, than one's wit to an echo. They can but reflect what we look and say—vain empty things if we are silent or unseen, and want a being.

Mirabell: Yet to those two vain empty things you owe the two greatest pleasures of your life.

Mrs. Millamant: How so?

Mirabell: To your lover you owe the pleasure of hearing yourselves praised, and to an echo the pleasure of hearing yourselves talk.

Witwoud: But I know a lady that loves talking so incessantly, she won't give an echo fair play; she has that everlasting rotation of tongue, that an echo must wait till she dies before it can catch her last words.

Mrs. Millamant: Oh, fiction!—Fainall, let us leave these men.

Mirabell: [*Aside to Mrs. Fainall.*] Draw off Witwoud.

Mrs. Fainall: Immediately.—[*Aloud.*] I have a word or two for Mr. Witwoud. [*Exeunt Witwoud and Mrs. Fainall.*]

Mirabell: [*To Mrs. Millamant.*] I would beg a little private audience too. —You had the tyranny to deny me last night, though you knew I came to impart a secret to you that concerned my love.

Mrs. Millamant: You saw I was engaged.

Mirabell: Unkind! You had the leisure to entertain a herd of fools—things who visit you from their excessive idleness, bestowing on your easiness that time which is the encumbrance of their lives. How can you find delight in such society? It is impossible they should admire you; they are not capable—or if they were, it should be to you as a mortification, for sure to please a fool is some degree of folly.

Mrs. Millamant: I please myself. Besides, sometimes to converse with fools is for my health.

Mirabell: Your health! Is there a worse disease than the conversation of fools?

Mrs. Millamant: Yes, the vapors; fools are physic for it, next to asafœtida.

Mirabell: You are not in a course of fools?

Mrs. Millamant: Mirabell, if you persist in this offensive freedom, you'll displease me.—I think I must resolve, after all, not to have you; we shan't agree.

Mirabell: Not in our physic, it may be.

Mrs. Millamant: And yet our distemper, in all likelihood, will be the same; for we shall be sick of one another. I shan't endure to be reprimanded nor instructed; 'tis so dull to act always by advice, and so tedious to be told of one's faults—I can't bear it. Well, I won't have you, Mirabell,—I'm resolved—I think—you may go.—Ha, ha, ha! What would you give, that you could help loving me?

Mirabell: I would give something that you did not know I could not help it.

Mrs. Millamant: Come, don't look grave, then. Well, what do you say to me?

Mirabell: I say that a man may as soon make a friend by his wit, or a fortune by his honesty, as win a woman by plain dealing and sincerity.

Mrs. Millamant: Sententious Mirabell! Prithee, don't look with that violent and inflexible wise face, like Solomon at the dividing of the child in an old tapestry hanging.

Mirabell: You are merry, madam, but I would persuade you for a moment to be serious.

Mrs. Millamant: What, with that face? No, if you keep your countenance, 'tis impossible I should hold mine. Well, after all, there is something very moving in a lovesick face. Ha, ha, ha!—Well, I won't laugh; don't be peevish—Heigho! now I'll be melancholy—as melancholy as a watch-light.[4] Well, Mirabell, if ever you will win me, woo me now.—Nay, if you are so tedious, fare you well; I see they are walking away.

Mirabell: Can you not find in the variety of your disposition one moment—

Mrs. Millamant: To hear you tell me Foible's married, and your plot like to speed? No.

Mirabell: But how came you to know it?

Mrs. Millamant: Without the help of

[4] A candle in a sick room.

the devil, you can't imagine—unless she should tell me herself. Which of the two it may have been I will leave you to consider; and when you have done thinking of that, think of me. [*Exit Mrs. Milla-mant.*]

Mirabell: I have something more!—Gone!—Think of you? To think of a whirlwind, though 'twere in a whirlwind, were a case of more steady contemplation—a very tranquillity of mind and mansion. A fellow that lives in a windmill, has not a more whimsical dwelling than the heart of a man that is lodged in a woman. There is no point of the compass to which they cannot turn, and by which they are not turned; and by one as well as another. For motion, not method, is their occupation. To know this, and yet continue to be in love, is to be made wise from the dictates of reason, and yet persevere to play the fool by the force of instinct.—Oh, here come my pair of turtles!—What, billing so sweetly! Is not Valentine's Day over with you yet? [*Enter Waitwell and Foible.*] Sirrah Waitwell; why, sure you think you were married for your own recreation, and not for my conveniency.

Waitwell: Your pardon, sir. With submission, we have indeed been solacing in lawful delights; but still with an eye to business, sir. I have instructed her as well as I could. If she can take your directions as readily as my instructions, sir, your affairs are in a prosperous way.

Mirabell: Give you joy, Mrs. Foible.

Foible: Oh, 'las, sir, I'm so ashamed!—I'm afraid my lady has been in a thousand inquietudes for me. But I protest, sir, I made as much haste as I could.

Waitwell: That she did indeed, sir. It was my fault that she did not make more.

Mirabell: That I believe.

Foible: But I told my lady as you instructed me, sir, that I had a prospect of seeing Sir Rowland, your uncle; and that I would put her ladyship's picture in my pocket to show him, which I'll be sure to say has made him so enamored of her beauty, that he burns with impatience to lie at her ladyship's feet and worship the original.

Mirabell: Excellent Foible! Matrimony has made you eloquent in love.

Waitwell: I think she has profited, sir; I think so.

Foible: You have seen Madam Millamant, sir?

Mirabell: Yes.

Foible: I told her, sir, because I did not know that you might find an opportunity; she had so much company last night.

Mirabell: Your diligence will merit more—in the meantime—[*Gives money.*]

Foible: O dear sir, your humble servant!

Waitwell: [*Putting forth his hand.*] Spouse.

Mirabell: Stand off, sir, not a penny!—Go on and prosper, Foible—the lease shall be made good and the farm stocked if we succeed.

Foible: I don't question your generosity, sir, and you need not doubt of success. If you have no more commands, sir, I'll be gone; I'm sure my lady is at her toilet, and can't dress till I come.—Oh, dear, [*looking out*] I'm sure that was Mrs. Marwood that went by in a mask! If she has seen me with you, I'm sure she'll tell my lady. I'll make haste home and prevent her. Your servant, sir.—Bye, Waitwell. [*Exit Foible.*]

Waitwell: Sir Rowland, if you please.—The jade's so pert upon her preferment she forgets herself.

Mirabell: Come, sir, will you endeavor to forget yourself, and transform into Sir Rowland?

Waitwell: Why, sir, it will be impossible I should remember myself.—Married, knighted, and attended all in one day! 'tis enough to make any man forget himself. The difficulty will be how to recover my acquaintance and familiarity with my former self, and fall from my transformation to a reformation into Waitwell. Nay, I shan't be quite the same Waitwell neither; for now, I remember me, I'm married and can't be my own man again.

Aye, there's the grief; that's the sad change of life,
To lose my title, and yet keep my wife. [*Exeunt.*]

NOTES AND QUESTIONS ON ACT II

We have seen how Act I is devoted largely to exposition and to establishing of tone. Act II really continues the process, for here we learn of the relations of Mirabell and Mrs. Fainall, of Mrs. Fainall and her husband, of Mrs. Marwood's relation to Mirabell and Fainall, and of Fainall's having an eye on Millamant's money. Indeed, the play may hardly be said to go forward in this act, for little "happens" except that Foible and Waitwell, having been married, report to Mirabell for orders. Mirabell's conspiracy—about which we learn more—is launched, though it does not really influence the action before Act III. And at best it is only a part of the main action—Mirabell's suit to Millamant.

Two questions will probably occur to the reader: (1) Is the play too slow in starting? (2) Does the plot become too much involved? Some people who saw the play in 1700 felt that the plot was too slight. We know, for example, that a Lady Marow wrote at the time to an acquaintance in the country: "'The Way of the World,' Congreve's new play, doth not answer expectation, there being no plot in it but many witty things to ridicule the Chocolate House, and the fantastical part of the world."

As for slowness: we may assume that Congreve wished to allow us ample time in which to become acquainted with the characters and their complex relationships. In the latter half of the play events occur with breath-taking rapidity; one reversal of situation hurries upon another. It may be argued that their effectiveness is increased by the rather leisurely beginning. A more important point, perhaps, is that the brilliant wit of a good deal of the first two acts is—as Congreve may have hoped—a partial compensation for our not having a sharper sense of forward movement. The wit offers a kind of tension and intellectual movement of its own. But the fact is that we still do not have as definite a sense of dramatic forces and direction as we might have.

As for complexity of plot: whatever Lady Marow may have meant by the "fantastical part of the world," certainly the complication of the love affairs to which we are introduced borders on the fantastical. The tangle is possible, of course, but it hardly seems probable. Yet this we should take into account: that Congreve is engaged in heightening and stylizing what is already a heightened and artificial world. He is not thereby freed, of course, from his responsibility to give us a world which has some relation to the world of human nature which we know; that is, there must be some level on which the world of the play is not merely a distorted and unnatural world. But, here again, noticing the special character of his material, we may be willing to suspend judgment and wait. A fine caricature may hit off a character as well as a fine portrait or a good photograph. We are willing to let the caricaturist falsify details—even violate the natural order of things—if he knows what he is doing and if his caricature as a whole does give us the subject.

Congreve is, as a matter of fact, using a sort of caricature as his method rather than attempting to give us a scientifically accurate picture of life among the upper classes in 1700. Petulant, for instance, is doubtless more foppish than any real fop. Mirabell is probably a little more studiedly detached than any lover is likely to be—then or now. Congreve is obviously laughing at his sophisticated world, and the tangle of relationships which he exhibits is one way of suggesting that that world is artificial, too devious, over-sophisticated. (The method, however, does not debar him from presenting the characters as laughing at themselves or as having depths beneath their surface raillery. In reading the rest of the play, indeed, the student should see to what extent such depths are suggested, especially in Mirabell and Millamant.)

Another aspect of the complexity of relationships, however, and one which equally demands our attention, is the purely technical problem of how clearly that complexity is conveyed to the reader. If the reader or audience remains constantly confused, that fact obviously militates somewhat against the total effectiveness of the work. At this point we are ready to note one part of Congreve's method which undoubtedly creates considerable difficulty for us: more than any playwright whom we have studied, he depends upon talk *about* characters and situations to present to us what we should know about them. In Act I, for instance, Mirabell and Fainall talk about *nine* other characters who are otherwise unknown to us. Nor is the talk idle chat: we are obviously meant to be identifying, and learning things about, these otherwise unknown characters. With *five* of them, we are not aided by a personal appearance until Act II; *two* do not appear until Act III. Thus Act I imposes an almost unbearable weight of attention upon the audience; and a reader is often called upon to go back, sort out, and study the various pieces of information which he has been given. In no other play in this book has an author demanded such active and intense collaboration from his readers. (We may observe, too, that the wit which is shared by almost all the characters, even some of the servants, tends to blur out such distinctions as are made among the characters. Compare *Lady Windermere's Fan*, where, from the start, we have a relatively "straight" character, Lady Windermere, as the focal point for a good deal of the action.)

By now it is clear, therefore, that the reader who wishes to cooperate successfully with the author must be unusually alert in looking for passages that convey important information. Of course, in all mature literature, a high degree of alertness is essential; here, however, it is required, not only for the *meaning*, but also for plain *matters of fact* which usually we may take for granted.

1. At the beginning of this act Mrs. Fainall and Mrs. Marwood dis-

cuss their attitudes toward Mirabell and toward the male sex generally. How do their speeches bear upon the central problem of the play?

2. Is the quarrel between Mrs. Marwood and Fainall in this act too bitter for the tone of a gay comedy? What is its function in the play? Does it contribute to the tone? Does it serve notice that the issues of this play are "serious" ones, after all?

3. What does the banter between Mirabell and Millamant (p. 405a, 44 ff.) reveal: that Millamant is really cruel? That she loves power, or that she is fearful that a wife has no power? Does Mirabell really believe that beauty is the gift of the lover, or is he, on the other hand, fearful lest this turn out to be true indeed? Are these people in love with each other? How seriously are we to take the speech which Mirabell utters just after Millamant has left him?

4. To Mirabell's question, "What, billing so sweetly! Is not Valentine's Day over with you yet?" Waitwell the servant answers: "With submission, we have indeed been solacing in lawful delights; but still with an eye to business, sir." In what ways does the speech make an ironic commentary on the concerns of the play: on the love affairs of the fashionable? On the way of the world? On the institution of marriage? On the hopes of Millamant and Mirabell?

5. What is ironic in the way in which Mr. and Mrs. Fainall address each other on their first meeting in the act (p. 401a, 33 ff.)?

6. How much insight into human motives and impulses does Fainall appear to have?

7. In the interview between Mirabell and Mrs. Fainall (p. 403b, 15 ff.), do you find anything in Mrs. Fainall's character difficult to explain? Is she too spiritless?

8. Analyze the source of the humor in Millamant's lines about pinning up her hair (p. 405a, 21 ff.). Beneath the fooling, is any serious discrimination among lovers implied?

9. Millamant openly says that she likes "to give pain" (p. 405b, 2–3). What does the fact that she says this tell us about her character?

10. What lines in the final speeches of Mirabell, Foible, and Waitwell are meant to direct our attention to coming actions?

11. Note how a series of witticisms sometimes develops from a single concept or image, e.g., "want of breath" (p. 404b, 29 ff.); and health and disease (p. 406a, 38 ff.).

ACT III

[SCENE: A room in Lady Wishfort's house.]

[*Lady Wishfort at her toilet, Peg waiting.*]

Lady Wishfort: Merciful! no news of Foible yet?

Peg: No, madam.

Lady Wishfort: I have no more patience.—If I have not fretted myself till I am pale again, there's no veracity in me! Fetch me the red—the red, do you hear, sweetheart?—An arrant ash-color, as I am a person! Look you how this wench stirs! Why dost thou not fetch me a little red? Didst thou not hear me, Mopus? [1]

10   [1] Cf. modern "dope."

Peg: The red ratafia, does your ladyship mean, or the cherry-brandy?

Lady Wishfort: Ratafia, fool! No, fool. Not the ratafia, fool—grant me patience!—I mean the Spanish paper,[2] idiot—complexion, darling. Paint, paint, paint!—dost thou understand that, changeling, dangling thy hands like bobbins before thee? Why dost thou not stir, puppet? Thou wooden thing upon wires!

Peg: Lord, madam, your ladyship is so impatient!—I cannot come at the paint, madam; Mrs. Foible has locked it up and carried the key with her.

Lady Wishfort: A pox take you both! —Fetch me the cherry-brandy then. [*Exit Peg.*] I'm as pale and as faint, I look like Mrs. Qualmsick, the curate's wife, that's always breeding.—Wench! Come, come, wench, what art thou doing? Sipping? Tasting?—Save thee, dost thou not know the bottle? [*Enter Peg with a bottle and china cup.*]

Peg: Madam, I was looking for a cup.

Lady Wishfort: A cup, save thee! and what a cup hast thou brought!—Dost thou take me for a fairy, to drink out of an acorn? Why didst thou not bring thy thimble? Hast thou ne'er a brass thimble clinking in thy pocket with a bit of nutmeg?—I warrant thee. Come, fill, fill!—So—again.—[*One knocks.*]—See who that is.—Set down the bottle first. —Here, here, under the table.—What, wouldst thou go with the bottle in thy hand, like a tapster? As I'm a person, this wench has lived in an inn upon the road before she came to me, like Maritornes the Asturian in *Don Quixote!*—No Foible yet?

Peg: No, madam, Mrs. Marwood.

Lady Wishfort: Oh, Marwood; let her come in.—Come in, good Marwood. [*Enter Mrs. Marwood.*]

Mrs. Marwood: I'm surprised to find your ladyship in dishabille at this time of day.

Lady Wishfort: Foible's a lost thing— has been abroad since morning, and never heard of since.

Mrs. Marwood: I saw her but now as I came masked through the park, in conference with Mirabell.

Lady Wishfort: With Mirabell!—You call my blood into my face, with mentioning that traitor. She durst not have the confidence! I sent her to negotiate an affair in which, if I'm detected, I'm undone. If that wheedling villain has wrought upon Foible to detect me, I'm ruined. Oh, my dear friend, I'm a wretch of wretches if I'm detected.

Mrs. Marwood: O madam, you cannot suspect Mrs. Foible's integrity.

Lady Wishfort: Oh, he carries poison in his tongue that would corrupt integrity itself! If she has given him an opportunity, she has as good as put her integrity into his hands. Ah, dear Marwood, what's integrity to an opportunity? Hark! I hear her! [*To Peg.*] Go, you thing, and send her in. [*Exit Peg.*] [*To Mrs. Marwood.*] Dear friend, retire into my closet, that I may examine her with more freedom.—You'll pardon me, dear friend; I can make bold with you.—There are books over the chimney—Quarles and Prynne, and *The Short View of the Stage,* with Bunyan's works, to entertain you. [*Exit Mrs. Marwood.*] [*Enter Foible.*]

Lady Wishfort: O Foible, where hast thou been? What hast thou been doing?

Foible: Madam, I have seen the party.

Lady Wishfort: But what hast thou done?

Foible: Nay, 'tis your ladyship has done, and are to do; I have only promised. But a man so enamored—so transported!—Well, if worshipping of pictures be a sin—poor Sir Rowland, I say—

Lady Wishfort: The miniature has been counted like—but hast thou not betrayed me, Foible? Hast thou not detected me to that faithless Mirabell?— What hadst thou to do with him in the Park? Answer me; has he got nothing out of thee?

Foible. [*Aside.*] So the devil has been

[2] Cosmetic.

beforehand with me. What shall I say? —[*Aloud.*]—Alas, madam, could I help it if I met that confident thing? Was I in fault? If you had heard how he used me, and all upon your ladyship's ac- 5 count, I'm sure you would not suspect my fidelity. Nay, if that had been the worst, I could have borne; but he had a fling at your ladyship too. And then I could not hold, but i'faith I gave him 10 his own.

Lady Wishfort: Me? What did the filthy fellow say?

Foible: Oh, madam! 'tis a shame to say what he said—with his taunts and 15 his fleers, tossing up his nose. Humh! (says he) what, you are a hatching some plot (says he), you are so early abroad, or catering (says he), ferreting for some disbanded officer, I warrant.—Half-pay 20 is but thin subsistence (says he)—well, what pension does your lady propose? Let me see (says he); what, she must come down pretty deep now, she's super- annuated (says he) and— 25

Lady Wishfort: Odds my life, I'll have him—I'll have him murdered! I'll have him poisoned! Where does he eat?—I'll marry a drawer [3] to have him poisoned in his wine. I'll send for Robin from 30 Locket's [4] immediately.

Foible: Poison him! poisoning's too good for him. Starve him, madam, starve him: marry Sir Rowland, and get him disinherited. Oh, you would bless your- 35 self to hear what he said!

Lady Wishfort: A villain! Superannu- ated!

Foible: Humh (says he), I hear you are laying designs against me too (says 40 he), and Mrs. Millamant is to marry my uncle (he does not suspect a word of your ladyship); but (says he) I'll fit you for that. I warrant you (says he) I'll hamper you for that (says he)—you and 45 your old frippery [5] too (says he); I'll handle you—

Lady Wishfort: Audacious villain!

Handle me, would he durst!—Frippery? old frippery! Was there ever such a foul-mouthed fellow? I'll be married to- morrow; I'll be contracted to-night.

Foible: The sooner the better, madam.

Lady Wishfort: Will Sir Rowland be here, sayest thou? When, Foible?

Foible: Incontinently, madam. No new sheriff's wife expects the return of her husband after knighthood with that impatience in which Sir Rowland burns for the dear hour of kissing your lady- ship's hand after dinner.

Lady Wishfort: Frippery! superannu- ated frippery! I'll frippery the villain; I'll reduce him to frippery and rags! a tatterdemalion! I hope to see him hung with tatters, like a Long-lane [6] pent- house or a gibbet thief. A slander- mouthed railer! I warrant the spend- thrift prodigal's in debt as much as the million lottery, or the whole court upon a birthday. I'll spoil his credit with his tailor. Yes, he shall have my niece with her fortune, he shall.

Foible: He! I hope to see him lodge in Ludgate [7] first, and angle into Black- friars for brass farthings with an old mitten. [8]

Lady Wishfort: Aye, dear Foible; thank thee for that, dear Foible. He has put me out of all patience. I shall never recompose my features to receive Sir Rowland with any economy of face. This wretch has fretted me that I am abso- lutely decayed. Look, Foible.

Foible: Your ladyship has frowned a little too rashly; indeed, madam. There are some cracks discernible in the white varnish.

Lady Wishfort: Let me see the glass.— Cracks, sayest thou?—why, I am ar- rantly flayed—I look like an old peeled wall. Thou must repair me, Foible, be- fore Sir Rowland comes, or I shall never keep up to my picture.

Foible: I warrant you, madam, a little art once made your picture like you, and

[3] Bartender. [4] A restaurant. [5] Junk; old clothes; second-hand clothing store.

[6] Long-lane: center of old clothes trade [7] Debtors' prison. [8] Using a cord, let down a mitten to collect alms.

now a little of the same art must make you like your picture. Your picture must sit for you, madam.

Lady Wishfort: But art thou sure Sir Rowland will not fail to come? Or will he not fail when he does come? Will he be importunate, Foible, and push? For if he should not be importunate, I shall never break decorums—I shall die with confusion if I am forced to advance.— Oh, no, I can never advance!—I shall swoon if he should expect advances. No, I hope Sir Rowland is better bred than to put a lady to the necessity of breaking her forms. I won't be too coy, neither.—I won't give him despair—but a little disdain is not amiss; a little scorn is alluring.

Foible: A little scorn becomes your ladyship.

Lady Wishfort: Yes, but tenderness becomes me best—a sort of dyingness—you see that picture has a sort of ::—ha, Foible? a swimmingness in the eye—yes, I'll look so.—My niece affects it, but she wants features. Is Sir Rowland handsome? Let my toilet be removed—I'll dress above. I'll receive Sir Rowland here.—Is he handsome? Don't answer me. I won't know; I'll be surprised. I'll be taken by surprise.

Foible: By storm, madam. Sir Rowland's a brisk man.

Lady Wishfort: Is he? Oh, then he'll importune, if he's a brisk man. I shall save decorums if Sir Rowland importunes. I have a mortal terror at the apprehension of offending against decorums. Oh, I'm glad he's a brisk man! —Let my things be removed, good Foible. [*Exit Lady Wishfort.*] [*Enter Mrs. Fainall.*]

Mrs. Fainall: Oh, Foible, I have been in a fright lest I should come too late! That devil Marwood saw you in the Park with Mirabell, and I'm afraid will discover it to my lady.

Foible: Discover what, madam?

Mrs. Fainall: Nay, nay, put not on that strange face! I am privy to the whole design and know that Waitwell,

to whom thou wert this morning married, is to personate Mirabell's uncle, and as such, winning my lady, to involve her in those difficulties from which Mirabell only must release her, by his making his conditions to have my cousin and her fortune left to her own disposal.

Foible: Oh, dear madam, I beg your pardon. It was not my confidence in your ladyship that was deficient, but I thought the former good correspondence between your ladyship and Mr. Mirabell might have hindered his communicating this secret.

Mrs. Fainall: Dear Foible, forget that.

Foible: O dear madam, Mr. Mirabell is such a sweet, winning gentleman—but your ladyship is the pattern of generosity.—Sweet lady, to be so good! Mr. Mirabell cannot choose but be grateful. I find your ladyship has his heart still. Now, madam, I can safely tell your ladyship our success: Mrs. Marwood had told my lady, but I warrant I managed myself. I turned it all for the better. I told my lady that Mr. Mirabell railed at her; I laid horrid things to his charge, I'll vow; and my lady is so incensed that she'll be contracted to Sir Rowland to-night, she says. I warrant I worked her up, that he may have her for asking for, as they say of a Welsh maidenhead.

Mrs. Fainall: O rare Foible!

Foible: Madam, I beg your ladyship to acquaint Mr. Mirabell of his success. I would be seen as little as possible to speak to him: besides, I believe Madam Marwood watches me. — She has a month's mind [9]; but I know Mr. Mirabell can't abide her.—[*Enter Footman.*] John, remove my lady's toilet.— Madam, your servant: my lady is so impatient I fear she'll come for me if I stay.

Mrs. Fainall: I'll go with you up the back stairs lest I should meet her. [*Exeunt.*] [*Enter Mrs. Marwood.*]

[9] Desire.

Mrs. Marwood: Indeed, Mrs. Engine, is it thus with you? Are you become a go-between of this importance?—Yes, I shall watch you. Why, this wench is the *passe-partout,* a very master-key to everybody's strong-box. My friend Fainall, have you carried it so swimmingly? I thought there was something in it, but it seems it's over with you. Your loathing is not from a want of appetite, then, but from a surfeit. Else you could never be so cool to fall from a principal to be an assistant,—to procure for him! A pattern of generosity, that, I confess. Well, Mr. Fainall, you have met with your match.—O man, man! Woman, woman! The devil's an ass: if I were a painter, I would draw him like an idiot, a driveller with a bib and bells. Man should have his head and horns,[10] and woman the rest of him. Poor simple fiend!—"Madam Marwood has a month's mind, but he can't abide her."—'Twere better for him you had not been his confessor in that affair, without you could have kept his counsel closer. I shall not prove another pattern of generosity; he has not obliged me to that with those excesses of himself! And now I'll have none of him.—Here comes the good lady, panting ripe, with a heart full of hope, and a head full of care, like any chemist[11] upon the day of projection. [*Enter Lady Wishfort.*]

Lady Wishfort: Oh, dear Marwood, what shall I say for this rude forgetfulness?—but my dear friend is all goodness.

Mrs. Marwood: No apologies, dear madam; I have been very well entertained.

Lady Wishfort: As I'm a person, I am in a very chaos to think I should so forget myself: but I have such an olio[12] of affairs, really I know not what to do. —[*Calls.*] Foible!—I expect my nephew, Sir Wilfull, every moment, too.—[*Calls again.*] Why, Foible!—He means to travel for improvement.

[10] Symbol of a man with an unfaithful wife.
[11] Alchemist. [12] Mixture; muddle.

Mrs. Marwood: Methinks Sir Wilfull should rather think of marrying than travelling, at his years. I hear he is turned of forty.

Lady Wishfort: Oh, he's in less danger of being spoiled by his travels—I am against my nephew's marrying too young. It will be time enough when he comes back and has acquired discretion to choose for himself.

Mrs. Marwood: Methinks Mrs. Millamant and he would make a very fit match. He may travel afterwards.—'Tis a thing very usual with young gentlemen.

Lady Wishfort: I promise you I have thought on't—and since 'tis your judgment, I'll think on't again. I assure you I will. I value your judgment extremely. On my word, I'll propose it. [*Enter Foible.*]

Lady Wishfort: Come, come, Foible— I had forgot my nephew will be here before dinner. I must make haste.

Foible: Mr. Witwoud and Mr. Petulant are come to dine with your ladyship.

Lady Wishfort: Oh, dear, I can't appear till I'm dressed! Dear Marwood, shall I be free with you again, and beg you to entertain 'em? I'll make all imaginable haste. Dear friend, excuse me. [*Exeunt Lady Wishfort and Foible.*] [*Enter Mrs. Millamant and Mincing.*]

Mrs. Millamant: Sure never anything was so unbred as that odious man!— Marwood, your servant.

Mrs. Marwood: You have a color; what's the matter?

Mrs. Millamant: That horrid fellow, Petulant, has provoked me into a flame: I have broken my fan.—Mincing, lend me yours. Is not all the powder out of my hair?

Mrs. Marwood: No. What has he done?

Mrs. Millamant: Nay, he has done nothing; he has only talked—nay, he has said nothing neither, but he has contradicted everything that has been said. For my part, I thought Witwoud and he would have quarrelled.

Mincing: I vow, mem, I thought once they would have fit.

Mrs. Millamant: Well, 'tis a lamentable thing, I swear, that one has not the liberty of choosing one's acquaintance as one does one's clothes.

Mrs. Marwood: If we had that liberty, we should be as weary of one set of acquaintance, though never so good, as we are of one suit, though never so fine. A fool and a doily stuff would now and then find days of grace, and be worn for variety.

Mrs. Millamant: I could consent to wear 'em if they would wear alike; but fools never wear out they are such *drap du Berri* [13] things. Without one could give 'em to one's chambermaid after a day or two!

Mrs. Marwood: 'Twere better so indeed. Or what think you of the playhouse? A fine, gay, glossy fool should be given there, like a new masking habit, after the masquerade is over and we have done with the disguise. For a fool's visit is always a disguise, and never admitted by a woman of wit but to blind her affair with a lover of sense. If you would but appear barefaced now, and own Mirabell, you might as easily put off Petulant and Witwoud as your hood and scarf. And indeed, 'tis time, for the town has found it; the secret is grown too big for the pretence. 'Tis like Mrs. Primly's great belly; she may lace it down before, but it burnishes [14] on her hips. Indeed, Millamant, you can no more conceal it than my Lady Strammel can her face—that goodly face, which, in defiance of her Rhenish-wine tea,[15] will not be comprehended in a mask.

Mrs. Millamant: I'll take my death, Marwood, you are more censorious than a decayed beauty or a discarded toast.— Mincing, tell the men they may come up.—My aunt is not dressing; their folly is less provoking than your

[13] Woollen cloth originally made at Berry, France. [14] Thrives; increases in size. [15] Rhine wine, taken to reduce corpulence.

malice. [*Exit Mincing.*]—The town has found it! what has it found? That Mirabell loves me is no more a secret than it is a secret that you discovered it to my aunt, or than the reason why you discovered it is a secret.

Mrs. Marwood: You are nettled.

Mrs. Millamant: You're mistaken. Ridiculous!

Mrs. Marwood: Indeed, my dear, you'll tear another fan if you don't mitigate those violent airs.

Mrs. Millamant: Oh, silly! ha, ha, ha! I could laugh immoderately.—Poor Mirabell! His constancy to me has quite destroyed his complaisance for all the world beside. I swear, I never enjoined it him to be so coy. If I had the vanity to think he would obey me, I would command him to show more gallantry— 'tis hardly well-bred to be so particular on one hand, and so insensible on the other. But I despair to prevail, and so let him follow his own way. Ha, ha, ha! Pardon me, dear creature, I must laugh —ha, ha, ha!—though I grant you 'tis a little barbarous ha, ha, ha!

Mrs. Marwood: What pity 'tis, so much fine raillery and delivered with so significant gesture, should be so unhappily directed to miscarry.

Mrs. Millamant: Ha! Dear creature, I ask your pardon. I swear, I did not mind you.

Mrs. Marwood: Mr. Mirabell and you both may think it a thing impossible, when I shall tell him by telling you—

Mrs. Millamant: Oh dear, what? for it is the same thing if I hear it—ha, ha, ha!

Mrs. Marwood: That I detest him, hate him, madam.

Mrs. Millamant: O, Madam! why, so do I—and yet the creature loves me— ha, ha, ha! How can one forbear laughing to think of it.—I am a sibyl if I am not amazed to think what he can see in me. I'll take my death, I think you are handsomer—and within a year or two as young; if you could but stay for me, I should overtake you—but that cannot be.—Well, that thought makes me melancholic.—Now I'll be sad.

Mrs. Marwood: Your merry note may be changed sooner than you think.

Mrs. Millamant: D'ye say so? Then I'm resolved I'll have a song to keep up my spirits. [*Enter Mincing.*]

Mincing: The gentlemen stay but to comb, madam, and will wait on you.

Mrs. Millamant: Desire Mrs.——that is in the next room to sing the song I would have learned yesterday.—You shall hear it, madam—not that there's any great matter in it, but 'tis agreeable to my humor.

Song

1

Love's but the frailty of the mind,
When 'tis not with ambition joined;
A sickly flame, which, if not fed, expires,
And feeding, wastes in self-consuming fires.

2

'Tis not to wound a wanton boy
Or amorous youth, that gives the joy;
But 'tis the glory to have pierced a swain,
For whom inferior beauties sighed in vain.

3

Then I alone the conquest prize,
When I insult a rival's eyes:
If there's delight in love, 'tis when I see
That heart, which others bleed for, bleed for me.

[*Enter Petulant and Witwoud.*]

Mrs. Millamant: Is your animosity composed, gentlemen?

Witwoud: Raillery, raillery, madam; we have no animosity—we hit off a little wit now and then, but no animosity. The falling out of wits is like the falling out of lovers. We agree in the main, like treble and bass. Ha, Petulant?

Petulant: Aye, in the main—but when I have a humor to contradict—

Witwoud: Aye, when he has a humor to contradict, then I contradict, too. What! I know my cue. Then we contradict one another like two battledores; for contradictions beget one another like Jews.

Petulant: If he says black's black—if I have a humor to say 'tis blue—let that

pass—all's one for that. If I have a humor to prove it, it must be granted.

Witwoud: Not positively must—but it may—it may.

Petulant: Yes, it positively must, upon proof positive.

Witwoud: Aye, upon proof positive it must; but upon proof presumptive it only may.—That's a logical distinction now, madam.

Mrs. Marwood: I perceive your debates are of importance and very learnedly handled.

Petulant: Importance is one thing, and learning's another. But a debate's a debate; that I assert.

Witwoud: Petulant's an enemy to learning; he relies altogether on his parts.

Petulant: No, I'm no enemy to learning. It hurts not me.

Mrs. Marwood: That's a sign indeed it's no enemy to you.

Petulant: No, no, it's no enemy to anybody but them that have it.

Mrs. Millamant: Well, an illiterate man's my aversion. I wonder at the impudence of any illiterate man to offer to make love.

Witwoud: That I confess I wonder at, too.

Mrs. Millamant: Ah! to marry an ignorant that can hardly read or write!

Petulant: Why should a man be any further from being married, though he can't read, than he is from being hanged? The ordinary's [16] paid for setting the psalm, and the parish priest for reading the ceremony. And for the rest which is to follow in both cases, a man may do it without book—so all's one for that.

Mrs. Millamant: D'ye hear the creature?—Lord, here's company, I'll be gone. [*Exeunt Mrs. Millamant and Mincing.*] [*Enter Sir Wilfull Witwoud in a country riding habit, and Servant to Lady Wishfort.*]

Witwoud: In the name of Bartlemew and his fair,[17] what have we here?

[16] Chaplain.   [17] Bartholomew Fair, held annually in Smithfield.

Mrs. Marwood: 'Tis your brother, I fancy. Don't you know him?

Witwoud: Not I. — Yes, I think it is he—I've almost forgot him; I have not seen him since the Revolution.

Servant: [*To Sir Wilfull.*] Sir, my lady's dressing. Here's company; if you please to walk in, in the meantime.

Sir Wilfull: Dressing! What, it's but morning here I warrant, with you in London; we should count it towards afternoon in our parts, down in Shropshire. — Why, then belike, my aunt han't dined yet,—ha, friend?

Servant: Your aunt, sir?

Sir Wilfull: My aunt, sir! Yes, my aunt, sir, and your lady, sir; your lady is my aunt, sir. — Why, what! Dost thou not know me, friend? Why, then send somebody hither that does. How long hast thou lived with thy lady, fellow, — ha?

Servant: A week, sir — longer than anybody in the house, except my lady's woman.

Sir Wilfull: Why, then belike thou dost not know thy lady, if thou seest her,—ha, friend?

Servant: Why, truly, sir, I cannot safely swear to her face in a morning, before she is dressed. 'Tis like I may give a shrewd guess at her by this time.

Sir Wilfull: Well, prithee try what thou canst do; if thou canst not guess, inquire her out, dost hear, fellow? And tell her, her nephew, Sir Wilfull Witwoud, is in the house.

Servant: I shall, sir.

Sir Wilfull: Hold ye; hear me, friend; a word with you in your ear. Prithee, who are these gallants?

Servant: Really, sir, I can't tell; here come so many here, 'tis hard to know 'em all. [*Exit Servant.*]

Sir Wilfull: Oons, this fellow knows less than a starling; I don't think a' knows his own name.

Mrs. Marwood: Mr. Witwoud, your brother is not behindhand in forgetfulness—I fancy he has forgot you too.

Witwoud: I hope so—the devil take him that remembers first, I say.

Sir Wilfull: Save you, gentlemen and lady!

Mrs. Marwood: For shame, Mr. Witwoud; why don't you speak to him?— [*To Sir Wilfull.*] And you, sir.

Witwoud: Petulant, speak.

Petulant: [*To Sir Wilfull.*] And you sir.

Sir Wilfull: No offense, I hope. [*Salutes Mrs. Marwood.*]

Mrs. Marwood: No, sure, sir.

Witwoud: [*Aside.*] This is a vile dog, I see that already. No offence! ha, ha, ha! —To him, to him, Petulant, smoke him.[18]

Petulant: [*Surveying him round.*] It seems as if you had come a journey, sir: —hem, hem.

Sir Wilfull: Very likely, sir, that it may seem so.

Petulant: No offence, I hope, sir.

Witwoud: [*Aside.*] Smoke the boots, the boots, Petulant, the boots! Ha, ha, ha!

Sir Wilfull: May be not, sir; thereafter, as 'tis meant, sir.

Petulant: Sir, I presume upon the information of your boots.

Sir Wilfull: Why, 'tis like you may, sir: if you are not satisfied with the information of my boots, sir, if you will step to the stable, you may inquire further of my horse, sir.

Petulant: Your horse, sir? your horse is an ass, sir!

Sir Wilfull: Do you speak by way of offence, sir?

Mrs. Marwood: The gentleman's merry, that's all, sir. — [*Aside.*] 'Slife, we shall have a quarrel betwixt an horse and an ass before they find one another out. — [*Aloud.*] You must not take anything amiss from your friends, sir. You are among your friends here, though it may be you don't know it.— If I am not mistaken, you are Sir Wilfull Witwoud.

---

[18] Compare "burn him up."

Sir Wilfull: Right, lady; I am Sir Wilfull Witwoud—so I write myself. No offence to anybody, I hope—and nephew to the Lady Wishfort of this mansion.

Mrs. Marwood: Don't you know this gentleman, sir?

Sir Wilfull: Hum! What, sure 'tis not —yea, by'r Lady, but 'tis—'sheart, I know not whether 'tis or no—yea, but 'tis, by the Wrekin,[19] Brother Anthony! What, Tony, i'faith!—what, dost thou not know me? By'r Lady, nor I thee, thou art so be-cravated, and so beperiwigged!—'Sheart, why dost not speak? art thou overjoyed?

Witwoud: Odso, brother, is it you? Your servant, brother.

Sir Wilfull: Your servant!—why yours, sir. Your servant again—'sheart, and your friend and servant to that— and a [*puff*]—and a—flap-dragon [20] for your service, sir! and a hare's foot and a hare's scut [21] for your service, sir! an you be so cold and so courtly.

Witwoud: No offence, I hope, brother.

Sir Wilfull: 'Sheart, sir, but there is, and much offence!—A pox, is this your Inns o'Court breeding, not to know your friends and your relations, your elders, and your betters?

Witwoud: Why, brother Wilfull of Salop,[22] you may be as short as a Shrewsbury-cake, if you please. But I tell you 'tis not modish to know relations in town. You think you're in the country, where great lubberly brothers slabber and kiss one another when they meet, like a call of sergeants [23]—'tis not the fashion here; 'tis not indeed, dear brother.

Sir Wilfull: The fashion's a fool; and you're a fop, dear brother. 'Sheart, I've suspected this—by'r Lady, I conjectured you were a fop since you began to change the style of your letters, and write on a scrap of paper gilt round the edges, no bigger than a *subpœna*. I might expect this when you left off

---

[19] A hill in Shropshire. [20] Term of contempt (from a game). [21] Tail. [22] Shropshire. [23] Call of a sergeant-at-law to the bar.

"Honored Brother," and "hoping you are in good health," and so forth—to begin with a "Rat me, knight, I'm so sick of a last night's debauch—'ods heart," and then tell a familiar tale of a cock and a bull, and a whore and a bottle, and so conclude.—You could write news before you were out of your time, when you lived with honest Pumple Nose, the attorney of Furnival's Inn—you could entreat to be remembered then to your friends round the Wrekin. We could have gazettes, then, and Dawks's Letter,[24] and the Weekly Bill,[25] till of late days.

Petulant: 'Slife, Witwoud, were you ever an attorney's clerk? of the family of the Furnivals? Ha, ha, ha!

Witwoud: Aye, aye, but that was but for a while—not long, not long. Pshaw! I was not in my own power then; an orphan, and this fellow was my guardian. Aye, aye, I was glad to consent to that man to come to London. He had the disposal of me then. If I had not agreed to that, I might have been bound 'prentice to a felt-maker in Shrewsbury; this fellow would have bound me to a maker of felts.

Sir Wilfull: 'Sheart, and better than to be bound to a maker of fops—where, I suppose, you have served your time, and now you may set up for yourself.

Mrs. Marwood: You intend to travel, sir, as I'm informed.

Sir Wilfull: Belike I may, madam. I may chance to sail upon the salt seas, if my mind hold.

Petulant: And the wind serve.

Sir Wilfull: Serve or not serve, I shan't ask licence of you, sir; nor the weathercock your companion. I direct my discourse to the lady, sir.—'Tis like my aunt may have told you, madam— yes, I have settled my concerns, I may say now, and am minded to see foreign parts—if an' how that the peace holds, whereby that is, taxes abate.

---

[24] A news sheet for country circulation. [25] Bill of Mortality for London, issued weekly.

Mrs. Marwood: I thought you had designed for France at all adventures.

Sir Wilfull: I can't tell that; 'tis like I may, and 'tis like I may not. I am somewhat dainty in making a resolution because when I make it I keep it. I don't stand shill I, shall I, then; if I say't, I'll do't. But I have thoughts to tarry a small matter in town to learn somewhat of your lingo first, before I cross the seas. I'd gladly have a spice of your French, as they say, whereby to hold discourse in foreign countries.

Mrs. Marwood: Here's an academy in town for that use.

Sir Wilfull: There is? 'Tis like there may.

Mrs. Marwood: No doubt you will return very much improved.

Witwoud: Yes, refined, like a Dutch skipper from a whale-fishing. [*Enter Lady Wishfort and Fainall.*]

Lady Wishfort: Nephew, you are welcome.

Sir Wilfull: Aunt, your servant.

Fainall: Sir Wilfull, your most faithful servant.

Sir Wilfull: Cousin Fainall, give me your hand.

Lady Wishfort: Cousin Witwoud, your servant; Mr. Petulant, your servant; nephew, you are welcome again. Will you drink anything after your journey, nephew, before you eat? Dinner's almost ready.

Sir Wilfull: I'm very well, I thank you, aunt—however, I thank you for your courteous offer. 'Sheart, I was afraid you would have been in the fashion, too, and have remembered to have forgot your relations. Here's your cousin Tony; belike, I mayn't call him brother for fear of offence.

Lady Wishfort: Oh, he's a rallier, nephew—my cousin's a wit. And your great wits always rally their best friends to choose.[26] When you have been abroad, nephew, you'll understand raillery better. [*Fainall and Mrs. Marwood talk apart.*]

[26] As they choose.

Sir Wilfull: Why then, let him hold his tongue in the meantime, and rail when that day comes. [*Enter Mincing.*]

Mincing: Mem, I am come to acquaint your la'ship that dinner is impatient.

Sir Wilfull: Impatient! why, then, belike it won't stay till I pull off my boots.—Sweetheart, can you help me to a pair of slippers?—My man's with his horses, I warrant.

Lady Wishfort: Fie, fie, nephew! you would not pull off your boots here!—Go down into the hall—dinner shall stay for you. [*Exit Sir Wilfull.*] My nephew's a little unbred; you'll pardon him, madam.—Gentlemen, will you walk? Marwood?

Mrs. Marwood: I'll follow you, madam—before Sir Wilfull is ready. [*Manent Mrs. Marwood and Fainall.*]

Fainall: Why then, Foible's a bawd, an arrant, rank, match-making bawd. And I, it seems, am a husband, a rank husband; and my wife a very errant, rank wife—all in the way of the world. 'Sdeath, to be an anticipated cuckold, a cuckold in embryo! Sure, I was born with budding antlers, like a young satyr or a citizen's child. 'Sdeath! to be out-witted, to be out-jilted—out-matrimony'd!—If I had kept my speed like a stag, 'twere somewhat—but to crawl after, with my horns like a snail, and be outstripped by my wife—'tis scurvy wedlock.

Mrs. Marwood: Then shake it off. You have often wished for an opportunity to part, and now you have it. But first prevent their plot—the half of Millamant's fortune is too considerable to be parted with to a foe, to Mirabell.

Fainall: Damn him! that had been mine, had you not made that fond discovery.[27]—That had been forfeited, had they been married. My wife had added lustre to my horns by that increase of fortune; I could have worn 'em tipped with gold, though my forehead had been furnished like a deputy-lieutenant's hall.

[27] Silly exposure.

Mrs. Marwood: They may prove a cap of maintenance [28] to you still, if you can away [29] with your wife. And she's no worse than when you had her—I dare swear she had given up her game before she was married.

Fainall: Hum! that may be.

Mrs. Marwood: You married her to keep you; and if you can contrive to have her keep you better than you expected, why should you not keep her longer than you intended?

Fainall: The means, the means?

Mrs. Marwood: Discover to my lady your wife's conduct; threaten to part with her! My lady loves her, and will come to any composition to save her reputation. Take the opportunity of breaking it just upon the discovery of this imposture. My lady will be enraged beyond bounds, and sacrifice niece, and fortune, and all, at that conjuncture. And let me alone to keep her warm; if she should flag in her part, I will not fail to prompt her.

Fainall: Faith, this has an appearance.

Mrs. Marwood: I'm sorry I hinted to my lady to endeavor a match between Millamant and Sir Wilfull; that may be an obstacle.

Fainall: Oh, for that matter, leave me to manage him. I'll disable him for that; he will drink like a Dane. After dinner I'll set his hand in.

Mrs. Marwood: Well, how do you stand affected towards your lady?

Fainall: Why, faith, I'm thinking of it.—Let me see—I am married already, so that's over. My wife has played the jade with me—well, that's over, too. I never loved her, or if I had, why, that would have been over, too, by this time. —Jealous of her I cannot be, for I am certain; so there's an end of jealousy: weary of her I am, and shall be—no, there's no end of that—no, no, that were too much to hope. Thus far concerning

[28] Heraldic term. The two points of the cap suggest cuckold's horns. Note the pun on *maintenance.* [29] Endure.

my repose; now for my reputation. As to my own, I married not for it, so that's out of the question; and as to my part ir my wife's—why, she had parted witl hers before; so bringing none to me, she can take none from me. 'Tis against all rule of play that I should lose to one who has not wherewithal to stake.

Mrs. Marwood: Besides, you forgot marriage is honorable.

Fainall: Hum, faith, and that's well thought on. Marriage is honorable, as you say; and if so, wherefore should cuckoldom be a discredit, being derived from so honorable a root?

Mrs. Marwood: Nay, I know not; if the root be honorable, why not the branches?

Fainall: So, so; why, this point's clear.—Well, how do we proceed?

Mrs. Marwood: I will contrive a letter which shall be delivered to my lady at the time when that rascal who is to act Sir Rowland is with her. It shall come as from an unknown hand—for the less I appear to know of the truth, the better I can play the incendiary. Besides, I would not have Foible provoked if I could help it—because you know she knows some passages—nay, I expect all will come out. But let the mine be sprung first, and then I care not if I am discovered.

Fainall: If the worst come to the worst, I'll turn my wife to grass. I have already a deed of settlement of the best part of her estate, which I wheedled out of her, and that you shall partake at least.

Mrs. Marwood: I hope you are convinced that I hate Mirabell. Now you'll be no more jealous?

Fainall: Jealous! No, by this kiss. Let husbands be jealous, but let the lover still believe; or, if he doubt, let it be only to endear his pleasure, and prepare the joy that follows when he proves his mistress true. But let husbands' doubts convert to endless jealousy; or, if they have belief, let it corrupt to superstition and blind credulity. I am single, and will herd no more with 'em. True, I wear the badge, but I'll disown the order. And since I take my leave of 'em, I care not if I leave 'em a common motto to their common crest: 5

All husbands must or pain or shame endure; The wise too jealous are, fools too secure.

[*Exeunt.*]

QUESTIONS ON ACT III

1. Meredith has characterized the language of Lady Wishfort as "boudoir Billingsgate." What does he mean? Illustrate from the first part of the act.

2. Compare the early part of the act, in which Marwood overhears the conversation of the other characters, with the "screen scene" in *The School for Scandal*. The function of the scene, to introduce a complication in the plot, is obvious. But is the scene discordant in tone? Is it too much in the nature of farce for such a comedy as this? Does it have any of the symbolic significance of Sheridan's screen scene?

3. What is the function of the song in the middle of the act? Does it reflect Millamant's real feelings? Does it reflect the fashionable feelings which she knows she is supposed to have? In what way, if any, does it stand as a commentary on the situation?

4. Sir Wilfull, it should be noted, has a double value. On one level he serves as a conventional "hick comedy" figure—that is, for the amusement that can be derived from placing an unpolished countryman in a polished urban society. But Sir Wilfull, it soon becomes apparent, is a great deal more than a simpleton: he has a certain wit and penetration of his own, and he is far from lacking courage in his own convictions. He has, therefore, an important function in giving us another perspective upon the polite world which otherwise we have so far had to take at its own evaluation. To what extent are we meant to sympathize with this new point of view? With whom is Sir Wilfull most sharply contrasted? Do the scenes with Sir Wilfull give us any new light on Lady Wishfort?

As you read the rest of the play, try to determine whether Sir Wilfull is meant to cut a better figure in contrast with some characters than in contrast with others.

5. What in the first part of Act III helps quickly to establish continuity with Act II?

6. Lady Wishfort characterizes Mirabell as having "poison in his tongue that would corrupt integrity itself." Does the speech help also to characterize her? Are we given elsewhere in the play anything to support or weigh against her characterization of him?

7. The books which Lady Wishfort recommends to Marwood are all by Puritans: two express great hostility to the theater. What is Congreve's purpose in mentioning them here?

8. What do we learn about the tone of the play and about the attitudes expressed in it from Millamant's speech, "I wonder at the impudence of any illiterate man to offer to make love"?

9. What matters mentioned in the last several pages of the act are very important for our comprehension of the various schemes which come to fruition in the rest of the play?

ACT IV

[Scene continues.]

[*Enter Lady Wishfort and Foible.*]

Lady Wishfort: Is Sir Rowland coming, sayest thou, Foible? And are things in order?

Foible: Yes, madam, I have put wax 10 lights in the sconces, and placed the footmen in a row in the hall, in their best liveries, with the coachman and postilion to fill up the equipage.

Lady Wishfort: Have you pulvilled [1] 15 the coachman and postilion, that they may not stink of the stable when Sir Rowland comes by?

Foible: Yes, madam.

Lady Wishfort: And are the dancers 20 and the music ready, that he may be entertained in all points with correspondence to his passion?

Foible: All is ready, madam.

Lady Wishfort: And—well—how do I 25 look, Foible?

Foible: Most killing well, madam.

Lady Wishfort: Well, and how shall I receive him? in what figure shall I give his heart the first impression? There is 30 a great deal in the first impression. Shall I sit?—no, I won't sit—I'll walk—aye, I'll walk from the door upon his entrance, and then turn full upon him—no, that will be too sudden. I'll lie,—aye, 35 I'll lie down—I'll receive him in my little dressing-room; there's a couch— yes, yes, I'll give the first impression on a couch.—I won't lie neither, but loll and lean upon one elbow with one foot a 40 little dangling off, jogging in a thoughtful way—yes—and then as soon as he appears, start, aye, start and be surprised, and rise to meet him in a pretty disorder—yes.—Oh, nothing is more 45

[1] Scented.

alluring than a levee from a couch, in some confusion; it shows the foot to advantage, and furnishes with blushes, and recomposing airs beyond compari- 5 son. Hark! there's a coach.

Foible: 'Tis he, madam.

Lady Wishfort: Oh, dear, has my nephew made his addresses to Millamant? I ordered him.

Foible: Sir Wilfull is set in drinking, madam, in the parlor.

Lady Wishfort: Odds my life, I'll send him to her. Call her down, Foible; bring her hither. I'll send him as I go.—When they are together, then come to me, Foible, that I may not be too long alone with Sir Rowland. [*Exit Lady Wishfort.*] [*Enter Mrs. Millamant and Mrs. Fainall.*]

Foible: Madam, I stayed here to tell your ladyship that Mr. Mirabell has waited this half-hour for an opportunity to talk with you—though my lady's orders were to leave you and Sir Wilfull 25 together. Shall I tell Mr. Mirabell that you are at leisure?

Mrs. Millamant: No. What would the dear man have? I am thoughtful, and would amuse myself—bid him come 30 another time. [*Repeating, and walking about.*]

There never yet was woman made
Nor shall, but to be cursed.[2]

35 That's hard!

Mrs. Fainall: You are very fond of Sir John Suckling to-day, Millamant, and the poets.

Mrs. Millamant: He? Aye, and filthy 40 verses—so I am.

Foible: Sir Wilfull is coming, madam. Shall I send Mr. Mirabell away?

Mrs. Millamant: Aye, if you please, Foible, send him away, or send him 45 hither—just as you will, dear Foible. I

[2] From a poem by Suckling.

think I'll see him—shall I? Aye, let the wretch come. [*Exit Foible.*] [*Repeating.*]

Thyrsis, a youth of the inspired train.³

Dear Fainall, entertain Sir Wilfull— 5
thou hast philosophy to undergo a fool.
Thou art married and hast patience—I
would confer with my own thoughts.

Mrs. Fainall: I am obliged to you that
you would make me your proxy in this 10
affair, but I have business of my own.
[*Enter Sir Wilfull.*] O Sir Wilfull, you
are come at the critical instant. There's
your mistress up to the ears in love and
contemplation; pursue your point now 15
or never.

Sir Wilfull: Yes; my aunt will have it
so—I would gladly have been encouraged
with a bottle or two, because I'm somewhat wary at first before I am ac- 20
quainted.—[*This while Millamant walks
about repeating to herself.*]—But I hope,
after a time, I shall break my mind—
that is, upon further acquaintance.—So
for the present, cousin, I'll take my 25
leave. If so be you'll be so kind to make
my excuse, I'll return to my company—

Mrs. Fainall: Oh, fie, Sir Wilfull!
What! You must not be daunted.

Sir Wilfull: Daunted! No, that's not 30
it; it is not so much for that—for if so be
that I set on't, I'll do't. But only for the
present, 'tis sufficient till further acquaintance, that's all—your servant.

Mrs. Fainall: Nay, I'll swear you 35
shall never lose so favorable an opportunity if I can help it. I'll leave you
together, and lock the door. [*Exit.*]

Sir Wilfull: Nay, nay, cousin—I have
forgot my gloves!—What d'ye do?— 40
'Sheart, a' has locked the door indeed, I
think. Nay, Cousin Fainall, open the
door! Pshaw, what a vixen trick is this?
—Nay, now a' has seen me too.—
Cousin, I made bold to pass through as 45
it were—I think this door's enchanted!

Mrs. Millamant. [*Repeating.*]

  I prithee spare me, gentle boy,
  Press me no more for that slight toy.

³ From Waller's "The Story of Phœbus
and Daphne Applied."

Sir Wilfull: Anan?⁴ Cousin, your
servant.

Mrs. Millamant:

  —That foolish trifle of a heart.—

Sir Wilfull!

Sir Wilfull: Yes—your servant. No
offence, I hope, cousin.

Mrs. Millamant: [*Repeating.*]

  I swear it will do its part,
  Though thou dost thine, employ'st thy power
    and art.

Natural, easy Suckling!

Sir Wilfull: Anan? Suckling. No such
suckling neither, cousin, nor stripling: I
thank heaven, I'm no minor.

Mrs. Millamant: Ah, rustic, ruder
than Gothic!

Sir Wilfull: Well, well, I shall understand your lingo one of these days,
cousin; in the meanwhile I must answer
in plain English.

Mrs. Millamant: Have you any business with me, Sir Wilfull?

Sir Wilfull: Not at present, cousin.—
Yes, I made bold to see, to come and
know if that how you were disposed to
fetch a walk this evening; if so be that I
might not be troublesome, I would have
sought a walk with you.

Mrs. Millamant: A walk! what then?

Sir Wilfull: Nay, nothing—only for
the walk's sake, that's all.

Mrs. Millamant: I nauseate walking;
'tis a country diversion. I loathe the
country, and everything that relates
to it.

Sir Wilfull: Indeed! ha! Look ye, look
ye—you do? Nay, 'tis like you may—
here are choice of pastimes here in town,
as plays and the like; that must be confessed, indeed.

Mrs. Millamant: Ah, *l'étourdi!* I hate
the town too.

Sir Wilfull: Dear heart, that's much—
ha! that you should hate 'em both! Ha!
'tis like you may; there are some can't
relish the town, and others can't away

⁴ Beg pardon.

with the country—'tis like you may be one of those, cousin.

Mrs. Millamant: Ha, ha, ha! yes, 'tis like I may.—You have nothing further to say to me?

Sir Wilfull: Not at present, cousin.—'Tis like when I have an opportunity to be more private, I may break my mind in some measure—I conjecture you partly guess—however, that's as time shall try—but spare to speak and spare to speed, as they say.

Mrs. Millamant: If it is of no great importance, Sir Wilfull, you will oblige me to leave me; I have just now a little business—

Sir Wilfull: Enough, enough, cousin: yes, yes, all a case.—When you're disposed, when you're disposed. Now's as well as another time, and another time as well as now. All's one for that—Yes, yes, if your concerns call you, there's no haste; it will keep cold, as they say. Cousin, your servant.—I think this door's locked.

Mrs. Millamant: You may go this way, sir.

Sir Wilfull: Your servant; then with your leave I'll return to my company. [*Exit.*]

Mrs. Millamant: Aye, aye; ha, ha, ha!

Like Phœbus sung the no less amorous boy.[5]

[*Enter Mirabell.*]

Mirabell: "Like Daphne she, as lovely and as coy." Do you lock yourself up from me, to make my search more curious, or is this pretty artifice contrived to signify that here the chase must end, and my pursuits be crowned? For you can fly no further.

Mrs. Millamant: Vanity! No—I'll fly, and be followed to the last moment. Though I am upon the very verge of matrimony, I expect you should solicit me as much as if I were wavering at the grate of a monastery, with one foot over the threshold. I'll be solicited to the very last—nay, and afterwards.

Mirabell: What, after the last?

Mrs. Millamant: Oh, I should think I was poor and had nothing to bestow, if I were reduced to an inglorious ease and freed from the agreeable fatigues of solicitation.

Mirabell: But do not you know that when favors are conferred upon instant [6] and tedious solicitation, that they diminish in their value, and that both the giver loses the grace, and the receiver lessens his pleasure?

Mrs. Millamant: It may be in things of common application; but never, sure, in love. Oh, I hate a lover that can dare to think he draws a moment's air, independent of the bounty of his mistress. There is not so impudent a thing in nature as the saucy look of an assured man, confident of success. The pedantic arrogance of a very husband has not so pragmatical [7] an air. Ah! I'll never marry unless I am first made sure of my will and pleasure.

Mirabell: Would you have 'em both before marriage? or will you be contented with the first now, and stay for the other till after grace?

Mrs. Millamant: Ah! don't be impertinent.—My dear liberty, shall I leave thee? my faithful solitude, my darling contemplation, must I bid you then adieu? Ay-h adieu—my morning thoughts, agreeable wakings, indolent slumbers, all ye *douceurs*, ye *sommeils du matin, adieu.*—I can't do't, 'tis more than impossible.—Positively, Mirabell, I'll lie abed in a morning as long as I please.

Mirabell: Then I'll get up in a morning as early as I please.

Mrs. Millamant: Ah! Idle creature, get up when you will—and d'ye hear, I won't be called names after I'm married; positively, I won't be called names.

Mirabell: Names!

Mrs. Millamant: Aye, as wife, spouse, my dear, joy, jewel, love, sweetheart, and the rest of that nauseous cant, in

---

[5] From Waller. See note 3.

[6] Insistent. [7] Dogmatic.

which men and their wives are so fulsomely familiar—I shall never bear that. Good Mirabell, don't let us be familiar or fond, nor kiss before folks, like my Lady Fadler and Sir Francis; nor go to Hyde Park together the first Sunday in a new chariot, to provoke eyes and whispers, and then never to be seen there together again, as if we were proud of one another the first week, and ashamed of one another ever after. Let us never visit together, nor go to a play together; but let us be very strange and well-bred. Let us be as strange as if we had been married a great while, and as well-bred as if we were not married at all.

Mirabell: Have you any more conditions to offer? Hitherto your demands are pretty reasonable.

Mrs. Millamant: Trifles—as liberty to pay and receive visits to and from whom I please; to write and receive letters, without interrogatories or wry faces on your part; to wear what I please, and choose conversation with regard only to my own taste; to have no obligation upon me to converse with wits that I don't like, because they are your acquaintance: or to be intimate with fools, because they may be your relations.— Come to dinner when I please; dine in my dressingroom when I'm out of humor, without giving a reason. To have my closet inviolate; to be sole empress of my tea-table, which you must never presume to approach without first asking leave. And lastly, wherever I am, you shall always knock at the door before you come in. These articles subscribed, if I continue to endure you a little longer, I may by degrees dwindle into a wife.

Mirabell: Your bill of fare is something advanced in this latter account.— Well, have I liberty to offer conditions —that when you are dwindled into a wife, I may not be beyond measure enlarged into a husband?

Mrs. Millamant: You have free leave. Propose your utmost; speak and spare not.

Mirabell: I thank you.—*Imprimis* then, I covenant that your acquaintance be general; that you admit no sworn confidante or intimate of your own sex —no she-friend to screen her affairs under your countenance, and tempt you to make trial of a mutual secrecy. No decoy-duck to wheedle you—a fop scrambling to the play in a mask—then bring you home in a pretended fright, when you think you shall be found out— and rail at me for missing the play and disappointing the frolic which you had, to pick me up and prove my constancy.

Mrs. Millamant: Detestable *imprimis!* I go to the play in a mask!

Mirabell: Item, I article, that you continue to like your own face, as long as I shall; and while it passes current with me, that you endeavor not to new-coin it. To which end, together with all vizards for the day, I prohibit all masks for the night, made of oiled-skins and I know not what hogs' bones, hares' gall, pig-water, and the marrow of a roasted cat. In short, I forbid all commerce with the gentlewoman in what-d'ye-call-it Court. *Item,* I shut my doors against all bawds with baskets, and pennyworths of muslin, china, fans, atlases,[8] etc. *Item,* when you shall be breeding—

Mrs. Millamant: Ah! name it not.

Mirabell: Which may be presumed, with a blessing on our endeavors—

Mrs. Millamant: Odious endeavors!

Mirabell: I denounce against all strait lacing, squeezing for a shape, till you mould my boy's head like a sugar-loaf, and instead of a man-child, make me father to a crooked billet. Lastly, to the dominion of the tea-table I submit—but with proviso, that you exceed not in your province, but restrain yourself to native and simple tea-table drinks, as tea, chocolate, and coffee; as likewise to genuine and authorized tea-table talk— such as mending of fashions, spoiling reputations, railing at absent friends,

_____
[8] A variety of satin.

and so forth—but that on no account you encroach upon the men's prerogative, and presume to drink healths, or toast fellows: for prevention of which I banish all foreign forces, all auxiliaries to the 5 tea-table, as orange-brandy, all aniseed, cinnamon, citron, and Barbadoes waters, together with ratafia, and the most noble spirit of clary, but for cowslip wine, poppy water, and all dormitives, 10 those I allow.—These provisos admitted, in other things I may prove a tractable and complying husband.

Mrs. Millamant: O horrid provisos! filthy strong-waters! I toast fellows! 15 odious men! I hate your odious provisos.

Mirabell: Then we're agreed. Shall I kiss your hand upon the contract? And here comes one to be a witness to the sealing of the deed. [*Enter Mrs. Fain-* 20 *all.*]

Mrs. Millamant: Fainall, what shall I do? Shall I have him? I think I must have him.

Mrs. Fainall: Aye, aye, take him, take 25 him; what should you do?

Mrs. Millamant: Well then—I'll take my death, I'm in a horrid fright.—Fainall, I shall never say it—well—I think— I'll endure you.

Mrs. Fainall: Fie! fie! Have him, have him, and tell him so in plain terms; for I am sure you have a mind to him.

Mrs. Millamant: Are you? I think I have—and the horrid man looks as if he 35 thought so too. Well, you ridiculous thing you, I'll have you—I won't be kissed, nor I won't be thanked—here, kiss my hand though.—So, hold your tongue now; don't say a word. 40

Mrs. Fainall: Mirabell, there's a necessity for your obedience; you have neither time to talk nor stay. My mother is coming, and in my conscience if she should see you, would fall into fits, 45 and maybe not recover time enough to return to Sir Rowland, who, as Foible tells me, is in a fair way to succeed. Therefore spare your ecstasies for another occasion, and slip down the back- 50 stairs, where Foible waits to consult you.

Mrs. Millamant: Aye, go, go. In the meantime I suppose you have said something to please me.

Mirabell: I am all obedience. [*Exit* 5 *Mirabell.*]

Mrs. Fainall: Yonder, Sir Wilfull's drunk, and so noisy that my mother has been forced to leave Sir Rowland to appease him; but he answers her only 10 with singing and drinking. What they may have done by this time I know not, but Petulant and he were upon quarreling as I came by.

Mrs. Millamant: Well, if Mirabell 15 should not make a good husband, I am a lost thing, for I find I love him violently.

Mrs. Fainall: So it seems, when you mind not what's said to you.—If you 20 doubt him, you had best take up with Sir Wilfull.

Mrs. Millamant: How can you name that superannuated lubber?—Foh! [*Enter Witwoud from drinking.*]

Mrs. Fainall: So! Is the fray made up, 25 that you have left 'em?

Witwoud: Left 'em? I could stay no longer. I have laughed like ten christ'n- ings—I am tipsy with laughing. If I had stayed any longer I should have burst— 30 I must have been let out and pieced in the sides like an unfixed camlet.[9]—Yes, yes, the fray is composed; my lady came in like a *noli prosequi*,[10] and stopped their proceedings. 35

Mrs. Millamant: What was the dispute?

Witwoud: That's the jest; there was no dispute. They could neither of 'em speak for rage, and so fell a sputtering 40 at one another like two roasting apples. [*Enter Petulant, drunk.*] Now, Petulant, all's over, all's well. Gad, my head begins to whim it about—Why dost thou not speak? Thou art both as drunk and 45 mute as a fish.

Petulant: Look you, Mrs. Millamant —if you can love me, dear nymph, say

[9] Unstiffened material. [10] Be unwilling to prosecute.

it—and that's the conclusion. Pass on, or pass off—that's all.

Witwoud: Thou hast uttered volumes, folios, in less than *decimo sexto*,[11] my dear Lacedemonian.[12] Sirrah Petulant, thou art an epitomizer of words.

Petulant: Witwoud—you are an annihilator of sense.

Witwoud: Thou art a retailer of phrases, and dost deal in remnants of remnants, like a maker of pincushions— thou art in truth (metaphorically speaking) a speaker of shorthand.

Petulant: Thou art (without a figure) just one-half of an ass, and Baldwin[13] yonder, thy half-brother, is the rest.— A Gemini[14] of asses split would make just four of you.

Witwoud: Thou dost bite, my dear mustard seed; kiss me for that.   20

Petulant: Stand off!—I'll kiss no more males—I have kissed your twin yonder in a humor of reconciliation, till he [*hiccup*] rises upon my stomach like a radish.   25

Mrs. Millamant: Eh! filthy creature! —What was the quarrel?

Petulant: There was no quarrel—there might have been a quarrel.

Witwoud: If there had been words enow between 'em to have expressed provocation, they had gone together by ears like a pair of castanets.

Petulant: You were the quarrel.

Mrs. Millamant: Me!

Petulant: If I have a humor to quarrel, I can make less matters conclude premises.—If you are not handsome, what then, if I have a humor to prove it? If I shall have my reward, say so; if not, fight for your face the next time yourself. I'll go sleep.

Witwoud: Do; wrap thyself up like a wood-louse, and dream revenge—and hear me; if thou canst learn to write by to-morrow morning, pen me a challenge. —I'll carry it for thee.

Petulant: Carry your mistress's mon-

key a spider!—Go, flea dogs, and read romances!—I'll go to bed to my maid. [*Exit Petulant.*]

Mrs. Fainall: He's horridly drunk. How came you all in this pickle?

Witwoud: A plot, a plot, to get rid of the knight—your husband's advice, but he sneaked off. [*Enter Lady Wishfort and then Sir Wilfull, drunk.*]

Lady Wishfort: Out upon't, out upon't! At years of discretion, and comport yourself at this rantipole rate!

Sir Wilfull: No offence, aunt.

Lady Wishfort: Offence! as I'm a person, I'm ashamed of you. Fob! how you stink of wine! D'ye think my niece will ever endure such a borachio! you're an absolute borachio.[15]

Sir Wilfull: Borachio?

Lady Wishfort: At a time when you should commence an amour and put your best foot foremost—

Sir Wilfull: 'Sheart, an you grudge me your liquor, make a bill—give me more drink, and take my purse—[*Sings.*]

Prithee fill me the glass,
    Till it laugh in my face,
With ale that is potent and mellow;
He that whines for a lass,
    Is an ignorant ass,
For a bumper has not its fellow.

But if you would have me marry my cousin—say the word, and I'll do't. Wilfull will do't; that's the word. Wilfull will do't; that's my crest—My motto I have forgot.

Lady Wishfort: [*To Mrs. Millamant.*] My nephew's a little overtaken, cousin, but 'tis with drinking your health.— O' my word, you are obliged to him.

Sir Wilfull: *In vino veritas*, aunt.—If I drunk your health to-day, cousin—I am a Borachio. But if you have a mind to be married, say the word, and send for the piper; Wilfull will do't. If not, dust it away, and let's have t'other round.— Tony!—Odds heart, where's Tony?— Tony's an honest fellow; but he spits

---

[11] Very small book. [12] Noted for saying little. [13] The ass in *Reynard the Fox.* [14] Twins.

[15] Drunkard

after a bumper, and that's a fault.—
[*Sings.*]

We'll drink and we'll never ha' done, boys,
  Put the glass then around with the sun, 5
    boys,
Let Apollo's example invite us;
  For he's drunk every night,
  And that makes him so bright,
That he's able next morning to light us.

The sun's a good pimple,[16] an honest
soaker; he has a cellar at your Antipodes. If I travel, aunt, I touch at your
Antipodes.—Your Antipodes are a good,
rascally sort of topsy-turvy fellows: if I 15
had a bumper, I'd stand upon my head
and drink a health to 'em.—A match or
no match, cousin with the hard name—
Aunt, Wilfull will do't. If she has her
maidenhead, let her look to't; if she has 20
not, let her keep her own counsel in the
meantime, and cry out at the nine
months' end.

  Mrs. Millamant: Your pardon,
madam, I can stay no longer—Sir Wil- 25
full grows very powerful. Eh! how he
smells! I shall be overcome, if I stay.
Come, cousin. [*Exeunt Mrs. Millamant
and Mrs. Fainall.*]

  Lady Wishfort: Smells! He would 30
poison a tallow-chandler and his family!
Beastly creature, I know not what to do
with him!—Travel, quotha! Aye, travel,
travel—get thee gone, get thee gone; get
thee but far enough, to the Saracens, or 35
the Tartars, or the Turks!—for thou art
not fit to live in a Christian commonwealth, thou beastly pagan!

  Sir Wilfull: Turks? No; no Turks,
aunt. Your Turks are infidels, and be- 40
lieve not in the grape. Your Mahometan,
your Mussulman, is a dry stinkard—no
offence, aunt. My map says that your
Turk is not so honest a man as your
Christian. I cannot find by the map that 45
your Mufti is orthodox—whereby it is
a plain case that orthodox is a hard
word, aunt, and [*hiccup*]—Greek for
claret.—[*Sings.*]

To drink is a Christian diversion,
  Unknown to the Turk or the Persian:
    Let Mahometan fools
    Live by heathenish rules,
And be damned over tea-cups and coffee.
  But let British lads sing,
  Crown a health to the king,
And a fig for your sultan and sophy!

Ah, Tony! [*Enter Foible, and whispers
Lady Wishfort.*]   10

  Lady Wishfort: [*Aside to Foible.*] Sir
Rowland impatient? Good lack! what
shall I do with this beastly tumbril?—
[*Aloud.*] Go lie down and sleep, you
sot!—or, as I'm a person, I'll have you
bastinadoed with broomsticks.—Call up
the wenches. [*Exit Foible.*]

  Sir Wilful: Ahey! wenches; where are
the wenches?

  Lady Wishfort: Dear Cousin Witwoud,
get him away, and you will bind me
to you inviolably. I have an affair of
moment that invades me with some
precipitation—you will oblige me to all
futurity.   25

  Witwoud: Come, knight.—Pox on him,
I don't know what to say to him.—Will
you go to a cock-match?

  Sir Wilfull: With a wench, Tony? Is
she a shakebag, sirrah? Let me bite your 30
cheek for that.

  Witwoud: Horrible! he has a breath
like a bagpipe—Aye, aye; come, will you
march, my Salopian?

  Sir Wilfull: Lead on, little Tony— 35
I'll follow thee, my Anthony, my
Tantony. Sirrah, thou shalt be my
Tantony, and I'll be thy pig.[17] [*Sings.*]

And a fig for your sultan and sophy.

[*Exeunt Sir Wilfull and Witwoud.*]

  Lady Wishfort: This will never do. It
will never make a match—at least before 45
he has been abroad. [*Enter Waitwell, disguised as Sir Rowland.*] Dear Sir Rowland,
I am confounded with confusion at the
retrospection of my own rudeness!—I

---

[16] Boon companion.

[17] St. Antony and the pig are associated
in legend.

have more pardons to ask than the pope distributes in the year of jubilee. But I hope, where there is likely to be so near an alliance, we may unbend the severity of decorums and dispense with a little ceremony.

Waitwell: My impatience, madam, is the effect of my transport; and till I have the possession of your adorable person, I am tantalized on the rack; and I do but hang, madam, on the tenter of expectation.

Lady Wishfort: You have excess of gallantry, Sir Rowland, and press things to a conclusion with a most prevailing vehemence.—But a day or two for decency of marriage—

Waitwell: For decency of funeral, madam! The delay will break my heart —or, if that should fail, I shall be poisoned. My nephew will get an inkling of my designs, and poison me; and I would willingly starve him before I die —I would gladly go out of the world with that satisfaction.—That would be some comfort to me, if I could but live so long as to be revenged on that unnatural viper!

Lady Wishfort: Is he so unnatural, say you? Truly, I would contribute much, both to the saving of your life and the accomplishment of your revenge—not that I respect myself, though he has been a perfidious wretch to me.

Waitwell: Perfidious to you!

Lady Wishfort: O Sir Rowland, the hours that he has died away at my feet, the tears that he has shed, the oaths that he has sworn, the palpitations that he has felt, the trances and the tremblings, the ardors and the ecstasies, the kneelings and the risings, the heart-heavings and the handgrippings, the pangs and the pathetic regards of his protesting eyes! Oh, no memory can register!

Waitwell: What, my rival! Is the rebel my rival?—a' dies!

Lady Wishfort: No, don't kill him at once, Sir Rowland; starve him gradually, inch by inch.

Waitwell: I'll do't. In three weeks he shall be barefoot; in a month out at knees with begging an alms.—He shall starve upward and upward, till he has nothing living but his head, and then go out in a stink like a candle's end upon a save-all.[18]

Lady Wishfort: Well, Sir Rowland, you have the way—you are no novice in the labyrinth of love; you have the clue. But as I am a person, Sir Rowland, you must not attribute my yielding to any sinister appetite, or indigestion of widowhood; nor impute my complacency to any lethargy of continence. I hope you do not think me prone to any iteration of nuptials—

Waitwell: Far be it from me—

Lady Wishfort: If you do, I protest I must recede—or think that I have made a prostitution of decorums; but in the vehemence of compassion, and to save the life of a person of so much importance—

Waitwell: I esteem it so—

Lady Wishfort: Or else you wrong my condescension.

Waitwell: I do not, I do not—

Lady Wishfort: Indeed you do.

Waitwell: I do not, fair shrine of virtue!

Lady Wishfort: If you think the least scruple of carnality was an ingredient,—

Waitwell: Dear madam, no. You are all camphire[19] and frankincense, all chastity and odor.

Lady Wishfort: Or that—[*Enter Foible.*]

Foible: Madam, the dancers are ready; and there's one with a letter, who must deliver it into your own hands.

Lady Wishfort: Sir Rowland, will you give me leave? Think favorably, judge candidly, and conclude you have found a person who would suffer racks in honor's cause, dear Sir Rowland, and will wait on you incessantly. [*Exit Lady Wishfort.*]

Waitwell: Fie, fie!—What a slavery

---

[18] A holder that will let a candle burn to the end. [19] Supposed to produce impotence.

have I undergone! Spouse, hast thou any cordial? I want spirits.

Foible: What a washy rogue art thou, to pant thus for a quarter of an hour's lying and swearing to a fine lady!

Waitwell: Oh, she is the antidote to desire! Spouse, thou wilt fare the worse for't—I shall have no appetite to iteration of nuptials this eight-and-forty hours.—By this hand I'd rather be a chairman in the dog-days than act Sir Rowland till this time to-morrow! [*Enter Lady Wishfort, with a letter.*]

Lady Wishfort: Call in the dancers.— Sir Rowland, we'll sit, if you please, and see the entertainment. [*A dance.*] Now, with your permission, Sir Rowland, I will peruse my letter.—I would open it in your presence, because I would not make you uneasy. If it should make you uneasy, I would burn it. Speak, if it does —but you may see by the superscription it is like a woman's hand.

Foible: [*Aside to Waitwell.*] By heaven! Mrs. Marwood's, I know it.— My heart aches—get it from her.

Waitwell: A woman's hand? No, madam, that's no woman's hand; I see that already. That's somebody whose throat must be cut.

Lady Wishfort: Nay, Sir Rowland, since you give me a proof of your passion by your jealousy, I promise you I'll make a return by a frank communication.—You shall see it—we'll open it together—look you here.—[*Reads.*]— "Madam, though unknown to you"— Look you there, 'tis from nobody that I know—"I have that honor for your character, that I think myself obliged to let you know you are abused. He who pretends to be Sir Rowland, is a cheat and a rascal."—Oh, heavens! what's this?

Foible. [*Aside.*] Unfortunate, all's ruined!

Waitwell: How, how! Let me see, let me see!—[*Reads.*] "A rascal, and disguised and suborned for that imposture,"—O villainy! O villainy!—"by the contrivance of—"

Lady Wishfort: I shall faint!—I shall die, I shall die!—Oh!

Foible. [*Aside to Waitwell.*] Say 'tis your nephew's hand—quickly, his plot, —swear it, swear it!

Waitwell: Here's a villain! Madam, don't you perceive it? Don't you see it? *Lady Wishfort:* Too well, too well! I have seen too much.

Waitwell: I told you at first I knew the hand.—A woman's hand! The rascal writes a sort of a large hand—your Roman hand.—I saw there was a throat to be cut presently. If he were my son, as he is my nephew, I'd pistol him!

Foible: O treachery!—But are you sure, Sir Rowland, it is his writing?

Waitwell: Sure? Am I here? Do I live? Do I love this pearl of India? I have twenty letters in my pocket from him in the same character.

Lady Wishfort: How!

Foible: Oh. what luck it is, Sir Rowland, that you were present at this juncture! This was the business that brought Mr. Mirabell disguised to Madam Millamant this afternoon. I thought something was contriving when he stole by me and would have hid his face.

Lady Wishfort: How, how!—I heard the villain was in the house, indeed; and now I remember, my niece went away abruptly when Sir Wilfull was to have made his addresses.

Foible: Then, then, madam, Mr. Mirabell waited for her in her chamber; but I would not tell your ladyship to discompose you when you were to receive Sir Rowland.

Waitwell: Enough; his date is short. *Foible:* No, good Sir Rowland, don't incur the law.

Waitwell: Law! I care not for law. I can but die and 'tis in a good cause.— My lady shall be satisfied of my truth and innocence, though it cost me my life.

Lady Wishfort: No, dear Sir Rowland, don't fight. If you should be killed, I must never show my face; or hanged— oh, consider my reputation, Sir Rowland!—No, you shan't fight.—I'll go in and examine my niece; I'll make her confess. I conjure you, Sir Rowland, by all your love, not to fight.

Waitwell: I am charmed, madam; I obey. But some proof you must let me give you; I'll go for a black box which contains the writings of my whole estate, and deliver that into your hands.

Lady Wishfort: Aye, dear Sir Rowland, that will be some comfort. Bring the black box.

Waitwell: And may I presume to bring a contract to be signed this night? May I hope so far?

Lady Wishfort: Bring what you will, but come alive, pray, come alive! Oh, this is a happy discovery!

Waitwell: Dead or alive I'll come— and married we will be in spite of treachery; aye, and get an heir that shall defeat the last remaining glimpse of hope in my abandoned nephew. Come, my buxom widow:
Ere long you shall substantial proofs receive,
That I'm an errant knight—
Foible: [*Aside.*] Or arrant knave.
[*Exeunt.*]

QUESTIONS ON ACT IV

1. Compare Lady Wishfort's conversation with Foible as she prepares to meet her lover (p. 422a, 7 ff.) and Millamant's later conversation with Mirabell (p. 424a, 35 ff.). Would it be fair to say that Lady Wishfort is very artfully preparing to appear artless and that Millamant reverses the process—that she is trying to appear more artful and designing than she really is?

2. The "bargaining scene" between Millamant and Mirabell is obviously balanced by the "love" scene between Lady Wishfort and the supposed Sir Rowland. What points of resemblance are there? What is the basic contrast? In what different ways, for example, do Millamant and Lady Wishfort dismiss any suggestion that their desires are in the least way "carnal"? What is the difference between the mind and personality shown, on the one hand, by Mirabell and Millamant, and, on the other, by Lady Wishfort?

3. Millamant stipulates that Mirabell must refrain after their marriage from all "nauseous cant." How does the scene between Lady Wishfort and the supposed Sir Rowland give point to her proviso?

4. Both the bargaining scene and the declaration of "Sir Rowland" to Lady Wishfort may be taken as parodies on the conventional proposal scene. In what way is each a parody?

5. How does the interview of the matter-of-fact, unsentimental Sir Wilfull with Millamant prepare for the bargaining scene which follows it?

6. An ironic complication in this act is the fact that in one respect the plans of Marwood and her lover Fainall are at cross purposes. Trace out the difficulty created for them by this fact.

7. As questions 2, 3, 4, and 5 suggest, the act is almost entirely concerned with "love" scenes. On the face of it the drunken scenes involving Witwood, Petulant, and Sir Wilfull may seem to violate the pattern; yet closer inspection reveals that they also fit into it. In view of this fact, could we venture any conclusion as to the sort of statement about love which is being made or implied by the act as a whole?

ACT V

[Scene continues.]

[*Lady Wishfort and Foible.*]

Lady Wishfort: Out of my house! Out of my house, thou viper, thou serpent, that I have fostered! thou bosom traitress, that I raised from nothing!—Begone, begone, begone, go! go!—That I took from washing of old gauze and weaving of dead hair, with a bleak blue nose over a chafing-dish of starved embers, and dining behind a traverse rag,[1] in a shop no bigger than a bird-cage!—Go, go! Starve again! Do, do!

Foible: Dear madam, I'll beg pardon on my knees.

Lady Wishfort: Away! out, out!—Go, set up for yourself again!—Do, drive a trade, do, with your three-pennyworth of small ware, flaunting upon a packthread under a brandy-seller's bulk, or against a dead wall by a ballad-monger! Go, hang out an old Frisoneer gorget,[2] with a yard of yellow colbertine[3] again, do! An old gnawed mask, two rows of pins, and a child's fiddle; a glass necklace with the beads broken, and a quilted night-cap with one ear! Go, go, drive a trade!—These were your commodities, your treacherous trull! this was the merchandise you dealt in when I took you into my house, placed you next myself, and made you governante of my whole family! You have forgot this, have you, now you have feathered your nest?

Foible: No, no, dear madam. Do but hear me; have but a moment's patience. I'll confess all. Mr. Mirabell seduced me. I am not the first that he has wheedled with his dissembling tongue; your ladyship's own wisdom has been deluded by him—then how should I, a poor ignorant, defend myself? O madam, if you knew but what he promised me, and how he assured me your ladyship

should come to no damage!—Or else the wealth of the Indies should not have bribed me to conspire against so good, so sweet, so kind a lady as you have been to me.

Lady Wishfort: No damage! What, to betray me, and marry me to a cast servingman! to make me a receptacle, an hospital for a decayed pimp! No damage! O thou frontless impudence, more than a big-bellied actress!

Foible: Pray, do but hear me, madam! He could not marry your ladyship, madam.—No, indeed; his marriage was to have been void in law, for he was married to me first, to secure your ladyship. He could not have bedded your ladyship; for if he had consummated with your ladyship, he must have run the risk of the law, and been put upon his clergy.[4]—Yes, indeed, I inquired of the law in that case before I would meddle or make.

Lady Wishfort: What, then I have been your property, have I? I have been convenient to you, it seems!—while you were catering for Mirabell, I have been broker for you! What, have you made a passive bawd of me?—This exceeds all precedent! I am brought to fine uses, to become a botcher of second-hand marriages between Abigails and Andrews. I'll couple you! Yes, I'll baste you together, you and your Philander. I'll Duke's-place[5] you, as I'm a person! Your turtle is in custody already: you shall coo in the same cage if there be a constable or warrant in the parish. [*Exit Lady Wishfort.*]

Foible: Oh, that ever I was born! Oh, that I was ever married!—A bride!—aye, I shall be a Bridewell-bride.[6]—Oh! [*Enter Mrs. Fainall.*]

Mrs. Fainall: Poor Foible, what's the matter?

Foible: O madam, my lady's gone for a constable! I shall be had to a justice

---

[1] A ragged curtain. [2] Worn over the bosom. [3] Cheap lace.

[4] Forced to plead benefit of clergy (tested by the ability to read) in order to escape hanging. [5] See Act 1, note 6. [6] House of correction.

and put to Bridewell to beat hemp. Poor Waitwell's gone to prison already.

Mrs. Fainall: Have a good heart, Foible; Mirabell's gone to give security for him. This is all Marwood's and my husband's doing.

Foible: Yes, yes; I know it, madam. She was in my lady's closet, and overheard all that you said to me before dinner. She sent the letter to my lady, and that missing effect, Mr. Fainall laid this plot to arrest Waitwell when he pretended to go for the papers, and in the meantime Mrs. Marwood declared all to my lady.

Mrs. Fainall: Was there no mention made of me in the letter? My mother does not suspect my being in the confederacy? I fancy Marwood has not told her, though she has told my husband.

Foible: Yes, madam, but my lady did not see that part; we stifled the letter before she read so far—Has that mischievous devil told Mr. Fainall of your ladyship, then?

Mrs. Fainall: Aye, all's out, my affair with Mirabell—everything discovered. This is the last day of our living together, that's my comfort.

Foible: Indeed, madam; and so 'tis a comfort if you knew all—he has been even with your ladyship, which I could have told you long enough since, but I love to keep peace and quietness by my goodwill. I had rather bring friends together than set 'em at distance. But Mrs. Marwood and he are nearer related than ever their parents thought for.

Mrs. Fainall: Sayest thou so, Foible? Canst thou prove this?

Foible: I can take my oath of it, madam; so can Mrs. Mincing. We have had many a fair word from Madam Marwood, to conceal something that passed in our chamber one evening when you were at Hyde Park, and we were thought to have gone a-walking, but we went up unawares—though we were sworn to secrecy, too; Madam Marwood took a book and swore us upon it, but it was but a book of poems. So long as it was not a Bible oath, we may break it with a safe conscience.

Mrs. Fainall: This discovery is the most opportune thing I could wish.— Now, Mincing! [*Enter Mincing.*]

Mincing: My lady would speak with Mrs. Foible, mem. Mr. Mirabell is with her; he has set your spouse at liberty, Mrs. Foible, and would have you hide yourself in my lady's closet till my old lady's anger is abated. Oh, my old lady is in a perilous passion at something Mr. Fainall has said; he swears, and my old lady cries. There's a fearful hurricane, I vow. He says, mem, how that he'll have my lady's fortune made over to him, or he'll be divorced.

Mrs. Fainall: Does your lady or Mirabell know that?

Mincing: Yes, mem; they have sent me to see if Sir Wilfull be sober, and to bring him to them. My lady is resolved to have him, I think, rather than lose such a vast sum as six thousand pounds. —Oh, come, Mrs. Foible, I hear my old lady.

Mrs. Fainall: Foible, you must tell Mincing that she must prepare to vouch when I call her.

Foible: Yes, yes, madam.

Mincing: Oh, yes! mem, I'll vouch anything for your ladyship's service, be what it will. [*Exeunt Mincing and Foible.*] [*Enter Lady Wishfort and Mrs. Marwood.*]

Lady Wishfort: Oh, my dear friend, how can I enumerate the benefits that I have received from your goodness! To you I owe the timely discovery of the false vows of Mirabell; to you I owe the detection of the imposter Sir Rowland. —And now you are become an intercessor with my son-in-law, to save the honor of my house and compound for the frailties of my daughter. Well, friend, you are enough to reconcile me to the bad world, or else I would retire to deserts and solitudes, and feed harmless sheep by groves and purling streams.

Dear Marwood, let us leave the world, and retire by ourselves and be shepherdesses.

Mrs. Marwood: Let us first dispatch the affair in hand, madam. We shall have leisure to think of retirement afterwards. Here is one who is concerned in the treaty.

Lady Wishfort: Oh, daughter, daughter! is it possible thou shouldst be my child, bone of my bone, and flesh of my flesh, and, as I may say, another me, and yet transgress the most minute particle of severe virtue? Is it possible you should lean aside to iniquity, who have been cast in the direct mould of virtue? I have not only been a mould but a pattern for you and a model for you, after you were brought into the world.

Mrs. Fainall: I don't understand your ladyship.

Lady Wishfort: Not understand? Why, have you not been naught?[7] have you not been sophisticated?[8] Not understand! here I am ruined to compound for your caprices and your cuckoldoms. I must pawn my plate and my jewels, and ruin my niece, and all little enough—

Mrs. Fainall: I am wronged and abused, and so are you. 'Tis a false accusation—as false as hell, as false as your friend there, aye, or your friend's friend, my false husband!

Mrs. Marwood: My friend, Mrs. Fainall! Your husband my friend? What do you mean?

Mrs. Fainall: I know what I mean, madam, and so do you; and so shall the world at a time convenient.

Mrs. Marwood: I am sorry to see you so passionate, madam. More temper would look more like innocence. But I have done. I am sorry my zeal to serve your ladyship and family should admit of misconstruction, or make me liable to affronts. You will pardon me, madam, if I meddle no more with an affair in which I am not personally concerned.

Lady Wishfort: O dear friend, I am so ashamed that you should meet with such returns!—[*To Mrs. Fainall.*] You ought to ask pardon on your knees, ungrateful creature; she deserves more from you than all your life can accomplish.—[*To Mrs. Marwood.*] Oh, don't leave me destitute in this perplexity! No, stick to me, my good genius.

Mrs. Fainall: I tell you, madam, you are abused.—Stick to you! aye, like a leech, to suck your best blood—she'll drop off when she's full. Madam, you shan't pawn a bodkin, nor part with a brass counter, in composition for me. I defy 'em all. Let 'em prove their aspersions; I know my own innocence, and dare stand a trial. [*Exit Mrs. Fainall.*]

Lady Wishfort: Why, if she should be innocent, if she should be wronged after all—ha! I don't know what to think—and I promise you her education has been unexceptionable—I may say it; for I chiefly made it my own care to initiate her very infancy in the rudiments of virtue, and to impress upon her tender years a young odium and aversion to the very sight of men. Aye, friend, she would ha' shrieked if she had but seen a man, till she was in her teens. As I am a person, 'tis true—she was never suffered to play with a male child, though but in coats; nay, her very babies[9] were of the feminine gender. Oh, she never looked a man in the face but her own father, or the chaplain, and him we made a shift to put upon her for a woman, by the help of his long garments and his sleek face, till she was going in her fifteen.

Mrs. Marwood: 'Twas much she should be deceived so long.

Lady Wishfort: I warrant you, or she would never have borne to have been catechized by him; and have heard his long lectures against singing and dancing, and such debaucheries; and going to filthy plays, and profane music-meetings, where the lewd trebles squeak nothing but bawdy, and the basses roar

---

[7] Naughty. [8] "Adulterated."   [9] Dolls.

blasphemy. Oh, she would have swooned at the sight or name of an obscene play-book!—and can 1 think, after all this, that my daughter can be naught? What, a whore? and thought it excommunication to set her foot within the door of a playhouse! O dear friend, I can't believe it. No, no! As she says, let him prove it —let him prove it.

Mrs. Marwood: Prove it, madam? What, and have your name prostituted in a public court—yours and your daughter's reputation worried at the bar by a pack of bawling lawyers? To be ushered in with an "Oyez" [10] of scandal, and have your case opened by an old fumbling lecher in a quoif [11] like a man-midwife; to bring your daughter's infamy to light; to be a theme for legal punsters and quibblers by the statute; and become a jest against a rule of court, where there is no precedent for a jest in any record—not even in Domesday Book; to discompose the gravity of the bench, and provoke naughty interrogatories in more naughty law Latin; while the good judge, tickled with the proceeding, simpers under a grey beard, and fidgets off and on his cushion as if he had swallowed cantharides, or sat upon cow-itch.—

Lady Wishfort: Oh, 'tis very hard!

Mrs. Marwood. And then to have my young revellers of the Temple take notes, like 'prentices at a conventicle, and after, talk it all over again in commons, or before drawers in an eating-house.

Lady Wishfort: Worse and worse!

Mrs. Marwood: Nay, this is nothing; if it would end here, 'twere well. But it must, after this, be consigned by the shorthand writers to the public press; and from thence be transferred to the hands, nay into the throats and lungs of hawkers, with voices more licentious than the loud flounder-man's, or the woman that cries grey peas. And this

you must hear till you are stunned—nay, you must hear nothing else for some days.

Lady Wishfort: Oh, 'tis insupportable! No, no, dear friend, make it up, make it up; aye, aye, I'll compound. I'll give up all, myself and my all, my niece and her all—anything, everything for composition.

Mrs. Marwood: Nay, madam, I advise nothing; I only lay before you, as a friend, the inconveniences which perhaps you have overseen. Here comes Mr. Fainall. If he will be satisfied to huddle up all in silence, I shall be glad. You must think I would rather congratulate than condole with you.

Lady Wishfort: Aye, aye, I do not doubt it, dear Marwood; no, no, I do not doubt it. [*Enter Fainall.*]

Fainall: Well, madam, I have suffered myself to be overcome by the importunity of this lady, your friend; and am content you shall enjoy your own proper estate during life, on condition you oblige yourself never to marry, under such penalty as I think convenient.

Lady Wishfort: Never to marry!

Fainall: No more Sir Rowlands; the next imposture may not be so timely detected.

Mrs. Marwood: That condition, 1 dare answer, my lady will consent to without difficulty; she has already but too much experienced the perfidiousness of men.— Besides, madam, when we retire to our pastoral solitude we shall bid adieu to all other thoughts.

Lady Wishfort: Aye, that's true; but in case of necessity, as of health, or some such emergency—

Fainall: Oh, if you are prescribed marriage, you shall be considered; I only will reserve to myself the power to choose for you. If your physic be wholesome, it matters not who is your apothecary. Next, my wife shall settle on me the remainder of her fortune not made over already, and for her maintenance depend entirely on my discretion.

Lady Wishfort: This is most in-

---

[10] The call made to open a session of court.
[11] Lawyer's cap.

humanly savage, exceeding the barbarity of a Muscovite husband.

Fainall: I learned it from his Czarish majesty's [12] retinue, in a winter evening's conference over brandy and pepper, amongst other secrets of matrimony and policy as they are at present practised in the northern hemisphere. But this must be agreed unto, and that positively. Lastly, I will be endowed, in right of my wife, with that six thousand pounds which is the moiety of Mrs. Millamant's fortune in your possession, and which she has forfeited (as will appear by the last will and testament of your deceased husband, Sir Jonathan Wishfort) by her disobedience in contracting herself against your consent or knowledge and by refusing the offered match with Sir Wilfull Witwoud, which you, like a careful aunt, had provided for her.

Lady Wishfort: My nephew was *non compos*, and could not make his addresses.

Fainall: I come to make demands—I'll hear no objections.

Lady Wishfort: You will grant me time to consider?

Fainall: Yes, while the instrument is drawing, to which you must set your hand till more sufficient deeds can be perfected—which I will take care shall be done with all possible speed. In the meanwhile I will go for the said instrument, and till my return you may balance this matter in your own discretion. [*Exit Fainall.*]

Lady Wishfort: This insolence is beyond all precedent, all parallel. Must I be subject to this merciless villain?

Mrs. Marwood: 'Tis severe indeed, madam, that you should smart for your daughter's wantonness.

Lady Wishfort: 'Twas against my consent that she married this barbarian, but she would have him, though her year was not out.—Ah! her first husband, my son Languish, would not have

carried it thus! Well, that was my choice, this is hers: she is matched now with a witness.—I shall be mad!—Dear friend, is there no comfort for me? must I live to be confiscated at this rebel-rate?—Here come two more of my Egyptian plagues too. [*Enter Mrs. Millamant and Sir Wilfull Witwoud.*]

Sir Wilfull: Aunt, your servant.

Lady Wishfort: Out, caterpillar! Call not me aunt! I know thee not!

Sir Wilfull: I confess I have been a little in disguise,[13] as they say.—'Sheart! and I'm sorry for't. What would you have? I hope I have committed no offence, aunt—and if I did I am willing to make satisfaction; and what can a man say fairer? If I have broke anything, I'll pay for't, and it cost a pound. And so let that content for what's past, and make no more words. For what's to come, to pleasure you I'm willing to marry my cousin; so pray let's all be friends. She and I are agreed upon the matter before a witness.

Lady Wishfort: How's this, dear niece? Have I any comfort? Can this be true?

Mrs. Millamant: I am content to be a sacrifice to your repose, madam, and to convince you that I had no hand in the plot, as you were misinformed. I have laid my commands on Mirabell to come in person and be a witness that I give my hand to this flower of knighthood; and for the contract that passed between Mirabell and me, I have obliged him to make a resignation of it in your ladyship's presence. He is without, and waits your leave for admittance.

Lady Wishfort: Well, I'll swear I am something revived at this testimony of your obedience, but I cannot admit that traitor—I fear I cannot fortify myself to support his appearance. He is as terrible to me as a gorgon, if I see him I fear I shall turn to stone, and petrify incessantly.

Mrs. Millamant: If you disoblige him, he may resent your refusal and insist

---

[12] Peter the Great visited England in 1697.   [13] Drunk.

upon the contract still. Then 'tis the last time he will be offensive to you.

Lady Wishfort: Are you sure it will be the last time?—If I were sure of that—shall I never see him again?

Mrs. Millamant: Sir Wilfull, you and he are to travel together, are you not?

Sir Wilfull: 'Sheart, the gentleman's a civil gentleman, aunt; let him come in. Why, we are sworn brothers and fellow-travellers.—We are to be Pylades and Orestes,[14] he and I. He is to be my interpreter in foreign parts. He has been overseas once already, and with proviso that I marry my cousin, will cross 'em once again only to bear me company.—'Sheart, I'll call him in. An I set on't once, he shall come in; and see who'll hinder him. [*Exit Sir Wilfull.*]

Mrs. Marwood: This is precious fooling, if it would pass; but I'll know the bottom of it.

Lady Wishfort: O dear Marwood, you are not going?

Mrs. Marwood: Not far, madam; I'll return immediately. [*Exit Mrs. Marwood.*] [*Re-enter Sir Wilfull and Mirabell.*]

Sir Wilfull: Look up, man, I'll stand by you. 'Sbud an she do frown, she can't kill you; besides—harkee, she dare not frown desperately, because her face is none of her own. 'Sheart, an she should, her forehead would wrinkle like the coat of a cream-cheese; but mum for that, fellow-traveller.

Mirabell: If a deep sense of the many injuries I have offered to so good a lady, with a sincere remorse and a hearty contrition, can but obtain the least glance of compassion, I am too happy. Ah, madam, there was a time!—but let it be forgotten—I confess I have deservedly forfeited the high place I once held, of sighing at your feet. Nay, kill me not, by turning from me in disdain. I come not to plead for favor—nay, not for pardon; I am a suppliant only for

your pity. I am going where I never shall behold you more—

Sir Wilfull: How, fellow-traveller! you shall go by yourself then.

Mirabell: Let me be pitied first, and afterwards forgotten.—I ask no more.

Sir Wilfull: By'r Lady, a very reasonable request, and will cost you nothing, aunt! Come, come, forgive and forget, aunt. Why, you must, an you are a Christian.

Mirabell: Consider, madam, in reality you could not receive much prejudice. It was an innocent device; though I confess it had a face of guiltiness, it was at most an artifice which love contrived —and errors which love produces have ever been accounted venial. At least think it is punishment enough that I have lost what in my heart I hold most dear, that to your cruel indignation I have offered up this beauty, and with her my peace and quiet—nay, all my hopes of future comfort.

Sir Wilfull: An he does not move me, would I may never be o' the quorum! An it were not as good a deed as to drink, to give her to him again, I would I might never take shipping!—Aunt, if you don't forgive quickly, I shall melt, I can tell you that. My contract went no farther than a little mouth glue, and that's hardly dry—one doleful sigh more from my fellow-traveller, and 'tis dissolved.

Lady Wishfort: Well, nephew, upon your account—Ah, he has a false insinuating tongue!—Well sir, I will stifle my just resentment at my nephew's request. I will endeavor what I can to forget, but on proviso that you resign the contract with my niece immediately.

Mirabell: It is in writing, and with papers of concern; but I have sent my servant for it, and will deliver it to you with all acknowledgments for your transcendent goodness.

Lady Wishfort: [*Aside.*] Oh, he has witchcraft in his eyes and tongue!—When I did not see him, I could have bribed a villain to his assassination; but

---

[14] Faithful friends in Greek legend.

his appearance rakes the embers which have so long lain smothered in my breast. [*Enter Fainall and Mrs. Marwood.*]

Fainall: Your date of deliberation, madam, is expired. Here is the instrument; are you prepared to sign?

Lady Wishfort: If I were prepared, I am not impowered. My niece exerts a lawful claim, having matched herself by my direction to Sir Wilfull.

Fainall: That sham is too gross to pass on me—though 'tis imposed on you, madam.

Mrs. Millamant: Sir, I have given my consent.

Mirabell: And, sir, I have resigned my pretensions.

Sir Wilfull: And, sir, I assert my right and will maintain it in defiance of you, sir, and of your instrument. 'Sheart, an you talk of an instrument, sir, I have an old fox [15] by my thigh shall hack your instrument of ram vellum to shreds, sir! It shall not be sufficient for a mittimus [16] or a tailor's measure. Therefore withdraw your instrument, sir, or by'r Lady, I shall draw mine.

Lady Wishfort: Hold, nephew, hold!

Mrs. Millamant: Good Sir Wilfull, respite your valor!

Fainall: Indeed! Are you provided of a guard, with your single beef-eater there? But I'm prepared for you, and insist upon my first proposal. You shall submit your own estate to my management, and absolutely make over my wife's to my sole use, as pursuant to the purport and tenor of this other covenant.—[*To Mrs. Millamant.*] I suppose, madam, your consent is not requisite in this case; nor, Mr. Mirabell, your resignation; nor, Sir Wilfull, your right. —You may draw your fox if you please, sir, and make a bear-garden flourish somewhere else, for here it will not avail. This, my Lady Wishfort, must be subscribed, or your darling daughter's turned adrift, like a leaky hulk, to sink

or swim, as she and the current of this lewd town can agree.

Lady Wishfort: Is there no means, no remedy to stop my ruin? Ungrateful wretch! dost thou not owe thy being, thy subsistence, to my daughter's fortune?

Fainall: I'll answer you when I have the rest of it in my possession.

Mirabell: But that you would not accept of a remedy from my hands—I own I have not deserved you should owe any obligation to me; or else perhaps I could advise—

Lady Wishfort: Oh, what?—what? To save me and my child from ruin, from want, I'll forgive all that's past; nay, I'll consent to anything to come, to be delivered from this tyranny.

Mirabell: Aye, madam, but that is too late; my reward is intercepted. You have disposed of her who only could have made me a compensation for all my services. But be it as it may, I am resolved I'll serve you! You shall not be wronged in this savage manner.

Lady Wishfort: How! Dear Mr. Mirabell, can you be so generous at last? But it is not possible. Harkee, I'll break my nephew's match; you shall have my niece yet, and all her fortune, if you can but save me from this imminent danger.

Mirabell: Will you? I'll take you at your word. I ask no more. I must have leave for two criminals to appear.

Lady Wishfort: Aye, aye;—anybody, anybody!

Mirabell: Foible is one, and a penitent. [*Enter Mrs. Fainall, Foible, and Mincing.*]

Mrs. Marwood: These corrupt things are brought hither to expose me. [*Aside.*] Oh, my shame! [*Mirabell and Lady Wishfort go to Mrs. Fainall and Foible.*]

Fainall: If it must all come out, why let 'em know it; 'tis but the way of the world. That shall not urge me to relinquish or abate one tittle of my terms; no, I will insist the more.

Foible: Yes, indeed, madam, I'll take my Bible oath of it.

Mincing: And so will I, mem.

---

[15] Sword.   [16] Writ of commitment to prison.

Lady Wishfort: O Marwood, Marwood, art thou false? My friend deceive me? Hast thou been a wicked accomplice with that profligate man?

Mrs. Marwood: Have you so much ingratitude and injustice to give credit against your friend to the aspersions of two such mercenary trulls?

Mincing: Mercenary, mem? I scorn your words. 'Tis true we found you and Mr. Fainall in the blue garret; by the same token, you swore us to secrecy upon Messalina's [17] poems. Mercenary? No, if we would have been mercenary, we should have held our tongues; you would have bribed us sufficiently.

Fainall: Go, you are an insignificant thing!—Well, what are you the better for this? Is this Mr. Mirabell's expedient? I'll be put off no longer.—You, thing that was a wife, shall smart for this! I will not leave thee wherewithal to hide thy shame; your body shall be naked as your reputation.

Mrs. Fainall: I despise you and defy your malice!—You have aspersed me wrongfully—I have proved your falsehood! Go, you and your treacherous—I will not name it, but, starve together. Perish!

Fainall: Not while you are worth a groat, indeed, my dear. Madam, I'll be fooled no longer.

Lady Wishfort: Ah, Mr. Mirabell, this is small comfort, the detection of this affair.

Mirabell: Oh, in good time. Your leave for the other offender and penitent to appear, madam. [*Enter Waitwell with a box of writings.*]

Lady Wishfort: O Sir Rowland!—Well, rascal!

Waitwell: What your ladyship pleases. I have brought the black box at last, madam.

Mirabell: Give it me. Madam, you remember your promise?

Lady Wishfort: Aye, dear sir.

Mirabell: Where are the gentlemen?

[17] Malapropism for *miscellaneous.*

Waitwell: At hand, sir, rubbing their eyes—just risen from sleep.

Fainall: 'Sdeath, what's this to me? I'll not wait your private concerns. [*Enter Petulant and Witwoud.*]

Petulant: How now! What's the matter? Whose hand's out?

Witwoud: Heyday! What, are you all got together like players at the end of the last act?

Mirabell: You may remember, gentlemen, I once requested your hands as witnesses to a certain parchment.

Witwoud: Aye, I do; my hand I remember—Petulant set his mark.

Mirabell: You wrong him. His name is fairly written, as shall appear.— [*Undoing the box.*] You do not remember, gentlemen, anything of what that parchment contained?

Witwoud: No.

Petulant: Not I; I writ, I read nothing.

Mirabell: Very well, now you shall know.—Madam, your promise.

Lady Wishfort: Aye, aye, sir, upon my honor.

Mirabell: Mr. Fainall, it is now time that you should know that your lady, while she was at her own disposal, and before you had by your insinuations wheedled her out of a pretended settlement of the greatest part of her fortune—

Fainall: Sir! pretended!

Mirabell: Yes, sir. I say that this lady while a widow, having, it seems, received some cautions respecting your inconstancy and tyranny of temper, which from her own partial opinion and fondness of you she could never have suspected—she did, I say, by the wholesome advice of friends and of sages learned in the laws of this land, deliver this same as her act and deed to me in trust, and to the uses within mentioned. You may read if you please—[*holding out the parchment.*] though perhaps what is written on the back may serve your occasions.

Fainall: Very likely, sir. What's here? —Damnation! [*Reads.*] "A deed of conveyance of the whole estate real of

Arabella Languish, widow, in trust to Edward Mirabell."—Confusion!

Mirabell: Even so, sir; 'tis the way of the world, sir,—of the widows of the world. I suppose this deed may bear an 5 elder date than what you have obtained from your lady?

Fainall: Perfidious fiend! then thus I'll be revenged. [*Offers to run at Mrs. Fainall.*]

Sir Wilfull: Hold, sir! Now you may make your bear-garden flourish somewhere else, sir.

Fainall: Mirabell, you shall hear of this, sir, be sure you shall.—Let me 15 pass, oaf! [*Exit Fainall.*]

Mrs. Fainall: Madam, you seem to stifle your resentment; you had better give it vent.

Mrs. Marwood: Yes, it shall have 20 vent—and to your confusion, or I'll perish in the attempt. [*Exit Mrs. Marwood.*]

Lady Wishfort: O daughter, daughter! 'Tis plain thou hast inherited thy 25 mother's prudence.

Mrs. Fainall: Thank Mr. Mirabell, a cautious friend, to whose advice all is owing.

Lady Wishfort: Well, Mr. Mirabell, 30 you have kept your promise—and I must perform mine.—First, I pardon, for your sake, Sir Rowland there, and Foible. The next thing is to break the matter to my nephew—and how to do that— 35

Mirabell: For that, madam, give yourself no trouble; let me have your consent. Sir Wilfull is my friend. He has had compassion upon lovers, and generously engaged a volunteer in this action for 40 our service, and now designs to prosecute his travels.

Sir Wilfull: 'Sheart, aunt, I have no mind to marry. My cousin's a fine lady, and the gentleman loves her, and she 45 loves him, and they deserve one another. My resolution is to see foreign parts—I have set on't—and when I'm set on't I must do't. And if these two gentlemen would travel too, I think 50 they may be spared.

Petulant: For my part, I say little—I think things are best off or on.

Witwoud: 'Ygad, I understand nothing of the matter; I'm in a maze yet, like a dog in a dancing-school.

Lady Wishfort: Well, sir, take her, and with her all the joy I can give you.

Mrs. Millamant: Why does not the man take me? Would you have me give myself to you over again?

Mirabell: Aye, and over and over again; [*kisses her hand*] I would have you as often as possibly I can. Well, Heaven grant I love you not too well; that's all my fear.

Sir Wilfull: 'Sheart, you'll have time enough to toy after you're married; or if you will toy now, let us have a dance in the meantime, that we who are not lovers may have some other employment besides looking on.

Mirabell: With all my heart, dear Sir Wilfull. What shall we do for music?

Foible: Oh, sir, some that were provided for Sir Rowland's entertainment are yet within call. [*A dance.*]

Lady Wishfort: As I am a person, I can hold out no longer. I have wasted my spirits so to-day already, that I am ready to sink under the fatigue, and I cannot but have some fears upon me yet, that my son Fainall will pursue some desperate course.

Mirabell: Madam, disquiet not yourself on that account; to my knowledge his circumstances are such he must of force comply. For my part, I will contribute all that in me lies to a reunion; in the meantime, madam—[*to Mrs. Fainall*] let me before these witnesses restore to you this deed of trust. It may be a means, well-managed, to make you live easily together.

From hence let those be warned who
    mean to wed,
Lest mutual falsehood stain the bridal
    bed;
For each deceiver to his cost may find
That marriage-frauds too oft are paid
    in kind.   [*Exeunt omnes.*]

EPILOGUE

After our epilogue this crowd dismisses,
I'm thinking how this play'll be pulled
  to pieces.
But pray consider, ere you doom its fall,
How hard a thing 'twould be to please
  you all.
There are some critics so with spleen
  diseased, 5
They scarcely come inclining to be
  pleased:
And sure he must have more than mortal
  skill,
Who pleases anyone against his will.
Then, all bad poets we are sure are foes,
And how their number's swelled, the
  town well knows: 10
In shoals I've marked 'em judging in
  the pit;
Though they're on no pretense for
  judgment fit,
But that they have been damned for
  want of wit.
Since when, they by their own offences
  taught,
Set up for spies on plays and finding
  fault. 15
Others there are whose malice we'd
  prevent;
Such who watch plays with scurrilous
  intent
To mark out who by characters are
  meant.

And though no perfect likeness they can
  trace,
Yet each pretends to know the copied
  face. 20
These with false glosses feed their own
  ill nature,
And turn to libel what was meant a
  satire.
May such malicious fops this fortune
  find,
To think themselves alone the fools de-
  signed!
If any are so arrogantly vain, 25
To think they singly can support a
  scene,
And furnish fool enough to entertain.
For well the learn'd and the judicious
  know
That satire scorns to stoop so meanly
  low
As any one abstracted fop to show.
For, as when painters form a matchless
  face, 31
They from each fair one catch some
  different grace,
And shining features in one portrait
  blend,
To which no single beauty must pre-
  tend;
So poets oft do in one piece expose 35
Whole *belles-assemblées* of coquettes and
  beaux.

NOTES ON *THE WAY OF THE WORLD*

I. THE COMPLEXITY OF THE PLOT

We have already seen (see the Notes on Act II) that some of the reader's difficulty with the play lies in the fact that he is, at the start, expected to learn about a fairly large number of characters almost entirely through the accounts given of them by others. A more important source of confusion is that most of the complex relationships among these characters are presented to us in *brief explanatory statements* rather than *fully developed by dramatic interaction* of the characters. And when these statements come, as they often do, in advance of actions which we as yet grasp only dimly, we are quite likely to overlook their importance. If we do happen to miss, or grasp inadequately, a brief line which provides the key to a later

action, we may very well go through a whole act in considerable uncertainty as to its relation to the general movement of the play. For example,
Mirabell's purpose in having Waitwell pretend to be a nobleman in love
with Lady Wishfort is described explicitly in only a few lines in Act II
(p. 404a, 18 ff.) and in Act III (p. 413b, 1 ff.); if their purport is not fully
caught, the whole business of the disguise and pretended love is likely to
seem more a mystery, even though amusing, than a significant part of the
plot.

Since Congreve uses this method, it is clear that actors and actresses on
the one hand, and readers on the other, have an unusual responsibility for
recognizing and giving special emphasis to such key lines. We may ask:
can an author legitimately impose such extra burdens? Congreve, we feel
rightly, does not give us enough help in keeping the plot straight. On the
other hand, the rights which an author has with respect to the reader depend pretty largely upon what he is giving in return for the labor expended.
If, like Plautus, he is giving us only farce (and in some ways Plautus's plot
is easier to keep straight than Congreve's), we may feel little inclined to
take much trouble in keeping clear about all the details of a complicated
plot. But if, like Congreve, he is giving us, whether on comic or tragic level,
a mature comment upon experience, then he may rightly ask us to follow
him in the method which he has chosen for that comment. As we shall see,
Congreve has a great deal to say that is worth our attention. Yet here we
run into another special quality of *The Way of the World:* although the
tangle of relationships is a means to an end (unlike Plautus's confusion,
which is an end in itself), it is not the only means. That is, although we will
do well to study out all the lines of action and keep them straight, in one
sense that is not essential; at least it is not the most important exercise
demanded of us. For, ultimately, Congreve speaks less by means of the
outcome of his various plots and counter-plots than by the *tone* created by
the speech, manner, and attitudes of the participants in, and the observers
of, the various actions. Not that the action can be ignored: it is important
that Mirabell and Millamant do find a successful solution to their problem:
but it is more important still that they do it in a certain *way* and with
complete maintenance of certain essential *attitudes* (which we shall discuss later). If it be argued that the play which we thus characterize must
be undramatic because it depends rather on *talk* than on *action*, the answer
is this: in a play where so much is accomplished by *tone*, the *talk* is a very
important kind of action. The talk develops attitudes which clash with
each other, and, still better, with conventional expectations; it develops
character by revelation of basic attitudes.

Such considerations should be kept in mind when we learn that the play
originally failed because of its plot and when we are given the standard
criticism that the plot is too confused. These are important facts: but
they still do not constitute a final condemnation of the play.

2. CONGREVE'S ATTITUDE TOWARD HIS CHARACTERS

When we come to the important problem of Congreve's comment upon experience, we must first judge his attitudes toward his characters—a task complicated by the fact that these attitudes are far from meeting conventional expectations. In this matter such a seasoned critic as W. M. Thackeray has failed by misreading Congreve as a cynic, that is, one who believes the worst of human beings. It is ironic that such a charge should result from Congreve's method, which compliments the reader by assuming that the reader can distinguish good and bad even when the distinction is not made obvious.

Congreve, for instance, does not divide his characters into heroes and villains. He does not underline the goodness of his more admirable characters. He does not burn with righteous indignation when he presents such bad characters as Mrs. Marwood and Fainall; instead, he treats them with detachment by giving due play to their motives, their insight into others, their quickness, etc. He does not utterly deride the boobies such as the fops and Sir Wilfull; he allows them a measure of wit and acuteness. He does not present Mirabell as a flawless hero; instead he shows Mirabell very emphatically in "the way of the world" in his not only having had an affair with Millamant's cousin but also having married her off to the unpalatable Fainall as a cover-up; Congreve neither conceals these facts nor attempts to present Mirabell, in his new love for Millamant, as a changed or "converted" man. Finally, Congreve does not make Millamant into an obviously "sweet" or lovely heroine; she knows her way about in the world; she enjoys coquetry and the exercise of power; to grasp her essential charm we must see more than the glittering surface of her manner.

This is characterization at an adult level, and a naïve reader may think that it makes sense only if we regard the author as a sardonic observer of an insoluble human muddle. Such a reader will think that Congreve ought to have had the characters whom he regards favorably reject the artificial life of society and embrace a more direct, spontaneous way of life—especially in the matter of love. The only character, however, who rejects society is Sir Wilfull; but, though we are meant to sympathize to some extent with Sir Wilfull's shrewdness and honesty, it is clear that his gaucheries are still meant to be comic. That is, he is also measured by the author's criterion; though he aids the lovers, he does not himself provide a criterion for their conduct.

Society has its shortcomings, then, and the country also has its shortcomings. But this fact does not mean that Congreve believes that nowhere are values to be found. The fact that we reject some things which the characters do, while at the same time we accept other things, shows that a system of values is operating in the play. Our critical problem is to define them—not altogether an easy task since, though they do not coincide with, they do not wholly differ from, the standards of conduct upon which fashionable society in the play preens itself. Yet we should not make the mistake of thinking that Congreve approvingly presents a picture of a cynically heartless society. Nor, on the other hand, does he give us, with the ease of the sentimentalist, conventional reassurances about "natural" and spontaneous love, the victory of good over evil, and the triumph of "pure love." In fact, the elimination of all traces of sentimentality is one of the striking achievements of the play.

3. CONGREVE'S SYSTEM OF VALUES

What, then, are Congreve's values? *The Way of the World,* we may say, represents *values as achieved by discipline.* Discipline means control, order, the rejection of extremes. What we should go on to observe, then, is how, through the action of the play, Congreve does reject extremes.

Manners Versus Emotions. We are not asked to choose between raw, uninhibited but sincere emotion on the one hand, and artificial, insincere manners on the other. Such a dilemma is oversimple and therefore false. But many of the characters are caught in this dilemma: Sir Wilfull is impaled on the former horn, Witwoud and Petulant on the latter. Sir Wilfull can say, "The *fashion's* a fool . . ."; Witwoud can say (of Millamant), "And for my part, but that it is almost a *fashion* to admire her, I should— \ark'ee—to tell you a secret, . . .—I shall never break my heart for her."

At one extreme, the matter-of-fact Sir Wilfull rejects romantic love, the niceties of courtship, gracefully extravagant compliments; when Millamant shows indifference to him, he dismisses the matter with: "When you're disposed, when you're disposed. Now's as well as another time, . . ." At the other extreme, the fops are for lovers' conventions as ends in themselves, for nicety, delicacy of taste, and wit. But their emphasis lies on the mastery of the mechanism rather than on anything to be achieved by the mechanism. For them, therefore, the poetry of courtship is really as meaningless as it is for Sir Wilfull.

Congreve presents a nice irony here: opposite extremes tend to coalesce. When drunk, Petulant and Sir Wilfull take precisely the same line. Petulant, drunk, can say to Millamant: "If you are not handsome, what then, if I have a humor to prove it? If I shall have my reward, say so; if not, fight for your face the next time yourself. . . . I'll go to bed to my maid." When his chivalrous manners are peeled off—and they are worn by him merely as a modish garment—he is exactly like Sir Wilfull, who scorns manners and cries out, at the mention of wenches, "Ahey! wenches; where are the wenches?"

Mirabell and Millamant. The problem of extremes also engages the hero and heroine, though for them discipline means not only the rejection of unsuitable extremes but also the reconciliation of objectives that, in the society in which they live, are usually found in opposition. Millamant, for instance, would like to marry Mirabell and save her fortune too (maybe she *would* sacrifice it; since this is comedy, she is not really tested). But much more important—the play really hinges on this issue—is that Millamant wants to save, not only her lover and her fortune, but romantic love and marriage too; to have marriage, but also a certain tone and dignity that, like romantic love—as she sees—do not always go with marriage.* The marriage is too often one of convenience, of money or social position; the poetry of love is dropped after courtship or hardened into a meaningless conventional form for appearance's sake. The problem of Mirabell and Millamant is to define and create a situation, to discover a discipline, whereby love and dignity and marriage may be combined.

Congreve highlights this problem in two places. When Lady Wishfort, disillusioned, takes refuge in the mawkish poetry of "I would retire to deserts and solitudes, and feed harmless sheep by groves and purling streams. Dear Marwood, let us leave the world, and retire by ourselves and be shepherdesses" she shows what is *not* the way out—escape, an undisciplined jumping from one extreme to another. On the other hand, the famous bargaining scene in Act IV shows Mirabell and Millamant dealing directly with their problem—seeking the terms, the discipline, by which they may realize their complex objective. The serious implications are all there, though the tone is that of the finest comedy—one of urbane and witty gaiety. Sentimentalists may miss the feeling, and moralists may miss the seriousness (just as neither may know how to deal with Falstaff and Hal); Congreve's achievement is, like that of his characters, the avoidance of both lushness and solemnity.

4. CONGREVE'S VARIATIONS ON THE THEME OF LOVE

Why is the bargaining scene so successful? For one thing, because the various stipulations and demands, though made in a manner that may suggest selfishness or indulgence of whim, actually embody sound critiques of conventional matrimony, of its trivialities and hypocrisies. Taken alone, this critique itself might make Mirabell and Millamant look vain, condescending, and persnickety; but it is largely justified by the rest of the play. In fact, the relationship of Mirabell and Millamant is to be seen in the context of all the relationships of the play, from which it receives considerable qualification.

The theme is love, of which Congreve has presented an amazing number of variations—not for variety's sake, but as the background which defines the central problem of the play. The Fainalls, for instance, had married without love at all—he for money, she to cover up an amour. Lady Wishfort, whose chief concern is sex, is offered pretended passion by Waitwell, a parody of romantic courtship. Fainall and Marwood carry on an illicit relationship, marred by his distrust and her halfheartedness. Marwood's passion for Mirabell offers another variation, unrequited love, though the

---

* The phrase "romantic love" perhaps needs further definition, for the word "romantic" has been used in so many meanings and the whole phrase has become so vulgarized in recent years that its use here may be misleading. Yet we need a term which will not only assert the retention of a certain personal dignity in the relationship—as opposed to "love" that is selfishly possessive—but also one which will denote the retention of a certain spontaneity and charm as opposed to a matter-of-fact, sober-sides domestic partnership.

"love" is largely a medley of desire, pride, pique, and the wish to make Fainall jealous. Here we have a sharp contrast between her and Mrs. Fainall, who with equanimity sees her former lover laying suit to another woman. The desire for the contrast may have influenced Congreve here, since he leaves us somewhat uncertain about Mrs. Fainall's character; perhaps we are to assume that the earlier affair has burned itself out into a kind of general amiability, but the evidence does not clarify the matter finally. Then there are the bachelors—Sir Wilfull, Petulant, and Witwoud—to whom love is either a fashion or a convenience, and the servants, Waitwell and Foible, whose marriage, like that of the Fainalls, is one of convenience—in this case, their betters' convenience. Yet there is a variation here, for the pair seem to be in love: Foible sounds sincere enough when, upon her husband's being arrested, she wails about becoming "a Bridewell bride."

Ironically enough, they are the only happy couple in the play. It is perhaps significant that they are outside the world of fashion and its temptations. They can see it in perspective, and Congreve definitely presents them as seeing the other characters as they are. Ironically, they are not at the mercy of the conventions because they are *beneath* the conventions. Mirabell and Millamant must recognize the conventions, within which they aim for the same working relationship. Waitwell and Foible, by showing the possibility of domestic harmony, offer a kind of dramatic intimation of what Mirabell and Millamant may achieve.

The Way of the World represents, then, almost a symphonic pattern in which the theme of love receives a variety of treatments, ranging from the somber—the Fainall-Marwood affair is bitter, perhaps, as Bonamy Dobrée has suggested, even verging on the tragic—to the burlesque, which we see in Waitwell's pretended assault on Lady Wishfort. Somewhere between those extremes Mirabell and Millamant must plot their course—facing the opposition not merely of the Marwoods who would "mar" their affair and of the Fainalls scheming to get their money, but, more importantly, of a society which, because of its own addiction to extremes (of conventionality, sentimentality, pretence, etc.), must naturally be opposed to their search for balance and discipline. But this latter struggle becomes also a struggle with themselves: have they the inner stamina to adhere to standards of their own? If not, Millamant will "dwindle into a wife" and Mirabell be "enlarged into a husband"—two phrases, by the way, which beautifully epitomize the stereotyped marital relationship in which the essential dignity of the individual is lost. The loss of that dignity is what Congreve shows in the others: Fainall is "enlarged," Mrs. Fainall is "dwindled," Marwood can talk independently to Fainall because she is not tied to him, Lady Wishfort is only too eager to dwindle.

Thus the way of the world gives meaning to the bargaining scene, in which the participants struggle with the world and with themselves. Millamant imposes conditions, but she is equally willing to have Mirabell impose conditions: "Speak and spare not," she says. Some of her chief injunctions regard their joint conduct rather than her own prerogatives. And if each one does speak at times for himself, how else could Congreve convey the terms of a self-imposed discipline? For each one to outline in detail his *own* schedule of good behavior would be very close to sentimentality. But the play does not become soft and effusive. Congreve always keeps the tone firm; the wit in the bargaining scene is conspicuous.

5. CONGREVE'S USE OF IRONY

Very important in Congreve's management of the bargaining scene— as well as in the whole treatment of the love-affair—is the irony. On one plane it is the irony of lovers doing the opposite of what is expected of them, namely, haggling over rights and privileges and working out itemized contracts. On another plane, there is the ironic contrast between the unimportance of many (not all) of the minutiae discussed and the real importance of the deeper implications. If the details are trivial, the realism of the lovers is not trivial; and there is a real wistfulness—intensified by and yet, at the same time, protected from sentimentality by, the humor—in Millamant's exclamation, "Let us be as strange as if we had been married a great while, and as well-bred as if we were not married at all."

Thus Congreve has Mirabell and Millamant approach all issues through teasing and banter. They are aware of each other's faults, as they well may be, for they are also aware of their own. The amusing little scene in Act I in which Mirabell says, "I like her with all her faults—nay, like her for her faults," is significant. Mirabell is laughing at his mistress and also being ironic about his infatuation for her. Note the climax, in which he says of her frailties, "They are now grown as familiar to me as my own frailties, and in all probability in a little time longer I shall like 'em as well." To like her faults risks the sentimental, but the risk is completely countered by the playful, and yet shrewdly realistic, statement of his devotion to his own faults. His love is real, but he remains ironically perceptive.

There should be no doubt of the underlying genuineness of feeling: for one thing, no one not a lover (or an outright enemy) would take so much trouble to tease and joke about someone else. But the feeling may be missed by someone who takes the speeches only at their surface meaning, or someone who demands a direct avowal of feeling and has not the sophistication to grasp the fact that emotion may be presented indirectly.

Congreve makes matters sure, however, when he has Millamant say outright, "Well, if Mirabell should not make a good husband, I am a lost thing, for I find I love him violently"; she makes her confession, true, but even that she balances with a realistic view of future possibilities. Congreve demands more of us in Mirabell's comparable line at the close of the play, "Well, Heaven grant I love you not too well; that's all my fear." Reflection is needed to show us that the ironic playfulness would be possible only to one completely sure of his own feelings.

Can you find other instances of the indirect conveyance of real feelings?

6. THE RELATION OF THE INTRIGUE PLOT TO THE COMEDY AS A WHOLE

We have already seen (cf. Sections 4 and 5) that Congreve has his main characters engaging in two struggles—one against external forces that would interfere with their marriage, the other against themselves, against their tendency to give in to the way of the world. Congreve has done a very interesting thing in combining two struggles that are on quite different levels: one is a familiar *intrigue* plot, common to light plays of the period; the other is *comedy of character*, growing out of the struggle to combine love and dignity and marriage, to give them a place in the world without conforming to the way of the world.

The question then arises: is there any real relationship between the two struggles? May they even be contradictory? (Compare the monetary "reward" in this play with that in *The School for Scandal*.) At best, it hardly seems that the qualities which Mirabell and Millamant exhibit in their struggle with themselves are in any way necessary in the intrigue plot: a gross Mirabell and a heartless and superficial Millamant might very well have succeeded in dealing with the obstacles set up by Fainall, Mrs. Marwood, and Lady Wishfort.

The Intrigue Plot as Symbol. In one sense the intrigue plot serves to indicate that the tone of the play is light rather than solemn. But a more important defense for using the intrigue plot and combining it with a study of character is that the former does symbolize on one level, if not a very high level, the more important victory which the lovers achieve in their struggle with themselves: the way of the world can be mastered; the happy ending can be achieved. If one can conquer the intrigues of the world, one may also be able to conquer its conventions. To gain the consent of Lady Wishfort, then, is of less importance in itself (the lovers might say farewell to the fortune; nothing in the play indicates that they would not do this if necessary) than as a symbol, as it were, of their self-mastery. For the paradox of the situation is that the lovers' ability to master the way of the world in their own private love—to come to terms with it without being brought to terms by it—allows them to override the outside obstacles to their marriage.

The Intrigue in Act V. This truth is well exemplified by a part of the action in the final act. Act V is burdened with immense complications, some of which, of course, we have been quite able to foresee—Lady Wishfort's angry disillusionment about Waitwell, her anguish at her daughter's adultery and at Fainall's demands, and her getting a truer picture of Marwood. But halfway through the act there is suddenly made the surprising discovery that Mirabell and Millamant are now prepared to resign each other, and Millamant to accept Sir Wilfull—all, apparently, to please Lady Wishfort. As a result, Lady Wishfort's wrath is mitigated, Mirabell is admitted to her and can further soften her by his personal charm; and finally he is able to effect a rescue which is the determining factor in causing

Lady Wishfort to decide to withdraw her opposition to his marrying Millamant. In one sense, of course, all this is in the mode of intrigue comedy —the bringing about of a desired end by skillful trickery. But note actually how much play of character there is in the device which Mirabell and Millamant use: they run the quite serious risk that Lady Wishfort may, despite everything, accept their resignation of each other (she has had enough reason to be vindictive). Their acceptance of this possibility gives evidence of a high degree of willingness to face the consequences, of discipline and control. Thus, as we have said, their self-mastery is the clue to their mastery of the external situation.

Mirabell's possession of the deed which prevents Fainall from securing his wife's property belongs of course in the category of *deus ex machina* (cf. the uncle's settling everything up in *The School for Scandal*). But there is this to be said for it: rather than being a mere scheme to make things "come out right," it does fit into and help exhibit the character of Mirabell. If he did marry Arabella to Fainall, he at least also took measures to protect her against Fainall; we see his forcefulness and his essential trustworthiness in the fact that she adopts his plan. Our feeling that the solution is brought about by a *deus ex machina*, then, is due less to Congreve's going outside of character than to his not warning us what is up, that is, to his using surprise instead of expectation.*

The Plot as an Index of Attitude. Actually the plot, flimsy and involved as it is, succeeds rather well in emphasizing the special problem which confronts Congreve's hero and heroine. The qualities in them which interest Congreve are those highly civilized virtues of insight, understanding, and a sense of proportion.

The person possessed of such virtues has too much knowledge to take seriously things which are finally unimportant; too much sense of humor, to take himself too seriously; and he has learned that his way through a brittle world of appearances and shows—the world of "society" in any age—is to maintain a lively sense of the transience of things and their relative unimportance. This is not to say that he believes in nothing—that he has no values. But his allegiance to those more permanent values in which he does believe he may express through understatement, or ironical observation, or jest. Take Millamant's delightful fooling about pinning up her hair with verse, never with prose (Act II). The banter is superficially in keeping with Witwoud's more heavy-footed wit; but it is not inanely frivolous. It speaks volumes about the merits of the usual verse of lovers and what it is good for, but it delightfully distinguishes between

---

* For some readers the surprise may be qualified somewhat by the following bit of "preparation." Mirabell, in preparing his scheme to ensnare Lady Wishfort by "marrying" her to the supposed Sir Rowland, took, as we remember, some pains to insure that the marriage would be void by having Waitwell legally married to Foible. Readers who have noticed the emphasis given to this aspect of the scheme in Acts I and II may not be too much surprised to hear that Mirabell, in arranging a marriage of convenience for Mrs. Fainall, has taken care that she will not lose her fortune if Fainall turns out badly. The shrewd foresight and the consideration are, after all, in character.

the lover who has written his love letter in prose and the one who has at least taken the trouble, doubtless by dint of biting his pen, to put his into verse; and lastly, it expresses Millamant's amused contempt for poor Witwoud, who is so proud of his wit and of his ability to speak entertainingly to a fine lady.

The Attitude of the Lovers. In general, Millamant and Mirabell throughout the play practice the Biblical injunction to "answer a fool according to his folly," but they are far from being fools themselves. They know, too, how thoroughly out of place would be a "lyric cry from the heart" in a world devoted to fashion and to keeping up appearances. Moreover, they know how easy it is to deceive oneself into thinking that maudlin sentimentality—if only it be one's own sentimentality—is really serious emotion. They prefer not to risk the expression of their love in statements that may, in their possible extravagance, be confused with the cant of affected gallantry, on the one hand, or with overlush sentimentality on the other. Their speech is continually bathed in irony; but their deeper feelings can survive the ironical and witty expressions in which they are expressed. Indeed, one can go further and say that their sincerity is guaranteed by the fact that in expressing their affection for each other, neither Mirabell or Millamant relaxes that keen awareness of the deviousness of the way of the world of which the irony is a symptom. The lovers, then, are not sensitive innocents immersed in a world of folly and knavery. If they maintain a kind of innocence, it is because they are able to carry out the Biblical injunction to be as "wise as serpents," though as "innocent as doves." This is the charm of the lovers, of Millamant in particular. She remains charming, high-spirited, gay, throughout the play: to be intelligent does not require that she become a cynic, and, being in love, on the other hand, does not require that she stifle her intelligence. If we as readers feel that the plot on which the play rests is a sort of tempest in a teapot—intrigue and counterintrigue, cluttered up with some rather ludicrous and farcical exposures, we may be sure that Mistress Millamant would be the first to agree with us. In its intrigue and in its farcical extravagance the plot is but a heightened form of the way of the world which she is able to see through, and thus triumph over. It calls for the ironic playfulness so neatly exemplified in Witwoud's line in the final scene: "What, are you all got together, like players at the end of the last act?"

QUESTIONS

1. What examples can you find, besides those already referred to, of key explanatory lines which the reader must not fail to understand fully if he is to follow successfully the details of subsequent action?

2. Study all the evidence on the attitude which Congreve takes to Sir Wilfull.

3. In the bargaining scene in Act IV, some of the demands made are trivial, some less so. Note which ones have to do directly with important matters.

4. What facts make the final disgrace of Marwood especially ironic?

5. Study Lady Wishfort's speech in Act V about the bringing-up of her daughter (p. 434b, 22 ff.). Some of her remarks sound very much like contemporary criticism of the theatre and of other modes of entertainment by the Rev. Jeremy Collier and others. What purpose might Congreve have had in thus reproducing their points of view?

6. What are the indications, throughout Acts IV and V, that Lady Wishfort, when she is outside the realm of her chief obsession, is not wholly unable to see things as they are? Is anything gained by giving her such ability?

7. We have already suggested that the adoption of the point of view of "the world" is one distinguishing mark of comedy. For another clue to the nature of comedy the reader might consult that part of the last act in which Mirabell appears. It is noteworthy that it is his personal charm, more than anything else, which influences the direction of events; on that ground he is largely forgiven various misdeeds. Might it be correct, then, to suggest that comedy is concerned with the realm of "personality" rather than, say, of morality or other extra-personal values? That personal charm is the chief standard of judgment? How would this apply to *The School for Scandal?*

8. The student may find it very useful to make some comparison of Mirabell and Charles Surface, since the latter also represents the way of the world. But note how much milder an example of the man of the world Charles Surface is. Is it correct to say that Mirabell also has some—not all—of the qualities of Joseph Surface? Might this thinning out of the character of Mirabell be partially responsible for our feeling that the treatment of Charles Surface does not escape sentimentality? Judging by the two plays, what inferences can you draw about the difference between comedy at the beginning and at the end of the eighteenth century? Likewise, compare Waitwell with old Rowley.

9. We have said that Mirabell's possession of the deed from Mrs. Fainall comes as a big surprise at the end. Can you find, however, any "buried" references which indicate that some sort of document is to be introduced? See the last part of Act IV.

10. Compare the treatment of the "unities" in this play with that in Ibsen's *Rosmersholm.* Note especially the tightening up of the unity of time in Congreve's play.

11. Bonamy Dobrée suggests that in the relationship between Fainall and Marwood Congreve moves toward the tragic. Do you find this a sound judgment? Compare, for instance, Marwood and Shakespeare's Cleopatra: does the former seem to have any of the greatness of the latter? To what extent is Marwood able to elicit our sympathy? Dobrée also sees in Lady Wishfort a kind of pathos. Do you accept this judgment?

12. Compare the final exit of Fainall and Marwood with the final exit of the "villains" at the end of *The School for Scandal.*

13. The last speech of the play hints the reconciliation of the Fainalls. Would this be possible in a problem play? In tragedy?

14. We have already pointed out two types of comedy to be discerned in this play: the intrigue level, and the level of comedy of character. Besides these we may observe farce (the drunken scenes), comedy of wit (even the fools make some very witty remarks), and parody (as in the Lady Wishfort courtship scenes). Which of these, if any, are ingredients in what is called "comedy of manners"? How does the comedy here differ from that in *Henry IV*? Or that in Shaw's *Major Barbara*? (See Appendix A.)

The Mirabell-Millamant affair is obviously the focal point of the various gradations of comedy in the play. How well does it bring them all into focus?

15. How many of the names of the *dramatis personæ* give some clue to their characters?

16. We have discussed the play as a symphonic pattern of variations on the theme of love. It may be possible, also, to discern other such patterns which serve as minor motifs in the play—motifs which support and amplify the main theme.

a. Note, for instance, the different variations upon the theme of age. Foible tells Lady Wishfort that Mirabell had called her "superannuated"; Millamant applies the same adjective to Sir Wilfull. Much, in fact, is made of the age of Sir Wilfull. In the middle of Act III Millamant makes some rather sharp remarks to Marwood on the subject of age (p. 415b, 48 ff.). Can you find any other references to age which would help support the hypothesis that there is a youth-and-age motif in the play?

b. Note, also, that the words which make up the title of the play are spoken at various times in the play. Find all the passages in question and see whether they shed any light on the total meaning. Does the phrase acquire a different tone as it is used by different characters? Note especially the variation in the final use by Mirabell near the end.

c. Finally, there are a number of variations in the language used by different characters, even though the language of wit is at one time or another used by almost all of them. There is, for instance, Lady Wishfort's "boudoir Billingsgate," of which we have already spoken. There is the rather gauche speech of Sir Wilfull. There is the sharp contrast between Waitwell's language as he "proposes" to Lady Wishfort and that addressed to Foible, his real wife. There are different levels of wit—that of Mirabell and Millamant, and that of Witwoud and Petulant. At different times we have effects dependent upon the repetition of the words of one character by another. Do you find other evidences of the special use of language? Do all such uses support the central theme of the play?

17. Might it be argued that the problem of Mirabell and Millamant with regard to the social world is in any way comparable to the problem of Prince Hal with regard to the political world? Note that both—the lovers in one play and the Prince in the other—must undergo certain disciplines, reconcile certain conflicting forces, avoid certain extremes. Does this parallel, if it holds good, shed further light on the nature of comedy? If the parallel does hold, what character in Congreve's play might be said to have a role or position comparable to Falstaff's?

PART FOUR

SPECIAL STUDIES
in the
TRAGIC MODE

1. Introduction

THE plays in this section are in general more difficult than any which have preceded, and in each one, also, we shall meet problems of a special sort. In the earlier sections we have gone rather thoroughly into comic types; we are now concerned with the tragic mode. Yet the plays do not represent a wholly new departure from their predecessors. In *Everyman, The London Merchant,* and *Rosmersholm* we have been at least on the periphery of tragedy and have had to consider tentatively some of the issues which tragedy introduces—for instance, the problem of the tragic hero, the tragic ending, focus, the nature of the conflict. Now we must deal directly, and as fully as possible, with these issues and with others like them.

Within the tragic mode we can find a great variety of examples, and the plays in this section have been chosen because they present a diversity of problems. At the same time, certain resemblances between the plays should not only provide a background against which to see the differences but also suggest, perhaps, certain procedures and assumptions common to tragedy generally.

Chekhov's *The Sea Gull* is not properly tragedy at all, perhaps, but in tone it has resemblances to tragedy and therefore poses a problem which is suitable to the present section. At the same time Chekhov's play has a partial thematic similarity to Congreve's *The Way of the World,* which we have just read. So *The Sea Gull* not only affords a convenient transition but also throws us immediately into rather complex matters of tone and structure.

With Marlowe's *The Tragical History of Dr. Faustus,* one of the best pre-Shakespearian plays, we come definitely into the realm of tragedy. Though it poses at least one special problem in structure, it is less complexly put together than Shakespearian tragedy. Hence it provides an especially suitable introduction to the study of poetic language in drama—a subject of high importance in the work of Shakespeare.

The *Oedipus Rex* of Sophocles, one of the most famous of Greek tragedies, is especially useful in the study of tragedy because it not only compels us to work through the difficulties offered by the fact that the play comes out of a different culture from our own, but also permits us to observe, behind all the differences in form and myth, the working of a concept of tragedy not unlike that of Shakespeare and indeed all great dramatists. Like Doctor Faustus, Oedipus is seen in relation to a religious tradition, and with this basic similarity of situation we can go on to investigate the kinds of reality from the contemplation of which tragedy emerges.

In *King Lear* we find the most complex of all the tragedies considered here—complex in its number of characters, in its involved plot, in its profound use of imagery and symbolism, and in its philosophical implications.

With the analysis of *King Lear* and with the shorter analyses of and questions on *Hamlet, Othello, Macbeth*, and *Antony and Cleopatra*, the present section should provide a useful approach to the study of Shakespearian tragedy.

2. Chekhov, *The Sea Gull*

*T*HE *SEA GULL* of Anton Chekhov (1860–1904) was first presented in St. Petersburg in 1896; thus it falls within the same decade as Ibsen's *Rosmersholm* and Wilde's *Lady Windermere's Fan*. As a point of departure, therefore, the student may find it convenient to see whether there are any parallels among these three nearly contemporary European plays. He will observe, for instance, that each of them is concerned, to a greater or less degree, with love affairs that fall outside the sanction of society. But once this similarity of situation has been observed, the real question arises: Is Chekhov's attitude toward his materials the same as that of Wilde or Ibsen?

This is the problem of *tone*. Chekhov calls his play a "comedy"; hence the reader will want to see whether he can detect any relationship to Wilde's play. If, on the other hand, he does not discover the flippancy or the wit or the prevalent gaiety of some of the other comedies he has read, but instead finds a large measure of bitter unhappiness, he will have to decide in what especial sense the word *comedy* is used. Perhaps he will find a clue in the statement of a distinguished actress, who has taken various parts in Chekhov plays, that it was Chekhov's genius to relish joys and smile at faults, to observe compassionately the necessary mixture of strength and weakness in man.

As he reads, the student should be attempting to deal with one other problem—the problem posed by criticisms sometimes made by newcomers to Chekhov's work: "Where's it all going? There's no plot." *Is* there a plot? If there is, what structural peculiarity obscures the fact from the casual reader? Keeping such questions in mind will aid the reader in determining the sources of dramatic effect in *The Sea Gull*.

THE SEA GULL [1]

DRAMATIS PERSONÆ

IRINA NIKOLAYEVNA ARKADIN (MA-
DAME TREPLEV), *an actress*
KONSTANTIN GAVRILOVITCH TREPLEV,
her son, a young man
PYOTR NIKOLAYEVITCH SORIN, *her
brother*
NINA MIHAILOVNA ZARETCHNY, *a young
girl, the daughter of a wealthy land-
owner*
ILYA AFANASYEVITCH SHAMRAEV, *a retired lieutenant,* SORIN'S *steward*

POLINA ANDREYEVNA, *his wife*
MASHA, *his daughter*
BORIS ALEXEYEVITCH TRIGORIN, *a
literary man*
YEVGENY SERGEYEVITCH DORN, *a doc-
tor*
SEMYON SEMYONOVITCH MEDVEDENKO,
a schoolmaster
YAKOV, *a labourer*
A MAN COOK
A HOUSEMAID

The action takes place in SORIN'S *house and garden. Between the Third and Fourth
Acts there is an interval of two years.*

ACT I

[Part of the park on Sorin's estate.
Wide avenue leading away from the
spectators into the depths of the park
toward the lake is blocked up by a platform roughly put together for private
theatricals, so that the lake is not visible.
To right and left of the platform, bushes.
A few chairs, a little table.]

[*The sun has just set. Yakov and other
labourers are at work on the platform behind the curtain; there is the sound of
coughing and hammering. Masha and
Medvedenko enter on the left, returning
from a walk.*]

Medvedenko: Why do you always wear
black?

Masha: I am in mourning for my life.
I am unhappy.

Medvedenko: Why? [*Pondering.*] I
don't understand . . . You are in good
health; though your father is not very
well off, he has got enough. My life is
much harder than yours. I only get
twenty-three roubles a month, and from

that they deduct something for the
pension fund, and yet I don't wear
mourning. [*They sit down.*]

Masha: It isn't money that matters.
A poor man may be happy.

Medvedenko: Theoretically, yes; but
in practice it's like this: there are my
two sisters and my mother and my little
brother and I, and my salary is only
twenty-three roubles. We must eat and
drink, mustn't we? One must have tea
and sugar. One must have tobacco. It's
a tight fit.

Masha: [*Looking round at the platform.*] The play will soon begin.

Medvedenko: Yes. Miss Zaretchny will
act: it is Konstantin Gavrilitch's play.
They are in love with each other and
today their souls will be united in the
effort to realize the same artistic effect.
But your soul and mine have not a
common point of contact. I love you, I
am so wretched I can't stay at home.
Every day I walk four miles here and
four miles back and I meet with nothing
but indifference from you. I can quite
understand it. I am without means and

[1] The Constance Garnett translation in the Modern Library text, used by courtesy of
Random House, Inc.

have a big family to keep. . . . Who would care to marry a man who hasn't a penny to bless himself with?

Masha: Oh, nonsense! [*Takes a pinch of snuff.*] Your love touches me, but I can't reciprocate it—that's all. [*Holding out the snuffbox to him*]. Help yourself.

Medvedenko: I don't feel like it. [*A pause.*]

Masha: How stifling it is! There must be a storm coming. . . . You're always discussing theories or talking about money. You think there is no greater misfortune than poverty, but to my mind it is a thousand times better to go in rags and be a beggar than . . . But you wouldn't understand that, though. . . .

[*Sorin and Treplev enter on the right.*]

Sorin: (*Leaning on his walking stick.*) I am never quite myself in the country, my boy, and, naturally enough, I shall never get used to it. Last night I went to bed at ten and woke up this morning at nine feeling as though my brain were glued to my skull, through sleeping so long. [*Laughs.*] And after dinner I accidentally dropped off again, and now I am utterly shattered and feel as though I were in a nightmare, in fact. . . .

Treplev: Yes, you really ought to live in town. [*Catches sight of Masha and Medvedenko.*] When the show begins, my friends, you will be summoned, but you mustn't be here now. You must please go away.

Sorin: [*To Masha.*] Marya Ilyinishna, will you be so good as to ask your papa to tell them to take the dog off the chain?—it howls. My sister could not sleep again last night.

Masha: Speak to my father yourself; I am not going to. Please don't ask me. [*To Medvedenko.*] Come along!

Medvedenko: [*To Treplev.*] So you will send and let us know before it begins. [*Both go out.*]

Sorin: So I suppose the dog will be howling all night again. What a business it is! I have never done as I liked in the country. In old days I used to get leave

for twenty-eight days and come here for a rest and so on, but they worried me so with all sorts of trifles that before I had been here two days I was longing to be off again. [*Laughs.*] I've always been glad to get away from here. . . . But now I am on the retired list, and I have nowhere else to go, as a matter of fact. I've got to live here whether I like it or not. . . .

Yakov: [*To Treplev.*] We are going to have a bath, Konstantin Gavrilitch.

Treplev: Very well; but don't be more than ten minutes. [*Looks at his watch.*] It will soon begin.

Yakov: Yes, sir. [*Goes out.*]

Treplev: [*Looking round the stage.*] Here is our theater. The curtain, then the first wing, then the second, and beyond that—open space. No scenery of any sort. There is an open view of the lake and the horizon. We shall raise the curtain at exactly half past eight, when the moon rises.

Sorin: Magnificent.

Treplev: If Nina is late it will spoil the whole effect. It is time she was here. Her father and her stepmother keep a sharp eye on her, and it is as hard for her to get out of the house as to escape from prison. [*Puts his uncle's cravat straight.*] Your hair and your beard are very untidy. They want clipping or something. . . .

Sorin: [*Combing out his beard.*] It's the tragedy of my life. Even as a young man I looked as though I had been drinking for days or something of the sort. I was never a favourite with the ladies. [*Sitting down.*] Why is your mother out of humor?

Treplev: Why? Because she is bored. [*Sitting down beside him.*] She is jealous. She is set against me, and against the performance, and against my play because Nina is acting in it, and she is not. She does not know my play, but she hates it.

Sorin: [*Laughs.*] What an idea!

Treplev: She is annoyed to think that even on this little stage Nina will have a triumph and not she. [*Looks at his watch.*] My mother is a psychological freak. Unmistakably talented, intelligent, capable of sobbing over a book, she will reel off all Nekrassov by heart; as a sick nurse she is an angel; but just try praising Duse in her presence! O-ho! You must praise no one but herself, you must write about her, make a fuss over her, be in raptures over her extraordinary acting in *La Dame aux Camélias* or the *Ferment of Life;* but she has none of this narcotic in the country, she is bored and cross, and we are all her enemies—we are all in fault. Then she is superstitious—she is afraid of three candles, of the number thirteen. She is stingy. She has got seventy thousand roubles in a bank at Odessa—I know that for a fact—but ask her to lend you some money, and she will burst into tears.

Sorin: You imagine your mother does not like your play, and you are already upset and all that. Don't worry; your mother adores you.

Treplev: [*Pulling the petals off a flower.*] Loves me, loves me not; loves me, loves me not; loves me, loves me not. [*Laughs.*] You see, my mother does not love me. I should think not! She wants to live, to love, to wear light blouses; and I am twenty-five, and I am a continual reminder that she is no longer young. When I am not there she is only thirty-two, but when I am there she is forty-three, and for that she hates me. She knows, too, that I have no belief in the theater. She loves the stage, she fancies she is working for humanity, for the holy cause of art, while to my mind the modern theater is nothing but tradition and conventionality. When the curtain goes up, and by artificial light, in a room with three walls, these great geniuses, the devotees of holy art, represent how people eat, drink, love, move about, and wear their jackets; when from these commonplace sentences and pictures they try to draw a moral—a petty moral, easy of comprehension and

convenient for domestic use; when in a thousand variations I am offered the same thing over and over again—I run away as Maupassant ran away from the Eiffel Tower, which weighed upon his brain with its vulgarity.

Sorin: You can't do without the stage.

Treplev: We need new forms of expression. We need new forms, and if we can't have them we had better have nothing. [*Looks at his watch.*] I love my mother—I love her very much—but she leads a senseless sort of life, always taken up with this literary gentleman, her name is always trotted out in the papers—and that wearies me. And sometimes the simple egoism of an ordinary mortal makes me feel sorry that my mother is a celebrated actress, and I fancy that if she were an ordinary woman I should be happier. Uncle, what could be more hopeless and stupid than my position? She used to have visitors, all celebrities—artists and authors—and among them all I was the only one who was nothing, and they only put up with me because I was her son. Who am I? What am I? I left the University in my third year—owing to circumstances "for which we accept no responsibility," as the editors say; I have no talents, I haven't a penny of my own, and on my passport I am described as an artisan of Kiev. You know my father was an artisan of Kiev, though he too was a well-known actor. So, when in her drawing room all these artists and authors graciously noticed me, I always fancied from their faces that they were taking the measure of my insignificance—I guessed their thoughts and suffered from the humiliation. . . .

Sorin: And, by the way, can you tell me, please, what sort of man this literary gentleman is? There's no making him out. He never says anything.

Treplev: He is an intelligent man, good-natured and rather melancholy, you know. A very decent fellow. He is still a good distance off forty, but he is already celebrated and has enough and to spare of everything. As for his writings . . . what shall I say? They are charming, full of talent, but . . . after Tolstoy or Zola you do not care to read Trigorin.

Sorin: Well, I am fond of authors, my boy. At one time I had a passionate desire for two things: I wanted to get married, and I wanted to become an author; but I did not succeed in doing either. Yes, it is pleasant to be even a small author, as a matter of fact.

Treplev: [*Listens.*] I hear steps . . . [*Embraces his uncle.*] I cannot live without her. . . . The very sound of her footsteps is lovely. . . . I am wildly happy. [*Goes quickly to meet Nina Zaretchny as she enters.*] My enchantress—my dream. . . .

Nina: [*In agitation.*] I am not late. . . . Of course I am not late. . . .

Treplev: [*Kissing her hands.*] No, no, no!

Nina: I have been uneasy all day. I was so frightened. I was afraid father would not let me come. . . . But he has just gone out with my stepmother. The sky is red, the moon is just rising, and I kept urging on the horse. [*Laughs.*] But I am glad. [*Shakes Sorin's hand warmly.*]

Sorin: [*Laughs.*] Your eyes look as though you have been crying. . . . Fie, fie! That's not right!

Nina: Oh, it was nothing. . . . You see how out of breath I am. I have to go in half an hour. We must make haste. I can't stay, I can't! For God's sake don't keep me! My father doesn't know I am here.

Treplev: It really is time to begin. We must go and call the others.

Sorin: I'll go this minute. [*Goes to the right, singing* "To France two grenadiers." *Looks round.*] Once I sang like that, and a deputy prosecutor said to me, "You have a powerful voice, your Excellency"; then he thought a little and added, "but not a pleasant one." [*Laughs and goes off.*]

Nina: My father and his wife won't

let me come here. They say it is so Bohemian here . . . they are afraid I shall go on the stage. . . . But I feel drawn to the lake here like a sea gull. 5 . . . My heart is full of you. [*Looks round.*]

Treplev: We are alone.

Nina: I fancy there is someone there.

Treplev: There's nobody. [*They kiss.*]

Nina: What tree is this? 10

Treplev: An elm.

Nina: Why is it so dark?

Treplev: It's evening; everything is getting dark. Don't go away early, I entreat you! 15

Nina: I must.

Treplev: And if I come to you, Nina, I'll stand in the garden all night, watching your window.

Nina: You can't; the watchman 20 would notice you. Trésor is not used to you, and he would bark.

Treplev: I love you!

Nina: Sh-h. . . .

Treplev: [*Hearing footsteps.*] Who is 25 there? You, Yakov?

Yakov: [*Behind the stage.*] Yes, sir.

Treplev: Take your places. It's time to begin. Is the moon rising?

Yakov: Yes, sir. 30

Treplev: Have you got the methylated spirit? Have you got the sulphur? When the red eyes appear there must be a smell of sulphur. [*To Nina.*] Go, it's all ready. Are you nervous? 35

Nina: Yes, awfully! Your mother is all right—I am not afraid of her—but there's Trigorin . . . I feel frightened and ashamed of acting before him . . . a celebrated author. . . . Is he young? 40

Treplev: Yes.

Nina: How wonderful his stories are.

Treplev: [*Coldly.*] I don't know. I haven't read them.

Nina: It is difficult to act in your 45 play. There are no living characters in it.

Treplev: Living characters! One must depict life not as it is, and not as it ought to be, but as we see it in our dreams. 50

Nina: There is very little action in

your play—nothing but speeches. And to my mind there ought to be love in a play. [*Both go behind the stage.*]
[*Enter Polina Andreyevna and Dorn.*]
Polina: It is getting damp. Go back and put on your galoshes.
Dorn: I am hot.
Polina: You don't take care of yourself. It's obstinacy. You are a doctor, and you know perfectly well that damp air is bad for you but you want to make me miserable; you sat out on the veranda all yesterday evening on purpose. . . .
Dorn: [*Hums.*] "Do not say that youth is ruined."
Polina. You were so absorbed in conversation with Irina Nikolayevna . . . you did not notice the cold. Own up . . . you are attracted by her.
Dorn: I am fifty-five.
Polina. Nonsense! That's not old for a man. You look very young for your age, and are still attractive to women.
Dorn: Well, what would you have?
Polina: All you men are ready to fall down and worship an actress, all of you!
Dorn: [*Hums.*] "Before thee once again I stand." If artists are liked in society and treated differently from merchants, for example, that's only in the nature of things. It's idealism.
Polina: Women have always fallen in love with you and thrown themselves on your neck. Is that idealism too?
Dorn: [*Shrugs his shoulders.*] Well, in the attitude of women to me there has been a great deal that was good. What they principally loved in me was a first-rate doctor. You remember that ten or fifteen years ago I was the only decent accoucheur in the district. Then, too, I have always been an honest man.
Polina: [*Seizes him by the hand.*] Dearest!
Dorn: Sh-h! They are coming.
[*Enter Madame Arkadin arm in arm with Sorin, Trigorin, Shamraev, Medvedenko, and Masha.*]
Shamraev: In the year 1873 she acted marvellously at the fair at Poltava. It

was a delight! She acted exquisitely! Do you happen to know, madam, where Pavel Semyonitch Tchadin, a comic actor, is now? His Rasplyuev was inimitable, even finer than Sadovsky's, I assure you, honoured lady. Where is he now?
Madame Arkadin: You keep asking me about antediluvians. How should I know? [*Sits down.*]
Shamraev: [*With a sigh.*] Pashka Tchadin! There are no such actors now. The stage has gone down, Irina Nikolayevna! In old days there were mighty oaks, but now we see nothing but stumps.
Dorn: There are few actors of brilliant talents nowadays, that's true; but the average level of acting is far higher than it was.
Shamraev: I can't agree with you. But, of course, it's a matter of taste. *De gustibus aut bene aut nihil.*
[*Treplev comes out from behind the stage.*]
Madame Arkadin: [*To her son.*] My dear son, when is it going to begin?
Treplev: In a minute. I beg you to be patient.
Madame Arkadin: (*Recites from Hamlet.*]
"Oh Hamlet, speak no more!
Thou turn'st mine eyes into my very soul;
And there I see such black and grained spots
As will not leave their tinct."
Treplev: (*Paraphrasing from Hamlet*).
"Then why do you yield to sin, seek love in the depths of wickedness?"
[*A horn is sounded behind the stage.*]
Treplev: Ladies and gentlemen, we begin! I beg you to attend. [*A pause.*] I begin. [*Taps with a stick and recites aloud.*] Oh, you venerable old shadows that float at nighttime over this lake, lull us to sleep and let us dream of what will be in two hundred thousand years!
Sorin: There will be nothing in two hundred thousand years.

Treplev: Then let them present that nothing to us.

Madame Arkadin: Let them. We are asleep.

[*The curtain rises; the view of the lake is revealed; the moon is above the horizon, its reflection in the water; Nina Zaretchny, all in white, is sitting on a big stone.*]

Nina: Men, lions, eagles and partridges, horned deer, geese, spiders, silent fish that dwell in the water, starfishes and creatures which cannot be seen by the eye—all living things, all living things, all living things, having completed their cycle of sorrow, are extinct. . . . For thousands of years the earth has borne no living creature on its surface, and this poor moon lights its lamp in vain. On the meadow the cranes no longer waken with a cry, and there is no sound of the May beetles in the lime trees. It is cold, cold, cold! Empty, empty, empty! Dreadful, dreadful, dreadful! [*A pause.*] The bodies of living creatures have vanished into dust, and eternal matter has transformed them into rocks, into water, into clouds, while the souls of all have melted into one. That world-soul I am—I. . . . In me is the soul of Alexander the Great, of Caesar, of Shakespeare, and of Napoleon, and of the lowest leech. In me the consciousness of men is blended with the instincts of the animals, and I remember all, all, all! And I live through every life over again in myself! [*Will-of-the-wisps appear.*]

Madame Arkadin: [*Softly.*] It's something decadent.

Treplev: [*In an imploring and reproachful voice.*] Mother!

Nina: I am alone. Once in a hundred years I open my lips to speak, and my voice echoes mournfully in the void, and no one hears. . . . You too, pale lights, hear me not. . . . The stagnant marsh begets you before daybreak and you wander until dawn, but without thought, without will, without the tremor of life. For fear that life should spring up in you

the father of eternal matter, the devil, keeps the atoms in you, as in the stones and in the water, in continual flux, and you are changing perpetually. For in all the universe nothing remains permanent and unchanged but the spirit. [*A pause.*] Like a prisoner cast into a deep, empty well I know not where I am and what awaits me. All is hidden from me but that in the cruel, persistent struggle with the devil—the principle of the forces of matter—I am destined to conquer, and, after that, matter and spirit will be blended in glorious harmony and the Kingdom of the Cosmic Will will come. But that will come only little by little, through long, long thousands of years when the moon and the bright Sirius and the earth are changed to dust. . . . Till then—terror, terror . . . [*A pause; two red spots appear upon the background of the lake.*] Here my powerful foe, the devil, is approaching. I see his dreadul crimson eyes. . . .

Madame Arkadin: There's a smell of sulphur. Is that as it should be?

Treplev: Yes.

Madame Arkadin: [*Laughs.*] Oh, it's a stage effect!

Treplev: Mother!

Nina: He is dreary without man——

Polina: [*To Dorn.*] You have taken your hat off. Put it on or you will catch cold.

Madame Arkadin: The doctor has taken his hat off to the devil, the father of eternal matter.

Treplev: [*Firing up, aloud.*] The play is over! Enough! Curtain!

Madame Arkadin: What are you cross about?

Treplev: Enough! The curtain! Let down the curtain! [*Stamping.*] Curtain! [*The curtain falls.*] I am sorry! I lost sight of the fact that only a few of the elect may write plays and act in them. I have infringed the monopoly. I . . . I . . . [*Tries to say something more, but with a wave of his hand goes out on left.*]

Madame Arkadin: What's the matter with him?

Sorin: Irina, you really must have more consideration for youthful vanity, my dear.

Madame Arkadin: What did I say to him?

Sorin: You hurt his feelings.

Madame Arkadin: He told us beforehand that it was a joke, and I regarded his play as a joke.

Sorin: All the same . . .

Madame Arkadin: Now it appears that he has written a great work. What next! So he has got up this performance and smothered us with sulphur not as a joke but as a protest. . . . He wanted to show us how to write and what to act. This is getting tiresome! These continual sallies at my expense—these continual pinpricks would put anyone out of patience, say what you like. He is a vain, whimsical boy!

Sorin: He meant to give you pleasure.

Madame Arkadin: Really? He did not choose an ordinary play, however, but made us listen to this decadent delirium. For the sake of a joke I am ready to listen to delirium, but here we have pretensions to new forms and a new view of art. To my thinking it's no question of new forms at all, but simply bad temper.

Trigorin: Everyone writes as he likes and as he can.

Madame Arkadin: Let him write as he likes and as he can, only let him leave me in peace.

Dorn: Jupiter! you are angry. . . .

Madame Arkadin: I am not Jupiter— I am a woman. [*Lights a cigarette.*] I am not angry—I am only vexed that a young man should spend his time so drearily. I did not mean to hurt his feelings.

Medvedenko: No one has any grounds to separate spirit from matter, seeing that spirit itself may be a combination of material atoms. [*With animation, to Trigorin.*] But you know someone ought to write a play on how we poor teachers live, and get it acted. We have a hard, hard life.

Madame Arkadin: That's true, but don't let us talk either of plays or of atoms. It is such a glorious evening! Do you hear? There is singing! [*Listens.*] How nice it is!

Polina: It's on the other side of the lake. [*A pause.*]

Madame Arkadin: [*To Trigorin.*] Sit down beside me. Ten or fifteen years ago there were sounds of music and singing on that lake continually almost every night. There are six country houses on the shores of the lake. I remember laughter, noise, shooting, and love affairs without end. . . . The *jeune premier* and the idol of all those six households was in those days our friend here, the doctor [*Motions with her head towards Dorn.*] Yevgeny Sergeitch. He is fascinating still, but in those days he was irresistible. But my conscience is beginning to trouble me. Why did I hurt my poor boy's feelings? I feel worried. [*Aloud.*] Kostya! Son! Kostya!

Masha: I'll go and look for him.

Madame Arkadin: Please do, my dear.

Masha: [*Going to the left.*] Aa-oo! Konstantin Gavrilitch! Aa-oo! [*Goes off.*]

Nina: [*Coming out from behind the stage.*] Apparently there will be no going on, and I may come out. Good evening! [*Kisses Madame Arkadin and Polina Andreyevna.*]

Sorin: Bravo! Bravo!

Madame Arkadin: Bravo! Bravo! We admired you. With such an appearance, with such a lovely voice, you really cannot stay in the country; it is a sin. You must have talent. Do you hear? It's your duty to go on the stage.

Nina: Oh, that's my dream! [*Sighing.*] But it will never be realized.

Madame Arkadin: Who knows? Here, let me introduce Boris Alexeyevitch Trigorin.

Nina: Oh, I am so glad . . . [*Overcome with embarrassment.*] I am always reading your . . .

Madame Arkadin: [*Making her sit down beside them.*] Don't be shy, my dear. He is a celebrity, but he has a simple heart. You see, he is shy himself.

Dorn: I suppose we may raise the curtain; it's rather uncanny.

Shamraev: [*Aloud.*] Yakov, pull up the curtain, my lad. [*The curtain goes up.*]

Nina: [*To Trigorin.*] It is a queer play, isn't it?

Trigorin: I did not understand it at all. But I enjoyed it. You acted so genuinely. And the scenery was delightful. [*A pause.*] There must be a lot of fish in that lake.

Nina: Yes.

Trigorin: I love angling. There is nothing I enjoy so much as sitting on the bank of a river in the evening and watching the float.

Nina: But I should have thought that for anyone who has known the enjoyment of creation, no other enjoyment can exist.

Madame Arkadin: [*Laughing.*] Don't talk like that. When people say nice things to him he is utterly floored.

Shamraev: I remember one evening in the opera theater in Moscow the celebrated Silva took the lower C! As it happened, there was sitting in the gallery the bass of our church choir, and all at once—imagine our intense astonishment—we heard from the gallery "Bravo, Silva!" a whole octave lower—like this: [*In a deep bass.*] "Bravo, Silva!" The audience sat spellbound. [*A pause.*]

Dorn: The angel of silence has flown over us.

Nina: It's time for me to go. Goodbye.

Madame Arkadin: Where are you off to? Why so early? We won't let you go.

Nina: My father expects me.

Madame Arkadin: What a man, really . . . [*Kisses her.*] Well, there is no help for it. I am sorry—I am sorry to let you go.

Nina: If you knew how grieved I am to go.

Madame Arkadin: Someone ought to see you home, my little dear.

Nina: [*Frightened.*] Oh, no, no!

Sorin: [*To her, in an imploring voice.*] Do stay!

Nina: I can't, Pyotr Nikolayevitch.

Sorin: Stay for an hour. What is there in that?

Nina: [*Thinking a minute, tearfully.*] I can't! [*Shakes hands and hurriedly goes off.*]

Madame Arkadin: Unfortunate girl she is, really. They say her mother left her father all her immense property—every farthing of it—and now the girl has got nothing, as her father has already made a will leaving everything to his second wife. It's monstrous!

Dorn: Yes, her father is a pretty thorough scoundrel, one must do him the justice to say so.

Sorin: [*Rubbing his cold hands.*] Let us go too, it's getting damp. My legs ache.

Madame Arkadin: They seem like wooden legs, you can hardly walk. Let us go, unlucky old man! [*Takes his arm.*]

Shamraev: [*Offering his arm to his wife.*] Madame?

Sorin: I hear that dog howling again. [*To Shamraev.*] Be so kind, Ilya Afanasyitch, as to tell them to let it off the chain.

Shamraev: It's impossible, Pyotr Nikolayevitch, I am afraid of thieves getting into the barn. Our millet is there. [*To Medvedenko, who is walking beside him.*] Yes, a whole octave lower: "Bravo, Silva!" And he not a singer—simply a church chorister!

Medvedenko: And what salary does a chorister get? [*All go out except Dorn.*]

Dorn: [*Alone.*] I don't know, perhaps I know nothing about it, or have gone off my head, but I liked the play. There is something in it. When that girl talked about loneliness and afterwards when the devil's eyes appeared, I was so excited that my hands trembled. It is fresh, naïve. . . . Here he comes, I believe. I want to say all the nice things I can to him.

Treplev: [*Enters.*] They have all gone.

Dorn: I am here.

Treplev: Mashenka is looking for me all over the park. Insufferable creature she is!

Dorn: Konstantin Gavrilitch, I liked your play extremely. It's a strange thing, and I haven't heard the end, and yet it made a strong impression! You are a gifted man—you must persevere.

[*Treplev presses his hand warmly and embraces him impulsively.*]

Dorn: Fie, what a hysterical fellow! There are tears in his eyes! What I mean is this. You have taken a subject from the realm of abstract ideas. So it should be, for a work of art ought to express a great idea. A thing is only fine when it is serious. How pale you are!

Treplev: So you tell me to persevere?

Dorn: Yes. . . . But write only of what is important and eternal. You know, I have had varied experiences of life, and have enjoyed it; I am satisfied, but if it had been my lot to know the spiritual heights which artists reach at the moment of creation, I should, I believe, have despised my bodily self and all that appertains to it and left all things earthly as far behind as possible.

Treplev: Excuse me, where is Nina?

Dorn: And another thing. In a work of art there ought to be a clear definite idea. You ought to know what is your aim in writing, for if you go along that picturesque route without a definite goal you will be lost and your talent will be your ruin.

Treplev: [*Impatiently.*] Where is Nina?

Dorn: She has gone home.

Treplev: [*In despair.*] What am I to do? I want to see her . . . I must see her. . . . I must go. . . .

[*Enter Masha.*]

Dorn: [*To Treplev.*] Calm yourself, my boy.

Treplev: But I am going all the same. I must go.

Masha: Come indoors, Konstantin Gavrilitch. Your mother wants you. She is worried.

Treplev: Tell her that I have gone away. And I beg you—all of you—leave me in peace! Let me alone! Don't follow me about!

Dorn: Come, come, come, dear boy. . . . You can't go on like that. . . . That's not the thing.

Treplev: [*In tears.*] Good-bye, doctor. Thank you . . . [*Goes off.*]

Dorn: [*With a sigh.*] Youth! youth!

Masha. When people have nothing better to say, they say, "Youth! youth!" . . . [*Takes a pinch of snuff.*]

Dorn: [*Takes her snuffbox from her and flings it into the bushes.*] That's disgusting! [*A pause.*] I believe they are playing the piano indoors. We must go in.

Masha: Wait a little.

Dorn: What is it?

Masha: I want to tell you once more. I have a longing to talk . . . [*Growing agitated.*] I don't care for my father . . . but I feel drawn to you. For some reason I feel with all my heart that you are very near me. . . . Help me, Help me, or I shall do something silly, I shall make a mock of my life and ruin it. . . . I can't go on. . . .

Dorn: What is it? Help you in what?

Masha: I am miserable. No one, no one knows how miserable I am! [*Laying her head on his breast, softly.*] I love Konstantin!

Dorn: How hysterical they all are! How hysterical! And what a lot of love. . . . Oh, the sorcery of the lake! [*Tenderly.*] But what can I do, my child? What? What?

CURTAIN.

QUESTIONS ON ACT I

1. Treplev says of his mother: "My mother is a psychological freak" (p. 459); ". . . my mother does not love me . . ., I am a continual reminder that she is no longer young" (p. 459); and "I love my mother . . . but she leads a senseless sort of life" (p. 459). These, as well as other remarks, indicate a certain complexity in Treplev's attitude to his mother. How may that attitude be defined?

2. Assuming that Madame Arkadin's quotation from *Hamlet* (p. 461) is half-amused, half-unthinking, Treplev's pat reply from *Hamlet* tells us what about his relations to his mother? About the intensity of his feelings toward his own play and his motive in presenting it? How far is his motive like Hamlet's motive in presenting his play before the court? About his attitude toward Trigorin? (The student will remember that Hamlet's mother, after his father's death, has married his uncle, and that, in the scene from which the *Hamlet* quotations come, Hamlet is bitterly reproaching his mother for her conduct and attempting to persuade her to repudiate his uncle, the king.)

3. How does Madame Arkadin's question and remark about the smell of sulphur indicate her attitude toward the play? Toward her son?

4. Is Treplev's burst of anger, with which he stops the play, properly motivated? In this connection consider his analysis of his mother's character, and his conversation with his uncle (pp. 458–59).

5. Notice how skillfully Chekhov has introduced his characters by means of some typical comment or action. (The student will find that many of the comments seem to be rambling and off the subject, apparently leading the reader away from the action in hand; but most of these actually serve to suggest the nature of the characters—the schoolmaster's preoccupation with himself and his salary, Dorn's good-natured cynicism, Shamraev's rambling reminiscences.) Note especially how Nina and Polina are characterized by their initial speeches.

6. How does Chekhov suggest the various conflicts and relationships in this act: Treplev's hostility toward Trigorin, Nina's anxiety to please Madame Arkadin, Masha's concern for Treplev, etc., etc.?

7. What is the point of Dorn's final comment: "How hysterical they all are! How hysterical! And what a lot of love!"? Has Chekhov indicated sufficiently the fact that practically all the characters are nervous—are in a state of tension? And has he suggested sufficiently the love patterns which exist among this group of people? Note carefully how many of these patterns there are.

ACT II

[A croquet lawn. The house with a big veranda in the background on the right; on the left is seen the lake with the blazing sun reflected in it.]

[*Flower beds. Midday. Hot. Madame Arkadin, Dorn, and Masha are sitting on a garden seat in the shade of an old lime tree on one side of the croquet lawn. Dorn has an open book on his knee.*]

Madame Arkadin: [*To Masha.*] Come, let us stand up. [*They both get up.*] Let us stand side by side. You are twenty-two and I am nearly twice as old. Yevgeny Sergeitch, which of us looks the younger?

Dorn: You, of course.

Madame Arkadin: There! And why is it? Because I work, I feel I am always on the go, while you stay always in the same place and have no life at all. . . . And it is my rule never to look into the future. I never think about old age or death. What is to be, will be.

Masha: And I feel as though I had been born long, long ago; I trail my life along like an endless train. . . . And often I have not the slightest desire to go on living [*sits down*]. Of course, that's all nonsense. I must shake myself and throw it all off.

Dorn: [*Hums quietly.*] "Tell her, my flowers."

Madame Arkadin: Then I am as particular as an Englishman. I keep myself in hand, as they say, my dear, and am always dressed and have my hair done *comme il faut*. Do I allow myself to go out of the house even into the garden in a dressing gown, or without my hair being done? Never! What has preserved me is that I have never been a dowdy, I have never let myself go, as some women do . . . [*Walks about the lawn with her arms akimbo.*] Here I am, as brisk as a bird. I could take the part of a girl of fifteen.

Dorn: Nevertheless, I shall go on.

[*Takes up the book.*] We stopped at the corn merchant and the rats. . . .

Madame Arkadin: And the rats. Read. [*Sits down.*] But give it to me, I'll read. It is my turn. [*Takes the book and looks in it.*] And rats. . . . Here it is. . . . [*Reads.*] "And of course for society people to spoil novelists and to attract them to themselves is as dangerous as for a corn merchant to rear rats in his granaries. And yet they love them. And so, when a woman has picked out an author whom she desires to captivate, she lays siege to him by means of compliments, flattery, and favors . . ." Well, that may be so with the French, but there is nothing like that with us, we have no set rules. Among us, before a woman sets to work to captivate an author, she is generally head over ears in love herself, if you please. To go no further, take Trigorin and me. . . .

[*Enter Sorin, leaning on his stick and with him Nina; Medvedenko wheels an empty bath chair in after them.*]

Sorin: [*In a caressing tone, as to a child.*] Yes? We are delighted, aren't we? We are happy today at last? [*To his sister.*] We are delighted! Our father and stepmother have gone off to Tver, and we are free now for three whole days.

Nina: [*Sits down beside Madame Arkadin and embraces her.*] I am happy! Now I belong to you.

Sorin: [*Sits down in his bath chair.*] She looks quite a beauty today.

Madame Arkadin: Nicely dressed and interesting. . . . That's a good girl. [*Kisses Nina.*] But we mustn't praise you too much for fear of ill luck. Where is Boris Alexeyevitch?

Nina: He is in the bathing house, fishing.

Madame Arkadin: I wonder he doesn't get sick of it! [*Is about to go on reading.*]

Nina: What is that?

Madame Arkadin: Maupassant's "Sur l'eau," my dear. [*Reads a few lines to herself.*] Well, the rest isn't interesting or true. [*Shuts the book.*] I feel uneasy. Tell me, what's wrong with my son?

Why is he so depressed and ill humored? He spends whole days on the lake and I hardly ever see him.

Masha: His heart is troubled. [*To Nina, timidly.*] Please, do read us something out of his play!

Nina: [*Shrugging her shoulders.*] Would you like it? It's so uninteresting.

Masha: [*Restraining her enthusiasm.*] When he reads anything himself his eyes glow and his face turns pale. He has a fine mournful voice, and the gestures of a poet.

[*There is a sound of Sorin snoring.*]

Dorn: Good night!

Madame Arkadin: Petrusha!

Sorin: Ah?

Madame Arkadin: Are you asleep?

Sorin: Not a bit of it. [*A pause.*]

Madame Arkadin. You do nothing for your health, brother, and that's not right.

Sorin. I should like to take something, but the doctor won't give me anything.

Dorn: Take medicine at sixty!

Sorin: Even at sixty one wants to live!

Dorn: [*With vexation.*] Oh, very well, take valerian drops!

Madame Arkadin. It seems to me it would do him good to go to some mineral springs.

Dorn. Well, he might go. And he might not.

Madame Arkadin. What is one to make of that?

Dorn. There's nothing to make of it. It's quite clear. [*A pause.*]

Medvedenko. Pyotr Nikolayevitch ought to give up smoking.

Sorin: Nonsense!

Dorn: No, it's not nonsense. Wine and tobacco destroy the personality. After a cigar or a glass of vodka, you are not Pyotr Nikolayevitch any more but Pyotr Nikolayevitch plus somebody else; your ego is diffused and you feel toward yourself as to a third person.

Sorin: [*Laughs.*] It's all very well for you to argue! You've lived your life, but what about me? I have served in the Department of Justice for twenty-eight years, but I haven't lived yet, I've seen and done nothing as a matter of fact, and very naturally I want to live very much. You've had enough and you don't care, and so you are inclined to be philosophical, but I want to live, and so I drink sherry at dinner and smoke cigars and so on. That's all it comes to.

Dorn: One must look at life seriously, but to go in for cures at sixty and to regret that one hasn't enjoyed oneself enough in one's youth is frivolous, if you will forgive my saying so.

Masha: [*Gets up.*] It must be lunchtime. [*Walks with a lazy, lagging step.*] My leg is gone to sleep. [*Goes off.*]

Dorn: She will go and have a couple of glasses before lunch.

Sorin: She has no personal happiness, poor thing.

Dorn: Nonsense, your Excellency.

Sorin: You argue like a man who has had all he wants.

Madame Arkadin: Oh, what can be more boring than this sweet country boredom! Hot, still, no one ever doing anything, everyone airing their theories. . . . It's nice being with you, my friends, charming to listen to you, but . . . to sit in a hotel room somewhere and learn one's part is ever so much better.

Nina: [*Enthusiastically.*] Delightful! I understand you.

Sorin: Of course, it's better in town. You sit in your study, the footman lets no one in unannounced, there's a telephone . . . in the streets there are cabs and everything. . . .

Dorn: [*Hums.*] "Tell her, my flowers."

[*Enter Shamraev, and after him Polina Andreyevna.*]

Shamraev: Here they are! Good morning! [*Kisses Madame Arkadin's hand and then Nina's.*] Delighted to see you in good health. [*To Madame Arkadin.*] My wife tells me that you are proposing to drive into town with her today. Is that so?

Madame Arkadin: Yes, we are thinking of it.

Shamraev: Hm! that's splendid, but how are you going, honoured lady? They are carting the rye today; all the men are at work. What horses are you to have, allow me to ask?

Madame Arkadin: What horses? How can I tell which?

Sorin: We've got carriage horses.

Shamraev: [*Growing excited.*] Carriage horses! But where am I to get collars for them? Where am I to get collars? It's a strange thing! It passes my understanding! Honoured lady! forgive me, I am full of reverence for your talent. I would give ten years of my life for you, but I cannot let you have the horses!

Madame Arkadin: But if I have to go! It's a queer thing!

Shamraev: Honoured lady! you don't know what farming means.

Madame Arkadin: [*Flaring up.*] That's the old story! If that's so, I go back to Moscow today. Give orders for horses to be hired for me at the village, or I'll walk to the station.

Shamraev: [*Flaring up.*] In that case I resign my position! You must look for another steward. [*Goes off.*]

Madame Arkadin: It's like this every summer; every summer I am insulted here! I won't set my foot in the place again. [*Goes off at left where the bathing shed is supposed to be; a minute later she can be seen entering the house. Trigorin follows her, carrying fishing rods and tackle, and a pail.*]

Sorin: [*Flaring up.*] This is insolence! It's beyond everything. I am thoroughly sick of it. Send all the horses here this minute!

Nina: [*To Polina Andreyevna.*] To refuse Irina Nikolayevna, the famous actress! Any wish of hers, any whim even, is of more consequence than all your farming. It's positively incredible!

Polina: [*In despair.*] What can I do? Put yourself in my position: what can I do?

Sorin: [*To Nina.*] Let us go to my sister. We will all entreat her not to go away. Won't we? [*Looking in the direction in which Shamraev has gone.*] Insufferable man! Despot!

Nina: [*Preventing him from getting up.*] Sit still, sit still. We will wheel you in. [*She and Medvedenko push the bath chair.*] Oh, how awful it is!

Sorin: Yes, yes, it's awful. But he won't leave, I'll speak to him directly. [*They go out; Dorn and Polina Andreyevna are left alone on the stage.*]

Dorn: People are tiresome. Your husband ought to be simply kicked out, but it will end in that old woman Pyotr Nikolayevitch and his sister begging the man's pardon. You will see!

Polina: He has sent the carriage horses into the fields too! And there are misunderstandings like this every day. If you only knew how it upsets me! It makes me ill; see how I am trembling. . . . I can't endure his rudeness. [*In an imploring voice.*] Yevgeny, dearest, light of my eyes, my darling, let me come to you. . . . Our time is passing, we are no longer young, and if only we could lay aside concealment and lying for the end of our lives, anyway . . . [*A pause.*]

Dorn: I am fifty-five; it's too late to change my life.

Polina: I know you refuse me because there are other women too who are as near to you. You can't take them all to live with you. I understand. Forgive me, you are tired of me.

[*Nina appears near the house; she is picking flowers.*]

Dorn: No, it's all right.

Polina: I am wretched from jealousy. Of course you are a doctor, you can't avoid women. I understand.

Dorn: [*To Nina, who comes up to them.*] How are things going?

Nina: Irina Nikolayevna is crying and Pyotr Nikolayevitch has an attack of asthma.

Dorn: [*Gets up.*] I'd better go and give them both valerian drops.

Nina: [*Gives him the flowers.*] Please take these.

Dorn: Merci bien. [*Goes toward the house.*]

Polina: [*Going with him.*] What charming flowers! [*Near the house, in a smothered voice.*] Give me those flowers! Give me those flowers! [*On receiving them tears the flowers to pieces and throws them away; both go into the house.*)

Nina: [*Alone.*] How strange it is to see a famous actress cry, and about such a trivial thing! And isn't it strange? A famous author, adored by the public, written about in all the papers, his photographs for sale, his works translated into foreign languages—and he spends the whole day fishing and is delighted that he has caught two gudgeon. I thought famous people were proud, unapproachable, that they despised the crowd, and by their fame and the glory of their name, as it were, revenged themselves on the vulgar herd for putting rank and wealth above everything. But here they cry and fish, play cards, laugh and get cross like everyone else!

Treplev: [*Comes in without a hat on, with a gun and a dead sea gull.*] Are you alone here?

Nina: Yes.

[*Treplev lays the sea gull at her feet.*]

Nina: What does that mean?

Treplev: I was so mean as to kill this bird today. I lay it at your feet.

Nina. What is the matter with you? [*Picks up the bird and looks at it.*]

Treplev: [*After a pause.*] Soon I shall kill myself in the same way.

Nina: You have so changed, I hardly know you.

Treplev: Yes, ever since the day when I hardly knew you. You have changed to me, your eyes are cold, you feel me in the way.

Nina: You have become irritable of late, you express yourself so incomprehensibly, as it were in symbols. This bird is a symbol too, I suppose, but forgive me, I don't understand it. [*Lays the sea gull on the seat*]. I am too simple to understand you.

Treplev: This began from that evening when my play came to grief so stupidly.

Women never forgive failure. I have burnt it all; every scrap of it. If only you knew how miserable I am! Your growing cold to me is awful, incredible, as though I had waked up and found this lake had suddenly dried up or sunk into the earth. You have just said that you are too simple to understand me. Oh, what is there to understand? My play was not liked, you despise my inspiration, you already consider me commonplace, insignificant, like so many others . . . [*Stamping.*] How well I understand it all, how I understand it! I feel as though I had a nail in my brain, damnation take it together with my vanity which is sucking away my life, sucking it like a snake . . . [*Sees Trigorin, who comes in reading a book.*] Here comes the real genius, walking like Hamlet and with a book too. [*Mimics.*] "Words, words, words." . . . The sun has scarcely reached you and you are smiling already, your eyes are melting in its rays. I won't be in your way. [*Goes off quickly.*]

Trigorin: [*Making notes in his book.*] Takes snuff and drinks vodka. Always in black. The schoolmaster is in love with her. . . .

Nina: Good morning, Boris Alexeyevitch!

Trigorin: Good morning. Circumstances have turned out so unexpectedly that it seems we are setting off today. We are hardly likely to meet again. I am sorry. I don't often have the chance of meeting young girls, youthful and charming; I have forgotten how one feels at eighteen or nineteen and can't picture it to myself, and so the young girls in my stories and novels are usually false. I should like to be in your shoes just for one hour to find out how you think, and altogether what sort of person you are.

Nina: And I should like to be in your shoes.

Trigorin: What for?

Nina: To know what it feels like to be a famous, gifted author. What does it feel like to be famous? How does it affect you, being famous?

Trigorin: How? Nohow, I believe. I have never thought about it. [*After a moment's thought.*] It's one of two things: either you exaggerate my fame, or it never is felt at all.

Nina: But if you read about yourself in the newspapers?

Trigorin: When they praise me I am pleased, and when they abuse me I feel out of humour for a day or two.

Nina: What a wonderful world! If only you knew how I envy you! How different people's lots in life are! Some can scarcely get through their dull, obscure existence, they are all just like one another, they are all unhappy; while others—you, for instance—you are one out of a million, have an interesting life full of brightness and significance. You are happy.

Trigorin: I? [*Shrugging his shoulders.*] Hm. . . . You talk of fame and happiness, of bright interesting life, but to me all those fine words, if you will forgive my saying so, are just like a sweetmeat which I never taste. You are very young and very good natured.

Nina: Your life is splendid!

Trigorin: What is there particularly nice in it? [*Looks at his watch.*] I must go and write directly. Excuse me, I mustn't stay . . . [*Laughs.*] You have stepped on my favourite corn, as the saying is, and here I am beginning to get excited and a little cross. Let us talk though. We will talk about my splendid bright life. . . . Well, where shall we begin? [*After thinking a little.*] There are such things as fixed ideas, when a man thinks day and night, for instance, of nothing but the moon. And I have just such a moon. I am haunted day and night by one persistent thought: I ought to be writing, I ought to be writing, I ought . . . I have scarcely finished one novel when, for some reason, I must begin writing another, then a third, after the third a fourth. I write incessantly, post haste, and I can't write in any other way. What is there splendid and bright in that, I ask you? Oh, it's an absurd life! Here I am with you; I am excited, yet every moment I remember that my unfinished novel is waiting for me. Here I see a cloud that looks like a grand piano. I think that I must put into a story somewhere that a cloud sailed by that looked like a grand piano. There is a scent of heliotrope. I hurriedly make a note: a sickly smell, a widow's flower, to be mentioned in the description of a summer evening. I catch up myself and you at every sentence, every word, and make haste to put those sentences and words away into my literary treasure house—it may come in useful! When I finish work I race off to the theater or to fishing; if only I could rest in that and forget myself. But no, there's a new subject rolling about in my head like a heavy iron cannon ball, and I am drawn to my writing table and must make haste again to go on writing and writing. And it's always like that, always. And I have no rest from myself, and I feel that I am eating up my own life, and that for the sake of the honey I give to someone in space I am stripping the pollen from my best flowers, tearing up the flowers themselves and trampling on their roots. Don't you think I am mad? Do my friends and acquaintances treat me as though I were sane? "What are you writing? What are you giving us?" It's the same thing again and again, and it seems to me as though my friends' notice, their praises, their enthusiasm—that it's all a sham, that they are deceiving me as an invalid and I am somehow afraid that they will steal up to me from behind, snatch me and carry me off and put me in a madhouse. And in those years, the best years of my youth, when I was beginning, my writing was unmixed torture. A small writer, particularly when he is not successful, seems to himself clumsy, awkward, unnecessary; his nerves are strained and overwrought. He can't resist hanging about people connected with literature and art, unrecognized and unnoticed by anyone, afraid to look anyone boldly in the face, like a passionate gambler without any money. I hadn't seen my reader, but for some reason I always imagined him hostile, and mistrustful. I was afraid of the public, it alarmed me, and when I had to produce my first play it always seemed to me that all the dark people felt hostile and all the fair ones were coldly indifferent. Oh, how awful it was! What agony it was!

Nina: But surely inspiration and the very process of creation give you moments of exalted happiness?

Trigorin: Yes. While I am writing I enjoy it. And I like reading my proofs, but . . . as soon as it is published I can't endure it, and I see that it is all wrong, a mistake, that it ought not to have been written at all, and I feel vexed and sick about it . . . [*Laughing.*] And the public reads it and says: "Yes, charming, clever. Charming, but very inferior to Tolstoy," or, "It's a fine thing, but Turgenev's *Fathers and Children* is finer." And it will be the same to my dying day, only charming and clever, charming and clever—and nothing more. And when I die my friends, passing by my tomb, will say, "Here lies Trigorin. He was a good writer, but inferior to Turgenev."

Nina: Forgive me, but I refuse to understand you. You are simply spoiled by success.

Trigorin: What success? I have never liked myself; I dislike my own work. The worst of it is that I am in a sort of delirium, and often don't understand what I am writing. I love this water here, the trees, the sky. I feel nature, it arouses in me a passionate, irresistible desire to write. But I am not simply a landscape painter; I am also a citizen. I love my native country, my people; I feel that if I am a writer I am in duty bound to write of the people, of their sufferings, of their future, to talk about science and the rights of man and so on,

and so on, and I write about everything. I am hurried and flustered, and on all sides they whip me up and are angry with me; I dash about from side to side like a fox beset by hounds. I see life and culture continually getting farther and farther away while I fall farther and farther behind like a peasant too late for the train; and what it comes to is that I feel I can only describe scenes and in everything else I am false to the marrow of my bones.

Nina: You are overworked and have not the leisure nor the desire to appreciate your own significance. You may be dissatisfied with yourself, but for others you are great and splendid! If I were a writer like you, I should give up my whole life to the common herd, but I should know that there could be no greater happiness for them than to rise to my level, and they would harness themselves to my chariot.

Trigorin: My chariot, what next! Am I an Agamemnon, or what? [*Both smile.*]

Nina: For such happiness as being a writer or an artist I would be ready to endure poverty, disappointment, the dislike of those around me; I would live in a garret and eat nothing but rye bread, I would suffer from being dissatisfied with myself, from recognizing my own imperfections, but I should ask in return for fame . . . real, resounding fame. . . . [*Covers her face with her hands.*] It makes me dizzy. . . . Ough!

[*The voice of Madame Arkadin from the house.*]

Madame Arkadin: Boris Alexeyevitch!

Trigorin: They are calling for me. I suppose it's to pack. But I don't want to leave here. [*Looks round at the lake.*] Just look how glorious it is! It's splendid!

Nina: Do you see the house and garden on the other side of the lake?

Trigorin: Yes.

Nina: That house was my dear mother's. I was born there. I have spent all my life beside this lake and I know every little islet on it.

Trigorin. It's very delightful here! [*Seeing the sea gull.*] And what's this? *Nina:* A sea gull. Konstantin Gavrilitch shot it. *Trigorin:* A beautiful bird. Really, I don't want to go away. Try and persuade Irina Nikolayevna to stay. [*Makes a note in his book.*] *Nina:* What are you writing? *Trigorin:* Oh, I am only making a note. A subject struck me. [*Putting away the notebook.*] A subject for a short story: a young girl, such as you, has lived all her life beside a lake; she loves the lake like a sea gull, and is as free and happy as a sea gull. But a man comes by chance, sees her, and having nothing better to do, destroys her like that sea gull here. [*A pause.*] [*Madame Arkadin appears at the window.*] *Madame Arkadin:* Boris Alexeyevitch, where are you? *Trigorin:* I am coming. [*Goes and looks back at Nina. To Madame Arkadin at the window.*] What is it? *Madame Arkadin:* We are staying. [*Trigorin goes into the house.*] *Nina:* [*Advances to the footlights; after a few moments' meditation.*] It's a dream!

CURTAIN.

QUESTIONS ON ACT II

1. In the conversation which opens the act Madame Arkadin gives Masha her recipe for maintaining youth and achieving success. On the surface level this is a merely casual conversation. Do these remarks of Madame Arkadin attain deeper significance as the act proceeds?

2. What do Nina's deprecation of Treplev's play and her desire to please Madame Arkadin tell us about her character?

3. What is the function of Sorin in this act? Are Sorin's sense of not having lived and his anxiety to achieve life and experience also characteristic of the others who hear his conversation? Do his comments, made generally, point up their special problems? Note that his particular frustrations—the physician's unwillingness to let him "take a cure at some springs," Medvedenko's advice to him to give up tobacco, Shamraev's refusal to let him have the horses—all these petty frustrations are evidently taken by him as symbolic of a larger frustration.

4. How does Shamraev serve as a foil to Sorin? How does his refusal to allow his master the use of the horses give an ironic indication as to the nature of Sorin's failure? Note that Shamraev's high-handed treatment of his employer is apparently habitual. What does this fact tell us about Sorin's interest in practical affairs? About his easygoing nature?

5. What is the significance of Nina's speech on page 470 beginning, "How strange it is to see a famous actress cry"? What light does this speech throw on Nina's naïvete?

6. The incident of the sea gull—particularly since it is to become one of the symbols of the play—deserves special consideration. Treplev's presentation of the dead sea gull to Nina is romantic and "melancholy," something in the manner of his moody experimental play. (One notices that Treplev is careful to ascertain that he and Nina are alone before he makes

his little speech to her about the sea gull.) But Nina is perfectly matter-of-fact in her rejection of his rather poetic approach to their relationship. "What's the matter with you?" she asks. Fascinated as she now is with the brilliant world of Trigorin and Madame Arkadin, she is not willing to play any longer at this game of symbols. How does the little incident manage to suggest the break in the earlier relations of Nina and Treplev?

7. What is the function of the reference to Hamlet made by Treplev on page 470? If it has been suggested that Madame Arkadin is like Hamlet's mother, is it suggested here that Nina is something like Ophelia (the sweet and delicate girl with whom Hamlet is in love and who is destroyed in the conflict of forces in that play)?

8. What is the relation of the scene between Nina and Trigorin to that between Nina and Treplev? What ironic contrasts are to be found in them? In what sense is Trigorin's use of the sea gull as a symbol conventionally "romantic"? But in what way is it more realistic than Treplev's?

9. Consider Trigorin's last speech to Nina (p. 473). Is he interested in Nina? Or in his idea for a story? What light does the speech shed on Nina herself?

10. What are the various meanings of Nina's last speech in the act: "It's a dream"?

ACT III

[*The dining-room in Sorin's house. Doors on right and on left. A sideboard. A medicine cupboard. A table in the middle of the room. A portmanteau and hatboxes; signs of prepa: ation for departure. Trigorin is having lunch; Masha stands by the table.*]

Masha: I tell all this to you as a writer. You may make use of it. I am telling you the truth: if he had hurt himself seriously I would not have gone on living another minute. But I have pluck enough all the same. I just made up my mind that I would tear this love out of my heart, tear it out by the roots.

Trigorin: How are you going to do that?

Masha: I am going to be married. To Medvedenko.

Trigorin: That's the schoolmaster?

Masha: Yes.

Trigorin: I don't understand what's the object of it.

Masha: To love without hope, to spend whole years waiting for some-thing. . . . But when I marry, there will be no time left for love, new cares will smother all the old feelings. And, anyway, it will be a change, you know. Shall we have another?

Trigorin: Won't that be too much?

Masha: Oh, come! [*Fills two glasses.*] Don't look at me like that! Women drink much oftener than you imagine. Only a small proportion drink openly as I do, the majority drink in secret. Yes. And it's always vodka or brandy. [*Clinks glasses.*] My best wishes! You are a good-hearted man; I am sorry to be parting from you. [*They drink.*]

Trigorin: I don't want to go myself.

Masha: You should beg her to stay.

Trigorin: No, she won't stay now. Her son is behaving very tactlessly. First, he shoots himself, and now they say he is going to challenge me to a duel. And whatever for? He sulks, and snorts, and preaches new forms of art. . . . But there is room for all—new and old—why quarrel about it?

Masha: Well, there's jealousy too. But it is nothing to do with me.

[*A pause. Yakov crosses from right to left with a portmanteau. Nina enters and stands by the window.*]

Masha: My schoolmaster is not very brilliant, but he is a good-natured man, and poor, and he is very much in love with me. I am sorry for him. And I am sorry for his old mother. Well, let me wish you all happiness. Don't remember evil against me. [*Shakes hands with him warmly.*] I am very grateful for your friendly interest. Send me your books and be sure to put in an inscription. Only don't write, "To my honoured friend," but write simply, "To Marya who belongs nowhere and has no object in life." Good-bye! [*Goes out.*]

Nina: [*Stretching out her arm toward Trigorin, with her fist clenched.*] Odd or even?

Trigorin: Even.

Nina: [*With a sigh.*] Wrong. I had only one pea in my hand. I was trying my fortune whether to go on the stage or not. I wish someone would advise me.

Trigorin: It's impossible to advise in such a matter. [*A pause.*]

Nina: We are parting and . . . perhaps we shall never meet again. Won't you please take this little medallion as a parting gift? I had your initials engraved on one side of it . . . and on the other the title of your book, *Days and Nights.*

Trigorin: How exquisite! [*Kisses the medallion.*] A charming present!

Nina: Think of me sometimes.

Trigorin: I shall think of you. I shall think of you as you were on that sunny day—do you remember?—a week ago, when you were wearing a light dress . . . we were talking . . . there was a white sea gull lying on the seat.

Nina: [*Pensively.*] Yes, a sea gull . . . [*A pause.*] We can't talk any more, there's someone coming. . . . Let me have two minutes before you go, I entreat you . . . [*Goes out on the left.*]

[*At the same instant Madame Arkadin, Sorin in a dress coat with a star of some* order on it, then Yakov, occupied with the luggage, enter on the right.*]

Madame Arkadin: Stay at home, old man. With your rheumatism you ought not to go gadding about. [*To Trigorin.*] Who was that went out? Nina?

Trigorin: Yes.

Madame Arkadin: Pardon, we interrupted you. [*Sits down.*] I believe I have packed everything. I am worn out.

Trigorin: [*Reads on the medallion.*] "Days and Nights, page 121, lines 11 and 12."

Yakov: [*Clearing the table.*] Am I to pack your fishing things too, sir?

Trigorin: Yes, I shall want them again. You can give away the hooks.

Yakov: Yes, sir.

Trigorin: [*To himself.*] Page 121, lines 11 and 12. What is there in those lines? [*To Madame Arkadin.*] Are there copies of my books in the house?

Madame Arkadin: Yes, in my brother's study, in the corner bookcase.

Trigorin: Page 121 . . . [*Goes out.*]

Madame Arkadin: Really, Petrusha, you had better stay at home.

Sorin: You are going away; it will be dreary for me at home without you.

Madame Arkadin: And what is there in the town?

Sorin: Nothing particular, but still . . . [*Laughs.*] There will be the laying of the foundation stone of the Zemstvo-hall, and all that sort of thing. One longs to shake oneself free from this stagnant existence, if only for an hour or two. I've been too long on the shelf like some old cigarette holder. I have ordered the horses for one o'clock; we'll set off at the same time.

Madame Arkadin: [*After a pause.*] Come, stay here, don't be bored and don't catch cold. Look after my son. Take care of him. Give him good advice. [*A pause.*] Here I am going away and I shall never know why Konstantin tried to shoot himself. I fancy jealousy was the chief cause, and the sooner I get Trigorin away from here, the better.

Sorin: What can I say? There were

other reasons too. It's easy to understand; he is young, intelligent, living in the country, in the wilds, with no money, no position and no future. He has nothing to do. He is ashamed of his idleness and afraid of it. I am very fond of him indeed, and he is attached to me, yet in spite of it all he feels he is superfluous in the house, that he is a dependent, a poor relation. It's easy to understand, it's *amour propre....*

Madame Arkadin: He is a great anxiety to me! [*Pondering.*] He might go into the service, perhaps.

Sorin: [*Begins to whistle, then irresolutely.*] I think that quite the best thing would be if you were to ... let him have a little money. In the first place he ought to be able to be dressed like other people and all that. Just look at him, he's been going about in the same wretched jacket for the last three years and he has no overcoat ... [*Laughs.*] It would do him no harm to have a little fun ... to go abroad or something. ... It wouldn't cost much.

Madame Arkadin: But all the same ... I might manage the suit, perhaps, but as for going abroad ... No, just at the moment I can't even manage the suit. [*Resolutely.*] I have no money!
[*Sorin laughs.*]

Madame Arkadin: No!

Sorin: [*Begins to whistle.*] Quite so. Forgive me, my dear, don't be cross. I believe you.... You are a generous, noble-hearted woman.

Madame Arkadin: [*Weeping.*] I have no money.

Sorin: If I had money, of course I would give him some myself, but I have nothing, not a half-penny [*laughs*]. My steward takes all my pension and spends it all on the land and the cattle and the bees, and my money is all wasted. The bees die, and the cows die, they never let me have horses. ...

Madame Arkadin: Yes, I have money, but you see I am an actress; my dresses alone are enough to ruin me.

Sorin: You are a kind, good creature

... I respect you. ... Yes ... but there, I got a touch of it again ... [*Staggers.*] I feel dizzy. [*Clutches at the table.*] I feel ill and all that.

Madame Arkadin: [*Alarmed.*] Petrusha! [*Trying to support him.*] Petrusha, my dear! [*Calling.*] Help! help!
[*Enter Treplev, with a bandage round his head, and Medvedenko.*]

Madame Arkadin: He feels faint!

Sorin: It's all right, it's all right! [*Smiles and drinks some water.*] It's passed off ... and all that.

Treplev: [*To his mother.*] Don't be frightened, Mother, it's not serious. Uncle often has these attacks now. [*To his uncle.*] You must lie down, Uncle.

Sorin: For a little while, yes. ... But I am going to the town all the same. ... I'll lie down a little and then set off. ... It's quite natural. [*Goes out leaning on his stick.*]

Medvedenko: [*Gives him his arm.*] There's a riddle: in the morning on four legs, at noon on two, in the evening on three. ...

Sorin: [*Laughs.*] Just so. And at night on the back. Thank you, I can manage alone. ...

Medvedenko: Oh come, why stand on ceremony! [*Goes out with Sorin.*]

Madame Arkadin: How he frightened me!

Treplev: It is not good for him to live in the country. He gets depressed. If you would be generous for once, mother, and lend him fifteen hundred or two thousand roubles, he could spend a whole year in town.

Madame Arkadin: I have no money. I am an actress, not a banker. [*A pause.*]

Treplev: Mother, change my bandage. You do it so well.

Madame Arkadin: [*Takes out of the medicine cupboard some iodoform and a box with bandaging material.*] The doctor is late.

Treplev: He promised to be here at ten, and it is midday already.

Madame Arkadin: Sit down. [*Takes the bandage off his head.*] It's like a turban. Yesterday a stranger asked in the kitchen what nationality you were. But you have almost completely healed. There is the merest trifle left. [*Kisses him on the head.*] You won't do anything naughty again while I am away, will you?

Treplev: No, Mother. It was a moment of mad despair when I could not control myself. It won't happen again. [*Kisses her hand.*] You have such clever hands. I remember, long ago, when you were still acting at the Imperial Theater—I was little then—there was a fight in our yard and a washerwoman, one of the tenants, was badly beaten. Do you remember? She was picked up senseless ... you looked after her, took her remedies and washed her children in a tub. Don't you remember?

Madame Arkadin: No. [*Puts on a fresh bandage.*]

Treplev: Two ballet dancers lived in the same house as we did at the time. ... They used to come to you and have coffee. ...

Madame Arkadin: I remember that.

Treplev: They were very pious. [*A pause.*] Just lately, these last days, I have loved you as tenderly and completely as when I was a child. I have no one left now but you. Only why, why do you give yourself up to the influence of that man?

Madame Arkadin: You don't understand him, Konstantin. He is a very noble character. ...

Treplev: And yet when he was told I was going to challenge him, the nobility of his character did not prevent him from funking it. He is going away. Ignominious flight!

Madame Arkadin: What nonsense! It is I who am asking him to go.

Treplev: A very noble character! Here you and I are almost quarreling over him, and at this very moment he is somewhere in the drawing room or the garden laughing at us ... developing Nina, trying to convince her finally that he is a genius.

Madame Arkadin: You take a pleasure in saying unpleasant things to me. I respect that man and beg you not to speak ill of him before me.

Treplev: And I don't respect him. You want me to think him a genius too, but forgive me, I can't tell lies, his books make me sick.

Madame Arkadin: That's envy. There's nothing left for people who have pretension without talent but to attack real talent. Much comfort in that, I must say!

Treplev: [*Ironically.*] Real talent! [*Wrathfully.*] I have more talent than all of you put together if it comes to that! [*Tears the bandage off his head.*] You, with your hackneyed conventions, have usurped the supremacy in art and consider nothing real and legitimate but what you do yourselves; everything else you stifle and suppress. I don't believe in you! I don't believe in you or in him!

Madame Arkadin: Decadent!

Treplev: Get away to your charming theater and act there in your paltry, stupid plays!

Madame Arkadin: I have never acted in such plays. Let me alone! You are not capable of writing even a wretched burlesque! You are nothing but a Kiev shopman! Living on other people!

Treplev: You miser.

Madame Arkadin: You ragged beggar! [*Treplev sits down and weeps quietly.*]

Madame Arkadin: Nonentity! [*Walking up and down in agitation.*] Don't cry. ... You mustn't cry. [*Weeps.*] Don't ... [*Kisses him on the forehead, on the cheeks and on the head.*] My dear child, forgive me. ... Forgive your sinful mother. Forgive me, you know I am wretched.

Treplev: [*Puts his arms around her.*] If only you knew! I have lost everything! She does not love me, and now I cannot write ... all my hopes are gone. ...

Madame Arkadin: Don't despair ... Everything will come right. He is going away directly, she will love you again.

[*Wipes away his tears.*] Give over. We have made it up now.

Treplev: [*Kisses her hands.*] Yes, Mother.

Madame Arkadin: [*Tenderly.*] Make it up with him too. You don't want a duel, do you?

Treplev. Very well. Only, Mother, do allow me not to meet him. It's painful to me—it's more than I can bear. [*Enter Trigorin.*] Here he is . . . I am going . . . [*Rapidly puts away the dressings in the cupboard.*] The doctor will do the bandaging now

Trigorin: [*Looking in a book.*] Page 121 . . . lines 11 and 12. Here it is. [*Reads.*] "If ever my life can be of use to you, come and take it."

[*Treplev picks up the bandage from the floor and goes out.*]

Madame Arkadin: [*Looking at her watch.*] The horses will soon be here.

Trigorin: [*To himself.*] "If ever my life can be of use to you, come and take it."

Madame Arkadin: I hope all your things are packed?

Trigorin: [*Impatiently.*] Yes, yes. [*Musing.*] Why is it that I feel so much sorrow in that appeal from a pure soul and that it wrings my heart so painfully? "If ever my life can be of use to you, come and take it." [*To Madame Arkadin.*] Let us stay one day longer.

[*Madame Arkadin shakes her head.*]

Trigorin: Let us stay!

Madame Arkadin: Darling, I know what keeps you here. But have control over yourself. You are a little intoxicated, try to be sober.

Trigorin: You be sober too, be sensible and reasonable, I implore you; look at it all as a true friend should. [*Presses her hand.*] You are capable of sacrifice. Be a friend to me, let me be free!

Madame Arkadin: [*In violent agitation.*] Are you so enthralled?

Trigorin: I am drawn to her! Perhaps it is just what I need.

Madame Arkadin: The love of a provincial girl? Oh, how little you know yourself!

Trigorin: Sometimes people sleep as they talk—that's how it is with me, I am talking to you and yet I am asleep and dreaming of her. . . . I am possessed by sweet, marvelous dreams. . . . Let me be free. . . .

Madame Arkadin: [*Trembling.*] No, no! I am an ordinary woman, you can't talk like that to me. Don't torture me, Boris. It terrifies me.

Trigorin: If you cared to, you could be not ordinary. Love—youthful, charming, poetical, lifting one into a world of dreams—that's the only thing in life that can give happiness! I have never yet known a love like that. . . . In my youth I never had time, I was always hanging about the editors' offices, struggling with want. Now it is here, that love, it has come, it beckons to me. What sense is there in running away from it?

Madame Arkadin: [*Wrathfully.*] You have gone mad!

Trigorin: Well, let me!

Madame Arkadin: You are all in a conspiracy together to torment me today! [*Weeps.*]

Trigorin: [*Clutching at his heart.*] She does not understand! She won't understand!

Madame Arkadin: Am I so old and ugly that you don't mind talking of other women to me? [*Puts her arms round him and kisses him.*] Oh, you are mad! My wonderful, splendid darling. . . . You are the last page of my life! [*Falls on her knees.*] My joy, my pride, my bliss! . . . [*Embraces his knees.*] If you forsake me even for one hour I shall not survive it, I shall go mad, my marvelous, magnificent one, my master. . . .

Trigorin: Someone may come in. [*Helps her to get up.*]

Madame Arkadin: Let them, I am not ashamed of my love for you. [*Kisses his hands.*] My treasure, you desperate boy, you want to be mad, but I won't have it, I won't let you . . . [*Laughs.*] You are mine . . . mine. . . .

This forehead is mine, and these eyes, and this lovely silky hair is mine too ... you are mine all over. You are so gifted, so clever, the best of all modern writers, you are the one hope of Russia ... You have so much truthfulness, simplicity, freshness, healthy humour. ... In one touch you can give all the essential characteristics of a person or a landscape, your characters are living. One can't read you without delight! You think this is exaggerated? That I am flattering you? But look into my eyes ... look. ... Do I look like a liar? You see, I am the only one who can appreciate you; I am the only one who tells you the truth, my precious, wonderful darling. ... Are you coming? Yes? You won't abandon me? ...

Trigorin: I have no will of my own ... I have never had a will of my own. ... Flabby, feeble, always submissive—how can a woman care for such a man? Take me, carry me off, but don't let me move a step away from you. ...

Madame Arkadin: [*To herself.*] Now he is mine! [*In an easy tone as though nothing had happened.*] But, of course, if you like, you can stay. I'll go by myself and you can come afterwards, a week later. After all, why should you be in a hurry?

Trigorin: No, we may as well go together.

Madame Arkadin: As you please. Let us go together then [*A pause.*]
[*Trigorin makes a note.*]
Madame Arkadin. What are you writing?

Trigorin: I heard a good name this morning, *The Maiden's Forest.* It may be of use. [*Stretches.*] So we are to go then? Again there will be railway carriages, stations, refreshment bars, mutton chops, conversations. ...

Shamraev: [*Enters.*] I have the honor to announce, with regret, that the horses are ready. It's time, honoured lady, to set off for the station; the train comes in at five minutes past two. So please do me a favor, Irina Nikolayevna,

do not forget to inquire what has become of the actor Suzdaltsev. Is he alive and well? We used to drink together at one time. ... In *The Plundered Mail* he used to play incomparably ... I remember the tragedian Izmaïlov, also a remarkable personality, acted with him in Elisavetograd. ... Don't be in a hurry, honored lady, you need not start for five minutes. Once they were acting conspirators in a melodrama and when they were suddenly discovered Izmaïlov had to say, "We are caught in a trap," but he said, "We are caught in a tap!" [*Laughs.*] A tap!

[*While he is speaking Yakov is busy looking after the luggage. The maid brings Madame Arkadin her hat, her coat, her umbrella, and her gloves; they all help Madame Arkadin to put on her things. The man cook looks in at the door on left and after some hesitation comes in. Enter Polina Andreyevna, then Sorin and Medvedenko.*]

Polina: [*With a basket.*] Here are some plums for the journey. ... Very sweet ones. You may be glad to have something nice. ...

Madame Arkadin: You are very kind, Polina Andreyevna.

Polina: Good-bye, my dear! If anything has not been to your liking, forgive it. [*Weeps.*]

Madame Arkadin: [*Embraces her.*] Everything has been nice, everything! But you mustn't cry.

Polina: The time flies so fast!

Madame Arkadin: There's no help for it.

Sorin: [*In a greatcoat with a cape to it, with his hat on and a stick in his hand, enters from door on left, crossing the stage.*] Sister, it's time to start, or you may be too late after all. I am going to get into the carriage. [*Goes out.*]

Medvedenko: And I shall walk to the station ... to see you off. I'll be there in no time ... [*Goes out.*]

Madame Arkadin: Good-bye, dear friends. ... If we are all alive and well, we shall meet again next summer. [*The*

maid, the cook, and Yakov kiss her hand.] Don't forget me. [Gives the cook a rouble.] Here's a rouble for the three of you.
   The Cook: We humbly thank you, madam! Good journey to you! We are very grateful for your kindness!
   Yakov: May God give you good luck!
   Shamraev: You might rejoice our hearts with a letter! Good-bye, Boris Alexeyevitch!
   Madame Arkadin: Where is Konstantin? Tell him that I am starting; I must say good-bye. Well, don't remember evil against me. [To Yakov.] I gave the cook a rouble. It's for the three of you.
   [All go out on right. The stage is empty. Behind the scenes the noise that is usual when people are being seen off. The maid comes back to fetch the basket of plums from the table and goes out again.]
   Trigorin: [Coming back.] I have forgotten my stick. I believe it is out there, on the veranda. [Goes and, at door on left, meets Nina, who is coming in.] Is that you? We are going. . . .

   Nina: I felt that we should see each other once more. [Excitedly.] Boris Alexeyevitch, I have come to a decision, the die is cast, I am going on the stage. I shall be gone from here tomorrow; I am leaving my father, I am abandoning everything, I am beginning a new life. Like you, I am going . . . to Moscow. We shall meet there.
   Trigorin: [Looking round.] Stay at the "Slavyansky Bazaar" . . . Let me know at once . . . Molchanovka, Groholsky House. . . . I am in a hurry . . . [A pause.]
   Nina: One minute more. . . .
   Trigorin: [In an undertone.] You are so lovely. . . . Oh, what happiness to think that we shall see each other soon! [She sinks on his breast.] I shall see again those wonderful eyes, that inexpressibly beautiful tender smile . . . those soft features, the expression of angelic purity. . . . My darling . . . [A prolonged kiss.]

                                   CURTAIN.

QUESTIONS ON ACT III

1. Is the frank confession made by Masha to Trigorin properly motivated? Do you think that she would pour out her heart in this way? Why?

2. Consider Sorin's speech on page 475 in which he tries to explain to Madame Arkadin that Treplev's attempted suicide was motivated by something more than jealousy. Why is it important for the reader's understanding of Treplev? Does the drama bear out Sorin's analysis?

3. What is the significance of the fact that Sorin attempts to intercede with his sister for Treplev, and Treplev tries to intercede with her for Sorin? Each, the student will notice, tries to persuade Madame Arkadin to give the other one a little money. Do the two men understand each other? To what extent is their plight similar?

4. Consider Treplev's analysis of Trigorin which he makes to his mother on page 477. How fair an analysis is it? What light does it throw upon Treplev himself? Why is the question of whether or not Trigorin possesses real talents important to Treplev?

5. Is Madame Arkadin actually jealous of Nina? Is she really in love with Trigorin? Why does she insist upon keeping Trigorin for herself? Why is it necessary for her to be sure of him?

6. The act closes with Nina's plans to follow Trigorin. In the light of

this fact, reconsider Trigorin's last speech to Nina in Act II (p. 473). What does the speech tell us of Trigorin's attitude toward Nina? Toward his literary career? About his honesty or lack of honesty?

ACT IV

[*Between the Third and Fourth Acts there is an interval of two years.*]

[*One of the drawing rooms in Sorin's house, which has been turned into a study for Konstantin Treplev. On the right and left, doors leading to inner apartments. In the middle, glass door 10 leading on to the veranda. Besides the usual drawing-room furniture there is, in corner on right, a writing table, near door on left, a sofa, a bookcase, and books in windows and on the chairs.* 15 *Evening. There is a single lamp alight with a shade on it. It is half dark. There is the sound of the trees rustling, and the wind howling in the chimney. A watchman is tapping.*]

[*Enter Medvedenko and Masha.*]

Masha: [*Calling.*] Konstantin Gavrilitch! Konstantin Gavrilitch! [*Looking* 25 *round.*] No, there is no one here. The old man keeps asking every minute, where is Kostya, where is Kostya? He cannot live without him. . . .
Medvedenko: He is afraid of being 30 alone. [*Listening.*] What awful weather! This is the second day of it.
Masha: [*Turns up the lamp.*] There are waves on the lake. Great big ones.
Medvedenko: How dark it is in the 35 garden! We ought to have told them to break up that stage in the garden. It stands as bare and ugly as a skeleton, and the curtain flaps in the wind. When I passed it yesterday evening, it seemed 40 as though someone were crying in it.
Masha: What next . . . [*A pause.*]
Medvedenko: Let us go home, Masha.
Masha: [*Shakes her head.*] I shall stay here for the night. 45
Medvedenko: [*In an imploring voice.*]

Masha, do come! Our baby must be hungry.
Masha: Nonsense. Matryona will feed him. [*A pause.*]
5 *Medvedenko:* I am sorry for him. He has been three nights now without his mother.
Masha: You are a bore. In old days you used at least to discuss general subjects, but now it is only home, baby, home, baby—that's all one can get out of you.
Medvedenko: Come along, Masha!
Masha: Go by yourself.
Medvedenko: Your father won't let me have a horse.
Masha: Yes, he will. You ask, and he will.
Medvedenko: Very well, I'll ask. Then 20 you will come tomorrow?
Masha: [*Taking a pinch of snuff.*] Very well, tomorrow. How you pester me.
[*Enter Treplev and Polina Andreyevna Treplev brings in pillows and a quilt, and* 25 *Polina Andreyevna sheets and pillowcases; they lay them on the sofa, then Treplev goes to his table and sits down.*]
Masha: What's this for, Mother?
Polina: Pyotr Nikolayevitch asked us 30 to make a bed for him in Kostya's room.
Masha: Let me do it. [*Makes the bed.*]
Polina: [*Sighing.*] Old people are like children. [*Goes up to the writing table* 35 *and, leaning on her elbow, looks at the manuscript; a pause.*]
Medvedenko: Well, I am going then. Good-bye, Masha. [*Kisses his wife's hand.*] Good-bye, Mother. [*Tries to kiss* 40 *his mother-in-law's hand.*]
Polina: [*With vexation.*] Come, if you are going, go.
Medvedenko: Good-bye, Konstantin Gavrilitch.
45 [*Treplev gives him his hand without speaking; Medvedenko goes out.*]

Polina: [*Looking at the manuscript.*] No one would have guessed or thought that you would have become a real author, Kostya. And now, thank God, they send you money from the magazines. [*Passes her hand over his hair.*] And you have grown good-looking too. . . . Dear, good Kostya, do be a little kinder to my Mashenka!

Masha: [*As she makes the bed.*] Leave him alone, Mother.

Polina: [*To Treplev.*] She is a nice little thing. [*A pause.*] A woman wants nothing, you know, Kostya, so long as you give her a kind look. I know from myself.

[*Treplev gets up from the table and walks away without speaking.*]

Masha: Now you have made him angry. What induced you to pester him?

Polina: I feel so sorry for you, Mashenka.

Masha: Much use that is!

Polina: My heart aches for you. I see it all, you know, I understand it all.

Masha: It's all foolishness. There is no such thing as hopeless love except in novels. It's of no consequence. The only thing is one mustn't let oneself go and keep expecting something, waiting for the tide to turn. . . . When love gets into the heart there is nothing to be done but to clear it out. Here they promised to transfer my husband to another district. As soon as I am there, I shall forget it all. . . . I shall tear it out of my heart.

[*Two rooms away a melancholy waltz is played.*]

Polina: That's Kostya playing. He must be depressed.

Masha: [*Noiselessly dances a few waltz steps.*] The great thing, Mother, is not to have him before one's yes. If they only give my Semyon his transfer, trust me, I shall get over it in a month. It's all nonsense.

[*Door on left opens. Dorn and Medvedenko wheel in Sorin in his chair.*]

Medvedenko: I have six of them at home now. And flour is two kopeks per pound.

Dorn: You've got to look sharp to make both ends meet.

Medvedenko: It's all very well for you to laugh. You've got more money than you know what to do with.

Dorn: Money? After thirty years of practice, my boy, troublesome work during which I could not call my soul my own by day or by night, I only succeeded in saving two thousand roubles, and that I spent not long ago abroad. I have nothing.

Masha: [*To her husband.*] You have not gone?

Medvedenko: [*guiltily.*] Well, how can I when they won't let me have a horse?

Masha: [*With bitter vexation in an undertone.*] I can't bear the sight of you.

[*The wheel chair remains in the left half of the room; Polina Andreyevna, Masha, and Dorn sit down beside it, Medvedenko moves mournfully to one side.*]

Dorn: What changes there have been here! The drawing room has been turned into a study.

Masha: It is more convenient for Konstantin Gavrilitch to work here. Whenever he likes, he can walk out into the garden and think there.

[*A watchman taps.*]

Sorin: Where is my sister?

Dorn: She has gone to the station to meet Trigorin. She will be back directly.

Sorin: Since you thought it necessary to send for my sister, I must be dangerously ill. [*After a silence.*] It's a queer thing, I am dangerously ill and here they don't give me any medicines.

Dorn: Well, what would you like to have? Valerian drops? Soda? Quinine?

Sorin: Ah, he is at his moralizing again! What an infliction it is! [*With a motion of his head toward the sofa.*] Is that bed for me?

Polina: Yes, it's for you, Pyotr Nikolayevitch.

Sorin: Thank you.

Dorn: [*Hums.*] "The moon is floating in the midnight sky."

Sorin: I want to give Kostya a subject for a story. It ought to be called "The Man who Wished"—*L'homme qui a voulu.* In my youth I wanted to become a literary man—and didn't; I wanted to speak well—and I spoke horribly badly [*mimicking himself*], "and all the rest of it, and all that, and so on, and so forth" . . . and I would go plodding on and on, trying to sum up till I was in a regular perspiration; I wanted to get married—and I didn't; I always wanted to live in town and here I am ending my life in the country—and so on.

Dorn: I wanted to become an actual civil councilor—and I have.

Sorin: [*Laughs.*] That I had no hankerings after. That happened of itself.

Dorn: To be expressing dissatisfaction with life at sixty-two is really ungracious, you know.

Sorin: What a persistent fellow he is! You might understand that one wants to live!

Dorn: That's just frivolity. It's the law of nature that every life must have an end.

Sorin: You argue like a man who has had enough. You are satisfied and so you are indifferent to life, nothing matters to you. But even you will be afraid to die.

Dorn: The dread of death is an animal fear. One must overcome it. A rational fear of death is only possible for those who believe in eternal life and are conscious of their sins. And you, in the first place, don't believe, and, in the second, what sins have you to worry about? You have served in the courts of justice for twenty-five years—that's all.

Sorin: [*Laughs.*] Twenty-eight. . . .

[*Treplev comes in and sits down on a stool at Sorin's feet. Masha never takes her eyes off him.*]

Dorn: We are hindering Konstantin Gavrilitch from working.

Treplev: Oh no, it doesn't matter. [*A pause.*]

Medvedenko: Allow me to ask you, doctor, what town did you like best abroad?

Dorn: Genoa.

Treplev: Why Genoa?

Dorn: The life in the streets is so wonderful there. When you go out of the hotel in the evening, the whole street is packed with people. You wander aimlessly zigzagging about among the crowd, backwards and forwards; you live with it, are psychologically at one with it and begin almost to believe that a world-soul is really possible, such as was acted by Nina Zaretchny in your play. And, by the way, where is she now? How is she getting on?

Treplev: I expect she is quite well.

Dorn: I was told that she was leading a rather peculiar life. How was that?

Treplev: That's a long story, doctor.

Dorn: Well, tell it to us shortly. [*A pause.*]

Treplev: She ran away from home and had an affair with Trigorin. You know that?

Dorn: I know.

Treplev: She had a child. The child died. Trigorin got tired of her and went back to his old ties, as might have been expected. Though, indeed, he had never abandoned them, but in his weak-willed way contrived to keep both going. As far as I can make out from what I have heard, Nina's private life was a complete failure.

Dorn: And the stage?

Treplev: I fancy that was worse still. She made her debut at some holiday place near Moscow, then went to the provinces. All that time I did not lose sight of her, and wherever she went I followed her. She always took big parts, but she acted crudely, without taste, screamingly, with violent gestures. There were moments when she uttered a cry successfully or died successfully, but they were only moments

Dorn: Then she really has some talent?

Treplev: It was difficult to make it out. I suppose she has. I saw her but she would not see me, and the servants would not admit me at the hotel. I understood her state of mind and did not insist on seeing her. [*A pause.*] What more can I tell you? Afterwards, when I was back at home, I had some letters from her—warm, intelligent, interesting letters. She did not complain, but I felt that she was profoundly unhappy; every line betrayed sick overstrained nerves. And her imagination is a little unhinged. She signed herself the Sea Gull. In Pushkin's *Mermaid* the miller says that he is a raven, and in the same way in her letters she kept repeating that she was a sea gull. Now she is here.

Dorn: Here? How do you mean?

Treplev: In the town, staying at an inn. She has been there for five days, I did go to see her, and Marya Ilyinishna here went too, but she won't see anyone. Semyon Semyonitch declares he saw her yesterday afternoon in the fields a mile and a half from here.

Medvedenko: Yes, I saw her. She went in that direction, toward the town. I bowed to her and asked her why she did not come to see us. She said she would come.

Treplev: She won't come. [*A pause.*] Her father and stepmother refuse to recognize her. They have put watchmen about so that she may not even go near the house. [*Walks away with the doctor toward the writing table.*] How easy it is to be a philosopher on paper, Doctor, and how difficult it is in life!

Sorin: She was a charming girl.

Dorn: What?

Sorin: She was a charming girl, I say. Actual Civil Councilor Sorin was positively in love with her for a time.

Dorn: The old Lovelace.

[*Shamraev's laugh is heard.*]

Polina: I fancy our people have come back from the station. . . .

Treplev: Yes, I hear mother.

[*Enter Madame Arkadin, Trigorin, and with them Shamraev.*]

Shamraev: [*As he enters.*] We all grow old and dilapidated under the influence of the elements, while you, honored lady, are still young . . . a light blouse, sprightliness, grace. . . .

Madame Arkadin: You want to bring me ill luck again, you tiresome man!

Trigorin: How do you do, Pyotr Nikolayevitch! So you are still poorly? That's bad! [*Seeing Masha, joyfully.*] Marya Ilyinishna!

Masha: You know me, do you? [*Shakes hands.*]

Trigorin: Married?

Masha: Long ago.

Trigorin: Are you happy? [*Bows to Dorn and Medvedenko, then hesitatingly approaches Treplev.*] Irina Nikolayevna has told me that you have forgotten the past and are no longer angry. [*Treplev holds out his hand.*]

Madame Arkadin: [*To her son.*] Boris Alexeyevitch has brought the magazine with your new story in it.

Treplev: [*Taking the magazine; to Trigorin.*] Thank you, you are very kind. [*They sit down.*]

Trigorin: Your admirers send their greetings to you. . . . In Petersburg and Moscow there is great interest in your work and I am continually being asked questions about you. People ask what you are like, how old you are, whether you are dark or fair. Everyone imagines, for some reason, that you are no longer young. And no one knows your real name, as you always publish under a pseudonym. You are as mysterious as the Iron Mask.

Treplev: Will you be able to make a long stay?

Trigorin: No, I think I must go back to Moscow tomorrow. I am obliged to. I am in a hurry to finish my novel, and besides, I have promised something for a collection of tales that is being published. It's the old story, in fact.

[*While they are talking, Madame*

Arkadin and Polina Andreyevna put a card table in the middle of the room and open it out. Shamraev lights candles and sets chairs. A game of lotto is brought out of the cupboard.]

Trigorin: The weather has not given me a friendly welcome. There is a cruel wind. If it has dropped by tomorrow morning I shall go to the lake to fish. And I must have a look at the garden and that place where—you remember?— your play was acted. I've got a subject for a story, I only want to revive my recollections of the scene in which it is laid.

Masha: [To her father.] Father, let my husband have a horse! He must get home.

Shamraev: [Mimicking.] Must get home—a horse! *[Sternly.]* You can see for yourself: they have just been to the station. I can't send them out again.

Masha: But there are other horses. *[Seeing that her father says nothing, waves her hand.]* There's no doing any-thing with you.

Medvedenko: I can walk, Masha. Really. . . .

Polina: [With a sigh.] Walk in such weather . . . *[Sits down to the card table.]* Come, friends.

Medvedenko: It is only four miles. Good-bye. *[Kisses his wife's hand.]* Good-bye, Mother. *[His mother-in-law reluctantly holds out her hand for him to kiss.]* I wouldn't trouble anyone, but the baby . . . *[Bows to the company.]* Good-bye . . . *[Goes out with a guilty step.]*

Shamraev: He can walk right enough. He's not a general.

Polina: [Tapping on the table.] Come, friends. Don't let us waste time, we shall soon be called to supper.

[Shamraev, Masha, and Dorn sit down at the table.]

Madame Arkadin: [To Trigorin.] When the long autumn evenings come on they play lotto here. Look, it's the same old lotto that we had when our mother used to play with us, when we

were children. Won't you have a game before supper? *[Sits down to the table with Trigorin.]* It's a dull game, but it is not so bad when you are used to it. *[Deals three cards to everyone.]*

Treplev: [Turning the pages of the magazine.] He has read his own story, but he has not even cut mine. *[Puts the magazine down on the writing table, then goes toward door on left; as he passes his mother he kisses her on the head.]*

Madame Arkadin: And you, Kostya?

Treplev: Excuse me, I would rather not . . . I am going out. *[Goes out.]*

Madame Arkadin: The stake is ten kopeks. Put it down for me, Doctor, will you?

Dorn: Right.

Masha: Has everyone put down their stakes? I begin . . . Twenty-two.

Madame Arkadin: Yes.

Masha: Three!

Dorn: Right!

Masha: Did you play three? Eight! Eighty-one! Ten!

Shamraev: Don't be in a hurry!

Madame Arkadin: What a reception I had in Harkov! My goodness! I feel dizzy with it still.

Masha: Thirty-four!

[A melancholy waltz is played behind the scenes.]

Madame Arkadin: The students gave me an ovation. . . . Three baskets of flowers . . . two wreaths and this, see. *[Unfastens a brooch on her throat and lays it on the table.]*

Shamraev: Yes, that is a thing. . . .

Masha: Fifty!

Dorn: Exactly fifty?

Madame Arkadin: I had a wonderful dress. . . . Whatever I don't know, I do know how to dress.

Polina: Kostya is playing the piano; he is depressed, poor fellow.

Shamraev: He is awfully abused in the newspapers.

Masha: Seventy-seven!

Madame Arkadin: As though that mattered!

Trigorin: He never quite comes off.

He has not yet hit upon his own medium. There is always something queer and vague, at times almost like delirium. Not a single living character.

Masha: Eleven!

Madame Arkadin: [Looking round at Sorin.] Petrusha, are you bored? *[A pause.]* He is asleep.

Dorn: The actual civil councilor is asleep.

Masha: Seven! Ninety!

Trigorin: If I lived in such a place, beside a lake, do you suppose I should write? I should overcome this passion and should do nothing but fish.

Masha: Twenty-eight!

Trigorin: Catching perch is so delightful!

Dorn: Well, I believe in Konstantin Gavrilitch. There is something in him! There is something in him! He thinks in images; his stories are vivid, full of color, and they affect me strongly. The only pity is that he has not got definite aims. He produces an impression and that's all, but you can't get far with nothing but an impression. Irina Nikolayevna, are you glad that your son is a writer?

Madame Arkadin: Only fancy, I have not read anything of his yet. I never have time.

Masha: Twenty-six!

[Treplev comes in quietly and sits down at his table.]

Shamraev: [To Trigorin.] We have still got something here belonging to you, Boris Alexeyevitch.

Trigorin: What's this?

Shamraev: Konstantin Gavrilitch shot a sea gull and you asked me to get it stuffed for you.

Trigorin: I don't remember! *[Ponaering.]* I don't remember!

Masha: Sixty-six! One!

Treplev: [Flinging open the window, listens.] How dark it is! I don't know why I feel so uneasy.

Madame Arkadin: Kostya, shut the window, there's a draught.

[Treplev shuts the window.]

Masha: Eighty-eight!

Trigorin: The game is mine!

Madame Arkadin: [Gaily.] Bravo, bravo!

5 *Shamraev:* Bravo!

Madame Arkadin: That man always has luck in everything. *[Gets up.]* And now let us go and have something to eat. Our great man has not dined today.

10 We will go on again after supper. *[To her son.]* Kostya, leave your manuscripts and come to supper.

Treplev: I don't want any, Mother, I am not hungry.

15 *Madame Arkadin:* As you like. *[Wakes Sorin.]* Petrusha, supper! *[Takes Shamraev's arm.]* I'll tell you about my reception in Harkov.

[Polina Andreyevna puts out the
20 *candles on the table. Then she and Dorn wheel the chair. All go out by door on left; only Treplev, sitting at the writing table, is left on the stage.]*

Treplev: [Settling himself to write; runs
25 *through what he has written already.]* I have talked so much about new forms and now I feel that little by little I am falling into a convention myself. *[Reads.]* "The placard on the wall proclaimed.
30 . . . The pale face in its setting of dark hair." Proclaimed, setting. That's stupid. *[Scratches out.]* I will begin where the hero is awakened by the patter of the rain, and throw out all the
35 rest. The description of the moonlight evening is long and overelaborate. Trigorin has worked out methods for himself, it's easy for him now. . . . With him the broken bottleneck glitters on
40 the dam and the mill wheel casts black shadow—and there you have the moonlight night, while I have the tremulous light, and the soft twinkling of the stars, and the faraway strains of
45 the piano dying away in the still fragrant air. . . . It's agonizing. *[A pause.]* I come more and more to the conviction that it is not a question of new and old forms, but that what matters is that a
50 man should write without thinking about forms at all, write because it

springs freely from his soul. [*There is a tap at the window nearest to the table.*] What is that? [*Looks out of window.*] There is nothing to be seen . . . [*Opens the glass door and looks out into the garden.*] Someone ran down the steps. [*Calls.*] Who is there? [*Goes out and can be heard walking rapidly along the veranda; returns half a minute later with Nina Zaretchny.*] Nina, Nina!

[*Nina lays her head on his breast and weeps with subdued sobs.*]

Treplev: [*Moved.*] Nina! Nina! It's you . . . you. . . . It's as though I had foreseen it, all day long my heart has been aching and restless. [*Takes off her hat and cape.*] Oh, my sweet, my precious, she has come at last. Don't let us cry, don't let us!

Nina: There is someone here.

Treplev: No one.

Nina: Lock the doors, someone may come in.

Treplev: No one will come in.

Nina: I know Irina Nikolayevna is here. Lock the doors.

Treplev: [*Locks the door on right, goes to door on left.*] There is no lock on this one. I'll put a chair against it. [*Puts an armchair against the door.*] Don't be afraid, no one will come.

Nina: [*Looking intently into his face.*] Let me look at you. [*Looking round.*] It's warm, it's nice. . . . In old days this was the drawing room. Am I very much changed?

Treplev: Yes . . . You are thinner and your eyes are bigger. Nina, how strange it is that I should be seeing you. Why would not you let me see you? Why haven't you come all this time? I know you have been here almost a week. . . . I have been to you several times every day; I stood under your window like a beggar.

Nina: I was afraid that you might hate me. I dream every night that you look at me and don't know me. If only you knew! Ever since I came I have been walking here . . . by the lake. I have been near your house many times and could not bring myself to enter it. Let us sit down. [*They sit down.*] Let us sit down and talk and talk. It's nice here, it's warm and snug. Do you hear the wind? There's a passage in Turgenev, "Well for the man on such a night who sits under the shelter of home, who has a warm corner in safety." I am a sea gull. . . . No, that's not it. [*Rubs her forehead.*] What was I saying? Yes . . . Turgenev . . . "And the Lord help all homeless wanderers!" . . . It doesn't matter. [*Sobs.*]

Treplev: Nina, you are crying again. . . . Nina!

Nina: Never mind, it does me good . . . I haven't cried for two years. Yesterday, late in the evening, I came into the garden to see whether our stage was still there. It is still standing. I cried for the first time after two years and it eased the weight on my heart and made it lighter. You see, I am not crying now. [*Takes him by the hand.*] And so now you are an author. . . . You are an author, I am an actress. . . . We too have been drawn into the whirlpool. I lived joyously like a child—I woke up singing in the morning; I loved you and dreamed of fame, and now? Early tomorrow morning I must go to Yelets third-class . . . with peasants, and at Yelets the cultured tradesmen will pester me with attentions. Life is a coarse business!

Treplev: Why to Yelets?

Nina: I have taken an engagement for the whole winter. It is time to go.

Treplev: Nina, I cursed you, I hated you, I tore up your letters and photographs, but I was conscious every minute that my soul is bound to yours for ever. It's not in my power to leave off loving you, Nina. Ever since I lost you and began to get my work published my life has been unbearable—I am wretched. . . . My youth was, as it were, torn away all at once and it seems to me as though I have lived for ninety years already. I call upon you, I kiss the earth on which you have walked;

Wherever I look I see your face, that tender smile that lighted up the best days of my life. . . .

Nina: [*Distractedly.*] Why does he talk like this, why does he talk like this?

Treplev: I am alone in the world, warmed by no affection. I am as cold as though I were in a cellar, and everything I write is dry, hard, and gloomy. Stay here, Nina, I entreat you, or let me go with you!

[*Nina rapidly puts on her hat and cape.*] *Treplev:* Nina, why is this? For God's sake, Nina! [*Looks at her as she puts her things on; a pause.*]

Nina: My horses are waiting at the gate. Don't see me off, I'll go alone. . . . [*Through her tears.*] Give me some water. . . .

Treplev: [*Gives her some water.*] Where are you going now?

Nina: To the town. [*A pause.*] Is Irina Nikolayevna here?

Treplev: Yes. . . . Uncle was taken worse on Thursday and we telegraphed for her.

Nina: Why do you say that you kissed the earth on which I walked? I ought to be killed. [*Bends over table.*] I am so tired! If I could rest . . . if I could rest! [*Raising her head.*] I am a sea gull. . . . No, that's not it. I am an actress. Oh, well! [*Hearing Madame Arkadin and Trigorin laughing, she listens, then runs to door on left and looks through the keyhole.*] He is here too. . . . [*Turning back to Treplev.*] Oh, well . . . it doesn't matter . . . no. . . . He did not believe in the stage, he always laughed at my dreams and little by little I left off believing in it too, and lost heart. . . . And then I was fretted by love and jealousy, and continually anxious over my little one. . . . I grew petty and trivial, I acted stupidly. . . . I did not know what to do with my arms, I did not know how to stand on the stage, could not control my voice. You can't understand what it feels like when one knows one is acting disgracefully. I am

a sea gull. No, that's not it. . . . Do you remember you shot a sea gull? A man came by chance, saw it, and, just to pass the time, destroyed it. . . . A subject for a short story. . . . That's not it, though. [*Rubs her forehead.*] What was I saying? . . . I am talking of the stage. Now I am not like that. I am a real actress, I act with enjoyment, with enthusiasm, I am intoxicated when I am on the stage and feel that I am splendid. And since I have been here, I keep walking about and thinking, thinking and feeling that my soul is getting stronger every day. Now I know, I understand, Kostya, that in our work —in acting or writing—what matters is not fame, not glory, not what I dreamed of, but knowing how to be patient. To bear one's cross and have faith. I have faith and it all doesn't hurt so much, and when I think of my vocation I am not afraid of life.

Treplev: [*Mournfully.*] You have found your path, you know which way you are going, but I am still floating in a chaos of dreams and images, not knowing what use it is to anyone. I have no faith and don't know what my vocation is.

Nina: [*Listening.*] 'Sh-sh . . . I am going. Good-bye. When I become a great actress, come and look at me. Will you promise? But now . . . [*presses his hand*] it's late. I can hardly stand on my feet. . . . I am worn out and hungry. . . .

Treplev: Stay, I'll give you some supper.

Nina: No, no. . . . Don't see me off, I will go by myself. My horses are close by. . . . So she brought him with her? Well, it doesn't matter. When you see Trigorin, don't say anything to him. . . . I love him! I love him even more than before. . . . A subject for a short story . . . I love him, I love him passionately, I love him to despair. It was nice in the old days, Kostya! Do you remember? How clear, warm, joyous, and pure life was, what feelings we had—feelings like tender, exquisite flowers. ... Do you remember? [*Recites.*] "Men, lions, eagles, and partridges, horned deer, geese, spiders, silent fish that dwell in the water, starfishes, and creatures which cannot be seen by the eye—all living things, all living things, all living things, have completed their cycle of sorrow, are extinct. ... For thousands of years the earth has borne no living creature on its surface, and this poor moon lights its lamp in vain. On the meadow the cranes no longer waken with a cry and there is no sound of the May beetles in the lime trees ..." [*Impulsively embraces Treplev and runs out of the glass door.*]

Treplev: [*After a pause.*] It will be a pity if someone meets her in the garden and tells mother. It may upset mother. ...

[*He spends two minutes in tearing up all his manuscripts and throwing them under the table; then unlocks the door on right and goes out.*]

Dorn: [*Trying to open the door on left.*] Strange. The door seems to be locked ... [*Comes in and puts the armchair in its place.*] An obstacle race.

[*Enter Madame Arkadin and Polina Andreyevna, behind them Yakov carrying a tray with bottles; Masha; then Shamraev and Trigorin.*]

Madame Arkadin. Put the claret and the beer for Boris Alexeyevitch here on the table. We will play as we drink it. Let us sit down, friends.

Polina: [*To Yakov.*] Bring tea too at the same time. [*Lights the candles and sits down to the card table.*]

Shamraev: [*Leads Trigorin to the cupboard.*] Here's the thing I was speaking about just now. [*Takes the stuffed sea gull from the cupboard.*] This is what you ordered.

Trigorin: [*Looking at the sea gull.*] I don't remember it. [*Musing.*] I don't remember.

[*The sound of a shot coming from right of stage; everyone starts.*]

Madame Arkadin: [*Frightened.*] What's that?

Dorn: That's nothing. It must be something in my medicine chest that has gone off. Don't be anxious. [*Goes out at door on right, comes back in half a minute.*] That's what it is. A bottle of ether has exploded. [*Hums.*] "I stand before thee enchanted again. ..."

Madame Arkadin: [*Sitting down to the table.*] Ough, how frightened I was. It reminded me of how ... [*Hides her face in her hands.*] It made me quite dizzy. ...

Dorn: [*Turning over the leaves of the magazine, to Trigorin.*] There was an article in this two months ago—a letter from America—and I wanted to ask you among other things [*puts his arm round Trigorin's waist and leads him to the footlights*] as I am very much interested in the question. ... [*In a lower tone, dropping his voice.*] Get Irina Nikolayevna away somehow. The fact is, Konstantin Gavrilitch has shot himself. ...

CURTAIN.

QUESTIONS ON ACT IV

1. Why does Chekhov give us the scene at the beginning of the act in which Masha refuses to go home? Is it a way of suggesting what has been happening to Treplev—that Masha senses his loneliness and defeat? What is the significance of Masha's statement (p. 482): "There is no such thing as hopeless love except in novels"?

2. Consider Sorin's speech (p. 483) beginning: "I want to give Kostya a subject for a story, etc." Granted that the speech is a commentary on Sorin's own disappointment, does it help to suggest the plight of Treplev?

3. Is the information about what has happened to Nina brought in naturally?

4. What do Treplev's speeches on the subject suggest? That he has lost interest in Nina? That he is trying to be objective? That he still loves her but is trying to conceal that fact from himself? Or what?

5. What is the significance of Trigorin's having brought Treplev a magazine with Treplev's latest story in it? Madame Arkadin apparently thinks that this present may pacify Treplev. Treplev himself notices that Trigorin has obviously not read the story. What is the significance of Trigorin's analysis of Treplev's style (pp. 485–86)?

6. Trigorin wins the game of lotto, and Madam Arkadin comments, "That man always has luck in everything." The comment is made casually as a bit of small talk, but does it take on a deeper significance in the context of the act?

7. Shamraev tells Trigorin that he has had the sea gull stuffed for him, but Trigorin cannot remember anything about it. What is the symbolic significance of this passage? If we remember that it was Treplev who shot the sea gull, may the little incident be taken as an allegory of the action of the play?

8. What is the significance of Treplev's disparaging analysis of his own literary style?

9. What does Nina mean when she tells Treplev (p. 487), "You are an author, I am an actress. We too have been drawn into the whirlpool"? Is there an implied contrast between the quiet lake, the proper haunt of the sea gull, and the whirlpool?

10. Is Nina still in love with Treplev? What is her attitude toward him? How do you know?

11. What is the importance of Treplev's speech (p. 489): "It will be a pity if someone meets her in the garden and tells mother. It may upset mother. . . ,"?

NOTES ON *THE SEA GULL*

I. THE VARIOUS CONFLICTS

Two special problems, as we have already suggested, are presented sharply to the student of Chekhov: the problem of tone and the problem of structure. The problem of tone, that is, of the play's relation to the comic or the tragic mode, is one which can be temporarily postponed until we have considered other issues which lead up to it. As for the problem of structure, several facts are obvious immediately. Chekhov's plays have the reputation of dealing with frustration, and in a sense this reputation is well founded. To say that *The Sea Gull* deals with frustration is perhaps to say that apparently "nothing happens"; that is, we do not find the conventional dramatic structure in which one or more characters develop and carry through a line of action by a traceable "forward movement." There is no clear objective toward which things seem to be moving and in terms of which the play ends. Hence, even though the play ends with a violent action—Treplev's suicide—we may very well feel that we have not seen a characteristic plot develop. Treplev may seem merely frustrated, a sad young man, who never succeeds in solving his problem and finds nothing to do but kill himself. But the fact is that we are always aware of a high state of tension in the play—the quality by which we identify drama. For we are constantly aware of the existence of conflict—indeed, of a multitude of conflicts.

In the introduction we spoke of a short story (p. 16) which is almost a play. Now, in *The Sea Gull*, we are at first glance tempted to find a novel presented on the stage and not a proper "drama" at all. It is true that the technique of this play shows the influence of techniques developed in fiction. For example, the play is not focused on one central character. There is rather a multiple focus of the sort which occurs more frequently in fiction and which in drama may be dangerous (cf. p. 181). But *The Sea Gull* is a drama in its own right and represents not a mixture of forms but dramatic form in the full sense of that term.

Perhaps the best approach which we can make to this problem is to begin with a consideration of the types of conflict to be found in the play and to attempt arbitrarily to relate them to one conflict, say Treplev's. There are many conflicts. There are so many that a careless reader may feel that there is no central conflict at all—that the struggles of the various characters merely cancel each other out. There is Treplev's conflict with his brilliant actress mother—a struggle, on the more superficial levels, for money, for literary reputation, for freedom to express himself. But this struggle is, on the deepest level, a struggle to *be* himself, and it involves, ultimately, the problem of defining himself. Now how may the other conflicts be related to this one? Is there any relation? Masha's conflict is internal: she is very much in love with Treplev, but recognizes that her love is hopeless and makes her decision to marry the dull schoolmaster. Other struggles seem less immediately related to Treplev's. There is Nina's struggle with her father and stepmother and with the stifling and meaningless respectability which they represent. There is Sorin's struggle to realize something out of life—to transcend the kind of existence in which nothing seems to happen—in which he seems to go through existence without having lived. There is even, in a lower key, Polina's attempt to persuade Dorn to agree to an open acknowledgment of their love for each other.

In all of these conflicts the protagonists are unsuccessful: but there are two characters who are so successful that one hesitates to characterize their efforts as "struggles" at all. Madame Arkadin maintains her equilibrium so easily that her success is hardly in doubt. Even Trigorin's defection from her is brief and qualified. Trigorin himself never agonizes—either for a literary reputation or for love. With no effort at all, he takes Nina away from Treplev and away from the lake.

We asked, in a tentative effort to organize the materials, how these various conflicts are related to Treplev's conflict. The two successful char-- acters, of course, we see in direct opposition to Treplev: Madame Arkadin and Trigorin represent some of the forces against which he struggles. But the unsuccessful struggles are also related to Treplev's: they tend to parallel and echo his own failure at one point or another. It is possible that they tend to define the ultimate nature of his struggle. But we shall see this more clearly if we postpone an answer until we have considered several of the themes which seem to emerge from the various conflicts.

2. THE LOVE THEME

The patterning of the love affairs in this play is quite as complicated as that in *The Way of the World*. We have ardent, idealistic young love (Treplev for Nina), glamor-struck love (Nina for Trigorin), unrequited, hopeless love (Masha for Treplev), furtive love (Polina for Dorn), the com- fortable "arrangement" (Madame Arkadin and Trigorin), etc. To illustrate the complications of the unrequited love theme: Medvedenko is in love with Masha, who is in love with Treplev, who is in love with Nina, who is in love with Trigorin, who is in love (at least in his own way) with Madame Arkadin, who is in love with herself. Needless to say, Chekhov has arranged this patterning for a different purpose than that of Congreve. Though he calls his play a comedy, what we sense is pathos, and perhaps tragedy. One of the most remarkable things about *The Sea Gull* is that Chekhov has made the patterning of the love affairs so intricate, and yet has man- aged to avoid the tone either of melodrama or of light comedy.

A definition of the tone actually achieved had best be deferred to a later section of this discussion where the whole problem of this play's relation to comedy and tragedy will be dealt with. But some of the other functions of the intricate patterning of the love affairs can be mentioned here. One func- tion is to supply a qualifying background for Treplev's particular problem. The other love affairs serve to define, sometimes by parallel, sometimes by contrast, Treplev's own situation. For example, other characters, like Treplev, suffer from unrequited love: Nina; Polina, in a sense; Masha, for Treplev himself. (Even though Masha's resignation—her sense of the unalterable nature of things—keeps her from struggling, yet it gives her dignity, and she has, in her very hopelessness, a kind of security, which Treplev lacks.)

Moreover, Treplev is aware, in part, of this background of love relation- ships. He is aware of the frustration of some of the others. This comprehen- sion increases Treplev's bitterness and restlessness. Treplev's knowledge, for example, of Trigorin's basic shallowness and even of his mother's final triviality influences all his actions profoundly.

3. THE ART THEME

Treplev's play, for example, is conditioned heavily by his sensitiveness to his mother's and her paramour's literary fame. In addition to his positive creative aims, he wants also to shock his mother; to declare his independence of the popular standards of art in terms of which she and Trigorin are famous. But his purpose, too, is to win his mother's respect, to make her see that he has not only independence but talent. And, too, the play is to define for himself what he thinks about life—what life *is*.

His play therefore is not merely an attempt at literary accomplishment. It springs actually from a deeper impulse toward self-expression; hence his hurt feelings. But, aside from his hope of approval, he has another motive: he must show his mother and her friends, including the second-rate artist Trigorin, that he has no illusions about what his mother's reputation as an actress really means or the kind of literature which she thinks is fine. But the play is a debacle, in part because he has failed at the beginning even to shock his mother seriously—she pigeonholes the effort as "decadent" poetry, and so is able to dismiss it. In part, the play fails because of Treplev's own honesty. The play represents an aspiration and not a fulfillment. Treplev is too honest to see it otherwise.

Attitudes to Art. But only one person who sees the play gets any sense of what Treplev has tried to do. Though Sorin, Treplev's uncle, is sympathetic with his nephew's effort, only Dorn expresses any liking for the play. Nina is worried because there are no living characters in it; Masha is interested merely in the author because she is in love with him; the schoolmaster takes only a pedantic interest—he questions some of the innovations. Trigorin says that he doesn't understand a word of it. All of them—possibly Dorn, who makes no pretensions to literature, excepted—see it only in personal terms or judge it by the standards of conventionally successful literary work.

As we have already seen, most of these people cannot communicate with each other—cannot express to one another what they yearn to express. Yet, most of them assume that literature is such expression. They feel that they have a story to tell—that there is material for a story in their lives, but they cannot comprehend Treplev's attempt at such expression.

The ironic contrasts between what people take art to be and what the conventionally successful artists make of it, is seen through the play. The romantic view which Nina takes of the artist applies, in a way, to Treplev, who wants to write "from his soul." Hence she exclaims: "I should have thought that for anyone who has known the enjoyment of creation, no other enjoyment can exist." But she attributes this kind of creation to *Trigorin*, whose attitude toward his work is that of a perfectly humdrum businessman. In the same way, poor Masha's attitude is comparable to Nina's: she feels free to pour out her sadness to Trigorin because he is a writer: "You might use it. I am telling you the truth: if he had hurt himself seriously I would not have gone on living another minute." Again, everyone feels that Madame Arkadin, as a great actress, is capable of sensitiveness and depth of feeling. They defer to her, not merely because she is charming, and not merely because she has won public acclaim, but because they feel that she is a great artist. And so she is; but her greatness as an actress is perfectly consonant with selfishness, pettiness, and a general incomprehension of the emotions that rack her son and brother.

We have seen how literature, as he conceives of it ideally, seems to offer to Treplev an escape from his frustration by giving him a means of expression. In much the same way Nina is attracted by the stage. The world of the stage represents a way of escape from her father's tyranny and a dull and frustrating environment in which she finds herself. But whereas Treplev's interest in the stage springs in part from an awareness of the distinction between what art ought to be and what conventionally successful art is, to Nina the stage is completely glamorous and represents a means of escape into a more satisfying world. And Trigorin, far from appearing to be a rather shallow popular author, appears to her quite genuinely to be a hero.

One may summarize therefore by saying that the stage and the world of practical writing, in contrast with literature as viewed ideally, acts in the case of both these young people as a disrupting force, though it carries them in opposite directions. Of the two, Nina is the less complicated, the more naïve, the more easily dazzled. But Chekhov makes no easy judgment in favor of one as opposed to the other. Nina's bedazzlement is perfectly natural in the circumstances, and the fact that Treplev can see through the illusion which has fascinated her simply adds to his own frustration.

Complication of Character. The ironic failure of the young people to fulfil their hopes is, in turn, in ironic contrast with the "success" of Madame Arkadin and Trigorin; in fact, the irony may even seem directed against the latter two. But the fact is that the play is not primarily, if at all, a satire on popular artistic success. Chekhov, we should observe, carefully refrains from turning Madame Arkadin and Trigorin into villainess and villain. They are genuinely successful, they possess some very real talent, and in a sense they are quite frank about themselves. Trigorin, for example, is perfectly honest in talking about the lack of glamor in his profession. He tells Nina quite truthfully that there is nothing spectacular or romantic about the business of writing, and he confesses with what is quite obvious sincerity that he is a minor writer. Actually, Trigorin is made to go about with his notebook, jotting down bits of material for his stories, in the most jog-trot, businesslike way. He dotes on fishing. By contrast it is Masha, the rather unattractive, vodka-drinking, snuff-taking girl who exhibits a romantic abandon in her attitude toward life.

Madame Arkadin, too, is sincere—at least as sincere as one can be who acts consistently off the stage as well as on the stage. It is very easy to oversimplify her character. There is a sense in which it is fair to say that she is merely a superficial and thoroughly selfish woman. She is wrapped up in her own concerns. She is vain. She makes little effort to understand her son, and her feelings toward both her son and her brother are essentially those of the sentimentalist.

Yet it is a triumph on the part of Chekhov that we feel the charm of the woman in spite of the fact that he has exposed her limitations so mercilessly. And she has real charm. There is no question of that. Even after we have discounted the conventional compliments and the flattery of the people who surround her, it is plain that the other characters, including her son, do find her quite definitely charming.

Madame Arkadin's Selfishness. This fact may suggest the need to analyze her selfishness a little further. There is a sense in which she quite really becomes panic-stricken when she thinks of giving up money. Her brother (p. 476a, ll. 33–36) apparently recognizes this. Moreover the adulation which she demands, like the money, is absolutely necessary to her sense of security. It is perhaps not too much to say that Madame Arkadin is really a great actress precisely because of her self-centered nature, because of the very superficiality of her emotions, because she is incapable of the kind of sincerity which, say, Nina or Masha possesses. Toward Madame Arkadin one must take, in part at least, the attitude that one takes toward a rather wayward and naughty but delightful and charming child. In part this is the pathos of her son's situation. His mother's selfishness is the cause of his own distress, and yet he himself simply cannot treat her as another adult person. We find him actually coaxing her and trying to reclaim her as one would a child.

In Act III, the scene of reconciliation between Madame Arkadin and Trigorin is a perfect epitome of their emotional versatility. Finding that Trigorin wishes to be free, she experiences a moment of alarm. But her acting, she finds, is still completely effective: Trigorin in a moment is begging her to take him with her and never to leave him. Reassured, she can immediately become perfectly casual. She can tell him: ". . . if you like, you can stay. . . . After all, why should you be in a hurry?" And Trigorin, a moment later, can be jotting down in his notebook more materials for a story.

To sum up—and perhaps to oversimplify—it is Madame Arkadin and Trigorin, those successful creatures of the brilliant world, those artists who deal daily in emotions, who turn out to be childish, immature, and impervious to the deeper emotions: on the other hand, it is the youthful characters like Nina and Treplev who, in their intensity and their participation in the real drama of experience, are destroyed.

4. THE THEME OF THE TRADITION

We have seen that an important aspect of Treplev's struggle is his attempt to realize himself—to come to terms with his own desires—to find what he wants, and attain it. We have seen how this attempt at self-realization involves the love theme and the art theme. For Treplev, art and love are in some way identified: for Trigorin, on the other hand, art is a craft, almost a trade. But there is a further theme, easy to overlook, which has its importance in Treplev's attempt to find himself. Treplev's mother and uncle are members of a landed aristocracy. Such a society is stable; it has come to terms with itself and lives by a code. Sorin has served the state as a member of such an aristocracy. He is now "Civil Councilor," an official who has, according to Mr. Stark Young's translation, the rank of a rear admiral or a major general. Madame Arkadin, it is true, has married an actor, Treplev's father, and has become an actress herself. But she evidently still thinks of herself as a great lady. Treplev, it is true, does not give himself the airs of an aristocrat. He is not the unthinking conservative. He is young and rebellious. He wants to strike out for himself. Still, he is the heir of a code, even though the code is apparently in decay. Thus, when he is frustrated in his attempt to expose to his mother the ignominy of her choice, and when Trigorin takes his sweetheart from him, the young man falls back on his code. Dishonored, his recourse is to challenge Trigorin to a duel. In terms of the code that is what he should do. But Trigorin refuses to fight: he feels no claim of the code. And Madame Arkadin, though she can mock her son by calling him a "Kiev shopman" when she is angry, does not respect the aristocratic code either. At any rate, she is unwilling to respect her son's appeal to the code. Trigorin, in refusing her son's challenge, does not, in her eyes, become a coward; she does not see her son as a man of honor issuing a challenge, but only as an over-wrought, foolish boy.

The Meaning of Sorin's Life. The decay of the tradition generally is suggested all along through the play by Sorin. Sorin, though he is hardly bitter, recognizes fully the emptiness of his life. He is the statesman who helps manage the state but is at the mercy of his own overseer; the man, living on his own acres, who is bored with the country; the man who has had honors and a "successful" career, but who feels that he has never lived. His frustration, accepted with a kind of genial resignation, serves as a counterpart to his nephew's. But it also suggests the background of Treplev's: for Treplev, the tradition is used up, is spent. He must make his mark as an individual, as a writer, not as a landholder, the representative of a code. But, as far as his experience indicates, the only alternative to the life of his Uncle Sorin, for whom he has sympathy, seems to be that of Trigorin, for whom he has only contempt.

5. THE MULTIPLE FOCUS

Thus far, we have discussed the play as if Treplev were at the center of it, observing how the various conflicts are related directly or indirectly to his conflict (see Section 1 of this analysis). But the student will have noticed that Chekhov himself has not overtly focused the play on Treplev. In his presentation, at least, Treplev does not dominate the play. Nina, Madame Arkadin, Trigorin—all come in for as much attention as Treplev does, and even characters like Masha and Dorn and Polina are much more than types—much more, too, than a mere chorus commenting upon the fortunes of the hero. Indeed, it is easy for the student to feel that Chekhov has failed altogether to provide a focus. Rather, he seems to have presented us with a confusion—a group of characters, each with his problem, at cross purposes with each other. Here, possibly, is the source of the frequent criticism that Chekhov does not have a "plot," that is, a discernible "forward action."

But before we conclude too hastily that the dramatist is confused, we ought to see what relationships emerge upon a sensitive reading or the witnessing of a sensitive presentation of the play on the stage. As we have already seen, important patternings do emerge: there are the frustrated characters and the "successful" ones, and the price paid for this success by the successful ones is pretty clearly suggested. Moreover, among the frustrated characters, there are counterpointings and contrasts. The nature of the frustration varies, and the response to it varies, too. Sorin's response is very different from Treplev's; Masha's, from Nina's.

Chekhov, by refusing to keep our attention mainly on Treplev, has perhaps made his play more difficult; but his method does give him some great advantages. The characters are very solid; some who, like Masha, are not presented at great length, yet appear very real. Moreover, since we learn about the various characters only from their attitudes toward each other— even in small talk, in connection with some casual event—we have no sense of the author's forcing some interpretation on us, oversimplifying a given situation in favor of some thesis about life. We have an unusual sense of the complexity of life as it is observed by the author.

6. COMEDY OR TRAGEDY

But the reader may conceivably feel that with all this complexity Chekhov has no interpretation himself, that the irony which is used so much in this play is an irresponsible and cynical irony. What is Chekhov's attitude toward his characters, after all? Does he see his play as a kind of comedy? Or does he see the general situation as tragic?

On one level, of course, it is thoroughly unimportant whether we decide to call the play a comedy or a tragedy. The play is what it is—good, if it is good; poor, if it is poor; and the affixing of a label, merely as a label, has little significance. But the question is worth answering in so far as it involves the matter of the dramatist's attitude and in so far as it gives us an opportunity to define and state that attitude.

Earlier discussions in this book (cf. p. 110) have already indicated that the mere fact that the play ends with Treplev's death does not in itself commit us to calling the play a tragedy. As we have seen, tragedy requires more than an unhappy ending. Moreover, we have seen that tragedy requires a dominant figure, a hero or protagonist, who is capable of meaningful struggle (cf. pp. 110, 312–14).

He must have a certain force. He must not be weak, merely the passive victim of external forces, but must be able to struggle powerfully with the forces with which he is in opposition. If we take Treplev to be the protagonist, he hardly measures up in this respect. He is sensitive; he realizes what is happening to him, but he hardly has the force or the maturity to make a real struggle of it. And his last act, an act which is decisive for him, is suicide and is therefore essentially negative.

So by these tests *The Sea Gull* is hardly a tragedy. Yet one hesitates to call it a comedy. Very serious issues are involved. If nothing happens to Madame Arkadin and to Trigorin, very much indeed happens to Nina and to Treplev. The lives of both of them are ruined. So, although the comedy contains some satire—that directed, for instance, at popular success in literature—it is still something which cuts much deeper than mere satire; and if it is comedy, it is a wry and sardonic comedy, not a gay and playful one.

What is Chekhov's attitude toward his characters? How seriously does he take them? How seriously does he expect us to take them? The questions are not easy, for the shadings of attitude are such that we shall have to answer with care if we are to give an accurate account of the attitudes. But the answers can be given, for the play itself suggests those attitudes plainly enough to the sensitive reader. And answers to these questions of attitude may allow us to state how the play is related to comedy and to tragedy.

Esthetic Distance. Perhaps the term which makes the best approach to Chekhov's attitude is "esthetic distance." This is not altogether a happy term, but it is difficult to hit upon one that is more accurate. Every dramatist, of course, stands apart from the scene which he portrays: all employ some measure of esthetic distance—some consciousness of the drama as it is viewed in perspective. But Chekhov has here employed a great deal of esthetic distance. As he uses it in this play, however, it is not what it sometimes becomes: a sense of reserve, a high degree of austerity and aloofness. The play gives the sense of informality rather than that of formality.

But in the matter of sympathetic *identification* with the characters, the dramatist holds himself (and his readers) at quite a remove. We are made constantly aware of the youthfulness of Nina and Treplev—of their essentially youthful enthusiasms and youthful despairs. We are constantly reminded that the appraisals of the situation made by these characters must be taken at a discount. Not that we do not "sympathize" with them; not that we feel that their responses are inadequately motivated. Perhaps it is just because we do know so fully the nature of their responses, that we have to discount them as giving "the whole truth."

Something of the same reserve applies also to the mature characters. Madame Arkadin, for example, is in many respects a magnificent woman, and we are willing to believe that she is a great actress: but we simply do not take her outbursts altogether seriously. There is something childlike and even "childish" about her emotional reactions, even though we are aware of the fact that she is self-centered and able to take care of herself in the world which she inhabits. In the same way we see through Trigorin quite as easily as we see through Madame Arkadin—even as Treplev sees through both of them—though we continue to be convinced that Trigorin is a successful writer and a plausible, self-sufficient, intelligent character.

One may sum up with reference to all the characters by saying that the dramatist stands above them all in his knowledge of them, even in a kind of patronage of them, so that the whole group of characters seems a little diminished and reduced. This does not mean that the characters are not real, nor does it mean, as is sometimes hinted, that Chekhov has bathed them in an atmosphere of hopelessness and lethargy. What it does mean is perhaps this: that Chekhov never invites us to identify ourselves with any one of them but rather to view them all from a vantage point of superior knowledge, as it were, with a mixture of pity and ironic understanding.

The Treatment of Dorn. Perhaps some exception from this generalization ought to be made for the character of Dorn. Dorn is more discerning than most of the other characters. It is he alone who senses what Treplev's abortive play was attempting to say. It is he who can comment at the end of the first act: "How hysterical they all are! How hysterical! And what a lot of love. . . . Oh, the sorcery of the lake! What can I do, my child? What? What?" It is he, significantly enough, who discovers Treplev's suicide and who has taken command of the situation as the play ends.

Moreover, it is Dorn alone of the characters who has no "problem" to solve; or, if he has a problem (Polina's love for him), he is the only character who has come to terms with it. (Shamraev, Sorin's steward, hardly counts here, for he is too insensitive, too easily satisfied with ordinary concerns, to have a problem, in any case.) This is not to say that Dorn is Chekhov's mouthpiece or that Chekhov invites us to identify Dorn's judgments with our own. Dorn never becomes a tragic chorus, commenting upon the action, suggesting to us what our response should be.

Indeed, Dorn himself does not fully understand the action which surrounds him. He is perhaps too ready to discount the depth of Polina's yearning, or the full urgency of Sorin's feeling that he has never lived; and, presumably, he too is taken by surprise when Treplev shoots himself. Yet Dorn, though not Chekhov's mouthpiece, can be used to give hints of Chekhov's final attitude. At least he can ward us off from certain misconceptions as to that attitude: that Trigorin is a shallow fool; that Madame Arkadin is merely a hard, selfish woman; that Sorin is just a tiresome valetudinarian, etc.

The dramatist has not played up the pathos. He has not insisted upon the pity of Treplev's plight or of Nina's ruin. But, on the other hand, his detachment is not that of the mere cynic. That is, Chekhov does not see the situation which works itself out with Treplev's death as a meaningless situation in which there are no values and to which the only proper response is a bitter and cynical laugh. Indeed, the sensitive reader may very well feel that the final attitude which the dramatist wishes us as audience to adopt is that of a wise pity—an attitude which takes into account the hurt and failure, and which is alive to the ironies implicit in the situation, and yet which refuses to delude itself [for a moment about the limitations of the pathetic characters as well as the trivialities of the "successful" characters.

QUESTIONS ON *The Sea Gull*

1. Mr. Joseph Wood Krutch has written of *The Sea Gull* that it "is not a mixture of comedy and tragedy. . . . Neither the spirit of tragedy nor the spirit of comedy could include all the variety of incident and character which the play presents. They can only be included within some mood less downright than that of tragedy and comedy, and one of Chekhov's originalities was just his success in creating such a mood." Comment upon this statement, illustrating your commentary from your reading of the play.

2. Can you arrive at a satisfactory symbolic definition of the sea gull? Some suggestion as to its meaning has already been made (Act IV, question 7). Note carefully all the characters who have anything to do with the sea gull. What do you make of Nina's repeatedly saying (in Act IV) that she is the sea gull and then promptly denying it?

3. Is it possible that the lake has a definable symbolic meaning? Note that it is the place where Yakov swims and Trigorin fishes; at the same time it is the backdrop of Treplev's play; and various characters react to it in different ways.

4. Is there any symbolism in the card game? In the storm, which is mentioned several times? In the recurrent problem of the horses? In the stage, especially in the contrast between its condition in Act I and its condition in Act IV? What is indicated about Chekhov's technique by the fact that there appears to be so much symbolic suggestiveness in his various materials? What other dramatist represented in this volume does he appear to resemble in this respect?

5. Would it be possible, in interpreting the play, to regard it largely as a commentary on literature and art? We have already seen, of course, the rather complex meanings implied in the conflict between Treplev and Trigorin. Do Nina and Madame Arkadin act as foils for each other in a similar fashion? Where does the parallelism between pairs or individuals, if there is any, obviously end? If we regard Madame Arkadin as a kind of embodiment of the world of the theater, what is said about that world by the treatment of her in the play? What character or characters seem to be entirely outside the world of art and letters?

6. What part does Sorin play in preventing the play from seeming to be a sardonic commentary on experience? We have seen that he is a kind of symbol of various failures. Yet has he in any way "succeeded," that is, come to any sort of achievement in personality or character which we may regard with considerable sympathy? In what ways is he like Dorn? Different from Dorn?

7. The final stress of our main analysis has been upon the "esthetic distance" of the play, upon the way in which we are invited to engage in a sympathetic and yet, so to speak, nonpartisan contemplation of the fates of the various characters. This result is secured, to a large extent, by a presentation, often ironic, of the pros and cons, that is, of all sides, of the characters. Note how our seeing all sides of the characters is accomplished,

in part, by the presentation of a variety of attitudes to each character. Observe, for instance, how all the characters view and respond to Madam Arkadin, and how Treplev himself changes in his feelings toward her from one moment to another. Make a study, also, of the diverse attitudes to Trigorin and to Treplev, including, in each case, the character's attitude to himself. What is shown by the widely different reactions to Treplev's play?

8. What is ironic in: (a) the relationship between the emotional situations of Masha and her mother? (b) Masha's resolving to tear out her love for Treplev by the roots? (c) Nina's and Treplev's attitude toward the future in Act IV?

9. Is there any consistency in Nina's parents' locking her in in Act I and locking her out in Act IV?

10. What seems to be the relationship between love and art in Treplev and Trigorin respectively?

11. Various characters in the play, notably Treplev and Nina, face "problems." Would it be suitable, however, to describe the play as a problem play? Is the play topical—that is, is it concerned with issues peculiar to a certain time and place? Or do its values transcend the historical and local?

The Sea Gull AND SHAKESPEARE'S Hamlet

In the text of The Sea Gull, as we have seen, there are several direct references to Hamlet (and these suggest questions which have already been asked). It is therefore clear that, to some extent at least, Chekov had Shakespeare's play in mind when he was working on his own play. Hence it should be profitable for the student to read Hamlet carefully and to try to see in what ways, if any, each play sheds some light on the other.

1. Allowing for all the differences of external detail, is there any essential resemblance between the situation of Hamlet and that of Treplev? Compare them in age, in temperament, in imaginative qualities, and in terms of the types of people against whom they must contend. What is it that leads them either to contemplate or to seek death? If we may say that both are frustrated characters, to what extent do the two frustrations differ from or resemble each other?

2. May it perhaps be said that in each play we see a young man of ideals coming to grips with an adult, actual world-as-it-is, with its compromises, its insensitiveness, and even its downright evil? If so, how does the practical, adult world of Shakespeare's play differ from that of Chekhov's play? How does the relationship between Claudius and Hamlet's mother differ from that between Trigorin and Madam Arkadin? Note, in this connection, the attitudes of other characters besides the sons to the mothers' relationships with men. What is it that Claudius and Gertrude really want of Hamlet at the start? See I. ii, 66 ff.

3. Compare the two mother-son relationships. Which mother is stronger, more able to control situations? Less sensitive or less impressionable?

4. Trigorin has not, of course, committed a murder as Claudius has. But is it possible to conceive of him as having killed something that Treplev has idealized in the same way that Hamlet idealizes his father? As we have already seen, Chekhov does not make Trigorin into a "villain," that is, in this case, into a stupid, wholly unprincipled writer. How does this parallel Shakespeare's treatment of Claudius? What does Shakespeare do to make Claudius something more than a melodrama villain?

5. We have spoken of Treplev as representing, to some extent, "tradition." In which of these two plays does tradition play a stronger part in forming the plot?

6. We have spoken of the possibility of considering the plays as studies in the clash of idealism and worldliness (always keeping in mind that the latter term has to be somewhat differently defined for each play). How does Polonius fit into the category of worldly people? May he be taken as a kind of parody of worldly prudence, as an example of the "practical" man gone completely to seed? How correctly does he perceive things in those situations in which he believes himself to be very discerning? Can he go beneath the surface? Does he get even the surface right? Note how we go from a ludicrous to a tragic extreme as we observe the different members in a chain relationship: Polonius checks up on Laertes, who checks up on Claudius and Hamlet, who are checking up on each other (compare the chain of unsuccessful lovers in *The Sea Gull*). What has Laertes' worldliness done to him? Notice that he is much concerned about the family "honor"; but is he much concerned to act honorably?

7. What is the difference between "the way of the world" as it is understood by Shakespeare and by Congreve? Does the difference in attitudes provide us with a basic means of distinguishing between comedy and tragedy?

8. Is there any relationship between the attitude of Nina's parents to her, and that of Polonius and Laertes to Ophelia? What have Nina and Ophelia in common? Which of the two characters is the stronger? With regard to Polonius' and Laertes' management of Ophelia's affairs, is their "worldly" view of Hamlet's attitude to her as sound as Ophelia's inexperienced, instinctive view of that attitude?

9. What is the irony of Treplev's referring to Trigorin as Hamlet in Act II (p. 470)? Is there still further irony in that Trigorin can on occasion exhibit a Hamlet-like introspective quality?

10. Which play appears to go further in suggesting profound problems of good and evil? Does either one tend to deal with its materials on the psychological rather than the moral level?

11. In view of the matters already discussed or suggested, may it be said that Chekhov has domesticated, and transposed into realistic middle-class terms, the Hamlet situation? That he has removed the violent and heroic, and to an extent the philosophical, aspects and thus worked toward some other effect than the tragic? What, then, is the value of the comparison with *Hamlet*? Can it be said to do two things: show us how Chekhov veers from tragedy, and give us additional clues to the meaning of *The Sea Gull*?

3. Marlowe, *Dr. Faustus*

CHRISTOPHER MARLOWE'S *The Tragical History of Doctor Faustus* (ca. 1588) is often spoken of as illustrating the author's remarkable skill (he was no more than twenty-four years old at the time) in the delineation of heroic character and in the use of blank verse, which became the standard verse form for Elizabethan tragedy. The student will of course find his attention focused primarily upon the development of the complex character of Doctor Faustus through the scenes in which his sharp inner conflict is especially observable. But the poetry, which has been much praised, should not be thought of as a separate matter. In fact, Marlowe's imagery is a very important means of presenting Faustus's psychological states, and the student should observe it carefully from the beginning. The questions which constitute a considerable part of the final discussion are intended especially to assist the student in tracing the patterns of imagery from scene to scene and in discovering their implications.

Instead of the classical five-act form which had come into general use by his time, Marlowe uses a form not unlike that of *Everyman*. The present arrangement of scenes is a conventional one which has been used since the nineteenth century. In view of the relative brevity of the scenes and of the play as a whole, it has seemed preferable to place all discussion of and questions on individual scenes at the end of the play.

THE TRAGICAL HISTORY OF DOCTOR FAUSTUS

DRAMATIS PERSONÆ

THE POPE
CARDINAL OF LORRAINE
THE EMPEROR OF GERMANY
DUKE OF VANHOLT
FAUSTUS
VALDES, } friends to FAUSTUS
CORNELIUS, }
WARNER, servant to FAUSTUS
CLOWN
ROBIN
RALPH
Vintner
Horse-courser
A Knight

An Old Man
Scholars, Friars, and Attendants
DUCHESS OF VANHOLT
LUCIFER
BELZEBUB
MEPHISTOPHILIS
Good Angel
Evil Angel
The Seven Deadly Sins
Devils
Spirits in the shapes of ALEXANDER THE GREAT, of his Paramour, and of HELEN OF TROY
Chorus

[Enter Chorus.]

Chorus: Not marching now in fields
of Thrasimene,[1]
Where Mars did mate [2] the Cartha-
ginians;
Nor sporting in the dalliance of love;
In courts of kings where state is over-
turned;
Nor in the pomp of proud audacious
deeds,   5
Intends our Muse to vaunt his heavenly
verse:
Only this, gentlemen—we must perform
The form of Faustus' fortunes, good or
bad:
To patient judgments we appeal our
plaud,[3]   9
And speak for Faustus in his infancy.
Now is he born, his parents base of
stock,
In Germany, within a town called
Rhodes:
Of riper years, to Wittenberg [4] he went,
Whereas [5] his kinsmen chiefly brought
him up.
So soon he profits in divinity,[6]   15
The fruitful plot of scholarism graced,
That shortly he was graced with doc-
tor's name,
Excelling all whose sweet delight dis-
putes
In heavenly matters of theology;
Till swoln with cunning, of a self-con-
ceit,[7]   20
His waxen wings did mount above his
reach,
And, melting, heavens conspired his
overthrow; [8]
For, falling to a devilish exercise,
And glutted now with learning's golden
gifts,   24
He surfeits upon cursed necromancy; [9]
Nothing so sweet as magic is to him,

[1] Italian lake, where Hannibal defeated
Romans in 217 B.C. [2] Ally himself with. [3] For
applause. [4] The university. [5] Where. [6] Advances in theology. [7] Self-confidently swollen
with learning. [8] Like Icarus of Greek legend,
Faustus attempted to fly too high. [9] Black
magic.

Which he prefers before his chiefest
bliss:
And this the man that in his study sits.
[Exit.]

SCENE I. FAUSTUS'S STUDY

[Faustus discovered.]

Faustus: Settle thy studies, Faustus,
and begin
To sound the depth of that thou wilt
profess: [1]
Having commenced, be a divine in
show,[2]
Yet level at the end of every art,[3]
And live and die in Aristotle's works.
Sweet Analytics,[4] 'tis thou hast ravished
me!   6
Bene disserere est finis logices.[5]
Is, to dispute well, logic's chiefest end?
Affords this art no greater miracle?
Then read no more; thou hast attained
that end.   10
A greater subject fitteth Faustus' wit:
Bid *ὀὐ καὶ μὴ ὀὐ* [6] farewell, and Galen [7]
come,
Seeing, *Ubi desinit philosophus, ibi in-
cipit medicus:* [8]
Be a physician, Faustus; heap up gold,
And be eternized for some wondrous
cure!   15
Summum bonum medicinae sanitas.
The end of physic is our body's health.
Why, Faustus, hast thou not attained
that end?
Is not thy common talk sound apho-
risms? [9]
Are not thy bills [10] hung up as monu-
ments,   20
Whereby whole cities have escaped the
plague,
And thousand desp'rate maladies been
eased?
Yet art thou still but Faustus, and a
man.

[1] Teach. [2] Public. [3] Aim at all knowledge.
[4] Logic. [5] To dispute well is the end of logic.
[6] Being and not being. [7] Greek medical writer
of second century. [8] Where the philospher
stops, the physician begins. [9] Medical rules.
[10] Prescriptions.

Couldst thou make men to live eternally,
Or, being dead, raise them to life again,
Then this profession were to be esteemed.   26
Physic, farewell! Where is Justinian? [11]
                    [*Reads*]
*Si una eademque res legatur duobus, alter
rem, alter valorem rei, etc.*[12]
A pretty case of paltry legacies! [*Reads.*]
*Exhaereditare filium non potest pater,
nisi, etc.*[13]   30
Such is the subject of the Institute,
And universal body of the law:
This study fits a mercenary drudge,
Who aims at nothing but external trash;
Too servile and illiberal for me.   35
When all is done, divinity is best:
Jerome's Bible,[14] Faustus; view it well.
                    [*Reads.*]
Stipendium peccati mors est.[15] Ha! *Stipendium, etc.*
The reward of sin is death: that's hard.
                    [*Reads.*]
*Si peccasse negamus, fallimur, et nulla
est in nobis veritas:* [16]   40
If we say that we have no sin, we deceive ourselves, and there's no
truth in us.
Why, then, belike,
We must sin, and so consequently die.
Aye, we must die an everlasting death.
What doctrine call you this, *Che sera,
sera:*   45
What will be, shall be? Divinity, adieu!
These metaphysics of magicians,
And necromantic books are heavenly;
Lines, circles, scenes, letters, and characters;
Aye, these are those that Faustus most
desires.   50
O, what a world of profit and delight,
Of power, of honor, of omnipotence,
Is promised to the studious artizan!

[11] Roman emperor who codified law. [12] If
one and the same thing is willed to two
people, one receives the thing, the other the
value of the thing, etc. [13] A father cannot
disinherit a son unless, etc. [14] Latin translation, called the Vulgate. [15] Romans 6:23.
[16] I John 1:8.

All things that move between the quiet
poles
Shall be at my command: emperors and
kings   55
Are but obeyed in their several provinces,
Nor can they raise the wind, or rend
the clouds;
But his dominion that exceeds [17] in
this,
Stretcheth as far as doth the mind of
man;
A sound magician is a mighty god: 60
Here, Faustus, try thy brains to gain a
deity!
Wagner!
                    [*Enter Wagner.*]
Commend me to my dearest friends,
The German Valdes and Cornelius;
Request them earnestly to visit me. 65
  Wagner: I will, sir.   [*Exit.*]
  Faustus: Their conference will be a
greater help to me
Than all my labors, plod I ne'er so fast.
  [*Enter Good Angel and Evil Angel.*]
  Good Angel: O, Faustus, lay that
damnéd book aside,
And gaze not on it, lest it tempt thy
soul,   70
And heap God's heavy wrath upon thy
head!
Read, read the Scriptures:—that is
blasphemy.
  Evil Angel: Go forward, Faustus, in
that famous art
Wherein all Nature's treasure is contained:
Be thou on earth as Jove is in the sky,
Lord and commander of these elements.
                    [*Exeunt Angels.*]
  Faustus: How am I glutted with conceit [18] of this!   77
Shall I make spirits fetch me what I
please,
Resolve me of all ambiguities,[19]
Perform what desperate enterprise I
will?   80
I'll have them fly to India for gold,
Ransack the ocean for orient pearl,

[17] Excels. [18] Thought. [19] Settle all problems.

And search all corners of the new-found
world
For pleasant fruits and princely deli-
cates;
I'll have them read me strange phi-
losophy,   85
And tell the secrets of all foreign kings;
I'll have them wall all Germany with
brass,
And make swift Rhine circle fair
Wittenberg;
I'll have them fill the public schools
with silk,
Wherewith the students shall be bravely
clad;   90
I'll levy soldiers with the coin they
bring,
And chase the Prince of Parma [20] from
our land,
And reign sole king of all our provinces;
Yea, stranger engines for the brunt of
war,
Than was the fiery keel at Antwerp's
bridge,[21]   95
I'll make my servile spirits to invent.
Come, German Valdes, and Cornelius,
And make me blest with your sage
conference!
[*Enter Valdes and Cornelius.*]
Valdes, sweet Valdes, and Cornelius,
Know that your words have won me at
the last   100
To practice magic and concealed arts:
Yet not your words only, but mine own
fantasy,
That will receive no object;[22] for my
head
But ruminates on necromantic skill.
Philosophy is odious and obscure;   105
Both law and physic are for petty wits;
Divinity is basest of the three,
Unpleasant, harsh, contemptible, and
vile:
'Tis magic, magic, that hath ravished
me.
Then, gentle friends, aid me in this
attempt;   110

And I, that have with concise syllogisms
Gravelled [23] the pastors of the German
church,
And made the flowering pride of
Wittenberg
Swarm to my problems,[24] as the infernal
spirits
On sweet Musaeus [25] when he came to
hell,   115
Will be as cunning as Agrippa [26] was,
Whose shadows made all Europe honor
him.
Valdes: Faustus, these books, thy wit,
and our experience,
Shall make all nations to canonize us.
As Indian Moors [27] obey their Spanish
lords,   12c
So shall the subjects of every element
Be always serviceable to us three;
Like lions shall they guard us when we
please;
Like Almain rutters [28] with their horse-
men's staves,
Or Lapland giants, trotting by our
sides;   125
Sometimes like women, or unwedded
maids,
Shadowing more beauty in their airy
brows
Than have the white breasts of the
queen of love:
From Venice shall they drag huge
argosies,
And from America the golden fleece
That yearly stuffs old Philip's treasury;
If learnéd Faustus will be resolute. 132
Faustus: Valdes, as resolute am I in
this
As thou to live: therefore object [29] it not.
Cornelius: The miracles that magic
will perform   135
Will make thee vow to study nothing
else.
He that is grounded in astrology,
Enriched with tongues, well seen [30] in
minerals,

[20] The Prince ruled the Netherlands for
Spain. [21] A fire ship used by the Dutch
against a Parma-held bridge. [22] Admit no
objection. [23] Put down, confounded. [24] Discussions.
[25] Poet; see *Aeneid* VI, 667. [26] Cornelius
Agrippa, 1486–1535, German philosopher
and physician. [27] American Indians. [28] German horsemen. [29] Bring up. [30] Learned.

Hath all the principles magic doth require:
Then doubt not, Faustus, but to be renowned, 140
And more frequented for this mystery
Than heretofore the Delphian oracle.
The spirits tell me they can dry the sea,
And fetch the treasure of all foreign wrecks,
Aye, all the wealth that our forefathers hid 145
Within the massy entrails of the earth:
Then tell me, Faustus, what shall we three want?
Faustus: Nothing, Cornelius. O, this cheers my soul!
Come, show me some demonstrations magical,
That I may conjure in some lusty [31] grove, 150
And have these joys in full possession.
Valdes: Then haste thee to some solitary grove,
And bear wise Bacon's [32] and Albanus' [33] works,
The Hebrew Psalter, and New Testament,
And whatsoever else is requisite 155
We will inform thee ere our conference cease.
Cornelius: Valdes, first let him know the words of art;
And then, all other ceremonies learned,
Faustus may try his cunning by himself.
Valdes: First I'll instruct thee in the rudiments, 160
And then wilt thou be perfecter than I.
Faustus: Then come and dine with me and, after meat,
We'll canvass every quiddity [34] thereof;
For, ere I sleep, I'll try what I can do:
This night I'll conjure, though I die therefore. [*Exeunt.*]

---

[31] Pleasant. [32] Roger Bacon (1214?-1294), philosopher and alchemist. [33] Reference uncertain. [34] Fine point.

SCENE II. BEFORE FAUSTUS'S HOUSE

[*Enter Two Scholars.*]

First Scholar: I wonder what's become of Faustus, that was wont to make our schools ring with *sic probo.*[1]
Second Scholar: That shall we know; for see, here comes his boy. 5
[*Enter Wagner.*]
First Scholar: How now, sirrah! where's thy master?
Wagner: God in heaven knows.
Second Scholar: Why, dost not thou know? 10
Wagner: Yes, I know; but that follows not.
First Scholar: Go to, sirrah! leave your jesting, and tell us where he is. 14
Wagner: That follows not necessary by force of argument, that you, being licentiate,[2] should stand upon 't: therefore acknowledge your error, and be attentive.
Second Scholar: Why, didst thou not say thou knewest? 21
Wagner: Have you any witness on 't?
First Scholar: Yes, sirrah, I heard you.
Wagner: Ask my fellow if I be a thief. 25
Second Scholar: Well, you will not tell us?
Wagner: Yes, sir, I will tell you: yet, if you were not dunces, you would never ask me such a question; for is not he *corpus naturale?*[3] and is not that *mobile?*[4] then wherefore should you ask me such a question? But that I am by nature phlegmatic, slow to wrath, and prone to lechery (to love, I would say), it were not for you to come within forty foot of the place of execution, although I do not doubt to see you both hanged the next sessions. Thus having triumphed over you, I will set my countenance like a precisian,[5] and begin to speak thus:—Truly, my dear brethren, my master is within at dinner, with

---

[1] Thus I prove. [2] Having a degree. [3] Physical body. [4] Movable. [5] Puritan.

Valdes and Cornelius, as this wine, if it could speak, it would inform your worships: and so, the Lord bless you, preserve you, and keep you, my dear brethren, my dear brethren! [*Exit.*]

First Scholar: Nay, then, I fear he is fallen into that damned art for which they two are infamous through the world. 52

Second Scholar: Were he a stranger, and not allied to me, yet should I grieve for him. But, come, let us go and inform the Rector,[6] and see if he by his grave counsel can reclaim him.

First Scholar: O, but I fear me nothing can reclaim him! 59

Second Scholar: Yet let us try what we can do. [*Exeunt.*]

SCENE III. A GROVE

[*Enter Faustus to conjure.*]

Faustus: Now that the gloomy shadow of the earth,
Longing to view Orion's drizzling look,
Leaps from th' Antarctic world unto the sky,
And dims the welkin with her pitchy breath,
Faustus, begin thine incantations, 5
And try if devils will obey thy hest,
Seeing thou has prayed and sacrificed to them.
Within this circle is Jehovah's name,
Forward and backward anagrammatized,[1]
The breviated names of holy saints, 10
Figures of every adjunct[2] to the heavens,
And characters of signs and erring[3] stars,
By which the spirits are enforced to rise:
Then fear not, Faustus, but be resolute,
And try the uttermost magic can perform.— 15

[6] Head of the university.
[1] Made into an anagram (by scrambling the letters). [2] Star. [3] Moving.

Sint mihi dei Acherontis propitii! Valeat numen triplex Jehovae! Ignei, aerii, aquatani spiritus, salvete! Orientis princeps Belzebub, inferni ardentis monarcha, et Demogorgon, propitiamus vos, ut appareat et surgat Mephistophilis. Quid tu moraris? Per Jehovam, Gehennam, et consecratam aquam quam nunc spargo, signumque crucis quod nunc facio, et per vota nostra, ipse nunc surgat nobis dicatus Mephistophilis![4] 26

[*Enter Mephistophilis.*]

I charge thee to return, and change thy shape;
Thou art too ugly to attend on me:
Go, and return an old Franciscan friar;
That holy shape becomes a devil best.

[*Exit Mephistophilis.*]

I see there's virtue in my heavenly words: 31
Who would not be proficient in this art?
How pliant is this Mephistophilis,
Full of obedience and humility! 34
Such is the force of magic and my spells:
No, Faustus, thou art conjuror laureat,
That canst command great Mephistophilis:

Quin regis Mephistophilis fratris imagine.[5]

[*Re-enter Mephistophilis like a Franciscan friar.*]

Mephistophilis: Now, Faustus, what wouldst thou have me do?

Faustus: I charge thee wait upon me whilst I live, 40
To do whatever Faustus shall command,
Be it to make the moon drop from her sphere,
Or th' ocean to overwhelm the world.

[4] May the Gods of Acheron be propitious to me. May the triple divinity of Jehovah work. Hail, spirits of fire, air, water. Belzebub, prince of the East, monarch of the burning lower world, and Demogorgon, we propitiate you, that Mephistophilis may appear and rise. Why do you delay? By Jehovah, Gehenna, and the holy water which I now sprinkle, and the sign of the cross which I now make, and by our prayers, may Mephistophilis himself, having been called, now rise to us. [5] Indeed you rule in the image of your brother Mephistophilis.

Mephistophilis: I am a servant to great Lucifer,
And may not follow thee without his leave: 45
No more than he commands must we perform.
  Faustus: Did not he charge thee to appear to me?
  Mephistophilis: No, I came hither of mine own accord.
  Faustus: Did not my conjuring speeches raise thee? speak.
  Mephistophilis: That was the cause, but yet *per accidens;* [6]   50
For, when we hear one rack [7] the name of God,
Abjure the Scriptures and his Savior Christ,
We fly, in hope to get his glorious soul;
Nor will we come, unless he use such means   54
Whereby he is in danger to be damned.
Therefore the shortest cut for conjuring
Is stoutly to abjure the Trinity,
And pray devoutly to the prince of hell.
  Faustus: So Faustus hath   59
Already done; and holds this principle,
There is no chief but only Belzebub;
To whom Faustus doth dedicate himself.
This word "damnation" terrifies him not,
For he confounds hell in Elysium: [8]   64
His ghost be with the old philosophers!
But, leaving these vain trifles of men's souls,
Tell me what is that Lucifer thy lord?
  Mephistophilis: Arch-regent and commander of all spirits.
  Faustus: Was not that Lucifer an angel once?
  Mephistophilis: Yes, Faustus, and most dearly loved of God.   70
  Faustus: How comes it, then, that he is prince of devils?
  Mephistophilis: O, by aspiring pride and insolence;

For which God threw him from the face of heaven.
  Faustus: And what are you that live with Lucifer?
  Mephistophilis: Unhappy spirits that fell with Lucifer,   75
Conspired against our God with Lucifer,
And are for ever damned with Lucifer.
  Faustus: Where are you damned?
  Mephistophilis: In hell.
  Faustus: How comes it, then, that thou art out of hell?   80
  Mephistophilis: Why, this is hell, nor am I out of it:
Think'st thou that I, who saw the face of God,
And tasted the eternal joys of heaven,
Am not tormented with ten thousand hells,   84
In being deprived of everlasting bliss?
O, Faustus, leave these frivolous demands,
Which strike a terror to my fainting soul!
  Faustus: What, is great Mephistophilis so passionate [9]
For being deprived of the joys of heaven?   89
Learn thou of Faustus manly fortitude,
And scorn those joys thou never shalt possess.
Go bear these tidings to great Lucifer:
Seeing Faustus hath incurred eternal death
By desp'rate thoughts against Jove's deity,   94
Say, he surrenders up to him his soul,
So he will spare him four and twenty years,
Letting him live in all voluptuousness;
Having thee ever to attend on me,
To give me whatsoever I shall ask,
To tell me whatsoever I demand,   100
To slay mine enemies, and aid my friends,
And always be obedient to my will.
Go and return to mighty Lucifer,
And meet me in my study at midnight,
And then resolve [10] me of thy master's mind.   105

[6] Incidentally. [7] Twist or torture; possibly, make an anagram of. [8] He cannot distinguish hell and Elysium—the abode, in Greek mythology, of blessed souls.

[9] Disturbed. [10] Inform.

Mephistophilis: I will, Faustus.

[*Exit.*]

Faustus: Had I as many souls as there be stars,
I'd give them all for Mephistophilis.
By him I'll be great emp'ror of the world,
And make a bridge thorough the moving air,　110
To pass the ocean with a band of men;
I'll join the hills that bind the Afric shore,
And make that country continent [11] to Spain,
And both contributory to my crown:
The Emp'ror shall not live but by my leave,　115
Nor any potentate of Germany.
Now that I have obtained what I desired,
I'll live in speculation of this art,
Till Mephistophilis return again.

SCENE IV. A STREET

[*Enter Wagner and Clown.*]

Wagner: Sirrah boy, come hither.
Clown: How, boy! swowns, boy! I hope you have seen many boys with such pickadevaunts [1] as I have. Boy, quotha!　5
Wagner: Tell me, sirrah, hast thou any comings in? [2]
Clown: Aye, and goings out too. You may see else.　9
Wagner: Alas, poor slave! see how poverty jesteth in his nakedness! the villain is bare and out of service, and so hungry, that I know he would give his soul to the devil for a shoulder of mutton, though it were blood-raw.　15
Clown: How! my soul to the devil for a shoulder of mutton, though 'twere blood-raw! not so, good friend: by'r lady, I had need have it well roasted, and good sauce to it, if I pay so dear.　20
Wagner: Well, wilt thou serve me, and

[11] Touching.
[1] Pointed beards. [2] Income.

I'll make thee go like *Qui mihi discipulus?* [3]
Clown: How, in verse?
Wagner: No, sirrah; in beaten silk and staves-acre. [4]　26
Clown: How, how, Knave's-acre! [5] aye, I thought that was all the land his father left him. Do ye hear? I would be sorry to rob you of your living.　30
Wagner: Sirrah, I say in staves-acre.
Clown: Oho, oho, staves-acre! why, then, belike, if I were your man, I should be full of vermin.　34
Wagner: So thou shalt, whether thou beest with me or no. But, sirrah, leave your jesting, and bind yourself presently unto me for seven years, or I'll turn all the lice about thee into familiars, [6] and they shall tear thee in pieces.　40
Clown: Do you hear, sir? you may save that labor; they are too familiar with me already: swowns, they are as bold with my flesh as if they had paid for my meat and drink.　45
Wagner: Well, do you hear, sirrah? hold, take these guilders.

[*Gives money.*]

Clown: Gridirons, what be they?
Wagner: Why, French crowns.　49
Clown: Mass, but for the name of French crowns, a man were as good have as many English counters. [7] And what should I do with these?
Wagner: Why, now, sirrah, thou art at an hour's warning, whensoever and wheresoever the devil shall fetch thee.
Clown: No, no; here, take your gridirons again.　58
Wagner: Truly, I'll none of them.
Clown: Truly, but you shall.
Wagner: Bear witness I gave them him.
Clown: Bear witness I gave them you again.
Wagner: Well, I will cause two devils presently to fetch thee away.—Baliol and Belcher!　67

[3] Who is my pupil (a song). [4] Larkspur, used to destroy lice. [5] A narrow London street. [6] Familiar spirits. [7] Counterfeit or debased coins.

Clown: Let your Baliol and your Belcher come here, and I'll knock them, they were never so knocked since they were devils: say I should kill one of them, what would folks say? "Do ye see yonder tall fellow in the round slop?[8] he has killed the devil." So I should be called Kill-devil all the parish over. 76

[*Enter two Devils; and the Clown runs up and down crying.*]

Wagner: Baliol and Belcher—spirits, away! [*Exeunt Devils.*]

Clown: What, are they gone? a vengeance on them! they have vile long nails. There was a he-devil and a she-devil: I'll tell you how you shall know them; all he-devils has horns, and all she-devils has clefts and cloven feet.

Wagner: Well, sirrah, follow me. 85

Clown: But, do you hear? if I should serve you, would you teach me to raise up Banios and Belcheos?

Wagner: I will teach thee to turn thyself to any thing, to a dog, or a cat, or a mouse, or a rat, or anything. 91

Clown: How! a Christian fellow to a dog, or a cat, a mouse, or a rat! no, no, sir; if you turn me into anything, let it be into the likeness of a little pretty frisking flea, that I may be here and there and everywhere. O, I'll tickle the pretty wenches' plackets; I'll be amongst them, i' faith.

Wagner: Well, sirrah, come. 100

Clown: But, do you hear, Wagner?

Wagner: How!—Baliol and Belcher!

Clown: O Lord, I pray, sir, let Banio and Belcher go sleep. 104

Wagner: Villain, call me Master Wagner, and let thy left eye be diametarily[9] fixed upon my right heel, with *quasi vestigias nostras insistere.*[10]
[*Exit.*]

Clown: God forgive me, he speaks Dutch fustian.[11] Well, I'll follow him; I'll serve him, that's flat. [*Exit.*]

[8] Loose breeches. [9] Diametrically. [10] As though to stand in our footsteps. [11] Jargon.

SCENE V. FAUSTUS'S STUDY

[*Faustus discovered.*]

Faustus: Now, Faustus, must
Thou needs be damned, and canst thou not be saved;
What boots it, then, to think of God or heaven?
Away with such vain fancies, and despair;
Despair in God, and trust in Belzebub:
Now go not backward; no, Faustus, be resolute: 6
Why waver'st thou? O, something soundeth in mine ears,
"Abjure this magic, turn to God again!"
Aye, and Faustus will turn to God again.
To God? he loves thee not; 10
The god thou serv'st is thine own appetite,
Wherein is fixed the love of Belzebub:
To him I'll build an altar and a church,
And offer lukewarm blood of new-born babes.

[*Enter Good Angel and Evil Angel.*]

Good Angel: Sweet Faustus, leave that execrable art. 15

Faustus: Contrition, prayer, repentance—what of them?

Good Angel: O, they are means to bring thee unto heaven!

Evil Angel: Rather illusions, fruits of lunacy,
That makes men foolish that do trust them most.

Good Angel: Sweet Faustus, think of heaven and heavenly things. 20

Evil Angel: No, Faustus; think of honor and of wealth.
[*Exeunt Angels.*]

Faustus: Of wealth!
Why, the signiory of Emden[1] shall be mine.
When Mephistophilis shall stand by me,
What god can hurt thee, Faustus? thou art safe: 25
Cast no more doubts.—Come Mephistophilis,
And bring glad tidings from great Lucifer;—

[1] Control of an important German city.

Is 't not midnight?—come, Mephistophilis,
Veni, veni, Mephistophile! [2]
[Enter Mephistophilis.]
Now tell me what says Lucifer, thy lord?   30
Mephistophilis: That I shall wait on Faustus while he lives,
So he will buy my service with his soul.
Faustus: Already Faustus hath hazarded that for thee.
Mephistophilis: But, Faustus, thou must bequeath it solemnly,
And write a deed of gift with thine own blood;   35
For that security craves great Lucifer.
If thou deny it, I will back to hell.
Faustus: Stay, Mephistophilis, and tell me, what good
Will my soul do thy lord?   39
Mephistophilis: Enlarge his kingdom.
Faustus: Is that the reason why he tempts us thus?
Mephistophilis: Solamen miseris socios habuisse doloris.[3]
Faustus: Why, have you any pain that [4] torture others?
Mephistophilis: As great as have the human souls of men.
But tell me, Faustus, shall I have thy soul?   45
And I will be thy slave, and wait on thee,
And give thee more than thou hast wit to ask.
Faustus: Aye, Mephistophilis, I give it thee.
Mephistophilis: Then, Faustus, stab thine arm courageously,
And bind thy soul, that at some certain day   50
Great Lucifer may claim it as his own;
And then be thou as great as Lucifer.
Faustus: [Stabbing his arm.] Lo, Mephistophilis, for love of thee,
I cut mine arm, and with my proper blood
Assure my soul to be great Lucifer's,

Chief lord and regent of perpetual night!   56
View here the blood that trickles from mine arm,
And let it be propitious for my wish.
Mephistophilis: But, Faustus, thou must
Write it in manner of a deed of gift.
Faustus: Aye, so I will. [Writes.]
But, Mephistophilis,   61
My blood congeals, and I can write no more.
Mephistophilis: I'll fetch thee fire to dissolve it straight.   [Exit.]
Faustus: What might the staying of my blood portend?
Is it unwilling I should write this bill?
Why streams it not, that I may write afresh?   66
Faustus gives to thee his soul: ah, there it stayed!
Why shouldst thou not? is not thy soul thine own?
Then write again, Faustus gives to thee his soul.
[Re-enter Mephistophilis with a chafer [5] of coals.]
Mephistophilis: Here's fire; come, Faustus, set it on.   70
Faustus: So, now the blood begins to clear again;
Now will I make an end immediately.
[Writes.]
Mephistophilis: O, what will not I do to obtain his soul?   [Aside.]
Faustus: Consummatum est; [6] this bill is ended,
And Faustus hath bequeathed his soul to Lucifer.   75
But what is this inscription on mine arm?
Homo, fuge: [7] whither should I fly?
If unto God, he'll throw me down to hell.
My senses are deceived; here's nothing writ:—   79
I see it plain; here in this place is writ,
Homo, fuge: yet shall not Faustus fly.
Mephistophilis: I'll fetch him some-

[2] Come, come, Mephistophilis. [3] The solace for the wretched is to have company in grief. [4] You is the antecedent of that.

[5] Heater. [6] It is finished; cf. John 19:30. [7] Man, fly.

what to delight his mind. [*Aside, and then exit.*]
[*Re-enter Mephistophilis with Devils, who give crowns and rich apparel to Faustus, dance, and then depart.*]
Faustus: Speak, Mephistophilis, what means this show?
Mephistophilis: Nothing, Faustus, but to delight thy mind withal,
And to show thee what magic can perform.   85
Faustus: But may I raise up spirits when I please?
Mephistophilis: Aye, Faustus, and do greater things than these.
Faustus: Then there's enough for a thousand souls.
Here, Mephistophilis, receive this scroll,
A deed of gift of body and of soul: 90
But yet conditionally that thou perform
All articles prescribed between us both.
Mephistophilis: Faustus, I swear by hell and Lucifer
To effect all promises between us made!
Faustus: Then hear me read them.
[*Reads.*] *On these conditions following. First, that Faustus may be a spirit in form and substance. Secondly, that Mephistophilis shall be his servant, and at his command. Thirdly, that Mephistophilis shall do for him, and bring him whatsoever [he desires]. Fourthly, that he shall be in his chamber or house invisible. Lastly, that he shall appear to the said John Faustus, at all times, in what form or shape soever he please. I, John Faustus, of Wittenberg, Doctor, by these presents, do give both body and soul to Lucifer prince of the east, and his minister Mephistophilis; and furthermore grant unto them that, twenty-four years being expired, the articles abovewritten inviolate, full power to fetch or carry the said John Faustus, body and soul, flesh, blood, or goods, into their habitation wheresoever.*   116
By me, JOHN FAUSTUS.
Mephistophilis: Speak, Faustus, do you deliver this as your deed?

Faustus: Aye, take it, and the devil give thee good on 't.
Mephistophilis: Now, Faustus, ask what thou wilt.   120
Faustus: First will I question with thee about hell.
Tell me, where is the place that men call hell?
Mephistophilis: Under the heavens.
Faustus: Aye, but whereabout?
Mephistophilis: Within the bowels of these elements,   125
Where we are tortured and remain for ever:
Hell hath no limits, nor is circumscribed
In one self place; for where we are is hell,
And where hell is, there must we ever be:
And, to conclude, when all the world dissolves,   130
And every creature shall be purified,
All places shall be hell that are not heaven.
Faustus: Come, I think hell's a fable.
Mephistophilis: Aye, think so still. till experience change thy mind.
Faustus: Why, think'st thou, then, that Faustus shall be damned? 135
Mephistophilis: Aye, of necessity, for here's the scroll
Wherein thou hast given thy soul to Lucifer.
Faustus: Aye, and body too: but what of that?
Think'st thou that Faustus is so fond to [8] imagine
That, after this life, there is any pain?
Tush, these are trifles and mere old wives' tales.   141
Mephistophilis: But, Faustus, I am an instance to prove the contrary;
For I am damned, and am now in hell.
Faustus: How! now in hell!
Nay, an [9] this be hell, I'll willingly be damned here: 145
What! walking, disputing, etc.
But, leaving off this, let me have a wife,
The fairest maid in Germany;

---

[8] Foolish as to. [9] If.

For I am wanton and lascivious,
And cannot live without a wife.　150
Mephistophilis: How! a wife!
I prithee, Faustus, talk not of a wife.
Faustus: Nay, sweet Mephistophilis,
fetch me one; for I will have one.
Mephistophilis: Well, thou wilt have
one. Sit there till I come:　155
I'll fetch thee a wife in the devil's
　name.　[*Exit.*]
[*Re-enter Mephistophilis with a
Devil dressed like a Woman, with
fireworks.*]
Mephistophilis: Tell me, Faustus, how
dost thou like thy wife?
Faustus: A plague on her for a hot
　whore!
Mephistophilis. Tut, Faustus,　160
Marriage is but a ceremonial toy;
If thou lovest me, think no more of it.
I'll cull thee out the fairest courtesans,
And bring them every morning to thy
　bed;
She whom thine eye shall like, thy
　heart shall have,　165
Be she as chaste as was Penelope,
As wise as Saba,[10] or as beautiful
As was bright Lucifer before his fall.
Hold, take this book, peruse it thor-
　oughly:　[*Gives book.*]
The iterating of these lines brings gold;
The framing of this circle on the ground
Brings whirlwinds, tempests, thunder,
　and lightning;　172
Pronounce this thrice devoutly to thy-
　self,
And men in armor shall appear to thee,
Ready to execute what thou desir'st.
Faustus: Thanks, Mephistophilis; yet
fain would I have a book wherein I
might behold all spells and incantations,
that I might raise up spirits when I
please.　180
Mephistophilis: Here they are in this
book.　[*Turns to them.*]
Faustus: Now would I have a book
where I might see all characters and
planets of the heavens, that I might
know their motions and dispositions.

[10] The Queen of Sheba.

Mephistophilis: Here they are too.
　[*Turns to them.*]
Faustus: Nay, let me have one book
more—and then I have done—wherein I
might see all plants, herbs, and trees,
that grow upon the earth.　190
Mephistophilis: Here they be.
Faustus: O, thou art deceived.
Mephistophilis: Tut, I warrant thee.
　[*Turns to them.*]

SCENE VI. IN THE HOUSE OF FAUSTUS

Faustus: When I behold the heavens,
　then I repent,
And curse thee, wicked Mephistophilis,
Because thou hast deprived me of those
　joys.
Mephistophilis: Why, Faustus,
Thinkest thou heaven is such a glorious
　thing?　5
I tell thee, 'tis not half so fair as thou,
Or any man that breathes on earth.
Faustus: How prov'st thou that?
Mephistophilis: 'Twas made for man,
　therefore is man more excellent.
Faustus: If it were made for man,
　'twas made for me:　10
I will renounce this magic and repent.
[*Enter Good Angel and Evil Angel.*]
Good Angel: Faustus, repent; yet God
　will pity thee.
Evil Angel: Thou art a spirit; God
　cannot pity thee.
Faustus: Who buzzeth in mine ears I
　am a spirit?
Be I a devil, yet God may pity me;　15
Aye, God will pity me, if I repent.
Evil Angel: Aye, but Faustus never
　shall repent.　[*Exeunt Angels.*]
Faustus: My heart's so hardened, I
　cannot repent:
Scarce can I name salvation, faith, or
　heaven,
But fearful echoes thunder in mine ears,
"Faustus, thou art damned!" Then
　swords, and knives,　21
Poison, guns, halters, and envenomed
　steel
Are laid before me to dispatch myself;

And long ere this I should have slain
myself,
Had not sweet pleasure conquered deep
despair.   24
Have not I made blind Homer sing to me
Of Alexander's love and Oenon's death?[1]
And hath not he,[2] that built the walls
of Thebes
With ravishing sound of his melodious
harp,
Made music with my Mephistophilis?
Why should I die, then, or basely
despair?   30
I am resolved; Faustus shall ne'er re-
pent.—
Come, Mephistophilis, let us dispute
again,
And argue of divine astrology.
Tell me, are there many heavens above
the moon?   34
Are all celestial bodies but one globe,
As is the substance of this centric [3]
earth?
Mephistophilis: As are the elements,
such are the spheres,
Mutually folded in each other's orb,
And, Faustus,
All jointly move upon one axletree,   40
Whose terminine [4] is termed the world's
wide pole;
Nor are the names of Saturn, Mars, or
Jupiter
Feigned, but are erring stars.
Faustus: But, tell me, have they all
one motion, both *situ et tempore?* [5]
Mephistophilis: All jointly move from
east to west in twenty-four hours upon
the poles of the world; but differ in their
motion upon the poles of the zodiac.
Faustus: Tush,   49
These slender trifles Wagner can decide:
Hath Mephistophilis no greater skill?
Who knows not the double motion of the
planets?
The first is finished in a natural day;
The second thus: as Saturn in thirty
years; Jupiter in twelve; Mars in four;
the Sun, Venus, and Mercury in a year;

the Moon in twenty-eight days. Tush,
these are freshmen's suppositions. But,
tell me, hath every sphere a dominion
or *intelligentia?* [6]   60
Mephistophilis: Aye.
Faustus: How many heavens or
spheres are there?
Mephistophilis: Nine; the seven
planets, the firmament, and the empyr-
eal heaven.   66
Faustus: Well, resolve me in this question: why have we not conjunctions,
oppositions, aspects, eclipses,[7] all at one
time, but in some years we have more,
in some less?   71
*Mephistophilis: Per inaequalem mo-
tum respectu totius.* [8]
Faustus: Well, I am answered. Tell
me who made the world?   75
Mephistophilis: I will not.
Faustus: Sweet Mephistophilis, tell me.
Mephistophilis. Move me not, for I
will not tell thee.
Faustus: Villain, have I not bound
thee to tell me any thing?   81
Mephistophilis: Aye, that is not
against our kingdom; but this is. Think
thou on hell, Faustus, for thou art
damned.   85
Faustus: Think, Faustus, upon God
that made the world.
Mephistophilis: Remember this.[9]
                                   [*Exit.*]
Faustus: Aye, go, accursed spirit,
to ugly hell!
'Tis thou hast damned distressed
Faustus' soul.
Is 't not too late?   90
[*Enter Good Angel and Evil Angel.*]
Evil Angel: Too late.
Good Angel: Never too late, if Faustus
can repent.
Evil Angel: If thou repent, devils
shall tear thee in pieces.
Good Angel: Repent, and they shall
never raze thy skin.
                           [*Exeunt Angels.*]

---

[1] Paris's love for Helen; Oenone, Paris's
wife, killed herself. [2] Amphion. [3] In the center
(of the cosmos). [4] End. [5] In place and time.
[6] An intelligence or ruling spirit. [7] Astronomical terms. [8] By motion unequal in respect to that of the whole. [9] Evidently the
bond.

Faustus: Aye, Christ, my Savior,   95
Seek to save distressed Faustus' soul!
[*Enter Lucifer, Belzebub, and Mephistophilis.*]
Lucifer: Christ cannot save thy soul, for he is just.
There's none but I have interest in the same.
Faustus: O, who art thou that look'st so terrible?
Lucifer: I am Lucifer,   100
And this is my companion-prince in hell.
Faustus: O, Faustus, they are come to fetch away thy soul!
Lucifer: We come to tell thee thou dost injure us:
Thou talk'st of Christ, contrary to thy promise:
Thou shouldst not think of God: think of the devil,   105
And of his dam too.
Faustus: Nor will I henceforth: pardon me in this,
And Faustus vows never to look to heaven,
Never to name God, or to pray to him,
To burn his Scriptures, slay his ministers,   110
And make my spirits pull his churches down.
Lucifer: Do so, and we will highly gratify thee.
Faustus, we are come from hell to show thee some pastime: sit down, and thou shalt see all the Seven Deadly Sins appear in their proper shapes.   116
Faustus: That sight will be as pleasing unto me,
As Paradise was to Adam, the first day
Of his creation.   119
Lucifer: Talk not of Paradise nor creation; but mark this show: talk of the devil, and nothing else.—Come away!
[*Enter the Seven Deadly Sins.*]
Now, Faustus, examine them of their several names and dispositions.   125
Faustus: What art thou, the first?
Pride: I am Pride. I disdain to have

any parents. I am like Ovid's flea; [10] I can creep into every corner of a wench. Sometimes, like a periwig, I sit upon her brow; or, like a fan of feathers, I kiss her lips. But, fie, what a scent is here! I'll not speak another word, except the ground were perfumed, and covered with cloth of arras.   135
Faustus: What art thou, the second?
Covetousness: I am Covetousness, begotten of an old churl in an old leathern bag; and, might I have my wish, I would desire that this house and all the people in it were turned to gold, that I might lock you up in my good chest. O my sweet gold!   143
Faustus: What art thou, the third?
Wrath: I am Wrath. I had neither father nor mother: I leapt out of a lion's mouth when I was scarce half-an-hour old; and ever since I have run up and down the world with this case of rapiers, wounding myself when I had nobody to fight withal. I was born in hell; and look to it, for some of you shall be my father.   153
Faustus: What art thou, the fourth?
Envy: I am Envy, begotten of a chimney-sweeper and an oyster-wife. I cannot read, and therefore wish all books were burnt. I am lean with seeing others eat. O, that there would come a famine through all the world, that all might die, and I live alone! then thou shouldst see how fat I would be. But must thou sit, and I stand? Come down, with a vengeance!   164
Faustus: Away, envious rascal!— What art thou, the fifth?
Gluttony: Who, I, sir? I am Gluttony. My parents are all dead, and the devil a penny they have left me, but a bare pension, and that is thirty meals a-day and ten bevers [11]—a small trifle to suffice nature. O, I come of a royal parentage! my grandfather was a Gammon of Bacon, my grandmother a Hogshead of Claret wine; my godfathers were these, Peter Pickle-herring and

[10] In a poem erroneously attributed to Ovid.   [11] Lunches between meals.

Martin Martlemas-beef;[12] O, but my godmother, she was a jolly gentlewoman, and well beloved in every good town and city; her name was Mistress Margery March-beer.[13] Now, Faustus, thou hast heard all my progeny; wilt thou bid me to supper? 183
Faustus: No, I'll see thee hanged; thou wilt eat up all my victuals.
Gluttony: Then the devil choke thee!
Faustus: Choke thyself, glutton!— What art thou, the sixth? 189
Sloth: I am Sloth. I was begotten on a sunny bank, where I have lain ever since; and you have done me great injury to bring me from thence: let me be carried thither again by Gluttony and Lechery. I'll not speak another word for a king's ransom. 196
Faustus: What are you, Mistress Minx, the seventh and last?
Lechery: Who, I, sir? I am one that loves an inch of raw mutton better than an ell of fried stockfish, and the first letter of my name begins with L. 202
Lucifer: Away, to hell, to hell!
[Exeunt the Sins.]
Now, Faustus, how dost thou like this?
Faustus: O, this feeds my soul! 205
Lucifer: Tut, Faustus, in hell is all manner of delight.
Faustus: O, might I see hell, and return again,
How happy were I then!
Lucifer: Thou shalt; I will send for thee at midnight.
In meantime take this book; peruse it thoroughly, 210
And thou shalt turn thyself into what shape thou wilt.
Faustus: Great thanks, mighty Lucifer!
This will I keep as chary as my life.
Lucifer: Farewell, Faustus, and think on the devil.

---

[12] St. Martin's Day, November 11, was the time for hanging up meat salted for the winter. [13] Beer brewed in March was considered very good.

Faustus: Farewell, great Lucifer.
Come, Mephistophilis. 216
[Exeunt omnes.]
[Enter Chorus.]
Chorus: Learned Faustus.
To know the secrets of astronomy
Graven in the book of Jove's high firmament,
Did mount himself to scale Olympus' top, 220
Being seated in a chariot burning bright,
Drawn by the strength of yoky dragons' necks.
He now is gone to prove cosmography,
And, as I guess, will first arrive at Rome,
To see the Pope and manner of his court, 225
And take some part of holy Peter's feast,
That to this day is highly solemnized. *[Exit.]*

SCENE VII. THE POPE'S PRIVY-CHAMBER

[Enter Faustus and Mephistophilis.]
Faustus: Having now, my good Mephistophilis,
Passed with delight the stately town of Trier,[1]
Environed round with airy mountaintops,
With walls of flint, and deep-entrenched lakes,
Not to be won by any conquering prince;
From Paris next, coasting the realm of France, 6
We saw the river Maine fall into Rhine,
Whose banks are set with groves of fruitful vines;
Then up to Naples, rich Campania,
Whose buildings fair and gorgeous to the eye. 10
The streets straight forth, and paved with finest brick,
Quarter the town in four equivalents;
There saw we learned Maro's[2] golden tomb,

---

[1] Treves. [2] Virgil, thought in the Middle Ages to be a magician.

The way he cut, an English mile in
length,
Thorough a rock of stone, in one night's
space;   15
From thence to Venice, Padua, and the
rest,
In one of which a sumptuous temple
stands,
That threats the stars with her aspiring
top.
Thus hitherto hath Faustus spent his
time:
But tell me now what resting-place is
this?   20
Hast thou, as erst I did command,
Conducted me within the walls of
Rome?
Mephistophilis: Faustus, I have; and,
because we will not be unprovided, I
have taken up his Holiness' privy-
chamber for our use.   26
Faustus: I hope his Holiness will bid
us welcome.
Mephistophilis: Tut, 'tis no matter,
man; we'll be bold with his good cheer.
And now, my Faustus, that thou may'st
perceive   31
What Rome containeth to delight thee
with,
Know that this city stands upon seven
hills
That underprop the groundwork of the
same:
Just through the midst runs flowing
Tiber's stream,   35
With winding banks that cut it in two
parts;
Over the which four stately bridges lean,
That make safe passage to each part of
Rome:
Upon the bridge called Ponte Angelo
Erected is a castle passing strong,   40
Within whose walls such store of
ordnance are,
And double cannons framed of carved
brass,
As match the days within one com-
plete year;
Besides the gates, and high pyramides,[3]

Which Julius Caesar brought from
Africa.   45
Faustus: Now, by the kingdoms of
infernal rule,
Of Styx, of Acheron, and the fiery lake
Of ever-burning Phlegethon,[4] I swear
That I do long to see the monu-
ments
And situation of bright-splendent Rome:
Come, therefore, let's away.   51
Mephistophilis: Nay, Faustus, stay:
I know you'd fain see the Pope,
And take some part of holy Peter's
feast,
Where thou shalt see a troop of bald-
pate friars,
Whose *summum bonum*[5] is in belly-
cheer.   55
Faustus: Well, I'm content to compass
then some sport,
And by their folly make us merriment.
Then charm me, that I
May be invisible, to do what I please,
Unseen of any whilst I stay in Rome.
[*Mephistophilis charms him.*]
Mephistophilis: So, Faustus; now   61
Do what thou wilt, thou shalt not be
discerned.
[*Sound a Sennet.*[6] *Enter the Pope and
the Cardinal of Lorraine to the banquet,
with Friars attending.*]
Pope: My Lord of Lorraine, will 't
please you draw near?
Faustus: Fall to, and the devil choke
you, an you spare!
Pope: How now! who's that which
spake?—Friars, look about.   65
First Friar: Here's nobody, if it like
your Holiness.
Pope: My lord, here is a dainty dish
was sent me from the Bishop of Milan.
Faustus: I thank you, sir.   70
[*Snatches the dish.*]
Pope: How now! who's that which
snatched the meat from me? Will no
man look?—My lord, this dish was sent
me from the Cardinal of Florence.
Faustus: You say true; I'll ha 't. 75
[*Snatches the dish.*]

[3] Apparently obelisks.

[4] Rivers in Hades. [5] Highest good. [6] Trumpet notes marking exit or entrance.

Pope: What, again?—My lord, I'll drink to your grace.

Faustus: I'll pledge your grace.
[*Snatches the cup.*]

Cardinal of Lorraine: My lord, it may be some ghost, newly crept out of purgatory, come to beg a pardon of your Holiness. 82

Pope: It may be so.—Friars, prepare a dirge to lay the fury of this ghost.— Once again, my lord, fall to.
[*The Pope crosses himself.*]

Faustus: What, are you crossing of yourself? 86
Well, use that trick no more, I would advise you.
[*The Pope crosses himself again.*]
Well, there's the second time. Aware the third;
I give you fair warning.
[*The Pope crosses himself again, and Faustus hits him a box of the ear; and they all run away.*]
Come on, Mephistophilis; what shall we do? 90

Mephistophilis: Nay, I know not: we shall be cursed with bell, book, and candle.[7]

Faustus: How! bell, book, and candle —candle, book, and bell—
Forward and backward, to curse Faustus to hell! 95
Anon you shall hear a hog grunt, a calf bleat, and an ass bray,
Because it is Saint Peter's holiday.
[*Re-enter all the Friars to sing the dirge.*]

First Friar: Come, brethren, let's about our business with good devotion.
[*They sing.*]
*Cursed be he that stole away his Holiness' meat from the table! maledicat Dominus![8] 102
Cursed be he that struck his Holiness a blow on the face! maledicat Dominus!
Cursed be he that took Friar Sandelo a blow on the pate! maledicat Dominus!
Cursed be he that disturbeth our holy dirge! maledicat Dominus! 108*

[7] Rite of excommunication. [8] May the Lord curse [him].

Cursed be he that took away his Holiness' wine! maledicat Dominus! Et omnes Sancti![9] Amen! 111
[*Mephistophilis and Faustus beat the Friars and fling fireworks among them; and so exeunt.*]

SCENE VIII. Near an Inn

[*Enter Robin the Ostler, with a book in his hand.*]

Robin: O, this is admirable! here I ha' stolen one of Doctor Faustus' conjuring-books, and i' faith I mean to search some circles for my own use. Now will I make all the maidens in our parish dance at my pleasure, stark naked before me; and so by that means I shall see more than e'er I felt or saw yet. 8
[*Enter Ralph, calling Robin.*]

Ralph: Robin, prithee, come away; there's a gentleman tarries to have his horse, and he would have his things rubbed and made clean: he keeps such a chafing with my mistress about it; and she has sent me to look thee out; prithee, come away. 15

Robin: Keep out, keep out, or else you are blown up, you are dismembered, Ralph: keep out, for I am about a roaring piece of work.

Ralph: Come, what doest thou with that same book? thou canst not read?

Robin: Yes, my master and mistress shall find that I can read, he for his forehead, she for her private study; she's born to bear with me, or else my art fails. 26

Ralph: Why, Robin, what book is that?

Robin: What book! why, the most intolerable book for conjuring that e'er was invented by any brimstone devil.

Ralph: Canst thou conjure with it?

Robin: I can do all these things easily with it; first, I can make thee drunk with ippocras[1] at any tabern[2] in Europe for nothing; that's one of my conjuring works. 36

[9] And all the saints. [1] Spiced wine. [2] Robin mispronounces *tavern.*

Ralph: Our Master Parson says that's nothing.

Robin: True, Ralph: and more, Ralph, if thou hast any mind to Nan Spit, our kitchen-maid, then turn her and wind her to thy own use as often as thou wilt, and at midnight. 43
Ralph: O, brave Robin! shall I have Nan Spit and to mine own use? On that condition I'll feed thy devil with horse-bread as long as he lives, of free cost.

Robin: No more, sweet Ralph; let's go and make clean our boots, which lie foul upon our hands, and then to our conjuring in the devil's name. [*Exeunt.*]

SCENE IX. The Same

[*Enter Robin and Ralph with a silver goblet.*]

Robin: Come, Ralph: did not I tell thee, we were for ever made by this Doctor Faustus' book? *Ecce signum!* [1] here's a simple purchase [2] for horse-keepers: our horses shall eat no hay as long as this lasts. 6
Ralph: But, Robin, here comes the Vintner.

Robin: Hush! I'll gull [3] him super-naturally. 10
[*Enter Vintner.*]
Drawer, I hope all is paid; God be with you!—Come, Ralph.

Vintner: Soft, sir; a word with you. I must yet have a goblet paid from you, ere you go. 15
Robin: I a goblet, Ralph, I a goblet!—I scorn you; and you are but a, etc.[4] I a goblet! search me.

Vintner: I mean so, sir, with your favor. [*Searches Robin.*]
Robin: How say you now? 21
Vintner: I must say somewhat to your fellow.—You, sir!

Ralph: Me, sir! me, sir! search your fill. [*Vintner searches him.*] Now, sir, you may be ashamed to burden honest men with a matter of truth. 27

[1] Behold the sign. [2] Advantage, profit. [3] Trick, fool. [4] The actor could "ad lib" his terms of abuse.

Vintner: Well, t' one of you hath this goblet about you.

Robin: You lie, drawer, 'tis afore me [*Aside.*]—Sirrah you, I'll teach you to impeach honest men;—stand by;—I'll scour you for a goblet;—stand aside you had best, I charge you in the name of Belzebub.—Look to the goblet, Ralph. [*Aside to Ralph.*] 36
Vintner: What mean you, sirrah?

Robin: I'll tell you what I mean. [*Reads from a book.*] *Sanctobulorum Periphrasticon* [5]—nay, I'll tickle you, Vintner.—Look to the goblet, Ralph [*Aside to Ralph.*]—[*Reads.*] *Polypragmos Belseborams framanto pacostiphos tostu, Mephistophilis, etc.*[5]

[*Enter Mephistophilis, sets squibs [6] at their backs, and then exit. They run about.*]

Vintner: O, *nomine Domini!*[7] what meanest thou, Robin? thou hast no goblet. 47
Ralph: *Peccatum peccatorum!*[8]— Here's thy goblet, good Vintner.

[*Gives the goblet to Vintner, who exit.*]
Robin: *Misericordia pro nobis!*[9] what shall I do? Good devil, forgive me now, and I'll never rob thy library more.

[*Re-enter Mephistophilis.*]
Mephistophilis: Monarch of hell, under whose black survey 53
Great potentates do kneel with awful fear,
Upon whose altars thousand souls do lie,
How am I vexed with these villains' charms!
From Constantinople am I hither come,
Only for pleasure of these damned slaves.

Robin: How, from Constantinople! you have had a great journey. Will you take sixpence in your purse to pay for your supper, and be gone? 62
Mephistophilis: Well, villains, for your presumption, I transform thee into an ape, and thee into a dog; and so be gone. [*Exit.*]
Robin: How, into an ape! that's

[5] Nonsense words. [6] Firecrackers. [7] In the name of the Lord. [8] Sin of sins. [9] Mercy on us.

brave: I'll have fine sport with the boys;
I'll get nuts and apples enow.
Ralph: And I must be a dog.   70
Robin: I' faith, thy head will never be
out of the pottage-pot.   [Exeunt.]
          [Enter Chorus.]
Chorus: When Faustus had with
     pleasure ta'en the view
Of rarest things, and royal courts of
     kings,
He stayed his course, and so returned
     home;   75
Where such as bear his absence but with
     grief,
I mean his friends and near'st com-
     panions,
Did gratulate his safety with kind
     words,
And in their conference of what befell,
Touching his journey through the
     world and air,   80
They put forth questions of astrology,
Which Faustus answered with such
     learned skill
As they admired and wondered at his
     wit.
Now is his fame spread forth in every
     land:
Amongst the rest the Emperor is one,
Carolus the Fifth, at whose palace
     now   86
Faustus is feasted 'mongst his noblemen.
What there he did, in trial of his art,
I leave untold—your eyes shall see
     performed.   [Exit.]

SCENE X. Court of Charles V

[Enter Emperor, Faustus, and a
Knight, with Attendants, among whom
Mephistophilis.]

Emperor: Master Doctor Faustus, I
have heard strange report of thy knowledge in the black art, how that none in
my empire nor in the whole world can
compare with thee for the rare effects
of magic: they say thou hast a familiar
spirit, by whom thou canst accomplish
what thou list. This, therefore, is my
request, that thou let me see some proof
of thy skill, that mine eyes may be wit-

nesses to confirm what mine ears have
heard reported: and here I swear to
thee, by the honor of mine imperial
crown, that, whatever thou doest, thou
shalt be no ways prejudiced or en-
damaged.   16
Knight: I' faith, he looks much like a
conjurer.   [Aside.]
Faustus: My gracious sovereign,
though I must confess myself far inferior to the report men have published,
and nothing answerable [1] to the honor
of your imperial majesty, yet, for that
love and duty binds me thereunto, I am
content to do whatsoever your majesty
shall command me.   26
Emperor: Then, Doctor Faustus,
     mark what I shall say.
As I was sometime solitary set
Within my closet, sundry thoughts arose
About the honor of mine ancestors,   30
How they had won by prowess such
     exploits,
Got such riches, subdued so many king-
     doms,
As we that do succeed,[2] or they that
     shall
Hereafter possess our throne, shall   34
(I fear me) ne'er attain to that degree
Of high renown and great authority:
Amongst which kings is Alexander the
     Great,
Chief spectacle of the world's pre-
     eminence,
The bright shining of whose glorious
     acts
Lightens the world with his reflecting
     beams,   40
As when I hear but motion [3] made of
     him,
It grieves my soul I never saw the man:
If, therefore, thou, by cunning of thine
     art,
Canst raise this man from hollow vaults
     below,
Where lies entombed this famous con-
     queror,   45
And bring with him his beauteous para-
     mour,

---

[1] Comparable. [2] Follow. [3] Mention.

Both in their right shapes, gesture, and
attire
They used to wear during their time of
life,
Thou shalt both satisfy my just desire,
And give me cause to praise thee whilst
I live.   50
Faustus: My gracious lord, I am ready
to accomplish your request, so far forth
as by art and power of my spirit I am
able to perform.
Knight: I' faith, that's just nothing at
all.   [*Aside.*]
Faustus: But, if it like your grace, it is
not in my ability to present before your
eyes the true substantial bodies of those
deceased princes, which long since are
consumed to dust.   61
Knight: Aye, marry, Master Doctor,
now there's a sign of grace in you, when
you will confess the truth.   [*Aside.*]
Faustus: But such spirits as can lively
resemble Alexander and his paramour
shall appear before your grace, in that
manner that they both lived in, in their
most flourishing estate; which I doubt
not shall sufficiently content your imperial majesty.   71
Emperor: Go to, Master Doctor; let
me see them presently.
Knight: Do you hear, Master Doctor?
you bring Alexander and his paramour
before the Emperor!   76
Faustus: How then, sir?
Knight: I' faith, that's as true as
Diana turned me to a stag.[4]
Faustus: No, sir; but, when Actaeon
died, he left the horns for you.—Mephistophilis, h˃ ⸺ .ᴇ.   82
                 [*Exit Mephistophilis.*]
⸺ night: Nay, an you go to conjuring,
I'll be gone.   [*Exit.*]
Faustus: I'll meet with you anon for
interrupting me so.—Here they are, my
gracious lord.   87
[*Re-enter Mephistophilis with Spirits
in the shapes of Alexander and his
Paramour.*]

⁴ Diana turned Actaeon into a stag who
was killed by his own hounds.

Emperor: Master Doctor, I heard this
lady, while she lived, had a wart or mole
in her neck: how shall I know whether
it be so or no?   91
Faustus: Your highness may boldly
go and see.
Emperor: Sure, these are no spirits,
but the true substantial bodies of those
two deceased princes. [*Exeunt spirits.*]
Faustus: Will 't please your highness
now to send for the knight that was so
pleasant with me here of late?   99
Emperor: One of you call him forth.
                       [*Exit Attendant.*]
[*Re-enter the Knight with a pair of
horns on his head.*]
How now, sir knight! Feel on thy head.
Knight: Thou damned wretch and
execrable dog,
Bred in the concave of some monstrous
rock,
How dar'st thou thus abuse a gentleman?
Villain, I say, undo what thou hast
done!   105
Faustus: O, not so fast, sir! there's no
haste: but, good, are you remembered
how you crossed me in my conference
with the Emperor? I think I have met
with [5] you for it.   110
Emperor: Good Master Doctor, at my
entreaty release him: he hath done
penance sufficient.
Faustus: My gracious lord, not so
much for the injury he offered me here
in your presence, as to delight you with
some mirth, hath Faustus worthily re-
quited this injurious knight; which
being all I desire, I am content to release him of his horns:—and, sir knight,
hereafter speak well of scholars.—Mephistophilis, transform him straight.
[*Mephistophilis removes the horns.*]—
Now, my good lord, having done my
duty, I humbly take my leave.   124
Emperor: Farewell, Master Doctor:
yet, ere you go,
Expect from me a bounteous reward.
        [*Exeunt Emperor, Knight, and At-
tendants.*]
⁵ Got even with.

Scene XI. A Green

Faustus: Now, Mephistophilis, the restless course
That Time doth run with calm and silent foot,
Short'ning my days and thread of vital life,
Calls for the payment of my latest years:
Therefore, sweet Mephistophilis, let us Make haste to Wittenberg.   6
Mephistophilis: What, will you go on horseback or on foot?
Faustus: Nay, till I'm past this fair and pleasant green, I'll walk on foot.
[*Enter a Horse-courser.[1]*]
Horse-courser: I have been all this day seeking one Master Fustian: mass, see where he is!—God save you, Master Doctor!   14
Faustus: What, horse-courser! you are well met.
Horse-courser: Do you hear, sir? I have brought you forty dollars for your horse.
Faustus: I cannot sell him so. If thou likest him for fifty, take him.   21
Horse-courser: Alas, sir, I have no more!—I pray you speak for me.
Mephistophilis: I pray you, let him have him: he is an honest fellow, and he has a great charge, neither wife nor child.   27
Faustus: Well, come, give me your money [*horse-courser gives Faustus the money*]: my boy will deliver him to you. But I must tell you one thing before you have him; ride him not into the water, at any hand.
Horse-courser: Why, sir, will he not drink of all waters?   35
Faustus: O, yes, he will drink of all waters; but ride him not into the water: ride him over hedge or ditch, or where thou wilt, but not into the water.
Horse-courser: Well, sir.—Now am I made man for ever: I'll not leave my horse for forty: if he had but the quality

[1] Horse dealer.

of hey-ding-ding, hey-ding-ding,[2] I'd make a brave living on him: he has a buttock as slick as an eel [*Aside.*]— Well, God b'wi'ye, sir: your boy will deliver him me: but, hark ye, sir; if my horse be sick or ill at ease, you'll tell me what it is?   49
Faustus: Away, you villain! what, dost think I am a horse-doctor?
[*Exit Horse-courser.*]
What art thou, Faustus, but a man condemned to die?
Thy fatal time doth draw to final end;
Despair doth drive distrust unto my thoughts:
Confound these passions with a quiet sleep: 55
Tush, Christ did call the thief upon the cross;
Then rest thee, Faustus, quiet in conceit.[3]   [*Sleeps in his chair.*]
[*Re-enter Horse-courser, all wet, crying.*]
Horse-courser: Alas, alas! Doctor Fustian, quotha? mass, Doctor Lopus[4] was never such a doctor: has given me a purgation, has purged me of forty dollars; I shall never see them more. But yet, like an ass as I was, I would not be ruled by him, for he bade me I should ride him into no water: now I, thinking my horse had had some rare quality that he would not have had me known of, I, like a venturous youth, rid him into the deep pond at the town's end. I was no sooner in the middle of the pond, but my horse vanished away, and I sat upon a bottle[5] of hay, never so near drowning in my life. But I'll seek out my doctor, and have my forty dollars again, or I'll make it the dearest horse!—O, yonder is his snipper-snapper.—Do you hear? you, heypass,[6] where's your master?   78
Mephistophilis: Why, sir, what would you? you cannot speak with him.
Horse-courser: But I will speak with him.

[2] If he can dance to music. [3] Thought.
[4] Doctor Lopez, executed in 1594 on a charge of having plotted to poison Queen Elizabeth.
[5] Bundle. [6] Juggler.

Mephistophilis: Why, he's fast asleep: come some other time. 84

Horse-courser I'll speak with him now, or I'll break his glass windows about his ears.

Mephistophilis: I tell thee, he has not slept this eight nights.

Horse-courser: An he have not slept this eight weeks, I'll speak with him. 92

Mephistophilis: See, where he is, fast asleep.

Horse-courser: Aye, this is he.—God save ye, Master Doctor, Master Doctor, Master Doctor Fustian! forty dollars, forty dollars for a bottle of hay!

Mephistophilis: Why, thou seest he hears thee not. 100

Horse-courser: So-ho, ho! so-ho, ho! [*Hollas in his ear.*] No, will you not wake? I'll make you wake ere I go. [*Pulls Faustus by the leg, and pulls it away.*] Alas, I am undone! what shall I do? 106

Faustus: O, my leg, my leg!—Help, Mephistophilis! call the officers!—My leg, my leg!

Mephistophilis: Come, villain, to the constable. 111

Horse-courser: O Lord, sir, let me go, and I'll give you forty dollars more!

Mephistophilis: Where be they?

Horse-courser: I have none about me: come to my ostry,[7] and I'll give them you. 117

Mephistophilis: Be gone quickly.

[*Horse-courser runs away.*]

Faustus: What, is he gone? farewell he! Faustus has his leg again, and the Horse-courser, I take it, a bottle of hay for his labor. Well, this trick shall cost him forty dollars more.

[*Enter Wagner.*]

How now, Wagner! what's the news with thee? 125

Wagner: Sir, the Duke of Vanholt doth earnestly entreat your company.

Faustus: The Duke of Vanholt! an honorable gentleman, to whom I must

be no niggard of my cunning.—Come, Mephistophilis, let's away to him. 131

[*Exeunt.*]

SCENE XII. The Court of the Duke of Vanholt

[*Enter the Duke of Vanholt, the Duchess, and Faustus.*]

Duke of Vanholt: Believe me, Master Doctor, this merriment hath much pleased me.

Faustus: My gracious lord, I am glad it contents you so well.—But it may be, madam, you take no delight in this. I have heard that great-bellied women do long for some dainties or other: what is it, madam? Tell me and you shall have it.

Duchess of Vanholt: Thanks, good Master Doctor; and, for I see your courteous intent to pleasure me, I will not hide from you the thing my heart desires; and, were it now summer, as it is January and the dead time of the winter, I would desire no better meat than a dish of ripe grapes. 17

Faustus. Alas, madam, that's nothing!—Mephistophilis, be gone. [*Exit Mephistophilis.*] Were it a greater thing than this, so it would content you, you should have it. 22

[*Re-enter Mephistophilis with grapes.*] Here they be, madam: will't please you taste on them?

Duke of Vanholt: Believe me, Master Doctor, this makes me wonder above the rest, that being in the dead time of winter and in the month of January, how you should come by these grapes.

Faustus: If it like your grace, the year is divided into two circles over the whole world, that, when it is here winter with us, in the contrary circle it is summer with them, as in India, Saba,[1] and farther countries in the east; and by means of a swift spirit that I have, I had them brought hither, as ye see.— How do you like them, madam? be they good? 39

[7] Hostelry.

[1] Arabia.

Duchess of Vanholt: Believe me, Master Doctor, they be the best grapes that e'er I tasted in my life before.
Faustus: I am glad they content you so, madam.   44
Duke of Vanholt: Come, madam, let us in, where you must well reward this learned man for the great kindness he hath showed to you.
Duchess of Vanholt: And so I will, my lord; and, whilst I live, rest beholding [2] for this courtesy.   51
Faustus: I humbly thank your grace.
Duke of Vanholt: Come, Master Doctor, follow us. and receive your reward.   [*Exeunt.*]

SCENE XIII. A Room in the House of Faustus

[*Enter Wagner.*]

Wagner: I think my master means to die shortly,
For he hath given to me all his goods:
And yet, methinketh, if that death were near,
He would not banquet, and carouse, and swill
Amongst the students, as even now he doth,   5
Who are at supper with such belly-cheer
As Wagner ne'er beheld in all his life.
See, where they come! belike the feast is ended.
[*Enter Faustus with two or three Scholars, and Mephistophilis.*]
First Scholar: Master Doctor Faustus, since our conference about fair ladies, which was the beautiful'st in all the world, we have determined with ourselves that Helen of Greece was the admirablest lady that ever lived: therefore, Master Doctor, if you will do us that favor, as to let us see that peerless dame of Greece, whom all the world admires for majesty, we should think ourselves much beholding unto you.
Faustus: Gentlemen,   20

For that I know your friendship is unfeigned,
And Faustus' custom is not to deny
The just requests of those that wish him well,
You shall behold that peerless dame of Greece,
No otherways for pomp and majesty
Than when Sir Paris crossed the seas with her,   26
And brought the spoils to rich Dardania.[1]
Be silent, then, for danger is in words.
[*Music sounds, and Helen passeth over the stage.*]
Second Scholar: Too simple is my wit to tell her praise,
Whom all the world admires for majesty.
Third Scholar: No marvel though the angry Greeks pursued   31
With ten years' war the rape [2] of such a queen,
Whose heavenly beauty passeth all compare.
First Scholar: Since we have seen the pride of Nature's works,
And only paragon of excellence,   35
Let us depart; and for this glorious deed
Happy and blest be Faustus evermore!
Faustus: Gentlemen, farewell: the same I wish to you.
[*Exeunt Scholars and Wagner.*]
[*Enter an Old Man.*]
Old Man: Ah, Doctor Faustus, that I might prevail
To guide thy steps unto the way of life,
By which sweet path thou may'st attain the goal   41
That shall conduct thee to celestial rest!
Break heart, drop blood, and mingle it with tears,
Tears falling from repentant heaviness
Of thy most vile and loathsome filthiness,   45
The stench whereof corrupts the inward soul
With such flagitious crimes of heinous sins
As no commiseration may expel,

---

[2] Indebted.   [1] Troy. [2] Abduction.

But mercy, Faustus, of thy Savior
sweet,
Whose blood alone must wash away thy
guilt.   50
Faustus: Where art thou, Faustus?
wretch, what hast thou done?
Damned art thou, Faustus, damned;
despair and die!
Hell calls for right, and with a roaring
voice
Says, "Faustus, come; thine hour is
almost come";
And Faustus now will come to do thee
right.   55
[*Mephistophilis gives him a dagger.*]
Old Man: Ah, stay, good Faustus,
stay thy desperate steps!
I see an angel hovers o'er thy head,
And, with a vial full of precious grace,
Offers to pour the same into thy soul:
Then call for mercy, and avoid despair.
Faustus: Ah, my sweet friend, I feel
Thy words to comfort my distressed
soul!   62
Leave me a while to ponder on my sins.
Old Man: I go, sweet Faustus; but
with heavy cheer,[3]
Fearing the ruin of thy hopeless soul.
                                    [*Exit.*]
Faustus: Accursed Faustus, where is
mercy now?   66
I do repent; and yet I do despair:
Hell strives with grace for conquest in
my breast:
What shall I do to shun the snares of
death?
Mephistophilis: Thou traitor, Faustus,
I arrest thy soul   70
For disobedience to my sovereign lord:
Revolt, or I'll in piece-meal tear thy
flesh.
Faustus: Sweet Mephistophilis, en-
treat thy lord
To pardon my unjust presumption,
And with my blood again I will confirm
My former vow I made to Lucifer.   76
Mephistophilis: Do it, then, quickly,
with unfeigned heart,
Lest greater danger do attend thy drift.

[*Faustus stabs his arm, and writes
on a paper with his blood.*]
Faustus: Torment, sweet friend, that
base and crooked age,
That durst dissuade me from thy
Lucifer,   80
With greatest torments that our hell
affords.
Mephistophilis: His faith is great; I
cannot touch his soul;
But what I may afflict his body with
I will attempt, which is but little worth.
Faustus: One thing, good servant,
let me crave of thee,   85
To glut the longing of my heart's
desire—
That I might have unto my paramour
That heavenly Helen which I saw of
late,
Whose sweet embracings may extinguish
clean
These thoughts that do dissuade me
from my vow,   90
And keep mine oath I made to Lucifer.
Mephistophilis: Faustus, this, or
what else thou shalt desire,
Shall be performed in twinkling of an
eye.
                          [*Re-enter Helen.*]
Faustus: Was this the face that
launched a thousand ships,   94
And burnt the topless towers of Ilium?—
Sweet Helen, make me immortal with a
kiss.—   [*Kisses her.*]
Her lips suck forth my soul: see where
it flies!—
Come, Helen, come, give me my soul
again.
Here will I dwell, for heaven be in these
lips,
And all is dross that is not Helena.   100
I will be Paris, and for love of thee,
Instead of Troy, shall Wittenberg be
sacked
And I will combat with weak Menelaus,[4]
And wear thy colors on my plumed
crest;
Yes, I will wound Achilles in the heel,[5]

[4] Helen's husband. [5] Achilles' vulnerable
spot, where Paris shot him with a poisoned
arrow.

[3] Spirits.

And then return to Helen for a kiss.
O, thou art fairer than the evening air
Clad in the beauty of a thousand stars;
Brighter art thou than flaming Jupiter
When he appeared to hapless Semele; [6]
More lovely than the monarch of the
sky   111
In wanton Arethusa's [7] azured arms;
And none but thou shalt be my para-
mour!   [*Exeunt.*]

[*Enter the Old Man.*]

Old Man: Accursed Faustus, miserable man,
That from thy soul exclud'st the grace
of heaven,   115
And fly'st the throne of his tribunal-
seat!

[*Enter Devils.*]

Satan begins to sift me with his pride:
As in this furnace God shall try my
faith,
My faith, vile hell, shall triumph over
thee.
Ambitious fiends, see how the heavens
smile   120
At your repulse, and laugh your state
to scorn!
Hence, hell! for hence I fly unto my God.
       [*Exeunt.*]

SCENE XIV. The same

[*Enter Faustus, with Scholars.*]

Faustus: Ah, gentlemen!
First Scholar: What ails Faustus?
Faustus: Ah, my sweet chamber-
fellow, had I lived with thee, then had I
lived still! but now I die eternally.
Look, comes he not? comes he not?   6
Second Scholar: What means Faus-
tus?
Third Scholar: Belike he is grown into
some sickness by being over-solitary. 10
First Scholar: If it be so, we'll have
physicians to cure him.—'Tis but a
surfeit; never fear, man.
Faustus: A surfeit of deadly sin, that
hath damned both body and soul.   15
Second Scholar: Yet, Faustus, look

[6] Mortal loved by Jupiter.   [7] See analysis
of this scene, page 538.

up to heaven; remember God's mercies
are infinite.
Faustus: But Faustus' offense can
ne'er be pardoned: the serpent that
tempted Eve may be saved, but not
Faustus. Ah, gentlemen, hear me with
patience, and tremble not at my
speeches! Though my heart pants and
quivers to remember that I have been
a student here these thirty years, O,
would I had never seen Wittenberg,
never read book! and what wonders I
have done, all Germany can witness,
yea, all the world; for which Faustus
hath lost both Germany and the world,
yea, heaven itself, heaven, the seat of
God, the throne of the blessed, the
kingdom of joy; and must remain in
hell for ever—hell, ah, hell, for ever!
Sweet friends, what shall become of
Faustus, being in hell for ever?   37
Third Scholar: Yet, Faustus, call on
God.
Faustus: On God, whom Faustus hath
abjured! on God, whom Faustus hath
blasphemed! Ah, my God, I would weep!
but the devil draws in my tears. Gush
forth blood, instead of tears! yea, life
and soul—O, he stays my tongue! I
would lift up my hands; but see, they
hold them, they hold them!   47
All: Who, Faustus?
Faustus: Lucifer and Mephistophilis.
Ah, gentlemen, I gave them my soul
for my cunning!
All: God forbid!
Faustus: God forbade it, indeed; but
Faustus hath done it: for vain pleasure
of twenty-four years hath Faustus lost
eternal joy and felicity. I writ them a
bill with mine own blood: the date is
expired; the time will come, and he will
fetch me.   59
First Scholar: Why did not Faustus
tell us of this before, that divines might
have prayed for thee?
Faustus: Oft have I thought to have
done so; but the devil threatened to
tear me in pieces, if I named God, to
fetch both body and soul, if I once gave
ear to divinity: and now 'tis too late.

Gentlemen, away, lest you perish with
me.　　　　　　　　　　　　　69
Second Scholar: O, what shall we do
to save Faustus?
Faustus: Talk not of me, but save
yourselves, and depart.
Third Scholar: God will strengthen
me; I will stay with Faustus.　　　75
First Scholar: Tempt not God, sweet
friend; but let us into the next room,
and there pray for him.
Faustus: Aye, pray for me, pray for
me; and what noise soever ye hear, come
not unto me, for nothing can rescue me.
Second Scholar: Pray thou, and we will
pray that God may have mercy upon
thee.　　　　　　　　　　　　84
Faustus: Gentlemen, farewell; if I
live till morning, I'll visit you; if not,
Faustus is gone to hell.
All: Faustus, farewell.
[Exeunt Scholars. — The clock strikes
eleven.]
Faustus: Ah, Faustus,　　　　　89
Now hast thou but one bare hour to live,
And then thou must be damned per-
petually!
Stand still, you ever-moving spheres of
heaven,
That time may cease, and midnight
never come;
Fair Nature's eye, rise, rise again, and
make　　　　　　　　　　　　94
Perpetual day; or let this hour be but
A year, a month, a week, a natural day,
That Faustus may repent and save his
soul!
O lente, lente currite, noctis equi![1]
The stars move still, time runs, the
clock will strike,
The devil will come, and Faustus must
be damned.　　　　　　　　　100
O, I'll leap up to my God!—Who pulls
me down?—
See, see, where Christ's blood streams
in the firmament!
One drop would save my soul, half a
drop: ah, my Christ!—

Ah, rend not my heart for naming of my
Christ!
Yet will I call on him: O, spare me,
Lucifer!—　　　　　　　　　105
Where is it now? 'tis gone: and see,
where God
Stretcheth out his arm, and bends his
ireful brows!
Mountains and hills come, come, and
fall on me,
And hide me from the heavy wrath of
God!
No, no!　　　　　　　　　　110
Then will I headlong run into the earth:
Earth, gape! O, no, it will not harbor
me!
You stars that reigned at my nativity,
Whose influence hath allotted death and
hell,　　　　　　　　　　　114
Now draw up Faustus, like a foggy mist,
Into the entrails of yon lab'ring clouds,
That, when you vomit forth into the
air,
My limbs may issue from your smoky
mouths,
So that my soul may but ascend to
heaven!
[The clock strikes the half-hour.]
Ah, half the hour is past! 'twill all be
past anon.　　　　　　　　　120
O God,
If thou wilt not have mercy on my soul,
Yet for Christ's sake, whose blood hath
ransomed me,
Impose some end to my incessant pain;
Let Faustus live in hell a thousand
years,　　　　　　　　　　125
A hundred thousand, and at last be
saved!
O, no end is limited to damned souls!
Why wert thou not a creature wanting
soul?
Or why is this immortal that thou hast?
Ah, Pythagoras' metempsychosis,[2] were
that true,　　　　　　　　　130
This soul should fly from me, and I be
changed
Unto some brutish beast! all beasts are
happy,

[1] Run slowly, O slowly, horses of the
night (Ovid, Amores, I, 13).

[2] Transmigration of souls from human
beings to animals.

For, when they die,
Their souls are soon dissolved in elements;
But mine must live still to be plagued in hell. 135
Cursed be the parents that engendered me!
No, Faustus, curse thyself, curse Lucifer
That hath deprived thee of the joys of heaven. [*The clock strikes twelve.*]
O, it strikes, it strikes! Now, body, turn to air,
Or Lucifer will bear thee quick to hell! [*Thunder and lightning.*]
O soul, be changed into little waterdrops, 141
And fall into the ocean, ne'er be found! [*Enter Devils.*]
My God, my God, look not so fierce on me!
Adders and serpents, let me breathe a while!

Ugly hell, gape not! come not, Lucifer!
I'll burn my books!—Ah, Mephistophilis! 146
[*Exeunt Devils with Faustus.*]
[*Enter Chorus.*]
Chorus: Cut is the branch that might have grown full straight,
And burned is Apollo's laurel-bough,
That sometime grew within this learned man.
Faustus is gone: regard his hellish fall,
Whose fiendful fortune may exhort the wise, 151
Only to wonder at unlawful things,
Whose deepness doth entice such forward wits
To practice more than heavenly power permits. [*Exit.*]
Terminat hora diem; terminat auctor opus.[3] 155

[3] The hour ends the day; the author ends his work.

NOTES ON *DR. FAUSTUS*

1. THE PROBLEM OF STRUCTURE: THE "MIDDLE"

To the reader who has just finished *Dr. Faustus* it will be apparent that the most important problem is one of structure, that is, the arrangement of events by which the initial situation is modified and developed until the final situation is brought about. There is an effective beginning (Faustus's making and carrying out his decision) and an effective ending (Faustus's having to fulfil his part of the contract), but between the two the course of events seems almost haphazard. The action appears to move rather irregularly and disconnectedly, and in some scenes there is a marked decline in quality. This is the problem of the "middle."

Aristotle said—and the statement is famous—that a play should have a beginning, a middle, and an end (see Aristotle's *Poetics*, 6, in the Glossary). A middle, he explained, naturally follows something else and is itself followed by something else (in *King Lear*, as we shall see, the middle is the conduct of Goneril and Regan after they are in power: this follows upon Lear's putting them in power and in turn is necessarily followed by the catastrophic results for all of them). For convenience we may phrase our problem thus: does Marlowe's tragedy actually have a "middle"? This question makes us consider two problems:

Marlowe has, strictly speaking, no "plot," that is, no single action, continuing from the first part of the play through the middle to the end, in terms of which we can see Faustus's development. Hamlet at the start faces a specific problem of revenge in Denmark, and he faces the same problem, with its ramifications, throughout the play; Macbeth seeks a throne, and his search leads to every other action throughout the play. But Faustus is not involved in a single situation which organically evolves to form the rest of the play. He gets his power, but then the action seems to stop; he is not engaged in some project whose development is the next phase of the plot. So the author must initiate a *new action* in which we see Faustus using his power; in this sense the middle does not "necessarily follow" from the beginning. Likewise none of the actions in which we see Faustus using his power *determines* the ending; that is, there is no direction connection between, say, the horse-courser episode and Faustus's being carried off by the devils. The ending seems rather to *spring directly from the early part of the play:* Faustus is carried off by the devils because he made a bargain with the devils.

The second phase of the problem of the middle has been implied by the preceding paragraph: in showing how Faustus uses his power, the author invents not one new action, but several different ones, thus increasing our sense of the discontinuity in the middle. His structure is "episodic" (see Glossary). Now episodes may be so used as to develop a plot, each acting as an irreplaceable part of the line of action leading to the end; thus we have a "linear" construction. But the middle of *Doctor Faustus* is not linear; the scenes are rather like separate radii from a single center, each illustrating in its own way Faustus's use of power. After each one we have to go back, meet new characters, and start all over again.

These structural difficulties, as well as weaknesses in the prose scenes, have led to the theory that another writer has revised Marlowe's original play; Dr. Paul Kocher believes that this reviser was Thomas Nashe. But we must deal with the play as it exists, and the question is whether a case can be made for the middle scenes of the play—whether they have a structural function. One thing seems sure: the author or authors did recognize the problem—namely, that the presentation of the mere making and fulfilling of a contract could not itself be effective drama. The end would grow out of the beginning; the conclusion would be foregone. Realizing this, the author has taken at least two steps to make the middle functional, that is, dramatically related to beginning and ending:

1. There is an obvious effort to present a *conflict* rather than a mere *record of events*. The clash within Faustus, which appears both in his serious inner disturbances and in his clashes with the devils, grows stronger rather than weaker after he has decided to practice magic and thus suggests that the decision itself—to practice magic—is a starting point rather than a final determining act. Further, the devils' great fear of losing him indicates that he still retains freedom of choice. If the contract is not unbreakable, it is not the making of the contract but the subsequent conduct of Faustus that determines the end. This leads us to the author's second step:

2. The author presents Faustus as undergoing a deterioration of character which accounts *in moral terms* for the ending. If Faustus lost his soul

merely on legal grounds, the play could be no more than a kind of court record. But the spectacle of his decline gives probability, dramatic acceptability, to the ending. The "middle" shows him as reaffirming his bargain and as making bad use of the power it brings him. These points require further consideration.

2. FAUSTUS'S CONFLICT

Faustus's inner conflict, upon which Marlowe mainly relies for dramatic force, presents a number of aspects for consideration:

1. The first suggestion that there are two sides in Faustus is the appearance of the angels in Scene i. Here the conflict is only potential, but later it becomes actual; Faustus's quarrel with himself is a continuing entity. The student should trace the fluctuations, which are one means of giving plausibility to the conflict.

2. Marlowe suggests the pervasiveness, the basic and inevitable nature of the conflict by presenting it on three different levels. First, it is presented directly in soliloquy, a Renaissance theatrical *convention* (see Glossary) on which Marlowe depends considerably in such scenes as i, iii, and xiv. Notice, also, further uses of soliloquy in v and vi. Second, Marlowe borrows from medieval drama the Good and Evil Angels, which we may consider as objectifications both of the conflicting elements in Faustus and of the principles of good and evil in the world. Do you think the angels "work," or would Marlowe have done better to suggest the same meanings by presenting a conflict between actual persons, say different kinds of scholars? Or do the angels accomplish anything that human beings could not? In this connection, consider the use of the Old Man in xiii, a fairly complex character. It is clear that on one level he represents Faustus's better self, like the Good Angel. What other meanings can you see in him? Why is he made an "old" man? What characteristics of age are to be attributed to him?

Third, Faustus's conflict appears most strikingly as a conflict with the devils. Here again we find two levels: the devils are of course actual demons, infernal creatures; but we sense, at the same time, that they are embodiments of one of the conflicting forces within Faustus. As with the Angels, he must resist both inner and outer enemies. Now, the tension of this situation is enhanced by another complexity: Mephistophilis is paradoxically both the ally and the enemy of Faustus. The situation would be much simpler, and less dramatic, if Mephistophilis were only a supernatural errand boy, like Aladdin's genius, or only an external enemy to be resisted. But for Faustus the especial complication of experience is that he cannot oppose the whole man to an outer enemy: he must resist not only the devils but also the demands of the part of himself that wishes for the pleasures to be provided by the devils; on the other hand, if he accepts the devils as allies, he must face his old beliefs, which are gradually making it explicit that his infernal ally is his destroyer. Thus Marlowe has hit upon a technical device for exhibiting powerfully the destructive conflict in which Faustus finds himself. And it is clear, at the same time, that the play becomes something more than the record of the making and fulfilment of a legal contract.

What is the significance of the contrast between Scene vi, where three devils oppose Faustus, and Scene xiii, where Mephistophilis alone controls him? Is the contrast dramatically effective?

3. A final aspect of Faustus's complex struggle is the irony with which it is presented: Faustus sells his soul with complete certainty, has that certainty shaken, and finally comes to another certainty, the antithesis of his early flippant assurance. Unlike the villain of melodrama, Faustus does not become a hardened sinner; instead, his original resolve, heroic in its way, dissolves. As he is transformed from superman to Everyman, his authentically tragic stature beccmes evident.

The irony is finally pointed in Scene iii: while Faustus denies all power above himself, Mephistophilis pointedly acknowledges his own subservience to Lucifer. He gives a lesson to the vain Faustus, who goes on with sophomoric jauntiness about "damnation" and "vain trifles of men's souls" and inquires in a detached, scientific way about Mephistophilis's origin. Marlowe develops the scene most shrewdly: Mephistophilis, thinking of his past, experiences a momentary renewal of his old love for Heaven and a sharpened sense of his present evil state (Marlowe in part applies the psychology of Boethius and Dante, "There is no greater sorrow than remembering, in misery, the happy times"). Thus Mephistophilis becomes more complex than a mere villain would be; for the moment he is far wiser than the callow Faustus. Marlowe pushes the situation to a brilliant paradox: the stealer of souls, in a moment of spiritual concern recovered from his past, urges Faustus to save his soul; and the man with a soul, in the ignorance which he takes for supreme knowledge, throws away his soul and sneers at the weakness of his adviser. The tension continues with further irony: neither of them maintains his uncharacteristic position.

3. THE MEANING OF FAUSTUS'S EXPERIENCE: HIS DEVELOPMENT

Faustus's conflict, we have seen, links the scenes in such a way as to create a continuous dramatic force. In a more subtle way the continuity is the product of an evolving commentary upon experience which becomes the more searching as the scenes progress; the episodes, in other words, are not merely interesting episodes in the life of Faustus, such as we find in some historical plays, but embody a meaningful development of the human being in a certain type of situation. Faustus is a specialized Everyman, and the growing symbolic force of his actions compensates for the absence of the conventional dramatic structure. The middle scenes, we find, make an important contribution to the total meaning.

That meaning becomes apparent in a deterioration which morally justifies the conclusion. The deterioration is presented in terms of *man's quest for knowledge and power*. Faustus makes an all-out quest for omniscience and omnipotence. But when the nature of true knowledge comes home to him, it is too late for him to do anything about it; and, after using his own great power badly, he ends up completely in the power of evil. He is the victim of a double irony.

Scene i. Faustus, the universal scholar, casts aside as inadequate the existing forms of knowledge. His climactic rejection of theology sets up the main irony of the play: he will not accept "The reward of sin is death" and "We must die an everlasting death." Here he can possess that knowledge—*free;* yet by selling his soul he will only, in the end, gain overpowering recognition that it is true knowledge. ". . . we deceive ourselves," he quotes from the New Testament as he goes on to become the victim of a complete self-deception. He denies knowledge that acts as a brake upon his sense of power.

Notice carefully the language of the scene. Pick out the words and phrases which suggest Faustus's interest in power. Do the words he uses to discuss other fields of knowledge suggest his leaning toward magic even before he speaks of it directly? Is there any evidence that he cannot forget about God and Heaven and everlasting life as easily as his denial of "divinity" might suggest? Examine his speeches carefully for evidence on this point. What is the significance of such lines as "necromantic books are *heavenly*" and "A sound magician is a mighty *God*"?

Scene iii. Faustus's denial of logic (i. 6 ff.) shows itself ironically in Faustus's logical inconsistency. The very oath with which ne summons Mephistophilis invokes the aid of the God whose doctrine he has denied; *i.e.*, man's quest for power leads him counter to both theology and logic. The fact that he has invoked the devil by "anagrammatizing" God's name "forward and backward" ought to suggest to Faustus that he is not really escaping God, and that magic is not an independent moral realm where he can irresponsibly enjoy self-indulgence. Further, he should consider the attitude of Mephistophilis to the deity and to men's souls—an attitude which Marlowe sets down in fine ironic contrast to Faustus's own.

Trace the verbal evidence which suggests that Faustus is becoming intoxicated with his new sense of power and is therefore incapable of clear thinking, and, indeed, willing to throw important problems out of the window. Consider especially Faustus's last two speeches. What connection can you find between the language of this scene and that of Scene i? Is the idea of eternity still conspicuously present? What is suggested by Faustus's jauntiness? What is the source of dramatic tension at this point?

Scene v. What is most obvious here is the heightening of the tension as the older heritage in Faustus's character begins to reassert itself in opposition to his new quest of power, and to appear in constantly more overt ways. The tension is increased by irony: Faustus *reasons* away his doubts and the Good Angel's arguments, but he fails to *reason* about the significance of his needing supernatural aid in conveying his soul (a fact which is very concretely dramatized)—namely, that it is not his to give away. Now, Faustus's ignoring what he wants to ignore—*repressing* it, as we have learned to say today—results in certain psychological disturbances, in his "seeing things" (l. 76 ff.). What does Mephistophilis do to "cure" Faustus?

The most powerful words in the scene are those with which Faustus indicates completion of the contract—*Consummatum est*, "It is finished," the very words which Christ used on the cross. What are the clear ironic contrasts between Faustus's giving up his soul and Christ's dying on the cross? At a deeper level, however, does Faustus's use of the words not show the action of his unconscious and, therefore, reveal his serious inner split? Here he gives testimony to the hold of the Christian world-view upon him; willy-nilly he belongs to a world of which redemption is a cardinal fact. Consciously he may deny that world, but he cannot escape it.

This is the state of the problem of knowledge which was the starting point of the play: even as Faustus is more thoroughly committed than ever to power-knowledge, the old knowledge keeps forcing itself upon him. What are the implications of his inquiries about hell? Consider, in this connection, Faustus's reasoning in iii, 65. Of the two books which he secures from Mephistophilis, which one, in the light of subsequent developments, is more interesting to him? What contribution is made to the meaning of the play by Mephistophilis's statement of the value of souls to him? By his comparing a woman's beauty to that of "Lucifer before his fall"?

Scene vi. The dramatic tension is heightened further as the psychological undercurrent which we have observed in Faustus grows stronger. Why do the Good and Evil Angels appear twice in this scene? Why do three devils appear to Faustus in the middle of the scene?

The student should observe the language pattern which first ties the scene to the preceding ones and then bears the major weight of the scene itself. Note how the talk of "heaven" in the early part of the scene establishes a tie with Scenes i, iii, and v and at the same time shows us the other element in Faustus that he cannot get rid of. But note especially the subtle use of the pattern in mid-scene, where Faustus's uncontrollable concern with *heaven* takes the form of an apparently detached discussion of the *heavens*. And what lies beneath the surface comes out when he suddenly asks, "Tell me who made the world." This is the crisis of the play as far as the central problem of knowledge is concerned. First we realize that for Faustus the power-knowledge for which he has given up everything is not enough: the eternal problems of the mind and spirit, whose reality he had denied, keep pressing back upon him. Ironically, he had long ago had an answer to the question which he now asks. The final irony is that now he can get no answer—a situation full of meaning. For Faustus can tell, from Mephistophilis's protective attitude to "our kingdom," that there are conflicting forces in the universe, a fact which by implication he had denied. And the ultimate truth is that knowledge depends upon point of view, upon attitude toward the materials of knowledge: Faustus has adopted the wrong point of view; his premises are wrong. He wants "power-knowledge" to give him knowledge of final, universal truth.

It is just at this moment that he has a bitter flash of recognition, like that which had led to his *Consummatum est* in Scene v; but this time it is open and entirely undisguised. "Think . . . upon god that made the world," he says, and he comes closer than at any other time to breaking his contract. Thus we can see the play dramatically advancing: Faustus's ultimate fate becomes the more meaningful as he struggles, but still is unable, to conquer his passion for power.

The parade of the Sins after Faustus has reaffirmed his loyalty to hell permits too great a reduction of tension, and this part of the scene is rather insipid. But does the scene have a dramatic function? Why do the devils introduce the Sins? Do they treat Faustus in a similar fashion earlier in the play? Does the exhibition of the Sins have, as might be expected, any moral significance? What is ironic about this situation? In one sense the Sins may be said to be the kind of knowledge the devils can give, and Faustus seems pleased with it. Is there anything ironic in this? Is such knowledge like that which he seeks earlier? If, then, this part of the scene may be said to be valid in conception, how might the author have given it more force and vitality?

The student should note the excellent irony of Faustus's lines before and after the Sins' parade. Before, he says it will be as pleasing to him "As Paradise was to Adam the first day." How is this line—in its imaginative evocations—related to other lines in the play—for instance, v, 74? What contrast does it suggest between Adam and Faustus? And, at the same time, what similarity between them? Did Adam also face a problem of knowledge? Afterwards Faustus exclaims, "O might I see hell, and return again. How happy were I then!" What are the ironies in this speech? Does it in any way add to the suggested parallel with Adam?

At the end Wagner says that Faustus is studying astronomy; that is, the *heavens* are still on his mind. But we see him asking no more questions: *he no longer seeks final truths.* His quest for knowledge is ended: from now on, until the last two scenes, he simply exercises power. When we recall that "all power corrupts, and absolute power corrupts absolutely," we expect deterioration.

Scenes vii, x, xi, xii. Here we see Faustus, having given up the quest for knowledge (except for the brief statement of the Chorus that he is skilled in astrology, an undramatic suggestion of his continuing interest in the *heavens*), merely exercising power. Note precisely what he does with his power in each of the scenes. Does he use it well? How does this Faustus compare with the earlier philosophical Faustus? Do these scenes constitute a commentary on Faustus's bargain with the devil? Do we feel that Faustus has driven a good bargain? Do these scenes also constitute a commentary upon man's use of power generally? Do the scenes suggest anything to us about the relationship between the value of power and the end for which it is used? What is the symbolic value of the class of people for whom Faustus performs? Does he ever use his power in behalf of the humble, or of the intellectually and spiritually distinguished?

Faustus's earlier qualms are noticeably missing. Does this fact help show the development of his character? How may we account for the absence of qualms? May it be said that the exercise of power is in itself a kind of intoxication? Is there any reason why Faustus's intellectual quest in the earlier part of the play should be more likely to stimulate his conscience than his present activities are?

Only in the middle of Scene xi (l. 52 ff.) is there a slight indication of a break in his enjoyment. What are the ironic implications of his question, ". . . what, dost think I am a horse-doctor?" Of "Tush, Christ did call the thief upon the cross"? How is the latter related to his use of *consummatum est* in Scene v? Do these few lines suggest a kind of fatal triviality in Faustus? Or might Marlowe—or his reviser—profitably have lengthened the passage?

In these scenes, also, the structure is markedly episodic. There is not a continuous narrative pattern, but new characters and new situations keep coming up and disappearing. The danger is that the reader will feel a series of minor, separated impacts instead of the single major impact of an integrated work. How serious is that danger here? Do these four scenes act as isolated units loosely held together by the fact that they all have the same central character? Or are there other ties? Is there a unity of theme overshadowing the fact that they are separate little adventures? Is there a common symbolic significance that counterbalances the separateness?

Scene xiii. This is a unifying scene in that it brings together the four scenes just discussed and the earlier scenes in the play. As in Scenes vii, x, xi, and xii, Faustus is using his power to do favors—though this time for his fellow scholars. What is the effect of this difference? What is the contrast between Faustus and the scholars? At the same time that he is using power, Faustus is also, as early in the play, suffering his inner conflict—verging on repentance, falling short of it, and sliding deeper into perdition than ever. Does Faustus come as close to repentance here as in Scene vi? How can you tell? What is the significance of this? What is shown by his calling the Old Man "Sweet friend" and then applying the same term to Mephistophilis? What is shown by Faustus's sudden hatred for the Old Man? Why does Mephistophilis want Faustus to commit suicide?

Note the careful structure of the scene: Faustus's pangs of conscience occur *between* the two appearances of Helen, so that there is an ironic contrast between them. To the Scholars the mere sight of Helen is an unalloyed pleasure, but for Faustus the gratification of desire with the traditionally most beautiful woman in the world is less an ecstasy then a need, indeed, a narcotic: it must "extinguish clean / These thoughts that do dissuade me from my vow . . . to Lucifer." He cannot have his pleasure undiluted: he has sold out to get the power that he must now use to help him forget that he has sold out. But before going further, we should note the complex meaning of Helen: at one level, obviously, she stands for physical pleasure. But, as the most beautiful woman, Helen has a special status; as her lover, Faustus is to be distinguished from Ralph, who is content with Nan Spit (viii, 44-47). Further, Helen is also admired by the other Scholars: she is, in part, a symbol of the classical civilization which in the Renaissance called forth such passionate devotion. When Faustus speaks, then, of "heavenly Helen," he is, of course, in terms of the play's dominant language pattern, showing that his *values have been turned upside down;* but we should be clear what he is substituting for the Heaven of old. The student should observe carefully how the *heaven* imagery connects this passage with the rest of the play.

We have already seen the importance of imagery in qualifying and enriching the meaning of drama (see IMAGERY in the Glossary and Index). Special analysis is called for by the imagery in Faustus's speech beginning, "Was this the face, etc.," which is deservedly the most famous in the play; for the imagery consistently conveys both the outer meaning of an intensely felt beauty which can be expressed only in terms of the heaven which it means to Faustus, and the ironic secondary meaning, or undertone, of the destruction to which the experience finally brings Faustus. Helen immediately suggests ("launch'd . . . ships"; "burnt . . . towers") the ten-year war and the destruction of Troy: Faustus is the modern Troy. Ilium was *topless;* in the Christian sense, Faustus's soul is *topless,* that is, lofty, of highest importance. The towers *burned;* Faustus *burns* with passion, and he is doomed to a *burning* hell. *Immortal,* carrying the theme further, functions in three ways. There is the immortality of fame—that of Menelaus and Paris. Then there is a kind of immediate physical immortality (Faustus's heaven): the ecstasy of the kiss will make the recipient feel superior to death. And since to gain Helen, so to speak, he has given up eternal life, what he has got is immortality in hell. In that sense her lips "suck forth my soul," as well as in the immediate sense that she gains his complete and consuming devotion. Thus can "Heaven be in these lips"; they are his religion, the final summary of his values. With these values he will be Paris, though Paris was not an admirable hero, and though Faustus can at the moment think of two of Paris's less heroic exploits. The theme of destruction here becomes overt: Wittenberg shall be sacked like Troy. Again the meaning is double: in one sense Faustus is imaginatively recreating the Troy story in a modern setting, savoring the rhetoric; in another sense, Wittenberg will be sacked by being deprived of its most eminent scholar. Then Faustus makes a very startling comparison —of Helen to Jupiter, and, by implication, of himself to a woman Jupiter had loved—Semele. Thus he expresses the transcendent magnificence of Helen. But he also does much more: Semele had wished to see Jupiter directly, in all his glory, as Faustus has desired Helen. To "hapless Semele" the vision was a brilliant flame which destroyed her. Now notice how completely this fits into and amplifies the context: Ilium was burned, Wittenberg sacked, and Semele destroyed by "flaming Jupiter." So Faustus is destroyed by his fiery vision—the fire of lust, and the fire of hell to which he is doomed. Then Marlowe draws together the two preceding comparisons, continuing with Jupiter, again as a lover. Arethusa is one of the Hesperides, who live in the west, on the borders of eternal darkness; Jupiter is again the sun, and his love of Arethusa is the sunset. The colors of sunset suggest the flames of the other fire images; the connection with "thou art fairer than the evening air" is obvious; and again the disappearance of sunset brilliance into night is in harmony with the idea of loss or destruction that runs throughout the speech and to which Faustus is committed: "And none but thou shalt be my paramour." The Old Man's following line is logical enough: "That from thy soul exclud'st the grace of Heaven." Note, finally, that Jupiter, considered as the sun, and "a thousand stars" are also heavens: what were once the objects of philosophical inquiry and, by extension, symbols of religious belief, have become metaphors of passion.

4. CONCLUSIONS ON STRUCTURE: THE "MORAL MIDDLE"

The middle of the play ends with the Helen scene. Our problem has been to see whether, since the ending (Faustus's payment of his debt) appears to spring directly from the beginning (Faustus's making the contract), the intervening scenes have really had any function besides filling out the play. Since, in investigating the problem, we have had to consider in detail the meaning of the different scenes, we can see how a study of meaning and a study of structure tend to coincide.

First, we have seen Faustus's inner conflict—his constant efforts to summon up the total renunciation by which he might break the contract, and his failure to do so. Hence he has to pay with his soul. In that sense the ending of the play logically follows, not upon the making of the pact with the devil, but upon the subsequent fidelity to the pact and, when he should know better, the reaffirmation of the pact.

Then, we have seen Faustus deteriorate from the quest of knowledge to the trivial exercise of power. Marlowe has given convincing dramatic substance to Faustus's line in Scene xiv: "For vain pleasure of twenty-four years hath Faustus lost eternal joy and felicity." Hence the middle scenes present the conduct by which Faustus comes to deserve his fate, and they become what we may call a "moral middle." Merely to make and carry out a contract is not itself the material of drama; the dramatic, imaginative power of the play depends not u,ۛon legal but upon moral cause and effect. Man does not get to Heaven by contract but has to deserve Heaven; from his struggle to deserve it we get such a play as *Everyman*. Similarly man does not get to hell by contract; he must deserve his fate. So Faustus's *continuing* choice, rather than his initial choice, of evil; his conduct after the making of the contract, rather than the making of the contract itself— is the real cause of the end of the play. The middle is integral.

Granted the case that can be made for the middle parts of the play, it is still true that Scenes vii, x, xi, and xii leave us with a considerable feeling of dissatisfaction. There is too much of the farcical in the presentation of a very serious matter. The triviality of Faustus is of course likely to produce some light moments, but we feel that there ought to be some contrasting material in the scenes, some more serious point of view by which the author may make clear his *attitude* to Faustus's conduct. Perhaps some such material dropped out in the process of revision. So we find in these scenes an unusual technical situation: the protagonist's conduct clearly demands a certain attitude in the author, and yet there is no overt evidence that such an attitude exists. The author seems to enter too wholeheartedly into the tomfoolery, as though the farce were an end in itself, and as if he had no responsibility for indicating its meaning. How might he have remedied this defect? Might he have shown us more of the inner development of Faustus? How might such a character as the Old Man have been utilized here?

5. THE FINAL SCENE

Marlowe has written a very effective ending. Faustus is again in the world of scholars with which he had once been dissatisfied but where he would now gladly stay; we have the ironic contrast of the stay-at-home scholars who have kept their souls and the more daring one who has ranged the world and lost everything. Note other details of this ironic contrast.

The extreme tension of the final soliloquy springs from the inability of a paralyzed will to respond to desires of maddening intensity: "O, I'll leap up to my God! Who pulls me down?" Note the concreteness of the imagery throughout the passage. Note the careful use of the time element to heighten the intensity. Note the pervasive irony, especially that of the line which Faustus quotes from a love poem by Ovid: "Horses of the night, run slowly, O slowly." The original speaker was a lover in the arms of his mistress, hoping for a tardy arrival of the morning which will end his ecstasy. Faustus, however, prays not for a continuation of ecstasy but for a delay of the tortures which even in anticipation make the present almost unbearable. Note the heightening of his terror, which leads him to think up desperately ingenious devices for punishment which will be all-horrible yet fall short of eternal damnation. Note, finally, the details of the language of the scene and the relation of the language to the total meaning of the play. Find the words which reflect the idea of *eternity*, and observe how they continue a theme from the early scenes of the play. Note the constant antiphony of the words *heaven* and *hell*, which underscore the double reality that Faustus had not wished to recognize (cf. iii, 65). Note the constant repetition of the word *soul* and compare this with Faustus's idea expressed in iii, 67. Observe how these regular word patterns are a further way of organizing the materials of the drama as a meaningful whole.

6. Dr. Faustus AS TRAGEDY

Before considering *Dr. Faustus* as tragedy, the student should review the remarks made on tragedy in the analyses of *Everyman* (p. 110), *The London Merchant* (pp. 182–3, 188), and *Rosmersholm* (pp. 312–314), and in the Glossary.

Is Faustus a satisfactory tragic hero? If the student will glance at points 11 and 12 in the outline of Aristotle's *Poetics* in the Glossary, he will find a description of the tragic hero which seems to fit Faustus. We do have a double feeling about Faustus: we recognize that he merits his punishment, that is, that he has a "flaw"; but we pity him as we can pity only a "good" man. That is, there are conflicting elements in his make-up, and we have seen him struggle between them.

Perhaps the most interesting question is this: in what sense is Faustus a "good" man, that is, one "whose misfortune is brought about not by vice and depravity"? First of all, Faustus does *not* do certain things that would evoke our hatred and revulsion; though he says he wants power "To slay mine enemies, and aid my friends," we do not see him slaying enemies or acting cruelly or treacherously. He wants to "live in all voluptuousness," but actually we see almost no unrelieved sensuality; his passion for Helen is certainly not commonplace and sordid, but involves rather a kind of quest, something more than a mere search for another mistress. Faustus is not unfaithful to his friends; he is not ungenerous; in Scene xiv, even under terrible pressure, he is considerate of his friends. Faustus never desires evil as such; rather he forgets the good. He is not so much vicious as misguided. If Faustus can for a while deceive himself by deadening his moral sense, it ultimately comes back to him in a very powerful form. And Faustus is an imaginative man, a "big" man, not a petty and contemptible one; he has tragic grandeur; only a "big" man could be thoroughly damned.

Unlike Barnwell, Faustus faces a moral issue alone; the play is not cluttered up by external matters such as the state of society and the emotions of observers. The structure of the play, the use of only two main characters, is a way of stressing the fact that the problem is private and spiritual. Marlowe omits the pity of others and the praise of Faustus's virtues.

Faustus, we have said, is a kind of Everyman; yet there is a sharp difference between this play and *Everyman*. Both, of course, deal with the problem of human beings who have made serious mistakes with regard to values, and both protagonists undergo penance for their errors. But Everyman's error is caught in time; he has the will to draw back and does draw back; the final stress is upon his achievement of heavenly rewards. In *Everyman* penance is an incident; in *Faustus* penance—here an unmitigable punishment—is the final uncompromising reality. Why? Because Marlowe, in his study of human potentialities for casting off all restrictions and gratifying the individual will, reaches a more profound and searching level. Marlowe goes to the bottom of things in identifying and bringing to light the quality in Everyman which makes him, despite his awareness of strong persuasive forces, unable to draw back. Marlowe's Everyman is daring and heroic; yet he has a familiarity and universality that make him eminently recognizable. In him we see the perennial human aspiration to reconstruct a universe in terms that will give the human being unlimited power with unlimited irresponsibility—indulgence without retribution. It is human both to aspire and in aspiring to lose sight of the limitations of humanity. Here is the center of the tragic irony. As in Sophocles' *Oedipus*, which we shall read later, the protagonist gradually becomes aware of a truth that, if he had had less self-assurance, less rashness, he might have recognized earlier. But when man aspires beyond his own power, he becomes inconsistent and illogical. Faustus denies the supernatural but at the same time invokes the supernatural. He sells his soul—this is either to admit its reality or to try to trick the devil, which would seem very rash in view of the devil's manifest power. But gradually he recognizes his error and understands that the devil implies God. He realizes that he has victimized himself.

Faustus, then, is the tragic hero—the struggling, representative man who is erring rather than vicious. Marlowe, it is worth noting, makes a final vigorous case for his "goodness," that is, for his ability to recover his insight into values which had lost their power to motivate his conduct. Suppose he had denied them: we would then no longer have the tragic hero, for error would have become principle, and the tragic flaw the whole spiritual reality.

FURTHER QUESTIONS ON *Dr. Faustus*

1. Scenes ii, iv, viii, and ix are clearly what is called "comic relief," [1] that is, materials added to entertain the members of an audience who find the tragic mode too exacting. The problem, with regard to such materials, is always to distinguish between "comic relief" which does nothing but afford a change of tone and theme, probably to the detriment of the unity of the work, and "comic relief" which is an integral part of the play, a kind of variation upon the theme of the play in a different tone. Try to determine into which category each of these scenes fits. Of the comic characters, which one has also some part in the serious scenes? Is there anything in Scene ii which has to do with the main plot? How many lines in Scene iv deal with the subject of the main plot? What is the relationship of the conjuring in Scenes iv, viii, and ix to that of the main plot? Is there any suggestion here of the influence of Faustus upon the people around him? Do

---

[1] "Comic relief" is at best a dubious term. As generally used, it seems to imply that even a first-rate dramatist such as Shakespeare deliberately interrupts the main dramatic business upon which he is engaged to introduce playful irrelevancies that will "relieve" the tension. Something of this kind may conceivably happen in inferior theatrical entertainments. But in first rate drama an apparent shift to comedy will be taken at face value only by a naïve audience or reader. In Shakespeare this "relief" will usually be found to be an important variation of the main theme, one which makes just as real and just as strong demands upon the reader as any other part of the play.

they seem improved by the new skills which are available to them? Are there any contrasts which help underline the meaning of the main plot? Compare, for instance, Faustus' desire for Helen of Troy with Robin's for "all the maidens in our parish" and Ralph's for Nan Spit.

2. In discussing *Everyman* we commented upon the play as parable, pointing out the ways in which the dramatic rendering of a theme is richer and more complex than a direct, didactic statement could have been. *Dr. Faustus* is like *Everyman* in that it has a theme which might be stated fairly simply and directly. Is it a simpler or a more complex play than *Everyman?* Why? Does it, like *Everyman*, contain any elements that seem purely didactic in intention? What matters does it go into which it might omit if the writer's intention were purely didactic?

3. Several times in the play Marlowe uses a Chorus. What is its function? By comparing the lines of the Chorus in this play with those of the Chorus in Sophocles' *Oedipus*, which follows, the student will be able to see how little of the original function of the Chorus is left in the 1590's.

4. Study the language of Faustus' soliloquy after the Good and Evil Angels disappear in Scene i. What does it show about his state of mind? Does it suggest that he will use his power well? What is suggested by the frequent repetition of the pronoun *I?*

5. What is the significance of Faustus' use of the verb *die* in his last speech in Scene i? Should it remind us of anything else in the scene?

6. Analyze Faustus' final speech in Scene iii. What does it show about his state of mind? Is the passage reminiscent of any passage earlier in the play?

7. Note the recurrence of the word *soul* in Scenes iii and v? How does the word help connect the scenes with the rest of the play? What is suggested by the constant repetition of the word?

8. We have already spoken of the antiphony of *hell* and *heaven* in Scene xiv. Note the preparation for this antiphony in the language of Scenes v, vi, and xiii.

9. Could Scenes vii, x, xi, and xii be arranged differently? If so, what else do we learn from this fact about the structure of this part of the play?

10. Why is Wagner presented as naïvely failing to understand Faustus's carousing and swilling before his death?

11. What is the function of the Old Man at the end of Scene xiii?

12. Why is the final scene more than a melodramatic thriller?

13. What kind of meaning might this play have—if any—to a reader who could not accept the religious framework? Would it be necessary for such a reader to dismiss the play as simply a rather competent presentation of an obsolete way of looking at life?

FURTHER READING

For a fuller discussion of some of the points raised here see Robert B. Heilman, "The Tragedy of Knowledge: Marlowe's Treatment of Faustus," *Quarterly Review of Literature*, II (1946), 316–332.

4. Sophocles, *Oedipus the King*

O*EDIPUS THE KING* (430 B.C. or 415 B.C. has been conjectured as its date) is usually regarded as Sophocles'
masterpiece, and, indeed, by many as the masterpiece
of all Greek tragedy. In this connection, it may be of significance that
Aristole, in his *Poetics*, refers to *Oedipus the King* more frequently than
to any other play in illustrating his comments on the nature of tragedy.

Before reading the play, the student would do well to read (or reread)
the sketch on classical drama (pp. 701 ff.) for an account of the way in
which a Greek drama was staged. There are other matters which the
student ought to know before embarking on the play—matters with which
Sophocles could assume his audience was familiar.

Many years before the time represented by this play, Oedipus as a
young man and a stranger had come to Thebes to find the Theban king,
Laius, recently dead and the city devastated by a monster, the Sphinx. To
all, she propounded the riddle: What is that which first goes on four feet,
then on two, then at last on three, yet is weakest when it uses most feet?
The Sphinx could be exorcised only by a man who could answer the riddle.
Oedipus answered correctly that the creature was man, who first crawls
on all fours, then walks on two feet, and at last must support himself with
a staff. At his answer, the Sphinx hurled herself off the rock on which she
crouched, and was killed. The city, in gratitude to its savior, offered the
crown to Oedipus, and he became king of Thebes, marrying Jocasta, the
widow of the slain Laius.

Oedipus has reigned in prosperity for many years when now, as the play
opens, his people come to beg him to save the city once more from a plague
which has overwhelmed it.

OEDIPUS THE KING [1]

CHARACTERS

Oedipus, King of Thebes
Priest of Zeus
Creon, brother of Jocasta
Teiresias, the blind prophet
Jocasta

First Messenger, a shepherd from
Corinth
A Shepherd, formerly in the service of
Laius
Second Messenger, from the house
Chorus of Theban Elders

Mute Persons

A train of suppliants (old men, youths, and children)
The children Antigone and Ismene, daughters of Oedipus and Jocasta

[1] The Jebb translation. There is some modernization of vocabulary and idiom.

[*Before the palace of Oedipus at Thebes. In front of the palace there is an altar of Zeus. A group of old men, youths, and young children are gathered around the altar in the attitude of suppliants. They are dressed in white and hold olive branches in their hands. The palace doors open; Oedipus enters, in the robes of a king, and speaks.*]

Oedipus: My children, latest born to Cadmus [2] who was of old, why are you set before me thus with wreathed branches of suppliants, while the city reeks with incense, rings with prayers for health and cries of woe? I considered it unfitting, my children, to hear these things from the mouth of others, and have come hither myself, I, Oedipus, renowned of all.

Tell me, then, venerable man—since it is your natural part to speak for these—in what mood are you placed here, with what dread or what desire? Be sure that I would gladly give all aid; hard of heart would I be, did I not pity such suppliants as these.

Priest of Zeus: Nay, Oedipus, ruler of my land, you see of what years we are who beset your altars—some, nestlings still too tender for flight; some, bowed with age, priests, as I of Zeus; and these, the chosen youth; while the rest of the folk sit with wreathed branches in the marketplaces, and before the two shrines of Pallas, and where Ismene gives answer by fire.

For the city, as you yourself see, is now too sorely vexed, and can no more lift her head from beneath the angry waves of death; a blight is on her in the fruitful blossoms of the land, in the herds among the pastures, in the barren pangs of women; and above all the flaming god, the malign plague, has swooped on us, and ravages the town; by whom the house of Cadmus is made waste, but dark Hades rich in groans and tears.

[2] The legendary founder of Thebes.

It is not as deeming you ranked with gods that I and these children are suppliants at your hearth, but as deeming you first of men, both in life's common chances, and when mortals have to do with more than man: seeing that you came to the town of Cadmus, and did free us from the tax that we rendered to the hard songstress; and this, though you knew nothing from us that could help you, nor had been schooled; no, by a god's aid, it is said and believed, did you uplift our life.

And now, Oedipus, king glorious in all eyes, we beseech you, all we suppliants, to find for us some succor, whether by the whisper of a god you know it, or perhaps as in the power of man; for I see that, when men have been proved in deeds past, the issues of their counsels, too, most often have effect.

On, best of mortals, again uplift our state! On, guard your fame, since now this land calls you savior for your former zeal; and never be it our memory of your reign that we were first restored and afterward cast down: nay, lift up this state in such a way that it may fall no more!

With good omen you gave us that past happiness; now also show yourself the same. For if you are to rule this land, even as you are now its lord, it is better to be lord of men than of a waste; since neither walled town nor ship is anything, if it is void and no men dwell within it with you.

Oedipus: Oh my piteous children, known, well known to me are the desires wherewith you have come; well know I that you suffer all; yet, sufferers as you are, there is not one of you whose suffering is as mine. Your pain comes on each of you for himself alone, and for no other; but my soul mourns at once for the city, and for myself, and for you.

So that you rouse me not, truly, as one sunk in sleep; no, be sure that I have wept very many tears, gone many ways in wanderings of thought. And the sole remedy which, well pondering, I could find, this I have put into act. I have sent the son of Menoeceus, Creon, my own wife's brother, to the Pythian house 5 of Phoebus,[3] to learn by what deed or word I might deliver this town. And already, when the lapse of days is reckoned, it troubles me what he is doing; for he delays strangely, beyond 10 the fitting time. But when he comes, then shall I be no true man if I do not do all that the god shows.

Priest: Nay, in season have you spoken; at this moment these sign to 15 me that Creon draws near.

Oedipus: O King Apollo, may he come to us in the brightness of saving fortune, even as his face is bright!

Priest: Indeed, to all appearance he 20 brings comfort; else would he not be coming crowned thus quickly with berry-laden bay.

Oedipus: We shall know soon; he is within hearing distance. [*Enter Creon.*] 25 Prince, my kinsman, son of Menoeceus, what news have you brought us from the god?

Creon: Good news. I tell you that even troubles hard to bear, if by chance all 30 goes well, will end in perfect peace.

Oedipus: But what is the oracle? So far, your words make me neither bold nor yet afraid.

Creon: If you wish to hear while these 35 are present, I am ready to speak, or else to go within.

Oedipus: Speak before all. The sorrow which I bear is for these more than for my own life.

Creon: With your permission, I will tell what I heard from the god. Phoebus our lord bids us plainly to drive out a defiling thing which, he says, has been harbored in this land, and not to harbor 45 it so that it cannot be healed.

Oedipus: By what rite shall we cleanse ourselves? What is the manner of the misfortune?

Creon: By banishing a man, or by bloodshed in payment of bloodshed, since it is that blood which brings the tempest on our city.

Oedipus: And who is the man whose fate he thus reveals?

Creon: Laius, king, was lord of our land before you were pilot of this state.

Oedipus: I know it well—by hearsay, for I never saw him.

Creon: He was slain, and the god now bids us plainly to wreak vengeance on his murderers, whoever they may be.

Oedipus: And where are they upon the earth? Where shall the dim track of this old crime be found?

Creon: In this land, said the god. What is sought for can be caught; only that which is not watched escapes.

Oedipus: And was it in the house, or in the field, or on strange soil that Laius met this bloody end?

Creon: It was on a visit to Delphi, as he said, that he had left our land; and he came home no more, after he had once set forth.

Oedipus: And was there none to tell? Was there no comrade of his journey who saw the deed, from whom information might have been gained, and used?

Creon: All perished, save one who fled in fear, and could tell for certain only one thing of all that he saw.

Oedipus: And what was that? One thing might show the clue to many, could we get but a small beginning for hope.

Creon: He said that robbers met 40 and fell on them, not with the strength of one man, but with very many hands.

Oedipus: How, then, unless there was some trafficking in bribes from here, should the robber have dared thus far?

Creon: Such things were surmised, but, Laius once slain, amid our troubles no avenger rose.

Oedipus: But, when royalty had fallen 50 thus, what trouble in your path can have hindered a full search?

[3] The oracle of Phoebus Apollo at Delphi.

Creon: The riddling Sphinx had made us let dark things go, and bade us think of what lay at our doors.

Oedipus: Well, I will start afresh, and once more make dark things plain. Right worthily has Phoebus, and worthily have you, bestowed this care on the cause of the dead; and so, as is fitting, you shall find me too leagued with you in seeking vengeance for this land, and for the god besides. On behalf of no far-off friend, no, but in my own cause, shall I dispel this taint. For whoever was the slayer of Laius might wish to take vengeance on me also with a hand as fierce. Therefore, in doing right to Laius, I serve myself.

Come, hasten my children, rise from the altar steps, and lift these suppliant boughs; and let some other summon hither the folk of Cadmus, warned that I mean to leave nought untried; for our health, with the god's help, shall be made certain—or our ruin.

Priest: My children, let us rise; we came at first to seek what this man himself promises. And may Phoebus, who sent these oracles, come to us therewith, our savior and deliverer from the pest.

[*Exeunt Oedipus and Priest. Enter Chorus of Theban elders.*]

Chorus: [*Singing.*]

Strophe 1

O sweetly-speaking message of Zeus, in what spirit have you come from golden Pytho to glorious Thebes? I am on the rack, terror shakes my soul, O Delian healer [4] to whom wild cries rise, in holy fear of you; what thing you will work for me, perchance unknown before, perchance renewed with the revolving years. Tell me, immortal voice, born of golden hope!

Antistrophe 1

First I call on you, daughter of Zeus, divine Athena, and on your sister,

[4] Apollo, whose birthplace was Delos.

guardian of our land, Artemis, who sits on her throne of fame, above the circle of our Agora, and on Phoebus the Fardarter: O shine forth on me, my three-fold help against death! If ever aforetime, to halt a ruin hurrying on the city, you drove a fiery pest beyond our borders, come now also!

Strophe 2

Woe is me, countless are the sorrows I hear; a plague is on all our host, and thought can find no weapon for defense. The fruits of the glorious earth grow not; by no birth of children do women surmount the pangs in which they shriek; and life on life may you see sped, like bird on nimble wing, aye, swifter than resistless fire, to the shore of the western god.

Antistrophe 2

By such deaths, past numbering, the city perishes; unpitied, her children lie on the ground, spreading pestilence, with none to mourn; and meanwhile young wives, and gray-haired mothers with them, uplift a wail at the steps of the altars, some here, some there, entreating for their weary woes. The prayer to the Healer rings clear, and, blent therewith, the voice of lamentation; for these things, golden daughter of Zeus, send us the bright face of comfort.

Strophe 3

And grant that the fierce god of death, who now with no brazen shields, yet amid cries as of battle, wraps me in the flame of his onset, may turn his back in speedy flight from our land, borne by a fair wind to the great deep of Amphitrite, or to those waters in which none find haven, even to the Thracian wave; for if night leave anything undone, day follows to accomplish this. O you who wield the powers of the fire-fraught lightning, O Zeus our father, slay him beneath your thunderbolt!

Antistrophe 3

Lycean [5] *King, gladly would I see your
shafts also, from your bent bow's string of
woven gol`, go abroad in their might, our
champions in the face of the foe; yea, and*

[5] Theban, after Lycus, a legendary king
of Thebes.

*the flashing fires of Artemis wherewith
she glances through the Lycian hills. And
I call him whose locks are bound with
gold, who is named with the name of this*
[5] *land, ruddy Bacchus to whom Bacchantes
cry, the comrade of the Maenads, to draw
near with the blaze of his blithe torch, our
ally against the god unhonored among gods.*

QUESTIONS [6]

1. What is the tone of the first speech of Oedipus? In this connection examine the whole speech and particularly the line "I, Oedipus, renowned of all." The speech is evidently that of a father of his people and it is a formal speech. What else does it suggest about the speaker?

2. Notice that the priest in his formal supplication to Oedipus states explicitly that they do not deem Oedipus "ranked with gods" but the "first of men." Yet does not the very carefulness of the priest indicate that there is a tendency to regard Oedipus almost as a divinity?

3. What is the effect of having the priest remind Oedipus of his former victory over the Sphinx?

4. At Creon's return Oedipus dismisses his suggestion that he relate the oracle to him privately and asks that it be given in the hearing of all. What does this suggest about Oedipus's virtues? About his confidence?

5. It is evident that Sophocles wishes to account for the fact that the investigation of the murder of Laius has been deferred for so long. Does Creon's answer, "The riddling Sphinx had made us let dark things go, and bade us think of what lay at our doors," account for the matter satisfactorily? Does the play suggest that Oedipus was sufficiently ambitious to have accepted the proffered throne without asking too many questions?

[*Oedipus enters during the closing strains of the choral song.*]

Oedipus: You pray, and in answer to your prayer—if you will give a loyal welcome to my words and minister to your own disease—you may hope to find succor and relief from woes. These words will I speak publicly, as one who has been a stranger to this report, a [10]

stranger to the deed, for I should not be as far on the track if I were tracing it alone, without a clue. But as it is, since it was only after the time of the [5] deed that I was numbered a Theban among Thebans, to you, the Cadmeans all, I do thus proclaim.

Whoever of you knows by whom Laius son of Labdacus was slain, I bid [10] him to declare all to me. And if he is

---

[6] The questions on the different parts of *Oedipus the King* are always placed after the choruses. These mark divisions of the play which are comparable to those made by the act divisions of Roman and modern drama.

afraid, I tell him to remove the danger of the charge from his path by denouncing himself; for he shall suffer no heavier penalty than to leave the land, unhurt. Or if anyone knows an alien, from another land, as the assassin, let him not keep silence; for I will pay his reward, and my thanks shall rest with him besides.

But if you keep silence—if anyone, through fear, shall seek to screen friend or self from my behest—hear what I then shall do. I charge you that no one of this land, of which I hold the power and the throne, give shelter or speak word unto that murderer, whoever he be, make him partner of his prayer or sacrifice, or serve him with the lustral rite; but that all ban him their homes, knowing that *this* is our defiling thing, as the oracle of the Pythian god has newly shown me. I am then in this manner the ally of the god and of the slain. And I pray solemnly that the slayer, whoever he be, whether his hidden guilt is lonely or has partners, may evilly, as he is evil, wear out his unblest life. And for myself I pray that if, with my cognizance, he should become an inmate of my house, I may suffer the same things which just now I called down upon others. And on you I lay it to make all these words good, for my sake, and for the sake of the god, and for our land's, thus blasted with barrenness by angry heaven.

For even if the matter had not been urged on us by a god, it was not fitting that you should leave the guilt thus unpurged, when one so noble, and he your king, had perished; rather were you bound to search it out. And now, since it is I who hold the powers which once he held, who possess his bed and the wife who bore offspring to him; and since, had his hope of issue not been frustrated, children born of one mother would have made ties betwixt him and me—but, as it was, fate swooped upon his head; but, by reason of these things will I uphold this cause, just as though it were the cause of my own father, and

will leave nothing untried in seeking to find him whose hand shed that blood, for the honor of the son of Labdacus and of Polydorus and elder Cadmus and Agenor who was of old.

And for those who obey me not, I pray that the gods send them neither harvest of the earth nor fruit of the womb, but that they be wasted by their lot that now is, or by one yet more dire. But for all you, the loyal folk of Cadmus to whom these things seem good, may Justice our ally, and all the gods be with you graciously forever.

Leader of the Chorus: As you have put me on my oath, my oath, O king, I will speak. I am not the slayer, nor can I point to him who slew. As for the question, it was for Phoebus, who sent it, to tell us this thing—who can have wrought the deed.

Oedipus: Justly said; but no man on earth can force the gods to do what they will not.

Leader: I would gladly say what seems to me next best after this.

Oedipus: If there is yet a third course, do not hesitate to show it.

Leader: I know that our lord Teiresias is the seer most like to our lord Phoebus; from whom, O king, a searcher into these things might learn them most clearly.

Oedipus: Not even this have I left out of my cares. On the hint of Creon, I have twice sent a man to bring him; and this long while I marvel why he is not here.

Leader: Indeed, the rumors are but faint and old.

Oedipus: What rumors are they? I look to every story.

Leader: Certain wayfarers were said to have killed him.

Oedipus: I, too, have heard it, but none sees him who saw it.

Leader: Nay, if he knows what fear is, he will not stay when he hears your curses, so dire are they.

Oedipus: When a man shrinks not from a deed, neither is he scared by a word.

Leader: Well, here is one to put him to the test. For here they bring at last the godlike prophet, in whom alone of men the truth lives.

[*Enter Teiresias, led by a boy.*]

Oedipus: Teiresias, whose soul grasps all things, the lore that may be told and the unspeakable, the secrets of heaven and the low things of earth, you feel, though you cannot see, what a plague 10 haunts our state, from which, great prophet, we find in you our protector and our only savior. Now Phoebus, if indeed you do not know it from the messengers, sent answer to our question 15 that the only riddance from the pest which could come was if we should learn aright the slayers of Laius, and slay them, or send them into exile from our land. Do you then, grudge neither voice 20 of birds nor any other way of seer-lore that you have, but rescue yourself and the state, rescue me, rescue all that is defiled by the dead. For we are in your hand; and man's noblest task is to help 25 others by his best means and powers.

Teiresias: Alas, how dreadful to have wisdom where it profits not the wise! Aye, I knew this well, but let it slip out of mind; else would I never have 30 come here.

Oedipus: What now? How sad you have come in.

Teiresias: Let me go home. Most easily will you bear your burden to the 35 end, and I mine, if you will consent.

Oedipus: Your words are strange, nor kindly to the state which nurtured you, when you withhold this response.

Teiresias: No, I see that you, on your 40 part, do not open your lips in season; therefore I do not speak, that I also may not have your misfortune.

Oedipus: For the love of the gods, turn not away, if you have knowledge; 45 all we suppliants implore you on our knees.

Teiresias: Aye, for you are all without knowledge; but never will I reveal my griefs, that I may not tell yours. 50

Oedipus: How say you? You know the secret, and will not tell it, but are minded to betray us and to destroy the state?

Teiresias: I will pain neither myself 5 nor you. Why vainly ask these things? You will never learn them from me.

Oedipus: What, basest of the base— for you would anger a stone itself—will you never speak out? Can nothing touch you? Will you never make an end?

Teiresias: You blame my mood, but do not see that to which you are wedded. No, you find fault with me.

Oedipus: And who would not be angry to hear the words with which you now slight this city?

Teiresias: The future will come of itself, though I shroud it in silence.

Oedipus: Then, seeing that it must come, you on your part should tell of it.

Teiresias: I will speak no further. Rage, if you will, with the fiercest anger that your heart knows.

Oedipus: Aye, indeed I will not spare, so angry am I, to speak all my thought. Know that you seem to me even to have helped in plotting the deed, and to have done it, short of slaying with your hands. If you had eyesight, I would have said, also, that the doing of this thing was yours alone.

Teiresias: Indeed? I charge you that you abide by the decree of your own mouth, and from this day speak neither to these elders nor to me; *you* are the accursed defiler of this land.

Oedipus: So brazen with your blustering taunt? And by what means do you trust to escape your due?

Teiresias: I have escaped: in my truth is my strength.

Oedipus: Who taught you this? It was not, at least, your art.

Teiresias: You—for you spurred me into speech against my will.

Oedipus: What speech? Speak again that I may learn it better.

Teiresias: Did you not grasp my 50 meaning before? Or are you tempting me in talk?

Oedipus: No, I did not grasp it so that I can call it known. Speak again.

Teiresias: I say that you are the slayer of the man whose slayer you seek.

Oedipus: Now you shall rue it that you have twice spoken words so dire.

Teiresias: Would you have me say more, that you may be more angry?

Oedipus: What you will; it will be said in vain.

Teiresias: I say that you have been living in an unguessed shame with your nearest kin, and see not to what woe you have come.

Oedipus: Do you indeed think that you shall always speak thus without smarting?

Teiresias: Yes, if there is any strength in truth.

Oedipus: Indeed there is—for all except you; for you that strength is not, since you are maimed in ear, and in mind, and in eye.

Teiresias: Aye, and you are a poor wretch to utter taunts which every man here will soon hurl at you.

Oedipus: Night, endless night has you in her keeping, so that you can never hurt me, or any man who sees the sun.

Teiresias: No, your doom is not to fall by *me.* Apollo is enough, whose care it is to work that out.

Oedipus: Are these Creon's schemes, or yours?

Teiresias: No, Creon is not a plague to you: you are your own.

Oedipus: O wealth, and empire, and skill surpassing skill in life's keen rivalries, how great is the envy which cleaves to you, if for the sake of this very power which the city has put into my hands, a gift unsought, Creon the trusty, Creon my old friend, has crept on me by stealth, yearning to thrust me out of it, and has suborned such a scheming juggler as this, a tricky quack, who has eyes only for his gains, but in his art is blind.

Come, now, tell me, where have you proved yourself a seer? Why, when the Watcher was here who wove dark song,[7] did you say nothing that could free this folk? Yet the riddle, at least, was not for the first comer to read. There was need of a seer's skill, and none such were you found to have, either by help of birds, or as known from any god. No, I came, I, Oedipus the ignorant, and made her mute, when I seized the answer by my wit, untaught by birds. And it is I whom you are trying to oust, thinking to stand close to Creon's throne. I think that you and the plotter of these things will regret your zeal to purge the land. Indeed, if you did not seem to be an old man, you would have learned to your cost how bold you are.

Leader: To our thinking, both this man's words and yours, Oedipus, have been said in anger. Not for such words is our need, but to seek how we shall best carry out the mandates of the god.

Teiresias: King though you are, the right of reply at least must be judged the same for both; of that I too am lord. Not to you do I live as servant, but to Loxias;[8] and so I shall not stand enrolled under Creon for my patron. And I tell you, since you have taunted me even with blindness, that you have sight, yet see not in what misery you are, nor where you dwell, nor with whom. Do you know of what stock you are? And you have been an unwitting foe to your own kin, in the shades, and on earth above; and the double lash of your mother's and your father's curse shall one day drive you from this land in dreadful haste, with darkness then on the eyes that now see true.

And what place shall not be harbor to your shriek, what of all Cithaeron shall not ring with it soon, when you have learned the meaning of the nuptials in which, within that house, you found a fatal haven after a voyage so fair? And you do not guess of a throng of other ills, which shall make you level with your true self and with your own brood.

[7] The Sphinx. [8] Apollo.

Therefore heap your scorn on Creon and on my message; for no one among men shall ever be crushed more miserably than you.

Oedipus: Are these taunts to be indeed borne from *him?* Hence, ruin take you! Hence, this instant! Back, away, go away from these doors!

Teiresias: I would never have come, not I, if you had not called me.

Oedipus: I did not know that you were about to speak folly, or it would have been long before I called you to my house.

Teiresias: Such am I—as you think, 15 a fool; but for the parents who begot you, sane.

Oedipus: What parents? Stay . . . and who of men is my father?

Teiresias: This day shall show your 20 birth and shall bring your ruin.

Oedipus: What riddles, what dark words you always speak.

Teiresias: But are you not most skilled in unraveling dark speech?   25

Oedipus: Make that my reproach in which you will find me great.

Teiresias: Yes, it was just that fortune that undid you.

Oedipus: But if I delivered this town, 30 I do not care.

Teiresias: Then I will go; so do you, boy, take me hence.

Oedipus: Aye, let him take you. While here, you are a hindrance, a trouble; 35 when you have vanished, you will vex me no more.

Teiresias: I will go when I have done my errand, fearless of your frown, for you can never destroy me. And I tell 40 you: the man of whom you have for a long time been in quest, uttering threats, and proclaiming a search into the murder of Laius—that man is here, in appearance an alien sojourner; but 45 presently he shall be found a native Theban, and shall not be glad of his fortune. A blind man, he who now has sight, a beggar, who now is rich, he shall make his way to a strange land, 50 feeling the ground before him with his staff. And he shall be found at once brother and father of the children with whom he consorts; son and husband of the woman who bore him; heir to his 5 father's bed, shedder of his father's blood.

So go in and think of that; and if you find that I have been at fault, say thenceforth that I have no understand- 10 ing in prophecy. [*Teiresias is led out by the boy. Oedipus enters the palace.*]

Chorus [*Singing.*]

Strophe 1

Who is he of whom the divine voice from the Delphian rock has spoken, as having wrought with red hands horrors that no tongue can tell?

It is time that he ply in flight a foot stronger than the feet of storm-swift steeds; for the son of Zeus is springing on him, all armed with fiery lightnings, and with him come the dread, unerring fates.

Antistrophe 1

Yea, newly given from snowy Parnassus, the message has flashed forth to make all search for the unknown man. Into the wild wood's covert, among caves and rocks he is roaming, fierce as a bull, wretched and forlorn on his joyless path, still seeking to put from him the doom spoken at Earth's central shrine; [9] *but that doom ever lives, ever flits around him.*

Strophe 2

Dreadly, indeed, dreadly does the wise augur move me, who approve not, nor am able to deny. How to speak, I know not; I am fluttered with forebodings; neither in the present have I clear vision, nor of the future. Never in past days, nor in these, have I heard how the house of Labdacus or the son of Polybus [10] *had, either against the other, any grief that I could bring as proof in assailing the public fame*

[9] At Delphi.   [10] Oedipus, who recognized Polybus, King of Corinth, as his father.

*f Oedipus, and seeking to avenge the line
*f Labdacus for the undiscovered murder.

Antistrophe 2

Nay, Zeus and Apollo are keen of
thought, and know the things of earth; but
that mortal seer wins knowledge above
mine, of this there can be no sure test,

though man may surpass man in lore.
Yet, until I see the word made good, nevei
will I assent when men blame Oedipus.
Before all eyes, the winged maiden came
5 against him of old, and he was seen to be
wise; he bore the test, in welcome service to
the state. Never, therefore, by the verdict oj
my heart shall he be judged guilty of crime.

QUESTIONS

1. Note the first speech of Oedipus in the preceding section of the play: "You pray, and in answer to your prayer—if you will give a loyal welcome to my words," etc. Does this passage suggest that Oedipus considers the prayer made by the chorus as a rather perfunctory ritual which one ought to observe but which can scarcely be productive of any actual good?

2. In his second speech Oedipus states that ". . . no man on earth can force the gods to do what they will not." Consider these lines in connection with the colloquy with Teiresias which follows. The lines may help account for Oedipus's suspicion of Teiresias: that is, Teiresias as a mere mortal cannot force the gods to speak and therefore may be lying. But do not the lines make an ironic comment upon Oedipus's own conduct toward Teiresias in which he tries to force the priest of the gods to speak against his will?

3. The first speech of Teiresias is highly interesting in terms of what follows in the play. Teiresias evidently believes that there can be a wisdom which "profits not the wise" and that the possessor of such wisdom is therefore miserable. Evidently Oedipus finds it difficult to believe that there can be a knowledge which profits nothing—in short, to believe that sometimes it may be folly to be wise. Does his reply to Teiresias' first speech indicate this view? Does his whole conduct through the first part of the play indicate it?

4. Of course Teiresias, when angered sufficiently, does speak. Is the loosening of his tongue properly motivated? If so, what light does this motive throw upon his original refusal to speak?

5. Among the taunts which Oedipus hurls at Teiresias is that Teiresias is "a tricky quack, who has eyes only for his gains, but in his art is blind." In part of course this is an obvious jibe at Teiresias's physical blindness. As a sarcasm, it is particularly ironic, since Teiresias is the priest of Apollo, god of the sun. Are there other senses in which the epithet is true or, in the course of the play, comes to be true?

6. Note that Oedipus, like his people, attaches great importance to his victory over the riddling Sphinx. Can it be said that this victory—achieved, as Oedipus says, "by my wit, untaught of birds"—has tended to blind Oedipus to possibilities which pure reason fails to see?

7. What is the particular dramatic function of the chorus which follows this angry argument between Oedipus and Teiresias? Is it in part to justify

the previous conduct of Oedipus as natural? Is it to reaffirm the fact that Apollo will track down the murderer, no matter how carefully he hides himself?

[Enter Creon.]
Creon: Fellow citizens, having learned that Oedipus the king lays dire charges against me, I am here, indignant. If, in the present troubles, he thinks that he 5 has suffered from *me*, by word or deed, anything that tends to harm, in truth I do not want my full term of years, when I must bear such blame as this. The wrong of this rumor touched me 10 not in one point alone, but has the largest scope, if I am to be called a traitor in the city, a traitor too by you and by my friends.

Leader of the Chorus: But this taunt 15 came under stress, perhaps, of anger, rather than from the purpose of the heart.

Creon: And the saying was uttered, that *my* counsels won the seer to utter 20 his falsehoods?

Leader: Such things were said—I know not with what meaning.

Creon: And was this charge laid against me with steady eyes and steady mind? 25

Leader: I know not. I see not what my masters do. But here comes our lord forth from the house.

[Enter Oedipus.]

Oedipus: Sirrah, how did you come 30 here? Have you a front so bold that you have come to my house, you who are the proved assassin of its master, the palpable robber of my crown? Come, tell me, in the name of the gods, was it 35 cowardice or folly that you saw in me, that you plotted to do this thing? Did you think that I would not note this deed of yours creeping on me by stealth, or that, aware of it, I would not ward 40 it off? Now is not your foolish attempt— to seek, without followers or friends, a throne—a prize which followers and wealth must win?

Creon: Mark me now. In answer to 45 your words, hear a fair reply, and then judge for yourself on the basis of knowledge.

Oedipus: You are apt in speech, but I have a poor understanding for your lessons, since I have found you my malignant foe.

Creon: Now first hear how I will explain this very thing—

Oedipus: But one thing, do not explain—that you are not false.

Creon: If you think that stubbornness without sense is a good gift, you are not wise.

Oedipus: If you think that you can wrong a kinsman and escape the penalty, you are not sane.

Creon: Justly said, I grant you. But tell me what is the wrong that you say you have suffered from me.

Oedipus: Did you advise, or did you not, that I should send for that reverend seer?

Creon: And now I am still of the same mind.

Oedipus: How long is it then, since Laius—

Creon: Since Laius . . .? I do not take your drift . . .

Oedipus: —was swept from men's sight by a deadly violence?

Creon: The count of years would run far into the past.

Oedipus: Was this seer, then, practicing his craft in those days?

Creon: Yes, skilled as now, and in equal honor.

Oedipus: Made he, then, any mention of me at that time?

Creon: Never, certainly, when I was within hearing.

Oedipus: But did you not hold a search concerning the murder?

Creon: Due search we held, of course, and learned nothing.

Oedipus: And how was it that this sage did not tell his story *then?*

Creon: I know not. Where I lack light, it is my wont to be silent.

Oedipus: Thus much, at least, you know, and could decleare with light enough.

Creon: What is that? If I know it, I will not deny it.

Oedipus: That, if he had not conferred with you, he would never have talked of *my* slaying Laius.

Creon: If he says so, you know it best; but I claim to learn from you as much as you now have learned from me.

Oedipus: Learn your fill; I shall never be guilty of the blood.

Creon: Say, then: you have married my sister?

Oedipus: The question does not allow denial.

Creon: And you rule the land as she does, with like sway?

Oedipus: She obtains from me all she desires.

Creon: And do not I rank as a third peer of you two?

Oedipus: Indeed, it is just there that you are seen as a false friend.

Creon: Not so, if you would reason with your own heart as I do with mine. And first weigh this: whether you think that any one would rather choose to rule amid terrors than in unruffled peace, granting that he is to have the same powers. Now I, for one, have no yearning in my nature to be a king rather than to do kingly deeds; no, nor has any man who knows how to keep a sober mind. For now I win all favors from you without fear; but, were I ruler myself, I should be doing much even against my own pleasure.

How, then, could royalty be sweeter for me to have than painless rule and influence? Not yet am I so misguided as to desire other honors than those which profit. Now, all wish me joy; now, every man has a greeting for me; now, those who have requests of you crave speech with me, since therein is all their

hope of success. Then why should I resign these things, and take those? No mind will become false while it is wise. Nay, I am no lover of such policy, and, if another put it into practice, I could never bear to act with him.

And, in proof of this, first, go to Pytho,[11] and ask if I brought you true word of the oracle; then next, if you find that I have planned anything in concert with the soothsayer, take and slay me, by the sentence not of one mouth, but of two—by my own no less than yours. But make me not guilty in a corner, on unproved surmise. It is not right to adjudge bad men good recklessly, or good men bad. I count it a like thing for a man to cast off a true friend as to cast away the life in his own bosom, which most he loves. But you will learn these things with sureness in time, for time alone shows a just man; but you could discern a knave even in one day.

Leader: Well has he spoken, O king, for one who takes care not to fall; the quick in counsel are not sure.

Oedipus: When the stealthy plotter is moving on me quickly, I too must be quick with my counterplot. If I await him in repose, his ends will have been gained, and mine missed.

Creon: What do you want, then? To cast me out of the land?

Oedipus: Not so. I desire your death—not your banishment—that you may show forth what kind of thing envy is.

Creon: You speak as one resolved not to yield or to believe?

[*Oedipus:* No, for you do not persuade me that you are worthy of belief.][12]

Creon: No, for I find you not sane.

Oedipus: Sane, at least, in my own interest.

Creon: But you should be so in mine also.

Oedipus: No, you are false.

Creon: But if you understand nothing?

Oedipus: Yet must I rule.

[11] Delphi. [12] Inserted by Jebb for a line which he believed had been lost.

Creon: Not if you rule ill.

Oedipus: Hear him, O Thebes!

Creon: Thebes is for me also—not for you alone.

[*Jocasta enters from the palace.*]

Leader: Cease, princes. And in good time for you I see Jocasta coming yonder from the house, with whose help you should settle your present feud.

Jocasta: Misguided men, why have you raised such foolish strife of tongues? Are you not ashamed, while the land is thus sick, to stir up troubles of your own? Come, go into the house [*to Œdipus*], and you, Creon, to your home—and forbear to make much of a petty grief.

Creon: Kinswoman, Oedipus your lord intends to do dread things to me, actually one or the other of two ills—to thrust me from the land of my fathers, or to slay me.

Oedipus: Yes, for I have caught him, lady, doing evil, by evil arts, against my person.

Creon: Now may I see no good, but perish accursed, if I have done to you any of what you charge me with!

Jocasta: O, for the gods' love, believe it, Oedipus—first for the sake of this awful oath to the gods, and then for my sake and for theirs who stand before you.

[*The following lines between the Chorus and Oedipus and between the Chorus, Jocasta, and Oedipus are chanted responsively.*]

Strophe 1

Chorus: Consent, reflect, hearken, O my king, I pray you.

Oedipus: What grace, then, would you have me grant you?

Chorus: Respect him who in other times was not foolish, and who is now strong in his oath

Oedipus: Now do you know what you crave?

Chorus: Yes.

Oedipus: Declare, then, what you mean.

Chorus: That you should never use an unproved rumor to cast a dishonoring charge on the friend who has bound himself with an oath.

Oedipus: Then be very sure that, when you seek this, for me you seek destruction, or exile from this land.

Strophe 2

Chorus: No, by him who stands in front of all the heavenly host, no, by the Sun! Unblest, unfriended may I die by the uttermost doom, if I have that thought! But my unhappy soul is worn by the withering of the land, and again by the thought that our old sorrows should be crowned by sorrows springing from you two.

Oedipus: Then let him go, though I am surely doomed to death, or to be thrust dishonored from the land. Your lips, not his, move my compassion by their plaint; but he, wherever he be, shall be hated.

Creon: You appear as sullen in yielding, as vehement in the excesses of your wrath; but such natures are justly most difficult for themselves to bear.

Oedipus: You will not leave me in peace, and be gone?

Creon: I will go my way. I have found you undiscerning, but in the eyes of these I am just.   [*Exit Creon.*]

Antistrophe 1

Chorus: Lady, why do you delay to take yonder man into the house?

Jocasta: I will do so when I have learned what has happened.

Chorus: Blind suspicion, bred of talk, arose; and, on the other side, injustice wounds.

Jocasta: It was on both sides?

Chorus: Both.

Jocasta. And what was the story?

Chorus: It is enough, I think, enough—when our land is already vexed, that the matter should rest where it ceased.

Oedipus: Do you see to what you have come, for all your honest purpose, in seeking to relax and blunt my zeal?

Antistrophe 2

Chorus: King, I have said it not once only: be sure that I should have been shown a madman, bankrupt in sane counsel, if I put you away—you who gave a true course to my beloved country when distraught by troubles, you who now also are likely to prove our prospering guide.

Jocasta: In the name of all the gods, tell me also, O king, on what account you have conceived this steadfast wrath.

Oedipus: That will I do, for I honor you, lady, above yonder men. The cause is Creon and the plots that he has laid against me.

Jocasta: Speak on—if you can tell clearly how the feud began.

Oedipus: He says that I stand guilty of the blood of Laius.

Jocasta: Of his own knowledge? Or on hearsay from another?

Oedipus: No, he has made a rascal seer his mouthpiece; as for himself, he keeps his lips wholly pure.

Jocasta: Then absolve yourself of the things of which you speak. Listen to me, and learn for your comfort that there is no mortal who can claim the gift of prophecy. I will give you solid proof of that.

An oracle came to Laius once—I will not say from Phoebus himself, but from his ministers—that the doom should overtake him to die by the hand of his child, who should spring from him and me.

Now Laius—as at least the rumor says—was murdered one day by foreign robbers at a place where three highways meet. And the child's birth was not three days' past, when Laius pinned its ankles together, and had it thrown, by others' hands, on a trackless mountain.

So, in that case, Apollo did not bring it about that the babe should become the slayer of his father, or that Laius should die—the dread thing which he feared—by his child's hand. Thus did the messages of seercraft map out the future. Do not pay any attention to

them. Whatever needful things the god seeks, he himself will easily bring to light.

Oedipus: What restlessness of soul, lady, what tumult of mind has come upon me since I heard you speak!

Jocasta: What anxiety has startled you, that you say this?

Oedipus: I thought I heard this from you: that Laius was slain where three highways meet.

Jocasta: Yes, that was the story; it has not died out yet.

Oedipus: And where is the place where this happened?

Jocasta: The land is called Phocis, and branching roads lead to the same spot from Delphi and from Daulia.

Oedipus: And what is the time that has passed since these things took place?

Jocasta: The news was published to the town shortly before you were first seen in power in this land.

Oedipus: O Zeus, what have you decreed to do to me?

Jocasta: And why, Oedipus, does this thing weigh upon your soul?

Oedipus: Ask me not yet, but tell me what was the stature of Laius, and how ripe his manhood.

Jocasta: He was tall, the silver just lightly strewn among his hair; and his form was not greatly unlike yours.

Oedipus: Unhappy that I am! I think I have been laying myself even now under a dread curse, and did not know it.

Jocasta: How say you? I tremble when I look on you, my king.

Oedipus: I have dread misgivings that the seer can see. But you will make it clearer if you will tell me one thing more.

Jocasta: Indeed, though I tremble, I will answer all that you ask, when I hear it.

Oedipus: Did he go in a small force, or with many armed followers, like a chieftain?

Jocasta: They were five in all—a herald one of them; and there was one carriage, which bore Laius.

Oedipus. Alas! It is now clear indeed. Who was it that gave you these facts, lady?

Jocasta: A servant, the sole survivor who came home.

Oedipus: Is he by chance at hand in the house now?

Jocasta: No, he is not. As soon as he came thence, and found you reigning instead of Laius, he supplicated me, with hand laid on mine, that I would send him to the fields, to the pastures of the flocks, that he might be far from the sight of this town. And I sent him; he was worthy, for a slave, to win even a greater favor than that.

Oedipus: Would, then, that he could return to us without delay!

Jocasta: It is easy. But why do you command this?

Oedipus: I fear, lady, that my own lips have been unguarded; and therefore I am eager to behold him.

Jocasta: Indeed, he shall come. But I too, I think, have a claim to learn what lies heavy on your heart, my king.

Oedipus: Yes, and it shall not be kept from you, now that my forebodings have advanced so far. Who indeed is more to me than you, to whom I should speak as I pass through such a fortune as this?

My father was Polybus of Corinth, my mother the Dorian Merope; and I was held first of all the people in that town, until something happened to me—worthy, indeed of wonder, though not worthy of my own heat concerning it. At a banquet a man full of wine cast it at me in his cups that I was not the true son of my father. And I, vexed, restrained myself for that day as best I might, but on the next I went to my father and mother, and questioned them; and they were angry for the taunt with him who let that word fly. So from them I had comfort; yet the thing was ever rankling in my heart, for it still crept abroad with strong rumor. And, unknown to mother or father, I went to Delphi; and Phoebus sent me

forth disappointed of that knowledge for which I came, but in his response set forth other things, full of sorrow and terror and woe—even that I was fated to defile my mother's bed, and that I should show unto men a brood which they could not endure to behold, and that I should be the slayer of the sire who begot me.

And I, when I had listened to this, turned to flight from the land of Corinth, thenceforth knowing of its region by the stars alone, to some spot where I should never see fulfilment of the infamies foretold in my evil doom. And on my way I came to the place in which you say that this prince perished. Now, lady, I will tell you the truth. When in my journey I was near to those three roads, there met me a herald, and a man seated in a carriage drawn by colts, as you have described; and he who was in front, and the old man himself, were for thrusting me rudely from the path. Then, in anger, I struck him who pushed me aside—the driver; and the old man, seeing it, watched the moment when I was passing, and, from the carriage, brought his goad with two teeth down directly upon my head. Yet he was paid with interest; by one swift blow from the staff in his hand he was rolled right out of the carriage, on his back; and I slew every man of them.

But if this stranger had any tie of kinship with Laius, who is now more wretched than the man before you? What mortal could prove more hated of heaven? Whom no stranger, no citizen, is allowed to receive in his house; whom it is unlawful that any one accost; whom all must repel from their homes! And this—this curse—was laid on me by no mouth but my own! And I pollute the bed of the slain man with the hands by which he perished. Tell me, am I vile? Oh, am I not utterly unclean?—seeing that I must be banished, and in banishment see not my own people, nor set foot in my own land, or else be joined in wedlock to my mother, and slay my sire, even Polybus, who begat and reared me.

Then would not he speak aright of Oedipus, who judged these things sent by some cruel power above man? Forbid, forbid, you pure and awful gods, that I should see that day! No, may I be swept from among men before I behold myself visited with the brand of such a doom!

Leader of the Chorus: To us, indeed, O king, these things are fraught with fear. Yet have hope, until at last you have gained full knowledge from him who saw the deed.

Oedipus: Hope, in truth, rests with me thus far alone; I can await the man summoned from the pastures.

Jocasta: And when he has appeared, what would you have of him?

Oedipus: I will tell you. If his story be found to tally with yours, I at least shall stand clear of the disaster.

Jocasta: And what of special note did you hear from me?

Oedipus: You were saying that he spoke of Laius as slain by robbers. If, then, he still speaks, as before, of several, I was not the slayer: a solitary man could not be identified with that band. But if he names one lonely wayfarer, then beyond doubt this guilt leans to me.

Jocasta: Be assured that thus, at least, the tale was first told. He cannot revoke that, for the city heard it, not I alone. But even if he should diverge somewhat from his former story, never, king, can he show that the murder of Laius, at least, is truly square with prophecy—of whom Loxias [13] plainly said that he must die by the hand of my child. Nevertheless that poor innocent never slew him, but perished first itself. So henceforth, for what concerns divination, I would not look to my right hand or my left.

Oedipus: You judge well. But nevertheless send someone to fetch the peasant, and do not neglect this matter.

Jocasta: I will send without delay. But let us come into the house; I will do nothing except at your good pleasure. [*Oedipus and Jocasta go into the palace.*] *Chorus:* [*Singing.*]

Strophe 1

May destiny still find me winning the praise of reverent purity in all words and deeds sanctioned by those laws of range sublime, called into life throughout the high clear heaven, whose father is Olympus alone; their parent was no race of mortal men, no, nor shall oblivion ever lay them to sleep; the god is mighty in them, and he grows not old.

Antistrophe 1

Insolence breeds the tyrant. Insolence, once vainly surfeited on wealth that is not fitting nor good for it, when it has scaled the topmost ramparts, is hurled to a dire room, wherein no service of the feet can serve. But I pray that the god never quell such rivalry as benefits the state; the god will I ever hold for our protector.

Strophe 2

But if any man walks haughtily in deed or word, with no fear of Justice, no reverence for the images of gods, may an evil doom seize him for his ill-starred pride, if he will not win his vantage fairly, nor keep him from unholy deeds, but must lay profaning hands on sanctities.

Where such things are, what mortal shall boast any more that he can ward the arrows of the gods from his life? In fact, if such deeds are in honor, why should we join in the sacred dance?

Antistrophe 2

No more will I go reverently to earth's central and inviolate shrine, no more to Abae's temple [14] or Olympia,[15] if these

---

[13] Apollo.

[14] A shrine in Phocis. [15] An oracle of Zeus.

oracles do not prove true, so that all men
shall point at them with the finger. Nay,
king, if you are rightly called, Zeus all-
ruling, may it not escape you and your
ever-deathless power!

The old prophecies concerning Laius
are fading; already men are setting them
at nought, and nowhere is Apollo glorified
with honors; the worship of the gods is
5 perishing.

QUESTIONS

1. Note the imagery of sight and blindness which runs through the first speeches of Creon. (This imagery, the student will have noticed, actually occurs in the previous scenes; indeed, such imagery runs throughout the play.) Creon asks (p. 553a, 25) whether Oedipus made the charge of treason "with steady eyes." Then the chorus goes on to say "I see not what my masters do." What is the effect of such passages coming after Oedipus's taunt at Teiresias that he is stone blind, and Teiresias's curse in which he predicts that Oedipus shall become blind? Notice further that the same imagery is at least implied in Oedipus's first speech to Creon: Creon's deed is a "creeping" upon him "by stealth," planned so that Oedipus would not be able to "ward it off."

2. May the whole scene between Creon and Oedipus be said to epito-mize the actions and attitudes of Oedipus throughout the play? That is, this scene displays the process of reasoning by which Oedipus concludes that Creon and Teiresias are plotting against him. It is a "reasonable" con-clusion for Oedipus to make, a natural conclusion; unfortunately, though "natural" and "reasonable," it just happens to be wrong.

3. What other functions does this angry scene between Creon and Oedipus serve? Does it help establish the character of Creon? Does it carry us deeper into a knowledge of Oedipus, the "successful" man? Does it suggest that deep below all of Oedipus's self-confidence there is a basic sense of insecurity and fear that the kingdom is not permanently his?

4. Jocasta's advice that Oedipus not conduct his affairs in public differs from Creon's tentative suggestion, made earlier, that he hear the oracle in private. Here, in public, the men are making a scene which will not do them or the state any good. Yet is there not some connection between Creon's advice and Jocasta's? Is it not possible that Oedipus needs to learn that there are some things best kept quiet and not explored publicly?

5. Jocasta apparently has never before told her husband Oedipus about the oracle's warning to Laius that he should perish by the hand of his own son. Is the fact that she reveals the oracle just at this time sufficiently motivated? Specifically, do not the quarrel between Creon and Oedipus and Oedipus's overwrought condition together account for the fact that she nows tells Oedipus something which evidently she had preferred not to talk about before?

6. Notice that Jocasta's speech (p. 556a, 51) is calculated to allay Oedipus's suspicion of Creon by damning Teiresias and oracles in general. Presumably Jocasta's argument, if completed, would go something like this: since

oracles are not to be trusted, Creon surely would be too wise to use as his instrument the prophecies of a "tricky quack"; but the argument, insofar as it would have exculpated Creon, is not completed, for Oedipus catches at Jocasta's statement that Laius was murdered at a spot where three roads meet. The speech which was to clear Oedipus of fear has actually, by reminding him of the man whom he killed at the meeting of three roads, given him for the first time a positive detail of evidence calculated to suggest that he is the murderer. This ironical pattern is repeated later in the play.

7. Notice how important the imagery of sight and blindness becomes in the speeches between Oedipus and Jocasta which close this scene. Oedipus fears that the "seer can see" after all; "It is now clear indeed"; "I am eager to behold" the shepherd; "in banishment see not my own people"; "Forbid, forbid . . . that I should see that day" etc., etc. What is the effect of this pattern of sight imagery?

8. As we approach the end of this scene Oedipus trembles with real fear that Teiresias's awful statement will prove true. He intends to summon the herdsman. He will play out the string to the end. But the play does not proceed in a straight line downward from this point. There is to be a false hope given in the next scene, and Oedipus and Jocasta are to exult in a kind of triumph before the doom becomes perfectly clear. What is the dramatic effect of the introduction of this false hope?

9. Note that Oedipus, though now alarmed, does *not* fear the fulfillment of the oracle prophesying that he would kill his father. He fears merely that he has incurred the curse which he himself has pronounced on the slayer of Laius. What is gained by indicating here the intensity of his horror at what amounts to the lesser of the two evils?

10. What is the function of the chorus which concludes this scene? Is the antistrophe meant to apply to Oedipus? If not, why does the Chorus voice such opinions here? What is the function of the second antistrophe? Is the reproach that "the old prophecies concerning Laius are fading" meant to apply to Oedipus? Or rather to the difficulties which Oedipus is having in tracing Laius's murderer?

[*Jocasta comes forth, bearing a branch, wreathed with festoons of wool, which, as a suppliant, she is about to lay on the altar of the household god, Lycean Apollo, in front of the palace.*]

Jocasta: Princes of the land, the thought has come to me to visit the shrines of the gods, with this wreathed branch in my hands, and these gifts of incense. For Oedipus excites his soul overmuch with all manner of alarms, nor, like a man of sense, judges the new things by the old, but is at the will of the speaker, if he speaks terrors.

Since, then, by counsel I can do no good, to you, Lycean Apollo, for you 5 are nearest, I have come, a suppliant with these symbols of prayer, that you may find us some riddance from uncleanness. For now we are all afraid, seeing *him* affrighted, even as they who 10 see fear in the helmsman of their ship.

[*While Jocasta is offering her prayers to the god, a Messenger, evidently a stranger, enters and addresses the Elders of the Chorus.*]

Messenger: Might I learn from you, strangers, where is the house of the king Oedipus? Or, better still, tell me 5 where he himself is, if you know.

Leader of the Chorus: This is his dwelling, and he himself, stranger, is within; and this lady is the mother of his children. 10

Messenger: Then may she be ever happy in a happy home, since she is his heaven-blest queen.

Jocasta: Happiness to you also, stranger! It is due your fair greeting. 15 But say what you have come to seek or to tell.

Messenger: Good news, lady, for your house and for your husband.

Jocasta: What is it? And from whom 20 have you come?

Messenger: From Corinth, and at the message which I will soon speak you will rejoice—doubtless, yet perhaps grieve.

Jocasta: And what is it? How does it 25 have a double potentiality?

Messenger: The people wish to make him king of the Isthmian land, as it was said there.

Jocasta: How then? Is the aged Polybus no more in power?

Messenger: No, in truth, for death holds him in the tomb.

Jocasta: How say you? Is Polybus 35 dead, old man?

Messenger: If I do not speak the truth, I am content to die.

Jocasta: O handmaid, away with all speed, and tell this to your master! 40 O you oracles of the gods, where do you stand now! This is the man whom Oedipus long feared and shunned, lest he should slay him; and now this man has died in the course of destiny, not 45 by his hand.

[*Oedipus enters from palace.*]

Oedipus: Jocasta, dearest wife, why have you summoned me forth from these doors?

Jocasta: Hear this man, and judge, 50 as you listen, to what the awful oracles of the gods have come.

Oedipus: And he, who may he be, and what news does he have for me?

Jocasta: He is from Corinth, to tell that your father Polybus no longer lives, but has perished.

Oedipus: How, stranger? Let me have it from your own mouth.

Messenger: If I must first make this news plain, know indeed that he is dead and gone.

Oedipus: By treachery, or by visit of disease?

Messenger: A light thing in the scale brings the aged to their rest.

Oedipus: Ah, he died, it seems, of sickness?

Messenger: Yes, and of the long years that he had counted.

Oedipus: Alas, alas! Why, indeed, my wife, should one look to the hearth of the Pythian seer, or to the birds that scream above our heads, on whose showing I was doomed to slay my father? But he is dead, and is already beneath the earth, and here am I, who have not put hand to spear. Unless, perhaps, he was killed by longing for me; thus, indeed, I should be the cause of his death. But the oracles as they stand, at least, Polybus has swept with him to his rest in Hades: they are worth nothing.

Jocasta: And did I not predict this to you long ago?

Oedipus: You did, but I was misled by my fear.

Jocasta: Now no more take any of these things to heart.

Oedipus: But surely I must needs fear my mother's bed?

Jocasta: Nay, what should mortal fear for whom the decrees of Fortune are supreme, and who has clear foresight of nothing? It is best to live at random, as one may. But do not fear concerning wedlock with your mother. Many men before now have so fared in dreams also, but he to whom these 50 things are as nothing bears his life most easily.

Oedipus. All these bold words of yours would have been well if my mother were not living; but as it is, since she lives, I must necessarily fear, though you speak reassuringly.

Jocasta: Nevertheless your father's death is a great sign to cheer us.

Oedipus: Great, I know, but my fear is of her who lives.

Messenger: And who is the woman about whom you fear?

Oedipus: Merope, old man, the consort of Polybus.

Messenger: And what is it in her that excites your fear?

Oedipus: A heaven-sent oracle of dread import, stranger.

Messenger: Lawful, or unlawful, for another to know?

Oedipus: Lawful, surely. Loxias once said that I was doomed to espouse my own mother, and to shed with my own hands my father's blood. Therefore my home in Corinth was long kept at a distance by me—with a fortunate outcome, indeed. Yet still it is sweet to see the face of parents.

Messenger: Was it indeed for fear of this that you were an exile from that city?

Oedipus: And because, old man, I did not wish to be the slayer of my father.

Messenger: Then why have I not freed you, king, from this fear, seeing that I came with friendly purpose?

Oedipus: Indeed you should have reward due from me.

Messenger: Indeed it was chiefly for this that I came—that, on your return home, I might reap some good.

| *Oedipus:* No, I will never go near my parents.

Messenger: Ah, my son, it is plain enough that you do not know what you are doing.

Oedipus: How, old man? For the gods' love, tell me.

Messenger: If for these reasons you shrink from going home.

Oedipus: Aye, I dread lest Phoebus prove himself true for me.

Messenger: You dread to be stained with guilt through your parents?

Oedipus: Even so, old man. It is this that always terrifies me.

5 *Messenger:* Do you know, then, that your fears are wholly groundless?

Oedipus: How so, if I was born of those parents?

Messenger: Because Polybus was 10 nothing to you in blood.

Oedipus: What do you say? Was Polybus not my father?

Messenger: No more than he who speaks to you, but just so much.

15 *Oedipus:* And how can my sire be equal with him who is as nothing to me?

Messenger: Indeed he did not beget you, any more than I.

Oedipus: Why then did he call me his 20 son?

Messenger: Know that he had received you as a gift from my hands long ago.

Oedipus: And yet he loved me so 25 dearly, who came from another's hand?

Messenger: Yes, his former childlessness brought him to it.

Oedipus: And you—had you bought me or found me by chance, when you 30 gave me to him?

Messenger: Found you in Cithaeron's winding glens.

Oedipus: And why were you roaming in those regions?

35 *Messenger:* I was there in charge of mountain flocks.

Oedipus: What, were you a shepherd, a wandering worker?

Messenger: But your preserver, my 40 son, in that hour.

Oedipus: What was my plight when you took me in your arms?

Messenger: The ankles of your feet might bear witness.

45 *Oedipus:* Ah me, why do you speak of that old trouble?

Messenger: I freed you when you had your ankles pinned together.

Oedipus: Aye, it was a dread brand of 50 shame that I took from my cradle.

Messenger: From that happening you

w:re called by the name which is still yours.

Oedipus: Oh, for the gods' love, was the deed my mother's or father's? Speak!

Messenger: I do not know. He who gave you to me knows that better than I. 5

Oedipus: What, you got me from another? You did not come upon me yourself?

Messenger: No. Another shepherd gave you to me.

Oedipus: Who was he? Can you tell clearly?

Messenger: I think he was called one 15 of the household of Laius.

Oedipus: The king who ruled this country long ago?

Messenger: The same. It was in his service that the man was a shepherd. 20

Oedipus: Is he still alive, that I might see him?

Messenger: Indeed, you people of the country should know best.

Oedipus: Is there any of you present 25 that knows the shepherd of whom he speaks, that has seen him in the pastures or the town? Answer! The hour has come when these things should finally be revealed.

Leader of the Chorus: It appears that he speaks of no other than the peasant whom you are already eager to see. But our lady Jocasta might best tell of that. 35

Jocasta: Why ask of whom he spoke? Pay no attention . . . don't waste a thought on what he said . . . it would be idle.

Oedipus: It must not happen that, 40 with such clues in my grasp, I should fail to bring my birth to light.

Jocasta: For the gods' sake, if you have any care for your life, give up this search! My anguish is enough. 45

Oedipus: Be of courage. Though I be found the son of a slave-mother—aye, a slave for three generations—*you* will not be proved baseborn.

Jocasta: Yet hear me, I implore you: 50 do not do it.

Oedipus: I must not hear of not discovering the whole truth.

Jocasta: Yet I wish you well. I advise you for the best.

Oedipus: These best counsels, then, vex my patience.

Jocasta: Ill-fated one! May you never come to know who you are!

Oedipus: Go, someone, fetch me the herdsman hither, and leave that woman to glory in her princely stock.

Jocasta: Alas, alas, miserable! That word alone can I say to you, and no other word henceforth forever.

[*She rushes into the palace.*]

Leader: Why has the lady gone, Oedipus, in a transport of wild grief? I fear a storm of sorrow will break forth from this silence.

Oedipus: Break forth what will! Be my race never so lowly, I must crave to learn it. That woman, for she is proud with more than a woman's pride, perhaps thinks shame of my base source. But I, who hold myself son of Fortune that gives good will, will not be dishonored. She is the mother from whom I spring, and the months, my kinsmen, have marked me sometimes lowly, sometimes great. Such being my lineage, never more can I prove false to it, or spare to search out the secret of my birth.

Chorus: [*Singing.*]

Strophe

If I am a seer or wise of heart, O Cithaeron, you shall not fail—by yonder heaven, you shall not—to know at tomorrow's full moon that Oedipus honors thee as native to him, as his nurse, and his mother, and that you are celebrated in our dance and song, because you are well pleasing to our prince. O Phoebus to whom we cry, may these things find favor in your sight!

Antistrophe

Who was it, my son, that of the race whose years are many bore you in wedlock with Pan, the mountain-roaming father?

Or was it a bride of Loxias that bore you?
For dear to him are all the upland pas-
tures. Or perhaps it was Cyllene's lord,[16]
   [16] Hermes.

or the Bacchantes' god, dweller on hilltops,
that received you, a newborn joy, from one
of the nymphs of Helicon, with whom he
most has pleasure.

QUESTIONS

1. What value inheres in the fact that Jocasta begins this section of the play with a prayer to Apollo? Is her prayer answered? How? Compare Jocasta's prayer to Apollo, the author of the oracle, with her flouting of oracles just before the song of the chorus (p. 558*b*, 47–49). Is there any inconsistency in her conduct?

2. The messenger from Corinth thinks of himself as the bearer of good news, and proceeds, when he finds what the situation is, to improve the goodness of the news: that is, he tells that Oedipus has not only inherited a kingdom but has escaped the doom foretold by the oracle. Oedipus and Jocasta are aware of the irony involved in the fact that news of the death should be good news. But what further ironies are involved in the situation?

3. May it be said that Oedipus's speech beginning "Alas, alas! Why, indeed, my wife, should one look to the hearth of the Pythian seer," etc. marks the height of his *hubris* or pride? Does Jocasta share his *hubris*?

4. What is the point of having Oedipus and Jocasta attempt to explain away the oracle as mere figurative language? Is this attempt part and parcel of the rationalizing mind which Oedipus displays? (Note that at least on the surface level it is an attempt to save the oracle by finding some meaning for it which has been fulfilled, even though the expected meaning has apparently not been fulfilled.)

5. The Greek dramatists sometimes used a device called stichomythy— that is, a spirited altercation or a riddling question and answer, each statement or question and each answer occupying respectively one line. Stichomythy occurs in the speech in the latter part of the conversation between Oedipus and the messenger beginning at p. 562*a*, 46. Does the device seem to be justified here? What effects does it produce?

6. What is the dramatic value of the messenger's going on to say too much—that is, going on to make his account convincing by adding details which, as they develop, point toward the horrible truth?

7. By p. 563*a*, 36, Jocasta knows the truth, knows that she is the mother of Oedipus. Does she show herself as maternal, as attempting to protect her child in this last appearance of hers on the stage? Is there anything ironic in her assuming such a role?

8. The dramatic value of Oedipus's misunderstanding Jocasta's attempt to make him desist from his questionings is quite obvious. Is the misunderstanding properly motivated as well?

9. May it be said that Oedipus attains his highest point of grandeur and of folly in his speech beginning "Break forth what will! Be my race never so lowly," etc.? Note that a lesser man would be content to let well enough

alone, would not gamble with fate, would decide, for perhaps cowardly reasons, that there can be such a thing as too much knowledge. Is Oedipus's speech, moreover, the speech of a "successful" man, a self-made man? And does it thus point to something very deep in his character and in his motivation—that is, does it point to the kind of essential insecurity which the self-made man so frequently feels?

10. How does the speech of the chorus extend and develop this statement of Oedipus's "pride," or lack of "pride"?

Oedipus: Elders, if it is for me to guess, who have never met with him, I think I see the herdsman of whom we have long been in quest; for in his venerable age he tallies with yonder 5 stranger's years, and besides I recognize those who bring him, I think, as servants of my own. But perhaps you may have the advantage of me in knowledge, if you have seen the herdsman before.

Leader: Yes, I know him, be sure; he 10 was in the service of Laius—trusty as any man in his shepherd's place.

[*The herdsman is brought in.*]

Oedipus: I ask you first, Corinthian 15 stranger, is this he whom you mean?

Messenger: The very man whom you behold.

Oedipus: Ho, you, old man, I would have you look this way and answer all 20 that I ask you. You were once in the service of Laius?

Herdsman: I was—a slave not bought, but reared in the house.

Oedipus: Employed in what labor, or 25 what way of life?

Herdsman: For the best part of my life I tended flocks.

Oedipus: And what were the regions that you mainly frequented?

Herdsman: Sometimes it was Ci- 30 thaeron, sometimes the neighboring ground.

Oedipus: Have you observed this man in those parts— 35

Herdsman: Doing what? . . . What do you mean? . . .

Oedipus: . . . this man here? Or have you ever met him before?

Herdsman: Not that I could speak of at once from memory.

Messenger: And no wonder, master. But I will bring clear recollection to his 5 ignorance. I am sure that he well knows of the time when we abode in the region of Cithaeron—he with two flocks, I his comrade with one—three full half-years, from spring to Arcturus; and then for 10 the winter I used to drive my flock to my own fold, and he took his to the fold of Laius. Did any of this happen as I say, or did it not?

Herdsman: You speak the truth, 15 though 'tis long ago.

Messenger: Come, tell me now: do you know of having given me a boy in those days, to be reared as my own foster son?

Herdsman: What now? Why do you 20 ask the question?

Messenger: That man there, my friend, is he who then was young.

Herdsman: Plague take you! Be silent once for all! 25

Oedipus: Ha! Chide him not, old man. Your words need chiding more than his.

Herdsman: And wherein, most noble 30 master, do I offend?

Oedipus: In not telling of the boy concerning whom he asks.

Herdsman: He speaks without knowledge; he is busy to no purpose.

Oedipus: You do not want to speak 35 with a good grace, but you shall under punishment.

Herdsman: No, for the gods' love, do not misuse an old man.

Oedipus: Ho, someone, pinion him this instant.

Herdsman: Alas, why? What more would you learn?

Oedipus: Did you give this man the child of whom he speaks?

Herdsman: I did, and would I had perished that day.

Oedipus: Well, you will come to that, unless you tell the honest truth.

Herdsman: No, I am much more lost, if I speak.

Oedipus: The fellow is bent, it seems, on more delays . . .

Herdsman: No, no. I said before that I gave it to him.

Oedipus: From where had you got it? In your own house, or from another?

Herdsman: It was not my own; I had received it from a man.

Oedipus: From whom of the citizens here? From what home?

Herdsman: Give up, master, for the gods' love; refrain from asking more.

Oedipus: You are lost if I have to question you again.

Herdsman: It was a child, then, of the house of Laius.

Oedipus: A slave? Or one born of his own family?

Herdsman: Alas, I am on the dreaded brink of speech.

Oedipus: And I of hearing; yet must I hear.

Herdsman: You must know, then, that it was said to be his own child, but your lady within could best say how these things are.

Oedipus: How? She gave it to you?

Herdsman: Yes, O king.

Oedipus: For what end?

Herdsman: That I should make away with it.

Oedipus: Her own child, the wretch?

Herdsman: Yes, from fear of evil prophecies.

Oedipus: What were they?

Herdsman: The tale ran that he must slay his father.

Oedipus: Why, then, did you give him up to this old man?

Herdsman: Through pity, master, thinking that he would bear him away to another land, whence he himself came; but he saved him for the direst woe. For if you are what this man says, know that you were born to misery.

Oedipus: Oh, oh! All brought to pass— all true! O light, may I now look my last upon you, I who have been found accursed in birth, accursed in wedlock, accursed in the shedding of blood!

[*He rushes into the palace.*]

Chorus: [*Singing.*]

Strophe 1

Alas, ye generations of men, how mere a shadow do I count your life! Where, where, is the mortal who wins more of happiness than just the seeming, and, after the semblance, a falling away? Yours is a fate that warns me—yours, yours, unhappy Oedipus—to call no earthly creature blest.

Antistrophe 1

For he, O Zeus, sped his shaft with peer-less skill, and won the prize of an all-prosperous fortune; he slew the maiden with crooked talons who sang darkly; he arose from our land as a tower against death. And from that time, Oedipus, you have been called our king, and have been honored supremely, bearing sway in great Thebes.

Strophe 2

But now whose story is more grievous in men's ears? Who is a more wretched captive to fierce plagues and troubles, with all his life reversed?

Alas, renowned Oedipus! The same bounteous place of rest sufficed you, as child and as father also, that you should make thereon your nuptial couch. Oh, how can the soil wherein your father sowed, unhappy one, have suffered you in silence so long?

Antistrophe 2

Time the all-seeing has found you out
in your despite; he judges the monstrous
marriage wherein begetter and begotten
have long been one.

Alas, child of Laius, would, would
that I had never seen you. I wail as one
who pours a dirge from his lips; truth to
tell, it was you that gave me new life,
5 and through you darkness has fallen upon
my eyes.

QUESTIONS

1. The reluctance of the herdsman to answer repeats a pattern which we have observed before in Oedipus's attempts to elicit information. Does it come here as a boringly repetitious device, or is the effect heightened because we are now familiar with the pattern?

2. Is Oedipus's irritability sufficiently accounted for by the repetition of delay and the heightened tension?

3. Observe the speech of the chorus very carefully (p. 566*b*, 17 ff.). Do they blame Oedipus in this speech? Whose is the guilt which has been revealed? Can there be such a thing as unintended guilt? Do they treat Oedipus as a man who has been apprehended in crime or as a man who is found to be infected with a disease? Do they call attention to a discrepancy between Oedipus's apparent seeming goodness and actual villainy, or do they stress the contrast between what has been his seeming health and actual lack of health?

[*Enter Second Messenger from the palace.*]

Second Messenger: You who are ever most honored in this land, what deeds shall you hear, what deeds behold, what burden of sorrow shall be yours, if, true to your race, you still care for the house of Labdacus! For I believe that not Ister nor Phasis [17] could wash this house clean, so many are the ills that it 10 shrouds, or will soon bring to light—ills wrought not unwittingly, but on purpose. And those griefs pain most which are seen to be of our own choice.

Leader: Indeed those which we knew 15 before fall not short of claiming sore lamentation. Besides them, what do you announce?

Second Messenger: This is the shortest tale to tell and to hear: Our royal lady 20 Jocasta is dead.

[17] The Danube and the Araxes rivers.

Leader: Alas, unfortunate one! From what cause?

Second Messenger: By her own hand. The worst of all that has happened is spared us, for there was none there to 5 see. Nevertheless, so far as my own memory allows me to speak, you shall learn that unhappy woman's fate.

When, frantic, she had passed within the vestibule, she rushed straight towards her nuptial couch, clutching her hair with the fingers of both hands; once within the chamber, she dashed the doors together at her back; then called on the name of Laius, long since a corpse, mindful of that son, begotten long ago, by whom the father was slain, leaving the mother to breed accursed offspring with his own.

And she bewailed the wedlock wherein, wretched, she had borne a twofold brood, husband by husband, children by her child. And how thereafter she perished is more than I know. For with a shriek Oedipus burst in, and suffered us not to watch her woe unto the end; on him, as he rushed around, our eyes were set. To and fro he went, asking us to give him a sword—asking where he should find the wife who was no wife, but a mother whose womb had borne alike himself and his children. And, in his frenzy, a power above man was his guide; for it was none of us mortals who were nigh. And with a dread shriek, as though some one beckoned him on, he sprang at the double doors, and from their sockets he forced the bending bolts, and rushed into the room.

There beheld we the woman hanging by the neck in a twisted noose of swinging cords. But he, when he saw her, with a dread, deep cry of misery loosed the halter whereby she hung. And when the hapless woman was stretched upon the ground, then was the sequel dread to see. For he tore from her raiment the golden brooches with which she was decked, and lifted them, and struck directly on his own eyeballs, uttering words like these: "No more shall you behold such horrors as I was suffering and working. Long enough have you looked on those whom you ought never to have seen, failed in knowledge of those whom I yearned to know. Henceforth you shall be dark."

To such dire refrain, not once alone but oft struck he his eyes with lifted hand; and at each blow the bloody eyeballs bedewed his beard, nor sent forth sluggish drops of gore, but all at once a dark shower of blood came down like hail.

From the deeds of two, such ills have broken forth, not one alone, but with mingled woe for man and wife. The old happiness of their ancestral fortune was once happiness indeed; but today lamentation, ruin, death, shame, all earthly ills that can be named—all, all, are theirs.

Leader: And hath the sufferer now any respite from pain?

Second Messenger: He cries for some

one to unbar the gates and show to all the Cadmeans his father's slayer, his mother's—the unholy word must not pass my lips—as purposing to cast himself out of the land, and abide no more, to make the house accursed under his own curse. However he lacks strength, and someone to guide his steps; for the anguish is more than man may bear. And he will show this to you also; for lo, the bars of the gates are withdrawn, and soon you shall behold a sight which even he who abhors it must pity.

[*The central door of the palace is now opened. Oedipus comes forth, leaning on attendants; the bloody stains are still upon his face. The following lines between Oedipus and the Chorus are chanted responsively.*]

Chorus: O dread fate for men to see, O most dreadful of all that have met my eyes! Unhappy one, what madness has come on you? Who is the unearthly foe that, with a bound of more than mortal range, has made your ill-starred life his prey?

Alas, alas, hapless one. No, I cannot even look on you, though there is much that I would eagerly ask, eagerly learn, much that draws my wistful gaze—with such a shuddering do you fill me.

Oedipus: Woe is me! Alas, alas, wretched that I am! Whither, whither, am I borne in my misery? How is my voice swept abroad on the wings of the air? Oh my Fate, how far have you sprung!

Chorus: To a dread place—dire in men's ears, dire in their sight.

Strophe 1

Oedipus: O horror of darkness that enfolds me, visitant unspeakable, resistless, sped by a wind too fair! Ay me! And once again, ay me! How is my soul pierced by the stab of these goads, and above all by the memory of sorrows.

Chorus: Yea, amid woes so many, a twofold pain may well be yours to mourn and to bear.

Antistrophe 1

Oedipus: Ah, friend, you still are steadfast in your care of me; you still have patience to care for the blind man. Ah me! Your presence is not hid from me. No, dark though I am, yet I know your voice very well.

Chorus: Man of dread deeds, how could you in such a manner quench your vision? What more than human power urged you?

Strophe 2

Oedipus: Apollo, friends, Apollo was he that brought these my woes to pass, these my miserable, miserable woes; but the hand that struck the eyes was none but mine, wretched that I am. Why was I to see, when sight could show me nothing sweet?

Chorus: These things are even as you say.

Oedipus: Say, friends, what can I more behold, what can I love, what greeting can touch my ear with joy? Haste, lead me from the land, friends, lead me hence, the utterly lost, the thrice accursed, yea, the mortal most abhorred of heaven!

Chorus: Wretched alike for your fate and for your sense of it, would that I had never so much as known you.

Antistrophe 2

Oedipus: Perish the man, whoever he was, who freed me in the pastures from the cruel shackle on my feet, and saved me from death, and gave me back to life— a thankless deed! Had I died then, to my friends and to your own soul I would not have been so heavy a grief.

Chorus: I also would have had it thus.

Oedipus: Then I would not have come to shed my father's blood, nor have been called among men the spouse of her from whom I sprang; but now I am forsaken by the gods, son of a defiled mother, successor to the bed of him who gave me my own wretched being; and if there be yet a woe surpassing woes, it has become the portion of Oedipus.

Chorus: I do not know how I can say that you have counseled well; for you would be better dead than living and blind.

Oedipus: Do not advise me further that these things are not best done thus; give me counsel no more. For, if I had sight, I do not know with what eyes I could even have looked on my father, when I came to the place of the dead, or indeed on my miserable mother, since against both I have sinned such sins as strangling could not punish. But do you think that the sight of children, born as mine were born, was lovely for me to look upon? No, no, forever not lovely to my eyes. No, nor was this town with its towered walls, nor the sacred statues of the gods, since I, thrice wretched as I am—I, noblest of the sons of Thebes— have doomed myself to know these no more, by my own command that all should thrust away the impious one— even him whom the gods have shown to be unholy, and of the race of Laius.

After bearing such a strain upon myself, was I to look with steady eyes upon this folk? No, in truth, no. Were there still a way to choke the fount of hearing, I would not have hesitated to make a fast prison of this wretched frame, that so I should have known neither sight nor sound; for it is sweet that our thought should dwell beyond the sphere of griefs.

Alas, Cithaeron, why did you have a shelter for me? When I was given to you, why did you not slay me immediately, that thus I might never have revealed my origin to men? Ah, Polybus, ah, Corinth, and you that were called the ancient house of my fathers, how fair in appearance was I your nursling, and what ills were festering beneath. For now I am found evil, and of evil birth. O you three roads, and you secret glen—you coppice and narrow way where three paths met—you who drank from my hands that father's blood which was my own—you remember, perhaps, what deeds I wrought for you to see, and then, when I came hither, what fresh deeds I went on to do?

O marriage rites, you gave me birth, and when you had brought me forth, again you bore children to your child; you created an incestuous kinship of fathers, brothers, sons—brides, wives, mothers—yea, all the foulest shame that is wrought among men. But indeed it is unfitting to name what it is unfitting to do. Hasten, for the gods' love, hide me somewhere beyond the land, or slay me, or cast me into the sea, where you shall never behold me more. Approach, consent to lay your hands on a wretched man; hearken, fear not, my plague can rest on no other mortal.

[Enter Creon.]

Leader: No, here is Creon, at an opportune time for your requests, be they for action or advice; for he alone is left to guard the land in your place.

Oedipus: Ah me, how indeed shall I accost him? What claim to belief can be found on my part? For in the past I have been found wholly false to him.

Creon: I have not come in mockery, Oedipus, nor to reproach you with any bygone fault. *[To the attendants.]* But you, if you respect the children of men no more, revere at least the all-nurturing flame of our lord the Sun; cease showing thus nakedly a pollution such as this, one which neither earth can welcome, nor the holy rain, nor the light. No, take him into the house as quickly as you can; for it best accords with piety that kinsfolk alone should see and hear a kinsman's woes.

Oedipus: For the gods' love—since you have done a gentle violence to my prediction, you who have come in a spirit so noble to me, a man most vile— grant me a favor. For your good I will speak, not for my own.

Creon: And what favor are you so eager to have from me?

Oedipus: Cast me out of this land with all speed, to a place where no mortal shall be found to greet me again.

Creon: This I would have done, be sure, but that I desired first to learn all my duty from the god.

Oedipus: No, his command has been set forth in full—to let me perish, the parricide, the unholy one that I am.

Creon: Such was the purport; yet, seeing to what a pass we have come, it is better to learn clearly what should be done.

Oedipus: Will you, then, seek a response on behalf of such a wretch as I am?

Creon: Yes, for you yourself will now surely put faith in the god.

Oedipus: Yes. And on you I lay this charge, to you will I make this entreaty: give to her who is within such burial as you yourself wish; for you will fittingly render the last rites to your own. But for me, never let this city of my father be condemned to have me dwelling in it while I live; no, let me abide on the hills, where yonder is Cithaeron, famed as mine, which my mother and father, while they lived, set for my appointed tomb, that thus I may die by the decree of them who sought to slay me. However, of this much I am sure: that neither sickness nor anything else can destroy me; for I would never have been snatched from death but in reserve for some strange doom.

No, let *my* fate go whither it will; but concerning my children, I pray you, Creon, take no thought for the care of my sons, for they are men, so that, wherever they may be, they can never lack the means to live. But my two girls, poor unfortunate ones, who never knew my table laid with food without their father's presence, but ever in all things shared my daily bread, I pray you, care for *them;* and, if you can, let me touch them with my hands and indulge my grief. Grant it, prince, grant it, you noble heart. Ah, could I but once touch them with my hands, I should think that they were with me, even as when I had sight . . .

[*Creon's attendants lead in the children Antigone and Ismene.*]

Ha? O you gods, can it be my loved ones that I hear sobbing? Can Creon have taken pity on me and sent for my children, my darlings? Am I right?

Creon: Yes, it is of my contriving, for I knew your joy in them of old, the joy that now is yours.

Oedipus: Then may you be blessed, and for reward of this act, may heaven prove to you a kinder guardian than it has to me. My children, where are you? Come here, here to the hands of him whose mother was your own, the hands whose acts have brought it about that your father's once bright eyes should be such orbs as these—his, who, seeing nothing, knowing nothing, became your father by her from whom he sprang. For you also do I weep—behold you I cannot—when I think of the bitter life in days to come which men will make you live. To what company of the citizens will you go, to what festival, from which you will not return home in tears, instead of sharing in the holiday? But when you are now come to years ripe for marriage, who will be he, who will be the man, my daughters, that will hazard accepting the reproaches which will be injurious alike to my offspring and to yours? For what misery is lacking? Your father killed his father, he had offspring from her who bore him, and begot you at the sources of his own being. Such are the taunts that will be cast at you, and who will then wed? The man lives not; no, it cannot be, my children, but you must wither in barren maidenhood.

Ah, son of Menoeceus, hear me—since you are the only father left to them, for we, their parents, are lost, both of us—allow them not to wander poor and unwed, who are your kinswomen, nor abase them to the level of my woes. No, pity them, when you see them at this tender age so utterly forlorn except for you. Signify your promise, generous man, by the touch of your hand. To you, my children, I would have given much advice, were your minds mature; but now I would have this to be your prayer—that you live where occasion permits, and that the life which is your portion may be happier than your father's.

Creon: Your grief has had large enough scope; now pass into the house.

Oedipus: I must obey, though it is in no way sweet.

Creon: Yes, for it is in season that all things are good.

Oedipus: Do you know, then, on what conditions I will go?

Creon: You shall name them; thus I shall know them when I hear.

Oedipus: See that you send me to dwell beyond this land.

Creon: You ask me for what the god must give.

Oedipus: No, to the gods I have become most hateful.

Creon: You shall have your wish presently.

Oedipus: So you consent?

Creon: It is not my habit to speak idly what I do not mean.

Oedipus: Then it is time to lead me hence.

Creon: Come, then, but let your children go.

Oedipus: No, do not take these from me.

Creon: Do not desire to be master in all things, for the mastery which you won has not followed you through life.

Chorus: [*Singing.*] *Dwellers in our native Thebes, behold, this is Oedipus, who knew the famed riddle, and was a man most mighty; on whose fortunes what citizen did not gaze with envy? Behold into what a stormy sea of dread trouble he has come.*

Therefore, while our eyes wait to see the destined final day, we must call no one happy who is of mortal race, until he has crossed life's border, free from pain.

QUESTIONS

1. What is accomplished in this last scene of the play, if anything? Is the scene merely a catalogue of horrors?

2. If we judge that something is accomplished in this last scene, do we not imply that Oedipus's self-knowledge, and not the overt action, is central to the play?

3. Does the reported action by the second messenger seem thin and "literary," or does it here give a sense of restraint? To put the matter in another way: would anything be gained by representing on the stage Oedipus's act of self-blinding? (Compare the blinding of Gloucester in *Lear*, which is shown upon the stage. Is one method better than the other; or can each be justified in terms of its context? Does the blinding of Gloucester help characterize other people in the scene?)

4. Notice that the comments of Oedipus have to do not merely with his present woe but with his past blindness and his new knowledge. (The knowledge has been bought at a bitter price, but it is knowledge just the same.) Are the references made by Oedipus to his blinded eyes merely an attempt to enforce the physical horror or, on the other hand, is the physical horror somewhat mitigated by being used meaningfully—that is, by being used to point up his previous blindness and his present insight? What is the relation of the frequent use, in earlier scenes, of images taken from seeing and blindness to the tissue of sight imagery used in p. 569b, 7–37? Does the earlier use prepare for this scene? Make a study of the imagery throughout the play, and note how it amplifies the meaning throughout.

5. Consider the speech of Creon at p. 570a, 30. Earlier in the play he had suggested to Oedipus that Oedipus come inside to hear privately the word from the oracle, and we remember that Jocasta, when Oedipus quarreled with Creon, tried to get him to come inside. Do these scenes bear upon this passage in which Creon cries shame upon the spectators with the statement that "it best accords with piety that kinsfolk alone should see and hear a kinsman's woes"? Moreover, is Creon's reference to hiding the sight from the sun—"the all-nurturing flame of our lord the Sun"—a glancing reference to Phoebus Apollo, the god of the sun, whose priest Teiresias is and who has finally brought out into the sunlight the darkest and most monstrous of secrets? How many references or prayers to Apollo have there been throughout the play?

6. Is the scene with the children intended merely as an appeal for sympathy and pity? Or is it in part justified by the fact that Oedipus is thus given an opportunity to show that his primary concern is no longer for himself but for his children, whom he regards as innocent victims?

7. Can one justify Creon's last speech? Does it seem to come as a reprimand to a man who is down?

8. Does the final comment of the chorus come as a pat moral tag? If it does not, why not?

NOTES ON *OEDIPUS THE KING*

I. THE PROBLEM OF MEANING

The primary difficulty with this play comes down to a matter of its meaning. The brilliance of the plot has frequently been praised. The handling of the elements of plot is masterly, and even a modern audience has little difficulty in seeing this. The present vogue of the detective story indicates that many a modern reader will appreciate the skillful use of suspense. But to what end is all the ingenuity? How can Oedipus be guilty of something which he has done unwittingly? And if one answers that he is guilty of *hubris*—that is, that he is too sure of himself, too confident in his own powers, a little unmindful of the gods most modern readers find this explanation hard to accept. To one kind of modern reader, the arrogance of Oedipus may seem slight, and even if proved to exist, could hardly account adequately for the miseries in which he is eventually overwhelmed. For such a modern reader, the punishment definitely does not fit the crime.

The Greek Context. Nor will it do to tell such a reader that the Greeks had certain ideas which made the guilt of Oedipus, for them at least, adequate to the punishment. This would be to save the play (as a documentation of Greek ideas and mores) at the price of robbing it of any significance which transcends a mere Greek parochialism. It is perfectly true that our understanding of a play may depend upon a knowledge of the ideas and customs of the period in which it was written. If we are, for example, to understand, in Sophocles' *Antigone*, the conflict between the claims of state and the claims of blood, we need to know the importance of Greek burial rites. If we do understand the fearful consequences for the dead man of his body's not receiving burial, then an adequate motive is supplied for Antigone's action. The problem and the *theme* of *Antigone*, then, are of universal importance: for the problem posed by the conflict between a religious and a secular law confronts us today just as it confronted the Greeks of Antigone's day.

Our real problem, then, with *Oedipus the King*, is to relate the particular ideas and customs utilized in the play to universal themes. In this connection, modern anthropology and psychology have been of some help. We do not refer primarily to the fact that Sigmund Freud has used Oedipus as a symbol for a complex of important emotional biases and attitudes. We have in mind this: that modern anthropology and psychology have shown that more value attaches to "myth" than men in the recent past have been inclined to think; that the human mind often works in devious ways; that the great symbolisms of the past are not exhausted in any merely rational "explanation" of them.

Sophocles inherited the story of Oedipus, which had survived because it had captured the imagination of the Greeks. For various Greek writers it perhaps meant various things. What did it mean to Sophocles?

Of several things, indeed, we may be sure at the outset: Sophocles was not interested in exploiting mere sensationalism, nor was he interested in presenting some conventional "message" with a kind of mechanical piety. On the one hand, *Oedipus* is not merely a detective story. Suspense there is, and beautifully handled suspense. But every Greek who saw the play, we must remember, knew beforehand the Oedipus story and its outcome. The dramatist intended a significance beyond that of mere melodrama. But on the other hand, the dramatist's meaning was not exhausted in some special "message" of concern merely to his particular audience. Some modern scholars have been tempted to veer to this extreme, and to consider that Sophocles was preoccupied with affirming the importance of the gods and of their oracles as a wholesome lesson to an audience which he feared was becoming increasingly skeptical. There is a sense in which this account may be true; but the student must not take the play to be a sort of horrible *exemplum* of what happens to skeptical people who disregard the oracles. As such, the play would have little to say to modern man, who of course owes no allegiance to the oracles. Does Sophocles' play make any universal statement?

2. THE PLAY AS A CRITIQUE OF RATIONALISM

Perhaps the easiest way for a modern audience to approach the play is to look at it as a *critique of the claims of rationalism*. We live in a period in which the claims of a complete rationalism have been energetically urged, and one in which the methods of rationalism have been pursued with an apparently overwhelming success. If the play bears upon the problem of rationalism in any fashion, then it may yield something for us at once—whatever our final judgment on the meaning of the play turns out to be.

The Character of Oedipus. Oedipus as presented in the play is certainly not a wicked man. He has ruled as a just king, and he has ruled with great success. More than that, he is considered to be the savior of the Theban state. On his arrival at Thebes, as a young man and as a stranger, he had found a headless state—the king having been killed—and a state that was living under a nightmare. The Sphinx preyed upon the city and could be driven away from the city only by the man who could give the correct answer to the riddle which she propounded. Oedipus answered correctly, and the Sphinx was thus exorcised. Oedipus, having been hailed as a hero, married the queen, and became the king of Thebes.

All this the Greek audience knew, and we must know it as well, if we are to understand the import of the tragedy. For what Oedipus had done in answering the Sphinx was to give an impressive demonstration of the power of the unaided human mind to dispel the darkness of irrationality. But the human intellect has its limitations. Fate is finally inscrutable. It is true that man must use his reason as best he can. (Sophocles apparently approves heartily of what Oedipus has done: reason is good, and is to be used.) But Oedipus has become too confident in his success, too sure of his own powers and of his own innocence, as his colloquies with Teiresias and with Creon indicate.

To say this is not to attempt to overemphasize Oedipus's "guilt." Sophocles himself has not stressed it too heavily. He has not tried to make of Oedipus a monster, with a towering pride in his own human powers. Oedipus shows respect to the gods. In his difficulty he appeals to the Delphic oracle. He has, as the play opens, already summoned the seer Teiresias. In general, then, he is a "good" man, whose actions are "reasonable" and understandable. The point worth stressing is not Oedipus's villainy, but rather the nature of the attitudes which he exemplifies.

When the people of Thebes appeal to Oedipus, as the play opens, it is not only the welfare of his people but his own reputation that is at stake. As the priest urges him: "Guard your fame, since . . . this land calls you Saviour for your former zeal." Save us once more. Again, when Oedipus asks why the murder of Laius was not followed up at the time of the murder, Creon explains that, immediately after the murder, the confusion brought upon the state by the Sphinx "made us let dark things go, and bade us to think of what lay at our doors." With these reminders of his former triumph, Oedipus goes on to say, "*I* will start afresh, and once more make dark things plain." It is a natural comment to make and perhaps, under the circumstances, hardly a boast. Yet the emphasis on *I* (the Greek text has 'ἐγώ, which in unemphatic usage would be omitted) would come with special ironic effect to an audience that knew what the sequel to Oedipus's investigation was to be.

X When the Chorus has prayed to the gods for deliverance, Oedipus remarks, "You pray, and in answer to your prayer—if you will give a loyal welcome to my words and minister to your own disease—you may hope to find succor and relief from woes." The provision is not so much arrogant as simply complacent. Oedipus believes in ritual: he acknowledges the necessity for observing the sacrifices, consulting oracles, and uttering prayers. But, though prayer is all very well, fulfillment of the prayer is somehow made to rest upon their heeding his words and acting upon them. Let us repeat: Sophocles has not inartistically made Oedipus a monster of insolence. All that Oedipus says is "natural"; yet he exhibits a kind of complacency with regard to his ability and good motives that becomes increasingly significant as the play develops.

A significant further hint as to the attitude with which Oedipus begins his search for the murderer is given in his formal appeal to the murderer to come forward and confess, and in his formal curse upon the murderer if he fails to come forward. Does Oedipus really expect the curse to bring forth the murderer? Evidently not, for when the Chorus suggests that the murderer will surely quail before the terror of the curse, Oedipus answers: "When a man shrinks not from a deed, neither is he scared by a word."

The appeal to the murderer has then been essentially formal and perfunctory. Plainly Oedipus expects to achieve results by gathering and sifting the evidence himself. And here he is very thorough indeed, taking every step that he can think of. In general, he shows himself as the energetic and practical leader of the state, who will do anything and everything—even offering clemency for confession—calculated to throw light on the murder. But it is obviously not on curses or pleas that Oedipus relies. It is on his own powers of reason—the powers that overthrew the Sphinx.

3. THE RATIONAL MAN'S EMOTIONS

✗ His very diligence, however, and his consciousness of his own clean hands and good intentions, provide his one blind spot: he will allow none of the evidence to reflect upon him in the slightest degree, and any delay or hesitancy by witnesses angers him. Irritated by Teiresias's reluctance to speak, he is prompt to assign the worst motives to him, and once he is really angry he can be quite unreasonable in attributing the worst possible motives to Creon. If it be objected that, as Sophocles presents it, all of Oedipus's conduct is quite "natural"—that no one in his position could possibly suspect himself, and that therefore the accusation leveled against him quite properly makes him furious, one can only agree. But this observation does not alter the fact that Oedipus is possessed by a kind of overweening confidence in the power of human reason—in this case, his own reason.

On the matter of his self-confidence, the anger of Oedipus is quite revealing: he has evidently never had too much faith in Teiresias as a prophet—which is why he is so easily convinced that Teiresias has trumped up a charge against him; he is very proud of his ability to solve riddles without help, for he taunts Teiresias with failing to answer the Sphinx and says proudly, "*I* came, I, Oedipus the ignorant, and made her mute, when I seized the answer by my wit, untaught by birds." He is prompt to suspect Creon and blame him bitterly for even having suggested appealing to Teiresias.

At the same time it is perfectly understandable that Teiresias is unwilling to reveal an unpalatable truth which he knows will be rejected by a man so confident in his own rightness as Oedipus is. The actions of both men are completely plausible in terms of their initial assumptions: it is the initial assumptions that clash, and this clash is pointed up in the angry words between the two men. Oedipus taunts Teiresias with being a mystery monger—"What riddles, what dark words you always speak." Teiresias taunts Oedipus in return for his confidence in rationality—"But are you not most skilled in unraveling dark speech?" And Oedipus accepts the compliment even though it be left-handed: "Make that my reproach in which you will find me great."

The chorus which follows this interchange (p. 551) is most interesting. The Chorus is quite confident that the murderer cannot escape, but they are troubled at the accusation which Teiresias has leveled squarely at Oedipus. Whereas they have complete confidence in the gods, they are not certain that Teiresias's utterance represents the truth of the gods: ". . .

but that a mortal seer wins knowledge above mine, of this there can be no sure test . . ." This is precisely Oedipus's own point: the gods *may* know; but when it comes to a mortal's claiming to be the mouthpiece of the gods, here he is unconvinced. It is significant that the Chorus closes its song with another reference to Oedipus's victory over the Sphinx. Ironically, the event dominates the feeling of the people of the city as it evidently dominates the thinking of Oedipus himself.

In his angry colloquy with Creon, Oedipus shows to disadvantage; he is unreasonable, suspicious, obstinate—traits which we hardly think of as characteristic of the rational man. But they spring from Oedipus's very confidence in his reason; and, in terms of his reasoning, his anger is quite justified. The kind of reasoning to which Oedipus pins his hopes (pp. 553–54) perfectly warrants the suspicion of Creon to which he gives free rein, and his reasoning is good—as far as it goes. Most men would desire the kingship (even though Creon says that he doesn't), and most men who had information about the death of a king would be all too happy to lay their information before a people anxious to find the murderer rather than bring it forward now after a lapse of years.

Whatever conflicts with Oedipus's "reasoned" conclusions must make way for them: the confidence that might have been engendered by long association—as with Creon; or the wisdom of an old and blind servant of the gods—as with Teiresias; or the ripe counsel of the Theban elders. Oedipus has a bright mind and is an able reasoner, but, as Creon says, he is not *wise:* he does not realize that in human affairs the simplest, or even the apparently most logical, explanation of the facts is not necessarily the true one.

This general confidence in reason shows in a better light in Oedipus's passionate eagerness to get the whole truth. He will not rest satisfied until he knows fully. The counsel to let well enough alone—counsel first given by Teiresias, then by the Chorus, and later by Jocasta—does not for a moment deter him. Sophocles has been quite fair to Oedipus here: if he trusts too confidently in his own ability to arrive at the truth, he at least does have a passionate devotion to the truth, and he refuses to hush up his doubts, once they have begun to arise.

4. JOCASTA'S RELATION TO THE THEME

It is of course one of the major ironies of the play that it is Jocasta's effort to reassure Oedipus that first shakes him with doubt. She argues that one need not pay attention to the oracles: "Listen to me, and learn for your comfort that there is no mortal who can claim the gift of prophecy." She illustrates her generalization by pointing out the complete failure of the oracle which had stated that Laius would be killed by his own son. The son died as an infant, and Laius was killed by a highwayman. But in saying this, she happens to describe the place where Laius was killed, and Oedipus remembers too well that he had killed a man of about Laius's age

at this spot and about the same time that Laius died. Jocasta tries to discourage him from seeking additional information, but Oedipus cannot rest
until he knows, for better or worse, whether or not he is guilty.

If we have been correct in approaching the play as a critique of rationalism, then this theme receives a strong reinforcement from the speeches
and actions of Jocasta. Fate, she believes, can be outwitted. Long ago, she
and Laius tried to circumvent the oracle's prediction concerning their offspring, and she is sure that they have succeeded. If that prophecy has
proved to be false, this prophecy concerning her husband may also be
meaningless. "You judge well," Oedipus tells her (p. 558).

We should notice, however, that Jocasta does not say that the gods are
powerless. She is careful to say of the oracle which she believes that she and
Laius have circumvented: ". . . I will not say [it was] from Phoebus himself, but from his ministers. . . ." She levels her attack, as Oedipus did in
his colloquy with Teiresias, against the ministers of the gods—not against
the gods themselves. Oedipus reveals himself as truly Jocasta's son: his
mother before him had come to rely on her own wit and her ability to bring
prophecies to naught.

The Chorus's Contribution. The song of the Chorus at this point is highly
significant (p. 558). The last speeches of Oedipus and Jocasta smack of an
irreverence toward the oracles from which the Theban citizens wish to
dissociate themselves. Hence the Chorus comments on the fact that insolence breeds tyranny, and goes on to make the distinction between the
tyrant and the true patriot. Does this mean that the Chorus now has
Oedipus in mind in its reference to "the tyrant" who has no "reverence
for the images of the gods"? Not precisely. It still retains its faith in
Oedipus, as its next song indicates. It certainly does not believe that he is
guilty of the murder of Laius. But the last colloquy between Oedipus and
his queen, as well as his insolence toward Creon, is clearly the occasion
which has prompted the Chorus's disturbed comments on insolence and
scorn of the divine images. And the last stanza of its song certainly comments very specifically on Jocasta's statement that she will henceforth
"look for what concerns divination" neither "to my right hand or my
left."

In a sense the Chorus's song is actually a prayer on behalf of Oedipus.
They have always regarded him as a true patriot, but still he requires
heaven's aid. To scorn it—and they evidently fear that Oedipus's present
attitude toward the oracles partakes of such scorn—and to trust to one's
own reasoning is not only to fail but even to risk becoming the proud
sinner.

The messenger from Corinth gives dramatic corroboration to Jocasta's
speeches on the falsity of the oracles: another prophecy has apparently
failed to come true. Polybus has not been killed by Oedipus but has died a
natural death. Jocasta's first thought is about this aspect of the message,
and she hastens to make Oedipus aware of it. Oedipus receives the news
with joy, and here he comes to his full expression of *hubris*. There is a kind

of exaltation in his exclamation: ". . . why should one look to the hearth of the Pythian seer, or to the birds that scream above our heads. . . . But the oracles as they stand at least, Polybus has swept with him to his rest in Hades: they are worth nothing." And Jocasta joins him in his exultation: "And did I not predict this to you long ago?" The man "to whom these things are nothing bears his life most easily."

The Irony of the Messenger. Yet Oedipus confesses that he retains one lingering fear: of the prophecy concerning his mother, for Merope is still alive. The Messenger endeavors to reassure him by telling him that Merope was never his mother, nor Polybus his father. But, eager as he is to give Oedipus joy and make possible his return to Corinth, the Messenger has failed to understand the earlier conversation, or else is very shortsighted and clumsy. By telling Oedipus that Polybus and Merope are not his parents, he does not invalidate the curse—he actually gives it a new vitality. For the prophecy has failed only if Polybus was the father of Oedipus. If he was not, then Oedipus may yet kill, or may already have killed, his father: the death of Polybus now proves nothing. In the same way, Oedipus has now been freed from fear of Merope—*but only at the price of having to fear every other woman old enough to be his mother.* Thus the Messenger, whose first words have filled Oedipus with a sense of triumph and exultation, ironically goes on to open up the abyss beneath Oedipus's feet.

When the Messenger goes on to say that the shepherd who gave the infant Oedipus to him was one of Laius's house, Jocasta knows all that she needs to know. She makes one last attempt to dissuade her husband from carrying on the search. But Oedipus again makes, with fine irony, the natural and "logical" deduction from her reluctance: Jocasta evidently is afraid to find that she has wedded a foundling, a man of no name. In expressing his scorn at what he imagines to be Jocasta's false pride, Oedipus ironically expresses his own pride—a pride which has in it a fine manliness as well as a kind of arrogance. He is, he boasts, Fortune's favorite child, and he is willing to stand by what Fortune can do to him. Fortune has brought him from a foundling origin to the point of highest power. He glories in the fact that he has become king not by the accident of birth but by achievement. It is what a man is that counts: "Nothing can make me other than I am." But to the audience, the statement comes with ironic force: it sets forth his noble independence but also his tragedy. Nothing can make Oedipus other than what he is, the son of Laius.

The apparently coincidental arrival of the herdsman is explained by the fact that he has already been summoned. But Oedipus has forgot his original reason for summoning him—to secure testimony on the death of Laius—in his eager interest in the more immediate question of his own birth. This forgetting, which the Chorus shares, is natural. As it comes about, the Herdsman will answer both questions. Yet, like Teiresias and Jocasta, the Herdsman would save Oedipus from the horrible knowledge if he could. But as before, Oedipus is ironically uncompromising in getting at the truth, and at the end he has his proof.

5. THE PROBLEM OF OEDIPUS'S GUILT

The speech of the Chorus (p. 566) is not only a noble poem. It serves to point the theme. Notice that the Chorus does not blame Oedipus. Instead, it comments upon the uncertainty of human life: the fact that "success" does not mean happiness, the fact that fate cannot be tricked. As we have seen, pity, cruelty, foresight, and bravery have all been employed in trying to circumvent fate, and have actually themselves been woven into the web of fate: the cruel decision of Laius and Jocasta to expose the babe, the pity of the Herdsman who found it, the decision of Oedipus to give up his life as a king's son by leaving Corinth—all have played their part in bringing about the fulfillment of the prophecy.

Yet, as we have remarked, the modern reader may remain dissatisfied with the meaning of the play. He tends to ask what Oedipus could have done to avoid the fate which overtakes him and, if he can find no such preventive step indicated, he feels that Oedipus is simply a passive, helpless victim of fate. The modern reader may also share a closely related feeling, that Oedipus is not a "guilty" man—does not deserve his fate. At least one modern classical scholar has recently put this view forcefully.

These possible objections relate to two very important elements in tragedy. As we have said (pp. 110, 312–13), the protagonist must not be "a virtuous man brought from prosperity to adversity" (see Aristotle's *Poetics* 12, Appendix). The nature of Oedipus's guilt has already been canvassed somewhat. But a final account of it depends upon our disposition of the other objection, that Oedipus is a "passive" character.

The Question of Focus. In the first place it is important to see that Sophocles might have written his play so as to have put the principal focus on some decisive act by which the protagonist causes his own ruin. Ibsen's *Ghosts*, for example, has such a focus. In that play Mrs. Alving, though her husband is a libertine and she feels that she ought to leave him, has yielded to the pressures of conventional society and, with the best of motives, has gone back to him and borne him a son. As the play opens, the son, now a young man, returns home, and the now widowed mother gradually learns with horror that her hopes for her carefully nurtured son have been wrecked. He has inherited his father's disease and, as the play ends, goes mad before her eyes. He is only a victim, a pathetic figure. The tragedy is Mrs. Alving's. She had chosen with good intentions, but she had chosen unwisely, and she now suffers the consequence of her choice.

One can conceive of Sophocles' play worked out in somewhat the same way, becoming instead of *Oedipus the King*, a sort of *Jocasta the Queen*. Jocasta, though she knew what the oracle had prophesied, would, in our supposed play, have gone on to bear Laius's child, and then have attempted, with Laius, to try to get around the consequences. She has even been willing to kill the child to forestall the horror of what he may do. She makes her decision—she commits herself to a course of action—which brings her doom upon her. So focused, the play would have an active pro tagonist and a decisive act. If it be objected that such a play would, by centering the play on Jocasta, turn Oedipus, like Ibsen's Oswald, into an essentially pathetic, not a tragic figure, one must certainly agree.

But this play Sophocles chose not to write; instead he preferred to give us the play as it stands, which may seem a play which lacks a specific focus on some decisive act, the well-intentioned but disastrous commitment to a course of action. For though we can argue, if we like, that Oedipus actually performed such an act when he ventured to kill Laius and another such act when he married Jocasta (if he had believed the oracle fully he would have dared kill no man, dared marry no woman), still, these events took place long before the action of the play. They are brought into focus only late in the play. Is *Oedipus the King*, then, a play which lacks emphasis on some decisive act committed by the protagonist, and which presents us, consequently, with what is essentially a passive, suffering protagonist?

The "Action" of the Play. As Sophocles has actually focused the play, the "action" consists in Oedipus's struggle for knowledge—a struggle first for knowledge of the evil that besets the state, but ultimately a struggle for self-knowledge. This knowledge does not overwhelm a passive Oedipus. He has to strive actively for it—against recalcitrant witnesses and against the pleas of well-wishers who try to dissuade him from the quest. The oracle does not simply "announce" that Oedipus is the murderer. Even the specific accusation made by Teiresias as the instrument of the god is qualified by the obvious anger in which it is spoken. The accusation does not convince the Theban elders, for instance; it does not constitute "proof." Oedipus has demanded proof. We must not forget that it is Oedipus, more than any other person in the play, who manages to get together this proof which damns him.

It may be helpful at this point to remind ourselves that whereas in many stories there is a decisive change in the fortunes of the protagonist (he wins his battle or he is killed), still, in many other stories, what "happens" to the protagonist is not some overt change, but an inner one: the protagonist comes to a new knowledge of himself—he comes to understand himself as he did not before. The outer event and the inner event may be intimately connected with each other: in *Oedipus the King*, for example, the intellectual illumination has tremendous repercussions in the field of overt action. Oedipus can no longer reign in Thebes; moreover, he cannot bear any longer to look at the world about him. He puts out his eyes and begs for banishment. But the inner change, even when not connected with a decisive overt action, can be as meaningful as the first, and it can be as "dramatic." To take an example from one of the plays in this book, something of the greatest importance has happened to Lear, even if he should come at the end to be restored to his throne and kingdom. He has gained— and this is also true of Faustus—a kind of knowledge which makes him a different man from the man whom we see at the beginning of the play.

Knowing as Action. Knowing, then, is a form of action. The gaining of knowledge can be the most important thing which happens to a character, and like other happenings it may either be stumbled upon by the weak and essentially passive character or it may be striven for heroically and tragically. Oedipus strives actively for the damning knowledge; he does not bury his head in the sand. It is his glory that he *must* know. But if his striving for knowledge is his glory, it is also his weakness. He is not only confident of his own powers to unriddle what is obscure: he cannot conceive what the implications of full knowledge of any event may be for the human being. Life for the successful Oedipus is rational and has no mysteries that lurk in dark corners. Oedipus cannot comprehend, as indeed few human beings ever can (Faustus, we have seen, is another example), that human eyes may be dazzled and blinded by a *complete* illumination of even those things which seem best known and most familiar.

The speeches and actions of Oedipus in this play represent thoroughly those traits which manifested themselves in his leaving Corinth, his killing of Oedipus, and his acceptance of Jocasta and the crown—the mixture of nobility, pride, calculation, self-confidence, and impetuosity. We see in action here the man who took these actions years before, and since Oedipus has realized, not evaded, his true nature, we can understand how he came to the decisions that he did; that is, we can see from Oedipus's present conduct that those earlier actions were "in character." But by presenting the Oedipus of years later, Sophocles has been able to focus attention, not so much on the problem of action, as on that of knowledge. That is, Sophocles has chosen for primary emphasis the ironic discrepancy between full knowledge and man's partial knowledge. Oedipus is dramatized for us primarily as thinker rather than as actor, though of course his past actions are necessarily involved.

Like Rosmer in Ibsen's play (or like Lear) Oedipus comes at the end to understand himself—and, again like them, only through the revelation of the superficiality of his former knowledge. We can go further and say that his final understanding is the product not of "success" but of suffering. It is a wisdom that contains and extends beyond mere rationalism, for it involves a deep-seated awareness of the limitations of rationalism.

Poetic Justice. What shall we say then to the reader who feels that Oedipus's punishment does not fit his crime? We may well take the line that Sophocles himself has the Chorus take at the end of the play. The appeal is to the facts. As a matter of fact, do the best-laid plans of mice and men often "gang a-gley," and do men incur penalties from life out of all proportion to their conscious infraction of the laws of life? The question is not: What is desirable or ideal human experience? but, What is general human experience?

Oedipus's punishment can scarcely be made to square with poetic justice —with getting his deserts—but that is just the point of the tragedy: that men do not actually experience poetic justice. Life does not follow the course that men think it will follow or ought to follow. The outcome of *Oedipus the King*, we may say, does not rest upon some thesis that Sophocles thought ought to be true, but on what Sophocles observed to be the actual state of affairs.

6. THE UNIVERSALITY OF *Oedipus the King*

Lest the reader feel that this is too dark and saturnine an account of the human situation, at least as it exists today, one needs only to appeal again to the facts. One need not read this play as a tract for the times of the atom bomb in order to suggest that the play has still something to say to our times—that it deals with a universal problem.

Our own age is one which has taken with the utmost seriousness the Faustian dictum that knowledge is power. We have sought knowledge passionately, and with remarkable success. Part of our motive has been the desire for power, but it would be unfair to deny that there has been a noble side to our motivation. We have been happy to garner even "useless" knowledge as somehow good in itself. We could not, we felt, have too many facts. We could not have too much knowledge. That is still the passionate faith of a great many of us, even at a time when the amount of knowledge which we have gained has become embarrassing to us.

It *has* become embarrassing—this is the testimony of the scientists themselves. And knowledge, as we are coming to see, is not the same thing as wisdom. At the moment when man has come to his fullest knowledge of how to manipulate the world of things—and his fellows, considered as objects of manipulation, considered as things—at just this moment he has come to see how little he knows himself, how nonlogical, how irrational the human mind itself is. To say all this is not to plunge into an obscurantism of despair. (A careful reading of Sophocles will indicate that Sophocles himself has offered no counsel of despair.) But we may actually be in a better position than recent generations have been to appreciate the general critique of rationalism which Sophocles offers us, for we have had the easy myth of automatic progress shaken for us as it was not shaken for them, and we have had a rather naïve faith in rationalism seriously questioned.

If the play does constitute a critique of rationalism, the ironics of the play become deeply meaningful. For the essence of irony is the contrast between the expected or the desired or the ideal experience and the actual experience. The ironic insight thus always shocks by reversing normal expectancies. As we have seen, this play is a tissue of such ironies: Oedipus, by attempting to circumvent his fate, has insured its realization; the Sphinx's riddle turns upon the question "What is man?" and Oedipus, who thought that he knew the answer, finds at the end that he did not know what he himself was; Oedipus, who saves Thebes from the Sphinx, cannot save himself—"Others he saved, himself he could not save"; Jocasta's attempts to assuage her husband's fears actually inflame those fears; the messenger from Corinth whose message "proves" that the oracle has been false unwittingly brings the real proof of its truth; Oedipus's curse upon the murderer of Laius has been unconsciously a curse on himself;

Oedipus attains the wisdom of Teiresias, whose blindness he has earlier mocked, only by becoming himself blind. But these ironic reversals are not used merely for the more superficial theatrical effects (though some of them function admirably as dramatic effects). Properly understood, they underline the critique of human knowledge which is made by the play as a whole.

For truth, Sophocles suggests, may slip up on the blind side of man: logical deduction may miss it, energy and diligence may fail to encompass it; it can run with the hounds as well as with the hare. The simplest explanation which covers all the facts may be the one which the human mind is necessarily constrained to accept; but the simplest explanation may not be the true explanation.

QUESTIONS ON *Oedipus the King*

1. The student should compare *Dr. Faustus* with *Oedipus the King*. Both plays make a critique of knowledge. In both of them the protagonist begins with a definite conception of what kind of knowledge is valuable, and in both, the protagonist comes to another sort of knowledge. Oedipus, of course, feels sure that the predicted curse cannot apply to him; on the other hand, Faustus invites the curse, as it were, with open eyes. Compare and contrast the meaning of the two plays. Consider the possibilities that are available to the dramatist in terms of the contrasting situations.

2. There is a sense in which *Oedipus the King* concerns itself with pride of family and pride of lineage. Oedipus possesses a noble independence which comes out when he discovers that he is not of royal blood, the son of King Polybus, as he had supposed he was, but a foundling, the mere child of fortune. But notice that, at the end of the play, Oedipus accepts his restoration to princely lineage as the child of King Laius, with touching pathos and yet with a fine ironic dignity when he says (p. 569) ". . . since I, thrice wretched as I am—I, noblest of the sons of Thebes—yet doomed myself to know these no more. . . ." What ironies are present in this reference to himself as the "noblest of the sons of Thebes"? What are some of the ways in which these ironic senses have been prepared for?

3. "Sophoclean irony" involves the discrepancy between what the character in a play thinks to be true and what, as the audience already knows, is actually true. Oedipus, for example, promises that he will conduct the investigation into the death of Laius as zealously as if Laius were his own father. The term "Sophoclean" derives, of course, from the brilliant use to which Sophocles put this device in his various tragedies. On the basis of a reconsideration of the play, can the student agree that *Oedipus the King* may be characterized as a tissue of "Sophoclean ironies"? (The Greek audience, of course, knew the story of Oedipus and its outcome before it sat down to view the play.) How skillfully has Sophocles made use of his audience's prior knowledge of the story? Does this prior knowledge kill the possibility of suspense? On the other hand, is it possible to argue that the play is more effective to a reader or audience which knows the plot

than to one which does not? Consider, in this connection, Herbert Read's contention that true drama and suspense about the outcome of the plot are incompatible.

4. Consider carefully the function of the Chorus in this play. Are the songs of the Chorus mere bits of "decoration"? May it be said that the Chorus serves as a device to control the attitudes of the audience throughout the play—to express its apprehension, its hope, its desire to advise the hero, or to warn the hero, etc.? Is the Chorus in this play something which could be dispensed with, or is it, on the other hand, an integral part of the play which performs highly important functions?

5. The student should read Sophocles' other play on the Oedipus theme, *Oedipus at Colonus*, which portrays the blind Oedipus during the last part of his life. We have considered *Oedipus the King* as a complete play, as indeed it is; and one need not read *Oedipus at Colonus* in order to complete the story. Yet *Oedipus at Colonus* may be more meaningful to us after a reading of *Oedipus the King*. What traits, if any, connect the older Oedipus with the character whom we have known in *Oedipus the King*? How is the older Oedipus different from the character in *Oedipus the King*? What has come out of Oedipus's sufferings, if anything? Why is Oedipus, at the end of his life, regarded as holy? Does this regard for him as holy spring merely from the prophecy told of him, or is this holiness with which he is credited manifested to the audience dramatically in terms of a revelation of traits of mind and character? In other words, is the contention between Thebes and Athens over which shall furnish the burial place for Oedipus motivated mechanically, or does the character in the play convince us dramatically that he does possess a special sanctity?

6. *Oedipus at Colonus* may seem to involve even less overt action than does *Oedipus the King*. Yet, there is a sense in which it may be argued that Oedipus in the play concerning his old age is more "active"—less the victim, less passive, than he was when he reigned at Thebes. Consider the matter and discuss it fully.

7. To what extent does *Oedipus at Colonus* depend upon our knowledge of *Oedipus the King*? Is *Oedipus at Colonus* a dramatically self-contained unit? Is the relationship between the two plays comparable to that between *Henry IV, Part One* and *Henry IV, Part Two*?

8. What may we learn about the nature of tragic experience from the change in attitude toward Oedipus, which is the subject of Question 5? Why is the experience not merely "unhappy," as the popular use of the word *tragic* would imply? Is there anything redemptive in the experience? Why should this be true?

FURTHER READING

The instructor may wish to take up, at this time, Shakespeare's *Macbeth*, which, in some very interesting points, has resemblances to and differences from *Oedipus the King*. The notes and questions on *Macbeth* may be found on pages 668 ff.

5. Shakespeare, *King Lear*

*K*ING LEAR (1605 or 1606) is one of the most complex of Shakespeare's tragedies; perhaps it is one of the most complex of all tragedies. Taken at the more obvious level, the complexity is the result of an apparently double plot and of complex interrelationships among an unusually large number of principal characters. In reading the play, the student should first strive to define the relationship among the parts. What is the connection between the Gloucester plot and the Lear plot? Does one simply echo the other, giving us a kind of double view of parental misunderstanding, or are they integrated in some fundamental way? In seeking an answer to this question, the student will inevitably find himself moving into the underlying problem of the meaning of the play. Here he will doubtless find it useful to see what he has learned in *Oedipus the King* that will throw light upon the tragic statement of *Lear*.

But the question of meaning will involve the reader also in a study of the system of imagery and symbols which Shakespeare uses. In *Henry IV, Part One* we have already seen how imagery is used to qualify meaning; in *King Lear* we have a tremendous fullness and variety of imagery which must be taken into account if the intent of the play is to be defined. Hence the imagery demands attention from the start.

KING LEAR

DRAMATIS PERSONÆ

LEAR, King of Britain	Doctor
KING OF FRANCE	Fool
DUKE OF BURGUNDY	OSWALD, Steward to Goneril
DUKE OF CORNWALL	A Captain employed by Edmund
DUKE OF ALBANY	Gentleman attendant on Cordelia
EARL OF KENT	A Herald
EARL OF GLOUCESTER	Servants to Cornwall
EDGAR, Son to Gloucester	GONERIL ⎫
EDMUND, Bastard Son to Gloucester	REGAN ⎬ Daughters to Lear
CURAN, A courtier	CORDELIA ⎭
Old Man, Tenant to Gloucester	

Knights of Lear's train, Captains, Messengers, Soldiers, and Attendants

SCENE—BRITAIN

ACT I

SCENE I—*King Lear's palace*

[*Enter Kent, Gloucester, and Edmund.*]

Kent: I thought the king had more affected [1] the Duke of Albany than Cornwall.

Glou.: It did always seem so to us: but now, in the division of the kingdom, it appears not which of the dukes he values most; for qualities are so weighed, that curiosity in neither can make choice of either's moiety.[2] 9

Kent: Is not this your son, my lord?

Glou.: His breeding, sir, hath been at my charge: I have so often blushed to acknowledge him, that now I am brazed to 't.

Kent: I cannot conceive you. 15

Glou.: Sir, this young fellow's mother could: whereupon she grew round-wombed, and had, indeed, sir, a son for her cradle ere she had a husband for her bed. Do you smell a fault? 20

Kent: I cannot wish the fault undone, the issue of it being so proper.

Glou.: But I have a son, sir, by order of law, some year elder than this, who yet is no dearer in my account: though this knave came something saucily to the world before he was sent for, yet was his mother fair; there was good sport at his making, and the whoreson must be acknowledged. Do you know this noble gentleman, Edmund? 31

Edm.: No, my lord.

Glou.: My lord of Kent: remember him hereafter as my honourable friend.

Edm.: My services to your lordship.

Kent: I must love you, and sue to know you better. 37

Edm.: Sir, I shall study deserving.

Glou.: He hath been out nine years, and away he shall again. The king is coming.

[*Sennet. Enter King Lear, Cornwall, Albany, Goneril, Regan, Cordelia, and Attendants.*]

[1] More liking for. [2] Extreme care by either cannot lead him to choose the other's share.

Lear: Attend the lords of France and Burgundy, Gloucester.

Glou.: I shall, my lord.

[*Exeunt Gloucester and Edmund.*]

Lear: Meantime we shall express our darker [3] purpose. 45
Give me the map there. Know that we have divided
In three our kingdom: and 't is our fast intent
To shake all cares and business from our age;
Conferring them on younger strengths, while we
Unburthen'd crawl toward death. Our son of Cornwall, 50
And you, our no less loving son of Albany,
We have this hour a constant will to publish
Our daughters' several dowers, that future strife
May be prevented now. The princes, France and Burgundy,
Great rivals in our youngest daughter's love, 55
Long in our court have made their amorous sojourn,
And here are to be answer'd. Tell me, my daughters,—
Since now we will divest us, both of rule,
Interest of territory, cares of state,—
Which of you shall we say doth love us most? 60
That we our largest bounty may extend
Where nature doth with merit challenge.[4] Goneril,
Our eldest-born, speak first.

Gon.: Sir, I love you more than words can wield the matter;
Dearer than eye-sight, space, and liberty; 65
Beyond what can be valued, rich or rare;
No less than life, with grace, health, beauty, honour;
As much as child e'er loved, or father found;
A love that makes breath poor, and speech unable;

[3] Underlying. [4] Natural qualities and merits both make claims.

Beyond all manner of so much I love
you.   70
Cor.: [*Aside.*] What shall Cordelia
speak? Love, and be silent.
Lear: Of all these bounds, even from
this line to this,
With shadowy forests and with cham-
pains rich'd,
With plenteous rivers and wide-skirted
meads,
We make thee lady: to thine and Al-
bany's issue   75
Be this perpetual. What says our second
daughter,
Our dearest Regan, wife to Cornwall?
Speak.
Reg.: I am made
Of that self metal as my sister,
And prize me at her worth. In my true
heart   80
I find she names my very deed of love;
Only she comes too short: that I profess
Myself an enemy to all other joys,
Which the most precious square of sense
professes; [5]
And find I am alone felicitate   85
In your dear highness's love.
    Cor.:   [*Aside.*] Then poor Cordelia!
And yet not so; since, I am sure, my
love's
More ponderous than my tongue.
Lear: To thee and thine hereditary
ever
Remain this ample third of our fair
kingdom;   90
No less in space, validity, and pleasure,
Than that conferr'd on Goneril. Now,
our joy,
Although our last and least; to whose
young love
The vines of France and milk of Bur-
gundy
Strive to be interess'd,[6] what can you
say to draw   95
A third more opulent than your sisters?
Speak.
Cor.: Nothing, my lord.
Lear: Nothing!
Cor.: Nothing.

[5] Which the most delicate sensibility
makes us aware of. [6] To have an interest in.

Lear: Nothing will come of nothing:
speak again.   100
Cor.: Unhappy that I am, I cannot
heave
My heart into my mouth: I love your
majesty
According to my bond; no more nor less.
Lear: How, how, Cordelia! mend your
speech a little,   104
Lest you may mar your fortunes.
    Cor.:   Good my lord,
You have begot me, bred me, loved me: I
Return those duties back as are right fit,
Obey you, love you, and most honour
you.
Why have my sisters husbands, if they
say
They love you all? Haply, when I shall
wed,   110
That lord whose hand must take my
plight shall carry
Half my love with him, half my care and
duty:
Sure, I shall never marry like my sisters,
To love my father all.
Lear: But goes thy heart with this?
Cor.:   Ay, my good lord.
Lear: So young, and so untender?
Cor.: So young, my lord, and true.
Lear: Let it be so; thy truth, then,
be thy dower:
For, by the sacred radiance of the sun,
The mysteries of Hecate,[7] and the night;
By all the operation of the orbs   121
From whom we do exist and cease to be;
Here I disclaim all my paternal care,
Propinquity and property of blood,
And as a stranger to my heart and me
Hold thee, from this, for ever. The
barbarous Scythian,
Or he that makes his generation messes
To gorge his appetite, shall to my bosom
Be as well neighbour'd, pitied, and re-
lieved,
As thou my sometime daughter.   130
    Kent: Good my liege,—
    Lear: Peace, Kent!
Come not between the dragon and his
wrath.

[7] Goddess of enchantments.

I loved her most, and thought to set my
rest
On her kind nursery. Hence, and avoid
my sight!
So be my grave my peace, as here I give
Her father's heart from her! Call
France; who stirs?   136
Call Burgundy. Cornwall and Albany,
With my two daughters' dowers digest
the third:
Let pride, which she calls plainness,
marry her.
I do invest you jointly with my power,
Pre-eminence, and all the large effects
That troop with majesty. Ourself, by
monthly course,   142
With reservation of an hundred knights,
By you to be sustain'd, shall our abode
Make with you by due turn. Only we
shall retain
The name, and all th' addition [8] to a
king;   146
The sway, revenue, execution of the rest,
Beloved sons, be yours: which to confirm,
This coronet part between you. [*Giving
the crown.*]
Kent: Royal Lear,
Whom I have ever honour'd as my king,
Loved as my father, as my master
follow'd,   151
As my great patron thought on in my
prayers,—
Lear: The bow is bent and drawn,
make from the shaft.
Kent: Let it fall rather, though the
fork invade
The region of my heart: be Kent un-
mannerly,   155
When Lear is mad. What wilt thou do,
old man?
Think'st thou that duty shall have
dread to speak,
When power to flattery bows? To plain-
ness honour's bound,
When majesty falls to folly. Reserve
thy state,[9]
And, in thy best consideration, check
This hideous rashness: answer my life
my judgement,[10]   161

[8] Titles. [9] Keep your power. [10] "I will
stake my life on my opinion" (Johnson).

Thy youngest daughter does not love
thee least;
Nor are those empty-hearted whose
low sounds
Reverb no hollowness.
Lear.   Kent, on thy life, no more.
Kent: My life I never held but as a
pawn   165
To wage against thine enemies; nor
fear to lose it,
Thy safety being the motive.
Lear: Out of my sight!
Kent: See better, Lear; and let me still
remain
The true blank [11] of thine eye.
Lear: Now, by Apollo,—
Kent: Now, by Apollo, king,
Thou swear'st thy gods in vain.
Lear: O, vassal! miscreant!
[*Laying his hand on his sword.*]
Alb. ⎱
Corn. ⎰ Dear sir, forbear.   172
Kent: Do;
Kill thy physician, and thy fee bestow
Upon thy foul disease. Revoke thy
gift;
Or, whilst I can vent clamour from my
throat,   176
I'll tell thee thou dost evil.
Lear: Hear me, recreant!
On thine allegiance, hear me!
Since thou hast sought to make us
break our vows,
Which we durst never yet, and with
strain'd pride   180
To come betwixt our sentences and our
power,
Which nor our nature nor our place
can bear,
Our potency made good, take thy reward.
Five days we do allot thee, for pro-
vision
To shield thee from diseases of the
world;   185
And on the sixth to turn thy hated back
Upon our kingdom: if, on the tenth day
following,
Thy banish'd trunk be found in our
dominions,

[11] The white center of a target.

The moment is thy death. Away! by Jupiter,
This shall not be revoked.   190
Kent: Fare thee well, king: sith thus thou wilt appear,
Freedom lives hence, and banishment is here.
[*To Cordelia.*] The gods to their dear shelter take thee, maid,
That justly think'st, and hast most rightly said!   194
[*To Regan and Goneril.*] And your large speeches may your deeds approve,
That good effects may spring from words of love.
Thus Kent, O princes, bids you all adieu;
He 'll shape his old course in a country new. [*Exit.*]
[*Flourish. Re-enter Gloucester, with France, Burgundy, and Attendants*]
Glou.: Here 's France and Burgundy, my noble lord.
Lear: My lord of Burgundy,   200
We first address toward you, who with this king
Hath rivall'd for our daughter: what, in the least,
Will you require in present dower with her,
Or cease your quest of love?
Bur.:   Most royal majesty,
I crave no more than hath your highness offer'd,   205
Nor will you tender less.
Lear: Right noble Burgundy,
When she was dear to us, we did hold her so;
But now her price is fall'n. Sir, there she stands:
If aught within that little seeming substance,   209
Or all of it, with our displeasure pieced,
And nothing more, may fitly like your grace,
She 's there and she is yours.
Bur.:   I know no answer.
Lear: Will you, with those infirmities she owes,[12]
Unfriended, new-adopted to our hate,

Dower'd with our curse, and stranger'd with our oath,   215
Take her, or leave her?
Bur.:   Pardon me, royal sir;
Election makes not up[13] on such conditions.
Lear: Then leave her, sir; for, by the power that made me,
I tell you all her wealth. [*To France.*]
For you, great king,
I would not from your love make such a stray,   220
To match you where I hate; therefore beseech you
To avert your liking a more worthier way
Than on a wretch whom nature is ashamed
Almost to acknowledge hers.
France: This is most strange,
That she, who even but now was your best object,   225
The argument of your praise, balm of your age,
The best, the dearest, should in this trice of time
Commit a thing so monstrous, to dismantle
So many folds of favour. Sure, her offence
Must be of such unnatural degree, 230
That monsters it, or your fore-vouch'd affection
Fall'n into taint:[14] which to believe of her,
Must be a faith that reason without miracle
Should never plant in me.
Cor.: I yet beseech your majesty,—
If for I want that glib and oily art, 235
To speak and purpose not,—since what I well intend,
I 'll do 't before I speak,—that you make known
It is no vicious blot, murder, or foulness,
No unchaste action, or dishonour'd step,
That hath deprived me of your grace and favour;   240

But even for want of that for which I
am richer,
A still-soliciting eye, and such a tongue
That I am glad I have not, though not
to have it
Hath lost me in your liking.
Lear: Better thou
Hadst not been born than not to have
pleased me better.   245
France: Is it but this,—a tardiness in
nature
Which often leaves the history unspoke
That it intends to do? My lord of Bur-
gundy,
What say you to the lady? Love 's not
love
When it is mingled with regards that
stand   250
Aloof from the entire point. Will you
have her?
She is herself a dowry.
Bur.:   Royal Lear,
Give but that portion which yourself
proposed,
And here I take Cordelia by the hand,
Duchess of Burgundy.   255
Lear: Nothing; I have sworn; I am
firm.
Bur.: I am sorry, then, you have so
lost a father
That you must lose a husband.
Cor.:   Peace be with Burgundy!
Since that respects of fortune are his
love,
I shall not be his wife.   260
France: Fairest Cordelia, that art
most rich, being poor;
Most choice, forsaken; and most loved,
despised!
Thee and thy virtues here I seize upon:
Be it lawful I take up what 's cast
away.
Gods, gods! 't is strange that from their
cold'st neglect   265
My love should kindle to inflamed re-
spect.
Thy dowerless daughter, king, thrown
to my chance,
Is queen of us, of ours, and our fair
France:
Not all the dukes of waterish Burgundy

Can buy this unprized precious maid of
me.   270
Bid them farewell, Cordelia, though
unkind:
Thou losest here, a better where to find.
Lear: Thou hast her, France: let her
be thine; for we
Have no such daughter, nor shall ever
see
That face of hers again. Therefore be
gone   275
Without our grace, our love, our beni-
son.
Come, noble Burgundy.
[*Flourish. Exeunt all but France,
Goneril, Regan, and Cordelia.*]
France: Bid farewell to your sisters.
Cor.: The jewels of our father, with
wash'd eyes
Cordelia leaves you: I know you what
you are;   280
And like a sister am most loath to call
Your faults as they are named. Love
well our father:
To your professed bosoms I commit him:
But yet, alas, stood I within his grace,
I would prefer him to a better place.
So, farewell to you both.   286
Reg.: Prescribe not us our duty.
Gon.:   Let your study
Be to content your lord, who hath re-
ceived you
At fortune's alms. You have obedience
scanted,
And well are worth the want that you
have wanted.   290
Cor.: Time shall unfold what plighted [15]
cunning hides:
Who cover faults, at last shame them
derides.
Well may you prosper!
France: Come, my fair Cordelia.
[*Exeunt France and Cordelia.*]
Gon.: Sister, it is not little I have to
say of what most nearly appertains to
us both. I think our father will hence
to-night.   297
Reg. That 's most certain, and with
you; next month with us.

---

[15] Folded, complicated.

Gon.: You see how full of changes his age is; the observation we have made of it hath not been little: he always loved our sister most; and with what poor judgement he hath now cast her off appears too grossly.   305

Reg.: 'T is the infirmity of his age: yet he hath ever but slenderly known himself.

Gon.: The best and soundest of his time hath been but rash; then must we look to receive from his age, not alone the imperfections of long-engraffed condition,[16] but therewithal the unruly waywardness that infirm and choleric years bring with them.   315

Reg.: Such unconstant starts are we like to have from him as this of Kent's banishment.

Gon.: There is further compliment of leave-taking between France and him. Pray you, let us sit together: if our father carry authority with such disposition as he bears, this last surrender of his will but offend [17] us.   324

Reg.: We shall further think on 't.

Gon.: We must do something, and i' the heat.   [*Exeunt.*]

SCENE II—*The Earl of Gloucester's castle*

[*Enter Edmund, with a letter.*]

Edm. Thou, nature, art my goddess; to thy law
My services are bound. Wherefore should I
Stand in the plague of custom,[1] and permit
The curiosity [2] of nations to deprive me,
For that I am some twelve or fourteen moonshines   5
Lag of a brother? Why bastard? wherefore base?
When my dimensions are as well compact,
My mind as generous, and my shape as true,

[16] Of long habit. [17] Hurt.
[1] Be injured by conventions. [2] Fastidiousness.

As honest madam's issue? Why brand they us
With base? with baseness? bastardy? base, base?   10
Who, in the lusty stealth of nature, take
More composition and fierce quality
Than doth, within a dull, stale, tired bed,
Go to the creating a whole tribe of fops,
Got 'tween asleep and wake? Well, then,
Legitimate Edgar, I must have your land: 16
Our father's love is to the bastard Edmund
As to the legitimate: fine word— *legitimate!*
Well, my legitimate, if this letter speed,
And my invention thrive, Edmund the base   20
Shall to [3] the legitimate: I grow; I prosper:
Now, gods, stand up for bastards!
          [*Enter Gloucester.*]

Glou.: Kent banish'd thus! and France in choler parted!
And the king gone to-night! prescribed [4] his power!
Confined to exhibition! [5] All this done
Upon the gad! [6] Edmund, how now! what news?   26

Edm.: So please your lordship, none.
          [*Putting up the letter.*]

Glou.: Why so earnestly seek you to put up that letter?

Edm.: I know no news, my lord.

Glou.: What paper were you reading?

Edm.: Nothing, my lord.   31

Glou.: No? What needed, then, that terrible dispatch of it into your pocket? the quality of nothing hath not such need to hide itself. Let 's see: come, if it be nothing, I shall not need spectacles.

Edm.: I beseech you, sir, pardon me: it is a letter from my brother, that I have not all o'er-read; and for so much as I have perused, I find it not fit for your o'er-looking.   41

Glou.: Give me the letter, sir.

[3] Come up to, conquer. [4] Limited, restricted. [5] An allowance. [6] Quickly; on the spur of the moment.

Edm.: I sh.ll offend, either to detain or give it. The contents, as in part I understand them, are to blame.   45

Glou.: Let 's see, let 's see.

Edm.: I hope, for my brother's justification, he wrote this but as an essay or taste of my virtue.

Glou.: [*Reads.*] "This policy and reverence of age makes the world bitter to the best of our times; keeps our fortunes from us till our oldness cannot relish them. I begin to find an idle and fond bondage in the oppression of aged tyranny; who sways, not as it hath power, but as it is suffered. Come to me, that of this I may speak more. If our father would sleep till I waked him, you should enjoy half his revenue for ever, and live the beloved of your brother, EDGAR."   63

Hum—conspiracy!—"Sleep till I waked him,—you should enjoy half his revenue,"—My son Edgar! Had he a hand to write this? a heart and brain to breed it in?—When came you to this? who brought it?   69

Edm.: It was not brought me, my lord; there 's the cunning of it; I found it thrown in at the casement of my closet.

Glou.: You know the character to be your brother's?   75

Edm.: If the matter were good, my lord, I durst swear it were his; but, in respect of that, I would fain think it were not.

Glou.: It is his.   80

Edm.: It is his hand, my lord; but I hope his heart is not in the contents.

Glou.: Has he never before sounded you in this business?   84

Edm.: Never, my lord: but I have heard him oft maintain it to be fit, that, sons at perfect age, and fathers declined, the father should be as ward to the son, and the son manage his revenue.

Glou.: O villain, villain! His very opinion in the letter! Abhorred villain! Unnatural, detested, brutish villain! worse than brutish! Go, sirrah, seek

him; I'll apprehend him: abominable villain! Where is he?   95

Edm.: I do not well know, my lord. If it shall please you to suspend your indignation against my brother till you can derive from him better testimony of his intent, you shall run a certain course; where, if you violently proceed against him, mistaking his purpose, it would make a great gap in your own honour, and shake in pieces the heart of his obedience. I dare pawn down my life for him, that he hath wrote this to feel my affection to your honour, and to no other pretence of danger.[7]   108

Glou.: Think you so?

Edm.: If your honour judge it meet, I will place you where you shall hear us confer of this, and by an auricular assurance have your satisfaction; and that without any further delay than this very evening.   115

Glou.: He cannot be such a monster—

Edm.: Nor is not, sure.

Glou.: To his father, that so tenderly and entirely loves him. Heaven and earth! Edmund, seek him out; wind me into him, I pray you: frame the business after your own wisdom. I would unstate myself, to be in a due resolution.[8]   123

Edm.: I will seek him, sir, presently; convey the business as I shall find means, and acquaint you withal.

Glou.: These late eclipses in the sun and moon portend no good to us: though the wisdom of nature can reason it thus and thus, yet nature finds itself scourged by the sequent effects: love cools, friendship falls off, brothers divide: in cities, mutinies; in countries, discord; in palaces, treason; and the bond cracked 'twixt son and father. This villain of mine comes under the prediction; there 's son against father: the king falls from bias [9] of nature; there 's father against child. We have seen the best of our time: machinations, hollowness, treachery, and all ruinous

[7] With no other dangerous intention. [8] Give up my position to be certain. [9] Tendency; *i.e.*, acts unnaturally.

disorders, follow us disquietly to our graves. Find out this villain, Edmund; it shall lose thee nothing; do it carefully. And the noble and true-hearted Kent banished! his offence, honesty! 'T is strange.   [*Exit.*]

Edm.: This is the excellent foppery of the world, that, when we are sick in fortune,—often the surfeit of our own behaviour,—we make guilty of our disasters the sun, the moon, and the stars: as if we were villains by necessity; fools by heavenly compulsion; knaves, thieves, and treachers,[10] by spherical predominance; drunkards, liars, and adulterers, by an enforced obedience of planetary influence; and all that we are evil in, by a divine thrusting on: an admirable evasion of whore-master man, to lay his goatish disposition to the charge of a star! My father compounded with my mother under the dragon's tail; and my nativity was under Ursa major; so that it follows, I am rough and lecherous. Fut, I should have been that I am, had the maidenliest star in the firmament twinkled on my bastardizing. Edgar—[*Enter Edgar*] and pat he comes like the catastrophe of the old comedy: my cue is villainous melancholy, with a sigh like Tom o' Bedlam.[11] O, these eclipses do portend these divisions! fa, sol, la, mi.   174

Edg.: How now, brother Edmund! what serious contemplation are you in?

Edm.: I am thinking, brother, of a prediction I read this other day, what should follow these eclipses.

Edg.: Do you busy yourself about that?   181

Edm.: I promise you, the effects he writes of succeed unhappily; as of unnaturalness between the child and the parent; death, dearth, dissolutions of ancient amities; divisions in state, menaces and maledictions against king and nobles; needless diffidences, banishment of friends, dissipation of cohorts, nuptial breaches, and I know not what.   190

[10] Traitors. [11] A beggar pretending madness.

Edg.: How long have you been a sectary astronomical?   [12]

Edm.: Come, come; when saw you my father last?

Edg.: Why, the night gone by.   195

Edm.: Spake you with him?

Edg.: Ay, two hours together.

Edm.: Parted you in good terms? Found you no displeasure in him by word or countenance?   200

Edg.: None at all.

Edm.: Bethink yourself wherein you may have offended him: and at my entreaty forbear his presence till some little time hath qualified the heat of his displeasure; which at this instant so rageth in him, that with the mischief of your person it would scarcely allay.[13]

Edg.: Some villain hath done me wrong.   210

Edm.: That 's my fear. I pray you, have a continent forbearance till the speed of his rage goes slower; and, as I say, retire with me to my lodging, from whence I will fitly bring you to hear my lord speak: pray ye, go; there 's my key: if you do stir abroad, go armed.

Edg.: Armed, brother!   218

Edm.: Brother, I advise you to the best; go armed: I am no honest man if there be any good meaning towards you: I have told you what I have seen and heard; but faintly, nothing like the image and horror of it: pray you, away.   225

Edg.: Shall I hear from you anon?

Edm.: I do serve you in this business.
                            [*Exit Edgar.*]

A credulous father! and a brother noble, Whose nature is so far from doing harms,
That he suspects none; on whose foolish honesty   230
My practices ride easy! I see the business.

Let me, if not by birth, have lands by wit:
All with me 's meet that I can fashion fit.   [*Exit.*]

[12] Student of astrology. [13] Even injury to you would not make it subside.

SCENE III—*The Duke of Albany's palace*

[*Enter Goneril, and Oswald, her steward.*]

Gon.: Did my father strike my gentleman for chiding of his fool?

Osw.: Yes, madam.

Gon.: By day and night he wrongs me; every hour
He flashes into one gross crime or other,
That sets us all at odds: I 'll not endure it: 5
His knights grow riotous, and himself upbraids us
On every trifle. When he returns from hunting,
I will not speak with him; say I am sick:
If you come slack of former services,
You shall do well; the fault of it I 'll answer. 10
Osw.: He 's coming, madam; I hear him. [*Horns within.*]
Gon.: Put on what weary negligence you please,
You and your fellows; I 'ld have it come to question:
If he distaste it, let him to our sister,
Whose mind and mine, I know, in that are one, 15
Not to be over-ruled. Idle old man,
That still would manage those authorities
That he hath given away! Now, by my life,
Old fools are babes again; and must be used
With checks as flatteries,—when they are seen abused. 20
Remember what I have said.
Osw.: Very well, madam.
Gon.: And let his knights have colder looks among you;
What grows of it, no matter; advise your fellows so:
I would breed from hence occasions, and I shall,
That I may speak: I 'll write straight to my sister, 25
To hold my very course. Prepare for dinner. [*Exeunt.*]

SCENE IV—*A hall in the same*

[*Enter Kent, disguised.*]

Kent: If but as well I other accents borrow,
That can my speech defuse,[1] my good intent
May carry through itself to that full issue
For which I razed my likeness.[2] Now, banish'd Kent,
If thou canst serve where thou dost stand condemn'd, 5
So may it come, thy master, whom thou lovest,
Shall find thee full of labours.

[*Horns within. Enter Lear, Knights, and Attendants.*]

Lear: Let me not stay a jot for dinner; go get it ready. [*Exit an Attendant.*] How now! what art thou? 10

Kent: A man, sir.

Lear: What dost thou profess? what wouldst thou with us?

Kent: I do profess to be no less than I seem; to serve him truly that will put me in trust: to love him that is honest; to converse with him that is wise, and says little; to fear judgement; to fight when I cannot choose; and to eat no fish. 20

Lear: What art thou?

Kent: A very honest-hearted fellow, and as poor as the king.

Lear: If thou be as poor for a subject as he is for a king, thou art poor enough. What wouldst thou? 26

Kent: Service.

Lear: Who wouldst thou serve?

Kent: You.

Lear: Dost thou know me, fellow? 30

Kent: No, sir; but you have that in your countenance which I would fain call master.

Lear: What 's that?

Kent: Authority. 35

Lear: What services canst thou do?

Kent: I can keep honest counsel, ride, run, mar a curious tale in telling it, and

[1] Disguise. [2] Destroyed my identity.

deliver a plain message bluntly: that which ordinary men are fit for, I am qualified in; and the best of me is diligence.   42
Lear: How old art thou?
Kent: Not so young, sir, to love a woman for singing, nor so old to dote on her for anything: I have years on my back forty-eight.   47
Lear: Follow me; thou shalt serve me: if I like thee no worse after dinner, I will not part from thee yet. Dinner, ho, dinner! Where 's my knave? my fool? Go you, and call my fool hither.   52
                          [*Exit an Attendant.*]
                          [*Enter Oswald.*]
You, you, sirrah, where 's my daughter?
Osw.: So please you,—   [*Exit.*]
Lear: What says the fellow there? Call the clotpoll back. [*Exit a Knight.*] Where 's my fool, ho? I think the world 's asleep. [*Re-enter Knight.*] How now! where 's that mongrel?
Knight: He says, my lord, your daughter is not well.   61
Lear: Why came not the slave back to me when I called him?
Knight: Sir, he answered me in the roundest manner, he would not.   65
Lear: He would not!
Knight: My lord, I know not what the matter is; but, to my judgement, your highness is not entertained with that ceremonious affection as you were wont; there 's a great abatement of kindness appears as well in the general dependants as in the duke himself also and your daughter.
Lear: Ha! sayest thou so?   75
Knight: I beseech you, pardon me, my lord, if I be mistaken; for my duty cannot be silent when I think your highness wronged.
Lear: Thou but rememberest me of mine own conception: I have perceived a most faint neglect of late; which I have rather blamed as mine own jealous curiosity than as a very pretence and purpose of unkindness: I will look further into 't. But where 's my fool? I have not seen him this two days.   87

Knight: Since my young lady's going into France, sir, the fool hath much pined away.
Lear: No more of that; I have noted it well. Go you, and tell my daughter I would speak with her. [*Exit an Attendant.*] Go you, call hither my fool. [*Exit an Attendant. Re-enter Oswald.*] O, you sir, you sir, come you hither, sir: who am I, sir?   97
Osw.: My lady's father.
Lear: "My lady's father"! my lord's knave: you whoreson dog! you slave! you cur!   101
Osw. I am none of these, my lord; I beseech your pardon.
Lear: Do you bandy looks with me, you rascal?   [*Striking him.*]
Osw. I 'll not be struck, my lord. 106
Kent: Nor tripped neither, you base foot-ball player. [*Tripping up his heels.*]
Lear: I thank thee, fellow; thou servest me, and I 'll love thee.   110
Kent: Come, sir, arise, away! I 'll teach you differences: away, away! If you will measure your lubber's length again, tarry: but away! go to; have you wisdom? so.   [*Pushes Oswald out.*]
Lear: Now, my friendly knave, I thank thee: there 's earnest of thy service.   [*Giving Kent money.*]
                          [*Enter Fool.*]
Fool: Let me hire him too: here's my coxcomb.   [*Offering Kent his cap.*]
Lear: How now, my pretty knave! how dost thou?   122
Fool: Sirrah, you were best take my coxcomb.
Lear: Why, my boy?
Fool: Why, for taking one's part that 's out of favour: nay, an thou canst not smile as the wind sits, thou 'lt catch cold shortly: there, take my coxcomb: why, this fellow has banished two on 's daughters, and did the third a blessing against his will: if thou follow him, thou must needs wear my coxcomb. How now, nuncle! Would I had two coxcombs and two daughters!   135
Lear: Why, my boy?
Fool: If I gave them all my living, i 'ld

keep my coxcombs myself. There 's mine; beg another of thy daughters.

Lear: Take heed, sirrah; the whip.

Fool: Truth 's a dog must to kennel; he must be whipped out, when Lady the brach[3] may stand by the fire and stink. 144

Lear: A pestilent gall to me!

Fool: Sirrah, I 'll teach thee a speech.

Lear: Do.

Fool: Mark it, nuncle:
Have more than thou showest,
Speak less than thou knowest, 150
Lend less than thou owest,[4]
Ride more than thou goest,[5]
Learn more than thou trowest,[6]
Set less than thou throwest; [7]
Leave thy drink and thy whore,
And keep in-a-door, 156
And thou shalt have more
Than two tens to a score.

Kent: This is nothing, fool.

Fool: Then 't is like the breath of an unfee'd lawyer; you gave me nothing for 't. Can you make no use of nothing, nuncle? 163

Lear: Why, no, boy; nothing can be made out of nothing.

Fool: [To Kent.] Prithee, tell him, so much the rent of his land comes to: he will not believe a fool. 168

Lear: A bitter fool!

Fool: Dost thou know the difference, my boy, between a bitter fool and a sweet fool?

Lear: No, lad; teach me. 173

Fool: That lord that counsell'd thee
To give away thy land,
Come place him here by me,
Do thou for him stand:
The sweet and bitter fool
Will presently appear;
The one in motley here, 180
The other found out there.

Lear: Dost thou call me fool, boy?

Fool: All thy other titles thou hast given away; that thou wast born with. 185

Kent: This is not altogether fool, my lord.

Fool: No, faith, lords and great men will not let me; if I had a monopoly out, they would have part on 't: and ladies too, they will not let me have all fool to myself; they 'll be snatching. Nuncle, give me an egg, and I 'll give thee two crowns. 194

Lear: What two crowns shall they be?

Fool: Why, after I have cut the egg i' the middle, and eat up the meat, the two crowns of the egg. When thou clovest thy crown i' the middle, and gavest away both parts, thou borest thy ass on thy back o'er the dirt: thou hadst little wit in thy bald crown, when thou gavest thy golden one away. If I speak like myself in this, let him be whipped that first finds it so. 205
[*Singing.*]
Fools had ne'er less grace in a year;
For wise men are grown foppish,
And know not how their wits to wear,
Their manners are so apish.

Lear: When were you wont to be so full of songs, sirrah? 211

Fool: I have used it, nuncle, ever since thou madest thy daughters thy mothers: for when thou gavest them the rod, and put'st down thine own breeches,
[*Singing.*]
Then they for sudden joy did weep,
And I for sorrow sung. 217
That such a king should play bo-peep,
And go the fools among.
Prithee, nuncle, keep a schoolmaster that can teach thy fool to lie: I would fain learn to lie. 222

Lear: An[8] you lie, sirrah, we 'll have you whipped.

Fool: I marvel what kin thou and thy daughters are: they 'll have me whipped for speaking true, thou 'lt have me whipped for lying; and sometimes I am whipped for holding my peace. I had rather be any kind o' thing than a fool: and yet I would not be thee, nuncle; thou hast pared thy wit o' both sides,

[3] A hound bitch. [4] Ownest. [5] Walkest.
[6] Believest, knowest. [7] Bet less than you win in a throw.

[8] If.

and left nothing i' the middle: here comes or e o' the parings. 234
[Enter Goneril.]
Lear: How now, daughter! what makes that frontlet [9] on? Methinks you are too much of late i' the frown.
Fool: Thou wast a pretty fellow when thou hadst no need to care for her frowning; now thou art an O without a figure: I am better than thou art now; I am a fool, thou art nothing. *[To Goneril.]* Yes, forsooth, I will hold my tongue; so your face bids me, though you say nothing. Mum, mum, 245
He that keeps nor crust nor crum,
Weary of all, shall want some.
[Pointing to Lear.] That 's a shealed peascod.[10]
Gon.: Not only, sir, this your all-licensed fool, 250
But other of your insolent retinue
Do hourly carp and quarrel; breaking forth
In rank and not-to-be-endured riots. Sir,
I had thought, by making this well known unto you,
To have found a safe redress; but now grow fearful, 255
By what yourself too late have spoke and done,
That you protect this course, and put it on
By your allowance; which if you should, the fault
Would not 'scape censure, nor the redresses sleep,
Which, in the tender of a wholesome weal, 260
Might in their working do you that offence,
Which else were shame, that then necessity
Will call discreet proceeding.[11]
Fool: For, you know, nuncle,

[9] Headband; *i.e.*, frown. [10] A pod with the peas taken out. [11] (Ll. 259–63) . . . nor the punishment fail, which, to preserve the public welfare, would necessarily seem justified, though otherwise it would appear a shameful injury to you.

The hedge-sparrow fed the cuckoo so long, 265
That it had it head bit off by it young.
So, out went the candle, and we were left darkling.
Lear: Are you our daughter?
Gon.: I would you would make use of your good wisdom,
Whereof I know you are fraught; and put away 270
These dispositions, which of late transport you
From what you rightly are.
Fool: May not an ass know when the cart draws the horse? Whoop, Jug! I love thee. 275
Lear: Doth any here know me? This is not Lear:
Does Lear walk thus? speak thus? Where are his eyes?
Either his notion [12] weakens, his discernings
Are lethargied—Ha! waking? 'Tis not so?
Who is it that can tell me who I am?
Fool: Lear's shadow. 281
Lear: I would learn that; for, by the marks of sovereignty, knowledge, and reason, I should be false persuaded I had daughters. 285
Fool: Which they will make an obedient father.
Lear: Your name, fair gentlewoman?
Gon.: This admiration, sir, is much o' the savour
Of other your new pranks. I do beseech you
To understand my purposes aright: 290
As you are old and reverend, you should be wise.
Here do you keep a hundred knights and squires;
Men so disorder'd, so debosh'd [13] and bold,
That this our court, infected with their manners,
Shows like a riotous inn: epicurism [14] and lust 295
Make it more like a tavern or a brothel

[12] Mental power. [13] Debauched. [14] Sensuality; gluttony.

Than a graced palace. The shame itself
  doth speak
For instant remedy: be then desired
By her, that else will take the thing she
  begs,
A little to disquantity your train;   300
And the remainder that shall still de-
  pend,
To be such men as may besort your age,
And know themselves and you.
    Lear: Darkness and devils!
Saddle my horses; call my train to-
  gether.
Degenerate bastard! I 'll not trouble
  thee: 305
Yet have I left a daughter.
    Gon.: You strike my people, and your
  disorder'd rabble
Make servants of their betters.
           [Enter Albany.]
    Lear: Woe, that too late repents,—
    [To Alb.] Is it your will? Speak, sir.
Prepare my horses.   310
Ingratitude, thou marble-hearted fiend,
More hideous when thou show'st thee
  in a child
Than the sea-monster!
    Alb.:   Pray, sir, be patient.
    Lear: *[To Goneril.]* Detested kite!
  thou liest:
My train are men of choice and rarest
  parts,   315
That all particulars of duty know,
And in the most exact regard support
The worships of their name. O most
  small fault,
How ugly didst thou in Cordelia show!
That, like an engine, wrench'd my frame
  of nature   320
From the fix'd place; drew from my
  heart all love,
And added to the gall. O Lear, Lear,
  Lear!
Beat at this gate, that let thy folly in,
          [Striking his head.]
And thy dear judgement out! Go, go,
  my people.
    Alb.: My lord, I am guiltless, as I am
  ignorant   325
Of what hath moved you.
    Lear: It may be so, my lord.

Hear, nature, hear; dear goddess, hear!
Suspend thy purpose, if thou didst in-
  tend
To make this creature fruitful!
Into her womb convey sterility!   330
Dry up in her the organs of increase;
And from her derogate [15] body never
  spring
A babe to honour her! If she must
  teem,
Create her child of spleen; that it may
  live
And be a thwart [16] disnatured torment
  to her!   335
Let it stamp wrinkles in her brow of
  youth;
With cadent tears fret channels in her
  cheeks;
Turn all her mother's pains and benefits
To laughter and contempt; that she
  may feel
How sharper than a serpent's tooth it is
To have a thankless child! Away, away!
          [Exit.]   341
    Alb.: Now, gods that we adore,
  whereof comes this?
    Gon.: Never afflict yourself to know
  more of it:
But let his disposition have that scope
That dotage gives it.   345
        [Re-enter Lear.]
    Lear: What, fifty of my followers at
  a clap!
Within a fortnight!
    Alb.   What 's the matter, sir?
    Lear: I 'll tell thee: *[To Goneril.]*
  Life and death! I am ashamed
That thou hast power to shake my man-
  hood thus;   350
That these hot tears, which break from
  me perforce,
Should make thee worth them. Blasts
  and fogs upon thee!
The untented [17] woundings of a father's
  curse
Pierce every sense about thee! Old fond
  eyes,
Beweep this cause again, I 'll pluck ye
  out,   355

[15] Denatured; degraded. [16] Cross-grained;
trouble-making. [17] Incurable.

And cast you, with the waters that you
loose,
To temper clay. Ha? Let it be so.
I have another daughter,
Who, I am sure, is kind and comfortable:
When she shall hear this of thee, with
her nails   360
She 'll flay thy wolvish visage. Thou
shalt find
That I 'll resume the shape which thou
dost think
I have cast off for ever.
  [Exeunt Lear, Kent, and Attendants.]
Gon.: Do you mark that?
Alb.: I cannot be so partial, Goneril,
To the great love I bear you,—   366
Gon.: Pray you, content. What,
  Oswald, ho!
[To the Fool.] You sir, more knave than
fool, after your master.
Fool: Nuncle Lear, nuncle Lear, tarry
and take the fool with thee.   370
  A fox, when one has caught her,
  And such a daughter,
  Should sure to the slaughter,
  If my cap would buy a halter:
So the fool follows after.   [Exit.]
Gon.: This man hath had good
  counsel:—a hundred knights!   376
'T is politic and safe to let him keep
At point a hundred knights: yes, that on
  every dream,
Each buzz, each fancy, each complaint,
  dislike,
He may enguard his dotage with their
  powers,   380
And hold our lives in mercy. Oswald, I
  say!
Alb.: Well, you may fear too far.
Gon.   Safer than trust too far:
Let me still take away the harms I
  fear,
Not fear still to be taken: I know his
  heart.
What he hath utter'd I have writ my
  sister: 385
If she sustain him and his hundred
  knights,
When I have show'd the unfitness,—
  [Re-enter Oswald.] How now, Os-
  wald!

What, have you writ that letter to my
  sister?
Osw.: Aye, madam.
Gon.: Take you some company, and
  away to horse: 390
Inform her full of my particular fear;
And thereto add such reasons of your
  own
As may compact it more. Get you gone;
And hasten your return. [Exit Oswald.]
  No, no, my lord,
This milky gentleness and course of
  yours   395
Though I condemn not, yet, under
  pardon,
You are much more at task for want of
  wisdom
Than praised for harmful mildness.
Alb.: How far your eyes may pierce I
  cannot tell:
Striving to better, oft we mar what 's
  well.   400
Gon.: Nay, then—
Alb.: Well, well; the event.[18]
                              [Exeunt.]

SCENE V—Court before the same

[Enter Lear, Kent, and Fool.]

Lear: Go you before to Gloucester
with these letters. Acquaint my daughter no further with any thing you
know than comes from her demand out
of the letter. If your diligence be not
speedy, I shall be there afore you.   6
Kent: I will not sleep, my lord, till I
have delivered your letter.   [Exit.]
Fool: If a man's brains were in 's
heels, were 't not in danger of kibes?[1]
Lear: Ay, boy.   11
Fool: Then, I prithee, be merry; thy
wit shall ne'er go slip-shod.
Lear: Ha, ha, ha!
Fool: Shalt see thy other daughter
will use thee kindly; for though she's
as like this as a crab 's[2] like an apple,
yet I can tell what I can tell.   18
Lear: What canst thou tell, boy?

18 Time will tell.
1 Sores. 2 Crab apple.

Fool: She will taste as like this as a crab does to a crab. Thou canst tell why one's nose stands i' the middle on 's face?

Lear: No. 23

Fool: Why, to keep one's eyes of either side 's nose; that what a man cannot smell out, he may spy into.

Lear: I did her wrong—

Fool: Canst tell how an oyster makes his shell?

Lear: No. 30

Fool: Nor I neither; but I can tell why a snail has a house.

Lear: Why?

Fool: Why, to put his head in; not to give it away to his daughters, and leave his horns without a case. 36

Lear: I will forget my nature. So kind a father! Be my horses ready?

Fool: Thy asses are gone about 'em. The reason why the seven stars are no more than seven is a pretty reason.

Lear: Because they are not eight? 42

Fool: Yes, indeed: thou wouldst make a good fool.

Lear: To tak 't again perforce! Monster ingratitude! 46

Fool: If thou wert my fool, nuncle, I 'ld have thee beaten for being old before thy time.

Lear: How 's that? 50

Fool: Thou shouldst not have been old till thou hadst been wise.

Lear: O, let me not be mad, not mad, sweet heaven!
Keep me in temper: I would not be mad! [*Enter Gentleman.*] How now! are the horses ready?

Gent.: Ready, my lord. 55

Lear: Come, boy. [*Exeunt.*]

Fool: She that 's a maid now, and laughs at my departure,
Shall not be a maid long, unless things be cut shorter.

QUESTIONS ON ACT I

1. Act I is one of the most compact opening acts that we have dealt with; we may almost say that it has to be compact if Shakespeare is to get off to a good start on one of his most complex plots. Note how Shakespeare plunges immediately into the exposition of the complex situation with which he intends to deal. In the few lines before Lear's entry in Scene i, what do we learn about the situation at court? Of the character of Gloucester? Do the characters who speak first seem to have been put here merely as mouthpieces for the exposition, or do they become vitally concerned in the matters about which they speak?

2. Does the language of the three daughters suggest their characters to us even before we have really seen them in action? Note that Goneril's speech on her love for her father is full of abstractions. What sort of effect do they have upon the careful reader? How does Cordelia's "according to my bond" contrast with this? Do the two speeches shed some light upon the relative effectiveness of hyperbole and of understatement?

3. What do we learn about Lear in Scene i? What does the dramatic evidence here tell us about his tragic flaw?

4. What immediate dramatic value is secured by Shakespeare's use of such a character as Kent?

5. What is gained, if anything, by the contrast of France and Burgundy? Does it carry on a contrast in values which has already been introduced? Does Lear's attitude toward France and Burgundy shed further light on Lear himself?

6. Notice the puns in France's speech beginning "Fairest Cordelia, thou art, etc." Do they merely show cleverness on France's part, or do they give greater fullness to his meaning?

7. How are we prepared for what Goneril and Regan say in their private talk at the end of Scene i? Do we now receive any further clues to their essential nature?

8. To what extent does the brief dialogue at the very beginning of Scene i prepare us for Edmund's soliloquy at the beginning of Scene ii?

9. In Scene ii we shift to a plot apparently quite distinct from the first: it is here that the complexity of the play first begins to become evident. But can the reader already sense some connectives in terms of theme? Is the Gloucester-Edmund-Edgar relationship in any way suggestive of Lear's relationship with his various daughters?

10. Gloucester's speech beginning "these late eclipses" and the following soliloquy by Edmund are undoubtedly meant to be taken together. Which of the two speeches is intellectually sounder, more rational? In general, of course, we are inclined to be sympathetic with the rational as against the superstitious. Yet with which of the two characters are we more sympathetic? Why? Do these facts suggest that Shakespeare may be making a not wholly favorable analysis of the rational man, or, in more general terms, of the values of rationalism? The student should keep this possibility in mind as he reads the rest of the play. Do the actions and statements of Goneril and Regan suggest they too may come under this analysis?

11. Scene iii is very compact. What clue does it give to future action? Are we surprised by what Goneril says, or does it seem plausible in her? Why? Oswald says almost nothing; yet do we get a clear picture of his relationship to Goneril?

12. Why is the relationship between Lear and his daughters developed so rapidly in Scenes iv and v? What does this show us about Goneril? About the center of Shakespeare's interest? Is he primarily interested in the political problem in Lear's kingdom?

13. The Fool does not play any direct part in the major actions. Is he therefore nonessential? Is he merely for "comic relief"? (See, in this connection, Question 1 on *Dr. Faustus*.) Does he really give Lear, or the reader, relief? What seems to be his relationship to Lear in Scene iv? How are we to understand the sharpness of his tone in speaking to Lear? Is his mind as keen as Lear's? As keen as those of Goneril and Regan? If, like them, he manifests an acute intelligence, what is the difference between the way he uses his and the way they use theirs? How, in other words, may he be contrasted at this point with both Lear and Lear's daughters? With Oswald? With Kent?

14. What is ironic about Lear's experience with his daughters? Is it intended that the reader sympathize with him by the end of Act I? Why is this true? With regard to his followers, it has been said by a critic that Lear does not really need one hundred men, and that what Goneril says in this connection is true enough. But do we agree with Goneril? Why? If the

retainers are not strictly necessary, what value do they have? Would the play be more or less effective if the retainers were necessary?
15. Why is Lear made to pray that he may not go mad?

ACT II

SCENE I—*The Earl of Gloucester's castle*

[*Enter Edmund, and Curan meets him.*]

Edm.: Save thee, Curan.
Cur.: And you, sir. I have been with your father, and given him notice that the Duke of Cornwall and Regan his duchess will be here with him this night.
Edm.: How comes that?   6
Cur.: Nay, I know not. You have heard of the news abroad; I mean the whispered ones, for they are yet but ear-kissing arguments?   10
Edm.: Not I: pray you, what are they?
Cur.: Have you heard of no likely wars toward, 'twixt the Dukes of Cornwall and Albany?   15
Edm.: Not a word.
Cur.: You may do, then, in time. Fare you well, sir.   [*Exit.*]
Edm.: The duke be here to-night? The better! best!
This weaves itself perforce into my business.   20
My father hath set guard to take my brother;
And I have one thing, of a queasy question,[1]
Which I must act: briefness[2] and fortune, work!
Brother, a word; descend: brother, I say!   [*Enter Edgar.*]
My father watches: O sir, fly this place;
Intelligence is given where you are hid;
You have now the good advantage of the night.   27
Have you not spoken 'gainst the Duke of Cornwall?
He's coming hither; now, i' the night, i' the haste,

[1] Of a delicate nature. [2] Promptness.

And Regan with him: have you nothing said
Upon his party 'gainst the Duke of Albany?   31
Advise yourself.
Edg.:   I am sure on 't, not a word.
Edm.: I hear my father coming: pardon me;
In cunning I must draw my sword upon you:
Draw; seem to defend yourself; now quit you well.   35
Yield: come before my father. Light, ho, here!
Fly, brother. Torches, torches! So, farewell.   [*Exit Edgar.*]
Some blood drawn on me would beget opinion   [*Wounds his arm.*]
Of my more fierce endeavour: I have seen drunkards
Do more than this in sport. Father, father!   40
Stop, stop! No help?
[*Enter Gloucester, and Servants with torches.*]
Glou.: Now, Edmund, where 's the villain?
Edm.: Here stood he in the dark, his sharp sword out,
Mumbling of wicked charms, conjuring the moon   44
To stand auspicious mistress,—
Glou.:   But where is he?
Edm.: Look, sir, I bleed.
Glou.: Where is the villain, Edmund?
Edm.: Fled this way, sir. When by no means he could—
Glou.: Pursue him, ho! Go after.   [*Exeunt some servants.*] By no means what?
Edm.: Persuade me to the murder of your lordship;
But that I told him, the revenging gods   50
'Gainst parricides did all their thunders bend;

Spoke, with how manifold and strong a
　bond
The child was bound to the father; sir, in
　fine,
Seeing how loathly opposite [3] I stood
To his unnatural purpose, in fell mo-
　tion,　　　　　　　　　　　　　55
With his prepared sword, he charges
　home
My unprovided body, lanced mine arm:
But when he saw my best alarum'd
　spirits,
Bold in the quarrel's right, roused to
　the encounter,　　　　　　　　59
Or whether gasted [4] by the noise I made,
Full suddenly he fled.
　　Glou.:　　　　　Let him fly far:
Not in this land shall he remain un-
　caught;
And found—dispatch. The noble duke
　my master,
My worthy arch and patron, comes to-
　night:
By his authority I will proclaim it,　65
That he which finds him shall deserve
　our thanks,
Bringing the murderous coward to the
　stake;
He that conceals him, death.
　　Edm.: When I dissuaded him from his
　intent,
And found him pight [5] to do it, with
　curst [6] speech　　　　　　　　70
I threaten'd to discover him: he replied,
"Thou unpossessing bastard! dost thou
　think,
If I would stand against thee, would the
　reposal
Of any trust, virtue, or worth in thee
Make thy words faith'd? No: what I
　should deny,—　　　　　　　　75
As this I would; ay, though thou didst
　produce
My very character,—I 'ld turn it all
To thy suggestion,[7] plot, and damn'd
　practice:
And thou must make a dullard of the
　world,

　[3] Loathingly opposed. [4] Frightened. [5] Determined. [6] Sharp. [7] Attribute it all to thy
instigation.

If they not thought the profits of my
　death　　　　　　　　　　　　80
Were very pregnant and potential
　spirits
To make thee seek it."
　　Glou.: O strong and fasten'd villain!
Would he deny his letter? I never got [8]
　him.　　　　　　　*[Tucket within.]*
Hark, the duke's trumpets! I know not
　where he comes.
All ports I 'll bar; the villain shall not
　'scape;　　　　　　　　　　　85
The duke must grant me that: besides,
　his picture
I will send far and near, that all the
　kingdom
May have due note of him; and of my
　land,
Loyal and natural boy, I 'll work the
　means
To make thee capable.[9]　　　　90
[Enter Cornwall, Regan, and Attendants.]
　　Corn.: How now, my noble friend!
　Since I came hither,
Which I can call but now, I have heard
　strange news.
　　Reg.: If it be true, all vengeance
　comes too short
Which can pursue the offender. How
　dost, my lord?
　　Glou.: O! madam, my old heart is
　crack'd, is crack'd!　　　　　95
　　Reg.: What, did my father's godson
　seek your life?
He whom my friend named? your
　Edgar?
　　Glou.: O! lady, lady, shame would
　have it hid.
　　Reg.: Was he not companion with the
　riotous knights
That tend upon my father?　　　100
　　Glou.: I know not, madam: 't is too
　bad, too bad.
　　Edm.: Yes, madam, he was of that
　consort.
　　Reg.: No marvel, then, though he were
　ill affected:
'T is they have put him on the old man's
　death,

　[8] Begot. [9] Able to inherit.

To have the expense and waste [10] of his revenues.   105
I have this present evening from my sister
Been well inform'd of them; and with such cautions,
That if they come to sojourn at my house,
I 'll not be there.
Corn.:   Nor I, assure thee, Regan.
Edmund, I hear that you have shown your father   110
A child-like office.[11]
Edm.:   'T was my duty, sir.
Glou.: He did bewray his practice;[12] and received
This hurt you see, striving to apprehend him.
Corn.: Is he pursued?
Glou.:   Ay, my good lord.
Corn.: If he be taken, he shall never more   115
Be fear'd of doing harm: make your own purpose,
How in my strength you please.[13] For you, Edmund,
Whose virtue and obedience doth this instant
So much commend itself, you shall be ours:
Natures of such deep trust we shall much need;   120
You we first seize on.
Edm.:   I shall serve you, sir.
Truly, however else.
Glou.:   For him I thank your grace.
Corn.: You know not why we came to visit you,—
Reg.: Thus out of season, threading dark-eyed night:
Occasions, noble Gloucester, of some prize,[14]   125
Wherein we must have use of your advice:
Our father he hath writ, so hath our sister,
Of differences, which I best thought it fit

To answer from our home; the several messengers
From hence attend dispatch. Our good old friend,   130
Lay comforts to your bosom; and bestow
Your needful counsel to our business,
Which craves the instant use.
Glou.:   I serve you, madam:
Your graces are right welcome.
      [*Exeunt.*]

SCENE II—*Before Gloucester's castle*

[*Enter Kent and Oswald, severally.*]

Osw.: Good dawning to thee, friend: art of this house?
Kent: Ay.
Osw.: Where may we set our horses?
Kent: I' the mire.   5
Osw.: Prithee, if thou lovest me, tell me.
Kent: I love thee not.
Osw.: Why, then, I care not for thee.
Kent: If I had thee in Lipsbury pinfold,[1] I would make thee care for me.
Osw.: Why dost thou use me thus? I know thee not.
Kent: Fellow, I know thee.   14
Osw.: What dost thou know me for?
Kent: A knave; a rascal; an eater of broken meats; a base, proud, shallow, beggarly, three-suited, hundred-pound, filthy, worsted-stocking knave; a lily-livered, action-taking [2] knave; a whoreson, glass [3]-gazing, superserviceable,[4] finical rogue; one-trunk-inheriting slave; one that wouldst be a bawd in way of good service, and art nothing but the composition [5] of a knave, beggar, coward, pandar, and the son and heir of a mongrel bitch: one whom I will beat into clamorous whining, if thou deniest the least syllable of thy addition.[6]   31
Osw.: Why, what a monstrous fellow

---

[10] Spending and wasting. [11] Filial conduct.
[12] Disclose Edgar's plot. [13] Make your own plans, using my authority. [14] Importance.

[1] Reference not clear; possibly the teeth.
[2] Going to law (instead of courageously fighting). [3] mirror. [4] Officious. [5] Combination. [6] Titles.

art thou, thus to rail on one that is neither known of thee nor knows thee!

Kent: What a brazen-faced varlet art thou, to deny thou knowest me! Is it two days ago since I tripped up thy heels, and beat thee before the king? Draw, you rogue: for, though it be night, yet the moon shines; I'll make a sop o' the moonshine of you: draw you whoreson cullionly [7] barber-monger, draw. [*Drawing his sword.*]

Osw.: Away! I have nothing to do with thee. 45

Kent: Draw, you rascal: you come with letters against the king; and take Vanity-the-puppet's part against the royalty of her father: draw, you rogue, or I'll so carbonado [8] your shanks: draw, you rascal; come your ways. 51

Osw.: Help, ho! murder! help!

Kent: Strike, you slave; stand, rogue, stand; you neat [9] slave, strike. [*Beating him.*]

Osw.: Help, ho! murder! murder! 55

[*Enter Edmund with his rapier drawn, Cornwall, Regan, Gloucester, and Servants.*]

Edm.: How now! What's the matter?

Kent: With you, goodman boy, an you please: come, I'll flesh [10] ye; come on, young master.

Glou.: Weapons! arms! What's the matter here? 61

Corn.: Keep peace, upon your lives: He dies that strikes again. What is the matter?

Reg.: The messengers from our sister and the king. 65

Corn.: What is your difference? speak.

Osw.: I am scarce in breath, my lord.

Kent: No marvel, you have so bestirred your valour. You cowardly rascal, nature disclaims in [11] thee: a tailor made thee. 71

Corn.: Thou art a strange fellow: a tailor make a man?

Kent: Ay, a tailor, sir: a stone-cutter or a painter could not have made him

so ill, though they had been but two hours at the trade. 77

Corn.: Speak yet, how grew your quarrel?

Osw.: This ancient ruffian, sir, whose life I have spared at suit of his gray beard,—

Kent: Thou whoreson zed! thou unnecessary [12] letter! My lord, if you will give me leave, I will tread this unbolted villain into mortar, and daub the wall of a jakes [13] with him. Spare my gray beard, you wagtail? 88

Corn.: Peace, sirrah!

You beastly knave, know you no reverence?

Kent: Yes, sir; but anger hath a privilege.

Corn.: Why art thou angry? 92

Kent: That such a slave as this should wear a sword,
Who wears no honesty. Such smiling rogues as these,
Like rats, oft bite the holy cords a-twain
Which are too intrinse [14] t' unloose; smooth every passion 96
That in the natures of their lords rebel;
Bring oil to fire, snow to their colder moods;
Renege, affirm, and turn their halcyon beaks
With every gale and vary of their masters, 100
Knowing nought, like dogs, but following.
A plague upon your epileptic visage!
Smile you my speeches, as I were a fool?
Goose, if I had you upon Sarum plain,
I'ld drive ye cackling home to Camelot.

Corn.: What, art thou mad, old fellow?

Glou.: How fell you out? say that.

Kent: No contraries hold more antipathy 108
Than I and such a knave.

Corn.: Why dost thou call him knave? What is his fault?

Kent: His countenance likes me not.

---

[7] Rascally; base. [8] Cut crosswise (used of a piece of meat before broiling). [9] Pure; unmixed. [10] Initiate (in hunting). [11] Disowns.

[12] Z (zed) was often omitted in contemporary dictionaries. [13] Outhouse. [41] Intricate; tightly drawn.

Corn.: No more, perchance, does mine, nor his, nor hers.

Kent: Sir, 't is my occupation to be plain:⠀⠀⠀⠀⠀⠀⠀⠀⠀⠀⠀113
I have seen better faces in my time
Than stands on any shoulder that I see
Before me at this instant.

Corn.:⠀⠀⠀⠀⠀This is some fellow,
Who, having been praised for bluntness, doth affect
A saucy roughness, and constrains the garb⠀⠀⠀⠀⠀⠀⠀⠀⠀⠀⠀118
Quite from his nature: [15] he cannot flatter, he;
An honest mind and plain, he must speak truth.
An they will take it, so; if not, he 's plain.
These kind of knaves I know, which in this plainness
Harbour more craft and more corrupter ends
Than twenty silly-ducking observants
That stretch their duties nicely.[16]⠀⠀⠀125

Kent: Sir, in good faith, in sincere verity,
Under the allowance of your great aspect,
Whose influence, like the wreath of radiant fire
On flickering Phoebus' front,—

Corn.:⠀⠀⠀⠀⠀What mean'st by this?

Kent: To go out of my dialect, which you discommend so much. I know, sir, I am no flatterer: he that beguiled you in a plain accent was a plain knave; which for my part I will not be, though I should win your displeasure to entreat me to 't.⠀⠀⠀⠀⠀⠀⠀⠀⠀136

Corn.: What was the offence you gave him?

Osw.: I never gave him any:
It pleased the king his master very late
To strike at me, upon his misconstruction;⠀⠀⠀⠀⠀⠀⠀⠀⠀⠀⠀141
When he, compact,[17] and flattering his displeasure,

[15] Carries his affected bluntness to an unnatural extreme. [16] Punctiliously carry out their duties. [17] Taking his part.

Tripp'd me behind; being down, insulted, rail'd,
And put upon him such a deal of man,
That worthied him, got praises of the king⠀⠀⠀⠀⠀⠀⠀⠀⠀⠀⠀145
For him attempting who was self-subdued;
And, in the fleshment [18] of this dread exploit,
Drew on me here again.

Kent: None of these rogues and cowards
But Ajax is their fool.[19]

Corn.:⠀⠀⠀⠀⠀Fetch forth the stocks!
You stubborn ancient knave, you reverent braggart,
We 'll teach you—

Kent:⠀⠀⠀⠀⠀Sir, I am too old to learn:
Call not your stocks for me: I serve the king;⠀⠀⠀⠀⠀⠀⠀⠀⠀⠀⠀152
On whose employment I was sent to you:
You shall do small respect, show too bold malice
Against the grace and person of my master,⠀⠀⠀⠀⠀⠀⠀⠀⠀⠀⠀155
Stocking his messenger.

Corn.: Fetch forth the stocks! As I have life and honour,
There shall he sit till noon.

Reg.: Till noon! till night, my lord; and all night too.

Kent: Why, madam, if I were your father's dog,⠀⠀⠀⠀⠀⠀⠀⠀⠀⠀⠀160
You should not use me so.

Reg.:⠀⠀⠀⠀⠀Sir, being his knave, I will.

Corn.: This is a fellow of the self-same colour
Our sister speaks of. Come, bring away the stocks!⠀⠀⠀[*Stocks brought out.*]

Glou.: Let me beseech your grace not to do so:
His fault is much, and the good king his master⠀⠀⠀⠀⠀⠀⠀⠀⠀⠀⠀165
Will check him for 't: your purposed low correction
Is such as basest and contemned'st wretches

[18] Under the stimulus. [19] Perhaps: a plain, blunt fellow such as Ajax is always the butt.

For pilferings and most common tres-
passes
Are punish'd with: the king must take
it ill,
That he, so slightly valued in his mes-
senger, 170
Should have him thus restrain'd.
Corn.: I 'll answer that.
Reg.: My sister may receive it much
more worse,
To have her gentleman abused, as-
saulted,
For following her affairs. Put in his legs.
[*Kent is put in the stocks.*]
Corn.: Come, my lord, away. 175
[*Exeunt all but Gloucester and Kent.*]
Glou.: I am sorry for thee, friend; 't is
the duke's pleasure,
Whose disposition, all the world well
knows,
Will not be rubb'd nor stopp'd: I 'll en-
treat for thee.
Kent: Pray, do not, sir: I have
watched and travell'd hard;
Some time I shall sleep out, the rest I 'll
whistle. 180
A good man's fortune may grow out at
heels:
Give you good morrow!
Glou.: The duke's to blame in this;
't will be ill-taken. [*Exit.*]
Kent: Good king, that must approve
the common saw,
Thou out of heaven's benediction com-
est 185
To the warm sun! [20]
Approach, thou beacon to this under
globe,
That by thy comfortable beams I
may
Peruse this letter! Nothing almost sees
miracles
But misery: I know 't is from Cordelia,
Who hath most fortunately been in-
form'd 191
Of my obscured course; and shall find
time
From this enormous state, seeking to
give

[20] Old saw or proverb, apparently de-
scribing a decline in fortune.

Losses their remedies. All weary and
o'er-watch'd,
Take vantage, heavy eyes, not to behold
This shameful lodging. 196
Fortune, good night: smile once more:
turn thy wheel! [*Sleeps.*]

SCENE III—*A wood*

[*Enter Edgar.*]

Edg.: I heard myself proclaim'd;
And by the happy hollow of a tree
Escaped the hunt. No port is free; no
place,
That guard, and most unusual vigi-
lance,
Does not attend my taking. Whiles I
may 'scape, 5
I will preserve myself: and am be-
thought
To take the basest and most poorest
shape
That ever penury, in contempt of man,
Brought near to beast: my face I 'll
grime with filth:
Blanket my loins; elf [1] all my hair in
knots; 10
And with presented nakedness out-face
The winds and persecution of the
sky.
The country gives me proof and pre-
cedent
Of Bedlam beggars, who, with roaring
voices,
Strike in their numb'd and mortified
bare arms 15
Pins, wooden pricks, nails, sprigs of
rosemary;
And with this horrible object, from low
farms,
Poor pelting villages, sheep-cotes, and
mills,
Sometime with lunatic bans,[2] sometime
with prayers,
Enforce their charity. Poor Turlygod!
poor Tom! 20
That 's something yet: Edgar I nothing
am. [*Exit.*]

[1] Tangle, in the manner of an elf. [2] Curses.

SCENE IV—*Before Gloucester's castle.*
Kent in the stocks

[*Enter Lear, Fool, and Gentleman.*]

Lear: 'T is strange that they should
so depart from home,
And not send back my messenger.
Gent.:   As I learn'd,
The night before there was no purpose
in them
Of this remove.
Kent: Hail to thee, noble master!
Lear: Ha!   5
Makest thou this shame thy pastime?
Kent.   No, my lord.
Fool: Ha, ha! he wears cruel garters.
Horses are tied by the heads, dogs and
bears by the neck, monkeys by the loins,
and men by the legs: when a man's
over-lusty at legs, then he wears wooden
nether-stocks.   12
    Lear: What 's he that hath so much
thy place mistook
To set thee here?
Kent: It is both he and she;
Your son and daughter.
Lear: No.
Kent: Yes.
Lear: No, I say.
Kent: I say, yea.
Lear: By Jupiter, I swear, no.   20
Kent: By Juno, I swear, ay.
Lear: They durst not do 't;
They could not, would not do 't; 't is
worse than murder,
To do upon respect such violent out-
rage:
Resolve me, with all modest haste,
which way
Thou mightst deserve, or they impose,
this usage,   25
Coming from us.
Kent: My lord, when at their home
I did commend your highness' letter to
them,
Ere I was risen from the place that
show'd
My duty kneeling, came there a reeking
post,
Stew'd in his haste, half breathless,
panting forth   30,

From Goneril his mistress salutations;
Deliver'd letters, spite of intermission,[1]
Which presently they read: on whose
contents,
They summon'd up their meiny,[2] straight
took horse;
Commanded me to follow, and attend
The leisure of their answer; gave me
cold looks: 36
And meeting here the other messenger,
Whose welcome, I perceived, had
poison'd mine,—
Being the very fellow which of late
Display'd so saucily against your high-
ness,—   40
Having more man than wit about me,
drew:
He raised the house with loud and
coward cries.
Your son and daughter found this
trespass worth
The shame which here it suffers.
Fool: Winter 's not gone yet, if the
wild-geese fly that way.   46
Fathers that wear rags
    Do make their children blind;
But fathers that bear bags
    Shall see their children kind.   50
Fortune, that arrant whore,
    Ne'er turns the key to the poor.
But, for all this, thou shalt have as
many dolours[3] for thy daughters as thou
canst tell in a year.   55
Lear: O, how this mother swells up
toward my heart!
Hysterica passio, down, thou climbing
sorrow,[4]
Thy element 's below! Where is this
daughter?
Kent: With the earl, sir, here within.
Lear: Follow me not;
Stay here.   [*Exit.*]
Gent.: Made you no more offence but
what you speak of?   62
Kent: None. How chance the king
comes with so small a number?
Fool: An thou hadst been set i' the

---

[1] Of interrupting me. [2] Company. [3] A pun
on *dolour*, sorrow, and *dollar*, the coin (peso).
[4] Lear describes symptoms of hysteria, called
then both *mother* and *hysterica passio*.

stocks for that question, thou hadst
well deserved it.
Kent: Why, fool? 68
Fool: We 'll set thee to school to an
ant, to teach thee there 's no labouring
i' the winter. All that follow their noses
are led by their eyes but blind men;
and there 's not a nose among twenty
but can smell him that 's stinking. Let
go thy hold when a great wheel runs
down a hill, lest it break thy neck with
following; but the great one that goes
up the hill, let him draw thee after.
When a wise man gives thee better
counsel, give me mine again: I would
have none but knaves follow it, since a
fool gives it. 82
That sir which serves and seeks for gain,
    And follows but for form,
Will pack when it begins to rain,
    And leave thee in the storm.
But I will tarry; the fool will stay,
    And let the wise man fly:
The knave turns fool that runs away;
    The fool no knave, perdy. 90
Kent: Where learned you this, fool?
Fool: Not i' the stocks, fool.
    [*Re-enter Lear, with Gloucester.*]
Lear: Deny to speak with me? They
are sick? they are weary?
They have travell'd all the night? Mere
fetches; [5]
The images of revolt and flying off. 95
Fetch me a better answer.
Glou.:   My dear lord,
You know the fiery quality of the duke;
How unremoveable and fix'd he is
In his own course.
    Lear: Vengeance! plague! death!
confusion! 100
Fiery? what quality? Why, Gloucester,
Gloucester,
I 'ld speak with the Duke of Cornwall
and his wife.
    Glou.: Well, my good lord, I have in-
form'd them so.
Lear: Inform'd them! Dost thou
understand me, man?
Glou.: Ay, my good lord. 105

[5] Evasions, tricks.

Lear: The king would speak with
Cornwall; the dear*father
Would with his daughter speak, com-
mands, tends,[6] service:
Are they inform'd of this? My breath
and blood!
Fiery? the fiery duke? Tell the hot duke
that— 109
No, but not yet: may be he is not well·
Infirmity doth still neglect all office [7]
Whereto our health is bound; we are
not ourselves
When nature, being oppress'd, com-
mands the mind
To suffer with the body: I 'll forbear;
And am fall'n out with my more headier
will,[8] 115
To take the indisposed and sickly
fit
For the sound man. Death on my state!
wherefore   [*Looking on Kent.*]
Should he sit here? This act persuades
me
That this remotion of the duke and her
Is practice only.[9] Give me my servant
forth. 120
Go tell the duke and 's wife I 'ld speak
with them,
Now, presently: bid them come forth
and hear me,
Or at their chamber-door I 'll beat the
drum
Till it cry sleep to death.
    Glou.: I would have all well betwixt
you.   [*Exit.*]
Lear: O me, my heart, my rising
heart! but, down! 126
Fool: Cry to it, nuncle, as the cockney
did to the eels when she put 'em i' the
paste alive; she knapped [10] 'em o' the
coxcombs with a stick, and cried
"Down, wantons, down!" 'T was her
brother that, in pure kindness to his
horse, buttered his hay. 133
    [*Enter Cornwall, Regan, Gloucester,
and Servants.*]
Lear: Good morrow to you both.

[6] Expects. [7] Duty. [8] Because of my impetuosity, I have done wrong to take, etc.
[9] That this removal is a stratagem. [10] Struck
sharply.

Corn.:   Hail to your grace!
    [*Kent is set at liberty.*]
Reg.: I am glad to see your highness.
Lear: Regan, I think you are; I know what reason
I have to think so: if thou shouldst not be glad,
I would divorce me from thy mother's tomb,
Selpulchring an adultress. [*To Kent.*]
  O, are you free?
Some other time for that. Beloved Regan,   140
Thy sister's naught: O Regan, she hath tied
Sharp-tooth'd unkindness, like a vulture, here: [*Points to his heart.*]
I can scarce speak to thee; thou 'lt not believe
With how depraved a quality—O Regan!
Reg.: I pray you, sir, take patience; I have hope   145
You less know how to value her desert
Than she to scant her duty.
Lear: Say, how is that?
Reg.: I cannot think my sister in the least
Would fail her obligation; if, sir, perchance
She have restrain'd the riots of your followers,   150
'T is on such ground, and to such wholesome end,
As clears her from all blame.
Lear: My curses on her!
Reg.:   O, sir, you are old;
Nature in you stands on the very verge
Of her confine: you should be ruled and led   155
By some discretion, that discerns your state
Better than you yourself. Therefore, I pray you,
That to our sister you do make return;
Say you have wrong'd her.
Lear: Ask her forgiveness?
Do you but mark how this becomes the house: 160
"Dear daughter, I confess that I am old; [*Kneeling.*]

Age is unnecessary: on my knees I beg
That you 'll vouchsafe me raiment, bed, and food."
Reg.: Good sir, no more; these are unsightly tricks:
Return you to my sister.
Lear: [*Rising.*] Never, Regan:
She hath abated me of half my train;
Look'd black upon me; struck me with her tongue   167
Most serpent-like, upon the very heart:
All the stored vengeances of heaven fall
On her ingrateful top! Strike her young bones,
You taking airs,[11] with lameness!
Corn.:   Fie, sir, fie!
Lear: You nimble lightnings, dart your blinding flames   172
Into her scornful eyes! Infect her beauty,
You fen-suck'd fogs, drawn by the powerful sun,
To fall and blister!
Reg.: O the blest gods! so will you wish on me,
When the rash mood is on.
Lear: No, Regan, thou shalt never have my curse:
Thy tender-hefted[12] nature shall not give
Thee o'er to harshness: her eyes are fierce; but thine   180
Do comfort and not burn. 'T is not in thee
To grudge my pleasures, to cut off my train,
To bandy hasty words, to scant my sizes,
And in conclusion to oppose the bolt
Against my coming in: thou better know'st   185
The offices of nature, bond of childhood,
Effects of courtesy, dues of gratitude;
Thy half o' the kingdom hast thou not forgot,
Wherein I thee endow'd.
Reg.:   Good sir, to the purpose.
Lear.: Who put my man i' the stocks?
    [*Tucket within.*]

---

[11] Infecting. [12] Delicately contructed.

Corn.:   What trumpet's that?
Reg.: I know't, my sister's: this approves her letter,   191
That she would soon be here.
        [*Enter Oswald.*]
                Is your lady come?
Lear: This is a slave, whose easy-borrow'd pride
Dwells in the fickle grace of her he follows.
Out, varlet, from my sight!
    Corn.:   What means your grace?
Lear: Who stock'd my servant?
Regan, I have good hope   196
Thou didst not know on't. Who comes here? O heavens, [*Enter Goneril.*]
If you do love old men, if your sweet sway
Allow obedience, if you yourselves are old,
Make it your cause; send down, and take my part!   200
[*To Goneril.*] Art not ashamed to look upon this beard?
O Regan, wilt thou take her by the hand?
    Gon.: Why not by the hand, sir?
How have I offended?
All's not offence that indiscretion finds
And dotage terms so.
    Lear: O sides, you are too tough;
Will you yet hold? How came my man i' the stocks?   206
Corn.: I set him there, sir: but his own disorders
Deserved much less advancement.
    Lear: You! did you?
Reg.: I pray you, father, being weak, seem so.
If, till the expiration of your month,
You will return and sojourn with my sister,   211
Dismissing half your train, come then to me:
I am now from home, and out of that provision
Which shall be needful for your entertainment.
    Lear: Return to her, and fifty men dismiss'd?   215
No, rather I abjure all roofs, and choose

To wage against the enmity o' the air;
To be a comrade with the wolf and owl,—
Necessity's sharp pinch! Return with her?
Why, the hot-blooded France, that dowerless took   220
Our youngest born, I could as well be brought
To knee his throne, and, squire-like, pension beg
To keep base life afoot. Return with her?
Persuade me rather to be slave and sumpter
To this detested groom.
                [*Pointing at Oswald.*]
Gon.:   At your choice, sir.
Lear: I prithee, daughter, do not make me mad: 226
I will not trouble thee, my child; farewell:
We'll no more meet, no more see one another:
But yet thou art my flesh, my blood, my daughter;
Or rather a disease that's in my flesh,
Which I must needs call mine: thou art a boil,   231
A plague-sore, or embossed carbuncle,
In my corrupted blood. But I'll not chide thee;
Let shame come when it will, I do not call it:
I do not bid the thunder-bearer shoot,
Nor tell tales of thee to high-judging Jove: 236
Mend when thou canst; be better at thy leisure:
I can be patient; I can stay with Regan,
I and my hundred knights.
    Reg.:   Not altogether so:
I look'd not for you yet, nor am provided   240
For your fit welcome. Give ear, sir, to my sister;
For those that mingle reason with your passion
Must be content to think you old, and so—
But she knows what she does.

Lear: Is this well spoken?
Reg.: I dare avouch it, sir: what, fifty
followers? 245
Is it not well? What should you need of
more?
Yea, or so many, sith that both charge
and danger
Speak 'gainst so great a number? How,
in one house,
Should many people, under two com-
mands,
Hold amity? 'T is hard; almost impos-
sible. 250
Gon.: Why might not you, my lord,
receive attendance
From those that she calls servants or
from mine?
Reg.: Why not, my lord? If then they
chanced to slack you,
We could control them. If you will
come to me,—
For now I spy a danger,—I entreat you
To bring but five-and-twenty: to no
more 256
Will I give place or notice.
Lear: I gave you all—
Reg.: And in good time you gave it.
Lear: Made you my guardians, my
depositaries;
But kept a reservation to be follow'd
With such a number. What, must I
come to you 261
With five-and-twenty, Regan? said
you so?
Reg.: And speak 't again, my lord; no
more with me.
Lear: Those wicked creatures yet do
look well-favour'd,
When others are more wicked; not
being the worst 265
Stands in some rank of praise. [*To
Goneril.*] I 'll go with thee:
Thy fifty yet doth double five-and-
twenty,
And thou art twice her love.
Gon.: Hear me, my lord:
What need you five-and-twenty, ten, or
five,
To follow in a house where twice so
many 270
Have a command to tend you?

Reg.: What need one?
Lear: O, reason not the need: our
basest beggars
Are in the poorest thing superfluous: [13]
Allow not nature more than nature
needs,
Man's life is cheap as beast's: thou art a
lady; 275
If only to go warm were gorgeous,
Why, nature needs not what thou
gorgeous wear'st,
Which scarcely keeps thee warm. But,
for true need,—
You heavens, give me that patience,
patience I need!
You see me here, you gods, a poor old
man, 280
As full of grief as age; wretched in both!
If it be you that stirs these daughters'
hearts
Against their father, fool me not so
much
To bear it tamely; touch me with noble
anger,
And let not women's weapons, water-
drops, 285
Stain my man's cheeks! No, you un-
natural hags,
I will have such revenges on you both,
That all the world shall—I will do such
things,—
What they are, yet I know not; but they
shall be
The terrors of the earth. You think
I 'll weep; 290
No, I 'll not weep:
I have full cause of weeping; but this
heart
Shall break into a hundred thousand
flaws,
Or ere I 'll weep. O fool, I shall go mad!
[*Exeunt Lear, Gloucester, Kent, and
Fool.*]
[*Storm and tempest.*]
Corn.: Let us withdraw; 't will be a
storm. 295
Reg.: This house is little: the old man
and his people
Cannot be well bestow'd.

[13] Have more than bare necessity.

Gon.: 'T is his own blame; hath put
himself from rest,
And must needs taste his folly.
Reg.: For his particular,[14] I 'll receive
him gladly, 300
But not one follower.
Gon.: So am 1 purposed.
Where is my lord of Gloucester?
Corn.: Follow'd the old man forth: he
is return'd.
[*Re-enter Gloucester.*]
Glou.: The king is in high rage.
Corn.: Whither is he going?
Glou.: He calls to horse; but will I
know not whither. 305
Corn.: 'T is best to give him way; he
leads himself.

[14] As for himself alone.

Gon.: My lord, entreat him by no
means to stay.
Glou.: Alack, the night comes on, and
the high winds
Do sorely ruffle; for many miles about
There 's scarce a bush.
Reg.: O, sir, to wilful men-
The injuries that they themselves pro-
cure 311
Must be their schoolmasters. Shut up
your doors,
He is attended with a desperate train;
And what they may incense him to,
being apt
To have his ear abused, wisdom bids fear.
Corn.: Shut up your doors, my lord;
't is a wild night: 316
My Regan counsels well: come out o' the
storm. [*Exeunt.*]

QUESTIONS ON ACT II

1. When Gloucester says of Edgar, "Let him fly far," what parallel is suggested between Gloucester and Lear? Does such a parallel help hold the plot together?

2. Trace the various ironies in Scene i. What are we to make of the fact that Regan tries to explain Edgar's supposed evil conduct by saying that he has associated with Lear's knights?

3. Is the conflict between Oswald and Kent in Scene ii simply so much byplay, or does it in any way contribute to the main action and theme of the play? Both men are in the service of a lord. Does their conduct contain any implication about the kind of service they are in?

4. What does Scene ii show about Cornwall? Is he in any way like Edmund? Does he, for instance, have Edmund's sharp intelligence? Compare his speech beginning "This is some fellow, / Who, etc." and Oswald's "I never gave him any," which are alike in that neither of them analyzes Kent correctly. But which of the two comments the more shrewdly upon human character?

5. Although Lear is not present in Scene ii, what does this scene show us about his status in the kingdom? What dramatic effect can Shakespeare secure later because Lear is not present in this scene?

6. In Scene iii, what bearing do Edgar's exile and madness have upon the main theme? What symbolic meaning is suggested here?

7. Act II presents some significant evidence on Gloucester. In Scene ii we see his sympathy for Kent. Notice, on the other hand, his speeches in Scene iv, "You know the fiery quality of the duke," and "I would have all well betwixt you." What is really Gloucester's basic trouble? Can we say that he "goes along with" the powers that be, and doesn't really discover

what his principles are until too late? Might it be said, also, that he doesn't
see what the issue is until it is too late?

8. What is ironic about Lear's attitude to Regan before Goneril enters in
Scene iv? How does the reader know that he is wrong?

9. What are the climactic pressures upon Lear which begin to make his
life unbearable? Follow through the passages which suggest his growing
feeling that the situation is almost too much for his sanity. Do these suggestions become stronger as the scene unfolds?

10. At the end of Act I we suggested that Lear's retainers had some
meaning beyond the possibility of their being literally needed. Note that
Lear begins his last speech in Act II: "O, reason not the need." That is, he
repudiates mere need as a standard of judgment of values. But note also
that the verb he uses is *reason,* and that *reasoning* with him is what the
daughters have been doing with him throughout the scene. But by *reason*
they do not arrive at a sense of values which enables them to deal con-
siderately with Lear; it appears that they may actually be using their
reason to conceal whatever grasp of the situation they may have and to
justify their own will. Note, for instance, the "reasoning" employed by
Regan in her last speech in the act: to her, "wisdom" consists in looking
out for herself, and devil take the hindmost. In the light of this evidence
review Act I, Question 10, which concerns Edmund's use of reason. Does it
appear by now that there is a close thematic relationship between Edmund
and the two sisters, and that in terms of their conduct Shakespeare may
be making a profound comment upon the way in which the human reason,
when it is left to its own devices, tends to work?

ACT III

Scene 1—*A heath*

[*Storm still. Enter Kent and a Gentleman, meeting.*]

Kent: Who's there, besides foul
weather?

Gent.: One minded like the weather,
most unquietly.

Kent: I know you. Where's the king?

Gent.: Contending with the fretful
elements;

Bids the wind blow the earth into the
sea, 5

Or swell the curled waters 'bove the
main,

That things might change or cease;
tears his white hair,

Which the impetuous blasts, with eyeless rage,

Catch in their fury, and make nothing
of;

Strives in his little world of man to out-
scorn 10

The to-and-fro-conflicting wind and
rain.

This night, wherein the cub-drawn bear
would couch,

The lion and the belly-pinched wolf
Keep their fur dry, unbonneted he runs,
And bids what will take all.

Kent: But who is with him?

Gent.: None but the fool; who labours
to outjest 16

His heart-struck injuries.

Kent: Sir, I do know you;

And dare, upon the warrant of my note,[1]
Commend a dear [2] thing to you. There
is division,

Although as yet the face of it be cover'd

[1] Upon the strength of my knowledge (of
facts, or, of you). [2] Important.

With mutual cunning, 'twixt Albany
and Cornwall;
Who have—as who have not, that their
great stars
Throned and set high?—servants, who
seem no less,
Which are to France the spies and
speculations [3]
Intelligent [4] of our state; what hath
been seen,   25
Either in snuffs and packings [5] of the
dukes,
Or the hard rein which both of them
have borne
Against the old kind king; or something
deeper,
Whereof perchance these are but
furnishings; [6]
But, true it is, from France there comes
a power   30
Into this scatter'd kingdom; who al-
ready,
Wise in our negligence, have secret feet
In some of our best ports, and are at
point
To show their open banner. Now to you:
If on my credit you dare build so far
To make your speed to Dover, you shall
find   36
Some that will thank you, making just
report
Of how unnatural and bemadding sor-
row
The king hath cause to plain.[7]
I am a gentleman of blood and breeding;
And, from some knowledge and assur-
ance, offer   41
This office to you.
  Gent.: I will talk further with you.
  Kent.:   No, do not.
For confirmation that I am much more
Than my out-wall,[8] open this purse, and
take   45
What is contains. If you shall see
Cordelia,—
As fear not but you shall,—show her
this ring;
And she will tell you who your fellow is

3 Observers. 4 Giving knowledge. 5 Quarrels and plots. 6 Indications. 7 Complain of.
8 Appearance.

That yet you do not know. Fie on this
storm!
I will go seek the king.   50
  Gent.: Give me your hand: have you
no more to say?
  Kent.: Few words, but, to effect, more
than all yet;
That, when we have found the king,—
in which your pain
That way, I 'll this,—he that first lights
on him
Holla the other. · [*Exeunt severally.*]

SCENE II—*Another part of the heath.
Storm still*

[*Enter Lear and Fool.*]

  Lear: Blow, winds, and crack your
cheeks! rage! blow!
You cataracts and hurricanoes, spout
Till you have drench'd our steeples,
drown'd the cocks!
You sulphurous and thought-executing
fires,
Vaunt-couriers [1] of oak-cleaving thun-
derbolts,   5
Singe my white head! And thou, all-
shaking thunder,
Smite flat the thick rotundity o' the
world!
Crack nature's moulds, all germens [2]
spill at once,
That make ingrateful man!   9
  Fool: O nuncle, court holy-water in a
dry house is better than this rain-water
out o' door. Good nuncle, in, ask thy
daughters' blessing: here 's a night pities
neither wise men nor fools.
  Lear: Rumble thy bellyful! Spit, fire!
spout, rain!   15
Nor rain, wind, thunder, fire, are my
daughters:
I tax not you, you elements, with unkindness;
I never gave you kingdom, call'd you
children,
You owe me no subscription [3]: then let
fall

1 Advance-messengers.   2 Germs of life.
3 Allegiance.

Your horrible pleasure; here I stand,
your slave,   20
A poor, infirm, weak, and despised old
man:
But yet I call you servile ministers,
That will with two pernicious daughters
join
Your high-engender'd battles 'gainst a
head   24
So old and white as this. O! O! 't is foul!
    Fool: He that has a house to put 's
head in has a good head-piece.
    The cod-piece that will house
      Before the head has any,
    The head and he shall louse;   30
      So beggars marry many.
    The man that makes his toe
      What he his heart should make
    Shall of a corn cry woe,
      And turn his sleep to wake.   35
For there was never yet fair woman but
she made mouths in a glass.
    Lear: No, I will be the pattern of all
patience; I will say nothing.
                [*Enter Kent.*]
    Kent: Who 's there?   40
    Fool: Marry, here 's grace and a cod-
piece; that 's a wise man and a fool.
    Kent: Alas, sir, are you here? things
that love night
Love not such nights as these; the
wrathful skies
Gallow [4] the very wanderers of the dark,
And make them keep their caves: since
I was man,   46
Such sheets of fire, such bursts of horrid
thunder,
Such groans of roaring wind and rain,
I never
Remember to have heard: man's nature
cannot carry
The affliction nor the fear.
    Lear: Let the great gods,
That keep this dreadul pudder [5] o'er
our heads,   51
Find out their enemies now. Tremble,
thou wretch,
That hast within thee undivulged
crimes,

Unwhipp'd of justice: hide thee, thou
bloody hand;
Thou perjured, and thou simular [6] of
virtue   55
That are incestuous: caitiff, to pieces
shake,
That under covert and convenient
seeeming
Hast practised on man's life: close pent-
up guilts
Rive your concealing continents,[7] and cry
These dreadful summoners grace. I am a
man   60
More sinn'd against than sinning.
    Kent: Alack, bare-headed!
Gracious my lord, hard by here is a
hovel;
Some friendship will it lend you 'gainst
the tempest:
Repose you there; while I to this hard
house—
More harder than the stones whereof 't
is raised;   65
Which even but now, demanding after
you,
Denied me to come in—return, and
force
Their scanted courtesy.
    Lear: My wits begin to turn.
Come on, my boy: how dost, my boy?
art cold?
I am cold myself. Where is this straw,
my fellow?   70
The art of our necessities is strange,
That can make vile things precious.
Come, your hovel.
Poor fool and knave, I have one part in
my heart
That 's sorry yet for thee.
    Fool: [*Singing.*]
He that has and a little tiny wit,—   75
    With hey, ho, the wind and the rain,—
Must make content with his fortunes fit,
    Though the rain it raineth every day.
    Lear: True, my good boy. Come, bring
us to this hovel.
            [*Exeunt Lear and Kent.*]
    Fool: This is a brave night to cool a
courtezan.   80

    [6] Pretender to. [7] Burst your concealing
containers.

---

[4] Frighten. [5] Turmoil.

I 'll speak a prophecy ere I go:
When priests are more in word than
    matter;
When brewers mar their malt with
    water;
When nobles are their tailors' tutors;
No heretics burn'd, but wenches'
    suitors;   85
When every case in law is right;
No squire in debt, nor no poor knight;
When slanders do not live in tongues;
Nor cutpurses come not to throngs;
When usurers tell their gold i' the
    field;   90
And bawds and whores do churches
    build;
Then shall the realm of Albion
Come to great confusion:
Then comes the time, who lives to
    see 't,   94
That going shall be used with feet.
This prophecy Merlin shall make; for I
live before his time.   [Exit.]

SCENE III—*Gloucester's castle*

[*Enter Gloucester and Edmund.*]

Glou.: Alack, alack, Edmund, I like
not this unnatural dealing. When I
desired their leave that I might pity
him, they took from me the use of mine
own house; charged me, on pain of their
perpetual displeasure, neither to speak
of him, entreat for him, nor any way
sustain him.   8
Edm.: Most savage and unnatural!
Glou.: Go to; say you nothing. There
is division between the dukes; and a
worse matter than that: I have received
a letter this night; 't is dangerous to be
spoken; I have locked the letter in my
closet: these injuries the king now bears
will be revenged home; there 's part of
a power already footed: we must incline
to the king. I will seek him, and privily
relieve him: go you and maintain talk
with the duke, that my charity be not
of him perceived: if he ask for me, I am
ill, and gone to bed. If I die for it, as no
less is threatened me, the king my old
master must be relieved. There is some

strange thing toward, Edmund; pray
you, be careful.   [*Exit.*]
    Edm.: This courtesy, forbid thee,[1]
    shall the duke   27
Instantly know; and of that letter too:
This seems a fair deserving, and must
    draw me
That which my father loses; no less
    than all:
The younger rises when the old doth
    fall.   [*Exit.*]

SCENE IV—*The heath. Before a hovel*

[*Enter Lear, Kent, and Fool.*]

Kent: Here is the place, my lord;
    good my lord, enter:
The tyranny of the open night 's too
    rough
For nature to endure.   [*Storm still.*]
Lear: Let me alone.
Kent: Good my lord, enter here.
Lear: Wilt break my heart?
Kent: I had rather break mine own.
    Good my lord, enter.   5
Lear: Thou think'st 't is much that
    this contentious storm
Invades us to the skin: so 't is to thee;
But where the greater malady is fixed,
The lesser is scarce felt. Thou 'ldst shun
    a bear;
But if thy flight lay toward the raging
    sea,   10
Thou 'ldst meet the bear i' the mouth.
    When the mind 's free,
The body 's delicate: the tempest in my
    mind
Doth from my senses take all feeling else
Save what beats there. Filial ingrati-
    tude!
Is it not as this mouth should tear this
    hand   15
For lifting food to 't? But I will punish
    home:
No, I will weep no more. In such a night
To shut me out! Pour on; I will endure.
In such a night as this! O Regan,
    Goneril!

---

[1] Kindness (to the King), which was forbidden thee.

Your old kind father, whose frank heart
   gave all,— 20
O, that way madness lies; let me shun
   that;
No more of that.
Kent: Good my lord, enter
   here.
Lear: Prithee, go in thyself; seek thine
   own ease:
This tempest will not give me leave to
   ponder
On things would hurt me more. But I 'll
   go in. 25
[*To the Fool.*] In, boy; go first. You
   houseless poverty,—
Nay, get thee in. I 'll pray, and then I 'll
   sleep. [*Fool goes in.*]
Poor naked wretches, whereso'er you
   are,
That bide the pelting of this pitiless
   storm,
How shall your houseless heads and
   unfed sides, 30
Your loop'd and window'd raggedness,
   defend you
From seasons such as these? O, I have
   ta'en
Too little care of this! Take physic,[1]
   pomp;
Expose thyself to feel what wretches
   feel,
That thou mayst shake the superflux to
   them, 35
And show the heavens more just.
Edg. [*Within.*] Fathom and half,
   fathom and half! Poor Tom!
    [*The Fool runs out from the hovel.*]
Fool: Come not in here, nuncle, here 's
a spirit. Help me, help me! 40
Kent: Give me thy hand. Who 's
there?
Fool: A spirit, a spirit: he says his
name 's poor Tom.
Kent: What art thou that dost grum-
ble there i' the straw? Come forth.
[*Enter Edgar disguised as a madman.*]
Edg.: Away! the foul fiend follows me!
Through the sharp hawthorn blow the
   winds. 48

Hum! go to thy bed, and warm thee.
Lear: Didst thou give all to thy
   daughters?
And art thou come to this?
   Edg.: Who gives any thing to poor
Tom? whom the foul fiend hath led
through fire and through flame, through
ford and whirlpool, o'er bog and quag-
mire; that hath laid knives under his
pillow, and halters in his pew; set rats-
bane by his porridge; made him proud
of heart, to ride on a bay trotting-horse
over four-inched bridges, to course his
own shadow for a traitor. Bless thy five
wits! Tom 's a-cold,—O, do de, do de,
do de. Bless thee from whirlwinds, star-
blasting, and taking![2] Do poor Tom
some charity, whom the foul fiend vexes:
there could I have him now,—and there,
—and there again, and there. 67
           [*Storm still.*]
Lear: Have his daughters brought him
   to this pass?
Couldst thou save nothing? Wouldst
   thou give 'em all?
Fool: Nay, he reserved a blanket, else
we had been all shamed.
Lear: Now, all the plagues that in the
   pendulous air
Hang fated o'er men's faults light on
   thy daughters!
Kent: He hath no daughters, sir.
Lear: Death, traitor! nothing could
   have subdued nature 75
To such a lowness but his unkind
   daughters.
Is it the fashion that discarded fathers
Should have thus little mercy on their
   flesh?
Judicious punishment! 't was this flesh
   begot
Those pelican[3] daughters. 80
   Edg.: Pillicock sat on Pillicock-hill:
Halloo, halloo, loo, loo!
Fool: This cold night will turn us all
to fools and madmen.
Edg.: Take heed o' the foul fiend: obey
thy parents; keep thy word's justice;
swear not; commit not with man's

[1] Medicine.

[2] Infections. [3] Young pelicans were believed to feed on their mothers' blood.

sworn spouse; set not thy sweet heart on proud array. Tom's a-cold.   89

Lear: What hast thou been?

Edg.: A serving-man, proud in heart and mind; that curled my hair; wore gloves in my cap; served the lust of my mistress' heart, and did the act of darkness with her; swore as many oaths as I spake words, and broke them in the sweet face of heaven: one that slept in the contriving of lust, and waked to do it: wine loved I deeply, dice dearly; and in woman out-paramoured the Turk: false of heart, light of ear, bloody of hand; hog in sloth, fox in stealth, wolf in greediness, dog in madness, lion in prey. Let not the creaking of shoes nor the rustling of silks betray thy poor heart to woman: keep thy foot out of brothels, thy hand out of plackets, thy pen from lenders' books, and defy the foul fiend.   109

Still through the hawthorn blows the cold wind:

Says suum, mun, nonny.

Dolphin my boy, boy, sessa! let him trot by.
                                    [*Storm still.*]

Lear: Thou wert better in thy grave than to answer with thy uncovered body this extremity of the skies. Is man no more than this? Consider him well. Thou owest the worm no silk, the beast no hide, the sheep no wool, the cat no perfume. Ha! here's three on's are sophisticated![4] Thou art the thing itself: unaccommodated man is no more but such a poor, bare, forked animal as thou art. Off, off, you lendings! come, unbutton here. [*Tearing off his clothes.*]

Fool: Prithee, nuncle, be contented; 't is a naughty night to swim in. Now a little fire in a wild field were like an old lecher's heart; a small spark, all the rest on's body cold. Look, here comes a walking fire.   130

[*Enter Gloucester, with a torch.*]

Edg.: This is the fiend Flibbertigibbet: he begins at curfew, and walks

[4] Adulterated.

till the first cock; he gives the web and the pin,[5] squints the eye, and makes the hare-lip; mildews the white wheat, and hurts the poor creature of earth.   136
Swithold[6] footed thrice the old[7];
He met the night-mare, and her ninefold;
  Bid her alight,
  And her troth plight,
And, aroint[8] thee, witch, aroint thee!

Kent: How fares your grace?   142

Lear: What's he?

Kent: Who's there? What is't you seek?

Glou.: What are you there? Your names?

Edg.: Poor Tom; that eats the swimming frog, the toad, the tadpole, the wall-newt and the water; that in the fury of his heart, when the foul fiend rages, eats cow-dung for sallets;[9] swallows the old rat and the ditch-dog; drinks the green mantle of the standing-pool; who is whipped from tithing to tithing,[10] and stocked, punished, and imprisoned; who hath three suits to his back, six shirts to his body, horse to ride, and weapon to wear;   157
But mice and rats, and such small deer,[11]
Have been Tom's food for seven long year.

Beware my follower. Peace, Smulkin; peace, thou fiend!   160

Glou.: What, hath your grace no better company?

Edg.: The prince of darkness is a gentleman:
Modo he's call'd, and Mahu.

Glou.: Our flesh and blood, my lord, is grown so vile,
That it doth hate what gets[12] it.   165

Edg.: Poor Tom's a-cold.

Glou.: Go in with me: my duty cannot suffer
To obey in all your daughters' hard commands:
Though their injunction be to bar my doors,

[5] Disease of the eye. [6] Probably St. Vitalis, invoked against nightmare. [7] Wold, plain. [8] Begone. [9] Salads, greens. [10] District. [11] Animals. [12] Begets.

And let this tyrannous night take hold
upon you, 170
Yet have I ventured to come seek you
out,
And bring you where both fire and food
is ready.
Lear: First let me talk with this
philosopher.
What is the cause of thunder?
Kent: Good my lord, take his offer;
go into the house. 175
Lear: I 'll talk a word with this same
learned Theban.
What is your study?
Edg.: How to prevent the fiend, and
to kill vermin.
Lear: Let me ask you one word in
private.
Kent: Importune him once more to
go, my lord;
His wits begin to unsettle. 180
Glou.: Canst thou blame him?
[*Storm still.*]
His daughters seek his death; ah, that
good Kent!
He said it would be thus, poor banish'd
man!
Thou say'st the king grows mad; I 'll
tell thee, friend,
I am almost mad myself: I had a son,
Now outlaw'd from my blood; he sought
my life, 187
But lately, very late: I loved him,
friend;
No father his son dearer: true to tell
thee,
The grief hath crazed my wits. What a
night's this!
I do beseech your grace,—
Lear: O, cry you mercy, sir.
Noble philosopher, your company. 192
Edg.: Tom 's a-cold.
Glou.: In, fellow, there, into the
hovel: keep thee warm.
Lear: Come, let's in all.
Kent: This way, my lord.
Lear: With him;
I will keep still with my philosopher.
Kent: Good my lord, soothe him;
let him take the fellow. 197
Glou.: Take him you on.

Kent: Sirrah, come on; go along with
us.
Lear: Come, good Athenian.
Glou.: No words, no words: hush.
Edg.: Child Rowland to the dark
tower came, 202
His word was still,—Fie, foh, and fum,
I smell the blood of a British man.
[*Exeunt.*]

SCENE V—*Gloucester's castle*

[*Enter Cornwall and Edmund.*]

Corn.: I will have my revenge ere I
depart his house.
Edm.: How, my lord, I may be cen-
sured, that nature thus gives way to
loyalty, something fears me to think of.
Corn.: I now perceive, it was not altogether your brother's evil disposition
made him seek his death; but a provoking merit, set a-work by a reprove-
able badness in himself.[1] 10
Edm.: How malicious is my fortune,
that I must repent to be just! This is the
letter he spoke of, which approves him
an intelligent party [2] to the advantages
of France. O heavens! that this treason
were not, or not I the detector! 16
Corn.: Go with me to the duchess.
Edm.: If the matter of this paper be
certain, you have mighty business in
hand. 20
Corn.: True or false, it hath made thee
Earl of Gloucester. Seek out where thy
father is, that he may be ready for our
apprehension.
Edm.: [*Aside.*] If I find him comforting [3] the king, it will stuff his suspicion
more fully.—I will persevere in my
course of loyalty, though the conflict
be sore between that and my blood. 29
Corn.: I will lay trust upon thee; and
thou shalt find a dear father in my love.
[*Exeunt.*]

[1] Edgar is "provoked" (stimulated) by
his own merit, set in operation by Gloucester's
badness, to seek Gloucester's death. [2] Proves
him to be well informed. [3] Helping.

SCENE VI—*A chamber in a farmhouse adjoining the castle*

[*Enter Gloucester, Lear, Kent, Fool, and Edgar.*]

Glou.: Here is better than the open air; take it thankfully. I will piece out the comfort with what addition I can; I will not be long from you.

Kent: All the power of his wits have given way to his impatience: the gods reward your kindness! [*Exit Gloucester.*]

Edg.: Frateretto calls me; and tells me Nero is an angler in the lake of darkness. Pray, innocent, and beware the foul fiend.   11

Fool: Prithee, nuncle, tell me whether a madman be a gentleman or a yeoman?

Lear: A king, a king!

Fool: No, he's a yeoman that has a gentleman to his son; for he's a mad yeoman that sees his son a gentleman before him.

Lear: To have a thousand with red burning spits
Come hissing in upon 'em,—   20

Edg.: The foul fiend bites my back.

Fool: He's mad that trusts in the tameness of a wolf, a horse's heels, a boy's love, or a whore's oath.

Lear: It shall be done; I will arraign them straight.   25
[*To Edgar.*] Come, sit thou here, most learned justicer;
[*To the Fool.*] Thou, sapient sir, sit here. Now, you she foxes!

Edg.: Look, where he stands and glares! Wantest thou eyes at trial, madam?   30
Come o'er the bourn, Bessy, to me,—

Fool: Her boat hath a leak,
And she must not speak
Why she dares not come over to thee.

Edg.: The foul fiend haunts poor Tom in the voice of a nightingale. Hopdance cries in Tom's belly for two white herring. Croak not, black angel; I have no food for thee.

Kent: How do you, sir? Stand you not so amazed: 40

Will you lie down and rest upon the cushions?

Lear: I'll see their trial first. Bring in the evidence.
[*To Edgar.*] Thou robed man of justice, take thy place;
[*To the Fool.*] And thou, his yoke-fellow of equity,
Bench by his side: [*To Kent.*] you are o' the commission,[1]   45
Sit you too.

Edg.: Let us deal justly.
Sleepest or wakest thou, jolly shepherd?
Thy sheep be in the corn;
And for one blast of thy minikin[2] mouth,   50
Thy sheep shall take no harm.
Pur! the cat is gray.

Lear: Arraign her first; 't is Goneril. I here take my oath before this honourable assembly, she kicked the poor king her father.   56

Fool: Come hither, mistress. Is your name Goneril?

Lear: She cannot deny it.

Fool: Cry you mercy, I took you for a joint-stool.[3]

Lear: And here's another, whose warp'd looks proclaim
What store her heart is made on. Stop her there!
Arms, arms, sword, fire! Corruption in the place!
False justicer, why hast thou let her 'scape?   65

Edg.: Bless thy five wits!

Kent: O pity! Sir, where is the patience now,
That you so oft have boasted to retain?

Edg.: [*Aside.*] My tears begin to take his part so much,
They'll mar my counterfeiting.   70

Lear: The little dogs and all,
Tray, Blanch, and Sweet-heart, see, they bark at me.

Edg.: Tom will throw his head at them. Avaunt, you curs!
Be thy mouth or black or white,   75

---

[1] Justice of the peace. [2] Dainty. [3] A proverbial expression, used in pretended apology. The Fool also alludes to Lear's hallucination.

Tooth that poisons if it bite;
Mastiff, greyhound, mongrel grim,
Hound or spaniel, brach [4] or lym,[4]
Or bobtail tike [4] or trundle-tail,[4]
Tom will make them weep and wail:
For, with throwing thus my head, 81
Dogs leap the hatch, and all are fled.
Do de, de, de. Sessa! Come, march to
wakes and fairs and market-towns.
Poor Tom, thy horn is dry.

Lear: Then let them anatomize
Regan: see what breeds about her
heart. Is there any cause in nature that
makes these hard hearts? [*To Edgar.*]
You, sir, I entertain [5] for one of my
hundred; only I do not like the fashion
of your garments. You will say they are
Persian; but let them be changed. 93

Kent: Now, good my lord, lie here and
rest awhile.

Lear: Make no noise, make no noise;
draw the curtains: so, so, so. We'll go
to supper i' the morning. So, so, so.

Fool: And I'll go to bed at noon.

[*Re-enter Gloucester.*]

Glou.: Come hither, friend: where is
the king my master? 100

Kent: Here, sir; but trouble him not,
his wits are gone.

Glou.: Good friend, I prithee, take
him in thy arms;
I have o'erheard a plot of death upon
him:
There is a litter ready; lay him in 't.
And drive toward Dover, friend, where
thou shalt meet 105
Both welcome and protection. Take up
thy master:
If thou shouldst dally half an hour, his
life,
With thine, and all that offer to defend
him,
Stand in assured loss: take up, take up;
And follow me, that will to some
provision 110
Give thee quick conduct.

Kent: Oppressed nature sleeps:
This rest might yet have balm'd thy
broken sinews,[6]

Which, if convenience will not allow,
Stand in hard cure. [*To the Fool.*] Come,
help to bear thy master:
Thou must not stay behind.

Glou.:   Come, come, away.

[*Exeunt all but Edgar.*]

Edg: When we our betters see bearing
our woes, 116
We scarcely think our miseries our foes.
Who alone suffers suffers most i' the
mind,
Leaving free things and happy shows
behind:
But then the mind much sufferance doth
o'erskip
When grief hath mates, and bearing
fellowship.
How light and portable my pain seems
now,
When that which makes me bend makes
the king bow; 123
He childed as I father'd! Tom, away!
Mark the high noises, and thyself
bewray [7]
When false opinion, whose wrong
thought defiles thee,
In thy just proof repeals and reconciles
thee.
What will hap more to-night, safe 'scape
the king!
Lurk, lurk.   [*Exit*]

SCENE VII—*Gloucester's castle*

[*Enter Cornwall, Regan, Goneril, Edmund, and Servants.*]

Corn.: Post speedily to my lord your
husband; show him this letter: the army
of France is landed. Seek out the traitor
Gloucester.

[*Exeunt some of the Servants.*]

Reg.: Hang him instantly. 5

Gon.: Pluck out his eyes.

Corn.: Leave him to my displeasure.
Edmund, keep you our sister company:
the revenges we are bound to take upon
your traitorous father are not fit for
your beholding. Advise the duke, where

---

[4] Types of dog. [5] Engage. [6] Strained
nerves.

[7] Identify yourself when misunderstandings about you are cleared up.

you are going, to a most festinate [1]
preparation: we are bound to the like.
Our posts shall be swift and intelligent
betwixt us. Farewell, dear sister: fare-
well, my lord of Gloucester.   16
        [*Enter Oswald.*]
How now! where 's the king?
    Osw.: My lord of Gloucester hath con-
        vey'd him hence:
Some five or six and thirty of his
    knights,
Hot questrists [2] after him, met him at
    gate;   20
Who, with some other of the lord's
    dependants,
Are gone with him toward Dover; where
    they boast
To have well-armed friends.
    Corn.:   Get horses for your mistress.
    Gon.: Farewell, sweet lord, and sister.
    Corn.: Edmund, farewell.
[*Exeunt Goneril, Edmund, and Oswald.*]
        Go seek the traitor Gloucester,
Pinion him like a thief, bring him before
us.   [*Exeunt other Servants.*]
Though well we may not pass upon his
    life   27
Without the form of justice, yet our
    power
Shall do a courtesy to our wrath, which
    men
May blame, but not control. Who 's
    there? the traitor?
[*Enter Gloucester, brought in by two
or three.*]
    Reg.: Ingrateful fox! 't is he.
    Corn.: Bind fast his corky [3] arms.   32
    Glou.: What mean your graces? Good
        my friends, consider
You are my guests: do me no foul play,
    friends.
    Corn.: Bind him, I say.
                [*Servants bind him.*]
    Reg.:   Hard, hard. O filthy traitor!
    Glou.: Unmerciful lady as you are,
        I'm none.   36
    Corn.: To this chair bind him. Villain,
        thou shalt find—
            [*Regan plucks his beard.*]
    [1] Hasty.   [2] Searchers.   [3] Shriveled (with
age).

    Glou.: By the kind gods, 't is most
        ignobly done
To pluck me by the beard.
    Reg.: So white, and such a traitor!
    Glou.:   Naughty lady,
These hairs, which thou dost ravish from
        my chin,   41
Will quicken, and accuse thee: I am your
        host:
With robbers' hands my hospitable
        favours
You should not ruffle thus. What will
        you do?
    Corn.: Come, sir. what letters had
        you late from France?   45
    Reg.: Be simple-answered, for we
        know the truth.
    Corn.: And what confederacy have
        you with the traitors
Late footed in the kingdom?
    Reg.: To whose hands have you sent
        the lunatic king?
Speak.
    Glou.: I have a letter guessingly set
        down,   50
Which came from one that 's of a neu-
        tral heart,
And not from one opposed.
    Corn.:   Cunning.
    Reg.:   And false.
    Corn.: Where hast thou sent the king?
    Glou.: To Dover.
    Reg.: Wherefore to Dover? Wast
        thou not charged at peril—   55
    Corn.: Wherefore to Dover? Let him
        answer that.
    Glou.: I am tied to the stake, and I
        must stand the course. [4]
    Reg.: Wherefore to Dover?
    Glou.: Because I would not see thy
        cruel nails
Pluck out his poor old eyes; nor thy
        fierce sister   60
In his anointed flesh stick boarish fangs.
The sea, with such a storm as his bare
        head
In hell-black night endured, would have
        buoy'd up,
And quench'd the stelled [5] fires:
    [4] Attack of the dogs in bear-baiting.
    [5] Starry; perhaps, fixed.

Yet, poor old heart, he holp the heavens
  to rain.   65
If wolves had at thy gate howl'd that
  stern time,
Thou shouldst have said "Good porter,
  turn the key.
All cruels else subscribe." [6] But I shall
  see
The winged vengeance overtake such
  children.
Corn.: See 't shalt thou never. Fel-
  lows, hold the chair.   70
Upon these eyes of thine I 'll set my
  foot.
Glou.: He that will think to live till
  he be old,
Give me some help! O cruel! O you
  gods!
Reg.: One side will mock another; the
  other too.
Corn.: If you see vengeance,—
First Serv.: Hold your hand, my lord:
I have served you ever since I was a
  child;   76
But better service have I never done you
Than now to bid you hold.
Reg.   How now, you dog!
First Serv.: If you did wear a beard
  upon your chin,
I 'd shake it on this quarrel. What do
  you mean?   80
Corn.: My villain!
            [*They draw and fight.*]
First Serv.: Nay, then, come on, and
  take the chance of anger.
Reg.: Give me thy sword. A peasant
  stand up thus!
[*Takes a sword, and runs at him behind.*]
First Serv.: O, I am slain! My lord,
  you have one eye left
To see some mischief on him. O! [*Dies.*]
Corn.: Lest it see more, prevent it.
  Out, vile jelly!   86
Where is thy lustre now?

  [6] Disputed passage. Perhaps: yield to all
cruel creatures.

Glou.: All dark and comfortless.
Where 's my son Edmund?
Edmund, enkindle all the sparks of
  nature,
To quit [7] this horrid act.
Reg.:   Out, treacherous villain!
Thou call'st on him that hates thee: it
  was he   91
That made the overture of thy treasons
  to us;
Who is too good to pity thee.
Glou.: O my follies! then Edgar was
  abused.
Kind gods, forgive me that, and prosper
  him!   95
Reg.: Go thrust him out at gates, and
  let him smell
His way to Dover.
          [*Exit one with Gloucester.*]
    How is 't, my lord? how look you?
Corn.: I have received a hurt: follow
  me, lady;
Turn out that eyeless villain; throw
  this slave   99
Upon the dunghill. Regan, I bleed apace:
Untimely comes this hurt: give me your
  arm. [*Exit Cornwall led by Regan.*]
Sec. Serv.: I 'll never care what wicked-
  ness I do,
If this man come to good.
Third Serv:.   If she live long,
And in the end meet the old course of
  death,
Women will all turn monsters.   105
Sec. Serv.: Let 's follow the old earl,
  and get the Bedlam [8]
To lead him where he would: his roguish
  madness
Allows itself to any thing.
Third Serv.: Go thou: I 'll fetch some
  flax and whites of eggs
To apply to his bleeding face. Now,
  heaven help him!   110
          [*Exeunt severally.*]

[7] Avenge. [8] The madman, *i.e.*, Edgar.

QUESTIONS ON ACT III

1. The chief element in Scene i is Kent's expository speech. Does the news of a military power that may help Lear seem very important? Is any tension derived from the expectation of a rescue? Or would that be a melodramatic effect? Have things gone too far by now to make external help of such value? Why?

2. Is the storm scene in Scene ii used merely because it is a frightening spectacle ("good theatre"), or is the scene meaningful? Do we see any change in Lear's mental state? Has the storm been prepared for? Is the storm merely a storm, or does it have a symbolic value? Do Lear's remarks spoken about and addressed to the storm show that he is achieving a fuller understanding of what has happened to him?

3. The chief purpose of Scene iii is, of course, to show the step by which Gloucester's downfall is brought about. Does the scene contribute also to our knowledge of Gloucester's character? Which side of him is here in the ascendancy? Perhaps the subtlest part of the scene is the suggestion that more than one motive has a share in Gloucester's decision. Which lines suggest that there may still be a trace of opportunism in Gloucester?

4. Scene iv may seem, at a superficial glance, only grotesque or terrifying. We should note, however, its dramatic accomplishments. At the most obvious level we see some change in Lear's physical situation because of Gloucester's help; we also see a further development in Gloucester. Tom's apparent madness, for which Lear can imagine but one cause, keeps Lear thinking of his own torment and thus leads him further along the road to madness. But note a further change in him: what is the significance of the lines beginning "O, I have ta'en / Too little care of this"? What is accomplished in terms of theme by bringing Edgar and Lear into juxtaposition? What sort of comment is thus made upon the state of the world which has exiled them? The combination of a fool, a pretended madman, and a man who is obviously going mad (and even Gloucester adds, "The grief hath crazed my wits") is not one from which one might expect much good sense. Yet are we not made to feel that in this group there is a high degree of understanding, and, perhaps, a sound grasp of values? If this is true, then we can see some powerfully ironic effects in the making. This irony is enhanced, too, if we consider the structural relation of this group of characters to other characters in the play. In Edmund, Goneril, Regan, and even Cornwall, we have suggested, Shakespeare is studying the way in which sharp minds may work; at one level, at least, their intelligence is unquestionable; but we have also seen that they may miss the main point very badly. At this stage in the play, what we apparently find is a contrast between shrewd, successful, worldly people and, on the other hand, those whom the world scorns and even drives mad. The student should observe how this contrast is developed.

5. When Gloucester finds Lear in Scene iv, he comes "with a torch." Once earlier in the play (II. i) he had searched in the dark with a torch.

Compare his understanding of the two situations. May it be said that he is here coming into a state of enlightenment?

6. In Scenes v and vii we see Cornwall giving way entirely to a vengeful hatred of Gloucester; he even admits that he will have only "the form of justice." Does he here show the same wisdom which we have already seen him to be capable of? Taken purely at the practical level, is his action sensible? If we compare his emotional frenzy with Lear's, which seems to take its possessor farther from a sense of values? Since we see Cornwall so likely to give way to emotional impulse, what are we to conclude about the usefulness of his analytical faculty? Note that most of these questions which have been asked about Cornwall may also be asked about Regan.

7. Trace the development of Gloucester's character in Scenes vi and vii. When does he reach his greatest heights as a man of courage and insight? Note that this achievement coincides with his being brutally tortured. Does the fact that he is tortured by being blinded have any special ironic significance? Could his tragic flaw be described as a lack of insight? What shocking enlightenment comes to him right after he has been blinded?

8. In one sense Lear's "trial" of his daughters in Scene vi is merely a mad scene, with Lear's central frenzy amplified in effect by the lines of Edgar and the Fool. But is the trial, itself so much nonsense, simply a way of showing that Lear has gone to pieces, or may we say that there is an essential rightness in Lear's attitude? To discover the real effectiveness of the scene, however, we must consider it in its structural relations. We should recall that in I. i Lear also held a trial of his daughters: what is the ironic contrast between that and this? Which is the more just? Is the mad Lear more "sensible" than the sane one? Even more marked in the relationship between Lear's arraignment of his daughters in Scene vi and Cornwall's arraignment of Gloucester in Scene vii; the two come so close together that we can hardly fail to take them, in part, as comments on each other. What do we learn from the comparison? Which is the more just? The more sane? What bearing would this have on the general theme of the play as suggested in Question 4?

9. What is the significance of the revolt of the servant against Cornwall in Scene vii?

ACT IV

SCENE I—The heath

[*Enter Edgar.*]

Edg.: Yet better thus, and known to
  be contemn'd
Than still contemn'd and flatter'd. To
  be worst,
The lowest and most dejected thing of
  fortune,

Stands still in esperance, lives not in
  fear:
The lamentable change is from the
  best;   5
The worst returns to laughter. Welcome,
  then,
Thou unsubstantial air that I embrace!
The wretch that thou hast blown unto
  the worst
Owes nothing to thy blasts. But who
  comes here?

[*Enter Gloucester, led by an Old Man.*]

My father, poorly led? World, world, O
world!　　　　　　　　　　　　10
But that thy strange mutations make
us hate thee,
Life would not yield to age.[1]
　Old Man: O, my good lord, I have
been your tenant, and your father's
tenant, these fourscore years.　　15
　Glou.: Away, get thee away; good
friend, be gone:
Thy comforts can do me no good at all;
Thee they may hurt.
　Old Man: You cannot see your way.
　Glou.: I have no way, and therefore
want no eyes;　　　　　　　　20
I stumbled when I saw: full oft 't is
seen,
Our means secure us, and our mere
defects
Prove our commodities.[2] O dear son
Edgar,
The food of thy abused father's wrath!
Might I but live to see thee in my
touch,　　　　　　　　　　　25
I 'ld say I had eyes again!
　Old Man: How now! Who 's there?
　Edg.: [*Aside.*] O gods! Who is 't can
say "I am at the worst"?
I am worse than e'er I was.
　Old Man:　　　　'T is poor mad Tom.
　Edg.: [*Aside.*] And worse I may be
yet: the worst is not
So long as we can say "This is the
worst."　　　　　　　　　　30
　Old Man: Fellow, where goest?
　Glou.:　　　　　Is it a beggar-man?
　Old Man: Madman and beggar too.
　Glou.: He has some reason, else he
could not beg.
I' the last night's storm I such a
fellow saw;
Which made me think a man a worm:
my son　　　　　　　　　　35
Came then into my mind; and yet my
mind
Was then scarce friends with him: I have
heard more since.

[1] If its vicissitudes did not make us hate
life, we would be unwilling to grow old. [2] Our
resources make us overconfident, and our
shortcomings turn out to be advantages.

As flies to wanton boys, are we to the
gods;
They kill us for their sport.
　Edg.:　　[*Aside.*] How should this be?
Bad is the trade that must play fool to
sorrow,　　　　　　　　　　40
Angering itself and others.—Bless thee,
master!
　Glou.: Is that the naked fellow?
　Old Man.　　　　　Ay, my lord.
　Glou.: Get thee away: if, for my
sake,
Thou wilt o'ertake us, hence a mile or
twain,
I' the way toward Dover, do it for
ancient love;　　　　　　　45
And bring some covering for this naked
soul,
Which I 'll entreat to lead me.
　Old Man:　　　Alack, sir, he is mad.
　Glou.: 'T is the times' plague, when
madmen lead the blind.
Do as I bid thee, or rather do thy
pleasure;
Above the rest, be gone.　　　50
　Old Man: I 'll bring him the best
'parel that I have,
Come on 't what will.　　　[*Exit.*]
　Glou.: Sirrah, naked fellow,—
　Edg.: Poor Tom 's a-cold. [*Aside.*] I
cannot daub [3] it further.
　Glou.: Come hither, fellow.　　55
　Edg.: [*Aside.*] And yet I must.—Bless
thy sweet eyes, they bleed.
　Glou.: Know'st thou the way to
Dover?
　Edg.: Both stile and gate, horse-way
and foot-path. Poor Tom hath been
scared out of his good wits: bless thee,
good man's son, from the foul fiend!
five fiends have been in poor Tom at
once; of lust, as Obidicut: Hobbidi-
dance, prince of dumbness; Mahu, of
stealing; Modo, of murder; Flibbertigibbet, of mopping and mowing, who
since possesses chambermaids and wait-
ing-women. So, bless thee, master!
　Glou.: Here, take this purse, thou
whom the heavens' plagues　　6c

[3] Dissemble.

Have humbled to all strokes: that I am
wretched
Makes thee the happier: heavens, deal
so still!
Let the superfluous [4] and lust-dieted
man,
That slaves [5] your ordinance, that will
not see
Because he does not feel, feel your
power quickly;
So distribution should undo excess, 75
And each man have enough. Dost thou
know Dover?
Edg.: Ay, master.
Glou.: There is a cliff, whose high
and bending head
Looks fearfully in the confined deep:
Bring me but to the very brim of it, 80
And I'll repair the misery thou dost
bear
With something rich about me: from
that place
I shall no leading need.
Edg.: Give me thy arm:
Poor Tom shall lead thee. *[Exeunt.]*

SCENE II—*Before the Duke of Albany's
palace*

[Enter Goneril and Edmund.]

Gon.: Welcome, my lord: I marvel our
mild husband
Not met us on the way. *[Enter Oswald.]*
Now, where's your master?
Osw.: Madam, within; but never man
so changed.
I told him of the army that was landed;
He smiled at it: I told him you were
coming; 5
His answer was "The worse": of
Gloucester's treachery,
And of the loyal service of his son,
When I inform'd him, then he call'd me
sot,
And told me I had turn'd the wrong side
out:
What most he should dislike seems
pleasant to him; 10
What like, offensive.

⁴ Having an over-abundance of things.
⁵ Contemns.

Gon. *[To Edm.]* Then shall you go no
further.
It is the cowish terror of his spirit,
That dares not undertake: he'll not
feel wrongs
Which tie him to an answer. Our wishes
on the way
May prove effects. Back, Edmund, to
my brother; 15
Hasten his musters and conduct his
powers:
I must change arms at home, and give
the distaff
Into my husband's hands. This trusty
servant
Shall pass between us: ere long you are
like to hear,
If you dare venture in your own behalf,
A mistress's command. Wear this; spare
speech; *[Giving a favour.]*
Decline your head: this kiss, if it durst
speak, 22
Would stretch thy spirits up into the air:
Conceive, and fare thee well.
Edm.: Yours in the ranks of death.
Gon.: My most dear Gloucester!
[Exit Edmund.]
O, the difference of man and man! 26
To thee a woman's services are due:
My fool usurps my body.
Osw.: Madam, here comes my lord.
[Exit. Enter Albany.]
Gon.: I have been worth the whistle.¹
Alb.: O Goneril!
You are not worth the dust which the
rude wind 30
Blows in your face. I fear your disposi-
tion:
That nature, which contemns it origin,
Cannot be border'd ² certain in itself;
She that herself will sliver and dis-
branch ³
From her material sap, perforce must
wither 35
And come to deadly use.
Gon.: No more; the text is foolish.
Alb.: Wisdom and goodness to the vile
seem vile:

¹ I was once worth your regard. ² Contained; *i.e.*, kept within certain limits
³ Break off and separate.

Filths savour but themselves. What
have you done?
Tigers, not daughters, what have you
perform'd?   40
A father, and a gracious aged man,
Whose reverence even the head-lugg'd [4]
bear would lick,
Most barbarous, most degenerate! have
you madded.
Could my good brother suffer you to
do it?
A man, a prince, by him so benefited!
If that the heavens do not their visible
spirits   46
Send quickly down to tame these vile
offences,
It will come,
Humanity must perforce prey on itself,
Like monsters of the deep.
    Gon.:   Milk-liver'd man!
That bear'st a cheek for blows, a head
for wrongs: 51
Who hast not in thy brows an eye dis-
cerning
Thine honour from thy suffering; that
not know'st
Fools do those villains pity who are
punish'd
Ere they have done their mischief.
Where 's thy drum?   55
France spread his banners in our noise-
less land,
With plumed helm thy state begins to
threat;
Whiles thou, a moral fool, sit'st still,
and criest
"Alack, why does he so?"
    Alb.:   See thyself, devil!
Proper deformity seems not in the fiend
So horrid as in woman.
    Gon.:   O vain fool! 61
    Alb.: Thou changed and self-cover'd
thing, for shame,
Be-monster not thy feature. Were 't my
fitness
To let these hands obey my blood,
They are apt enough to dislocate and tear
Thy flesh and bones: howe'er thou art a
fiend,   66
A woman's shape doth shield thee.
    [4] Dragged by the head.

Gon.: Marry, your manhood! mew!
    [*Enter a Messenger.*]
Alb.: What news?
Mess.: O, my good lord, the Duke of
Cornwall's dead;   70
Slain by his servant, going to put
out
The other eye of Gloucester.
    Alb.:   Gloucester's eyes!
Mess.: A servant that he bred,
thrill'd with remorse,
Opposed against the act, bending his
sword
To his great master; who, thereat en-
raged,   75
Flew on him, and amongst them fell'd
him dead;
But not without that harmful stroke,
which since
Hath pluck'd him after.
    Alb.:   This shows you are above,
You justicers, that these our nether
crimes
So speedily can venge! But, O poor
Gloucester!   80
Lost he his other eye?
    Mess.:   Both, both, my lord.
This letter, madam, craves a speedy
answer;
'T is from your sister.
    Gon.: [*Aside.*] One way I like this
well;
But being widow, and my Gloucester
with her,   85
May all the building in my fancy
pluck [5]
Upon my hateful life; another way,
The news is not so tart.[6]—I 'll read, and
answer.   [*Exit.*]
Alb.: Where was his son when they
did take his eyes?
Mess.: Come with my lady hither.
Alb.:   He is not here.
Mess.: No, my good lord; I met him
back again.   91
Alb.: Knows he the wickedness?
Mess.: Ay, my good lord; 't was he
inform'd against him;

[5] Wreck my air castles. [6] Sour, disagreeable. "Another way" is, of course, the same
as "one way" of the first line of her speech.

And quit the house on purpose, that
their punishment
Might have the freer course.
Alb.:   Gloucester, I live
To thank thee for the love thou show'dst
the king,
And to revenge thine eyes. Come hither,
friend:
Tell me what more thou know'st.   98
[*Exeunt.*]

SCENE III—*The French camp near Dover*

[*Enter Kent and a Gentleman.*]

Kent: Why the King of France is so
suddenly gone back know you the
reason?
Gent.: Something he left imperfect in
the state, which since his coming forth
is thought of; which imports to the
kingdom so much fear and danger, that
his personal return was most required
and necessary.   9
Kent: Who hath he left behind him
general?
Gent.: The Marshall of France, Monsieur La Far.
Kent: Did your letters pierce the
queen to any demonstration of grief?
Gent.: Ay, sir; she took them, read
them in my presence;   16
And now and then an ample tear trill'd
down
Her delicate cheek: it seem'd she was a
queen
Over her passion, who, most rebel-like,
Sought to be king o'er her.
Kent: O, then it moved her.
Gent.: Not to a rage: patience and
sorrow strove   21
Who should express her goodliest. You
have seen
Sunshine and rain at once: her smiles
and tears
Were like, a better way: those happy
smilets,
That play'd on her ripe lip, seem'd not
to know   25
What guests were in her eyes; which
parted thence,

As pearls from diamonds dropp'd. In
brief,
Sorrow would be a rarity most beloved,
If all could so become it.
Kent: Made she no verbal question?
Gent.: 'Faith, once or twice she
heaved the name of "father"   30
Pantingly forth, as if it press'd her
heart;
Cried "Sisters! sisters! Shame of ladies!
sisters!
Kent! father! sisters! What, i' the storm?
i' the night?
Let pity not be believed!" There she
shook
The holy water from her heavenly eyes,
And clamour moisten'd; then away she
started   36
To deal with grief alone.
Kent: It is the stars,
The stars above us, govern our condi-
tions;
Else one self mate and mate [1] could not
beget
Such different issues. You spoke not
with her since?   40
Gent.: No.
Kent: Was this before the king re-
turn'd?
Gent.:   No, since.
Kent: Well, sir, the poor distress'd
Lear 's i' the town;
Who sometime, in his better tune, re-
members
What we are come about, and by no
means   45
Will yield to see his daughter.
Gent.:   Why, good sir?
Kent: A sovereign shame so elbows
him: his own unkindness,
That stripp'd her from his benediction,
turn'd her
To foreign casualties,[2] gave her dear
rights
To his dog-hearted daughters, these
things sting   50
His mind so venomously, that burning
shame
Detains him from Cordelia.

[1] The same husband and wife. [2] Risks
abroad.

Gent.:   Alack, poor gentleman!
Kent: Of Albany's and Cornwall's
powers you heard not?   53
Gent.: 'T is so, they are afoot.
Kent: Well, sir, I 'll bring you to our
master Lear,
And leave you to attend him: some dear
cause
Will in concealment wrap me up awhile;
When I am known aright, you shall not
grieve
Lending me this acquaintance. I pray
you, go   59
Along with me.   [*Exeunt.*]

Scene IV — *The same. A tent*

[*Enter, with drum and colours, Cordelia, Doctor, and Soldiers.*]

Cor.: Alack, 't is he: why, he was met
even now
As mad as the vex'd sea; singing aloud;
Crown'd with rank fumiter and furrow-
weeds,
With   hor-docks,   hemlock,   nettles,
cuckoo-flowers,
Darnel, and all the idle weeds that grow
In our sustaining corn. A century[1] send
forth;   6
Search every acre in the high-grown
field,
And bring him to our eye. [*Exit an
Officer.*] What can man's wisdom
In the restoring his bereaved sense?
He that helps him take all my outward
worth.   10
Doct.: There is means, madam:
Our foster-nurse of nature is repose,
The which he lacks; that to provoke in
him,
Are many simples operative, whose
power
Will close the eye of anguish.
Cor.:   All blest secrets,
All you unpublish'd virtues of the earth,
Spring with my tears! be aidant and
remediate   17
In the good man's distress! Seek, seek
for him;

[1] Sentry.

Lest his ungovern'd rage dissolve the
life
That wants the means to lead it.
[*Enter a Messenger.*]
Mess.:   News, madam;
The British powers are marching hither-
ward.   21
Cor.: 'T is known before; our prepara-
tion stands
In expectation of them. O dear father
It is thy business that I go about;
Therefore great France   25
My mourning and important[2] tears
hath pitied.
No blown ambition doth our arms in-
cite,
But love, dear love, and our aged
father's right:
Soon may I hear and see him!   29
[*Exeunt.*]

Scene V—*Gloucester's castle*

[*Enter Regan and Oswald.*]

Reg.: But are my brother's powers set
forth?
Osw.:   Ay, madam.
Reg.: Himself in person there?
Osw.:   Madam, with much ado:
Your sister is the better soldier.
Reg.: Lord Edmund spake not with
your lord at home?
Osw.: No, madam.   5
Reg.: What might import my sister's
letter to him?
Osw.: I know not, lady.
Reg.: 'Faith, he is posted hence on
serious matter
It was great ignorance, Gloucester's
eyes being out,
To let him live: where he arrives he
moves   10
All hearts against us: Edmund, I think,
is gone,
In pity of his misery, to dispatch
His nighted life; moreover, to descry
The strength o' the enemy.
Osw.: I must needs after him, madam,
with my letter.   15

[2] Importunate.

Reg.: Our troops set forth to-morrow:
stay with us;
The ways are dangerous.
Osw.: I may not, madam:
My lady charged my duty in this busi-
ness.
Reg.: Why should she write to Ed-
mund? Might not you
Transport her purposes by word? Be-
like, 20
Something—I know not what: I 'll love
thee much,
Let me unseal the letter.
Osw.: Madam, I had rather—
Reg.: I know your lady does not love
her husband;
I am sure of that: and at her late being
here
She gave strange œilliads [1] and most
speaking looks 25
To noble Edmund. I know you are of
her bosom. [2]
Osw.: I, madam?
Reg.: I speak in understanding; you
are, I know 't:
Therefore I do advise you, take this
note: [3]
My lord is dead; Edmund and I have
talk'd, 30
And more convenient is he for my
hand
Than for your lady's: you may gather
more.
If you do find him, pray you, give him
this;
And when your mistress hears thus
much from you,
I pray, desire her call her wisdom to
her. 35
So, fare you well.
If you do chance to hear of that blind
traitor,
Preferment falls on him that cuts him
off.
Osw.: Would I could meet him,
madam! I should show
What party I do follow.
Reg.: Fare thee well. [*Exeunt.*]

[1] Amorous glances. [2] In her confidence.
Take note of this.

SCENE VI—*Fields near Dover*

[*Enter Gloucester, and Edgar dressed
like a peasant.*]

Glou.: When shall we come to the top
of that same hill?
Edg.: You do climb up it now: look,
how we labour.
Glou.: Methinks the ground is even.
Edg.: Horrible steep.
Hark, do you hear the sea?
Glou.: No, truly.
Edg.: Why, then, your other senses
grow imperfect 5
By your eyes' anguish.
Glou.: So may it be, indeed:
Methinks thy voice is alter'd; and thou
speak'st
In better phrase and matter than thou
didst.
Edg.: You 're much deceived: in noth-
ing am I changed
But in my garments.
Glou.: Methinks you 're better spoken.
Edg.: Come on, sir; here 's the place:
stand still. How fearful 11
And dizzy 't is, to cast one's eyes so
low!
The crows and choughs that wing the
midway air
Show scarce so gross as beetles: half way
down
Hangs one that gathers sampire, [1]
dreadful trade! 15
Methinks he seems no bigger than his
head:
The fishermen, that walk upon the
beach,
Appear like mice; and yond tall anchor-
ing bark,
Diminish'd to her cock; her cock, [2] a
buoy
Almost too small for sight: the murmur-
ing surge, 20
That on the unnumber'd idle pebbles
chafes,
Cannot be heard so high. I 'll look no
more,

[1] Herb growing on sea cliffs. [2] Cock-boat,
small boat.

Lest my brain turn, and the deficient
  sight
Topple down headlong.
  Glou.:   Set me where you stand.
Edg.: Give me your hand: you are
  now within a foot   25
Of the extreme verge: for all beneath
  the moon
Would I not leap upright.
  Glou.:   Let go my hand.
Here, friend, 's another purse; in it a
  jewel
Well worth a poor man's taking: fairies
  and gods
Prosper it with thee! Go thou farther off;
Bid me farewell, and let me hear thee
  going.   31
Edg.: Now fare you well, good sir.
Glou.:   With all my heart.
Edg.: Why I do trifle thus with his
  despair
Is done to cure it.
Glou.: [*Kneeling.*] O you mighty gods!
This world I do renounce, and, in your
  sights,   35
Shake patiently my great affliction off:
If I could bear it longer, and not fall
To quarrel with your great opposeless
  wills,
My snuff [3] and loathed part of nature
  should
Burn itself out. If Edgar live, O, bless him!
Now, fellow, fare thee well.
                    [*He falls forward.*]
Edg.:   Gone, sir: farewell.
And yet I know not how conceit [4] may rob
The treasury of life, when life itself 43
Yields to the theft: had he been where
  he thought,
By this had thought been past. Alive or
  dead?
Ho, you sir! friend! Hear you, sir! speak!
Thus might he pass indeed: yet he
  revives.
What are you, sir?
  Glou.:   Away, and let me die.
Edg.: Hadst thou been aught but
  gossamer, feathers, air,
So many fathom down precipitating, 50

Thou 'dst shiver'd like an egg: but thou
  dost breathe;
Hast heavy substance; bleed'st not;
  speak'st; art sound.
Ten masts at each [5] make not the
  altitude
Which thou hast perpendicularly fell!:
Thy life 's a miracle. Speak yet again.
  Glou.: But have I fall'n, or no?   56
Edg.: From the dread summit of this
  chalky bourn.[6]
Look up a-height; the shrill-gorged
  lark so far
Cannot be seen or heard: do but look
  up.
Glou.: Alack, I have no eyes.   60
Is wretchedness deprived that benefit,
To end itself by death? 'T was yet some
  comfort,
When misery could beguile the tyrant's
  rage,
And frustrate his proud will.
  Edg.:   Give me your arm:
Up: so. How is 't? Feel you your legs?
  You stand.   65
Glou.: Too well, too well.
Edg.:   This is above all strangeness.
Upon the crown o' the cliff, what thing
  was that
Which parted from you?
  Glou.:   A poor unfortunate beggar.
Edg.: As I stood here below, me-
  thought his eyes
Were two full moons; he had a thousand
  noses,   70
Horns whelk'd [7] and waved like the en-
  raged sea:
It was some fiend; therefore, thou
  happy father,
Think that the clearest gods, who make
  them honours
Of men's impossibilities, have preserved
  thee.
Glou.: I do remember now; henceforth
  I 'll bear   75
Affliction till it do cry out itself
"Enough, enough," and die. That thing
  you speak of,
I took it for a man; often 't would say

---

[3] Smouldering wick of a candle; worthless
remainder. [4] Imagination, illusion.

[5] End to end. [6] Boundary (of the sea).
[7] Rough, rugged.

"The fiend, the fiend": he led me to that place.

Edg.: Bear free and patient thoughts. But who comes here? 80

[*Enter Lear, fantastically dressed with wild flowers.*]

The safer sense [8] will ne'er accommodate His master thus.

Lear: No, they cannot touch me for coining; I am the king himself.

Edg.: O thou side-piercing sight! 85

Lear: Nature's above art in that respect. There's your press-money. That fellow handles his bow like a crow-keeper: draw me a clothier's yard. Look, look, a mouse! Peace, peace; this piece of toasted cheese will do 't. There's my gauntlet; I 'll prove it on a giant. Bring up the brown bills. O, well flown, bird! i' the clout, i' the clout: hewgh! Give the word. 95

Edg.: Sweet marjoram.

Lear: Pass.

Clou.: I know that voice.

Lear: Ha! Goneril, with a white beard! They flattered me like a dog; and told me I had white hairs in my beard ere the black ones were there. To say "ay" and "no" to every thing that I said!— "Ay" and "no" too was no good divinity. When the rain came to wet me once, and the wind to make me chatter; when the thunder would not peace at my bidding; there I found 'em, there I smelt 'em out. Go to, they are not men o' their words: they told me I was every thing; 't is a lie, I am not ague-proof. 112

Glou.: The trick of that voice I do well remember: Is 't not the king?

Lear: Ay, every inch a king: When I do stare, see how the subject quakes. 115

I pardon that man's life. What was thy cause? [9]

Adultery?

Thou shalt not die: die for adultery! No:

[8] Sounder sense: sanity. [9] What were you charged with?

The wren goes to 't, and the small gilded fly

Does lecher in my sight. 120

Let copulation thrive; for Gloucester's bastard son Was kinder to his father than my daughters Got 'tween the lawful sheets.

To 't, luxury, pell-mell! for I lack soldiers.

Behold yond simpering dame, 125

Whose face between her forks presages snow; [10]

That minces [11] virtue, and does shake the head

To hear of pleasure's name;

The fitchew,[12] nor the soiled horse, goes to 't

With a more riotous appetite. 130

Down from the waist they are Centaurs, Though women all above:

But to the girdle do the gods inherit, Beneath is all the fiends';

There 's hell, there 's darkness, there is the sulphurous pit, 135

Burning, scalding, stench, consumption; fie, fie, fie! pah! pah! Give me an ounce of civet; good apothecary, sweeten my imagination: there 's money for thee.

Glou.: O, let me kiss that hand! 140

Lear: Let me wipe it first; it smells of mortality.

Glou.: O ruin'd piece of nature! This great world Shall so wear out to nought. Dost thou know me?

Lear: I remember thine eyes well enough. Dost thou squiny [13] at me? No, do thy worst, blind Cupid; I 'll not love. Read thou this challenge; mark but the penning of it.

Glou.: Were all thy letters suns, I could not see one.

Edg.: I would not take this from report; it is, 150

And my heart breaks at it.

Lear: Read.

Glou.: What, with the case [14] of eyes?

[10] Face suggests virtue. Forks: perhaps hands, or hair-supports. [11] Coyly affects. [12] Polecat. [13] Squint. [14] Sockets.

Lear: O, ho, are you there with me? [15]
No eyes in your head, nor no money in
your purse? Your eyes are in a heavy
case, your purse in a light: yet you see
how this world goes.　　　　　　158
Glou.: I see it feelingly.
Lear: What, art mad? A man may see
how this world goes with no eyes. Look
with thine ears: see how yond justice
rails upon yond simple thief. Hark in
thine ear: change places; and, handy-
dandy, which is the justice, which is the
thief? Thou hast seen a farmer's dog
bark at a beggar?　　　　　　　167
Glou.: Ay, sir.
Lear: And the creature [16] run from the
cur? There thou mightst behold the
great image of authority: a dog's
obeyed in office.
Thou, rascal beadle, hold thy bloody
　　hand!
Why dost thou lash that whore? Strip
　　thine own back;
Thou hotly lust'st to use her in that
　　kind　　　　　　　　　　　175
For which thou whipp'st her. The
　　usurer hangs the cozener.
Through tatter'd clothes great vices do
　　appear;
Robes and furr'd gowns hide all. Plate [17]
　　sins with gold,
And the strong lance of justice hurtless
　　breaks;
Arm it in rags, a pigmy's straw does
　　pierce it.　　　　　　　　　180
None does offend, none, I say, none;
　　I'll able 'em;
Take that of me, my friend, who have
　　the power
To seal the accuser's lips. Get thee glass
　　eyes;
And, like a scurvy politician, seem
To see the things thou dost not. Now,
　　now, now, now:　　　　　　185
Pull off my boots: harder, harder: so.
Edg.: O, matter and impertinency
　　mix'd!
Reason in madness!

[15] Is that the point?　[16] Human being.
[17] *Plate* is a modern emendation. The Folio
place might mean, "put into office."

Lear: If you wilt weep my fortunes,
　　take my eyes.
I know thee well enough; thy name is
　　Gloucester:　　　　　　　　190
Thou must be patient; we came crying
　　hither:
Thou know'st, the first time that we
　　smell the air,
We wawl and cry. I will preach to thee:
　　mark.
Glou.: Alack, alack the day!
Lear: When we are born, we cry that
　　we are come　　　　　　　195
To this great stage of fools: this' a good
　　block; [18]
It were a delicate stratagem, to shoe
A troop of horse with felt: I'll put t in
　　proof;
And when I have stol'n upon these
　　sons-in-law,
Then, kill, kill, kill, kill, kill, kill!　200
[*Enter a Gentleman, with Attendants.*]
Gent.: O, here he is; lay hand upon
　　him. Sir,
Your most dear daughter—
Lear: No rescue? What, a prisoner? I
　　am even
The natural fool of fortune. Use me well;
You shall have ransom. Let me have
　　surgeons;　　　　　　　　205
I am cut to the brains.
Gent.:　　　You shall have any thing.
Lear: No seconds? all myself?
Why, this would make a man a man of
　　salt,
To use his eyes for garden water-pots,
Ay, and laying autumn's dust.
Gent.:　　　　　　　Good sir,—
Lear: I will die bravely, like a smug
　　bridegroom. What!　　　　211
I will be jovial: come, come; I am a
　　king,
Masters, know you that.
Gent.: You are a royal one, and we
　　obey you.
Lear: Then there's life in 't. Come,
and you get it; you shall get it by run-
ning. Sa, sa, sa, sa.　　　　217
[*Exit running; Attendants follow.*]
[18] Perhaps a hat block or a mounting
block.

Gent.: A sight most pitiful in the meanest wretch,
Past speaking of in a king! Thou hast a daughter,
Who redeems nature from the general curse 220
Which twain have brought her to.
Edg.: Hail, gentle sir.
Gent.: Sir, speed you: what's your will?
Edg.: Do you hear aught, sir, of a battle toward?
Gent.: Most sure and vulgar: [19] every one hears that,
That can distinguish sound.
Edg.: But, by your favour,
How near's the other army? 226
Gent.: Near and on speedy foot; the main descry
Stands on the hourly thought. [20]
Edg.: I thank you, sir; that's all.
Gent.: Though that the queen on special cause is here,
Her army is moved on.
Edg.: I thank you, sir. [*Exit Gent.*]
Glou.: You ever-gentle gods, take my breath from me; 231
Let not my worser spirit tempt me again
To die before you please!
Edg.: Well pray you, father.
Glou.: Now, good sir, what are you?
Edg.: A most poor man, made tame to fortune's blows; 235
Who, by the art of known and feeling sorrows,
Am pregnant [21] to good pity. Give me your hand,
I'll lead you to some biding.
Glou.: Hearty thanks:
The bounty and the benison of heaven
To boot, and boot! [22] 240
[*Enter Oswald.*]
Osw.: A proclaim'd prize! Most happy!
That eyeless head of thine was first framed flesh
To raise my fortunes. Thou old unhappy traitor,

[19] Commonly known. [20] Sight of the main army is hourly expected. [21] Disposed. [22] In addition (to thanks) and (the benison of heaven) help (you). (Herford)

Briefly thyself remember: the sword is out 244
That must destroy thee.
Glou.: Now let thy friendly hand
Put strength enough to 't.
[*Edgar interposes.*]
Osw.: Wherefore, bold peasant,
Darest thou support a publish'd traitor? Hence;
Lest that the infection of his fortune take
Like hold on thee. Let go his arm.
Edg.: Chill [23] not let go, zir, without vurther 'casion. 251
Osw.: Let go, slave, or thou diest!
Edg.: Good gentleman, go your gait, and let poor volk pass. An chud ha' bin zwaggered out of my life, 't would not ha' bin zo long as 't is by a vortnight. Nay, come not near th' old man; keep out, che vor ye, or ise try whether your costard or my ballow be the harder: chill be plain with you. [24] 260
Osw.: Out, dunghill!
Edg.: Chill pick your teeth, zir: come; no matter vor your foins. [25]
[*They fight, and Edgar knocks him down.*]
Osw.: Slave, thou hast slain me: villain, take my purse: 264
If ever thou wilt thrive, bury my body;
And give the letters which thou find'st about me
To Edmund earl of Gloucester; seek him out
Upon the British party: O, untimely death!
Death! [*Dies.*]
Edg.: I know thee well: a serviceable villain 270
As duteous to the vices of thy mistress
As badness would desire.

[23] I will. Edgar uses the dialect generally given to rustics in Elizabethan drama. [24] Good gentleman, go your way, and let poor folk pass. If I could have been swaggered (intimidated) out of my life, it would not have been so long as it is by a fortnight. Nay, come not near the old man; keep out, I warn you, or I'll try whether your apple (*i.e.*, head) or my cudgel be the harder. I'll be plain with you. [25] Thrusts.

Glou.:   What, is he dead?
Edg.: Sit you down, father; rest you.
Let 's see these pockets: the letters that
     he speaks of
May be my friends. He 's dead; I am
     only sorry   275
He had no other death's-man. Let us see:
Leave, gentle wax; and, manners,
     blame us not:
To know our enemies' minds we rip
     their hearts;
Their papers, is more lawful.   279
     [*Reads.*] "Let our reciprocal vows be
remembered. You have many oppor-
tunities to cut him off: if your will want
not, time and place will be fruitfully
offered. There is nothing done, if he
return the conqueror: then am I the
prisoner and his bed my gaol; from the
loathed warmth whereof deliver me,
and supply the place for your labour.
     "Your—wife, so I would say—
          "Affectionate servant,[26]
                    "GONERIL."
O undistinguish'd space of woman's
     will![27]   292
A plot upon her virtuous husband's
     life;
And the exchange my brother! Here, in
     the sands,
Thee I 'll rake up, the post unsanctified
Of murderous lechers: and in the ma-
     ture time   296
With this ungracious paper strike the
     sight
Of the death-practised[28] duke: for him
     't is well
That of thy death and business I can tell.
     Glou.: The king is mad: how stiff[29]
is my vile sense,   300
That I stand up, and have ingenious[30]
     feeling
Of my huge sorrows! Better I were dis-
     tract:
So should my thoughts be sever'd from
     my griefs,
And woes by wrong imaginations lose
The knowledge of themselves.

[26] Lover. [27] Indefinable extent of woman's
desire. [28] Whose death was intrigued for.
[29] Obstinate. [30] Conscious.

Edg.:   Give me your hand:
                    [*Drum afar off.*]
Far off, methinks, I hear the beaten
     drum: 306
Come, father, I 'll bestow you with a
     friend.   [*Exeunt.*]

SCENE VII—*A tent in the French camp*

[*Enter Cordelia, Kent, Doctor, and
Gentleman.*]

     Cor.: O thou good Kent, how shall I
     live and work,
To match thy goodness? My life will be
     too short,
And every measure fail me.
     Kent.: To be acknowledged, madam,
     is o'erpaid.   4
All my reports go with the modest truth;
Nor more nor clipp'd, but so.
     Cor.:   Be better suited:
These weeds are memories of those
     worser hours:
I prithee, put them off.
     Kent: Pardon, dear madam;
Yet to be known shortens my made
     intent:[1]
My boon I make it, that you know me
     not   10
Till time and I think meet.
     Cor.: Then be 't so, my good lord.
     [*To the Doctor.*] How does the
     king?
     Doct.: Madam, sleeps still.
     Cor.: O you kind gods,
Cure this great breach in his abused
     nature!   15
The untuned and jarring senses, O,
     wind up
Of this child-changed father!
     Doct.:   So please your majesty
That we may wake the king: he hath
     slept long.
     Cor.: Be govern'd by your knowledge,
     and proceed
I' the sway of your own will. Is he
     array'd?   20
     [*Enter Lear in a chair carried by
Servants.*]

[1] Interferes with my plans.

Gent.: Ay, madam; in the heaviness of
sleep
We put fresh garments on him.
Doct.: Be by, good madam, when we
do awake him;
I doubt not of his temperance.[2]
Cor.:   Very well.
Doct.: Please you, draw near. Louder
the music there!   25
Cor.: O my dear father! Restoration
hang
Thy medicine on my lips; and let this
kiss
Repair those violent harms that my
two sisters
Have in thy reverence made!
Kent: Kind and dear princess!
Cor.: Had you not been their father,
these white flakes   30
Did challenge pity of them. Was this
a face
To be opposed against the jarring
winds?
To stand against the deep dread-bolted
thunder?
In the most terrible and nimble stroke
Of quick, cross lightning? to watch—
poor perdu![3]—   35
With this thin helm? Mine enemy's dog,
Though he had bit me, should have
stood that night
Against my fire; and wast thou fain,
poor father,
To hovel thee with swine, and rogues
forlorn,
In short and musty straw? Alack,
alack!   40
'T is wonder that thy life and wits at
once
Had not concluded all. He wakes; speak
to him.
Doct.: Madam, do you; 't is fittest.
Cor.: How does my royal lord? How
fares your majesty?
Lear: You do me wrong to take me
out o' the grave: 45
Thou art a soul in bliss; but I am bound
Upon a wheel of fire, that mine own
tears

Do scald like molten lead.
Cor.:   Sir, do you know me?
Lear: You are a spirit, I know: where
did you die?
Cor.: Still, still, far wide![4]   50
Doct.: He's scarce awake: let him
alone awhile.
Lear: Where have I been? Where am
I? Fair daylight?
I am mightily abused. I should e'en die
with pity,
To see another thus. I know not what
to say.
I will not swear these are my hands:
let's see;   55
I feel this pin prick. Would I were as-
sured
Of my condition!
Cor.:   O, look upon me, sir,
And hold your hands in benediction o'er
me:
No, sir, you must not kneel.
Lear: Pray, do not mock me:
I am a very foolish fond old man,   60
Fourscore and upward, not an hour
more nor less;
And, to deal plainly,
I fear I am not in my perfect mind.
Methinks I should know you, and know
this man;
Yet I am doubtful: for I am mainly
ignorant   65
What place this is; and all the skill I
have
Remembers not these garments; nor I
know not
Where I did lodge last night. Do not
laugh at me;
For, as I am a man, I think this lady
To be my child Cordelia.
Cor.:   And so I am, I am.
Lear: Be your tears wet? yes, 'faith.
I pray, weep not: 71
If you have poison for me, I will drink it.
I know you do not love me; for your
sisters
Have, as I do remember, done me wrong:
You have some cause, they have not.
Cor.:   No cause, no cause.

---

[2] Sanity.   [3] Lost one.   [4] Wandering in his mind.

Lear: Am I in France?
Kent: In your own kingdom, sir.
Lear: Do not abuse me.   77
Doct.: Be comforted, good madam:
the great rage,[5]
You see, is kill'd in him: and yet it is
danger
To make him even o'er [6] the time he has
lost.
Desire him to go in: trouble him no more
Till further settling.
   Cor.:   Will 't please your highness
walk?   82
Lear: You must bear with me:
Pray you now, forget and forgive: I am
old and foolish.
[*Exeunt all but Kent and Gentleman.*]

[5] Madness. [6] Inform him about.

Gent.: Holds it true, sir, that the Duke
of Cornwall was so slain?   86
   Kent: Most certain, sir.
   Gent.: Who is conductor of his
people?
   Kent: As 't is said, the bastard son of
Gloucester.   91
   Gent.: They say Edgar, his banished
son, is with the Earl of Kent in Germany.
   Kent: Report is changeable. 'T is time
to look about; the powers of the kingdom approach apace.   97
   Gent.: The arbitrement is like to be
bloody. Fare you well, sir.   [*Exit.*]
   Kent: My point and period will be
thoroughly wrought,
Or well or ill, as this day's battle's
fought.   [*Exit.*]

QUESTIONS ON ACT IV

1. What is the irony of the relationship established between Edgar and Gloucester in Scene i?

2. We have suggested that there is a special significance in Gloucester's being blinded rather than maltreated in some other way. In this connection consider the significance of his speech in Scene i beginning "I have no way . . ."

3. Aside from a new insight into a specific situation which he had misjudged, what enlightenment of a general sort comes to Gloucester? Note his speech beginning, "Here, take this purse," and compare it with Lear's lines beginning "Poor naked wretches" in III. iv.

4. Note that in Scene ii a double contrast is worked out—that between Albany and Goneril, and that between Albany and Edmund. With the development of the character of Albany, what new note comes into the play? Note how Goneril's reception of the news of Cornwall's death is consistent with what we have already seen of her. But in what way is her passion for Edmund a new development? Is she still the same shrewd calculator of advantage? Are there any signs here of danger for her? What is the relationship of the materials in Scene v to those in Scene ii?

5. Can you suggest any reason why Shakespeare reports (Scene iii) Cordelia's attitude to Lear as well as presents it directly (Scene iv)? Consider these matters: (1) it is a long time since we have seen Cordelia; (2) she has good reason to be unfriendly to Lear. What contrast is immediately suggested by Cordelia's attitude?

6. What is the relationship between the roles of Edgar and Cordelia in this act? A version of *King Lear* which had a long popularity made Edgar and Cordelia happy lovers. Would this addition really improve the play?

7. In Scene iv compare Cordelia's lines on the war with those on her father. Which is she the more interested in? How does this fact amplify the contrast between her and her sisters?

8. Lear's climactic mad scene (Scene vi) comes after we have already seen Cordelia and a doctor ready to take care of him. Does this arrangement make these occurrences an ironic commentary upon what happened in the first scene of the play? How?

9. The student should compare the first part of Scene vi (Gloucester and Edgar) with I. ii and II. i, in which the main characters are Gloucester and Edmund, for the full effectiveness of IV. vi depends upon the parallelism with the earlier scenes. At the most obvious level Edgar is saving his father from despair. But note that Edgar may be said to be "working on" his father just as Edmund did, and doing it by much the same means—leading him to make inferences from what he believes to be the facts. Thus we have one of the skillful structural echoes in which the play abounds. Show how each of these scenes sheds light on the other. Notice, also, one of the statements attributed by Edmund to Edgar in I. ii, "fathers declining, the father should be as a ward to the son . . ." The events of Act IV make what sort of ironic commentary upon the accusation?

10. The second part of Scene vi is Lear's climactic mad scene; it is one of the best known in the play. Are Lear's speeches simply nonsensical? Why does Edgar say "Reason in madness"? See how much meaning you can trace in his speeches, how much accurate commentary upon the world of the play. What have we seen that would give meaning to his lines on justice? To his line, "A man may see how the world goes with no eyes"? Analyze his metaphor for his daughters: ". . . they are Centaurs."

11. Does the letter which Edgar finds on Oswald come as a surprise. Why?

12. What change of tone occurs in Scene vii? Why can the reader not feel at this point that all is coming out well for Lear?

ACT V

SCENE I—*The British camp near Dover*

[*Enter, with drum and colours, Edmund, Regan, Gentlemen, and Soldiers.*]

Edm.: Know of the duke if his last purpose hold,
Or whether since he is advised by aught
To change the course: he's full of alteration
And self-reproving: bring his constant pleasure.[1]
   [*To a Gentleman, who goes out.*]

Reg.: Our sister's man is certainly
   miscarried.   5
Edm.: 'T is to be doubted,[2] madam.
Reg.:   Now, sweet lord,
You know the goodness I intend upon
   you:
Tell me—but truly—but then speak
   the truth,
Do you not love my sister?
Edm.   In honour'd love.
Reg.: But have you never found my
   brother's way   10
To the forfended place?
Edm.:   That thought abuses you.

[1] Final decision.

[2] Feared.

Reg.: I am doubtful that you have been conjunct
And bosom'd with her, as far as we call hers.
Edm.: No, by mine honour, madam.
Reg.: I never shall endure her: dear my lord,　　15
Be not familiar with her.
Edm.:　　　　Fear not:
She and the duke her husband!
[*Enter, with drum and colours, Albany, Goneril, and Soldiers.*]
Gon.: [*Aside.*] I had rather lose the battle than that sister
Should loosen him and me.
Alb.: Our very loving sister, well be-met.　　20
Sir, this I heard; the king is come to his daughter,
With others whom the rigour of our state
Forced to cry out. Where I could not be honest,
I never yet was valiant: for this business,
It toucheth us,[3] as France invades our land,　　25
Not bolds [4] the king, with others, whom, I fear,
Most just and heavy causes make oppose.
Edm.: Sir, you speak nobly.
Reg.:　　　　Why is this reason'd?
Gon.: Combine together 'gainst the enemy;　　29
For these domestic and particular broils
Are not the question here.
Alb.:　　　　Let's then determine
With the ancient of war [5] on our proceeding.
Edm.: I shall attend you presently at your tent.
Reg.: Sister, you 'll go with us?
Gon.: No.　　35
Reg.: 'T is most convenient; pray go with us.
Gon.: [*Aside.*] O, ho, I know the riddle.—I will go.
[*As they are going out, enter Edgar disguised.*]

[3] It concerns me. [4] Not as it encourages.
[5] Experienced soldiers.

Edg.: If e'er your grace had speech with man so poor.
Hear me one word.
Alb.:　　　　I 'll overtake you, Speak.
[*Exeunt all but Albany and Edgar.*]
Edg.: Before you fight the battle, ope this letter.　　40
If you have victory, let the trumpet sound
For him that brought it: wretched though I seem,
I can produce a champion that will prove
What is avouched there. If you miscarry,
Your business of the world hath so an end,　　45
And machination ceases. Fortune love you!
Alb.: Stay till I have read the letter.
Edg.:　　　　I was forbid it.
When time shall serve, let but the herald cry,
And I 'll appear again.
Alb.: Why, fare thee well: I will o'erlook thy paper. [*Exit Edgar.*]
[*Re-enter Edmund.*]
Edm.: The enemy 's in view; draw up your powers.　　51
Here is the guess of their true strength and forces
By diligent discovery; but your haste
Is now urged on you.
Alb.: We will greet the time.[6] [*Exit.*]
Edm.: To both these sisters have I sworn my love;　　55
Each jealous of the other, as the stung
Are of the adder. Which of them shall I take?
Both? one? or neither? Neither can be enjoy'd,
If both remain alive: to take the widow
Exasperates, makes mad her sister Goneril;　　60
And hardly shall I carry out my side,
Her husband being alive. Now then we 'll use
His countenance [7] for the battle; which being done,

[6] Face what happens. [7] Authority.

Let her who would be rid of him devise
His speedy taking off. As for the mercy
Which he intends to Lear and to Cor-
delia, 66
The battle done, and they within our
power,
Shall never see his pardon; for my state
Stands on me to defend, not to debate.
[*Exit.*]

SCENE II—*A field between the two camps*

[*Alarum within. Enter, with drum and
colours, Lear, Cordelia, and Soldiers,
over the stage; and exeunt.*]

[*Enter Edgar and Gloucester.*]

Edg.: Here, father, take the shadow of
this tree
For your good host; pray that the right
may thrive:
If ever I return to you again,
I'll bring you comfort.
   Glou.:   Grace go with you, sir!
                  [*Exit Edgar.*]
[*Alarum and retreat within. Re-enter
Edgar.*]
   Edg.: Away, old man; give me thy
hand; away! 5
King Lear hath lost, he and his daughter
ta'en:
Give me thy hand; come on.
   Glou.: No farther, sir; a man may rot
even here.
   Edg.: What, in ill thoughts again?
Men must endure
Their going hence, even as their coming
hither: 10
Ripeness is all: come on.
   Glou.: And that's true too. [*Exeunt.*]

SCENE III—*The British camp near Dover*

[*Enter, in conquest, with drum and
colours, Edmund; Lear and Cordelia,
prisoners; Captain, Soldiers, &c.*]

   Edm.: Some officers take them away:
good guard,
Until their greater pleasures first be
known

That are to censure them.
   Cor.:   We are not the first
Who, with best meaning, have incurr'd
the worst.
For thee, oppressed king, I am cast
down; 5
Myself could else out-frown false for-
tune's frown.
Shall we not see these daughters and
these sisters?
   Lear: No, no, no, no! Come, let's
away to prison:
We two alone will sing like birds i' the
cage:
When thou dost ask me blessing, I'll
kneel down, 10
And ask of thee forgiveness: so we'll
live,
And pray, and sing, and tell old tales,
and laugh
At gilded butterflies, and hear poor
rogues
Talk of court news; and we'll talk with
them too,
Who loses and who wins; who's in,
who's out; 15
And take upon 's the mystery of
things,
As if we were God's spies: and we'll
wear out,
In a wall'd prison, packs and sects of
great ones,
That ebb and flow by the moon.
   Edm.:   Take them away.
   Lear: Upon such sacrifices, my
Cordelia, 20
The gods themselves throw incense.
Have I caught thee?
He that parts us shall bring a brand
from heavens,
And fire us hence like foxes.[1] Wipe thine
eyes;
The good-years shall devour them,[2]
flesh and fell,
Ere they shall make us weep: we'll see
'em starv'd first. 25
Come.
[*Exeunt Lear and Cordelia, guarded.*]
   Edm.: Come hither, captain; hark.

[1] A reference to smoking foxes out of their
holes. [2] Equivalent to "Devil take them."

Take thou this note [*giving a paper*];
go follow them to prison:
One step I have advanced thee; if thou
dost
As this instructs thee, thou dost make
thy way
To noble fortunes: know thou this, that
men   30
Are as the time is: to be tender-minded
Does not become a sword: thy great
employment
Will not bear question: either say thou
'lt do 't,
Or thrive by other means.
    Capt.:   I 'll do 't, my lord.
    Edm.: About it; and write happy when
        thou hast done.   35
Mark, I say, instantly; and carry it so
As I have set it down.
    Capt.: I cannot draw a cart, nor eat
dried oats;
If it be man's work, I 'll do 't. [*Exit.*]
    [*Flourish. Enter Albany, Goneril,
Regan, another Captain, and Soldiers.*]
    Alb.: Sir, you have show'd to-day
        your valiant strain,   40
And fortune led you well: you have the
captives
Who were the opposite of this day's
strife:
We do require them of you, so to use
them
As we shall find their merits and our
safety
May equally determine.
    Edm.:   Sir, I thought it fit
To send the old and miserable king   46
To some retention and appointed
guard;
Whose age has charms in it, whose title
more,
To pluck the common bosom on his
side,
And turn our impress'd lances [3] in our
eyes   50
Which do command them. With him I
sent the queen;
My reason all the same; and they are
ready

To-morrow, or at further space, to ap-
pear
Where you shall hold your session. At
this time
We sweat and bleed: the friend hath
lost his friend;   55
And the best quarrels, in the heat, are
cursed
By those that feel their sharpness:
The question of Cordelia and her father
Requires a fitter place.
    Alb.:   Sir, by your patience,
I hold you but a subject of this war,   60
Not as a brother.
    Reg.: That 's as we list to grace him.
Methinks our pleasure might have been
demanded,
Ere you had spoke so far. He led our
powers;
Bore the commission of my place and
person;
The which immediacy [4] may well stand
up,   65
And call itself your brother.
    Gon.:   Not so hot:
In his own grace he doth exalt himself,
More than in your addition.[5]
    Reg.:   In my rights,
By me invested, he compeers the best.
    Alb.: That were the most, if he should
husband you.   70
    Reg.: Jesters do oft prove prophets.
    Gon.:   Holla, holla!
That eye that told you so look'd but
a-squint.
    Reg.: Lady, I am not well; else I
should answer
From a full-flowing stomach.[6] General,
Take thou my soldiers, prisoners,
patrimony;   75
Dispose of them, of me; the walls are
thine:
Witness the world, that I create thee
here
My lord and master.
    Gon.:   Mean you to enjoy him?
    Alb.: The let-alone lies not in your
good will.
    Edm.: Nor in thine, lord.

---

[3] Lancers pressed into service.

[4] Closeness to my own authority. [5] The
title you give him. [6] Deep emotion.

Alb.:   Half-blooded fellow, yes.
Reg.: [*To Edmund.*] Let the drum strike, and prove my title thine.   81
Alb.: Stay yet; hear reason. Edmund, I arrest thee
On capital treason; and, in thy arrest,
This gilded serpent. [*Pointing to Goneril.*] For your claim, fair sister,
I bar it in the interest of my wife;   85
'T is she is sub-contracted to this lord,
And I, her husband, contradict your bans.
If you will marry, make your loves to me,
My lady is bespoke.
Gon.:   An interlude! [7]
Alb.: Thou art arm'd, Gloucester: let the trumpet sound: 90
If none appear to prove upon thy person
Thy heinous, manifest, and many treasons,
There is my pledge [*throwing down a glove*]; I 'll make it on thy heart,[8]
Ere I taste bread, thou art in nothing less
Than I have here proclaim'd thee.
Reg.:   Sick, O, sick!
Gon.: [*Aside.*] If not, I 'll ne'er trust medicine.   96
Edm.: There 's my exchange [*throwing down a glove*]: what in the world he is
That names me traitor, villain-like he lies:
Call by thy trumpet: he that dares approach,
On him, on you, who not? I will maintain   100
My truth and honour firmly.
Alb.: A herald, ho! Trust to thy single virtue; [9] for thy soldiers,
All levied in my name, have in my name
Took their discharge.
Reg.:   My sickness grows upon me.
Alb.: She is not well; convey her to my tent. [*Exit Regan, led. Enter a Herald.*] Come hither, herald,—Let the trumpet sound,—And read out this.

[7] A play; probably, a comedy; that is, a jest. [8] Make it undeniable; print indelibly. [9] Valor alone.

Her.: [*Reads.*] "If any man of quality or degree within the lists of the army will maintain upon Edmund, supposed Earl of Gloucester, that he is a manifold traitor, let him appear by the third sound of the trumpet: he is bold in his defence."   115
Edm.: Sound!   [*First trumpet.*]
Her.: Again!   [*Second trumpet.*]
Her.: Again!   [*Third trumpet.*]
    [*Trumpet answers within.*]
[*Enter Edgar, armed, with a trumpet before him.*]
Alb.: Ask him his purposes, why he appears
Upon this call o' the trumpet.
Her.:   What are you?
Your name, your quality? and why you answer   121
This present summons?
Edg.:   Know, my name is lost;
By treason's tooth bare-gnawn, and canker-bit: [10]
Yet am I noble as the adversary
I come to cope.
Alb.:   Which is that adversary?
Edg.: What 's he that speaks for Edmund Earl of Gloucester?   126
Edm.: Himself: what say'st thou to him?
Edg.:   Draw thy sword,
That, if my speech offend a noble heart,
Thy arm may do thee justice: here is mine.
Behold, it is the privilege of mine honours,   130
My oath, and my profession: I protest,
Maugre [11] thy strength, place, youth, and eminence,
Despite thy victor sword and fire-new fortune,
Thy valour and thy heart, thou art a traitor;
False to thy gods, thy brother, and thy father;   135
Conspirant 'gainst this high-illustrious prince;
And, from the extremest upward of thy head

[10] Eaten by the caterpillar. [11] In spite of.

To the descent and dust below thy foot,
A most toad-spotted traitor. Say thou
"No,"
This sword, this arm, and my best
spirits, are bent   140
To prove upon thy heart, whereto I
speak,
Thou liest.
   Edm.: In wisdom I should ask thy
name;
But, since thy outside looks so fair and
warlike
And that thy tongue some say of
breeding breathes,   145
What safe and nicely I might well de-
lay
By rule of knighthood, I disdain and
spurn: ⸴ ·.
Back do I toss these treasons to thy
head;
With the hell-hated lie o'erwhelm thy
heart;
Which, for they [12] yet glance by and
scarcely bruise,   150
This sword of mine shall give them in-
stant way,
Where they shall rest for ever. Trumpets,
speak!
   [*Alarums. They fight. Edmund falls.*]
Alb.: Save him, save him!
   Gon.:   This is practice,[13] Gloucester:
By the law of arms thou wast not bound
to answer
An unknown opposite; thou art not
vanquish'd,   155
But cozen'd and beguiled.
   Alb.:   Shut your mouth, dame,
Or with this paper shall I stop it.
Hold, sir;
Thou worse than any name, read thine
own evil:
No tearing, lady; I perceive you know it.
   [*Gives the letter to Edmund.*]
   Gon.: Say, if I do, the laws are mine,
not thine: 160
Who can arraign me for 't?   [*Exit.*]
   Alb.:   Most monstrous! oh!
Know'st thou this paper?
   Edm.:   Ask me not what I know.
   [12] Because the treasons and the lie. [13] A
plot, trickery.

Alb.: Go after her: she's desperate;
govern her.
   Edm.: What you have charged me
with, that have I done;
And more, much more; the time will
bring it out: 165
'T is past, and so am I. But what art
thou
That hast this fortune on me? If thou 'rt
noble,
I do forgive thee.
   Edg.:   Let's exchange charity.
I am no less in blood than thou art,
Edmund;
If more, the more thou hast wrong'd
me.   170
My name is Edgar, and thy father's son.
The gods are just, and of our pleasant
vices
Make instruments to plague us:
The dark and vicious place where thee
he got
Cost him his eyes.
   Edm.:   Thou hast spoken right,
't is true;   175
The wheel is come full circle; I am here.
   Alb.: Methought thy very gait did
prophesy
A royal nobleness: I must embrace thee:
Let sorrow split my heart, if ever I
Did hate thee or thy father!
   Edg.:   Worthy prince, I know 't.
   Alb.: Where have you hid yourself?
How have you known the miseries of your
father?   182
   Edg.: By nursing them, my lord. List
a brief tale;
And when 't is told, O, that my heart
would burst!
The bloody proclamation to escape,
That follow'd me so near,—O, our
lives' sweetness!
That we the pain of death would hourly
die
Rather than die at once!—taught me to
shift
Into a madman's rags; to assume a
semblance
That very dogs disdain'd: and in this
habit   190
Met I my father with his bleeding rings,

Their precious stones new lost; became
his guide,
Led him, begg'd for him, saved him from
despair;
Never,—O fault!—reveal'd myself unto
him,
Until some half-hour past, when I was
arm'd: 195
Not sure, though hoping, of this good
success,
I ask'd his blessing, and from first to last
Told him my pilgrimage: but his flaw'd
heart,—
Alack, too weak the conflict to sup-
port! —
'Twixt two extremes of passion, joy and
grief, 200
Burst smilingly.
   Edm.:   This speech of yours hath
moved me,
And shall perchance do good: but speak
you on;
You look as you had something more
to say.
   Alb.: If there be more, more woeful,
hold it in;
For I am almost ready to dissolve, 205
Hearing of this.
   Edg.:   This would have seem'd a
period [14]
To such as love not sorrow; but another,
To amplify too much, would make much
more,
And top extremity.
Whilst I was big in clamour came there
in a man, 210
Who, having seen me in my worst estate,
Shunn'd my abhorr'd society; but then,
finding
Who 't was that so endured, with his
strong arms
He fasten'd on my neck, and bellow'd
out
As he 'ld burst heaven; threw him on my
father; 215
Told the most piteous tale of Lear and
him
That ever ear received: which in re-
counting

[14] End.

His grief grew puissant, and the strings
of life
Began to crack: twice then the trumpets
sounded,
And there I left him tranced.
   Alb.:   But who was this?
   Edg.: Kent, sir, the banish'd Kent;
who in disguise 221
Follow'd his enemy king, and did him
service
Improper for a slave.
   [*Enter a Gentleman, with a bloody knife.*]
   Gent.: Help, help, O, help!
   Edg.:   What kind of help?
   Alb.:   Speak, man.
   Edg.: What means this bloody knife?
   Gent.:   'T is hot, it smokes;
It came even from the heart of—O,
she's dead! 226
   Alb.: Who dead? speak, man.
   Gent.: Your lady, sir, your lady: and
her sister
By her is poisoned; she confesses it.
   Edm.: I was contracted to them both:
all three
Now marry in an instant.
   Edg.:   Here comes Kent. [*Enter
Kent.*]
   Alb.: Produce the bodies, be they
alive or dead. 232
   [*The bodies of Goneril and Regan are
brought in.*]
This judgement of the heavens, that
makes us tremble,
Touches us not with pity. [*Sees Kent.*]
O, is this he?
The time will not allow the compliment
Which very manners urges.
   Kent: I am come
To bid my king and master aye good
night. 237
Is he not here?
   Alb.:   Great thing of us forgot!
Speak, Edmund, where 's the king? and
where 's Cordelia?
See'st thou this object, Kent?
                  [*Points to Edmund.*]
   Kent: Alack, why thus?
   Edm.:   Yet Edmund was beloved:
The one the other poison'd for my sake,
And after slew herself.

Alb.: Even so. Cover their faces.

Edm.: I pant for life: some good I
    mean to do, 245
Despite of mine own nature. Quickly
    send,—
Be brief in it,—to the castle; for my writ
Is on the life of Lear and on Cordelia:
Nay, send in time.

Alb.:   Run, run, O, run!

Edg.: To who, my lord? Who has
    the office? [15] send 250
Thy token of reprieve.

Edm.: Well thought on: take my
    sword,
Give it the captain.

Edg.:   Haste thee for thy life.
        [*Exit a Captain.*]

Edm.: He hath commission from thy
    wife and me 254
To hang Cordelia in the prison, and
To lay the blame upon her own despair,
That she forbid herself.[16]

Alb.: The gods defend her! Bear him
    hence awhile. [*Edmund is borne off.*]
    [*Re-enter Lear, with Cordelia dead in
    his arms; Captain and others following.*]

Lear: Howl, howl, howl, howl! O, you
    are men of stones:
Had I your tongues and eyes, I 'ld use
    them so 260
That heaven's vault should crack. She 's
    gone for ever!
I know when one is dead, and when one
    lives;
She 's dead as earth. Lend me a looking-
    glass;
If that her breath will mist or stain
    the stone, 264
Why, then she lives.

Kent: Is this the promised end?

Edg.: Or image of that horror? [17]

Alb.:   Fall, and cease!

Lear: This feather stirs: she lives! if it
    be so,
It is a chance which does redeem all
    sorrows
That ever I have felt. 269

Kent: [*Kneeling.*] O my good master!

Lear: Prithee, away.

[15] Duty. [16] Committed suicide. [17] The end
of the world.

Edg.: 'T is noble Kent, your friend.

Lear: A plague upon you, murderers,
    traitors all!
I might have saved her; now she 's gone
    for ever!
Cordelia, Cordelia! stay a little. Ha!
What is 't thou say'st? Her voice was
    ever soft, 275
Gentle, and low, an excellent thing in
    woman.
I kill'd the slave that was a-hanging thee.

Capt.: 'T is true, my lords, he did.

Lear: Did I not, fellow?
I have seen the day, with my good biting
    falchion
I would have made them skip: I am old
    now, 280
And these same crosses spoil me. Who
    are you?
Mine eyes are not o' the best: I 'll tell
    you straight.

Kent: If fortune brag of two she loved
    and hated,
One of them we behold.

Lear: This is a dull sight.[18] Are you
    not Kent?

Kent: The same,
Your servant Kent. Where is your
    servant Caius? 286

Lear: He 's a good fellow, I can tell
    you that;
He 'll strike, and quickly too: he 's dead
    and rotten.

Kent: No, my good lord; I am the
    very man,—

Lear: I 'll see that straight. 290

Kent: That, from your first of differ-
    ence and decay,[19]
Have follow'd your sad steps.

Lear: You are welcome hither.

Kent: Nor no man else: all 's cheerless,
    dark, and deadly.
Your eldest daughters have fordone
    themselves,
And desperately are dead.

Lear: Ay, so I think.

Alb.: He knows not what he says:
    and vain is it 296
That we present us to him.

[18] My eyesight is dull. [19] Beginning of
your change of fortune and your downfall.

Edg.: Very bootless.
[*Enter a Captain.*]
Capt.: Edmund is dead, my lord.
Alb.: · That 's but a trifle here.
You lords and noble friends, know our
intent.
What comfort to this great decay [20] may
come 300
Shall be applied: for us, we will re-
sign,
During the life of this old majesty,
To him our absolute power. [*To Edgar
and Kent.*] You, to your rights;
With boot, and such addition [21] as your
honours
Have more than merited. All friends
shall taste 305
The wages of their virtue, and all foes
The cup of their deservings. O, see,
see!
Lear: And my poor fool [22] is hang'd!
No, no, no life!
Why should a dog, a horse, a rat, have
life,
And thou no breath at all? Thou 'lt
come no more, 310
Never, never, never, never, never!
Pray you, undo this button: thank you,
sir.

[20] Catastrophe; or, this destroyed Lear.
[21] Rewards and increments. [22] Term of affection, applied here to Cordelia.

Do you see this? Look on her, look, her
lips,
Look there, look there! [*Dies.*]
Edg.: He faints! My lord, my lord!
Kent: Break heart; I prithee, break!
Edg. Look up, my lord.
Kent: Vex not his ghost: O, let him
pass! he hates him much 316
That would upon the rack of this tough
world
Stretch him out longer.
Edg.: He is gone, indeed.
Kent: The wonder is, he hath en-
dured so long:
He but usurp'd his life. 320
Alb.: Bear them from hence. Our
present business
Is general woe. [*To Kent and Edgar.*]
Friends of my soul, you twain
Rule in this realm, and the gored state
sustain.
Kent: I have a journey, sir, shortly
to go;
My master calls me, I must not say no.
Edg.: The weight of this sad time we
must obey; 326
Speak what we feel, not what we ought
to say.
The oldest hath borne most: we that
are young
Shall never see so much, nor live so long.
[*Exeunt, with dead march.*]

QUESTIONS ON ACT V

1. What is the purpose of the short dialogue between Edmund and Regan at the beginning of Scene i?

2. What further development of Albany do we see in Act V?

3. Why does Shakespeare show us the brief interchange between Edgar and Albany in Scene i? How does this prevent the possibility of a melo-dramatic effect later?

4. What is the significance of Edmund's soliloquy that closes Scene i? What has happened to Edmund since Act I? Is he still the shrewd analyst and schemer? Or does he seem to be giving up before the complexity of the situation? If so, what comment does this scene then make upon the rational-ism which has been conspicuous in Edmund and in Lear's elder daughters? Do they manifest, at the end of the play, the same cool, rational control of circumstances that they practiced earlier? If not, why not? Where was their code deficient?

5. Lear's first speech in Scene iii shows what changes in him?

6. What is ironic about the Captain's line, after Edmund has given him instructions in Scene iii, "If it be man's work, I'll do 't"?

7. Examine Goneril's speeches to Regan in the scene before Regan's collapse. Since Goneril speaks with knowledge of Regan's physical condition, in what tone must she speak?

8. What development has taken place in Edgar during the play? Has any previous action indicated the resourcefulness which he shows here?

9. What complication in the character of Edmund does Shakespeare exhibit in Scene iii? Consider his acceptance of Edgar's challenge, his subsequent attitude to Edgar, his comment on the dead sisters, his line, "Some good I mean to do . . ." Is Edmund's last-minute conduct consistent with the principles of action which he set up for himself early in the play? If not, what comment does the play make upon his earlier principles?

10. Lear's speeches upon the death of Cordelia might easily have fallen into melodramatic ranting. Study his lines to see why they do not take on such a tone. Consider the following matters: Is there any indication that Lear endeavors to control himself? Is his speech at any time quieter than at others, or do his speeches constitute one long outburst? How does his recollection of the past help give concreteness to the expression of his emotions in the present? What is the effect of his careful effort to see whether Cordelia is still alive? Of his confused remarks to Kent?

11. What is suggested, near the end of the play, by such figures as "the rack of this tough world" and "the gored state"?

12. Edgar says of his father, "I . . . saved him from despair"; Edmund says that the killer of Cordelia was "To lay the blame upon her own despair, . . ." Show how the brothers' attitude to despair is a way of heightening the contrast between them.

13. Compare Kent's "Break, heart; I prithee, break!" with Lucy's line, "Break, break, my heart!" at the end of *The London Merchant*. Which is the more effective? Why?

NOTES ON *KING LEAR*

I. COMPLEXITY OF THE PLOT

In *King Lear* we come to the most complex of the plays which we have studied and one which therefore presents a number of special problems. The reader becomes aware immediately of the complexity of the plot, and besides this there is, as various questions on the individual scenes have suggested, a considerable complexity of patterns of meaning. The student's problem is to see how the manifold materials of this drama—words, single events and experiences, and fully developed plot elements—merge in a unified tragedy of very powerful effect.

Lear Compared with Other Plays. There is an obvious structural contrast between *King Lear*, on the one hand, and, on the other, such plays as *Everyman* and *Dr. Faustus*, with their single central characters to whom everything else in the play is so sharply subordinated that they almost give us the effect of appearing alone. At first sight, however, we might expect to find some main similarity between *King Lear* and such plays as *Rosmers-holm, Oedipus the King*, and *The London Merchant:* in each of them other characters besides the tragic protagonist have some prominence, and, what is more important, in each of them the private situation of the protagonist is partially identified with a public situation. But as we go further we begin to see differences: in *The London Merchant* the subsidiary interests receive so much attention, and the tone is so inconsistent, that the play seems never to have a tragic center; in *Rosmersholm* the tragic issue wavers between Rosmer and Rebecca enough to leave us feeling that, despite the obvious merits of the play, focus is never quite achieved; in *Oedipus the King*, despite the King's public situation, the plot materials are considerably more restricted than in *King Lear*, and Oedipus is always unmistakably the central character.

Interweaving of Plot Elements. Our first problem is to see how the elements of a very full and variegated plot work together so that the final effect is not one of diffuseness and lack of focus. At the simplest level, of course, the diverse ingredients are held together by the close interrelationship of the various characters in terms of plot: (1) Gloucester, who appears at first only as one of the men at Lear's court, becomes an associate of the usurpers and then a devoted helper of the king and then a victim of the usurpers; thus his own actions become almost a part of the main plot. (2) The tracing of Edgar's fate is brought close to the main plot by Edgar's association with Lear, his aiding Gloucester, and, of course, his important contributions to the working out of the plot in Act V, Scene iii. (3) Edmund's plotting against Edgar and Gloucester, which might easily become a separate line of action, is woven closely into the main pattern by the two sisters' falling in love with Edmund. (4) The public and private are bound together, at the plot level, by the fact that the working out of the private emotion and the resolution of the private conflicts—between parents and children, between rival lovers—also determine the state of affairs in the kingdom.

To understand further Shakespeare's technique, we should also observe what, in the interest of unity, he has excluded: (1) We see nothing of France and Burgundy after the scene of Cordelia's betrothal, a scene which exists chiefly as a commentary on Lear's obtuseness. (2) Kent and Cordelia we see only in relation to Lear; a less accomplished playwright might have introduced something of the "private life" of each. (3) Likewise Cornwall and Albany are shown only in their relationship to major characters. (4) The Fool's wit relates only to the dramatic materials of the play.

But still, we must admit, these relationships are of a somewhat mechanical sort, and, although they are structurally effective enough to make the

2. THE SOURCES OF UNITY

play more of a piece, say, than *The London Merchant* ever comes to be, they still are not the ultimate source of the unity which we feel in *King Lear*. To define that more precisely, we need to go beneath the plot surface and seek out the meaning to which, we may assume, all the characters contribute.

As a first step we may examine the Gloucester plot, since it contains the largest portion of the dramatic materials not immediately identified with the main action, to see how it combines with and works together with the Lear plot. Certain similarities we see immediately: each parent is deceived by one child or children and thus made to mistreat another child, who, ironically, later returns to treat his unkind parent with especial loving kindness. There are enough differences in detail—the student will probably want to outline them for himself—so that Shakespeare is not merely playing the same tune twice or doubling the volume to get his effect. Furthermore, the Gloucester plot gets under way after, and ends before, the Lear plot, so that, by its shorter duration, the Gloucester plot is subordinated to the other and hence seems not a mere parallel to it but a kind of amplification or extension of it.

The Tragic Flaws. To go a step further, we observe that Lear and Gloucester both fall into the pattern of the "tragic hero" (see Glossary) whom we have already studied in connection with other plays: with both we feel profoundly sympathetic even while we recognize that their sufferings have a logical connection with their "tragic flaws." What is the tragic flaw? May we not say that with each man it is a kind of error of understanding? *Oedipus the King*, we suggested, might be read as a study of the claims of the human reason; in one respect, *King Lear* appears to push the same study still further. Lear, of course, is not the sort of consciously rational man that Oedipus is; yet, like Oedipus, he does reason about certain phenomena in question, and he draws the wrong conclusion. In fact, we may say that he starts off a whole train of troubles by insisting on an untenable proposition: that love can be measured, measured as if it were a material quantum with a certain shape or size. He makes the intellectual mistake of applying the wrong standards; deeds, rather than words, are the symbol of love, and Lear could find the answer to his question, not in verbal formulas but in the lives of daughters whom he had observed from infancy. Yet on that vast and perhaps roughly outlined evidence he will not rely, just as Oedipus will not trust his long knowledge of Creon and Teiresias; he insists on neat little statements, which can come only from the application of irrelevant standards. Lear's second mistake is his misinterpretation of the attempted measurements which his demands exact: in the opening scene he overestimates the meaningless abstractions and hyperboles of Goneril and Regan, and wholly misses the import of Cordelia's precise metaphor. He might have tested their language by his instinctive sense, so to speak, of their character, his nonrational awareness of their worth. But he has chosen to be a sort of detective and, since his mind is not up to the role, he makes so profound an error that he comes to unbearably bitter experiences.

Now, when we return to the Gloucester plot, we see the situation varied in that initiative is taken by the deceptive child rather than by the muddled father: but again we find the father as detective, reasoning faultily from the evidence, and conspicuously failing—like Oedipus and Lear—to consult his own experienced sense of Edgar's worth, to consult what we might call "the Edgar tradition." He thinks badly and acts unjustly. But this is only part of Gloucester's story; we have other evidence on the nature of his "flaw." For one thing, we are not allowed to forget that Edmund is illegitimate, and in V. iii Edgar specifically connects Gloucester's suffering with his adulterous act: "The dark and vicious place where thee he got / Cost him his eyes." Also, as we have already seen (Act II, Question 7), Gloucester, although he does not wholly approve of the conduct of the new lords of the realm, is inclined to accept them and to try "to do business with" them. Now, as we look closer, can we not conclude that Gloucester's conduct is all of a piece? We can say, perhaps, that Gloucester is too ready to "fall in with" whatever influences are brought to bear upon him. In Act I we see him referring jauntily to Edmund's illegitimacy: he had fallen in easily with the worldly attitude that takes sexual morality lightly. Then we see him falling in with Edmund's suggestions, and, next, inclined to fall in with the new rulers; even when he finally goes to help Lear, it is not wholly clear that he is doing more than falling in with the faction that appears to him more likely to win—although once he is committed and sees Lear, it is clear that his positive sympathies are definitely aroused. Indeed, as his speech beginning "These late eclipses" (I. ii) indicates, Gloucester is even inclined to charge all evil events up to astrological forces which he must fall in with because he can't do anything else. On the different occasions referred to, Gloucester might have been moved by the code of sexual morality, by his prior knowledge of Edgar, by his sworn loyalty to the king, by his sense of decency and right. But on those occasions when we see him making positive choices, he thinks faultily about the data he has to work with, even though he feels wise enough. Not that he would ever voluntarily do anything which he felt to be evil, but he too easily falls in with that in which he ought to see evil.

Lear and Gloucester as Complements. Lear, without ever questioning his own rightness, imposes his will upon others; Gloucester falls in with the will of others without questioning their rightness. Thus Gloucester becomes, structurally, not a duplicate, but the complement, of Lear; in the two men we see shown, with remarkable fullness, the different basic forms that may be taken by the tragic error in understanding. One imposes error, the other accepts; and the latter has, quite logically, the secondary role. We should note, too, the consistency of the roles—as active and passive—throughout the play. At one moment, it is true, Gloucester is goaded to a direct attack upon the sisters, and, through this positive act of his, his character gains enough in complexity to give him a tragic stature and to keep him from being merely an allegorical figure. But after he is blinded, Gloucester gives up, so to speak, before his misery; his impulse to suicide is essentially negative; Shakespeare appears, very fittingly, to have thought of him as falling into the Christian sin of despair. But Lear is always a vigorous, aggressive figure; he fights his daughters to the bitter end; even in his madness he imposes his personality upon the others. He becomes quiescent only in the brief scenes with Cordelia, and then, in the final expression of anguish, he becomes again a commanding, dominating figure beside whom the others seem small.

Symbolic Relation of Parents and Children. To pass to another aspect of structural relationships: the element of kinship in the story has a symbolic function by which the different characters are bound still more tightly together. For not only are the different children of each of the old men individuals who behave in different ways, but they also represent the *different elements which are in conflict in the fathers.* Is not Edmund, with his resolve to get on in the world by whatever means he can, that is, as he says, to "have lands by wit," an extension of Gloucester's own tendency to substitute worldly codes for stronger, but less tangible, imperatives? And is Edgar's gullibility not the same as his father's; and his kindness to his father the same as his father's ultimate kindness to Lear? But this extension of inner conflicts into characters who in part objectify the conflicting subjective elements is most marked in Lear's family. In Cordelia we see, at the start, the sharp insight into people and grasp of values which Lear comes to have when, in practical terms, it is too late; and in her there is also the tenderness which at times Lear is capable of exhibiting. Cordelia and Kent, both in their opposition to the others and in their candor to Lear, in a sense symbolize the sound side of Lear trying to assert itself; later in the play they are completely identified with the Lear to whom insight has at last come.

But more important is the link between Lear and his elder daughters, for here is the central irony of the play and a very important clue to the thematic bearing of the play. Lear's tragic flaw is their whole being. For Lear, in dividing the land, is introducing a principle which Goneril and Regan then carry on to logical extremes; at one level, therefore, they may be said to show what happens when one element in him gains the upper hand. Lear, as we have already said, forces the use of the principle of measurement where it is not applicable; he introduces a spirit of calculation; and he is ruthless in punishing what does not contribute to his proposed advantage. Thus Goneril and Regan come to power. And what comes to power with them is the spirit of calculation: in fact, throughout the rest of the play we see Shakespeare tracing the history of three people—for, in another unifying stroke which is convincingly logical, Edmund has become an ally of the sisters—in whom the cold calculation of worldly advantage has almost totally excluded adherence to any other values. That history the student should follow in detail—through the treatment of Lear, the treatment of Gloucester, the intended treatment of Albany, and, in the ironic climax, the treatment of the sisters by each other.

Ironic Reversals. Lear and Gloucester both come to the disillusionment which, as a part of the ironic effect of the play, the reader could from the start see was due them. Just after he is blinded Gloucester is told (III. vii) about his error—in a whiplash statement that is Regan's final contribution to his torture. To Lear the truth comes gradually in the course of several scenes (I. iv; I. v; II. iv) which, because of their importance to the thematic development of the play, deserve a little further attention here. The chief material of these scenes is the haggling over the number of retainers Lear shall have. Now these scenes must be read as the complement of the first scene of the play, in which Lear may be said to be haggling with his daughters about the amount of their love for him. There, he had insisted upon an inappropriate calculation; here, he is the victim of an inappropriate calculation by the very daughters who had profited from his own misapplied arithmetic. The daughters' love required a different kind of estimate from that which Lear proposed; likewise his demand for a hundred retainers needs to be estimated by another standard than the rational one of necessity. Both realities would have to be grasped by extrarational means. Hence, "Reason not the need," Lear exclaims in defense of what we would call the symbolic value of his retainers; it is his final speech at court, and it is a magnificent summation of the issue. "I cannot reason my love," Cordelia might similarly have said to Lear.

3. THE MEANING OF THE PLAY

Now, if we attempt to pull together the implications of the materials thus far examined, we can perhaps lay our hands on the general structure of the play. In the present discussion we have pointed out that the early activities of Lear and Gloucester might be read as a commentary upon the efficacy of human reason. In certain questions on the individual acts (I. Questions 10 and 13; II. Question 10; III. Questions 4 and 5; IV. Question 10; V. Questions 4 and 9), we have suggested that parts of the play appear to be an examination of the workings of the rationalistic mind. Lear and Gloucester, by making serious errors of understanding, open the door to the careers of Goneril, Regan, and Edmund. Now the striking quality of each of these three is coolness of blood—for a time at least—and sharpness of mind. It is quite significant that Shakespeare has not made any one of them stupid and loutish; they are all quick, shrewd, penetrating—especially in observing the workings of other minds. Their sense is in one aspect a liberating sharpness; it becomes the debunking spirit in Edmund, who sneers at his father's astrological superstitions. Similarly Goneril and Regan analyze their father's folly in disinheriting Cordelia. What common conclusions do they—in effect, if not in fact—draw? That in a foolish world they must look out for themselves, and that there is nothing reasonable to hold them back. And in a short time they go a long way; they do have remarkable "success."

The Mad Group. In the meantime the men who have made possible their careers have suffered ironic enlightenment and torture at their hands.

Lear has gone mad; he is in the company of the Fool, who by men of the world would be amiably tolerated, of course, but in any serious context would be regarded as a contemptible creature; and of fugitive Edgar, who can secure a miserable existence only by pretending insanity (for a while Gloucester, feeling that his grief may drive him mad, is with them). Beneath all the specific clashes brought about by the manifold movements of plot, may we not say that the tension of the play is between the rational, worldly characters and these irrational and quasi-irrational characters who cannot get on in the world? By all the usual standards of judgment, Lear and his associates are indeed a sorry company, deserving sympathy, of course, but hardly exacting respect. The callous person of little insight might say, "Yes, it's too bad, but that's the way the world goes." The more sensitive person of little insight—and this is the class into which many secondary artists fall—might be content to leave the play at that, merely inviting hatred for the cruel, stressing the pathos of the injured, and perhaps ending with a considerable measure of "poetic justice."

But thus to fall into melodrama is precisely the temptation which Shakespeare avoids; he never loses firmness of tone. The reader is free to hate the cruel if he wishes, but he is compelled to remember what the cruelty means. Things have gone too far, the issues are too deep, for poetic justice. And in the treatment of Lear and his associates Shakespeare is intent, not upon securing pathos at all but, instead, upon showing the fine insight which exists in, or comes to, those characters who live in an air of mental incompetence. From the start it is apparent that the Fool is not merely a brilliant wit but a sound judge of human beings and of the meaning of their actions; his fierce ironies sharpen Lear's growing awareness of what he has done. Edgar for a while speaks nonsense—although a careful examination of his lines will show that a number of them reflect the state of the world where so much evil is at work. But the mind which produces these desperate irrelevancies begins gradually to emerge as a deeply comprehending one, and by the end of the play Edgar has become a philosophical commentator upon his world. Lear, however, is the most important of the three—for the madness which is in part brought on by his realization of his terrible error is not an *escape*, as it might be, from unbearable reality but, if anything, an intensification of his awareness of the state of the world. Here, indeed, Lear fully possesses the insight which he needed, but could not find, at the beginning of the play; this is most strikingly apparent in the latter half of Act IV, Scene vi, where Lear, in several long speeches—in which, the student should observe, he brings together the storm, the sex theme which has belonged to the play from the start, Gloucester's blindness, and the animal imagery which is so frequent throughout the play—incisively analyzes the human forces that he has come to understand. So, instead of being content merely to invoke pity for the mistreated, Shakespeare has chosen to present a brilliant paradox of insight where it might least be expected—a paradox stressed by Edgar's overt statement of it, "Reason in madness."

The Sane Group. And is not the more inclusive paradox of the play the fact that the "reasonable" people—Goneril, Regan, and Edmund— are the ones who are really mad? In one sense they are the embodiment of worldly sanity: they have understood how to get hold of the world, they have practically got hold of it, they have won a decisive battle. But they have lost all grasp of moral and spiritual values; they have understood much, but they have not understood the final realities. They have madly tried to make a world without essential ingredients. Ironically, they come to be understood better than they ever understand; they never grasp the issues involved in their dealings with Lear and Gloucester. And the final ironic flick is that their code is not good even at the low level where it might seem most efficacious—the practical level; for, ultimately, the rational worldlings do not even understand themselves. Goneril's and Regan's passion for Edmund is inconsistent with their code, and in the interest of political success they ought to put it behind them in the same way in which they put behind them whatever else is not conducive to practical advantage. But in this perverse way the irrational in them reasserts itself; they cannot control their passion; they try to realize it by their conspiratorial technique, which has now become their only way of dealing with life; and it destroys them.

Kent and Cordelia. With the irrational devotion of Goneril and Regan to Edmund we should compare the equally irrational devotion of Cordelia and Kent to Lear. In worldly terms they might have saved their skins by deserting a king who was clearly on the way out. They do not desert him, however, and they go down. But unlike Goneril and Regan, they go down in an honorable and a meaningful way; their lives are integrated at the highest possible level; and thus they are in fine dramatic contrast with Goneril and Regan. This contrast extends deep into the realm of values, for, whereas Goneril and Regan use their minds independently, opportunistically, and with indifference to any restraints upon them in their own pursuits, Kent and Cordelia make their decisions in terms of loyalties which are a restraint upon both their casual preferences and their hope of profit. In Act I they are keen enough to distinguish between a superficial, erring Lear and an essential Lear, a man of integrity who embodies the values to which they must subject themselves. Goneril and Regan play upon the former to their own profit; Kent and Cordelia stand by the latter. At first exiled—the exile tends to become a symbol of Lear's loss of his grip on values—they are later identified, in their acts of unqualified devotion, with the essential Lear. They have chosen in terms of traditional loyalties—the loyalty of daughter to father, the loyalty of subject to lord, and, more profoundly still, the loyalty of the sensitive human being to the forces outside himself whose rightness he cannot ignore. Kent is no less sharp-minded than Goneril and Regan; but *all his intelligence is exercised in the service of Lear*. Theirs has escaped such a discipline.

The later rapport of Lear with Kent and Cordelia, and likewise of Gloucester with Edgar, is a dramatic symbol of the recovery of insight which we have seen manifested directly in the words of Lear and Gloucester, just as their early alliance, if so we may call it, with Goneril and Regan and Edmund was a symbol of the introduction of, or reliance upon, rational processes which are not of themselves capable of supplying man with the values he needs. But this early alliance liberated forces which exact a terrible toll before they are played out, and which are the means by which nemesis comes to the tragic protagonists. Thus, as we analyze the relationships, both dramatic and symbolic, among the various characters, we see emerging both the structure and the theme of the play. *King Lear* is one of the most complex of tragedies, but we can observe a remarkably skillful integration of its numerous parts in a controlled form that, as it evolves, becomes the fitting expression of a profound theme that cannot be simply set forth.

4. TONE

Our statement that Lear, although he proceeds from an obtuse calculation to a brilliant imaginative grasp of human forces, has initiated a kind of thinking which later returns bitter punishment upon him, poses a final question: what is the tone of the play? Is the drama a bitterly disillusioned statement that if mankind has got off on the wrong foot, made a basic error, nothing can save him? Or, since Lear's imagination is most penetrating when he is mad, is the play merely an ironic laudation of madness? A cynical insistence that in such a world only madness makes sense?

It seems clear that Shakespeare does not view the human situation as desperate. The play repudiates Gloucester's despair, and through the pity and therapeutic efforts of the others we are never allowed to forget that Lear's madness, whatever insights it may bring, is nevertheless a pathological state. But, the student may ask, if the play is not to be considered a sardonic presentation of human confusion, where does Shakespeare give dramatic evidence of the fact? It is true that the play does not offer the more obvious forms of encouragement which we find in popular literature: it demands, instead, that we distinguish between the grasp of values and "success." What is really significant is that Lear and Gloucester *do* come to a finer insight than they had before; they finally did not compromise with what must have looked like a very successful political order. They made mistakes, but they did not become vicious. And Kent and Cordelia never did lose their grasp of values; Albany developed from uncertainty in a difficult situation of conflicting loyalties, and Edgar from gullibility, to an active comprehension of their world. What the play reaffirms, is, on the one hand, the tragic consequences of the human failure of understanding, and, on the other hand, the human ability to regain, or retain, understanding in the face of violent temptations to make bargains and save one's skin. The really bitter play would show a world completely enslaved to the uninhibited rational scheming which is the Goneril-Regan way of life.

Do not our final three tragedies all, in fact, concern themselves with the capacity of man for a kind of spiritual rehabilitation? In each case the tragic protagonist is the person who, with no vicious intention, opens the door that brings retribution upon himself. Faustus and Oedipus, in their different ways, exhibit pride in powers of reason that lead them to skepticism of religious traditions; but to the validity of the tradition, whatever it may mean in suffering, both come to bow. Lear, in applying a rational standard when it is grossly out of place, opens the door to an assault upon the whole traditional order of his society. But the old values have their adherents, and Lear comes to understand his error and what it has meant. Perhaps it is of the nature of tragedy to reaffirm man's ability to recover the insights by which he may endure.

QUESTIONS ON *King Lear*

(Most of the following questions call for a rather full examination of the text of the play, and it may be, therefore, that they will be dealt with most effectively as individual student papers or full-length reports.)

1. So far we have discussed the main structural design of the play. But the structure is so complex that we find relationships established by still other means than those already examined. The blinding of Gloucester, for example, may seem at first glance like simply a chance product of official anger, interchangeable with any other physical injury that might have been inflicted. But examination reveals that it is more than that. Notice the time at which Gloucester is blinded: is there anything ironic in this? Is there any suggestion in earlier scenes that Gloucester has suffered a kind of blindness before he is actually blinded? Consider carefully the language of I. ii. Likewise study the language of III. vii to see what it suggests about Gloucester's power of seeing. How is the meaning of blindness given emphasis by part of the dialogue in IV. i?

Further, note how the blindness pattern is used to establish another relationship between Gloucester and Lear. Note the lines I. i and I. iv which suggest that Lear does not see so well as he ought. Does the darkness of the stormy night make any contribution to the pattern? What lines in V. iii comment on Lear's powers of sight? Do any of these carry us back to early events in the play?

Again, are images of sight so used as to contribute to the characterization of the sisters? Note what Lear says about their eyes—*i.e.*, their ways of looking at things—in II. iv. How is the sight pattern utilized in IV. v and V. iii to comment on their passion for Edmund? Compare with the comments on Goneril and Regan those which refer to Cordelia's weeping, and note how these lines amplify the contrast between them.

In view of what we have said about the tragic flaws of Lear and Gloucester, how does the sight pattern contribute to the central meaning of the play? Would sight be a good symbol for insight? Is there a double meaning in such lines as those of Edgar in IV. vi beginning "I 'll look no more"?

2. In a previous question (III. 8) we have pointed out that various episodes in the play are related to each other in that, whatever their

external form, they are all really trial scenes—Lear's trial of his daughters in Act I, his suit against Goneril and Regan (the sisters are both defendant and judge) in Acts I and II, his "arraignment" of them in III. vi, and the trial of Gloucester in III. vii. Do any other scenes belong to this series? What does the series suggest about the state of justice in the world of the play? What lines of Lear in the second half of IV. vi amplify the justice theme, if we may so call it? Do the characters in the play believe generally that justice has disappeared from the world, or do they have faith that it will again become dominant? Study the lines carefully for evidence on this point, especially those in the final scene.

3. Is Edgar's nakedness a solitary phenomenon, or are other elements in the play related to it? Are his changing fortunes in any way symbolized by his dress? Why does Lear want to take off his clothes when he sees Edgar? Does this episode remind you in any way of his action in I. i, when he "divests" himself of his royal power? What other disguises are there in the play besides Edgar's? Are different kinds of personal disguises contrasted? Do any lines about clothes and nakedness deal with the subject? Does the fool ever talk about the subject? See I. iv and II. iv. Consider Lear's speech beginning "Poor naked wretches" in III. iv, and his garb in IV. iv. Go through the play and find all the lines which refer to clothes or which use clothes images, and see whether they constitute a pattern which appears to contribute to the meaning of the play.

4. Miss Caroline Spurgeon has already pointed out the wide use of animal imagery in *King Lear*. There is room, however, for a thorough study of the uses which are made of it. In general, we may suggest, there are two: the characterization of individuals, and the definition of man's fate in the world. Which characters are presented more completely by means of animal imagery? What tone appears to be created by the regular use of animal imagery in the presentation of the world of the play? What does it imply about human potentialities?

5. We have already discussed the way in which Goneril and Regan "break down," so to speak, in their rationally worked out lives and let their passion for Edmund be their undoing. Does Edmund love either of them in return? Is there some corresponding breakdown in Edmund? Can you find a point at which he appears to stop taking firm steps and to begin letting things drift? Does he go further than the sisters in reacting from his scheming career? What traditional or emotional responses appear in him in the latter part of the play? What do his reactions in V. iii suggest about his code of life? That it is unsatisfactory in any way?

6. Many critics have pointed out the ironic correspondence between the storm which beats about Lear's head and the inner storm which leads to his madness. Is the storm put there simply because it is a parallel to Lear's mental storm? Is it prepared for in advance? What other meanings might it have besides the one already suggested? Might it also symbolize the moral state of the world of the play? What comparisons occur to Lear when he talks about the storm?

7. Are Edgar's concluding lines in V. iii merely convenient couplets, or do they make any contribution to the meaning of the play? Do they fit into any of the language patterns?

8. Some critics have suggested that in Cordelia there is at least a suggestion of a tragic flaw—a certain proud inflexibility in the face of Lear's request. Does this argument seem tenable? Does Cordelia have a large enough part in the play to be considered of really tragic stature? Ascertain how many scenes she actually appears in.

9. We have spoken of the "rational" quality in Goneril, Regan, and Edmund. On the other hand, how much "rationalization" (in the psychological sense) is there in Edmund's speech in I. ii? How much rationalization appears in any of the three of them otherwise?

10. What is the irony of Edmund's lines to his father in I. ii beginning, ". . . if you violently contend against him"?

11. Notice Gloucester's speech early in IV. i in which he says, apostrophizing Edgar, "Might I but live to see thee in my touch, / I 'ld say I had eyes again!" Compare this with Oedipus's speech, just before Antigone and Ismene are led in almost at the end of *Oedipus the King:* "Ah, could I but touch them with my hands, I should think that they were with me, even as when I had sight." Does the resemblance between the speeches. written independently in different civilizations, tell us anything about the working of the artistic imagination? Does it suggest that, in comparable situations, certain symbolic modes of expression are likely to recur?

FURTHER READING

A more elaborate discussion of many of the points raised here may be found in Robert B. Heilman's *This Great Stage* (Baton Rouge: Louisiana State University Press, 1948).

NOTES AND QUESTIONS ON *OTHELLO*

(Line numbers in references to *Othello*, *Macbeth*, and *Antony and Cleopatra* are those used in the Globe, Arden, Yale, and Kittredge editions.)

1. The student will quickly recognize certain similarities between *Othello* and *King Lear*. Perhaps the most obvious likeness is that between Iago and Edmund, between Iago's psychological manipulation of Othello and Edmund's of Gloucester; and in his hard, unprincipled aggressiveness Iago is also clearly related to Goneril and Regan. We have already used the term *rationalist* to describe the evil characters in *Lear*. In Iago we again see a sharp sense of fact, a shrewd observation of how people respond to stimuli and how their minds work, and a complete exclusion of any "irrational" considerations—such as duty or loyalty or honor—which might interfere with his using, to his own advantage, the human facts of which he is a master. In certain ways, then, a knowledge of *Lear* gives a good start in the understanding of *Othello*. What kind of conclusion about Shakespeare is suggested by the occurrence of similar motifs in these two

plays? Do they indicate that he had a rather sharply defined conception of the nature of evil, or at least of one of the sources of evil?

2. In *King Lear* we found the rationalist characters occasionally "rationalizing," that is, finding apparently reasonable justifications for conduct they had already determined on. Does Iago ever rationalize in this sense of the word? What about his several statements that his wife had been unfaithful to him with Othello? Some critics have regarded these statements as evidence of a belief honestly held by Iago. Is Iago, however, the kind of person to rest in a suspicion? To be unable to secure information if he really wants it? Do his brief statements of his suspicion indicate any real perturbation? Compare the language of Othello when Othello really comes to think that Desdemona is unfaithful. Or again, may Iago's suspicion be explained, as one critic has suggested, simply as the product of his general cynicism about human beings? But if it is that, what ground does he have for his apparent resentment? If Iago really thought that Emilia had been unfaithful, might he not be expected sooner or later to make some direct accusation of her, especially, perhaps, in the final scene when he is very angry at her and might by so doing attempt to impeach her testimony?

What other motive might account for Iago's conspiracy? Does jealousy of Cassio seem an adequate explanation? Or must we, at least in part, regard Iago on the symbolic level, and consider him as an embodiment of the evil in the world, apparently existing spontaneously and becoming a kind of natural antithesis to the goodness of Othello? Study, in this connection, some of Iago's longer speeches, especially the soliloquies. Notice that in I. iii, lines 373 and 392, he says, "I hate the Moor." Since Othello is presented primarily as a lover, may not this antithesis of love and hate symbolize the opposition of good and evil?

3. To look a little further at the possible parallels with *King Lear*, we might suggest that Iago's cold, hard reason, like that of the rationalists in *King Lear*, is not enough, even for merely practical purposes; Iago's sense of fact never includes a sense of moral or spiritual fact. Hence, he is really an example of "madness in reason." Yet this particular formulation of Iago's failure hardly occurs to us, because there is not a developed madness pattern as there is in *King Lear*. But it is worth noting that in one place Othello says (V. ii, 107–109) that the "error of the moon" (*i.e.*, the deviation of the heavenly body associated with both love and insanity) "makes men mad." This seems almost like a germ of the structural pattern used in *King Lear* (which very probably was written somewhat later than *Othello*). What does this fact suggest about the relationship of the two plays? In which one is Shakespeare more concerned with the problem of knowledge? Which one develops more complexly the potentialities of the materials?

4. If the opposition between Iago and Othello does not turn on the paradox of madness, it is of course clearly developed in other terms. Othello, for instance, is conspicuously lacking in Iago's sense of fact—in, we

might almost say, Iago's scientific sense; Othello gets his facts badly confused; he mistakes appearances for evidence, and then makes the wrong inferences. He is a well-meaning, but muddled man; in some ways he does not fall very far short of a human type for whom we are likely to have contempt. And here we come to another problem: if Iago resembles Edmund, does Othello resemble Gloucester? If he does, is he suited to be a tragic hero? Is he anything more than the pitiable victim? Gloucester, as we have said, is generally a passive character; he is always *giving in to* various pressures. Does Othello, then, merely give in and, at the end, despair? Or does he act with the positiveness of the tragic hero? If, unlike Iago, Othello constantly errs with regard to the facts, where is he, so to speak, correct, accurate? What does he have that Iago lacks? What ultimately determines his course of action? May we not call it the moral sense, or perhaps the sense of justice? Othello, we observe, is generally presented as a strong, upright, commanding person who evokes the admiration and affection of his associates; the killing of Desdemona by such a person becomes, then, something more than mere murder or private revenge or wanton brutality. This is not to defend the murder, but it is important to understand it; and what we should see is the sense of a *violated code* which lies behind Othello's act. The student should examine carefully Othello's lines in V. iii for evidence that Othello's emotions are interfused with a sense of the principle involved. Thus, acting in a way that seems justified and necessary, he acts positively; and the tragic irony is of course that he is bringing about his own doom. But what is especially important for the understanding of Othello is that he invokes his principles not only to punish Desdemona but also to punish himself. This is the important difference between Othello's suicide and Gloucester's attempted suicide; Gloucester acts in despair, but Othello acts in justice. How is this apparent in his lines just before he stabs himself (V. ii, 350–55)? Why is it important that, although Othello does try to attack Iago, the final scene is focused rather on what he does to himself than on what he does to Iago? In our impression of Othello, what is the significance of his confessing his deed (V. ii, 128) when it might have been technically possible for him to evade the issue?

5. Although Gloucester and Othello are both victimized by cunning, Gloucester is a more "worldly" person than Othello, who might be an allegorical figure of innocence. In Iago and Othello, indeed, we see the serpent and dove (compare the final paragraph of Question 2). Here Shakespeare introduces a very effective irony: innocence is usually thought of as the antithesis of evil, yet here evil comes, at least in part, from or through innocence. Othello's innocence, his unsuspectingness, his failure to test the facts, is a part of his tragic flaw. In what way does Desdemona's innocence—and, indeed, her sense of her own innocence—contribute ironically to the tragic outcome? Tragedy can be identified by its concern with the reality of the flaw, and with the complications that attend upon the operation of apparent virtues. Given the same initial situation, how

might a melodrama have developed the tension between Iago and Othello?

6. If Othello is only partly like Gloucester, to what extent does he become a tragic hero of the same stamp as Lear? Note the relationship between their decisive acts which bring about their downfall. Yet in *Lear* we see so much more time devoted to the consequences of the tragic act; in *Othello* most of the emphasis is upon the plotting which leads up to the tragic act, upon Iago's misleading of Othello. What does this fact suggest about the relationship between the plays? Is there any difference in tone? Which seems to penetrate more deeply into the human sufferings produced by the evil to which man is not immune? Does Iago's "working on" Othello ever seem tediously drawn out?

7. In *King Lear* and *Oedipus the King*, which we have dealt with at length, as well as in *Macbeth*, which is treated briefly in the present section, and in the *Oresteia*, which is discussed in Appendix A, we have seen a public action—that is, a tragic experience of certain individuals which transcends their own lives and has repercussions throughout the societies in which they are public figures. In *Othello*, however, the situation is essentially private, even though Othello himself is a public figure of some importance. Does this fact seem at all to narrow the interest and significance of the play?

To return to Question 6, in which we were distinguishing between the tragedy which is concerned with the preparation for the tragic act, and that which is concerned with the consequences of the tragic act: can we say that the latter is in the main of the "public" rather than the "private" type?

8. How far does Othello come to understand what he has done? To what extent is this consistent with the tragdies which we have examined? Does the evidence justify our saying that self-knowledge, especially self-knowledge which is achieved too late, is a characteristic experience of the tragic hero? To what extent does the tragic experience appear to be accompanied by an awareness of having by one's own action thrown away a good? Might it be argued, perhaps, that the illumination to which the tragic hero comes is one of the ways by which tragedy achieves its effect, that is, becomes quieting and reassuring rather than disturbing and depressing? If so, we might argue that this illumination is essential to tragic meaningfulness and that what may seem, at first glance, an "unhappy" ending becomes something quite different because of the element of understanding. Conversely, the really depressing and unhappy ending would be that on the "darkling plain . . . Where ignorant armies clash by night," or, we may add, where there is merely an illusion of understanding.

9. We spoke, in Question 2, of Iago's rationalism. Note how, in various speeches to Roderigo (I. iii and II. i), Iago reasons about love—about Roderigo's own passion for Desdemona and about the probable outcome of the Othello-Desdemona relationship. What is ironic about Iago's reasoning? Aside from such irony, however, we observe a kind of antithesis between

Iago's reason and Othello's love as the source of their attitudes to experience (perhaps, looking back at Question 3, we might say that Othello's love is the equivalent of Lear's madness). In fact, it may be possible to consider love the basic theme in the play and to find in the variegated treatment of love an organic pattern. There is, of course, the central passion of Othello and Desdemona. This is set off against Iago's constant protestation of love for Othello, and Othello's reiteration of belief in Iago's love: here we have hate ironically disguised as love (compare the suggestions made in the final paragraph of Question 2). Othello's love for Desdemona is contrasted, in another way, with the hysterical passion of Roderigo, and Desdemona's deep feeling for Othello with her friendly affection for Cassio ("the love I bear to Cassio"). The Othello-Desdemona relationship is partly paralleled by that between Cassio and Bianca, and is contrasted with that between Iago and Emilia, whose matter-of-fact unemotional collaboration gives way, under the impulse of Emilia's devotion to Desdemona, to mutual contempt and hatred. Against all the love is Iago's rationalistic disbelief in love as a value.

The central irony is that nearly all these relationships end badly, almost as if to justify Iago. Love, which "conquers all," fails to bring about a single peaceful and harmonious relationship. The student should note, in addition, all the ironies of detail, some of which have already been mentioned. Further, what is ironic about Cassio's not wanting to be seen with Bianca for fear Othello will not like it (III. iv, 192 ff.)? About Bianca's and Desdemona's being called "strumpet" and other such terms? What kind of comment on such terms is made by the final conduct of each young woman? What is the irony of III. iv, 26 ff.?

Is Shakespeare's attitude one of ironic and cynical disillusionment? Is Othello's "loved not wisely but too well" a way of saying that wisdom in love consists of withholding a safe share of devotion and looking out for oneself? Or is some other definition of *wisely* implied? Are we to believe that Iago's materialistic definition of love is wise? How does our attitude to Iago influence our conception of the meaning of the play? Even if love does not bring about happy endings, do other values persist which keep the play from seeming cynical?

In case the success with which Iago misleads Othello should itself seem to be merely a cynical commentary upon the blindness of love, ought we not also to take into account the special circumstances of the relationship between Desdemona and Othello? Is not Shakespeare really making a shrewd psychological analysis of their particular situation? Note that each is to the other something of an exotic: he, a Moor, experienced in war from boyhood; she, the delicate and sheltered Venetian girl. In this connection, recall Othello's speech telling how he won her (I. iii, 128 ff.). The point is not that these people are not in love with each other, not that they are merely infatuated; nor that their love is not deep and sincere; nor even that love is necessarily foolish. Should we not rather understand that the fact that neither of the principals as yet "knows" the other fully plays into

Iago's hands? If they had been married for a number of years, would Iago have found his task more difficult?

A final clue to the tone of the play may rest in a comparison of *Othello* with two other plays in this book which present many variations upon the love theme—*The Way of the World* and *The Sea Gull*. Note that the three different treatments involve quite different tones. From which of the two other plays does *Othello* most differ? Why? May *Othello* be distinguished from the other two in that Othello's problem does not have the social aspect with which both Congreve and Chekhov are concerned? Show how, in *Othello* more than in the other two plays, the problem is almost entirely an inner one for the protagonist, not one that involves a struggle against outer forces. Does this fact help in identifying *Othello* as a tragedy rather than another type of play?

10. In considering the tone of the play, the problem raised in Question 9, the student should take into account the imagery of the play. Miss Caroline Spurgeon (*Shakespeare's Imagery*) has pointed out that there are a great many images reflecting animality and sexuality, sometimes in combination. The student should make a collection of these images and see how they work. Do they appear to reflect the author's view of human life, or are they dramatic expressions of the point of view of one character or another? Do they grow out of the momentary mood or the mental habits of the character? Are we invited to sympathize with or to respect the character's point of view?

The student will notice, also, the use of the word *poisons* in V. ii, 363. There are a number of other uses of this word or related words. How does such repeated usage affect the tone? Does it suggest that the ill success of love is an inevitable occurrence or that it becomes inevitable only under certain circumstances?

11. Does the play make much use of contrasting images of light and dark? What purpose do such images serve? Are they ever used ironically?

12. Is there any resemblance between Emilia of *Othello* and Albany of *Lear*?

13. Some critics have argued that it is inconsistent for Othello to be persuaded by Emilia in V. ii when in IV. ii he remains unmoved by her insistence that Desdemona is chaste. Can you defend the apparent change in Othello? How might the fact that he has killed Desdemona affect his susceptibility to persuasion?

14. What is the function in the play of the events of Act I, in which Iago makes his first and unsuccessful effort to get Othello into trouble? Act I, of course, shows how cunning and unscrupulous Iago is, and how much honor and dignity Othello possesses. But it also shows Othello managing a situation much better than he does later in the play. Is this misleading? On reflection, however, we note that here (1) Othello knows all the facts; (2) Brabantio, his antagonist, is an excitable, unscheming sort of person with whom it is not too difficult to deal; (3) the Duke, if only in a small way, aids the cause of justice by acting as moderator. When we see,

then, how everything happens to Othello's advantage, and see also how thoroughly unprincipled Iago is, do we not anticipate, even in the midst of Othello's initial triumph, the danger which lies ahead for him?

15. What is the irony of I. iii, 292–97?

16. In what way does II. iii, 223 ff. suggest the technique of Edmund in making Gloucester suspicious of Edgar? Also III. iii, 35 ff. and 96 ff.? Note Iago's daring in III. iii, 165 ff., and point out the comparable daring in Edmund.

17. Analyze Othello's figure of speech in III. iii, 454 ff.

18. It has been charged that some of Othello's language is too rhetorical to be wholly effective. One of the figures of speech likely to produce a rhetorical effect is hyperbole. Notice Othello's use of hyperbole in III. iii, 443–4, 454 ff.; IV. i, 186; V. ii, 74–5. Can you make a case for these figures as doing justice to the intensity of Othello's feeling? Or must the passages be considered merely "rhetorical"?

19. A famous, though not respected, critique of *Othello* is that of Thomas Rymer in *A Short View of Tragedy* (1693). Rymer's criticism is an extreme example of the application of the "rules" (see Index); it also exemplifies a kind of critical attitude to Shakespeare which recurs in the seventeenth and eighteenth centuries. Below are some of Rymer's criticisms. How would you answer them?

a. The language is not suitable to the characters and circumstances. The words in II. i, 67 ff. are not those of "the exchange or insuring office."

b. To call Othello "the Moor of Venice" gives him a "pre-eminence which neither history nor heraldry can allow him."

c. The only moral is that girls should not "run away with Blacka moors" "without their parents' consent" and that wives should "look well to their linen."

d. It is improbable that a Moor would rise to such position in the state or win a wife of such distinction.

e. Othello does not act like a general except perhaps in "killing himself to avoid a death the law was about to inflict upon him." "His love and his jealousy are no part of a soldier's character unless for comedy."

f. Iago is "most intolerable"; *i.e.*, he is incredible as a soldier. Shakespeare was using "something new and surprising, against common sense and nature."

g. Iago and Roderigo have no right, no provocation, to be as familiar with Brabantio as they are in I. i.

h. The hearing of Brabantio's case in the middle of the night is improbable.

i. The change of place to Cyprus in Act II is bad; the author "had it never in his head to make any provision of transport ships" for the audience (see *Unities* in Glossary and Index).

j. In II. i, 83 ff. Cassio shows too great intimacy with Desdemona and Emilia; he is unsoldierlike.

k. At Cyprus, the general conduct is incredible in "a town of war."

l. Othello's jealousy is improbable.

m. Concerning the vituperative language Othello uses to Desdemona: ". . . for his excellency, a my lord general, to serenade a senator's daughter with such a volley of scoundrel filthy language is sure the most absurd maggot that ever bred from any poet's addle brain."

NOTES AND QUESTIONS ON *MACBETH*

1. For the student using this book, an obvious way in which to approach *Macbeth* is through certain resemblances between *Macbeth* and *Oedipus the King:* both plays deal with a prophecy and the realization of that prophecy; and in both, the protagonist's attitude toward fate becomes of paramount importance.

In *Oedipus the King* the prophecy is a double one (the oracle given to Laius and that given to Oedipus), neither aspect of which Oedipus wishes to see realized, but both of which, he finds, are realized in the end—the two prophecies ultimately coming to the same thing. In *Macbeth*, the prophecy is also a double one, that giving the crown to Macbeth, which Macbeth is anxious to see realized; and the other, giving the succession to Banquo's children, which Macbeth hopes to frustrate. But in *Macbeth*, as in *Oedipus the King*, the two prophecies become finally one: the protagonist's efforts to bend fate to his will actually fulfill the prophecy. What other parallels, if any, exist between the two plays? Granting the great differences between Lady Macbeth and Jocasta, do they have any traits in common? Compare their attitudes toward supernatural revelations. Compare the attitude of each toward her husband.

2. What is accomplished by the first short scene involving the witches? The scene introduces the witches, it is true, but does it do anything to establish the mood of the play? What is suggested by the statement of the third witch that they intend "to meet with Macbeth"? (As we shall see, they also meet Banquo, and they have something to say to him also.)

3. Note carefully the difference between the reactions of Macbeth and Banquo to the speeches of the witches. Which speaker is the more interested? Which takes them the more seriously? How do you know? Compare also the different reactions of Macbeth and Banquo to the confirmation of the prophecy that Macbeth shall become the Thane of Cawdor.

4. Shakespeare has been highly praised for the fine psychology displayed in the gradual development of Macbeth's decision to kill the king: first, a lively, though still innocent, ambition for the throne; then ambition coupled with hope; then guilty fantasy, which horrifies his conscience; and finally the broaching of the matter to Lady Macbeth—even though at this point he still is not committed to a decision. Find the lines in I. iii and I. iv which justify this account of the stages of his guilt. Does this account leave out any stages? If so, fill them in.

5. How thoroughly does Lady Macbeth understand her husband's nature? How do the antecedent scenes serve to give us confidence in her

analysis made here (I. v)? Does her understanding of her husband serve to justify her precipitancy here in resolving on the murder? Lady Macbeth tells Macbeth that his "face . . . is as a book where men / May read strange matters" (I. v, 63–64). What does she mean? In what way is this observation justified subsequently in the play (*e.g.*, see III. iv)?

6. Read carefully the speech of Macbeth at I. vii, 1–28. Are Macbeth's scruples sincere? Is the fact that he has scruples at the last moment in character? Note the basic reproach which Lady Macbeth levels at him: that he is a weakling, a baby, not a man. Notice that the point recurs throughout the play: Macbeth asks the assassins of Banquo whether they are men (III. i, 101–68) and later exclaims (III, iv, 99–107) "What man dare, I dare. . . . Why so: being gone, I am a man again." Can it be said that Macbeth's essential damnation resides in his attempt to steel himself against pity and to assume the inhuman manliness which Lady Macbeth urges on him? Is Macbeth a sensitive and imaginative man? How do you know?

7. In reassuring her overwrought husband, Lady Macbeth says that "'tis the eye of childhood / That fears a painted devil" (II. ii, 54–55) and "A little water clears us of this deed" (II. ii, 67). Does she believe this herself? Is she trying to believe it? (cf. II. ii, 13–14 and V. i, 38 ff.). Is Lady Macbeth a coarse and insensitive woman? Or is she a woman of a great deal of sensitivity who keeps herself under an iron control? Justify your answer.

8. Is the drunken jesting of the porter (II. iii) beneath the level of a serious play? Or if it is justified, in what terms: as providing contrast? In relaxing the tension of Scene ii so that we may feel the tightening of tension once more with the discovery of the murder? Or what?

9. What are the motives which make Macbeth resolve to kill Banquo? Fear that Banquo suspects him of Duncan's murder? The fact that the upright Banquo is a standing rebuke to his own conduct? Banquo's "royalty of nature," "valor," and "wisdom"? The fact that the witches have promised that Banquo's sons shall inherit the throne? Note that if Macbeth were anxious only to have the throne for himself—if he had no desire to found a dynasty—he would probably act most prudently by committing no additional murders. Note also, in this general connection, (1) the general and almost intangible quality of Macbeth's fear of Banquo, and (2) the fact that it is just after the appearance of Banquo's ghost at the banquet that Macbeth resolves to seek the counsel of the witches once more.

10. How does III. ii, with its account of the terrible dreams that afflict both Macbeth and Lady Macbeth, prepare for what happens in Scene iv? Lady Macbeth had said (II. ii), "These deeds must not be thought / After these ways; so, it will make us mad." Have they been successful in avoiding thoughts of their deeds "after these ways"? Does Scene ii bear on the motivation for Banquo's murder: that is, is it possible that Macbeth feels that the murder of Banquo will somehow solve matters?

11. What is the significance of Macbeth's refusal to tell Lady Macbeth of his arrangement to dispose of Banquo (III. ii, 45–46)? Is he trying to show that he can plan and execute a murder independently of her help?

12. When Macbeth sees Banquo's ghost, Lady Macbeth immediately accounts for it as the product of Macbeth's fear: "This is the very painting of your fear: / This is the air-drawn dagger, which, you said, / Led you to Duncan" (III. iv, 61–63), and she goes on to reproach her husband for being a baby, not a real man. (Compare her reproaches in Acts I and II.) May it be said that, in part at least, Macbeth's tragedy is just this: he has too much imagination, too much sensitivity, too much conscience to assume the "manliness" which his wife urges on him? Is he shocked that, even after his wife's tutelage, he still finds himself looking on his world with "the eye of childhood / That fears a painted devil"? Analyze the irony involved in Macbeth's bewildered comment: "the times have been / That, when the brains were out, the man would die, / And there an end" (III. iv, 78–80). Has he really adopted his wife's overbrittle rationalism? Consider Macbeth's last speech in Act III (iv, 142–4). Is it ironically pathetic? Does he believe in his explanation? How does it testify to his essential damnation?

13. Why is it appropriate that we should see the beginning of the rally against Macbeth (Act IV. vi) so soon after the scene in which Macbeth's demoralization is shown?

14. Why does Macbeth return to the witches? Does he really expect them to recall their prophecy concerning Banquo's children? May one state his dilemma in this way: if the witches really know the future, then the future is fixed and it cannot be altered by having the witches unsay what they have prophecied concerning Banquo's children; if the witches do not know the future, then a comforting prophecy from them is of no value anyway? Or, may one put the matter thus: Macbeth wants to eat his cake and have it: he wants the witches to tell the truth with regard to his fortunes—but falsehoods with regard to Banquo's? Macbeth in his disappointment curses the witches: "And damn'd all those that trust them" (IV. i, 137–38). But does he not continue to trust them? Does he not, like Oedipus, thus pronounce a curse upon himself? Granted that Macbeth's logic with regard to the witches involves a contradiction, what of Shakespeare's treatment of his psychological states? Is the psychology sound?

15. What is the general purpose of IV. ii? Why does Macbeth order the slaughter of Macduff's wife and children? Is the innocent prattling of the child intended merely to call forth pathos? When the murderers enter, Lady Macduff speaks what amounts to a prayer for her husband's safety, and the little boy denounces the charge of treason against his father as a lie. How are these speeches related to their conversation earlier in the scene? Is the child's defiance of Macbeth's murderers symbolic? What does it symbolize, if anything?

16. Scene iii (IV) depicts the gathering of the forces that are to unseat Macbeth. Why does Malcolm traduce himself before Macduff as he does? Notice the use of understatement to indicate the anguish with which

Macduff hears the news of the murder of his wife and children. How is this incident used to suggest the intensity and resolution which is coming to possess Macbeth's enemies abroad?

17. In Act V there is a rising tempo, as one misfortune after another falls upon Macbeth until he is swept to his death. In attempting to account for the effect of crescendo that is given, consider the following factors: (1) the alternation of scenes inside Macbeth's castle and outside it, in which his enemies are portrayed as coming steadily nearer the castle; (2) the succession of scenes in which his inner defenses crumble—Lady Macbeth's madness, her death, Macbeth's increasing feeling of loneliness and even listlessness; and (3) the gradual crumbling of his trust in the witches' prophecies as one after another is realized in an unexpected sense.

18. How have Lady Macbeth's sleepwalking and reenactment of the murder been prepared for? Why is it especially ironic? Remember her earlier confidence: "A little water clears us of this deed" and her sarcastic reference to "the eye of childhood / That sees a painted devil." Why is it dramatically more effective to portray her, rather than her husband, as cracking under the strain?

19. Compare Macbeth's hanging on to the last shreds of hope afforded by the witches' prophecies with Oedipus's clinging to the hope that the herdsman may prove him innocent. Can Macbeth hope further? Is the psychology involved in his desperate clinging to hope good psychology?

20. In V. iii, Macbeth, in speaking of Scotland, ironically uses the same comparison that Macduff and Malcolm use in IV. iii: Scotland is like a wounded or sick human being. Macbeth tells the physician that if he could "find the disease, / And purge it to a sound and pristine health, / I would applaud thee to the echo. . . ." Macbeth, of course, is himself the disease that must be purged away. Compare the situation with that of Oedipus, who is himself the curse from which Thebes suffers; note, also, the literal state of "disease" in Thebes.

21. In V. v, Macbeth says: "I have supp'd full of horrors: / Direness, familiar to my slaughterous thoughts, / Cannot once start me." He is apparently telling the truth: he is not afraid. He has at last succeeded in putting on the inhuman manliness which Lady Macbeth has urged him to put on. But what has been the price he has paid for this desperate bravery? Connect this with what Macbeth has to say about the meaninglessness of life in his next speech.

22. *Macbeth*, as compared with *Oedipus the King*, seems a play bursting with overt action. Does it also show itself to be, nonetheless, a play about the acquisition of knowledge? What knowledge about fate does Macbeth gain in the play? About human beings in general? About himself? May Act V, though filled with exciting action as it is, be said to occupy itself with stripping off one layer after another of Macbeth's illusions? In this connection consider the following speeches of Macbeth: "my way of life / Has fall'n into the sere," etc. (V. iii, 22–28); "Canst thou not minister to a mind diseas'd" (V. iii, 40–45); "Tomorrow and tomorrow" etc. (V. v,

18–28)," "[I] begin to doubt the equivocation of the fiend / That lies like truth" (V. v, 42–44); "And be these juggling fiends no more believ'd, / That palter with us in a double sense" (V. vii, 48–49). Compare what Macbeth learns, not only with what Oedipus learns, but with what Rosmer, Faustus, and Lear learn.

23. Note that the witches do not overtly influence the action in any way: that is, they do not force events to come about by spells or magic. Their influence is exerted in the play entirely through human agency. Note also that they do not lie: they tell the literal truth, although Macbeth manages to deceive himself by it. (They do not deceive Banquo: they do not precipitate him into an action which he would not otherwise have taken.) We need not argue then that Shakespeare intended us to consider the witches to be merely creatures of Macbeth's own imagination. (Banquo also sees the witches, though only Macbeth sees the air-drawn dagger and Banquo's ghost.) Shakespeare, in so far as this play is concerned, evidently does not question the existence of the witches any more than Sophocles, in *Oedipus the King*, questions the reality of the oracles and the gods whose messages the oracles gave. Yet what is gained by refusing to let the witches act directly to bring about events, and limiting their prophecies to literal truth, thus throwing the whole burden of the interpretation of what they say and the actions which spring from these interpretations, on the human being Macbeth? Compare, in this regard, the relation of natural and supernatural in *Oedipus the King*.

24. By the end of the play, Macbeth has suffered great degeneration. Malcolm refers to him at the end as "this dead butcher." Yet may it be said that Macbeth, in some sense, holds our admiration to the end? Why? Is his unflagging bravery a sufficient reason for his claim on our admiration? If not, what further qualities make him, for us, something more than a bloody tyrant, a ruthless butcher?

25. Some of Shakespeare's greatest poetry is to be found in this play. A full understanding of the play, indeed, requires an understanding of the poetry. Some of the recurring images, such as those of blood and darkness, take on a symbolic value as they are used. But there are other symbols, the meaning of which is less easily seen: Miss Spurgeon has pointed out the number of images in this play having to do with old clothes. Collect these, and consider with them the large number of images involving masks, false faces, etc. What symbolic value, if any, attaches to them? Consider also how many times in the play the image of the child occurs, sometimes as a figure of helplessness, sometimes as a symbol of growth and development, sometimes as the image of weakness and tenderness which Macbeth must put aside in favor of being a bold and resolute "man." What patterns of imagery emerge? How are they related to other aspects of the play?

26. Another of the elements in the play which, as has often been pointed out, is used a great deal to help produce the total effect, is sleep. Note all the uses of sleep, in fact or in the words, and try to determine what they contribute to the play.

FURTHER READING

There is further discussion of some of the points raised here in Caroline Spurgeon's *Shakespeare's Imagery* and in Chapter II of Cleanth Brooks's *The Well Wrought Urn* (New York, 1947).

QUESTIONS ON *ANTONY AND CLEOPATRA*

We have already gone lengthily into the problem of imagery in discussing *Dr. Faustus* and *King Lear*. With this rather elaborate start, the student should be able to go on and investigate problems of imagery in other plays. Several such problems in *Antony and Cleopatra* are suggested in the following questions.

1. Professor Leo Kirschbaum has pointed out the function of food imagery in indicating attitudes of the characters to each other. A typical passage is I. v, 29–31. See how many other such passages you can find and what they tell about the speaker or the person spoken to or of.

2. Professor Kirschbaum also points out the prevalence of erotic imagery, especially in the characterization of Cleopatra. Find the relevant passages and see what light they shed on the character of Cleopatra. (It should be recalled at this point that the character of Cleopatra has been a matter of much disagreement among critics. Some think she is inconsistently presented by Shakespeare. This is a possibility which the student should explore for himself.)

3. Miss Caroline Spurgeon says that our attention is especially attracted by "images of the world, the firmament, the ocean and vastness generally," and that these determine the tone of the play. The student should make a collection of such images and attempt to describe their influence on the tone. Is there anything in the characters, or in the action of the play, that would correspond to the largeness of which we are constantly reminded by the terminology?

4. Miss Spurgeon likewise finds that the play makes considerable use of the imagery of movement. After finding some of the illustrative passages, consider the question of how suitable such imagery is to the dramatic content of the play.

5. Several passages in V. ii are especially worthy of detailed analysis. Study lines 76–100, 206–220, 279–312.

6. How does the Soothsayer in I. ii and II. iii differ from the witches in *Macbeth*?

7. Is the Clown in V. ii in any way reminiscent of the Fool in *King Lear*? What obvious differences are there between them?

8. Does the play in general represent Antony's relationship with Cleopatra as a fulfilling or a wasting of his potentialities? (Do the materials referred to in Question 3 shed any light on this question?) Or is there any simple answer to the question? Does the consideration of this problem give any clue to the essential nature of tragedy?

9. What does Octavius stand for in the world of the play?

10. An excellent problem in connection with *Antony and Cleopatra* is the difference between it and Dryden's *All for Love*. Using essentially the same materials, Dryden undertook to write a play in conformity with the neoclassical "rules." (Compare the basis of Rymer's criticism of *Othello*.) Notice how Dryden handles the unities. Study, also, his poetry. What kind of imagery does he use? Does he use an imagery as complex and rich as that of Shakespeare?

APPENDIXES

APPENDIX A

Other Plays—Analyses and Questions

THESE exercises on additional plays are intended to provide opportunity for a more complete study of the drama than is made possible by the plays which can be printed in a volume of this size. The instructor may wish to assign the plays discussed here to students for individual reports or to have the class as a whole read, in the library, some or all of the plays and work them out with the aid of the exercises. In order to facilitate library work, we have given lists of some of the texts or editions in which the various plays may be found.

An instructor who prefers a historical approach will doubtless wish to use the plays in chronological order (Appendix B will show their relationship to the historical pattern). The instructor who uses simply a critical approach to different types of drama might either take up these plays after he has finished the body of the text or else use these plays along with the others. In general, of course, the plays (which are arranged alphabetically by author) may be taken up in any order which the instructor prefers. The following table merely suggests an order which seems profitable to the editors. It indicates at what stage in a course the plays may, in their opinion, most suitably be used and, where possible, connections—by resemblance or contrast—that may be made between these plays and those printed in the body of the text.

SIMPLER TYPES

Shakespeare, *Comedy of Errors* (Plautus, *Menaechmi*—a source of Shakespeare's play)

Second Shepherds' Play (Plautus, *Menaechmi*—farce; *Everyman*—religious drama)

Morton, *Speed the Plough* (Plautus, *Menaechmi*—farce; Lillo, *The London Merchant*—melodrama)

INTERMEDIATE

Maugham, *The Circle* (Wilde, *Lady Windermere's Fan*—similar plot and tone)

Rice, *Street Scene* (Ibsen, *Rosmersholm*—problem play)

Rostand, *Cyrano de Bergerac* (Congreve, *Way of the World*—treatment of love; Shakespeare, *Henry IV*—treatment of character)

Lope de Vega, *The King the Greatest Alcalde* (Shakespeare, *Henry IV*, and Ibsen, *Rosmersholm*—political problem, poetry)

Shaw, *Major Barbara* (Sheridan, *School for Scandal*, and Congreve, *Way of the World*—comedy types)

Howard, *The Silver Cord* (Ibsen, *Rosmersholm*—problem play, psychological interest)

1

MORE COMPLEX TYPES

Aeschylus, *Oresteia* (Sophocles, *Oedipus*—problems in Greek tragedy; Shakespeare, *King Lear*—relations of parents and children as a tragic theme)

Eliot, *Murder in the Cathedral* (*Everyman* and *Dr. Faustus*—drama based on Christian tradition; *I Henry IV*—treatment of history)

Euripides, *Hippolytus* (Sophocles, *Oedipus*—problems in Greek tragedy; Chekhov, *The Sea Gull*—treatment of love theme)

O'Neill, *Mourning Becomes Electra* (Sophocles, *Oedipus*—classical drama and "modernized" treatment of classical theme; *King Lear*—family relationships)

Racine, *Phaedra* (Chekhov, *The Sea Gull*—treatment of love: contrast in interpretation of young men)

Synge, *Riders to the Sea* (Chekhov, *The Sea Gull;* Ibsen, *Rosmersholm*—symbolism)

ORESTEIA

By AESCHYLUS

and

MOURNING BECOMES ELECTRA *

By EUGENE O'NEILL

It will be interesting and valuable for the student to make a detailed comparison of *The Oresteia* with *Mourning Becomes Electra*. In a sense it may seem an unrewarding task (and one which may be unfair to either dramatist), since the two trilogies are so far removed from each other in time and since their relations to their respective civilizations are so different. Moreover, as the perceptive student will soon realize, the purposes of the authors are radically different.

But this last statement provides the best justification for making the comparison. Through such a comparison the student may perhaps best arrive at each author's intention, a subject which is interesting and important to any student of drama. One may go on to point out that the later dramatist has definitely invited a comparison: his theme at least superficially resembles that of Aeschylus, and his characters balance those of Aeschylus—Mannon: Agamemnon; Christine: Clytemnestra; Lavinia: Electra; Brant: Aegisthus; Orin: Orestes, etc. Indeed, even details of the stage set are reminiscent of Greek tragedy: O'Neill describes the Mannon house as "a large building of the Greek temple type that was in vogue in the first half of the nineteenth century."

* Of the rather numerous translations of the *Oresteia*, only the later ones are mentioned here. That of E. H. Plumptre is in Vol. 2 of *Tragedies and Fragments*, Boston, n.d.; of Lewis Campbell, in *Seven Plays*, The World's Classics, Oxford, n.d.; that of Herbert Weir Smith in Vol. 2 of the Loeb Library edition of Aeschylus, New York, 1926–1927; that of Gilbert Murray in *Ten Greek Plays*, ed. Lane Cooper, New York, 1930, and in *Fifteen Greek Plays*, ed. Lane Cooper, New York, 1943; that of E. D. A. Morshead in Vol. 1 of *The Complete Greek Drama*, eds. W. S. Oates and Eugene O'Neill, Jr., New York, 1938.

Mourning Becomes Electra was published in New York, 1931, and appears also in *Nine Plays*, New York, 1932, and in Vol. 2 of *Plays*, New York, 1941.

Perhaps the best way to manage such a comparison is to observe the relationship between the comparable parts of the two trilogies.

Agamemnon and Homecoming

1. Compare the motivation of Clytemnestra and Christine. Is each dramatist fair to his character? Aeschylus makes primary, of course, Clytemnestra's desire for vengeance for Agamemnon's killing of their child, but he also gives Agamemnon a trace of "hubris," pride (in his own power), and has him order Clytemnestra to welcome Cassandra, whom he has brought back as concubine. O'Neill makes Christine's love for Brant primary, though he does suggest a psychological explanation for her earlier estrangement from Mannon. What difference of general intention is shown by the two treatments of this motivation? What is the effect upon the dramatic "stature" of each woman? Presumably Clytemnestra once loved her husband, whereas Christine has never loved hers. Does this fact render her deed more terrible and ironic than Christine's?

2. Aeschylus does not introduce Electra in this play at all. Why does O'Neill bring Lavinia into his? What function does she perform?

3. The threats to Clytemnestra and the suggestions of the vengeance that will fall upon her are voiced, in the *Agamemnon*, by the Chorus of old men; in *Homecoming* the threats are spoken by Lavinia. What is the difference in effect? Does the method make O'Neill's play less general and public, more private and "psychological"?

4. One of the finest passages in the *Agamemnon* is Cassandra's prophecy as she stands before the doomed house of Atreus and describes the Furies which she sees settled upon its roof. Is there any comparable passage in O'Neill's play? O'Neill too sees his House of

Mannon living under a curse. What is the nature of that curse? Does O'Neill succeed in making it more inward and intangible than that which haunts the House of Atreus? Is the interpretation of the curse given by Aeschylus more primitive and therefore more gross?

The Libation-Pourers and The Hunted

1. The motive of Electra in wishing to avenge her father is relatively more straightforward: she grieves for him and she hates his murderers. The motive of Lavinia is complex. Why has O'Neill complicated it? In the interest of plausibility? In the interest of "psychology"?

2. Orin is decidedly weaker than is Orestes. His mother and sister struggle over Orin, each trying to win him to her side. Why has O'Neill felt it necessary to make this basic change in the character? What is the motive, conscious or unconscious, which decides him to kill?

3. Is Orestes in the scene in which his mother begs for her life implausibly cool and unfeeling? Does the following comment of the Chorus help suggest the struggle that goes on in his mind? Does his speech following his execution of his mother and her paramour suggest the struggle? (The speech of triumph breaks down into an argument that he *has* been justified, and this in turn into his horrified vision of the Furies.)

4. Is the psychology here subtle enough? Notice that the Furies are not seen by the members of the Chorus, who attempt to assure Orestes that these are merely "fancies," at which he bursts out with "Can you not see them?"

5. In O'Neill's play the revulsion of Orin at his mother's death is given a great deal of prominence. Does it involve a more subtle psychology than that of Orestes? Why has O'Neill found it necessary to complicate it with jealousy?

The Eumenides and The Haunted

With these final plays in the trilogies the dramatists move much further apart, and their radical difference in intention becomes very clear indeed. In *The Eumenides* the curse is purged away, the deities of heaven and the lower world are reconciled, and a new order of justice is established. The trilogy ends "publicly" with a religious rite and with a song of rejoicing on the lips of the worshippers. Good has come out of Evil, though not without great suffering: the warring claims of reason and instinct come into harmony.

In *The Haunted* the curse is confirmed. Lavinia gives up her hopeless struggle to lay the ghosts of guilt. She orders the shutters of the Mannon house to be nailed up and walks into the house, closing the door behind her. She intends to "punish" herself "until the curse is paid out and the last Mannon is let to die."

In a sense, therefore, the O'Neill play may seem to be darker, more bitter, and *therefore* more "tragic" than that of Aeschylus, which, indeed, ends on a note of triumph—is indeed one of the Greek "happy tragedies." But before we draw any such hasty conclusion, it will be wise to see with what, ultimately, each dramatist is concerned.

It ought to be apparent that Aeschylus is throughout the three plays concerned with the moral meaning of the actions which he describes. Each of the characters is caught between warring claims—Clytemnestra between a desire to avenge her daughter and her vows to her husband; Orestes, between the necessity to avenge his father and his filial ties to his mother; Agamemnon, between his love for his daughter Iphigenia and his position as commander of the Greek host. Even the deities are so caught: Apollo would assert the right of *lex talionis;* the Eumenides, the claims of blood-guilt incurred by the murder of one close in blood. Whether or not Aeschylus has reconciled these conflicting claims, or whether, having reconciled them for his day and time, he has also provided the modern reader with a satisfying reconciliation, he has at least been concerned with the nature of justice. The action interests him in terms of moral significance. He continually raises the question of *why* as he explores the evils which come from the house of Atreus.

O'Neill, on the other hand, clearly seems interested in the "psychological how"—the tangled web of complexes that accounts for the actions of his characters. Here he has drawn heavily upon the discoveries of students of abnormal psychology like Freud. But does his drama transcend the "case history"? Does his interest become more than "clinical"?

The student should ponder these questions before trying to decide the issue of which trilogy is more nearly typical of tragedy. The conclusion of the *Oresteia* may seem "happier" than that of *Mourning Becomes Electra,* but the former attempts to arrive at a sort of equilibrium of moral forces—an equilibrium achieved in other Greek plays by the death or ruin of the protagonist; and tragedy, considered historically, has always manifested such a concern.

1. Why, in terms of the dramatist's purpose, can Electra be left out of *The Eumenides* completely while Lavinia comes to dominate *The Haunted?*

2. Is Orestes let off too lightly in *The Eumenides?* If he is justified, in what terms is he justified, and what is the nature of the qualifications which, the dramatist suggests, surround his justification?

3. Granted, in the case of both the Greek and the American play, that the circumstances depicted are most unusual, which play is the less "special" of the two? Which the more universal?

4. At the end of Act III of *The Haunted* Lavinia, who has hated her

mother, exclaims, "I'm Mother's daughter—not one of you. I'll live in spite of you!" How does O'Neill account for this *volte face?* Point out other shifts of the sort in the sympathies of the two Mannon children, and account for them.

5. In *The Eumenides* Orestes, after the verdict in his favor, leaves the scene, though the debate between the deities is far from settled. Does his retirement point to the fact that the problem in which he is involved is larger than his own fate, and that the dramatist wants to put the final emphasis on a general principle, not upon the fate of a particular individual?

6. The deities who take the stage in *The Eumenides* are moved by the passions of human beings: they quarrel, become angry, maintain their rights, etc. Yet do they succeed in symbolizing principles? If so, what principle does Apollo symbolize? The Eumenides? Zeus? Athene?

7. Does the use of the Chorus give Aeschylus any special advantage over O'Neill? What particular function is carried out by the Chorus in each of the three plays? Does it ever aid in presenting the "psychology" of character? In pointing up the moral problems and the moral significances?

8. How fair has Aeschylus been in presenting the claims of his various opposed characters? Why is fairness necessary in terms of his general purpose? How fair has O'Neill been in presenting the claims of his opposed characters? How necessary is fairness in terms of his purpose?

9. How heavily does O'Neill's trilogy lean upon that of Aeschylus? That is, does O'Neill utilize the reader's knowledge of the *Oresteia* in building up the effects of his own play?

10. Are the conflicting principles represented by Apollo and the Eumenides analogous in any way to the conflicting principles in *Rosmersholm?* Could we compare the Eumenides with the White Horses in Ibsen's play?

11. A student who wishes to go outside the plays in this book might compare the management of the guilty conscience in *Macbeth* with that in *The Eumenides*, especially in the scenes in which Macbeth and Orestes see the apparitions not visible to the others.

12. Another excursion into additional plays might profitably take the student to T. S. Eliot's *The Family Reunion*, in which, as in the *Oresteia*, the Eumenides not only are actually present but also undergo the same transformation into a source of good. Work out the details of the parallel. The comparison between Eliot's and O'Neill's adaptation of classical materials should be a significant one.

MURDER IN THE CATHEDRAL *

By T. S. ELIOT

Since *Murder in the Cathedral* is a play in verse, the student will have to attend carefully to the poetry, which is not to be thought of as a kind of outer coating, a kind of decoration which is external to the action of the play. Rather, it is in terms of the poetry that we shall

* This play was published in New York in 1935.

come into an experience of the really important dramatic action that makes the play.

We shall understand why this must be so when we reflect that the main action is that within Thomas himself, an internal struggle; indeed, with regard to the external conflict with the knights who murder him, Thomas will seem to be passive; and one of the knights, later in the play, actually accuses him of inviting his own death. Moreover, Eliot has chosen as his chorus (who comment upon the action and who indicate most specifically the impingement of Becket's murder upon the people) a group of old women, creatures who are helpless and can affect the action in no way at all. The poetry spoken by the Chorus and by Thomas thus has a very heavy burden placed upon it: it must convey with subtlety and power that which is important and dramatic but which, from the nature of things, can hardly be conveyed by external action.

It is possible, even so, that the student may conclude that the play is too "passive" to be effective drama, and that the death of a martyr is a hopeless subject for a drama. In attempting to judge this matter, the student might take into account the questions which follow. But as he embarks on an exploration of this question, he may note that Mr. Eliot himself is quite aware of the problem. Becket himself reflects upon it, as this passage in his sermon indicates: ". . . we do not think of a martyr simply as a good Christian who has been killed because he is a Christian: for that would be solely to mourn. We do not think of him simply as a good Christian who has been elevated to the company of the Saints: for that would be simply to rejoice. . . . Saints are not made by accident. Still less is a Christian martyrdom the effect of a man's will to become a Saint . . ."

1. How do the speeches of the Three Priests (after the Herald's announcement) provide exposition? How do they look forward to the events to come? Consider particularly the comments on Thomas's "pride."

2. Consider carefully the speeches of the first three Tempters. In what ways, if at all, have they been anticipated by the Three Priests? In what ways do they anticipate the speeches of the Three Knights?

3. Thomas expects the first three Tempters; he does not expect the fourth. What is the relation of the Fourth Tempter to Thomas? What is the effect of having the Fourth Tempter paraphrase Thomas's earlier speech, "We do not know very much of the future," etc.?

4. Why does the author end this part of the play by having the Three Priests and the Chorus *join* the Tempters in an appeal to Thomas?

5. What is the function of the Interlude? Does the sermon in which it consists break the dramatic pattern? Does it contribute to the dramatic pattern?

6. What is the function of the chorus spoken after the Knights have left for the first time? Has the poet adequately suggested the sense of ultimate confusion in which things seem to turn into their opposites and all fixed relations are dissolved? Why is it dramatically "right" that the Chorus should feel this at this time?

7. Thomas demands that the Priests unbar the door and admit the murderers. This decision keeps him from seeming merely passive in this crisis; yet the author must not make him seem to invite his own death—seizing upon martyrdom as a pure act of the will out of pride. Has the author succeeded in making Thomas an active protagonist and yet freed him from the charge that he has "sought" martyrdom? How?

8. In the course of the play Eliot at several points faces quite explicitly the matter of the meaning of the death of Thomas to a modern audience. The Fourth Tempter glances at what will happen to the memory of Thomas in future ages.

> . . . when men will not hate you
> Enough to defame or to execrate you,
> But pondering the qualities that you lacked
> Will only try to find the historical fact.

At the end of Part One, Thomas actually addresses the modern audience directly. But the most violent shift, out of the historical pattern of the events portrayed into the present, occurs in the passage in which the Knights defend their action in modern journalistic prose. Is the shift too violent? Why has Eliot ventured to make it? What does it tell us about the central intention of the play?

9. Are the passages which follow the Knights' defense—the speeches of the First and Third Priest and the final Chorus—"modern" or medieval? Do they succeed in conveying the sense of something "eternal"?

10. Is the function of the chorus substantially different from that in the plays by Euripides and Racine, or that in Aeschylus's *Oresteia?*

11. *Murder in the Cathedral* and *Everyman* may both be said to be Christian plays. *Everyman*, as we saw earlier, is much more than a sermon in dramatic form. What qualities in *Murder in the Cathedral* indicate that it is more than a tract?

12. Since this play is a poetic drama, we shall do well to attend carefully to the poetry, particularly to the poetry of the choruses. An obvious starting point in a study of this poetry is an examination of the imagery. For example, in the last chorus of Part I, animals dominate the imagery: "Puss-purr of leopard, footfall of padding bear," etc. But animal imagery dominates even more obviously the next chorus ("I have smelt them," etc.). Animals are mentioned once more in the final chorus, though here they are no longer exotic creatures like the leopard and the ape, but native like the wolf, hawk, and finch, and domestic, like the lamb. What governs the choice of these images? What are the varying effects? Why is the sense of smell so important in the earlier choruses and ignored in the final one? These questions should suggest others to the student, and he should not be satisfied until he feels that he understands the poetry of the play, not only for itself, but for the qualifications which it exerts on the total effect of the play.

HIPPOLYTUS *

By EURIPIDES

Since Euripides and Racine † are dealing with the same theme, a study of the differences between the two should amplify our understanding of dramatic method.

1. In what way is Euripides' emphasis

* The *Hippolytus* of Euripides is available in the Woodhull translation in the Everyman Library edition, 1908; in the Arthur S. Way translation, Loeb Classical Library, New York and London, 1912; in the E. P. Coleridge translation in *The Complete Greek Drama*, eds. W. J. Oates and Eugene O'Neill, Jr.; in the Gilbert Murray translation in *Fifteen Greek Plays*, ed. Lane Cooper, New York, 1943.

† Note. This play should be studied in connection with Racine's *Phaedra;* the exercises below presuppose familiarity with the discussion of Racine's play. See pp. 468–470 for a discussion of the *Phaedra.*

different from Racine's? How is the importance of Phaedra reduced and that of Hippolytus increased? Does Euripides make as much of Phaedra's inner conflict as does Racine?

2. Racine could hardly have given Hippolytus the central importance which he has here, for, as we saw, Racine's Hippolytus was largely a victim of circumstances. How does Euripides keep Hippolytus from seeming a victim of circumstances? What part does his own character play in the fate which he meets? What is the "tragic flaw" in terms of which his fate becomes meaningful and therefore tragic rather than melodramatic? Consider, for instance, the description of himself in his last long speech:

> I who devoutly worshipped
> The gods, and all the human race excelled
> In chastity, . . .

What is the significance of the scene between Hippolytus and the palace officer early in the play? Of Hippolytus' last speech to the nurse about the middle of the play? Would it seem plausible to define Hippolytus' fundamental error as one of stress: overstressing one aspect of life, and underemphasizing a relationship of fundamental importance?

3. If we may assume some such conception to have underlain Euripides' handling of his materials, the next question is whether Euripides has successfully transmitted it to us in dramatic terms. He uses Venus as the agent or voice of the determining principle of action. How favorably does he present her? Does he admit, in his portrayal of her, elements which are likely to diminish our acceptance of her point of view? What is the effect of what is said about her by other characters in the play? Consider, in this connection, the treatment of Diana in the play. Does Euripides, on the other hand, adequately present that aspect of Hippolytus which must be used to justify his suffering? Or is Euripides inclined to portray him oversympathetically? Do you feel that any of the author's effects verge upon the sentimental?

4. In this connection it may be worth noting that in his play *The Frogs*, Aristophanes, the Greek writer of comedy, makes Aeschylus, a slightly older writer of tragedy, say of Euripides,

> Thou bastard of the earth,
> With thy patch'd robes and rags of sentiment
> Raked from the streets . . . .

Does the *Hippolytus* provide any justification of the charge? Compare the death of Hippolytus here with that in Racine's play. Does Euripides appear to be "holding" the scene? Does it remind you in any way of the death scenes in Lillo's *The London Merchant?*

5. If we now return to Phaedra, we can see that her part in the play is that of an instrument of divine intentions. In view of this fact, Euripides might have been satisfied to make her simply a fill-in character who performs the necessary function of falling in love with Hippolytus. But Euripides is not satisfied with this simple procedure; he prefers, instead, to proceed more complexly by developing Phaedra fully as a character. How does he do this?

6. We see in Euripides as in Racine a certain use of the imagery of light and dark. Which playwright makes more consistent use of such imagery?

7. How does Euripides secure suspense in the first scene between Phaedra and the nurse? Could the nurse be said to be "practical" in somewhat the same way that Falstaff is? If so, do we feel the same way about them? Why?

8. Does Phaedra's accusation of Hippolytus seem wholly consistent with the rest of Euripides's treatment of her? Might the accusation have come just as well from the nurse? Compare Racine's treatment of this matter.

9. Does Euripides, the classical dramatist, observe the "rule" of stage decorum as carefully as Racine, the neoclassical dramatist? What conclusion about the "rule" might this fact suggest?

10. The opening speech of Venus exemplifies the expository prologue which is often used in classical plays, especially those of Euripides. Does this convention seem to interfere seriously with the "suspense"? To destroy our interest in what follows? Why?

11. Compare the treatment of illicit love in this play with that in Lillo's *The London Merchant*—the analysis of character, the consequences, the retribution. Which author deals with his situation in the more complex and mature way?

THE SILVER CORD *

By SIDNEY HOWARD

1. Howard's exposition is accomplished very succinctly: we are speedily introduced to the leading characters, the more important aspects of their backgrounds are sketched in, and their dominant characteristics, which will lead to the conflict of the play, are made clear. Is the exposition managed plausibly as well as speedily? At what point does the exposition end, would you say, and the forward movement begin?

2. Hester is obviously a foil for Christina, Robert for David. This obvious use of foils is extremely helpful in providing variety within the small cast. On the other hand, is the pairing off of characters too neat? Does it oversimplify the minor characters?

3. Is Mrs. Phelps plausible? Her obsession with her children—her possessiveness, her jealousy of her sons' sweethearts and wives—is doubtless found in some women. But is the degree to which such emotions dominate Mrs. Phelps plausible? Has the author heightened these traits too much in his anxiety to make his point? Has he turned Mrs. Phelps into a monster? Consider, for example, her calling to her sons to get their sweaters as they rush to rescue Hester from drowning.

4. What is the basic struggle in the play? How are the special aspects of it defined? Consider Hester's struggle with Mrs. Phelps, Robert's struggle with her, David's struggle with her, Christina's struggle with her. Is *struggle* too emphatic a word for some of these cases?

* This play is available in *Contemporary Drama: Nine Plays*, eds. E. B. Watson and B. Pressey, New York, 1931 ff.; *Dramas of Modernism and Their Forerunners*, ed. M. J. Moses, Boston, 1931 ff.; *Modern American and British Plays*, ed. S. M. Tucker, New York, 1933; *Representative Modern Dramas*, ed. C. H. Whitman, New York, 1936.

5. In the overt conflict between Christina and Mrs. Phelps at the end of the play, does the author take some pains to see that Mrs. Phelps's side is presented? Why? May Christina's analysis of the situation be taken to be the author's own? How far may Christina be said to be the author's mouthpiece?

6. Are the sons in the play too weak? Waiving the case of Robert, one can see that even David, at the end of the play, is being fought over by two women while he himself is relatively passive in the struggle. What does this fact suggest about the emphasis intended in the play?

7. A psychological explanation for the mother's attitude toward her sons and of the sons' attitude toward their mother is suggested throughout the play and is given specific statement in the final speeches of Christina. Yet, how far is the psychological account incorporated in the play itself, that is, dramatized? As the play stands, some readers will feel that the author is primarily interested, not in *how the situation came about*—in the crucial choices which Mrs. Phelps made, in the decisions which she came to which committed her and her sons to their emotional imbroglio—but rather in *the ways out of the situation* in which they have all become involved. In other words, the play is not primarily interested in dealing dramatically with cause and effect but with effect and remedy. (This may suggest to you a comparison with *Lady Windermere's Fan*, in parts of which Wilde seemed to become more interested in *rescuing* Lady Windermere than in *studying* her.) What effect does such a method—if this is Howard's method—have upon the tone of a play? Does it look toward tragedy or comedy? Toward melodrama?

8. In what senses is *The Silver Cord* a

"problem play"? What would be its interest as a play in a civilization in which the problem did not exist? What would be its interest in a civilization in which the problem has been eliminated? Is it intended to direct people's attention to the problem? Does it suggest remedies? Can you defend the play against the charge that it is primarily a tract—an essay calling attention to the evils of a social problem with a view to its elimination? Consider whether the author transcends the issues of the immediate problem and thus opens a wider area of meaningfulness.

9. What is "the silver cord"?

THE KING THE GREATEST ALCALDE *

By LOPE DE VEGA

In the last speech of the play Sancho refers to *The King the Greatest Alcalde* as a "comedy." A critic points out, however, that Lope developed the *comedia* as a form which combined numerous elements ranging from tragedy to farce. Perhaps, then, instead of merely treating the play as a kind of comedy, we should examine the various elements which compose it and see what kinds of effect they produce.

1. The class-dispute which appears in the central action suggests the problem play, although other elements fall outside the problem—some of the actions of Pelayo and Nuno, and the love affair itself, which, instead of being taken for granted as a starting-point, is presented with great gayety and vivacity. But insofar as aristocratic injustice is the central issue, the question that arises is this: Does the problem "date" the play? I.e., is it no longer of interest because of the disappearance of the feudalism from which it stems? Or does Lope give his materials more than historical significance? Does he generalize, as it were, the problem of injustice? Does he go beyond social problems into problems of character? Consider especially the treatment of Don Tello.

* This play, as translated by John G. Underhill, may be found in *Four Plays by Lope de Vega*, New York, 1936, and in *World Drama*, ed. Barrett Clark, New York, 1933.

2. Again, some elements suggest melodrama—the external conflict, the abduction and imprisonment, flight and pursuit, rape, the *deus ex machina*, punishment of the "villain." But is Lope willing to stop at the "thriller" stage? Let us consider some of the following points:

a. Is the king altogether a *deus ex machina?* He is an all-powerful outside force, but is his final action unprepared for? Is he really an outside force, or does Lope consider him an integral part of the play? Does he have any symbolic value? Why is so much pressure put upon him in the final scene?

b. There is a "happy ending," which is certainly too easy and ready-made. Yet in another sense the king's rescue comes too late. Does this not show Lope in part willing to let his materials *take their logical course* instead of merely managing a melodramatic escape?

c. Is Don Tello merely a "straight" villain, or does Lope try to make him a plausible, developed character? Note how he is presented at the beginning and at the end. Note, most of all, how he behaves after abducting Elvira. Are not his continual efforts to rationalize his act subtle signs of an inner disturbance? Might we say, perhaps, that Lope is taking a character who is not wholly bad and investigating the effect upon him of circumstances which bring out certain evil tendencies?

d. The treatment of Feliciana is especially important, for Lope might have treated her sentimentally in either of two ways—as the hateful lady who aids her brother's villainy, or as the kind woman who repudiates her brother completely. How does Lope avoid both of these extremes? What is the effect of his method?

e. Pelayo might be considered the farcical element that is often found in melodrama (cf. Morton's *Speed the Plough*). But is he merely the comically stupid oaf? Or does he have some resemblance to the fool of Elizabethan drama, who is capable of sharp insights into the way of the world? Consider, for instance, the lines (in the scene with Don Tello in Act I) in which he repeats Sancho's lines "hind-end first." Again, is Pelayo's constant talk about pigs only an end in itself, or does it suggest other meanings? Does the motif of "piggishness" occur elsewhere in the play? Do Pelayo's lines ever serve to qualify the tone? Consider the farewell scene (early in Act II) as Sancho and Pelayo leave to call upon the king. Finally, does the use of Pelayo help give a more complex picture of peasant life?

f. Is Sancho merely the honest rustic of melodrama, or is he made an interesting individual? Note, for instance, his appeal to Don Tello early in Act II; rather than a simple demand, it is imaginative, subtle, skillful. What interesting use of symbolic language does it contain?

g. Is Elvira, likewise, merely a pathetic victim, or is she made interesting in her own right?

3. Such points suggest that the play must be considered more than a melodrama. Does it, however, become a tragedy? Can we properly regard Sancho and Elvira as tragic characters, or are they simply victims? Aside from the happy ending, would their situation lead to tragedy or pathos? Do they have a "tragic flaw"? Or any quality that

Lope might have developed as a tragic flaw? (Cf. the pride of Hippolytus in Euripides' play.)

On the other hand, might Don Tello be the tragic protagonist? He is not wholly evil; we see his evil conduct, indeed, as a kind of "tragic flaw" after we have seen him in another light (note that he has a certain relationship to Macbeth and to Phaedra). But is the play so focused as to make it Don Tello's tragedy? Is our attention primarily upon him?

4. After study of such points the reader will conclude, perhaps, that if the play falls short of tragedy, it at least improves upon melodrama and avoids some of the pitfalls of the problem play. And there are other qualities which suggest that Lope, if in parts he is commonplace, is in some ways reaching a moderately high literary level.

a. What is the effect of the wit which appears in different parts of the play? Note the various examples of wordplay. Does the tone ever suggest that of Congreve?

b. Observe the irony that pervades the play. Don Tello's part has an entirely ironic origin; the student should trace all the details that contribute to the ironic effect. The well-intending Nuno has an inclination toward obvious conclusions which often leads to ironic effect: note his original attitude to Tello, his attitude to Elvira after her detention, his view of the visiting Alcalde's success. Trace the irony throughout the play.

c. Finally, there is some excellent poetry in the play: note the imagery in Sancho's speech to Don Tello in Act II, already mentioned; in Sancho's speech to Tello beginning "Great my Lord, the years pass by" in Act I (note how what he says here about the morning is picked up later in the Act, when he several times refers to the dawn). The student should give especial attention to the animal imagery in Don Tello's first long speech in Act I and in Sancho's last iong speech in the same act and again in Don Tello's speech beginning "No, she is a woman" in Act II; and to Sancho's speech beginning "Wrongs are like children" in Act II.

Several images or terms recur throughout the play in a way that suggests something more than coincidence. Note the various references to the sun, to Elvira's hair, and to swords and see whether they in any way suggest or reflect the changes of situation which constitute the play. But most of all trace the references to flowers and blossoms, which appear in Sancho's first speech and in Elvira's last speech in the play, as well as to trees and plants. These appear clearly to be not decorative but a means of suggesting a certain *natural* order of things and of pointing up a violation of that order. See to what extent you can relate the passages to the whole meaning of the play.

OTHER QUESTIONS

5. How successfully are exposition and foreshadowing managed?
6. Why are Don Tello and Feliciana made to talk about marriage in the first scene in which they appear?
7. Why does Lope have Don Tello develop a passion for Elvira very rapidly instead of tracing a gradual development? Does this show how he intends to handle and stress his materials?
8. Is Lope on the right track in having Don Tello constantly looking for reasons to be angry at Sancho?
9. Compare the treatment of the political problem in this play with that in Shakespeare's *Henry IV*. Are the authors' points of view the same? Is one more mature than the other? Is the Pelayo comedy as integral to the play as the Falstaff comedy is to its play?

THE CIRCLE *

By SOMERSET MAUGHAM

Because it deals with the same basic situation—that of a woman who is deciding whether to leave her husband for another man—Maugham's play invites comparison with Wilde's *Lady Windermere's Fan*. But the comparison immediately leads to the perception of differences, and the tracing of these differences is very useful: it shows us how two treatments of a situation may become quite different because the authors have *different attitudes to the material.*

First we see that Maugham and Wilde conceive of the problem quite differently.

* This play is available in Montrose J. Moses, *Dramas of Modernism and Their Forerunners*, 1931; S. M. Tucker, *Twenty-Five Modern Plays*, 1931; *My Best Play*, London, 1934; E. B. Watson and B. Pressey, *Contemporary Drama: Nine Plays* New York, 1931 ff

Lady Windermere is in love with her husband; Elizabeth is not. How does this alter the moral situation? Is Elizabeth's eloping a different matter from Lady Windermere's? Could you justify the point that it would be less moral to remain with her husband than to leave him? What difference, also, is brought about by the fact that Lady Windermere has a child, whereas Elizabeth does not? Is the difference between Lord Windermere and Arnold of any significance here?

But both authors are writing comedy and are therefore not primarily concerned with moral issues at all. We are invited to consider, not whether Lady Windermere and Elizabeth are *doing the wrong thing*, but whether they are *doing the expedient thing:* (1) How will they make out against a hostile society? (2) What will be the effect on them of the special kind of life which they will have to lead? The issue is really a psychological one.

The dramatists are alike in their focusing of these questions: each protagonist must make her answer by the aid of an object lesson provided by the preceding generation. Lady W. not only decides to stay with her husband but also gains a broader understanding of character: this is the crux of the play. But Elizabeth decides to leave—even after seeing, in Lady Kitty, a product of unconventional life who is considerably inferior to Mrs. Erlynne in maturity, dignity, and understanding. The problem then is: what does Maugham wish us to think about this decision?

One *might* describe Maugham as a romantic, one who believes in the primacy of love, whatever the circumstances and results. Does he, however, take steps to keep the Teddie-Elizabeth affair from seeming merely a romantic idyl? Is there anything "realistic" in the relationship? Are we meant to feel that, despite their enthusiasm and certain "poetic" lines, they have their feet on the ground? Finally, does Maugham's attitude to love, as shown by his treatment of other characters, seem a wholly romantic one?

The answer to this last question may suggest that Maugham's attitude is essentially ironic rather than romantic. If this is true, we must then determine whether it is bitterly ironic or whether it is the irony of a detached, amused, but nevertheless sympathetic observer. To consider the first option: is Maugham, in terms of the play, merely stating that people are always emotional fools who will never use sense or learn by experience? By a certain reading of the evidence we might make this reading fit almost every character in the play. But is it not too narrow? Is there not something to be said for the decision which Elizabeth makes? Does Maugham suggest, also, that there is really something to be said for Kitty and Lord Porteous?

Is there any intimation that, had the latter pair lived conventional lives, they might perhaps have fallen far short of the bright hopes which in periods of recrimination they still recall?

Is it possible, then, that once again we have something like the mature comedy of *Henry IV, Part I*—comedy which views experience in perspective and finds that "there is much to be said on both sides"? (If Maugham is shallower than Shakespeare because his characters are less profoundly conceived and because his situation is less inevitable, still he does touch on the broad subject of the usefulness of others' experience as a guide to action.) What does Maugham do to suggest that Kitty and Porteous, however lacking in charm and dignity they are at their worst, perhaps did not make the worst possible choice? Champion-Cheney is a delightful cynic: but how does Maugham show that he does not have a totally effective key to a wise and serene life? There is, of course, his miscalculation as to how things will work out. But note, additionally, the implications of his speech in Act II: "It's a matter of taste. I love old wine, old friends, and old books, but I like young women. On their twenty-fifth birthday I give them a diamond ring and tell them they must no longer waste their youth and beauty on an old fogey like me." Does this not suggest, perhaps, a certain immaturity, comparable to that of Kitty and Porteous at their least restrained? Is it possible that he has never grown up to something which they have experienced?

Again, as the deserted husband, Arnold would naturally claim our sympathy: but by what means does Maugham—from the start—indicate that a man must be more than a legal husband if he is to be a satisfactory mate whom we can admire? Finally, we are by no means sure that the young lovers are, under the stress of their emotion, making a bad choice. As a matter of fact, their romantic passion is presented favorably. But note that, finally, Maugham does not commit himself as to how things will go with them. How does he show that, for better or worse, their future lies with them? What, in the last analysis, does Maugham "believe" in?

Do we not here once again have the essence of the comic situation: that there are no perfect choices? But Maugham views this fact with a sympathetic, not a disillusioned irony: by making Teddie and Elizabeth disavow expectations of a perfect future, he gives them the best start he can in their gamble against the conventions.

QUESTIONS

1. What is the importance of Teddie's speech in Act III which begins, "But I wasn't offering you happiness," in determining the tone of the play? Does this make the tone more or less "romantic"?

2. Would you agree that Maugham maintains a more consistently comic tone than Wilde? If so, can it still be argued that the choice faced by Elizabeth is a more "real" one than that faced by Lady Windermere?

3. Do you find any witty aphorisms which resemble those in Wilde's play?

4. Does Maugham use any devices which suggest the technique of the "well-made" play as employed by Wilde? Do any of his devices for giving characters information or for getting them moved about have the air of artificiality which characterizes some of Wilde's methods?

5. Does Maugham in any way suggest parallels between the younger and older pair of lovers—parallels which indicate that the younger *may* come to resemble the older? Consider, for instance, Teddie's manner of speaking to Elizabeth.

6. Could Maugham's play be considered, like Congreve's, a pattern of variations upon the theme of love? What variations are there? What is the

relationship of the other variants to Teddie and Elizabeth? Does their problem in any way resemble that of Mirabell and Millamant?

7. Maugham has developed his third act almost entirely by means of irony. Find the various instances of it. Note especially the contrast between Arnold and Teddie. Arnold almost wins Elizabeth back by his gentle considerateness. What winning quality of Teddie's is contrasted with this?

8. How is the choice of the lovers affected by the fact that it is always a "career" or a "place in society" which is presented as the alternative. Does this kind of alternative make the romantic impulse seem more or less trustworthy?

9. How does Maugham's observance of the unities compare with Wilde's?

10. Though much is said about Arnold's career, we never take it very seriously. Why?

11. Compare Arnold's gamble in Act III with Mirabell's gamble in Act V. Is it logical, in view of the total situations, that one should succeed and the other fail?

12. How successfully is the exposition managed in Act I? Note especially the dialogue between Elizabeth and Arnold. Before the avowal between Elizabeth and Teddie, what suggestions are given us that the relationship between them is not wholly casual? Maugham has managed this rather skillfully, and his methods are worth some attention.

13. What provides the sense of progression in Act I? Note how the act gradually builds towards its climax.

14. Does Arnold's antique chair have any symbolic value? Is Kitty's mistake about "Sheraton" a mere comic malapropism, or does the mention of *The School for Scandal* have ironic overtones?

15. Does Maugham have Champion-Cheney return at the end of Act I just for the shock? Or is the return plausible in terms of Champion-Cheney's character?

16. What is the function of false teeth throughout the play?

17. Do we find as many varieties of comedy as we found in Congreve? Is there any farce? Does Maugham ever permit a too trivial tone?

18. What is shown by Elizabeth's annoyance at her father-in-law for his attitude to Kitty and Porteous? (Act II).

19. In Wilde's play we saw that the structure of several acts was determined partly by the use of contrasting panels of action. Is there any suggestion of the same scheme here? Especially within Acts II and III you may find evidence of balanced or contrasting scenes. Does the use of such scenes help give perspective?

20. Compare the Elizabeth-Kitty interview in Act III with the comparable scene between Lady Windermere and Mrs. Erlynne. What is the difference in tone? Which scene verges more toward melodrama? Why? What does Maugham do to keep Kitty's character consistent and balanced during this scene?

SPEED THE PLOUGH (1800) *

By THOMAS MORTON

Speed the Plough combines farce and melodrama (hence it may conveniently be studied in connection with such plays as *The Twin Menaechmi* and *George Barnwell*); it tries for a variety of effects in a way often found in popular entertainments—for instance, the movies. In fact, it is as if it had been worked over by a "gag man" who had schemes to meet every taste. Therefore it shows us what happens when the author is trying to please everybody.

1. How good is the focus of the play? Is the reader's attention upon one central action, or divided among a multitude of activities? How many plots or themes can you find in the play? Is the complexity of the play like that of Congreve's *Way of the World*? Or does it rather suggest a three-ring circus?

2. In this play we see enormous quantities of action—even more than in *The Twin Menaechmi*. Does much of the action appear to be meaningful?

* This play may be found in *Lesser English Comedies of the Eighteenth Century*, The World's Classics Series, Oxford, 1927, and in *English Plays 1660–1820*, ed. A. E. Morgan, New York and London, 1935. It also appeared in a 19th-century edition and in Mrs. Inchbald's *British Theatre*, Vol. 25.

What is the effect of such matters as the mortgage, the ploughing match, castle mysteries, an explosion and fire? Could Morton have used any of the given materials in such a way as to produce a mature and serious drama? Might he, for instance, have used the theme of the influence of past upon present, as Ibsen did in *Ghosts* and, in a sense, Shakespeare in *Hamlet*? What opportunity does he have for psychological studies? Might he have presented variations upon the theme of the relationship between the sexes, as Congreve does in *The Way of the World*? It is even possible that Morton thought he was doing some of these things. Why, then, does his way of doing things produce an effect of vast triviality?

3. Is Morton's characterization very thorough? What characters seem to be only conventional types? Analyze the effect of superficiality produced by the treatment of Susan and Bob Handy in Act V. i. Is the character of Bob Handy consistent throughout the play? Could you defend the argument that Morton's fondness for *matters of fact* (the "whodunit" style) leads him away from real problems of character? Compare him, in this respect, with Wilde.

4. In what instances does Morton's desire for a happy denouement lead him to use a *deus ex machina*—that is, to refuse to deal seriously with the implications of a situation? In the satire on science we can see one motif that simply drops out of sight. Are there others? How about the satire on matrimony?

5. To what extent do other kinds of comedy than farce appear in the play? Note the satirical tendencies and see how fully they are carried out. Is there any comedy of character? Consider, in this connection, Dame Ashfield's attitude to Mrs. Grundy (who, by the way, was first heard of in this play). There is some influence, also, of the "comedy of humors"—a type dependent upon a character's possession of a special "humor" or dominant characteristic. The danger of the form is that characters may become freaks. Does Morton escape the danger?

6. After a comic start, Morton first asks us to take things seriously in Act I. iii. How are we affected by the "Grove," a character "wrapt in a great coat," whistles as signals, cryptic remarks? Why do such details fail to suggest fundamental seriousness? What of Henry's gestures and style of speech? Does his language ever remind you of the sort of thing Sheridan was satirizing in *The School for Scandal?* Is the serious language of the play ever marked by clichés? Study the language of Scenes i and ii in Act III.

7. What is the effect of the introduction of patriotic speeches in Act III. ii and elsewhere? Aristotle says that each kind of art should have the kind of effect appropriate to it. Is patriotism fitting here, or must we conclude that Morton is simply trying to drag in every effect he can? Is such an author sure of himself?

8. Is there a perceptible relationship between serious and comic effects, as in *Henry IV* or *Lady Windermere's Fan* or even *The King the Greatest Alcalde?* How does Morton's treatment of interclass relationships compare with Lope de Vega's?

PHAEDRA *

By JEAN RACINE

Racine's *Phaedra* (1677), which we have already compared to Euripides' *Hippolytus*, also poses certain problems like those of Ibsen's *Rosmersholm*, and thus we may get at the essential qualities of the play by considering the general similarities with Ibsen's play.

1. First the question comes up: whose tragedy is it? Although Phaedra is the title character, Hippolytus re-

* The English translation by Robert Boswell is available in *The Chief European Dramatists*, ed. Brander Matthews, Boston, 1916, and in *Types of World Tragedy (World Drama Series)*, ed. Robert M. Smith, New York, 1928; Robert Henderson's translation is in *A Treasury of the Theatre*, eds. Burns Mantle and John Gassner, New York, 1935.

ceives almost as much of our attention as she does, and he is certainly treated very sympathetically. But is he more than a good character who meets an unhappy fate? Is he, so to speak, a victim of circumstances? Is there, in him, even as much conflict as we saw in Rosmer? Do we see him really struggle, or make vital decisions on which future developments hinge? Do we not, in his situation, find *pathos* rather than a genuinely tragic effect?

It seems clear, in fact, that Racine has played down one aspect of the story which might have brought Hippolytus into tragic pre-eminence—his love for Aricia. In what serious conflict might this have involved Hippolytus? (Compare *Romeo and Juliet*, or, in a somewhat different way, the *Antigone* of Sophocles.) Notice, however, that Theseus does not even believe that Hippolytus really loves Aricia. What effect is secured by the incredulity of Theseus?

As for the death of Hippolytus—is it used primarily for its effect on us, or for its effects on other characters in the play? What are those effects? Does Hippolytus's death really have as much significance as Rosmer's? Why does Aricia have only a small part at the end?

2. Like Ibsen's Rebecca, then, Phaedra is the tragic protagonist—but Racine is clear about his objective from the start. Beginning with Act I, our attention is centered on Phaedra's problem. Despite the large parts assigned other characters, the focusing is well managed (compare, in this respect, *The London Merchant*). What is Phaedra's conflict? How does Racine endeavor to keep our sympathy for her? How does he show us that she is struggling? Although her passion for Hippolytus is unique, do we feel that hers is merely a "case history"? Or is she universalized? If so, how? May her passion for Hippolytus be regarded as symbolic of a kind of general human experience? Is this similarly true of her willingness to have him wrongly accused? How are we made to feel that her remorse is real? What does she not do that would wholly alienate our sympathy?

3. As we have seen, Ibsen was interested, at least at the start of his play, in certain social problems. Does Racine manifest any similar interest? Does he take the matter of the succession to Theseus's throne, even while it still appears to be a real problem, very seriously? Would it be correct to say that the political problem merely provides a way of analyzing the characters further? If so, would this indicate that Racine is further away from, or closer to, tragic effects?

4. The materials with which Ibsen works include, very importantly, the characters' "sense of the past," the influence of tradition. Is such an influence also at work in Racine's play? In this connection, study carefully all that is said about the ancestry of Theseus, Phaedra, and Aricia. How do these characters regard such facts? As mere family history? As something to escape from? As a "fate" which is part of their heritage and with which they must deal? Are they merely passive? Do they gain or lose dignity because of their attitude to what has gone before? (We recall that George Barnwell is inclined to talk about what he is "fated" to do. Perhaps the lack of impressiveness of what he says may be illuminated by contrasting his situation with that of Racine's characters.)

5. Whereas in Ibsen we discerned a tendency to conform to the "unities," we see in Racine a dramatist who observed the unities on principle; in fact, his play is a good example of the neoclassical "rules" tragedy which was the ideal of European dramatists for a century or more. In a larger sense, the play illustrates the tendency of all drama to deal simply with the crisis of a situation. What important events, for instance, have taken place before the opening of the play? (Compare Lillo, who tries to record a whole situation, from beginning to end, in *The London Merchant*.) Does the observance of the unities make the play seem cramped? Or is it possible that Racine, by a certain vagueness as to time and place, makes us tend to lose consciousness of such matters?

6. One of the neo-classical "rules" was that of stage decorum, in accordance with which violent deaths or other acts of violence never occurred on the stage but were reported by other characters. Hence some critics call this play "declamatory," as if the play consisted merely of formal speeches *about* events. Is this a sound judgment? Does the

play seem undramatic? Or does the dialogue generate a definite tension of its own? To what extent do we see actual conflicts within and between characters? Would the play necessarily be improved by our seeing directly some of the reported death scenes?

7. We have seen that many of Ibsen's effects depend upon irony. Is this also true of Racine's? Make a careful study of the play to discover the extent of his use of ironic effects. It is well to recall, in this connection, that Racine was modeling his play upon Greek tragedy, which often relied heavily upon irony.

8. In Shakespeare we have seen certain suggestions made, or certain concepts stressed, by the repetition of, or by variations played upon, certain images and figures. It is highly possible that Racine is using such devices to amplify the meaning of his play. Note that, upon her first appearance in Act I, Phaedra says a farewell to the sun; and that, at the end of Act V, she speaks of "Death, from mine eyes veiling the light of heav'n." Returning to Act I, we find that, after Oenone and Phaedra have both spoken of Phaedra's seeking the "light," Phaedra wishes for "the forest's shade"—associated, for her, with Hippolytus. Trace the imagery of light and darkness throughout the play and see whether the contrast seems to support and amplify the general intention of the play. Note, in this connection, the reference to the "torch of life" and the "flames of love." Do you find any paradox here?

9. Racine's technical craftsmanship has been very much admired. How well does he prepare for future events? Find all the passages which prepare us, in one way or another, for the reported death of Theseus, for the return of Theseus, and especially for the death of Hippolytus. Note how all the references to Hippolytus's chariot or "car" are introduced. How well is the exposition managed in Acts I and II?

10. Several of the acts seem to be constructed by means of parallel scenes. In Act I, for instance, what similarities are there between the Hippolytus-Theramenes scene and the Phaedra-Oenone scene? What ironic differences? In Act II, what is the relationship between the Hippolytus-Aricia scene and the Hippolytus-Phaedra scene? What ironic resemblance is there between Phaedra's attitude to Hippolytus and Aricia's?

11. Phaedra's confidante Oenone is an interesting character. At one level she is merely the faithful servitor who becomes the ironic victim of Phaedra's ingratitude. In what sense, however, may she be said to deserve her fate? Is she in any way a symbolic character? Does she represent a part of Phaedra herself? Is her rationalism in any way like that of Ibsen's Rebecca? Does she resemble Lady Macbeth?

12. What ironic use is made of the familiar motif of the hostile stepmother?

13. To what extent does pride become an auxiliary motif in the play? Is pride ever treated ironically?

14. How is the fact that Theseus and Hippolytus are father and son reflected in the workings of Phaedra's mind?

15. What symbolic use is made of Hippolytus's sword in Acts II, III, and IV? Is the technique in any way reminiscent of Wilde's in his use of Lady Windermere's fan?

16. How is Phaedra's attitude to Hippolytus complicated by various events?

17. Dryden complains that Racine has transformed his original Greek character, a vigorous out-of-doors young man, into "Monsieur Hippolyte." Is the charge justified? Does anything in Act IV suggest that Aricia might be called "Mlle. Arice"?

18. Consult question 11 on Euripides' *Hippolytus*, and then work out a complete study of the treatment of illicit love by Racine, Euripides, and Lillo. Note, further, the variations of the theme which are found in Ibsen's *Rosmersholm*.

STREET SCENE *

By ELMER RICE

1. Has the author successfully distinguished among his large number of characters? In answering this question, consider the use made of (1) uniforms—of the letter-carrier, the ambulance-men—and of (2) dialect—of the Swede, the Italian, etc. Why has the author used so many *dramatis personæ?*

2. How is the exposition managed—of the situation of the Maurrant family, the particular problem in which the family is now involved, the conflict which must soon be brought to a head?

3. Is the action confused? Assuming that the basic line of action is that of the fortunes of the Maurrant family, do the concerns of the other characters obscure this line? How would you justify the statement that these subsidiary happenings actually bear upon the main line of the action?

4. The first act may seem to present no more than a "slice of life"—the welter of experience presented higgledy-piggledy, with a certain convincing realism, yet without any clear pattern or meaning. Is this, however, a fair account of the matter? Does a forward movement appear before the act ends? What is it?

5. What is the author's attitude toward Mrs. Maurrant? Toward Frank Maurrant? Does he see them endowed with moral responsibility, or, primarily, as victims of environment?

6. Why, in the second act, does the author insist upon the helplessness of Rose? What is he doing besides foreshadowing later events? Is he helping bring out the theme of his play here?

7. Sam Kaplan's family situation seems to differ radically from that of Rose, but what do the two situations have in common? How, again, does this fact support the theme of the play?

8. What do we learn about the intentions of the play from the fact that the shooting of Mrs. Maurrant occurs in the *second* act, not the third? "Whose play" is it? What is the function of the third act?

9. Is Rose a *tragic* character? Is she victim or protagonist? What measure of free will is accorded to her by the dramatist? What measure of moral responsibility? Is she placed in the play to *determine*—or at least to attempt to determine—events, or simply to feel and respond to events?

10. Does Rose make a good central character? Assuming that one character can typify completely the problems and feelings of the whole community, is Rose a good choice for such a character? How typical is she? How untypical? The fortunes of how many of the other characters are tied in with hers?

11. Does the dramatist have any "solution" for the problems which he poses? Should he have any? In what sense, if any, is *Street Scene* to be regarded as a "problem play"?

12. In considering an answer to question 11, notice that the author has a number of characters express through the play their own "philosophies of life." Do any of these speeches serve to represent the author's own views? Do any of them obviously reflect views with which you would regard him as unsympathetic? How is his lack of sympathy indicated dramatically?

13. Notice how many "walk-on" characters there are—characters who simply walk across the scene and say a few words which have little or nothing to do with the action. Granted that some

* This play was published separately, New York, 1929; it is also available in *Contemporary Drama: Nine Plays*, eds. E. B. Watson and B. Pressey, New York, 1931 ff.; *Twentieth Century Plays*, ed. F. W. Chandler, New York, 1934; *Pulitzer Prize Plays*, eds. K. C. and W. H. Cordell, New York, 1935.

of them have been chosen merely for the sake of variety or realism, are there some who contribute symbolic effects to the play?

14. In Act III, why is the discovery of the chicken which Mrs. Maurrant has been cooking effective? Does it make an ironic commentary on the events that have occurred during the morning? What is that commentary?

15. Why has the author chosen the little episode which he uses for the ending of the play? It, too, makes an ironic comment on the whole action that has occurred. What is the meaning of that comment?

16. Is *Street Scene* better focused, or less well focused, than *Rosmersholm?*

17. In which play (*Street Scene* or *Rosmersholm*) do the forces that move the characters come largely from within the characters? From the environment? Which, therefore, appears to give a more profound version of human character? Which comes closer to tragedy?

18. When *Street Scene* was first produced, its setting was considered to be very original; it was indeed strikingly different from the realistic interiors which had long been the vogue in American drama. Does this setting, however, in any way resemble that of Plautus's play? Are the settings used in a comparable fashion?

CYRANO DE BERGERAC *

By EDMOND ROSTAND

In this essentially romantic play, Cyrano has the attractiveness of the brave man who lives for honor and yet who possesses a sense of humor, of the man who has a poet's sensitiveness but a sensitiveness which he must conceal behind an exterior of bravado. Moreover, he has the final attractiveness of the hero who is not perfect, and who is conscious of his defect. He has an overlarge nose, but he does not protect himself by slinking into obscurity; he brazens

* This play was published in the Brian Hooker translation, in New York, 1923; in the *Plays*, translated by Henderson Norman, New York, 1921; in the Howard Kingsbury translation in *A Treasury of the Theatre*, ed. Burns Mantle, New York, 1935; in the Gertrude Hall translation in *Chief Contemporary Dramatists*, Second Series, ed. T. H. Dickinson, Boston, 1921; *Modern Continental Plays*, ed. S. M. Tucker, New York, 1929; *Twenty-Five Modern Plays*, ed. S. M. Tucker, New York, 1931; *Contemporary Drama: Nine Plays*, eds. E. B. Watson and B. Pressey, New York, 1931 ff.; *Representative Modern Dramas*, ed. C. H. Whitman, New York, 1936.

out the situation. His reaction to Valvert's insult is typical: Cyrano beats him in the duel but at the same time shows Valvert how much more stinging and original insults might have been made.

1. What has the author done to prevent Cyrano's action in Act I from seeming that of a bully? How do the following serve to counteract such an impression: the duel with Valvert? Cyrano's confession to Le Bret (at the end of the act) of his true reason for hustling the player off the stage?

2. How does Ragueneau, the poetical baker, serve as a foil for Cyrano? In what respects does he present a parallel?

3. What is the tone of the first two acts? Is it plainly comic? But what, more precisely, is the nature of the comedy? Does it have an element of fantasy, a kind of spirit of make-believe which keeps us from measuring the characters and actors against the world of reality?

4. How heavily does Rostand rely on the fantastic in the scene under Roxane's balcony in Act III? Even

assuming that Cyrano would generously help Christian win the woman he himself loves, is the scene very probable? Would not Cyrano have to have rather marked gifts as a ventriloquist for Roxane to be deceived? Would not Roxane have to be rather undiscerning not to suspect that something was wrong? Do we, by the way, ever learn anything about Roxane except that she has a pretty face and appreciates an eloquent and handsome lover?

5. If we are willing to accept improbabilities because of the general tone of fantasy and because the author is obviously being playful, what about the scene in which Cyrano renounces Roxane forever in Act IV? (After Roxane has said that she would love her husband even if he were disfigured, even if he were grotesquely ugly, because of his soul, and after Cyrano has begun to hope, Le Bret whispers to him that Christian has just been killed.) Do the melodramatic turns and improbable situations stand up when the issues (as here) become serious and we are required to take them seriously?

6. At the end of Act IV Rostand gives the following stage directions for Cyrano's last speech: "Declaiming, as he stands in the midst of flying bullets." Could this stage direction be carried out? What does it tell about Rostand's attitude toward realism and toward his play in general?

7. Is the ending of the play sentimental? What is the attitude which the author wants us to take toward Cyrano's final heroics? Are his last speeches sufficiently salted with wit? Or do some of them become self-regarding and ludicrous if we refuse to take them sentimentally? For example, why is "I believe she is looking at me . . . that she dares to look at my nose, the bony baggage who has none" successful, whereas "Ah, you are there too, you bloated and pompous Silliness! I know

full well that you will lay me low at last. . . . No matter: whilst I have breath, I will fight you, I will fight you, I will fight you" is emptily theatrical? Could it be fairly said that Cyrano actually falls a victim to silliness here? That his wit and capacity for self-irony which make him delightful in the first act desert him here?

8. Taking the play as a whole, in what scenes is Cyrano most plausible? Least plausible? In what scenes is he most attractive? Least attractive?

9. What is the quality of his love for Roxane? Is it based on any meeting of minds, on any comprehension of her personality? (Does Roxane, by the way, have a personality?) Or is Cyrano's love for her the love for something completely remote and unreal?

10. What is the total intention of the play? Is it successfully realized? Taking the previous questions into account, write a full analysis of the play. How much must your judgment of the play be influenced by the changes of tone implied by questions 3, 5, and 7? Do the changes in tone suggest uncertainty in the author's intention?

11. The balcony scene, as well as other aspects of this play, is somewhat suggestive of Shakespeare's *Romeo and Juliet*. How far do the similarities go? What are the fundamental differences? Is Shakespeare's play "romantic" in the same way that Rostand's is?

12. To what extent might Cyrano be compared with Falstaff (they both have physically grotesque characteristics that are laughed at, both have a sense of humor, etc.)? What is the difference between the attitudes of the respective authors toward these characters? Which author views his character more objectively? Sees him more complexly?

13. Compare the treatment of love in Rostand's play with that in Congreve's *Way of the World,* in which love is also a central theme.

THE SECOND SHEPHERDS' PLAY *

The Second Shepherds' Play (a late medieval drama) presents some useful points of comparison with Plautus's *Menaechmi*, since it also belongs to the category of farce. As a matter of fact, the English play in some ways seems even more primitive than the Latin one.

1. Does *The Second Shepherds' Play*, however, depend primarily upon coincidence or upon character? To what extent can you trace the central events to the character of the shepherds? Of Mak? Of Mak's wife?

2. In one sense the three shepherds might be said to function as one character. Does the author, however, try to differentiate them? Examine their lines in the opening scene and, more impor-

* *The Second Shepherds' Play* may be found in the Riverside Literature Series, ed. C. G. Child, Boston, 1910; in *The Story of the Drama*, ed. Joseph R. Taylor, Boston, 1930, Vol. 2; *British Prose and Poetry*, eds. Lieder, Lovett, and Root, Boston, 1938, Vol. 1; and *The Literature of England*, eds. Woods, Watt, and Anderson, Chicago, 1936, Vol. 1.

tantly, in the scene in which they visit Mak.

3. How good a technician is the author? Does he generally prepare us for what is going to happen later in the play? What early evidence is there of Mak's cleverness? Of his acting ability? Why are we not surprised by his thievery? By the mode of concealment of the stolen lamb?

4. Is there any irony in the play? Consider especially the discovery scene.

5. Is there any real wit in the scene preceding the discovery? Are there any puns?

6. The play as a whole shows how secular material was replacing Biblical material at this late period in the development of the so-called Miracle Plays. Does the author, in adding his original comic story, in any way connect it with the Biblical story? Some of the characters, of course, are the same, but, beyond that, is there what might be called a comic version of the serious theme?

COMEDY OF ERRORS

By WILLIAM SHAKESPEARE

Since Shakespeare's *Comedy of Errors* is based partly on Plautus's *The Twin Menaechmi*, it should be interesting to compare the two plays.

1. **Shakespeare's Farce.** The use of the two sets of twins presents a more extreme version of farce than *The Twin Menaechmi* (the idea may have come from Plautus's *Amphitryon*). Does this seem to you to make for funnier or cleverer situations? Is it a valid rule that, the greater the possibility of mistaken identity, the greater the potential comic effect? Or must other matters be considered? To what extent would comic effects be diminished by the probable state of confusion of the audience?

Would the audience feel inclined to make the effort necessary to keep things straightened out?

Yet Shakespeare adds other external complications—the problem of the twins' parents and of Aegeon's saving his life; the Adriana-Antipholus-Luciana triangle plot; the merchant-Angelo complication in Act IV. i. Note how, as he multiplies his attractions, Shakespeare intensifies his problem of winning our assent, our "willing suspension of disbelief." Note to what extent the main plot, as well as occurrences along the way, depends upon coincidence. Is there much effort to motivate the very important meetings of wrong people?

Again, is there any logical reason why Antipholus of Ephesus and his Dromio, when they are trying to get into the former's house in Act III. i, should be able to get absolutely no attention from within? The essential problem of probability, of course, lies in the attitude of characters to the situations which confront them. Does Shakespeare satisfactorily explain their lack of suspicion and rational inquiry? Note what Antipholus says about his servant in Act I. ii, and what, in general, the Syracusans believe—that they are bewitched. Compare this with Menaechmus II's effort to rationalize his experiences. Does Shakespeare work out his method as thoroughly as Plautus? Does the reader have to make too many concessions? Does he find sufficient return in the combination of juggling act (how long can the confusion be kept up?), the grotesque (Dromio's description of the maid in Act III. ii), and pie-throwing farce—the beatings of the Dromios (why do these not seem serious?)? Compare the effort required by Congreve's *Way of the World*

2. **The Change from Farce.** Yet the play actually *tends*—not very successfully, of course—to be something more than farce, and we can profitably observe how certain devices bring about changes in tone.

For instance, Aegeon's being in danger of losing his life suggests melodrama or even the problem play. What is accomplished by the amount of space allotted to Aegeon's tale? By the fact that Antipholus of Syracuse falls in love with Luciana? By the fact that the courtesan appears, not as the mistress of Antipholus of Ephesus, but only in an incidental role?

There is an important movement toward drama of character in the change of Plautus's shrewish wife into an Adriana who has some sensitiveness and intelligence. In Act II. i, the lateness of the husband, instead of calling forth

farcical rage, introduces some discussion of marital relations—in the manner of the problem play. The difference of opinion serves partly to characterize both sisters, and the contrast between them attracts the interest that in a straight farce might be directed toward vituperation against the missing husband. Adriana is still more interesting, however, in the second part of Act II. ii, where she speaks partly in grief, partly in incredulity, but chiefly with a desire to grasp the fundamental implications of the situation. As she examines infidelity in the light of the doctrine that man and wife are one, she develops the paradoxical position that his adultery becomes hers. We are invited to study and understand rather than to laugh. How consistently does Shakespeare keep the treatment of Adriana at this level?

How does the tendency away from farce appear at the end of Act III. i? In what ways does Balthazar actually suggest the atmosphere of the comedy of manners? Note especially these lines:

Her sober virtue, years, and modesty,
    Plead on her part some cause to you unknown.

Here he (1) thinks in terms of character and (2) suggests that there may be a rational explanation of the mystery. Are such actions characteristic of farce? In Act III. ii what serves to make Luciana a developed rather than a blank or passive character? Is her relation to Antipholus used merely for "love interest," or is the love motivated? Note that the romantic element heads off another farcical possibility. When Adriana takes Antipholus of Syracuse home, there is a situation which could lead naturally to "bedroom farce," the kind which skirts the possibility of adultery. But Shakespeare eliminates this possibility by his partly serious treatment of Adriana and by focusing the visiting Antipholus's attentions directly on Luciana. Of course, the conflict of tones makes a totally satisfactory handling of the Luciana-Antipholus scene practically impossible. If she makes the logical recognition that this is another Antipholus, the play ends; if she accepts Antipholus, her position is inconsistent and immoral; if she rejects him, the later rapprochement is less plausible. What is called for is a treatment of conflict within Luciana, but this is barely suggested; if the treatment were complete, the play would be quite different.

This, then, is the chief problem of the play: in attempting to do several different things, Shakespeare cannot do them all completely or consistently. Do you feel that this is a basic defect or that the interest of the work is increased by giving it to some extent an appeal more mature than that of farce?

OTHER QUESTIONS

3. Trace out Adriana's reaction to the apparent arrest, madness, and immuring of her husband. Is the effect here that of farce or of something else?

4. To what extent does Act IV. ii develop an inner conflict in each of the sisters?

5. Study the different elements in Act V which contribute to a tone of farce or to other tones.

6. What change is effected, if any, by the dropping of Plautus's parasite? Who might be said to replace him?

7. Do the various puns, like that upon *marks* in Act I. ii. 81 ff., and the witticisms, like those in Act II, suggest the effects of farce or of some other kind of comedy?

8. Does Shakespeare handle his exposition differently from Plautus? How useful is the situation in Act I. i for exposition? Does Shakespeare ever rely on Plautus's device of having a character make explanations directly to the audience?

9. Do the Ephesus-Syracuse legal relations, since they affect only a small part of the action, receive disproportionate attention?

10. How does Shakespeare try to rationalize the co-existence of the two sets of twins? Does he do anything about the recurrence of the names (note Plautus's handling of this)?

11. Why, in Act III. i, is the conversation between those inside the house and those outside so managed that no one in either party sees anybody in the other? Is there any effort to make this plausible? Would you say that the scene typifies the procedures of farce?

MAJOR BARBARA *

By G. B. SHAW

In certain regards *Major Barbara* resembles Ibsen's *Rosmersholm*. Like *Rosmersholm*, Shaw's play deals with the disillusionment of an idealist who is forced to see that the springs of human action are other than she has supposed

and to realize that the ideals in which she has believed are either masks for ugly realities or are warped by realities into travesties of themselves.

But, whereas Ibsen's play is worked out as a tragedy. Shaw's is developed as a kind of comedy. The difference is pervasive: it has much to do with the fact that one play has an "unhappy" ending and the other an "optimistic" ending. It shows itself in a number of ways: in the brisk tone of Shaw's play,

---

* This play was printed separately in London, 1912, and New York, 1912; it may also be found in *John Bull's Other Island and Major Barbara*, New York, 1918, and in Vol. XI of the *Collected Works*, New York, 1930 ff.

in its concern for ideas as such, in the lack of preoccupation with the individual and in the concern with society, in the use of fantastic plot situations, swift reversals of situation, etc.

As his preface indicates, Shaw is obviously interested in ideas for their own sake. Does he sacrifice any qualities of the play to his concern for presenting ideas? Is the play merely an extension of the preface? Or does the play as a whole transcend the ideas?

(There can certainly be no objection to the author's using any method he wishes as a means of expressing his ideas—tract, billboard, or play. But if we are trying to judge the status of a play as a play, it is important to determine whether or not the play is being used merely as a vehicle for something else, and whether or not it is an effective vehicle. Moreover, if the play should turn out to be primarily a tract, then we have a right, of course, to apply to it the criteria which one applies to tracts. Every play, of course, deals with a problem, with human problems. The issue is whether it treats them in the manner of a tract or digests and assimilates them to its own being as a great drama does.)

1. Which characters are real? That is, which impress us as being humanly complex? Which are oversimplified to caricatures? Are the caricatures good caricatures? That is, in which are the simplifications and distortions justified?

2. Is the initial situation fantastic or realistic? In answering this question, take into account the probability of the Undershaft method of inheritance and the probability of Lady Britomart's having a daughter in the Salvation Army.

3. Does the plot ever border on farce? Can you justify the dramatist's use of surprise and coincidence? For example, Bill's girl happens to have fallen in love with Todger Fairmile, the wrestler, who, it turns out, has recently been converted by the Salvation Army, and, last of all, it comes out that Todger Fairmile is the brother-in-law of the brother of Shirley who has just come into the Salvation Army hut for the first time and gets into talk with Bill. This set of coincidences obviously makes Barbara's job of pacifying Bill considerably simpler. Has the dramatist oversimplified her task too much?

4. What does Undershaft represent? Is he plausible? Is he consistent? Obviously, Shaw is using him to make some of the points which he is anxious to make. Does Shaw simply "state" the points, as an essayist might do, or does he embody them, dramatize them? For example, Undershaft says, "I said, 'Thou shalt starve ere I starve'; and with that word I became free and great. . . . That is the history of most self-made millionaires, I fancy." Yet, Undershaft is not self-made: he was adopted into the firm. Again, Undershaft demands that Cusins abide by the Armourers' Faith to sell to any man with the price. Yet Cusins is to be adopted and taken into the firm so that he may use the power which the firm represents in order to save society.

5. Is Undershaft the author's mouthpiece at any points in the play? Is Barbara? Where?

6. What is the function of Cusins? Is there any reason to believe that he will be a successful armaments maker? Why does Undershaft adopt him as his heir?

7. It is sometimes said that in reading a Shaw play one should pay no attention to the plot but simply listen to the amusing talk. In that case, why should Shaw have put his talk into a play at all? Is the dramatic mode justified? How?

8. Assuming that the talk is brilliant, is it brilliant merely from moment to moment, or does the brilliance spring from profound insights into the way that human beings and the society in which they live behave? That is, do the charac-

ters ever shift position for the sake of scoring a point? Do later speeches ever contradict earlier speeches? Or are the characters ultimately consistent? For example, Undershaft hates poverty for himself and takes means to insure himself against it. Does his single-minded devotion to this end allow room for a desire to eliminate poverty for all men? What motivates his desire to entice Cusins and Barbara into the firm? To increase his own wealth? To have about him people whom he likes? To put power into the hands of idealists for the betterment of the world?

9. Consider the play as a satire. What types of people and what institutions are attacked? How effective is the satire? Illustrate.

10. How does the comedy of Shaw differ from that of Congreve and Sheridan? Are the latter two concerned primarily with the problems of Society or with the private problems of individuals in a society which the authors, though they may laugh at some aspects of it, in the main accept?

11. Insofar as the plot borders on farce, does it tend to resemble the farce of Plautus? Or is there still a fundamental distinction?

RIDERS TO THE SEA *

By JOHN M. SYNGE

Perhaps the most remarkable thing about this play is the intensity of effect it achieves in proportion to its unusual brevity. The intensity, no doubt, is the result of a number of factors. The student might investigate the following matters, however, in an effort to see how the play gains its power.

1. The plot (which at first reading may seem over-simple) is actually very tightly packed: it deals with the last day of a long, long struggle which the old mother has waged against the sea. On this day the body of her son Michael is identified, and the last son, Bartley, is drowned. The struggle is over. How do these events gain power from the struggle which they suggest? How does the identification of Michael's body

* This play is available in a separate edition, Boston, 1911; in Synge's *Works*, Boston, 1912, and in the *Complete Works*, New York, 1935; in *A Book of Modern Plays*, Lake Library, ed. George R. Coffman, Chicago, 1925; *A Treasury of the Theatre*, ed. R. B. Mantle, New York, 1935; *The Atlantic Book of Modern Plays*, ed. S. A. Leonard, Boston, 1934; and *Representative Modern Dramas*, ed. C. H. Whitman, New York, 1936.

prepare for, or "set up," the death of Bartley?

2. Notice that the play is finally Maurya's play; the tragedy, if it is a tragedy, her tragedy. How is attention directed to her from the very beginning of the play? How do the speeches of the girls focus attention on her reaction to events rather than on their own? Does her reaction to Bartley's death, which comes as a surprise to the girls, constitute the surprise ending of the play? Or does Bartley's death constitute the surprise ending? Is it his death or her reaction to it that focuses the theme of the play?

3. It ought to be apparent that the play gives little scope for full development of the characters. The persons in the play tend to remain types. How does the author make a virtue of this fact, one which would usually be considered a drawback? May it be said that the characters tend to be symbolic? If so, what do they symbolize?

4. What other means of symbolism are used in the play? Consider the white boards, for instance. How do they point

the implications of the play—at the beginning and at the end?

5. It may be said that *Riders to the Sea* consistently uses symbol rather than direct statement, or, in more general terms, understatement rather than overstatement. How does the ending of the play illustrate this method?

6. Is there sufficient struggle in this play? It is true that Maurya tries to keep Bartley from going to the boat. But does her action constitute enough conflict to allow the play to be considered a tragedy? Could it be said that this conflict really has its function in pointing to a deeper conflict, of which it is merely one aspect? What is this deeper struggle?

7. Is Maurya too passive to be a tragic protagonist? How would one go about defending the play on this point?

8. Consider the appropriateness of the dialogue to the effect of the play. The speech of these peasants, which is removed from the dialogue of the everyday world, serves what function in the play? Is it, however, too "poetical," that is, unnaturally elevated or prettified? If not, why not?

9. With regard to the importance of the part played by the sea, this play may be compared with Racine's *Phaedra* and Euripides' *Hippolytus*. There is, however, a sharp difference in the meanings given the sea. How do those meanings vary from play to play? How does the meaning of the sea influence the tragic quality of the different plays?

10. What is the difference between the deaths by drowning in *Riders to the Sea* and those in *Rosmersholm?*

APPENDIX B

Historical Sketch of the Drama

As the word *sketch* indicates, the following account is but a very brief and incomplete outline of the development of classical and modern drama. It is intended chiefly for classes in which the instructor wishes to combine the analysis of dramatic forms with the use of historical perspectives. Its principal function is to indicate how the plays discussed in this volume (either in the body of the text or in Appendix A) fit into or illustrate a historical pattern. The names of such plays are preceded by an asterisk.

CLASSICAL DRAMA

Both classical and modern drama are of religious origin, and in part, therefore, the history of both is a record of the evolution from ritualistic beginnings.

Greek drama grew out of the worship of Dionysus, god of fertility; the original form was a hymn of praise (dithyramb) sung by a chorus which also engaged in a

ritual dance. The first step toward tragedy, it is usually assumed, was the chorus leader's coming to have a separate part and carrying on a "dialogue" with the chorus; then the leader impersonated Dionysus or some other character in a story about Dionysus. Thus he became the "first actor," supposedly the creation of Thespis in the sixth century B.C. Aeschylus added the "second actor" and Sophocles the third, in the fifth century B.C. Thus, there came about a great increase in the importance of dialogue, and hence of plot and character, and a corresponding decrease in the importance of the chorus.

But the chorus remained, always an integral part of Greek drama; the drama retained its original religious association, the presentation of plays being part of extensive and complex religious services; the "plots" came almost entirely from traditional stories about certain families and individuals and their experiences in a world in which divine agency was always present. In the drama, then, religion and all its imaginative and cultural manifestations were brought to a focus. The religious festival to which the drama belonged took place in the spring, a week-long holiday; it was a community activity and experience; part of the expenses were borne by the state; a strict discipline was observed. At the theatre the audience sat on semicircular benches on a slope; before them danced the chorus on a circular *orchestra* ("dancing place"), in the center of which was an altar of Dionysus; the acting was on the dancing place and possibly on a raised platform behind it. To the rear was the *skene* or tent (for dressing); its wall could be painted to create a *scene*.

Such plays as survive indicate that the fifth century was the high period of Greek drama. During the religious festival tragic poets presented their dramas in competition (there were separate competitions for comic and dithyrambic poets); each competitor had to present a tetralogy—a tragic trilogy plus a less serious "satyr-play." The *Oresteia* of Aeschylus (525–455 B.C.) is the sole surviving trilogy; it illustrates not only the various formal aspects of Greek tragedy, but also the severe tone and high moral concern of Aeschylus. Of his approximately 90 play, 7 survive; he won 13 first prizes. Sophocles (495–405 B.C.) wrote about

125 plays, of which 7 survive; he won 20 first prizes. In his *Antigone* we observe a characteristic conflict of forces to which humanity is subject; in his *Oedipus Rex*, the irony for which Sophocles is distinguished. Euripides (480–406) wrote about 90 plays, won only 4 first places, but became very popular later, as is shown by the survival of 18 of his plays. He was a "modern," so to speak: rather a skeptic of the values which Aeschylus took for granted, somewhat of a psychological analyst, and, in Browning's words, "The Human with his droppings of warm tears." These characteristics all have some part in his *Hippolytus.

Greek comedy had a separate evolution from Dionysiac ritual. The surviving comedies are later than the tragedies. In the fifth century B.C. there flourished "Old Comedy," characterized by sharp satire of institutions and individuals, obscenity, lustiness, colorful language and farcical effects. The type is brilliantly represented by the 11 surviving plays of Aristophanes (448?–388?), who wrote 40; the 11 are the only complete Greek comedies extant. A conservative, Aristophanes constantly satirized the new and the present—in *The Banqueters*, the New Education; in *The Wasps*, the passion for law courts; in *The Acharnians*, the war with Sparta; *The Frogs*, by the way, shows a preference for Aeschylus over Euripides. Of Middle Comedy, no examples are extant; New Comedy, which flourished in the fourth century, is represented by many fragments of Menander. It was milder in tone than Old Comedy, dealt with types rather than individuals, and used a wide variety of emotional effects, showing the influence of Euripides. Menander's work can be conjecturally estimated from that of Terence, the Roman dramatist who borrowed from him.

Developing partly from primitive native models and to a greater extent by imitation of Greek models, Roman drama began in the third century B.C. Presentations originally took place on ceremonial occasions, some of them historically religious in significance; but in Rome the secularization of the drama was completed. The great period of Roman drama came early—in the third and second centuries. Of the tragedy of that period—imitated from the Greeks, especially from Euripides, and using largely the traditional subjects of Greek drama—only isolated passages survive. But comedy is well represented: of the 100 plays ascribed to Plautus (254?–184?), 20 survive, and all 6 of those by Terence (195?–159?) are extant. Plautus's plays are marked by lively farce, rapid movement, boisterous language, the confusions resulting from mistaken identity and other such external matters. These characteristics appear in *The Twin Menaechmi* and in *Amphitryon*, both of which influenced Shakespeare's *Comedy of Errors*. Terence, who also uses rather stereotyped situations, produces a less lively play but one with more characterization and wider emotional appeal. Influenced by Menander, he himself was enormously influential on Renaissance dramatists throughout Europe. *The Woman of Andros* is perhaps his best known play.

The only surviving Roman tragedies are the 10 ascribed to Seneca (B.C. 4?–65 A.D.), which show the influence of Euripides and are all on Greek subjects (e.g., *Medea, Phaedra, Oedipus, Agamemnon*). Inferior to Greek tragedy, they are marked by their effort to do Greek themes in purely human terms, by scenes of horror, declamatory passages, epigrammatic lines, the use of supernatural forces such as ghosts, and of themes such as revenge and hatred.

With the decline of the drama, the Roman theatre finally came to house a form of entertainment comparable to that of modern circuses, burlesque, and vaudeville; it was attacked by the Christians and finally put out of business by the invaders from the North. But centuries later, Roman drama was rediscovered and had a vast influence on the European theatre.

MODERN DRAMA

The classical Roman drama that was so much admired and copied in the Renaissance exerted its influence upon a new dramatic stream that had its origin in the Middle Ages—in the Roman Church. We can trace a linear development from Christian ritual to the contemporary stage. In fact, the progress from the ninth century, when the first known dramatic additions to the liturgy appear, to the end of the sixteenth century, when Shakespeare was in the middle of his career, is roughly comparable to the progress from the early Dionysiac dithyramb to the age of Aeschylus, Sophocles, and Euripides.

The development of drama was roughly the same throughout the Christian world. The first step appears to have been the addition of certain lines, called a "trope," to the Easter Mass, to be spoken by members of the clergy in assumed roles. The earliest extant trope, the *Quem Quaeritis*, is four lines long; three are spoken by the Angels, one by the Marys. Apparently roles were added, lines expanded, and actions developed until the various aspects of the Easter story were fully presented by the clergy and constituted an important part of the services. Then the events connected with the birth of Christ were also dramatized, as well as other phases of the life of Christ; finally various episodes in the New Testament, and then in the Old, were added to the repertory. The term *Mystery* is generally used to denote plays on Biblical themes, and the term *Miracle* to denote those based on Saints' lives—a very popular source of drama.

As a result of the growing popularity of such plays, they were finally presented outside instead of inside the church; the Latin, which was the universal language of the Church and hence of the drama, gave way to the vernacular (English, French, etc.); finally the Church gave up all connection with the plays, and they fell into the hands of, and were highly developed by, the Guilds (trade and professional associations). The Guilds of different towns worked up collections of plays known as Cycles—series which presented the Christian world from Creation to Doomsday. The York Cycle, the most complete of the few extant cycles, contains 49 plays. Under the Guilds such plays continued to be popular even through the sixteenth century.

Long before that, however, other important developments had taken place. The basic element in the total secularization of the drama was of course the secularization of the materials; gradually the Biblical stories began to be treated with considerable freedom and originality, and to be expanded by the addition of non-Biblical elements. Noah and his wife, for instance, were often used to provide domestic comedy of a sort analogous to the Jiggs comedy of today. One of the best examples of the almost complete displacement of Biblical by secular material is *The Second Shepherds' Play* (1400?). A considerable broadening of the materials available to drama was accomplished by the Morality Play, a new form which came into prominence in the fifteenth century. It was a dramatic allegory, which is conventionally described as a battle between the Virtues and Vices for the soul of man. Despite the use of abstract characters, the Morality was often very concrete in detail, and, applied to current educational and political themes, it was popular throughout the sixteenth century. The best example of the Morality Play is *Everyman* (ca. 1500?).

The next step toward completely secular themes and toward secularized and individualized characters may be seen in the comic plays of John Heywood (called Interludes) in the first third of the sixteenth century. By this time, however, the spread of classical learning, which was the most conspicuous feature of the Renaissance, was bringing about considerable familiarity with the Roman drama, and from it were learned lessons about form, plot, and characterization. Full-length five-act plays appeared, with more complex plots and more mature characterization. Roman influence appears strongly in such a comedy as Nicholas Udall's *Ralph Roister Doister* (ca. 1540?) and such a tragedy as Sackville and Norton's *Gorboduc* (ca. 1560?). After the mid-sixteenth century, then, the English drama, open to all kinds of materials and characters, and growing constantly more familiar with the fully developed classical forms, was ready for the perfecting touch of skilled artists. This development from fairly primitive to rather mature forms was largely the work of a set of brilliant young graduates of the universities—usually called "The University Wits"—who began writing for the theatre in the 1580's. Such men as George Peele, John Lyly, Christopher Marlowe, Robert Greene, and Thomas Kyd not only gave the drama a more skillful management of plot and a profounder characterization than it had known before, but also created the various comic and tragic types which Shakespeare and his later contemporaries were to use so brilliantly.

Shakespeare, who did most of his writing between 1590 and 1610, began his career with simpler types such as the *Henry VI* plays and *Comedy of Errors* (1591). Then he went on to develop the comic genre in such plays as *The Merchant of Venice* and *As You Like It*, and, in the *Henry IV* plays, to develop the "chronicle" play as very successful mature comedy. To his third period, the first decade of the seventeenth century, belong the tragedies— *Lear*,

Hamlet, Othello, Macbeth; and at the end came such plays as *The Tempest.* The plays are in verse form; they represent the wedding of great drama with great poetry. Poetic brilliance also characterizes other Elizabethan dramatists—Webster, Tourneur, Middleton, Rowley, Shirley, Ford in tragedy (even when sensationalism and sentimentalism begin to make inroads); Dekker, Massinger, Marston, Middleton, and Shirley in comedy. Notable in the period also are the romantic comedies of Beaumont and Fletcher, the "humors" comedy of Jonson, and the domestic drama of Heywood. The age finally ends with the closing of the theatres by the Puritans in 1642.

In other countries in Europe drama developed from its medieval phase by steps analogous to those which occurred in England. The Renaissance drama was brilliant in both Spain and France. In Spain Lope Felix de Vega Carpio (1562–1635) is said to have written two thousand plays. He is well known for the romantic "cape and sword" play exemplified by *The Star of Seville* and for a more mature type in which is found a mixture of comedy, tragedy, and the problem play—as in *The King the Greatest Alcalde.* Pedro Calderón de la Barca (1600–1681) wrote romantic drama often considered to be philosophical, such as *Life is a Dream.* The great period of the French drama was the seventeenth century, when, under the influence of the French Academy, the "classical rules" became much more important than they ever were in England. In tragedy the chief names are Pierre Corneille (1606–1684) and Jean Racine (1639–1699); working within the neo-classical conventions, the latter produced a poetic drama in which human nature is penetratingly grasped. His *Phaedra* is one of his best known plays. Molière (Jean Baptiste Poquelin, 1622–1673) wrote brilliant satirical comedies such as *Les Précieuses Ridicules* and *Tartuffe.* Classicism held on

tenaciously in the French drama, finally giving way, in the eighteenth century, to the domestic drama of Diderot and others, and, in the nineteenth, to the romantic and historical plays of Victor Hugo.

After the Restoration in 1660, the brilliance of Elizabethan tragedy is gone. We find instead the so-called "heroic drama" of Dryden and others—a romantic rhetorical genre frequently hingeing on such conflicts as that between love and honor; the tragedy of Otway and others in which pathos is stressed; "classical" or "rules" tragedy, successfully practiced in Dryden's *All for Love* (1678) and then declining for the next century. Restoration drama reached its peak in comedy of manners—the gay, witty, satirical presentations of the sophisticated world which we see in Etherege, Wycherley, Congreve, Vanbrugh, and Farquhar. Actually, the most famous play from the group, Congreve's *The Way of the World,* as well as much of the work of Vanbrugh and Farquhar, falls in the eighteenth century, which then sees the gradual disappearance of comedy of manners and the rise of sentimental comedy. Exemplified in such plays as Richard Steele's *The Conscious Lovers,* this type tends to substitute the admiration of virtue for the ridicule of folly; its influence extends even to Sheridan, whose *The School for Scandal* is a late-century effort to rehabilitate the comedy of manners. The bourgeois influence, to which the change in comedy is generally ascribed, also affects tragedy: in Lillo's *The London Merchant,* moralizing is joined with sentimental and melodramatic effects. With the decline of both tragic and comic perception, the turn of the century sees drama at a new low; Morton's *Speed the Plough* illustrates the combination of farce and melodrama which dominated much of the nineteenth-century theatre.

In the meantime the Romantic poets

were writing a good deal of closet drama; some Romantic work—plays by Goethe, Schiller, and Victor Hugo, for instance—had considerable influence upon the theatre; Shelley's tragedy *The Cenci* and Goethe's philosophical *Faust* have been of continuing literary interest. The Romantic impulse is always more or less present, of course, and we find it, in a specialized manifestation, in Rostand's *Cyrano de Bergerac* (1897).

In the last seventy-five years, however, the dominant force in the drama may be said to have been the "problem"—the special issue arising out of contemporary economic, social, and political conditions. The strongest influence has been that of the Norwegian Ibsen in such plays as *The Doll's House*, *Ghosts*, and *The Enemy of the People;* at his best, as in *Rosmersholm*, we see Ibsen approaching tragedy. In France, problem plays were written by Brieux; in England, by a succession of dramatists including T. W. Robertson, Sir A. W. Pinero, Henry Arthur Jones, John Galsworthy, Granville Barker, etc. Two witty Irishmen have dealt with problems in a special way. Oscar Wilde has combined the problem play with the epigrammatic comedy of manners, as *Lady Windermere's Fan* indicates. George Bernard Shaw embodies his treatment of the problem in an argumentative realistic comedy which specializes in turning accepted points of view upside down. *Major Barbara* sheds light upon his methods. It is impossible to list here the innumerable contemporary writers of problem plays. Suffice it to say that Maugham's *The Circle* shows a rather witty treatment of a problem in

personal conduct, while Rice's *Street Scene* illustrates an American handling of a problem of society. In recent years there has been a special concern with psychological problems, such as that treated in Howard's *The Silver Cord*. It is of course not fair to the varied productions of Eugene O'Neill to describe him wholly in such terms, but *Mourning Becomes Electra*, at least, does exhibit the psychological interest at an extreme—the reduction of an ancient myth to terms of modern abnormal psychology.

A special feature of twentieth-century drama has been the Irish drama, which, with its stress upon Irish themes and language, exemplifies a rather widespread modern tendency to find special expression for national and local themes. The chief figures in the Irish movement were Yeats, Lady Gregory, and Synge, whose *Riders to the Sea* is one of the most popular Irish plays. In the Irish plays, too, we find a good deal of the symbolism which, from Ibsen on, has had a regular if minor place in modern drama, and of the use of poetic form with which there has been a good deal of experimentation. In America it is especially Maxwell Anderson who has essayed the poetic drama. T. S. Eliot's *Murder in the Cathedral* is a very interesting example of the type.

Perhaps the coincidence of O'Neill's reducing an ancient drama of moral and religious significance to terms of abnormal psychology, and Eliot's returning both to the religious theme and the poetic form which originally belonged to all drama—perhaps this coincidence indicates that we are coming or have come to the end of some kind of definable cycle.

GLOSSARY

I. SOME PRINCIPLES OF DRAMA

CERTAIN ASPECTS of drama are here given slightly longer definitions than can be conveniently fitted into the usual short glossary. This arrangement also makes possible a connected discussion of several related terms.

ARISTOTLE'S POETICS

Aristotle's discussion of tragedy has been mentioned frequently in this book. Some of his important points—this is far from a complete list—are the following *:

1. Tragedy represents men "as better than in actual life."

2. It "endeavours, as far as possible, to confine itself to a single revolution of the sun, or but slightly to exceed this limit."

3. ". . . through pity and fear" it effects "the proper purgation of these emotions."

4. ". . . most important of all is the structure of the incidents. . . . Hence the incidents and the plot are the end of a tragedy; and the end is the chief thing of all."

5. "Character is that which reveals moral purpose, showing what kind of things a man chooses or avoids."

6. "A whole is that which has a beginning, a middle, and an end. A beginning is that which does not itself follow anything by causal necessity, but after which something naturally is or comes to be. An end, on the contrary, is that which itself naturally follows some other thing, either by necessity, or as a rule, but has nothing following it. A middle is that which follows something

as some other thing follows it. A well constructed plot, therefore, must neither begin nor end at haphazard, but conform to these principles."

7. "Unity of plot does not . . . consist in the unity of the hero. . . . The plot, being an imitation of an action, must imitate one action and that a whole, the structural union of the parts being such that, if any one of them is displaced or removed, the whole will be disjointed and disturbed."

8. Tragedy presents not "what has happened, but what may happen." It "tends to express the universal," that is, "how a person of a certain type will on occasion speak or act, according to the law of probability or necessity. . . ."

9. "Of all plots and actions the episodic are the worst. I call a plot 'episodic' in which the episodes or acts succeed one another without probable or necessary sequence."

10. The effect of pity and terror "is best produced when the events come on us by surprise; and the effect is heightened when, at the same time, they follow as cause and effect."

11. An aid to the proper effect of tragedy is the reversal, "by which the action veers round to its opposite, subject always to our rule of probability or necessity" (this is really a definition of *dramatic irony*).

12. The proper effect is not produced by "the spectacle of a virtuous man

* Quotations in Butcher's translation.

brought from prosperity to adversity," nor by "that of a bad man passing from adversity to prosperity," nor by "the downfall of the utter villain. . . ."

13. The proper tragic hero is "a man who is not eminently good and just, yet whose misfortune is brought about not by vice or depravity, but by some error or frailty" (the "tragic flaw").

14. Tragedy must not depend upon spectacle, upon extraneous aids, or upon the "monstrous," "for we must not demand of Tragedy any and every kind of pleasure, but only that which is proper to it."

15. Character must be good, true to life, consistent with itself and with the class to which the person belongs; the dramatist should aim at the necessary and the probable.

16. The "unravelling of the plot, no less than the complication, must arise out of the plot itself; it must not be brought about by the *Deus ex Machina* . . ."

17. Recognitions, of persons or facts, are worst when brought about by signs such as birthmarks; best when they arise "from the incidents themselves, where the startling discovery is made by natural means."

18. The chorus "should be regarded as one of the actors; it should be an integral part of the whole, and share in the action, in the manner not of Euripides but of Sophocles."

19. "With respect to the requirements of art, a probable impossibility is to be preferred to a thing improbable and yet possible."

CONVENTIONS

In the study of all arts we hear a good deal about certain "conventions." In understanding the drama we need to know something about its conventions.

A story is told of a woman who, when a theatrical performance produced in her a stronger emotional response than she liked, toned down her feelings by assuring herself, "But this is only a play." Now what she was doing was deliberately destroying the *illusion* upon which a work of art depends. It is obvious that if a spectator is going to say, "This is only a play," or "These are only words on a printed page," or "This is only paint upon a canvas," the play or poem or painting cannot "work" for him, cannot exist as forms which have a reality greater than and different from the bare physical elements of which they are composed. For a work of art to have a reality of its own—or, in other critical terms, to give an illusion of reality—there are two fundamental necessities: the spectator must be capable of exercising, and willing to exercise, his imagination (the suspension of disbelief, Coleridge called it), and the work itself must do certain things to engage his imagination. The former needs no discussion here, but the latter needs amplification.

Note that at the start the normal theatregoer accepts, as part of the *artistic reality*, certain conditions which do not conform to everyday reality. At the movies he sees only certain combinations of light and color, which he accepts as the equivalents of people in action. Furthermore, he sees only a two-dimensional representation, to which he himself adds depth. At a puppet-show he sees six-inch figures which he accepts as actual persons of full-size—so successfully that at the end the operator who steps into the stage seems like a grotesque giant. At the legitimate theatre he does see people like himself, but their actions take place in a generally three-sided place which is supposedly a normal outdoor or indoor scene. This discrepancy he is not bothered by, however; he takes walls away or adds them, as necessary, and he transforms himself from a physically present intruder into an invisible spectator whose presence can be no bar to the carrying on of very private actions and conversations.

We always make these adjustments, even without being aware of it; that is, we accept certain *conventions*. A convention is a common agreement—either arrived at arbitrarily, like the ground rules at a baseball game, or resulting from long practice, like certain phases of etiquette. Conventions save questions, quibbles, needless argument; they are conveniences, and we do not demand that they be rational in the way that a debate, for instance, should be rational.

All kinds of dramatic and theatrical entertainments depend fundamentally upon conventions—that is, upon our willing acceptance of certain conventional substitutions for everyday reality. It is agreed at the outset that we will use our imaginations to make the jump from the partial representation to the complete reality.* Now, given this initial situation, the drama can go on to engage the imagination, by every means available, in much more complex and far-reaching activities. Of course its chief means is *character*, the center of all narrative forms of literature. The author must use the *concrete;* actions and characters must be consistent; causes must be adequate to explain effects. Unless he is striving for the special effects of fantasy, the author must work preponderantly from the known world. Using the terms in the broadest sense, the devices by which he bids for the reader's acceptance are *realistic* and *logical*.

Once we have said that, however, we must immediately qualify it by saying that the dramatist also has available many devices which in the ordinary sense are not realistic and logical at all.

* Only in the neoclassical period did critics generally insist that the stage ought to duplicate, as minutely as possible, all the characteristics of the actions it was representing, and to choose for representation only such actions as it could reproduce with slavish fidelity. Such a prescription disregarded the function of the imagination.

These we can again describe by the word "conventions." Conventions vary greatly from age to age, but in one way they are all alike: they are accepted as legitimate parts of the writer's machinery, whether or not they cohere with our experience in the "real" world.

Since the conventions of an alien stage, because of their unfamiliarity are easier to perceive than our own, the student may find it convenient here to read the account of the conventions of the Roman stage in Part 2 of the analysis of Plautus's *The Twin Menaechmi* (p. 141). Several of the conventions of the Plautine drama are in wide general use—*asides*, for instance, the speeches heard by the audience but not by the characters on the stage. These were much used in Shakespeare's day and continued to appear in succeeding centuries. Note that they appear especially in comedy and in the melodrama that developed in the nineteenth century. In our day Eugene O'Neill has employed them in a very special and elaborate way—using them regularly throughout a play to denote a character's real thoughts as contrasted with what he says in his regular speeches.

Another familiar convention is the *soliloquy*, which may be used very skillfully (as in Shakespeare) to analyze an individual's state of mind or very awkwardly to convey information (that is, for *exposition*) which the author is not skillful or conscientious enough to present in more dramatic terms. Conventions regarding *stage settings* vary a good deal: in classical and Elizabethan days they were simple and suggestive, whereas early in the twentieth century there developed a cult of minute accuracy which allowed the imagination as limited a function as did neo-classical conceptions of time and place. More recently we have seen reversions to simplicity and the wider use of the symbolic. Conventions in *costume* are not consistent: in his own day Shakespeare's characters appeared in contemporary dress, but in our day they are costumed according to the period depicted by the play. Again there are varying conventions with regard to language: in comic writing there has always been much more use of prose and the prosaic, of the rhythm and vocabulary of actual speech, whereas until the last century tragedy was regularly done in the *language of poetry* (whether good poetry or bad poetry). There have even been different conventions of poetic language: for instance, Dryden, Addison, and Johnson in different degrees thought it highly improper to use the wide vocabulary and complex figurative language that Shakespeare used. Other dramatic genres function in terms of other conventions: a *romantic* work, for instance, in general depends upon our acceptance of a simpler kind of characterization than is necessary for tragedy or high comedy.

Obviously, any dramatist is in some way or other dependent upon conventions. His problem is to utilize them as necessary or helpful in the construction of his individual dramatic view of things, but to avoid depending on them so fully that he turns out a machine-made job, perhaps momentarily acceptable on a certain level, but doomed to rejection by sharper minds or by everyone when conventions change. If for exposition or for display of inner conflicts or for other effects he relies too largely on soliloquies or asides, he shirks the dramatist's main technical obligation. If he writes tragedy in verse because it is the convention to do so, but lacks the command of metaphor and other devices which mark the distinction between poetry and metrical prose, he fails. If he characterizes according to certain conventions—creating, for instance, the simple hero and villain of melodrama—his result is a stereotype. In other words, to rely unduly on accepted attitudes and procedures is to end in a lifeless *conventionality*. Conventions are useful; complete conventionality is deadly.

In leaving this subject, we find three things that we ought to keep in mind:

1. Drama, like other art forms, depends at the start upon certain conventions, certain terms agreed on by both the dramatist and his audience; and individual plays are always developed partly by means of certain conventional devices. To question these, to say, "This is not like life," is to be rather naïve. On the other hand, not to recognize conventions as such and not to understand their role, is not to be fully informed about the nature of drama.

2. We should always be aware of the fluctuating line between the acceptable utilization of conventions and an undiscriminating reliance on them. The commonplace in literature is largely the result of overworked conventionalism. Conventions may be used brilliantly: Shakespeare took over the standard blank verse of Elizabethan drama and made it an instrument of great poetry. Thus he provides the key to the difficult task facing any writer who looks beyond the box-office: though he must depend, unless he is the rare innovator who achieves high excellence, largely on the materials and methods both of his age and of the form in which he writes, he must transcend these conventions—through them rise to a quality which will be apparent to periods with different expectations.

3. A convention may actually embody a principle which at first glance we may not recognize as such. T. S. Eliot argues that the language of tragedy is poetry. If that is true, what appears on one level as a convention is on a deeper level a formal necessity, an essential quality.

MOTIVATION

Motivation, a word that is widely used in the discussion of drama (and likewise of other narrative forms), has a number of connotations. At the most literal level an author has "motivated" an action when he has presented an adequate "motive" for it: here the question is really one of successful characterization. If the reader feels that A's hatred of B is well accounted for and is consistent with A's character, or that A's shift to indifference toward B is acceptable in terms of what has happened and of what we know of A, then the hatred, or the disappearance of the hatred, is said to be "well motivated." But note that we are not willing to have an author depend, for his motivation, upon mere *stock responses*, that is, to make too easy appeals to patriotism, mother love, "loyalty," and so on. Anybody can do that. So we do not accept A's being devoted to B merely because they are related, or because A is indebted to B ("He gave me my start"), or because they come from the same state, or because the devotion is "nice" or makes unguarded people "feel warm inside." We expect the dramatist to present *concrete* evidence (actions, thoughts) that accounts specifically for this devotion; this will be interpretative, and will not merely rely upon our thinking that devotion is a fine thing but will indicate the quality and significance of the devotion —as misguided, unselfish, unwilling, sentimental, despairing, cynical, profit-seeking, fanatical. In other words, devotion (and so hate or curiosity or any other expression of character) varies in individual cases, and it is only by a consciousness and understanding of individual variations—and thus a repudiation of general, stereotyped reactions— that an author can present a case with the convincing accurateness that will deserve the term "well motivated." In this sense, motivation leads us into a fairly complex problem of the author's grasp of meanings and values; we really get down to the ultimate excellence or badness of the play. What he has

done with a character depends upon the skill with which he can express his discriminations in concrete dramatic forms.

Motivation, however, is also widely used with reference to dramatic events and happenings aside from the human forces, decisions, or choices (evidences of character) involved in them. When events and occurrences appear to lack a proper cause, reason, or justification, we call them "unmotivated." We all are familiar with certain types of unmotivated action: the unexpected death which conveniently removes troublesome characters; the legacy which solves all financial problems; the character who suddenly shows up to straighten out difficult situations—the *deus ex machina*, as he is called (the rich uncle, the lost brother, the detective, etc.); the *coincidence* by which things happen, or people meet, or don't meet, at just the right time—in immediate theatrical terms, the vast number of exits and entrances which are very convenient but not at all logical (note how large the problem looms in the *Menaechmi*). Even at this level, where things are simpler than those discussed in the preceding paragraph, we get somewhat into the realm of meanings and values: obviously an author who believes that vital issues can be dealt with in terms of legacies and sudden deaths is not one whose interpretation of experience we can take very seriously.

Notice that we can almost equate "unmotivated" and "unexpected." That is, if action or conduct is reasonable and logical, we can, at least in a general way, anticipate it. And we anticipate it because in some way or other we have been given advance notice of it. Obviously, an author does not say outright that such-and-such a thing is going to happen (we are all familiar with the crude "But as we shall see, he would live to rue this unjust victory"). He suggests it; he gives us information which will lead us to make certain inferences. If a character is ill or is given to taking great risks, his death will seem probable. If a character has shown skill in acting and deception, we can accept easily his carrying out of a great hoax (see the *Second Shepherds' Play*). Evidence of habitual reckless driving can "motivate" an automobile accident; of generosity, a benefaction; of sensitiveness, abnormally defensive behavior. If we are going to have a man drown or fall off a cliff, we need to know in advance that the river or cliff is there; if we are going to have a screen scene, we must know about the screen (see *The School for Scandal*); if a character is going to be called away suddenly by financial problems, we must know about the financial problems in advance. If a character is going to be detained somewhere and thus make possible a scene which his presence would prevent, we should have good reason to expect his detention. It has been said, concerning well-planned and articulated plays of our day, that if you see a gun in Act I, you know that there is going to be a suicide or murder in Act III. This sort of thing naturally can become too easy, and planning in terms of character is still fundamental; but it is well to keep in mind that Act III needs also to be set up in mechanical terms.

The process of leading up to subsequent events and situations is sometimes simply referred to as "preparation," sometimes also as *dramatic foreshadowing*. The latter term is also used to describe the creation of an *atmosphere* —for instance, ominousness—which will in itself suggest developments of a certain kind. This could be managed very awkwardly (by the use of "omens," superstitions, lighting effects, etc.) or quite skillfully (in terms of character— as in *Macbeth*, for instance). However managed, dramatic foreshadowing thus conceived takes us over into another extensive subject—*tone*. *Tone* may be defined as the reflection in the artist's work of the artist's attitude toward his materials. The tone of a literary work,

for example, may be playful or solemn, ironic or naïve, etc. A full discussion of tone would, indeed, be extensive, for the tone of a play, in its most inclusive sense, may be considered merely the working out of the author's attitude toward the world which he portrays. Rather than elaborating a full discussion of tone at that level, however, we are here simply indicating that consistency of tone is a kind of index of the way in which things are going and thus an aspect of motivation. If an author shifts his tone, evokes responses that do not support each other (as in many musical shows), we may feel either that he is inept or that he is sacrificing everything to a presumably astonishing variety. Or he may carefully build up a single consistent impression— that the whole thing is playful, perhaps, or that it is all of quite serious import. Necessary as this is, it will not cover up other limitations: a farce such as the *Menaechmi* may be admirably consistent in tone but still entirely lack treatment of character and hence motivation in mature human terms.

It may be convenient, in summary, to divide motivation into two parts: (1) the adequate provision, usually by advance notice of some kind, for all materials, mechanical matters, occurrences, and non-voluntary actions that the author is going to make use of; (2) the adequate provision for all actions which spring from character—that is, consistency, thoroughness, and individuality of characterization, made apparent in concreteness of presentation from the beginning of the play on. If a playwright fails in the former, he will seem careless or awkward, and he will certainly lack finish, perhaps to a degree that will seriously interfere with the success of his work. But if he fails in the latter, he will fail in the fundamental quality on which the work depends.

Note, finally, that as a well motivated work may be distinguished by the quality of expectedness, any work which depends for its effect upon unexpectedness is going to pay very little attention to motivation. That is, it is of the very nature of *farce* and *melodrama*, which rely upon speed, surprise, and shock, to keep the audience uninformed, and to present characters so superficially that the author can at any time have them do almost anything he may want for effect (cf. the *Menaechmi* and *Speed the Plough*). And here we come to two great ironies of literary study: unexpectedness itself tends to become stereotyped, and farce and melodrama, when not done by the most skillful hand, can become the most tediously *conventional* forms of drama. But drama which depends upon expectation rather than surprise (to repeat Coleridge's praise of Shakespeare) really gains the virtue of being unexpected: in the hands of a first-rate artist a profound treatment of character, with the unerring consistency that is the best motivation, inevitably comes across with the freshness of something wholly new.

TEMPO

Tempo is the pace or speed at which a given scene or a whole work moves, and in a play it will obviously depend upon certain aspects of the dialogue. But since all authors are concerned with tempo, the problem of the dramatist can be illuminated by some comparison of plays and fiction.

The importance of tempo is something that we all instinctively recognize, though we may not be specifically aware of it as such. We all know, for instance, how a single joke can be spoiled by improper timing. We need time for certain effects to sink in, and too much speed may spoil a good point. Contrariwise, too much delay may wear suspense thin. An interruption—though it may not, for instance, interfere with the logical progress of a story—may seriously mar the effect because the time-relationship of the parts is disrupted. Some such consideration is often behind the request, "Come on, let's start over again."

In a play, actors may vary the pace of speeches, and stage directions like "Slowly" or "Rapidly" may cause the reader to make some adjustments; but in general we have the impression of moving from speech to speech at a rather constant speed. A storywriter can more easily make his material appear to move at different speeds. He is free to break up a dialogue at any point by a descriptive or analytical passage, which can affect the tempo in two ways. If the inserted passage is a brief summary of a part of the conversation, the author will speed up the movement by making us feel that we have covered a period of time in less time than the original events took. But if the inserted passage is a description of the feelings or thoughts or sensations of one speaker, and if this passage does not replace dialogue, but is, as it were, simply put in between two speeches which otherwise would come one right after the other, we would obviously have a sense of being slowed down. That is, a short period of time in the action takes a relatively long period of time for the reader to experience it.

The principle involved can be presented more concretely in a comparison of two actual passages. Let us first look at part of a scene from a play:

Trowbridge: Can we count on you, then, or can't we?
Maxon: I told you I'm not sure.
Trowbridge: You've had plenty of time to make up your mind.
Maxon: I know, but making up your mind is not as easy as talking about it.
Trowbridge: If you don't make up your mind, it's because you don't want to face the issue.
Maxon: That's not fair. I've faced—
Trowbridge: What you did once doesn't prove anything now. If you don't come along, it's because you won't face it when the heat is on. This is the only chance to beat them.
Maxon: That's what you say.

Trowbridge: All right, I'm finished. This is the end. Are you coming or aren't you?
Maxon: [*After long pause*]. I guess not.

Now notice the same scene as handled in fiction, with the speeches kept intact to facilitate the comparison.

"Can we count on you, then, or can't we?" Trowbridge was angry, and his moving toward the door seemed less an act of departure than a move necessary to use up the physical energy that his emotion had released. In a less forceful man, it might have been a retreat; with him, it was a threat. Maxon followed, but more slowly. He looked down. He was unwilling. Had he not looked in good enough health—tanned, his jersey revealing heavy muscles—he would have struck you as a sick man dragging himself off to the medicine cabinet. "I told you I'm not sure." It was a complaint; not a statement of fact. He might have been an amateur gambler mourning a fate that had done him no justice. Trowbridge said, holding himself in, "You've had plenty of time to make up your mind." The condemnation was unspokenly profane. Maxon twisted the string of the hall lamp. So his own efforts twisted him about before his judge. "I know, but making up your mind is not as easy as talking about it." Trowbridge moved closer again. When he stood still, he talked louder. "If you don't make up your mind, it's because you don't want to face the issue." Maxon whipped up a shadow of resentment. "That's not fair. I've faced—" "What you did once doesn't prove anything now." Trowbridge charged in. "If you don't come along, it's because you won't face it when the heat is on. This is the only chance to beat them." "That's what you say." Like a schoolboy. "All right, I'm finished. This is the end." Half turned to the door, he was relaxed again. But he was inexorable. "Are you coming or aren't you?" This was the minute. No delay any more. No stalling. You could get off the track or be hit. It was impossible to be where something was going on and still be an innocent bystander. If you had only been a bystander in the past—yes. But then the problems had

not seemed too hard. The boys had all pretty much stuck together. They hadn't been going after much. It was not that it had been safe, but that no real decisions had been asked. No bridge-burning. He had fallen in. He hadn't been a bystander. There hadn't been many bystanders. A wormy crowd, he had thought them. But not wormy through and through; just some bad spots here and there. The boys hadn't paid them enough attention to work up bad names for them—well, this wasn't then. The worm turns. Joke, eh. This was different. He wasn't different. He was the same. He hadn't had to face this sort of thing before. He was standing in fire, shriveling bit by bit. He wasn't surprised to hear his febrile gasp, "I guess not."

With the same dialogue, the fiction form comes to triple the length of the drama form, and it could, without padding, be still longer. That is to say that in general it moves more slowly. In one sense, indeed, drama is always going to move "faster" than fiction: it selects briefer and fewer aspects of a total experience to deal with, and it presents them in a more compressed form.

To go back to the piece of prose fiction above, we can see that there are variations of pace even *within* this little episode. We see that the first three or four speeches are accompanied by descriptive passages: the writer is trying to convey the total effect of the scene, and so he takes it more slowly. In the middle of the piece, however, he cuts the description to a bare minimum, and consequently the pace is accelerated. Thus he gets both variety and a sense of heightened tension. Further, he builds up to the climax of the scene, Maxon's definite answer. He wants this to sink in—the difficulty and importance of it, and so he withholds Maxon's answer while we read auxiliary material, this time not a description of external appearances but an analysis of what is going on in Maxon's mind. So the author "holds" this part of the incident, slows it up almost to a standstill.

Just as in other matters, so in timing

the novelist has greater resources than the dramatist. In fact, the ways in which he can "time" a scene are almost infinite. But the dramatist is limited. As we have seen, he cannot describe, nor, except with difficulty, analyze mental operations.

Does this mean that he is entirely without resources? No, it does not. He can, at the simplest level, use typographic devices freely. He can have a speech printed like this:

Maxon: Well—[*he pauses, as if to get breath*]. Well—[*another effort at speech also fails*]. I don't—I don't [*he grabs for words, but they don't come*]. I don't—see [*Trowbridge keeps a set expression*], I don't see . . . [*voice trails off*].

Plainly, however, this is an artificial device which must be used very sparingly. A related procedure—really an amplification of this—would be to insert descriptive passages between speeches, that is, to enlarge and prolong stage directions. More recent plays do this more frequently than older ones. But such passages, for one thing, are really outside the play; and, in so far as they do become integrated, the play is really being transformed into a novel. The dramatist is not facing his problem but avoiding it. It is easy to see that the dramatist, instead of doctoring up his play with devices borrowed from another form, can do better by using several potentialities of his own medium.

1. One of these potentialities is the length and structure of speeches. Shortening them will speed them up; one's eye literally runs down a page in which each speech is composed of only a word or two. Or, if the subject of the dialogue does not easily permit this sort of treatment, different kinds of structure within a speech will appreciably affect its tempo. Compare these two speeches:

If you can assist, and are willing to, the problem, though it may not be solved, will at least have begun to assume clear outlines.

Come on, let's get to work. You can be a lot of help. Show us how to organize it. Lend us a hand. Let's go.

Both speeches contain the same number of words. But the former, with its longer units and more involved structure, tends to hold us up and thus to give us the impression of a leisurely, considered manner of speech. The latter, broken up into five sentences and using the imperative mood, gives us the impression of haste and impatience. Thus the *rhetorical structure*, as we may call it, greatly influences the tempo (as well as other qualities) of the speech.

2. As the dramatist can vary the structure of a single speech and can vary the length of speeches with respect to each other, so can he vary larger units. Two characters A and B can speak to each other a short time in comparison with the time that C and D speak to each other, or A can speak to B longer than to C. Regardless of internal structure, the shorter scene will seem to move more quickly.

3. But the preceding point does not hold absolutely, for the "density" of a speech may outweigh the length in influencing sense of speed. A complexly metaphorical speech may be of such weight as to slow up a scene very effectively. In fact, a 50 or 75-word speech so composed may move more slowly than 200 words or more of direct, matter-of-fact statement. The "Tomorrow and tomorrow" speech of Macbeth is short, but its pace is very deliberate.

But as we examine the subject a little more closely, another fact comes into view: the dramatist cannot arbitrarily use these devices to lengthen or shorten speeches and scenes. Changes in tempo, though they help produce a necessary variety, *cannot be used merely for the sake of that variety.* They are subject to a rigorous *logic:* tempo is a way of interpreting materials, and these latter will determine what goes fast and what slow. A failure in tempo is actually an indication of faulty understanding in the writer. Too much speed means either that the writer has underestimated the stress which a scene ought to have or has not properly adjusted the dialogue to the function it must perform. Correspondingly, a sense of slowness means an overdevelopment of a theme or a failure to make minor alterations in style as a combination of over-emphasis of some parts and under-emphasis of others, so that all tend to have the same weight and movement.

Thus tempo, we may say, is *functional* —a part of the complex of means by which the author says what he has to say. Therefore tempo is not really separable from other aspects of the dramatic process; with minor exceptions it cannot be changed independently, that is, without making changes in, for instance, emphasis. The Maxon-Trowbridge dialogue is really a different thing from the Maxon-Trowbridge scene as described in fiction form. In the former, our attention is focused exclusively on a central aspect of the conflict, its expression in words; in the latter we see, besides the conflict in verbal form, the physical surroundings, certain physical aspects of conflict, including some analysis of the relation of past to present. In other words, the process of slowing down the movement is the same as making a more elaborate interpretation of, and therefore radically changing, a scene. Just as the length of a scene is a criterion (though not the only possible one) of its significance, so the structure of each speech must represent more than an effort to secure variety of movement. For it must be related, as we have seen before, to the character and to the immediate situation: an inarticulate or unlearned person is not likely ever to launch into flowing periods, nor a well-disciplined individual to break down into unrelated interjections. Both length and density of a speech vary according to the individual and the situation which he is in; stresses cannot be

added unless they are logical in these terms.

In summary, then, we find the matter of tempo embedded in a complex set of interrelationships. At a rather simple level, of course, the dramatist can effect certain changes of pace by the skillful use of mechanical devices. But success or failure in the superficial manipulation of these devices will not ultimately be able to produce profound excellence or inflict fatal damage. For the means by which a writer produces a sense of changed tempo must be used with respect to more fundamental matters. If there is to be a contrast in length of scenes, it must be justified by the extent and importance of the materials to be dealt with in these scenes. Similarly with the length, density, and other rhetorical devices in the individual speeches. When the parts of a play are so timed that we have a sense not only of variety but also of appropriateness of movement, we know that the author has assessed his material competently, proportioning stress to importance by extended treatment or other devices, securing modulation by arrangement of scene, and so presenting his conflict in human terms that the contrast itself is developed in the timing.

TYPES: FARCE AND MELODRAMA

Farce and *melodrama* depend upon action that is unrelated to character or at best stems from characters so superficial or stereotyped that they are incapable of voluntary action of any importance. Farce, if it succeeds at all, evokes laughter; melodrama plays upon a variety of emotions—excitement, fear, horror, righteous indignation, satisfaction in the due punishment of evil or rewarding of good.

Of course, *farce* and *high comedy* both evoke laughter, and the line between them cannot be exactly drawn; any play dealing with the transitory and the relative, as comedy does (see the analysis of *Lady Windermere's Fan*), is going to tend toward one extreme or the other. It has been argued that comic situations are those which produce in the spectator a feeling of superiority (comedy, said Aristotle, represents people as being worse than they are). If we apply this criterion also to farce, we can perhaps distinguish it from comedy by noting the different ways in which each produces the sense of superiority. There are different levels on which a character may be made to look ridiculous. At the simplest, of course, he can be put into a ridiculous physical situation, as in a pie-throwing farce. The efforts of the Merry Wives of Windsor to make a fool of Falstaff do not depart very far from this category. But we begin to move from farce toward a higher grade of comedy when we find, first, that the character's situation is brought about less by some one else's scheming and more by his own qualities, and, second, that the situation moves toward the psychological or social and away from its dependence on the physical. Thus in *The School for Scandal* Joseph Surface fails in various plans and is publicly embarrassed for his hypocrisy; in Jonson's *Volpone* the greedy characters suffer legal punishment. But in *Lady Windermere's Fan*, Society—which may be said to be a comic character in the play—is merely made the object of witticisms, and Lady Berwick is merely *presented* as a loquacious, managerial opportunist. Her punishment, if we may call it that, is the subtlest: it consists merely in the attitude of the reader to her.

An author may set out to write farce; or he may aspire to comedy, but by sheer ineptitude land in farce. Shakespeare's *Comedy of Errors* is based upon several cases of confused identity—a situation which obviously cannot go much beyond the farcical. Jonson's *Volpone* is a satire of greed in which the characters come through so clearly that we have almost no feeling of a depend-

ence on mere situation. If the author of the late medieval *Second Shepherds' Play* had known the terms, he would doubtless have called his work a farce; yet the humorous situation of the play grows enough out of the characters to make some approach to comedy. On the other hand, while Morton in *Speed the Plough* must have felt that he was achieving real comic effects, he constantly falls into farce (See the notes on that play in Appendix A).

Some light is shed on the meaning of the word *farce* by our very common expression "It's a farce," which we use to describe almost anything that in a ridiculous way fails to achieve its intentions.

TYPES: MELODRAMA, PROBLEM PLAY, AND TRAGEDY

Like farce, *melodrama* may be described as unmotivated in terms of character, and also like farce, it may result from an unsuccessful effort to write something else, such as *tragedy* or a *problem play*. When the author fails to present characters profoundly enough and individually enough conceived, what results may be dull or laughable or possibly even exciting in a way. In so far as it avoids ideas and skims over characters, it is melodrama. *Speed the Plough* provides a very good example of the kind of melodrama that results when the author is unwilling to treat his characters and situations seriously enough. When it turns out that the central situation is due to a misunderstanding, that there is no real moral or psychological issue, the author has really run out on his problem: all he has left is such suspense as he can get by keeping the bare facts of the case in the dark.

We should, however, guard against seeing *melodrama* merely as *tragedy* which doesn't come off. Tragedy may fail to come off and yet not be melodrama, viz., Dr. Johnson's *Irene*. Or an author may aim only at melodrama, and what he does may be good or bad melodrama. That which is based entirely on cliché situations and stereotyped characters—"Western" stories, for instance—can certainly make no appeal at all at the adult level. But it is possible to have plots with originality, and characters which show some psychological penetration, and these may be entertaining enough at their own level. The participants in an adventure story need not be stock characters; they may be so complexly presented that the work *tends* toward the problem play or the tragedy.

Such a transition is difficult, though, for the melodrama really deals in escape, whereas at a more serious level escape is impossible. The essence of tragedy is the inescapability of the issue; Hamlet and Phaedra and Orestes, regardless of what happens to them, go on to deal uncompromisingly with the crises their lives present. Note further that the possibility of escape depends at least partly on the kind of situation the character is in. In melodrama he has to escape from ambush, from the sheriff, from different kinds of physical dangers; granted good luck or sufficient strength and adroitness—with which the author usually provides his characters—escape usually takes place. The situations are physical. In problem plays, the situation is likely to be a social one, as in various plays by Ibsen, Chekhov and Galsworthy: the individual has in some way to deal with the conventions or the modes of conduct or attitudes of a society. Either side may be right, or the merits may be divided, but at any rate a solution is not easily arrived at if the social context is to be taken seriously. Strength and adroitness cannot easily provide escape from a society set in motion. Unlike melodrama, the end is not predictable. But in *tragedy* the problem is still more difficult: the situation is moral, and the individual, we

may say, has to cope with a universe. The universe appears, naturally, not on the stage (like society) but in the mind of the protagonist; though the conflicting elements may have an external symbolic form, the conflict is essentially internal. The protagonist has a sense of moral order—the universal with which he must deal. It is none the less real for existing in his mind; indeed, it is the more real for not being a physical or personal enemy that can be destroyed, or a society that may disintegrate and thus perhaps justify the individual. In its intangibility lies its indestructibility, its universality. There is no escape, and it is in this sense that tragedy may be said to be concerned with fate or destiny.

In the light of the foregoing we ought to be better able to understand the unsatisfactoriness of the popular use of the word *tragedy* today. Whenever someone is killed in an automobile accident, newspapers speak of the "tragedy," but clearly there is no tragedy at all; there is no voluntary or meaningful action (though an automobile crash conceivably *could* be used to express a tragic issue). Too, such accidents are spoken of as "fatal," though in no acceptable sense is fate involved at all; *fatal*, as used, means that someone has died, though actually "fate" may bring many kinds of experience besides death. Again, we find *tragedy* used of unhappy experiences of children, though obviously tragedy is only an adult experience. Often, too, we hear unhappy endings, in life or literature, spoken of as "tragic." Yet, as a matter of fact, the kind of dealing with the moral universe that constitutes tragedy need not end "unhappily," as we can see from Aeschylus's trilogy the *Oresteia;* and, on the other hand, there are "unhappy endings" that are *not* necessarily tragic—the death or punishment, let us say, of criminal or vicious people ("His tragic career came to an unhappy end"), the results of illness, injury, fire, economic disaster, etc. It is possible that a

dramatist or novelist *might* use such
events to indicate the kind of values an
individual has and the kind of choices
he makes; but they are not tragic simply
because they are unpleasant and un-
desirable experiences.

By way of summary: melodrama
grows out of physical and material
difficulties, and escape from danger is
the characteristic process, although its
effects may depend upon injury and
death, either as events that fail to attain
a desired tragic quality, or as means
that the author uses deliberately for
their own sake; the problem play is
characteristically concerned with situations in the broadest sense social, where
various kinds of solutions may be worked
out or suggested, but where, since we
are working with more fully characterized and developed people than in
melodrama, mere "escape" would be
a trivial evasion of the issue; tragedy is
concerned with universal moral issues
which the individual has to face largely
alone and which he can in no sense
escape. Of course such definitions are
not to be regarded as final, for you will
be able to think of types of situations
which are usable in various ways. Take,
for instance, legal difficulties: in general
a conflict with the law is likely to be
melodramatic, with stress on escape
(the unexpected evidence at the trial,
the last-minute reprieve, etc.). On the
other hand, in such a play as Galsworthy's *The Silver Box*, which deals
with the varying statuses of rich and
poor before the law, a legal matter is
the basis of a problem play. And in
Sophocles' *Antigone* we have a tragedy
in which the situation, or one aspect of
it, is "legal": but here we have the law
in conflict with a higher imperative, and
it is this latter which really defines the
quality of the play. Obviously, then,
the raw materials do not in themselves
predetermine the mood of the play, for
they can be used in different ways (we
have already stressed the importance
of the author's attitude). But this must

be said: certain raw materials in general
do yield more readily to one type of
treatment than another, just as rubber
and iron, for instance, whatever the
diversity of the uses to which each may
be put, are not exactly interchangeable.
By and large, situations involving
danger, threats, violence, etc., furnish
very great problems to the writer who
wants to use them for something superior to melodrama. He will require
much more than ordinary skill to make
such situations function symbolically
instead of one-dimensionally. Conversely, if he wants merely to "entertain" or to "thrill" his audience, he has
his composition almost ready-made.

We might attempt a further distinction of types in terms of the kind of
effect produced by each. We have said
above that melodrama "entertains" or
"thrills"; in a sense, of course, all drama
does that. If it does not entertain, if it
does not afford pleasure, it—as well as
all other literature—fails. Obviously it
must evoke the reader's emotions and
stimulate his imagination. But then
we come to other questions: how do
this? to what end?

Compare, for instance, the kind of
emotional experience one has at a good
athletic contest with that called for by
a piece of "good" literature. The one
gives a kind of tenseness and exhilara-
tion at the moment, and that is the end
of it. The latter likewise elicits a state
of concentration and absorption, perhaps longer or shorter than the former,
but this is only the beginning; the experience is capable of repetition, enlargement, revision; it is accompanied
by and stimulates reflection. The game
is pleasurable at one level; but it means
nothing. The literary work is pleasurable too; but it is likewise meaningful;
it is a commentary on life, and in so far
as it is fully grasped, it has the effect of
knowledge; it may heighten observation, change attitudes, and widen understanding; it brings a kind of growth.
Similarly there are levels within

literature itself, and that of melodrama is really the game level: excitement, tension, suspense for their own sake, for the kind of pleasure those things bring, and nothing left over. You discard all your powers of apprehension except curiosity about the outcome; you do not ask, Is it worthwhile? or, What does it mean? In the problem play, however, the conflict is not for the conflict's sake (as in the game or melodrama). The conflict introduces issues and, consequently, a sense of right and wrong, or at least of better and worse. One's emotional response comes to involve reflection upon the situation represented by the plot, and one may well acquire a modified or clarified view of the situation. Hence the problem play leaves a sort of residue, as the melodrama does not. If the melodrama is analogous to the game, perhaps the problem play is analogous to an election or some other form of civic or political activity: the emotional experience is closely tied to an awareness of the issues involved, and the issues endure after the election or campaign.

In tragedy, finally, one's emotional concern is also identified with one's sense of a problem; but the concern is infinitely more intense and profound because of the greater importance, universality, and pervasiveness of the problem; because, in a word, it is a problem not of a group or society but of all people, one which they must face at all times, not in the easier form of an outer problem which they can combat, but as an aspect of themselves with which they must, at bottom, deal privately, though our attention may be focused (as in *Hamlet*) upon the outer situations which reflect the private transactions. Perhaps we may say that tragedy grows out of the nature of man, out of the conflict of good and evil in which he is always engaged. Hence the durability of tragedy as compared with the problem play, which, because of the forceful impact of any immediate prob-

lem, may seem overwhelmingly intense in its day but which, unless it by some miracle transcends the temporary, must surely fade into forgetfulness as a new day brings forth new problems.

Perhaps we may learn something about ourselves from the fact that tragedy is not "popular." It is the form which makes man face the most serious issues instead of escaping from them; he is brought face to face with himself, with the complexities of his own nature; a high quality of attention is demanded of him; and he is fed no splendid illusions, no sugary optimism, to make reality look simpler or more manageable than it is. What, on the other hand, does he find in "escape literature"? Several things, perhaps: (1) characters who escape; Good always triumphantly escapes from Evil—an outside force which is disposed of as if it were a sort of pest; (2) escape for the reader—from the commonplace into a charming and exciting world where achievement is easy; (3) most seriously, escape from the adult realm of responsibility, where the logic of human character must be met, where experience must be seen fully, and evil dealt with as an intimate and goading reality.

"Escape literature" has a place— though not too large a one—which it would be unduly solemn to deny. The danger is not in enjoying it on occasion but in mistaking escape for interpretation, taking opium for food. To see only the good is very bad indeed. Perhaps the worst fault is that of writers who trade in charm and optimism, distorting experience to please the unsuspecting and the uncritical.

In the evaluation of the different levels of literature, the equipment of the reader is of course important. A person without literary experience or critical habits may honestly take clichés, stereotypes, the simple and easy, the superficial and sentimental, for the real thing. But experience and the critical habit can both be acquired, and one need not long be taken in by the false and pretentious. It goes without saying, of course, that the will to discriminate is essential: a person usually content with any play that boasts a "plot," regardless of its triteness or obviousness or improbability, or a person who regards literature merely as the pleasurable repetition of well-worn patterns, will have to work to recognize (1) that some plots represent the natural workings of fully developed characters and thus come to be humanly significant; (2) that some authors try to do this but fail; and (3) that others don't even try.

II. SHORTER DEFINITIONS

ALLEGORY: Narrative in which the persons and events stand for a system of ideas. The characters are often personifications of objects or abstractions, as in *Everyman*. *Parable* implies, perhaps, a briefer, more obvious, less systematic allegorical story. The distinction should not be pressed too sharply. See pp. 100 ff.

ANTICLIMAX: A disappointing loss of tension or force; a "let down"; a failure to reach an expected intensity. See *climax*.

ASIDE: See pp. 30 and 487.

ATMOSPHERE: Mood or feeling created by events, places, and situations. Compare with, and distinguish from, *tone*. See p. 490.

ATTITUDE: This volume is often concerned with the attitude of the author to his materials, that is, his understanding and interpretation of them. His attitude expresses itself in the use of the comic or tragic mode, in the use or non-use of *irony*, in the *tone* and *form* of the work, etc. See pp. 75, 248 ff., 383 ff., and 443-4.

CHORUS: A singing and dancing group from whose words, in Dionysiac ritual, Greek drama evolved. Used, later, to comment on or interpret the action; to help create tone; to dramatize the universal significance of the conflict. The classical studies of the Renaissance led to wide use of the chorus in drama since 1500. See pp. 458-9 and 479-80; *Aristotle's Poetics*, 18.

CHRONICLE PLAY: A play on a historical or biographical theme. The term usually implies a chronological *structure*, which is often loosely knit or *episodic*. The chronicle play is hardly to be conceived of as a special type, however; the problem of the author's ultimate attitude toward his material is the same as in any other play. See pp. 376-7.

CLICHÉ: A worn-out expression such as "shaking like a leaf." A cliché, however, may be an effective part of a characterization. A cliché situation is a stereotyped one—the last-minute rescue, and so on. A cliché plays for the *stock response*. See *Aristotle's Poetics*, 10.

CLIMAX: The most intense moment of conflict; the turning point. See *denouement*. For a discussion of the arrangement of materials in climactic order, see pp. 54-55 and 143.

CLOSET DRAMA: Drama intended to be read rather than produced.

COINCIDENCE: In drama, simultaneous occurrence of two events, such as two people's happening to come to the same place at the same time, etc. Although it may be used functionally—for instance, to create an ironic effect—coincidence frequently indicates inability to work out a plot in terms of character. See pp. 64-65 and 489.

COMEDY: A term so loosely and variously used, and conventionally applied to so wide an area of dramatic writing, that extended discussion would be required to formulate a satisfactory definition. In this book, however, comedy is treated as that form of drama which has its orientation in "the way of the world" rather than in ultimate moral problems; which is concerned with man's relation to society rather than to immutable truths; which deals with experience at a level where expediency and compromise are suitable rather than questionable; and where the best judgment of society rather than one's own conscience provides the criterion of conduct. For elaborations see pp. 78–79, 242–54, 385–7, 448 ff., and 494–5. Compare *farce*. See also *high comedy, comedy of manners, comedy of humors, intrigue comedy*.

COMEDY OF HUMORS: A kind of comedy of character based upon the "humor" or dominant trait (avarice, jealousy, trickiness, etc.) of character. The danger of the method is oversimplification—the freakish and farcical. Comedy of humors was at its best in the hands of Ben Jonson; it has appeared sporadically ever since.

COMEDY OF MANNERS: Used in several senses. In the more restricted usage, comedy which wittily portrays fashionable life. But *manners* also means "moral actions" and hence "character." Thus "comedy of manners" becomes "comedy of character," in contrast with "comedy of situation" or "intrigue comedy."

CONCENTRATION: An effect of compactness and intensity; getting to the "center" of things. See *focus*. *Unity* is essential to, but does not guarantee, concentration. The *unities* have been defended as a means of concentration. There is, indeed, a special aid to concentration in the mechanical limitations of the drama. See pp. 27 ff. and 45.

CONCRETE: Expressed by means of actions and words that are characterizing and meaningful, that is, specific and original rather than stereotyped and conventional. See pp. 487 and 489.

CONVENTIONS: Techniques that are accepted by common agreement. See pp. 486–8. Conventions are necessary, but good drama avoids *conventionality*, which results from excessive reliance upon conventions of character, plot, etc. See p. 488.

COSTUME, CONVENTIONS OF: See pp. 487 ff.

DENOUEMENT: The resolution or "unravelling" or "working out" of the plot. This may be almost identical with *climax*, as in *Rosmersholm*, where the outcome of the conflict is not determined until the very end; or the climactic moment of decision may leave other matters for solution, as in *Lady Windermere's Fan*. See *Aristotle's Poetics*, 16.

DEUS EX MACHINA: "God out of a machine." In Greek drama a God, lowered to the stage by a mechanical device, often intervened at the end of a play to work out a situation. Hence, any rescuing or saving agency introduced to bring about a desired end. Use of the term generally implies that logic of situation and character has been ignored. See p. 489 and *Aristotle's Poetics*, 16.

DRAMATIC: Having the quality of drama, that is, presented by means of characters in action and marked by the tension of conflict. Does *not* mean *surprising, unusual, shocking, striking, coincidental*, or *melodramatic*. See *theatrical*.

EPISODE: A loose term for any unit of action in a play, such as the "robbery episode" in *Henry IV*. However, a play composed of a series of episodes not causally united in a single action is said to have *episodic structure*. See *chronicle play* and *Aristotle's Poetics*, 9.

EPISODIC STRUCTURE: See *episode*.

EXPOSITION: See pp. 30 and 487.

FARCE: See pp. 137 ff. and 494–5.

FIGURATIVE LANGUAGE: See *imagery*.

FOCUS: The directing of the reader's attention primarily to one character, situation, or concept, and the subordination of other interests to the central one. Focus is an evidence of unity. A play may be said to lack focus if the author has not succeeded in giving a primary position to one character or action or element (see pp. 180, 467). The focus may be such as to produce one kind of effect rather than another, as in *Rosmersholm*. In such a case the focus may be functionally related to the author's attitude—a means of indicating his point of view. See p. 245.

FORESHADOWING, DRAMATIC: See *Motivation;* see pp. 489 ff.

FORM: The total organization of materials—ideas, characters, situations, scenes, etc.; the arrangement of all the parts to create a desired effect; the *way* in which the author sets forth his *theme.* Hence it includes *structure, style,* the use or non-use of *symbols, irony, coincidence, unities,* and all other available devices; it will involve questions of *focus, tone, probability,* etc. In some ways *form* is almost synonymous with *method,* though *method* usually implies a process of the author, and *form* a quality of the work. See pp. 100 ff. and 244.

FUNCTIONAL: Having a definite function to perform in the development of the play; helping carry out the author's intention; not merely conventional, or decorative, or existing for its own sake. See p. 494.

HERO, TRAGIC: See *Aristotle's Poetics,* 12, 13, 15.

HEROIC DRAMA: A form of drama, popular in the late seventeenth century, which often involved a conflict between love and honor, and which was characterized by language at times poetic but generally highflown and bombastic.

HIGH COMEDY: A general term roughly denoting the mature effects of comedy of character. Rather than depending upon farce, intrigue, or other kinds of situation, the author derives his effects from a complex view of character. See pp. 494–5.

IMAGERY: The use of images; the conveying of meaning through appeal to the various senses; communication by means of the *concrete* and the particular. Imagery includes direct and literal description; *figurative language* such as *similes,* which are comparisons using *as* or *like,* and *metaphors,* which identify the two things being compared; and *symbols.* Although in any drama the writer may employ more or less imagery, a reader's awareness of imagery becomes especially important when the dramatist makes primary use of poetic language. See pp. 32, 185 ff., 312, 330–1, and 346 ff.

INTRIGUE COMEDY: Comedy of situation characterized by stratagem and conspiracy, generally in amorous matters. See pp. 448 ff.

IRONY: *Verbal irony* or *irony of statement* is a manner of expression by which the reader, in order that he may be made to grasp the discrepancies of experience, is compelled to infer a good deal more than the words say; the writer may use *understatement,* in which he says less than he means; or *paradox,* in which he stresses the apparently self-contradictory; or, most frequently, the device of saying what he does mean. In this book, however, we have been mainly concerned with *dramatic irony* or *irony of situation,* in which the outcome is different from what is expected or from what may seem fitting. This should not be confused with the "surprise ending," for which the author manipulates materials to keep the reader guessing. *Dramatic irony* involves rather a discrepancy between what a character expects or plans and what happens. The reader is generally "in on it." The purpose of such irony is not primarily to surprise but to create a profound impression of the contradictoriness and complexity of human experience. It is functional, therefore, in a mature view of experience, and is to be contrasted with the comparatively "straight" development characteristic of more superficial literary works. See *Aristotle's Poetics*, 10, 11, 12, and pp. 284, 299, 308, 386–7, and 447.

INTERIOR MONOLOGUE: A character's meditating with himself; the equivalent of *soliloquy*.

LOGICAL: As applied to drama or other literary works, consistent with the terms of character, situation, and mood which the author has adopted. See pp. 489 ff.

MELODRAMA: See pp. 491 and 494 ff.

METAPHOR: See *imagery*.

METHOD: All the procedures which the author uses to accomplish his end. See *form;* also pp. 15 and 20 ff.

MOTIVATION: Logical accounting for the behavior of the *dramatis personae*, primarily in terms of "motives" but also by means of other devices which produce anticipation of future events. See pp. 24, 44 and 488 ff.

NEO-CLASSICAL: Applied to certain beliefs and practices of the European literary world of the sixteenth, seventeenth, and eighteenth centuries. In drama, neo-classicism was marked by devotion to the "rules": the three unities, the use of a chorus, the avoidance of violence on the stage, the use of only royal or noble characters in tragedy, a severe "correctness" in language, etc. The rules were believed (with only partial correctness) to be derived from ancient practice and Aristotelian precept. See *unities*, p. 315 and p. 469.

OBJECTIVE: *Objective* and *subjective* are less applicable in drama than in other literary forms in that the dramatist must speak entirely through the characters and therefore has less opportunity for the direct comment and expression of personal feelings and views which we call *subjective*. He can of course treat one character purely as his mouthpiece, and when the words of such a character outweigh the *logical* demands of character and situation, the work may be called subjective. As applied to the manner of characterization, *objective* and *subjective* also find less use in drama in that the form of drama—speech and action—by its nature makes for an objective method. By such devices as *soliloquy*, of course, it is possible to get within a character, but this is still far removed from the direct presentation of thought and feeling—the *subjective* method—which is possible in fiction.

PARABLE: See *allegory*.

PARADOX: A statement or an occurrence which is apparently self-contradictory but at the same time profoundly logical. See *irony*.

PATHOS: Literally "suffering"; hence, the quality of a situation that evokes compassion or sympathy. Pathos usually implies weakness, helplessness, insurmountable difficulties. (1) An author may represent a legitimately pathetic situation; (2) he may attempt to evoke a sense of pathos which the characters and situation do not justify and thus fall into *sentimentality;* (3) he may aim at *tragedy* but, by failure to endow his protagonist with adequate will or strength to struggle, may achieve merely the pathetic. See *Aristotle's Poetics*, 12 and 13, and pp. 312–3.

PERSONIFICATION: Presenting as an animate character something inanimate, such as an object or an abstraction. See *allegory*.

PLOT: The structure of the action. See *Aristotle's Poetics*, 4, 6, 7, 9, 16, and 17.

POETIC DRAMA: Drama in which the lines make regular use of the devices of poetry—rhythm, metaphor, other kinds of *imagery*, etc. Poetic drama is not to be thought of as a special or unique mode but rather as the form toward which all drama, by the demands of its own nature, logically moves. See pp. 23 ff.

POETRY, LANGUAGE OF: See *imagery;* also pp. 23–4, 186–7, 312, and 488.

PROBABILITY: Logicalness; consistency with the terms of character and situation that are used. Probability is often said to rely upon an author's grasp of the "universal," that which is characteristic of human experience, that which "may" happen. Aristotle recurrently insists upon the probable. See *Aristotle's Poetics,* especially points 8 and 19, but also 9, 11, and 15.

PROBLEM PLAY: See *theme;* also pp. 81, 314–5, and 494 ff.

PROGRESSION: Forward movement; the development of the situation. See pp. 29 ff. 44, and 286–7.

PROPAGANDA: See *theme, sentimentality.*

REALISTIC: Characterized by fidelity to the generally observed facts of experience. Compare *romantic.* See p. 487.

RHETORICAL STRUCTURE: Arrangement of the words of the *dramatis personae.* See p. 493.

ROMANTIC: Implies that which is different from everyday experience: unusual, remote, exotic, idyllic, etc. Compare *realistic.* As used in this book, *romantic* does not apply to the Romantic Movement and is not contrasted with *classical.* See under Some Principles of Drama, p. 488.

RULES: See *neo-classical.*

SELECTION: The author's choice of the materials with which he must create the effects he desires. The problem is especially pointed in drama because of the limitations imposed by the form. See pp. 27 ff. and 74.

SENTIMENTALITY: In a person, emotional response in excess of the occasion; in a literary work, the effort to secure an emotional response not prepared for, or not justified by, the character and situation. Compare *pathos.* Emotions frequently played upon are grief, pity, and love of goodness (compare *stock response*). Hence *sentimental comedy,* which plays up to the reader's love of goodness rather than to his sense of the ridiculous (see pp. 248 ff.). Such comedy tends to split good and evil and put them into separate characters where they can be easily loved and hated. Note that this simplification of character is also characteristic of *propaganda* literature; the doctrinaire and the sentimental tend to go hand in hand, just as they did in the eighteenth century. *Sentimental tragedy* subordinates its grasp of moral issues and complexity of character to the more obvious appeals to pity and other emotional responses. See pp. 183 ff., also *Aristotle's Poetics,* 12, 13, 15.

SIGNIFICANT VARIATION: A type of structure in which the effect is secured by an alteration in a pattern of action which has become familiar by repetition. See pp. 10 ff and 108.

SIMILE: See *imagery.*

SOLILOQUY: An "alone-talk"; the "thinking aloud" of one character; a speech which is not part of a dialogue. See pp. 30–1 and 487.

STAGE SETTINGS, CONVENTIONS OF: See p. 487.

STOCK RESPONSE: The immediate, standard, predictable reaction of an uncritical reader to the conventional appeal of a stereotyped character, situation, or emotion. See *cliché, sentimentality,* and p. 489.

STRUCTURE: The arrangement of the larger elements, especially the *episodes* and the details of action within episodes; structure is functional in that it is an important means of presenting *theme.* See pp. 54–6, 63–6, 104 ff., 244 ff., 283–4, 307–8, and 308–9; also *Aristotle's Poetics,* 4, 6, 9, 10, 11, 17.

STYLE: Usually denotes the selection and arrangement of words. In drama, the language is determined to a considerable extent by the requirements of character. Characters may of course speak wittily or metaphorically or prosaically, etc., and their language may change somewhat as situations change. For the relation of witty language to theme, see p. 78; for the implications of imagery and word-play, pp. 330-1, 348-9, and 381, and the notes on the plays by Euripides, Lope de Vega, and Racine in Appendix A; for other comments on the significance of language, pp. 143, 185-7, and 312; also *imagery*, *poetic drama*.

SUBJECTIVE: See *objective*.

SUSPENSE: A combination of uncertainty about and intense interest in the outcome of an action or the way in which the outcome is to be brought about.

SYMBOL: An object or incident which stands for something else, frequently, something limited and concrete which stands for something inclusive and abstract. For notes on symbols, see the analysis of *Rosmersholm*, *passim*. A specific dramatic situation representing universal or recurrent human relationships may be said to be symbolic (see pp. 75 ff). A plot itself may be a symbol (see p. 448).

TEMPO: See pp. 490 ff.

THEATRICAL: Literally, characteristic of the theatre. Although it might appear to be synonymous with *dramatic*, which is often mistakenly used for it (and indeed "good theatre" is always dramatic), *theatrical* has come to mean artificially contrived effects, implausible situations introduced merely because they are "striking" or spectacular, contrasts and clashes which exist for their own sake rather than as the logical products of theme and character. The theatrical situation is melodramatic rather than dramatic; it is external and showy, and often coincidental; it is "sensational"—for instance, breaking up the wedding ceremony before a church full of guests. Theatrical speech is characterized by inappropriate elevation, excessive emphasis, clichés, pompousness instead of inherent seriousness, rant instead of emotional force, the highfalutin instead of the truly poetic. Hence, a

"theatrical manner" suggests exaggeration, self-consciousness, posturing. A person of perception will dismiss as "theatrical" what a naïve observer is likely to consider "so dramatic."

THEME: In one sense, the general subject with which a work is concerned—for instance, in *Everyman*, salvation; in *Rosmersholm*, the relation of tradition and reason. See also p. 444. In another sense, the "meaning" implied by the drama; what the author is "saying"; his interpretation of experience. See pp. 77, 101 ff., 244. *Thesis* is sometimes also used in this sense, but "thesis play" or "purpose play" usually suggests a drama of which the primary intention is to set forth or imply a specific program of action. Such an intention implies the subordination of character and structure to the "message" that the author wishes to deliver. This is the risk always run by the *problem play*, and rarely avoided by literature of *propaganda*, with its devotion to bringing about courses of action.

THESIS: See *theme*.

TONE: General effect produced by an author's selection and treatment of materials—as comic, tragic, gay, etc. A product of the author's attitude to his materials and his skill in conveying that attitude to the reader. More inclusive than but not wholly distinguishable from *atmosphere*. See p. 490.

TRAGEDY: A term so much debated that a satisfactory brief definition is impossible. In general, this book treats tragedy as that form of drama in which the protagonist undergoes a morally significant struggle; in which the conflict is rather within a character than between characters or between a character and external forces (though the conflicting elements may be symbolized in external form); and in which the protagonist, although treated sympathetically, incurs guilt of which the expiation (by suffering, death, or other means) is part of the dramatic problem. In the main this book relies upon the Aristotelian account of tragedy; for this, see pp. 485–486. For other details see pp. 109–10, 180–ff., and 312–4. For the distinctions among Melodrama, the Problem Play, and Tragedy, see pp. 495 ff.

TRAGIC FLAW: See *Aristotle's Poetics*, 13.

UNDERSTATEMENT: See *irony*.

UNITIES: The "unities" of time, place, and action were considered essential by Renaissance critics: of time, that the action take place within a day; of place, that the action take place within one building or city; of action, that there be a single plot of limited extent. See *unity*, *concentration*. Many dramatists, such as Shakespeare, paid little attention to the unities of time and place. Racine was more attentive to them. Various modern dramatists—Ibsen is one—are in practice comparatively faithful to the unities, although only unity of action is generally considered to have theoretical justification. See pp. 27 ff., 314; also *Aristotle's Poetics*, 2, 7.

UNITY: "One-ness." In general, the quality of a literary work in which all the characters, action, language, etc. are functionally related to a single objective. *Unity* may mean *unity of theme*, by which different strands of action may be bound together; see pp. 180–4, 376–7, 386–7. *Unity* is sometimes restricted to the meaning of *unity of action*, the most important of the three "unities." See *unities*; see *Aristotle's Poetics*, 6, 7.

WELL-MADE PLAY: An influential nineteenth-century type of drama, chiefly the work of the French dramatist Scribe, in which all details of the action were supposed to be very realistically worked out, with especial reference to cause and effect. Many of the devices now seem artificial and even melodramatic. See p. 80.

INDEX

This index does not include Part II of the Glossary.

(Appendix pages are referred to in boldface; references to pages after 452 concern the 12-play edition.)

R